HENRI BERGSON: A BIBLIOGRAPHY

Revised Second Edition

BIBLIOGRAPHIES OF FAMOUS PHILOSOPHERS

The Philosophy Documentation Center is publishing a series of "Bibliographies of Famous Philosophers," Richard H. Lineback, general editor. Published bibliographies include:

Alfred North Whitehead: A Primary-Secondary Bibliography

Edmund Husserl and His Critics: An International Bibliography (1894-1979)

Jean-Paul Sartre and His Critics: An International Bibliography (1938-1980), Second Edition

Martin Heidegger: Bibliography and Glossary

Hobbes Studies (1879-1979): A Bibliography

George Santayana: A Bibliographical Checklist (1880-1980)

Paul of Venice: A Bibliographical Guide

José Ortega y Gasset: A Bibliography of Secondary Sources

A Bibliography of Vico in English (1884-1984)

Henri Bergson: A Bibliography, Revised Second Edition

HENRI BERGSON: A BIBLIOGRAPHY
Revised Second Edition

P. A. Y. Gunter

Published by

**PHILOSOPHY DOCUMENTATION CENTER
BOWLING GREEN STATE UNIVERSITY
BOWLING GREEN, OHIO 43403-0189
U.S.A.**

CONTENTS

PART I

INTUITION AND ITS EXPRESSIONS: AN INTRODUCTION TO THE "BERGSON LITERATURE"

Henri Louis Bergson (1859-1941) is the most prominent French philosopher of the last hundred years. The literature, psychology and religious thought of our time have all felt the transforming impact of his conceptions, while few aspects of contemporary philosophy remain unaffected by his critiques of analytical method, mathematical time, and scientific materialism, or by his concepts of intuition, duration and creative evolution. While Bergson's philosophy has—consistently with its impact—produced an immense, often highly interesting secondary literature, sheer size and diversity have sometimes made access to that body of writing a difficult matter. The present work—a second, enlarged edition of the Bergson bibliography published by the Philosophy Documentation Center in 1974—attempts to remove any of the obstacles which stand in the way of the appreciation and use of the "Bergson Literature."

To remove such obstacles has not been in all respects a simple task. The Bergson literature now spans nearly a century of interpretation and response. Standard bibliographic sources—particularly philosophic sources—fail to provide a full account of its contents. To approach a philosophical literature which is interdisciplinary in nature, it is necessary to search widely, often in sources which would seem to have little to do with philosophy *per se*. Many items in this bibliography are the result of extensive non-standard searches.

The extreme diversity of the Bergson literature is due in part to the popular vogue which his thought enjoyed in the first decades of this century. To an unusual extent for an academician, Bergson reached beyond the confines of academic philosophy. Political leaders, journalists, writers, literary critics—to name a few—felt called upon to write about his "new philosophy". Their articles, in newspapers, books, and popular magazines, were often enthusiastic but imprecise, and they lent a "literary", "high fashion" aura to Bergson's thought which scarcely conveyed its true content. Nevertheless, though it is uneven in tenor and fragmentary in viewpoint, no satisfactory catalogue of the Bergson literature can neglect "Popular Bergsonism." It is included here.

Usually with greater caution, professional philosophers also felt compelled to answer the challenge of Bergson's thought. During the years 1900-1925 philosophical journals bristled with articles concerning his philosophy, while books detailing or discounting his ideas issued regularly from the press. The impact on contemporary philosophy was decisive, though often hard to characterize in detail. On the occasion of Bergson's visit to Columbia University, in 1912, John Dewey concluded:

> "No philosophic problem will ever exhibit the same face and aspect that it presented before Professor Bergson invited us to look at it in its connexions with duration as a real and vital fact."[1]

The correctness of Dewey's insight is attested by the presence in this bibliography not only of items by the majority of the most eminent philosophers of our time, but by an abundance of items by philosophers of all ranks, nationalities, and viewpoints.

There is a danger, however, in becoming a symbol of the *Zeitgeist*. Philosophical fashions are notoriously unstable, and their ebb is liable to be as devoid of balanced reflection as their flood. World War I was decisively to end the Bergson vogue. In the aftermath of that cultural disaster, prewar verities—especially those with an optimistic ring—seemed hollow indeed. In the words of the novelist D. H. Lawrence, after the war there were "no more big words." Interest in Bergson did not vanish in the new atmosphere, however. Instead it gradually but perceptibly waned, even where the diffuse but still recognizable influence of his ideas persisted.

Meanwhile, though he was to continue to write, Bergson's health declined, sapped by a crippling arthritis which reduced him to the status of a near invalid. Commentary on his philosophy was to continue throughout his life, though largely in diminished volume. In spite of predictions to the contrary, it continues today. Much of this more recent literature exhibits a profounder balance and a clearer understanding than that produced during the years of his popularity.

Explanations of the structure and conventions utilized in this bibliography (style, annotation, range, etc.) are certainly called for. But before entering into such explanations, it will be helpful to provide a brief sketch of the development and fundamental assumptions of Bergson's philosophy. This sketch should make Bergson's contentions clear to those otherwise unfamiliar with his thought. It will also help explain the relevance of his ideas to many of the writers mentioned—and included—below.

I

What did Bergson say that so won the interest of his contemporaries? In part his appeal stemmed from the subjects with which he dealt. The unconscious mind, biological evolution, dreams, laughter, psychological time, memory, the revolt against mechanism—all were in the air around the turn of the century. In part his impact stemmed from the contrast he drew between different sorts of knowledge and the different sorts of reality to which he believed they correspond. Real knowledge, Bergson insists, is attained through "intuition." But intuition must be contrasted with "analysis"—the portrayal of experience in static, spatial terms. Analysis is extremely useful; indeed, it is the very paradigm of the pragmatic approach. But its static concepts prevent it from successfully grasping the dynamics of change, i.e. of "duration," the special object of intuition.

From the vantage-point of analysis the world appears repetitious, stable, predictable. For intuition, however, the world is experienced as an ongoing process giving rise to novel, unpredictable events. The goal of philosophy, for Bergson, is systematically to approach, via intuition, as closely as possible the "stream of reality." To do so philosophy must get beyond the artificial symbolization of reality to reality itself. "Metaphysics," Bergson teaches, "is the science which claims to dispense with symbols."[2]

The terms intuition and analysis were first used by Bergson in *An Introduction to Metaphysics* (1903). His earlier studies, however—*Time and Free Will* (1889) and *Matter and Memory* (1896)—had made implicit use of these terms by the contrast they drew between the experience of duration and the static concepts through which we represent it. In what follows, brief sketches of these earlier studies will be given, along with a survey of some major ideas of *Creative Evolution* (1907), the work which was to make Bergson famous almost over night. Though these descriptions will explore the dualities which are fundamental to Bergsonism, the will do so only briefly. More extensive treatments of Bergson's major works are provided in the section of this bibliography (Part II) dealing with Bergson's writings.

In *Time and Free Will* the experience of inner duration is examined from a phenomenological and psychological standpoint. This duration, Bergson shows, is qualitative, heterogeneous, and dynamic. No two of its successive moments are identical, while its components at any moment are so profoundly interrelated that to isolate them (as psychological "states" or "sensations") is both to deform them and render them static. Thus when we try to describe our mental life by means of spatial symbolism we shatter it, transforming wholeness into fragmentation, novelty into repetition, freedom into determinism. Such habitual misrepresentation may have very real effects on our behavior, for, having lost touch with or freedom, we may cease to exercise it. Yet, Bergson insists, we are free, at least in those moments when we cast aside our "spatialized" and "superficial" self and express the deeper self which underlies it. Such free acts are the result of a long personal history or reflection, hesitation, and effort, and are hence relatively rare. But though rare, they are decisive. And since they express something individual, novel, and unrepeatable, they are in principle incapable of being predicted.

This dynamic and indeterminist concept of personal freedom is retained in *Matter and Memory*. But it is reshaped there to show how freedom exists as an integral yet ultimately controlling factor in the human body. Almost since the time of Descartes scientific study of the brain and nervous system has been taken as proving that the body is closed to influence from the mind. More recently, neurophysiology has been used to support the thesis that mind-states are so many ghostly, ineffectual "reflections" of the brain. If this latter, epiphenomenalist, theory is true, then it makes no sense to say that the mind can originate novel, unpredictable acts. (Indeed, it makes no sense to say that the mind can originate anything at all.) If the former theory is true then no such act, even assuming that it exists, can be expressed through the body.

Bergson's approach to these difficulties shows a characteristic blend of common sense intelligence and speculative daring. All modern formulations of the mind-body problem, Bergson points out, presuppose that the brain has a disinterested, purely speculative function. This assumption seems plausible, but even a cursory examination reveals its weakness. The brain and perceptual organs are structured *adaptively*. That is, they are formed so as to enable us to relate effectively to the most easily manipulable aspects of the world around us. They help us to cope. The nervous system is an instrument—a tool or set of tools—and like all tools, it has a highly specialized and therefore limited function. The fundamental character prevents it from picturing, mirroring, or otherwise replicating external reality in any comprehensive sense. Its function is selective, not reduplicative.

It does not follow from this, Bergson is quick to point out, that we are somehow cut off by our perceptual and neurophysiological apparatus from our environment. Far from it. In "pure perception," he holds, we participate directly in the processes of the world around us. (We thus have an underlying intuition of matter.) What needs to be explained, therefore, is not that we perceive, but that we perceive so little; not that we are directly aware of the world but that our sense organs select and represent to us so little of it: and, it must be added, represent this little in a schematic, essentially static way.

If the pragmatic, instrumental function of the brain forbids any thoroughgoing one-to-one correspondence between brain state and external physical reality, it must equally, Bergson contends, forbid any one-to-one correspondence between the state of consciousness and the state of the brain. The brain does not, Bergson observes, give rise to consciousness. It does not, as one materialist contended "secrete thought in the way that the liver secretes bile."

Rather, the function of the brain is to "limit" consciousness, enabling, even forcing, us to attend to the demands of life. Our nervous system (and sense organs) channel our awareness towards particular objects, permitting us to recall only those of our memories which help us to deal with them. Without such limitations, Bergson speculates, we might gain a fuller intuition of the rich inter-relatedness of the world or of our own unconscious memories. But we would live in reverie: diffuse, undirected, devoid of focus. Bergson terms the brain therefore, the "organ of attention to life."[3] By being forced to attend to life, we are coerced not only into focal awareness but into focused effort. The free inner self of *Time and Free Will*, it turns out, can exist only over and against a brain and nervous system which are both its opposite and its instrument.

If this concept of mind-body relationships is correct, we would be ill-advised to look for the mind's higher functions within the adaptive mechanisms of the nervous system. We should instead, to use more recent terminology, look there for the complex of "cybernetic" systems which enable us—often automatically—to act on and cope with our surroundings. Thus Bergson states:

> He who could penetrate into the interior of a brain and see what happens there, would probably obtain full details of... sketched-out, or prepared movements; there is no proof he would learn anything else.[4]

At the time *Matter and Memory* was written the most fully investigated brain function was memory, particularly the maladies of memory, the aphasias. Intensive study of the literature of aphasiology reinforced Bergson's conviction that memories are not stored in the brain.

This statement must be qualified since, Bergson contends, there are two contrasting sorts of memory. What the neurophysiologist studies, and can be ascribed to the brain, is "rote" or "habit" memory (for example, the ability to repeat a poem or a number which we have made the effort, through repetition, to memorize). Such memories are present performances, and have no intrinsic reference to the past. But when it comes to memories of the past *per se*—reminiscences, Proustian recollections—the brain may limit what we can recall, but does not create or contain the recollections themselves. These are preserved automatically and remain in the psychological unconscious, little noticed but potentially active.

The focus of Bergson's writings from the publication of *Time and Free Will* until 1900 explains in large degree the number of items in this bibliography concerned with neurology, psychopathology, and general psychology. It also explains the presence of items devoted to literary and artistic topics. Bergson's psychological theories, including those developed in *Laughter* (1901), have had a profound effect on many poets, novelists, dramatists, painters and critics of our time. Bergson thus belongs to the psychologists, painters and *littérateurs* as well as to the philosophers.

But he belongs to the biologists as well. *Creative Evolution* (1907) contains both Bergson's critique of mechanistic biologies and a metaphysical vision on a grand scale. Since Charles Darwin's *Origin of Species* evolutionary theory had been taken as supporting a mechanistic and materialistic metaphysics according to which life is "nothing but" its material constituents: a string of fortunate coincidences preserved through natural selection. Bergson, however, was not satisfied with this explanation. Not only does it fail to fully explain the emergence of new biological forms, it relies unconsciously on a spatialized, static, and therefore contradictory concept of time. In the universe of neo-Darwinism (especially when interpreted as an extension of the Newtonian world-view) nothing exists but empty space, internally changeless particles, and random motion: with motion itself conceived, strictly, as a series of instantaneous positions and as reversible. What is left of duration—of real time—in such a universe? Only a word uttered by theorists. But those who use the word

fall back unconsciously (and, Bergson insists, inconsistently) on actual experienceable duration in order to give that word real meaning. The basic goal of *Creative Evolution* is,
therefore, to replace the abstract, homogeneous, merely verbal time of neo-Darwinism with
an ongoing, organically interrelated, creative process: a real duration.

There are different ways of carrying out this program. (One thinks of similar proposals
by Alfred North Whitehead, Samuel Alexander, and Pierre Teilhard de Chardin, all of whom
took up Bergson's basic project but suggested concepts of evolution which diverged significantly from his.) Basic to Bergson's scheme is a contract between life and non-living matter,
a contrast reminiscent of the mind-matter duality of *Matter and Memory*. While biological
evolution proceeds in the direction of organisms having increased diversity, efficiency, and
activity, non-living matter drifts in the opposite direction: towards homogeneity, repetition,
passivity. Put simply: life and entropy proceed in opposite directions.

In *Creative Evolution* this difference of direction is explicated through the notion of a
"life force", which drives evolution along radically new paths. This force or tendency must
contend with the resistance of matter, which presents itself initially as an obstacle to biological
creativity. Not every project undertaken by life has succeeded: witness the number of species
which have stagnated, degenerated, or become extinct. Those main directions in which life
has succeeded, however, exhibit successes which have been possible thanks to the obstacle
presented by matter. For Bergson matter is both a resistance and a material to be shaped.

Evolution is a divergent process (Bergson was not the first to assert this, but was one
of the first to stress it.) branching out from an initial starting-point to create an extraordinary
diversity of species. Animal life itself has developed in two contrasting directions: the
vertebrates, culminating in the higher primates and man, and the arthropods, culminating in
the highly coordinated societies of the social insects. Insect societies, unlike those of human
beings, depend essentially on "instinct", an unlearned knowledge which Bergson holds, is
primarily attuned to life. A wasp (the sphex, for example) "knows" how to sting a caterpillar
on its nerve centers so as to paralyze it without killing it; many other similar examples could
be given. While instinct may by remarkably precise in its manifestations, it is both extremely
conservative and restricted in scope. Insect societies seem to possess no history[5]: through
countless millennia they show no signs of innovation; instinct in the sphex is limited to
specific prey and to these alone. These limitations do not change.

The contrast between human and insect societies is striking. Man is distinguished as a
species primarily through his capacity to construct new tools and machines; he should be
termed not *homo sapiens* but *homo faber*. This penchant for dealing not with life *per se* but
with matter, which can be shaped so as to harness natural forces, is the culmination of a
tendency fundamental to vertebrates. But while the emergence of man as an intelligent,
tool-using creature is treated by Bergson as a triumph of life over entropy, he points out that
human intelligence has a specialized biological function and therefore, like instinct, also
possesses inherent limitations. Man has payed a price for his success, not only in the instability
of his history but in a relentless one-sidedness. Man spatializes in order to control.

It is not surprising, then, that human intelligence, which has developed by adapting
itself more and more accurately to non-living matter, should begin to understand evolution
materialistically and mechanistically. But such a viewpoint, rooted as it is in the notion of
a spatialized time, must fail to do justice to the dynamic of the evolutionary advance. To
understand evolution we must employ our entire conceptual capacity. Besides intelligence
we must employ intuition, which is:

> ...instinct that has become disinterested, self-conscious, capable of reflecting on its object and
> enlarging it indefinitely.[6]

Intuition is not raw instinct, as we would find in in a bee hive or a termite colony: limited to specific biological objects and harnessed to specific pragmatic tasks. It is not intelligence, limited to the analysis of its object in spatial terms and always with an eye for practical use. Intuition joins the reflectiveness of intelligence with the immanence of instinct; it is a mode of reflection uniquely capable of following the dynamics of evolution without "freezing" or fragmenting it.

II

Bergson's philosophy contains a rich harvest of ideas, many novel, many controversial. Given the intrinsic interest of his notions, as well as their consonance with the *Zeitgeist*, it is not surprising that his philosophy was to have such a widespread impact. There was, as noted above, the vogue associated with the phrase "fashionable Bergsonism": an aura of subtly nuanced anti-intellectualism which came to be associated with his philosophy in spite of his protests. But a far profounder influence sprang from Bergson's thought, an influence derived from Bergson's efforts to bring his readers to reexamine their ideas, to develop new concepts, and explore new directions. The present bibliography is in no sense limited to detailing this latter influence—as the briefest examination of the text will show. But it does embody a special effort to make this influence known.

Before providing a general sketch of some of the main lines of Bergson's influence it will be helpful to explain the manner in which he believed his philosophy was capable of having a conceptually constructive—that is, a creative—influence. Those who, like Bertrand Russell or George Santayana, attacked Bergson for introducing intuition as a veritable mode of knowledge, have done so not only because Bergson's intuitionism seems to lead to a dangerous kind of anti-intellectualism but because it also seems to culminate in a conceptually baffling, inexpressible experience: a conceptual *cul de sac* from which there is no semantic of syntactical exit. Does not Bergson depict intuition as leading us to "dispense with symbolism"? And does not symbolism not include both ordinary as well as formal (mathematical) language?

Such objections are understandable. (Indeed, Bergson's manner of speaking has sometimes led to their being urged.) But, though understandable, they are mistaken. Paradoxical as it might at first appear, the capacity to provoke conceptual creativity was one of Bergson's primary goals, and was at the heart of what he meant by intuition. Intuition as he understood it could, by ever more radically and completely approaching the fundamental phenomenon of change (duration) throughout the range of its existence, lead to new conceptual schemes, including new symbols and symbol-systems. It can lead to new fields, as well as new methods, of investigation.

Intuition had already been applied fruitfully—through not methodically—Bergson held, in the origins of modern science. He cites a pivotal case in the history of science, the infinitesimal calculus of Isaac Newton and G. W. Leibniz, as being based on a more adequate intuition of duration.[7] At the very roots of the calculus is the concept of acceleration, a notion which the Greeks were never able to crystallize, and without which the Newtonian synthesis would have been unthinkable. It would not have been possible to develop the calculus without taking seriously the notion of acceleration, and investigating change *per se*. The result was not only a transformation of received notions of change but the creation of a new mathematical symbolism. Intuition as Bergson understood it is thus a fundamental ingredient in paradigm shifts: scientific aesthetic, or religious. It is a "generative principle" through which new approaches to experience are created.

If this intended heuristic function of intuition was misunderstood by many of Bergson's contemporaries, there were others who appropriated one or another of his basic insights and applied them to specific disciplines. What follows is a survey of the work of some of those individuals. Like much of the present bibliography, this survey is incomplete. Further research in the history of ideas might cause some of the claims made below to be restricted; but it would also, almost certainly, cause new names to be added to the list.[8]

The relevance of Bergson's philosophy to psychology is clear. Indeed, it is sometimes difficult to discern Bergson the psychologist from Bergson the philosopher. Not surprisingly, then, some psychologists were to adopt an explicitly Bergsonian approach. Among these are Georges Dwelshauvers, Albert Bazaillas, Emile Lubac, Georges H. Luquet and Raoul Mourgue. Other psychologists, who can not be described as exclusively Bergsonian, nonetheless developed an applied certain of Bergson's ideas: G. Finnbogason, Henri Delacroix, Henri Wallon, Albert Spaier, Constantin von Monakow, and Jean Piaget.[9] Contemporary American psychologists sympathetic to Bergson include Frank X. Barron and the experimental psychologists Frederick T. Melges and Endel Tulving.

Turn of the century Europe, besides seeing the birth of psychology as an independent science, also witnessed the emergence of what Henri Ellenberger has termed "dynamic psychiatry".[10] Bergson's concepts of unconscious memory and its repression by the cerebral mechanism and the demands of ordinary life placed him very near to the main currents of "psychoanalysis" during the years of its formulation. Here again two groups of psychiatrists can be singled out. Eugene Minkowski applied Bergsonism directly to psychiatry, as did Charles Blondel (who also owed a significant debt to to sociology of Emile Durkheim) and, again, Albert Bazaillas. Others in dynamic psychiatry who appropriated aspects of Bergson's thought are Pierre Janet, Wilhelm Reich, Carl Gustav Jung[11], and in America James Jackson Putnam, William Alanson White, L. E. Emerson, and in very specific respects, Harry Stack Sullivan and Sandor Rado. More recently Bergson's viewpoint has been broadly appropriated by "humanistic psychotherapy, and has been explicated for English-speaking psychologists by Richard E. Johnson.

There is another current of thought, which might be termed psychobiological, which in varying measure bears the imprint of Bergson's inspiration. Here one should mention, in France, Albert Vandel, Albert Bourloud, Raymond Ruyer, and Maurice Pradines, and, in Britain, William McDougall. McDougall's name might also have been added to the list of psychologists noted above.

From psychobiology to biology is but a short step. Here again there is a contrast between Bergsonians in biology and those whose debts to the Bergsonian corpus are partial or even indirect. James Johnstone and Alexis Carrel must be interpreted as applying Bergsonism directly to biology, as must Pierre Lecomte du Noüy (in his studies of the "cicatrization" of wounds.[12] So, for his study of evolutionary rates, must François Meyer. These scientists were significant pioneers in chronobiology: The study of biological time. In English-speaking countries, while *Creative Evolution* made few outright converts, it did persuade many biologists that mechanistic interpretations of neo-Darwinism should be dropped in favor of interpretations (often grouped under the heading of "emergent evolutionism") stressing evolutionary creativity and unpredictability. Among those biologists so influenced are J. Arthur Thompson, Julian S. Huxley, Ronald A. Fisher, C. Lloyd Morgan, Theodosius Dobzhansky, Sewall Wright, and William Morton Wheeler.

While Bergson's critiques of mechanistic concepts and his notions of psychological and biological time would seem to lend themselves naturally to investigations in psychology and biology, his resolute insistence on the first-person standpoint and his consequent determined defense of the reality of the human individual would seem to preclude the application of his ideas to sociology. But while French sociology has largely adhered to its Durkheimian inheritance, there have been significant Bergsonian contributions as well. George Gurvitch's concept of social time is owed directly to Bergson, as are the similar ideas on social and historical time of Pitrim A. Sorokin (though a debt here appears be be also owed by Sorokin to Nicolai Lossky). Daniel Essertier and Emile Lasbax developed explicitly Bergsonian sociologies in the 1920's and 30's, while Pierre Janet, working from a little appreciated side of Bergson's philosophy, developed a system of social behaviorism similar to that of George Herbert Mead. The social psychology of Alfred Schutz was shaped in part by Schutz's Bergsonian affiliation, as, to a lesser degree, was the anthropology of Claude Levi-Strauss. Recently G. B. Milner, in Britain, has found in Bergson the resolution of fundamental dilemmas of anthropology.

Among historians and historiographers we find Adriano Tilgher, who takes from Bergson the notion of the centrality of work in human history, and Lewis Mumford and Eric Veogelin, who derive from Bergson the notion of an "axial period" in human spiritual development. Arnold Toynbee's "challenge-response" model of world history is nourished by the Bergsonian faith in human creativity. In not quite the same context, George Sorel's appropriation of Bergsonian concepts in the formulation of syndicalist theory should not be neglected.

When we pass from Bergson's influence on the sciences to his impact on the arts we find a better known and more generally recognized phenomenon. This is certainly understandable. Not only did Bergson's explorations of time, imagery, dreams, memory suggest to artists fresh directions, new modes of symbolization; they affirmed, in a milieu saturated with scientism and the myth of the machine, the artist's capacity, *via* intuition, to explore reality itself. If creative—and rebellious—artists were drawn to French intuitionism, it was also because that philosophy could scarcely have been better timed or placed to attract them. Paris during Bergson's tenure at the Collège de France was not only the recognized world capital of art, it was the matrix from which post-impressionist art was so explosively to emerge.

In the context of such a ferment of ideas and feelings, theories and counter-theories, the tracing of "influences" becomes an especially difficult affair. Dozens of "isms" were to bloom and fade in Paris between turn of century fauvism and the surrealism of the 1920's and 1930's. Though Bergson seems to have taken part in the formation of the prevailing climate of opinion in Paris, the lines of influence leading from his philosophy to any one "ism" are usually vague, diffuse. An indefinite boundary indeed separates the philosopher here from the *Zeitgeist*. In what follows, therefore, only those figures will be cited for whom a strong case has been made. The inclusion of other figures must be contingent on further—and sceptical—investigation.

Bergson's influence on literature and literary criticism is by far the best documented component of his aesthetic impact. Among the french critics who used Bergsonism to interpret literature are Albert Thibaudet, Charles Du Bos, Georges Poulet, and Charles Péguy. In Britain John Middleton Murray, F. S. Flint, and Thomas Ernest Hulme were Bergsonian literary critics. Hulme made Bergson the source of Anglo-American imagism. Among the writers (novelists, dramatists, poets...) profoundly inspired by Bergson's philosophy are Charles Péguy, Nikos Kazantzakis, George Rostrevor Hamilton, William Faulkner, René Arcos, and Marcel Proust. Other writers for whom a partial Bergsonian influence may plausibly be claimed are Antonio Machado, Virginia Woolf, Eugene Ionesco, André Gide, Alfred Jarry, Osip Mandel'shtam, Jorge Louis Borges, O. V. de Milosz, T. S. Eliot, Robert

Frost, William Golding, Henry Miller, James T. Farrell, Walker Percy, Pedro Salinas, and Wallace Stevens. It would be worth investigating to see if the names of St. John Perse, Gertrude Stein, Thomas Wolfe, or James Joyce might be included here.

Among post-impressionist art movements Bergson's thought received an appreciative but selective reception. Italian futurism (more in the case of Umberto Boccioni than in that of F. T. Marinetti) embraced the forward vector of Bergson's creative evolution while disregarding his stress upon the efficacy of memory and the immortality of the past. Recent scholarship has revealed a Bergsonian ferment in pre-revolutionary Russian aesthetic circles. Russian futurism, acmeism (Nikolai Gumilev, Osip Mandel'shtam), suprematism (Kasimir Malevich), formalism (Victor Shklovsky, Yury Tyanov) and symbolism all avowed a debt to the views expressed in *Creative Evolution* and *An Introduction to Metaphysics*. The situation in Russian artistic circles was in part a response to the aesthetic revolution already taking place in Paris, where Bergson's ideas had challenged "les esprits forts". A partial factor in the formulation of fauvism (as later of surrealism), he was to have a deeper impact on the development of cubism. In the United States the Photo-Secessionists grouped around Alfred Steiglitz regularly discussed Bergson, who was condemned by conservative critics as the source of American post-impressionism. In England the influential art critic Herbert Read remained on certain basic issues an "unrepentant Bergsonian" throughout his career.

It must be pointed out again, at the risk of tedious repetition, that no claim is made in the compiling of these lists that all movements or individuals were shaped in the same way or the same extent by Bergson's intuitionism. If the stream of consciousness novel was profoundly shaped by the central ideas of Bergson (and William James), André Gide seems to have appropriated only certain aspects of Bergson's *Le Rire (Laughter*, 1910). If Surrealism made use primarily of Bergson's treatment of philosophical imagery in *An Introduction to Metaphysics*, post-impressionism generally was able to take inspiration from the (anti-representationalist) critique of spatial representation found in all of Bergson's works.

III

The quarter century between *Creative Evolution* (1907) and *The Two Sources of Morality and Religion* (1932) was a time of relative silence for Bergson. A crippling arthritis, which began in the early 1920's, confined him physically and limited his writing time, in his own words, to "hours, even minutes," per day.[13] *Mind-Energy* (1919) and *The Creative Mind* (1934) are almost exclusively reissues of previously published essays. (Exceptions—and they are important exceptions—are the two prefaces in *The Creative Mind*, which, along with *An Introduction to Metaphysics*, constitute Bergson's Discourse on Method.) *Duration and Simultaneity* (1922), a criticism of Einstein's special theory of relativity, evidences Bergson's long-standing interest in the problems and concepts of modern physics and reveals much about his concepts of physical time and space, concepts which brought him, as physicist Louis de Broglie points out, very close to the basic ideas of quantum physics. Yet *Duration and Simultaneity* is a program piece, a response to specific objections urged at a specific time, and is not a central part of the overall development of his thought. The culmination of Bergsonism is to be found in the expansive religious vision of *The Two Sources of Morality and Religion*, with its distinction between "two religions" and its active, enduring God.

Classical Christian theology has traditionally emphasized the "timeless," i.e. eternal and unchanging, aspects of God. Bergson, by contrast, emphasizes those respects in which God can be understood as active and dynamic. Christian theology has often relied on highly rationalistic proofs of God's existence and nature. For Bergson, however, any proposed proof pertaining to God must depend upon the confirmation provided by mystical experience: mystical experience and, it must be pointed out, its human, social expressions. It is the mystic who achieves the fullest, most immediate awareness (in the broadest sense, an intuition) of the divine. But the object of the mystic's intuition is dynamic, moving Eternity, the source and character of whose creativity must be described as active love. Bergson persistently points out, therefore, that fully attained mystical intuition leads to action and expresses a creative concern for one's fellow man. He also insists that this intuition, which leads to the formulation of the *concepts* through which it can be expressed, is "supra" and not "infra"-rational. It must never be confused with blind irrationality.

If the mystic's message is indeed what Bergson claims that it is, there must be a profound resistance to it on the part of human societies. The true mystic—the moral and religious genius—would draw mankind into the "open society"; men prefer instead the "closed society", whose loyalties they profess and whose existence they defend.

> Never shall we pass from the closed society to the open society, from the city to humanity, by any mere broadening out. The two things are not of the same essence.[14]

The mystic, the prophet, must grapple with and attempt to overcome, so to speak, the moral entropy of society. The difficulties in his way must necessarily be enormous, but *The Two Sources of Morality and Religion* embodies Bergson's belief that human social evolution exhibits the gradual triumph of the open over the closed society. It is clear from Bergson's discussion that this triumph—which is partial, and never absolutely secure—is rendered possible only through the counterpoise of the closed society, which provides both a necessary negation and a field of possibilities for the divine love. Of the major world religions it is Christianity—itself, Bergson well understood, the fulfillment of Judaism—which has most fully embodied an impetus towards the open society and offered a creative ethics to mankind. In the teachings of Jesus and the Christian mystics we find God's love most profoundly fulfilled.

This brief survey of the development of Bergson's thought scarcely does justice to the variety of subjects with which he dealt or the originality of many of his conclusions. The sketch of Bergson, his philosophy and his influence offered above does make clear the basic topics to be covered in this bibliography. It also, along with the descriptions provided of the international "Bergson vogue" of the early decades of this century and the phenomenon of Bergson's constructive influence, helps to suggest some of the problems involved in collecting and organizing the Bergson literature.

IV

The introduction to the first edition of this bibliography contains the following claim:

> This bibliography almost certainly contains the bulk of the Bergson literature, or at least that part of it published in French, English, German, Spanish, Italian, Portuguese, and possibly the Scandinavian languages as well.[15]

The optimism expressed in this passage was based on strong factors: recourse to all previous Bergson bibliographies, to several major libraries, and to numerous standard bibliographic sources. Nonetheless, a decade of further experience calls for several corrections. Since the present edition contains an additional two thousand entries over and above those presented in 1974, and since at least three hundred more incomplete entries still lie, in various stages of disarray, on the bibliographer's desk, it is clear that any claim of completeness should be qualified. This edition contains the bulk of the essentially or exclusively *philosophical* Bergson literature in the major European languages. It possibly does not contain the major portion of the Bergson literature outside of philosophy *per se*: that is, in fields like literature or the arts, or the natural and behavioral sciences. In both cases, philosophical and "extaphilosophical", and particularly in the latter, much remains to be done, in a field which appears inexhaustible.

Several matters of detail concerning this bibliography should also be printed out. For one, no attempt has been made to edit out items which are of doubtful value, or extreme brevity, or which concern Bergson only tangentially or in part. Any one of these might prove useful to some scholar concerned with Bergson or his times. For the same reason, some articles or even quotes have been included simply because they provide valuable sidelights on Bergson's ideas or the general impression conveyed by them. (Some quotes have been presented simply because the author does not think a sense of humor should be excluded even from bibliographic research.)

While all relevant materials encountered in the course of compiling this reference work have been included, certain classes of entries have been left largely incomplete. No effort has been made to locate the majority of newspaper or magazine articles concerning Bergson or his philosophy, though some of these might prove interesting. The same is true for reviews, particularly those dealing with the secondary literature. Unpublished articles or talks on Bergson are in general not cited unless mentioned in other bibliographic sources. Nor has there been an attempt to include previously unpublished letters by, to, or concerning Bergson. It has, however, been possible to add some previously published Bergson correspondence to the already full collection of correspondence published recently in France (Cf. below, *Mélanges*). It is this researcher's impression that quite a bit of Bergson's correspondence remains to be collected and published. He has found dozens of unpublished letters by and to Bergson sequestered in libraries, archives, and personal collections. In this context it is useful to point out the existence of the Bergson Library (Le Fonds Bergson in the Bibliothèque Jaques Doucet, 8, place du Panthéon, Paris, France) which contains Bergson's papers and private library along with translations of his writings, a collection of secondary literature, and memorabilia.

A few words should be said concerning the relative size of the present work. The Bergson bibliography published in 1913 by Columbia University contains 496 items, 86 by Bergson. The Bergson bibliography of 1941, edited by Alfredo Coviello and published in Argentina, contains 1056 items, of which Bergson is the author of 198. Since 1941 several Bergson bibliographies have appeared (Cf. Index: Sources Used in Compiling This Bibliography). Most of these are small in comparison with the above two volumes. The bibliography published by the *Revue Internationale de Philosophie* in 1950 contains 215 items; the bibliographies published in *Les Etudes Bergsoniennes*, Volume 4, contain 205 items. The exception is the bibliography in Rose-Marie Mossé-Bastide's *Bergson éducateur* (1955), which contains 1796 items, 288 of which are by Bergson. By contrast, while the first edition of the present bibliography contains 4381 items (472 by Bergson) the present edition contains 6396—6662 if translations, which are not numbered in the text, are included. (It should be noted here that while items are included for 1984 and 1985, the bibliography for these years is significantly incomplete, while items for 1982 and 1983 will no doubt continue to surface. These gaps are due in large measure to the need to shift from the task of collecting the subject matter to that of processing it.)

Numbers by themselves provide only the most abstract indication of quality or usefulness. But there are other factors, beyond the quantitative, which should be singled out. It has been possible to correct and complete many erroneous and/or incomplete entries found in earlier bibliographies. This is particularly relevant to the Coviello bibliography, which contains many incomplete, misspelled, or otherwise enigmatic items. (A concerted effort has been made—largely through work in the Latin American collection at the University of Texas at Austin—to include as much of the Latin American Bergson literature as possible. The bibliographer can only record his frustration at not being able to accomplish more along these lines.[16] It has also been possible to include items from categories poorly represented previously: masters theses and doctoral dissertations (particularly, though not exclusively, in English); translations of works by Bergson; psychology journals; literary sources; general humanities and sociology bibliographic sources.

Of the previous Bergson bibliographies only one (Columbia University, 1913) contains annotations of Bergson's writings. Only one contains annotations of items concerning Bergson. This is the bibliographic material published in the *Giornale di metafisica* in 1959 and subsequently in the proceedings of the Congrès Bergson. The 1974 bibliography was therefore the first to attempt to annotate items both by and about Bergson. But (to deal first with the secondary literature) the results were not entirely satisfactory. Annotations were relatively infrequent, and, when provided, were often brief. Important items were passed over; less important items were explicated. The present edition attempts to make up for this unevenness by adding a number of annotations to the contents of the first edition, by generously annotating newly-added items, and by improving previous annotations where possible. Cross-referencing has also been added in order to point out important items or conceptual relationships. Once again the results are far from perfect. Many items remain unannotated, unreferenced—a fact regretted by this editor. But at least it can be said that the present edition provides a far more satisfactory entrance to the secondary literature than its predecessor. It should be pointed out, in connection with cross-referencing, that the index to this bibliography, because of its structure, implicitly cross-references many writers and concepts. That is, under an author's name are included not only his or her writings but reviews of and responses to his or her writings or ideas. This method of indexing is somewhat cumbersome. But it has the merit of focusing networks of and opinions which would otherwise be scattered and, hence, more likely to be overlooked.

The situation with regard to the annotation and cross-referencing of items written by Bergson is similar to that involving the secondary literature: similar, though not identical. As is often not the case with the secondary literature, there is no difficulty in gaining access to Bergson's writings. This ease of access is due to the availability of the centenary edition of his works (first published 1959, cited below as *Edition du Centenaire*) and the more recent *Mélanges* (1972) which includes *Durée et simultanéité* and a translation of Bergson's Latin thesis as well as a remarkably complete collection of correspondence, reviews, talks and articles.[17] The present bibliography presents all items included in *Mélanges* and the *Edition du Centenaire*, plus some minor items (primarily letters and translations) by Bergson not included there.

Annotation of the primary literature in the first edition was extensive, covering all major works and explaining the content of many letters, reviews, talks, etc. The same incompleteness and unevenness present in the annotation of the first edition secondary literature was evident here too, however. The present bibliography therefore expands the annotations of Bergson's major works, while adding annotations to many of his less well known essays. It adds cross-references where these appear particularly useful. The result is a far more adequate account of Bergson's thought: an introduction to his philosophy which, at the same time, explains many of the debates evident in the secondary literature.

In matters of punctuation, capitalization, and form *The MLA Style Sheet*, Second Edition, has been followed here as in the original edition. This has provided consistency, but has necessitated making changes in numerous entries. For example, colons have been substituted for commas, dashes, semicolons, and other punctuations which separate titles and subtitles. This has been done even in the "borderline cases", in which it is questionable whether the latter part of title is a subtitle or not, e.g., in cases where a title is followed not by a subtitle in the ordinary sense, but by dates. In languages other than French, English, German, Italian, Spanish, or Portuguese, however, entries have been left in the form in which they have been found. This includes Swedish, Danish, Dutch, Russian, Czech, Polish, Rumanian, Finnish, Japanese, Latvian, Arabic, Hebrew and Turkish language entries. Other deviations from MLA conventions are the result of efforts to achieve visual clarity. (For example, abbreviations like "p." or "pp." are sometimes included in order to distinguish page numbers from year, issue, or volume numbers.) All entries, both in the section containing items by Bergson and in the section containing items about him, are arranged in chronological order annually, and alphabetically within any given year. Throughout the bibliography titles beginning with Bergson's name (e.g. Enrico Bergson, Henri Bergson, M. Bergson, Professor Bergson) are alphabetized under 'B'.

It might well be thought that bibliographic research is tedious. The clerical labor necessary to render a bibliography as precise and as extensive as possible is certainly done without exhilaration. But the study of intellectual history, so deeply involved in bibliography, provides a real and persistent fascination. The expressions of Bergson's intuitions in philosophy, the arts, the sciences have been extraordinarily diverse. The fate of his ideas has often been surprising, often ironic. The extent to which his ideas have been utilized—often, utilized and forgotten as such—continues to strike this researcher as remarkable.

But in Bergson's case this usefulness is intended, is an expected result of his philosophical method. No less than Sir Francis Bacon, René Descartes, or Gottfried W. Leibniz, he offered his way of doing philosophy as one which can lead to new discoveries. No less than his friend William James, therefore, he believed in fruitfulness as a criterion of truth. A metaphysician and, in the broadest sense, an idealist, he was also in the broadest sense a positivist and a verificationist as well. In his case the history of ideas bears on the very heart of the Bergsonian logic, and on the truth or falsehood of his philosophy as well.[18]

I would like to thank North Texas State University for research grant aid, which has made it possible to employ research assistants and utilize interlibrary loans. Without this help the present Bibliography would have been much delayed and far less extensive. Mr. Joseph P. Lowry, Mr. Stephen Da Silva, and Mr. David Williams are due a vote of thanks for their work as research assistants. I would also like to thank Professor Thomas Preston, Dean of Arts and Sciences at North Texas State University, for financial assistance which has helped defray word-processor typing expenses. Thanks are also du to Cathy Copeland, secretary of the North Texas State University Department of Philosophy, for her help typing bibliographic entries and for her omnipresent cheerfulness. Ms. Kathryn Bode and Ms. Renate Roberts are due my gratitude for the patience and tenacity with which they mastered the IBM Personal Editor software system and transferred this mammoth manuscript to computer discs. Thanks go to Francis Baumli for help with 'typos' and for bibliographic suggestions. Finally, I wish to thank Milič Čapek and Mary Markovsky for their bibliographic suggestions, most but not all of which are presented below.

Pete A. Y. Gunter
Department of Philosophy
North Texas State University
Denton, Texas 76203

Notes

1. John Dewey, "Preface." *A Contribution to a Bibliography of Henri Bergson* (New York: Columbia University Press, 1912), xii.

2. Henri Bergson, "An Introduction to Metaphysics" in *The Creative Mind* (New York: Philosophical Library, 1946), p. 191.

3. Henri Bergson, "Introduction" *Matter and Memory* (London: Allen & Unwin, 1950), xviii.

4. Ibid.

5. The reference here is to historical, not to evolutionary time. Insect societies have evolved, and in *this* sense may be said to have histories.

6. Henri Bergson, *Creative Evolution*. Intro. Pete A. Y. Gunter (Lanham, Maryland: University Press of America, 1984), p. 194.

7. Bergson thus contends that an intuition, which is qualitative in nature, may lead to new quantitative concepts. Cf. on this point esp. Jean Milet, *Bergson et le calcul infinitésimal* (Paris: Presses Universitaires de France, 1974), 184.

8. The appropriation of Bergson's thought was not, as the above remarks might suggest, limited to those in the sciences or, as remarks made below might indicate, to those in the arts. Among those in philosophy significantly indebted to Bergson are: William James, Alfred North Whitehead, Samuel Alexander, Gabriel Marcel, Edouard Le Roy, Maurice Merleau-Ponty, Henry Nelson Wieman, and Max Scheler.

9. The case Piaget-Bergson is both complex and paradoxical. Piaget notes that he derived the idea for a genetic epistemology from Bergson, but was to revolt strongly against the Bergsonian idea that logic and mathematics can not be applied to life. Cf. Jean Piaget, "Lettre." *Revue de Theologie et de Philosophie*, 9, No. 1, 1959, 44-47.

10. Henri Ellenberger, *The Discovery of the Unconscious* (New York: Basic Books, 1970), 932 pp.

11. In an extremely special respect the name of Sigmund Freud might be added to this list. Freud was to use certain of Bergson's ideas to complete his explanation of laughter (i. e. of wit). One might wonder, also, whether Freud's metapsychology, with its distinction between *eros* and *thanatos* owed anything to Bergson's analogous distinction between life and entropy.

12. Pierre Lecomte du Noüy was urged to the study of physiological time by Alexis Carrel, then his immediate superior in the French medical service. Carrel was an avowed Bergsonian.

13. Floris Delattre, "Les Dernières Années de Bergson." *Revue Philosophique de la France et de l'Etranger*, 131, Nos. 2-3, 1941, 125-138.

14. Henri Bergson, *The Two Sources of Morality and Religion* (Garden City, New York: Doubleday, 1954), p. 267.

15. Pete A. Y. Gunter, "Introduction." *Henri Bergson: A Bibliography* (Bowling Green, Ohio: Philosophy Documentation Center, 1974), p. 11.

16. A full-scale account of Bergson's influence in Latin America has never been attempted. What follows here, as in the rest of this bibliography, is thus an admittedly incomplete but suggestive list of Latin American thinkers who significantly took Bergson into account in their thinking and writing: Mexico: Antonio Caso, José Vasconcelos, Joaquín Xirau, Samuel Ramos; Brasil: Romano Galeffi, Candido Mota Filho, Sílvio de Macedo, Leonardo Van Acker; Argentina: Alejandro Korn, Francisco Romero, Alfredo Coviello, Coriolino Alberini, Angel Vasallo; Peru: Alejandro O. Deustua, Mariano Iberico; Puerto Rico: Roberto Murillo Zamora; Uruguay: Carlos Vaz Ferreira. Those who would add to this list are cordially invited to do so.

17. Henri Bergson. *Oeuvres*. Textes Annotés par André Robinet. Intro. Henri Gouhier (Paris: Presses Universitaires de France, 1959) 1602 pp. Henri Bergson. *Mélanges*. Ed. André Robinet (Paris: Presses Universitaires de France, 1972), 1692 pp.

18. On this point Cf. the writings of Milič Čapek and Vittorio Mathieu. Cf. also my "Introduction" to *Bergson and the Evolution of Physics* (Knoxville: University of Tennessee Press, 1969), pp. 3-42.

Erratum

In the last stage of preparing this manuscript for publication, a numbering error was found in the text. Number 2146 has been changed to 2146-56 to remedy this error. Numbers 2147 through 2156 were not used; no information has been omitted.

PART II

WORKS BY BERGSON

1877

1   "Solution d'un problème mathématique." *Nouvelles Annales Mathématiques*, 11,
17, 1878, 266-276; *Ecrits et paroles*,1, 3-9; *Mélanges*, 247-256. This is
Bergson's solution of a mathematical problem, for which he won first prize in
the "Concours générale de 1877" pour la classe de mathématiques élementaires."

1878

2   "Essay Written at the Ecole Normale. 1878-1881." In Jean Guitton, *La Vocation
de Bergson*. Paris: Gallimard, 1960, 229-241. This essay deals with the relationship between an author and his audience. "A son insu et sans le savoir, l'auteur
pense pour le publique, écrit pour les habiles. Comme auteur, il tient compte
des lettres; homme, il relève avant tout de l'humanité tout entière."

3   "Essay Written at the Ecole Normale. 1878-1881." In Jean Guitton, *La Vocation
de Bergson*. Paris: Gallimard, 1960, 242-255. This essay examines the weaknesses of the "penetrating mind." "Un esprit pénétrant peut ne point arriver à
la vérité... Il n'a pas encore cette souplesse, cette mobilité par lequel nous
sortons un instant de nous-mêmes, et pensons par autrui" (p. 255).

4   "Sur Un Problème de Pascal." *Etude sur Pascal et les géomètres contemporaines,
suivi de plusieurs notes scientifiques et littéraires*. Ed. Adolphe Desboves. Paris:
Delagrave, 1878, 129-130. Also in *Mélanges*, 254-255. This is a solution by
Bergson of a mathematical problem first posed by Pascal.

1882

5   "La Spécialité." Angers: Lachèse et Dolbeau, 1882, 16. Also in *Journal de Maine-
et-Loire*, No. 182, 4 août 1882, 264; M. Antier. *Le Lycée David d'Angers
depuis ses origines jusqu'à nos jours*. Angers: Editions de l'Ouest, 1947, 137-
142; *Ecrits et paroles*, 1, 10-16; fiMélanges, 257-264. In this talk, given at the
distribution of prizes at Angers on August 3, 1882, Bergson discusses the dangers
of specialization.

1883

6   *Extraits de Lucrèce: Avec un commentaire des notes et une étude sur la poésie,
la philosophie et la langue de Lucrèce*. Paris: Delagrave, 1883, 159. Also in
Ecrits et paroles, 1, 17-56 (L'Avantpropos); *Mélanges*, 265-310. This is
Bergson's translation of Lucretius' philosophical poem *De Rerum Natura*, with
commentary.

7 *Lucrèce: Extraits de Lucrèce: Avec un commentaire, des notes et une étude sur la poésie, la philosophie, la physique, le texte et la langue de Lucrèce.* 2e éd. Paris: Delagrave, 1955, x-viii, 160.

Translations

"Lucrecio." *Enciclopedia de educación.* Trans. Emílio Oribe. Montevideo. Enero 1946, 3-93.

The Philosophy of Poetry. Ed., trans., and in part recast by Wade Baskin. New York: Wisdom Library, 1959, 83. This work consists of Bergson's notes on Lucretius' poetry and on the nature of poetry in general. It does not contain Bergson's translation of Lucretius.

8 "Traduction de l'ouvrage de James Sully. *Les Illusions des sens et de l'esprit.*" Paris: Ballière et Cie., 1883. There is in this edition no mention of Bergson's name as translator. For notes concerning Bergson's translation Cf. *Mélanges*, 311.

1884

9 "Le Rire: De qui rit-on? Pourquoi rit-on?" *Moniteur du Puy-de-Dôme*, 21 février 1884. Also in *Mélanges*, 313-315. This is a journalistic account of Bergson's talk which is signed P.M. Here for the first time Bergson discusses the nature and causes of laughter. Cf. his *Laughter (Le Rire)* 1900.

1885

10 "Cours à la Faculté de Clermont-Ferrand." *Bulletin Mensuel de l'Académie de Clermont*, No. 77, décembre 1885, 147. Also in *Mélanges*, 332. This is an outline of two courses taught by Bergson. The course on the history of philosophy included Aristotle, Malebranche, and Spinoza. The course on general philosophical topics included discussions of matter, mind, the principal proofs of God's existence, and basic systems of ethics, including utilitarianism.

11 "La Politesse." *Palmarès du Lycée Clermont-Ferrand, distribution des prix du 30 juillet 1885.* Ed. Colbert. 1885. Also in *Moniteur du Puy-de-Dôme*, 6 août 1885; *Mélanges*, 317-332. For later version Cf. entry under 1892.

1886

12 "Cours à la Faculté de Clermont-Ferrand." *Bulletin Mensuel de l'Académie de Clermont*, No. 86, septembre 1886, 40-41. Also in *Mélanges*, 342. This is an outline of two courses taught by Bergson. The course on general philosophical topics included lectures on psychology, the attributes of God, scepticism, and idealism. The course on the history of philosophy included lectures on Aristotle's ethics and politics, Stoicism and Epicureanism, modern British empiricism, and ninteenth-century French philosophy.

13 "Une Inspection générale." Dauphin Meunier. "Une Leçon de M. Henri Bergson en 1886." *Le Figaro*, Supplément littéraire, 21 février 1914, p. 3, col. 3-4.

Also in *Mélanges*, 341. This is a brief mention of a lecture by Bergson on
pessimism.

14   "De La Simulation inconscient dans l'état d'hypnotisme." *Revue Philosophique de
        la France et de l'Etranger*, 22, 69-75; *Ecrits et paroles*, 1, 69-75; *Mélanges*,
        333-341. This is a sceptical critique of thought-reading experiments carried on
        by hypnotized subjects. Bergson suggests that hypnotized subjects may be able
        to read, print reflected in their hypnotists' cornea, and use their own eyes as
        magnifiers. (Cf., in the secondary literature, F. W. H. Myers, 1887, 1954)

1887

15   "Cours à la Faculté de Clermont-Ferrand." *Bulletin Mensuel de l'Académie de
        Clermont*, No. 98, septembre 1887, 40. Also in *Mélanges*, 343. This is an
        outline of two courses taught by Bergson. The course on general philosophical
        topics included lectures on psychophysics, habits, freewill and determinism,
        and philosophical method. The course on the history of philosophy included
        lectures on F. Bacon, N. Malebranche, and G. W. Leibniz.

1888

16   "Cours à la Faculté de Clermont-Ferrand." *Bulletin Mensuel de l'Académie de
        Clermont*, No. 108, juillet 1888, 363. Also in *Mélanges*, 345. These two lectures,
        one on philosophical psychology and the other on the history of philosophy,
        were never given.

1889

17   *Essai sur les données immédiates de la conscience*. Paris: Félix Alcan, 1889, viii,
        185 (Bibliothèque de philosophie contemporaine).

        The first of Bergson's major works, the *Essai sur les données immédiates de
        la conscience (Time and Free Will*, in English translation) contains most of the
        basic ideas developed in the course of his intellectual carreer. In particular, it
        introduces his all-important distinction between inner duration and space. Inner
        duration is qualitative, heterogeneous and dynamic. No two of its moments are
        identical, and its future states are unpredictable. By contrast, space is quantitative,
        homogeneous and static. Its parts are identical, while states described by it are
        in principle predictable. In duration we live, act and are free; in space we behave
        mechanically, "are acted" instead of acting, and thus neglect our freedom.

        Unfortunately, Bergson teaches, both ordinary and scientific modes of thought
        tend to "spatialize" the dynamics of inner duration, depicting *durée* as composed
        of static elements subjected to quasi-mechanical laws and therefore as lacking
        any substantial cohesion or wholeness. Thus we come to view the human self
        (Bergson here has 19th century associationist psychology in mind.) as a sort of
        complex machine for grinding out thoughts and behavior.

        To grasp the fallacy behind this viewpoint, Bergson insists, it is only necessary
        to see how completely it is based on a confusion between outer, spatial distinctions

and the actual qualitative nature of perception. The *Essai* is a detailed and exhaustive assault on what we might term "the dogma of quantitative perception:" that is, the deeply engrained idea that experience whether "inner" or "outer", consists of quantitative units or parts. It is at the same time a concerted effort to recover the immediate data of consciousness: the vague, qualitative, fugitive yet fundamental data which ground perception and of which, so to speak, we are made.

The first chapter of the *Essai* consists of a painstaking examination of the data of experience, from deep-seated psychic states (desire, hope, joy, sorrow) to "outer" sensations like muscular effort, pressure, and sensations of sight. This phenomenology of perception reveals, beneath a crust of spatialized representations and attitudes, a common qualitative character. Bergson's survey of perception concludes with a critique of psychophysics, a branch of the theory of perception which treats visual contents as quantitative in nature. (Thus, one white surface would be perceived as twice or three times as bright as another and all perceptual differences would be presumed to be additive). What the psychophysicist would interpret as a quantitative difference (expressed in terms of the Weber-Fechner law) is for Bergson qualitative difference which admits of no mathematical formulation.

In his second chapter Bergson, having cleared away the conceptual debris which have concealed the true data of experience, prepares to demonstrate the crucial contrast between inner duration and space. His demonstration begins, perhaps unexpectedly, with an analysis of mathematical (i.e., arithmetic) thought. We forget, Bergson holds, because we exibit the results of such elementary operations as addition or subtraction in space, that we have *performed* these operations in a subjective and qualitative duration. Typically, while the results are clear, distinct and static, we overlook the dynamic and continuous process which has brought them into being. The conclusion which Bergson draws from what is in fact a lengthy and difficult account of mathematical constructions is that all notions of "quantitative multiplicity" are derived, consciously or unconsciously, from the representation of space.

Once the connection between quantity and space is made clear, Bergson finds it possible to explore (for the first time, he believes) our inner, purely psychological duration. Here we discover:

...below the numerical multiplicity of conscious states, a qualitative multiplicity; below the self with well-defined states, a self in which *succeeding each other* means *melting into one another* and forming an organic whole. (TFW 128)

Inner duration exhibits no sharp (i.e. spatial) breaks from one moment to the next. Its components (our different memories, passions, sensations) interpenetrate and can not be sharply distinguished. Duration can therefore not be measured. And we should not expect that its progress should be predictable.

The notion of unpredictability leads Bergson, in his third and final chapter, to confront the time-honored and vexed question of human freedom. That the question of freedom should have been "vexed" is, Bergson asserts, not surprising. Basic questions of freedom have unwittingly been framed in terms of space and not in terms of duration. The very concept of psychological determinism is imported from theoretical (i.e. Newtonian) physics into psychology, and hence depends upon a spatialized, mechanical model for its intelligibility. It is no wonder that philosophers and psychologists persuaded by this model have described the self as "determined" by its states, as if the self were being pressed by "forces" acting on it from without. But the "parts" on the self are not so many external forces. They *are* the self. Moreover, they interpenetrate, so that each is changed by the others, and all taken together constitute a "whole". To say that we are "compelled" by our psychological states or by psychological forces (if these states or forces cohere deeply enough with our character) is thus to say that we are self-determined.

But there is another "spatializing" fallacy, commited by both opponents and defenders of freedom, which stands in the way. That is, the free act has been viewed as a choice between pre-existing alternatives, much in the way that a road is pictured as divided and leading off in two contrasting pre-existing directions. This abstract, spatial metaphor in fact tells us very little about the human self, which lives and develops by means of its very hesitations, until its free acts finally emerge naturally and without hesitation. That is, our freedom is more radical than has been assumed. We do not, in the profound issues of our lives, choose between possibilities: we *create* possibilities. In the free act we create ourselves; and this is a very different thing from saying that we merely choose, so to speak, between two previously determined alternatives.

It is clear that Bergson does not believe that free acts in this sense are very common. Some persons, he believes, live their entire lives without expressing themselves in any profound sense and hence without having known true freedom. The rest of us behave, for the most part, as creatures of physical and social habit: being "acted" instead of acting, living through our social and conventional, rather than through our profound selves. Only rarely are we self-possessed to such an extent that our acts are substantially free. Only then can our acts be said to derive from a cumulative qualitative progress which, by its very nature, escapes prediction. Bergson believes that the possibility of this freedom must be grounded on the distinction between qualitative, heterogenous, nonrepetitive duration and its "refraction" by means of language into a homogeneous, static, measurable space.

18   *Essai sur les données immédiates de la conscience.* Pref. Albert Thibaudet. Evreux: C. Herissey, 1927, xii, 295. (L'Intelligence. No. 6)

19   *Essai sur les données immédiates de la conscience.* Hersg. von Hans Kinkel. Bielefeld: Velhagen und Klasing, 1928, xx, 138. (Velhagen and Klasings Sammlung französich und engl. Schulausgaben. Prosateurs français, Vol. 238)

20   *Essai sur lès données immédiates de la conscience.* Genève: Skira, 1946, 190.

21   *Essai sur les données immédiates de la conscience.* Paris: Presses Universitaires de France, 1948, viii, 184. A new edition. (Bibliothèque de Philosophie contemporaine)

22   *Essai sur les données immédiates de la conscience* in *Oeuvres.* Ed. André Robinet. Paris: Presses Universitaires de France, 1959, 1-156.

23   *Essai sur les données immédiates de la conscience. .* Paris: Presses Universitaires de France, 1982, 180. (Quadrige, 31)

Translations

Ensayo sobre los datos inmediatos de la conciencia. Trans. Domingo Barnés. Madrid: Francisco Beltrán, 1919, 184. (Biblioteca Moderna de Filosofía y Ciencias Sociales)

Ensayo sobre los datos inmediatos de la conciencia. 2nd Ed. Trans. Domingo Barnés. Madrid: F. Beltrán, 1925, 192.

Ensayo sobre los datos inmediatos de la conciencia. 2e Ed. Trans. Domingo Barnés. Madrid: Francisco Beltran, 1944, 192. (Biblioteca Moderna de Filosofía y Ciencias Sociales)

Ensayo sobre los datos inmediatos de la conciencia, con un juicio critico de Mario A. Silva García. Montevideo: C. García y cía, 1944, 288.

"El Sentimento de lo Bello." *Revista de Ideas Estéticas,* 1, No. 3, 1943, 138-142. This is a passage from Chapter 1 of *L'Essai.* Trans. M.C. Iracheta.

Los Sentimientos Estéticos: La Gracia." Revista de Ideas Estéticas, 1, No. 3, 1943, 136-138. This is a passage from Chapter 1 of *L'Essai.* Trans. M.C. Iracheta.

O bezpośrednich danych świadomości: z upoważniena autora przelozyla K. Bobrowska. Warzawa: Wende, 1913, xi, 167.

Jikan to jiiyû. Trans. Yoshio Takeuchi. Tokyo: Kawade shobô, 1955, 225.

Jikan to jiyû. Trans. Hirai Hiroyuki. Tokyo: Hakusui-sha, 1974, 235.

Jikan to jiyû. Aristoteles no bashoron. Trans. Hirai Hiroyuki, Muraji Yoshinari, and Hirokawa Yoichi. Tokyo: Hakusuisha, 1965, 342. (...zenshû, No. 1) This is a translation of the *Essai* and *Quid Aristoteles de loco senserit.*

Jikan to jiyû. Sôzôteki shinka. Trans. Nakamura Yûjiro et al. Tokyo: Kawade shobo, 1967, 422. This is a translation of the *Essai* and *L'Évolution créatrice.*

Saggio sui dati immediati della conscienza. "Traduzione e Note Cura di Niso Ciusa." Torino: S.E.I., 1951, xxviii, 85.

Saggio sui dati immediati della concienza: A cura di Vittorio Mathieu. Torino: Casa Paravia, 1951, xviii, 189. (Biblioteca di Filosofia e Pedagogia)

Saggio sui dati immediati della conscienza. Trans. Giuseppe Cavallaro. Roma: Signorelli, 1957, 99. (Classici della filosofia)

Saggio sui dati immediati della conscienza. Trans. G. Bartoli. Torino: Boringhieri, 1964, 231. (Enciclopedia di autori classici, 85)

Suur'un bilâ vasite mûtalari hakkinda. Trans. Halil Nimetullah. Istanbul: Devlet Matbaasi, 1928.

Suur'un dořudan dořuya verileri. Trans. Mustafa Sekip tunc. Istanbul: Millî eītum basṁevi, 1950, 242. (Dünya edebiyatṅdan tercümeler. Fransiz klâsikleri: 180)

Time and Free Will: An Essay on the Immediate Data of Consciousness. Auth. Trans. F.L. Pogson. London: Swan Sonnenschein and Co., Ltd.; New York: Macmillan, 1910, xxiii, 252 (Library of Philosophy).

Time and Free Will: An Essay on the Immediate Data of Consciousness. Auth. Trans. F.L. Pogson. New York: Harper. 1960, xiii, 262. (Harper Torchbacks, TB1021).

Time and Free Will: An Essay on the Immediate Data of Consciousness. Auth. Trans. F.L. Pogson. London: G. Allen & Unwin; New York: Humanities Press, 1971, xxvii, 252. (Muirhead Library of Philosophy).

Vremia i svoboda voli. Trans. C.I. Hessen. Moscow: Русская ммсль, 1910, 238.

Vremia i svoboda voli: S prilozheniem traktata togo zhe avtora Vvedenie v metafiziku: Trans. S. Hessen and M. Grünwald. St. Petersburg: Russkaia mysl', 1912, 238.

Ý-thúrc luân. Trans. L.M. Cao-Văn-Luân. Hué: Nha xuát-bán Dai-Hoc, 1962, 154. This is a Vietnamese translation.

Zeit und Freiheit: Eine Abhandlung über die unmittelbaren Bewussteinstatsachen. Auth. Trans. Paul Fohr. *Jena: Diederichs, 1911, 189.*

Zeit und Freiheit: Eine Abhandlung über die unmittelbaren Bewusstseinstatsachen. Meisenheim am Glan: West Kultuverlag Hain, 1949, 200.

24   *Quid Aristoteles de loco Senserit.* Thesim Facultati Litterarum Parisiensi, proponebat H. Bergson, Scholae Normalis olim Alumnus, Lutetiae Parisorum, Edebat F. Alcan, Bibliopola, MDCCCLXXXIX, 82.

This is an analysis and criticism of Aristotle's concept of "place".

While most modern philosophers tend to distinguish physical bodies from an empty space which contains them, Aristotle combined these two concepts. The result is the concept of place defined as the inner surface of a body, insofar as it contains another body. (Thus, for example, if a body is in the air, the air—its interior surface— is the body's place.) Rather than deal satisfactorily with the concept of space, Bergson concludes, Aristotle seeks with his concept of place to cut short discussions dealing with the concept of space. He thus arrives at paradoxical concepts of place which do not appear defensible. Bergson's thesis on Artistotle was never included by him among his major works. It is significant, however, for the light it casts on the *Essai* (*Time and Free Will*) as well as on Bergson's understanding of Plato, G. W. Leibniz, I. Kant and, of course, Aristotle. (Cf., in the secondary literature, J. M. Staudenmaier, 1964, and C. J. Chambers, 1974.)

Translations

"L'Idée de lieu chez Aristotle." Trans. Robert Mossé-Bastide. *Les Etudes Bergsoniennes*, 2, 29-104.

"L'Idée de lieu chez Aristotle." Trans. Robert Mossé-Bastide in *Mélanges*. Ed. André Robinet. Paris: Presses Universitaires de France, 1972, 2-56.

"Aristotle's Concept of Place," in *Ancients and Moderns*. Ed. and Trans. John K. Ryan. Washington: Catholic University of America, 1970, 12-72.

Jikan to jiyû. Aristoteles no bashoron. Trans. Hirai Hiroyuki, Muraji Yoshinari, and Hirokowa Yoichi. Tokyo: Hakusuisha, 1965, 342. (...zenshû, No. 1) This is a translation of the *Essai* and *Quid Aristotles de loco senserit.*

1891

25   "Compte rendu de *La Genèse de l'idée de temps* de G. Guyau." *Revue Philosophique de la France et de l'Etranger*, 31, No. 1, janvier 1891, 185-190. Also in *Ecrits et paroles*, 1, 75-82; *Mélanges*, 349-356. This is a thorough analysis and criticism of Guyau's thesis that the concept of time is derived from that of space.

26   "Lettre à L. Dauriac: 6 juillet 1891." *Ecrits et paroles*, 3, 196 (résumé). Also in *Mélanges*, 356; Bibl. Victor-Cousin. This letter is concerned with Dauriac's *Croyance et réalité* and his concept of substance.

27 "Lettre à Félix Ravaisson: 2 novembre 1891." *Revue de Métaphysique et de Morale*, 45, No. 2, avril 1938, 195-196. Also in *Mélanges*, 357. Here Bergson thanks Ravaisson for a copy of an article on pedagogy.

1892

28 "La Politesse." *Palmarès du Lycée Henri-IV, distribution des prix du 30 juillet 1892*, 17-27. Also in *Ecrits et paroles*, 1, 57-68; *Mélanges*, 317-332.

29 *Discours sur la politesse*. Paris: Editions Colbert, 1945, 45.

1895

30 "Le Bon Sens et les études classiques: Discours prononcé lors de la distribution du Concours général, 30 juillet 1895." *Palmarès général*, 5-17. Also: *Concours général. Distribution des prix, année 1895*. Paris: Delalain, 1895, 5; *Le Bon Sens et les études classiques*. Clermont-Ferrand: L'Epervier, 1947, 74. Suivi d'un propos par Blaise Romeyer; "Bon Sens et justice." *La Nef*, 4, No. 32, juillet 1947, 61-72; *Mélanges*, 359-372. In this eassay Bergson considers what we ought to mean when we say that someone has "good sense," as opposed to mere "common sense." There are many similarities between "good sense" and what Bergson later came to identify as "intuition." (Cf., in the secondary literature, F. Fabre Luce de Gruson, 1959.)

Translation

"El buen sentido y los estudios clásicos." Trans. Armando D. Delucchi. *Revista de Filosofia*, (Argentina) 22, Nos. 12-13, 1963, 83-92.

31 "Lettre à O. Gréard: 15 avril 1895." *Ecrits et paroles*, 1, 83. Also in *Mélanges*, 359. The definition of "bon sens" (good sense) is discussed in this letter.

1896

32 "Cours sur Descartes." Rose-Marie Mossé-Bastide. *Bergson éducateur*. Paris: Presses Universitaires de France, 1955, 336-337. Also in *Mélanges*, 374. This is a general description by Bergson of a course taught by him concerning the philosophy of René Descartes.

33 *Matière et mémoire: Essai sur la relation du corps avec l'esprit*. Paris: Félix Alcan, 1896, iii, 279. (Bibliothèque de philosophie contemporaine)

Matière et mémoire "Matter and Memory", as Ian Alexander states, is the "bedrock of Bergsonism." The most central and also the most difficult of Bergson's works, it prolongs the essential insights of the *Essai "Time and Free Will)* while attempting to resolve some of that work's most serious difficulties. While the *Essai* had probed the character of perception and of the inner self with profound originality, it had driven an almost Cartesian wedge between duration and space: between the inner self and its world, between mind and body. The goal of *Matter and Memory* is to overcome this gap by developing, at once, a new theory of perception (mind-object) and of mind-body relationships. On the basis of this theory both mind and body and perceptual awareness and matter will be shown to have common characteristics and to be coherently relatable.

The first chapter of *Matter and Memory* explores the nature of perception, but from a "practical" standpoint: in terms of our manipulation of and adaptation to the world around us. ("Failure to study perception on these terms", Bergson holds, has prejudiced previous theories of perception, whether realist or idealist.) Our actual experience of the world, Bergson states, is of "objects" which are neither perfectly objective nor entirely subjective. He terms these entities "images", meaning by this to suggest that they have both pictorial (perspectival) and factual (objective) characteristics.

The pictorial, perspectival aspect of the world is, Bergson asserts, our own contribution. Largely the result of our sense organs, which eliminate characters of things which do not interest us and accentuate those characteristics which do, the pictorial character of "images" (desks, tables, chairs, trees) has its roots in the pragmatism of the observer. The objective side of the world, however, derives from the things themselves. Idealists, concentrating on the human contribution to ordinary perception, have concluded that the world is subjective, mind-dependent. Realists, concentrating on the objectivity of the world as revealed in ordinary perception, have asserted the existence of "matter" underlying the images encountered in perception, and have conceived matter on the model of the distinct images encountered there in terms of distinct objects, "atoms").

Failure both to recognize the inherently ambiguous nature of the "objects" of ordinary experience and to clearly distinguish the very different contributions made by the observer and the observed, has led according to Bergson to serious difficulties. Both idealism and realism, from their different perspectives, have paradoxically concluded that the world is experienced as subjective: idealism explicitly, realism implicitly, through its belief that the data of perception are first experienced as subjective, and are then "projected" onto the world.

The way out of this labyrinth, Bergson concludes, involves a new distinction between "pure perception" and "pure memory". In "pure perception", which underlies and grounds ordinary perception, we are in direct contact with the pulsations of physical matter. In "pure memory" we are aware of consciousness *per se*" a conservative, dynamic, creative existence whose rhythms are more prolonged than those of matter. Matter and memory, though both are present in ordinary perception, are very different in character, and can be studied separately.

The second chapter of *Matter and Memory* introduces Bergson's distinction between two different sorts of memory. The first, memory *par excellence*, is spontaneous or representative memory. It is the recollection of specific past events in their concrete richness of detail. The second is habit-memory, a present performance, established through an effort of attention and stored in the brain (as for example, in the recall of a poem or street address learned by rote repetition). The latter sort of memory has a physiological existence; the former, Bergson hypothesizes, does not. Bergson supports his distinction between two sorts of memory through a thorough analysis of the literature of aphasia: the disorders of verbal memory. An impartial analysis of the aphasias supports the distinction between two sorts of aphasia: those created by a psychological shock and those created by physical damage to the brain. In the case of psychologically induced aphasia, memories are not lost, and indeed, appear to continue to act, influencing present recollection and behavior. In the second, what seems to be destroyed is not memories but the motor mechanisms necessary to realize them. Recognition is thus a complex process which, beginning with pure memories, proceeds gradually through the materialization of memory-images towards physical acts. Memory is not, as might appear, a journey by our mind into the past. It is a dynamic progression of our past into our present, made possible by the adjustment and readjustment of our physiological (especially our neurophysiological) apparatus. Our brain is an organ which makes it possible for memories to materialize: to become present, and actual.

Chapter three of *Matter and Memory* develops the basic distinctions introduced in chapter two, with particular reference to the nature of unconscious memory and the part it plays in mental equilibrium. Our present, Bergson affirms, is sensori-motor; it consists of practical, behavioral choices. Our past, by contrast, consists of our accumulated memories. These are mental, rather than sensori-motor, in nature. Just as in present practical situations we must focus our attention on one part of our environment rather than another, so in recollection our recall is partial, touching on only a portion of our past. It is no more strange to assert that our memories (our unconscious mind) exist unpercieved than it is to assert that unpercieved physical objects exist. In this respect our relations with memory and matter are precisely analogous.

But though Bergson asserts (like Freud) that all memories are automatically preserved, he also asserts that they continue to have a practical function, which relates them again to the present. In perception, memories (i.e. spontaneous recollections) return, offering guidance to the sensori-motor mechanisms (i.e. physiological, "habit" memory). These two sorts of memory under normal circumstances offer each other mutual support. Mental illness occurs, however, when the equilibrium between the two kinds of memory is disrupted, and coping behavior ("attention to life") is no longer, or only sporadically, possible. In such cases, as in dreams or drug-unduced states, memory is cut off from realization in the present, the effort to live is blocked, thought and awareness are distracted. As in the case of the aphasias, Bergson finds two different causes for mental pathology, both stemming from damage to the brain.

In his fourth and final chapter Bergson confronts the general problem of mind-body dualism: the basic problem which he had set out, in *Matter and Memory*, to solve. This problem has been rendered insoluble in the past, he states, by the joint supposition that mind is entirely unextended while matter is entirely extended, i.e. geometrical. But the mind, Bergson protests, is partially extended. How else could memories "materialize, become present" in the brain, and in the field of perception? How else could "pure perception" be possible? Bergson also insists that the geometrical and mechanical concept of matter is false. Matter, rather than consisting of hard, unchanging particles (a concept wrongly borrowed from the imagery of ordinary human perception) actually consists of pulses of energy of extreme brevity, bound together by a thread of memory. Matter is more wave or field like than it is particulate, while motion consists in the transformation of an entire spatiotemporal situation rather than the movement of a distinct body through an empty space. Matter, like mind, is thus a mode of duration.

Once the common characteristics of mind and matter are understood, the question of their interrelations—of how either can effect the other— is in its general terms no longer insoluble. The durations of mind can approximate to those of matter; mind and body have certain essential characteristics in common. We can thus understand how in "pure perception" mind is within matter, in the fullest sense. We can also understand how "spontaneous memory" can participate in the structures of the nervous system and how damage to the nervous system could inhibit the functioning of mind.

34   *Matière et mémoire; essai sur la relation du corps a l'esprit.* 2nd ed. Paris: Félix Alcan, 1900, iii, 249.

35   *Matière et mémoire: Essai sur la relation du corps avec l'esprit.* Genève: Skira, 1946, 262.

36   *Matière et mémoire; essai sur la relation du corps a l'esprit.* Paris: Presses Universitaires de France, 1946, 280. (Bibliothèque de philosophie contemporaine)

37   *Matière et mémoire; essai sur la relation du corps a l'esprit,* in *Oeuvres.* Ed. André Robinet. Paris: Presses Universitaires de France, 1959, 161-379.

38   *Matière et mémoire; essai sur la relation du corps avec l'esprit.* 7ed. Paris: Presses Universitaires de France, 1965, 280. (Bibiothèque de philospphie contemporaine)

39   *Matière et mémoire.* Reéd. Paris: Presses Universitaires de France, 1982, 288. (Quadrige, 29)

Translations

Al-mādat w-al thakirat. Trans. A.A. Darkaoui. Damas: Eds. Min. de la Culture, 1967, 265.

Busshitsu to Kioku. Trans. Satomi Takahashi. Tokyo: Iwanami shoten, 1953, 322.

Busshitsu to Kioku. Trans. Tajimo Setsuo. Tokyo: Hakusuisha, 1965, 301. (...zenshû, No. 2)

Materie und Gedächtnis: Essays zur Beziehung zwischen Körper und Geist. Trans. with Intro. W. Windelband. Jena: Diederichs, 1908, xvi, 264.

Materie und Gedächtnis: Eine Abhandlung über die Beziehung zwischen Körper und Geist. Trans. Julius Frankenberger. Jena: Diederichs, 1919, 264.

Materie und Gedächtnis und andere Schriften. Trans. R. von Bendemann, Julius Frankenberger and Eugen Lerch. Frankfurt a. M.: S. Fischer, 1964, 489. (Fischer Paperbacks)

Materie und Gedächtnis. Trans. Julius Frankenberger. Ungekürzte Ausg. Frankfurt a. M., Wien: Ullstein, 1982, vii, 250.

Materia y memoria: Ensayo sobre la relación del cuerpo con el espíritu. Trans. Martín Navarro. Madrid, 1900, vii, 336.

Materia y memoria, ensayo sobre la relácion del cuerpo con el espiritu. Trans. Martín Navarro. La Plata, Argentina: C. Calomino, 1943, 269.

Matter and Memory. Auth. Trans. Nancy Paul and W. Scott Palmer. London: Swan Sonnenschein and Co.; New York: Macmillan, 1911, xx, 359 (Library of Philosophy). Bergson wrote a special introduction to this translation of *Matter and Memory.*

Matter and Memory. Auth. Trans. Nancy Margaret Paul and W. Scott Palmer. Garden City, N.Y.: Doubleday, 1959, xviii, 255. (Doubleday Anchor Books, A172)

Matter and Memory. Auth. Trans. Nancy Margaret Paul and W. Scott Palmer. London: G. Allen and Unwin; New York: Humanities Press, 1970, xxiv, 339. (Muirhead Library of Philosophy.)

vât chát và ký-c. Trans. L.-M. Cao-Vǎn-Luân. Hué: Nhà xuát-bán ai-hoc, 1963, 216.

40   "Mémoire et reconnaissance." *Revue Philosophique de la France et de l'Etranger*, 41, 1896, 255-248, 380-399. Cf. apparat critique, *Edition du Centenaire*, 1491-1496, 1496-1501. This essay is republished in chapter 2, *Matière et mémoire*.

41   "Perception de matière." *Revue de Mètaphysique et de Morale*, 4, No. 2, mai 1896, 257-277. Cf. "apparat critique," *Edition du Centenaire*, 1501-1502. Appears in *Matière et mémoire*.

1897

42   "Compte rendu des *Principes de métaphysique et psychologie* de Paul Janet." *Revue Philosophique de la France et de l'Etranger*, 44, novembre 1897, 526-551. Also in *Ecrits et paroles*, I, 98-128; *Mélanges*, 375-410.

43   "Lettre á G. Lechalas." in G. Lechalas, "Compte rendu de *Matière et mémoire*." *Annales de Philosophie Chrétienne*, 36, 1897, 154, 328, 333. Also in *Ecrits et paroles*, I, 95-97; *Mélanges*, 410-413. Bergson deals here with the relations between consciousness and matter, between sensations and images, and with the nature of "virtual perception."

1900

44   "Bergson au Congrès international de philosophie: 2 août 1900." *Revue de Métaphysique et de Morale*, 8, 1900, 525, 531, 532. Also in *Mélanges*, 417-418. This essay includes a discussion of F. Evellin's "antinomies."

45   "Bergson au Congrès international de philosophie: 3 août 1900." *Revue de Métaphysique et de Morale*, 8, 1900, 566, 574, 575, 582. Also in *Mélanges*, 418. This essay includes a discussion of the nature if idealism, and of Edouard Le Roy's paper on science and liberty.

46   "Communication au VIe Congrès internationale de psychologie." *Revue de Métaphysique et de Morale*, 8, 1900, 803. *Mélanges*, 435. This is a brief mention of Bergson's address on intellectual effort. It occurs in an article by N. Vaschide. (Cf. Bergson's "L'Effort intellectuel," 1902.)

47   "Lettre à L. Dauriac: 4 décembre 1900." *Etudes Bergsoniennes*, 3, 196. Also in *Mélanges*, 436-437. Bergson's concept of laughter is discussed in this letter.

48   "Note sur les origines psychologiques de notre croyance à la loi de causalité." *Bibliothèque du congrès international de philosophie*, I. *Philosophie générale et métaphysique*. Paris: Armand Colin, 1900, 1-15. Also in *Ecrits et paroles*, I, 129-137; *Mélanges*, 419-428. Belief in the law of causality, Bergson holds, is based on the coordination of our tactile impressions with our visual impressions. The continuation of visual impressions into tactile impressions generates motor

habits which are tendencies to action.

49   "Note sur les origines psychologiques de notre croyance à la loi de causalité."
        Revue de Métaphysique et de Morale, 8, 1900, 655-664. *Mélanges*, 428-435.
        This is an abstract of Bergson's paper followed by a discussion.

50   "Le Rire." *Revue de Paris*, 7, Nos. 23 et 24, 1899, 512-514, 759-790; No. 1,
        1900, 146-179.

        This is Bergson's classic study of the phenomenon of laughter. We laugh,
        Bergson holds, when we observe clumsiness, inelasticity, unadaptability—that
        is, whenever we find tendencies towards mechanism in the behavior of living,
        presumably vital, human beings. The romantic dreamer, unaware of reality; the
        miser, unaware of the character and the results of his greed; the systematically
        absent-minded character in general: all behave repetitiously rather than spontane-
        ously and adaptably. The mechanical nature of laughable behavior explains the
        abstract, impersonal, almost formulaic nature of comic characters, who are
        portrayed not as unique individuals but as types, and whose foibles are as
        predictable as they are unconscious.

        Just as the laughable involves a broadly social lack of adaptation to circumstances,
        so, Bergson asserts, laughter is clearly a social phenomenon. It is, in fact, a
        social weapon used against minor flaws of character: flaws which, developed
        to the extreme, would lead to serious moral consequences. Wherever society
        discerns inelasticity of character, it finds a veiled threat to its customs and
        implied rules. It responds to the social threat with a social gesture: laughter.
        Laughter is intended to change behavior, as well as attitudes.

        Equipped with these basic distinctions, Bergson explores the various sources of
        laughter: the comic in situations, the comic in words, and the comic in character.
        Situation comedies clearly demostrate the "encrustation" of the mechanical on
        the vital. The principles underlying this encrustation are repetition, inversion,
        and the "reciprocal interference of series" (a situation belonging to two indepen-
        dent series of events at once.) The comic element in words fits into a similar
        threefold classification.

        The comic in character is a profounder source of laughter than situation or verbal
        comedy. This kind of comedy involves three conditions: unsociability in the
        performer, lack of feeling in the spectator, and automatism. The comic character
        is inevitably inattentive both to himself and to others; he becomes comic to the
        spectator as soon as the spectator's feelings cease to involve hime. But even in
        the highest comedy of character (say, Don Quixote) we do not penetrate to the
        depths of human personality. That is left to the tragedian, who momentarily
        lifts the veil that hides us from ourselves and allows us to see ourselves, through
        the tragic figure, as unique.

51   *Le Rire: Essai sur la signification du comique.* Paris: Félix Alcan, 1900, vii, 204.
        (Bibliothèque de philosophie contemporaine)

52   *Le Rire; essai sur la signification du comique.* 23rd ed. Paris: Félix Alcan, 1924,
        viii, 208. (Bibliothèque de philosophie contemporaine)

53   *Le Rire; essai sur la signification du comique.* 57ed. Paris: Presses Universitaires
        de France, 1941, viii, 157. (Bibliothèque de philosophie contemporaine)

54   *Le Rire: Essai sur la signification du comique.* Genève: Skira, 1945, 134.

55   *Le Rire: Essai sur la signification du comique*. Paris: Fequet et Boudier, 1947, 107.

56   *Le Rire: Essai sur la signification du comique*, in *Oeuvres*. Ed. André Robinet. Paris: Presses Universitaires de France, 1959, 381-485.

57   *Le Rire: Essai sur la signification du comique*. Paris: Presses Universitaires de France, 1981, viii, 157 (Quadrige, 11)

Translations

Der gelekhter. Warsaw: "Glorja", 1928, 155.

Gülme. Trans. Mustafa Sekip Tunc. [komiğin anlamĭ üzerinde deneme] Istanbul: Millî gğitim basĭmevi, 1945, iii, 145. (Dünya edebiyatĭndan tercümeler. Fransĭz klâsikleri: 96)

Hatzekhok. Trans. Jacob Levy. Jerusalem: Rubin Hass., 1947, 123.

Ha-Zehoq. Trans. Yaakow Levi. Jerusalem: R. Mass, 1975, 127.

Das Lachen. Trans. J. Frankenberger and W. Fränzel. Jena: E. Diederichs, 1914, 134.

Das Lachen. Trans. J. Frankenberger and W. Fränzel. Jena: Diederichs Verlag, 1921, 135.

Das Lachen. Trans. Julius Frankenberger and W. Fränzel. Meissenheim am Glan: Westkulturverlag A. Hain, 1949, 112.

Das Lachen: Ein Essay über die Bedeutung des Komischen. Trans. Roswitha Plancherel-Walter. Zürich: Verlag der Arche, 1972, 141.

Latteren. Trans. Evan Wyller. Oslo: Tanum, 1971, 132.

Laughter: An Essay on the Meaning of the Comic. Auth. Trans. Cloudesly Brereton and Fred Rothwell. London and New York: Macmillan, 1911, vii, 200.

Laughter: An Essay of the Meaning of the Comic. Trans. C. Brereton and F. Rothwell. London: Macmillian, 1935, 200. (New Eversley Series)

"Laughter" in *Comedy*. Intro. and Appendix Wylie Sypher. Garden City, New York: Doubleday and Company, Inc., 1956, 61-190.

"Laughter." in *The Comic in Theory and Practice*. Eds. Enck, J. J.; Forter, E. T. and Whitley, A. New York: Appleton-Century Crofts, 1960, 43-64.

"The Individual and the Type," In Rader, Melvin, *A Modern Book of Aesthetics*, 5th Ed. New York: Holt, Rinehart and Winston, 1979, 73-80. This is a selection from *Laughter*. It is preceded (pp. 71-72) by a brief introduction.

"What is the Object of Art?" *Camera Work*, No. 37, 1912, 22-26. This is a lenghtly excerpt from the English translation of *Laughter*.

"Why do we Laugh? in *Great Essays by Nobel Prize Winners*. Eds. L. Hamalian and E.L. Volpe. New York: Noonday Press, 1960, 171-188.

A nevetés. Trans. Nańdor Szavái. Budapest: Gondolat Kiadó, 1968, 164.

A nevetés. 2nd ed. Trans. Nańdor Szavái. Budapest: Gondolat Kiadó, 1971, 164.

La risa: Ensayo sobre la significación de lo cómico. Valencia: Promoteo, 1914, ix, 219. (Biblioteca de Cultura Contemporánea)

La risa: Ensayo sobre la significación de lo cómico. Trans. Amalia Haydée Raggio. Buenos Aires Losada, 1939, 154. (Biblioteca Contemporánea, 55)

La risa: Ensayo sobre la significación de lo cómico. 4th ed. Trans. Amalia Haydée Raggio. Buenos Aires: Editorial Losada, 1962, 151. (Biblioteca contemporanea, No. 55)

La risa: Ensayo sobre la significación de lo cómico. Trans. P. Girosi. Buenos Aires: Tor, 1939.

La Risa. Valencia: Ediciones Prometo, 1971, 158.

La risa; ensayo sobre la significacion de lo comico. Trans. María Louisa Pérez Torres. Madrid: Espasa-Calpe, 1973, 164. (Collección austral, 1534)

"El Arte: Lo Individual en el Arte." *Revisita de Ideas Estáeticas*, 1, No. 3, 1943, 135-136. This is a passage from chapter 3 of *Le Rire*. Trans. M. C. Iracheta.

"El Arte: Realismo e Idealismo." *Revista de Ideas Estéticas*, 1, No. 3, 1943, 130-135. This is a passage from chapter 3 of *Le Rire*. Trans. M.C. Iracheta.

"Lo Cómico en sus tres Aspectos Fundamentales." *Revista de Ideas Estéticas*, No. 4, 1943, 111-113. This is a passage from chapter 1, section 1 of *Le Rire*. Trans. M.C. Iracheta.

"Especies de lo cómico: La Exageración, La Ironía y el humor." *Revista de Ideas Estéticas*, 1, No. 4, 1943, 114-116. This is a passage from chapter 2, section 2, of *Le Rire*. Trans. M.C. Iracheta.

Tagore, Rabandrinath; Hamsun, Kunt. *(Tagore:) Gitanjali; (Hamson:) La ciudad de Segelfoss*; Vives, Amalia Aydee. Barcelona: G.P., 1963, 504.

Il riso: Saggio sul significato del comico. Trans. A. Cervesato and C. Gallo. Bari: Laterza e Figli, 1916. (Biblioteca di cultura moderna)

Il riso: Saggio sul significato del comico. Trans. F. Stella. Milano: Rizzoli, 1961, 166. (Biblioteca iniversale Rizzoli, 1707-1708)

O riso. Trans. G. de Castilho. Lisbon: Guimarães, 1960, 150.

Skrattet: En undersokning av Komikens vasen. Trans. Algot Ruhe. Stockholm, 1910, 172.

Smiech: esej o komizmie. Trans. Stanisalw Cichowicz. Intro. Stefan Morawski. Krakow: Wydaw. Liter., 1977.

Smiech: Esej o význame knomična. Trans. Anton Vantuch. Bratislava: Tatran, 1966, 149.

Smiech: Studyum o komicie. "Wiedza i zycie; zagadniena z pradu wspołćzesnego w dziedzinie wiedzy, sztuki i zycia społcecznego." Ser. 2, vol. 2, 1902.

O smijehu: Esejo značenju smiješnoga. Trans. Srećko Dźamonja. Sarajevo: Veselin Maslesa, 1958, 120.

O smekhu; esej o znachenú smeshnoga. Beograd. S. B. Tsvijannović, 1920, 147.

Smiekh v zhizni i na stsenie. Trans. А.Е. ЯновскагоSt. Petersburg: X.X. Vyek, 1900, 181.

Tiếng cu'ờ'i hay lu'o'c' kháo vê ý nghĩa cúa hài-tính. Trans. Pham-Xuân-Dô. Saigon: Bô Quõc-Gia Giáo-Duc, 1960, 163.

To gelio. Trans. Nikos Kazantzakis. 1914; rpt. Athens: Ekdot. Oikos G. Phexē, 1965, x, 121.

Warai. Trans. Tatsuo Hayashi. Tokyo: Iwanami shoten, 1951, 211.

Warai. Trans. Tatsuo Hayashi. Tokyo: Iwanami shoten: 1976, 255.

1901

58   "Collège de France: Cours de M. Bergson sur l'idée de cause." *Revue de Philosophie*, 1, No. 3, avril 1901, 385-388. *Mélanges*, 439-441. This article is signed "J.C."

59   "Cours du Collège de France: 26 décembre 1901." *Archives du Collège de France*, 1, 1901, 71-72. Also in *Mélanges*, 512. Brief mention is made of a course on the idea of time and on Plotinus' sixth *Ennead* in this essay.

60   "Cours du Collège de France: Philosophie grecque et latine." *Archives du Collège de France*, 1, 1901, 55-56. Also in *Ecrits et paroles*, 1, 138; *Mélanges*, 438. Bergson discusses here the concept of causality held by both ancients and moderns.

61   "Le Rêve." *Bulletin de l'Institut Général Psychologique*, 1, No. 3, mai 1901, 97-122.

This brief essay extends the basic ideas of *Matter and Memory* into the field of dream research. Dreams and dream-perception, Bergson insists, are really not different in structure from ordinary waking experience and perception. In both cases there are contributions from the mind (i.e., from memory, primarily) and from matter (i.e. from objects in the world and from the body). What is lacking in the dream but present in everyday life, is the effort necessary for precise and practical adaptation to specific features of the world. In the dream we find a different, often a strange marriage between our memories and our vaguely perceived sensations. Our waking minds operate similarly, but in terms of specifically chosen, useful sensations and memories called up specifically to interpret them.

Bergson concludes his masterful analysis of the nature and structure of dreams with two specific suggestions. We ought, he urges, to study deep sleep for the clues it may give us to our deeply buried memories—unconscious memory. (Here Bergson points in the direction of "psychoanalysis".) Similarly, we ought to study deep sleep for what it may reveal to us about psychic phenomena.

Bergson does not, in this essay, mention the name of René Descartes or the skeptical arguments which Descartes based on dreams. It is clear, however, that on Bergson's view, dreams always require a basis in real perception, however vague. This realization undercuts the Cartesian assumption that dreaming is a purely mental, perfectly subjective experience.

62   "Le Rêve." *Revue Scientifique*, 4e Sér. 15, No. 23, 8 juin 1901, 705-715.

63   "Le Rêve." in *L'Energie Spirituelle: Essais et conférences*. Paris: Félix Alcan, 1919. This version of "Le Rêve", and those which follow, were significantly emended by Bergson.

64   "Le Rêve." in *Oeuvres*. Ed. André Robinet. Paris: Presses Universitaires de France, 1959, 878-897. (Cf. notes, 1566-1568)

65   "Le Rêve," in *Etudes Bergsoniennes*, 6, 61-86.

66   "Le Rêve," in *Mélanges*. Ed. André Robinet. Paris: Presses Universitaires de France, 1972, 443-463.

Translations

"Dreams". *Bergson's Mind-Energy*. Trans. H. W. Carr. New York: Holt, 1920, 104-133.

Dreams. Trans. with Intro. Edwin Emery Slosson. New York: B.W. Huebsch, 1914, 57.

Dreams. Trans. with Intro. Edwin E. Slosson. London: T.F. Unwin, 1914, 62.

"The Origin and Birth of the Dream." *The World of Dreams: An Anthology*. Ed. Ralph l. Woods. New York: Random House, 1947, 947, 254-260.

"Such Stuff as Dreams are Made on: A study of the Mechanism of Dreaming." *Independent*, 76, Nos. 3396-3387, October 23 and October 30, 1913, 160-163, 200-203.

The World of Dreams. Trans. Wade Baskin. New York: The Wisdom Library, 1958, 58.

"Der Traum." in *Festchrift Walter Merz. Zum 60. Geburtstag dargebracht von Freunden und Verehrern*. Aarau: Sauerländer, 1928, vii, 242.

67   Bergson, Henri Louis. "Le Parallélisme psycho-physiologique et la métaphysique positive." *Bulletin de la Société française de philosophie*, 1, No. 2, juin 1901, 33-71. Also in *Ecrits et Paroles*, 1, 139-167 (in part); *Mélanges*, 463-502. This is an extended discussion, at the Société Française de Philosophie, of Bergson's mind-body theory, especially as it relates to his critique of the thesis that mind and body are "parallel". On pp. 464-471 M. Belot develops a detailed criticism of Bergson's views; on pp. 472-488 Bergson replies to these criticisms. A discussion follows on pp. 488-502. (Cf. Bergson's "Le Paralogisme psycho-physiologique," 1904.)

68   Bergson, Henri Louis. "Rapport sur le maintein d'un chaire de psychologie expérimentale et comparée." *Archives du Collège de France*, 112, Bergson, manuscript autographe. Also in *Mélanges*, 507-509. Bergson here briefly surveys the history of recent psychology and argues for continued support for a chair of experimental and comparative psychology at the Collège de France. This report was given November 10, 1901.

69   Bergson, Henri Louis. "Lettre du group d'études de phénomènes psychiques: 3 décembre 1901." *Bulletin de l'Institute generale psychologique*, 2, No. 1, 1902, 3-4. Also in *Mélanges*, 509-510. This letter, signed by Bergson and six other savants, announces the formation of a study group dedicated to the investigation of psychic phenomena. The investigation of such phenomena will require precise observation and rigorous experiment.

70   "Election à l'Académie des sciences morales et politiques: 14 décembre 1901." *Séances et Travaux de l'Académie des Sciences Morales et Politiques*, 157, 1902, p. 289. Also in *Mélanges*, 511.

71   "Réception à l'Académie des sciences morales et politiques: 21 décembre 1901." *Séances et Travaux de l'Académie des Sciences Morales et Politiques*, 157, 1902, p. 291. Also in *Mélanges*, 511.

1902

72   "Collège de France: Cours de M. Bergson." *Revue de Philosophie*, 2, No. 6, octobre 1902, 828-832. Also in *Mélanges*, 513-517. Here an account is given of a course on the concept of time.

73   "Cours du Collège de France." *Revue de Philosophie*, 4, No. 1, janvier 1904, 105-111. Also in *Mélanges*, 573-578. An article by Léonard Constant on

Bergson's course (1902-1903) on the history of the concept of time.

74 "Cours du Collège de France: Philosophie grecque et latine." *Archives du Collège de France*, 3, 1903, p.96. Also in *Ecrits et paroles*, 1, p. 191; *Mélanges*, 572. A brief account is given of courses presented in 1902-1903 on book two of Aristotle's *Physics* and on the history of the idea of time.

75 "Discussion à la Sociètè française de philosophie: La Place et le caractère de la philosophie dans l'enseignement secondaire par M. Belot." *Bulletin de la Société Française de Philosophie*, 3, 2 février 1903, 44-66. Also in *Ecrits et paroles*, 1, 187-190; *Mélanges*, 568-571. This discussion concerns the place of philosophy in secondary education.

76 "Discussion à la Société française de philosophie: Le Vocabulaire philosophique." *Bulletin de la Société française de Philosophie*, 2, juillet 1902, pp. 157, 160, 161. Also in *Ecrits et paroles*, 1, p. 174; *Mélanges*, 551-552. This discussion is concerned with an analysis of the terms "evidence" and "absolute." By absolute Bergson means real, complete, known in itself apart from any symbolic interpretation. This term (absolute) appears in Bergson's *An Introduction to Metaphysics* (1903).

77 "L'Effort intellectuel." *Revue Philosophique de la France et de l'Etranger*, 5, janvier 1902, 1-27. This is Begson's study of the way in which intuitive conceptions are developed into discursive, analytic form (whether scientific, literary or other). Intellectual creativity involves both a "dynamic schema" and a set of concrete images through which the schema is embodied. The movement from abstract idea to concrete imagery may meet with resistance from idea, images, or both. Insofar as this resistance causes hesitation, there is a feeling of resistance and of effort characteristic of intellectual endeavor.

78 "L'Effort intellectuel." in *L'Energie spirituelle: Essais et conferences*. Paris: Presses Universitaires de France, 1919. (Cf. *Mind-Energy*, 1920, 186-230.) This version of "L;Effort intellectuel", was significantly emended by Bergson. It is reproduced in the following editions.

79 "L'Effort intellectuel." *Oeuvres*. Ed. André Robinet. Paris: Presses Universitaires de France, 1969, 930-959. (Notes, 1568-1569)

80 "L'Effort intellectuel." *Etudes Bergsoniennes*, 6, 97-126.

81 "L'Effort intellectuel." *Mélanges*. Ed. André Robinet. Paris: Presses Universitaires de France, 1972, 519-550.

82 "De L'Intelligence." *Palmarès du Lycée Voltaire*, 6, No. 75, 1902, 1-9. Also in *Bulletin de l'Union pour la Vérité*, 21, No. 6, 15 avril 1914, 424-436; *Ecrits et paroles*, 1, 175-181; *Mélanges*, 553-560. In this talk Bergson defines intelligence, in a broad sense, as the collaboration of "intuition" and "intellect." Intelligence succeeds, Bergson holds, through an effort of concentration. These distinctions figure prominently in Bergson's *An Introduction to Metaphysics* (1903).

83 "Philosophie grecque et latine." *Archives du Collège de France*, 2, 1902, 49-50. Also in *Ecrits et paroles*, 1, p. 173; *Mélanges*, 512-513. A brief description of a course on Plotinus' sixth *Ennead* and the concept of time is given in this item.

84 "Rapport sur la Fondation Carnot; 6 décembre 1902." *Séances et Travaux de l'Académie des Sciences Morales et Politiques*, 159, 1903, 52-62. Also in *Ecrits et paroles*, 1, 182-186; *Mélanges*, 561-566.

1903

85   "Cause et raison chez Cournot." *Bulletin de la Société Française de Philosophie*,
         1, No. 8, août 1903, 209. Also in G. Tarde. *La Philosophie sociale de Cournot*,
         229; *Ecrits et paroles*, 1, p. 199; *Mélanges*, 589. This is a brief discussion by
         Bergson of A. A. Cournot's distinction between cause (actual casual factors)
         and reason (principle of explanation).

86   "Compte rendu de *An Essay on Laughter* de. J. Sully." *Revue Philosophique de
         la France et de l'Etranger*, 56, octobre 1903, 402-410. Also in *Ecrits et paroles*,
         1, 213-221; *Mélanges*, 594-603. Bergson analyzes Sully's concept of laughter
         and subjects it to a brief criticism. Sully, Bergson holds, has two distinct concepts
         of laughter but does not provide a clear transition between them.

87   "Cours du Collège de France: Histoire des Théories de la mémoire." *Revue de
         Philosophie*, 4, No. 12, décembre 1904, 801-814. Also in *Mélanges*, 614-625.
         The brain as a memory-bank, the association of ideas, the function of the brain,
         memory   versus   perception,   different   kinds   of   memory,   aphasias,
         epiphenomenalism, etc., are discussed in this account of a course given by
         Bergson in 1903-1904.

88   "Cours du Collège de France: Philosophie grecque et latine." *Archives du Collège
         de France*, 4, 1904, p. 77. Also in *Mélanges*, 613; *Ecrits et paroles*, 1, p. 222.
         This is a brief account of courses on 'Book Lambda' of Aristotle's *Physics* and
         on the evolution of concepts of memory.

89   "Discussion au groupe d'études des phénomènes psychiques." *Bulletin de l'Institut
         Général Psychologique*, 4, No. 1, janvier 1904, 28-31. Also in *Ecrits et paroles*,
         1, 209-212; *Mélanges*, 606-609. This discussion concerns high frequency radi-
         ation emitted by the nervous system and light penumbras surrounding the human
         body purportedly seen by "sensitives."

90   "Introduction à la métaphysique." *Revue de Métaphysique et de Morale*, 29, janvier
         1903, 1-36.

         This brief essay is both an outline of Bergson's theory of knowledge and a
         statement of his philosophical method. There are, he states, two different ways
         of knowing. The first can be termed "analysis": it involves an atomistic, piece-by-
         piece account of a subject-matter, and deals with static concepts. The second
         can be called "intuition": a term which Bergson introduces systematically here
         for the first time. Where analysis is atomistic, intuition is holistic. Intuition
         (defined as "intellectual sympathy") grasps realities as a whole and as dynamic
         continua. The fundamental goals of *An Introduction to Metaphysics*, having
         once sharply distinguished these two modes of knowledge, are to show both
         how they interrelate and how they jointly make possible an approach to a new
         metaphysics.

         Intuition has as its object the mobility of duration, while analysis attempts to
         understand its object with spatial concepts. The priviledged case of intuition is,
         Bergson states, the inner self: our own personality in its flowing through time.
         Empiricists have tried to understand the self by analyzing it into pieces and
         relating the pieces (mental states, supposed "atoms" of mental life) through laws
         of association. Rationalists have attempted to coordinate this numerical plurality

of mental states with a purely abstract formulation, the "unity of the ego", a unity imposed from without upon data created by the empiricist's atomistic mode of analysis. But the problem of the nature of the self has in both cases been approached wrongly. In order to truly understand the nature of the self we must use intuition, and intuition reveals that while the self is both multiple and single, its unity and plurality are not spatial (i.e. arithmetic) in nature.

Intuition, however, is not limited merely to the knowledge of the self. The human self exhibits only one "tension" of duration. There are many others, reaching down to brief pulsations of matter and, at the other, reaching upwards towards a more intense, more extended duration than our own. We thus must deal with a universe of differing sorts of durations, each on a different scale, each possessing a unique span of its own, from the nearly-spatial, nearly-homogeneous durations of matter to the richer, broader durations of the human self, to the ultimate duration, "containing" all others, which Bergson terms "Eternity".

Bergson is convinced that the study of this all-encompassing "continuity of durations" is the goal of both philosophy and the sciences, philosophy operating largely with intuition, science primarily with analysis. He stresses the fact, however, that in its revolutionary stages, in which it has created new symbol-systems and new modes of analysis, science has had need of and has always utilized intuition. The infinitesimal calculus of G. W. Leibniz and I. Newton, like Galileo's laws of falling bodies, were clear examples of the use of intuition by scientists, and depended upon an increased and more focused awareness of duration. The goal of philosophy is to apply this intuition methodically, where in the past it has been utilized "by accident."

Science and metaphysics thus come together in intuition, Bergson concludes. While intuition participates in (knows) duration as an "absolute", science transforms duration into space by means of symbols which, through "relative" from the viewpoint of metaphysics, are in pragmatic terms extraordinarily useful. Science requires from intuition its new intuitions, which may then be developed analytically; intuition requires from science the basic knowledge from which philosophy begins but which it must transcend in order to know the world and its contrasting durations more fully— and more fruitfully. Science maintains its time-honored goal of practical effectiveness, but broadens its horizons; while metaphysics becomes "integral experience."

91   "Introduction à la métaphysique." in *Oeuvres*. Ed. André Robinet. Paris: Presses Universitaires de France, 1959, 1392-1432. (Notes 1537-1539).

92   "Introduction à la métaphysique." in *La Pensée et le mouvant: Essais et conférences*. Paris: Félix Alcan, 1934.

Translations

Einführung in die Metaphysik. Auth. Trans. M. Susmann. Jena: Diederichs, 1909, 58.

La filosofia dell'intuizione: Introduzione alla metafisica, ed. estratti altre opera, a cura di Giovanni Papini. Lanciano, Italy: Carabba, 1908, 126.

"Innforing i metafysikken." in *Hva er metafysik*. Trans. Skirne Helg Bruland. Olso: J. G. Tanum, 1962, 138. (Ide og tanke)

"Introducción a la metafísica." Trans. C. M. Onetti. *Valoraciones* (Argentina), No. 12, 1928.

Introducción a la metafísica. Trans. Carlos Sabat Ercasty. Montivideo: García y Cía, 1944, 65.

Introduccíon a la metafísica. Trans. Rafael Moreno. México: Centro de estudios filosoficos, Universidad nacional autónoma de México, 1960, 50. (Cuadernos del Centro de Estudios Filosóficos, 8)

Introcucción a la metafísica y la intuición filosófica. Trans. M. Héctor Alberti. Buenos Aires: Siglo Veinte, 1966, 144. (Nueva colección siglo veinte)

Introducción a la metafísica y la intuicion filosofica. Trans. M. Héctor Alberti. 1966; rpt. Buenos Aires, 1973, 141.

Introduction à la métaphysique. Trans. B. Fogarasi. Budapest: Politzer, 1910, 41.

Introduction to Metaphysics. Auth. Trans. T. E. Hulme. New York: Putnam's Sons, 1912, iv, 92.

Introduction to Metaphysics. Auth. Trans. T. E. Hulme. London: Macmillan, 1913, vi, 79.

"Introduction to Metaphysics." *The Creative Mind.* Trans. Mabelle L. Andison. New York: Philosophical Library, 1946, 187-237.

Introduction to Metaphysics. Trans. Mabelle L. Andison. New York: Philosophical Library, 1961, 84.

Introduction to a New Philosophy: Introduction à la Métaphysique. Trans. Sidney Littman. Boston: John W. Luce and Co., 1912, 108.

"An Introduction to Metaphysics." In *Philosophy in the Twentieth Century: An Anthology.* Vol. III. Ed. with intro. William Barrett and Henry D. Aiken. New York: Random House, 1962, 303-332.

"An Introduction to Metaphysics." in *The Pleasures of Philosophy.* Ed. Charles Frankel. New York and Scarborough, Ontario, 1972, 287-294. This is a short passage from the T. E. Hulme translation of Bergson's *An Introduction to Metaphysics.*

"An Introduction to Metaphysics." in *Process Philosophy: Basic Writings.* Eds. Jack R. Sibley and Pete A. Y. Gunter. Lanham, Maryland: University Press of America, 1978, 27-48.

"An Introduction to Metaphysics." in *The Search for Being: Essays. Eds. Jean T. Wilde and Wm. Kimmel. Pref. Martin C. D'Arcy. New York: Twayne Publishers, 1962, 178-216.*

"Knowledge is Ultimately Intuitive." In *Classic Philosophical Questions.* Ed. James A. Gould. Third Ed. Columbus, Ohio: Charles E. Merrill Publishing Company, 1979, 237-248. This is a selection from *An Introduction to Metaphysics.*

Introduzione alla metafisica, a cura di Oddino Montiani. Lancio: R. Carabba, 1940, 110. (Classici del pensiero e dell'educazione, 4)

Introduzione alla metafisica. Ed. B. Brunello. Bologna: Zanichelli, 1949, 95.

Introduzione alla metafisica. Trans. Oddino Montiani. Lanciano: R. Carabba, 1949, 110. (Classici del pensiero dell'educazione, No. 34)

Introduzione alla metafisica. Trans. Vittorio Mathieu. Bari: Laterza, 1957, 103. (Piccola biblioteca filosofica)

Introduzione alla metafisica. 2nd Ed. Trans. Armando Vedaldi, Firenze: Sansoni, 1958, iv, 135. (Collana scolastica di testi filosofici)

Introduzione alla metafisica. Traduzione, introduzione e note di Giancarlo Penati. Brescia: La Scuola, 1970, xlvii, 69. (Il Pensiero)

Introduzione alla metafisica. 3rd ed. Trans. V. Mathieu. Bari: Laterza, 1970, lll. (Piccolo biblioteca filosofica Laterza, No. 53)

Intuition och intelligence: Inledning till metafysiken. Trans. Algot Ruhe. Stockholm: 1911. "Med ett forord ab professor Axel Herrlin."

Intuition og verdensankuelse. Trans. Knud Ferlov. Copenhagen: Gad, 1914, 76.

Keijijôgaku josetsu. Trans. Tokuo Sakata. Tokyo: Misuzu shobô, 1954, 231.

Nizām al-Athinīyīn. Trans. Tahā Husayn. al-Qāhirah: Dār al-Ma'ārif, 1966, 192.

Sôzô-teki shinka; keijijo-gaku nyûmon. Trans. Kosaku Matsuura; Keisaburô Masuda. Tokyo: Kawade shobô, 1953, 330. This contains translations of *L'Evolution créatrice* and *Introduction à la métaphysique.*

Wstep do metafizyki. Trans. Kazimir Bteszyński. Kraków: Gebethner, 1910, 104. (Ksiaznica naukowa i artystyczna)

93   "Lettre à M. L. Brunschvig: 26 février 1903." *Bulletin de la Sociét Française de Philosophie,* 3, 1903, 101-103. Also in *Ecrits et paroles,* 1, 194-196; *Mélanges,* 585-587. The concept of "moral liberty" is discussed in this letter.

94   "Lettre à A. Dayot." *Le Livre d'or de Renan.* Paris: Joanin, 1903, p. 137. Also in *Mélanges,* 610. Bergson here accepts a position on a committee to build a monument to Ernest Renan.

95   "Lettre à W. James: 6 janvier 1903." *Revue des Deux Mondes,* 15 octobre 1933, 797-798. Also in *Ecrits et paroles,* 1, 192-193; *Mélanges,* 587-589. In this letter Bergson discusses *Matter and Memory* and its difficulties.

96   "Lettre à Ch. Péguy: 22 février 1903." *Etudes Bergsoniennes,* 8, p. 14. Also in *Mélanges,* 582-583. Bergson politely critizes Péguy in this letter for publishing "An Introduction to Metaphysics" in *Cahiers de la Quinzaine.* Metaphysics, Bergson holds, does not always mix well with political and social thought.

97   "Préface à l'Esquisse d'un système de psychologie rationelle d'E. Lubac. *Esquisse d'un système de psychologie rationelle.* Paris: Félix Alcan, 1903, vvi-x. Also is *Ecrits et paroles,* 1, 204-207; *Mélanges,* 610, 612. This is a discussion of intuitive method in psychology.

98   "Rapport sur le concours pour le prix Halphen, à décerner en 1903." *Séances et Travaux de l'Académie des Sciences Morales et Politiques,* 160, 1903, 540-544. Also in *Ecrits et paroles,* 1, p. 200-203; *Mélanges,* 590-594. Bergson awards a prize to Boirac and Magendie for their *Leçons de psychologie appliquée à l'éducation.*

99   "Rapport sur *l'Esquisse d'un système de psychologie rationelle* d'E. Lubac." *Séances et Travaux de l'Académie des Sciences Morales et Politiques,* 161, 1904, p. 337. Also in *Ecrits et paroles,* 1, p. 208; *Mélanges,* 605-606. Bergson treats Lubac's treatise as a series of suggestions, some highly penetrating, for the study of psychological phenomena.

1904

100   "Le Paralogisme psycho-physiologique." *Revue de Métaphysique et de Morale,* 12, No. 6, novembre 1904, 859-908. This paper was read originally at the International Congress of Philosophy at Geneva in 1904. It was republished, slightly emended, as "Le Cerveau et la pensée." Bergson argues here that all

attempts to posit either the identity of or a parallelism between mind states and brain states imply a fundamental self-contradiction. This contradiction is rooted in an illicit ambiguity in the terms used to assert the identity or parallelist thesis. Without realizing it, we pass from idealist to realist interpretations of mental and physical notation-systems, and *vice versa*.

101   "Le Cerveau et la pensée." in *L'Energie spirituelle: essais et conférences*. Paris: Félix Alcan, 1919. (Cf. *Mind-Energy*, 1920, 231-255.)

102   "Le Cerveau et la pensée." in *Oeuvres*. Ed. André Robinet. Paris: Presses Universitaires de France, 1959, 959-974. (Notes, 1530-1531)

103   "Cours du Collège de France: Philosophie moderne." *Archives du Collège de France*, 5, 1905, p. 90. Also in *Ecrits et paroles*, 1, p. 234; *Mélanges*, 648-649. These are courses which were given in 1904-1905 on the evolution of the concept of liberty and on Spencer's *First Principles*, particularly Spencer's concept of "force."

104   "Demande de transfert à la chaire de philosophie moderne." *Mélanges*, 637-638.

105   "Discussion au Groupe d'études des phénomènes psychiques: Les Courbes respiratoires pendant l'hypnose." *Bulletin de l'Institut Général Psychologique*, 5, No. 2, mars 1905, 155-164. Also in *Ecrits et paroles*, 1, 225-228; *Mélanges*, 639-642. A discussion of breathing rhythms during successive stages of hypnosis.

106   "Discussion à la Société française de philosophie: Binet, Esprit et matière." *Bulletin de la société Française de Philosophie*, 5, No. 3, mars 1905, 94-99. Also in *Ecrits et paroles*, 1, 229-233; *Mélanges*, 643-648. A discussion of agreements and disagreements of Bergson and Binet on the function of the nervous system in perception. Bergson denies that his theory transforms sensory nerves into motor nerves.

107   "Lettre à Ch. Péguy: 19 juillet 1904." *Etudes Bergsoniennes*, 8, 15-16. Also in *Mélanges*, 630-631. This letter is concerned with obtaining a scholarship for a young friend of Péguy.

108   "Lettre à Ch. Péguy: 23 novembre 1904." *Etudes Bergsoniennes*, 8, p. 17. Also in *Mélanges*, 642-643. This letter is concerned with Bergson's courses on the evolution of the problem of liberty and on passages in Herbert Spencer's *First Principles*.

109   "Rapport sur un ouvrage de Victor Mortet: *Notes sur le texte des 'Institutions' de Cassiodore*." *Séances et Travaux de l'Académie des Sciences Morales et Politiques*, 162, octobre 1904, p. 485. Also in *Ecrits et paroles*, 1, p. 223; *Mélanges*, 628-629. This account is brief and expository.

110   "Rapport sur un ouvrage de J. Ruskin: *La Bible d'Amiens*: Préface et traduction de Marcel Proust." *Séances et Travaux de l'Académie des Sciences Morales et Politiques*, 162, octobre 1904, 491-492. Also in *Ecrits et paroles*, 1, p. 224; *Mélanges*, 629-630. Bergson lauds Marcel Proust's interpretation of Ruskin's thought.

111   "Réplique à E. Faguet." *Journal des Débats*, Feuilleton, La Semaine dramatique, 10 octobre 1904. Also in *Mélanges*, 631-637. This is a reply to Faguet's criticisms of Bergson's concept of laughter. According to Bergson, Faguet oversimplifies his "definition" of laughter.

112   "La Vie et l'oeuvre de Ravaisson." *Séances et Travaux de l'Académie des Sciences Morales et Politiques*, 161, 1904, 673-708. Here Bergson follows the development of Félix Ravaisson's philosophy while chronicling the events of Ravaisson's life. Ravaisson's philosophy is in certain respects vague, Bergson concedes, but that is because its form "is the form of an inspiration."

113 "La Vie et l'oeuvre de Ravaisson." *Mémoires de l'Académire des Sciences Morales et Politiques*, 25, 1907, 1-43.

114 "La Vie et l'Oeuvre de Ravaisson." in *La Pensée et le mouvant: Essais et conférences*. Paris: Presses Universitaires de France, 1934. (Cf. *The Creative Mind*, 1946, 261-300.)

115 "La Vie et l'oeuvre de Ravaisson." *Oeuvres*. Ed. André Robinet. Paris: Presses Universitaires de France, 1959, 1450-1481. (Notes, 1539)

1905

116 "Bergson et le médium Eusapia Palladino." *Bulletin de l'Institut Général Psychologique*, 8, No. 5-6, 1908, 415-546. Also in *Mélanges*, 673-674.

117 "Lettre à W. James: 15 février 1905." *Revue des Deux Mondes*, 15 octobre 1933, 798-799. Also in *Ecrits et paroles*, 2, 235-236; *Mélanges*, 651-652. This letter concerns radical empiricism and Bergson's concept of the unconscious.

118 "Lettre à W. James: 20 juillet 1905." *Revue des Deux Mondes*, 15 octobre 1933, 802-804. Also in *Ecrits et paroles*, 2, 241-242; *Mélanges*, 671-672. Bergson here discusses James' essay, "How Two Minds Can Know One Thing." He mentions his letter to the editor of the *Revue Philosophique* denying James' influence on his notion of pure duration.

119 "Lettre au directeur de la *Revue Philosophique* sur sa relation à James Ward et à William James." *Revue Philosophique de la France st de l'Etranger*, 60,août 1905, 229-231. Also in *Ecrits et paroles*, 2, 239-240; *Mélanges*, 656-658. Bergson denies any influence of William James on the development of his concept of "durée réelle." William James' notion of the stream of consciousness was developed in the context of psychological considerations; Bergson's notion of "durée réelle" was developed in a context of mathematical and physical preoccupations.

120 "Rapport sur *L'Ame et le corps* d'Alfred Binet." *Séances et Travaux de l'Académie des Sciences Morales et Politiques*, 165, 1906, 166-167. Also in *Ecrits et paroles*, 2, 251-252; *Mélanges*, 671-672. Binet's theories of matter and perception are discussed in this essay.

121 "Rapport sur un ouvrage de M. Ossip-Lourié: *Le Bonheur et l'intelligence*." *Séances et Travaux de l'Académie des Sciences Morales et Politiques*, 164, juillet 1905, 114 (Séance du 1er avril 1905). Also in *Ecrits et paroles*, 2, 237; *Mélanges*, 653-654. This is a brief account of a book which attempts to define the nature of happiness.

122 "Rapport sur le Prix Bordin à décerner en 1905: Mémoires sur Maine de Biran." *Séances et Travaux de l'Académie des Sciences Morales et Politiques*, 165, janvier 1906, 152-162 (Séance du 8 novembre 1905). Also in *Ecrits et paroles*, 2, 243-250; *Mélanges*, 662-671. Here Bergson examines two studies of the philosophy of Maine de Biran, assessing the strengths and weaknesses of each. First prize is awarded to a study titled *La Vie de l'esprit commence avec le premier effort voulu*.

1906

123 "Cours au Collège de France sur les théories de la volonté." *Revue de Philosophie*, 7, No. 7, 1er juillet 1907, 70-91. Also in *Mélanges*, 685-704. These are notes by P. Fontana on Bergson's course given in 1906-1907. In this essay on the theory of volition Bergson considers scientific materialism and the positions of

A. Schopenhauer and William James. He deals in particular with the nature of voluntary attention and muscular effort.

124 "Cours au Collège de France sur les théories de la volonté: Suite." *Revue de Philosophie*, 7, No. 10, 1er octobre 1907, 407-428. Also in *Mélanges*, 704-722. These are notes by P. Fontana on Bergson's course which was given in 1906-1907. In this essay on the nature of volition (the continuation of a previous essay) Bergson considers the effects of volition on the entire mental life, both in the case of particular mental acts and in the case of longer periods of time. In the latter case, Bergson holds that they have to do with character.

125 "Cours du collège de France: Philosophie moderne." *Archives du Collège de France*, 7, 1907, p. 80. Also in *Ecrits et paroles*, 2, p. 259; *Mélanges*, 684. Bergson's courses in 1906-1907 on the concept of volition an on Herbert Spencer's *Principles of Psychology* are discussed here.

126 "L'Idée de néant." *Revue Philosophique de la France et de l'Etranger*, 31, No. 10, octobre 1906, 449-466. This essay is republished in Ch. IV of *L'Evolution créatrice*. Bergson holds here that the idea of "nothing" is a pseudo-idea, involving an illicit transport of notions derived from practical behavior into the realm of pure theory. The idea of nothing is relative to some specific object for which we are searching. When we do not find that object we say we have found "nothing." But what we have found is a something, which we did not want. Negation itself, Bergson holds, is an "affirmation of the second degree." (Cf., in the secondary literature M. Couche, 1959 and V. Descombes, 1980.)

127 "Lettre à A. Bourgeois: 9 mai 1906." *Etudes Bergsoniennes*, 9, p. 21. Also in *Mélanges*, 681. This concerms Charles Péguy's *Cahiers de la Quinzaine*.

128 "Lettre à Ch. Péguy: 9 mai 1906." *Etudes Bergsoniennes*, 8, p. 20. Also in *Mélanges*, 680-681. This concerms Charles Péguy's *Cahiers de la Quinzaine*.

129 "Rapport sur un ouvrage de M. Jacques Bardoux: *Essai d'une psychologie de l'Angleterre contemporaine: Les Crises belliqueuses.*" *Séances et Travaux de l'Académie des Sciences Morales et Politiques*, 165, mai 1906, 683-684 (Séance du 10 février 1906). Also in *Ecrits et paroles*, 2, 253-254; *Mélanges*, 676-678. This is a rather brief examination of a study of industrial and political factors in Great Britain during the late nineteeth and early twentieth centuries and of the British attitude towards war.

130 "Rappport sur un ouvrage de P. Gaultier: *Le Sens de l'art*. Préface d'Émile Boutroux." *Séances et Travaux de l'Académie des Sciences Morales et Politiques*, 167, mars 1907, 425-426 (Séance du 24 novembre 1906). Also in *Ecrits et paroles*, 2, 257-258; *Mélanges*, 682-684. This concerns the place of emotion in aesthetics.

131 "Rapport sur un ouvrage de G. H. Luquet: *Idées générales de psychologie.*" *Séances et Travaux de l'Académie des Sciences Morales et Politiques*, 168, 1907, 425-426 (Séance du 5 mai 1906). Also in *Ecrits et paroles*, 2, 255-256; *Mélanges*, 679-680. This is a brief discussion of Luquet's Bergsonian psychology.

1907

132 "Enquête sur l'enseignement de la philosophie: Discussion avec Binet sur l'influence de la philosophie de Bergson sur les élèves des lycées." *Bulletin de la Société Française de Philosophie*, 8, janvier 1908, 12, 14, 21-22 (Séance du 28 novembre 1907). Also in *Ecrits et paroles*, 2, 277-278; *Mélanges*, 746-747. Here Bergson

protests strongly against anti-scientific interpretations of his thought. His philosophy seeks a rapprochement between science and metaphysics with no loss to either.

133   *L'Evolution créatice*. Paris: Félix Alcan, 1907, 403. (Bibliothèque de philosophie contemporaine)

Creative Evolution is an application both of the mind-matter duality of *Matter and Memory* (1896) and of the concept of philosophical method developed in *An Introduction to Metaphysics* (1903). Above all, it is a sustained reflection on and critique of turn of the century concepts of biological evolution, especially neo-Darwinism. All mechanistic theories of evolution including neo-Darwinism are, according to Bergson, insufficient to account for evolution in its richness and complexity. Such theories need to be supplemented by a more comprehensive philosophical explanation.

Bergson begins the first chapter of *Creative Evolution* by distinguishing living things from non-living. All things, living and non-living, endure. But, he cautions, living things embody a cumulative memory which makes it impossible for them to repeat the same state twice, while the memory which binds the successive states of non-living matter appears more repetitive than cumulative. We may therefore need different explanations for living than for non-living things, for biological evolution as opposed to physics and physical cosmology.

Evolutionary theories traditionally divide into two sorts, mechanistic and finalistic. Mechanism attempts to explain life through the chance coming together of material particles, while finalism attempts to explain life through the pursuit of definite, pre-ordained goals. Both explanations fail to account for the phenomenon of life, Bergson insists, because both ignore the fact of duration; both assume that *all is given* at the beginning. The two most important scientific theories of evolution are Lamarckianism and neo-Darwinism. Bergson rejects Lamarckianism on the grounds that no conclusive case of the inheritance of acquired characteristics has ever been demonstrated. He rejects neo-Darwinism on the basis of what he believes to be its fatal dilemma. For neo-Darwinism *either* evolution occurs through very gradual changes (In which case, how are the useful changes retained, in the right order, in order that new organs or organisms can evolve?); *or* it occurs through abrupt, radical changes (In which case we fall back on a miraculous happenstance: a sudden convergence of elements in just the right order, of the right kind, to produce a new organism.)

This argument is, Bergson believes, difficult to answer successfully in the case of specific organs and organisms. It is impossible to answer, he concludes, if we consider phenomena of evolutionary convergence: that is, the appearance, on distant branches of the evolutionary tree, of like organs in unlike organisms. The example which Bergson chooses is the existence in man and in the pectin (a mollusc) of an eye virtually identical in all basic structures: inverted retina, cornea, lens, etc. Accidental causes, operating by chance on widely varying evolutionary lines, can not produce this strange identity. An adequate explanation would involve the hypothesis on an "élan vital": a vital impetus, containing within itself the possibilities of a multiplicity of life-forms.

In the second chapter of *Creative Evolution* Bergson describes the evolutionary development of the vital impetus as it diverges to shape the world of living things. Bergson finds three main directions of evolutionary development (unless, he speculates, the fungi are to be considered as a fourth direction): the plants, which exist in a state of "torpor"; the vertebrates, which have more and more emphasized intelligence in the course of their development; and the arthropods, which have stressed instinct. Animal evolution thus culminates in two contrasting sorts of animal societies, each emphasizing a different sort of knowledge. Human societies emphasize intelligence (the capacity to shape tools out of matter) and insect societies utilize instinct (an innate knowledge of living things, but extremely limited in scope—to what is useful to a particular species).

The contrast between vertebrate intelligence and insect instinct suggests, Bergson continues, a combined reflection both on the theory of knowledge and on the categories of metaphysics. In each case we discover fundamental, essentially parallel dualities. Instinct is a kind of sympathy, which knows life "from within"; but it is limited, even in the most advanced insect societies, to very specific biological objects. Intelligence can deal with any sort of object; but it does so in spatial, abstract terms. The dilemma posed by the opposition of these two incomplete modes of knowledge can be resolved only by intuition, a mode of knowledge capable of grasping life itself, and which unites the flexibility, extensibility and self-consciousness of intelligence with the sympathy and interiority of instinct. Intuition is instinct become self-conscious, disinterested, capable of reflecting on its object and extending it indefinitely.

In the third chapter of *Creative Evolution* Bergson explores the analogy between the contrasting tendencies of evolution and non-living matter and the two directions of human thought, intuition (which is clearly not mere instinct) and intellect. The upward thrust of the human mind, the creation of new ideas, new possibilities, is for Bergson the work of intuition; the interruption of the intuitive effort produces an inverse phenomenon, the increasingly complex conceptual arsenal of the human intellect, with its spatialized expression of the intuitive insight. Similarly, life as it ascends towards more and more fully developed forms and increasingly conscious behavior must contend with non-living matter which (as described in terms of thermodynamics) descends in the direction of greater entropy, homogeneity, repetition. Intuition and life thus share a common *élan* while intellect and matter share a common direction. This is why man, *homo faber*, has succeeded so quickly and so conclusively as a scientist and engineer. But it is also why he has neglected the intuitive capacities which have underlain his scientific success. The development of human intuition and its application to the evolutionary process point, as Bergson sees it, to an important conclusion. In man alone, for the first time in the course of evolution, consciousness, originally present in the vital impetus, has regained itself; in this respect man is the goal of evolution.

Bergson concludes *Creative Evolution* with a reflection (taking up most of the fourth chapter) on the history of philosophy and of science. Greek philosophy (in Plato and Aristotle) sought to explain change through timeless form; to that extent, it tended to degrade change into something comparatively unreal. Modern science, though it borrows from Greek intellectualism, differs from Greek science and philosophy in its effort to consider its object not at a priviledged moment (its achievement of form) but at any moment whatever. Such a science is bound to consider time as a fundamental reality, but will nonetheless continue to conceive time as made up of static instants into which dynamic transitions will somehow be introduced. (Bergson calls this procedure the ćinematographic fallacy.") The result has been, from René Descartes to Immanual Kant and Herbert Spencer, a fundamental commitment to mechanistic concepts and to a homogeneous, spatialized time which now stands in the way of both philosophy and science. We must get beyond the scholasticism that has grown up around the physics of Galileo, just as early modern science and philosophy found it necessary to go beyond a scholasticism that had grown up around the physics of Aristotle.

134 *LÉvolution créatrice*. 52e ed. Paris: Presses Universitaires de France., 1940, x, 372. (Bibliotèque de philosophie contemporaine)

135 *L'Evolution créatrice*. Genève: Skira, 1946, 374.

136 *L'Evolution créatrice*. in *Oeuvres*. Ed. André Robinet. Paris: Presses Universitaires de France, 1959, 489-809.

137 *L'Évolution créatrice*. Nouv. éd. Paris: Presses Universitaires de France, 1981, xi, 372. (Quadrige, 8)

Translations

Creative Evolution. Auth. Trans. Arthur Mitchell. New York: Holt and Co., 1911, 407.

Creative Evolution. Auth. Trans. Arthur Mitchell. Foreword Irwin Edman. New York: The Modern Library, 1944.xxv, 453.

Creative Evolution. Auth. Trans. Arthur Mitchell. London: The Macmillian Co., 1954, xv, 425.

Creative Evolution. Auth. Trans. Arthur Mitchell. Foreword Irwin Edman. 1944: rpt. Westport, Conn.: Greenwood Press, 1975, xxv, 453.

Creative Evolution. Auth. Trans. Arthur Mitchell. Intro. Pete A. Y. Gunter. Lanham, Maryland: University Press of America, 1983, li, 407.

"The Evolution of Life." In *Philosophers of Science*. New York: Carlton House, 1947, 274-293.

"An Extract from Bergson." *Camera Work*, No. 36, October, 1911, 20-21. This excerpt concerns instinct, intelligence, and intuition.

"Form and Becoming." In *The Philosophy of Time: A Collection of Essays*. Ed. Richard M. Gale. Garden City, New York: Doubleday, 1967, 397-405. (Doubleday Anchor Originals, No. A573). This excerpt concerns Zeno's paradoxes.

"The Ideal Genesis of Matter and the Meaning of Evolution." in *Process Philosophy: Basic Writings*. Eds. Jack R. Sibley and Pete A. Y. Gunter. Lanham, Maryland: University Press of America, 1978, 151-171.

"The Philosophy of Ideas." *New Freewoman*, 1, No. 13, 1913, 246-248. This is an excerpt from *Creative Evolution*, pp. 329 *et seq*.

"Time in the History of Western Philosophy." In *Philosophy in the Twentieth Century: An Anthology*. Vol. III. Ed. with intro. William Barrett and Henry D. Aiken. New York: Random House, 1962, 331-363.

A evolução criadora. Trans. Adolfo Casais Monteiro. Intro. Jean Guitton. Rio de Janeiro: Ópera Mundi, 1971, 361.

A evolução criadora. Trans. Natanael Caixeiro. Rio de Janeiro: Zahar, 1979, 317 pp.

Evolución creadora. 2 Vols. Trans. Carlos Malagarriga. Madird: Renacimiento, 1912, 276, 251. This translation includes Alfredo Coviello, "Bergson en América", Francisco G. Calderon, "El Bergsonismo". (Los Grandes Filósofos)

La evolución creadora. Trans. Carlos Malagarriga. Intro. F. G. Calderon. Montevideo: Garcia, 1942, 385.

La evolución creadora. Trans. María Luisa Pérez Torres. Madrid: Espasa-Calpe, 1973, 319. (Collección austral, No. 1519)

Evólución creadora: Abreviatura de Fernando Vela. Buenos Aires: Revista de Occidenta Argentina, 1947, 192.

"Significado de la evolución." *Atlántida*, 9, No. 27, 1913, 348-379. This is taken from C. Malagarriga's translation.

L'evoluzione creatrice. Introduzione e Commento a Cura di Paolo Serini." Milano-Verona: Mondadori, 1935, 282. (Collana di Testi Filosofici)

L'evoluzione creatrice. Trans. U. Segre. Milano: Corbaccio, 1936, 226. (Collana univ. moderna, 61) The first edition was published in 1925.

L'evoluzione creatrice. Napoli: Libreria scientifica, 1947, 208. (Biblioteca di filosofia)

Evoluzione creatrice. Trans. L. Ferrarino. Bari: Laterza, 1949, 242.

L'evoluzione creatrice. Trans. amd Intro. Armando Vedaldi. Firenze: Sansoni, 1951, v, 224.

L'evoluzione creatrice, a cura di Francesco Albergamo. Mazara, Italy: Società Editrice Siciliana, 1952, 84.

L'evoluzione creatrice: Antologia a cura di Vittorio Mathieu. Bari, Italy: Laterza, 1957, 210. (Piccola biblioteca filosofica)

L'evoluzione creatrice: Estratti. Trans. L. Ferrarino. Bari, Italy: Laterza, 1959, iv, 242. (Piccola Biblioteca Filosofica)

L'evoluzione creatrice. Trans. Armando Vedaldi. Firenze: Sansoni, 1963, 224. (Collana scolastica di testi filosofica)

L'evoluzione creatrice. Trans. Giancarlo Penati. Brescia, Italy: La Scuola, 1961, 140.

L'evoluzione creatrice. Trans. Leonella Alano Podini. Milano: Fabbri, 1966, 396.

L'evoluzione creatrice. 3e ed. Trans. Giancarlo Penati. Brescia, Italy: La Scuola, 1968, 136.

Ewolucja twórcza. Warszawa: Gebethner & Wolff, 1913, ii, 310.

Ewolucja twórcza. Trans. Florian Znaniecki. Warsaw: Ksiązka i Wiedza, 1957, 318. This is a new edition preceded by an essay by Leszek Kołakowski, "Bergson, the Antinomy of Practical Reason."

Ha-Hitpathut ha-yotseret. Trans. Yosef Ur. Yerusalem: Magnes, 1974, 251.

La Nociono di la tempo: Unesma pagini de la Kreante eveluciono. Trans. Paulo Dienes. Budapest: Ido-editerio, 1919, 20. (Biblioteko dil internaciona kulturo. No. 7)

Schöpferische Entwicklung. Auth. Trans. Gertrud Kantorowicz. Jena: Diederichs, 1912, 373.

Schöpferische Entwicklung. Auth. Trans. Gertrud Kantorowicz. Zürich: Coron-Verlag, 1967, 365.

Den skapende utveckling. Trans. Algot Ruhe. Stockholm: 1911, 345.

Den skabende udvikling. Auth. Trans. Knud Ferlov. Copenhagen: Gad, 1914.

Sôzô-teki shinka; Keijijo-gaku nyûmon. Trans. Kosaku Matsuura; Keisaburô Masuda. Tokyo: Kawade shobô, 1953, 330. This contains translations of *L'Evolution créatrice* and *Introduction à la métaphysique.*

Sôzô-teki shinka. Trans. Notimichi Magata. Tokyo: Iwanami shoten, 1954, 231.

Sôzôteki shinka. Trans. Notimichi Magata. Tokyo: Iwanami shoten, 1961, 253.

Sôzôteki shinka. Trans. Matsunami Shinzaburô and Takahashi Masaaki. Tokyo: Hakusuisha, 1966, 434.

Jikan to jikû. Sôzôteki shinka. Trans. Nakamura Yûjiro et al. Tokyo: Kawade shobo, 1967, 422. This is a translation of the *Essai* and *L'Évolution créatrice.*

Al-Tatawwur al-khālig. Trans. Muhammad Qāsim. al-Qāhirah: Dār al-Fikr al-'arabī. 1961-1962.

Teremto fejlodés. Forditotta és bevezetéssel elláta dr. Dienes Valéria. Budapest: A Magyar tudományos akadémia, 1930, xvi, 338. (Az Akadémia filozófai könyvtára. Kiadja a magyar tudományos akadémia filozófai bizottsága. 2.)

138   "Lettre à W. James: 27 juin 1907." *Revue de Deux Mondes*, 15 Octobre 1933, 808-809. Also in *Ecrits et paroles*, 2, 260-261; *Mélanges*, 726-272.

139   "Lettreà E. J. Lotte: 26 août 1907. *Bulletin Joseph Lotte*, 104, mars 1940, 281-282. Also in Quoniam. *De La Sainteté*, 75-76; *Etudes Bergsoniennes*, 8, p. 22; *Mélanges*, 735. This is about Lotte's article on *L'Evolution créatrice.*

140   "Lettre à G. Papini." *Nouvelles Littéraires*, 15 décembre 1928. Also in *Ecrits et paroles*, 1, p. 204; *Mélanges*, 736. This letter, written in 1907, expresses Bergson's regrets concerning the cessation of publication of *Leonardo.*

141   "Lettre au directeur de la *Revue du Mois après l'article de Le Dantec sur L'Evolution créatrice.*" *Revue du Mois*, 4, No. 9, 10 Septembre 1907, 351-354. Also in *Ecrits et paroles*, 2, 264-267; Le Dantec. *Science et conscience*, Ch. VI; *Mélanges*, 731-735. This is a discussion of Le Dantec's misinterpretation of Bergson's theory of evolution: absolute and relative motion, epiphenomenalism, mathematism, and "élan vital."

142   "Rapport sur le concours pour le Prix Le-Dissez-de-Penanrun: Ouvrage de F. Evellin: *La Raison pure et les antinomies* et ouvrage de G. Belot: *Etudes de morale positive*". *Séances et Travaux de l'Académie des Sciences Morales et Politiques*, 169, janvier 1908, 91-102 (Séances du 26 octobre 1907). Also in *Ecrits et paroles*, 2, 262-263; *Mélanges*, 268-276; *Mélanges*, 736-746. Kant's antinomies are discussed here along with Belot's utilitarianism.

143   "Rapport sur un ouvrage de J. Bardoux (suite): *Essai d'une psychologie de l'Angleterre contemporaine: Les Crises politiques: Protectionnisme et radicalisme.*" *Séances et Travaux de l'Académie des Sciences Morales et Politiques, 169*, janvier 1908, 105-107 (Séance du 29 juin 1997). Also in Ecrits et paroles, 2, 262-263; *Mélanges*, 728-730. This is an account of a study of protectionism and free trade in Britain.

144   "Réponse à Frédéric Charpin sur la question religieuse." *Mercure de France*, 69, No. 241, 15 juillet 1907, 34. Also in Frédéric Charpin. *La Question religieuse.* Paris: 1908, p. 272; *Ecrits et paroles*, 2, 308; *Mélanges*, 730-731. Bergson claims here that religious feeling is not destined to fade away.

145   "Résumé par Bergson de ses cours sur *Formation et valeur des idées générales* et
        sur *Principes de la connaissance* de Berkeley." *Archives du collège de France*,
        7, 1907, p. 89. Also in *Ecrits et paroles*, 2, 279; *Mélanges*, 748. In this
        description of two courses given at the Collège de France, Bergson mentions
        problems concerning the relations between language and thought and concerning
        the different possible kinds of general ideas. Bergson's course on Berkeley
        included an attempt to define idealism and an analysis of Berkeley's theory of
        general ideas. Cf. Bergson's essay "L'Intuition philosophique" (1911) for
        Bergson's interpretation of Berkeley.

1908

146   "A Propos de *L'Evolution de l'intelligence géométrique*: Réponse à un article d'E.
        Borel." *Revue de Métaphysique et de Morale*, 16, No. 1, janvier 1908, 28-33.
        Also in *Ecrits et paroles*, 2, 280-285; *Mélanges*, 753-758. In this essay Bergson
        denies Borel's claim that he conceives mathematics and geometry not to have
        changed since the Greeks. Mathematics have indeed changed—witness the
        emergence of non-Euclidean geometries. But certain characteristics of mathema-
        tics remain constant. This item is important for the light it casts on Bergson's
        philosophy of mathematics.

147   "Discussion à propos du *Vocabulaire philosophique*: Interventions à propos des
        mots 'immédiat' et 'inconnaisable'." *Bulletin de la Société Française de
        Philosophie*, 8, août 1908, 331-333, 340-341. Also in *Ecrits et paroles*, 2,
        300-303; *Mélanges*, 771-772. Here Bergson gives his definitions of the words
        "immediate" and "unknowable."

148   "Lettre à Alfred Binet: 30 mars 1908." *Année Psychologique*, 14, 1908, 230-231.
        Also in *Ecrits et paroles*, 2, 292-293; *Mélanges*, 762-763. This letter is about
        Bergson's method of writing and the difficulties of introspection.

149   "Lettre à H. Wildon Carr." *Proceedings of the Aristotelian Society*, N.S. 9, 1908-
        1909, 59-60. This is about Zeno, the nature of motion, the future of the sciences,
        and the limitations of "intelligence."

150   "Lettre à L. Dauriac: 2 décembre 1908." *Etudes Bergsoniennes*, 3, p. 96 (in part).
        Also in *Mélanges*, 781 (complete). Bergson discusses agoraphobia, dreams, and
        abnormal psychology in this brief letter.

151   "Lettre à W. James: 9 mai 1908." *Revue des Deux Mondes*, 8. Sér. 17, No. 20,
        15 octobre 1933, 810-811. Also in *Ecrits et paroles*, 2, 294-295; *Mélanges*,
        765-766. This is about the early history of Bergson's thought. Bergson's ideas
        changed significantly from 1881 through 1883 at Angers.

152   "Lettre à W. James: 23 juillet 1908." *Revue des Deux Mondes*, 8, Sér. 17, No.
        20, 15 octobre 1933, 813-814. Also in *Ecrits et paroles*, 2, 304-305; *Mélanges*,
        775-777. In this letter Bergson comments favorably on an essay written about
        him by James. This essay appears in James's *A Pluralistic Universe*.

153   "Lettre à G. Sorel: Avril 1908." *Etudes Bergsoniennes*, 3, p. 48n. Also in *Mélanges*,
        764. This is a brief fragment concerning the difficulty of conceiving evolution
        through concepts.

154 "Lettre à J. de Tonquédec: 12 mai 1908." *Etudes par des Péres de la Compagnie de Jésus*, 130, No. 1, 1912, 156. Also in J. de Tonquédec. *Sur La Philosophie bergsonienne*, 1936, 60-61; *Ecrits et paroles*, 2, p. 269; *Mélanges*, 766-767. In this letter Bergson states that he is not a pantheist.

155 "Rapport sur un ouvrage d'A. Bazaillas: *Musique et inconscience.*" *Séances et Travaux de l'Académie des Sciences Morales et Politiques*, 169, juin 1908, 719-720 (Séances du ler février 1908). Also in *Ecrits et paroles*, 2, 288-289; *Mélanges*, 759-760. This is an expository review of Bazaillas' study of music, A. Schopenhauer, and the unconscious.

156 "Rapport sur un ouvrage de Boirac: *La Psychologie inconnue.*" *Séances et Travaux de l'Académie des Sciences Morales et Politiques*, 170, juillet 1908, 119-120 (Séance du 28 mars 1908). Also in *Ecrits et paroles*, 2, 290-291; *Mélanges*, 769-770. Brain and consciousness, the unconscious, and introspection are discussed in this essay.

157 "Rapport sur un ouvrage de J. Merlant: *Sénancour.*" *Séances et Travaux de l'Académie des Sciences Morales et Politiques*, 169, juin 1908, 720-721 (Séance du 18 janvier 1908). Also in *Ecrits et paroles*, 2, 286-287; *Mélanges*, 751-752. This is a brief description of a book on the poet and religious thinker Sénancour (1770-1846).

158 "Rapport sur un ouvrage de J. P. Nayrac: *La Fontaine.*" *Séances et Travaux de l'Académie des Sciences Morales et Politiques*, 170, septembre 1908, 484 (Séance du 23 mai 1908). Also in *Ecrits et paroles*, 2, 297; *Mélanges*, 768-769. Here Bergson discusses a psychological and literary study of the writer La Fontaine.

159 "Remarque sur l'organisation des congrés de philosophie aprés de compte rendu fait par H. Delacroix sur le Congrès international de philosophie de Heidelberg." *Bulletin de la Société Française de Philosophie*, 19 janvier 1909, 11-12 (Séance du octobre 1908). Also in *Ecrits et paroles*, 2, 306-307; *Mélanges*, 779-780. Here Bergson suggests that papers read at the next philosophical congress be confined by and large to general philosophical topics instead of concentrating on problems in the philosophy of particular sciences.

160 "Résumé par Bergson de ses cours sur *Nature de l'esprit et rapport de l'esprit à l'action cérébrale*et sur le *Siris* de G. Berkeley, p. 76. Also in *Ecrits et paroles*, 2, p. 209; *Mélanges*, 782. Here Bergson gives a general account of two courses. The first is concerned with the mind-body problem, the second with Berkeley's later thought as expressed in his book *Siris*. These courses were given in 1908-1909.

161 "Le Souvenir du présent et la fausse reconnaissance." *Revue Philosophique de la France et de l'Etranger*, 66, No. 4, décembre 1908, 561-593.

Here Bergson proposes an explanation of the phenomenon "déjà vu" (false recognition), in which the observer seems to perceive present circumstances as if he had experienced them in detail previously. Surveying the literature on the subject, Bergson concludes that two sets of theories may be useful in explaining the phenomenon: those that posit a "doubling" of psychological imagery and those which connect "déjà vu" with a general slackening of "attention to life." Referring to *Matter and Memory* (1896), Bergson argues that the memory of the present moment is created concomitantly with the occurrence of that moment, but is ordinarily—normal consciousness being focussed on the future and attempting to adapt to circumstances—not noticed. If, however, we were to become aware of this memory *as it is being formed*, we would have paradoxically, a "memory of the present"—*in the present*. This awareness of present memory, Bergson holds, accounts for "déjà vu". It occurs when there is a failure of "attention to life", in which the effort to cope is enfeebled and the memory of the present is thereby able to become conscious. Bergson speculates that the false recognition is an effort to limit the flagging of attention to life to specific, brief intervals, thus preventing more serious pathologies.

162   "Le Souvenir du présent et la fausse reconnaissance." *L'Energie spirituelle: Essais et conférences.* Paris: Presses Universitaires de France, 1919. This version contains numerous changes and corrections by Bergson. (Cf. *Mind-Energy*, 1920, 134-185.)

163   "Le Souvenir du présent et la fausse reconnaissance." *Oeuvres.* Ed. André Robinet. Paris: Presses Universitaires de France, 897-930. (Notes, 1523-1528)

Translation

"La imrpresión de 'ya visto'." *Estudios*, 27, No. 315, 1937, 27-76. Trans. L. M. Ravagnan.

1909

164   "Discours sur Gabriel Tarde: 12 septembre 1909." *Mélanges*, 799-801. This is a speech delivered on the occasion of the dedication of a monument to Tarde.

165   "Discussion à propos de l'ouvrage de Georges Dwelshauvers: *L'Inconscient dans la vie mentale.*" *Bulletin de la Société Française de Philosophie*, 10, No. 2, janvier 1910, 31-46 (Séance du 25 novembre 1909). Also in *Ecrits et paroles*, 2, 325-331; *Mélanges*, 803-810. In this highly interesting discussion, which includes an exchange between Bergson and Dwelshauvers, the terms "conscious" and "unconscious" are clarified.

166   "Discussion à propos du *Vocabulaire philosophique*: Intervention à propos du mot 'intuition'." *Bulletin de la Société Française de Philosophie*, 9, 1909, p. 274 (Séance du ler juillet 1909). Also in *Ecrits et paroles*, 2, p. 322; *Mélanges*, 796-797. This is a discussion of scientific knowledge as a precondition of intuition.

167   "Lettre à A. Bourgeois: 6 juillet 1909." *Etudes Bergsoniennes*, 8, p. 23, Also in *Mélanges*, 797. This brief note concerns *Cahiers de la Quinzaine*.

168   "Lettre à W. James: 21 janvier 1909." *Revue des Deux Mondes*, 8, Sér. 17, No. 20, 15 octobre 1933, 816-817. Also in *Ecrits et paroles*, 2, p. 310; *M"elanges*, 785-786. This concerns G. Fechner's *Zend-Avesta* and the hypothesis of a world-soul.

169   "Lettre à W. James: 9 avril 1909." *Revue des Deux Mondes*, 8, Sér. 17, No. 20, 15 octobre 1933, p. 817. Also in *Ecrits et paroles*, 2, p. 315; *Mélanges*, 790. Bergson congratulates James for his article in the *Hibbert Journal* on the philosophy of Bergson. This article appears in James' *A Pluralistic Universe*.

170   "Lettre à W. James: 30 avril 1909." *Revue des Deux Mondes*, 8, Sér. 17, No. 20, 15 octobre 1933, 817-818. Also in *Ecrits et paroles*, 2, 316-317; *Mélanges*, 791. In this letter Bergson discusses G. Fechner's *Zend-Avesta* and certain of

W. James' ideas concerning the philosophy of religion.

171 "Lettre à W. James: 28 octobre 1909." *Revue des Deux Mondes*, 8, Sér. 17, No. 20, 15 octobre 1944, 818-819. Also in *Ecrits et paroles*, 2, 323-324; *Mélanges*, 801-802. In this letter Bergson comments on James's *The Meaning of Truth* and upon the difficulties which James' philosophy will find in being understood.

172 "Lettre à Giuseppe Prezzolini: 12 juillet 1909." *Il tempo della voce*. Ed. Giuseppe Prezzolini. Milano e Firenze: Coedizione Longanese e Vallecchi, 1960, 239-242.

173 "Lettre à N. Söderblom: 27 juillet 1909." H. Sunden. *La Théorie bergsonienne de la religion*, 37. Also in *Mélanges*, 797-798. In this letter Bergson declines an invitation to give lectures at Uppsala on the philosophy of religion. His views on the subject are not yet precise and formulable.

174 "Préface aux *Pages choisies* de Gabriel Tarde, par ses fils." Paris: Michaud, 1909, 223. (Collection *Les Grands Philosophes*). Also in *Ecrits et paroles*, 2, 332-334; *Mélanges*, 811-813. Bergson here presents the basic ideas of the sociologist G. Tarde.

175 "Rapport sur un ouvrage de J. H. Boex-Borel (J. H. Rosny-aîné): *Le Pluralisme: Etude sur la discontinuité et l'hétérogénéité des phénomènes.*" *Séances et Travaux de l'Académie des Sciences Morales et Politiques*, 172, 1909, 517-519 (Séance du juin 1909). Also in *Ecrits et paroles*, 2, 319-321; *Mélanges*, 794-796.

176 "Rapport sur un ouvrage de Georges Bohn: *La Naissance de l'intelligence.*" *Séances et Travaux de l'Académie des Sciences Morales et Politiques*, 172, 1909, 144-145 (Séance du 1er mai 1909). Also in *Ecrits et paroles*, 2, 317-318; *Mélanges*, 792-793. This is about comparative psychology, intelligence, and tropisms.

177 "Rapport sur un ouvrage de M. Henri Delacroix: *Etudes d'histoire et de psychologie du mysticisme.*" *Séances et Travaux de l'Académie des Sciences Morales et Politiques*, 171, mai 1909, 670-671 (Séance du 20 janvier 1909). Also in *Ecrits et paroles*, 2, 313-314; *Mélanges*, 788-790. This is a brief, expository review of Delacroix's study of mysticism. Delacroix's ideas undoubtedly had an important influence on Bergson's philosophy of religion. (Cf., in the secondary literature, H. Gouhier, 1961.)

178 "Rapport sur un ouvrage de M. Emile Meyerson: *Identité et réalité.*" *Séances et Travaux de l'Académie des Sciences Morales et Politiques*, 171, mai 1909, 664-666 (Séance du 23 janvier 1909). Also in *Ecrits et paroles*, 2, 332-312; *Mélanges*, 786-788. This is a résumé of Meyerson's position in *Identity and Reality*.

1910

179 "Cours au Collège de France: La Théorie de la personne d'après Bergson." *Etudes par des pères de la Compagnie de Jésus*, 129, No. 4, 1911, 449-485. Also in *Mélanges*, 847-875. These notes were taken by Jules Grivet in 1910-1911. This lecture provides significant insights into Bergson's psychology and his interpretation of the psychology of his era. Bergson deals particularly with the problem of multiple personality. (Cf. Bergson's précis of his unpublished Gifford Lectures on the problem of personality, 1914.)

180   "Discussion pour le *Vocabulaire philosophique* sur le mot 'liberté'." *Bulletin de la Société Française de Philosophie*, 10, No. 7, 1910, 164-166 (Séance du 7 juillet 1910). Also in *Ecrits et paroles*, 2, p. 349; *Mélanges*, 833-834. In this item liberty is discussed as involving both self-determination and interdetermination; liberty is "situated" between these two terms.

181   "'Une Heure chez Henri Bergson' par Georges Aimel." *Paris-Journal*, 11 décembre 1910. Also in *Ecrits et paroles*, 2, 354-355; *Mélanges*, 843-844. Here Bergson discusses philosophy and art, literary creativity, symbolism, and his liking for the music of Claude Debussy.

182   "Lettre à I. Benrubi: 14 juin 1910." I. Benrubi. *Essais et témoignages*, 373. Also in *Mélanges*, 832. This letter is about Benrubi's articles concerning Bergson, F. Nietzsche, and J. J. Rousseau.

183   "Lettre à W. James: 21 mars 1910." *Revue des Deux Mondes*, 8, Sér. 17, No. 20, 15 octobre 1933, 819-820. Also in *Ecrits et paroles*, 2, 335-336; *Mélanges*, 816-817. This letter is about James' "The Moral Equivalent of War" and "A Suggestion about Mysticism." Bergson discusses a dream he has experienced as a possible "uncovering."

184   "Lettre à E. J. Lotte: 15 juillet 1910." *Bulletin Joseph Lotte*, 104, mars 1940, p. 282. Also in Quoniam. *De La Sainteté*, 76; "Etudes Bergsoniennes, 8, p. 30. Also in *Mélanges*, 834. In this letter Bergson praises Lotte's articles concerning *L'Evolution créatrice*.

185   "Lettre à E. J. Lotte: 20 septembre 1910." *Etudes Bergsoniennes*, 8, p. 30. Also in *Mélanges*, 835. In this letter Bergson regrets that he is unable to see M. Lotte at the present time.

186   "Lettre à Ch. Péguy: 14 janvie 1910." *Etudes Bergsoniennes*, 8, p. 24. *Mélanges*, 815-816. Bergson suggests a time at which he and Péguy might meet.

187   "Lettre à Ch. Péguy: 4 juin 1910." *Feuillets de l'Amitié Charles Péguy*, 30, p. 9. Also in *Etudes Bergsoniennes*, 8, p. 27; *Mélanges*, 828. In this letter Bergson arranges a meeting with Péguy.

188   "Lettre à Ch. Péguy: 20 juin 1910." *Feuillets de l'Amitié Charles Péguy*, 30, 9-10. Also in *Etudes Bergsoniennes*, 8, p. 29; *Mélanges*, 832-833. In this letter Bergson returns, with regrets, a manuscript by E. Berth.

189   "Lettre à Ch. Péguy." *Etudes Bergsoniennes*, 8, p. 31. Also in *Mélanges*, 842. Bergson discusses a recent issue of Péguy's *Cahiers de la Quinzaine*.

190   "Rapport pour le concours Charles-Lévêque à décerner en 1910: L'Ouvrage d'Hannequin: *Etudes d'histoire des sciences et d'histoire de la philosophie*." *Séances et Travaux de l'Académie des Sciences Morales et Politiques*, 174, 1910, 496-501 (Séance du 22 octobre 1910). Also in *Ecrits et paroles*, 2, 350-353; *Mélanges*, 835-839. Here Bergson awards a prize to a posthumously published study of modern philosophy.

191   "Rapport pour le concours de *Coenobium*." *Coenobium*, 6, No. 1, janvier 1912, 176-192. Also in *Ecrits et paroles*, 2, 350-353; *Mélanges*, 840-841. In these notes, written in 1910, Bergson discusses the relative merits of several works, some valuable, some not.

192   "Rapport sur un ouvrage de Lionel Dauriac: *Le Musicien poète R. Wagner; Etude de psychologie musicale*." *Séances et Travaux de l'Académie des Sciences Morales et Politiques*, 173, juin 1910, 803-805 (Séance du 16 avril 1910). Also

in *Ecrits et paroles*, 2, 337-339; *Mélanges*, 818-820. This is an expository review of Dauriac's book on Richard Wagner.

193   "Rapport sur un ouvrage de M. André Joussain: *Le Fondement psychologique de la morale.*" *Séances et Travaux de l'Académie des Sciences Morales et Politiques*, 173, juin 1910, 816-817 (Séance du 14 mai 1910). Also in *Ecrits et paroles*, 2, 340-341; *Mélanges*, 825-826. This is about an attempt to found morality on "sentiment."

194   "Rapport sur un ouvrage de Barret Wendell: *La France d'aujourd'hui.* 2e éd." Trans. G. Grappe. *Séances et Travaux de l'Académie des Sciences Morales et Politiques*, 174, juillet 1910, 146-148 (Séance du 11 juin 1910). Also in *Ecrits et paroles*, 2, 346-348; *Mélanges*, 829-831. In this brief essay, Bergson discusses a book about the French national character and its basic "seriousness."

195   "Réponse à l'article de W. B. Pitkin, 'James and Bergson'." *Journal of Philosophy, Pyschology, and Scientific Methods*, 7, No. 14, July 7, 1910, 385-388. Also in *Ecrits et paroles*, 2, 342-345; *Mélanges*, 820-824. In this article Bergson defends himself against Pitkin's anti-scientific interpretation of his thought.

196   "Résumé par Bergson de ses cours sur *La Personnalité*, et sur le *Traité de la réforme de l'entendement.*" *Archives du Collège de France*, 11, 1910, 114. Also in *Ecrits et paroles*, 2, 356-357; *Mélanges*, 845-846. This is a brief account by Bergson of lectures on the problem of personality and on the philosophy of Spinoza. (Cf. Bergson's précis of his unpublished Gifford Lectures on personality, 1914.)

1911

197   *Choix de textes*. Notice par René Gillouin. Paris: Louis Michaud, 1911, 222. (Les Grandes Philosophes français et étrangers)

198   "Entretien avec E.J. Lotte: 21 avril 1911." *Bulletin Joseph Lotte*, 104, mars 1940. 282-285. Also in *Études Bergsoniennes*, 8, 37-41; *Mélanges*, 879-882. This is about Bergson's proposed book on morality, mysticism, and the decadence of Europe.

199   "Interview par Jacques Morland: 19 août 1911." *L'Opinion*, 4e Année, No. 33, 19 août 1911, 241-242. Also in *Mélanges*, 939-944. Here Bergson discusses his divergent influence, his philosophical method, syndicalism, positivism, and the younger generation.

200   "L'Intuition philosophique." *Revue de Métaphysique et de Morale*, 19, No. 6, 1911, 809-827. In this talk, first given at the Congrès de Philosophie de Bologne on April 11, 1911, Bergson evaluates the part which intuition plays in the thought of philosophers and the method which should be used in interpreting a philosopher's thought.

Two mistakes should be avoided, Bergson warns, in interpreting the thought of a philosopher. We should not try to understand his thought by piecing together a picture of his thought derived from the externals of his system; and we should not try to derive his thought from the philosophies or the thought-tendencies of his predecessors. To fully interpret a philosopher we must strive to put ourselves within the basis of his thought.

Bergson applies this precept to the interpretation of philosophies of Baruch

Spinoza and George Berkeley, and to the relations bewteen philosophy and the sciences. When Berkeley's fourfold conceptual scheme is reduced to its essentials we find an image, of matter as a mere film, a thin surface, veiling a spiritual reality. Behind this image lies a single, simple intuition.

201   *L'Intuition philosophique.* Paris: Armand Colin, 1911, 19. This is a very limited edition, reprinted from the *Revue de Métaphysique et de Morale*, 1911.

202   *L'Intuition philosophique. Communication faite au Congrès philosophique de Bologne le x avril M.CM.XI. Paris: Helleu et Sergent, 1927, 93. (Collection philosophes et moralistes, V.8. La partie contemporaine)*

203   "L'Intuition philosophique." *La Pensée et le mouvant: Essais et conférences.* Paris: Félix Alcan, 1934. (Cf. *The Creative Mind*, 1946, 126-152.)

204   "L'Intuition philosophique." *Oeuvres.* Ed. André Robinet. Paris: Presses Universitaires de France, 1959, 1345-1365. (Notes, 1534-1535)

Translations

Introducción a la metafísca y la intuición filosófica. Buenos Aires: Leviathan, 1957, 144.

Introducción a la metafísica y la intuición filosófica. Buenos Aires: Siglo veinte, 1966, 144. (Neuva colección Siglo veinte)

Introcucción a la metafísica y la intuicion filosofica. Trans. M. Héctor Albert. 1966; rpt. Buenos Aires, 1973, 141.

La Intuicion filosofica. Trans. Emilio Oribe. Montevideo, Uruguay: Centro Ariel, 1931, 58.

205   "Lettre à Madame W. James: Juin 1911." *Revue des Deux Mondes*, 15 octobre 1933, p. 821. Also in *Mélanges*, 939. This is about Bergson's introduction to James' *Pragmatism*.

206   "Lettre à E. J. Lotte: 19 avril 1911." *Etudes Bergsoniennes*, 8, p. 36. Also in *Mélanges*, 879. Bergson arranges a meeting with Lotte in this letter.

207   "Lettre à E. J. Lotte: 20 septembre 1911." *Etudes Bergsoniennes*, 8, 45. Also in *Mélanges*, 944. Bergson here suggests that Lotte may be able to visit with him in Paris.

208   "Letter à Ch. Péguy: 3 février 1911." *Etudes Bergsoniennes*, 8, 33. Also in *Mélanges*, 878. This letter is about financial backing for C. Péguy's *Cahiers de la Quinzaine.*

209   "Lettre à Ch. Péguy: 3 mai 1911." *Etudes Bergsoniennes*, 8, 43-44. Also in *Mélanges*, 883-884. This letter is about C. Péguy's *Pages choisies.*

210   "Lettre à F. Znianiecki: 3 décembre 1811." *Ecrits et paroles*, 3, p. 654. Also in *Mélanges*, 960. This is about the Polish translation of *L'Evolution créatrice* and Bergson's opinion of the difficulties encountered in translating this work. Difficulties with the German translation are also mentioned.

211   "Life and Consciousness." *Hibbert Journal*, 10, Part 1, October, 1911, 22-41. This is the Huxley Lecture, delivered May 29, 1911 at the University of Birmingham. This version contains some materials added by Bergson after his address. In general this is a restatement of the basic theses of *Creative EVolution* (1907), with particular attention being payed to the relations between freedom, consciousness and choice. Everything takes place as if evolution sought to create organisms

capable of making real choices, thus expressing real freedom. Three "lines of fact" support this contention: the temporal structure of consciousness, which exhibits the preservation of memories with a view to action; the structure of the central nervous system, which is increasingly capable of choice and which can command an animal body which conserves energy, and thus makes motion possible; and the duration of consciousness,which is able, through its greater breadth, to "command" the infinitely briefer durations of matter.

Translations

"La Conscience et la vie." *L'Energie spirituelle: Essais et conférences*. Paris: Presses Universitaires de France, 1919. (Cf. *Mind-Energy*, 1920, 3-36.)

La Conscience et la vie. Hrsg. Max Höhn. Bielefeld: Velhagen und Klasing, 1933, xiv, 30. (Velhagen und Klasings franz. und engl. Schulausg. Prosateurs fran-çaise, vol. 263)

"La Conscience et la vie." *Oeuvres*. Ed. André Robinet. Paris: Presses Universitaires de France, 1959, 815-836.

"La Conscience et la vie." *Etides bergsoniennes*, 6, 5-36.

"La Conscience et la vie." *Mélanges*. Ed. André Robinet. Paris: Presses Universitaires de France, 1972, 915-938.

212   "On the Nature of the Soul." *Etudes Bergsoniennes*, 7, 9-16.

This article consists of four lectures delivered, respectively, on October 20, 21, 27, and 28, 1911 at Leeds University. This is a restatement of the basic theses of *Matter and Memory* concerning the relations between mind and body. This essay contains, in brief form, Bergson's responses to both scientific and philosophical criticisms of his dualistic and interactionist viewpoint.

213   "On the Nature of the Soul." *Mélanges*, Ed. André Robinet. Paris: Presses Universitaires de France, 1972, 944-959.

214   *La Perception du changement: Conférences faites à l'université d'Oxford les 26 et 27 mai 1911*. Oxford: Clarendon Press, 1911, 37.

This essay consists of two lectures delivered at Oxford University. The first lecture deals with Bergson's concept of philosophical method. In place of the methods of rationalism and traditional empiricism Bergson proposes an intuitive method. His comparison of intuition in art and in philosophy adds to his previous discussions of this relationship. The second lecture deals especially with the contrast between the continuity of change (for example, of motions or of sounds) as perceived and the discontinuity of change as conventionally conceptualized. It requires a real and difficult transformation of viewpoint in order to understand that all real change is continuous, that change is self-sufficient (that movement, for example, does not entail a *thing* which moves), and that cumulative memory plays a fundamental role in the continuity of the inner life.

215   "La Perception du changement" *La Pensée et le mouvant: Essais et conférences*. Paris: Félix Alcan, 1934. (Cf. *The Creative Mind*, 1946, 153-186.)

216   "La Perception du changement." *Oeuvres*. Ed. André Robinet. Paris: Presses Universitaires de France, 1959, 1365-1392. (Notes, 1576)

217   "La Perception du changement." *Etudes Bergsoniennes*, 6, 133-168.

218   "La Perception du changement." *Mélanges*. Ed. André Robinet. Paris: Presses Universitaires de France, 1972, 888-914.

Translations

Filosofen och livet. Trans. Algot Ruhe. Stockholm: Fyra föredrag, 1911, 77.

Vosprüatie izmiēnchivosti. Trans. V. A. Flerov. St. Petersburg, 1912.

219 "Les Réalités que la science n'atteint pas." *Foi et vie*, 14, No. 14, 16 juillet 1911, 421-422. Also in *Ecrits et paroles*, 2, 359-360; *Mélanges*, 885-887. In this essay Bergson claims that, though limited in scope, science possesses certainty. Philosophy, however, has its own method and object.

220 "Résumé de ses cours sur *L'Idée d'évolution* et sur *Les Principes généraux de la philosophie de Spinonza.*" *Archives du Collège de France*, 12, 1912, p. 38. Also in *Ecrits et paroles*, 2, p. 361; *Mélanges*, 961. This is a general description by Bergson of courses on the idea of evolution and on Spinoza's philosophy. These were given in 1911-1912.

1912

221 "Vérité et réalité: Introduction." *Le Pragmatisme, par William James*. Paris: Flammarion, 1911, i-xvi.

This is Bergson's introduction the French translation of William James' *Pragmatism*. Bergson cautions that we must change our ordinary conception of the world if we are to understand William James' philosophy. For James reality is fluctuating and the "things" which make it up are fluid. Equally, we must not confuse James' theory of knowledge with conventional (correspondence) theories of truth. For James, truth is not a process of discovery but a process of conceptual creativity. The True, according to James, is not a copy of what is or has been; it prepares our action upon what is going to be.

222 "Sur le pragmatisme de William James: Vérité et réalité." *La Pensée et le mouvant: Essais et conférences*. Paris: Félix Alcan, 1934. (Cf. *The Creative Mind*, 1946, 248-260.)

223 "Sur le pragmatisme de William James: Vérité et réalité." *Oeuvres*. André Robinet. Paris: Presses Universitaires de France, 1959, 1440-1450. (Notes 1539)

224 "Avant-propos à l'ouvrage de Rudolph Eucken: *Le Sens et la valeur de la vie.*" Paris: Félix Alcan, 1912, i-iv. Also in *Ecrits et paroles*, 2, 371-372; *Mélanges*, 971-973. In this foreward Bergson discusses, in very general terms, the significance and character of Eucken's thought.

225 "Conférence à *Foi et vie* sur l'âme et le corps." in *Le Materialisme actuel*. Ed. Gustave Le Bon. Paris: Flammarion, 1913, 7-48.

This a presentation, in simplified form, of the mind-body theory developed in *Matter and Memory*. Bergson concludes this talk with the claim that the survival of the soul after death is probable.

226 "L'Ame et le corps." *L'Energie spirituelle: Essais et conférences*, Paris: Presses Universitaires de France, 1919. (Cf. *Mind-Energy*, 1920, 37-74.)

227 *L'Ame et le corps*. Mit Einleitung und Anm. Max Müller. Frankfurt a.M.: M. Diesterweg, 1928, iv, 72. (Diesterwegs neusprachl. Schulausgaben m. deutschen Anm. Französ. Reihe. Vol. 16)

228 "L'Ame et le corps." *Oeuvres.* Ed. André Robinet. Paris: Presses Universitaires de France, 1959, 836-860. (Notes 1517-1520)

Translations

"El alma y el cuerpo." in *El materialismo actual.* Ed. Gustav Le Bon. Trans. E. González Blanco. Madrid: Gutemberg, 1915, 9f.

"Leib und Seele." *Neue Rundschau,* 24, No. 12, 1913, 889-908.

229 "Discours prononcé sur la tombe d'Henri Franck: 27 févirer 1912." *Henri Franck, 2 décembre 1888-25 février 1912,* Paris, 1912. Also in *Ecrits et paroles,* 2, p. 367; *Mélanges,* 965-966. This is a brief yet eloquent funeral oration.

230 "Letter of Recommendation for T. E. Hulme. 1912." T.E. Hulme. *Speculations.* London: Routledge and Kegan Paul, 1949, 271, viii. Bergson asserts here that Hulme will pursue a creative career in modern art.

231 "Lettre à L. Dauriac: 26 mai 1912." *Etudes Bergsoniennes,* 3, 196-197. Also in *Mélanges,* 968. This is a résumé of a letter. It is about Bergson's attitude towards I. Kant.

232 "Lettre à L. Dauriac: 18 août 1912." *Etudes Bergsoniennes,* 3, p. 197. This is a résumé of a letter on J. Meyerbeer.

233 "Lettre à Gilbert Maire." Cited in Gilbert Maire. "La Philosophie de G. Sorel." *Cahiers du Cercle Proud'hon,* 2, mars-avril 1912, 65. Also in *Ecrits et paroles,* 2, p. 370; *Mélanges,* 971. Bergson denies here that G. Sorel is one of his disciples.

234 "Lettre à Ch. Péguy: 21 mai 1912." *Feuillets de l'Amitié Charles Péguy,* 30, p. 11. Also in *Etudes Bergsoniennes,* 8, 45-46; *Mélanges,* 967. This letter concerns the possible publication of "L'Ame et le corps" in *Cahiers de la Quinzaine.*

235 "Lettre à M. Edouard Le Roy à la suite de deux articles parus dans la *Revue des Deux Mondes* sur la philosophie nouvelle, ler et 15 février 1912." *Ecrits et paroles,* 2, 364. Also in the preface to E. Le Roy. *Une Philosophie nouvelle.* Paris: Félix Alcan, 1912, iv-v. In this fragment of a letter Bergson congratulates Le Roy for his interpretation of his (i.e., Bergson's) philosophy.

236 "Lettre à J. de Tonquédec: 20 février 1912." *Etudes par des Pères de la Compagnie de Jésus,* 130, 20 février 1912, 514-516. Also in *Sur La Philosophie bergsonienne.* Paris: Beauchesne, 1946, 59-60; *Ecrits et paroles,* 2, 365-366; *Mélanges,* 963-964. This is about Bergson's philosophical method.

237 "Réponse à l'enquête de Jules Bertaut sur la jeunesse." *Le Gaulois,* 15 juin 1912. Also in H. Massis. *Les Jeunes Gens d'aujourd'hui.* Paris: Plon, 1913, 284-286; *Ecrits et paroles,* 2, 368-369; *Mélanges,* 968-970. Here Bergson holds that there is a profound change in the youth of France—a sort of moral renaissance.

1913

238 "The Bergson Lectures." *Columbia Alumni News,* 4, No. 26, 21 March 1913, 397-399. lso *Mélanges,* 978-981. These general notes on Bergson's lectures were taken by W.T. Bush. The lectures outline Bergson's epistemology and his ideas on the mind-body dualism.

239 "Cours à Columbia University: Spirituality and Liberty." *The Chronicle,* 13, March 6, 1913, 214-220. Also in *Mélanges,* 981-989. The following topics are discussed in this lecture: the need of a new philosophy, free will as moral health, memory as having no special home in the brain, the relations of vital phenomena to

science, life mentally and morally an effort, immortality.

240   "Discours au Comité France-Amérique." *France-Ameérique*, juin 1913, 341-350.
          Also in *Revue Internationale de l'Enseignement*, 33, No. 7, juillet 1913. 95-105;
          Ecrits et paroles, 2, 378-388; *Mélanges*, 990-1001. Here Bergson gives his
          impressions of New York, of Columbia University, and of Franco-American
          idealism.

241   "'Phantasms of the Living' and 'Psychical Research'." *Proceedings of the British
          Society for Psychical Research*, 26, 1913-462-479.

          This is Bergson's presidential address before the British Society for Psychical
          Research. It is essentially an application of the mind-body theory developed in
          Matter and Memory (1896) and the cosmology sketched in *Creative Evolution*
          (1907) to the problems of what we would now term parapsychology. If telepathy,
          for example, or clairvoyance, are real, they must be natural. They must be being
          repeated at all times, though we are not aware of them.

          Bergson argues that just as the brain is structured so as to block out the bulk of
          our memories, so our sense organs are structured so as to block out much of
          the physical world. We live among magnetic and other influences which mankind
          was late to discover. It may be that our minds, rather than being distinct and
          separate in space, are constantly "intercommunicating." Analogously, there may
          be phenomena of which we are not normally aware but which psychical research
          may some day discover.

Translations

"Fantômes de vivants et recherche psychique." *Annales des Sciences Psychiques*,
23e Année, No. 11-12, 1913, 321-329. This is a free translation.

"Les Phénomènes de l'inconnu." *La Revue*, 106, 15 fevrier 1914, 562-563. This
contains passages from the version in the *Annales des Sciences Psychique*.

"'Fantômes de vivants' et 'Recherche psychique'." *L'Energie Spirituelle: Essais
et conférences*." Paris: Presses Universitaires de France, 1919. This translation
differs significantly from those cited immediately above. (Cf. *Mind-Energy*,
1920, 75-103.)

"'Fantômes de vivants' et 'Recherche psychique'." *Oeuvres*. Ed. André Robinet.
Paris: Presses Universitaires de France, 1959, 870-878. (Notes 1566)

"'Fantômes de vivants' et 'Recherche psychique'." *Etudes Bergsoniennes*, 6, 37-60.

"'Fantômes de vivants' et 'Recherche psychique'." *Mélanges*. Ed. André Robinet.
Paris: Presses Universitaires de France, 1972, 1002-1019.

"Okkultismus und Naturwissenschaft." *Zentralblatt für Psychologie und
Psychologische Pädagogik*, 2, 1917, 197f.

"Science psychique et science physique." *Zeitschrift für Pathopsychologie*, 2, 1914,
570f.

242   "Lettre à I. Benrubi: 14 juillet 1913." I Benrubi. *Souvenirs sur Henri Bergson*,
          86. Also in Henri Bergson, *Essais et témoignages*, page de garde; *Mélanges*,
          1024. This letter is on creativity as the goal of human life.

243   "Lettre à L. Dauriac: 19 mars 1913." *Etudes Bergsoniennes*, 3, p. 197 résumé.
          Also in *Mélanges*, 990. This letter is about Bergson's concept of "vie en profon-
          deur' and the philosophy of music.

244 "Lettre à Fr. Grandjean: 12 juin 1913." Fr. Grandjean. *La Doctrine de M. Henri Bergson*. Also in *Mélanges*, 1020. This letter concerns Grandjean's book on Bergson.

245 "Lettre à Fr. Grandjean: 22 août 1913." Henri Bergson. *Essais et témoignages*, 372-373. Also in *Mélanges*, 1024-1025. Bergson affirms his decision, in this letter, not to allow publication of opinions expressed in conversation.

246 "Lettre à Marie-Anne Léon: 12 mars 1913." Catalogue Henri Bergson de la Bibliotèque Nationale, cote 273. Also in *Mélanges*, 989.

247 "Lettre à A. Mitchell." A. Mitchell. "Studies in Bergson's Philosophy." *Bulletin of the University of Kansas*, January 1914. Also in *Mélanges*, 1030-1031. This letter is a discussion of intuition as the basis for the posing of philosophical problems, the status of matter and of rest, and the unity of action and knowledge.

248 "Lettre à Thureau-Dangin: 25 septembre 1913." *Archives de l'Académie Française*, Série A. Also in *Mélanges*, 1025. In this letter Bergson proposes his candidacy for the French Academy.

249 "Letter sur le jury de cour d'assises: 19 octobre 1913." *Le Temps*, 19 octobre 1913, p. 4, col. 2-3. Also in *Ecrits et paroles*, 2, 389-392; *Mélanges*, 1026-1030. Here Bergson (who had served on a Parisian jury) discusses the "theatrical" weakness of French juries and their overindulgence towards "crimes of passion."

250 "Mission à l'Université Columbia." *Archives du Collège de France*, 13, 1913, 87-88. Also in *Ecrits et paroles*, 2, 373-374; *Melanges*, 976-977. This is a discussion of a course for students at Columbia University in New York titled "Esquisse d'une théorie de la connaissance." The public course was titled "Spiritualité et liberté."

251 "La Philosophie de Claude Bernard." *Annuaire du Collège de France*. Paris: Leroux, 1914, 46-52.

In this essay Bergson discusses the thought of the great French physiologist and student of scientific method, Claude Bernard. Bernard, Bergson points out, denied that any one scientific theory can be final and argued that philosophy and science can not be "systematic." He also argued that physiology was a science in its own right, independent of physics and chemistry. In these respects Bernard's philosophy resembles Bergson's.

252 "La Philosophie de Claude Bernard." *La Pensée et le mouvant: Essais et conférences*. Paris: Félix Alcan, 1934. This version differs significantly from the one listed above. (Cf. *The Creative Mind*, 1946, 238-247.)

253 "La Philosophie de Claude Bernard." *Claude Bernard: Extraits de son oeuvre*. Ed. E. Dhurout. Paris: Félix Alcan, 1939, 19-32.

254 "La Philosophie de Claude Bernard." *Oeuvres*. Ed. André Robinet. Paris: Presses Universitaires de France, 1959, 1433-1440. (Notes 1539)

Translation

"The Philosophy of Claude Bernard." *Bulletin of the History of Medicine*, 4, No. 1, 1936, 15-21.

255 "Rapport sur un ouvrage de J. M. Baldwin: *Le Darwinisme dans les sciences morales*." Also in *Séances et Travaux de l'Académie des Sciences Morales et Politiques*, 180, 1913, 329-331 (Séance du 14 juin 1913); *Ecrits et paroles*, 2, 375-377; *Mélanges*, 1020-1023. This is a discussion of Darwinism in psychology, A. Weissman's theory of "intra-selection," and the theory of "organic selection."

1914

256   "Discours de Bergson élu président de l'Acadéime des sciences morales et
        politiques." *Séances et Travaux de l'Académie des Sciences Morales et
        Politiques*, 181, 1914, 130-133 (Séance du 10 janvier 1914). Also in *Ecrits et
        paroles*, 2, 393-395; *Mélanges*, 1034-1037. This essay is on the importance of
        moral and political sciences.

257   "Discours prononcé à l'Académie des sciences morales et politiques." *Séances et
        Travaux de l'Académie des Sciences Morales et Politiques*, 192, 1914, p. 325.
        Also in *Le Figaro*, 9 août 1914, *Le Temps*, 8 août 1914; *Mélanges*, 1102.
        Bergson here conveys the thanks and the admiration of the French people for
        Belgium's brave struggle against the German invader.

258   "Discours prononcé à l'occasion du décès de Ludovic Beauchet." *Séances et
        Travaux de l'Académie des Sciences Morales et Politiques*, 181, 1914, 327-328
        (Séance du 17 jannvier 1914). Also in *Ecrits et paroles*, 2, 396-397; *Mélanges*,
        1044-1045. This is a brief review of the life and writing of a French legal scholar.

259   "Discours prononcá à l'occasion du décès de Charles Waddington." *Ecrits et
        paroles*, 11, 398-400. Also in *Séances et Travaux de l'Académie des Sciences
        Morales et Politiques*, 181, 1912, 441-445 (Séance du 21 mars 1914); *Ecrits et
        paroles*, 2, 398-400; *Mélanges*, 1046-1049. This is an account of the life and
        writings of a French philosopher and historian of philosophy.

260   "Discours sur la signification de la guerre." *Séances et Travaux de l'Académie des
        Sciences Morales et Politiques*, 183, 1915, 139-168. Also in (among many
        others) *Revue Universitaire*, 23, No. 10, 19 décembre 1914, 233-242; *La Sig-
        nification de la guerre*. Paris: Bloud et Gay, 1915, 7-29; *Le Châtiment*. Paris:
        Delagrave, 1915, 9-24; *La Revue*, 26, No. 3-4, 1915, 369-377; *Mélanges*,
        1107-1129.

        This is Bergson's concluding speech as president of the Academy of Moral and
        Political Sciences. The opening and closing sections express Bergson's attitude
        towards the First World War. The middle section includes necrologies, the award
        of prizes, etc.

        Bergson argues that Germany, once the home of philosophy and the arts, has
        become Prussianized. The result is a mechanization of life and of the German
        spirit which need not have taken place, had the German nation taken time to
        mature gradually. The First World War is a struggle of French "esprit" against
        German mechanism. Esprit shall prevail.

Translations

Krigets betydelse. Trans. Algot Ruhe. Stockholm: Wahlstrom & Widstrand, 1915,
    63.

Bergson, Henri Louis. "Germany Has Been Prussianized." *New York Times*, 64,
    No. 20, 805, January 10, 1915, pt. 5, p. 3:1.

"Life and Matter at War." *Hibbert Journal*, 13, No. 3, 1915, 465-475.

"Life and Matter at War." *The Meaning of the War*. Auth. T.H. Wildon Carr.
    London: Fisher Unwin, 1916, 47.

261   "La Force qui s'use et celle qui ne s'use pas." *Bulletin des Armées de la République*, No. 42, 4 novembre 1914, p. 1. Also in *La Signification de la guerre*, 40-42; *Mélanges*, 1105-1106. This is a discussion of French "force morale" versus German "force matérielle."

Translations

"The Force Which Wastes and that Which Does not Waste." *The Meaning of War.* Trans. H. Wildon Carr. London: Fisher Unwin, 1916, 47.

"The Vital Energies of France." *The New York Times Current History of The European War.* Vol. I. *August-December, 1914.* New York: The New York Times Company, 1917, 152-153.

262   "Hommage à Ribot." *Séances et Travaux de l'Académie des Sciences Morales et Politiques*, 182, 1914, p. 468. Also in *Mélanges*, 1104. In this essay Bergson works to prevent expulsion of German members from the Academy.

263   "Hommage au roi Albert et au peuple belge." *Daily Telegraph*, London. Also in *La Signification de la guerre*, 45-46; *Mélanges*, 1129-1130. Here Bergson expresses his admiration for the Belgian defense against Germany.

264   "Interview recueillie par Gremil: 16 février 1914." *La Dépêche de Toulouse*, 16 février 1914. Also in *Mélanges*, 1038-1040. This interview includes a brief account of Bergson's early life, a discussion of the place of system in philosophy, of determinism in history, etc.

265   "Lettre à A. Bourgeois: 19 septembre 1914." *Feuillets de l'Amitie Charles Péguy*, 1, p. 5. Also in *Etudes Bergsoniennes*, 8, p. 57; *Mélanges*, 1103. In this letter Bergson asks M. Bourgeois for the address of Mme. Péguy.

266   "Lettre à A. Bourgeois: 21 septembre 1914." *Feuillets de l'Amitié Charles Péguy*, 1, p. 5. Also in *Etudes Bergsoniennes*, 8, p. 57; *Mélanges*, 1104. In this letter Bergson conveys the news of Péguy's death.

267   "Lettre à E.J. Lotte: 12 février 1914." *Archives Charles Péguy.* Also in *Ecrits Bergsoniennes*, 8, p. 47; *Mélanges*, 1038. Bergson here thanks Lotte for some kind words.

268   "Lettre à Ch. Péguy: 27 février." *Feuillets de l'Amitié Charles Péguy*, 30, p. 12. Also in *Esprit*, 1953, 337; *Etudes Bergsoniennes*, 8, p. 49; *Mélanges*, 1042. This letter concerns a personal misunderstanding between Bergson and Péguy.

269   "Lettre à Ch. Péguy: 4 mars 1914.: *Etudes Bergsoniennes*, 8, p. 51. Also in *Mélanges*, 1043. This letter concerns the arranging of a meeting between Bergson and Péguy.

270   "Lettre à Ch. Péguy: 10 mars 1914." *Etudes Bergsoniennes*, 8, p. 52. Also in *Mélanges*, 1044. Here Bergson sets a time for a meeting with Péguy.

271   "Lettre à Ch. Péguy: 21 avril 1914." *Etudes Begsoniennes*, 8, 52-53. Also in *Mélanges*, 1086-1087. This concerns an issue of Péguy's *Cahiers de la Quinzaine* to be dedicated to Bergson.

272   "Lettre à Ch. Péguy: 4 mai 1914." *Etudes Bergsoniennes*, 8, 53-54. Also in *Mélanges*, 1087. In this letter Bergson thanks Péguy for his "Note sur philosophie bergsonienne."

273   "Lettre à Ch. Péguy: 17 mai 1914." *Etudes Bergsoniennes*, 8, 54-55. Also in *Mélanges*, 1088. This letter is about Péguy's "Note sur la philosophie bergsonienne."

274   "Lettre à Ch. Péguy: 9 juillet 1914." *Etudes Bergsoniennes*, 9, p. 56. Also in
       Mélanges, 1094. This letter is about the Bergson edition of *Cahiers de la
       Quinzaine.*

275   "Lettre à F. Vandérem: 27 février 1914." *Le Figaro*, 29 février 1914, p. 1, col.
       6. Also in *Mélanges*, 1040-1041. This letter contains replies to criticisms, a
       discussion of Bergson's lectures, his philosophical method, and the character
       of his conclusions.

276   "The Problem of Personality." *Etudes Bergsoniennes*, 7, 65-88. Also in *La Nature
       de l'âme: Le Problème de la personnalité.* André et Martine Robinet. Paris:
       Presses Universitaires de France, 1966, 231; *Mélanges*, 1051-1086. These are
       the never-completed Gifford Lectures for 1914-1915, lectures which were inter-
       rupted by the outbreak of the First World War. Only an English-language précise
       of the first half of these lectures is known to exist.

       In the first lecture Bergson states that the problem of personality is the basic
       problem of philosophy. This has been overlooked due to the tendency of Western
       philosophy, both ancient and modern, to look for unified system before seeking
       to deal with real individuality.

       In the second lecture Bergson deals with Plotinus, in whose thought we find
       the summation of Greek philosophy. Plotinus sought to understand both the
       unity and the plurality of human personality.

       In the third lecture Bergson sketches Plotinus' concept of the self, which is *de
       facto* in time but *de jure* in eternity. In becoming temporalized, the self becomes
       pluralized, losing its original unity. Action is thus less than contemplation,
       movement less than immobility. This notion of the self permeated western
       philosophy until and even after the time of Kant.

       In the fourth lecture Bergson argues that Plotinus' psychology has become
       weakened in modern times, largely through its being juxtaposed with a
       mechanistic concept of nature. Kant sought to save Plotinus'psychology by
       making existence in time relative to our faculty of knowing and placing human
       freedom outside of time. In doing so he believed he had also shown the impos-
       sibility of metaphysics.

       In the fifth lecture Bergson criticizes Kant's concept of personality, arguing that
       the unity of the self can be perceived, in time. To do this, however, would
       involve reforming mental habits which involve regarding the timeless as more
       real than time.

       In the sixth lecture Bergson moves to study the human self in time. He begins
       with the notion of *unconscious memory.*" *The idea of the "unconscious psychi-
       cal" is a consistent, defensible idea.*

       In the seventh lecture Bergson describes the self as a continuity of change, a
       continual forward movement which gathers up the past and creates the future.

       The eight and ninth lectures are devoted to the description and interpretation of
       disorders of personality. There are two basic components of personality: memory
       (the unconscious) and an impulse forward (the will). To attain these functions
       has cost humanity an effort, just as it costs us an effort to sustain them. To be
       a human being is a strain. Hence the disorders of personality, which derive
       either from memory or from will.

       Many cases of amnesia and most cases of multiple personality can be understood
       as failures in the effort required to "keep in view" the entirety of the personal
       past. Failures of the impulse towards the future give rise to "the disorder of
       doubt" (psychasthenia). Berson cites the phenomenon of false recognition as a

mild example of these disorders.

In the tenth lecture Bergson reviews the mind-body theory of *Matter and Memory*, which he believes proves the independence of mind *vis a vis* the body.

In the eleventh lecture Bergson considers his mind-body theory in the light of evolution. Evolution is a mechanism for creating personalities, which are creative forces.

277   "Rapport sur un ouvrage de Jacques Bardoux: *Croquis d'outremanche.*" *Ecrits et paroles*, 11, 401-402. Also in *Séances et Travaux de l'Académie des Sciences Morales et Politiques*, 182-1914, 94-95 (Séance du 28 mars 1914); *Ecrits et paroles*, 2, 401-402; *Mélanges*, 1049-1051. This concerns a study of Great Britain.

278   "Rapport sur un ouvrage de Jacques de Coussange: *La Scandinavie: Le Nationalisme scandinave.*" *Séances et Travaux de l'Académie des Sciences Morales et Politiques*, 183, 1915, 229-231 (Séance du 11 juillet 1914). Also in *Ecrits et paroles*, 2, 410-412; *Mélanges*, 1098-1101. This is a review of a book on the revival of nationalism in the Scandinavian nations.

279   "Rapport sur un ouvrage d'Edouard Dolléans: *Le Chartisme.*" *Ecrits et paroles*, 11, 407-409. Also in *Séances et Travaux de l'Académie des Sciences Morales et Politiques*, 183, 1915, 117-119 (Séance du 11 juillet 1914); *Ecrits et paroles*, 2, 406-409; *Mélanges*, 1085-1098. This is a discussion of English political and social movements of the early nineteenth century.

280   "Rapport sur un ouvrage de Jean Finot: *Progrès et bonheur.*" *Séances et Travaux de l'Académie des Sciences Morales et Politiques*, 182, 1914, 448-451 (Séance du 27 juin 1914). Also in *Ecrits et paroles*, 2, 403-406; *Mélanges*, 1090-1095. The conditions of happiness and the reality of progress are discussed in this review.

1915

281   "Discours à l'Académie des sciences morales et politiques: Renouvellement du bureau de l'Académie." *Séances et Travaux de l'Académie des Sciences Morales et Politiques*, 183, 1915, 133-135. Also in *La Signification de la guerre*, 33-35; *Le Temps*, 17 janvier 1915, in modified form; *Mélanges*, 1131-1133. This is a discussion of French "esprit" and German mechanism.

282   "Discours sur la guerre et la littérature de demain." *Revue Bleue*, 8-15 mai 1915, 162-164. Also in *Mélanges*, 1151-1156. Here Bergson states that the future cannot be predicted, that it depends on choices made in the present.

283   "Lettre à Jacques Chevalier: 14 mars 1915." Chevalier. *Bergson*, 64. Also in *Mélanges*, 1146. This letter gives an account of Bergson's preoccupation with the events of the First World War.

284   "Lettre à P. Grimanelli: 6 février 1915." *Revue Positiviste Internationale*, No. 2, 15 février 1915, 94-95. Also in *Mélanges*, 1144-1145. This letter contains Bergson's opinion of Auguste Comte, the founder of positivism.

285   "Lettre à A. Hébrard: 19 janvier 1915." *Le Temps*, 24 janvier 1915, p. 1. Also in *Mélanges*, 1136-1141. This is a correction of the account in *Le Temps* of Bergson's speach before the Académie des sciences morales et politiques. It includes a reply to Bergson by the editors of *Le Temps*.

286   "Lettre à Harald Höffding: 15 mars 1915." Höffding. *La Philosophie de Bergson*, 157-165. Also in *Ecrits et paroles*, 3, 455-458; *Mélanges*, 1146-1150. In this much-quoted letter Bergson points out that the concept of duration preceded the concept of intuition in the development of his thought and is far more fundamental to his philosophy.

287   "Lettre à H. M. Kallen: 28 octobre 1915." *Journal of Philosophy, Psychology, and Scientific Methods*, 12, No. 22, October 1915, 615-616. Also in Riley. *Le Bergsonisme en Amérique.*" *Revue Philosophique de la France et de l'Etranger*, 1921, 92-93; Descoqs. *Praelectiones Theologiae naturalis*, 1, p. 397; *Ecrits et paroles*, 3, p. 433 in shortened form; *Mélanges*, 1191-1194. Bergson objects here to H. M. Kallen's attempt to liken his views to those of traditional Greek metaphysics and to distance his views from those of William James. Bergson does not make unity prior to or more real than plurality, or propose a timeless eternity. Bergson and James see a common accord between science and experience.

288   "Lettre à Giuseppe Prezzolini: 3 juillet 1915." *Il tempo della voce*. Ed. Giuseppe Prezzolini. Milano e Firenze: Coedizione Longanese e Vallecchi, 1960, 689.

289   "La Philosophie française." *Revue de Paris*, 3, mai-juin 1915, 236-256. Also in *La Science française*. Paris: Larousse, 1915, 1, 15-37, *La Philosophie*. Paris: Larousse, 1915, 27; Reedited with e. E. LeRoy. *La Science française*. Paris: Larousse, 1933, 1-26 (many corrections); *Ecrits et paroles*, 2, 413-436; *Mélanges*, 1157-1189. Bergson claims in this essay that France has been the great initiator of new ideas in the evolution of modern philosophy.

Translation

De Fransche Wijsbegeerte. Trans. Antoon Vloemans. Rotterdam: De Voorpost, 1934.

290   "Progrès matériel et progrès moral." *Le Temps*, 19 janvier 1915, p. 1. Also in *Mélanges*, 1134-1136. This is a report of Bergson's speech at the Académie des sciences morales et politiques, 16 January 1915, by A. Hébrard.

291   "Rapport sur *La Science française* publié par le Ministère de l'instruction publique." *Séances et Travaux de l'Académie des Sciences Morales et Politiques*, 185, 1916, 103-104. Also in *Ecrits et paroles*, 3, 453-454; *Mélanges*, 1189-1191.

1916

292   "Au Périodique *La Razón*." *La Razón*. (Madrid), No. 70, 14 mayo 1916. Also in *Mélanges*, 1236. This essay concerns the relations between France and Spain.

293   "Conférence de Madrid: La Personnalité." *España* (weekly), 6 mayo 1916. Also in *Etudes Bergsoniennes*. 9, 57-118; *Mélanges*, 1215-1235. This is a general account of Bergson's theory of personality: mind and brain, artistic creativity, unity of states of consciousness, personal effort, dissociation of personality, fatigue, and creation and life.

294   "Conférence de Madrid sur l'âme humaine." *España* (weekly), 2 mayo 1916. Also in *Etudes Bergsoniennes*, 9, 11-56; *Mélanges*, 1200-1215. This is a general exposition of essential aspects of Bergson's philosophy: science and philosophy, creative evolution, conservation of energy, mind-body parallelism, the aphasias, etc.

295   "Discours pronocé à la Résidence des Etudiants à Madrid. le ler mai 1916." Manuel G. Morente. *La Filosofía de Henri Bergson*. Madrid: Residencia de Estudiantes,

1917, 15-23. Also in *Ecrits et paroles*, 3, 445-448; *Mélanges*, 1195-1200. This essay is about philosophical method and about the relations between France and Spain.

296   "Rapport sur un ouvrage de Jacques Chevalier: *La Notion du nécessaire chez Aristote et chez ses prédécesseurs.*" *Séances et Travaux de l'Académie des Sciences Morales et Politiques*, 185, 1916, 484-486 (Séance du ler juillet 1916). Also in *Ecrits et paroles*, 3, 451-452; *Mélanges*, 1238-1240. This is about necessity vs. contingency in Aristotle. Aristotle is unable to make these concepts consistent, Chevalier holds, because he lacks the idea of creation.

297   "Rapport sur un ouvrage de Paul Gaultier: *La Mentalité allemande et la querre.*" *Séances et Travaux de l'Académie des Sciences Morales et Politiques*, 195, 1916, 483-484 (Séance du ler juillet 1916). Also in *Ecrits et paroles*, 3, 449-450; *Mélanges*, 1236-1238. The German mystique of force is discussed here.

1917

298   "L'Amitié franco-américaine." *L'Amérique*, Nos. 3-4, 17-24 juin 1917, 15-17. Also in *France-Amérique*, 1967, 7-10; *Mélanges*, 1257-1268. This is a discussion of America, its idealism, and its entry into World War I.

299   "Article sur les Etats-Unis." *Le Petit Parisien*, 4 juillet 1917. Also in *Mélanges*, 1269-1270. This is a discussion of the idealistic motivations which led the United States to enter World War I.

300   "Communication à l'Académie des sciences morales et politiques." *Le Figaro*, 10 juin 1917, 1, col. 1-2. Also in *Mélanges*, 1253-1256. This is a report by Gabriel Hanotaux of Bergson's speech before the Academy concerning his diplomatic mission in the United States.

301   "Compte rendu de la séance du 9 juin 1917 à l'Académie des sciences morales et politiques." *Le Temps*, 11 juin 1917, 2, col. 6. Also in *Mélanges*, 1256-1257. This is an unsigned newspaper report of Bergson's speech. Bergson discusses the American attitude towards the First World War.

302   "Discours au banquet de la Société France-Amérique, à New York." *France-Amérique*, 1917, 8-16. Also in *Mélanges*, 1243-1248. This is a rousing speech on behalf of the Allied war effort.

303   "Lettre à Alfred Loisy: 20 juillet 1917." Cited in Loisy. *Mémoires pour servir l'histoire religieuse de notre temps*. Paris: Emile Nourry, 1931, 3, 348. Also in *Ecrits et paroles*, 3, p. 460; *Mélanges*, 1270. This letter is a discussion of Bergson's philosophy of religion, which indicates the importance of mystical experience.

304   "Lettre à Agenor Petit: 27 janvier 1917." A. Petit. *Bergson et le rationalisme*. 1921. Also in *Ecrits et paroles*, 3, p. 459; *Mélanges*, 1241-1242. The intelligence, Bergson holds, has a role to play both in philosophy and in metaphysics.

305   "Lettre: 16 août 1917." *Labyrinthe*, 2, No. 13, 1945, p. 7. Also in *Mélanges*, 1271-1272. This is about the possibility of a League of Nations.

306   "La Mission française en Amérique." "Préface à Viviani." *La Mission française en amérique*. Paris, 1917, 1-7. This article concerns Bergson's attempt to influence America to enter the First World War.

1918

307   "Allocution au Centre interallié pour le Mother's Day." *Mélanges*, 1306-1307. This was originally in an article by Georges Drouilly. *Le Gaulois*, 13 mai 1918. The topic discussed is the American intervention in the First World War.

308   "Discours de réception de Bergson à l'Académie française: 24 janvier 1918." *Institut de France, Académie française*. Paris: F. Didot, 1918, 3-41; Libraire Académique, Paris: Perrin, 1918, 1-44. Also in *Journal Officiel de la République Française*, 50, No. 25, 1918, 961-966; *Ecrits et paroles*, 3, 461-484; *Mélanges*, 1275-1302. This is Bergson's acceptance speech before the French Academy. As is customary his speech concerns the life and objectives of his predecessor in the Academy, in this case Emile Ollivier.

309   "Lettre à Albert Adès: 20 avril 1918." *Adès chez Bergson*. Paris, 1949, 130-131. Also in *Mélanges*, 1304. Here Bergson opposes the use of statements on philosophical subjects made in conversation.

310   "Lettre à Albert Adès: 26 avril 1918." *Adès chez Bergson*. Paris, 1949, 132-133. Also in *Mélanges*, 1305-1306. In this letter Bergson expresses his unwillingness to be quoted in interviews.

311   "Lettre à P. Imbart de la Tour: 2 décembre 1918." *La Bibliothèque de Louvain: Séance commemorative du quatrième anniversaire de l'incendie*. Paris: Perrin, 1919. Also in *Mélanges*, 1308-1310. This letter is about Belgian resistance to German aggression and the burning of the library of Louvain University.

312   "Notes pour Adès." *Adès chez Bergson*, 1949, 124-125. Also in *Mélanges*, 1302-1303. This is a point by point criticism of Adès' article *La Philosophie de Bergson dans la vie.*" Unity of the self, relations of past and present, self and society, concept of God, and anarchism are some of the ideas discussed.

1919

313   *L'Amitié indestructible: 2 mars 1919." Vie Universitaire*, mai 1919, 3-5. Also in C. Bouglé and P. Gastinel. *Qu'est-ce que l'esprit française?* Paris: Garnier. 1920, 63-66 in shortened form; *Ecrits et paroles*, 3, 485-488; *Mélanges*, 1312-1316. The topic discussed here is France, the United States, and their common idealism.

314   "French Ideals in Education and the American Student." *Living Age*, 303, No. 3938, December 1919, 775-777.

315   "A Propos de la nature du comique: Notes et discussions." *Revue du Mois*, 20, No. 119, 1919, 514-517. This is Bergson's reply to criticisms of his concept of laughter by Y. Delage.

316   "Conférence à Strasbourg 'Sur l'âme humaine'." *Journal d'Alsace et de Lorraine*, No. 122, 13 mai 1919. Also in *Mélanges*, 1316-1319. This is an account by A. Birckel of Bergson's talk. Bergson claims that the spiritual in man must overcome the mechanical. Other topics discussed are Germany, minds and bodies, psychic research, and the function of the intellect.

317   "L'Energie spirituelle: Essais et conférences. Paris: Félix Alcan, 1919, 227. (Bibliothèque de philosophie contemporaine)

This is a collection of essays and talks: "La Conscience et la vie" (1911), "L'Ame et le corps" (1912), "Fantômes de vivants et recherche psychique" (1913), "Le Rêve" (1901), "Le Souvenir du présent et la fausse reconnaissance" (1908),

"L'Effort intellectuel" (1902), and "Le Cerveau et la pensée" (1904). A brief sketch of each of these items is provided in this bibliography under the year in which it first appeared.

318   *L'Energie spirituelle: Essais et conférences*. Genève: Skira, 1946, 202.

319   *L'Energie spirituelle: Essais et conférences* in Oeuvres. Ed. André Robinet. Paris: Presses Universitaires de France, 1959, 811-977.

320   *L'Énergie spirituelle*. 161 éd. Paris: Presses Universitaires de France, 1982, 214. (Quadrige, 36)

Translations

Al taka arrouhia. Trans. Sami Aldroubi. Damas: Institut des Antiquités, 1964, 200.

Al-Tāqah Al-Rūhiyah. Tans. Sāmi Al-Durūbi. Al-Qāhirah: Al-Hay'ah Al-Misriryah Al-'Ammah Lil-Ta'lif Wa Al-Nashr, 1971, 197.

La energía espiritual: Ensayos y conferencias. Trans. Eduardo Ovejero y Maury. Madrid: Daniel Jorro, 1928, 324. (Bibliotheca Científico-Filosófica)

La energía espiritual: Ensayos y conferencias. Trans. Mario A. Silva García. Montevideo: C. Garcia, 1945.

Energiyah rubanith. Trans. Jacob M. Levy. Tel Aviv, 1943-1944, 200. (Ligevulam)

Henkinen tarmo. 2nd Ed. Trans. J. A. Hollo. Porvoo-Helsinki: Werner Söderström, 1958, 208.

Henkinen tarmo. 3rd Ed. Trans. J. Hollo. Helsinki: Werner Söderström, 1963, 208.

Mind-Energy: Lectures and Essays. Auth. Trans. H. Wildon Carr. New York: Henry Holt; London: Macmillan, 1920, x, 262.

Mind-Energy: Lectures and Essays. Auth. Trans. H. Wildon Carr. 1920; rpt. Westport, Conn.: Greenwood Press, 1975, x, 262.

"Myśl i ruch. Wstep do metafizyki. Intuicja filozoficzna. Postrzeznie zmiany, Dusca i ciato. Trans. Pauwel Beylin and Kazimierz Blezyński. Intro. Pawet Bewlin. Warsawa: Páństwowe Wydawnictwo Naukowe, 1963, 163. This is a collection of articles from *Mind-Energy* and *The Creative Mind*.

Năng-lure tinh-thän. Trans. L. M. Cao-Văn-Luân. Hue: Dai-Hoc. 1962. 155.

Die seelische Energie. Trans. Eugen Lerch. Jena: Diederichs, 1928, 190.

Seishin no energy. Trans. Watanabe Shû. Tokyo: Hakusuisha, 1965, 253. (...zenshû, No. 5)

Själslig kraft: Studier och föredrag. Trans. Algot Ruhe. Stockholm: Wahlstrom and Widstrand, 1921, 181.

Zihin Kudreti. Trans. Miraç Katircioğlu. Istanbul: Maarif Basimevi, 1959, 236.

321   "Letter to Ralph Tyler Flewelling, April 24, 1919." In Daniel S. Robinson, "The Bergson-Flewelling Correspondence, 1914-1940," *Corranto*, 10, No. 2, 1977, 22-23. In this letter, which is written in English, Bergson responds to criticisms of his philosophy by Ralph Tyler Flewelling. Bergson states that he has not had a chance to examine Flewelling's arguments in detail and that he will do so in the future. He criticizes Flewelling's method, which involves "accepting, as if they were final, the ordinary ready-made concepts."

1920

322   "Letter to Ralph Tyler Flewelling, November 20, 1920." In Daniel S. Robinson, "The Bergson-Flewelling Correspondence, 1914-1940," *Coranto*, 10, No. 2, 1977, 25-26. In this letter Bergson turns down an invitation to lecture at the University of Southern California. Though he would like, Bergson states, to accept the invitation, his present obligations (some of which date from before the First World War) make this impossible.

323   "Fragment d'une lettre à G. Sorel: 1920." *Etudes Bergsoniennes*, 3, p. 52. Also in *Mélanges*, 1326. Bergson finds Sorel's conclusions favorable towards religious emotion.

324   "Lettre à Jacques Chevalier: 28 avril 1920." Chevalier. *Bergson*. Paris: Plon, 1934, 296, 304. Also in *Ecrits et paroles*, 3, 489; *Mélanges*, 1322. In this letter Bergson explains the terms "intelligence," "intellectual," and "supra-intellectual." The latter term defines intuition.

325   "Lettre à M. Proust: 30 septembre 1920." J. Guitton. *Vocation de Bergson*, 40-41. Also in *Mélanges*, 1326. This is about Marcel Proust's success and the acuity of his introspective method.

326   "Lettre à l'administrateur de Collège de France: 3 octobre 1920." *Mélanges*, 1327. In this letter Bergson expresses his desire to retire from teaching.

327   "Le Possible et le réel." *La Pensée et le mouvant: Essais et conférences*. Paris: Félix Alcan, 1934. (Cf. *The Creative Mind*, 1946, 107-125.)

        This lecture was delivered at Oxford in 1920 and has never been published as a whole. Bergson argues here that "pseudo-problems" encountered by philosophers derive from poorl -stated questions, which are created by transporting terms which are pragmatically useful into the sphere of pure theory. The problem of the nature of "nothing" is one example of a pseudoproblem. Another is the supposition that possibility precedes actuality in the form of an idea. This is a notion which fits procedures of fabrication, where the blueprint precedes the product. The opposite, however, is true of evolution and of man's creative acts. Here the real precedes the possible. We abstract what is possible from the newly-created present and project it illicitly into the past.

328   "Le Possible et le réel." *Oeuvres*. Ed. André Robinet. Paris: Presses Universitaires de France, 1959, 1331-1345.

329   "Le Possible et le réel." *Etudes Bergsoniennes*, 7, 127-132.

330   "Le Possible et le réel." *Mélanges*. Ed. André Robinet. Paris: Presses Universitaires de France, 1972, 1322-1326. This is a résumé.

Translations

        "Creation as Unpredictable." in *The Creativity Question*. Eds. Albert Rotherberg and Carl R. Hausman. Durham, N.C.: Duke University Press, 1976, 366.

        "Skapandet och det nya." Trans. Mgr. Söderblom. *Nordisk tidskrift for vetenskap*, N.S., arg 6, 1930, 441-456.

1921

331   "Henri Bergson on Moral Values and Other Subjects." *Personalist*, 62, No. 2, 1961, 178-180. This article contains replies by Bergson to various questions posed to him by R.F. Piper in 1921.

332 "Lettre à *Le Figaro*: 25 février 1921." *Le Figaro*, 25 février 1921. Also in *Mélanges*, 1331-1332. Here Bergson denies any participation in a committee to aid Russian refugees.

333 "Préface." Woodbridge Riley. *Le Génie américain: Penseurs et hommes d'action*. Paris: Félix Alcan, 1921, i-iv. Also in *Ecrits et paroles*, 3, 495-496; *Mélanges*, 1336-1338. This is a review of a book on important thinkers and early religious movements in the United States.

334 "Rapport sur un ouvrage de René Gillouin: *Une Nouvelle Philosophie de l'historie moderne et française.*" *Séances et Travaux de l'Académie des Sciences Morales et Politiques*, 196, 1921, 167-170 (Séance du 9 juillet 1921). Also in *Ecrits et paroles*, 3, 492-494; *Mélanges*, 1333-1336. This is an exposition of the mystique of imperialism.

335 "Rapport sur un ouvrage d'Ossip-Lourié: *La Graphomanie: Essai de psychologie morbide.*" *Séances et Travaux de l'Académie des Sciences Morales et Politiques*, 196, 1921, 520-522 (Séance du 12 février 1921). Also in *Ecrits et paroles*, 3, 490-491; *Mélanges*, 1330-1331. Bergson claims that the study of the irresistible desire to write does not necessarily enlighten psychology.

1922

336 "Appel...en faveur des travailleurs intellectuels autrichiens et de la vie intellectuelle en Autriche." *Archives de l'Unesco*, C. 731, M. 443, 1922, XII, 1-2. Also in *Ecrits et paroles*, 3, 520-522; *Mélanges*, 1363-1366. Various means of aiding Austria's distressed intellectual community are suggested here.

337 "Avant-propos." J. Alexander Gunn. *Modern French Philosophy, a study of the Development since Comte*. London: Fisher Unwin, 1922, 8-9. Also in *Ecrits et paroles*, 2, 536-537; *Mélanges*, 1387-1388. Bergson gives a general account of the structure and subject matter of Gunn's book.

338 "Comment doivent écrire les philosophes? Ce que pensent... M. Henri Bergson." *Monde Nouveau*, 4e Sér., 6, No. 25, 15 décembre 1922, 228-233. Also in Bourquin, Ed. *Comment doivent écrire les philosophes?* Paris: Editions du Monde Nouveau, 1923, 166.

339 "Commission internationale de coopération intellectuelle: Questions relatives à la propriété scientifique, artistique et littéraire." *Archives de l'Unesco*, A. 61, 1922, XII et C. 559, 1922, XII, p. 33. Also in *Mélanges*, 1348. This concerns the need for international copyright laws.

340 "Commission international de coopération intellectuelle: Rapport de la Commission approuvé par le Conseil de la S.D.N. le 13 septembre 1922." *Archives de l'Unesco* A. 61, 1933, XII et C. 559, 1922, XII, 1-6. Also in *Ecrits et paroles*, 3, 504-515; *Mélanges*, 1352-1363. In this essay there is a general enquiry into the state of intellectual life, a discussion of possible help for nations in which intellectual life is menaced, of an international organization for scientific documentation, and of international cooperation in scientific research, etc.

341 "Commission internationale de coopération intellectuelle: Rapport sur la première session tenue à Genève du 1er au 6 août 1922." *Société des Nations*, 1922, 2-6. Also in *Ecrits et paroles*, 3, 504-515. Bergson intervenes at several points during this discussion.

342 "Commission internationale de coopération intellectuelle: Résolution du Président concernant les recherches archéologiques." *Archives de l'Unseco*, A. 61, 1922, XII et C. 559, 1922, XII, p. 28. Also in *Mélanges*, 1347-1348. Here Bergson

calls for international cooperation to preserve archeological treasures.

343   "Commission internationale de coopération intellectuelle: Sous-Commission de bibliographie: Première séance à Paris 20 décembre 1922." *Archives de l'Unesco*, C.I.C.I./B./P.V.I. Also in *Mélanges*, 1379-1383. Here Bergson discusses the problem of world libraries and international bibliographic libraries.

344   "Commission internationale de coopération intellectuelle: Sous-Commission de bibliographie: 21 décembre 1922." *Archives de l'Unesco*, C.I.C.I./B./P.V.I. Also in *Mélanges* 1383-1386. Here Bergson discusses, with Mme. Curie and others, the problems of creating an international bibliographic index.

345   "Discours de clôture du président de la Commission internationale de coopération intellectuelle: Genève, 5 août 1922." *Première session de la Commission internationale de coopération intellectuelle*. Genève, 1922, 36-37. Also in *Ecrits et paroles*, 3, 516-519; *Mélanges*, 1349-1352. This is a general discussion of the goals and the accomplishments of the Commission.

346   *Durée et simultanéité: A propos de la théorie d'Einstein*. Paris: Félix Alcan, 1922, viii, 245. (Bibliothèque de philosophie contemporaine)

This is Bergson's criticism of Albert Einstein's special theory of relativity. According to Bergson relativity theory is more an operational device used to bring order into our mathematical descriptions of the world than a straightforward description of reality, as Einstein believed. In particular, the space and time effects of relativity theory are fictions or conventions, rather than accurate descriptions of actual space and time.

In the first chapter of *Duration and Simultaneity* Bergson describes a halfway house between Newtonian physics and relativity theory proper which he terms Half-Relativity ("Demi-relativité). Half-Relativity retains the absolute space, motion and rest of Newtonian physics while adding new factors, a spatial contraction in the direction of motion and a slowing-down (dilatation) of time in moving objects. The spatial contraction is, on this theory, a real contraction relative to absolute space, the temporal retardation is a real retardation relative to absolute time. The simultaneity of events here also becomes relative: but in absolute time. For an observer stationary in absolute space, therefore, it will still be possible to correct for these strange space and time effects and determine the true lengths and times of observed events. One has thus introduced relativistic effects only to cancel them out.

In the second chapter Bergson examines complete relativity: Einstein's view. From the vantage-point of complete relativity there is complete reciprocity of motion. That is, there is no preferred "reference system" at rest in absolute space, as there is in Half-Relativity. All reference systems are equivalent; there is mutual displacement, without any one reference system being at rest.

Unfortunately, relativity physics is not able to sustain its postulate of the complete reciprocity of motion. Given two reference systems S and S', the physicist must choose one as the vantage-point from which he must make his observations and calculations. As soon as he does this, however, he has inadvertently reintroduced half-relativity, making his system (S) motionless, putting the other system (S') into motion. His own system will then show no relativistic space or time effects, while the other will embody them perfectly. The contradiction thus becomes apparent: we have proclaimed a symmetrical relationship in theory, only to introduce a mathematical asymmetry in practice.

Before showing the implications of this contradiction for our understanding of time and space, Bergson, in chapter three, discusses the all-important differences between experienced duration and spatialized, "clock" time. His discussion is a review of positions already taken in *Matter and Memory* (1896), *Creative Evolution* (1907) and other works. What is real, Bergson argues, is a qualitative, continuous, experienced or experienceable duration. What is symbolic, not ultimately real, is a mathematical and homogeneous time made up of (static) instants.

Armed with these distinctions, Bergson, in chapters four and five, undertakes to show that the relativistic space and time effects are not real effects. They are mathematical "perspectives": perspectives which depend upon a more fundamental experienced duration. Thus if we imagine two reference systems S and S', in motion relative to each other, if S is taken as the basic reference system, the relativistic space and time effects (spatial contraction, temporal dilatation, dislocation of simultaneity) occur in system S'. But if we choose S' as the basic reference system, the relativistic effects occur not in S' but in S. Actual living physicists, then, never experience relativistic effects in their own reference systems; these effects are always imputed to other reference systems, peopled not by real but by "fantasmal" physicists. The special theory of relativity thus contains an internal contradiction. It can not successfully maintain the perfect equivalence of all reference systems, for in it the observer's system is always "privileged."

In chapter six Bergson examines the formulation of the special theory of relativity in terms of a four-dimensional space-time. The results reinforce his previous conclusions. Formulation in terms of space-time geometries does not remove the contradictions inherent in relativity.

In a final note Bergson briefly explores differences between special and general relativity. The two relativity theories require significantly different interpretations. In particular, the (non-Euclidean) space of general relativity is observable and real.

Though a broadly Bergsonian, process-oriented interpretation of relativity theory remains possible, most physicists have not concurred with Bergson's interpretation of relativity theory. *Duration and Simultaneity* should not be taken simply as a philosophical reflection on physics, however. It also remains valuable for its profound phenomenology of experiential time and space and for the light which it sheds on Bergson's philosophy.

347 *Durée et simultanéité: A propos de la théorie d'Einstein.* 2e ed. Paris: Félix Alcan, 1923, 289. (Bibliothèque de philosophie contemporaine) This edition contains three appendices, which are replies to criticisms of Bergson's interpretation of relativity physics: "Le Voyage en boulet", "Réciprocité de l'accélération", and "Ligne d'Univers." The first appendix deals with criticisms of Bergson's contention that the space and time effects of special relativity are not real effects. The second and third appendices extend Bergson's reflections into the sphere of the general theory of relativity where, he argues, the same difficulties which haunt the special theory arise again.

348 *Durée st simultanéité: A propos de la théorie d'Einstein.* 3e ed. Paris: Félix Alcan, 1923, 289. (Bibliothèque de philosophie contemporaine)

349 *Durée et simultanéité: A propos de la théorie d'Einstein.* 7e ed. Paris: Presses Universitaires de France, 1968, 216. (Bibliothèque de philosophie contemporaine)

350 *Durée et Simultanéité: A propos de la théorie d'Einstein.* in *Mélanges.* Ed. André Robinet. Paris: Presses Universitaires de France, 1972, 57-244. (Notes 1599-1600)

Translations

Duration and Simultaneity. Trans. Leon Jacobson. Intro. Herbert Dingle. Indianapolis, Indiana: Bobbs-Merrill, 1965, x-v, 190. (Library of Liberal Arts)

"Time and Lived Duration." in *The Human Experience of Time: The Development of Its Philosophical Meaning.* Ed. Charles M. Sherover. New York: New York University Press, 1975, 218-238. This is chapter three of *Duration and Simultaneity.*

351 "Les Etudes gréco-latines et la réforme de l'enseignement secondaire." *Séances et Travaux de l'Académie des Sciences Morales et Politiques,* 199, 1923, 60-71. Also in *Revue de Paris,* 30, No. 9, ler mai 1923, 5-18; *Ecrits et paroles,* 3, 523-534; *Mélanges,* 1366-1379. This is a discussion of the vital role of classical studies in French education.

352 "Lettre à Karen Stephen: 1922." Karen Stephen. *The Misuse of Mind.* London: Kegan Paul, 1922, 107. Also in *Ecrits et paroles,* 3, p. 535; *Mélanges,* 1386-1387. This is a preface to Karen Stephen's *Misuse of Mind.* In it, Bergson praises Stephen's logical rigor.

353 "Préface à *La Fierté de vivre* de Pierre-Jean Ménard." *Mélanges,* 1389-1391. This is an introduction to the notes of a physican-philosopher killed in World War I. It discusses the place of heroism in human affairs.

354 "Remarques sur la théorie de la relativité." *Bulletin de la Société Française de Philosophie,* 22, No. 3, juillet 1922, 102-113 (Séance du 6 avril 1922). Also in *Ecrits et paroles,* 3, 497-503; *Mélanges,* 1340-1347; *La Pensée,* No. 210, 1980, 12-29. This article has been translated, with an introduction, in *Bergson and the Evolution of physics,* (1969). Ed. Pete A. Y. Gunter, 123-135. This is a criticism of relativity theory made by Bergson, in Einstein's presence, at a meeting of the Société française de philosophie. It states the basic arguments of *Duration and Simultaneity.*

1923

355 "Commission internationale de coopération intellectuelle: L'Enseignement de l'Esperanto: 31 juillet 1923." *Archives de l'Unesco,* C. 570, M. 224, 1923, XII, p. 40. Also in *Mélanges,* 1414-1416. Here Bergson discusses both the advantages and the drawbacks of an artificial international language.

356 "Commission internationale de coopération intellectuelle: Rapport sur la deuxième session tenue à Genève du 26 juillet au 2 août 1923. 15 août 1923." *Société des Nations,* A. 31, 1923, 12, 3-10. Also in *Ecrits et paroles,* 3, 542-559; *Mélanges,* 1398-1414. This is a detailed account of the work to be accomplished by the Commission and the problems it will encounter.

357 "Discours d'ouverture du président de la Commission internationale de coopération intellectuelle: 26 juillet 1923." *Deuxième session de la Commission internationale de coopération intellectuelle,* 1923, Procès-verbaux, 7. Also in *Ecrits et paroles,* 3, 540-541; *Mélanges,* 1397-1398. Here Bergson welcomes back the members of the Commission and urges them to seek practical goals.

358 "Discours prononcé au banquet offert à Xavier Léon pour le trentième anniversaire de la *Revue de Métaphysique et de Morale.*" *Trentenaire de la Revue de Métaphysique et de Morale. Hommage à M. Xavier Léon.* Paris: Presses Universitaires de France, 1924. Also in *Ecrits et paroles,* 3, 566-569; *Mélanges,*

1425-1428. This talk was given December 27, 1923. Bergson congratulates Xavier Léon for his great contribution to French philosophy.

359 "Lettre à Floris Delattre: 9 mai 1923." *Revue Philosophique de la France et de l'Etranger*, 1941, p. 134. Also in *Mélanges*, 1394. In this fragment Bergson discusses his ill health, particularly his insomnia.

360 "Lettre à Floris Delattre: 23 ou 24 août 1923." *Revue Anglo-américaine*, 13, No. 5, juin 1936, 392-393. Also in *Ecrits et paroles*, 3, 560-561; *Mélanges*, 1417-1418. Here Bergson describes his "durée" as being more continuous than William James' "stream of thought." James compared his stream of thought to the flight of a bird, containing "places of flight" and "places of rest." For Bergson, however, there is only flight.

361 "Lettre à R. de Flers: 27 avril 1923." *Le Figaro*, 28 avril 1923, 1, col. 3. Also in *Mélanges*, 1394. In this letter Bergson denies any knowledge of or influence by Laggrond.

362 "Lettre à A. Suarès: 1923." M. Dietschy. *Le Cas André Suarès*, p. 292. Also in *Mélanges*, 1429. In this fragment of a letter Bergson thanks Suarès for one of his books.

363 "Proposition de crédit supplémentaire pour la Commission de coopération intellectuelle." *Journal Officiel de la Société des Nations*, 1923. *Suppléments Spéciaux*, No. 17, 78-80. "Rapport de M. Bergson devant la Commission financière de l'Assemblée de la Société des Nations, Genève, le 26 septembre 1923." Also in *Ecrits et paroles*, 3, 562-566; *Mélanges*, 1419-1424. This is about the financial affairs of the commission.

364 "Rapport sur un ouvrage d'Alfred Tarde: *Le Maroc: Ecole d'énergie*." *Séances et Travaux de l'Académie des Sciences Morales et Politiques*, 201, 1924, 435-436 (Séance du 30 juin 1923). Also in *Ecrits et paroles*, 3, 538-539; *Mélanges*, 1395-1396. This is about the "first chapter" of a philosophy of colonialism.

365 "Réunion du conseil supérieur de l'éducation nationale: 3 juillet 1923." Mossé-Bastide. *Bergson éducateur*, p. 171. Also in *Mélanges*, 1395. This article is about the importance of a classical education.

1924

366 "Appel en faveur de la vie intellectuelle en Hongrie: 5 novembre 1924." *Journal Officiel de la Société des Nations*, 2, 1924, 1811. Also in *Ecrits et paroles*, 3, 581-582; *Mélanges*, 1459-1461. Here Bergson makes a plea for journals, books, and research funds for Hungary.

367 "Commission internationale de coopération intellectuelle: Ouverture de la session: 25 juillet 1924." *Archives de l'Unesco*, A. 20, 1924, XII, p. 9. Also in *Mélanges*, 1454-1455. Bergson welcomes Albert Einstein to the Commission and congratulates him on his success as a scientist.

368 "Commission internationale de coopération intellectuelle: Sous-Commission de bibliographie." *Archives de l'Unesco*, C.I.C.I./6e session/P.V.3. Also in *Mélanges*, 1452-1454. This article is a discussion of the possibility of an international bibliography for the social sciences.

369 "Letter to Marcus M. Marks." *Review of Reviews*, 70, No. 5 1924, 506. This letter concerns the international exchange of students.

370   "Lettre à Fl. Delattre: 3 décembre 1924." *Revue Philosophique de la France et de l'Etranger*, mars, 1941, 134. Also in *Mélanges*, 1462. This concerns Bergson's rheumatoid arthritis, which began towards the end of 1924.

371   "Lettre à E. Peillaube: Juillet, 1924." *Revue de Philosophie*, 24, No. 4, juillet 1924, 440. Also in *Mélanges*, 1462. Translated in *Bergson and the Evolution of Physics*, (1969) Ed. Pete A. Y. Gunter, 189-190. Bergson insists here that André Metz has failed to understand his criticisms of relativity theory. Under such circumstances Bergson can add nothing more to the discussion.

372   "Lettre du président de la Commissons au secrétaire de la Confédération internationale des travailleurs intellectuels: 26 juillet 1924." *Procès-verbal de la quatrième session de la Commission internationale de coopération intellectuelle*, Annexe 1, 50. Also in *Ecrits et paroles*, 3, 579; *Mélanges*, 1456-1457. In this letter Bergson discusses the fact that the Confédération internationale des travailleurs intellectuels has been denied permission to send a voting member to the C.I.C.I. meetings. A non-voting member, however, is to be allowed to attend.

373   "Lettre du président de la Commission de coopération intellectuelle à l'Association internationale des journalistes: 28 juillet 1924." *Procès-verbal de la quatrième session de la Commission internationale de coopération intellectuelle.* Annexe 7. Also in *Ecrits et paroles*, 3, 580; *Mélanges*, 1457-1458. This is a discussion of the fact that journalists were not allowed to attend meetings of C.I.C.I. However, a public session of the Commission is planned.

374   "Mémoire sur l'échange international des publications." *Journal de la Société des Nations*, janvier-juin 1924, Annexe 607a, 576-580. Also in *Ecrits et paroles*, 3, 570-578; *Mélanges*, 1463-1470. In this document, the findings of the International Commission for Intellectual Cooperation on the possibility of the free international exchange of publications are summarized.

375   "Préface." Floris Delattre. *Extraits de correspondance de W. James*. Paris: Payot, 1924, 7-12. Also in*Ecrits et Paroles*, 3, 583-586; *Mélanges*, 1470-1474. In this brief essay Bergson discusses the vision and personality of William James.

376   "Rapport sur *La Révolution physique et la science* de J. Sageret." *Séances et Travaux de l'Académie des Sciences Morales et Politiques*, 205, 1926, 300-301. Here Bergson points out parallels in the scientific thinking of Le. Dantec, Einstein, and J. H. Rosny-aîné. In all these cases, he shows, becoming triumphs over being.

377   "Les Temps fictifs et le temps réel." *Revue de Philosophie*, 24, mai 1924, 241-260. Also in *Mélanges*, 1432-1439. Translated, with an introduction, in *Bergson and the Evolution of Physics*. (1969) Ed. P. A. Y. Gunter, 165-186. This is a reply to criticisms of *Duration and Simultaneity* by André Metz. Bergson claims that Metz fails to understand the reciprocity of reference systems in the special theory of relativity and the reciprocity of acceleration in the general theory. The experiments which Metz appeals to, further, are incapable of proving his point. (Cf., in the secondary literature, A. Metz, 1923, 1924.)

1925

378   "Letter to the editor of the London *Times*, August 21, 1925." *The Times*, No. 44,049, August 25, 1925, p. 11. In this letter (written at Saint-Cergue, Switzerland) Bergson corrects an erroneous report in the *Times* that he is "so seriously ill that he is virtually a condemned man." That he has been visited by fourteen doctors recently is true, Bergson concedes, but several of these visited simply

as personal friends. (He has nonetheless been told that his constitution must be very strong to be able to withstand fourteen doctors.) A special rheumatic infection due to overwork does continue to affect him, and he will be required, when convalescent, to take the greatest care with his health.

379 "Lettre: 1925." *Mélanges*, 1477. This is a fragment which states: "Quand on a passé sa vie à chercher le vrai, on s'aperçoit qu'on l'eût mieux employée à faire du bien."

380 "Lettre de retraite de la Commission internationale de coopération intellectuelle: 27 juillet 1925." *Archives de l'Unesco*, C.I.C.I./C.A./1re Session/P.V.1. Also in *Mélanges*, 1476-1477. Here Bergson presents his regrets at his inability to attend sessions of the commission. He also discusses various suggestions regarding the commission's affairs.

1926

381 "Lettre à I. Benrubi: 21 novembre 1926." Benrubi. *Souvenirs sur Henri Bergson*, 110-111. Also in *Mélanges*, 1480. This is a discussion of Benrubi's *Contemporary Thought of France*.

1927

382 "Lettre à Léon Brunschvicg à l'occasion de la commémoration du deux cent cinquantième anniversaire de la mort de Spinoza: 12 février 1927." *Bulletin de la Société Française de Philosophie*, 27 juin 1927, p. 26. Also in *Ecrits et paroles*, 3, 587-588; *Mélanges*, 1482-1483. Here Bergson characterizes Spinoza's theory of knowledge as "connaissance intérieure."

383 "Lettre à de la Vallette-Montbrun, secrétaire général de l'Association des amis de Maine de Biran: 30 septembre 1927." *Revue Maine de Biran*, 1, No. 1, 1929, 1-2. Also in *Ecrits et paroles*, 3, 589; *Mélanges*, 1484. Here Bergson gives his very high opinion of Maine de Biran and his philosophy.

384 "Lettre à Wilfred Monod: 27 janvier 1927." W. Monod. *Le Problème du bien*, 2, p. 76. Also in H. Sunden. *La Théorie bergsonienne de la religion*, 13; *Mélanges*, 1481-1482. Here Bergson claims that the problem of God is a moral problem and discusses the possible relation between God and creation.

385 "Remerciement pour le Prix Nobel de littérature de 1928: L'Évolution créatrice." *Les prix Nobel 1928*, 57-59. Also in *Ecrits et paroles*, 3, 590-591; *Mélanges*, 1488-1490; Jean Guitton, *La Vie et l'oeuvre de H. Bergson*. Paris: Presses due Compagnonage, 1962, 349. (Guilde des Bibliophiles, collection des Prix Nobel de littérature). The latter volume contains a reception speech by Per Hallström and an introduction by Kjell Strömberg. This is Bergson's Nobel Prize for Literature acceptance speech.

Translations

L'evoluzione creatrice. Trans. L. Alano. Milano: Fabbri, 1966, 396 (I premi Nobel per la letteratura, 28).

Miguel Angel Asturas, Jacinto Benavente & Henri Bergson: Nobel Prize Library. New York: A. Gregory, 1971, 378.

386 "Lettre à I. Benrubi: 12 juin 1928." Benrubi. *Souvenirs sur Henri Bergson*, 112-114. Also in *Mélanges*, 1486-1487. Here Bergson congratulates Benrubi on his *Philosophische Stroemungen in Frankreich*. He also issues a warning concerning the difficulties involved in assigning "influence" to philosophers.

387 "Lettre à Fl. Delattre: 16 janvier 1928." *Revue philosophique de la France et de l'Etranger*, 1941, p. 134. *Mélanges*, 1485. This is a brief fragment concerning Bergson's health.

388 "Lettre à V. Jankélévitch: 7 juillet 1928." Jankélévitch. *Bergson,* (1959) 253. Also in *Mélanges*, 1487. Here Bergson agrees that there are similarities between his own philosophy and that of Spinoza.

389 "Lettre à L. Lévy-Bruhl: 22 novembre 1928." *Séances et Travaux de l'Académie des Sciences Morales et Politiques*, 1929, p. 374. Also in *Mélanges*, 1490. This letter is about the congratulations of the French Academy for Bergson's Nobel Prize.

390 "Lettre au Duc de la Force: 22 novembre 1928." *Mélanges*, 1491. Here Bergson thanks the French Academy for kind words concerning his Nobel Prize.

1929

391 "Lettre à Fl. Delattre: 11 mars 1929." *Revue de Philosophie*, mars 1941, 134. Also in *Mélanges*, 1493. This letter is about Bergson's health. He now has only minutes, rather than hours, in which he can work each day.

1930

392 "Lettre à Vladimir Jankélévitch: 6 août 1930." Vladimir Jankélévitch. *Bergson*. Paris: Félix Alcan, 1931, v; Nouvelle édition, 1959, 253. Also in *Ecrits et paroles*, 3, 592; *Mélanges*, 1487. Here Bergson congratulates Jankélévitch on his book, *Bergson*.

1931

393 "Lettre à Jeanne Hersch: 22 juillet 1931." *Archives de Psychologie*, 23 août 1931, 97. Also in *Mélanges*, 1498. In this letter, Bergson thanks Mlle. Hersch for her study of his philosophy.

394 "Lettre à Albert Kahn pour le 25e anniversaire de la fondation du cercle'Autour du Monde': 12 juin 1931." Alain Petit. "Le Premier Elève de Bergson: Un Précurseur alsacien de l'Unesco." *Revue Hommes et Mondes*, novembre 1949, 418 et 422. Also in *Mélanges*, 1497-1498. In these passages Bergson discusses the importance of the exchange of students between nations.

1932

395 *Les Deux Sources de la morale et de la religion*. Paris: Félix Alcan, 1932, 346. In *The Two Sources of Morality and Religion* Bergson applies the fundamental concepts of his philosophy to the traditional problems of morals and religion.

His approach is broadly sociological and anthropological, though he continues to defend the freedom and creativity of the individual. Behind Bergson's interpretation of sociology and anthropology stands his evolutionary vision. Though a distinctive and original study in its own right, *The Two Sources* is also an extension of the basic these of *Creative Evolution* (1907) into the interpretation of human history.

Fundamental to Bergson's sociology is his distinction between the open and the closed society. The closed society, in both its ethics and its religion, is turned inward upon itself. Its social rules are intended to maintain order in society and to defend a particular society against others. The connections between the closed society and the institution of war are clear. The open society, on the other hand, reaches out to all people, all societies. It offers a broadening and deepening of humanity across the boundaries of class and race, and gives to human life a purpose and an ultimate significance. The closed society tends towards social stasis and is intransigeantly conservative, the open society is the locus of moral and religious creativity, and strives to overturn institutions based on closure. The interaction bewteen these two social tendencies (openness and closure) defines the course of human history.

Bergson begins his study of morality and religion with an examination of the phenomenon of obligation. Obligation (the sense of "oughtness") derives not from pure reason but from social pressure. It is bound up with habits and entails obedience to society. Beneath social pressures and the habitual responses which they have built up lies, Bergson proposes, a social instinct, the residue of an instinctive potentiality which has reached its fullest development in insect societies, but which is nonetheless present in man, in spite of the acquisitions of his intelligence and of a higher morality. In spite of its instinctive roots, however, the morality of the closed society is expressed in clear, distinct percepts: in lists of do's and don't's whose social functions are clear.

In the second chapter Bergson explores a fundamental expression of the closed society, static religion. There are pressing reasons for the appearance of static religion. Social pressure, powerful and subtle though it may be, can not by itself create either sufficient social cohesion or sufficient personal incentive to ensure the survival of society. The great enemy of social cohesion is egoism, and human beings are tempted to egoism as soon as they begin to use their intelligence. Static religion responds by creating deities which forbid self-centered behavior: which forbid and chastize. The great enemy of incentive, of morale, in human beings is the thought of death, a thought which so far as we can tell only human beings can entertain. To this negative, disrupting thought primitive religion opposes a counter-thought: the survival of the self after death. Static religion is a "defensive reaction" of nature against the concept of the inevitability of death.

A third source of static religion is the notion of the "depressing margin of the unexpected between the initiative taken and the effect desired." The best laid plans of mice and men all to clearly can go astray. Against the depressing effects of this realization, static religion opposes the image of a helping, powerful deity who can defend against harm as well as bring good fortune.

The three main sources of static religion reinforce each other, in roughly equal proportions, but do not produce the same results everywhere. Bergson notes the fact, obvious to anthropologists and historians of religion, that though static religions may present themselves as permanent and unchanging, the gods of the static religions "evolve." Throughout man's history his gods have changed with his circumstances. Insofar as we are dealing with static religions, however, one constant remains amid countless variations: the gods are responses to the negative or dissolvent power of human intelligence.

Bergson has aleady made it clear, however, that the analysis of static religion does not exhaust the varieties of religous experience. There is a second sort of religion which brings with it a different ethics, based not on social pressure and felt obligation but on aspiration and idealism. In his third chapter Bergson investigates this second sort of spirituality, which he terms dynamic religion.

Dynamic religion represents a different way of acheiving "attachment to life" than does static religion. Static religion uses man's myth-making function to heal psychological wounds inflicted by intelligence; the result is social order and stability. Another means of acheiving this attachment was always possible, however; man can turn back and recapture the creative impetus which has brought man and the other forms of life into existence. This is the mystic's task: to break with the closed society and its point of view, as with human intelligence and its narrow pragmatism, and to seek to recover an inspiration prior to and more fundamental than either.

Such a project would require, Bergson is quick to point out, both great psycholog- ical strength and profound nobility of spirit. But it remains always possible, and it has been pursued at all times in all societies. We find this, in the West, in the Elusinian and Orphic mysteries, and in Pyhagoreanism and in Plato; it reoccurs again in Plotinus. In the Orient we find the mystic way in Hinduism, in Sufism, in Buddhism. But, Bergson insists, profound and significant as all of these religions were, they still represent an incomplete mysticism, which remained at the stage of reflection. A complete mysticism, though it too must forsake the city of man and its all-too-municipal deities, must go beyond the mystic exstasy: it must *act*. Paradoxically, a complete mysticism expresses itself in social action.

It is in the Judeo-Christian tradition that one finds the emergence and continuation of a complete, active mysticism, a mysticism which reaches its fullest expression in the figure of Jesus of Nazareth, and in the Christian mystics (St. Paul, St. Teresa, St. Francis, Joan of Arc...) who followed him. Dynamic religion, a profound manifestation of the life force, is a means of producing man's forward leap beyond the limits of the closed society for which nature intended him and into the open society which is the brotherhood of man.

In his final remarks (chapter four) Bergson explores the gap between the humanity of the closed society and the higher, more inclusive society of the mystics and moral geniusses. In spite of the accretions of civilization, basic—indeed, primi- tive—human character remains what it has always been. It is not democratic. Indeed, if it could proclaim itself in a motto its motto might be "authority, hierarchy, immobility." Democracy, exemplified in the Declaration of Indepen- dence or the rights of man, goes counter to this psychological bedrock. It is the result of, the political expression of, the dynamic mysticism of the Gospels, and points away from the exclusiveness and the warlike character of the primitive in man. What democracy fundamentally seeks is brotherhood.

Bergson ends his study with a meditation on the phenomenon of war. The cultivation of luxury, the expansion of population, the neglect of agriculture: all these, he states, are practical problems which form obstacles to peace between nations, but which might find practical solutions. But in order for man to resolve to use these solutions something more is necessary than ordinary practicality. What is needed is an ever-spreading mystic intuition: a joy before which our pleasures would pale, and our mutual divisions appear as minor obstacles.

396   *Les Deux Sources de la morale et de la religion.* Genève: Skira, 1946, 310.

397   *Les Deux Sources de la morale et de la religion* in *Oeuvres.* Ed. André Robinet. Paris: Presses Universitaires de France, 1959, 981-1247.

398   *Les Deux Sources de la morale et de la religion.* 217éd. Paris: Presses Universitaires de France, 1982, 340. (Quadrige, 34)

Translations

Ahlâk ve dinin iki kaynaği. Tercüme eden Mehmet Emin. Istanbul: Devlet Matbaasi, 1933.

Ahlâk ili dinin iki kaynaği. 2nd ed. Trans. Mehmet Keresen. Ankara: Millî Eğitim Basimevi, 1962, xvi, 410.

Ahklâk île dinin iki kaynaği. Trans. Mehmet Karasan, Istanbul: Millî Eğitim Basimevi, 1967, xii, 399.

Die beiden Quellen der Moral und der Religion. Trans. Eugen Lerch. Jena: Diederichs, 1933, 317.

Die beiden Quellen der Moral und der Religion. Trans. Eugen Lerch. Olten, Freiburg i. Br.: Walter, 1980, 317.

Las dos fuentes del la moral y de la religión. Montevideo: Ed. Claudio Garcia, 1944, 346.

Las dos fuentes de la moral y de la religión. Trans. Miguel González Fernández. Intro. José Ferrater Mora. Buenos Aires: Ed. Sudamericana, 1946, 390.

Los dos fuentos de la moral y de la religión. 2ed ed. Trans. Miguel González Fernández. Intro. José Ferrater Mora. Buenos Aires: Editorial Sudamericana, 1962, 303. (Collecion piraqua, No. 62)

"Emoción y Creación." *Revisita de Ideas Estéticas*, 1, No. 4, 1943, 109-110. This is a passage from Chapter 1 of *Les Deux Sources.* Trans. M. C. Iracheta.

Mecánica y mística. [San Sebastian] 1941, 14. (Supplemento literario de *Vértice*, marzo 1941) "Capítulo de su libro 'Les Deux Sources de la morale et de la religion.'"

Dôtoku to shûkyô no ni-gensen. Trans. Hirayama Takaji. Tokyo: Iwanami shoten, 1953, 401.

Dôtoku to shûkyô no nigensen. Trans. Nakamura Yûjiirô. Tokyo: Hakusùisha, 1965, 390. (Zenshū, No. 6)

Dôtoku to shûkyô no nigensen. Trans. Hirayama Takaji. Tokyo: Iwanami Shoten, 1977, 390.

Dôtoku to shûkyô no nigensen, Trans. Nakamura Yûjirô. Tokyo: Hakusuisha, 1978, 388.

Le due fonti della morale e della religione. Trad. Mario Vinciguerra. Milano: Ed. di Comunità, 1947, 348; 2ed., 1950, 352; 3e ed., 1962, 311; 4e ed., 1966, 311.

Le due fonti della morale e della religione. 5 ed. Trans. Mario Vinciguerra. Milano: Edizioni di Comunità, 1973, 270. (Saggi di cultura contemporanea, No. 105)

L'obbligazione morale: De le due fonti della morale e della religione. Trans. Luigi Pinto. Napoli: Ediz. Glaux, 1961, xxxvi, 141.

Oi duo pēges tēs ēthikēs kai tēs thrēskeias. Trans. B. Tatakis. Athens: G. Papadēmētrios, 1951.

Dvoji pramen mravnosti a náboženstvi. Trans. Václav Černý. Prague: Jan Laichter, 1936, x, 313. (Laichterova filosofická knihovna, No. 16).

Manb'ā Al-Akhlāq Wa Al-Din. Trans. Sāmī Al-Durūb. Al-Qāhirah: Al-Hay'ah Al-Misriyah Al-'Āmmah Lil-Ta'lif Wa Al-Nashr, 1971, 341.

De to kilder for moral og religion. Trans. Aasmund Brynildsen. Oslo: Bokhjornet, 1967, 287.

The Two Sources of Morality and Religion. Trans. R. Ashley Audra and Cloudesly Brereton with W. Horsfall Carter. New York: H. Holt and Company, 1935, viii, 308.

The Two Sources of Morality and Religion. Trans. R. Ashley Audra and Cloudesly Brereton, with W. Horsfall Carter. Garden City, New York: Doubleday, 1954, 320. (Doubleday Anchor Books, No. A28)

The Two Sources of Morality and Religion. Trans. R. Ashley Audra and Cloudesly Brereton, with W. Horsfall Carter. 1935; rpt. Westport, Conn.: Greenwood Press, 1974, viii, 308.

The Two Sources of Morality and Religion. Trans. R. Ashley Audra and Cloudesly Brereton, with W. Horsfall Carter. 1954; rpt. Notre Dame, Indiana: University of Notre Dame Press, 1977, 320.

"The Two Sources of Morality and Religion." in *Landmarks for Beginners in Philosophy.* Ed. Irwin Edman and Herbert W. Schneider. New York: Holt, 1941, 920-977.

"Mysticism, Action and Philosophy." in *Understanding Mysticism.* Ed. Richard Woods. Garden City, New York: Image Books, 1980, 357-378. This is a selection from "Dynamic Religion", Part III of *The Two Sources.*

"Dynamic Religion." in *Contemporary Religious Thinkers from Idealist Metaphysicians to Existential Theologians.* Ed. John Macquarrie. New York: Harper and Row, 1968, 133-139.

Freedom and Obligation." in *Freedom: Its Meaning.* Ed. Ruth N. Anshen. New York: Harcourt Brace and Co., 1940, 612-613. This consists of the initial pages of the first chapter of *The Two Sources.*

"The Concept of Freedom; The Open and the Closed Society," in *The Nature of Man.* Ed. Erich Fromm and Ramón Xirau. New York: The Macmillian Company; London: Collier-Macmillian Limited, 1968, pp. 254-259. The editors present brief passages from *Time and Free Will* and *The Two Sources.*

399   "Lettre á Guy-Grand: 11 juin 1932." *Bulletin de l'Union pour la Vérité,* 40, No. 7-8, avril-mai 1933, 331-332. Also in *Ecrits et pa*
es, 3, p. 597; *Mélanges,* 1504. This is about talks on Bergson's *Two Sources* given at the Union pour la vérité.

400   "Lettre à Xavier Léon: 28 mai 1932." *Bulletin de la Société Française de Philosophie,* 32, No. 4, octobre 1932, 122-123. Also in *Mélanges,* 1502-1503. This is a letter written on the occasion of the Commémoration Jules Lachelier.

401   "Lettre à A. Suarès: 22 novembre 1932." Dietschy. *Le Cas Suarès*, 282. Also in
       Mélanges, 1500. In this letter Bergson denies that he has been reduced to
       publishing *The Two Sources of Morality and Religion* at his own expense.

402   "Lettre-préface." Raoul Mourgue. *Neurobiologie de l'hallucination*. Bruxelles:
       Lamertin, 1932, 1-2. Also in *Ecrits et paroles*, 3, 594-595; *Mélanges*, 1501-
       1502. In this letter Bergson discusses method in psychology.

1933

403   "Lettre à A. Suarès: 16 juillet 1933." Mossé-Bastide. *Bergson éducateur*, 74. Also
       in *Mélanges*, 1507. This is about the nature of art.

404   "Lettre au P. Blaise Romeyer: 24 mars 1933." Blaise Romeyer. "Autour du prob-
       lème de la philosophie chrétienne." *Archives de Philosophie*, 10, No. 4, 1934,
       478. Also in *Ecrits et paroles*, 3, 596; *Mélanges*, 1507. This is about the issue
       of theodicy in *The Two Sources*.

405   "Lettre à Raimundo Lida." *Nosotros*, 27, No. 295, 1933, 447-448. Bergson con-
       gratulates R. Lida for his article "Bergson, Filosofo del Lenguaje," (*Nosotros*,
       No. 292, 1933) which, he states, is an important article accurately describing
       his concept of "the projection of thought in language."

406   "Letter to Ralph Tyler Flewelling, April 6, 1933." In Daniel S. Robinson, "The
       Bergson-Flewelling Correspondence, 1914-1920," *Coranto*, 10, No. 2, 1977,
       29. In this letter Bergson thanks Flewelling for an issue of the *Personalist*
       dedicated to his philosophy. He concurs with Flewelling's interpretation of his
       philosophy in its relations to personalism but criticizes Herman Hausheer's article
       likening Bergson's philosophy to that of Schelling.

407   "La Philosophie française." *La Science française*. Paris: Larousse, 1933, 1-26.
       Also in *Mélanges*, 1157-1189. This second version was written with the collab-
       oration of E. Le Roy.

1934

408   "Lettre à J. Chevalier: Fin 1934." *Le Van*, No. 169, janvier 1935, 29. Also in
       Entretiens avec Bergson, 222-223; *Mélanges*, 1518. This is about Chevalier's
       interpretation of *Les Deux Sources*. Bergson states: "Combien je souhaite que
       ces pages soient lues et méditées!"

409   "Lettre au Jury du Prix Nobel de la Paix: 9 janvier 1934." A. Heurgon-Desjardins.
       Paul Desjardins et les décades de Pontigny, 387-388. Also in *Mélanges*, 1509-
       1511. In this letter Bergson urges the candidacy of Paul Desjardins for the Nobel
       Peace Prize.

410   *La Pensée et le mouvant: Essais et conférences*. Paris: Félix Alcan, 1934, 322.
       (Bibliothèque de philosophie contemporaine).

       Most of the essays in this work were published previously. Brief sketches of
       these have been provided in the present bibliography, in the year in which they
       appeared. These are: "Le Possible et le réel" (1920), "L'Intuition philosophique"
       (1911), "La Perception du changement" (1911), "Introduction à la métaphysique"
       (1903), "La Philosophie de Claude Bernard" (1913), "Sur le pragmatisme de
       William James: Vérité et réalité" (1911), and "La Vie et l'oeuvre de Ravaisson"

(1904). Two of the essays published here were written especially for this volume, and are of great importance for the understanding of Bergson's thought. Taken together with his "Introduction to Metaphysics" they constitute his Discourse on Method: the central gateway to his philosophy. These essays are: "Croissance de la vérité: Mouvement rétrograde du vrai" ("Growth of Truth: Retrograde Movement of the True") and "De la position des problèmes" ("The Stating of Problems")

In the first of these ("Growth of Truth: Retrograde Movement of the True") Bergson argues as in "The Possible and the Real" against the notion that possibilities precede and structure the course of events. In fact, the opposite is the case. Possibilities and truth itself—do not precede actuality; rather, actuality—the creative course of events—creates new possibilites. History is thus not a choice between possibilities but the creation of possibilities, which are then projected onto the past. Truth is not in this sense prospective, it is retrospective: it has a retrograde movement. Once a new system emerges, we necessarily restructure and reconceive our past in terms of it. Bergson's discussion of these problems is accompanied by his intellectual autobiography. Above all he sought to introduce precision into philosophy.

In the second of these essays ("The Stating of Problems") Bergson argues that philosophers have often failed because they have stated problems wrongly. Once a problem is stated correctly, it is already virtually solved. Bergson here explores the factors which have lead him to seek for new ways of stating problems. Among the problems which he considers are the concepts of intuition, intelligence, clarity, intelligence, intellect, mysticism, and the manner in which philosophy and science should be related. Bergson's discussion of the manner in which philosophy and the sciences should be related clears away many of the confusions which have surrounded the interpretation of this all-important component of his philosophy. Far from being anti-scientific, Bergson protests, he has sought to create a philosophy which can help science progress.

411   *La Pensée et le mouvant: Essais et conférences*. 12e èd. Paris: Presses Universitaires de France, 1941, 291. (Bibliothèque de Philosophie Contemporaine).

412   *La Pensée et le mouvant: Essais et conférences* in *Oeuvres*. André Robinet. Paris: Presses Universitaires de France, 1959, 1249-1482. (Notes, 1574-1578).

Translations

The Creative Mind. Trans. Mabelle L. Andison. New York: Philosophical Library, 1946, 307.

An Introduction to Metaphysics: The Creative Mind. Trans. Mabelle L. Andison. Totowa, New Jersey: Littlefeild, Adams & Co., 1965, 252. (The Famous Classic, 164)

The Creative Mind. Trans. Mabelle L. Andison. New York: Greenwood Press, 1968, 307.

Denken und schöpferisches Werden: Aufsätze und Vorträge. Trans. and Intro. Leonore Kottje. Meisenheim am Glan: Westkulturverlag, 1948, 279.

Duşünce ve devingen. Trans. Miraç Katircioğlu. Istanbul: Maarif Basimevi, 1959, 343.

Mah'shava u-tenua. Trans. Yakov Levi. Jerusalem: Mosad Bailik, 1953, 170.

Myśl i ruch. Wstep do metafizyki. Intuicja filozoficzna. Postrzeznie zmiany, Dusca i ciato. Trans. Pauwel Beylin and Kazimierz Bézyñski. Intro. Pawel Beylin. Warsawa: Pañstwowe Wydawnictwo Naukowe, 1963, 163. This is a collection of esays from *Mind-Energy* and *The Creative Mind.*

El pensamiento y lo moviente. Trans. Heliodoro García García. Madrid: Espasa-Calpe, 1976, 232. (Collección Austral, 1615)

Shisô to ugokumono. Trans. Yoichi Kôno. Tokyo: Iwanami shoten ,1952, 102.

Shisû to ugokumono. Trans. Yanaihara Isaku. Tokyo: Hakuṡuisha, 1965, 328. (...zenshû, No. 7).

Shisô to ugokumono. 2 Vols. Trans. Yoichi Kôno. Tokyo: Iwanami shoten, 1953.

Tetsugaku nyûmon: Henka no chikaku. Trans. Yoichi Kôno. Tokyo: Iwanami shoten, 1953, 102.

Tetsugaku no hôhô. Trans. Yoichi Kôno. Tokyo: Iwanami shoten, 1955, 112.

413 "Quelques mots sur la philosophie française et sur l'esprit française." *Entretiens philosophiques, Conférences radio-diffusées du Poste National Radio-Paris.* Paris: Imprimerie 111 rue du Mont-Cenis, 1934, 5-9. Also in *Mélanges*, 1513-1517. Bergson claims here that science, form, and moral insight define French philosophy and the French spirit.

1935

414 "L'Académie française vue de New York par un de ses membres." *Trois Siècles de l'Académie française: 1635-1935.* Paris: Firmin-Didot, 1935, 473-485. Also in *Ecrits et paroles*, 3, 606-615; *Mélanges*, 1529-1539. Bergson here discusses American attitudes towards the Académie française.

415 "Lettre à Léon Bopp: 9 juillet 1935." *Mélanges*, 1519. In this letter Bergson thanks Bopp for a copy of *Esquisse d'un traité du roman.* Interesting views of aesthetics and the mechanism of artistic production conclude Bergson's remarks.

416 "Lettre à Fl. Delattre: décembre 1935." *Revue Philosophique de la France et de l'Etranger*, mars 1941, 131. Also in *Mélanges*, 1522. In this letter Bergson discusses modesty in philosophy.

417 "Lettre à Fl. Delattre: décembre 1935." *Revue Anglo-américaine*, 13, No. 5, juin 1936, 395-401. Also in *Ecrits et paroles*, 3, 600-605; *Mélanges*, 1522-1528. In this letter Bergson gives his (remarkably high) opinion of Samuel Butler.

418 "Lettre à A. Suarès: 4 juillet 1935." Dietschy. *Le Cas Suarès*, 84. Also in *Mélanges*, 1518. In this letter Bergson congratulates Suarès for his writings.

419 "Lettre à A. Suarès: ler octobre 1935." *Mélanges*, 1521. Bergson congratulates Suarès on the reception of an award.

420 "Lettre au P. Gorce: 16 août 1935." *Sophia* (Naples), 3, 1935. Also in *La Croix*, 21 septembre 1935, 3; *Ecrits et paroles*, 3, 598-599; *Mélanges*, 1520-1521. In this letter Bergson concurs with Gorce's interpretation of his thought, and adds that he is able to accept the essentials of those passages of Aquinas' philosophy which he has read.

1936

421   "Lettre à L. Bopp: 28 avril 1936." *Mélanges*, 1546. In this letter Bergson thanks Bopp for his "portrait de notre cher Thibaudet."

422   "Lettre à Jacques Chevalier: février 1936." "Publiée à la suite de l'article de Jacques Chevalier," "William James et Bergson," dans le receuil d'études, *Harvard et la France*, édité par les soins de la *Revue d'Histoire Moderne*, 1936, 117-121." Also in *Ecrits et paroles*, 3, 617-620; *Mélanges*, 1542-1545. In this letter Bergson gives his evaluation of William James and states that James' "spiritualism" explains his pragmatism and pluralism.

423   "Lettre à Jeanne Hersch: 25 novembre 1936." *Mélanges*, 1570-1571. This is a discussion of Hersch's *L'Illusion philosophique*.

424   "Lettre à Jean Labadie: 12 février 1936." Jean Labadie. "Aux Frontières de l'au-delà." *Choses vécues*. Paris: Grasset, *1939, 7-8*. Also in *Ecrits et paroles*, 3, 616; *Mélanges*, 1541. In this letter Bergson discusses Labadie's study of psychical research, which he commends.

425   "Lettre à A. Suarès: 27 juillet 1936." Dietschy. *Le Cas Suarès*, 302. Also in *Mélanges*, 1553-1554. Here Bergson sees in Suarès' *Valeurs* an aesthetic, a philosophy, and a "morale."

426   "Lettre au professeur Spearmann." Citée par R. Millet. *Le Temps*, 15 novembre 1936. Also in *Ecrits et paroles*, 3, 642; *Mélanges*, 1571. In this letter Bergson agrees that he is the enemy of dry rationalism but not of the exercise of reason.

427   "Mes Missions 1917-1918: 24 août 1936." *Hommes et Mondes*, No. 12, juillet 1947, 359-375. Also in *Ecrits et paroles*, 3, 627-641; *Mélanges*, 1554-1570. Here Bergson discusses his missions to the United States during World War I, his relations to Colonel House, Woodrow Wilson, and America's idealism. (Bergson had sought to bring the United States into the war on the side of the Allies.)

428   "Quelques mots sur Thibaudet critique et philosophe." *Nouvelle Revue Française*, 47, juillet 1936, 7-14. Also in *Ecrits et paroles*, 3, 621-626; *Mélanges*, 1547-1553. In this brief essay Bergson lauds A. Thibaudet's critical method, his originality, and his generosity.

1937

429   "Lettre à R. Jolivet: 1937." *Studia Catholica*, 14, No. 1, 1938, 55-60. Also in *Mélanges*, 1579. Bergson insists in this brief letter that his thought does not support anti-substantialism.

430   "Lettre à A. Suarès: 1937." Dietschy. *Le Cas Suarès*, 303. Also in *Mélanges*, 1580. Bergson has kind words to say here concerning Suarès' writings.

431   "Lettre au Père A.D. Sertillanges: 19 janvier 1937." Citée à la suite de l'article d'A.D. Sertillanges. "Le Libre Arbitre chez Saint Thomas et chez M. Bergson." *Vie Intellectuelle*, 49, No. 1, 10 avril 1937, 268-269. Also in *Ecrits et paroles*, 3, 643-644; *Mélanges*, 1573-1574. In this letter Bergson discusses his philosophy and its relationship to Thomism.

432   "Message au Congrès Descartes." *Nouvelles Littéraires*, No. 778, 11 septembre 1937, 1. Also in *Ecrits et paroles*, 3, 645-649; *Mélanges*, 1574-1579. Bergson here discusses René Descartes and his philosophy, as well as the part which

philosophy must play in the modern world.

1938

433   "Lettre à Léon Bopp: 22 septembre 1938." *Mélanges*, 1582-1583. Bergson thanks Bopp for a copy of *Liaisons du Monde*. The "devenir" of *L'Evolution créatrice*, Bergson insists, does not suggest anarchism or revolution, for "...un principe d'explication n'est pas une maxime de conduite."

434   "Lettre à Milič Čapek: 3 juillet 1938." Milič Čapek. *Bergson and Modern Physics*. Dordrecht, Holland, 1971, 401. Bergson agrees that his concepts of the physical world anticipated current ideas in physics, and congratulates the young scholar for clarifying this point.

435   "Lettre à Georges Goyau: 3 mars 1938." *Mélanges*, 1581. Bergson congratulates Goyau on his election as "secrétaire perpétuel" of the Academy.

436   "Lettre à A. Suarès: 17 mars 1938." Dietschy. *Le Cas Suarès*, 304. Also in *Mélanges*, 1581. In this letter Bergson defines the character of Suarès' determined optimism.

437   "Témoignage sur l'Angleterre." *Le Figaro*, 19 juillet 1938. Also in *Ecrits et paroles*, 3, 650; *Mélanges*, 1582. Sooner or later, Bergson holds, France and England should become one nation.

1939

438   "Letter to Paul Arthur Schilpp. 10 Mars 1939." In *The Philosophy of Alfred North Whitehead*. The Library of Living Philosophers, No. 3, Ed. Paul Arthur Schilpp, Evanston and Chicago: Northwestern University Press, 1941, xii. Bergson thanks Professor Schilpp for the invitation to participate in a volume dedicated to his philosophy. Old age, illness, and already established projects, however, make this impossible.

439   "Lettre à I. Benrubi: 15 juillet 1939." Benrubi. *Souvenirs sur Henri Bergson*, 133. Also in *Mélanges*, 1588-1589. Here Bergson discusses his writings. He denies the intention to write another book.

440   "Lettre à J. Chastenet: décembre 1939." *Le Temps*, 8 janvier 1940, p. 2, col. 6. Also in *Le Temps*, 13 janvier 1940, p. 3, col. 1-2; *Mélanges*, 1591. In this letter Bergson reiterates his 1914 opinion of Bismarckian Germany and finds it applicable to the contemporary scene.

441   "Lettre à Halévy en Souvenir de Péguy: 25 janvier 1939." J. Gualmier. *Péguy et nous*. Beyrouth, 1944, 53-55; *Le Temps*, 25 janvier 1939; *L'Aube*, 12 janvier 1945; *Feuillets de l'Amitié Charles Péguy*, 30, 13-14; *Etudes Bergsoniennes*, 8, 58-60. Also in *Ecrits et paroles*, 3, 651-653; *Mélanges*, 1585-1587. In this brief essay Bergson pays homage to Charles Péguy.

442   "Lettre à M. Nédoncelle: 1939." *Oeuvres philosophiques de Newman*. Paris: Aubier, 1945, 16-17. Also in *Mélanges*, 1592. In this letter Bergson comments on Cardinal Newman's philosophical background—or lack of it.

443   "Lettre à B. Romeyer: 7 août 1939." *Archives de Philosophie*, 17, No. 1, 1947, 46. Also in *Mélanges*, 1589. Bergson here replies that no celebration of his

eightieth birthday should be attempted.

444 "Lettre à S. Suarès: 28 mai 1939." Dietschy. *Le Csa Suarès*, 303. Also in *Mélanges*, 1588. Here Bergson congratulates Suarès for his moral and ethical concern.

445 "Lettre à l'Université de Lausanne: 1939." A. Raymond. "Henri Bergson." *Gazette de Lausanne*, 12 janvier 1941. Also in *Mélanges*, 1590. Bergson thanks the University of Lausanne for the award of an honorary degree.

446 "Une Pensée. 1939." *Mélanges*, 1591. Bergson here remarks briefly on the difficulty of doing philosophy.

1940

447 "Lettre à A. Billy: 1940 (?)." *Le Figaro*, 3 août 1940. Also in *Mélanges*, 1593. Bergson here recalls his years as a young professor at Clermont.

Fragments Without Dates

448 "Annotations sur un article de G. Maire." J. Guitton. *Vocation...*, 38. Also in *Mélanges*, 1597. Here Bergson discusses his relations with J. Lachelier and E. Boutroux. His opinion of J. Jaurès is that he was "éloquent et généreux."

449 "Lettre à A.O. Lovejoy." Arthur Oncken Lovejoy. *The Reason, the Understanding, and Time*. Baltimore, Maryland: Johns Hopkins, 1961, 185-202. In this letter Bergson explains the basic characteristics of duration to a sceptical Lovejoy.

450 "Lettre à H. Wildon Carr." in H. Wildon Carr. *The Philosophy of Change*. London: Macmillan, 1914, vii-viii. Bergson here states that when science is more advanced it may be possible to measure the creation of physical energy by the mind.

451 "Sur L'Effort créatrice." *Le Figaro Littéraire*, 11 janvier 1941. Also in *Mélanges*, 1597. Here Bergson discusses the difficulties of embodying a creative idea.

Various Collections, Anthologies

452 *Antologia. A cura di Giovanni Palumbo*. Palermo: G. B. Palumbo, 1955, 127. (Letture filosofiche, No. 12).

453 *Bereugeusong*. Trans. Le Mun tto. Seoul: Daeyang, 1971, 530.

454 *Bergson: Med indlendnig*. Ed. Peter Kemp. København; Berlingske, 1968, 233. (De Store Taenkere).

455 *Henri Bergson: Memoria y vida*. Trans. Mauro Armiño. Madrid: Alianza Editorial, 1977, 164.

456 *Cartas, conferências e outros escritos*. Trans. Franklin Leopoldo e Silva. And Bachelard, Gaston. *A filosofia do não; Filosofia do novo espírito científico*. Trans. José Moura Ramos. Sao Paulo: Abril Cultural, 1974, 514.

457 *Filozofické eseje*. Trans. Anton Vantuch. Bratislava: Slov. spis., 1970, 448. This is a translation of the *Essai, L'eñergie spirituelle*, and *Les Deux Sources*.

458 *Filosofische Geschriften*. Eds. A.M.W. Beerling, Gerard Wijdeveld, *et al.* Haar-

lem: Toorts, 1963, 396; Hasselt: Heideland, 1963, 396. This item contains writings by Rudolf Eucken and Bertrand Russell, as well as Bergson.

459 *Keijijôgaku nyûmon. Tetsugaku teki chokkan. Ishiki to seimei*, etc. Trans. Sakata Tokuo *et al*. Tokyo: Chûôkôronsha, 1969, 554. (Sekai no meicho, No. 53) This is a translation of *Introduction à la metaphysique, L'intuition philosophique, La Conscience et la vie*.

460 "Losse Passages." *Mens en Kosmos*, 15, No. 6, 1959, 251, 272-273. This is a series of quotes from the *Essai, L'Evolution créatrice, "Le Fausse Reconnaissance."*

461 *Obras escogidas. Ensayo sobre los datos immediatos de la conciencia. Materia y memoria. La évolucion creadora. La energía espirituel. Pensamiento y movimiento*. Trans. and Pref. José Antonio Mínguez. Madrid: Aguilar, 1963, 1288. (Biblioteca Premios Nobel).

462 *Mémoire et vie (Textes choisis par Gilles Deleuze)*. Paris: Presses Universitaires de France, 1957, 152.

463 *Mémoire et vie par Henri Bergson: Textes choisis par Gilles Deleuze*. 3e éd. Paris: Presses Universitaires de France, 1968, 156. ("Les Grands Textes"; bibliothèque classique de philosophie).

464 *Le opere: Il riso, L'evoluzione creatrice, Le due fonti della morale e della religione*. Enzo Paci. Trans. Carmine Gallo, Paolo Serini, Mario Vinciguerra. Torino: UTET, 1979, xxxiv, 596 (Scrittori del mondo: i Nobel).

465 *Páginas escogidas de filosofía: Platon, Kant, Bergson; noticias bio-bibliográficas y anotaciones*. Ed. José Pereira Rodriguez. Montevideo, Uruguay: A. Monteverde y cía, 1940.

466 *Réflexions sur le temps, l'espace et la vie*. Paris: Payot, 1929, 122. (Bibliothèque miniature, No. 4).

467 *Saggi pedagogici*. A cura di Francesco Cafaro. Torino: Paravia, 1962, xx, 73.

468 *Selección de textos precedidos de un estudio de J. Benrubi*. Trans. Demetrio Nuñez. Buenos Aires: Ed. Sudamericana, 1942, 225.

469 *Shôronshû*. Vol. 2. Trans. Kakeshita Eiishirô, Tominaga Atsushi and Akeida Shigeo. Tokyo: Hakusuisha, 1965, 317. (...zenshû, No. 9) This is a translation of *Écrits et Paroles*.

470 *Shôronshû*. Trans. Hanada Keisuke and Kâto Seiji. Tokyo: Hakusuisha, 1966, 383. This is a translation of *Écrits et paroles*.

PART III

WORKS CONCERNING BERGSON

1880

1   Evellin, François. *Infini et quantité: Etude sur le concept de l'infini en philosophie et dans les sciences.* Paris: Baillère, 1880. This work was utilized by Bergson in writing *Time and Free Will.*

1884

2   M.,P. "Le Rire: Conférence de M. Bergson." *Moniteur de Puy-de-Dôme*, 21 février 1884. Also in *Mélanges*, 313-315. This is a report of a talk on the nature of laughter. It is the predecessor of Bergson's *Le Rire* (1900).

1887

3   Myers, F. W. H. "On a Case of Alleged Hypnotic Hyperacuity of Vision." *Monde*, 12, No. 45, January, 1887, 156-158. The author comments on an article in the November, 1886 *Revue Philosophique* by Henri Bergson in which a presumed case of thought transference is explained through hypnotically-induced "hyperacuity" of vision. (The clairvoyant, Bergson asserted, could actually read letters in a book in the hypnotist's hand *reflected on the hypnotist's cornea.*) The author notes further experiments by Bergson demonstrating the supposed "clairvoyant's" hyperacuity of vision, and cites a personal letter by Bergson explaining details of these experiments. (Cf. the author, 1954.)

1890

4   Belot, Gustave. "Une Théorie nouvelle de la liberté." *Revue Philosophique de la France et de l'Etranger*, 30, No. 10, octobre 1890, 360-392. This is an appreciative review of *Time and Free Will.*

5   Couture, Léonce. "Review of *Essai sur les données immédiates* by Henri Bergson." *Polybiblion*, 2e Série, 31 (Partie littéraire), 1890, 303-304.

6   "Review of *Essai sur les données immédiates de la conscience* by Henri Bergson." *Revue Philosophique de la France et de l'Etranger*, 19, 1890, 519-538.

7   Ferri, Luigi. "Review of *Essai sur les données immédiates de la conscience* by Henri Berson." *Rivista italiana di filosofia*, 5, No. 2, marzo-aprile 1890, 248-249.

8   Herr, Lucien. "Review of *Essai sur les données immédiates de la conscience* by Henri Bergson." *Revue Critique*, N.S. 30, No. 52, 29 décembre 1890, 517-519. This is a brief mention, along with several other books.

9   Levy-Bruhl, Lucien. "Revue critique de l'*Essai*, anonyme." *Revue Philosophique de la France et de l'Etranger*, 29, No. 5, mai 1890, 519-538. This is a thorough-going, perceptive analysis.

10   Pillon, François. "Review of *Essai sur les données immédiates de la conscience* by Henri Bergson." *Année Philosophique*, 1, 1890, S.E. Suppl. 133.

11   Stout, George Frederick. "Free Will and Determinism." *Speaker*, 1, 10 May 1890, 520. This is a review of Bergson's *Essai sur les données immédiates de la conscience*.

1892

12   Beurlier, E. "Review of *Essai sur les données immédiates* by Henri Bergson." *Bulletin Critique*, 2e Sér., 10 ler juillet 1892.

1894

13   Sorel, Georges. "L'Ancienne et la Nouvelle Métaphysique." L'Ere nouvelle, 2, 1894.

1896

14   Bently, I. M. "Review of '*Mémoire et reconnaissance*' by Henri Bergson." *Philosophical Review*, 5, No. 4, 1896, 424-425.

15   Couturat, Louis. "Etudes sur l'espace et le temps de MM. Lechalas, Poincaré, Delboeuf, Bergson, L. Weber, et Evellin." *Revue de Métaphysique et de Morale*, 4, 1896, 646-669. The author is entirely critical of Bergson's duration and its contrast with mathematical time: "Si l'on analysait le temps psychologique de M. Bergson comme l'espace sensible de M. Poincaré, en verrait que l'un n'est pas plus le temps que l'autre n'est l'espace." (p. 663)

16   Fouillée, Alfred. *Le Mouvement idéaliste et la réaction contre la science positive.* Paris: Félix Alcan, 1896, 331. Bergson is discussed here on pp. 198-206.

17   Gardiner, H. N. "Mémoire et reconnaissance." *Psychological Review*, 3, No. 3. September 1896, 578-580.

18   Lechalas, Georges. *Etude sur l'espace et le temps.* Paris: Félix Alcan, 1896, 201. 2e éd, 201. Paris: Félix Alcan, 1909, 327.

19   Pillon, François." Review of *Matière et mémoire* by Henri Bergson." *Année Philosophique, 7, 1896, 190-192.*

20   Tarozzi, Giuseppe. *Della necessità del fatto naturale ed umano.* 2 Vols. Torino: Ermanno Loescher, 1896-1897.

1897

21   Lechalas, Georges. "Matière et mémoire: D'Après un nouveau livre de M. Bergson." *Annales de Philosophie Chrétienne*, N.S. 26, 1897, 146-164, 314-334.

22   Maisonneuve, L. "Review of *Matière et mémoire* by Henri Bergson." *Polybiblion*, 2e Série, 45 (Partie Littéraire), 1897, 497-499.

23   Margerie, Amedil de. "La Philosophie de M. Fouillée." *Annales de Philosophie Chrétienne*, N.S. 36, 1897, 147-164, 314-334.

24   Pilzecker, A. "Mémoire et reconnaissance." *Zeitschrift für Psychologie und Physiologie der Sinnesorgane*, 13, 1897, 229-232. This is a review of Bergson's article in the *Revue Philosophique*.

25   Alexander, Samuel. "Review of *Matière et mémoire* by Henri Bergson." *Mind*, 22, No. 24, October 1897, 572-573.

26   Weber, Louis. "Review of *Matière et mémoire* by Henri Bergson." *Mercure de France*, 23, No. 7, juillet 1897, 150-152.

1898

27   Jacob, B. "La Philosophie d'hier et celle d'aujourd'hui." *Revue de Métaphysique et de Morale*, 6, 1898, 170-201.

28   "Obituary: Professor Michael Bergson." *The Jewish Chronicle*, March 18, 1898, p. 13. This is an obituary recounting the details of the life of Bergson's father.

29   Ziehen, Theodor. "Review of *Matière et mémoire* by Henri Bergson." *Zeitschrift für Philosophie und philosophische Kritik*, N.S. 113, No. 12, Dezember 1898, 295-299.

1899

30   Le Roy, Edouard. "Science et philosophie." *Revue de Métaphysique et de Morale*, 7, 1899, 375-425, 503-562, 708-731; 8, 1900, 37-72. Bergson cites this study of relativism in scientific knowledge in *Creative Evolution*, p. 218. (*Oeuvres*, p. 680)

31   Masci, Filippo. "L' idealismo indeterminista." *Naples Academia di Scienze Moral e Politiche*, 30, No. 1, 1899, 35-184.

32   Nodet, Victor. *Les Agnoscies: La Cécité psychique en particulier*. Paris: Félix Alcan, 1899, 220.

33   Noël, Léon. *La Conscience du libre-arbitre*. Louvain: Institut supérieur de philosophie; Paris: Lethielleux, 1899, 288.

34   Rauh, Frédéric. *De La Méthod dans la psychologie des sentiments*. Paris: Félix Alcan, 1899, 397.

1900

35   Barzelloti, G. *La Philosophie de H. Taine*. Trans. Auguste Dietrich. Paris: F. Alcan, 1900, 448. (Bibliothéque de philosophie contemporaine) The author discusses similarities between Bergson and Taine on pp. 165-167.

36   Bos, Camille. "Contribution à la théorie psychologique du temps." *Revue Philosophique de la France et de l'Etranger*, 50, No. 12, décembre 1900, 594-610.

37   Brunschvicg, Léon. "L'Idéalisme contemporain." *Bibliothèque du Congrès international de philosophie: Philosophie générale et métaphysique*. Paris: Armand Colin, 1900, 39-57.

38   Coutrat, Louis. "Contre Le Nominalisme de M. Le Roy." *Revue de Métaphysique et de Morale*, 8, No. 1, janvier 1900, 87-93. The author criticizes Le Roy's concept of measurement and of number, including Cantorian infinite numbers. M. Le Roy was a well known disciple of Bergson.

39   Dauriac, Lionel. "Review of *Le Rire* by Henri Bergson." *Revue Philosophique de la France et de l'Etranger*, 50, No. 12, décembre 1900, 665-670.

40   Derselbe. *La Science positive et les philosophes de la liberté*. 1900.

41   Farges, Albert. *Le Cerveau, l'âme et les facultés*. 6e éd. Paris: Berche et Tralin, 1900, 491.

42   Hirsch, Charles-Henry. "Review of 'Le Rire' by Henri Bergson." *Mercure de France*, 34, No. 4, avril 1900, 223-227.

43   Le Roy, Edouard. "Réponse à M. Couturat." *Revue de Métaphysique et de Morale*, 8, 1900, 223-233. The author replies to Couturat's criticism of "Science et philosophie."

44   Mensch, L. "Review of *Le Rire* by Henri Bergson." *Polybiblion*, 2e Sér., 52 (Partie littéraire), 1900, 326-327.

45   Morselli, Emilio. *Un nuovo idealismo: H. Bergson*. Udine: Tosoline e Jacob, 1900.

46   Paulhan, François. "Contemporary Philosophy in France." *Philosophical Review*, 9, No. 1, January 1900, 42-69.

47   Petrone, Igino. *I limiti del determinismo scientifico: Saggio*. Modena, Italy: Vincenzie Nipoti, 1900, 139.

48   Pillon, Francois. "Review of *Le Rire* by Henri Bergson." *Année Philosophique*, 11, 1900, 135-138.

49   "Review of *Le Rire: Essai sur la signification du comique* by Henri Bergson." *Wiener Zeitung*, 1900.

50   Weber, Louis. "Review of *Le Rire* by H. Bergson." *Mercure de France*, 35, No. 7, juillet 1900, 225-227.

1901

51   Binet, Alfred. "H. Bergson: Note sir la conscience de l'effort intellectuel." *Année Psychologique*, 14, 1908, 229-230.

52   Brunschvicg, Léon. "La Philosophie nouvelle et l'intellectualisme." *Revue de Métaphysique et de Morale*, 9, 1901, 433-478.

53   C., J. "Collège de France: Cours de M. Bergson sur l'idée de cause." *Revue de Philosophie*, 1, No. 3, avril 1901, 358-388.

54   Grosse, Ernst. "Review of *Le Rire* by Henri Bergson." *Deutsche Literaturzeitung*, 21, No. 1, 1901, 13-14.

55   Heymans, Gérard. "Review of *Le Rire* by Henri Bergson." *Zeitschrift für Psychologie und physiologie der Sinnesorgane*, 25, 1901, 155-156. This is an

expository, congratulatory review. It is very brief.

56   Landormet Paul Charles Reed. "Remarques sur la philosophie nouvelle et sur ses rapports avec l'intellectualisme." *Revue de Métaphysique et de Morale*, 9, 1901, 478-486. The author insists that Bergson is anti-intellectual, M. Le Roy notwithstanding.

57   Le Roy, Edouard. "De La Valeur objective des lois physiques." *Bulletin de la Société Française de Philosophie*, 1, (Séance du 28 mars 1901), 1901, 5-32.

58   Le Roy, Edouard. "Un Positivisme nouveau." *Revue de Métaphysique et de Morale*, 9, 1901, 138-153.

59   Le Roy, Edouard. "Sur Quelques Objections adressées à la nouvelle philosophie." *Revue de Métaphysique et de Morale*, 9, 1901, 292-327; 407-432.

60   Marin, F. "Sur L'Origine des espèces." *Revue Scientifique*, 4e Sér., 16, No. 19, 1901, 577-588. This is an early attempt to apply Bergsonism to biology, prior to *Creative Evolution*.

61   Parodi, D. "Review of *Le Rire* by Henri Bergson." *Deutsche Literatur-Zeitung*, 22, January 1901, 13-14.

62   Parodi, Dominique. "Review of *Le Rire* by Henri Bergson." *Revue de Métaphysique et de Morale*, 9, No. 2, mars 1901, 224-236.

63   Sarlo, François de. "Le correnti filosofiche del Secolo XIX." *Flegrea*, 3, No. 6, 10 settèmbre 1901, 531-554.

64   Tufts, J. H. "Humor." *Psychological Review*, 8, No. 1, January 1901, 98-99. This is a brief review of *Laughter*.

65   Wilbois, Joseph. "L'Esprit positif." *Revue de Métaphysique et de Morale*, 9, 1901, 154-209, 597-645; 10, 1902, 69-105, 334-370, 565-612.

1902

66   Couchoud, Paul-Louis. "La Métaphysique nouvelle: *Matière et mémoire* de M. Bergson." *Revue de Métaphysique et de Morale*, 10, 1902, 225-243. This essay is a generally laudatory account of Bergson's philosophical method.

67   Giessler. "Review of 'Le Rire' by Henri Bergson." *Zeitschrift für Psychologie und Physiologie der Sinnesorgane*, 29, 1902, 231. The author is critical of Bergson's concept of laughter.

68   Izquierdo, G. "El esfuerzo intelectual segun H. Bergson." *Revista de Aragón*, 3, No. 2, februario 1902.

69   Leclere, Albert. "Le Mouvement catholique kantien en France." *Kant-studien*, 7, No. 2, 1902, 300-363. This article contains references to Bergson and his followers.

70   Mac Donald, M. S. "Review of 'L'Effort intellectuel' by Henri Bergson." *Philosophical Review*, 11, No. 4, July 1902, 416-417.

71   Moisant, Xavier. "La Notion de multiplicité dans la philosophie de Bergson." *Revue de Philosophie, 2, No. 6, juin 1902, 447-465. Bergson's position is virtually identical with scholasticism's, according to the author.*

72   Steeg, T. "Henri Bergson: Notice biographique avec protrait." *Revue Universelle*, 12, No. 1, janvier 1902, 15-16.

1903

73 Cantecor, G. "La Philosophie nouvelle et la vie de l'esprit." *Revue Philosophique de la France et de l'Etranger*, 55, No. 3, mars 1903, 252-277. This article is a critique of Bergson from a Kantian viewpoint.

74 Giessler. "Review of 'L'Effort intellectuel' by Henri Bergson." *Zeitschrift für Psychologie und Physiologie der Sinnesorgane*, 32, 1903, 128-129.

75 Gurwitsch, Aron. "Die französische Metaphysik der Gegenwart: H. Bergson." *Archiv für systematische Philosophie*, N.S. 9, No. 4, 1903, 463-490.

76 Höffding, Harald. *Philosophische Probleme*. Leipzig: O.R. Reisland, 1903, viii, 109. For references to Bergson, see pp. 28, 104.

77 Janet, Pierre. *Les Obesessions et la psychasthénie*. Paris: Félix Alcan, 1903. (Travaux du laboratoire de Psychologie de la clinique à la Salpêtrière. Troisième série) Cf. "La Perte de la fonction réel," pp. 431-439; pp. 477-488, "La Hiérarchie des phénomènes psychologiques"; and especially "La Tension psychologique" pp. 488-497 for Janet's use (perhaps independently of Bergson) of concepts developed in Bergson's *Matter and Memory* (1896). Cf. Bergson's introduction to the English translation of *Matter and Memory*.

78 Levi, Adolofo. *Sulle ultime forme dell'indeterminismo francese*. Firenze: Civelli, 1903.

79 Lubac, Emile. Esquisse d'un système de psychologie rationelle: leçons de psychologie. Préf. Henri Bergson. Paris: F. Alcan, 1903, xvi, 248. (Bibliothèque de philosophie contemporaine).

80 Petrone, Igino. *I limiti del determinissmo scientifico: Saggio*. 2nd ed. Roma: Società di Cultura, 1903, 144.

81 Tarde, Gabriel. *The Laws of Imitation*. 2dn ed. Trans. E. C. Parsons. Pref. F. H. Giddings. New York: Holt, 1903, 404. This book was first published in 1901; its second edition appeared in 1895. The author refers to Bergson in a footnote on p. 145; "We may admit that there are other quantitions in the soul; we may concede to the psycho-physicists, for example, in spite of M. Bergson's remarkable study on the *Données immédiates de la conscience*—which conforms so well in other respects to my own point of view on this subject—that the intensity of sensations... lends itself to experimental measurements."

1904

82 Bazaillas, Albert. *La Vie personnelle: Etude sur quelques illusions de la perception intérieure*. Paris: F. Alcan, 1904, 305.

83 Blum, Eugène. "Le IIe Congrès international de philosophie: Genève, 4-8 septembre 1904." *Revue Philosophique*, 58, No. 11, novembre 1904, 509-519. This article contains an account of Bergson's critique of psycho-physical parallelism on p. 509-510.

84 Boucaud, Charles. "L'Histoire de droit et la philosophie de M. Bergson." *Revue de Philosophie*, 4, No. 2, ler mars 1904, 229-306.

85   Cartier, E. "Discussion de Bergson's 'paralogism psycho-physiologique'." *Revue de Métaphysique et de Morale*, 12, No. 6, 1904, 1027-1037.

86   Coignet, Clarisse. "Kant et Bergson." *Revue Chrétienne*, 4e Sér., 1, No. 7, juillet 1904, 27-41.

87   Constant, Léonard. "Cours de M. Bergson sur l'histoire de l'idée de temps." *Revue de Philosophie*, 4, No. 1, janvier 1904, 105-111. The author provides a summary of Bergson's course on the history of the concept of time.

88   Lubac, E. *Esquisse d'un système de psychologie rationelle*. Paris: Félix Alcan, 1904, 245. "Préface par Henri Bergson." This is a Bergsonian psychology.

89   Prezzolini, Giuseppe. *Del linguaggio come causa di errore: H. Bergson*. Firenze: Spinelli, 1904.

90   Rauh, Frédéric. "Sur La Position du problème du libre arbitre." *Revue de Métaphysique et de Morale*, 12, No. 6, novembre 1904, 977-1006.

91   Visan, Tancrède de. *Paysages introspectifs: Poésies: Avec un essai sur le symbolisme*. Paris: Jouve, 1904, 152.

92   "Vtoroi mezhdmarodnyi filosofskii kongress." *Vesy*, 1, No. 10, October, 1904, 59-62.

93   Ziehen, Theodor. "Review of *Le Rire* by Henri Bergson." *Zeitschrift für Philosophie und philosophische Kritik*, N.S. 123, 1904, 215-216.

1905

94   Aliotta, Antonio. "La misura in psycologia sperimentale." Diss. Florence, 1905, 253.

95   Bazailllas, Albert. *La Vie personnelle: Etude sur quelques illusions de la vie intérieurs*. Paris: Félix Alcan, 1905, 305. The author's psychology is influenced by Bergson, though at points he is critical of Bergson's philosophy.

96   Brunschvicg, Léon. *L'Idéalisme contemporain*. Paris: Félix Alcan, 1905, 185.

97   Chide, Alphonse. *L'Idée de rythme*. Digne, France: Chaspoul, 1905, 184.

98   Dwelshauvers, Georges. "Raison et intuition: Etude sur la philosophie de M. Bergson." *Belique Artistique et Littéraire*, Ire Année, 1905, 185-199, 316-331; 2e Année, 1906, 17-35. This is an exposition of the basic ideas of Bergson's philosophy, stressing its psychological content.

99   "Review of 'Introduction à la métaphysique' by Henri Bergson. *Jeunese Laque*, No. 37, 1905, 223-232.

100   Jahn, M. Frantz. *Das Problem des Komischen*. Potsdam, Germany: Astein, 1905, 130.

101   Janet, Pierre. "A Propos du ‹‹Déjà vu››." *Journal de Psychologie Normale et Pathologique*, 2, No. 3 (1905), 289-307. The author traces theories of false recognition from the mid-nineteenth century until 1905. Intellectualist theories by Wigan and others have been succeeded by the "impressionist" theories of Höffding, James, and Bergson, which describe false recognition as a malady of perception. These theories at least focus attention on the troubles of perception; but they suffer from vagueness. They do not explain the recognition of the object whose existence is affirmed for the second time. The explanation which the author gives of false regognition, however, is almost identical with Bergson's.

False recognition and its associated phenomena stem from the failure of the individual *to attend to present reality* and present acts: "il y a un abaissment, une chute de la tension nerveuse et de la tension psychologique qui suprime cette fonction "elevée et ne laisse subsister que les fonctions inferieures" (pp. 303-304).

102   Le Roy, Edouard. "Sur La Logique de L'invention." *Revue de Métaphysique et de Morale*, 13, No. 2, 1905, 193-223.

103   Levi, Adolofo. *Sulle ultime forme dell' indeterminismo francese*. Firenze: Civelli, 1903.

104   Moisant, Xavier. "Dieu dans la philosophie de N. Bergson." *Revue de Philosophie*, 6, No. 5, mai 1905, 495-518. The author indicates how Bergson argues from the experience of duration to the existence of God.

105   Rageot, Gaston. "Le Congrès international de psychologie." *Revue Philosophique de la France et de l'Etranger*, 60, No. 7, juillet 1905, 67-87. The author suggests that Bergson drew his concept of duration from the ideas of W. James and J. Ward.

106   Rageot, Gaston. "Correspondance avec M. Bergson sur sa relation à M.W. James." *Revue Philosophique de la France et de l'Etranger*, 50, No. 8, août 1905, 229-231. Here Bergson denies that he derived his concept of duration from the writings of James Ward and William James.

107   Varisco, Bernardino. "La filosofia della contingenza." *Revisita filosofica*, 8, No. 1, 1905, 3-37. This is a short criticism of recent defenders of indeterminism, chiefly Bergson.

1906

108   Blum, Jean. "La Philosophie de M. Bergson et la poésie symboliste." *Mercure de France*, 73, No. 222, 15 septembre 1906, 201-207.

109   Ceresole, P. "Le Parallésime psycho-physiologique et l'argument de M. Bergson." *Archives de Psychologie*, 5, No. 2, 1906, 112-120. The author holds that to refute parallelism by Bergson's argument one must show as a matter of fact the external world may be modified without modification of the nervous system.

110   Courtney, J. W. "Review of 'A Propos du ‹‹Déjà vu››' by Pierre Janet." *Journal of Abnormal Psychology*, 1, No. 3 (1906), 149-150. The author recounts Janet's criticisms of Bergson's "impressionist" theory of false recognition.

111   Dwelshauvers, Georges. "Raison et intuition: Etude sur la philosophie de M. Bergson." *Revue Hebdomadaire des Cours et des Conférences*, 15, No. 4, 1906-07, 175-181; No. 8, 1906-07, 366-374; No. 10, 1906-07, 462-471; No. 13, 1906-07, 585-590; No. 16, 1906-07, 732-736; No. 17, 1906-07, 804-809.

112   Faguet, Emile. *Propos de théâtre: Troisième Série*. Paris: Société Française d'Imprimerie et de Librairie, 1906, 376. Bergson's theory of laughter is discussed on pp. 343-374. This essay was published first in *Journal des Débats*, 26 September 1904 and was republished 3 October 1904.

113   Jung, Carl Gustav. "The Psychology of Dementia Praecox." *Collected Works*, Vol. III, 1906, 3-151. In this study the author refers on pp. 65-66 to Bergson's theory of dreams, in conjunction with Edouard Claparède's "Esquisse d'une théorie

bioloqique de la sommeil." (*Archives Psychologique de la Suisse Romande*, 4, (1904-1905), 245-349). Jung refers to Bergson's and Claparède's notion of sleep as "disinterest in the present situation."

114   Lalande, André. "Philosophy in France, 1905." *Philosophical Review*, 15, No. 3, May 1906, 241-266.

115   Luquet, Georges Henri. *Idées générales de psychologie*. Paris: Félix Alcan, 1906, 295. This is a Bergsonian psychology. See Bergson's review, 1906.

116   Lux, Jacques. "Nos Philosophes: M. Henri Bergson." *Revue Politique et Littéraire, Reuve Bleue*, 5e Série, 6, No. 22, ler décembre 1906, 703-704.

117   Mamelet, A. "L'Idée de rythme par A. Chide." *Revue de Métaphysique et de Morale*, 14, No. 5, juillet 1906, 733-745.

118   Sauvage, George M. "The New Philosophy in France." *Catholic University Bulletin*, 12, No. 4, April 1906, 147-159; 14, No. 3, March 1908, 268-286.

1907

119   Aliotta, Antonio, "L'Evoluzione creatrice." *La Cultura Filosófica*, 1, No. 9, 1907, 235-240.

120   Balthasar, Nicholas. "Le Problème de Dieu d'après la philosophie nouvelle." *Revue Néo-scolastique de Philosophie*, 14, No. 4, novembre 1907, 449-489; 15, No. février 1908, 90-124.

121   Berthelot, René. "Discussion: Sur la nécessité, la finalit; et la liberté chez Hegel." *Bulletin de la Société Française de Philosophie*, 7, No. 2, avril 1907, 119-140. Bergson is discussed on pp. 136-138. This article is reprinted, with changes, in the author's *Evolutionisme et platonisme* (1908).

122   Besse, Clément. "Lettre de France: Pour l'intellectualisme." *Revue Néo-scolastique de Philosophie*, 14, No. 3 août 1907, 281-303.

123   Borel, Emile. "L'Evolution de l'intelligence géométrique." *Revue de Métaphysique et de Morale*, 15, No. 6 1907, 747-754. Borel charges Bergson with neglecting non-Euclidean geometry and giving a static picture of the human intellect. See Bergson's conclusive reply in the same journal, January, 1908.

124   Boyd, W. "Review of *L'Evolution créatrice* by Henri Bergson." *Review of Theology and Philosophy*, 3, No. 10, October 1907, 249-251.

125   Calderon, Francisco García. "Dos filósofos franceses: Bergson y Boutroux." *El Comercio*, 5 mayo 1907.

126   Caló, Giovanni. *Il problema delle libertà nel pensiero contemporaneo*. Milano: Sandron, 1907, 228.

127   Challaye, Félicien. "Le Syndicalisme révolutionnaire." *Revue de Métaphysique et de Morale*, 15, No. 1, janvier 1907, 103-127; No. 2, mars 1907, 256-272.

128   Dwelshauvers, Georges. "M. Bergson et la méthode intuitive." *Revue du Mois*, 4, No. 9, 10 septembre 1907, 336-350. This article also appeared in *Samedi*, No. 44, 1907. The author considers the problem of method in psychology. He compares Bergson's intuitive method with J. Lagneau's method of reflection.

129   Fontana, Paul. "Cours de M. Bergson au Collège de France: Théories de la volonté." *Revue de Philosophie*, 11, No. 7, juillet 1907, 70-91; No. 10, octobre 1907,

407-427.

130 Guieysse, Charles. "La Métaphysique de M. Bergson." *Pages Libres*, No. 355, 19 octobre 1907, 405-412; No. 356, 20 octobre 1907, 413-419.

131 Höffding, Harald. *Lehrbuch der Geschichte der neueren Philosophie.* Leipzig: Reisland, 1907, 286. This study contains a critique of *L'Essai sur les donnés immédiates.*

132 Hollard, A. "Review of *L'Evolution créatrice* by Henri Bergson." *Foi et vie*, 10, No. 18, 16 septembre 1907, 545-550.

133 Janssens, Edgar. "Review of 'Raison et intuition: Etude sur la philosophie de M. Henri Bergson' by Georges Dwelshauvers." *Revue Néo-scolastique de Philosophie*, 14, No. 1, février 1907, 140-142.

134 Le Dantec, Félix. "La Biologie de M. Bergson." *Revue du Mois*, 4, No. 8, août 1907, 230-241. This essay is republished as Chapter VI of Le Dantec, *Science et Conscience.* The author criticizes Bergson's biology in order to warn those who might otherwise be seduced by it. Cf. Bergson's reply in same number of this journal, 1907.

135 Le Dantec, Félix. "Review of *L'Evolution créatrice* by Henri Bergson." *Revue du Mois*, 4, No. 8, août 1907, 351-354. The author gives a critique of Bergson's biology.

136 Le Dantec, Félix. *De l'homme à la science: Philosophie du XIXe siècle.* Paris, Flammarion, 1907, 296. (Bibiliothèque de philosophie scientifique)

137 Le Roy, Edouard. "Comment se pose le problème de Dieu." *Revue de Métaphysique et de Morale*, 15, No. 2, 1907, 129-178; No. 4, 1907, 470-523.

138 Maisonneuve, L. "Review of *L'Evolution créatrice* by Henri Bergson." *Polybiblion*, 2e Série, 71 (Partie Littéraire), 1907, 405-406.

139 Noël, Léon. "Bulletin d'épistémologie: Le Pragmatisme." *Revue Néo-scolastique de Philosophie*, 14, No. 2, mai 1907, 220-243.

140 Pillon, François. "Review of *L'Evolution créatrice* by Henri Bergson." *Année Philosophique*, 19, 1907, 182-184.

141 Prins, Adolphe. "L'Evolution et la conception matérialiste de l'univers." *Revue de l'Université de Bruxelles*, 13, No. 4, octobre 1907, 29-67.

142 Rageot, Gaston. "Review of *L'Evolution créatrice* by Henri Bergson." *Revue Philosophique de la France et de l'Etranger*, 64, No. 7, juillet 1907, 73-85. This is an appreciative review of *L'Evolution créatrice.*

143 Sorel, Georges. "Review of *L'Evolution créatrice* by Henri Bergson." *Mouvement Socialiste*, 12, No. 191, 15 octobre 1907, 257-282; No. 193, 15 décembre 1907, 478-494; 13, No. 194, 15 janvier 1908, 34-52; No. 196, 15 mars 1908, 184-194; No. 197, 15 avril 1908, 276-294.

144 Tarde, G. de. "Une Nouvelle Métaphysique de M. Bergson." *Vie Contemporaine*, 1, novembre 1907.

145 Tonquédec, Joseph de. "La Notion de vérité dans la philosophie nouvelle." *Etudes par des Pères de la Compagnie de Jésus*, 110, 20 mars 1907, 721-749; juillet 1907, 68-82; 5 août 1907, 335-361.

146 Visan, Tancrède de. "L'Idéal symboliste: Essai sur la mentalité lyrique contemporaine." *Mercure de France*, 69, No. 241, 15 juillet 1907, 193-208. The author stresses a basic agreement of Bergson and symbolism on pp. 206-208.

147   Weber, Louis. "Review of *L'Evolution créatrice* by Henri Bergson." *Revue de Métaphysique et de Morale*, 15, No. 5, septembre 1907, 620-670. This is a lengthy exposition of Bergson's views.

1908

148   Aimel, Georges. "Individualisme et philosophie bergsonienne." *Revue de Philosophie*, 12, No. 6, juin 1908, 582-593.

149   Ardigo, Roberto. "Un pretesa pregiudiziale contro il positivismo." *Rivista di filosofia e scienzi affini*, 18, Nos. 1-2, 1908, 1-46. Reprinted in Ardigó's collected works, Vol. 10. Bergson and others are criticized here for failure to understand science and scientific philosophy.

150   Batault, Georges. "La Philosophie de M. Bergson." *Mercure de France*, 72, No. 258, 16 mars 1908, 193-211.

151   Bazaillas, Albert. *Musique et inconscience: Introduction à la psychologie de l'inconscient*. Paris: Félix Alcan, 1908, 320. The author gives a highly suggestive account of Bergson's psychology. Cf. Bergson's review, 1908.

152   Berthelot, René. *Evolutionisme et platonisme: Mélanges d'histoire de la philosophie et d'histoire des sciences*. Paris: Félix Alcan, 1908, 326. Bergson is discussed on pp. 131-138.

153   Binet, Alfred. "Une Enquête sur l'évolution de l'enseignement de la philosophie." *Année Psychologique*, 14, 1908, 229-230. See Bergson's reply to Binet, 1908, same journal. Binet had recorded antiscientific tendencies in Bergson's teaching. Bergson categorically denies this.

154   Bode, Boyd Henry. "Review of *L'Evolution créatrice* by Henri Bergson." *Philosophical Review*, 17, No. 1, January 1908, 84-89.

155   Borel, Emile. "Lettre à l'éditeur (Discussions)." *Revue de Métaphysique et de Morale*, 16, No. 2, 1908, 244-245. Borel here finds himself in essential agreement with Bergson as regards "l'intelligence géométrique."

156   Boutroux, Émile. "La Philosophie en France depuis 1867." *Revue de Métaphysique et de Morale*, 16, No. 6, 1908, 683-716. Bergson's concept of laughter is mentioned on p. 708; his attack on psycho-physical parallelism is cited on p. 689; the ideas of Edouard LeRoy are noted on pp. 701 and 706; those of Albert Bazaillas are mentioned on pp. 689-709.

157   Carr, Herbert Wildon. "Bergson's Theory of Knowledge." *Proceedings of the Aristotelian Society*, N.S. 9, 1908-09, 41-60. This is an account of Bergson's epistemology as developed in *L'Evolution créatrice*. It also contains a reply by Bergson to criticisms of this work. Cf. Bergson's letter to the author, 1908.

158   Chaumeix, André. "La Philosophie de M. Bergson." *Journal des Débats*, 24 mai 1908, 1027-1032. This article is reprinted in *Pragmatisme et modernisme*. Ed. J. Bourdeau. Paris: Félix Alcan, 221-236.

159   Chide, Alphonse. *Le Mobilisme moderne*. Paris: Félix Alcan, 1908, 292 (Bibliothèque de Philosophie Contemporaine).

160   Chide, Alphonse. "Pragmatisme et intellectualisme." *Revue Philosophique de la France et de l'Etranger*, 65, No. 4, avril 1908, 367-388.

161 Crespi, Attilio. "La metafisica di H. Berson." *Coenobium*, 2, No. 5, 1908, 46-51.

162 Cristiani, Léon. *Le Problème de Dieu et la pragmatisme*. Paris: Bloud et Cie., 1908, 62.

163 Decoster, Paul. "La Philosophie de M. Bergson." *Pages Amies*, No. 6, 20 janvier 1908.

164 Driesch, Hans. "Bergson, der biologische Philosoph." *Zeitschrift für den Ausbau der Entwicklungslehre*, 2, Nos. 1-2, 1908, 48-55. This is a chapter by chapter analysis of *L'Evolution créatrice*.

165 Duprat, Em. "Estudios de filosofía contemporánea: La filosofía de H. Berson." *Cultura Española*, Año 3, No. 1, 1908, 185-202; No. 2, 1908, 567-584.

166 Duprat, Em. "La filosofía francesa en 1907." *Nosotros*, 2, No. 15, octubre 1908, 156-160. The author discusses *Creative Evolution* and its impact.

167 Dwelshauvers, Georges. "De L'Intuition dans l'acte de l'esprit." *Revue de Métaphysique et de Morale*, 16, No. 1, janvier 1908, 55-65. This article is reprinted in the author's *La Synthèse mentale*.

168 Dwelshauvers, Georges. *La Synthèse mentale*. Paris: Félix Alcan, 1908, 276. Cf. Bergson's review, 1908. (Bibliothèque de philosophie contemporaine) This study, like most of the author's writings, is strongly influenced by Bergson's thought. Cf. Bergson's review, 1908.

169 "Review of *L'Evolution créatrice* by Henri Bergson." *Hibbert Journal*, 6, No. 1, January 1908, 435-442.

170 Gebert, K. "Philosophie der Innerwelt: Deutsche Üebertragg. der Philosophie Bergsons." *Das 20. Jahrhundert*, No. 48, November 1908.

171 Hébert, Marcel. *Le Pragmatisme: Etude de ses diverses formes, anglo-américaines, françaises et italiennes et de sa valeur religieuse*. 1-2 éds. Paris: Emile Nourry, 1908, 105, 168. Chapter four of this study concerns Bergson.

172 James, William. "Letter to James Jackson Putnam, August 19, 1908." In *James Jackson Putnam and Psychoanalysis*. Ed. Nathan G. Hale, Jr., Cambridge, Mass.: Harvard University Press, 1971, 74-75. James states: "The program you sketch is, I think, the form which the more spiritualistic philosophy of the future is bound more and more to assume, tho I fancy it will always be dogged more or less by a more materialist or mechanistic-determinist enemy. Bergson will have been the decisive initiator, but the necessary vagueness from the conceptual or intellectualist point of view of so many of his ideas will make it long ere the *general* mind swings over to his doctrines" (p. 74).

173 Keyserling, Herman Von. "Bergson." *Beilage zur Allgemeinen Zeitungen*, No. 35, 28 November 1908.

174 Kodis, J. "Philosophie de Bergson." *Przeglad Filozoficzny*. 1, No. 4, 1908.

175 Lalande, André. "Philosophy in France, 1907: I. Philosophy in the Universities." *Philosophical Review*, 17, No. 3, May 1908, 291-306.

176 Lebreton, Jules. *L'Encyclique et la théologie moderniste*. Paris: Beauchesne, 1908, 802.

177 Le Dantec, Félix. *Science et conscience: Philosophie du XXe siècle*. Paris: Flammarion, 1908, 328. The author develops various criticisms of Bergson's philosophy in Chapter 6 of this work.

178 Legendre, Maurice. "M. Bergson et son *Evolution créatrice*." *Bulletin de la Semaine*, 6 mai 1908.

179   Lenoble, Eugène. "Review of *L'Evolution créatrice* by Henri Bergson." *Revue de Clergé Français*, 53, No. 316, 15 janvier 1908, 180-208.

180   Lenoble, E. "La Philosophie de M. Bergson." *Revue du Clergé Français*, 1908, 620-622.

181   Le Roy, Edouard. "Philosophy in France, 1907: I. Philosophy in the Universities. II. Philosophy of Religion." *Philosophical Review*, 17, No. 3, May 1908, 291-315.

182   Leroy, Maxime. *La Loi, essai sur la théorie de l'authorité dans la démocratie.* Paris: V. Giard & E. Briêre, 1908, 351. This contains a brief discussion (pp. 238-242) of E. Le Roy's Catholic modernist *Dogme et critique*.

183   Loveday, Thomas. "Review of *L'Evolution créatrice* by Henri Bergson." *Mind*, 17, No. 67, July 1908, 402-408.

184   Mitchell, Arthur. "Review of *L'Evolution créatrice* by Henri Bergson." *Journal of Philosophy, Psychology, and Scientific Methods*, 5, No. 22, 22 October 1908, 603-612.

185   Mondain, G. "Remarques sur la théorie matérialiste." *Foi et Vie*, 11, No. 12, 15 juin 1908, 369-373.

186   Palmer, William Scott. "Presence and Omnipresence: A Christian Study Aided by the Philosophy of Monsieur Bergson." *Contemporary Review*, 93, No. 6, June 1908, 734-742. This study extends Bergson's thought to religious experience.

187   Parodi, Dominique. "Les Tendances de la philosophie contemporaine en France." *Petit Messager Belge*, No. 421, 1908, 50-51.

188   Pegnes, Thomas M. "Review of *L'Evolution créatrice* by Henri Bergson." *Revue Thomiste*, 16, No. 3, mai-juin 1908, 137-163.

189   Piéron, Henri. "Les Problèmes actuels de l'instinct." *Revue philosophique de la France et de l'Etranger*, 66, Octobre, 1908, 329-369.

190   Piat, Clodius. *Insuffisance des philosophies de l'intuition.* Paris: Plon-Nourrit et Cie., 1908, 319.

191   Prezzolini, Giuseppe. "La filosofia di Enrico Bergson." *Rassegna contemporanea*, 4, No. 11, 1908, 287-314.

192   Rageot, Gaston. "Le Problème expérimental du temps." *Revue Philosophique de la France et de l'Etranger*, 66, No. 7, 1908, 23-50.

193   Rageot, Gaston. *Les Savants et la philosophie.* Paris: Félix Alcan, 1908, 179. (Bibliothèque de la philosophie contemporaine) On pp. 147-179 the author examines "La métaphysique de la psychologie. Henri Bergson", describing Bergson's thought as a psychology of feeling, which already appears dated.

194   Ross, G. R. T. "The Satisfaction of Thinking." *Proceedings of the Aristotelian Society*, N.S. 9, 1908-1909, 119-140. Mathematical and intuitive accounts of motion are compared on pp. 127-132; Bergson's biology is discussed on pp. 134-135. The author is generally critical.

195   Ross, G. R. T. "A New Theory of Laughter." *Nation* (London), 4, 1908, 348-349. This is a review of *Le Rire*.

196   Rousselot, P. *L'Intellectualism de St. Thomas.* Paris: F. Alcan, 1908, xxv, 256. (Collection historique des grands philosophes).

197   Schoen, H. "Review of *L'Evolution créatrice* by Henri Bergson." *Zeitschrift für Philosophie und Pädogogik*, 15, No. 1, 1908, 39-41.

198   Setzer, Ambrosio. "Conceito do homem no sistema metafisico de Bergson." *Vozes de Petrôpolis*, 2, No. 3, 1908.

199   Silberstein. "Review of *L'Evolution créatrice* by Henri Bergson." *Przeglad filozoficzny*, 1, 1908.

200   Smith, Norman Kemp. "Subjectivism and Realism in Modern Philosophy." *Philosophical Review*, 17, No. 2, March, 1908, 138-148. The author concludes that: "The two most courageous and thoroughgoing attempts to establish realism have been those of Avenarius and Bergson." (139).

201   Sorel, Georges. *Réflexions sur la violence*. Paris: "Pages libres," 1908, 257. Numerous references to Bergson may be found throughout this study, a basic source of "radical syndicalism."

202   Steenbergen, A. "Henri Bergsons intuitive Philosophie." Diss. Rudolfstadt, 1908, iii, 46.

203   Tonquédec, Joseph de. "Comment interpréter l'ordre du monde?" *Etudes par des Pères de la Compagnie de Jésus*, 114, 5 mars 1908, 577-597.

204   Tonquédec, Joseph de.*Comment interpréter l'ordre du monde à propos du dernier ouvrage de M. Bergson*. Paris: Beauchesne, 1908.

205   Tonquédec, Joseph de. *La Notion de la vérité dans la philosophie nouvelle*. Paris: Beauchesne, 1908, 150. The author offers numerous criticisms of Bergson and Le Roy.

206   Trouché, H. "Review of *L'Evolution créatrice* by Henri Bergson." *Revue de Philosophie*, No. 11, novembre 1908, 520-534.

207   Tyrrell, George. "Review of *L'Evolution créatrice* by Henri Bergson." *Hibbert Journal*, 6, No. 1, January 1908, 435-442. This is a lengthy, mainly expository review.

208   Varisco, Bernardino. "La creázióne." *Rivista filosofica*, 11, No. 2, marzo-aprile 1908, 149-180. This is a review of *L'Evolution créatrice*. It consists largely of quotations.

209   Villassère, H. "Review of L'Evolution créatrice by Henri Bergson." *Bulletin Critique*, 3e Sér., 2, septembre 1908, 392-411. This is an exposition of the major arguments developed by Bergson in *L'Evolution créatrice*.

210   Windelband, Wilhelm. "Preface." *Materie und Gedächtnis*. Jena: Diederichs, 1908, 264, I-XV.

211   Wolf, A. "Natural Realism and Present Tendencies in Philosophy." *Proceedings of the Aristotelian Society*, 9, 1908-1909, 141-182. Bergson and several other philosophers are mentioned on p. 146 as representatives of a new tendency towards "realism."

1909

212   Baylac, Jacques. "La Philosophie de M. Bergson." *Bulletin de Littérature Ecclésiastique*, 11, No. 5, octobre 1909, 329-341.

213   "Bergson's New Idea." *Current Literature*, 47, No. 6, December 1909, 650-651.

214   Boer, Tjitze J. de. "De filosofie van Henri Bergson." *Beweging*, 3, 1909, 225-244.

215   Bohn, Georges. *La Naissance de l'intelligence*, Paris: Flammarion, 1909, 350.
       Cf. Bergson's review of this work of comparative psychology, 1909.

216   Bouglé, Célestin. "Syndicalistes et Bergsoniens." *Revue du Mois*, 6, No. 4, 10
       avril 1909, 403-416. The author distinguishes the "Bergsonians of the left"
       (syndicalists) from the "Bergsonians of the right." Both owe to Bergson their
       anti-intellectualism and passion for action. Dubious of the absolute verity of
       syndicalism, the author nonetheless commends syndicalists for their effort to
       see social and economic problems freshly.

217   Carr, Herbert Wildon. "Bergson's Theory of Instinct." *Proceedings of the Artistote-
       lian Society*, N.S. 10, 1909-10, 93-114. This article is an account of Bergson's
       theory of instinct. The author attempts to meet specific objections to Bergson's
       theory on pp. 111-114.

218   Challaye, Félicien. *Syndicalisme révolutionnaire et syndicalisme réformiste*. Paris:
       Félix Alcan, 1909, 156.

219   Coignet, Clarisse. "La Vie d'après M. Bergson." *Bericht über den III. inter-
       nationalen Kongress für Philosophie zu Heidelberg*. Hrsg. von Th. Elsenhans.
       Heidelberg: Carl Winters Universität Buchhandlung, 1909, 358-364.

220   Duprat, Em. "La filosofía francesa en 1908." *Nosotros*, 3, Nos. 2-3, julio y agosto
       1909, 324-328.

221   "Review of *L'Evolution créatrice* by Henri Bergson." *Nation*, 89, September 30,
       1909, 298-300.

222   Farges, Albert. "L'Erreur fondamentale de la philosophie nouvelle." *Revue
       Thomiste*, 17, No. 2, mars-arvril 1909, 182-197; No. 3, mai-juin 1909, 299-312.

223   Farges, Albert. *Etudes philosophiques pour vulgariser les théories d'Aristote et de
       Saint Thomas et montrer leur accord avec les sciences: I. Théorie fondamentale
       de l'acte et la puissance ou du mouvement: Le Devenir, sa causalité, sa finalité:
       Avec La Critique de la philosophie "nouvelle" de MM. Bergson et Le Roy, ou
       du modernisme philosophique*. Paris: Berche et Tralin, 1909-1910, 443.

224   Farges, Albert. "Le Problème de la contingence d'après M. Bergson." *Revue
       Pratique d'Apologétique*, 8, No. 86, 15 avril 1909, 115-122.

225   Ferrar, W. "Review of L'Evolution créatrice by Henri Bergson." *Commonwealth*,
       December 1909, 636-637.

226   Garrigou-Lagrange, Reginald. *Le Sens commun, la philosophie de l'être et les
       formules dogmatiques*. Paris: Desclée De Brouwer et Cie., 1909, 350. The
       author asserts that Bergson's philosophy is an "evolutionary monism."

227   Goldstein, Julius. "Henri Bergson und der Zeitlosigkeitsidealismus." *Literaturblatt
       der Frankfurter Zeitung*, 2 Mai 1909.

228   Grivet, Jules. "Henri Bergson: Esquisse philosophique." *Etudes par des Pères de
       la Compagnie de Jesus*, 121, 5 octobre 1909, 31-50; 20 novembre 1909, 454-478;
       124, 20 juillet 1910, 153-184.

229   Hulme, Thomas Ernest. "Bergson and Bax." *New Age*, N.S. 5, No. 12, July 22,
       1909, 259. This is a letter.

230   Hulme, Thomas Ernest. "The New Philosophy." *New Age*, N.S. 5, No. 10, July
       1, 1909, 198-199.

231   Hulme, Thomas Ernest. "Searchers After Reality: I. Bax." *New Age*, N.S. 5, No.
       13, July 29, 1909, 265-266.

232   James, William. "The Philosophy of Bergson." *Hibbert Journal*, 7, No. 3, April
       1909, 562-577. This essay is reprinted as "Bergson and His Critique of Intellec-
       tualism," Lecture VI in *A Pluralistic Universe*. New York: Longmans, Green
       and Company, 1919, 223-272.

233   Kodis, J. "Die schöpferische Evolution von Bergson." *Przeglad Filozoficzny*, 2,
       1909. (Poln. Sprache).

234   Leclère, Albert. *Pragmatisme, modernisme, protestantisme*. Paris: Bloud et Cie.,
       1909, 296.

235   Lovejoy, Arthur Oncken. "The Metaphysician of the Life-Force." *Nation*, 89, No.
       2309, September 30, 1909, 298-301. This is a review of *L'Evolution créatrice*.

236   Mokievski, P. "Философия Анти Бетгсона." *Русское Оогатстфо*, 6, 1909,
       153-158.

237   Momigliano, Attilio. "L'origine del comico." *Cultura filosofica*, 3, No. 4, 1909,
       406-433.

238   Palmer, William Scott. "Life and the Brain." *Contemporary Review*, 96, No. 10,
       October, 1909, 474-484. This review considers mind-brain and life-matter rela-
       tions in *Creative Evolution*.

239   Palmer, William Scott. "Thought and Instinct." *Nation*, 5, June 5, 1909, 341-342.

240   Pierce, Charles Sanders. "Letter to William James. March 9, 1909." In Ralph
       Barton Perry, *The Thought and Character of William James*. Vol. III. Boston:
       Little, Brown and Company, 1935, 437-438. In this letter Pierce complains
       against being compared with Bergson. "...that philosophy is either a science or
       is balderdash, and that a man who seeks to further science can hardly commit
       a greater sin than to use the terms of his science without anxious care to use
       them with strict accuracy, it is not very grateful to my feelings to be classed
       along with a Bergson who seems to be doing his prettiest to muddle all distinc-
       tions..." (p. 438).

241   Plekhanov, G. "Anri Bergson." *Sovremennyi mir*, 3, No. 2, 1909, 118-122.

242   Prezzolini, Giuseppe. "Giorgio Sorel e il sindacalismo: Le grandi teorie sindacaliste
       e la filosofia de E. Bergson." *Bolletino filosofico*, No. 2, 1909.

243   Prezzolini, Giuseppe. *La teoria sindacalista*. Napoli: Francesco Perella, 1909, 338.
       Bergson is discussed here on pp. 281-335.

244   Putnam, James Jackson. "Letter to Ernest Jones, November 22, 1909." In *James
       Jackson Putnam and Psychoanalysis*. Ed. Nathan G. Hale, Jr. Cambridge,
       Mass.: Harvard University Press, 1971, 211-212. On p. 211 Putnam informs
       Jones that he is going to read a paper comparing Bergson's and Freud's theories
       of the unconscious mental life at an upcoming meeting of the American
       Psychological Association.

245   Putnam, James Jackson. "Personal Impressions of Sigmund Freud and His Work,
       with Special Reference to His Recent Lectures at Clark University." *Journal of
       Abnormal Psychology*, 4, No. 5, 1909-1910, 293-310. The author introduces
       Freud's ideas to an American audience. On pp. 297-298 he likens Freud's idea
       that repressed feelings remain active to Bergson's notion that memories remain
       living and active forces. On p. 298 he mentions Bergson's belief that perceptions
       are really "nine parts memory."

246   Raymond, Marcel. "La Philosophie de l'intuition et la philosophie du concept." *Etudes Franciscaines*, 21, No. 2, juin 1909, 669-687.

247   Ross, G. T. "The Philosophy of Vitalism." *Nation*, (London), 4, March 13, 1909, 902-903.

248   Sabatier, Paul. *Les Modernistes: Note d'histoire religieuse contemporaine.* Paris: Fischlacher, 1909, liv, 256.

249   Seillière, Ernest. "L'Allemagne et la philosophie bergsonienne." *L'Opinion*, 11, No. 27, 3 juillet 1909, 13-14.

250   Seliber, G. "Der Pragmatismus und seine Gegner: Auf dem III. internationalen Kongress für Philosophie." *Archiv für systematische Philosophie*, N.S. 15, No. 3, 1909, 287-298.

251   Steenbergen, Albert. *Henri Bergsons intuitive Philosophie.* Iena: Diederichs, 1909, 110.

252   Taylor, Alfred Edward. Review of *A Pluralistic Universe*, by William James. *Mind*, N.S. 18, No. 72, 1909, 576-588. The reviewer finds William James' adherence to Bergson surprising. Unlike Bergson, James does not dive into the stream of experience. In general, this is a scathingly critical review.

1910

253   Antoniade, C. "Filosofia lui Henri Bergson." *Studii filosofice*, 5, No. 1, 1910, 24-59; No. 2, 1910, 113-169. This article is in Rumanian.

254   Bach, Salomon. *Depuis Renan: Propos bergsoniens.* Toulouse: "Poésie," 1910, 109.

255   Becher, Erich. "Review of *Materie und Gedächtnis*, by Henri Bergson." *Literarisches Centralblatt für Deutschland*, 61, No. 28, 9 Juli 1910, 917-918.

256   Benrubi, Isaac. "Henri Bergson." *Die Zukunft*, 18, No. 36, 4 Juni 1910, 318-322.

257   Benrubi, Isaac. "Review of *Henri Bergsons Intuitive Philosophie* by Albert Steenbergen." *Revue Philosophique de la France et de l'Etranger*, 69, No. 2, février 1910, 204-206. This is a critical review which defends Bergson while tending to concur with certain of Steenbergen's criticisms.

258   "Henri Bergson." *Coenobium*, 4, 1910, 141.

259   Berthelot, René. "L'Espace et le temps chez les physiciens." *Revue de Métaphysique et de Morale*, 17, No. 6, juin 1910, 774-775.

260   Bornhausen, Karl. "Die Philosophie H. Bergsons und ihre Bedeutung für den Religionsbegriff." *Zeitschrift für Theologie und Kirche*, 6, No. 6, 1910, 39-77.

261   Bosanquet, Bernard. "On a Defect in the Customary Logical Formulation of Inductive Reasoning." *Proceedings of the Aristotelian Society*, N.S. 11, 1910-11, 24-40. The author pursues a careful criticism of Bergson's concept of the intellect. "With tautological identity as the principle of intelligence, all systematic coherence, between term and term, equally as between judgment and judgment, inevitably vanishes." (31-32).

262   Bosanquet, Bernard. "The Prediction of Human Conduct: A Study in Bergson." *International Journal of Ethics*, 21, No. 1, October 1910, 1-15. In this address delivered at University College, Cardiff, Bosanquet attempts to make clear to a general audience Bergson's position on certain questions.

263   Boutroux, Émile. "William James." *Revue de Métaphysique et de Morale*, 18, No. 6, 1910, 711-743. This article was written on the occasion of James' death. It is a general review of his career and philosophy. On pp. 733-735, the author examines Bergson's influence on James.

264   Bovet, Pierre. "La Conscience de devoir dans l'introspection provoqué." *Archives de Psychologie*, 9, 1910, 304-369. Cf. pp. 310-311.

265   Carr, Herbert Wildon. "The Philosophy of Bergson." *Hibbert Journal*, 9, Part 2, July 1910, 873-883.

266   Carr, Herbert Wildon. "The Theory of Psycho-physical Parallelism as a Working Hypothesis in Psychology." *Proceedings of the Aristotelian Society*, N.S. 11, 1910-11, 129-143. This is a criticism of the theory of mind-body parallism based on Bergson's "Le Paralogisme psychophysiologique.

267   Carr, H. Wildon. "III. Instinct and Intelligence." *British Journal of Psychology*, 3, Part 3, 1910, 230-236. In this paper, presented at a symposium in July, 1910, at a joint meeting of the Aristotelian Society, British Psychological Society, and *Mind* Association, Carr explains Bergson's view of the relations between instinct and intelligence. The criticisms of Bergson's philosophy based on the fact that some instintive actions can be improved by practice and imitation only show that in some cases of instinctive action intelligence is present in some degree. But Bergson holds that intelligence and instinct are never present in pure forms but are both always present in some degree. That instinct can be "converted into intelligence" in some cases only proves that instinct, like intelligence, is a kind of cognition.

268   Chaumeix, André. "Les Critiques du rationalisme: A Propos des idées de M. Bergson et M. William James." *Revue Hebdomadaire*, 19e Année, No. 1, ler janvier 1910, 1-33.

269   Chiapelli, Allesandro. *Della critica al nuovo idealismo.* Torino: Fratelli Boca, 1910, 300.

270   Chiappelli, Allesandro. "Les Tendances vives de la philosophie contemporaine." *Revue Philosophique de la France et de l'Etranger*, 69, No. 3, mars 1910, 217-248.

271   Corbière, Charles. "Le Dieu de M. Bergson." *Revue de Théologie et des Questions Religieuses*, 19e Année, No. 2, ler mars 1910, 176-187.

272   Desaymard, Joseph. *H. Bergson à Clermont-Ferrand.* Clermont-Ferrand: Bellet, 1910, 40. This mémoire was published originally in *Bulletin Historique et Scientifique de l'Auvergne*, May 30, 1910, 204-216, and June 1910, 243-267. It provides many insights into Bergson's early career.

273   Dienes, V. and P. "Bemerkungen zur Metaphysik Bergsons." *Husz. szás*, 1910. (Ungar. Sprache).

274   Dolson, Grace Neal. "The Philosophy of Henri Bergson." *Philosophical Review*, 19, No. 6, November, 1910, 579-596; 20, No. 1, January, 1911, 46-48.

275   Dwelshauvers, Georges. "Discussion with Henri Bergson concerning the terms 'conscious' and 'unconscious'. November 25, 1909." *Bulletin de la Société Française de Philosophie*, 10, No. 2, 1910, 31 *et seq. Mélanges*, 803-10; *Ecrits et Paroles*, 2, 325-331.

276   Eschbach, V. "Henri Bergson." *Kölnische Volkszeitung*, 20 January 1910.

277   Florence, Jean. "La Philosophie de M. Bergson, jugée par M. Lasserre." *Phalange*, 5, No. 51, 20 septembre 1910, 218-269. This article concerns Pierre Lasserre's articles in the right wing *L'Action Française* on Bergson.

278   Freud, Sigmund. "Letter to James Jackson Putnam, March 10, 1910." in Nathan G. Hale, Jr. *James Jackson Putnam and Psychoanalysis*. Cambridge, Massachusetts: Harvard University Press, 1971, 96-97. The author replies to Jackson's letter (Feb. 15, 1910) urging Bergson's concept of the unconscious and the brain: "I make bold to say that from the beginning I have agreed with Bergson's view of the matter."

279   Freud, Sigmund. "Letter to James Jackson Putnam, September 29, 1910." in Nathan G. Hale, Jr. *James Jackson Putnam and Psychoanalysis*. Cambridge, Massachusetts: Harvard University Press, 1971, p. 108. The author responds to Putnam's argument for the *élan vital*: "I do not wish to comment at length about your letter of September 1. It does you a great credit. I only regret that my own thoughts do not reach such heights."

280   Fritzsche, Richard. "Review of *Materie und Gedächtnis* and *Einführung in die Metaphysik* by Henri Bergson and *Henri Bergsons intuitive Philosophie* by Steenbergen." *Vierteljahrschrift für wissenschaftliche Philosophie und Soziologie*, 34, No. 4, 1910, 353-357.

281   Gaultier, Jules de. "Le Réalisme du contenu." *Revue Philosophique de la France et de l'Etranger*, 69, No. 1, janvier 1910, 39-64. This essay deals with problems of continuity and discontinuity in Bergson.

282   Gibson, W. B. "The Intuition of Bergson." *Quest*, 2, 1910, 201-228.

283   Gillouin, René. *Henri Bergson: Choix de textes avec étude du système philosophique*. Paris: Louis-Michaud, 1910, 222.

284   Goldstein, Julius. "Henri Bergson und die Sozialwissenschaft." *Archiv für Sozialwissenschaft und Sozialpolitik*, 31, No. 1, Juli 1910, 1-22. This is a study of Bergson's philosophy (understood as *Lebensphilosophie*) and its relations to G. Sorel and syndicalism. The author also notes Bergson's relations to Catholic modernism.

285   Hibben, John Gries. "The Philosophical Aspects of Evolution." *Philosophical Review*, 18, No. 2, March 1910, 113-116.

286   "Instinct and Intelligence." *British Journal of Psychology*, 3, Part 3, 1910, 209-270. This is a symposium held at a joint meeting of the Aristotelian Society, British Psychological Society, and *Mind* Association in London, July 1910. It includes papers by Charles S. Myers, C. Lloyd Morgan, H. Wildon Carr, G. F. Stout, and William McDougall, with a reply by Charles S. Myers. Bergson's conceptions of instinct and intelligence are at issue throughout.

287   Jacks, Lawrence Pearsall. *The Alchemy of Thought*. New York: Holt, 1911; London: Williams and Nordgate, 1910, 349.

288   Jacoby, Gunther. "Review of *Einführung in die Metaphysik* by Henri Bergson; and *Henri Bergsons intuitive Philosophie* by Albert Steenbergen." *Archiv für die gesamte Psychologie*, 18, 1910, 19-20.

289   James, William. "Bradley or Bergson?" *Journal of Philosophy*, 7, No. 2, January 20, 1910, 29-33.

290   James, William. "A Great French Philosopher at Harvard." *Nation*, 90, No. 2335, March 31, 1910, 312-314.

291   James, William. *Philosophie de l'expérience*. Trans. E. Le Brun and M. Paris. Paris: Flammarion, 1910, 368. This is the French translation of *A Pluralistic Universe*.

292   James, William. "Letter to James Jackson Putnam, June 4, 1910." In *James Jackson Putnam and Psychoanalysis*. Ed. Nathan G. Hale, Jr. Cambridge, Mass.: Harvard University Press, 1971, 75-78. James mentions having attended a meeting of the Académie des sciences morales and having had two lunches with Bergson: "it is a pleasure to associate with a *really first* class mind" (p. 77).

293   Jeannière, René. "La Théorie des concepts chez M. Bergson et M. James." *Revue de Philosophie*, 17, No. 12, décembre 1910, 578-598. The author deals with interpretations of concepts and intuition in W. James and Bergson by H. M. Kallen, W. B. Pitkin, and W. P. Montague. Intuition is necessary, he concludes, but concepts also can attain to reality.

294   Joel, Karl. "Neues Denken." *Neue Rundschau*, 21, No. 2, 1910, 549-588.

295   Joussain, André. *Romantisme et religion*. Paris: Félix Alcan, 1910, 179.

296   Kallen, Horace M. "James, Bergson and Mr. Pitkin." *The Journal of Philosophy*, 7, No. 13, June 23, 1910, 353-357. The author defends William James' interpretation of Bergson.

297   Kostylev, N. "Le-Dantek i Bergson." *Vestnik Evropy*, No. 261, 1910, p. 89.

298   Kroner, Richard. "Henri Bergson." *Logos*, (Tübingen), 1, No. 1, 1910, 125-150.

299   Lalande, André. "Philosophy in France, 1909." *Philosophical Review*, 19, No. 4, July 1910, 241-266.

300   Lanczi, E. "Bemerkungen zur Metaphysik Bergsons." *Husz. száz*, 1910, (Ungar. Sprache).

301   Lasserre, Pierre. "La Philosophie de M. Bergson." *L'Action Française*, 6, août et septembre 1910.

302   Lasson, Adolf. "Henri Bergson." *Deutsche Literaturzeitung*, 31, No. 22, 28 Mai 1910, 1364-1366. This article is a report of an address on Bergson by Adolf Lasson.

303   Le Dantec, Félix. "Réflexions d'un philistin sur la métaphysique." *Grande Revue*, 62, No. 13, 10 juillet 1910, 1-16. This is a review of *La Philosophie de l'expérience (A Pluralistic Universe)* by William James. The reviewer critiques James' concepts of the will to believe, intellectualism, consciousness, and Bergson. He also attacks Bergson.

304   Leighton, J. A. "On Continuity and Discreteness." *Journal of Philosophy, Psychology and Scientific Methods*, 7, No. 9, April 28, 1910, 231-238. This is reprinted in the author's *Contre la métaphysique*, 1912.

305   "Review of *Materie und Gedächtnis* by Henri Bergson." *Literarisches Zentralblatt für Deutschland*, 61, Juli 1910, 917-918.

306   McDougall, William. "V. Instinct and Intelligence." *British Journal of Psychology*, 3, Part 3, 1910, 250-266. This paper was given during July, 1910, at a joint meeting of the Aristotelian Society, the British Psychological Society, and the *Mind* Association. The author criticizes Bergson's contention that instinct is a special kind of cognition. Intelligence and instinct are the same sort of activity, distinguished only by instinct's being the result of innate, and intelligence of

learned, factors. The studies by the Peckhams of the solitary wasps show, against Bergson and Fabre (who is described as having a "theological bias") that these wasps do not behave with perfect precision and have, therefore, no unerring vision of their object. Similarly, the intelligent behavior of such wasps under certain circumstances indicates that Bergson's distinction between the intelligent vertebrates and the instinctive arthropods is far from being established. The basic difference between arthropods and vertebrates is that the former have a very brief "youth" and little experience to draw on, while the latter have an extended youth and ample occasion to learn from experience. Furthermore, how instinct as a supposedly special kind of knowledge can specifically guide a wasp in the stinging of its prey or a bee in building its honeycomb is almost impossible to understand (pp. 253-358). In other respects the author is in agreement with Bergson; however, "I hold that the instincts are differentiations of 'l'élan vital' by means of which it pushes along diverging paths."

307   Mitchell, Arthur. "Freedom and Intuition in Henri Bergson's Philosophy." Diss. Harvard, 1910.

308   Montague, William Pepperel. "A Pluralistic Universe and the Logic of Irrationalism." *Journal of Philosophy*, 7, No. 6, 1910, 141-155. This is a review of *A Pluralistic Universe* by William James. The reviewer finds James' critique of "absolutism" convincing, but does not accept James' defense of Bergson's critique of "intellectualism."

309   Morgan, C. Lloyd. "II. Instinct and Experience." *British Journal of Psychology*, 3, Part 3, 1910, 219-229. The author argues that instinct and intelligence are not two different ways of regarding the same process but are distinguishable sorts of processes. Those who, like Bergson, draw upon the behavior of the solitary wasps for examples of perfect instinctive adaptation, should carefully study the recent observations of Dr. and Mrs. Peckham on the subject. (On this point Cf. R. Ruyer, 1959.)

310   Müller-Freienfels, Richard. "Review of *Materie und Gedächtnis* by Henri Bergson." *Zeitschrift für Psychologie und Physiologie der Sinnesorgane*, 56, No. 1-2, 1910, 126-129.

311   Myers, Charles S. "Instinct and Intelligence. A Reply." *British Journal of Psychology*, 3, No. 3, 1910, 267- 270. This is a reply to criticisms of a paper previously delivered during July, 1910, at a joint meeting of the Aristotelian Society, the British Psychological Society, and the *Mind* Association. (This paper appears in the same number of this journal, pp. 209-218). The author criticizes Bergson's concept of instinct, as defended by H. Wildon Carr on pp. 268-269. If Bergson and Carr are correct, the author states, then instinct is a special sort of consciousness of which we can have no concept: "We are endowing insects with a mental possession, of the nature of which we have not, and can never have, the faintest glimmering" (p. 268).

312   "A Philosophy of Freedom." *London Times Literary Supplement*, 9, No. 454, September 22, 1910, 336. This is a favorable and very clear exposition of the basic concepts of *Time and Free Will*.

313   Pitkin, Walter B. "James and Bergson: Or, Who is against Intellect?" *Journal of Philosophy*, 7, No. 9, April 28, 1910, 225-231. The author argues that Bergson's and James' anti-intellectualisms differ profoundly. Bergson does not reject con-

ceptual thought. Cf. Bergson's response, 1910.

314 Prager, Hans. "Henri Bergsons metaphysische Grundanschauung." *Archiv für systematische Philosophie*, 16, No. 3, 1910, 310-320.

315 Prezzolini, Giuseppe. *Bergson*. Firenze: Aldino, 1910, 4.

316 Prezzolini, Giuseppe. "H. Bergson." *Voce*, Anno 3, No. 4, 6 gennaio 1910, 239-240.

317 "Professor Bergson on Freewill." *Spectator*, 105, No. 4291, September 24, 1910, 465-466. This is an exposition of Bergson's position in *Time and Free Will*.

318 Putnam, James Jackson. "Freud's and Bergson's Theories of the Unconscious." *Psychological Bulletin*, 7, No.2, 1910, 44-45. This is an abstract of a talk. Putnam explains Freud's views and Bergson's as being closely similar as regards the distinction between conscious and unconscious mental processes.

319 Putnam, James Jackson. "Letter to Sigmund Freud, February 15, 1910." in Nathan G. Hale, Jr. *James Jackson Putnam and Psychoanalysis*. Cambridge, Massachusetts: Harvard University Press, 1971, p. 94. The author urges Bergson's concept of the unconscious as proving that the mind is not contained in the brain. Cf. Freud's reply March 10, 1910.

320 Putnam, James Jackson. "Letter to Sigmund Freud, September 1, 1910." in Nathan G. Hale, Jr. *James Jackson Putnam and Psychoanalysis*. Cambridge, Massachusetts: Harvard University Press, 1971, 106-107. The author argues for Bergson's concept of *élan vital* as a full explanation of human life. Cf. Freud's reply, September 29, 1910.

321 Review of *Einleitung in die Philosophy* by W. Jerusalem. *Revue de Métaphysique et de Morale*, 18, No. 2 (Supplement), 1910, 18-19.

322 Royce, Josiah. "The Reality of the Temporal." *International Journal of Ethics*, 20, No. 3, 1910, 257-271. This is a criticism of Bergson's concept of duration by a prominent American philosopher. Cf. M. Čapek, 1967.

323 Shepherd, Queen L. "Review of 'Le Souvenir du présent et la fausse reconnaissance' by Henri Bergson." *Psychological Bulletin*, 7, No. 9, September 15, 1910, 307.

324 Sobieski, Michal. "H. Bergson." *Kurier Warsawski*, 20 January 1910.

325 Sorel, Georges. *Réflexions sur la violence*. 2nd ed. Paris: Marcel Rivière, 1910, 412. Études sur le devenir social, No. 4.

326 Sorel, Georges. "Vues sur les problèmes de la philosophie." *Revue de Métaphysique et de Morale*, 18, No. 5, 1910, 581-613; 19, No. 1, 1911, 64-99.

327 Stout, G. F. "IV. Instinct and Intelligence." *British Journal of Psychology*, 3, Part 3, 1910, 237-249. The author argues that intelligent actions are not instinctively determined, and that every instinctive action is determined by intelligence. He also argues (pp. 243-245) against Bergson and H. Wildon Carr that instinct is not "a peculiar way of knowing, distinct from what is ordinarily called intelligence." There is nothing in the instinctive behavior of animals which can not be accounted for by a combination of intelligence and purely biological factors.

328 "Review of *Time and Free Will* by Henri Bergson." *Athenaeum*, No. 4330, October 13, 1910, 483-484.

329 "Review of *Time and Free Will: An Essay on the Immediate Data of Consciousness* by Henri Bergson." *Nation*, 91, No. 2369, November 24, 1910, 499-500. This is a general summary of Bergson's position in *Time and Free Will*.

330 "Review of *Time and Free Will: An Essay on the Immediate Data of Consciousness*, by Henri Bergson." *Saturday Review* (London), 90, No. 2866, October 1, 1910, 430.

331 Visan, Tancrède de. "La Philosophie de M. Bergson et le lyrisme contemporain." *Vers et Prose*, 6, No. 21, avril 1910, 125-140.

1911

332 *Athenaeum*, No. 4384, November 4, 1911, 560. This is a brief report on Bergson's concluding lectures on the nature of the self at University College, London.

333 Babynin, B. N. "Filosofiia Bergsona." *Voprosy filosofii i psikhologii*, 22, No. 3, 1911, 251-290; No. 4, 1911, 472-516.

334 Balfour, Arthur J. "Creative Evolution and Philosophic Doubt." *Hibbert Journal*, 10, Part 1, October 1911, 1-23. Reprinted in *Living Age*, 271, No. 3511, 2 December 1911, 515-527. Cf. also *Revue de Métaphysique et de Moralé*, 20, juillet 1912, 27.

335 "Mr. Balfour's Objection to Bergson's Philosophy." *Current Literature*, 51, No. 6, December 1911, 659-661. "When a former Prime Minister of England is in controversy with the leading philosophic thinker of our day over the deepest questions of human life and destiny, it behooves all the world to listen." (659). The author's account of Lord Balfour's objections to Bergson's philosophy is, however, superficial.

336 "Mr. Balfour and M. Bergson." *Spectator*, 1907, No. 4347 1911, 633-634.

337 Balsillie, David. "Professor Bergson on Time and Free Will." *Mind*, N.S. 20, No. 79, July 1911, 357-378. Reprinted as Chapter I of *An Examination of Professor Bergson's Philosophy*.

338 Baruzi, Joseph. *La Volonté de métamorphose*. Paris: Grasset, 1911, 202. Bergson's influence is found throughout this book.

339 Benrubi, Isaac. "La Renaissance de la philosophie en France." *Revue de Métaphysique et de Morale*, 19, No. 4, juillet 1911, 499-503. This article also appears in *Atti del IV Congresso Internazionali di Filosofia*, 1912.

340 Benrubi, Isaac. "Die Renaissance des Idealismus in Frankreich." *Deutsche Rundschau*, 149, October-Dezember 1911, 388-406.

341 "Bergson in English." *Nation* (New York), 92, No. 2400, 29 June 1911, 648-649. This is a review of *Matter and Memory*, translated by N. M. Paul and W. S. Palmer and of *Creative Evoluiton*, translated by Arthur Mitchell. An essentially critical review, it developes interesting comparisons of Bergson, Wm. James, and Fr. Pillon.

342 "M. Bergson and Others." *Spectator*, 106, No. 4323, 1911, 689-690. This is an impressionistic review of *Matter and Memory* and *Creative Evolution*.

343 "M. Bergson et le caractère quotidien de la philosophie." *Spectateur*, décembre 1911.

344 "M. Bergson on the Soul." *Spectator*, 107, No. 4349, 1911, 734-735. This article is a brief account of Bergson's lectures at London University.

345 "Bergson's Wonder-Working Philosophy." *Current Literature*, 50, No. 5, May 1911, 518-520. This article contains reviews of *Creative Evolution*, *Matter and Memory*, and *Time and Free Will*.

346 Björkman, Edwin. "Henri Bergson: The Philosopher of Actuality." *Forum*, 46, No. 3, September 1911, 268-276. This is a very general discussion of Bergson's philosophy.

347 Björkman, Edwin. "Henri Bergson: Philosopher or Prophet?" *Review of Reviews*, 54, No. 2, August 1911, 250-252.

348 Björkman, Edwin. "Is There Anything New Under the Sun?" *Forum*, 46, No. 1, July 1911, 11-21. The author gives a "popularized" account of Bergson's thought.

349 Björkman, Edwin. *Is There Anything New Under the Sun?* New York and London: Kennerly, 1911, 259.

350 Blanché, A. "Review of 'A Propos d'un article de Mr. Walter Pitkin intitulé James et Bergson by Henri Bergson." *Revue des Sciences Philosophiques et Théologiques*, 5, No. 1, 1911, 128-130.

351 Braun, Otto. "Review of *Wandlungen in Philosophie der Gegenwart*, by Julius Goldstein." *Kant-Studien*, 16, No. 4, 1911, 480-482.

352 Brunschvicg, Léon. "La Notion moderne de l'intuition et la philosophie des mathématiques." *Revue de Métaphysique et de Morale*, 19, No. 2, 1911, 145-176.

353 Carr, Herbert Wildon. "Review of *The Philosophy of Bergson* by A. D. Lindsay." *Mind*, N.S. 20, No. 80, October 1911, 560-566.

354 Cockerell, T. D. A. "The New Voice of Philosophy?" *Dial*, 51, No. 607, October 1, 1911, 253-255. This is a review of *Creative Evolution*.

355 Coignet, Clarisse. *De Kant à Bergson: Réconciliation de la religion et de la science dans un spiritualisme nouveau.* Paris: Félix Alcan, 1911, 155. (Bibliothèque de philosophie contemporaine) Cf. esp. 85-155.

356 "Review of *Creative Evolution* by Henri Bergson." *A.L.A. Booklist*, 7, No. 10, 1911, 409. The reviewer concludes: "One of the most important books in its field that has appeared in twenty years, but too technical for readers other than advanced students in philosophy."

357 "Review of *Creative Evolution* by Henri Bergson." *Athenaeum*, 1, No. 4355, April 1911, 411-412.

358 "Review of *Creative Evolution* by Henri Bergson." *Bookman* (New York), 34, No. 2, October 1911, 206.

359 "Review of *Creative Evolution* by Henri Bergson." *British Medical Journal*, 2, No. 2642, 19 August 1911, 380.

360 "Review of *Creative Evolution* by Henri Bergson." *Nature*, 87, No. 475, 1911, 475.

361 "Review of *Creative Evolution* by Henri Bergson." *Saturday Review* (London), 91, No. 2901, 3 June 1911, 695-689.

362 Crespi, Angelo. "Balfour e Bergson alle prese." *Coenobium*, 6, No. 10, 1911.

363 David, J. Wł. "O intuicyi w filozofii." *Krytyka*, 13, Nos. 3-4, September-October 1911, 92-101, 166-173. This is republished as *O intuicyi w filozofii Bergsona*. Kraków: Gebethner, 1911.

364 Delfour. "Le Style de M. Bergson." *L'Univers*, 19 avril 1911.

365   Delvolvé, Jean. "L'Influence de la philosophie de M. Bergson. I." *Mouvement Socialiste*, 29, 230, avril 1911, 267-268.

366   Dolson, Grace Neal. "Review of *Time and Free Will* by Henri Bergson." *Philosophical Review*, 20, No. 3, 1911.

367   Draghicesco, D. "L'Influence de la philosophie de M. Bergson. V." *Mouvement Socialiste*, 30, No. 235, novembre 1911, 266-269.

368   "Everyman's Philosophy." *Academy*, 80, No. 2034, 1911, 545. This is a review of *Matter and Memory* and *Creative Evolution*.

369   Fawcett, Edward Douglas. "Review of *Time and Free Will* by Henri Bergson." *Quest*, 2, 1911, 492-496.

370   Finnbogason, Guðmundur. *Den sympatiske forstaaelse*. København og Kristiana: Gyldenalske boghandel, Nordsik forlag, 1911, 175. Cf. the author, 1913.

371   Flournoy, Théodore. *La Philosophie de William James*. Paris: Saint-Blaise, 1911, 219.

372   Forsyth, T. "Review of *Time and Free Will* by Henri Bergson." *Review of Theology and Philosophy*, 6, 1911, 565-570.

373   Fouillée, Alfred. "L'Influence de la philosophie de M. Bergson. II." *Mouvement Socialiste*, 29, No. 230, avril 1911, 269.

374   Fouillée, Alfred. *La Pensée et les nouvelles écoles anti-intellectualistes*. Paris: Félix Alcan, 1911, xvi, 415.

375   Gaultier, Paul. *La Pensée contemporaine: Les Grands Problèmes*. Paris: Hachette, 1911, 312.

376   Gaultier, Paul. "Le Mouvement Philosophique: La Vie intérieure." *Revue Politique et Littéraire, Revue Bleue*, 49, No. 8, 25 février, 1911, 244-251. This is a review of l'*Essai, Matière et Mémoire* and *Morceaux choisis* by René Gillouin. The author provides a careful, accurate exposition of Bergson's psychology and epistemology.

377   Gibson, A. Boyce. "The Intuition of Bergson." *Quest*, 3, No. 1, January 1911.

378   Gillouin, René. *La Philosophie de M. Bergson*. Paris: Grasset, 1911, 187.

379   Gillouin, René. "La Philosophie de M. Bergson." *Parthénon*, 1, No. 1, octobre 1911.

380   Gillouin, René. "La Philosophie de M. Henri Bergson." *Revue de Paris*, 18e Année, No. 19, 1er octobre 1911, 528-558; No. 20, 15 octobre 1911, 847-875.

381   Goldstein, Julius. *Wandlungen in der Philosophie der Gegenwart: Mit besonderer Berücksichtigung des Problems von Leben und Wissenschaft*. Leipzig: W. Klinkhardt, 1911, vii, 171. The author deals with four basic topics: rationalism, and the philosophies of William James, Henri Bergson, and Rudolph Eucken.

382   Gould, F. J. "Bergson and Balfour." *Literary Guide and Rationalist Review*, N.S. No. 185, November 1911, 163-164.

383   Gourmont, Jean de. "Iziashchnaia slovesnost' Frantsii." *Apollon*, 2, No. 7, 1911, 70-71.

384   Grivet, Jules. "La Théorie de la personne d'après Henri Bergson." *Etudes par des Pères de la Compagnie de Jésus*, 129, No. 4, 1911, 449-485. This is an account of Bergson's lectures at the Collège de France on the concept of personality. It is reprinted in *Mélanges*, Ed. André Robinet, pp. 847-875. (Cf. P. Soulez, 1976)

385   Guy-Grand, Georges. *La Philosophie syndicaliste.* Paris: Grasset, 1911, 237.
       Bergson is discussed on pp. 34-51, 123-124, 144-147, and elsewhere.

386   Guy-Grand, Georges. *Le Procès de la démocratie.* Paris: Armand Colin, 1911,
       326. The materials which make up this book were published in *Revue de
       Métaphysique et de Morale* in January, March, July, and September 1910.

387   Höffding, Harald. *Der menschliche Gedanke, sein Formen und seine Aufgaben,*
       Leipzig: O. R. Reisland, 1911, vi, 430. For references to Bergson Cf. pp. 18,
       35, 144, 321 ff.

388   Hoppenot, Henri. "Le Cours de M. Bergson." *Bulletin de la Semaine*, 8, No. 6,
       8 février 1911, 71-72. This is an account of Bergson's lectures on personality
       at the Collège de France.

389   Hulme, Thomas Ernest. "Mr. Balfour, Bergson and Politics." *New Age*, N.S. 10,
       November 9, 1911, 38-40. This is a letter.

390   Hulme, Thomas Ernest. "Bax on Bergson." *New Age*, N.S. 9, No. 14, August 3,
       1911, 328-330.

391   Hulme, Thomas Ernest. "Bergsonism." *New Age*, N.S. 10, No. 2, November 23,
       1911, 46-47. This is a letter.

392   Hulme, Thomas Ernest. "Bergsonism." *New Age*, N.S. 10, November 23, 1911,
       94. This is a letter.

393   Hulme, Thomas Ernest. "Bergsonism." *New Age*, N.S. 10, No. 4, 1911, 11.

394   Hulme, Thomas Ernest. "Bergsonism in Paris." *New Age*, N.S. 9, No. 8, July 22,
       1911, 189-100. This is a letter.

395   Hulme, Thomas Ernest. "Notes on Bergson. I." *New Age*, N.S. 9, No. 25, 1911,
       587-588.

396   Hulme, Thomas Ernest. "Notes on Bergson. II." *New Age*, N.S. 9, No. 26, 1911,
       610-611.

397   Hulme, Thomas Ernest. "Notes on Bergson. IV." *New Age*, N.S. 10, No. 5, 1911,
       110-112.

398   Hulme, Thomas Ernest. "Notes on the Bologna Congress." *New Age*, N.S. 8, No.
       26, 1911, 607-608.

399   Jacobsson, Malte. *Henri Bergson's intuitions filosofi.* Lund, Sweden: Lindstedt,
       1911, 40.

400   James, William. *Le Pragmatisme.* Bibliothèque de philosophie scientifique. Trans.
       E. Le Brun. Paris: Flammarion, 1911, 312. This book contains an introduction
       by Henri Bergson.

401   Jerusalem, William. *Introduction to Philosophy.* Trans. C. F. Saunders. London:
       Macmillian, 1911, 402.

402   Joussain, André. "Edouard Schuré et la renaissance de l'idéalisme romantique."
       Revue Politique et Littéraire, Revue Bleue, 49e Année, No. 1, ler juillet 1911,
       21-26.

403   Joussain, André. "L'Idée de l'inconscient et l'intuition de la vie." *Revue
       Philosophique de la France et de l'Etranger*, 71, No. 5, mai 1911, 467-493.
       The author discusses the concept of the unconscious, relating it to music and
       to poetry.

404   Landquist, John. "Henri Bergson." *Ord och Bild*, 20, 1911, 541-550. Also in
       Revue Scandinave, 2, 1911.

405   Langevin, Paul. "L'Evolution de l'espace et du temps." *Revue de Métaphysique et de Morale*, 19, No. 4, 1911, 455-466. This article is an analysis of the paradoxes of the Special Theory of Relativity. Possibly it influenced Bergson's attitudes in *Duration and Simultaneity*.

406   "Latest of Philosophers: Three Works Which Have Given Berson Wide Repute Among the World Thinkers." *New York Times Review of Books*, 60, No. 19,566, August 20, 1911, 503. This is a review of *Time and Free Will, Matter and Memory*, and *Creative Evolution*.

407   Legendre, Maurice. "L'Influence de la philosophie de M. Bergson. VI." *Mouvement Socialiste*, 30, No. 233, juillet août 1911, 120-123.

408   Levi, Adolfo. "La filosofia dell'esperienza: La filosofia dell'intuizione indifferenziata (Bergson e James)." *Rivista di psicologia applicata*, 7, No. 1, gennaio-febbraio 1911, 47-75.

409   Lindsay, Alexander Dunlap. *The Philosophy of Bergson*. London: Dent and Sons, Ltd., 1911, 274.

410   Lovejoy, Arthur Oncken. "The Meaning of Vitalism." *Science*, 33, No. 851, January-June 1911, 610-614. Bergson's "psycho-vitalism" is discussed on p. 614.

411   Lovejoy, Arthur Oncken. "Schopenhauer as an Evolutionist." *Monist*, 21, No. 2, April 1911, 195-222. References to Bergson may be found in this article.

412   Mabie, Hamilton W. "Some Books Worth Reading." *Outlook*, 99, No. 13, 25 November 1911, 781-785. This article contains (p. 783) a brief review of *Laughter* by Henri Bergson.

413   Maritain, Jacques. "L'Evolutionnisme de M. Bergson." *Revue de Philosophie*, 19, Nos. 9-10, septembre-octobre 1911, 467-540.

414   Maritain, Jacques. *L'Evolutionnisme de M. Bergson*. Montligeon, France: Imprimerie-Librairie de Montligeon, 1911, 76. "Extrait de la *Revue de Philosophie*, octobre 1911."

415   Mason, Joseph Warren Teets. "Professor Bergson's Principle." *Nation*, 93, No. 2402, July 1911, 13. This is a letter to the editor criticizing a review of *Matter and Memory*.

416   Review of *Matter and Memory* by Henri Bergson. *A.L.A. Booklist*, 7, No. 10, 1911, 409-410.

417   "Review of *Matter and Memory* by Henri Bergson." *Expository Times*, 22, No. 6, 1911, 265.

418   Review of *Matter and Memory* by Henri Bergson. *Monist*, 21, No. 2, 1911, 318-320.

419   "Review of *Matter and Memory* by Henri Bergson." *New York Times*, 16, August 20, 1911, 503.

420   McCabe, Joseph. "The Anti-rationalism of Bergson." *Literary Guide and Rationalist Review*, N.S. No. 184, October 1911, 147-149.

421   Ménard, Alphonse. *Analyse et critique des Principes de la psychologie de W. James*. Lyon: Imprimeries réunis, 1910; Paris: Félix Alcan, 1911, 466. The author argues on pp. 409-417 that James differs from Bergson over the nature of memory, recognition, and attention. James' preference for sensory-motor explanations of mental phenomena accounts for these differences.

422   Mentré, F. "La Tradition philosophique." *Revue de Philosophie*, 18, No. 2, 1911, 69-76.

423   Morland, Jacques. "Une Heure chez M. Bergson." *L'Opinion,*, 4e Année, No. 33, 19 août 1911, 241-242. This article is quoted in *Mercure de France*, 93, 16 septembre 1911, 413ff.

424   Muirhead, J. H. "Philosophy of Bergson." *Hibbert Journal*, 9, No. 4, July 1911, 895-907. This is a review of *Time and Free Will, Matter and Memory*, and *Creative Evolution*.

425   Müller, Aloys. *Problem des absoluten Raumes und seine Beziehung zum allgemeinen Raumproblem.* Braunschweig, Germany: Vieweg und Sohn, 1911, 154. Bergson is discussed on p. 56 and following.

426   Müller, Jean. "Henri Bergson, philosophe d'une renaissance ou ce que nous devons à Bergson." *Renaissance Contemporaine*, 24 avril 1911, 409-416.

427   Murry, John Middleton. "Art and Philosophy." *Rhythm*, 1, No. 1, Summer 1911, 9-12. The author, a leader in English *avant garde* literary and artistic affairs, here proposes one of the earliest explanantions, written in English, of the implications of Bergsonian philosophy for aesthetic theory. The author states: "The philosophy of Bergson has of late come to a tardy recognition in England. In France it is a living artistic force. It is the open avowal of the supremacy of the intuition, of the spiritual vision of the artist in form, in words and meaning." (p. 55).

428   "On the Nature of the Soul." *Athenaeum*, No. 4383, October 28, 1911, 524. This is a brief report on Bergson's first two lectures on the nature of the self at University College, London.

429   "New Conception of God as Creative Evolution." *Current Literature*, 51, No. 2, August 1911, 182-183. This is a review of recent articles on Bergson in England.

430   Palante, Georges. "L'Influence de la philosophie de M. Bergson. III." *Mouvement Socialiste*, 29, No. 230, avril 1911, 270-271.

431   Parodi, Dominique. "Intuition et raison." *Revue de Métaphysique et de Morale*, 19, No. 4, juillet 1911, 555-559.

432   "Review of *La Perception du changement* by Henri Bergson." *Athenaeum*, No. 4379, September 30, 1911, 387. This is a brief expository review which likens Bergson's philosophy to an artistic vision.

433   "Philosophie de Bergson." *Revue de la Solidarité*, juillet 1911.

434   "Review of *The Philosophy of Bergson* by A. D. Lindsay." *Athenaeum*, No. 4369, July 22, 1911, 96-97.

435   Pitkin, Walter B. "Review of *Time and Free Will* by Henri Bergson." *Psychological Bulletin*, 8, No. 5, 1911, 176-180. This review is both critical and highly affirmative. The author lauds Bergson's treatment of subjective time and of the free act, but criticizes Bergson's sharp distinction between quality and quantity, duration and space: "Bergson establishes the rich reality of time, but, alas! thinks it can be done only by virtually eviscerating space! Some day, perhaps, philosophers will not maltreat either" (p. 180).

436   "Professor Bergson on Laughter." *London Times Literary Supplement*, 10, No. 513, November 9, 1911, 445. This is a review of *Laughter* by Henri Bergson.

437   Rageot, Gaston. "Henri Bergson." *Le Temps*, No. 18263, 2 juillet 1911, 3.

438   Rey, Abel. "Le Congrès international de philosophie, Bologne, 6-11 avril 1911." *Revue Philosophique de la France et de l'Etranger*, 72, No. 7, juillet 1911, 1-22. The author discusses Bergson's address on philosophical intuition.

439   Roosevelt, Theodore. "The Search for Thruth in a Reverent Spirit." *Outlook*, 99, 2 December 1911, 819-826. This is a general account of Bergson's thought by a former American president.

440   Rougue, Alberto. "Le 4e Congrès international de philosophie." *Voprosy filosofii i psikhologii*, 22, 1911.

441   Roustan, Désiré. *Psychologie*. Vol. I of *Leçons de philosophie*. Paris: Delagrave, 1911, 510. The author's psychology is permeated with Bergson's ideas, especially those of *Matter and Memory*, as well as by those of Wm. James. Cf. esp., imagery, pp. 26-28; psychophysics, pp. 54-57; attention, pp. 101-104; memory, pp. 269-277; instinct, pp. 489-491.

442   Ruckmich, Christian A. "Summary of 'La Théorie des concepts chez M. Bergson et M. James' by René Jeanniere." *Philosophical Review*, 20, No. 5, 1911, 577-578.

443   Sabatier, Paul. *L'Orientation religieuse de la France actuelle*. Paris: Armand Colin, 1911, 320.

444   Schnippenkötter, J. "Henri Bergson und seine Philosophie." *Akademische Monatsblätter*, 23, 1911, 170.

445   Segond, Joseph. *La Prière: Essai de psychologie religieuse*. Paris: Félix Alcan, 1911, 364.

446   Séverac, J.-B. "Enquêtes: Influence de la philosophie de M. Bergson." *Mouvement Socialiste*, 29, No. 229, mars 1911, 183-184.

447   Sheffer, Henry M. "Freud and Bergson." *The Jewish Review*, 1, No. 6, 1911, 529-543.

448   Slosson, Edwin Emery. "Twelve Major Prophets of Today: Henri Bergson." *Independent*, 70, No. 3262, June 8, 1911, 1246-1261. This is a general account of Bergson's philosophy, containing many photographs.

449   Solomon, Joseph. *Bergson*. London: Constable and Co., 1911, 128. (Philosophies Ancient and Modern, No. 16)

450   Solomon, Joseph. "Review of *Creative Evolution* by Henri Bergson." *Mind*, 20, No. 79, July 1911, 432-433. This review includes a negative assessment of A. Mitchell's translation.

451   Solomon, Joseph. "Philosophy of Bergson." *Mind*, 20, No. 1, 1911, 15-40.

452   Solomon, Joseph. "The Philosophy of Bergson." *Fortnightly Review*, N.S. 90, No. 539, November 1, 1911, 1014-1031. This is a general review of Bergson's thought.

453   Sorel, Georges. "Sur L'Evolution créatrice." *L'Indépendant*, 1, mai 1911. The author defends Bergson against attacks by the right-wing Action française.

454   Stewart, J. McKellar. *Critical Exposition of Bergson's Philosophy*. New York: Macmillan, 1911, 304.

455   "Students Flock to Bergson to Learn New Philosophy." *New York Times*, 60, No. 19573, 27 August 1911, pt. 5, p 6:1. This concerns the popularity of Bergson's lectures at the Collège de France.

456 "Successo di Enrico Bergson." *Rivista di filosofia neoscolastica*, 3, No. 6, dicembre 1911, 614-630.

457 Taylor, Alfred Edward. "Review of *Matter and Memory* by Henri Bergson." *International Journal of Ethics*, 22, No. 1, October 1911, 101-107. The author criticizes Bergson's "lack of thorough grounding in epistemological criticism."

458 Taylor, Alfred Edward. "Review of *Time and Free Will* by Henri Bergson." *International Journal of Ethics*, 21, No. 3, April 1911, 350-352. The author denies Bergson's thesis that "spatial" and "measurable" are equivalent.

459 Thompson, J. Arthur. "Biological Philosophy." *Nature*, 86, No. 2189, october 12, 1911, 475-477. This is a laudatory review of the English translation of *Creative Evolution* by a leading British biologist. The author states the major assumptions of Bergson's biology, concluding that while Bergson's "nature poetry" is in no sense biology, it may be "a very important complement."

460 Review of *Time and Free Will* by Henri Bergson. *A.L.A. Booklist*, 7, No. 10, 1911, 410.

461 "Über die gegenwärtige Aufgabe der Philosophie." *Logos*, 2, No. 1, 1911-1912, 126-127. This is a review of Bergson's address on philosophical intuition at the 4th International Philosophical Congress.

462 Visan, Tancrède de. *L'Attitude du lyrisme contemporain*. Paris: Mercure de France, 1911, 476. The last chapter of this study concerns Bergson and symbolism and appears on pp. 125-140.

463 Visan, Tancrède de. "Review of *Kant: Choix de textes* by René Gillouin and *H. Bergson: Choix de textes* by René Gillouin." *Revue de Philosophie*, 18, No. 1, janvier 1911, 101-102.

464 W., B. C. A. "Review of *Creative Evolution* by Henri Bergson." *Dublin Review*, 149, No. 298, 1911, 392-395.

465 *Westminster Review*, 175, No. 6, 1911, 699. The reviewer comments chiefly on A. Mitchell's translation of *Creative Evolution*, which he commends.

466 Walker, Leslie J. "L'Evolutionisme dans la théorie de la connaissance et de la vérité." *Revue de Philosophie*, 19, Nos. 9-10, septembre-octobre 1911, 417-466.

467 Ward, James. *The Realm of Ends*. Cambridge, England: University Press, 1911, 490. Bergson is mentioned on pp. 306-307.

468 Wize, K. F. "Der vierte Kongress für die Philosophie in Bologna." *Vierteljahrschrift für wissenschaftliche Philosophie*, 35, No. 4, 1911, 459-483. Bergson is discussed on pp. 464-466.

469 Wolf, A. "The Philosophy of Bergson." *The Jewish Review*, 2, No. 3, 1911, 204-233.

470 Zanta, Léontine. "La posizione del Bergson di frontragli studi psichici." *Luce e ombra*, 11, No. 2, febbrao 1911.

1912

471 Aliotta, Antonio. *La reazione idealistica contro la scienza*. Palermo: Casa editrice "Optima," 1912, 526.

472 Antonelli, E. "Bergson et le mouvement social contemporaine." *Neue Schweizer Rundschau*, 1912, 627-635, 809-816. This study is devoted to a discussion of Bergson and syndicalism, Marxism, and neo-Catholicism.

473 "Art. VI. Laughter" *Edingburgh Review*. 215, No. 440, April, 1912, 383-404. This is a review of several books, including *Laughter* by Henri Bergson.

474 Babbit, Irving. "Bergson and Rousseau." *Nation*, 95, No. 2472, 1912, 452-455.

475 Babbit, Irving. "Bergson et Rousseau." (Trans. Jeanne Scaltiel.) *Revue Bleue*, 50, No. 2, 1912, 725-730.

476 Baeumker, Claus. "Philosophie." *Philosophisches Jahrbuch der Görresgesellschaft*, 25, No. 1, 1912, 1-23.

477 Baeumker, Clemens. *Anschauung und Denken*. Paderborn: Schöningh, 1912 viii, 156.

478 Baldwin, James Mark. "Intuition." *American Year Book*. New York and London: Appleton and Company, 1912, 673-674. This is a brief, general account of Bergson's thought.

479 Baldwin, James Mark. "Psychology and Philosophy." In *The American Yearbook*. New York and London: D. Appleton & Co., 1912, 671-675. On pp. 673-675, the author explains Bergson's "alogism" and his concept of intuition. He emphasizes differences between Bergson's "alogism" and pragmatism.

480 Balsillie, David. *An Examination of Professor Bergson's Philosophy*. London: Williams and Nordgate, 1912, xii, 228.

481 Baratona, A. "L'ultimo libro di Bergson." *Rivista de filosofia*, Anno 4, No. 3, 1912.

482 Barr, Nann Clark. "The Dualism of Bergson." *Philosophical Review*, 22, No. 6, 1912, 629-652. The author argues that Bergson seeks to overcome his dualism in the mutual dependence of life and matter. But for a real synthesis life and matter must be processes constitutive of a self.

483 Baumker, Claus. "Über die Philosophie von Henri Bergson." *Philosophisches Jahrbuch der Gutberletgesellschaft*, 25, 1912, 1-23.

484 Benda, Julien. *Le Bergsonisme ou une philosophie de la mobilité*. Paris: Mercure de France, 1912, 134. This is the first of numerous attacks on Bergson, extending over many years, by the author.

485 *Review of Bergson*, by Joseph Solomon." *Athenaeum*, No. 4394, January 13, 1912, 37.

486 "Bergson and Balfour Discuss Philosophy." *Review of Reviews*, 44, No. 1, January 1912, 107-108.

487 "Bergson and a Critic." *Spectator*, 108, No. 4359, January 13, 1912, 61. This is a review of *Laughter* and of J. M. Stewart's *Critical Exposition*.

488 "Bergson on Comedy." *Living Age*, 272, No. 3526, February 3, 1912, 315-317. This review of *Laughter* by Henri Bergson was published originally in *The Outlook*. The reviewer concludes that "M. Bergson has chosen to illustrate his thesis in large part—indeed mainly—by reference to the theater, and he does not move with his accustomed mastery in the theater" (p. 317).

489 "Bergson Says World Needs a New System of Ethics." *New York Times*, 61, No. 19769, 10 March 1912, pt. 5, p. 6:1. This is an interview with Bergson, in Paris, by an unnamed New York Times reporter. Bergson here discusses his still unfinished study of ethics, his concept of philosophical method, his belief that the thoughts of philosophers in the long run rule the world. Bergson denies

that the ethical theory at which he may ultimately arrive will be either utilitarian or Kantian. He especially criticizes Kant, pointing out that the concept of a "universal law" is puzzling, while the question "What is duty?" remains unanswered. Concerning his study of ethics he states: "Similarly, now that I am studying ethics, there is a vast amount of work before me. I must study political economy and sociology—sociology, by the way, is very chaotic, I suppose, because it is so new. I believe it has a great future, but it may have to split into several different parts, as philosophy had long ago." A sketch of Bergson is included.

490 "Bergson's Intuitional Philosophy Justified by Sir Oliver Lodge." *Current Literature*, 52, No. 4, 1912, 433-445.

491 Bernard, E. "Bergson's Lebensbegriff und die moderne Umschau." *Tat*, 4, 1912, 239f.

492 Berrod, P. "La Philosophie de l'intuition." *Revue Philosophique de la France et de l'Etranger*, 74, No. 9, septembre 1912, 283-289.

493 Blacklock, W. "Bergson's Creative Evolution." *Westminster Review*, 177, No. 2, March 1912, 343-347.

494 Bode, Boyd Henry. "Review of *Creative Evolution* by Henri Bergson", translated by A. Mitchell." *American Journal of Psychology*, 23, No. 2, April 1912, 333-335.

495 Bonnet, Henri. "A Propos des théories de M. Bergson." *Société Nouvelle*, 2e Série, 46, No. 4, octobre 1912, 26-37. The author is highly critical of Bergson's theories.

496 Bosanquet, Bernard. *The Principle of Individuality and Value*. London: Macmillan, 1912, 409. Bergson is discussed on pp. 32-34, 54n, 94, 102n, 107n, 134, 137, 150, 168n, 172, 177n, 204-208, 230, 259, and 355.

497 Bourdeau, Jean. *La Philosophie affective: Nouveaux courants et nouveaux problèmes de la philosophie contemporaine: Descartes et Schopenhauer, W. James et M. Bergson, M. Th. Ribot et Alf. Fouillée, Tolstoi et Leopardi*. Paris: Félix Alcan, 1912, 181.

498 Bréhier, Émile. "La Philosophie d'Henri Bergson." *Revue Hebdomadaire des Cours et des Conférences*, 20, No. 2, 2 mai 1912, 337-346. This is a lecture given at the Université d'Oviedo, March 1912.

499 Bréhier, Émile. *Schelling*. Paris: Félix Alcan, 1912, 314. (Les Grands Philosophes) The author concludes that thought Schelling was a "positivistic intuitionist", his philosophy was incomplete, unproductive. Schelling too often sought to follow the continuity of becoming through the identity of its moments. "Il manqua à Schelling, pour remplir ces tâches, le goût et le sens de le psychologie qui caractérisent en France le fondateur d'un positivisme des données immédiates de la conscience, M. Bergson." (p. 306).

500 Brown, William. "The Philosophy of Bergson." *Church Quarterly Review*, 74, No. 2, April 1912, 126-142. This is a review of *Time and Free Will*, *Matter and Memory*, *Creative Evolution*, Stewart's *Critical Exposition of Bergson's Philosophy*, and Balsillie's *Examination of Professor Bergson's Philosophy*.

501 Calcagno, Alberto. "Henri Bergson e la cultura contemporaneo." *Rivista filosofica*, 4, No. 4, luglio-ottobre 1912, 407-431. This article maintains that the paradoxical

success of Bergson's philosophy is due to its apparent success in providing a new synthesis of nature and spirit, so long and so unhappily separated since their union in Greek thought.

502   Caldecott, A. "Review of *The Philosophy of Bergson* by A. D. Lindsay." *The Sociological Review*, 5, No. 1, 1912, 68-69. This is an expository, largely favorable review. The reviewer concludes that "the sociologist will see something of how higher intuitions effectually inform and guide the process of moulding into scientific knowledge the manifold..." (p. 69).

503   Calkins, Mary Whiton. "Henri Bergson: Personalist." *Philosophical Review*, 21, No. 6, November 1912, 666-675. The author protests against the "abstractness" of many evaluations of Bergson.

504   Carlile, William W. "Perception and Intersubjective Intercourse." *Mind*, 21, No. 84, October 1912, 508-521. On pp. 513 the author discusses James Ward's views with reference to Bergson.

505   Carr, Herbert Wildon. "Review of *Modern Science and the Illusions of Professor Bergson* by Hugh S. R. Elliot." *Mind*, 21, No. 84, October 1912, 579-581. The author is highly critical of Elliot's criticisms of Bergson.

506   Carr, Herbert Wildon. *Henri Bergson: The Philosophy of Change*. London: T. C. and E. C. Jack, 1912, 91. (People's Books, No. 26)

507   Carus, Paul. "The Anti-intellectual Movement of Today." *Monist*, 22, No. 3, July 1912, 397-404.

508   Chiappelli, Allesandro. *Idee e figure moderne*. Ancona: Puccini e Figli, 1912, 175. Spencer, Tolstoi, James, Bergson, and others are discussed in this study.

509   Clark, H. "Review of *Laughter* by Henri Bergson." *Review of Theology and Philosophy*, 7, 1912, 509.

510   Coimbra, Leonardo. *O criacionismo: Esboço de um sistema filosófico*. Pôrto: Biblioteca da Renascença, 1912, 311.

511   Cor, Raphaël. *Essais sur la sensibilité contemporaine: Nietzsche: De M. Bergson à M. Bazaillas: M. Claude Debussy*. Paris: Falque, 1912, 209.

512   Costelloe, Karin (née Stephen). "What Bergson Means by 'Interpenetration'." *Proceedings of the Aristotelian Society*, 13, 1912-1912, 131-155. It is argued here that the notion of interpenetration is absolutely essential to Bergson's philosophy.

513   "Review of 'Creative Evolution and the Philosophic Doubt' by Arthur J. Balfour in *Hibbert Journal*." *Revue de   étaphysique et de Morale*, 20, No. 4, 1912, Supplément, 27-29.

514   "Review of *Creative Evolution* by Henri Bergson." *Lancet*, 181, 10 February 1912, 1710-1711. The reviewer states: "The scientific atmosphere is thus especially favourable to the acceptance, or at all events to the consideration of Bergson's views..." p. 1711. Cf. Letters to the editor by R. F. Licorish, George Henslow and Ch. Walker, 1912.

515   Crespi, Angelo. "Lo spirito della filosofia de Bergson: I. L'analisi bergsoniana." *Cultura contemporanea*, 4, Nos. 7-8, 10-11, 1912.

516   "Review of *Critical Exposition of Bergson's Philosophy* by J. M. K. Stewart." *London Quarterly Review*, 118, No. 2, April 1912, 358-359.

517   "Review of *A Critical Exposition of Bergson's Philosophy* by J. McKellar Stewart."
       Saturday Review, 113, No. 2944, March 30, 1912, 398-399.

518   Croce, Benedetto. "Noterelle di estetica: 3. Bergson e Taine." *Critica*, 10, No. 6,
       1912, 479-481.

519   David, J. WŁ. "Okolo Bergsonismu." *Krytyka*, 14, No. 12, 1912, 344-353; 15,
       Nos. 1-2, 1912, 1-10; No. 3, 1912, 99-111; No. 4, 1912, 181-189; No. 5,
       1912, 239-252; No. 6, 1912, 311-326.

520   Davidson, W. T. "Bergson in England." *London Quarterly Review*, 117, No. 1,
       January 1912, 123-126.

521   De Laguna, Theodore. "Review of *La Pensée et les nouvelles écoles anti-intellec-
       tualistes* by Alfred Fouillée." *Journal of Philosophy*, 9, No. 16, 1 August 1912,
       498-500.

522   Della Seta, U. "L'intuizione della filosofia de Enrico Bergson." *Ultra*, 6, 1912.

523   Desaymard, Joseph. *La Pensée de Bergson*. Paris: Mercure de France, 1912, 78.
       (Les Hommes et les idées, No. 25)

524   Dewey, John. "Perception and Organic Action." *The Journal of Philosophy*, 9,
       No. 24, November 1912, 645-668. Dewey, in this essay, makes a critical analysis
       of Bergson's theory of perception, as expressed in *Matter and Memory*.

525   Dewey, John. "Review of *Modern Science and the Illusions of Professor Bergson*
       by Hugh Elliot." *Philosophical Review*, 21, 1912, 705-707. In this review Dewey
       criticizes a mechanistic critic of Bergson's philosophy.

526   Dimnet, Ernest. "Another French View of Laughter." *Saturday Review*, 113, No.
       2945, April 6, 1912, 420-422. This article is a critical response to a review of
       Bergson's *Laughter* by John Palmer in the March 23, 1912, issue of the *Saturday
       Review*. The author argues that Palmer misunderstands the French, who are
       quite capable of non-cerebral laughter, and that Bergson is by no means a typical
       Frenchman.

527   Dimnet, Ernest. *Edinburgh Review*, 215, No. 440, 1912, 383-404. This is a review
       of books on laughter by William Hazlitt, Herbert Spencer, George Meredith,
       James Sully, and Henri Bergson. The author concludes that "M. Bergson has
       been so struck by a certain aspect or part of the comic that he has taken it to
       cover the whole" (p. 397).

528   Dolson, Grace Neal. "Review of *De Kant à Bergson* by C. Coignet." *Philosophical
       Review*, 21, No. 3, May 1912, 380-381.

529   Dumesnil, Georges. "La Sophistique contemporaine." *Amitié de France*, février-
       avril, mai-juillet, août-octobre 1912.

530   Dumesnil, Georges. *La Sophistique contemporaine: Petit Examen de la philosophie
       de mon temps: Métaphysique, science, morale, religion*. Paris: Beauchesne,
       1912. The author presents many criticisms of Bergson and Bergsonism.

531   Durban, William. "The Philosophy of Henri Bergson." *Homiletic Review*, 63, No.
       1, January 1912, 20-23.

532   Dwelshauvers, Georges. "Evolution et durée dans la philosophie de Bergson."
       Revue de l'Université de Bruxelles, 18, No. 1, octobre 1912, 21-66. In the first
       half of this article the author describes the main outlines of Bergson's philosophy.
       In the second half he evaluates its significance.

533   Eisler, Rudolf. *Philosophen-lexicon*. Berlin: Siegfried Müller und Sohn, 1912,
       889. Bergson is discussed on pp. 57-60.

534   Elliot, Hugh S. R. *Modern Science and the Illusions of Professor Bergson*. Pref. Sir Ray Lankester. London: Longmans, Green and Company, 1912, 257. The author is highly critical. He assumes a mechanistic view of science and denies that Bergson's philosophy has any foundation in fact.

535   Eucken, Rudolph. *Main Currents of Modern Thought*. Trans. Meyrick Booth. London and Leipzig: Unwin, 1912, 488. Bergson and Oliver Lodge are discussed on pp.185-189.

536   Ewald, Oscar. "Philosophy in Germany in 1911." *Philosophical Review*, 21, No. 5, September 1912, 499-526. Bergson is discussed on pp. 523-525.

537   "Review of *Examination of Professor Bergson's Philosophy* by David Balsillie." *Revue de Métaphysique et de Morale*, 20, No. 4, 1912, Supplément, 25.

538   "Review of *An Examination of Professor Bergson's Philosophy* by David Balsillie." *Athenaeum*, No. 4401, 2 March 1912, 249.

539   Farges, Albert. "La Notion bergsonienne du temps." *Revue Néo-scolastique de Philosophie*, 19, No. 75, 1912, 337-378.

540   Farges, Albert. *La Philosophie de M. Bergson, professeur au Collège de France: Exposé et critique*. Paris: Maison de la Bonne Presse, 1912, 491.

541   Fawcett, Edward Douglas. "Matter and Memory." *Mind*, 21, No. 82, April 1912, 201-232. This is a discussion of Bergson's mind-body dualism, with special emphasis on the "spatiality" of matter.

542   Flint, F. S. "Contemporary French Poetry." *The Poetry Review*, 1, No. 8, August 1912, 357-414. The author introduces French Poetry of the pre-1914 generation to an English audience. He credits Bergson with having formulated the "intuitive" philosophy of this generation. He cites René Arcos as a poet strongly influenced by Bergson.

543   Florence, Jean. "Nature et méthode de la philosophie." *Phalange*, 7, 20 juillet 1912, 1-15.

544   Florence, Jean. "Réponse à M. Julien Benda." *Phalange*, 7, 20 septembre 1912, 278-285.

545   Forsyth, T. "Review of *Matter and Memory* by Henri Bergson." *Review of Theology and Philosophy*, 7, 1912, 451-455.

546   Gagnebin, Samuel. *La Philosophie de l'intuition: Essai sur les idées de M. Edouard Le Roy*. St. Blaise, France: Foyer Solidariste, 1912, 240. The first third of the book is devoted to the philosophy of Bergson. It is reviewed in *Revue de Philosophie*, 12, 7 août 1912.

547   Gardiner, H. N. "Review of *Laughter: An Essay on the Meaning of the Comic* by Henri Bergson." *Psychological Bulletin*, 9, No. 9, 1912, 354-358. This review is both explanatory and critical. The essentials of Bergson's theory of laughter are explained. On p. 358, the reviewer states: "And if comic laughter has a social function, as it doubtless has, and its spirit is akin to that of play, is it not at least as plausible to find that function in the serviceable relaxation it affords to the strain and stress of life as in the chastisement it inflicts on lapses from its 'requirements'?"

548   Gaudeau, B. "La Philosophie de M. Bergson détruit la liberté." *L'Univers*, 16 juin 1912.

549   Gaultier, Paul. "L'Oeuvre philosophique de M. Emile Boutroux." *Revue des Deux Mondes*, 11, No. 6, 15 octobre 1912, 837-871.

550   Gerrard, Thomas John. "Bergson, Newman and Aquinas." *Catholic World*, 96, No. 576, March 1912, 748-762.

551   Gillouin, René. *Idées et figures d'aujourd'hui*. Paris: Grasset, 1912, 267. The concluding chapter of this book concerns Henri Bergson.

552   Gillouin, René. "L'Influence de la philosophie de M. Bergson. VII." *Mouvement Socialiste*, 31, No. 238, février 1912, 132-133.

553   Goblot, Edmond. "A Propos de la philosophie de Bergson." *Le Volume*, 24, No. 34, 18 mai 1912, 537-539.

554   Goetz, Philip Becker. "Bergson." *Open Court*, 26, No. 9, September 1912, 572. This is a poem.

555   Goldbeck. "Review of *Einführung in die Metaphysik* by Henri Bergson." *Zeitschrift für den physikalischen und chemikalischen Unterricht*, 25, 1912, 66f.

556   Guastella, Cosmo. *L'infinito*. Palermo: Libreria Internazionale, Alberto Reber, 1912, 172. Criticisms of Bergson's concept of continuity are offered on pp. 121-123 and 129. The author argues against Bergson that reality is essentially discrete and continuity is only a metaphysical chimera.

557   Gundolf, Ernst. "Die Philosophie Henri Bergsons." *Jahrbuch für die geistige Bewegung*, 1912, 32-92.

558   Guy-Grand, Georges. "Un Grand Philosophe de la vie: M. Bergson." *La Vie*, 1, 4 mai 1912.

559   Harper, James Wilson. *Christian Ethics and Social Progress*. London: James Nisbet and Co., 1912, 285. This study contains chapters on Bergson.

560   Hébert, Marcel. "M. Bergson et son affirmation de l'existence de Dieu." *Revue de l'Université de Bruxelles*, 17, Nos. 8-9, mai-juin 1912, 609-616. This essay concerns Bergson's mention of God in *Creative Evolution*. It was also published in *Coenobium*, June 1912, 1-7.

561   Hébert, Marcel. *M. Bergson et son affirmation de l'existence de Dieu*. Brüssel: Weissenbruch, 1912, 8. This appeared first in *Revue de l'Université de Bruxelles*, May-June 1912.

562   "Review of *Henri Bergson: The Philosophy of Change* by H. Wildon Carr." *Athenaeum*, No. 4401, 2 March 1912, 249.

563   Henry, J. "Pragmatisme anglo-américain et philosophie nouvelle." *Revue Néo-Scholastique de Philosophie*, 19, No. 2, Mai 1912, 264-272. The author distinguishes sharply between the pragmatism of William James and F. C. S. Schiller and the "new philosophy" associated with Henri Bergson. Pragmatism begins with epistemology and is compatible with different sorts of metaphysics. Bergson, by contrast, begins with a metaphysics: radical evolutionism.

564   Henslow, George. "M. Bergson's *Creative Evolution*." *Lancet*, 182, 17 February 1912, 456. The author cites those who have dealt with the "new teleology" other than Bergson, namely, Henslow himself, H. H. Church, and Alfred Russell Wallace. This is a letter to the editor.

565   Hermann, E. *Eucken and Bergson: Their Significance for Christian Thought*. London: James Clark and Co., 1912, 244.

566   Hermit of Prague (Pseud.). "Review of *Modern Science and the Illusions of Professor Bergson* by Hugh S. R. Elliot." *Bedrock*, 1, No. 3, July 1912, 277-280.

567   Heymans, Gérard. "Die philosophie van Henri Bergson." *Tijdschrift voor Wijsbegeerte*, 5, No. 2, 1912, 205-238.

568   Hicks, G. Dawes. "The Nature of Willing." *Proceedings of the Aristotelian Society*, 13, 1912-1913, 27-65. This essay calls attention to "certain fundamental considerations in the psychology of volition that have important bearing upon the positions...of James and Bergson." The nature of volition does not entail anti-intellectualism, according to the author.

569   Hicks, G. Dawes. "Survey of Recent Philosophical and Theological Literature: Philosophy." *Hibbert Journal*, 10, No. 2, January 1912, 477-488. Recent Bergson literature is discussed on pp. 479-480.

570   Hocking, William Ernest. *The Meaning of God in Human Experience*. New Haven, Connecticut: Yale University Press; London: Henry Frowde, 1912, 586. Bergson, logic, and space are discussed on pp. 80-89.

571   Hoernlé, R. F. A. "The Analysis of Volition: Treated as a Study of Psychological Principles and Methods." *Proceedings of the Aristotelian Society*, N.S. 13, 1912-1913, 156-189. Bergson is discussed on pp. 163-167 and 180-181.

572   Hookham, George. "Further Notes on Bergson's Philosophy." *National Review*, 69, No. 350, April 1912, 325-336.

573   Hookham, George. "Professor Bergson as a Critic of Darwin." *National Review*, 69, No. 349, March 1912, 100-118.

574   Hugel, Baron Friedrich von. *Eternal Life: Its Implications and Applications*. Edinburgh: Clark, 1912, 443. Bergson is discussed on pp. 288-302 and elsewhere.

575   Hulme, Thomas Ernest. "Bergson in English." *Cambridge Magazine*, 1, No. 10, April 27, 1912, 265. This is a letter.

576   Hulme, Thomas Ernest. "Bergson in English." *Cambridge Magazine*, 1, No. 12, May 18, 1912, 353. This is a letter.

577   Hulme, Thomas Ernest. "Notes on Bergson." *New Age*, N.S. 10, No. 17, 1912, 359.

578   Hulme, Thomas Ernest. "Notes on Bergson. V." *New Age*, N.S. 10, No. 17, 1912, 401-403. Cf. Bergson's letter of recommendation for Hulme, 1912.

579   Hunt, Harriet E. *The Psychology of Auto-education: Based on the Interpretation of Intellect Given by Henri Bergson in his "Creative Evolution": Illustrated in the Work of Maria Montessori*. Syracuse, New York: Bardeen, 1912, 82.

580   Husband, Mary Gilliland. "Review of *L'Evolution créatrice* by Henri Bergson." *International Journal of Ethics*, 22, No. 4, July 1912, 462-467. This review gives a very general account of Bergson's position in *L'Evolution créatrice*.

581   "Review of *An Introduction to Metaphysics* by Henri Bergson." *Boston Transcript*, December 4, 1912, p. 25.

582   "Review of *An Introduction to Metaphysics* by Henri Bergson." *Independent*, 73, No. 3339, November 28, 1912, p. 1259. This is a review of both English translations (by Hulme and by Littman) of *An Introduction to Metaphysics*.

583   "Is the Bergson Philosophy that of a Charlatan?" *Current Literature*, 52, No. 2, February 1912, 198-199. The author provides a balanced assessment of Bergson's popularity.

584   Jacoby, Gunther. "Bergson, Pragmatism and Schopenhauer." *Monist*, 22, No. 3, October 1912, 593-611.

585   Jordan, Bruno. "Kant and Bergson." *Monist*, 22, No. 3, July 1912, 404-414. This article is translated from German.

586   Joussain, André. "L'Expansion du bergsonisme et la psychologie musicale." *Revue Politique et Littéraire, Revue Bleue*, 50e Année, No. 24, 15 juin 1912, 758-763. This is a discussion of contemporary French romanticism, with special reference to A. Schopenhauer, Bergson, and Bergson's "disciple" Albert Bazaillas. The author briefly discusses Bazaillas' conception of the unconscious, discusses the development of modern music.

587   Joussain, André. "Review of *La Philosophie de l'intuition: Essai sur les idées de M. Edouard Le Roy* by Samuel Gagnebin." *Revue Philosophique de la France et de l'Etranger*, 74, No. 8, août 1912, 191-193.

588   Kallen, Horace M. "Review of *Laughter: An Essay on the Meaning of the Comic* by Henri Bergson." *The Journal of Philosophy*, 9, No. 11, May 23, 1912, 303-305.

589   Keller, H. "Review of *Materie und Gedächtnis* by Henri Bergson." *Archiv für die gesamte Psychologie. Referate*, 23, 1912, 98-100.

590   Keyserling, Herman Graf. "Das Wesen der Intuition und Ihre Rolle in der Philosophie." *Logos*, 3, No. 1, 1912, 59-79.

591   Khlopov, I. "K voprosu o prirode intuitsii." *Voprosy filosofi f psikhologii*, 23, No. 5, 1912, 667-703.

592   Lalande, André. "Philosophy in France, 1911." *Philosophical Review*, 21, No. 1912, 279-302.

593   Larsson, Hans. *Intuitionsproblemet: Särskilt med hänsyn till Henri Bergsons teori*. Stockholm: Bonnier, 1912, 84.

594   "Laughter." *Edinburgh Review*, 285, No. 440, April 1912, 383-404. Five books on the subject of laughter are discussed in this review. Bergson's views are discussed on pp. 392-397.

595   "Review of *Laughter: An Essay on the Meaning of the Comic* by Henri Bergson." *North American Review*, 195, June 1912, 859-861.

596   "Review of *Laughter* by Henri Bergson." *American Journal of Psychology*, 23, No. 2, April 1912, 342.

597   "Review of *Laughter* by Henri Bergson." *Athenaeum*, No. 4393, 1912, 5. This is a perceptive, critical review. The reviewer concludes:"But, rather than laugh at others' lameness, why not laugh at our own superabundant energy which bids us, instead of walking, seek to fly in the air? And, meanwhile, let us, as men and philosophers, none the less seek to fly. There is a lightness inherent in laughter of the purer kind that may suffice to save us from any serious fall."

598   "Review of *Laughter* by Henri Bergson." *Dial*, 52, No. 616, February 16, 1912, 136.

599   "The Laughter of the French." *Saturday Review*, 113, No. 2943, Marhc 23, 1912, 362-363. The reviewer argues that Bergson has explained not the laughter of humanity, but the laughter of the "highly intellectual" French.

600   Le Dantec, Félix. *Contre la métaphysique: Question de méthode*. Paris: Félix Alcan, 1912, 255. (Bibliothèque de philosophie contemporaine) On pp. 227-239 the author attacks the crucial distinction (made by G. Bohn and Bergson) between intelligence, found essentially among vertebrates, and instinct, a faculty found

among arthropods.

601 Lee, Vernon. *Vital Lies: Studies of Some Varieties of Recent Obscurantism.* 2 Vols. London: John Lane, 1912. Bergson's name appears often in this study, especially in connection with the syndicalist doctrines of Georges Sorel. The author, however, does not examine Bergson's philosophy in detail. (Vernon Lee is a synonym for Violet Paget.)

602 Lenoble, Eugène. "Bergson." *Revue du Clergé Français*, 69, No. 416, 15 mars 1912, 715-725. This is a review of Bergson's "L'Intuition philosophique."

603 Le Roy, Edouard. "A Propos de l'intuition bergsonienne." *Revue du Mois*, 13, No. 78, 10 juin 1912, 733-735. Le Roy replies to Julien Benda's criticisms of Bergson's concept of intuition.

604 Le Roy, Edouard. "Une Philosophie nouvelle: M. Henri Bergson: I. La Méthode. II. La Doctrine." *Revue des Deux Mondes*, 6e période, 7, ler février 1912, 551-580; 15 février 1912, 800-833. Cf. Bergson's affirmative response to Le Roy, 1912.

605 Licorish, R. F. "Bergson's *Creative Evolution* and the Nervous System in Organic Evolution." *Lancet*, 182, February 10, 1912, 391-392. Lamarckian criticisms of Bergson are proposed in this article.

606 Lippman, Walter. "Bergson's Philosophy." *New York Times Review of Books*, 62, No. 20021, Part 6, November 17, 1912, 665-666. This is a review of *An Introduction to Metaphysics.*

607 Lippmann, Walter. "The Most Dangerous Man in the World." *Everybody's Magazine*, 27, No. 1, July 1912, 100-101. The author proposes that: "Bergson is not so much a prophet as a herald in whom the unrest of modern times has found a voice." (100).

608 Lodge, Sir Oliver. "Balfour and Bergson." *Hibbert Journal*, 10, No. 2, January 1912, 290-307. This article is reprinted in Sir Oliver Lodge, *Modern Problems.*

609 Lodge, Sir Oliver. "Bergson's Intuitional Philosophy Justified." *Current Literature*, 52, No. 4, April 1912, 443-445.

610 Lodge, Sir Oliver. *Modern Problems.* London: Methuen; New York: Doran, 1912, 348. An essay entitled "Balfour and Bergson" appears on pp. 26-57.

611 Lovejoy, Arthur Oncken. "The Problem of Time in Recent French Philosophy: I. Renouvier and Recent Temporalism." *Philosophical Review*, 21, No. 1, January 1912, 10-31.

612 Lovejoy, Arthur Oncken. "The Problem of Time in Recent French Philosophy: II. Temporalism and Anti-intellectualism : Bergson." *Philosophical Review*, 21, No. 3, May 1912, 322-343. The author argues that Bergson's concept of time is paradoxical and makes him an extreme anti-intellectual. But Bergson also has a quantitative conception of time, which is more acceptable. Cf. Lovejoy's *The Reason, the Understanding, and Time* (1961) for Bergson's response.

613 Lovejoy, Arthur Oncken. "The Problem of Time in Recent French Philosophy: III. Time and Continuity: Pillon, James." *Philosophical Review*, 21, No. 4, September 1912, 527-545. According to the author, Pillon's notion of time, with which Lovejoy agrees, eliminates Bergson's "difficulties" and agrees with one of James' three concepts of time.

614   Low, Sidney. "Mr. Balfour in the Study." *Edinburgh Review*, 216, No. 442, October 1912, 257-278. Bergson is discussed on pp. 268-271.

615   Lubac, Jean. *La Valeur du spiritualisme*. Paris: Grasset, 1912, 337.

616   Maire, Gilbert. "La Philosophie de Georges Sorel." *Cahiers du Cercle Proudhon*, 2, No. 2, mars-avril 1912, 57-81. This article contains part of a letter from Bergson explaining his relationship to Sorel. Cf. Henri Bergson, mars-avril 1912.

617   Maizière, G. "Une Philosophie moderne: M. Bergson." *Le Gaulois*, 1912.

618   Marcel, Gabriel. "Les Conditions dialectiques de la philosophie de l'intuition." *Revue de Métaphysique et de Morale*, 20, No. 5, 1912, 638-652. The author contends that intuition can have meaning only insofar as it is tested, verified.

619   Marchioli, E. "L'anima e l'evoluzione secondo Bergson." *Critica sociale*, No. 8, 1912.

620   Maritain, Jacques. "Les Deux Bergsonismes." *Revue Thomiste*, 20, No. 4, juillet-août 1912, 433-450.

621   Maritain, Jacques. *Les Deux Bergsonismes*. Toulouse, France: Edition Privat, 1912. The author distinguishes a "Bergsonism of fact" from a "Bergsonism of intention". Bergson's intentions may be excellent, but his philosophy, in fact, is insufficient.

622   Martin, Seymour. "Bergson: Creative Evolution." *Princeton Theological Review*, 10, No. 1, January 1912, 116-118.

623   "Review of *Materie und Gedächtnis* by Henri Bergson." *Zeitschrift für Pathopsychologie*, 1, 1912, 603-639.

624   Mayer, Willy. "Über die Störungen des 'wiederkennens': Eine kritische Untersuchung im Anschluss an *Matière et mémoire* von Henri Bergson." *Zeitschrift für Pathopsychologie*, 1, Mai 1912, 603-639. Bergson's theories of memory and perception are examined in this essay, which contains a criticism of Bergson's data, a search for verification by means of observations, a summary, and conclusion.

625   McGilvary, Evander Bradley. "Review of *Philosophy and Bergson* by A. D. Lindsay and *Critical Exposition of Bergson's Philosophy* by J. McKellar Stewart." *Philosophical Review*, 21, No. 5, September 1912, 598-602.

626   McGilvary, Evander Bradley. "The Two Theories of Consciousness in Bergson." *Journal of Philosophy*, 9, No. 13, 1912, 354-355.

627   Mellone, S. H. "Review of *La Perception du changement* by Henri Bergson." *Review of Theology and Philosophy*, 7, 1912, 647-654.

628   Meredith, J. C. "Critical Side of Bergson's Philosophy." *Westminster Review*, 167, No. 1, February 1912, 194-206.

629   Meyer, Adolf. "Pathopsychology and Psychopathology." *Psychological Bulletin*, 9, No. 4, 1912, 129-145. "English and French philosophy (Maudsley, Taine and Ribot, and lately also Bergson) has long appreciated the importance of pathology for psychology..." (p. 130).

630   Meyerson, Emile. *Identité et réalité*. 2e éd. Paris: Félix Alcan, 1912, 242. Cf. Bergson's review of the 1st edition, 1909.

631   "Review of *Modern Science and the Illusions of Professor Bergson* by Hugh S. R. Elliot." *Contemporary Review*, 101, No. 6, June 1912, 905-906.

632   "Review of *Modern Science and the Illusions of Professor Bergson* by Hugh S. R. Elliot." *Educational Review*, 44, No. 7, 1912, 210-211.

633   Moore, Addison W. "Bergson and Pragmatism. *Philosophical Review*, 21, No. 4, July 1912, 397-414. The author argues that Bergson is not a pragmatist. He suggests many criticisms of Bergson from a pragmatist standpoint.

634   Moore, Charles Leonard. "The Return of the Gods." *Dial*, 53, No. 634. November 16, 1912, 371-372.

635   Morgan, Conwy Lloyd. *Instinct and Experience*. New York: Macmillan; London: Methuen, 1912, 299. See especially Chapter VII, "The Philosophy of Instinct," 204-240.

636   Mories, A. S. "Bergson and Mysticism." *Westminster Review*, 177, No. 3, June 1912, 687-689.

637   Müller, Ernst. "Henri Bergson." *Archiv für systematische Philosophie*, N.S. 18, No. 2, 1912, 185-194.

638   Nève, Paul. *Le Pragmatisme et la philosophie de M. Bergson*. Louvain: Institut supérieur de philosophie, 1912, 38. This study is reprinted from *Annales de l'Institut Supérieur de Louvain*, 1912.

639   Nève, Paul. "Le Pragmatisme et la philosophie de M. Bergson." *Annales de l'Institute supérieur de Louvain*, 1, 1912, 173-210.

640   Overstreet, Harry Allen. "Mind and Body." *Psychological Bulletin*, 9, No. 1, 1912, 13-20. In this brief article the author reviews various recent attempts, including Bergson's, to deal with the mind-body problem. Bergson's concept of the self as ceaseless change is mentioned on p. 14; on pp. 17-18 his position is explained in general terms. The author states that "the one view which departs in a marked manner from the conventional modes of treatment of the problem is that of Bergson. The novelty of his view is due to his thought of perception as a means, not to knowledge, but to action" (p. 17).

641   Overstreet, Harry Allen. *Nation*, 94, No. 2432, 1912, 139-140. This is an expository review, which, however, contains some criticisms of the English translation of *Le Rire*.

642   Péladan, Joséphin. "L'Impressionisme philosophique: Le Bergsonisme." *Soleil*, 22 août 1912.

643   Peleger, André. "Le Bergsonisme en pratique." *Le Penseur*, 9, No. 4, 1912, 197-140; No. 6, 1912, 217-222; No. 7, 1912, 260-264. This is a rather satirical look at Bergson's philosophy.

644   "Review of *La Perception du changement* by Henri Bergson." *Revue de Métaphysique et de Morale*, 20, No. 2 (Supplément) 1912, 2.

645   "Periodical Literature. French." *The Sociological Review*, 5, No. 1, 1912, 81-82. The author recounts the substance of the article by Bergson in the November issue of the *Revue de Métaphysique et de Morale*, "L'Intuition philosophique." He also quotes from a "Bergsonian" article by Fr. d'Hautefeuille in the September issue of the *Revue de Métaphysique et de Morale*: "Morale normative et morale scientifique.

646   Perry, Ralph Barton. *Present Philosophical Tendencies*. New York: Longmans, Green, and Co., 1912, 383. A section entitled "Immediatism vs. Intellectualism" is on pp. 222-241; Bergson's concept of law is criticized on pp. 255-254; Bergson's theory of mind is discussed on pp. 299-301. These criticisms are

largely taken from the *Journal of Philosophy*, 1911.

647 "Review of *La Philosophie de l'intuition: Essai sur les idées de M. Edouard Le Roy* by Samuel Gagnebin." *Revue de Philosophie*, 12, No. 8, 1912, 463-466.

648 "The Philosophy of Henri Bergson." *Quarterly Review*, 216, No. 430, 1912, 152-177. This is a survey of Bergson's major writings.

649 Poulton, E. B. "Darwin and Bergson on the Interpretation of Evolution." *Bedrock*, 1, No. 2, April 1912, 48-65. This is a criticism of Bergson's vitalism and his concept of instinct. It contains a discussion of "mimicry."

650 Prager, Hans. "Schriften von Henri Bergson." *Zeitschrift für Philosophie und philosophische Kritik*, 145, No. 1, 1912, 88-93.

651 "Pressing forward into Space." *Nation*, 94, No. 2411, 11 April 1912, 355-356. This is a polemic against the current revolt among young American intellectuals obsessed with Henri Bergson's philosophy: "But when the Futurist paints a baby it is a metaphysical baby born in the Bergsonian philosophy and bred in revolt" (p. 356).

652 "Review of *The Principle of Individuality and Value* by Bernard Bosanquet." *The Sociological Review*, 5, No. 4, 1912, 368-370. The reviewer stresses Bosanquet's critique of Bergson's concepts of "intuition and "intellect." Intellect is according to Bosanquet neither repetitive nor analytic. The reviewer lauds Bosanquet's criticisms.

653 "Professor Bergson on the Soul." *Educational Review*, 43, No. 1, January 1912, 1-16. This is a summary of four lectures on the immortality of the soul given by Bergson in October, 1911, at the University of London. It is taken from articles in the London *Times*. (Cf. Henri Bergson, 1911, for bibliographic data and translations.)

654 "Professor Henri Bergson." *Open Court*, 26, No. 9, September 1912, 573.

655 Prout, F. R. "Review of 'L'Intuition philosophique' by Henri Bergson." *Philosophical Review*, 21, No. 2, March 1912, 295.

656 Robinson, Arthur. "Memory and Consciousness." *Proceedings of the Aristotelian Society*, 13, 1912-1913, 313-327. Several interesting criticisms of Bergson's concepts of memory and intelligence are offered by the author.

657 Rosenberg, Maximilian. "Die Erinnerungstäuschungen der 'reduplizierenden Paramnesie' und des 'déjà vu'" Ihre klinische Differenzierung und ihre psychologische Beziehung zueinander." *Zeitschrift für Pathopsychologie*, 1, Mai 1912, 561-602.

658 Roz, Firmin. "Review of *La Pensée contemporaine* by Paul Gaultier." *Correspondant*, N.S. 213, No. 4, 25 novembre 1912, 793-798.

659 Ruggiero, Guido de. *Filosofia contemporanea*. Bari, Italy: Laterza e Figli, 1912, 485. The articles "Bergson," which appears on pp. 203-214, and "I bergsoniani," on pp. 214-218, appeared originally in *La Cultura*, 1912.

660 Ruggiero, Guido de. *Lo svolgimento della filosofia di Bergson*. Trani, Italy: Ditta Vecchi, 1912, 12.

661 Ruggiero, Guido de. "Lo svolgimento della filosofia di Enrico Bergson." *La Cultura*, No. 4, 15 febrero 1912.

662 Russell, Bertrand. "On the Notion of Cause." *Proceedings of the Aristotelian Society*, 13, 1912-1913, 1-26. The author argues that Bergson misconstrues the

notion of causality which scientists actually use. Hence his "attack on science" fails.

663   Russell, Bertrand. "The Philosophy of Bergson." *Monist*, 22, No. 3, July 1912, 321-347. This is a famous criticism of Bergson's philosophy by a prominent English philosopher. The author holds that Bergson's intuition is mere instinct and therefore rooted in the past, unable to adapt to new circumstances and inimical to the intellect. Bergson's condemnation of mathematical conceptions of motion and time fails in the light of the new (Cantorian) concept of mathematical continuity. There is no reason to believe Bergson's philosophy is true. Cf. H. Wildon Carr. "Reply to Bertrand Russell" 1914. Cf. also Milič Čapek. *Bergson and Modern Physics*, 1971, pp. 335-345.

664   Russell, Bertrand. *The Philosophy of Bergson*. With a Reply by Mr. H. Wildon Carr, and a rejoinder by Mr. Russell. Chicago: Open Court, 1912, 27.

665   Russell, John E. "Bergson's Anti-intellectualism." *Journal of Philosophy*, 9, No. 3, February 1, 1912, 128-131. The author replies to Ralph Barton Perry's earlier criticisms of Bergson in the *Journal of Philosophy*.

666   Sanborn, Alvan F. "Henri Bergson: Pronounced 'The Foremost Thinker of France': His Personality, His Philosophy, and His Influence." *Century*, 85, No. 2, December 1912, 172-176. The author suggests insights into Bergson's character and personal life.

667   Schoen, H. "Heinrich Bergsons philosophischen Anschauungen." *Zeitschrift für Philosophie und philosophische Kritik*, 145, No. 2, Februar 1912, 40-129.

668   Schrecker, Paul. *Henri Bergsons Philosophie der Persönlichkeit*. München: Reinhardt, 1912, 61 (Schriften des Vereins für freie psychoanalytische Forschung, 3). Written by a disciple of Alfred Adler, this study suggests close parallels between Bergson and Adler, particularly as concerns Adler's and Bergson's concepts of memory.

669   Scott, J. W. "The Pessimism of Bergson." *Hibbert Journal*, 11, No. 1, October 1912, 99-116.

670   Segond, Joseph. "Les Antithèses du bergsonisme." *Annales de Philosophie Chrétienne*, 165, août 1912, 449-474.

671   Ségur, Nicolas. "La Philosophie à la mode: Le Bergsonisme." *Le Matin*, 25 juillet 1912.

672   Seta, Ugo della. *L'intuizione nella filosofia d Enrico Bergson*. Roma: Voghera, 1912, 26.

673   Smith, Norman Kemp. "Review of *Laughter* by Henri Bergson." *Hibbert Journal*, 11, No. 1, 1912, 220-225. The reviewer states that "the present work, as I shall try to show, is an excellent illustration both of the striking merits and of many doubtfully praiseworthy features in Bergson's thinking" (p. 220). The reviewer criticizes Bergson's method of exposition which, he holds, does not deal with recalcitrant facts and conceals basic assumptions—making them, therefore, immune to proof. The reviewer, however, agrees with the basic assumption underlying *Laughter*, i.e., that "tension and elasticity are the two complementary forces that life sets in play" (p. 223). He also commends Bergson's "essentially critical" attitude towards humor.

674 "Some Works on Philosophy." *Contemporary Review*, 192, No. 59, 1912, 290-295. This is a "review" of twelve books, most of them written by or about Bergson and William James. It is a collection of brief impressions. Bergson's *Time and Free Will*, James' *Some Problems of Philosophy* and *Memories and Studies* are among those works mentioned.

675 Stebbing, Lizzie Susan. "The Notion of Truth in Bergson's Theory of Knowledge." *Proceedings of the Aristotelian Society*, 13, 1912-1913, 224-256. The author argues against Bergson that philosophy is not "life" but "the interpretation of life by means of reason."

676 Stebbing, Lizzie Susan. Review of *Creative Evolution* by Henri Bergson. *The Sociological Review*, 5, No. 2, 1912, 161-166. The reviewer explains the basic features of Bergson's metaphysics and epistemology on pp. 161-165. On pp. 165-166 she advances criticisms of Bergson's method and conclusions: "What is the value of the method? From the point of view of metaphysical theory, it would seem to have no value at all. By definition, intuition is individual and incommunicable" (p. 165.).

677 Steinsilber, E. *Essai critique sur les idées philosophiques contemporaines*. Paris: Gauthier, 1912, xiv, 391.

678 Stewart, Herbert Leslie. *Questions of the Day in Philosophy and Psychology*. London: Edward Arnold, 1912, 284. Bergson's critique of psychophysics is discussed on pp. 24-25 and Bergson's attack on intellectualism on pp. 150-158.

679 Sujol, A. "Le Nouveau Spiritualisme de M. Henri Bergson." *Le Protestant*, 27e Année, No. 45, 9 novembre 1912, 353-355.

680 Sypkens, D. "De Evolutieleer van Henri Bergson." *Theologish Tijdschrift*, 46, Nos. 1-2, 1912, 158-190.

681 Taylor, Alfred Edward. "Creative Evolution by Henri Bergson." *International Journal of Ethics*, 22, No. 4, July 1912, 467-469. This is a largely appreciative review of Arthur Mitchell's translation with, however, certain criticisms of it.

682 Taylor, E. "Henri Bergson: A French Impression of the Philosopher." *Quest*, 4, No. 1, 1912, 328-334.

683 Tilgher, Adriano. "Io, libertà, e moralità nella filosofia di Enrico Bergson." *La Cultura*, 31, Nos. 22 and 23, 1912.

684 Tilgher, Adriano. *Io, libertà, e moralità nella filosofia di Enrico Bergson*. Trani, Italy: Ditta Vecchi, 1912, 16.

685 Titchener, Edward Bradford. "Review of *Laughter: An Essay on the Meaning of the Comic* by Henri Bergson." *American Journal of Psychology*, 23, No. 1, January 1912, 146-147. This is a review of the English translation of *Le Rire* with critical comments.

686 Tonquédec, Joseph de. "M. Bergson: Est-il moniste?" *Etudes par des Pères de la Compagnie de Jésus*, 130, No. 1, 10 février 1912, 506-516. This article is summarized in the *Revue de Philosophie*, avril 1912. Cf. Bergson's response, 1912. (Cf. Bergson's letters to the author May 12, 1908 and February 20, 1912. Bergson denies he is a pantheist.)

687 Townsend, James G. "Bergson and Religion." *Monist*, 22, No. 3, July 1912, 392-397.

688 Tuttle, J. R. "Review of 'Creative Evolution and Philosophic Doubt' by A. J. Balfour in *Hibbert Journal*, 11, 1-23." *Philosophical Review*, 22, No. 1, January

1912, 122-123.

689   Tuttle, J. R. "Review of 'Life and Consciousness' by Henri Bergson in *Hibbert Journal*, 11, 24-44," *Philosophical Review*, 21, No. 1, January 1912, 125-126.

690   Underhill, Evelyn. "Bergson and the Mystics." *English Review*, 10, No. 2, February 1912, 551-522. This study is republished in *Living Age*, 272, No. 3532, March 16, 1912, 668-675. This is a suggestive account of the relevance of Bergson's thought to mysticism.

691   Underhill, Evelyn. *Mysticism*. New York: Dutton, 1912, 600. Bergson is discussed on pp. 31-36.

692   Van Teslaar, J. S. *Review of Laughter: An Essay on the Meaning of the Comic* by Henri Bergson. *Journal of Abnormal Pyschology*, 7, No. 5, 1912-1913, 373-374. This is a congratulatory review, presenting an outline of Bergson's concept of laughter.

693   Vernede, Louis. "Le Bergsonisme ou une philosophie de la mobilité." *Phalange*, 7, No. 72, 1912, 485-507.

694   Vettard, Camille. "Review of *Le Bergsonisme ou une philosophie de la mobilité* by Julien Benda." *Nouvelle Revue Française*, 8, 1er novembre 1912, 940-944.

695   "Review of *La Vie Personnelle* by Albert Bazaillas." *Revue de Métaphysique et de Morale*, 13, No. 2 (Supplément), mars 1912, 62-64.

696   Viétroff, J. "L'Influence de la philosophie de M. Bergson. VI." *Mouvement Socialiste*, 31, No. 237, janvier 1912, 62-64. The author, writing from Russia, explains why Bergson's influence on contemporary philosophy is as great as Kant's on previous Modern philosophy.

697   W., B. C. A. "Review of *Laughter* by Henri Bergson." *Dublin Review*, 151, No. 302, July 1912, 181-184.

698   Wahl, Jean. "Deux Ouvrages récents sur la philosophie de M. Bergson." *Revue du Mois*, 7, No. 4, août 1912, 153-180. This is a critical discussion on *Le Bergsonisme* by Julien Benda and *Une Philosophie nouvelle* by E. Le Roy.

699   Walker, Charles. "M. Bergson's *Creative Evolution*." *Lancet*, 182, February 17, 1912, 456. In this letter to the editor, Walker criticizes R. F. Licorish's neo-Lamarckian interpretation of Bergson and criticizes Bergson for his failure to understand Darwinism.

700   Wasserberg, J. "Irracjonalizm Bergsona." *Przeglad Filozoficzny*, 16, No. 2, 1912, 145-160.

701   Waterlow, Sydney. "The Philosophy of Bergson." *London Quarterly Review*, 76, No. 3292, January 4, 1912, 152-176.

702   Wilbois, Joseph. *Devoir et durée: Essai de morale sociale*. Paris: Félix Alcan, 1912, 408. Written by a disciple of Bergson, to some degree this work foreshadows ideas to be developed by Bergson in *The Two Sources of Morality and Religion*.

703   Wolf, A. "Mr. Balfour on Teleology and Creative Evolution." *Hibbert Journal*, 10, Part 1, January 1912, 469-472. The author concludes that: "Not teleology, but only an externally imposed and completely determined teleology, is incompatible with creative evolution." (472).

704   Wolf, A. "The Philosophy of Probability." *Proceedings of the Aristotelian Society*, 13, 1912-1913, 328-361. Bergson is discussed on pp. 328, 336-337, and 360-361.

705 Yushkevich, Pavel Solomonovich. *Мировоззрение и мировоззрения.* Петербутг: 1912, 194. This contains a section on Bergson.

1913

706 Abbott, Lyman. "Philosophy of Progress." *Outlook*, 103, No. 8, Feburayr 22, 1913, 388-391.

707 Alexander, Hartley B. "Socratic Bergson." *Mid-West Quarterly*, No. 4, October 1913, 32-43.

708 Alexander, Samuel. "Freedom." *Proceedings of the Aristotelian Society*, N.S. 1913-1914, 322-354. Freedom and "durée" are discussed on pp. 329-336; mind and neural processes on pp. 341.

709 Alpern, Henry. *The March of Philosophy*. New York: Dial, 1913, 381. Bergson is discussed on pp. 301-318.

710 Andres, Cyril Bruyn. *Life, Emotion, and Intellect*. London and Leipzig: Fisher Unwin, 1913, 95.

711 Antonelli, E. *Bergson et le mouvement social contemporain*. Zürich: Wissen und Leben, 1913.

712 Arréat, L. "Review of *Vital Lies*, by Vernon Lee." *Revue Philosophique de la France et de l"Etranger*, 75, No. 6, 1913, 635-638.

713 "Believes In Intuition." *New York Times*, 62, No. 20, 103, February 7, 1913, p. 10. col. 6. In his lecture, delivered in English, Bergson states that the belief in intuition is one step towards "philosophical solutions."

714 Benda, Julien. *Une Philosophie pathétique*. Paris: Cahiers de la Quinzaine, 1913, 139 (Série 15, Cahier 2). This is a thoroughgoing criticism of Bergson's philosophy.

715 Benda, Julien. "Répense au défenseur de bergsonisme." *Mercure de France*, 204, ler juillet 1913, 5-41; 16 juillet 1913, 283-309.

716 "Bergson and Eucken under Fire." *Current Opinion*, 54, No. 4, April, 1913, 307-308.

717 "Bergson Here to Lecture." *New York Times*, 62, No. 20, 099, February 3, 1913, p. 5, col. 1.

718 "Bergson Lauds Us As Idealist Race." *New York Times*, 62, No. 20175, April 20, 1913, pt 3, p. 1:1,2. This Article reports remarks made by Bergson after his return from America to France. Bergson holds that though America is a mechanistic nation it is also an idealistic nation—the most idealistic on earth at this time. Americans are not greedy, but ambitious and high-spirited. The article notes that Bergson's remarks are in response to an attack on America, Americans and Mechanism by René Doumic. Doumic, in turn, was attacking a lecture given by an Englishman he thought was an American.

719 Bergson on Psychical Research." *Educational Review*, 46, September 1913, 208-212. This is under the category "Notes and News."

720 "Bergson Stands By Will." *New York Times*, 62, No. 20, 101, February 5, 1913, p. 8, col. 3. This brief article describes Bergson's lecture at Columbia University.

Bergson is reported as stating that 'will' is the master of intelligence.

721   "Bergson to Reply to Church Attack." *New York Times*, 62, No. 20, 308, August 31, 1913, pt. 3, p. 1, col. 5. This brief article reports that Bergson will give a series of lectures in response to the Roman Catholic Church's denunciation of his philosophy. Bergson is here reported as stating that his philosophy can be religiously interpreted.

722   "Bergson's Lectures." *Outlook*, 103, No. 7, February 15, 1913, 336.

723   "Bergson's New Idea of Evolution." *Literary Digest*, 46, No. 9, March 1, 1913, 454.

724   "Bergson's Own Introduction to His Own Philosophy." *Dial*, 55, No. 641, March 1, 1913, 185-186. This is a brief review of *An Introduction to Metaphysics* by Henri Bergson.

725   "Bergson's Reception in America." *Current Opinion*, 54, No. 3, March 1913, 226.

726   Bernardis, P. de. "La Philosophie nouvelle et le problème religieux." *Annales de Philosophie Chrétienne*, 4e Série, 16, mai-juin 1913.

727   Bernstein, Herman. *With Master Minds*. New York: University Series Publishing Co., 1913, 243. Bergson here comments on his Jewishness.

728   Berthelot, René. *Un Romantisme utilitaire: Etude sur le mouvement pragmatiste.* Vol. 2. *Le Pragmatisme chez Bergson.* Paris: Félix Alcan, 1913, 364. This is an exposition of Bergson's philosophy followed by a lengthy critique of Bergson's basic contentions in mathematics, physics, biology, and psychology. The author compares Bergson's pragmatism to those of F. Nietzsche, H. Poincaré, searches for the origins of Bergson's philosophy in 19th century utilitarianism and empiricism, and in the philosophies of F. Ravaisson and F. Schelling. This is a classic critique of Bergson's philosophy.

729   Björkman, Edwin. *Voices of Tomorrow: Critical Studies of the New Spirit in Literature.* New York and London: Kennerly, 1913, 328. Bergson is discussed on pp. 205-223.

730   Blum, Léon. "La Prochaine Génération littéraire." *Revue de Paris*, 20, No. 2, févier 1, 1913, 519-536. On pp. 526-530 the author describes the parallels between Bergson's philosophy and contemporary literary movements in France. Both Bergsonism and the new literary movements oppose tendencies in classical French thought.

731   Bonhoff, K. "Aus Bergsons Hauptwerken." *Protestantische Monatshefte*, 17, 1913, 168-181.

732   Bornstein, Benedykt. "Kant i Bergson." *Przeglad Filozoficzny*, 16, No. 2-3, 1913, 129-199.

733   Bornstein, Benedykt. *Kant i Bergson: Studyum o zasadniczym problemacie teoryi.* Warsaw: Wende, 1913.

734   Bouché, J. "La Philosophie de M. Bergson." *Questions ecclésiastiques*, 6, février 1913.

735   Boule, L. "Les Localizations cérebrales et la philosophie spiritualiste." *Revue des Questions Scientifiques*, 3e Sér., 23, 1913, 192-228, "et à suivre."

736   Broad, Charley Dunbar. "Note on Achilles and the Tortoise." *Mind*, 23, No. 86, April 1913, 318-319. The author insists: "...it is important even at this time of day to settle the controversy finally, because it and Zeno's other paradoxes have

become the happy hunting-ground of Bergsonians and like contemners of the human intellect." (318).

737 Brown, A. Barratt. "Intuition." *International Journal of Ethics*, 24, No. 3, 1913-1914, 282-293. This is a discussion of the meaning of intuition, including a critical comparison of Bergson's concept of intuition with that of F. H. Bradley.

738 Buccazo. "L'Intellectualisme de M. Bergson." *Parthénon*, 3, 5 août 1913.

739 Burns, Cecil Delisle. "Bergson: A Criticism of his Philosophy." *North American Review*, 197, No. 688, March 1913, 364-370. The author proposes various criticisms of "intuition."

740 Burroughs, John. "A Prophet of the Soul." *Atlantic Monthly*, 113, No. 1, January 1913, 120-132.

741 Bush, W. T. "The Bergson Lectures." *Columbia University Quarterly*, 15, No. 3, June 1913, 254-257.

742 Caldwell, Dr. William. *Pragmatism and Idealism*. New York: Macmillan; London: A. and C. Black, 1913, 268. Chapter 9 is entitled "Pragmatism and Idealism in the Philosophy of Bergson" and appears on pp. 234-261.

743 Carr, Herbert Wildon. "Life and Logic." *Mind*, 22, No. 88, October 1913, 484-492. This is a critique of Bosanquet's criticisms of Bergson in *The Principle of Individuality and Value*.

744 Carr, Herbert Wildon. *The Problem of Truth*. London and Edinburgh: T. C. and E. C. Jack, 1913, 93. Chapter seven is on Bergson and B. Croce.

745 Cochin, Denys. *Descartes*. Paris: Félix Alcan, 1913, 279. (Les Grands Philosophes) On pp. 192-279 the author outlines and criticizes Bergson's philosophy, proposing a Cartesian viewpoint in its place.

746 "Columbia Honors Bergson." *New York Times*, 62, No. 20, 100, February 4, 1913, p. 4, col. 2. This brief article notes the award of an honorary degree to Bergson by Columbia University.

747 Columer, A. "De Bergson à Bonnot: De Bergson au banditisme." *L'Action d'art*, 1913.

748 Cooke, Harold P. "Ethics and New Intuitionists. *Mind*, 22, No. 85, January 1913, 82-86.

749 Corey, Charles E. "Bergson's Intellect and Matter." *Philosophical Review*, 22, No. 5, 1913, 512-519. According to the author, Bergson is primarily interested in division and analysis; the work of integration is seldom done with equal care so that a distinction of a kind is apt to appear, later in his system, as one of degree only.

750 Cox, Marian. "Bergson's Message to Feminism." *Forum*, 49, No. 5, May 1913, 548-559. The author states: "...a definite message is in his insistent demand that we turn away from the intellectualism of life to life itself, and this also is the aim of feminism." (548).

751 "Review of *Critical Exposition of Bergson's Philosophy* by J. M. Stewart." *International Journal of Ethics (Ethics)*, 23, No. 1, January 1913, 211-216.

752 Desaymard, Joseph. "La Pensée d'Henri Bergson." *Vieille Auvergne*, mars 1913.

753 Dewey, John. "Introduction." *A Contribution to a Bibliography of Henri Bergson*. New York: Columbia University Press, 1913, ix-xii.

754   Dodson, George Rowland. *Bergson and the Modern Spirit: An Essay in Constructive Thought.* Boston: American Unitarian Association, 1913, 296.

755   Douglas, George William. "Christ and Bergson." *North American Review,* 197, No. 689, April 1913, 433-444.

756   Emerson, L. E. "The Case of Miss A: A Preliminary Report of a Psychoanalytic Study and Treatment of a Case of Self-Mutilation." *Psychoanalytic Review,* 1, No. 1, 1913, 41-54. "The necessary function of psychoanalysis implies an ethical and philosophical foundation. In this respect it is interesting to note the close correspondence between the psychoanalytic theories and the Bergsonian doctrines. Here, too, should be mentioned the work and doctrines of William James. But this paper is no place to develope these suggestions so they will be merely mentioned" (p. 53). The author footnotes Bergson's *Matière et mémoire* and *L'évolution créatrice.*

757   "Review of *Eucken and Bergson* by Mrs. E. Hermann." *Independent,* 74, No. 3350, February 13, 1913, 368-370.

758   "Eucken, Bergson, To-Day." *New York Times,* 62, No. 20, 119, February 23, 1913, pt. 7, p. 98, cols. 1, 2. This is a review of *Eucken and Bergson: Their Significance For Christian Thought* by E. Hermann.

759   Evans, Serge. "La Vie et l'intelligence." *Renaissance Contemporaine,* 24 juin 1913. This concerns Bergson and A. Schopenhauer.

760   Ewald, Oskar. "Henri Bergson als Neuromantiker." *Literarische Echo,* 15, No. 8, 1913, 517-521.

761   Ewald, Oskar. "Philosophie." in *Das Jahr 1913.* Leipzig: Teubner, 1913, p. 550.

762   Faguet, Emile. "Un Historien du symbolisme." *La Revue,* Sér. 6, 24e Année, Vol. C, 1er janvier 1913, 37-47. This article concerns Tancrède de Visan and Bergson.

763   Farges, Albert. "La Cosmologie bergsonienne." *Revue du Clergé Française,* 15 mars 1913, 740-741. This is a letter to the editor criticizing a review of the author's *La Philosophie de Bergson.* Bergson's is a philosophy of non-being, not of being. His concept of God is "scandalous," and his philosophy can not be made consistent with Thomism.

764   Feuling, Daniel Martin. "Bergson und der Thomismus." *Jahrbuch für Philosophie und spekulative Theologie,* 25, 1913, 33-55.

765   Finnabogason, Guðmundur. *L'Intelligence sympathique.* Trans. André Courmont, Paris: Félix Alcan, 1913, 244. (Bibliothèque de philosophie contemporaine) The author opposes "sympathetic intelligence" to "scientific intelligence". Scientific intelligence utilizes the principle of identity, deals with repetitive phenomena, can assure our survival. Sympathetic intelligence proceeds through imitation, explores the unique and particular, and strives for greater "richness of life."

766   Florence, Jean. "M. Bergson et Renouvier." *Phalange,* 8, No. 86, 1913, 97-104.

767   Garrigou-Lagrange, R. P. "Chronique de métaphysique: Autour du Blondelisme et du Bergsonisme." *Revue Thomiste,* 21, No. 5, 1913, 351-377. This article contains a general review of books on Bergson by A. Farges, F. LeDantec, G. Dumesnil and Pierre Lasserre. The reviewer is pleased with recent criticisms of Bergson.

768   Gerrard, Thomas John. "Bergson and Divine Fecundity." *Catholic World,* 98, No. 581, August 1913, 631-648.

769   Gerrard, Thomas John. "Bergson and Finalism." *Catholic World*, 98, No. 579, June 1913, 374-382.

770   Gerrard, Thomas John. "Bergson and Freedom." *Catholic World*, 97, No. 578, May 1913, 222-231.

771   Gerrard, Thomas John. "Bergson's Philosophy of Change." *Catholic World*, 96, No. 574, January 1913, 433-448.

772   Gerrard, Thomas John. "Bergson's Philosophy of Change: His Intuitive Method." *Catholic World*, 96, No. 575, February 1913, 602-616.

773   Granberry, J. "Bergson and his Philosophy." *Methodist Review*, 1, No. 1, 1913, 3-19.

774   Grandjean, Frank. *Une Révolution dans la philosophie*. Genève: Atar, 1913, 168.

775   Gurwitsch, A. *Философские исследования и очетки*. Москфа: Труд, 1913, xxxi, 311.

776   Heinichen, O. "Review of *Schöpferische Entwicklung* by Henri Bergson." *Tat*, 5, 1913, 188-194.

777   "He is Only a Parlor Professor." *New York Times*, 62, No. 20, 306, August 29, 1913, p. 8:4. This is an anti-Bergson editorial. Bergson, the writer states, "has taken care that the news of the Pope's condemnation of *Creative Evolution* should be accompanied by the announcement that this Winter he will deliver a course of lectures answering this redoubtable judge and critic." Thus Bergson secures an audience for himself that will be "large and fashionable." Those who read Bergson's books must suspect that "the truths in them are all old and the novelties false." "The fact is," the writer continues, "that Bergson passes for a bold and original thinker, a shaker of pillars and a disturber of foundations, only among those to whom the languages of science and philosophy are entirely unfamiliar, and for whom big words, adroitly used, are deeply impressive."

778   Heymans, Gèrard. "Les Deux   émoires de M. Bergson." *Année Psychologique*, 19, 1913, 66-74. The author proposes criticisms of Bergson's concept of memory. He denies Bergson's dualistic conclusions.

779   Hicks, G. Dawes. "Are the Intensity Differences of Sensation Qualitative?" *British Journal of Psychology*, 6, No. 2, 1913-1914, 155-174.

780   Hocking, William Ernest. "Significance of Bergson." *Yale Review*, N.S. 3, No. 1, 1913-1914, 303-326.

781   Hübener, Gustav. "Husserl, Bergson, George." *Die Güldenkammer*, 3, 1913, 212-221.

782   "Human Will Makes Energy." *New York Times*, 62, No. 20, 107, February 11, 1913, p. 24, col. 4. Bergson is reported as dismissing as absurd in this lecture theories of constant quantities of mental energy.

783   Huneker, James Gibbson. *The Pathos of Distance*. New York: Scribner's, 1913, 394. Bergson is characterized as the playboy of western philosophy on pp. 367-385.

784   Huneker, James Gibson. "The Playboy of Western Philosophy." *Forum*, 49, No. 3, March 1913, 257-268.

785   "An Introduction to Bergson." *Spectator*, 110, No. 4426, April 26, 1913, p. 719. This is a brief review of *An Introduction to Metaphysics* by Henri Bergson.

786   Review of *An Introduction to Metaphysics* by Henri Bergson. *A.L.A. Booklist*, 9, No. 6, 1913, 230.

787   Review of *An Introduction to Metaphysics* by Henri Bergson. *Contemporary Review*, 103, No. 67, 1913, 590-593.

788   "Review of *An Introduction to Metaphysics* by Henri Bergson." *Dial*, 54, No. 641, March 1, 1913, 185-186.

789   "Review of *An Introduction to Metaphysics* by Henri Bergson." *Spectator*, 110, No. 4426, 1913, 719. This is a brief, expository review. The reviewer concludes: "Not the permanent but the mutable is the quest of the new philosophy."

790   Jaspers, Karl. "Review of *Schöpferische Entwicklung* by Henri Bergson." *Zeitschrift für die gesamte Neurologie und Psychologie*, 6, 1913, 885-886. The reviewer asserts that a reading of *Schöpferische Entwicklung (Creative Evolution)* is necessary to an understanding of Bergson's earlier, more psychological works (*Time and Free Will, Matter and Memory, An Introduction to Metaphysics*). He contends that a definitive reading of Bergson's philosophy is not yet possible, but remarks that Bergson's tendency to approach psychological qualities directly, through intuition—without which psychology *per se* is impossible—is quite meaningful, and coincides with many contemporary efforts. Bergson's *Creative Evolution* brings together many of the psychological needs of the times. As a stimulus and a means towards clarity, Bergson's philosophy is useful, but one must warn against taking it as a model, and trying to resolve psychological and psychopathological problems through intuition. Bergson's interweaving of inexpressible metaphysical experience with clever logical arguments is irresolvable (unauflöslich). An article by Richard Kroner in *Logos*, 1913, is cited in this regard.

791   Jeliffe, Smith Ely. Review of *Creative Evolution* by Henri Bergson. *Journal of Nervous and Mental Disease*, 40, 1913, 485-488.

792   Jennings, H. S. "Moderne Wissenschaft und die Illusion von Bergson von H. Elliot." *Archiv für Hydrobiologie*, 9, 1913, 648-655.

793   Jerusalem, William. *Einleitung in die Philosophie*. Vienna and Leipzig: Braumiller, 1913, 402.

794   Jevons, Frank Byron. *Personality*. London: Methuen and Co., 1913, 171. Bergson is discussed on pp. 78-124 and elsewhere. The views of Hume, James, Bergson, and others are criticized in this study.

795   "The Jewishness of Bergson." *Literary Digest*, 46, No. 13, March 29, 1913, 712.

796   Johnston, Charles. "Where Bergson Stands." *Harper's Weekly*, 57, No. 2934, 15 March 1913, 16. The author offers a general account of Bergson's philosophy.

797   Johnstone, James. "Bergson's Philosophy of Organism." *Proceedings of the Liverpool Biological Society*, 26-27, 1913, 3-34.

798   Jones, H. Gordon. "Bergson et l'évolution: L'Evolution créatrice." Trans. Pierre Hilleman. *Revue Positiviste Internationale*, 8, No. 5, 1er octobre 1913, 311-320. This article appeared originally in *Positivist Review*, 1 August 1912. The author examines the biological doctrines of *L'Evolution créatrice*. He concedes that extreme forms of mechanism and finalism cannot account for evolution but denies that Bergson's "élan vital" can explain cellular differentiation, evolutionary convergence, or the wholeness of life.

799   Jourdain, Philip E. B. "Review of *L'infinito* by Cosmo Guastella." *Mind*, 22, No. 87, July 1913, 438-439.

800   Jung, Carl Gustav. "A Contribution to the Study of Psychological Types." In
        Collected Papers on Analytical Psychology. 2nd ed. Ed. Constance E. Long.
        London: Balliere, Tindall and Cox, 287-298. This paper was given in 1913, p.
        293, the author likens his concept of *libido* to Bergson's *élan vital*, and utilizes
        a concept of "crystallization" which, he states, is similar to Bergson's. He
        connects Bergson's metaphysics with the aesthetic theory of Worringer. This
        essay appears in French in *Archives de Psychologie*, 13, 1913, 289-299. It
        appears in C. G. Jung, *Collected Works*, 6, 499-509, where references to Bergson
        are found on p. 504.

801   Jung, Carl Gustav. "Letter to Dr. Löy, March, 1913." In "On Some Crucial Points
        in Psychoanalysis." In *Collected Papers on Analytical Psychology*. 2nd ed. Ed.
        Constance E. Long. London: Balliere, Tindall and Cox, 1922, 236-277. On pp.
        274-275, the author states that "the purely causal, not to say materialistic con-
        ception of the preceeding decades, would conceive the organic formation as the
        reaction of living matter, and this doubtless provides a position heuristically
        useful, but, as far as any real understanding goes, leads only to a more or less
        ingenious and *apparent* reduction of the problem. Let me refer you to Bergson's
        excellent criticism of this conception. From external forces but half the result,
        at most, could ensue; the other half lies within the individual disposition of the
        living material, without which it is obvious the specific reaction-formation could
        never be achieved. This principle must be applied also in psychology." This
        exchange of letters appears again in C. G. Jung's *Collected Works*, 4, 252-289.
        The reference to Bergson is found on p. 287.

802   Jung, Carl Gustav. "On Psychoanalysis." In *Collected Papers on Analytical
        Psychology*. 2nd ed. Ed. Constance E. Long. London: Balliere, Tindall and
        Cox, 1922, 226-235. In this paper, given in London in 1913, the author states
        that "from a broader standpoint libido can be understood as vital energy in
        general, or as Bergson's *élan vital*" (p. 231). This essay is retranslated as
        "Psychoanalysis and Neurosis" in C. G. Jung's *Collected Works*, 4, 243-251.
        For Jung's reference to *élan vital*, see p. 248.

803   Kehr, Theodor. "Bergson und die Probleme von Zeit und Dauer." *Archiv für die
        gesamte Psychologie*, 26, No. 1, 1913, 137-154.

804   Keller, Adolf. "Die Philosophie des Lebens." *Wissen und Leben*, 7, 1913, 89-97,
        194-284, 292-305.

805   Kitchin, Darcy Herworth. *Bergson for Beginners*. London: Allen and Company,
        Ltd. 1913, 225.

806   Kohler, Joseph. "Bergson und die Rechtswissenschaften." *Archiv für Rechts und
        Wirtschafts-Philosophie*, 7, No. 1, 1913, 56-69.

807   Lalande, André. "Philosophy in France, 1912." *Philosophical Review*, 22, No. 4,
        July 1913, 357-374.

808   Landquist, John. *Essayer: Ny samling*. Stockholm: A. Bonnier, 1913, 420. This
        work contains a section on Bergson.

809   "Lankester on Bergson." *New York Times*, 62, No. 20,309, September 1, 1913,
        p. 4, col. 5. This is a letter to the editor by Sir Ray Lankester. Sir Lankester
        comments: "Bergson is neither great, nor French, nor a philosopher, but verifies
        the humorous comparison applied to a metaphysician: a blind man in a dark
        room hunting for a black cat which is not there."

810   Lasserre, Pierre. "Que nous veut Bergson?" *L'Action Française*, 6, No. 173, 22 juin 1913, 3-4.

811   Lasserre, Pierre. *La Doctrine officielle de l'université*. Paris: Mercure de France, 1913, 506. The author describes Bergson as a pluralistic pantheist and regrettable anti-intellectual.

812   Le Roy, Edouard. *The New Philosophy of Henri Bergson*. Trans. Vincent Benson. New York: Holt and Company; London: Williams and Nordgate, 1913, 235.

813   Levine, Louis. "The Philosophy of Henry Bergson and Syndicalism." *New York Times*, 62, No. 20,091, January 26, 1913, pt. 5, p. 4, col. 1.

814   Lewkowitz, Julius. *Die Philosophie H. Bergsons: Wissenschaftliche Vereinigung jüdischer Lehrer und Lehrerinnen zu Berlin*. Berlin: Rosenthal & Co., 1913, 16. Beilage zum Jahresbericht für 1913.

815   Libby, Malanchthon F. "The Continuity of Bergson's Thought." *University of Colorado Studies*, 9, No. 4, September 1913, 147-202.

816   Losski, N. "Nedostatki gnossologii Bergsona i vliianie na ego metafiziki." *Voprosy filosofii i psikhologii*, 24, No. 118, 1913, 224-235.

817   Lotte, Joseph. "Lettre du 10 nov. 1912 à la *Revue de la Jeunesse*." *Bulletin des Professeurs Catholiques de l'Université*, 25 juin 1913.

818   Lovejoy, Arthur Oncken. "The Practical Tendencies of Bergsonism, I and II." *International Journal of Ethics*, 53, No. 3, April 1913, 253-275; No. 4, July 1913, 419-443. This is a thoroughgoing criticism of Bergson and his followers, with special emphasis on the relations between Bergson's thought and both syndicalism and Roman Catholic "modernism."

819   Lovejoy, Arthur Oncken. "Some Antecedents of the Philosophy of Bergson." *Mind*, 22, No. 88, October 1913, 645-492. F. Ravaisson, Lionel Dauriac, and G. Noël were precursors of Bergson, according to the author.

820   Ludovici, August. *Das genetische Prinzip: Versuch einer Lebenslehre*. München: Bruckman, 1913, 299.

821   Macintosh, Douglas C. "Bergson and Religion." *Biblical World*, 41, No. 1, January 1913, 34-40.

822   Maire, Gilbert. "Systèms philosophiques d'écoles littéraires: L'Utilisation du contresens." *Revue Critique des Idées et des Livres*, 20, No. 117, 25 février 1913, 430-444.

823   Malagarriga, Carlos. "Significado de la evolución por Henri Bergson." *Atlantida*, 9, No. 27, marzo 1913, 348-379. See the note on p. 475.

824   Marck, Siegfried. "Philosophie." *Nord und Süd*, 37, No. 5, Mai 1913, 201-213.

825   Maritain, Jacques. "L'Intuition. Au sens de conaissance instinctive ou d'inclination." *Revue de Philosophie*, 23, No. 3, juillet, 1913, 5-13.

826   Mason, Joseph Warren Teets. "The Bergson Method Confirmed." *North American Review*, 197, No. 686, January 1913, 90-104.

827   Massis, Henri. "La Philosophie de M. Bergson critiquée par Pie X." *Le Temps*, No. 19044, 25 août 1913, 3.

828   "Review of *Le Materialisme actuel* by Henri Bergson and others." *Edinburgh Review*, Vol. 218, No. 446, 1913, 417-434. The reviewer warns against the wordy infection which Bergson and like thinkers have injected into Great Britain.

829   Maury, Lucien. "Le Bergsonisme." *Revue Politique et Littéraire, Revue Bleue*, 51e Année, No. 4, 25 janvier 1913, 120-123. This is a review of J. Benda's *Bergsonisme*.

830   McCabe, Joseph. *Principles of Evolution*. Baltimore, Warwicke, and York, 1913, 264. Criticisms of Bergson may be found on pp. 247-253.

831   Mercier, Désiré. "Vers L'Unité." *Revue Néo-scolastique de Philosophie*, 20e Année, No. 3, 1913, 253-278. The author views Bergson as a monist and pantheist.

832   Miloradovich, K. M. "Dva uchenii o vremeni Kanta i Bergsona." *Ministerstvo narodnogo prosveshcheniia, Zhurnal*, 18, 1913, 323-329.

833   Montagne, H.-A. "Bergson et ses plus récents commentateurs." *Questions Actuelles*, 114, No. 20, 17 mai 1913, 631-638. This essay was first published in *Revue Thomiste*, 1913.

834   Montagne, F. H.-A. "Chronique d'histoire de philosophie." *Revue Thomiste*, 21, No. 3, 1913, 237-244. This is a review of books on Bergson by A. Farges, R. Gillouin, J. Segond and R. Cor.

835   Moore, Jared S. "Duration and Value." *Philosophical Review*, 22, No. 3, 1913, 304-306. The author argues that an analogy between Bergson's theories and Munsterberg's view of the relations between metaphysics and psychology may be applied to the problem of time. Time is psychologically discrete; but from the standpoint of value it is continuous.

836   Morrison, David. "The Treatment of History by Philosophers." *Proceedings of the Aristotelian Society*, N.S. 14, 1913-1914, 291-321. Bergson and individual personality are discussed on pp. 308-311.

837   Murry, John Middleton. "French Books." *Blue Review*, 1, No. 1, May, 1913, 56-62. The author remarks, in a discussion of Julien Benda's *L'Ordination*, that this work states a problem Bergson glosses over: "'Instinct' or 'intuition' is no panacea for the realities of life. The intellect and the desires of the intellect are as potent and as valuable to their possessor as instinct and the blind impulses of instinct. It has not been given to M. Bergson in the twentieth century to solve the difficulties and quiet the groanings of St. Paul." (p. 56).

838   Nys, Désirée. *La Notion du temps*. 2e éd. Louvain: Institut supérieur de philosophie, 1913, 308.

839   O'Keef, D. "Bergson's Critical Philosophy." *Irish Theological Studies*, No. 2, April 1913, 178-189.

840   Ostertag, H. "Bergson." *Neue kirchliche Zeitschrift*, 25, 1913, 991-1006.

841   Osty, Eugène. *Lucidité et intuition; étude expérimentale*. Paris: Félix Alcan, 1913, xxxix, 477.

842   Palmer, John. "French and English Laughter." *Saturday Review*, 114, No. 2946, April 13, 1913, 461. The author replies to criticisms of his interpretation of French character and of Bergson's concept of laughter by Ernest Dimnet in an erlier number of the *Saturday Review*. He admits that it is wrong to generalize about national character—yet concludes that, nonetheless, the French have never understood Shakespeare.

843   Papini, Giovanni. *Sul pragmatismo: Saggi e ricerche*. Milano: Milanese, 1913, 163.

844   Paulhan, Françoise. "La Lutte Philosophique et la division des croyances." *Revue Philosophique de la France et de l'Étranger*, 76, No. 10, 1913, 409-422. This is a review of *Le Materialisme actuel* by Henri Bergson, Henri Poincaré, Charles Gide and others.

845   Perry, Ralph Barton. "Philosophy." *The American Yearbook, 1912*. New York and London: D. Appleton & Co., 1913, 692-694. On p. 692 the author notes the increasing vogue of Bergson's philosophy in the United States, as well as criticisms of Bergson by Bertrand Russell and others.

846   "Pope Denounces Bergson." *New York Times*, 62, No. 20, 305, August 28, 1913, p. 1, col. 2. This article briefly recounts a denunciation of Bergson's philosophy, as expressed in *Creative Evolution*, by the Pope of the Roman Catholic Church. The Pope states that Bergson's philosophy is even more poisonous because it is "sugarcoated, subtle, and seductive in nature."

847   "Professor Bergson at City College." *Outlook*, 103, No. 9, March 1, 1913, 467.

848   "Professor Bergson's Concept of the Absolute." *Contemporary Review*, 103, No. 67, April 1913, 590-593. This is a review of Bergson's *Introduction to Metaphysics*.

849   "Professor Bergson: The College and Democracy." *Outlook*, 103, No. 9, 1913, 468.

850   "Professor Bergson on Psychical Research." *Educational Review*, 46, September, 1913, 208-212. This is an account of Bergson's speech before the British Society for Psychical Research in May, 1913.

851   Proust, Marcel. "Lettre au Temps." *Le Temps*, No. 19124, 13 novembre 1913, 2. This letter concerns the function of voluntary and involuntary memory in Bergson and Proust. Proust denies Bergson's influence.

852   Prudencio Bustillo, Ignacio. *Al margen del bergsonismo*. Sucre, Bolivia, 1913.

853   Quick, Oliver. "Bergson's Creative Evolution and the Individual." *Mind*, 22, No. 86, April 1913, 217-230. The author discusses problems related to the "vital impetus."

854   Reymond, Arnold. *La Philosophie de M. Bergson et le problème de la raison*. Lausanne: Impr. coopérative "La Concorde," 1913, 19.

855   Reymond, Arnold. "Philosophie de Bergson et problème de la raison." *Revue de Théologie et de Philosophie*, N.S. 1, 1913, 329-343.

856   Rolland-Gosselin, Marie-Dominique. "L'Intuitionisme bergsonien et l'intelligence." *Revue des Sciences Philosophiques et Théologiques*, 7, No. 3, 1913, 389-411.

857   Rougemont, E. de. "Portraits graphologiques: M. Henri Bergson." *Mercure de France*, 101, 16 février 1913, 736-756. This article contains an analysis of Bergson's handwriting.

858   Rozenfel'd, I. "Intuitivizm i futurizm" *Maski*, 6, 1913-1914, 17-26. The author discusses the profound influence of Bergson's philosophy on the futurist movement in contemporary art. He makes no distinction between Russian and Italian futurism.

859   Sanborn, Alvan F. "Bergson: Creator of a New Philosophy." *Outlook*, 1913, 103, No. 7, 353-358.

860   Santayana, George. *Winds of Doctrines: Studies in Contemporary Opinion*. London: Dent and Sons; New York: Scribner's, 1913, 215. Chapter three, "The Philosophy of M. Henri Bergson," is found on pp. 58-109. This is one of the most

celebrated critiques of Bergson's philosophy by an English-speaking philosopher.

861 Schaxel, Julius. "Bergsons Philosophie und die biologische Forschung." *Die Natur-wissenschaften*, 1-2, No. 83, 1913, 795-796. The author attacks Bergson's "biological philosophy." He concludes, "Bergson darf bei den Naturforschern auf keinen Beifall rechnen. Um so sicherer ist ihm der Erfolg bei denen, denen nichts an den einzelnen Resultaten der Forschung, alles an ihrem allgemeinsten Facit liegt. Sie sind heute wieder einmal einige Jahrzehnte von dem unerfüllten Versprechen einer Weltanschauung hingehalten, die sich ganz im Rahmen der Wissenschaft halten will, und des Wartens müde" (p. 796).

862 Schoen, H. "Review of *La Philosophie de M. Henri Bergson* and *Henri Bergson: Choix du texte avec étude du système philosophique* by René Gillouin." *Zeitschrift für Philosophie und Pädagogique*, 20, 1913, 542.

863 Schrecker, Paul. "Die individualpsychologische Bedeutung der ersten Kindheit-serinnerungen." *Zbl. Psychoanalytische Psychiater*, 4, 1913-1914, 121-130. For English translation and annotation Cf. the author, 1973.

864 Schultze, Martin. *Das Problem der Wahrheitserkenntnis bei William James und Henri Bergson*. Erlangen, Germany: Junge und Sohn, 1913, 81. This is the author's inaugural dissertation.

865 "The Science of Dreams." *The Independent*, 76, No. 3386, 1913, 153. This is a comment by the editors on the English translation of Bergson's "Le Rêve," published in *The Independent*. The similarities between Bergson's concept of dreams and Freud's are noted. The editors conclude, however, that Bergson's view is more balanced than Freud's.

866 Scott, J. W. "The Pessimism of Creative Evolution." *Mind*, 22, No. 87, July 1913, 344-360.

867 Segond, Joseph. *L'Intuition bergsonienne*. 1-2 ed. Paris: Félix Alcan, 1913, 1930, 158. (Bibliothèque de philosophie contemporaine)

868 Segur, Nicolas. "Bergson et bergsonisme." *La Revue*, 23e Année, 1er octobre 1912, 297-315. This essay also appears in *Wetenschap Bladen*, 1913, 82-108.

869 Seillière, Ernest. "Schätzung und Wirkung d. Philosophie i. heut. Frankreich." *Internationale Monatsschrift für Wissenschaft*, 7, No. 1, 1913, 42-58.

870 Sewall, Frank. *Is the Universe Self-centered or God-centered? An Examination of the Systems of Eucken and Bergson: Presidential Address Delivered to the Swedenborg Scientific Association*. Philadelphia, Pennsylvania: Swedenborg Scientific Association, 1913, 13.

871 Shastri, Prablu Datta. *The Conception of Freedom in Hegel, Bergson and Indian Philosophy*. Calcutta: Albion Press, 1913, 26.

872 Shimer, Hervey W. "Bergson's View of Organic Evolution." *Popular Science Monthly*, 82, No. 2, February 1913, 163-167. This is a review of the English translation of *Creative Evolution*. It is a general exposition of Bergson's views.

873 Shotwell, James T. "Bergson's Philosophy." *Political Science Quarterly*, 28, No. 1, March 1913, 130-135. Bergson has difficulties with intuition, value, and anti-intellectualism, according to the author.

874 Singer, Kurt M. "Von der Sendung des Judentums: Ideen zur Philosophie H. Bergsons." in *Vom Judentum: Ein Sammelbuch*. Leipzig, 1913, 71-100.

875   Slater, Mary White. "Vision of Bergson." *Forum*, 52, No. 6, December 1913, 916-932.

876   Slosson, Edwin Emery. "Recent Developments of Bergson's Philosophy." *Independeant*, 74, No. 3368, 19 June 1913, 1383-1385.

877   Smith, Richard. "Review of *Critical Exposition of Bergson's Philosophy* by J. M. Stewart." *International Journal of Ethics*, 23, No. 1, January 1913, 211-216.

878   Smith, Richard. "Review of *Laughter: An Essay on the Meaning of the Comic* by Henri Bergson." *International Journal of Ethics*, 22, No. 2, January 1913, 216-218. This is a critical but appreciative review. The author denies the incompatibility of feeling and laughter.

879   "Spiritual Philosopher." *Review of Reviews*, 47, No. 3, March 1913, 299.

880   Spurgeon, Caroline Frances Eleanor. *Mysticism in English Literature.* New York: Putman's Sons; Cambridge, England: University Press, 1913, 168. This is an account of mysticism based on Bergson's conceptions.

881   Stickers, Joe. "Bergson und sein Intuitionismus." *Das monistische Jahrhundert*, 4, 1913, 635-641, 653-663.

882   Stork, T. B. "Bergson and his Philosophy." *Lutheran Quarterly*, 47, 1913, 248-258.

883   "Tea For Henri Bergson. *New York Times*, 62, No. 20,116, February 20, 1913, p. 11, col. 5. This brief article recounts the circumstances of a tea given for Bergson by Columbia University faculty wives.

884   Thibaudet, Albert. *Trente ans de vie française*: Vol. 3. *Le Bergsonisme*. Paris: Nouvelle Revue Française, 1913, 2 vols., 256 et 253.

885   Thilly, Frank. "Romanticism and Rationalism." *Philosophical Review*, 22, No. 2, 1913, 107-132. This is the author's presidential address before the American Philosophical Society in 1912. It is an attack on "romantic" tendencies in philosophy, as represented by the thought of G. W. Hegel, F. W. Schelling, Bergson, William James and others. The author characterizes Bergson on pp. 116-118 as an anti-intellectual possessing tendencies towards Cartesian dualism.

886   Tonquédec, Joseph de. "Bergson et la scolastique." *Revue Critique des Idées et des Livres*, 23, No. 137, 25 décembre 1913, 651-670.

887   Visan, Tancrède de. "La Philosophie de M. Henri Bergson et l'esthétique contemporaine." *Vie et Lettres*, 1, No. 21, avril 1913, 124-137.

888   "Visiting French Philosopher." *Literary Digest*, 46, No. 1193, March 1, 1913, 460-461. This is a report on Bergson's lectures at Columbia University.

889   Waterlow, Sydney. "Review of *An Introduction to Metaphysics* by Henri Bergson." *International Journal of Ethics*, 24, No. 1, 1913-1914, 100-102. The author states: "From the premise that no whole is merely the sum of its parts, the conclusion that no whole is composed of parts,—that there are no parts at all,—does not follow." (102)

890   Willcox, Louise Collier. "Impressions of M. Bergson." *Harper's Weekly*, No. 2933, 8 March 1913, 6. This is a brief discussion of Bergson's lectures at Columbia University.

891   Wilm, Emil Carl. "Bergson and Philosophy of Religion." *Biblical World*, N.S. 42, No. 5, November 1913, 279-283.

892   Wolfe, James J. "Review of *Creative Evolution* by Henri Bergson." *South Atlantic Quarterly*, 12, No. 2, April, 1913, 184-186.

1914

893   "Academy Salutes Belgium." *New York Times*, 63, No. 20, 652, August 10, 1914,
        p. 3, col. 3. This article reports the substance of a speech to the Académie des
        Sciences Morales et Politiques on August 8 in which Bergson praises Belgium
        for its courage in the face of German invasion. Cf. Bergson, 1914.

894   Aliotta, Antonio. *The Idealistic Reaction Against Science*. Trans. W. Agnes McCas-
        kill. London: Macmillan and Co., Ltd., 1914, 483. Cf. "Bergson's Doctrine of
        Intuition," 127-137. The author is critical of Bergson's "exaggerations," particu-
        larly as concerns the failings of the intellect.

895   Altmann, Bruno. "Bergsons Welterfolg." *Die Aehre*, 19-20, 1914-1915.

896   Antal, Illés. "Bergson und Schopenhauer." *Drittes Jahrbuch der Schopenhauer
        Gesellschaft*, 1914, 3-15.

897   Armstrong, A. C. "Bergson, Berkeley, and Philosophical Intuition." *Philosophical
        Review*, 23, No. 4, July 1914, 430-438. Bergson's interpretation of Berkeley
        is discussed in this article.

898   Armstrong, A. C. "The Philosophy of Bergson." *Methodist Magazine*, 96, 1914,
        839-850.

899   Balmer, W. T. "Bergson and Eucken in Mutual Relation." *London Quarterly
        Review*, 122, No. 3, July 1914, 84-99.

900   "The Banning of Bergson," *Independent*, 79, No. 3424, July 20, 1914, 85-86.
        This brief article concerns the placing of Bergson's works on the Roman Catholic
        "Index". The author states: "...although the Catholic laity are thus prevented
        from finding out for themselves what Bergsonism is by reading it in its original
        form, they nevertheless cannot escape its influence, for it is in the air nowadays
        and they cannot be sheltered from it if they read at all." p. 86.

901   Bazaillas, Albert. "La Philosophie de M. Bergson." *Renaissance Politique et Lit-
        téraire*, 21 février 1914.

902   Benda, Julien. *Sur Le Succès du bergsonisme: Précédé d'une réponse au défenseurs
        de la doctrine*. Paris: Mercure de France, 1914, 250. This study contains "Une
        Philosophie pathétique."

903   Benito y Duran, Angel. "San Augustín y Bergson: La conciencia psicológia punto
        de partida de metafísicas divergentes." *Augustinus*, 4, No. 1, 1914, 95-134.

904   "Bergson and Psychical Research." *Unpopular Review*, 1, No. 1, 1914, 63-111.
        This is a general discussion of psychical research with brief references to Bergson.

905   "Bergson Elected Member of the French Academy." *New York Times*, February
        13, 1914, 4, col. 2.

906   "M. Bergson Gets His Reward." *New York Times*, 63, No. 20,475, February 14,
        1914, p. 10, col. 4. This is an editorial lauding Bergson's election to the French
        Academy.

907   "Bergson on Germany's Moral Force." *Literary Digest*, 49, No. 1287, 19 December
        1914, 1223.

908   "M. Bergson on Dreams." *Dial*, 56, No. 672, June 16, 1914, 510-511. This is a
        review of *Dreams* by Henri Bergson.

909 Beth, K. "Review of *Einführung in die Metaphysik* and *Schöpferische Entwicklung* by Henri Bergson." *Ungarische Rundschau*, 3, 1914, 262.

910 Beyer, Friedrich. "Bergsons Rückkehr zu Wildentum." *Der Türmer*, 17, No. 1, Oktober 1914, 107-109. This article contains a reply to Bergson's criticisms of the German mentality and the German war-machine.

911 Beyer, Thomas Percival. "Creative Evolution and the Woman's Question." *Educational Review*, 47, No. 1, January 1914, 22-27.

912 Bleszynski, K. "Ostatnia pracn Wl. Dawida o Bergsonie." *Krytyka*, 16, No. 5, 1914, 143-150.

913 Blondel, Charles. *La Conscience morbide: Essai de psychopathologie générale.* Paris: Félix Alcan, 1914, 342. The author's psychology is strongly influenced by Bergson. The consciousness of mentally disturbed patients is morbidly spatialized, de-temporalized.

914 Bobromska, K. "Bergsonizm ozyli filozofja zmiennosoi prodrug J. Bendy." *Przeglad Filozoficzny*, 18, No. 3, 1914, 374-384.

915 Bohn, Georges. *La Naissance de l'intelligence.* Paris: Flammarion, 1914, 350. (Bibliothèque de la philosophie scientifique).

916 Boine, Giovanni. "La novità di Bergson." *Nouva ontologia*, Ser. 5, 173, No. 1025, 1914, 24-37.

917 Bonus, Arthur. "Bergson muss es wissen!" *März*, 7, No. 3, 5 September 1914, 312-314. This article is a criticism of Bergson's attack on the German mentality and German militarism.

918 Botti, Luigi. "Mentre Bergson é messo all'indice." *Rassegna nazionale*, 36, No. 192, 1914, 187-194.

919 Briach, R. "Bergsons Entwicklung Theorie." *Kosmos*, 49, 1914.

920 Bricout, J. "M. Bergson à l'Index." *Revue du Clergé Français*, 20e Année, No. 474, 15 août 1914, 451ff.

921 Brink, L. "Review of *The Meaning of God in Human Experience* by William Ernest Hocking." *The Psychoanalytic Review*, 1, No. 4, 1914, 472-479. On p. 479 the reviewer contrasts Bergson's concept of the unconscious mind with Hocking's, holding that Bergson's is much truer to fact: "Not alone much simpler but more true to the fact is Bergson's picture of the unconscious, an undivided whole, the vast deposit of the conscious life admitted beyound the portals of conciousness only in so far as it is useful for our present purposes. As such a deposit, a product of our conscious life, it is a product of our character, too, but is not that character itself, which has rather risen upon and beyond it."

922 Bruce, H. Addington. "The Soul's Winning Fight with Science." *American Magazine*, 77, No. 3, March 1914, 21-26. W. James, Bergson, O. Lodge, and others are discussed in this article.

923 Burand, Georges. "L'Origine scolastique de la théorie de la perception extérieure de Bergson." *Entretiens Isreélites*, janvier 1914.

924 Bury, R. de. "Les Confidences de M. Bergson avec M. Gremil." *Mercure de France*, 108, 15 mars 1914, 397-398.

925 Cappellazzi, A. "Il pensiero filosofico e la filosofia di Bergson." *Scuola cattolica*, 2 Ser., 5, No. 6, 1914.

926 "A. Capus e. H. Bergson all' Academia francese" *Nouva Antologia*, 254, No. 1014, 1914, 363-365.

927   Carr, Herbert Wildon. "Review of *Bergson for Beginners* by Darcy B. Kitchen." *Mind*, 23, No. 92, October 1914, 612-163.

928   Carr, Herbert Wildon. "The Philosophical Aspects of Freud's Theory of Dream Interpretation." *Mind*, 23, No. 91, July 1914, 321-334. A comparison of Bergson's and Freud's concepts of dreams is made on pp. 324-325.

929   Carr, Herbert Wildon. "Review of *Pragmatism and Idealism* by William Caldwell." *Mind*, 23, No. 90, April 1914, 268-271. Bergson and pragmatism are discussed on pp. 270-271.

930   Carr, Herbert Wildon. "Reply to Bertrand Russell." Bertrand Russell. *The Philosophy of Bergson*. Cambridge: Bowes and Bowes, 1914, 36.

931   Caso, Antonio. *Filosofiá de la intiución*. México: The Author, 1914, 11. The author was to be a strong proponent of Bergson in Latin American philosophy. He dealt especially with Bergson's aesthetics.

932   Castro, Antonio. *Algunas anotaciones a la logica viva*. Montevideo, 1914. The author developes Thomist criticisms of Bergson and Vas Ferreira. Cf. Vaz Ferreira, 1920.

933   Célide, G. "Philosophe à la mode." *Gazette de France*, ler février 1914.

934   Célide, G. "Le Sorcier d'Israël." *Gazette de France*, 22 février 1914.

935   Cheydleur, Frédéric D. "Essai sur l'évolution des doctrines de M. Georges Sorel." Diss., Grenoble, 1914, 174. This is a "doctorat d'Université."

936   Colonna, Louis. "M. Bergson et son enseignement." *Revue Hebdomadire des Cours et des Conférences*, 22, No. 8, 5 mars 1914, 798-809.

937   Conrad, W. "Review of *Das Lachen* by Henri Bergson." *Zeitschrift für Aesthetik*, 9, 1914, 284-286.

938   Corrance, Henry C. "Bergson's Philosophy and the Idea of God." *Hibbert Journal*, 12, No. 46, January 1914, 374-388. The author argues that at this date Bergson neither affirms nor denies the reality of God.

939   Costelloe, Karin (née Stephen). "An Answer to Mr. Bertrand Russell's Article on the Philosophy of Bergson." *Monist*, 24, No. 1, January 1914, 145-155.

940   Costelloe, Karin (née Stephen). "Complexity and Synthesis: A Comparison of the Data and Philosophical Methods of Mr. Russell and M. Bergson." *Proceedings of the Aristotelian Society*, N.S. 15, 1914-1915, 271-303. This is a very carefully thought out analysis which is critical of Russell.

941   Cunningham, Gustavus Watts. "Bergson's Concept of Duration." *Philosphical Review*, 23, No. 6, November 1914, 525-539.

942   Cunningham, Gustavus Watts. "Bergson's Concept of Finality." *Philosophical Review*, 23, No. 6, 1914-1915, 648-663.

943   D., E. "Review of *Une Philosophie pathetique* by Julien Benda." *Nouvelle Revue Français*, 11, mai 1914, 885-890. The reviewer accuses the author of systematically misrepresenting Bergson's position.

944   Dauriac, Lionel. "Le Mouvement bergsonien." *Revue Philosophique de la France et de l'Etranger*, 75, No. 4, avril 1914, 400-414. This is a review of books on Bergson by Benda, Segond, Wilbois, Schrecker, and Le Roy.

945   Dauriac, Lionel. "Review of *La Philosophie bergsonienne* by Jacques Maritain." *Revue Philosophique de la France et de l'Etranger*, 77, No. 6, 1914, 631-634.

946 Dearborn, George V. N. "Review of *La Vie inconsciente et les mouvements* by Theodule Armand Ribot." *Journal of Abnormal Psychology*, 9, No. 4, 1914-1915, 361-362. The reviewer notes concerning Ribot's conception of the relations between the unconscious and mental activity, that "it opens up vistas of conjecture which Bergson and the philosophy of Heraclitus himself can not at present traverse" (p. 361). "The chapter on the general relations of motor ideas to the mental process does not require extended analysis. It is inherently in line with much recent thought (that, for example, of Bergson) in enlarging on the proof that every state of consciousness is a complex of which the kinesthetic elements form the stable and resistant part. If a metaphor be allowed, they are its skeleton. They assure its permanence" (p. 361).

947 Dimnet, Ernest. "The Meaning of M. Bergson's Success." *Saturday Review* (London), 116, No. 3045, March 7, 1914, 300.

948 "Does Henri Bergson Believe in Ghosts?" *New York Times*, 63, No. 20,700, September 27, 1914, pt. 6, p. 2:4. This article is a report of Bergson's acceptance speech as president of the British Society for Psychical Research. Bergson is reported as believing in telepathy and spirit messages and as holding that the burden of proof is on the shoulders of those who do not believe in psychic phenomena and not on the shoulders of those who do.

949 "Review of *Dreams* by Henri Bergson." *A.L.A. Booklist*, 11, No. 1, September, 1914, p. 5. This review is reprinted from *The Independent*.

950 "Review of *Dreams* by Henri Bergson." *Dial*, 56, No. 672, June 16, 1914, 510-511.

951 "Review of *Dreams* by Henri Bergson." *New York Times*, 63, No. 20,595, June 14, 1914, pt. 6, p. 274:2.

952 "Review of *Dreams* by Henri Bergson." *Spectator*, 113, No. 4507, November 14, 1914, p. 676.

953 "Review of *Dreams* by Henri Bergson." *Springfield Republican*, June 4, 1914, p. 5.

954 Driesch, Hans. *The History and Theory of Vitalism*. Trans. C. K. Ogden. London: Macmillan and Co., Ltd., 1914, 239. Bergson is discussed on pp. 66-92, 132-137, and 162-163.

955 Dubray, C. A. "The Philosophy of Henri Bergson." *Bulletin of the Catholic University of Washington*, 20, April 1914, 317ff.

956 "Editorial." *New York Times*, 22, February 1914, Sect. 5, p. 4, col. 1.

957 Farges, Albert. *La Philosophie de M. Bergson, professeur au Collège de France: Exposé et critique*. 2e éd. Paris: Impr. Feron-Vrau, 1914, 527. This edition includes replies to critics.

958 Farges, Albert. "Le Sens commun et son amputation par l'école bergsonienne." *Revue Néo-scolastique de Philosophie*, 21, No. 84, novembre 1914-1919, 440-479.

959 Flewelling, Ralph Tyler. "Bergson, Ward and Eucken in Their Relation to Bowne." *Methodist Magazine*, 96, 1914, 374-383.

960 Florian, Mircea. *Der Begriff der Zeit bei Henri Bergson*. Diss., Greifswald, 1914, 126. Greifswald, Germany: Bruncken and Co., 1914, 126.

961 Gauché, M. "Autour d'Henri Bergson." *Belgique Artistique et Littéraire*, 34, 1914, 332-341.

962 "George Brandes, 'Big, Strong, Unamiable, Yet Loveable'." *New York Times*, 63, No. 20, 581, May 31, 1914, pt. 5, p. 3:1. This article reports an interview with

the Danish critic, translator and literary historian, George Brandes, who took the occasion to criticize Bergson. Among Brandes' remarks are the following: "Pah, he does not exist!", "Bergson says nothing that Schelling did not say.", and "He says nothing new. If he had said anything new, he would be hated. But he pleases the crowd. He flatters them, because he does not let them know how stupid they are."

963   Gerrard, Thomas John. *Bergson: An Exposition and Criticism From the Point of View of Saint Thomas Aquinas*. London: Herder, 1914, 208. The author is thoroughly critical of Bergson.

964   Gilbert, Pierre. "Sur La Critique du bergsonisme." *Revue Critique des Idées et des Livres*, 24, No. 140, 10 février 1914, 374-375.

965   Gillouin, René. "La Philosophie de M. Henri Bergson." *L'Olivier*, 3e Année, No. 1, janvier 1914, 3-13.

966   Gremil, M. "Figures du temps présent: M. Henri Bergson." *La Dépêche de Toulouse*, 16 février 1914.

967   Gronau, Gotthard. *Henri Bergson: Ein Beitrag zur Philosophie der Gegenwart*. Wolfenbüttel, Germany: Ernst Fischer, 1914, 38.

968   Gronau, Gotthard. "Henri Bergson: Ein Beitrag zur Philosophie der Gegenwart." *Wissenschaftliche Beilag zum Jahresbericht des Städtischen Lyzeums Fräulein-Marien Schule zu Rüstingen*. Oldenburg, Germany, 1914.

969   Grossman, I. "Bakunin i Bergson." *Zavety*, No. 5, 1914, 47-62.

970   Hatheyer, F. "Review of *Das Lachen* by Henri Bergson." *Zeitschrift für Katholische Theologie*, 38, 1914, 162.

971   Hazay, Olivér von. "Ist intuitive Philosophie möglich?" *Zeitschrift für Philosophie und Philosophische Kritik*, 154, No. 2, 1914, 168-188.

972   Heilborn, Ernst. "Review of *Das Lachen* by Henri Bergson." *Literarische Echo*, 6, No. 15, 1914, 939-940.

973   Hinkle, Beatrice M. "Jung's Libido Theory and the Bergsonian Philosophy." *New York Medical Journal*, 99, 1914, 1080-1086." The author cites similarities between Bergson's philosophy and Jung's analytical psychology.

974   Höffing, Harald. *Henri Bergson's filosofi*. Kopenhagen: Glyendal, 1914, 70.

975   Iushkevich, P. S. "Bergson i ego filosofiia intuitsii." *Russkoe bogatstvo*, 11, No. 2, 1914, 33-59; No. 3, 1914, 47-67.

976   Janet, Pierre. "Psychoanalysis: III. Traumatic Memories Relative to Sexuality." *The Journal of Abnormal Psychology*, 9, No. 2, 1914-1915, 153-187. On p. 178, the author states of the various attempts to broaden the concept of sexual desire by Jung, Putnam, Jones, and others, "one fact stands out clearly; all the terms employed by the psychoanalysts, such as 'sexual instinct,' 'cravings of sexual gratification,' 'libido,' etc., designate simply the 'élan vitale' of metaphysicans." But the use of such words by psychologists to explain everything can be very dangerous. On p. 180, he states that "such confusion is not favorable either to the study of the 'élan vital' or to that of sexual phenomena in humanity."

977   Jary, Jacques. "Ce que nous devons au bergsonisme." *Renaissance Politique, Littérarie et Artistique*, 2, fvrier 1914, 28-29. This is a comment on an article by T. de Visan which appeared in the February 1914 issue of *Temps Présent*.

148   BERGSON BIBLIOGRAPHY

978   Johnstone, James. *The Philosophy of Biology.* Cambridge, England: University Press, 1914, 391. This study is a thoroughgoing attempt to apply Bergson's philosophy to the basic problems and concepts of biology.

979   Jones, Llewellyn. "The Meaning of Bergsonism. *Little Review*, 1, No. 1, March, 1914, 38-41.

980   Jung, Carl Gustav. "The Content of the Psychoses. Part II, 1914." *Collected Papers in Analytical Psychology.* Ed. C. E. Long. London: Balliere, Tindall and Cox, 1923, 336-351. Also in *Collected Works*, 3, 153-178. On p. 351 (*Collected Papers*) the author states, "I realize that my views are parallel with those of Bergson, and that in my book (*The Psychology of the Unconscious*) the concept of the libido which I have given is a concept parallel to that of *élan vital*; my constructive method corresponds to his intuitive work. When I first read Bergson a year and a half ago I discovered to my great pleasure everything which I had worked out practically, but expressed by him in consummate language and in wonderfully clear philosophical style." On pp. 347-348 (n), he again likens his concept of *libido* to Bergson's *élan vital.*

981   Jung, Carl Gustav. "On Psychological Understanding." *Journal of Abnormal Psychology*, 9, No. 6, 1914-1915, 385-389. In this essay, written in 1914, and delivered July 24, 1914, in London to the Psycho-Medical Society, the author likens his concept of *libido* to Bergson's *élan vital* on pp. 396 and 399. This essay appears again in C. G. Jung, *Collected Works*, 3, 179-193. In this new translation, I am able to find only one reference to Bergson, on p. 190.

982   Kallen, Horace M. "James, Bergson, and Traditional Metaphysics." *Mind*, 23, No. 90, April 1914, 207-239. The author argues that Bergson is a proponent of "traditional metaphysics," with its system-building tendencies, its distinction between appearance and reality, and its assumption that reality is "compensatory." James, he insists, is not.

983   Kallen, Horace M. *William James and Henri Bergson: A Study in Contrasting Theories of Life.* Chicago: University of Chicago Press, 1914, 248.

984   Keller, Adolph. *Eine Philosophie des Lebens.* Jena: Diederichs, 1914, 46. The author was the first to introduce C. G. Jung to the ideas of Bergson. Cf. C. G. Jung, 1916.

985   Kiefer, D. "Über die Bergsons Philosophie." *März*, 7, No. 2, 1914, 745-748.

986   Kronenberg, Moritz. "Bergson und Hegel." *Das literarische Echo*, 16, No. 13, 1914, 877-881.

987   Lanessan, Jean Marie de. *Transformation et créationisme.* Paris: Félix Alcan, 1914, 349.

988   Lepercq, Daniel. "La Philosophie bergsonienne." *Revue de la Jeunesse*, 5e Année, No. 10, 25 février 1914, 543-554.

989   Lepercq, Daniel. "A Propos du livre de M. Maritain." *Revue Thomiste*, 22, No. 2, 1914, 213-218. This is a review of *La Philosophie bergsonienne* by Jacques Maritain. The reviewer congratulates Maritain for "unmasking" the "perverse" Bergsonian philosophy.

990   Le Roy, Edouard. *Une Philosophie nouvelle: Henri Bergson.* Paris: Félix Alcan, 1914, 210. (Bibliothèque de philosophie contemporaine)

991   Levine, Louis. "The Philosophy of Bergson." *New York Times*, 22 February 1914, Sect. 5, p. 4, col. 1.

992 Levine, Louis. *Syndicalism in France.* New York: Columbia University, 1914, 299. The irrationalist influence of Bergson's ideas on the French Syndicalist movement is discussed in this study.

993 Lewis, Clarence Irving. "Bergson and Contemporary Thought." *University of California Chronicle,* 16, No. 2, 1914, 181-197.

994 Lewkowitz, Julius. *Die Philosophie H. Bergsons: Veröffentlichung der wissenschaftlichen Vereinigung jüdischer Lehrer und Lehrerinnen zu Berlin.* Berlin: Poppelauer, 1914, 16.

995 Lossky, Nikolai O. *Интуитивная философія Бетгсона.* Moscow: "Пумь", 1914, iii, 115.

996 Lovejoy, Arthur Oncken. *Bergson and Romantic Evolutionism.* Berkeley, California: University of California, 1914, 61.

997 Maire, Gilbert. "Bergsoniens contre Bergson." *La Revue,* 6e Sér., 106, 1er février 1914, 316-330.

998 Maritain, Jacques. *La Philosophie bergsonienne: Etudes critiques par Jacques Maritain.* Paris: M. Rivière et Cie., 1914, 477. This is a determined criticism of Bergson's philosophy by a Catholic philosopher and former student of Bergson's. The superiority of Aquinas' views is stressed.

999 Maritain, Jacques. "L'Esprit de la philosophie moderne." *Revue de Philosophie,* 24, No. 3, juin 1914, 601-625.

1000 Marot, Jean. "Le Cours de M. Bergson." *Renaissance Politique et Littéraire,* 2, 31 janvier 1914.

1001 "Review of *Le Matérialisme actuel* by Henri Bergson and Others." *L'Année Philosophique,* 24, 1914, 189f.

1002 Mellor, Stanley Alfred. *Religion as Affected by Modern Science and Philosophy.* London: Lindsey Press, 1914, 256. (Handbooks of Religion) Bergson is discussed on pp. 147-166.

1003 Messer, August. "Bergsons 'intuitive' Philosophie." *Zeitschrift für christliche Erziehungswesen,* 7, 1914, 74ff.

1004 Mignard. "Automatisation et spontanéité: Pathologie mentale et psychologie bergsonienne." *Journal de Psychologie Normale et Pathologique,* 11, 1914, 199-220. The author examines the case of Mlle Clemence P., a hysteric exhibiting partial dissociation of personality. He argues that her behavior can be explained by Bergson's psychology, as an example of "automatisation".

1005 Mills, Ernest Lyman. "A Comparison of the Main Points in the Epistemological Theories of Borden Parker Bowne and Henri Bergson." Diss. Boston 1914.

1006 Minkowski, Eugène. "Betrachtungen im Anschluss an das Prinzip des psychophysischen Parallelismus." *Archiv für die gesamte Psychologie,* 31, 1914, 132-243.

1007 "Mise à l'Index des oeuvres de Bergson." *Acta Apostolicae Sedis,* June 12, 1914, 314-315. Also in *Mélanges,* 1089. *Time and Free Will, Matter and Memory,* and *Creative Evolution* are in this proclamation placed on the Roman Catholic Index."

1008 Mitchell, Arthur. *Studies in Bergson's Philosophy.* Lawrence, Kansas: University Press, 1914, 115.

1009   Nagel."Bergsons Rede." *Die übersinnliche Welt*. Berlin, 1914, 94-109.

1010   "Les Nouveaux à l'Académie française." *Revue Hebdomadaire des Cours et des Conférences*, N.S. 10, No. 8, 21 février 1914, 4 pp. (no pagination).

1011   Olgiati, Francesco. *La filosofia di Enrico Bergson*. Torino: Fratelli Bocca, 1914, xix, 317. (Piccola Biblioteca di Scienze Moderne, No. 230.)

1012   Ott, Emil. *Henri Bergson: Der Philosoph moderner Religion*. Berlin and Leipzig: Teubner, 1914, 131. This is from *Natur und Geisteswelt*, 480.

1013   Péguy, Charles. *Note sur M. Bergson et la philosophie bergsonienne*. Paris: 8, rue de la Sorbonne, 1914, 105. *Cahiers de la Quinzaine*, 8e cahier, 15e Série. This is a famous interpretation and defense of Bergson's philosophy. The author stresses the pragmatic side of Bergson's thought and attacks characterizations of it as anti-intellectual.

1014   Péguy, Charles. "Note sur M. Bergson et la philosophie bergsonienne." *Grande Revue*, 84, No. 8, 25 avril 1914, 613-631.

1015   Péguy, Charles. *Note sur M. Bergson et la philosophie bergsonienne*. Paris: Emile Paul, 1914, 101.

1016   Perry, Ralph Barton. "Philosophy." In *The American Yearbook, 1913*. New York and London: D. Appleton and Company, 1914, 707-709. On p. 707 the author cites criticisms of Bergson's philosophy by Frank Thilly and others.

1017   Picard, Gaston and Tautain, Gustave-Louis. "Enquête sur M. Henri Bergson et l'influence de sa pensée sur la sensibilité contemporaine." *Grande Revue*, 83, No. 3, 10 février 1914, 544-560; 25 février 1914, 744-760; 84, No. 5, 10 mars 1914, 11-128; No. 6, 25 mars 1918, 309-328; No. 7, 10 avril 1914, 513-528.

1018   Pioli, G. "Tendenze religiose nella filosofia del Bergson e la condamna dell' 'Indice'. *Bilychnis*, 3, No. 8, 1914, 77-85.

1019   Pitkin, Walter B. "Time and Pure Activity." *Journal of Philosophy*, 11, No. 19, September 10, 1914, 521-526.

1020   Putnam, James Jackson. "Dream Interpretation and the Theory of Psychoanalysis." *Journal of Abnormal Psychology*, 9, No. 1, 1914-1915, 36-60. On p. 47 the author mentions Bergson's "poussée vitale." On p. 49 he states, "It has long been recognized as a sound psychological proposition (a proposition made great use of by Bergson in his careful reasonings) that everything a man does, or thinks, so far from standing alone, or having only a short history, has a history at least as long as the man's life. Not only does each act or thought of the adult rest, in part, upon the experiences of the child, in the sense that the boy is, to speak broadly, the father of the man; but the life of the man actually contains the experiences of the boy, as integral and (virtually) active elements of its own essence.

1021   Robinson, Arthur. "Review of *A Critical Exposition of Bergson's Philosophy* by J. McKellar Stewart." *Mind*, 23, No. 91, July 1914, 443-444.

1022   Robinson, Arthur. "Review of *An Introduction to Metaphysics* by Henri Bergson." *Mind*, 23, No. 90, April 1914, 285. This is a review of T. E. Hulme's translation of the *Introduction to Metaphysics*.

1023   Rolland-Gosselin, Marie-Dominique. "Bergsonisme." *Revue des Sciences Philosophiques et Théologiques*, 8, No. 2, 1914, 308-312. This is a review of Bergson's address on parapsychology and of books on Bergson by Grandjean, Maritain, and Berthelot.

1024   Rolland-Gosselin, Marie-Dominique. "La Perception extérieure d'après M.
        Bergson." *Revue des Sciences Philosophique et Théologiques*, 8, No. 3. 1914,
        397-422.

1025   Rouveyre, André. "Henri Bergson." *Egoist*, 1, No. 5, 1914, 88. This brief article
        contains a photograph.

1026   Ruhe, Algot Henrik Leonard. *Henri Bergson: Tänkesattet Bergson i dess.
        grunddrag*. Stockholm: Wahlstrom and Widstrand, 1914, 174.

1027   Ruhe, Algot, and Nancy Margaret Paul. *Henri Bergson: An Account of his Life
        and Philosophy*. London: Macmillan & Co., 1914, vii, 245.

1028   Russell, Bertrand. "Mysticism and Logic." *Hibbert Journal*, 12, No. 48, July
        1914, 780-803.

1029   Russell, Bertrand. *The Philosophy of Bergson: With a Reply by Mr. H. Wildon
        Carr, and a Rejoinder by Mr. Russell*. Cambridge, England: Bowes and Bowes;
        London: Macmillan; Glasgow: MacLehose, 1914, 36. This article is reprinted
        from the *Monist*, 1912.

1030   Sait, Una Mirrieless (Bernard). *The Ethical Implications of Bergson's Philosophy*.
        New York: The Science Press, 1914, 183.

1031   Sait, Una Mirrieless Bernard. "The Ethical Implications of Bergson's Philosophy."
        Diss. Columbia 1914, 183.

1032   Sanborn, Alvan F. "The New Nationalism in France." *Forum*, 51, No. 2, January
        1914, 9-26. Bergson's opinions of French youth are mentioned on pp. 21 of
        this article.

1033   Saussure, René de. "Le Temps en général et le temps bergsonien en particulier."
        Archives de Psychologie, 14, août 1914, 277-296. The author concedes the
        importance of time and agrees that philosophers, prior to Bergson, had neglected
        it. He argues, however, that time is both homogeneous and given-all-at-once
        like space. Time, thus, does not move: we move trough time. The author
        concludes that there are three sorts of existence: (1) space, (2) time, and (3)
        events, conceived as the operation of forces.

1034   Saussure, René de. "Réponse à M. Lutoslawski." *Archives de Psychologie*, 14,
        1914, 298-299. This is a response to a criticism of the author's talk "Le Temps
        en général et le temps bergsonien en particulier." The author explains his distinc-
        tion between qualitative and quantitative, and comments on Lutoslawski's equ-
        ation of duration with God's creative aspect.

1035   Schaefke, Friedrich. "Bergsons' 'L'Evolution créatrice'in den Hauptpunkten
        dargestellt und beurteilt." Diss., Göttingen, 1914, 79.

1036   Scott, J. W. "Ethical Pessimism in Bergson." *International Journal of Ethics*, 24,
        No. 2, January 1914, 147-167. The author discusses Bergson's concept of
        laughter and its negative implications.

1037   Segond, Joseph. "Bergson." *Chronique*, 22 février 1914. Possibly this journal is
        Chronique, published in London, 1899-1924.

1038   Seillière, Ernest. "Welche Moralphilosphie lässt Bergson erwarten?" *Internationale
        Monatsschrift für Wissenschaft, Kunst und Technik*, 8, 1914, 191-210.

1039   Sidis, Boris. *The Foundations of Normal and Abnormal Psychology*. Boston:
        Richard G. Badger, 1914, 416. The author, a student of William James, depre-
        cates Bergson for his "metaphysical" viewpoint, but on pp. 139-141 he stresses

Bergson's distinction between memory image and percept. On pp. 203-205 he criticizes Bergson's theory of the unconscious, asserting that it should be replaced with the concept of "subconscious consciousness." On pp. 372-374 he both utilizes and criticizes Bergson's theory of memory.

1040   Simmel, Georg. "La Philosophie d'Henri Bergson." *Die Güldenkammer*, 4, No. 6, Juni 1914.

1041   Slosson, Edwin Emery. *Twelve Major Prophets of Today*. Boston: Little, Brown and Company, 1914, xiii, 299.

1042   Solomon, Meyer. "On 'The Analysis and Interpretation of Dreams Based on Various Motives and on the Theory of Psychoanalysis,' a reply to Dr. James J. Putnam, with Critical Remarks on the Theory and Practice of Freudian Psychoanalysis." *The Journal of Abnormal Psychology*, 9, No. 2, 1914-1915, 98-138. Cf. pp. 117-118 for an application of Bergson's theory of the unconscious to dream phenomena.

1043   Stebbing, Lizzie Susan. *Pragmatism and French Voluntarism*. Cambridge, England: University Press, 1914, 168.

1044   Storck, Karl. "An Romain Rolland, Meaterlinck, Bergson, Shaw und Genossen! And die neutral. Protestler." *Der Türmer*, 17, No. 3, November 1914, 162-172.

1045   "Such Stuff As Dreams are Made On." *The Outlook*, 107, No. 10, July 4, 1914, 520-522. This is a review of *Dreams* by Henri Bergson.

1046   Tautain, Gustave-Louis and Picard, Gaston. "Enquête sur M. Henri Bergson et l'influence de sa pensée sur la sensibilité contemporaine." *Grande Revue*, 83, No. 3, 10 février 1914, 544-560; No. 4, 25 février 1914, 744-760; 84, No. 5, 10 mars 1914, 111-128; No. 6, 25 mars 1914, 309-328; No. 7, 10 avril 1914, 513-528.

1047   Theodorescu, Constantin A. *Die Erkenntnislehre Bergsons*. Jena: Frommansche, 1914, 56. This is an inaugural dissertation presented at the University of Jena. It is translated by the author from Rumanian.

1048   "Threatened Collapse of the Bergson Boom in France." *Current Opinion*, 56, No. 5, May 1914, 371-372.

1049   Truc, Gonzaque. "M. Benda et le bergsonisme." *Revue Critique des Idées et des Livres*, 24, No. 138, 10 janvier 1914, 33-41.

1050   Ugarte de Ercilla, E. "Bergson: Idolo de la filosofía francesa contemporánea." *Razón y Fe*, 39, No. 2, 1914, 298-311.

1051   Ugarte de Ercilla, E. "Boletín de filosofía contemporánea: Movimiento bergsoniano." *Razón y Fe*, 38, No. 4, 1914, 486-491.

1052   Vesper, Noël. *Anticipations à une morale du risque*. Pref. Jules Bois. Paris: Perrin et Cie, 1914. In some respects this study anticipates conclusions worked out by Bergson in *The Two Sorces of Morality and Religion*.

1053   Visan, Tancrède de. "Ce que nous devons à Bergson." *Temps Présent*, 1, 2 février 1914, 153-163.

1054   Vorst, B. van. "M. Bergson et les Américains." *Le Gaulois*, le février 1914.

1055   Werner, Charles. "Réunion des Philosophes de la Suisse Romande. Rolle, 25 juin 1914." *Archives de Psychologie*, 14, 1914, 296-299. The author gives an account of a discussion of René de Saussure's article "Le Temps en générale et le temps bergsonien en particulier" before the philosophical society of French-speaking

Switzerland. The discussions revolved around the question of whether or not time is spatial. Professors Grandjean and Lutoslawski (a Polish philosopher), in particular, contributed to the debate. Lutoslawski concludes that time is God, in God's creative aspect.

1056 Werner, H. "Review of *Das Lachen* by Henri Bergson." *Zentralblatt für Psychologie und Psychologische Pädagogik*, 1, 1914, 496-498.

1057 White, E. M. "Bergson and Education." *Educational Review*, 47, No. 5, May 1914, 433-443. This article is reprinted from the *London Journal of Education*. It is a general and speculative attempt to formulate a Bergsonian pedagogy.

1058 White, William A. "The Unconscious." *Psychoanalytic Review*, 2, No. 1, 1914, 12-28. On pp. 15-16, 25-27 the author proposes a Bergsonian concept of the unconscious.

1059 Whittaker, Albert L. "Bergson: First Aid to Common Sense." *Forum*, 51, No. 3, March 1914, 410-414.

1060 Willcox, Louise Collier. "Implications of Bergson's Philosophy." *North American Review*, 199, No. 700, March 1914, 448-451.

1061 Williams, T. Rhonnda. "Syndicalism in France and its Relation to the Philosophy of Bergson." *Hibbert Journal*, 12, No. 46, February 1914, 389-403. The author criticizes syndicalists for misinterpreting Bergson's concept of the intellect.

1062 Wilm, Emil Carl. *Henri Bergson: A Study in Radical Evolution*. New York: Sturgis and Walton Company, 1914, 193.

1063 Yushkevich, Pavel S. "Бергсон и его философия интуиции." *Русское богатство*, No. 2, 1914, 33-59; No. 3, 1914, 47-67.

1064 *Zoological Studies*. Aberdeen: Printed for the University of Aberdeen, 1914, 138. Articles by J. Arthur Thomson, J. J. Simpson, J. Alexander Innes, and A. Landsborough Thomson are contained in this volume.

1915

1065 Akely, Lewis Ellsworth. "Bergson and Science." *Philosophical Review*, 24, No. 3, May 1915, 270-287. The author holds that: "Science may possibly have something to learn from a great modern philosophy such as that of Bergson." (270). The author stresses the place of intuition in science and the need for a new philosophy of science education.

1066 "Aspects of Dream Life." *Journal of Abnormal Psychology*, 10, No. 2, 1915-1916, 100-119. The author states, "Bergson at the close of his essay on dreams hints that the mind may transcent its conjectured limits and be influenced in profound slumber by telepathy. This is but a hypothesis which must long await verification" (p. 118). The author's own dreams which forecast the future have been largely erroneous.

1067 Benda, Julien. "A Propos de 'La Philosophie française'." *Mercure de France*, 112, No. 417, 1915, 186-188. The author holds that Bergson does not understand French philosophy, with its rationalistic devotion to clear and distinct ideas.

1068 "Bergson Looking Backward." *Literary Digest*, 50, No. 1292, January 13, 915, 149-150. This is an account of Bergson's interpretation of German militarism.

1069   Beveridge, Albert J. *What is Back of the War*. Indianapolis: Bobbs-Merrill, 1915,
        430. An interview with Bergson, titled "The Prophet of the New Philosophy,"
        appears here on pp. 268-295. In this interview Bergson expresses his fear for
        the continued existence of French civilization. (A letter from Bergson and his
        corrections of Beveridge's interview are in the Library of Congress in the
        Beveridge papers.)

1070   Bönke, H. *Plagiator Bergson: Membre de l'Institut*. Charlottenburg, Sweden:
        Huth, 1915, 47.

1071   Borgese, Giuseppe Antonio. *Studî di letterature moderne*. Milano: Fratelli Treves,
        1915, 383.

1072   Braun, O. "Review of "Materie und Gedächtnis by Henri Bergson." *Archiv für
        Gesamte Psychologie*, 15, No. 4, 1915, 13-15. This review is brief, general,
        and highly favorable.

1073   Bruers, An. "Il principio di creazione del Bergson e la metapsichica." *Luce e
        ombra*, 15, No. 6, 1915.

1074   Bunge, C. "El pragmatismo." *Nosotros*, 9, No. 75, julio 1915, 17-19.

1075   Carr, Herbert Wildon. "Review of *Henri Bergson: An Account of his Life and
        Philosophy* by Algot Ruhe and Nancy Margaret Paul." *Mind*, 24, No. 93, January
        1915, 117-119.

1076   Carr, Herbert Wildon. "Bergson's Theory of Memory." *Athenaeum*, No. 4567,
        May 8, 1915, 427-429; No. 4568, May 15, 1915, 448-450. This article is a
        report of a lecture given by the author at King's College, London on May 5, 1915.

1077   Carr, Herbert Wildon. "Review of *The Ethical Implications of Bergson's Philosophy*
        by Una Bernard Sait." *Mind*, 24, No. 93, January 1915, 119-120.

1078   "Mr. Wildon Carr and Philosophy of Change." *Quest*, 7, No. 2, 1915, 568-574.
        This is a review of H. W. Carr's *The Philosophy of Change*.

1079   Caso, Antonio. *Problemas filosóficos*. México: Porrúa hermanos, 1915, 296. The
        chapter in this work entitled "La filosofía de la intuición" concerns Bergson's
        philosophy.

1080   Cérésole, Pierre. "L'Irréductibilité de l'intuition des probabilités et l'existence de
        propositions mathématiques indemonstrables." *Archives de Psychologie*, 15,
        1915, 225-305. The author argues against Henri Poincaré that the intuition of
        probability can not be reduced to an objective and formal probability calculus.

1081   Croce, Benedetto. *What is Living and What is Dead of the Philosophy of Hegel*.
        3rd ed. Trans. Douglas Ainslie. London: Macmillan & Co., 1915, 217. On pp.
        213-215, after an incisive analysis and criticism of Hegel's philosophy, the
        author notes the emergence of a new romanticism as one condition for a true
        understanding of Hegel's philosophy. He sees the new romantics as setting up
        the old Schellingian ideal of aesthetic contemplation: "Thus Bergson, one of
        the writers who have attached themselves to his movement, advocates as a
        metaphysic of the absolute, an intuitive knowledge 'qui s'installe dans le mouve-
        ment et adopte la vie même des choses.' But was not this just what Hegel
        demanded, and the point from which he began—to find a form of mind, which
        should be mobile as the movement of the real..."(p. 214). The author adds,
        however, that for Hegel such a view was only a starting point, not a conclusion.
        "The renunciation of thought would have been asked of Hegel in vain" (p. 214).

1082   D'Arcy, Charles F. *God and Freedom in Human Experience*. London: Edward
        Arnold, 1915, 312. This work is strongly influenced by Bergson.

1083   "Review of *Dreams* by Henri Bergson." *Athenaeum*, No. 4550, January 9, 1915,
        p. 35.

1084   Dunne, M. A. "Plato and Bergson: A Comparison and a Contrast." *American
        Catholic Quarterly Review*, 40, No. 159, July 1915, 442-449.

1085   Gates, R. Ruggles. "Evolutionism of Bergson." *Monist*, 25, No. 4, October 1915,
        537-555.

1086   Gehlke, Charles Elmer. *Emile Durkheim's Contributions to Sociological Theory*.
        New York: Columbia University, 1915, 188. The author discusses Durkheim
        and Bergson on pp. 88-92. Not without uneasiness, he cites many similarities
        between them. (Columbia University Studies in History, Economics, and Public
        Law, 63, No. 1)

1087   Gemelli, Agostino. "Henri Bergson e la néoscolastica italiana." *Rivista di filosofia
        neoscolastica*, 7, No. 2, 1915, 574-579. This is a review of Olgiati, *La filosofia
        de Henri Bergson*.

1088   Gramzow, Otto. "Bergson." *Westermanns illustrierte deutsche Monatshefte*, 69,
        No. 8, August 1915, 795-800.

1089   Hilpert, Constantin. "Die Unterscheidung der intuitiven Erkenntnis von der Analyse
        bei Bergson." Diss., Breslau, 1915, xix, 98.

1090   Höffding, Harald. *Modern Philosophers and Lectures on Bergson*. Auth. Trans.
        Alfred C. Mason. London: Macmillan, 1915, 317. This in an exposition and
        criticism of Bergson's basic theses. The author holds: "...Bergson rather paves
        the way towards a sort of artistic perception than towards a higher science."
        (238). The "Lectures on Bergson" occur on pp. 229-302; notes, on 313-317.

1091   Hoogveld, J. *Die nieuwe Wijsbegeerte: Een studie over Bergson*. Utrecht, Nether-
        lands: Dekker and van de Vegt, 1915, viii, 194.

1092   Horton, Lydiard H., "Scientific Method in the Interpretation of Dreams." *Journal
        of Abnormal Psychology*, 10, No. 6, 1915-1916, 369-399. On pp. 378, 379 and
        386, the author criticizes the us of *élan vital* as an explanatory concept in
        psychology.

1093   Imbart de la Tour, Pierre. "Le Pangermanisme et la philosophie de l'histoire: Lettre
        à M. Henri Bergson." *Revue des Deux Mondes*, 6e Sér., 30, No. 3, 1er décembre
        1915, 481-520.

1094   "Impressive French Honors to America." *New York Times*, 64, No. 20,945, May
        30, 1915, pt. 2, p. 4:5. This article includes a quote from Bergson lauding
        American idealism.

1095   Jelliffe, Smith Ely. "The Technique of Psychoanalysis." *Psychoanalytic Review*,
        2, No. 2, 1915, 191-199. On pp. 192-193, the author urges psychoanalysts to
        utilize Bergson's concepts of the unconscious and repression.

1096   Jones, Ernest. Review of *Laughter: An Essay on the Meaning of the Comic*, by
        Henri Bergson. *Journal of Abnormal Psychology*, 10, No. 2, 1915-1916, 219-
        222. The reviewer compares Bergson's concept of laughter with that of Freud.
        This is a very insightful brief study.

1097   "Mr. Kallen on Bergson." *North American Review*, 201, No. 710, January 1915,
        94-97.

1098	Khoroshko, V. "Философия Бергсона из точки зрения медиика." *Русская мысль*, 26, No. 2, 1915, 93-118. The title of this work translates into English as "Bergson's Philosophy from a Physician's Point of View."

1099	Klimke, Fr. "Bergson: Die Philosophie des Lebens." *Stimmen der Zeit*, 89, 1915, 223-236.

1100	Lovejoy, Arthur Oncken. "Review of *William James and Henri Bergson: A Study in Contrasting Theories of Life* by Horace M. Kallen." *Nation*, 100, No. 2597, 1915, 388-390.

1101	Macaskill, John. "Intellect and Intuition: A Footnote to Bergson and Bradley." *Contemporary Review*, 108, No. 7, July 1915, 91-99. The author cites interesting similarities between Bergson and F. H. Bradley.

1102	"Review of *The Meaning of the War* by Henri Bergson." *Aus der Nacht zum Licht*, 13, 1915-1916, 118.

1103	Mercanti, Pietro. *Il pensiero filosofico contemporaneo e la psicologia del Bergson*. Pref. Ernesto Buonaiuti. Roma: Angelo Signorelli, 1915, 151.

1104	Miller, Lucius Hopkins. "Bergson and Religion." *Biblical World*, N.S. 46, No. 5, November 1915, 285-293.

1105	Miller, Lucius Hopkins. "The Religious Implications of Bergson's Doctrine Regarding Intuition and the Primacy of Spirit." *The Journal of Philosophy*, 12, No. 23, 1915, 617-632. The author holds that Bergson's thought leads to the primacy of spirit and hence to a religious outlook.

1106	Mitchell, Arthur. "Studies on Bergson." *Bulletin of the University of Kansas*, 20, No. 4, 1915, 1-115.

1107	Paul, Nancy Margaret and Ruhe, Algot Henrik Leonard. *Henri Bergson: An Account of his Life and Philosophy*. London: Macmillan, 1914, 245.

1108	Perry, Ralph Barton. "Philosophy." *The American Yearbook, 1914*. New York and London: D. Appleton & Co., 1915, 677-679. On pp. 678-679, the author notes several criticisms of Bergson by H. M. Kallen, A. O. Lovejoy and others. He agrees with Kallen that Bergson is "a metaphysical absolutist" very different from William James. He notes that speculation about Bergson's religious philosophy should be deferred until Bergson's Gifford lectures on the concept of personality are available. (These lectures were never completed. Cf. Henri Bergson, "The Problem of Personality", April-May, 1914.)

1109	"Plagiator Bergson." *Monatshefte d. Comeniusgesellschaft für Kultur und Geistesleben*, N.S. 7, 1915, 185ff.

1110	"Review of *Plagiator Bergson* by H. Bönke." *Monatshefte der Comeniusgesellschaft für Kultur und Geistesleben*, N.S. 7, 1915, 185-186.

1111	Playne, Caroline. *Bergson and Free Will*. London: Headley, 1915.

1112	"Poet and Philosopher on the War." *Spectator*, 115, No. 4547, August 21, 1915, p. 248. This consists of two brief reviews, of Verhaeren's *Belgium's Agony* and Bergson's *The Meaning of the War*.

1113	Powell, Webster Hezekiah. "A Discussion of Henri Bergson's Metaphysical Views According to the Philosophy of Borden P. Bowne." Diss. Boston 1915.

1114	"Professor Henri Bergson Defines War." *New York Times*, 64, No. 21,043, September 5, 1915, pt. 5, p. 317:1. This is a brief unsigned expository review of *The Meaning of the War* by Henri Bergson.

1115   Robinson, Arthur. "Review of *The Philosophy of Change* by H. Wildon Carr."
        Mind, 24, No. 96, October 1915, 550-555.

1116   Simmel, Georg. "Bergson und d. deutsche 'Zynismus'. *Internationale
        Monatsschrift*, 9, 1915, 197ff.

1117   Strange, E. "Bergson's Theory of Intuition." *Monist*, 25, No. 3, July 1915, 466-470.

1118   Symons, Norman J. "Bergson's Theory of Intellect and Reality." *Queen's Quar-
        terly*, 24, No. 2, 1915, 177-192.

1119   Van der Brugh, Emmanuel Johannes. "De Philosophie van Bergson." *Vragen van
        den Dag*, 30, 1915.

1120   Velez, Pedro. M. *Dos lecturas filosóficos-teológicos: Bergson y el Indice, Pio X,
        el modernismo y Santo Tomás*. "Con las licencias necesarias." Lima: Impr. de
        "La Union," 1915, 30.

1121   Visenot. "Review of 'La Signification de la guerre' by Henri Bergson." *Polybiblion*,
        2e Série, 81 (Partie littéraire), 1915, 317-318.

1122   W., B. C. A. "Review of *Dreams* by Henri Bergson." *Dublin Review*, 156, No.
        312, 1915, 398-399.

1123   Werner, Alfred. "Henri Bergsons Philosophie." *Internationale Monatsschrift für
        Wissenschaft*, 9, 1915, 1431.

1124   Withof, A. "Een nieuwe wijsbegeerte: H. Bergson." *Het Nieuwe Levens*, 1, 1915.

1125   Woodbridge, Riley Isaac. *American Thought from Puritanism to Pragmatism*. New
        York: Henry Holt & Co., 1915, viii, 375. John Fiske is viewed as a predecessor
        of Bergson on pp. 215-216; Bergson's pragmatic and empiricist affinities with
        William James and Charles Sanders Pierce are noted on p. 333; Bergson and
        Emile Boutroux are detailed on p. 335 as philosophers whose ideas are sym-
        pathetic to American thought; differences between Bergson and American neo-
        realists are explained on p. 348; W. Pitkin's criticisms of Bergsonian and Driesc-
        hian biology are detailed on pp. 352-353.

1126   Wyant, G. G. "Bergson and his Philosophy." *Bookman*, 41, No. 1, March 1915,
        22-27.

1916

1127   "Allies Stand Firm as New Year Opens." *New York Times*, 65, No. 21,162, January
        2, 1916, pt. 2, p. 3, col 4. Bergson is here reported as stating that a "revivified
        France" will emerge victorious from the struggles of World War I.

1128   Anastasiadis, Ilias K. *Savigny, Thering, Bergson*. Athènes: 1916, 40.

1129   "Beard of the Poilu Must be Discarded." *New York Times*, 65, No. 21, 398, August
        25, 1916, p. 2, col. 7. This is a collection of witty quotes from French notables
        on the occasion of an order by the French high command that all infantryman
        must shave their beards. Bergson is quoted saying: "I am not afraid to go so
        far as to say that the visage is matter, while the beard is mind."

1130   Bennett, C. A. "Bergson's Doctrine of Intuition." *Philosophical Review*, 25, No.
        1, January 1916, 45-48.

1131   Brockdorf, Cay von. *Die Wahrheit über Bergson*. Berlin: Curtuis, 1916, 55.

1132   Burroughs, John. *Under the Apple-Trees*. Boston and New York: Houghton Mifflin
        Company, 1916, 315. Cf. pp. 197-227 for "Prophet of the Soul."

1133 Cunningham, Gustavus Watts. *A Study in the Philosophy of Bergson*. New York: Longmans, Green and Co., 1916, 212.

1134 Delle Piane, Arístides L. *La filosofía y su enseñanza*. Montevideo, 1916. Bergson and pragmatism are discussed in this book.

1135 Delbos, Victor. *L'Esprit philosophique de l'Allemagne et la pensée française*. Paris: Bloud et Gay, 1916, 43. (On cover: "Pages actuelles," 1914-1915, No. 40.)

1136 Dennert, E. "Bergson als Plagiator." *Unsere Welt*, 8, 1916, 217ff.

1137 Fonsegrive, George. "De Taine à Péguy." *Correspondant*, 10 novembre 1916, 529-534.

1138 Freud, Sigmund. *Wit and its Relation to the Unconscious*. New York: Moffat, Yard and Company, 1916, 383. References to Bergson's *Laughter* may be found on pp. 301-360. The author uses Bergson's theory of laughter to account for cases in which laughter is caused by repetitive, mechanized behavior.

1139 Gregory, J. "Dreams as Psychical Explosions." *Mind*, 25, No. 98, April 1916, 193-205. The author proposes criticisms of Bergson's theory of dreams.

1140 Hager, Wilhelm. *Bergson als Neu-Romantiker mit besonderer Berücksichtigung von M. Maeterlinck*. München: Frölich, 1916, viii, 81. This is an inaugural dissertation.

1141 Heidegger, Martin. "Der Zeitbegriff in der Geisteswissenschaft." Zeitschrift für *Philosophische Kritik*, 161, 1916, 173-188. The author distinguishes time in the social sciences from time in the natural sciences. The former is qualitative, the latter is quantitative; the former flows, the latter is fragmented; the former has no spatial quality, the latter is space. No mention is made of Bergson, but the distinctions are drawn by the author in Bergsonian terms. Cf. Martin Heidegger, 1927, 1978.

1142 Heymans, Gérard. "Een Nederlandsch boek over Bergson door Hoogveld: Di Nieuwe Wijsbegeerte." *Gids*, Ser. 4, 33, No. 1, 1916, 161-171.

1143 Hoeber, F. "Erlebnis der Zeit und Willensfreiheit: Versuche über Bergsons intuitive Philosophie." *Die weissen Blätter*, 4, No. 12, 1916, 185-198.

1144 Höffding, Harald. *La Philosophie de Bergson*. Trans. avec avant-propos Jacques de Coussange. Paris: Félix Alcan, 1916, ix, 165. (Bibliothèque de philosophie contemporaine) This book contains an important letter by Henri Bergson (March, 195) in which Bergson stresses the centrality of the concept of duration in his philosophy. The concept of duration was developed first, the concept of intuition subsequently, and in terms of that of duration.

1145 Horton, Lydiard H. "The Apparent Inversion of Time in Dreams." *Journal of Abnormal Psychology*, 11, No. 1, 1916-1917, 48-58. On pp. 53-55, the author distinguishes his theory of dreams from Bergson's. The author proposes an entirely neurological explanation of time-inversion: the "principle of apperceptive delay."

1146 Horton, Lydiard H. "On the Irrelevancy of Dreams." *Journal of Abnormal Psychology*, 11, No. 3, 1916-1917, 143-171. The author criticizes both Bergson's and Freud's theories of dreams in this article. His own concept of the dream is highly mechanistic, and is based on neurophysiology.

1147 Iberico y Rodriguez, Mariano. *La filosofía de Enrique Bergson*. Lima, 1916.

1148   Imbart de la Tour, Pierre. *Le Pangermanisme et la philosophie de l'histoire: Lettre à M. Bergson.* Paris: Perrin, 1916, 76.

1149   Jacoby, Gunther. "Bergson und A. Schopenhauer." *Internationale Monatsschrift für Wissenschaft*, 10, 1916, 454-479.

1150   Jones, Tudor. *The Spiritual Ascent of Man.* London: University of London Press, 1916.

1151   Jung, Carl Gustav. "The Conception of the Unconscious." *Collected Papers on Analytical Psychology*, 2nd ed. Ed. Constance E. Long. London: Balliere, Tindall and Cox, 1922, 445-474. In this talk, given in 1916 at the Zurich School for Analytical Psychology, the author states, "Special thanks are due to Bergson for having broken a lance for the right of the irrational to exist. Psychology will probably be obligated to acknowledge and to submit to a plurality of principles, in spite or the fact that this does not suit the scientific mind. Only so can psychology be saved from shipwreck" (p. 464). This talk appears again in C. G. Jung's *Collected Works*, 7, 269-304. The reference to Bergson appears on p. 288.

1152   Jung, Carl Gustav. *The Psychology of the Unconscious.* Trans. Beatrice M. Hinkle. New York: Dodd, Mead and Co., 1916, 566. This is the first English translation of Jung's *Wandlungen und Symbole der Libido*. On pp. 495-496, in footnote 30 to Part 1, p. 78, Jung thanks Dr. (Adolph) Keller of Zurich for bringing Bergson's "durée créatrice" to his attention. This footnote is attached to a passage describing "the driving force of the libido." On p. 314, Part 2, Jung uses Bergson's "durée créatrice" to explain mythological concepts of creation through time. *Wandlungen und Symbole der Libido* is retranslated by R. F. C. Hull as *Symbols of Transformation*. This new translation appears in C. G. Jung's *Collected Works*, 5, 1-557.

1153   Kerler, Dietrich Heinrich. "Bergson's Bildertheorie und das Problem des Verhältnisses zwischen Leib und Seele." *Vierteljahrsschrift für wissenschaftliche Philosophie*, 152, 1916, 349-362.

1154   Klimke, F. "Plagiator Bergson: Eine Kulturfrage." *Stimmen der Zeit*, 90, 1916, 422.

1155   Levinger, Lee Joseph. "The Philosophy of Henri Bergson and Judaism." *Central Conference of American Rabbis Yearbook*, 26, 1916, 269-290. A discussion by L. L. Mann and M. Ransom follows.

1156   Marshall, Henry Rutgers. "Retentiveness and Dreams." *Mind*, 25, N.S. 98, April 1916, 207-202. The author considers the views of Marshall, Freud, and Bergson on dreaming.

1157   "Review of *The Meaning of the War* by Henri Bergson." *A.L.A. Booklist*, 12, No. 6, March 1916, p. 277.

1158   Miller, Lucius Hopkins. *Bergson and Religion.* New York: Henry Holt and Company, 1916, 275.

1159   Molina, Enrique. *La filosofía de Bergson.* Santiago, Chile: Imprenta Barcelona, 1916, 128.

1160   Molina, Enrique. "La verdad y el método de Bergson." *Revista de Filosofía*, 2, No. 6, noviembre 1916, 321-341.

1161   Oesterreich, Konstantin, Ed. *Überweg's Grundriss der Geschichte der Philosophie.* 11th Ed. Vol. 4. Berlin: E. S. Mittler, 1916, Bergson's philosophy is examined on pp. 413f, his writings on pp. 534-536. Writings about Bergson are reviewed on pp. 769, 711, 818, 820, 825, 858. Cf. also pp. 530, 873, 875, 877.

1162   Palante, Georges. "Sur Le Succès du bergsonisme." *Mercure de France*, Sér. moderne 116, 16 juillet, 1916, 306-308. This is a review of Benda's *Sur Le Succès du bergsonisme.*

1163   Palcos, Alberto. "José Ortega y Gasset: El sentido de la filosofía." *Nosotros*, 10, No. 88, agosto 1916, 204.

1164   Pincherel, Salvatore. "Il calcolo delle probabilità e l'intuizione." *Scientia*, 10, No. 6, 1916, 417-426. A French translation of this article is given on pp. 193-203.

1165   Radhakrishnan, Sarvapalli. "Bergson's Idea of God." *Quest*, 8, No. 4, October 1916, 1-8.

1166   Rayner, Ernest A. "The Origin and Developement of Persons." *Philosophical Review*, 25, No. 6, November 1916, 788-800. The author pursues a critique of both Bergson and B. Bosanquet.

1167   Roure, Lucien. "Un Livre danois sur M. H. Bergson." *Etudes par des Pères de la Compagnie de Jésus*, 149, 5 novembre 1916, 398-403.

1168   Sagot du Vaurox, Mgr. Charles Paul. *Du subjectivisme allemand à la philosophie catholique*. Paris: Bloud et Gay, 1916. (Pages actuelles No. 89)

1169   Sarolea, Charles. *The French Renascence*. London: Allen and Unwin, 1916, 302. Bergson's part in the "French Renascence" is discussed on pp. 271-284.

1170   Seydl, E. "Henri Bergson." *Allgemeine Literaturbericht*, 25, No. 3, 1916, 65-70.

1171   Seydl, Ernest. "Henri Bergsons intuitive Philosophie." *Das neue Oesterreich*, 1, No. 1, 1916, 49-54.

1172   Sorel, Georges. *Reflections on Violence*. Trans. T. E. Hulme. London: Allen and Unwin, 1916, 299.

1173   Symons, Norman J. "Bergson's Theory of Intellect and Reality." *Scientific American Supplement*, 82, No. 2936, December 9, 1916, 370-371; 2137, December 16, 1916, 390-391. This is a highly critical analysis of Bergson's biology.

1174   Thompson, J. Arthur. "Professor Henri Bergson's Biology." *Royal Physical Society for the Promotion of Zoology and other Branches of Natural History* (Proceedings). Edinburgh, 19, 1916, 79-92. The author, a prominent British biologist, urges those in biology to profit from Bergson's conceptual standpoint. Bergson is correct to insist on the historical nature of the organism. His theory of instinct can not be brushed aside, his treatment of Lamarckianism is ingenious.

1175   Van Ginneken, T. "Nova et vetera." *Studiën*, 86, 1916, 582-584.

1176   Woodbridge, Frederick James Eugene. *The Purpose of History: Reflections on Bergson, Dewey and Santayana*. New York: Columbia University Press, 1916, 89.

1917

1177   "Address by Professor Bergson." *New York Times*, 66, No. 21,594, March 9, 1917, p. 6:7. This article reports Bergson's lecture before the American Academy of Arts and Letters concerning the French Academy. Bergson states that in France a man is not expected to be absorbed in one specialty. This penchant for eclecticism allows a man to remain a man, and prevents the "shrinking or cramping of the moral sense."

1178   "American Idealism." *New York Times*, 66, No. 21,659, May 13, 1917, pt. 2, p. 2, col. 4. This is an editorial supporting Bergson's claim that the United States is a nation of idealists.

1179   "Are Americans Money Worshippers? Bergson's Opinion." *Outlook*, 117, No. 4, September 1917, 119.

1180   "Bergson and the Art World." *Art World*, 2, No. 2, May 1917, 106-109. This is an unsigned editorial.

1181   "Dr. Henri Bergson Here." *New York Times*, 66, No. 21, 570, February 13, 1917, p. 7:2. This brief article notes Bergson's unheralded arrival in New York. (Bergson was on a diplomatic mission representing the French government. Cf. H. Bergson, "Mes Missions", 1936)

1182   "Henri Bergson Honored." *New York Times*, 66, No. 21, 598, March 13, 1917, p. 8, col. 3. This article notes that Bergson was the guest of honor at a luncheon, given by the France-America Society, at which both Bergson and France were praised by Joseph Choate.

1183   "Bergson Thanks America." *New Republic*, 13, No. 164, December 1917, 207-209. This is a speech by Bergson to the American and English Red Cross, October 28, 1917, delivered in Paris.

1184   Bermann, Gregorio. "Las orientaciones de la filosofía contemporánea." *Nosotros*, 11, No. 99, julio 1917, 428.

1185   Bönke, H. "Bergsons Bedeutung." *Unsere Welt*, 9, 1917, 85-92.

1186   Bussy, Gertrude Carman. "Typical Recent Conceptions of Freedom." Diss., Northwestern, 1917.

1187   Caso, Antonio. *Filosofiá francesa contemporánea*. México, 1917.

1188   Corrance, Henry C. "Bergson's Idea of God." *Quest*, 9, No. 1, January 1917, 340-342. This is a discussion of Prof. Radhakrishnan's gravamen against Bergson's philosophy.

1189   Drever, James. *Instinct in Man*. Cambridge, Massachusetts: University Press, 1917, 316. Bergson's views on instinct are discussed on pp. 82-110. "Instinct is the'life impulse'becoming conscious as determinate conscious impulse." (88).

1190   Garcia Morente, Manuel. *La filosofía de Henri Bergson: Con el discurso pronunciado por M. Bergson en la Residencia de Estudiantes el 10 de mayo de 1916*. Madrid: Publicaciones de la Residencia de Estudiantes, 1917, 150. (Collec. Austral) This item contains a talk given by Bergson during a diplomatic mission to Spain. (Cf. H. Bergson "Mes Missions," 1936.)

1191   Grandjean, Frank. *Esquisse d'une pédagogie inspirée du bergsonisme*. Genève: Atar, 1917, iv, 31. This essay was published originally in *Bulletin de la Société Pédagogique Genevoise*.

1192   Höffding, Harald. *La Philosophie de Bergson*. 2nd ed. Trans. Jacques de Coussange. Paris: Félix Alcan, 1917, ix, 165 (Bibliothèque de philosophie contemporaine).

1193   Jäger, Georg. "Das Verhältnis Bergsons zu Schelling." Diss., Leipzig, 1917, 64.

1194   Jäger, Georg. *Das Verhältnis Bergsons zu Schelling: Ein Beitrag zur Erörterung der Prinzipien einer organischen Weltauffassung*. Hamburg: Lütck & Wulff, 1917, 64.

1195 Joergensen, Joergen Fr. *Henri Bergson' Filosofi i omrids*. Kjoebenhavn: Forf., 1917, 88.

1196 Kerler, Dietrich Heinrich. *Henri Bergson und das Problem des Verhältnisses zwischen Leib und Seele; Kritische Anmerkungen zu Bergson's Buch "Materie und Gedächtnis."* Ulm: H. Kerler, 1917, 18.

1197 Laird, John. *Problems of the Self: An Essay Based on the Shaw Lectures Given in the University of Edinburgh March 1914*. London: Macmillan and Co., 1917, 375. The author compares Bergson and Fichte on pp. 168-170, noting that both insist on the centrality of activity and deny that space can be true basis of reality. The author compares Bergson and A. Schopenhauer on pp. 183-184, arguing that their conclusions diverge radically. On pp. 184-190 he examines Bergson's "voluntarism", concluding that Bergson is not a voluntarist.

1198 Lazarev, A. "Filosofia Bergsona." *Mysl' i slovo*, 1, 1917, 177-214.

1199 Lote, René. *Les Leçons intellectuelles de la guerre*. Paris: Perrin et Cie, 1917, 199. The author argues that Germany has succeeded to the extent that it has through the disciplined use of scientific intelligence. He subjects prewar French mentality (mystical and Bergsonian) to scathing criticism for not having prepared France for combat.

1200 "Lowly in France Rise to War Ideals." *New York Times*, 66, No. 21,596, March 11, 1917, pt. 1, p. 7:5. This is a report of Bergson's talk, on March 8, 1917, before the Academy of Arts and Letters concerning the French Academy, whose activities, Bergson states, express "something vital in the French spirit."

1201 Meckauer, Walter. "Der Intuitionismus und seine Elemente bei Henri Bergson." Diss., Breslau: H. Flieschmann, 1916, Leipzig: Meiner, 1917, 160.

1202 Molina, Enrique. "El espíritu según Bergson." *Revista de Filosofía*, 3, No. 2, marzo 1917, 203-214.

1203 Peckham, George William. *Logic of Bergson's Philosophy*. Diss., Columbia, 1917, 68. New York: Columbia University Press, 1917, 68. The author is highly critical of Bergson's dualistic tendencies. This dissertation was supervised by John Dewey.

1204 Radhakrishnan, Sarvapalli. "Is Bergson's Philosophy Monistic?" *Mind*, 25, No. 103, July 1917, 329-339. The author views Bergson as a monist.

1205 Robinson, Arthur. "The Philosophy of Bergson." *Modern Churchman*, 3e Ser., 7, No. 3, March 1917.

1206 Scott, J. W. "Bergsonism in England." *Monist*, 27, No. 2, April 1917, 179-204. The author concludes that Bergson's philosophy "...differs from other idealism in an essentially philosophical way only when it has something to say which is indefensible..." (204).

1207 Segond, Joseph. "L'Intellectualisme et la philosophie bergsonienne." *Revue Philosophique de la France et de l"Etranger*, 84, No. 2, juillet-décembre 1917, 77-95. The author reviews Höffding, *Philosophie de Bergson* and Grandjean, *Une Révolution dans la philosophie*. In general, he defends Bergson against criticisms.

1208 Seillière, Ernest. "L'Avenir de la philosophie bergsonienne." *Revue Politique et Littéraire, Revue Bleue*, 55, ler semestre, No. 8, 1917, 235-239; No. 9, 1917, 261-266; No. 10, 1917, 299-304.

1209   Sinclair, May. *A Defense of Idealism*. London: Macmillan, 1917, 396. Chapter II, entitled "Vitalism," appears on pp. 51-74. It is a discussion of Bergson's philosophy.

1210   Stephen, Karin. "Thought and Intuition." *Proceedings of the Aristotelian Society*, N.S. 18, 1917-1918, 38-74.

1211   Thayer, V. T. "God, and the Knowledge of God, According to Bergson and Spinoza." *Journal of Philosophy*, 14, No. 14, July 5, 1917. This is an abstract of a talk. The author stresses close similarities between Bergson and Spinoza.

1212   Tummers, F. "Bergson en de vrije wil." *Tijdschrift voor Wijsbegeerte*, 11, 1917, 488-504.

1213   Tyrrell, Henry. "Bergson." *Art World*, 2, No. 6, September 1917, 520-521. This is a poem dedicated to Bergson.

1214   Van Riper, Benjamin W. "On Cosmic Reversibility." *The Philosophical Review*, 26, No. 4, 1917, 361-380.

1215   Viviani, René. *La Mission française en Amérique, 24 avril-13 mai 1917*. Pref. Henri Bergson. Paris: Flammarion, 1917, 264.

1216   Zeifel, Eugène. "Jules Romains und H. Bergson." *Das literarische Echo*, 20, No. 2, 1917-1918, 84-87.

1918

1217   "Académie française: Réception de M. Henri Bergson: Discours de M. Bergson: Réponse de M. René Doumic." *Le Petit Temps*, 25 janvier 1918.

1218   Adès, Albert. "La Philosophie de Bergson dans la vie." *Grande Revue*, No, 2, 1918, 647-665; No. 3, 1918, 75-94; No. 4, 1918, 279-293.

1219   Adolph, K. "Bergsons Philosophie." *Pastor Bonus*, 30, 1918, 219-228.

1220   Benda, Julien. *Belphégor: Essai sur l'esthétique de la présente société française*. Paris: Emile Paul, 1918, 214. This is one of many books and articles by Benda devoted in part or as a whole to criticism of Bergson's philosophy.

1221   Boine, Giovanni. *La novità di Bergson*. Roma: Nuova Antologia, 1918, 16.

1222   Bouvier, Eugène Louis. *La Vie psychique des insects*. Paris: E. Flammarion, 1918, 299. (Bibliothèque de philosophie scientifique) Cf. the translation of this work, 1922.

1223   Carr, Herbert Wildon. "L'Interaction de l'esprit et du corps." *Revue de Métaphysique et de Morale*, 25, No. 1, janvier 1918, 25-59.

1224   Carr, Herbert Wildon. *"Time" and "History" in Contemporary Philosophy: With Special Reference to Bergson and Croce*. London: Milford, Oxford University Press, 1918, 19 (Proceedings of the British Academy, VIII, 20 March 1918). The author claims that from different standpoints Bergson and Benedetto Croce reach closely similar dynamic conceptions of reality.

1225   Carr, Herbert Wildon. "What Does Bergson Mean by Pure Perception?" *Mind*, 28, No. 108, October 1918, 472-474. The author replies to an earlier discussion of the same topic by Mr. Harward.

1226   Croce, Benedetto. "Bergson e Taine." *Conversazioni critiche*. Bari: Laterza, 1918.

1227   Dauzats, Charles. "Réception de M. Henri Bergson à l'Académie." *Le Figaro*, 3e Sér., 64, No. 25, 25 janvier 1918, 3.

1228   Delacroix, Gilbert. "La Réception de M. Bergson par M. Doumic." *Revue Heb-domadaire*, N.S. 14e Année, No. 5, 2 février 1918, 132-134.

1229   Delaunay, Lois. "Henri Bergson et Plotin." *Revue des Facultés Catholiques de l'Ouest*, 27, 1918, 344-362, 622-645.

1230   "Deluge of Letters Starts." *New York Times*, 67, No. 22, 024, May 13, 1918, p. 7:2. This article notes Bergson's speech, on Mother's Day, commending the American army.

1231   Doumic, René. "Réponse à Bergson." *Journal Officiel de la République Française*, 10, No. 5, 26 janvier 1918, 966-970. This is a talk given on the occasion of Bergson's reception into the Académie française.

1232   Doumic, René. *Séance de l'Académie française du 24 janvier 1918: Discours de réception de M. Henri Bergson: Réponse de M. René Doumic*. Paris: Perrin et Cie., 1918, 79.

1233   Eichthal, Eugène d'. "Des Rapports de la mémoire et de la métaphysique." *Revue Philosophique de la France et de l'Etranger*, 85, Nos. 3-4, mars-avril 1918, 177-201. This is a criticism of Bergson's concept of memory.

1234   Enoch, Maurice. "Réception de M. Henri Bergson à l'Académie française: Biographie." *Larousse Mensuel*, 4, No. 134, avril 1918, 409-410.

1235   Falkenfeld, Hellmuth. "Das Verhältnis von Zeit und Realität bei Kant und Bergson." Diss., Humboldt (Berlin), 1918, 48.

1236   Forster, H. "Henri Bergson." *Overland*, N.S. 71, No. 3, April 1918, 358.

1237   Foster, Frank Hugh. "Some Theistic Implications of Bergson's Philosophy." *American Journal of Theology*, 22, No. 2, April 1918, 274-299.

1238   Gaultier, Paul. "Henri Bergson." *Revue Politique et Littéraire, Revue Bleue*, 56e Année, No. 10, 1918, 297-302; No. 11, 1918, 331-336; No. 12, 1918, 360-365; No. 13, 1918, 389-394; No. 14, 1918, 428-431; No. 15, 1918, 469-472.

1239   "Germany Twice Guilty." *New York Times*, 67, No. 21,918, January 27, 1918, pt. 1, p. 13:2. This article cites Bergson's speech, on his election to the French Academy, attacking Germany.

1240   Giraud, Victor. *Le Miracle français: Trois Ans après*. Paris: Hachette, 1918, 362.

1241   Harward, J. "What Does Bergson Mean by Pure Perception?" *Mind*, Vol. 27, No. 106, 1918, 203-207. The author asserts: "On pp. 26-30 of *Matter and Memory* Bergson considers 'how conscious perception may be explained.' It is very difficult to assign any precise meaning to the contents of these pages." (203).

1242   Hébrard, Dom. *La Vie intérieure: Esquisse d'une philosophie religieuse de la vie intérieure et de l'action*. Paris: Beauchesne, 1918, xxxix, 596.

1243   Inge, William Ralph. *The Philosophy of Plotinus*. London, New York: Longmans, Green and Co., 1918, I, 270. Bergson's concept of time is discussed on pp. 174-177; Bergson's concept of consciousness on pp. 242-244.

1244   Jacquemont, P. "M. Bergson à l'Académie française." *La France Illustrée*, 2 février 1918.

1245   Jaloux, Edmond. "Henri Bergson." *Le Gaulois*, 24 janvier 1918.

1246   Larrosa, Juan R. "Del filósofo Bergson al Mariscal Joffre." *La Nación*, 8 septiembre 1918.

1247   Leighton, J. A. "Temporalism and the Christian Idea of God." *Chronicles*, 18, 1918, 283-288, 339-344.

1248   Macaskill, John. "Bergson and a Philosophical Peace." *Calcutta Review*, 2nd Ser., 6, No. 3, April 1918, 215-222.

1249   Mourgue, Raoul. "Néo-vitalisme et sciences physiques." *Revue de Métaphysique et de Morale*, 25, No. 4, 1918, 419-431. The author defends vitalism on the basis of physics, cites the work of J. Johnstone (1914), a biologist "qui s'inspire beaucoup de Bergson."

1250   Papini, Giovanni. *Stroncature*. 3rd ed. Firenze: Librería della voce, 1918, 398. Bergson and B. Croce are discussed on pp. 51-56.

1251   Pelca, G. "M. Henri Bergson à l'Académie: L'Eloge d'Emile Ollivier: La Réception de M. Bergson: La Réponse de M. Doumic." *Le Gaulois*, 26 janvier 1918. This is an account of Bergson's reception into the Académie française.

1252   Penido, Maurilio Teixeira-Leite. *La Méthode intuitive de M. Bergson: Essai critique*. Paris: Félix Alcan, 1918, 220.

1253   Rageot, Gaston. "Henri Bergson." *Revue de Paris*, 25, No. 3, 1er février 1918, 540-563.

1254   Rageot, Gaston. "Henri Bergson académicien." *Illustration*, 76, No. 3903, 2 février 1918, 103.

1255   Russell, Bertrand. *Proposed Roads to Freedom: Socialism, Anarchism, and Syndicalism*. London: George Allen, 1918; New York: Henry Holt and Company, 1919, 218. Bergson and syndicalism are mentioned on p. 68.

1256   Scott, J. W. "Realism and Politics." *Proceedings of the Aristotelian Society*, N.S. 18, 1918, 224-246. The author summarizes his article as follows: "The per is intended to show how little surprising it is that the speculations of M. Bergson and Mr. Russell, in practice, should work out in the same way; that people in the more advanced social movements of the present time should think to draw inspiration from both sources. The thesis is that there is something common to both the ways of thinking, that with this part of themselves they touch social movements, and that the feature in which they at once touch social movements and touch each other is their realism." (p. 224).

1257   Segond, Joseph. *La Guerre mondiale et la vie spirituelle*. Paris: Félix Alcan, 1918, 167, This study is an attempted explanation of war based in part on *L'Evolution créatrice*.

1258   Segond, Joseph. *Intuition et amitié*. Paris: Félix Alcan, 1918, 180 (Bibliothèque de philosophie contemporaine).

1259   Selden, Charles. "Bergson Confident of Allied Victory." *New York Times*, 67, No. 22,040, May 29, 1918, p. 2:6. Assured of Allied victory, Bergson states that the outcome of the First World War is evident to everyone but the German leaders.

1260   Sheldon, Wilmon Henry. *Strife of Systems and Productive Duality*. London: Humphrey Milford, 1918, 528. In "Intuition and Mysticism", pp. 287-316, the author discusses relations between Bergson's theory of knowledge and the truth-claims of various mystics. He identifies Bergson's *élan vital* with God.

1261   Smith, Norman Kemp. *Commentary to Kant's Critique of Pure Reason*. London: Macmillan, 1918, 651. Bergson is discussed on pp. 86, 142, 359-360n, and 587n.

1262   Sorley, W. R. *Moral Values and the Idea of God*. Cambridge, England: Cambridge University Press, 1918. Intuition and the vital impulse are discussed in this study.

1263   Souday, Paul. "Réception de M. Henri Bergson." *Le Temps*, No. 20657, 26 janvier 1918, 3.

1264   Troilo, Erminio. *La conflagrazione: Indagini sulla storia dello spirito contemporaneo*. Roma: Formiggini, 1918, 353.

1265   Troilo, Erminio. *Figure e studi di storia della filosofia*. Roma: Impr. Polyglotte l'Universelle, 1918, 324. This is a highly critical study of Bergson, James, Vailati, Bergi, and others.

1266   Truc, Gonzague. "La Guerre et le bergsonisme." *L'Opinion*, lle Année, No. 36, 7 septembre 1918, 180-181.

1267   Wechsler, I. S. "The Role of the Emotions in the Genesis of Insanition and Insanity from the Standpoint of Evolution." *Journal of Abnormal Psychology*, 12, No. 6, 1918, 375-389. "Every philosopher, from Thales to Bergson, has sought to explain the oneness of things" (p. 375). But now *science* is on the march.

1919

1268   Batault, Georges. *La Guerre absolue: Essai de philosophie de l'histoire*. Paris: Payot, 1919, 278.

1269   Boll, Marcel, "Sur La Durée, la liberté, et autres 'intuitions'." *Mercure de France*, 122, ler février 1919, 385-410.

1270   Carr, Herbert Wildon. *Henri Bergson: The Philosopy of Change*. London: T. C. and E. C. Jack, 1919, 126. (People's Books, No. 26)

1271   Carr, Herbert Wildon. "Review of *L'Energie spirituelle* by Henri Bergson." *Hibbert Journal*, 18, No. 1, 1919, 184-187.

1272   Decoster, Paul. *La Réforme de la conscience*. Bruxelles: Lamertin, 1919, 91.

1273   Delage, Yves. "Sur la Nature du comique." *Revue du Mois*, 20, No. 118, 10 août 1919, 337-354. Delage holds in oposition to Bergson that laughter arises through perception of disharmony between cause and effect. (See Bergson's response to the author in the next issue of the *Revue du Mois*, 1919.)

1274   Delaunay, Louis. *Monsieur Bergson at Plotin*. Angers: Siraudeau, 1919, 43.

1275   García Calderón, Francisco. *Ideas é impresiones: Precede un estudio Francisco García Calderón por Gonzalo Paris*. Madrid: América, 1919, 257. (Biblioteca de Ciencias Políticas y Sociales).

1276   Grubb, Edward. *The Religion of Experience*. London: Headley Brothers, Ltd., 1919, 202. Chapter IV concerns Bergson and intuition.

1277   Halévy, Daniel. *Charles Péguy et les Cahiers de la Quinzaine*. Paris: Payot, 1919, 267.

1278   Harward, J. "What Does Bergson Mean by Pure Perception?" *Mind*, Vol. 28, No. 112, 1919, 463-470. This is a response to H. Wildon Carr's reply to Harward's earlier discussion. It is very effective.

1279   Helms, Paul. *Fra Plato til Bergson: Idealistisk Taenken gennem Tiderne*. Copenhagen: Madsen, 1919, 276.

1280   Hermant, Abel. "Review of *L'Energie spirituelle* by Henri Bergson." *Le Figaro*, 3e Sér., 65, No. 179, 29 juin 1919, 4.

1281   Isaachsen-Dudok van Heel, Valborg. "Henri Bergson." *Groot-Nederland*, 17, 1919, 584-594.

1282   Knudsen, Peter. "Ist Bergson ein Plagiator Schopenhauers?" *Archiv für Geschichte der Philosophie*, 32, No. 1, 1919, 89-107.

1283   Lalande, André. "La Psychologie, ses divers objets et ses méthodes." *Revue Philosophique de la France et de l'Etranger*, 87, Nos. 3-4, mars-avril 1919, 117-221.

1284   Landquist, Johan. *Det levande förflutna: Betraktelser over samtida fragor*. Stockholm: A. Bonnier, 1919, 255. This book contains a section titled: "Bergson och de politiska partierna."

1285   Lenoir, Raymond. "Réflexions sur le bergsonisme." *Nouvelle Revue Française*, 13, No. 12, ler décembre 1919, 1077-1089.

1286   Narsy, R. "Review of *L'Energie spirituelle* by Henri Bergson." *Journal des Débats*, 11 août 1919.

1287   Parodi, Dominique. *La Philosophie contemporaine en France: Essai de classification des doctrines*. Paris: Félix Alcan, 1919, 302 (Bibliothèque de philosophie contemporaine).

1288   Radhakrishnan, Sarvepalli. "Bergson and Absolute Idealism." *Mind*, 28, No. 109, 1919, 41-53; No. 111, 1919, 275-296. The author concludes that: "Bergsonism must have absolute idealism as a foundation."

1289   Rageot, Gaston. "Review of *L'Energie spirituelle* by Henri Bergson." *Revue Hebdomadaire des Cours et des Conférences*, 28e Année, No. 51, 20 décembre 1919, 331-350.

1290   Reinke, Johannes. *Die Schaffende Natur: Mit Bezugnahme auf Schopenhauer und Bergson*. Leipzig: Verlag von Quelle und Meyer, 1919, 153. Bergson is discussed on pp. 111-129.

1291   Roure, Lucien. "Notes sur la psychologie de M. Bergson: *L'Energie spirituelle*." *Etudes par des Pères de la Compagnie de Jésus*, 161, 5 novembre 1919, 295-303.

1292   Scheler, Max. *Vom Umsturtz der Werte: Die Abhandlungen und Aufsätze*. Leipzig: Der Neue Geist Verlag, 1919, II, 345.

1293   Schinz, Albert. "Intellectualism Versus Intuitionism in French Philosophy Since the War." *Psychological Review Index*, 29, 1919, 393f. The author mentions J. Benda and René Lote as critics of "intuition" who blamed France's unpreparedness for the First World War on philosophers like Bergson.

1294   Schneeweiss, A. J. "Time and Speculative Philosophy." *Monist*, 28, No. 3, October 1919, 601-610.

1295   Scott, J. W. *Syndicalism and Philosophical Realism: A Study in the Correlation of Contemporary Social Tendencies*. London: A. and C. Black, Ltd., 1919. Bergson and syndicalism are discussed on pp. 88-160.

1296   Seligmann, Raphael. "Die Entwicklungstheorie Bergsons." *Sozialistisches Monatsheft*, 1919, 462-472.

1297   Smith, Mary, and McDougall, William. "Some Experiments in Learning and Retention." *British Journal of Psychology*, 10, Parts 2 and 3, 1919-1920, 199-209. The authors conclude, "In this paper we have adduced experimental evidence in support of Prof. Bergson's distinction between habit and memory; we have illustrated the great importance of effort or volition in rendering repetition effective in memorizing..." (p. 209).

1298   Thayer, V. T. "Comparison of Bergson and Spinoza." *Monist*, 29, No. 1, January 1919, 96-105.

1299   Truc, Gonzague. "Belphégor ou le monde bergsonien." *L'Opinion*, 12e Année, No. 17, 26 avril 1919, 373-374.

1300   Truc, Gonzague. "Troisième Lettre à une institutrice sur la culture de l'esprit: Bergson." *L'Ecole et la Vie*, 3, No. 10, 20 décembre 1919, 207-208. This is a general overview of Bergson's philosophy which mentions *L'Energie spirituelle* in passing.

1301   Vandérem, Fernand. "Review of *L'Energie spirituelle* by Henri Bergson." *Revue de Paris*, 26e Année, No. 16, 15 août 1919, 867-872.

1302   Voorthuisen, Th. "H. Bergson." *De Opbouw*, 2, 1919.

1303   Whitehead, Alfred North. *An Enquiry Concerning the Principles of Natural Knowledge* Cambridge: At the University Press, 1919, 200. Cf. pp. vii-viii. The author distinguishes "durations," as ultimate constituents of nature, from "instants." He uses three basic terms (duration, passage, and rhythm) drawn from Bergson's writings. Cf. also Ch. 18 "Rhytms", pp. 195-200.

1920

1304   Abbott, Lyman. "Four Books Reviewed." *Outlook*, 126, No. 17, December 29, 1920, p. 767. This article contains a brief review of *Mind-Energy* by Henri Bergson.

1305   Alexander, Samuel. *Space, Time and Deity: The Gifford Lectures at Glasgow 1916-1918*. 2 vols. London: Macmillan and Co., 1920. Bergson's concept of time is discussed on pp. i, 36, 44, 140; the spatialization of time on p. 148; Bergson and Heraclitus on p. 150; not-being on p. 199; motion as unitary on p. 321; change on p. 329; the intensity of sensations in Vol. 2, p. 1621.

1306   "Bergson on Mind." *London Times Literary Supplement*, No. 981, November 4, 1920, p. 715. This is an unsigned review of *Mind-Energy*. The reviewer concentrates on Bergson's concept of the brain and its functions.

1307   C., F. W. "Review of *Mind-Energy* by Henri Bergson." *Boston Transcript*, September 22, 1920, p. 4.

1308   Carr, Herbert Wildon. "The Concept of Mind Energy." *Mind*, 29, No. 113, 1920, 1-10. The author presents an exposition of of Bergson's *Mind-Energy*.

1309   Carr, Herbert Wildon. *The General Principle of Relativity*. London: Macmillan and Co., Ltd., 1920. The author discusses Bergson's and Russell's concepts of motion and continuity on pp. 34-39.

1310   Carr, Herbert Wildon. "What Does Bergson Mean by Pure Perception?" *Mind*, 26, No. 113, January 1920, 123. This is a further reply to Mr. Harward. (Cf. J. Harward, 1919)

1311   Chevalier, Jacques. "A Propos de la philosophie bergsonienne: Bergson et Aristote." *Les Lettres*, 8, No. 6, 1 juin 1920, 179-201. The author criticizes Jacques Maritain for quoting Bergson's statements concerning God out of context, and for failing to see that Bergson's intuition is close to Aquinas *intellectus*. Maritain's treatment of Aristotle is, moreover, erroneous.

1312 Chevalier, Jacques. "Discussion avec Jacques Maritain sur 'Aristote et Bergson'." *Les Lettres*, 8, No. 4, 1er avril 1920, 79-118.

1313 Chevalier, Jacques. "Le Point de vu: de M. Jacques Chevalier (Lettre ouverte à Gaëtan Bernouille, 24 Février 1920)" *Les Lettres*, 8, No. 4, 1 avril, 1920, 88-91. The author defends Bergson against Thomist criticisms urged in earlier numbers of this journal.

1314 Chiapelli, Alessandro. "L'energia spiruale: A proposito del nouvo libro di Enrico Bergson." *Nuova antologia*, Ser. 6, 205, No. 3, 1 marzo 1920, 3-13.

1315 Cochet, Marie-Anne. *L'Intuition et l'amour: Essai sur les rapports métaphysiques d l'intuition et de l'instinct avec l'intelligence et la vie*. Paris: Perrin, 1920, 263.

1316 Cory, Charles E. "A Subconscious Phenomenon." *Journal of Abnormal Psychology*, 14, No. 16, 1920, 369-375. The author begins his article as follows: "In his essay on Dreams, Henri Bergson makes the statement that the great discoveries of the last century were in the physical order, and that those of the twentieth century will probably be in the realm of the subconscious" (p. 369). The author agrees with this prophecy and gives a case history, involving automatic sketches.

1317 De Laguna, Theodore. "Review of *An Enquiry Concerning the Principles of Natural Knowledge* by Alfred North Whitehead." *Philosophical Review*, 29, No. 3, 1920, 269-275. The reviewer asserts on p. 269 that Whitehead is clearly influenced by Bergson, but that Whitehead attempts to reformulate science so that it will no longer be open to Bergson's criticisms.

1318 Dolson, Grace Neal. "Review of *L'Energie spirituelle* by Henri Bergson." *Philosophical Review*, 29, No. 2, 1920, 202-203.

1319 Dumas, Georges. "Introduction à la psychologie." *Nouveau Traité de psychologie*. Vol. 1. Ed. Georges Dumas. Paris: Félix Alcan, 1920, 335-366. Bergson and the history of French psychology are discussed on pp. 342-350, 355-356, and 362. Bergson's critique of associationism led associationists to look for dynamic, non-atomistic explanations, and to seek associations not in images and ideas but in directions and tendencies. Psychologists were led by Bergson's critique of mind-body parallelism to seek "adaptive" explanations of thought and behavior.

1320 Dwelshauvers, Georges. *La Psychologie française contemporaine: La Psychologie de Bergson*. Paris: Félix Alcan, 1920, 256. (Bibliothèque de philosophie contemporaine) Cf. chapter 5, "La Psychologie de Bergson," pp. 198-232. The author holds that Bergson's concept of "rational" is too narrow, but finds many of his solutions ingenious and useful. Once Bergson's anti-intellectual tendencies are compensated for, his approach provides a sound basis for psychology.

1321 Flewelling, Ralph Tyler. *Bergson and Personal Realism*. New York and Cincinnati, Ohio: The Abingdon Press, 1920, 304. The author criticizes Bergson's philosophy for lacking a personalistic standpoint. (Cf. the author, 1977.)

1322 Gentile, Giovanni. "Review of *L'Energie spirituelle* by H. Bergson." *Critica*, 18, No. 1, 1920, 107-112.

1323 Grandjean, Frank. *La Raison et la vue*. Paris: Félix Alcan, 1920, 374. This is a critique of the influence of the sense of sight on the formation of human reason. The influence of Bergson on this study is both apparent and professed.

1324 Gunn, John Alexander. *Bergson and His Philosophy.* London: Methuen and Co., Ltd., 1920, 190.

1325 Horton, Lydiard H. "What Drives the Dream Mechanism?" *Journal of Abnormal Psychology,* 15, No. 4, 1920-1921, 224-258. Criticisms of Bergson's theory of dream images are given here on pp. 248, 250-251, and 253.

1326 Johannet, R. "Discussion avec J. Maritain et Joseph de Tonquédec sur Bergson." *Les Lettres,* 8, No. 2, 1er février 1920, 24-32.

1327 Kanning, Fritz. "Rationales und intuitives Erkennen nach Henri Bergson. I. Rationale Grundbegriffe." Diss., Tübingen. 99.

1328 Kleiner, Juliusz. "Z zagadnien bergsonizmu i romantyzmu." *Przeglad Filozoficzny,* 24, No. 2, 1920, 140-148.

1329 Kuntze, F. "Bergson und die Not der Gegenwart." *Die Westmark, Rheinische Monatsschrift,* 1, 1920, 35-45.

1330 Lasserre, Pierre. *Les Chapelles littéraires, Claudel, Jammes, Péguy.* Paris: Garnier frères, 1920, ix-xxxix, 252. This book contains an essay severely critical of Bergson. Lasserre was a leader of the right-wing Action Française.

1331 Legendre, Maurice. "Réponse de Maurice Legendre à Jacques Maritain." *Les Lettres,* 8, No. 6, 1 juin 1920, 201-207. The author urges Maritain to quote from Aristotle concerning the creation of the world and the immortality of the soul, not from Aquinas. Maritain understands neither Aristotle nor Bergson.

1332 Legendre, Maurice. "Remarques sur le nouveau livre de M. Bergson, *L'Energie spirituelle.*" *Les Lettres,* 8, No. 1, 1er janvier 1920, 1-15.

1333 Legendre, Maurice. "Réponse." *Les Lettres,* 8, No. 3, 1er mars 1920, 55-60; No. 4, 1er avril 1920, 79-118. The author replies to criticisms of his review of *L'Energie spirituelle.*

1334 Lindsay, James. "Review of *Henri Bergson: A Bibliography.*" *Archiv für Geschichte der Philosophie,* 32, Nos. 3-4, 1920, 226.

1335 Maritain, Jacques. "Discussion avec Jacques Chevalier sur 'Aristote et Bergson'." *Les Lettres,* 8, No. 4, 1er avril 1920, 79-118.

1336 Maritain, Jacques. "Discussion avec de Tonquédec et R. Johannet sur Bergson." *Les Lettres,* 8, No. 2, 1er février 1920, 24-32.

1337 Mathewson, Louise. *Bergson's Theory of the Comic in the Light of English Comedy.* Lincoln, Nebraska: University of Nebraska Press, 1920, 27 (University of Nebraska Studies in Language, Literature, and Criticism, No. 5).

1338 "Review of *Mind-Energy* by Henri Bergson." *American Journal of Psychology,* 31, No. 4, October 1920, 410.

1339 Mourgue, Raoul. "Le Point de vue neuro-biologique dans l'oeuvre de M. Bergson et les données actuelles de la science." *Revue de Métaphysique et de Morale,* 27, No. 1, janvier-mars 1920, 27-70.

1340 Ovink, Bernard Jan Hendrik. *Henri Bergson.* Baarn, Netherlands: Hollandia-drukkerij, 1920. (Groote Denkers, 4th Ser., No. 1).

1341 Pentimalli, Giuseppi. *Bergson: La dottrina della durata reale e i suoi precedenti storici.* Torino: Fratelli Boca, 1920, 190.

1342 Pimenoff, L. L. "Freedom in the World-Soul: A Plea for Bergsonism." *Monist,* 30, No. 3, July 1920, 460-473.

1343 "Portrait of Bergson." *Outlook*, 126, December 29, 1920, 767. This is a review of *Mind-Energy*.

1344 Prezzolini, Giuseppe. *Uomini 22 e città 3*. Firenze: Vallecchi, 1920, 313. Bergson is discussed on pp. 41-66.

1345 Radhakrishnan, Sarvepalli. *The Reign of Religion in Contemporary Philosophy*. London: Macmillan and Co., Ltd., 1920, 463. Chapters 4 and 5 of this study ("M. Bergson and Absolute Idealism") as well as Chapter 7 ("Bergson's Idea of God") are journal articles published previously. References to Bergson may be found throughout this book.

1346 Rickert, Heinrich. *Die Philosophie des Lebens*. Tübingen, Germany: Mohr, 1920, 196.

1347 Rivers, W. H. R. *Instinct and the Unconscious*. Cambridge University Press, 1920, 252.

1348 Rolland-Gosselin, Marie-Dominique. "Bergsonisme." *Revue des Sciences Philosophiques et Théologiques*, 9, Nos. 1-2, janvier-avril 1920, 187-190. This is a review of *L'Energie spirituelle* and of books on Bergson by Olgiati, Höffding, and Penido.

1349 Royère, Jean. "Le Rire et l'art." *Renaissance Politique et Littéraire*, 27 novembre 1920.

1350 Sageret, Jules. *La Vague mystique: Henri Poincaré, Energétisme (W. Ostwald), Néo-thomisme (P. Duhem), Bergsonisme, Pragmatisme, Emile Boutroux*. Paris: Flammarion, 1920, 180.

1351 Schiller, Ferdinand Channing Scott. "Review of *L'Energie spirituelle* by Henri Bergson." *Mind*, 29, N.S. No. 115, July 1920, 350-354. This is a careful, generally laudatory review.

1352 Schinz, Albert. *French Literature of the Great War*. London and New York: D. Appleton and Co., 1920, 433. On pp. 239-248 the author characterizes Bergson's philosophy of "unmanly sentimentality" as having led France, unprepared, into the First World War.

1353 Selincourt, Basil de. "Music and Duration." *Music and Letters*, 1, No. 4, 1920, 286-293.

1354 Simon, Paul. *Der Pragmatismus in der modernen französischen Philosophie*. Paderborn, Germany: Schoningh, 1920, 158.

1355 Snell, Laird Wingate. "'Creative Evolution' and the Christian Faith." *Anglican Theological Review*, 2, No. 2, March 1920, 255-289.

1356 Sommer, P. "H. Bergson." *Warte*, 15, No. 2, 15 Januar 1920, 93-97.

1357 Thibaudet, Albert. "Réflexions sur la littérature: Lettre à Marcel Proust." *Nouvelle Revue Française*, 20, No. 3, Mars, 1920, 426-441. The author speaks of Proust's "ultra-bergsonisme."

1358 Tilgher, Adriano. "L'estetica di Enrico Bergson." *Nuova antologia*, 6e Ser., 219, No. 6, 16 novembre 1920, 163-168.

1359 Tonquédec, Joseph de. "Discussion avec J. Maritain et R. Johannet sur Bergson." *Les Lettres*, 8, No. 2, ler février 1920, 24-32.

1360 Vaz Ferreira, Carlos. *Lógica viva*. Montevideo: Talleres gráficos, 1920, 304. This work shows Bergson's and James' influence.

1361   Vignon, Paul. "Review of *L'Energie spirituelle* by Henri Bergson." *Revue de Philosophie*, 27, No. 4, 1920, 361-376.

1362   Ward, James. *Psychological Principles*. Second Edition. Cambridge, England: Cambridge University Press, 1920, 478 pp. On pp. 218-219 the author argues that psychological duration is not made up of instants. On p. 418 he remarks concerning the contrasts between changing evolution and unchanging physical law: "During all this long history, with its ever accelerating though devious progress, not a single physical law has ever changed. The whole stupendous drama of *l'élan vital*, as Bergson calls it, has nevertheless inserted itself into this—abstractly regarded—purely mechanical framework, producing a pattern which it cannot account for; but there it is to be accounted for somehow."

1363   Zulen, Pedro Salvino. *La filosofía de lo inexpresable: Bosquejo de una interpretación y una crítica de la filosofía de Bergson*. Lima: Impreso en los talleres tipográficos de Sanmarti y Cía., 1920, 62.

1921

1364   Albee, Ernest Kelley. "Review of *Mind-Energy* by Henri Bergson." *Philosophical Review*, 30, No. 6, 1921, 636.

1365   d'Amato, Ferdinando. *Il pensiero di Enrico Bergson*. Città di Castello: Casa Ed. il Solco, 1921, 390.

1366   Askowith, H. "Dr. Miller's Article on Bergson." *New Republic*, 26, No. 337, May 18, 1921, 356-357. This is a letter to the editor defending Bergson against Dickinson S. Miller's article in the April 20, 1921 *New Republic*.

1367   Balfour, Arthur J. B. *Essays, Speculative and Political*. New York: G. H. Doran, 1921, 241. Cf. pp. 99-134, "Bergson's Creative Evolution."

1368   Balz, Albert G. A. "Review of *Mind-Energy* by Henri Bergson." *The Journal of Philosophy*, 18, No. 23, 1921, 634-643.

1369   Beck, Heinrich. "Henri Bergsons Erkenntnistheorie." Diss., Leipzig, 1921, 89.

1370   "M. Bergson Retires." *Living Age*, 310, No. 4026, September 3, 1921, 617.

1371   "Review of *El Bergsonismo en la doctrina espiritista* by Gregorio Giménez." *Revista de Filosofía*, 7, No. 6, 1921, 463-466.

1372   Bourquin, Constant, "Sur La Prétention philosophique du symbolisme." *Belles-lettres*, 3, No. 28, octobre 1921, 337-349.

1373   Brown, Slater. "Review of *Mind-Energy* by Henri Bergson." *Dial*, 70, April 1921, 462-465. The reviewer is skeptical and mildly sarcastic.

1374   Calderon, Francisco García. "Los proyectos de un filósofo." *La Nación*, 1921.

1375   Carline, Armando. *La vita dello spirito*. Florence: Valecchi, 1921, 225. This study deals with Bergson, M. Blondel, B. Croce, and G. Gentile.

1376   D'Amato, Ferdinando. *Il pensiero di Enrico Bergson*, Città di Castello: Casa Ed. il Solco, 1921, 390.

1377   Gaultier, Paul. *Les Maîtres de la pensée française*. Paris: Payot et Cie., 1921, 271. Henri Bergson's philosophy is discussed on pp. 96-197.

1378   "Graphomania Described by a French Savant." *New York Times*, 70, No. 23,032, February 14, 1921, p. 9, col. 4. This is a not too coherent report of Bergson's review of *La Graphomanie, essai de psychologie morbide* by Ossip-Lourié, for the Académie des Sciences Morales et Politiques.

1379   Hocking, William Ernest. "The Dilemma in the Conception of Instinct, As Applied to Human Psychology." *The Journal of Abnormal Psychology and Social Psychology*, 16, Nos. 2-3, 1921, 73-95. "Why does Bergson, thinking of organic evolution, appeal for explanation to a vital principle? Is it not because independent series of organic forms, having different intermediaries, nevertheless converge to similar results? In the processes which eventuate in the eye of the pectin and the eye of the vertebrate, Bergson can only see a single experimental impulse operating with widely variant means." (p. 80)

1380   Holk, Lambertus Jacobus van. *De beteekenis van Bergson voor de philosophische theologie*. Leiden, Netherlands: Sijthoff, 1921, vi, 179.

1381   Joussain, André. *Esquisse d'une philosophie de la nature*. Paris: Félix Alcan, 1921, 197.

1382   Kerler, D. H. "Review of *Schöpferische Entwicklung* by Henri Bergson." in *Die Auserstandene Metaphysik*. Ulm: H. Kerler, 1921, 168-197.

1383   Lenoir, Raymond. "La Prévision et la nouveauté." *Revue de Métaphysique et de Morale*, 28, No. 2, janvier-mars 1921, 100-103. The author provides an account of Bergson's talk given at the "Meeting d'Oxford" which, minimally rewritten, became the article "Le Possible et le réel, 1920."

1384   Menegoz, Fernand. "La Philosophie de Bergson et la théologie protestante." *Revue d'histoire et de Philosophie religieuses*, 1, No. 4, 1921, 345-362.

1385   Mennicken, Peter. "Die Philosphie Henri Bergsons und der Geist moderner Kunst." Diss., Köln, 1921, 116.

1386   Miller, Dickinson S. "Mr. Bergson's Theories: What is Their Importance?" *New Republic*, 26, No. 333, 20 April 1921, 242-246. This is a highly critical review of *Mind-Energy*.

1387   "Review of *Mind-Energy* by Henri Bergson." *A.L.A. Booklist*, 17, No. 4, January, 1921, p. 137.

1388   Nicolardot, Firmin. *A Propos de Bergson: Remarques et esquisses*. Paris: Vrin, 1921, 174.

1389   Peña y Prado, Juan Manuel. "Bergson y el problema de la memoria." Diss., Arequipa, Peru, 1921.

1390   Petit, Agénor. *M. Bergson et le rationalisme*. Prague: Impr. d'E. Grégr et fils, 1921, 24. This study is followed by a letter from Bergson explaining the use of intelligence in both science and metaphysics.

1391   Riese. "Review of *Seelische Energie* by Henri Bergson." *Allgemeine ärztl. Zentralblatt für Psychotherapie*, 2, 1921, p. 181.

1392   Riley, Woodbridge. "La Philosophie française en Amérique: III, Le Bergsonisme." *Revue Philosophique de la France et de l'Etranger*, 91, No. 1-2, 1921, 75-107; No. 3-4, 1921, 234-271.

1393   Rostrevor, George. *Bergson and Future Philosophy: An Essay on the Scope of Intelligence*. London: Macmillan and Co., Ltd., 1921, 152. The author is George Rostrevor Hamilton. (Cf. G. R. Hamilton, 1965.)

1394   Savelli, Rodolfo. *Il pensiero di Henri Bergson*. Città di Castello: Il Solco, 1921.

1395   Souday, Paul. "La Retraite de M. Bergson." *Le Temps*, No. 21875, 24 juin 1921, 1.

1396   Spirito, Ugo. *Il pragmatismo nella filosofia contemporanea*. Firenze: Vallecchi, 1921, 222. (Il Pensiero Moderno, 5) Bergson is discussed on pp. 167-179.

1397   Stephen, Karin. "The Misuse of Mind." *Psyche*, 2, No. 4, October 1921, 127-137. This is an extract from the author's book, *The Misuse of Mind*.

1398   Saussure, Raymond de. "Review of *La Psychologie française contemporaine* by Georges Dwelshauvers." *Imago*, 7, No. 1, 1921, 216-217. The reviewer concludes his brief survey with the following statements concerning the forerunners of psychoanalysis: "Man könnte einen interessanten Vergleich ziehen zwischen dem, was er symbolische Assoziationen nennt und dem, was Bleuler autistisches Denken genannt hat. Mit Ribot erscheint zum erstenmal die Bedeutung der Affektivität. Gar manches in den Ideen Janets und Bergsons nähert uns dem Arbeitsgebiete Freuds noch mehr" (p. 217).

1399   T., C. F. "Review of *Mind-Energy* by Henri Bergson." *International Journal of Ethics*, 31, No. 31, April, 1921, p. 347.

1400   Talbott, E. Guy. "Eucken and Bergson: Two Modern Prophets." *Methodist Review*, 104, No. 6, November-December 1921, 940-943.

1401   Tredici, Giacinto. "New Tendencies in Contemporary Philosophy." *Scuola cattolica*, 49, No. 1, 1921. Blondel, Boutroux, Bergson, Varisco, Gentile, and Croce are discussed in this article.

1402   Truc, Gonzague. "Le Spiritualisme bergsonien et la raison moderne." *Revue de la Semaine Illustrée*, 9, No. 38, 23 septembre 1921, 425-441.

1403   Turquet-Milnes, Gladys Rosaleen. *Some Modern French Writers: A Study in Bergsonism*. New York: McBride and Company, 1921, 302.

1404   Vandérem, Fernand. *Le Miroir des Lettres: L'Energie spirituelle*. Paris: Flammarion, 1921, 251.

1922

1405   Asnaourow, Félix. "Progresos de la psicología." *Nosotros*, 16, No. 152, enero 1922, 55-59. This brief article concerns the importance of the unconscious mind in the functioning of human personality. The discovery of the unconscious and its function is credited to Pierre Janet, A. Binet, and Bergson in France, and to Freud and his disciples. The essay concludes with an account of S. Freud's former disciple, Alfred Adler.

1406   Baudouin, Charles. *Studies in Psychoanalysis: An Account of Twenty-Seven Concrete Cases Preceded by Theoretical Exposition*. Trans. Eden Paul and Cedar Paul. London: George Allen & Unwin Ltd., 1922, 352. Bergson is cited in this work on pp. 6, 24, 42, 58, 59, 60, 61, 73, 92, 238, 306, 307, 309, 335.

1407   "Review of *Bergson and Future Philosophy* by George Rostrevor." *Psyche*, N.S. 2, No. 3, 1922, 274.

1408   Boll, Marcel. *Attardés et précurseurs*. Paris: Chiron, 1922, 283. This study contains a critical discussion of Bergson and E. Boutroux.

1409   Bouvier, Eugène Louis. *The Psychic Life of Insects*. Trans. L. O. Howard. London: T. Fisher Unwin, 1922, 377. Bergson's concept of instinct is discussed here on pp. 353-362.

1410 Brown, William. *Suggestion and Mental Analysis*. London: University of London Press, 1922, 167. (2nd Ed. 1922, 172pp.) Bergson is discussed on pp. 127-167. This is an largely exposition of Bergson's philosophy with a few criticisms.

1411 Burroughs, John. "Sundown Papers." *Last Harvest*. New York: Houghton Mifflin, 1922, 264-288.

1412 Delattre, Floris. "Le Bergsonisme et la littérature." *Revue de l'Enseignement des Langues Vivantes*, 29, No. 6, juin 1922, 252-257.

1413 Desprechins, Emile. "M. Bergson et le féminisme." *Femme Belge*, 5, No. 8, janvier 1922, 763-766.

1414 Deustua, Alejandro O. "La actividad estetica." *Revista de Filosofia* (Buenos Aires), 8, No. 2, marzo 1922, 208-220. The author opposes Bergson's aesthetic theories to those of Charles Lalo.

1415 Du Bos, Charles. *Approximations*. 7 vols. Paris: Plon-Nourrit, 1922, 266; Crés et Cie., 1927, 238; Le Rouge et le Noir, 1929, 316; Corrêa, 1930, 327; Corrêa, 1932, 326; Corrêa, 1934, 448; Corrêa, 1947, 420. Du Bos' literary criticism is thoroughly impregnated with Bergson's thought.

1416 Du Bos, Charles. Cours inédit sur Bergson, donné devant un auditoire privé les 20 février, 23 février et 2 mars 1922. Archives de Mme. C. Du Bos.

1417 Dunan, Renée. "Author d'Einstein." *Monde Nouveau*, 4, Nos. 19-20, 15 septembre et ler octobre 1922, 290-295. Bergson is discussed on pp. 290-291.

1418 Dyrssen, Carl. *Bergson und die Deutsche Romantik*. Marburg, Germany: Elwert, 1922, 56.

1419 Einstein, Albert. "Remarques sur la théorie de la relativité." *Bulletin de la Société Française de Philosophie*, 20, No. 3, juillet 1922, 102-113. Also in *Ecrits et paroles*, 3, 497-503; *Mélanges*, 1340-1347; Translated, with an Introduction, in *Bergson and the Evolution of Physics*, Ed. P. A. Y. Gunter, 133. Relativity deals, Enstein holds, with objective reality, not subjective time. When it comes to objective reality there are many time series, not one, as Bergson holds. (Cf. Bergson's remarks, 1922.)

1420 Gentile, Giovanni. "Il pensiero di Enrico Bergson secondo Ferdinando D'Amato." *Critica*, 20, No. 1, 1922, 42-44.

1421 Gillouin, René. "La Philosophie de M. Henri Bergson." *Monde Nouveau*, 4e Année, No. 19-20, 1922, 164-171; No. 21, 1922, 357-364; No. 22, 1922, 29-37.

1422 Guillaume, Edouard. "La Question du temps, d'après M. Bergson." *Revue Générale des Sciences*, 33, 30 octobre 1922, 573-582. This is an expository account of Bergson's *Durée et simulanéité*.

1423 Iberico, Mariano. *Une filosofía estética*. Lima, 1922. This study contains a chapter entitled "Bergson." It was originally the author's thesis, completed in 1919.

1424 Ingarden, Roman. "Intuition und Intellekt bei Henri Bergson." *Jahrbuch für Philosophie und phänomenologische Forschung*, 5, 1922, 285-461. This is an excellent, carefully thought out study of Bergson's critique of intellectual analysis and of Bergson's concept of duration. The author was urged to undertake this study by Edmund Husserl. (Cf. Ingarden, 1959)

1425 Joad, Cyril Edward Mitchinson. "The Problem of Free Will in the Light of Recent Developments in Philosophy." *Proceedings of the Aristotelian Society*, N.S. 23, 1922-1923, 121-140. The author maintains that: "For Bergson this reality is a continuous flow or change. It is a pure becoming without marks of features of any kind, the distinctions and individuations we discern in it being due to the discriminating, selecting and cutting-up operations of our intellect... Beyond the 'élan vital' there is nothing." (125).

1426   Joad, Cyril Edwin Mitchinson. *Common-Sense Theology*. London: T. F. Unwin, 1922, 288. A section titled "Bergson and the Philosophy of Change," appears on pp. 13-39. For other references see the index.

1427   Kallen, Horace M. "La Methode de l'intuition et la méthode pragmatiste." *Revue de Métaphysique et de Morale*, 29, No. 1, janvier-mars 1922, 35-62. The author contrasts Bergson's philosophy, with its appeal to direct intuition, with pragmatism, for which knowledge is "indirect."

1428   Koch, Artur. "Das Zweierlei-Vorurteil im Bergsonischen Intuismus." Diss., Greifswald, 1922, 163.

1429   Koyré, Alexander. "Bemerkungen zu den Zenonischen Paradoxen." *Jahrbuch für Philosophie und phänomenologische Forschung*, 5, 1922, 603-627. The author deals with Bergson's account of Zeno's paradoxes on pp. 610-612. Cf. also 627.

1430   Lalou, René. *Histoire de la littérature française contemporaine: 1870 à nos jours.* Paris: G. Crès et Cie, 1922, 707. The author examines relations between Bergson's philosophy and various contemporary authors including Charles Péguy (pp. 365-373), Georges Sorel (pp. 620-623), Julien Benda (pp. 624-625) and André Suarez (p. 625). The author is critical of Bergson's vitalism and its influence. He does not link Bergson and Marcel Proust.

1431   Landquist, John. "Interview with Bergson." *Living Age*, 315, No. 4085, October 21, 1922, 222-224. This article was published in Vienna *Neue Freie Presse*, 19 August 1922. This article contains interesting remarks on Bergson's philosophy of history.

1432   Lenoir, Raymond *et al. La Tradition philosophique et la pensée française*. Paris: Félix Alcan, 1922. This collection contains an article by René Gillouin on Bergson.

1433   Lewkowitz, Albert. "Zur Religionsphilosophie der Gegenwart: II. Philosophie des Lebens: Darwin, Bergson, Simmel." *Monatsschrift für Geschichte und Wissenschaft des Judentums*, 66, N. 10-12, 1922, 250-268.

1434   Losski, N. O. *Intuitivnaia filosofiia Bergsona*. Petrograd: 1922, 109.

1435   Luce, Arthur Aston. *Bergson's Doctrine of Intuition*. New York and Toronto: The Macmillan Co., 1922, 112.

1436   McDougall, William. "A New Theory of Laughter." *Psyche*, N.S. 2, No. 3, 1922, 292-303, Cf. esp. 293-294.

1437   Maitra, Shishir Kumar. *The Neo-Romantic Movement in Contemporary Philosophy*. Pref. Ludwig Stein. Calcutta: The Book Company, 1922, 268. This study deals with Nietzsche, Chamberlain, Keyserling, and Bergson. It is highly critical.

1438   McGilvary, Evander Bradley. "James, Bergson, and Determinism." *University of California Publications, Modern Philology Section* (Gayley Anniversary Papers), 11, 1922, 23-30.

1439   Montfort, Eugène. *Vingt-cinq ans de littérature française*. Vol. 1. Paris: Librairie de France, 1922, 389. Bergson is discussed on pp. 108-113.

1440 Müller-Freienfels, Richard. *Irrationalismus: Umrisse einer Erkenntnislehre*. Leipzig: Felix Meiner, 1922, 300. This is an epistemological study which reaches conclusions very close to Bergson's.

1441 Olgiati, Francesco. *La filosofia di Enrico Bergson*. 2nd Ed. Torino: Fratelli Bocca, 1922, xxxvii, 311. (Piccola Biblioteca di Scienze Moderne, No. 230).

1442 Piéron, Henri. "Remarques sur la théorie de la relativité." *Bulletin de la Société Française de Philosophie*, 22, No. 3, juillet 1922, 102-113. Also in *Ecrits et paroles*, 3, 497-503; *Mélanges*, 1340-1347. This item is translated, with an introduction, in *Bergson and the Evolution of Physics*, Ed. P. A. Y. Gunter, 133-135. The author, arguing from psychological errors in ascribing succession to physical events, concludes that psychological time must be uncorrelatable with physical time. (Bergson [1922] responded that Piéron's reasoning is circular.)

1443 Rodrigues, Gustave. *Bergsonisme et moralité*. Paris: Chiron, 1922, 156.

1444 Roellenbleck, Ewald. "Beitrag zur Theorie des Komischen: Mit besonderer Berücksichtigung von Bergson, Jean Paul, Lipps." Diss., Köln, 1922, 66.

1445 Serini, Paulo. "Bergson e lo spiritualismo francese des secolo XIX." *Logos*, 5, No. 2-3, luglio-decembre 1922, 315-357; 6, No. 1, gennaio-marzo 1923, 78-104. This monograph relates Bergson's thought to the philosophies of Victor Cousin, Maine de Biran, Félix Ravaisson, Hyppolite Taine, Renan, and Jules Lachelier. It was republished in book form, 1923.

1446 Simmel, Georg. *Zur Philosophie der Kunst: Philosophische und Kunst philosophische Aufsätze*. Potsdam: Gustav Kiepenheuer Verlag, 1922, 173. An essay on Bergson appears here on pp. 126-145.

1447 Stephen, Karin. *The Misuse of Mind: A Study of Bergson's Attack on Intellectualism*. Pref. Henri Bergson. London: Kegan Paul, Trench, Trubner and Co., Ltd.; New York: Harcourt, Brace, and Company, 1922, 107. This is a careful study of Bergson's criticism of the intellect. It is a response primarily to Bertrand Russell's attack (1912, 1914) on Bergson's concepts of intuition, duration, analysis.

1448 Vivante, Leone. *Della intelligenza nell'espressione*. Roma: Maglione e Strini, 1922, 229. Bergson's concept of the function of the brain is discussed on pp. 48-61; his concept of concrete duration on pp. 166-167.

1449 Voisine, G. "La Durée des choses et la relativité: A Propos d'un livre récent de M. Bergson." *Revue de Philosophie*, 22, No. 5, septembre 1922, 498-522. This is an exposition of Bergson's general position in *Duration and Simultaneity*. The reviewer agrees that Einstein's multiple times are fictitious.

1450 Wheeler, Olive Annie. *Bergson and Education*. New York: Longmans, Green and Co., 1922, 130.

1451 Whitehead, Alfred North. *The Principle of Relativity: With Applications to Physical Science*. Cambridge: The University Press, 1922, 190. On p. 16 the author states that "I use the term 'limitation' for the most general conception of finitude. In a somewhat more restricted sense Bergson uses the very convenient term 'canalization'. This Bergsonian term is a useful one to keep in mind as a corrective to the misleading associations of the terms 'external' and 'internal', or of the terms 'whole' and 'part'." The author uses the term 'canalization' again on p. 24. See also pp. 38-39.

1923

1452 Abbagno, Nicola. *Sorgenti irrazionali del pensiero.* Napoli: F. Perella, 1923, 174. F. H. Bradley, J. Royce, H. Bergson, G. Gentile, and A. Aliotta are discussed in this study.

1453 Alberini, Coriolano. "Curso intensivo sobre el Bergsonismo." *Humanidedes,* 6, 1923, 318-319. This is an outline of a course. It includes an introduction, an account of Bergson's philosophy and critics, and a conclusion.

1454 Alexander, Hartley Burr. "Socratic Bergson." *Nature and Human Nature.* Chicago: Open Court, 1923, 301-318.

1455 Barat, L., und P. Chaslin. "Le Langage." *Traité de psychologie.* Vol. I. Ed. Georges Dumas. Paris: Félix Alcan, 1923, 733-768.

1456 Becquerel, Jean. "Critique de l'ouvrage *Durée et simultanéité.*" *Bulletin Scientifique des Etudiantes de Paris,* 10, No. 2, mars-avril 1923, 18-29. Cf. Appendix III, *Durée et simultanéité,* 2ᵉ ed. 1923, for Bergson's response to Becquerel's criticisms.

1457 Bourquin, Constant, Ed. *Comment doivent écrire les philosophes? Ce qu'en pensent: M. Henri Bergson, MM. André Lalande et Ernest Sellière, Antoine Albalat (et autres).* Paris: Editions du Monde Nouveau, 1923, 166.

1458 Carr, Herbert Wildon. "The Problem of Simultaneity." *Proceedings of the Aristotelian Society,* Supplementary Volume, 2, 1923, 15-25. The author is in essential agreement with Bergson's position in *Duration and Simultaneity.*

1459 Challaye, Félicien. *Philosophie scientifique et philosophie morale.* Paris: Nathan, 1923, 652.

1460 Crémieux, Benjamin. "Note sur la mémoire chez Proust." *Nouvelle Revue Française,* 20, No. 1, Janvier 1, 1923, 188-194. The author contends that Bergson's and Marcel Proust's views are closely similar: "Bergson a certainment aidé Proust a s'orienter décisivement et c'est le langage bergsonien qui rendra le mieux compte de son genre de mémoire..." p. 191.

1461 Curtuis, Ernst Robert. *Die Literarischen Wegbereiter des Neuen Frankreich.* Potsdam: Kiepenheur, 1923, 344. See the introduction for a statement of the influence of Bergson on French literature before 1914.

1462 Delattre, Floris. "William James bergsonien." *Revue Anglo-américaine,* 1, No. 2, 1923-1924, 135-144.

1463 D'Hautefeuille, François. *Le Privilège de l'intelligence.* Paris: Editions Brossard, 1923, 251. The author proposes a different concept of intuition than Bergson; he also makes some interesting criticisms of Bergson's version of intuition.

1464 Dorward, Alan, "Review of *The Misuse of Mind* by Karen Stephen." *Mind,* 32, No. 125, January 1923, 100-103.

1465 Dunan, Renée. "Bergson contre Einstein." *Vie des Lettres,* No. 1, janvier 1923.

1466 Fabre, Lucien. "Au Sujet du Valéry de Thibaudet." *Nouvelle Revue Française,* 19, No. 12, décembre 1923, 662-676. The author discusses Bergson's influence on A. Thibaudet on pp. 671-672.

1467 Fenichel, Otto. "Psychoanalyse und Metaphysik: Eine kritische Untersuchung." *Imago,* 9, No. 3, 1923, 318-343. The author attempts to refute the notion that

Freudian metapsychology and metaphysics have anything in common. His immediate target is those psychoanalysts (Otto Pfister, James Jackson Putnam, Carl Gustav Jung, and Alphonse Maeder) who have tried to render psychoanalysis metaphysical. His more general target is the philosophy of Bergson which, he says, many psychoanalysts have tried to utilize on the basis of its presumed similarity with Freud's ideas. While "intuition" is indeed indispensable to psychoanalysis, submersion in so-called "pure duration" is impossible. The unconscious is timeless, and the extension of characteristics observed in the "I" to the external world is impossible. The author's "refutation" of Bergsonism shows little appreciation of either the metaphysical elements in Freud's metapsychology or the psychoanalytic content of Bergson's philosophy. He spends most of his article developing a notion of intuition which is Freudian but (presumably) not Bergsonian.

1468 Fenichel, Otto. Review of "Medizin und Philosophie" by Kurt Hildebrandt. *Imago*, 9, No. 3, 1923, 394. The reviewer complains concerning Hildebrandt's article in the *Monatsschrift für Psychologie und Neurologie*, 51, No. 1, that there are those who, reacting against the mechanistic notions of psychoanalysis, try to base their thought on "phantastischen Übertreibungen. Man kann sagen, das sein unberichtiger Erfolg ebenso beschämend für die offizielle Psychologie war wie der berichtige! *Schopenhauer, Nietzsche, Bergson* seien leidenschaftlicher und anschaulicher als alle spezialistische Fachliteratur."

1469 Forti, Edgard. "La Psychologie bergsonienne et les survivances actuelles de l'associationisme." *Revue de Métaphysique et de Morale*, 30, No. 4, octobre-décembre 1923, 509-537. The author defends Bergson's approch to psychology against the of E. Rignano and H. Piéron.

1470 Garcia Morente, Manuel. "Europa en decadencia?" *Revista de Occidente*, Año 1, No. 2, agosto 1923, 177.

1471 Gautier, Henri. "Simples Remarques sur le *Valéry* de M. Thibaudet." *L'Ane d'or*, 2, No. 12, 1923, 349-351. The author commends those who criticize Thibaudet's tendency to "Bergsonize" Paul Valéry.

1472 Gunn, John Alexander. *Modern French Philosophy: A Study of Development Since Comte*. Pref. Henri Bergson. New York: Dodd, Mead and Company, 1922; London: Fisher Unwin, 1923, 358.

1473 Hasselmann, Karl B. "Das Problem der Willensfreiheit, unter besonderer Berücksichtigung der Theorien Münsterbergs, Bergsons und Joels." Diss., Halle, 1923, 159.

1474 Henry, J. "Bergsonisme et morale." *Revue Néo-scolastique de Philosophie*, 25, No. 98, mai 1923. The author concludes that Bergsonism leads, not to anarchy, but to the individual's contributing to the march of evolution as a whole.

1475 Ingenieros, José. "Encuesta sobre cooperación intelectual." *Revista de Filosofía*, 9, No. 4, julio 1923, 1-11.

1476 Jaloux, Edmond. *L'Esprit des livres*. Paris: Plon, 1923, 257. Bergson is discussed on pp. 101-107.

1477 Jones, William Thomas. "Working Philosophy of Life." *Discovery*, 4, No. 11, November 1923, 287-290.

1478 Klimke, Fridericus. *Institutiones Historiae Philosphiae*. Vol. 2. Romae: Sumptibus Universitatis Gregorianae; Friburg Brisg.: Herder & Co., 1923, 452. Cf.

Articulus II "Intuitionimus systematicus," 205-210.

1479   Landes, Margaret Winifred. "A Suggested Interpretation of Bergson's Doctrine of Intuition." Diss. Yale 1923.

1480   Leone, Enrico. *Anti-Bergson*. Napoli: Casa editrice La Luce del Pensiero, 1923.

1481   Metz, André. *La Relativité: Exposé élémentaire des théories d'Einstein et réfutation des erreurs contenues dans les ouvrages les plus notoires*. Pref. Jean Becquerel. Paris: Chiron, 1923, 156. In the second part of this book Metz criticizes critics of relativity theory, including Bergson.

1482   Minkowski, Eugène. "Étude psychologique et analyse phénomenologique d'un cas de mélancolie schizophrenique." *Journal de Psychologie normale et pathologique*, 20, 1923, 543-558.

1483   Müller-Freienfels, Richard. *Die Philosophie des zwanzigsten Jahrhunderts in Ihren Hauptströmungen*. Berlin: E. S. Mittler, 1923, 138. Cf. Zweiter Teil, 111. Irrationale Erkenntnismöglichkeiten (pp. 83-86) and VI. Die irrationale Metaphysik des Lebens (pp. 96-105).

1484   Nicolardot, Firmin. *Un Pseudonyme bergsonien? Ou le présage inaperçu*. Paris: Vrin, 1923, 242. The author suggests that a book entitled *L'Univers, la force et la vie*, published in 1884 under the pseudonym A. Laggrond, is an early work by Bergson. See the author's retraction of this view, 1924.

1485   Oesterreich, Travgott K. *Friedrich Überwegs Grundriss der Geschichte der Philosophie* Vol. 5. *Die Philosphie des Auslandes vom Beginn des 19. Jahrhunderts bis auf Die Gegenwart*. 1923, pp. xxix-xxx, 56-58.

1486   Paasen, Carl Richard van. *De antithisen in de philosphie von Henri Bergsons*. Haarlem: Kleijnenberg and Co., 1923, xvi, 128.

1487   Picard, Gabriel. *Le Problème critique fondamental*. Paris: G. Beauchesne, 1923, 94. (Half-title: *Archives de Philosophie*, 1, No. 2.) Bergson's concept of intuition is discussed here on pp. 50 ff.

1488   "Poetess Stirs France By Refusing Honors." *New York Times*, 72, No. 23,926, July 28, 1923, p. 3:7. This article notes the coming award to Bergson of the Legion of Honor. (The poetess is Garard d'Houville.)

1489   Proust, Robert. "Marcel Proust intime." *Nouvelle Revue Française*, 20, No. 1, 1 janvier, 1923, 24-26. The author discusses the influence of Alphonse Darlu on Marcel Proust. He notes that Marcel Proust later came under the influence of Desjardins and Bergson: "Cette influence de Darlu fut certainement sur lui considérable, comme celle de Paul Desjardins et ultérieurement celle de Bergson." p. 25.

1490   Prudencio Bustillo, Ignacio. *Ensayo de una filosofía jurídica*. Sucre, Bolivia: Universidad de San Francisco Javier, 1923. This work contains "referencias fundamentales a Bergson."

1491   Randall, John Herman. "Review of *Bergson's Doctrine of Intuition* by A. A. Luce and *Une Pseudonyme Bergsonien?* by Firmin Nicolardot." *Journal of Philosophy*, 20, No. 26, 1923, 718-719.

1492   Reik, Theodor. "Review of *Die Philosophie des zwanzigsten Jahrhunderts in ihren Hauptströmungen* by Richard Müller-Freienfels." *Imago*, 9, No. 3, 1923, 394-395. The reviewer deals primarily with Müller-Freienfels' interpretation of psychoanalysis as an application of "Verstehens" to man's irrational potentialities: "Ihm scheint die psychoanalytische Bewegung mehr und mehr zu einer Metaphysik des Lebens hinzuführen, aus einer therapeutischen Methode sei zu einer Art Kulturphilosophie erwachsen, die einseitige Einstellung auf das Sexuelle trete zurück, der Begriff der Libido werde Bergson's élan vital angenähert" (p. 394).

1493   Rency, Georges. "La Vie littéraire: Paul Valéry." *L'Indépendance Belge*, 94, No. 252, 1923, 4. This is a review of *Paul Valéry* by Albert Thibaudet. The reviewer concludes that "entre Valéry et Bergson, il n'y a que l'épaisseur d'un technique."

1494   Rignano, Eugenio. *The Psychology of Reasoning*. New York: Harcourt, Brace and Co., Inc.; London: Kegan Paul, Trench Trubner and Co., Ltd., 1923, 325. Various references to Bergson's theory of dreams may be found on pp. 40, 297, 303, and 310.

1495   Serini, Paulo. *Bergson e lo spiritualismo francese del secolo XIX*. Genova: Perella, 1923, 68.

1496   Stewart, J. McKellar. "The Notion of the Unconscious in the New Psychology." *Australasian Journal of Psychology and Philosophy*, 1, No. 3, 1923, 191-196. The author reproaches psychoanalysts for constructing notions of the unconscious on the analogy of conscious processes. He counters with the concept of the "pre-conscious" inspired by Bergson's dynamism.

1497   Thibaudet, Albert. "Conclusions sur le bergsonisme." *Nouvelle Revue Française*, 21, No. 9, septembre 1923, 257-271. This article is quoted from the concluding pages of Thibaudet's *Bergson*.

1498   Thibaudet, Albert. "Les Figures bergsoniennes de l'histoire." *Revue de Genève*, 7, No. 38, août 1923, 129-150.

1499   Thibaudet, Albert. *Paul Valéry*. Paris: Grasset, 1923, 189. The author here provokes a lively controversy by treating P. Valéry as a Bergsonian. The general consensus is that the author is wrong.

1500   Thibaudet, Albert. "Marcel Proust et la tradition française." *Nouvelle Revue Française*, 20, No. 1, Janvier 1, 1923, 130-139. The author compares the "mobilisme" of Proust to that of Montaigne and Bergson on p. 139.

1501   Tilgher, Adriano. *Voci del tempo*. Roma: Libr. di Sc. e Lettere, 1923, 224. Bergson is discussed on pp. 190-203.

1502   Truc, Gonzague. "Le Bergsonisme et le mouvement." *Revue Hebdomadaire des Cours et des Conférences*, 32e Année, No. 1, 3 mars 1923, 61-68. This is purportedly a review of *Durée et simultanéité*. In it the author merely takes the occasion to attack insidious Bergsonism.

1503   Turner, J. "The Future of Bergsonism." *Monist*, 33, No. 2, April 1923, 219-239.

1504   Vettard, Camille. "Proust et le temps." *Nouvelle Revue Française*, 20, No. 1, 1 janvier, 1923, 204-211. The author likens Marcel Proust's novels to Henri Bergson's philosophy.

1505   Vetter, Johannes. "Das Ästhetische in der Wirklichkeitslehre Bergsons." Diss., Erlangen, 1923, 69.

1506   Vujić, Vladimir. *Нови хуманизам, etc.* Огледи: Беозраб, 1923, 203, Chapters I-III and appendix I by V. Vujić and Chapter IV-V and appendix II by Prvoš Slankamenac concern the philosophies of Henri Bergson and William James.

1507   Wheeler, William Morton. *Social Life Among the Insects: Being a Series of Lectures Delivered at the Lowell Institute in Boston in March 1922*. New York: Harcourt, Brace & Co., 1923, 375. Lecture Two of this series, "Wasps Solitary and Social" (pp. 43-89), contains several references to Bergson. On p. 45 the author asserts that while Bergson and other authors (e.g., Wm. McDougall) have exaggerated the abilities of the wasps, "the wasp's psychic powers compared to those of most other insects or even of many of the lower vertebrates seem to me, nevertheless, to be sufficiently remarkable." The egg-laying and blood-sucking activities of parasitoid wasps are described on pp. 48-49 by the author (against Fabre and Bergson) as reflex behavior. Cf. also p. 59.

1508   Whitehead, Alfred North. "The Problem of Simultaneity." *Proceedings of the Aristotelian Society*, Supplementary Volume, 3, 1923, 34-41. Here Whitehead presents his alternative to Bergson's criticism of relativity theory. In essence, he accepts the time and space effects of relativity, but treats relativity theory as describing a world of process.

1924

1509   Asmodée. "Silhouette: Henri Bergson." *Revue Française*, 19e Année, No. 2, ler juin 1924.

1510   Bernstein, Hermann. "Henri Bergson." *Celebrities of Our Time*. New York: Lawren, 1924, 143-153.

1511   Bernstorff, Elizabeth Gräfin. "Eine Bergson-Spengler Parallele." Diss., Münster, 1924, 91.

1512   Bremond, Henri. "L'Américanisme de W. James." *Revue de France*, 4, No. 21, ler novembre 1924, 181-188.

1513   Carr, Herbert Wildon. "Review of *Le Bergsonisme* by Albert Thibaudet." *Mind*, 33, No. 131, July 1924, 332-334. This review contains an interesting mention of Bergson's philosophical endeavors *circa* 1924.

1514   Carr, Herbert Wildon. *The Scientific Approach to Philosophy*. London: Macmillan and Co., Ltd., 1924, 278.

1515   Carteron, Henri. "Remarques sur la notion de temps d'après Aristote." *Revue Philosophique de la France et de l'Etranger*, 98, No. 7-8, 1924, 68-81. This article deals with the concept of time in Aristotle, Kant, and Bergson.

1516   Chevalier, Jacques. "Le Continu et le discontinu." *Proceedings of the Aristotelian Society*, Supplementary Volume, 4, 1924, 174-196. Also in *Annales de l'Université de Grenoble*, N.S. 2, No. 1, 1924. The author argues, in Bergsonian fashion, that: "La continuité que nous présente l'univers en sa totalité, et dans chacune de ses parties distinctes, individualisées, est la continuité d'un rythme..." (196). Continuity is thus to be understood in terms of duration.

1517   Crémieux, Benjamin. *XXᵉ siècle*. Paris: Editions de la Nouvelle revue française, 1924, 251. The author parallels Bergson's concept of intuition with Proust's literary theories.

1518   Cresson, André. *La Position actuelle des problèmes philosophiques*. Paris: Stock, 1924, 127.

1519   Cunningham, Gustavus Watts. "Bergson's Doctrine of Intuition; Reply to M. W. Landes." *Philosophical Review*, 33, No. 6, November 1924, 604-606.

1520   Delattre, Floris. *William James bergsonien*. Paris: Presses Universitaires de France,
        1924, 34. Cf. Bergson's letters to the author, 1923 and 1924.

1521   "Discuss New Institute." *New York Times*, 73, No. 24, 342, September 16, 1924,
        p. 6, col. 5. Bergson is reported here as favoring the creation of an international
        institute for intellectual cooperation, to be directed by the League of Nations.
        He was later to lead this "institute".

1522   Edgell, Beatrice. *Theories of Memory*, Oxford: At the Clarendon Press, 1924,
        174pp. Chapter V of this work, "The Conception of Memory in the Philosophy
        of M. Bergson", pp. 114-133, concludes with the following remarks: "We may
        grant that [Samuel Butler] wrestled and failed to make memory-images intellig-
        ible by a theory of ensouled vibrations, but where Butler gave us one mystery,
        M. Bergson presents us with three: the impersonal memory of an ensouled body,
        the individual memory of a spirit mind, and the relation between them." p. 133.
        The author parallels Bergson's concept of instinct with his concept of personal
        memory, his concept of "intellect" with his concept of impersonal memory. The
        parallel is dubious.

1523   Fernandez, Ramon. "La Garantie des sentiments et les intermittences du coeur."
        Nouvelle Revue Française, 22, No. 4, 1 avril, 1924, 389-408. The author states
        that, Proust does have "une manière toute bergsonienne de prendre contact aven
        sa durée...mais les réactions de son intelligence sur sa sensibilité, qui déterminent
        son oeuvre, l'orientent plutôt vers une spatialization du temps et de la mémoire."
        400-40ln.

1524   Garcia Morente, Manuel. "Review of *Le Bergsonisme* by Albert Thibaudet." *Revista
        de Occidente*, 4, No. 2, abril 1924, 120-123.

1525   Janeff, Janko. "Das Leben und das Überlegendige: Eine kritische Untersuchung
        der Metaphysik Bergsons." Diss., Heidelberg, 1924, 99.

1526   Jankélévitch, Vladimir. "Deux Philosophes de la vie: Bergson, Guyau." *Revue
        Philosophique de la France et de l'Etranger*, 97, No. 6, juin 1924, 402-449.

1527   Johnstone, James. "Does the Demonstration of Physical Continuity in the Germ-
        Plasms of Successive Generations of Animal Organisms Also Demonstrate the
        Transmission of Mental Characters?" *Proceedings of the Aristotelian Society*,
        Supplementary Volume, 4, 1924, 130-137.

1528   Lafontaine, Albert-P. *La Culture française: La Philosophie de Bergson*. Paris:
        Vrin, 1924, 80. This is a general survey of Bergson's thought.

1529   Landes, Margaret W. "A Suggested Interpretation of Bergson's Doctrine of Intui-
        tion." *Philosophical Review*, 33, No. 5, September 1924, 450-462. This essay
        is part of a Ph. D. thesis presented at Yale University. The author attempts to
        reconcile intellectualist and anti-intellectualist interpretations of Bergson's intui-
        tion. Bergson meant to attack only Kant's concept of "intellect."

1530   Laporte, Jean. "Maine de Biran et Bergson." *Revue de France*, 4, No. 15, ler août
        1924, 620-625.

1531   Lefèvre, Frédéric. "Une Heure avec M. Paul Valéry." *Les Nouvelles Littéraires*,
        3, No. 103, 1924, 1-2; No. 104, 1924, 4; No. 105, 1924, 6. The third part of
        this interview concerns Bergson. This interview forms the main part of Lefèvre's
        Entretiens avec Paul Valéry (1926). Valéry here denies that he is a Bergsonian.

1532   Maritain, Jacques. *Réflexions sur l'intelligence et sur sa vie propre*. 2nd Ed. Paris: Nouvelle librarie nationale, 1924, 388.

1533   Marks, Marcus M. "Hour with Dr. Henri Bergson: Discussion of Study and Travel Plan for College Students." *Review of Reviews*, 70, No. 5, November 1924, 505-506. This involves plans for the international exchange of students, as a means to world peace.

1534   Mead, George Herbert. "The Genesis of the Self and Social Control." *International Journal of Ethics*, 35, No. 3, 1924-1925, 251-257. The author examines Bergson's theory of perception on pp. 254-256, nothing that it is a move towards freeing psychology from Cartesian dualism. He refers to Bergson's concept of instinct on pp. 262-266, distinguishing the sociability of insects from that of human beings. On p. 263, he states, "I wish, however, to restrict the social act to the class of acts which involve the cooperation of more than one individual, and whose object as defined by the act, in the sense of Bergson, is a social object." See also p. 274.

1535   Metz, André. "Un Dernier Mot d'André Metz." *Revue de Philosophie*, 31, No. 4, 1924, 440. This is the author's final reply to Bergson concerning the interpretation of relativity theory. It includes a brief remark by A. Einstein. It is translated, with an introduction, in *Bergson and the Evolution of Physics*, Ed. and Trans. with Intro. P. A. Y. Gunter, 189-190. See Bergson's (brief) rejoinder, 1924.

1536   Metz, André. "Le Temps d'Einstein et la philosophie: A Propos de l'ouvrage de M. Bergson, *Durée et simultanéité*." *Revue de Philosophie*, 31, No. 1, 1924, 56-58. This criticism of Bergson's thought is translated, with an introduction, in *Bergson and the Evolution of Physics*, Ed. P. A. Y. Gunter, 135-265. Cf. Bergson's reply, 1924. This is a criticism of Bergson's critique of relativity theory in the second edition of *Duration and Simultaneity*. Bergson confuses "proper" dimensions with "coordinate" dimensions. He fails to see that Langevin's voyager makes two trips, not one. He fails to account for the result of well-known experiments by Fizeau, Bucherer, Michelson. See Bergson's reply, 1924.

1537   Mornet, Daniel. *Histoire de la littérature et de la pensée françaises*. Paris: Bibliothèque Larousse, 1924, 263. Cf. section 2 (1870-1925) pp. 38-40, 92, 107-108.

1538   Nabert, Jean. *L'Expérience intérieure de la liberté*. Paris: Presses Univeritaires de France, 1924, 334.

1539   Nathanson, William. "Spinoza and Bergson." *Guardian*, 1, No. 2, December 1924, 15-16.

1540   Nicolardot, Firmin. *Flore de Gnose: Laggrond, Pellis et Bergson: Complément de l'étude intitutlée "Un Pseudonyme bergsonien?"* Paris: L'Auteur, 1924, 136. The author concludes that *L'Univers, la force et la vie* was not written by Bergson but by Auguste Glardon and E. Pellis.

1541   Nicolardot, Firmin. *A Propos de Bergson: Remarques critiques et esquisse d'un symbolisme de l'essai*. 2nd Ed. Paris: Chez l'auteur, 1924, 272.

1542   Nordmann, Charles. *Notre Maître le temps: Les Astres et les heures: Einstein ou Bergson?* Paris: Hachette, 1924, 223. This is a popularization of relativity theory, and of the Bergson-Einstein debate.

1543   Péguy, Charles. "Note sur M. Bergson et la philosophie bergsonienne." *Oeuvres complètes*. Vol. 9. *Oeuvres posthumes*, Paris: Nouvelle Revue Française, 1924, 335.

1544 Poyer, G. "Activité mentale, travail intellectuel et fatigue." *Traité de psychologie.* Vol. II. Ed. Georges Dumas. Paris: Félix Alcan, 1924, 608-632.

1545 Rageot, Gaston. "Le Rôle historique du bergsonisme." *Le Temps*, No. 22862, 13 mars 1924, 3.

1546 Recouly, Raymond. "Algunos recuerdos sobre H. Bergson." *La Nación*, noviembre 1924.

1547 Rey, Abel. "L'Invention artistique, scientifique, pratique." *Traité de psychologie.* Vol. II. Ed. Georges Dumas. Paris: Félix Alcan, 1924, 426-475.

1548 Sageret, Jules. *La Révolution philosophique et la science: Bergson, Le Dantec, J.-H. Rosny aîne.* Paris: Félix Alcan, 1924, 252. The author finds a basic similarity in the thought of Bergson, A. Einstein, F. Le Dantec, and J.-H. Rosny-Ainé. All tend to replace the ancient notion of substance with the idea of "history" or "duration". On pp. 1-83 he compares the ideas of Bergson and Le Dantec.

1549 Segond, Joseph. "Le Rationalisme de Bergson." *Revue Politique et Littéraire, Revue Bleue*, 62e Année, No. 8, 19 avril 1924, 263-266.

1550 Scheffer, Henry M. "Review of *Durée et Siumultanéité* by Henri Bergson." *Isis*, 6, No. 19, 1924, 570-571.

1551 Souday, Paul. "Les Livres." *Le Temps*, 14 août 1924, 3. The author, on the occasion of a reprinting of Albert Thibaudet's *Paul Valéry*, discounts the notion that Valéry was influenced by Bergson.

1552 "Tearing the Mask from Bergson." *Living Age*, 320, No. 4157, 8 March 1924, 479. This is a brief mention of Enrico Leone's *Anti-Bergson* (1923).

1553 Thomas, James Bishop. *A Guide to Bergson.* Girard, Kansas: Handelman-Julius Company, 1924, 64 (Little Blue Book No. 508). This is a brief popular essay.

1554 Thompson, J. Arthur. *The System of Animate Nature: The Gifford Lectures Delivered in the University of St. Andrews in the Years 1915 and 1916.* New York: Henry Holt & Co., 1924, 687. The author makes various references to Bergson, on pp. 21, 32, 38, 99, 169, and 234. On pp. 207-210, he deals with Bergson's concept of instinct as one of the three major views of instinct. (The other two are the reflex theories and the theories which make instinct a kind of intelligent behavior.) On pp. 209-210 he states, "The position that instinctive behavior is on a different evolutionary tack from intelligent behavior may be defended apart from Professor Bergson's particular view of the difference. When we observe a spider executing an extraordinarily complex and sharply punctuated series of movements which result in a web and doing this effectively for the very first time, we seem to be in a world different from that of intelligence. And again when we observe insects continuing to go through a laborious routine which has lost all its point, and from bondage to which the least modicum of intelligence would deliver them, we seem to be in a world very different from that of intelligence."

1555 Trnka, Tomáš. *Moderní filosofie ve slepe ulicce.* Prague: Ot. Storch-Marien, 1924, 60. (Edice Aventium, 78).

1556 Vandérem, Fernand. "Le Bergsonisme." *Revue de France*, 4, No. 7, 1er avril 1924, 621-626. This is a review of A. Thibaudet's *Le Bergsonisme.*

1557   Zdanowicz, C. "Molière and Bergson's Theory of Laughter." *University of Wisconsin Studies in Literature*, 20, No. 1, 1924, 99-125.

1925

1558   Alberini, Coriolano. "El problema ético en la filosofiá de Bergson." *Annales del Instituto Popular de Conferencias de "La Prensa,"* 11, 1925, Buenos Aires. Originally in "La Prensa" Septiembre 26, 1925.

1559   "Bergson Quits League Body." *New York Times*, 74, No. 24, 675, August 15, 1925, p. 5:5. This article reports Bergson's resignation (purportedly due to illness) from the League of Nations Commission on International Intellectual Cooperation.

1560   Bourquin, Constant. *Julien Benda: Ou, Le Point de vue de Sirius*. Intro. Jules de Gaultier. Paris: Editions du Siècle, 1925, 250.

1561   Brock, F. H. Cecil. "Implications of Bergson's Philosophy." *Proceedings of the Aristotelian Society*, N.S. 26, 1925-1926, 279-298.

1562   Calkins, Mary Whiton. *The Persistent Problems of Philosophy: An Introduction to Metaphysics Through the Study of Modern Systems*. New York: Macmillan, 1925, 601. Bergson is discussed on pp. 437-441.

1563   Caramelia, Santino. *Enrico Bergson*. Milano: Athena, 1925, 112.

1564   Challaye, Félicien. *Psychologie et métaphysique*. Paris: Nathan, 1925, 766.

1565   Chevalier, Jacques. *Le Continu et le discontinu*. Grenoble: Allier, 1925, 39.

1566   De Vleechauwer, H.-J. "De voorges-chiedenis van het Bergsonisme." *Vlaamsche Arbeid*, 1925-1926, 20-21.

1567   Drake, Durant. *Mind and its Place in Nature*. New York: Macmillan, 1925, 259. There are numerous references in this book to Bergson, on pp. 110, 111, 120, 140, 146, 153, 154, 155, 158, 233. On pp. 120-121 the author describes Bergson as one who holds that "qualitative heterogeneity is reducible to quantitative differences." On pp. 233 he states that because "voluntary action is simply a refinement on reflex action" Bergson is wrong to speak of free will.

1568   Driesch, Hans. *The Crisis in Psychology*. Princeton, N. J.: Princeton University Press, 1925, 275. The author makes references to Bergson on pp. 4, 24, 95-96, 154-155, 243, and 244. On p. 155 he states, "I recommend most intensively the thorough study of his *Matière et mémoire*, one of the profoundest, if not the profoundest, book of modern psychology."

1569   Durant, William James. *Contemporary European Philosphers: Bergson, Croce, and Bertrand Russell*. Girard, Kansas: Haldeman-Julius Company, 1925, 64.

1570   Dwelshauvers, Georges. *Les Mécanismes subconscients*. Paris: Félix Alcan, 1925, 146.

1571   Gilson, Etienne. "Review of *Le Bergsonisme* by Albert Thibaudet." *Revue Philosophique de la France et de l'Etranger*, 39, No. 5, septembre-octobre 1925, 308-310.

1572   Gunn, John Alexander. "Great Thinkers, II. Henri Bergson." *Australasian Journal of Psychology and Philosophy*, 3, No. 4, 1925, 277-286. Much interesting historical comment is contained in this article.

1573 Hammond, Albert L. "Some Alleged Incapacities of Intellect." *Philosophical Review*, 34, No. 6, November 1925, 557-559. The author attacks F. H. Bradley and Wm. James as well as Bergson for their intellectual (hence inconsistent) attack on the human intellect.

1574 "He Admits Only the Fourteen." *New York Times*, 74, No. 24,700, September 9, 1925, p. 24:6. This article reports a rumor that fourteen doctors had visited the ailing Bergson and that all had "condemmed" him. In a letter to the London Times Bergson had admitted that he had been visited by fourteen doctors, but pointed out that most of these visits were social calls.

1575 "Henri Bergson Denies Illness." *New York Times*, 74, No. 24,687, August 27, 1925, p. 7, col. 1.

1576 Herte, François. "Bergson." *Revue du Néo-positivisme* (Editon spéciale), 5, 15 mai-juin 1925, 92-144.

1577 Lalande, André. "Philosophy in France, 1924." *Philosophical Review*, 34, No. 6, November 1925, 533-557. Bergson is discussed on pp. 533-534.

1578 Larsson, Hans. *Intuition problemet: Särskilt med hänsyn till Henri Bergsons teori.* 2nd Ed. Stockholm: Bonnier, 1925, 80.

1579 Lenoble, Eugène. "H. Bergson." *Dictionnaire pratique des connaissances religieuses.* Vol. 1. Paris: Letouzey, 1925, 750-759.

1580 Macdonald, Niel Douglas. "Method in Religious Education as Affected by Certain Phases of the Philosophy of Bergson." Diss. Hartford Seminary 1925. (50083 in *Hartford Seminary Foundation, Doctoral Dissertations*, 1908-1935).

1581 Marcel, Gabriel. "Bergsonisme et musique." *Revue Musicale*, 6e Année, No. 5, ler mars 1925, 220-229.

1582 Molina, Enrique. *Dos filósofos contemporáneos: Guyau, Bergson.* 1-2 ed. Santiago, Chile: Nascimento, 1925, 1948, 389, 283.

1583 Nordmann, Charles. *The Tyranny of Time: Einstein or Bergson?* Trans. E. E. Fournier d'Albe. London: Unwin, Ltd., 1925, 216.

1584 Pacotte, Julian. *La Pensée mathématique contemporaine.* Paris: Félix Alcan, 1925, 126. The author concludes that Bergson's metaphysics best conforms to the spirit of contemporary mathematical physics.

1585 Paliard, Jacques. *Intuition et réflexion: Esquisse d'une dialectique de la conscience.* Paris: Félix Alcan, 1925, 464. This study is an attempted resolution of the "opposition entre Bergson et Hamelin" concerning the nature of thought.

1586 Parodi, Dominique. "La Philosophie française de 1918 à 1925." *Revue Philosophique de la France et de l'Etranger*, 15, Nos. 11-12, novembre-décembre 1925, 359-383.

1587 Perego, Luigi. *La dinamica dello spirito nella conoscenza: Saggio di critica e sintesi nel neo-dualismo gnoseologico del Bergson.* Bologna: Zanichelli, 1925, xii, 140.

1588 Perry, Ralph Barton. *Philosophy of the Recent Past: An Outline of European and American Philosophy since 1860.* New York: Scribner's, 1925, 230. The chapter entitled "The Impulse to Life: Bergson" is found on pp. 174-182.

1589 Pierre-Quint, Léon. *Marcel Proust: L'Homme, sa vie, son oeuvre.* Paris: Editions du Sagittaire, 1925, III. Bergson is discussed on p. 33.

1590   Pierre-Quint, Léon. *Marcel Proust: Sa vie, son oeuvre.* Nouvelle Edition, revue et augmentée. Paris: Simon Kra, 1925, 386. The previous edition of this book was titled *Le Comique et le mystère chez Proust.* The author enrolls Proust as a disciple of Bergson. Cf. the author, 1927.

1591   Quercy, Pierre. "Remarques sur la théorie bergsonienne de l'aphasie sensorielle." *Encéphale*, 5e Année, 1925, 89-98. The author, after reviewing recent scientific work relating to Bergson's concept of "sensory aphasia", concludes (p. 98) that it is already possible to extract precise questions which neurologists should investigate. A positive critique of Bergson's ideas can now begin.

1592   Quercy, Pierre. "Remarques sur une théorie bergsonienne de l'hallucination." *Annales Médico-psychologiques*, 2, 1925, 242-259. This is a careful, highly accurate account of Bergson's theory of hallucination (in the context of his mind-body theory). Bergson's mind-body theory does not exclude a particular theory of brain localization: i.e. of localized motor areas in the brain. For Bergson, unlike for traditional philosophy (e.g. H. Taine), hallucination is a false perception, and there is no perception without an object.

1593   Rabaud, Étienne. "Les Phénomenes de convergence en biologie." *Revue Philosophique de la France et de l'Etranger*, 99, Janvier-Juin, 1925, 5-50.

1594   Sinéty, Robert de. "Le Problème psychophysique. Les Variations de l'intensité des sensations est-elle measurable?" *Archives de Philosophie*, 3, No. 2, 1925, 1-41. The author deals with Bergson's objections to psychophysics on pp. 27-41.

1595   Strowski, Fortunat. "Le Bergsonisme en littérature." *Renaissance Politique, Littéraire, et Artistique*, 13, 9 juin 1925, 14-15.

1596   Strowski, Fortunat. *Tableau de la littérature française au XIXe siècle et au XXe siècle.* Paris: Mellottée, 1925, 722. Ch. Maurras and Bergson are discussed on pp. 670-676.

1597   Sturt, Mary. *The Psychology of Time.* London: Kegan Paul, Trench, Trubner and Co., Ltd., 1925, 152.

1598   Uznadze, D. "Bergsons Monismus." *Archiv für Geschichte der Philosophie*, 37, No. 1, 1925, 26-40.

1599   Van Suchtelen, N. "Over Bergson's *Schappende Evolutie.*" *Wil en Weg*, 4, 1925.

1600   Wilm, Emil Carl. *Theories of Instinct.* New Haven, Connecticut: Yale University Press, 1925, 188. Bergson's evolutionary theory is discussed on pp. 177-179.

1601   Wordsworth, John Crawford. *Adventures in Philosophy.* London: George Allen and Unwin, Ltd., 1925, 345. Chapter ten, "The Philosophy of Bergson," is found here on pp. 215-307.

1926

1602   Adam, Margarete. "Die intellektuelle Anschauung bei Schelling in ihrem Verhältnis zur Methode der Intuition bei Bergson." Diss. Hamburg, 1926.

1603   Baker, Arthur Ernest. *How to Understand Philosophy: From Socrates to Bergson.* New York: George H. Doran Co., 1926, 231. (Doran Modern Reader's Bookshelf)

1604   Benrubi, Isaac. *The Contemporary Thought of France.* Trans. E. B. Dickes. London: Williams and Nordgate, 1926, 214.

1605   Binet, Alfred. *L'Ame et le corps*. Paris: Flammarion, 1926, 286. Bergson's theory
        of perception is discussed on p. 48; Bergson's influence on Binet on pp. 85-87n;
        Bergson and Berkeley on the brain on pp. 234-235; Bergson and Binet on the
        function of the brain on pp. 236-241 and 268.

1606   Blondel, Charles. "The Morbid Mind." *Psyche*, N.S. 6, No. 24, April, 1926,
        73-86. The author describes the influence of Bergson and E. Durkheim on his
        La Conscience morbide. Both Bergson and Durkheim made psychology aware
        of the influence on the individual mind of society and of language.

1607   Braunschvig, Marcel. *La Littérature française contemporaine étudiée dans les
        textes (1850-1925)*. Paris: Armand Colin, 1926, 356. The first section of this
        book contains selections from Bergson and many others.

1608   Brinkgreve, M.-R.-J. "Bergson." *Tijdschrift voor Wijsbegeerte*, 20, No. 2, 1926,
        211-226.

1609   Campbell, Clarence A. "Bergson's Doctrine of Freedom." Diss., Washington (St.
        Louis), 1926.

1610   Chevalier, Jacques. *Bergson*. Paris: Plon, 1926, 317. This is a well-known com-
        prehensive account of Bergson's philosophy by a close personal acquaintance
        and disciple. Cf. English trans. 1928, Italian trans. 1937.

1611   Chevalier, Jacques. "Bergson et son époque." *Revue Hebdomadaire des Cours et
        des Conférences*, 27, No. 8, 1926, 673-681; No. 9, 1926, 18-26; No. 10, 1926,
        142-148; No. 11, 1926, 193-202; No. 13, 1926, 308-417; No. 14, 1926, 552-560;
        No. 15, 1926, 596-607. These articles appear in the author's *Bergson*.

1612   Chevalier, Jacques. *Les Maîtres de la pensée française: Bergson*. Paris: Plon,
        1926, xii, 317, "Nouvelle édition revue et augmentée." Paris: Plon, 1934, 357.

1613   "Committees for Intellectual Cooperation." *Current History*, 24, No. 3, June 1926,
        413-415.

1614   "Datos biogrficos sobre Bergson." *La Prensa*, enero 1926.

1615   Dreyfus, Robert. *Souvenirs sur Marcel Proust*. Paris: Grasset, 1926, 341. Memory
        in Bergson and Proust is discussed on pp. 287-292.

1616   Durant, William James. *The Story of Philosophy: The Lives and Opinions of the
        Greater Philosophers*. New York: Simon and Schuster, 1926, xii, 577. Bergson's
        philosophy is described in this book on pp. 487-507.

1617   Fleuriot de Langle, Paul. *Les Sources du comique dans la "Farce de Maître
        Pathelin."* Angers: Librairie du Roi René, 1926, 31.

1618   Forsyth, T. M. "Bergson's and Freud's Theories of Laughter: A Comparison and
        a Suggestion." *South African Journal of Science*, 23, 1926, 987-995.

1619   Franck, Henri. *Lettres à quelques amis*. Pref. André Spire. Paris: Grasset, 1926,
        303. Bergson is discussed on pp. 83, 84, 85, 90, and 141.

1620   Gatti, Pasquale. "Philosophy of Language." *Logos*, 12, Nos. 2, 3 e 4, 1926.
        Against H. Bergson and B. Croce, the author holds that language is a valid
        expression of thought.

1621   Georges-Michel, Michel. *En Jardinant avec Bergson, en junglant avec Kipling,
        en chassant le crocodile avec Sara Bernhardt, en boxant avec Maeterlinck...*
        Paris: Albin Michel, 1926, 349. This book contains an interview with Henri
        Bergson.

1622   Gsell, Paul. "La Vraie Pensée d'Henri Bergson." *Revue Mondiale*, 11e Sér., 27e Année, 15 février 1926, 349-369.

1623   Gunn, John Alexander. "Bergson and Einstein." *Australasian Journal of Psychology and Philosophy*, 4, No. 3, 1926, 215-218. This is a review of *Durée et simultanéité*. The author disagrees with both Einstein and Bergson over the nature of time.

1624   Gunn, John Alexander. "Time and Modern Metaphysics." *Australasian Journal of Psychology and Philosophy*, 4, No. 4, 1926, 258-267. M. J. Guyau, Bergson, S. Alexander, C. D. Broad, B. Russell, E. Cassirer, and A. N. Whitehead are considered in this article.

1625   James, William. *The Letters of William James*. Ed. Henry James. Boston: Little, Brown and Company, 1926, 384. This collection includes correspondence later published in Perry's *Thought and Character of William James*.

1626   Habert, O. *Le Primat de l'intelligence dans l'Histoire le la Pensée: Initiation à la philosphie*. Paris: Beauchesne, 1926, 448.

1627   Koechlin, Charles. "Les Temps et la musique." *Revue Musicale*, 7, No. 3, 1926, 45-62. The author distinguishes (on p. 46) four kinds of time: (1) "La durée pure, donnée de notre conscience profonde..."; (2) "Le temps psychologique"; (3) "Le temps mesuré par les moyens mathématiques"; (4) "temps musical." The author identifies "le temps musical" with "le temps auditif," and argues that an auditory, musical time always has some relationship with space, since it appears to us to be measurable and divisible. In dealing with musical time we are dealing with a "*spatialization* du temps, mais fort differente de celle (basée sur la vue) que considere M. Bergson" (p. 46).

1628   Kramer, F. "Bergsonische Intuitionsphilosophie: Bedeutung d., für d. moderne Schule." *Pädagogische Rundschau*, 2, No. 1, 1926, 34.

1629   Lalande, André. *Vocabulaire technique et critique de la philosophie*. 2 Vols. Paris: Félix Alcan, 1926, 1065. For annotation Cf. the author, 1947.

1630   Lefèvre, Frédéric. *Entreteins avec Paul Valéry: Précédés d'une preface de Henri Bremond, de l'Académie Française*. Paris: Le Livre, 1926, 376.

1631   Lefèvre, Frédéric. "Une Heure avec Raymond Poincaré." *Les Nouvelles Littéraires*, 5, No. 192, 1926, 1-2. Poincaré states: "Un Pays qui peut s'enorgueillir en même temps d'un Henri Bergson et d'un Paul Valéry demeure sans contredit le vrai foyer de le haute culture internationale."

1632   Maire, Gilbert. "Henri Bergson: Son Oeuvre." *Nouvelle Revue Critique*, 10, 1926.

1633   Maitra, Sisirkumar. "Rabandrinath Tagore and Bergson." *Calcutta Review*, 3rd Ser., 17, No. 3, May-June 1926, 189-295.

1634   Maritain, Jacques. *Réflexions sur l'intelligence*. 2nd Ed. Paris: Desclée de Brouwer, 1926, 388.

1635   Mason, Joseph Warren Teets. *Creative Freedom*. New York and London: Harper Brothers, 1926, 538. This book presents itself as a history of human spiritual evolution. The author explains: "Readers of this book, familiar with Bergson's writings, will realize how much the author owes to him." (xii).

1636   Maynial, Edouard. *Précis de la littérature française moderne et contemporaine (1715-1925)*. Paris: Delagrave, 1926, 268. Bergson is discussed on pp. 228-229.

1637   Metz, André. "Relativité et relativism." *Revue Philosophique de la France et de l'Etranger*, 51, Nos. 1-2, janvier-février 1926, 63-87. This essay is a criticism of *Duration and Simultaneity*.

1638   Minkowski, Eugene. "Bergson's Conceptions as Applied to Psychopathology."
Trans. F. J. Farnel. *Journal of Nervous and Mental Diseases*, 63, No. 6, 1926,
553-568. The author considers general paralysis and schizophrenia from a Bergsonian viewpoint. General paralytics experience rapid, superficial future-orien-
tation, believing in their own omnipotence; schizophrenics, by contrast, suffer
from "morbid geometrism." They attempt to remain in immobile isolation, reject
both dynamism and matters of degree. Observation of schizophrenics verifies
Bergson's psychology in this respect.

1639   Mulford, Henry Jones. "What is Intuition?" *Monist*, 26, No. 2, 1926, 307-312.

1640   Nogué. J. "Le Symbolisme spatial de la qualité." *Revue Philosophique de la France
et de l'Etranger*, 51, Nos. 7-8, juillet-août 1926, 70-106; Nos. 9-10, octobre-
novembre 1926, 267-298. The author defends spatial symbolization of consciousness.

1641   Osborn, Henry Fairfield. "Dr. Osborne State's Evolution's New Problem." *New
York Times*, 75, No. 24921, April 18, 1926, pt. 9, p. 5. This rather long article
was written at the request of the *Times* after its author had spoken on Bergson
at Cornell University. The author holds that evolution does not account for the
spiritual qualities of man. He states that while Bergson's concept of evolution
is "deductive", the "new" basis for evolution is based on induction.

1642   Oxenstierna, Gunnar Gabriel. *Tids-och intuitionsproblem i Bergsons filosofi*.
Uppsala, Sweden: Akademisk avhandlung, 1926, viii, 153.

1643   Russell, Bertrand. "Science, Relativity and Religion." *Nation and Athenaeum*, 39,
No. 8, 1926, 206-207. This is a review of *Science and the Modern World* by
A. N. Whitehead. The author compares Bergson and A. N. Whitehead on p.
207. Whitehead, Russell says, "is profoundly influenced by Bergson's belief in
interpenetration." Whitehead's philosophy, he states, consists of two parts, "a
logical construction leading to physics from a new set of non-material fundamentals, wholly admirable and profound; on the other hand, a metaphysic believed
by the author to be bound up with his logical construction, but in fact—again
I speak with deference—separable from it." This metaphysics, which is not
new, is approximately that of Plotinus or Bergson.

1644   Streeter, Burnett Hillman. *Reality: A New Correlation of Science and Religion*.
New York: Macmillan, 1926, 350. Cf. Chapter 5, "The Life-force, the Absolute,
or God," pp. 116-142.

1645   Thibaudet, Albert. "Réflexions sur la littérature: Poésie." *Nouvelle Revue Française*, 26, No. 148, 1926, 104-113. The author defends his Bergsonian view of
Paul Valéry.

1646   Valéry, Paul. "Henri Bergson et la Philosophie." in *Entretiens avec Paul Valéry*.
Pref. Henri Bremond. Ed. Frédéric Lefèvre. Paris: Le Livre, 1926, 77-79. Cf.
also 209-210.

1647   Ward, Mary. "James Ward on Sense and Thought." *Mind*, N.S. 35, No. 140,
October 1926, 452-456. Bergson and Ward agree on the nature of experienced
duration, according to the author.

1648   Williams, Ernest. "Religious Bearing of Bergson's Philosophy." *Hibbert Journal*,
24, No. 2, January 1926, 264-269.

1927

1649   Aliotta, Antonio. *Le origini dell'irrazionalismo contemporaneo*. Naples: Perella, 1927, 101. (Biblioteca di filosofia)

1650   Aveling, Francis. *Directing Mental Energy*. London: University of London Press, 1927, 276.

1651   Benda, Julien. "Reponse à Gabriel Marcel." *Nouvelle Revue Française*, 29, No. 171, décembre 1927, 855-856.

1652   "Bergson et le bergsonisme." *Chronique des Lettres Française*, 5, 1927, 264-265. Here A. Thibaudet discusses Jacques Chevalier's *Bergson*.

1653   Bergson's Philosophy." *London Times Literary Supplement*, 28, No. 1407, January 17, 1927, 35. This is a highly laudatory review of the English translation of *Bergson* by Jacques Chevalier.

1654   "Blondel y Freud," *Revista de Filosofia*, 13, 1, 1927, 110-123. This is a report of a lecture by Charles Blondel. See pp. 119-120 for a comparison of Bergson's and Freud's psychologies.

1655   Bonnefon, Daniel and Charles. *Les Ecrivains modernes de la France*. Paris: Fayard, 1927, 715.

1656   Bosanquet, Bernard. *Science and Philosophy and other Essays*. London: G. Allen and Unwin, 1927, 446. Cf. pp 223-235 for "Prediction of Human Conduct: A Study in Bergson."

1657   Brown, William. *Mind and Personality: An Essay in Psychology and Philosophy*. New York and London: G. P. Putnam's Sons, 1927, 256. Chapter nineteen, "Personality and Evolution," pp. 241-263, is an exposition of Bergson's philosophy with reference to its psychological content. On p. 20 the author remarks that *Matter and Memory* may almost be looked on as a textbook in general psychology. The author discusses time and eternity in Bergson on pp. 326-330.

1658   Brunschvicg, Léon. *Le Progrès de la conscience dans la philosophie occidentale*. Paris: Félix Alcan, 1927, II, 441. Part 4 is entitled "La Philosophie de la conscience de Condillac à Bergson."

1659   Carr, Herbert Wildon. *Changing Backgrounds in Religion and Ethics*. London: Macmillan and Co., Ltd., 1927, 224. Carr attempts to build a religious and ethical philosophy on the foundation of Bergsonian evolutionism.

1660   Carr, Herbert Wildon. "Life and Matter." *Personalist*, 8, No. 1, January 1927, 5-24.

1661   Cresson, André. *Les Courants de la pensée philosophique française*. 2 Vols. Paris: Armand Colin, 1927, 210 and 212. French philosophic thought from Montaigne to Bergson is discussed in this study. The discussion of Bergson is brief.

1662   D'Abro, Arthur. *Bergson ou Einstein*. Paris: Gaulon, 1927, 320. This is a polemic directed against Bergson's criticisms of relativity theory.

1663   D'Abro, Arthur. *The Evolution of Scientific Thought*. New York: Dover Publications, 1927, 481. Bergson's criticisms of Einstein are declared erroneous on pp. 214-217.

1664   Delattre, Floris. "La Personnalité d'Henri Bergson et l'Angleterre." *Revue de Littérature Comparée*, 7, No. 2, avril-juin 1927, 300-315.

1665   Durant, William James. *The Story of Philosophy*. Garden City, N. Y.: Garden City, 1927, 592. Cf. pp. 487-529.

1666   Eliot, T. S. "Mr. Middleton Murry's Synthesis." *The Criterion*, 6, No. 4, 1927, 340-347. On p. 346 the author asserts that "the Bergson time doctrine...reaches the point of fatalism which is wholly destructive."

1667   Essertier, Daniel. *Psychologie et sociologie: Essai de bibliographie critique*. Paris: F. Alcan, 1927, 234. (Publications du Centre de documentation sociale). In this introduction the author contrasts the ideas of E. Durkheim, the leader of 20th century French sociology, with those of Bergson. The cornerstone of Durkheim's thought is the same as Bergson's: the realization that knowledge (in sociology, in Durkheim's case) can not be based on conventional psychology. Durkheim derives from this insight a new method, which was the "generating intuition" of his system; but he fails. By transforming society into a collective mind with collective representations, he transforms a rule of method into a statement about nature of things. There is no basis for making the collective mind more "real" than the individual mind.

1668   Gray, Carlo. "Intuizionismo bergsoniano e intuizione dell'essere rosminiana." *Revista rosminiana*, 21, Nos. 1 et 4, 1927.

1669   Hausheer, Herman. "Bergson's Critique of Scientific Psychology." *Philosophical Review*, 36, No. 5, September 1927, 450-461. The author suggests that Bergson is similar to H. Rickert in opposing the scientific faith that science can comprehend the whole universe with its concepts. The psychical is free and creative. It displays two aspects: directly or by refraction through space. No psychological datum ever appears twice the same. The psychical is not a quantity and hence cannot be measured. It is subjective and cannot be an object. Its inner nature can be grasped by intuition, but not by symbols and concepts.

1670   Heymans, Gérard. "Les Deux Mémoires de Bergson." *Gesammelte Kleinere Schriften zur Philosophie and Psychologie*: Vol. 2. *Allgemeine Psychologie, Ethic und Aesthetik*. Den Haag, Netherlands: Nijhoff, 1927, 291-330.

1671   Hocking, William Ernest. "Contemporary Philosophy." in *Present-Day Thinkers and the New Scholasticism: An International Symposium*. Ed. John S. Zybura. St. Louis and London: B. Herder, 1927, 7-11. The author notes three alternatives in contemporary philosophy: the new realism, pragmatism, and Bergsonism. He states: "Bergson supplies a third alternative, more significant than that of neo-realism: for Bergson is pragmatical with respect to the living world. And through the essential instability of the intuitionist standpoint, the path of the next years leads to an internal rationalization of the content of intuition; that is, to a reaffirmation of metaphysical idealism on new grounds." (pp. 10-11).

1672   Hunter, W. S. "Abstract of *Bergson* by Jacques Chevalier." *Psychological Abstracts*, 1, No. 12, 1927, 617. The abstract notes: "A comprehensive account of Bergson's philosophy."

1673   Huxley, Julian. "Mind Considered From the Point of View of Biology." *Journal of Philosophical Studies (Philosophy)*, 2, No. 7, July 1927, 330-348. Bergson is discussed on pp. 33, 343-344, and 346-347.

1674   Iberico, Mariano. "Bergson y Freud." *Revista de Filosofía*, Año 13, No. 3, 1927, 375-378. The author discusses assumptions which Bergson and Freud have in common, namely, the importance of instinct and the unconscious mind in human behavior and development.

1675   Korn, Alejandro. "Filosofía Argentina." *Nosotros*, 21, Nos. 219-220, agosto 1927, 61.

1676   Lasbax, Emile. *La Cité humaine; Esquisse d'une Sociologie dialectique*. Vol. 1. *Histoire des systémes sociologiques*. Vol. 2. *Cinématique, statique et dynamique sociales*. Paris: J. Vrin, 1927, 311, 369. (Librarie philosophique). The author applies Bergsonism, carefully interpreted, to sociology. He hopes that this approach can fill the void left by the decline of the Durkheimian school.

1677   Le Roy, Edouard. *L'Exigence idéaliste et le fait de l'évolution*. Paris: Boivin et Cie., 1927, 270.

1678   Lotte, Joseph. *Lettres et entretiens*. Paris: L'Artisan du Livre, 1927, 215 (*Cahiers de le Quinzaine*, 18e Série, ler cahier). Letters and talks concerning Bergson are on pp. 119-120 and 154-155.

1679   Malagarriga, Carlos. "Filosofía bergsoniana y Catolicismo." *Nosotros*, 21, No. 221, octobre 1927, 5-13.

1680   Marcel, Gabriel. *Journal Métaphysique*. 15e ed. Paris: Librarie Gallimard, 1927, 342. (Bibliothèque des Idées) This intellectual "diary" (1914-1923) is dedicated to Henri Bergson and W. E. Hocking. Cf. pp. 9, 130-131, 195-197, 204, 243-247, 252.

1681   Marcel, Gabriel. "En marge de'La Trahison des clercs." *Nouvelle Revue Française*, 29, No. 171, Décembre, 1927, 831f. The author responds to J. Benda's critique of Bergsonism. Cf. Benda's reply, Dec. 1927.

1682   Meyerson, Emile. *De L'Explication dans les sciences*. Paris: Payot, 1927, 784. Bergson is cited on pp. 32, 191, 198, 220, 333, 511, 512, 527, 586, 674, and 681.

1683   Minkowiski, Eugène. *La Schizophrénie: Psychopathologie des schizoïdes et des schizophrènes*. Paris: Payot, 1927, 268.

1684   Morgan, C. Lloyd. *Emergent Evolution: The Gifford Lectures Delivered in the University of St. Andrews in the Year 1922*. New York: Holt; London: Williams and Nordgate, 1927, 313. The author examines and criticizes Bergson's concept of memory, imagery and cognition on pp. 148-172.

1685   Nordmann, Charles. "L'Ame immortelle, M. Bergson et la biologie." *L'Illustration*, 85, pt. 2, 15 octobre 1927, 416-418.

1686   Noulet, Émilie. *Paul Valéry*. Bruxelles: L'Oiseau blue, 1927, 88. See pp. 61-78, "Paul Valéry et la philosophie."

1687   Noulet, Emilie. "Valéry et la philosophie." *Flambeau*, 10, No. 3, 1927, 195-208. Parallels between Bergson and Valéry are developed on pp. 199-208.

1688   Nyman, Alfred. "Einstein-Bergson-Vaihinger: Ein Abwägungsversuch" *Annalen der Philosophie*, 6, 1927, 178-204. The author considers interpretations of relativity theory, including Bergson's.

1689   "La Personnalité d'Henri Bergson et l'Angleterre." *Chronique des Lettres Françaises*, 5, 1927, 703-705.

1690   Piéron, Henri. *Thought and the Brain*. Trans. C. K. Ogden. New York: Harcourt, Brace and Co.; London: Kegan, Paul, 1927, 262. In Part 3, "The Verbal Function and Thought," the author states "At present, in an atmosphere of thought impregnated with Bergson's powerful critique, so quickly assimilated that it has become impersonal, it is the intellectual analysis of the function of language, such as that attempted by Head, which has come to the front, and we are returning to the profound views of Hughlings Jackson." (pp. 151-152) Cf. also 205n.

1691   Pierre-Quint, Léon. *Marcel Proust: His Life and Work*. Trans. Hamish and Sheila Miles. New York: Alfred A. Knopf, 1927, 256. This is a translation of the author's *Marcel Proust: Sa vie, son oeuvre* (Paris: Simon Kra, 1925) The author treats Proust as a disciple of Bergson and as utilizing Bergsonian concepts of duration, the unconscious, language, expression, and memory. Cf. pp. 24-25, 133-134, 150, 218-219, 236-238, 248.

1692   Prvost, J. "Review of *L'Intuition philosophique* by Henri Bergson." *Europe*, 15, No. 60, 1927, 574-576.

1693   Prévost, Jean. "Spinoza à la Sorbonne." *Les Nouvelles littéraires*, Vol. 6, No. 299, 5 mars 1927, p. 1. On February 26, 1927 Paul Valéry had addressed celebrations at the Sorbonne concerning Spinoza. Valéry, presiding over the ceremonies, read a letter from Bergson, who was unable to attend.

1694   Ryder, H. Osborne. "The Philosophy of Change." *Personalist*, 8, No. 4, October 1927, 246-254. This is an analysis of Bergson's two lectures at Oxford in 1911 on "The Perception of Change."

1695   Souday, Paul. "Dialogues critiques." *Le Mansucrit Autographe*, 2, No. 9, 1927, 135-140. The author responds here to Thibaudet's "Lettre à Paul Valéry."

1696   Souday, Paul. *Marcel Proust*. Paris: S. Kra, 1927, 106. The author denies Proust's originality: "Ses idées ne sont pas nouvelles, et souvent elles sont fausses. Ce que l'on peut concéder, c'est que le bergsonisme et le freudism n'avaient pas encore exploités littérairement avant lui d'un façon aussi méthodique et aussi brillante." (pp. 105-106)

1697   Spaier, Albert. *La Pensée concrète: Essai sur le symbolisme intellectuel*. Paris: F. Alcan, 1927, 446. Cf. pp. 42-44 ("l'Intuition bergsonienne"), pp. 101-131 (a Bergsonian treatment of images, including memory images), pp. 328-333 ("La Libérte selon M. Bergson"). J.-P. Sartre cites Spaier as a Bergsonian psychologist, particularly in his treatment of imagery. (*Imagination*, 1936, p. 78)

1698   Taylor, Alfred Edward. "Dr. Whitehead's Philosophy of Religion." *Dublin Review*, 181, No. 362, 1927, 17-41. The author compares Bergson's and Whitehead's philosophies on pp. 34-37. He likens Whitehead's concept of creativity in nature to Bergson's *élan vital*, and confesses that he can make no sense of such an entity.

1699   Thibaudet, Albert. "Bergson et le bergsonisme." *Candide*, 4, No. 4, 20 janvier 1927.

1700   Thibaudet, Albert. "Lettre à Paul Valéry." *Le Manuscrit Autographe*, 2, No. 8, 1927, 44-49.

1701   Truc, Gonzague. "Bergsonisme et catholicisme." *L'Opinion*, 20e Année, No. 21, 21 mai 1927, 16-17.

1702   Twardowski, Kazimierz. *Rozprawy i artykuly filozoficzne*. Lwów: "Ksiaznica-Atlas," 1927, 447. This collection of essays and lectures, put together by the author's students, contains an article on Bergson.

1703   Vertesi, Frigyes. *Bergson: Rendelmélete*. Pécs, Hungary: 1927, 40.

1704   Vivante, Leone. *Notes on the Originality of Thought*. Trans. Brodrick-Bullock. London: John Lane, 1927, 227, Bergson is discussed on pp. 92 and 208n.

1705   Wilson, Edmund. "A. N. Whitehead: Physicist and Prophet." *New Republic*, 51, No. 654, 1927, 91-96. On p. 96 the author notes similarities and contrasts between Whitehead and Bergson. Whitehead, he asserts, "admires Bergson but has something in common with him." But Whitehead keeps logic, while Bergson throws it out.

1928

1706   Angioletti, Giovanni Batista. *Scrittori d'Europa*. Milano: Libr., d'Italia, 1928, 185. Bergson is discussed on pp. 61-71.

1707   Assmus, W. "Bergson: Advocat d. Intuitionsphilosophie: Bergson und seine Kritik d. Intellectualismus." *Unter dem Banne des Marxismus*, 2, No. 1, 1928, 8-43.

1708   Aubert, Louis. "Henri Bergson." *Bulletin de la Société Autour du Monde*, 15, 31 décembre 1928, 13-21.

1709   Baillot, A. "Bergson et Schopenhauer." *Mercure de France*, 208, 15 décembre 1928, 513-529.

1710   Bandas, Rudolph G. "The Bergsonian Conception of Science and Philosophy." *New Scholasticism*, 2, No. 3, July 1928, 215-235. Bergson's distinction between intuition and intellect is untenable, according to the author.

1711   Benda, Julien. *The Treason of Intellectuals*. Trans. Richard Aldington. New York: W. Morrow and Co., 1928, 244. This is a translation of *La Trahison des Clercs*. The author here attacks romanticisms of all kinds, particularly the practical, utilitarian romanticisms of Bergson and Nietzsche.

1712   Benrubi, Isaac. *Philosophische Strömungen der Gegenwart in Frankreich*. Leipzig: Meiner, 1928, 529.

1713   "Bergson." *Kinotechnik*, 10, 1928, 68.

1714   "Bergson et la vie contemplative: Lettre d'une prieure du Carmel." *Nouvelles Littéraires*, No. 322, 15 décembre 1928, 4.

1715   Berrueta, Juan Dominguez. "L'Intuition bergsonienne." *Nouvelles Littéraires*, No. 322, 15 décembre 1928, 3.

1716   Billy, André. "Review of *Henri Bergson* by Jacques Chevalier." *L'Oeuvre*, No. 4799, 20 novembre 1928, 4.

1717   Blondel, Charles. *La Conscience morbide*. 2nd ed. Paris: Félix Alcan, 1928, ii, 402. This edition contains an appendix not found in the first edition. Blondel was one of the first to apply Bergsonian ideas to psychopathology.

1718   Blondel, Maurice. *L'Itinéraire philosophique de Maurice Blondel*. Propos recueillis par Frédéric Lefèvre. Paris: Editions Spes, 1928, 283. Cf. pp. 47-51.

1719   Bojinoff, Assen. *Ist eine Metaphysik des Absoluten möglich? Die zwei Grundtypen aller Metaphysik: (Gegen) Antike Skepsis, Positivismus, Henri Bergson, Hans Driesch*. Sofia: Tschiepeff, 1928, 148.

1720   Bouglé, M. "Bergson y Durkheim." *La Nación*, 4 septiembre 1928, p. 8, col. 2a.

1721   Brunschvicg, Léon. "H. Bergson: Lauréat du Prix Nobel." *Revue de Paris*, 25e Année, No. 23, 1er décembre 1928, 671-686.

1722   Brunschvicg, Léon. "Le Bergsonisme dans l'histoire de la philosophie." *Nouvelles Littéraires*, No. 322, 15 décembre 1928, 1, 6.

1723 Casares, Tomás D. "Bergson." *Criterio*, 1, No. 39, 29 noviembre 1928, 268-269.

1724 Chevalier, Jacques. *Henri Bergson*. Authorized Trans. Lilian A. Clare. New York: Macmillan, 1928, 351.

1725 Chevalier, Jacques. *Henri Bergson: Suivi de pages inédites et de l'histoire de 7e fauteuil: Portrait de Bergson par Henri de Nolhac: Bibliographie: Autographe*. Paris: Servant, 1928, 103. This is a Nobel Prize commemorative.

1726 Chevalier, Jacques. "L'Intellectualisme d'Henri Bergson." *Nouvelles Littéraires*, No. 322, 15 décembre 1928, 5.

1727 Curtuis, Ernst Robert. *Marcel Proust*. Trans. Armand Pierhal. Paris: Editions de La Revue Nouvelle, 1928, 154. The author holds that temporal continuity is one of the basic traits of Proust's literature. He notes the influence of Alphonse Darlu on Proust, but adds on p. 43: "Plus tarde, la pensée bergsonienne eut sur lui une influence incontestable."

1728 D'Antonio, F. "La dottrina di Bergson e il diritto penale." *Rivista penale*, Anno 109, No. 1-2, 1928.

1729 Decoster, Paul. *Acte et synthèse: Esquisse d'une critique de la pensée pure*. Bruxelles: Lamertin, 1928, 158.

1730 Delteil, Joseph. "Bergsonisme grammatical ou la pêche à la ligne." *Nouvelles Littéraires*, No. 313, 13 octobre 1928, 1-2.

1731 D'Ors, Eugenio. "Allo, Madrid!" *Nouvelles Littéraires*, No. 322, 15 décembre 1928, 3.

1732 Dujovne, León. "La energía espiritual." *Síntesis*, 1, No. 12, mayo 1928, 117. This is a note concerning the Spanish translation of *L'Energie spirituelle* published in Madrid in 1928.

1733 Dwelshauvers, Georges. "Recherches expérimentales sur la pensée implicite." *Revue de Philosophie*, 28, No. 3, 1928, 217-255.

1734 Einstein, Albert. "A Propos de la déduction relativiste de Meyerson." *Revue Philosophique de la France et de l'Etranger*, 105, Nos. 3-4, mars-avril 1928, 161-166. Einstein agrees with Meyerson and Bergson that time should not be spatialized. This is a surprising admission, hardly consistent with others of Einstein's statements concerning time.

1735 Elliott, W. Y. *The Pragmatic Revolt in Politics*. New York: Macmillan, 1928, 540. Cf. pp. 111-113, 115, 119-120. The author denies that George Sorel's "Bergsonism" is deeply founded.

1736 Erckmann, R. "Bergson und Hanns Hörbiger." *Schlüssel zum Weltgeschehen*, 4, 1928, 364-369.

1737 Ferlov, Knud. "De Kierkegaard á Bergson." *Nouvelles Littéraires*, No. 322, 15 décembre 1928, 3.

1738 G., H. (Henri Gouhier?). "Entretien avec E. Le Roy, successeur de Bergson au Collège de France." *Nouvelles Littéraires*, No. 322, 15 décembre 1928, 6.

1739 Godmé, J. P. "Henri Bergson ou l'angélisme expérimental." *Cahiers d'Occident*, 2e Sér., 2, No. 1, 1928, 118-147. This article compares Bergson and Pascal. It is highly critical.

1740 Gsell, Paul. "Bergson est-il passé de mode?" *Revue Mondiale*, 187, 15 décembre 1928, 355-374.

1741 Höffding, Harald. *Les Conceptions de la vie.* Trans. A. Koyré. Paris: Félix Alcan, 1928, 170. Bergson is discussed on pp. 67-68 in this work.

1742 Janet, Pierre. *L'Evolution de la mémoire et de la notion du temps.* Paris: Chahine, 1928, 619. On pp. 155-159 the author distinguishes his concept of duration from that of Bergson. (Durations without memory are possible, he argues.) On pp. 195-202 he criticizes Bergson's concept of the two types of memory. (The existence of "pure memory" can not be proved.) Cf. also pp. 305-310, 516-518 for critiques of Bergson's notion of the present and of Bergson's critique of mathematical time. (Cf. C. M. Prévost, 1973.)

1743 Jankélévitch, Vladimir. "Prolégomènes au bergsonisme." *Revue de Métaphysique et de Morale,* 35, No. 4, octobre-décembre 1928, 437-490.

1744 Jolivet, Régîs. "Le Mouvement philosophique en France en 1926-1927." *New Scholasticism,* 2, No. 2, April 1928, 138-161. Bergson and psychology are discussed on pp. 148-149.

1745 Jung, Carl Gustav, "Instinct and the Unconscious." In *Contributions to Analytical Psychology.* Trans. H. G. and Cary F. Barnes. New York: Harcourt, Brace and Co., 1928. In this talk, first delivered in July, 1919, before a joint meeting of the British Psychological Society, the Aristotelian Society, and the Mind Association, the author criticizes the neo-Darwinian account of the life-cycle of the yucca moth, and adds, "but such an explanation is far from being satisfactory. Bergson's philosophy suggests another way of explanation, where the factor of 'intuition' comes in. Intuition, as a psychological function, is also an unconscious process" (p. 274). He adds that while instinct and intuition are analogous, they are by no means identical. On p. 280 he claims that Bergson discovered an "archetype" in his "durée créatrice." This essay appears, retranslated so as to put more distance between Jung's ideas and Bergson, in C. G. Jung's *Collected Works,* 8, 129-138. It was published in its original form in the *British Journal of Psychology,* 10, No. 1, 1919, 15-26.

1746 Jung, Carl Gustav. "On Psychical Energy." In *Contributions to Analytical Psychology.* Trans. H. G. and Cary F. Barnes. New York: Harcourt, Brace and Co., 1928, p. 32. Here Jung mentions Aristotle's *hormé,* Schopenhauer's "will," and Bergson's *élan vital,* and states, "from these concepts I have taken only the graphic or perceptual character of my term, not the definition of the concept." This paper appears in C. G. Jung's *Collected Works,* 8, pp. 3-66.

1747 Kappstein, Theodor. "Philosoph als Nobelpreisträger." *C. V. Zeitung Blätter für Deutschtum und Judentum,* 7, 1928, 675.

1748 Knudsen, Peter. "Die Bergsonische Philosophie in ihrem Verhältnis zu Schopenhauer." *Jahrbuch der Schopenhauer Gesellschaft,* 16, 1928, 3-44.

1749 Kuki, Shuzo. "Bergson au Japon." *Nouvelles Littéraires,* No. 322, 15 décembre 1928, 6.

1750 Landquist, Johan. *Henri Bergson: En populär framställling av hans filosofi.* Trans. L. Welhaven. Oslo: Aas and Wahls, 1928, 79.

1751 Laporte, Jean. "Témoignage." *Nouvelles Littéraires,* No. 322, 15 décembre 1928, 4.

1752 Laporte, Jean. "L'Oeuvre de Bergson." *Revue de France,* 8, No. 24, 15 décembre 1928, 725-733.

1753   Larsson, Hans. "Spinoza och Bergson: Utkast i anknyting till ett Spinozabrev." in *Festskrift tllägnad Axel Hägerström*. Uppsala: Almqvist & Wiksells, 1928, 229-236.

1754   Lasserre, Pierre. "Le Destin de Bergson." *Nouvelles Littéraires*, No. 294, 2 juin 1928, 1.

1755   Leroux, Emmanuel. "Témoignage." *Nouvelles Littéraires*, No. 322, 15 décembre 1928, 4.

1756   Lefèvre, Frédéric. *L'Itinéraire philosophique de Maurice Blondel*. Paris: Spes, 1928, 283. Cf. esp. 46-51 for a comparison of M. Blondel and Bergson.

1757   Lévy-Bruhl, Lucien. "Henri Bergson à l'Ecole normale." *Nouvelles Littéraires*, No. 322, 15 décembre 1928, 1.

1758   Lewis, Wyndham. *Time and Western Man*. New York: Harcourt, Brace and Company, 1928, 400; London: Chatto and Windus, 1927, 487. Highly critical references to Bergson are given throughout this largely literary study. The author cites Bergson, along with J. Joyce and others, as part of a wave of flabby, confused thinking that is destroying the Western intellect.

1759   Lossky, Nickolai. *L'Intuition, la matière et la vie*. Paris: Félix Alcan, 1928, 177. A sketch of Bergsonian theory of perception is given on pp. 23-24; his concept of symbolism on p. 49.

1760   Luchaire, Julien. "Bergson à Genève." *Nouvelles Littéraires*, No. 322, 15 décembre 1928, 4.

1761   Macwilliam, John. *Criticism of the Philosophy of Bergson*. Edinburgh: Clark, 1928, xii, 336.

1762   Maire, Gilbert. *Henri Bergson: Son Oeuvre*. Paris: Nouvelle Revue Critique, 1928, 72.

1763   Malagarriga, Carlos. "Bergson." *La Nación*, Suppl., 11 noviembre 1928.

1764   Malagarriga, Carlos. "Bergson." *La Nación*, Sec. II, 3, 18 noviembre 1928.

1765   Marcel, Gabriel. "Clairière." *Nouvelles Littéraires*, No. 322, décembre 1928, 3.

1766   Martinetti, Pietro. *La Libertà*. Milano: Libreria editrice Lombarda, 1928.

1767   Massis, Henri. "M. Henri Bergson ou le modernisme philosophique." *Cahiers d'Occident*, 2e Sér., 2, No. 4, 1928, 161-170. This is a series of notes on Bergson's philosophy written originally in December, 1913.

1768   Meyerson, Emile. "Dans la lignée des grands créateurs." *Nouvelles Littéraires*, No. 322, 15 décembre 1928, 1.

1769   Minkowski, Eugène. "Les Idées de Bergson en psychopathologie." *Nouvelles Littéraires*, No. 324, 29 décembre 1928, 7. Cf. the author, 1926.

1770   Mourgue, Raoul. "Bergson et la biologie du système nerveux." *Nouvelles Littéraires*, No. 322, 15 décembre 1928, 5. Discoveries by neurologists Pierre Marie, C. von Monakow, and Henry Head, have led most students of the nervous system to concur with the position taken by Bergson in *Matter and Memory*: mental phenomena (including memory images) are not localized in the brain. Bergson's position in *Creative Evolution* can aid in the creation of a new neurology. The author cites a recently published work by himself and C. von Monakow, *Introduction biologique à l'étude de la neurologie et de la psycho-pathologie*.

1771   Mourgue, Raoul and von Monakow, Constantin. *Introduction biologique à l'étude de la neurologie et de la psychopathologie, intégration et désintégration de la fonction.* Paris: Félix Alcan, 1928, xi, 420. This book applies Bergsonian ideas to neurology and psychology.

1772 Müller-Freienfels, Richard. "Die Philosophie Bergsons als Ausdruck französischer Mentalität." *Zwiebelfisch,* 20, No. 11-12, 1928, 399-404.

1773 Noailles, Anna, Comtesse de. l"La Renommée d'Henri Bergson." *Nouvelles Littéraires,* No. 322, 15 décembre 1928, 1.

1774 "Nobel Prize for Literature for 1927." *London Mercury,* 19, No. 108, December 1928, 124.

1775 Papini, Giovanni. "Mes Recontres avec Bergson." *Nouvelles Littéraires,* No. 322, 15 décembre 1928, 3.

1776 Pfister, Charles. "Bergson, élève de l'Ecole normale." *Nouvelles Littéraires,* No. 322, 15 décembre 1928, 4.

1777 Picard, Gaston. "Au Temps où naissait la gloire d'Henri Bergson." *Le Figaro Littéraire,* 17 novembre 1928.

1778 Pierre-Quint, Léon. "Le Prix Nobel à Bergson." *Revue de France,* 8e Année, No. 24, 15 décembre 1928, 701-708.

1779 Politzer, Georges. *La Fin d'une parade philosophique: Le Bergsonisme.* Paris: Les Revues, 1928, 120. This is a Marxist critique of Bergson. The author insists that Bergsonism is a rationalization of bourgeoise interests. For an evaluation of Politzer's critique Cf. A. Cornu, 1968 and A. Joussain, 1956. Politzer's critique of Bergson has been often reprinted.

1780 "Premio Nobel a Bergson." *La Prensa,* 14 noviembre 1928.

1781 Prévost, Jean. "Review of 'L'Intuition philosophique' by Henri Bergson." *Nouvelle Revue Française,* 16, No. 183, 1er décembre 1928, 860-862.

1782 "Le Prix Nobel à M. Bergson." *L'Action Française,* 21e Année, No. 320, 15 novembre 1928, 4.

1783 Rageot, Gaston. "Le Bergsonisme et le monde moderne." *Illustration,* 86, Pt. 2, 24 novembre 1928, 597-598.

1784 Rageot, Gaston. "Souvenirs d'un bergsonien." *Annales Politiques et Littéraires,* 72e Année, No. 2323, 1er décembre 1928, 493-494.

1785 Recouly, Raymond. "Honors Come to Bergson, Philosopher." *New York Times,* 78, No. 25, 894, December 16, 1928, pt. 5, pp. 7, 22. This is a portrait of Bergson by a friend and former pupil.

1786 "Redacción de 'El premio Nobel." *Síntesis,* 2, No. 19, diciembre 1928, 117-118.

1787 Rey, Abel. "French Philosophy in 1926 and 1927." *Philosophical Review,* 37, No. 6, November 1928, 527-556. The author claims that Bergsonism and Scholasticism have largely given to French philosophy its present characteristics.

1788 Richard, Gaston. "Nouvelles tendances sociologiques, en France et en Allemagne." *Revue Internationale de Sociologie,* Vol. 36, Nos. 11-12, novembre-décembre 1928. The author deals with the Bergsonian sociology of Daniel Essertier.

1789 Rignano, Eugenio. "Ce que la biologie doit à Bergson." *Nouvelles Littéraires,* No. 322, 15 décembre 1928, 3. The author holds that Bergson is responsible for broadening the concepts which biologists use to comprehend life.

1790 Roldan, Sánchez Eleazar. "A propósito de Bergson." *Revista de Filosofía,* 14, No. 1, enero 1928, 117-123.

1791   "Review of *Seelische Energie* by Henri Bergson." *Hippokrates*, 1, 1928, 523.

1792   Sertillanges, Antonin Gilbert. "Bergson devant le catholicisme." *Nouvelles Littéraires*, No. 322, 15 décembre 1928, 1.

1793   Soderblom, Mgr. (Archevêque d'Upsal). "Hommage." *Nouvelles Littéraires*, No. 322, décembre 1928, 3.

1794   Souday, Paul. "Le Prix Nobel." *Annales Politiques et Littéraires*, No. 2323, 1er décembre 1928, 501.

1795   Souday, Paul. "Le Prix Nobel à M. Bergson." *Le Temps*, No. 24564, 19 novembre 1928, 1.

1796   Souday, Paul. "Taine, Bergson et M. Thibaudet." *Le Temps*, No. 24452, 30 juillet 1928, 1.

1797   Talvart, Hector and Place, Joseph. "Henri Bergson." *Bibliographie des auteurs modernes de langue française*. Paris: Chronique des Lettres Françaises, 1928, i, 432. Bibliographic materials concerning Bergson may be found on pp. 379-389.

1798   Taylor, Alfred Edward. *A Commentary on Plato's Timaeus*. Oxford: Clarendon Press, 1928, 700. Bergson's concept of measurement is criticized on pp. 689-691. Cf. also pp. 61, 159n.

1799   Teran, Sisto. "Filosofía y metáfora." *Nosotros* 22, No. 224, enero 1928, 5-32.

1800   Thibaudet, Albert. "Henri Bergson écrivain." *Candide*, 5, 15 novembre 1928.

1801   Thibaudet, Albert. "Henri Bergson écrivain." *Messidor*, 15, No. 11-12, novembre-décembre 1928.

1802   Thibaudet, Albert. "Le Style intérieur d'une philosophie." *Nouvelles Littéraires*, No. 322, 15 décembre 1928, 1-2.

1803   Thibaudet, Albert. "Taine, Bergson et M. Souday." *Nouvelles Littéraires*, No. 302, 28 juillet 1928, 1.

1804   Wahl, Jean. "Témoignages." *Nouvelles Littéraires*, No. 322, 15 décembre 1928, 4.

1805   Warren, Lanning. "Bergson Surprised to Get Nobel Prize." *New York Times*, 78, No. 25, 880, December 2, 1928, p. 7, col. 3. This article briefly summarizes Bergson's career, his surprise at receiving the Nobel Prize for Literature.

1806   Whyte, Lancelot Law. *Archimedes or The Future of Physiscs*. New York: E. P. Dutton & Co., 1928. Chapter Two is titled "A Modern Duel: Einstein and Eddington v. Bergson and Whitehead."

1807   Zanta, Léontine. "Le Rayonnement de la philosophie française." *Journal des Débats*, 35, Pt. 2, 15 novembre 1928, 863-864.

1929

1808   Balthasar, Nicholas. "La Philosophie moderne et sa critique." *Revue Néo-scolastique de Philosophie*, 2e Sér., 31, No. 21, février 1929, 53-80. The author follows Decoster in criticism of criteriological principles in R. Descartes, B. Spinoza, I. Kant, J. Fichte, G. W. F. Hegel, and Bergson.

1809   Bayart, Pierre. *Une Application du bergsonisme à la science économique et comptable*. Paris: Librairie du "Ruceil Sirey," 1929, 16. "Extrait de la *Revue d'Economie Politique*, No. 5, 1929."

1810   Benrubi, Isaac. "H. Bergson." *Deutsche-französische Rundschau*, 2, 1929, 1018-1026.

1811   "Henri Bergson: Echo der Zeitungen z. Bergsons 70. Geburtstag." *Das literarische Echo*, 31, No. 3, 1929, 152.

1812   Brunschvicg, Léon. "Henri Bergsons Philosophie." *Revue Rhénane*, (Rhein Blätter) 9, No. 4, 1929, 4-12. Trans. C. Knoertzer.

1813   Buchenau, A. "Review of *Seelische Energie* by Henri Bergson." *Neue Jahrbücher für Wissenschaft und Jugendbildung*, 5, 1929, 744.

1814   Burnett, Etienne. *Essences*. Paris: Seheur, 1929, 252. Bergson and Proust are discussed on pp. 165-252.

1815   Burzio, Filippo. "Cinque maestri." *Ritratti*. Torino: Ribet, 1929.

1816   Černý, Václav. *Ideové kořeny současného umění: Bergson a ideologie současného romantismus*. Praha: O. Girgai, 1929, 102.

1817   Challaye, Félicien Robert. *Bergson*. Paris: Mellottée, 1929. (Les Philosophes)

1818   Conger, George Perrigo. *New Views of Evolution*. New York: The Macmillan Company, 1929, 235 pp. Cf. pp. 186-191, "Creative Evolution: Bergson". This discussion consists almost entirely of quotes from "Creative Evolution. The author concludes: "The effect of Bergson's philosophy, with its inner way of looking at things and its suggestion (not elaborated in detail) of a spirit operative in the cosmos, has been much more favorable to philosophies of religion than was the older evolutionism of Spencer. But Bergson remains virtually committed to vitalism which means that his philosophy is open to criticisms of the extreme evolutionists." (p. 191)

1819   Crémieux, Benjamin. *Du côté de Marcel Proust, suivi de lettres inédites de Marcel Proust à Benjamin Crémieux*. Paris: Lemarget, 1929, 172. The author contends on p. 10 that Bergson helped orient Proust's conception of memory and that Bergson's language best explicates memory as it functions in Proust's experience.

1820   Croce, Benedetto. "Note Concerning Bergson's Philosophy." *Critica*, 27 Juli 1929, 276. The author maintains that Bergson again took up a critique of abstract intelligence already begun by Hegel. But Hegel went beyond intuition through his "concept of the concept." Croce and Bergson conversed on this topic at the Congrès de Bologne in 1911.

1821   Danckert, Werner. "Impressionistische Gehalte in der Philosophie Bergsons." *Deutsche Vierteljahrsschrift für Literaturwissenschaft*, 7, No. 1, 1929, 154-156.

1822   Dibblee, George Binney. *Instinct and Intuition: A Study in Mental Duality*. London: Faber and Faber, 1929, 394. The author states that: "Dating back to...Descartes I must acknowledge my immense obligations to may philosophers of the French school, of whom I can only mention the most modern: MM. Henri Bergson, Maurice Blondel, and my friend M. Jacques Chevalier..." (8).

1823   Driesch, Hans. *The Science and Philosophy of the Organism*. 2nd ed. London: A. and C. Black, 1929, 344. Bergson and convergent evolution are discussed on pp. 182-183; *Matter and Memory* on 219; Bergson on mind and brain on 309; and Driesch and Bergson on "élan vital" on 328.

1824   Dujovne, León. "Bergson." *Síntesis*, 2, No. 20, enero 1929, 201-211.

1825   Dujovne, León. "Un numéro de 'Les Nouvelles Littéraires' dedicado a Bergson." *Síntesis*, 2, No. 22, marzo 1929, 117-119.

1826   Durant, William James. *Die grossen Denker*. Zürich: Orell Füssli, 1929, 557. Bergson is discussed on pp. 427-444.

1827   Essertier, Daniel. *Philosophes et savants français du XXe siècle: Extraits et notices*. Paris: Félix Alcan, 1929, 251.

1828   Fedi, R. "Lo spiritualismo de Enrico Bergson." *Bilychnis*, Anno 20, No. 2, 1929.

1829   "Filosofía Bergsoniana y Catolicismo de Carlos Malagarriga." *Revista de Filosofía*, 14, No. 4, 1929, 106. This is a comment on an article in the July 1928, issue of *Nosotros*.

1830   Gillouin, René. "Réflexions sur Bergson et le bergsonisme." *Monde Nouveau*, 10, No. 11, janvier-février 1929, 808-816.

1831   Gunn, John Alexander. *The Problem of Time*. London: Allen and Unwin, Ltd., 1929, 460.

1832   Gurwitsch, A. "Phänomenologie der Thematik und das reine Ich: Studien über Beziehungen von Gestalt Theorie und Phänomenologie." *Psychologische Forschung*, 12, 1929, 279-381. The author notes Bergson's concept of the self as non-spatialized on p. 369; he discusses Bergson's concept of psychological duration on pp. 372-373.

1833   Heidegger, Martin. *Sein und Zeit*. Vol. 1. Halle: Max Niemeyer, 1929, xi, 438. This work was first published in the *Jahrbuch für Philosophie und Phänomenologische Forschung*, 1927. Here, in a concluding footnote, the author attacks Bergson for his presumed Aristotelianism. Cf. M. Heidegger, 1962, for annotation.

1834   Hingston, R. W. G. *Instinct and Intelligence*. Intro. Bertrand Russell. New York: Macmillan, 1929, 296. This book is written in defense of the view that instinct is "lapsed intelligence" and against (Bergson's) view that instinct is a quasi-intuitive mode of knowledge. The author is able to show that insects often vary their behavior intelligently, to fit new situations, and sometimes acquire new "instincts." (Bergson did not deny any of these factors, however. Cf. R. Ruyer, 1959.)

1835   Hirschbeld, Peter. "Proust und Bergson." *Zeitschrift für Ästhetik und allgemeine Kunstwissenschaft*, 23, No. 2, 1929, 165-184.

1836   Hocking, William Ernest. "Bergson." Types of Philosophy. New York: Scribner's, 1929, 188-212.

1837   "Hommage à Henri Bergson." *Chronique des Lettres Françaises*, 7, 1929, 94-106.

1838   Huxley, Julian. *Essays of a Biologist*. New York: Alfred A. Knopf, 1929, 304. On pp. 32-35 the author briefly examines Bergson's biology, concluding: "There "is" an "urge of life": and it is, as a matter of fact, urging life up the steps of progress. But to say that biological progress is explained by the *élan vital* is to say that the movement of a train is 'explained' by an *élan locomotif* of the engine." (p. 33) Huxley's biology is, however, clearly similar to Bergson's. Cf. also pp. 177, 202, 303.

1839   Ivanoff. *Les Deux Aspects du bergsonisme*. Paris: Croville-Morant, 1929, 15.

1840   Janet and Seailles. *Histoire de la philosophie: Les Problèmes et les écoles* (Supplément: *Période contemporaine*, par Parodi, Tisserand, Dugas, Dorolle et Abel Rey). Paris: Delagrave, 1929, 240.

1841   Jankélévitch, Vladimir. "Bergsonisme et biologie: à propos d'un ouvrage récent." *Revue de Métaphysique et de Morale*, 36, No. 2, avril-juin 1929, 253-256. This is a review of *Introduction biologique à l'étude de la neurologie et de la psychopathologie* by Von Monakow and Mourgue.

1842   Keeling, Stanley V. "Bergson: Some Recent Appreciations in Philosophy in France." *Journal of Philosophical Studies*, 4, No. 15, July, 1929, 379-386. This is a review both of an edition of *Nouvelles Littéraires* dedicated to Bergson and of writings by Chevalier. It contains interesting comments on the fate of Bergsonianism in England.

1843   Knight, George Wilson. "Bergson and Shakespeare." *London Times Literary Supplement*, 28, No. 1407, January 17, 1929, 44. Close similarities between Bergson and Shakespeare are stressed in this essay.

1844   Krakowski, Edouard. "Bergson et Plotin." *Documents de la Vie Intellectuelle*, 3, No. 3, 20 juin 1930, 582-583. This study was published originally in *Une Philosophie de l'amour et de la beauté*. Paris: de Boccard, 1929, 236-237.

1845   Krakowski, Edouard. *L'Esthétique de Plotin et son influence*. Paris: de Boccard, 1929, 272. The author asserts that the influence of Plotinus extends to Maine de Biran, F. Ravaisson, and Bergson.

1846   Lasserre, Pierre. *Faust en France et autres études*. Paris: Calmann-Lévy, 1929, 235. Bergson is discussed on pp. 120-131.

1847   Laurilla, Kaarle Sanfrid. *La Théorie du comique de M. Henri Bergson*. Helsinki: Libr. academ., 1929, 66 (Suomalaisen Tiedeakatemian toimituksia, sarja B. nid. 23, No. 2). This study is a criticism of Bergson's concept of laughter.

1848   Le Bidois, Robert. "Autour du Prix Nobel: H. Bergson, écrivain." *Flambeau*, 12, No. 1, 1929, 73-88; No. 2, 1929, 152-153.

1849   Le Breton, Maurice. *La Personnalité de William James*. Paris: Hachette, 1929, 383. James and Bergson are discussed on pp. 151-164.

1850   Lerch, Emil. "Bergson in einer Nuss." *Volk und Heimat*, 5, No. 2, 1929, p. 1. This is a brief overview of Bergson's philosophy.

1851   Le Roy, Edouard. *La Pensée intuitive*: Vo. 1. *Au delà du discours*. Paris: Boivin et Cie., 1929, 204.

1852   Liebert, Arthur. "Review of *Seelische Energie* by Henri Bergson." *Kantstudien*, 34, No. 1-2, 1929, 184-186.

1853   Lubac, Emile. *Les Niveaux de conscience et d'inconscient et leurs intercommunications*. Paris: F. Alcan, 1929, 148.

1854   Maire, Gilbert. *Aux Marches de la civilisation occidentale: Henri Bergson, etc.* Paris: Baudinière, 1929, 224. Cf. esp. Ch. I, "Un Témoignage sur Henri Bergson."

1855   Marcuse, (Herbert?). "Review of *Einführung in die Metaphysik* by Henri Bergson." *Zeitschrift für Sexualwissenschaft und Sexualpolitik*, 16, No. 6, 1929, 427. The reviewer is very critical of Bergson's "philosophischen Mystizismus."

1856   Maritain, Jacques. "Bergsonisme et métaphysique." *Chroniques (huitième numéro de)*. Paris: Plon, 1929, 5-131.

1857   Maritain, Jacques. "Bergsonisme et métaphysique." *Le Roseau d'Or*, 24, No. 6, 1929, 5-131.

1858   Maritain, Jacques. "Bergsonismo y metafísica." *Criterio*, 2, No. 70, 1929, 297-301; No. 71, 1929, 329-332; No. 72, 1929, 361-363; No. 74, 1929, 425-429.

1859   Maritain, Jacques. "Sur La Critique Bergsonienne de l'intelligence." *La Vie Intel-lectuelle*, Vol. 2, Juin, 1929, 1004-1013. This is a section from part 2, Chapter VI of Maritain's *La Philosophie Bergsonienne*. (1914)

1860   Massis, Henri. "La declinación del bergsonismo." *Criterio*, Año 1, No. 15, junio 1929, 457-460.

1861   "Massis, Henri. 'La declinación del bergsonismo'." *Humanidades*, 19, 1929, 276. This is a brief mention of Massis' article in *Criterio*.

1862   Meyerson, Ignace. "Les Images." *Journal de Psychologie Normale et Pathologique*, 26, 1929, 625-709. For annotation cf. the author, 1932.

1863   Minkowski, Eugène. "La Notion du temps en psychiâtrie." *L'Évolution psychiat-rique*, 1, No. 2, 1929, 65-85. The author distinguishes two basic kinds of mental illness: schizophrenia (corresponding to Bergson's "intellect") and manic-depre-ssion (corresponding to "intuition"). He introduces two new concepts into the study of manic-depression: temporal unfolding and felt synchrony. The manic-depressive has lost the capacity to make a present; he has, equally, lost the capacity for felt synchrony. The melancholiac has lost the sense of the future.

1864   Minkowski, Eugène. "Les Idées de Bergson en psychopathologie." *Annales Medico-psychologiques*, 87, No. 1, 1929, 234-246.

1865   Molina, Garmendia (Enrique). "Scienza e filosofia nel pensiero di Henri Bergson." *Annuario Liceo-ginnasio Giovanni Plana in Alessandria*, 1929-1934.

1866   Moresco, Gino. "Intellectualismo y espiritualidad." *Criterio*, 2, No. 79, 5 sep-tiembre 1929, 11.

1867   Olgiati, Francesco. "Il concetto di sostenza." *Rivista di filosofia neoscolastica*, 21, No. 3, maggio-agosto 1929. The author analyzes the concept of substance in J. Locke, G. Berkeley, D. Hume, J. S. Mill, H. Taine, and Bergson.

1868   Palgon, Rudolf. *Die Weltanschauung Henri Bergsons*. Breslau, Germany: Priebatsch, 1929, 148.

1869   Palhories, Fortuné. *Vies et doctrines des grands philosophes*. Paris: Lanore, 1929, 111, 399. The final sections of this book concern W. James, F. Nietzsche, and Bergson.

1870   "Photograph of Bergson." *Scientific Monthly*, 28, No. 6, June 1929, 571.

1871   Pignato, Luca. "L'estetica mistica di Enrico Bergson." *Bilychnis*, Anno 20, No. 2, 1929.

1872   Pignato, Luca. *L'ottocento francesi: L'estetica mistica di Bergson*. Palermo: Cic-lope, 1929, 140. (I Libre della tradizione)

1873   Politzer, Georges. *Le Bergsonisme: Une Mystification philosophique*. Paris: Les Revues, 1929, 128.

1874   "Portrait of Bergson." *Current History*, 29, No. 4, January 1929, 604. This article concerns the award of a Nobel Prize to Bergson.

1875   Reynaud, Louis. *La Crise de notre littérature: Des Romantiques à Proust, Gide et Valéry*. Paris: Hachette, 1929, 256. Cf. pp. 125-126, 192-206. The author considers Bergson to be a disciple of Schopenhauer and Proust to be a disciple of Bergson.

1876   Richter, Johannes Rudolf. *Intuition und intellectuelle Anschauung bei Schelling und Bergson*. Ohlau, Germany: Schles., 1929, 88.

1877 Romanowski, Henryk. *Nowa filozofja: Studium o bergsonizmie.* Lublin: Towarzystwo Wiedzy Chrześjańskeij, 1929, 192. (Towarzystwo Wiedzy Chrześjańskeij Lublin, No. 4)

1878 Ruggiero, Guido de. "L'ultimo Bergson." *Critica*, 27, No. 4. luglio 1929, 264-277. The author proposes an idealistic, rationalistic interpretation of Bergson.

1879 Russell, Bertrand. *Mysticism and Logic.* London: George Allen; New York: Norton, 1929, 234.

1880 "Review of *Seelische Energie* by Henri Bergson." *Die Hilfe*, 35, 1929, 484.

1881 Steuer, A. "Review of *Seelische Energie* by Henri Bergson." *Literarische Handweiser*, 65, 1929, 668.

1882 Tarozzi, Giuseppe. "Enrico Bergson." *Cultura moderna*, Anno 28, No. 1, 1929.

1883 Teissonière, Paul. *La Génie de l'évolution créatrice.* Bruxelles: Foyer de l'âme, 1929, 282. (Les Principes de la nouvelle Reformation) This book explores the basic problemes of theology from the vantage-point of Bergson's *Creative Evolution.*

1884 Teran, Sisto. "Sobre la difusión de la filosofía." *Criterio*, 2, No. 83, octubre 1929, 150, 212.

1885 Terhaar, J. "Review of *Seelische Energie* by Henri Bergson." *Grütli-Kalender für 1925 und 1926*, 23, 1929, 425f.

1886 Thibaudet, Albert. "Bergson et Proust." *Journal de Genève*, 18 février 1929, p. 1. This is a review of *Essences* by E. Burnett.

1887 Tilgher, Adriano. *Homo faber: Storia del concetto del lavora nella civiltà occidentale.* Roma: Bardi, 1929, 200. (Liberia di scienze e lettre) Bergson's influence is found throughout this study of the part which work has played in the evolution of the human race.

1888 Turquet-Milnes, Gladys Rosaleen. "Bergson and Tragedy." *Contemporary Review*, 136, August 1929, 205-212. Bergson construes the tragic emotion as an affirmation of life, according to the author.

1889 Uchenko, Andrew. *The Logic of Events: An Introduction to a Philosophy of Time.* Berkeley: University of California Press, 1929, 180. Many philosophers are criticized in this study, including Bergson, B. Russell, B. Croce, G. Gentile, A. N. Whitehead, and Samuel Alexander.

1890 Villegas, Angel Camilo. *Bergson y la filosofía clásica.* Intro. F. de la Vega. Bogotá: Tip. Mogollón, 1929, 69.

1891 Whitehead, Alfred North. *Process and Reality: An Essay in Cosmology.* New York: The Macmillan Company; Cambridge, England: The University Press, 1929, 545. The author refers to Bergson on pp. vii, 49, 65, 174, 319, 336, 428, and 489. On p. vii the author states, "I am also greatly indebted to Bergson, William James, and John Dewey. One of my preoccupations has been to rescue their type of thought from the charge of anti-intellectualism, which rightly or wrongly has been associated with it." On pp. 49-50, the author notes certain respects in which his theory of intuition differs with Bergson's. On p. 319, the author states, "on the whole, the history of philosophy supports Bergson's charge that the human intellect 'spatializes the universe;' that is to say, that it tends to ignore the fluency, and analyze the world in terms of static categories." He adds that, unlike Bergson, he does not believe spatialization to be an intrinsic vice of the intellect. On p. 489, the author asserts that "spatialization" is a "real factor in the physical constitution of every actual occasion..."

1930

1892   Basu, P. S. *Bergson et le Vedânta*. Montpellier: Librairie Nouvelle, 1930, 147. Thèse Lettres, Montpellier.

1893   "Henri Bergson." *Documents de la Vie Intellectuelle*, 1, No. 4, 20 janvier 1930, 38-40. This was originally published in *Nouvelles Littéraires*, 15 December 1928.

1894   "Bibliographie de Bergson." *Documents de la Vie Intellectuelle*, 1, No. 4, 20 janvier 1930, 69-72.

1895   "Bibliographie des ouvrages relatifs à Bergson." *Documents de la Vie Intellectuelle*, 2, No. 5, 20 février 1930, 278-279.

1896   "Bibliographie des ouvrages relatifs à Bergson." *Documents de la Vie Intellectuelle*, 3, No. 3, 20 juin 1930, 583-588.

1897   Brunschvicg, Léon. "Bergson et l'intelligence." *Documents de la Vie Intellectuelle*, 2, No. 5, 20 février 1930, 246-254. This article appeared originally in *Progrès de la conscience dans la philosophie occidentale*. Vol. 2, Chs. 21-22.

1898   Cardone, Domenico Antonio. "Il concetto della natura ed il valore dell'umanità nella filosofia de H. Bergson." *Rivista internazionale de filosofia del diritto*, 10, No. 2, 1930.

1899   Chaix, J. *De Renan à Jacques Rivière: Dilettantisme et amoralisme*. Paris: Bloud et Gray, 1930, 223. (Cahiers de la Nouvelle Journée, No. 16) Cf. "V. L'influence bergsonienne", pp. 78-85. "et voilà comment, par un detour inattendu, la philosophie de M. Bergson, pour avoir trop médit de l'intelligence, rous ramène à l'amoralisme." p. 83. This remark appeared two years before the publication of Bergson's *Les Deux Sources*.

1900   Chevalier, Jacques. "L'Opinion de M. Jacques Chevalier." *Documents de la Vie Intellectuelle*, 2, No. 5, 20 février 1930, 256-261. This article was originally published in *Nouvelles Littéraires*, 15 décembre 1928.

1901   Chevalier, Jacques. "La Portée métaphysique de la pensée bergsonienne." *Documents de la Vie Intellectuelle*, 3, No. 3, 20 juin 1930, 562-568. This was originally Chapter VII of the author's *Bergson*.

1902   Chevalley, Abel. "Letter from France." *Saturday Review of Literature*, 6, No. 29, 8 February 1930, 720. This note concerns the influence of Bergson on literature.

1903   Dandieu, Arnaud. "Le Conflit du réel et du rationel dans la psychologie du temps et de l'espace." *Revue Philosophique de la France et de l'Etranger*, 110, Nos. 7-8, 1930, 448f.

1904   Dollard, Stewart E. "Two Schools of Becoming." *Modern Schoolman*, 6, No. 3, March 1930, 47-49. The author compares Bergson and Heraclitus.

1905   Figueroa, Ernesto L. *Bergson: Exposición de sus ideas fundamentales*. La Plata, Argentina: Biblioteca Humanidades, 1930, 299. (Biblioteca humanidades, 11)

1906   Fite, Warner. *The Living Mind*. New York: Dial, 1930, 317. Bergson is discussed on pp. 99-103, 146, and 154-156.

1907   "Review of *Le Génie de l'évolution créatrice* by Paul Teissonière." *Revue de Métaphysique et de Morale*, 37, No. 2, 1930, 3-4. (Supplement)

1908   George, André. "Bergson et Einstein." *Documents de la Vie Intellectuelle*, 1, No. 4, 20 janvier 1930, 52-60. This essay recapitulates the Bergson-Einstein debate.

1909   George, André. "Bergson et les livres récents de M. Edouard Le Roy." *Documents de la Vie Intellectuelle*, 1, No. 4, 20 janvier 1930, 60-64. This article is signed "A. G.".

1910   George, André. "Bergson et Thibaudet." *Documents de la Vie Intellectuelle*, 3, No. 3, 20 juin 1930, 578-582.

1911   Iliev, Athanasse. *Le Bergsonisme: Une Philosophie Prospective*. Sofia, 1930's, 166 pp.

1912   J., B. "Review of *Seelische Energie* by Henri Bergson." *Zeitschrift für Buddhismus*, 9, No. 1, 1930, 188-189.

1913   Jaensch, Erich R. "Grundsätzliches zur Typenforschung und empirisch vorgehenden philosophischen Anthropologie." *Zeitschrift für Psychologie*, 116, No. 1, 1930, 107-116.

1914   Jankélévitch, Vladimir. "Prolégomènes au bergsonisme." *Documents de la Vie Intellectuelle*, 1, No. 4, 20 janvier 1930, 40-62.

1915   "Jugements sur Bergson." *Documents de la Vie Intellectuelle*, 1, No. 4, 20 janvier 1930, 35-72; No. 5, 20 février 1930, 245-279; No. 3, 20 juin 1930, 541-588. This is a series of articles and passages on Bergson, most published elsewhere.

1916   Jurévičs, Paulis. *Le Problème de la connaissance dans la philosophie de Bergson*. Paris: Vrin, 1930, 278.

1917   K., A. "Review of *Bergson: Exposición de sus ideas fundamentales* by Ernesto L. Figueroa." *Humanidades*, 22, 1930, 241-242. The reviewer is probably Alejandro Korn.

1918   Krakowski, Edouard. "Bergson et Plotin." *Documents de la Vie Intellectuelle*, 3, No. 3, 20 juin 1930, 582-583. This study was published originally in *Une Philosophie de l'amour et de la beauté*. Paris: de Boccard, 1929, 236-237.

1919   Krakowski, Edouard. "L'Intuition antique et son destin moderne: Platon, Plotin et les contemporains." *Mercure de France*, 221, No. 770, 15 juillet 1930, 317-358. Bergson's influence on French literature is discussed on pp. 353-356.

1920   Lalande, André. *Les Illusions évolutionnistes*. Paris: Félix Alcan, 1930, 464. The author accepts the distinction between biological evolution and entropy but argues that reason, not intuition, must guide the development of man.

1921   Lalande, Andr. "La Psychologie, ses divers objects et ses méthodes." *Nouveau Traité de psychologie*. Vo. 1. Ed. Georges Dumas. Paris: Félix Alcan, 1930, 367-419. Bergson's influence on introspective psychology is discussed on pp. 380-382.

1922   Le Roy, Edouard. *La Pensée intuitive*: Vol. 2. *Invention et vérification*. Paris: Boivin et Cie., 1930, 297.

1923   Maire, Gilbert. "Philosophie et biologie." *Documents de la Vie Intellectuelle*, 1, No. 4, 20 janvier 1930, 66-67. This article also appears in *Aux Marches de la civilisation occidentale*, Badin, 1929.

1924   Malagarriga, Carlos. "Notas lexicológicas de un traductor." *Nosotros*, 24, No. 253, junio 1930, 322-338. The author explains the terminology used in his Spanish translation of *Creative Evolution* (1912).

1925 Marcel, Gabriel. "Carence de la spiritualité." *Documents de la Vie Intellectuelle*, 3, No. 3, 20 juin 1930, 574-578. This article appeared originally in *Nouvelle Revue Française*, March 1929.

1926 Maritain, Jacques. "La Métaphysique du bergsonisme." *Documents de la Vie Intellectuelle*, 3, No. 3, 20 juin 1930, 568-574. This essay was published originally in *La Métaphysique bergsonienne*, 2nd. ed.

1927 Maritain, Jacques. "L'Opinion de M. Jacques Maritain." *Documents de la Vie Intellectuelle*, 2, No. 5, 20 février 1930, 261-271. This essay was published originally in "Bergsonisme et métaphysique," *Le Roseau d'Or*.

1928 Maritain, Jacques. *La Philosophie bergsonienne: Etudes critiques par Jacques Maritain*. 2-3e ed. Paris: Librairie Tequi, 1930, 1948, 467. The third edition of this work is revised and enlarged.

1929 Maxence, Jean. *Positions: Valeur de l'inquiétude: Henri Bergson: Nécessité d'un dogmatisme: Pour continuer Jacques Rivière: Hiérarchie de la connaissance*. Paris: Saint-Michel, 1930, 247.

1930 Mayou, Jean-Jacques. "Le Roman de l'espace et du temps Virginia Woolf." *Revue Anglo-Americaine*, 7, No. 2, avril 1930, 312-326.

1931 Messer, August. *La filosofía actual*. 3rd Ed. Trans. Joaquin Xirau. Madrid: Revista de Occidente, 1930, 182, Cf. pp. 151-162 for ad description of Bergson's philosophy as a philosophy of life, intuition and action.

1932 Metz, Andre. "Un Prochain Ouvrage sur Bergson." *Documents de la Vie Intellectuelle*, 1, No. 4, 20 janvier 1930, 67-68.

1933 Meyerson, Emile. *Identity and Reality*. London: Allen and Unwin; New York: Macmillan, 1930, 495. Bergson's concept of absolute motion is discussed on p. 131; his ideas concerning the ether on p. 257; on the relativity of sense qualities on p. 296; on the electromagnetic theory of light on p. 296; on memory on pp. 354-355; on the "segmentation of reality" on pp. 356-357; on constants and variables on pp. 436-440.

1934 Munnynck, Marc de. "Henri Bergsons Philosophie." *Schweizerische Rundschau*, 31, 1930, 909-924, 995-1011.

1935 Munnynck, Marc de. "Examen de la philosophie bergsonienne." *Revue Catholique des Idées et des Faits*, No. 1, 24 janvier, 1930, 9-13.

1936 Munnynck, Marc de. "Examen de la philosophie bergsonienne." *Documents de la Vie Intellectuelle*, 3, No. 3, 20 juin 1930, 542-562. This appeared originally in *Revue Catholique des Idées et des Faits*, 1930.

1937 Ogden, Charles Kay and Richards, I. A. *The Meaning of Meaning: A Study of the Influence of Language Upon Thought and of the Science of Symbolism*. 3rd Edition. New York: Harcourt Brace and Company, 1930, 363. On pp. 153-159 the authors explore what they term Bergson's "disguized discussion" of the emotive function of language. Cf. also pp. 45, 238, 255-256.

1938 Proust, Marcel. *Correspondance générale*. "Publiée par Robert Proust et Paul Brach." Paris: I-IV, 1930-1936. See Volume III, p. 195, for Marcel Proust's remarks concerning his relation to Bergson.

1939 Quercy, Pierre. *L'Hallucination: Vol. 2. Philosophes et mystiques*. Paris: Félix Alcan, 1930, 381. Bergson's theory of hallucination is analyzed on pp. xxiii-xxvii and 141-172.

1940   Rabeau, Gaston. "Fait psychologique et intuition." *Documents de la Vie Intellectuelles*, 2, No. 5, 1930, 271-277. This study was published originally in *Réalité et relativité*. Paris: Rivière, 1927, 191-200.

1941   Rádl, Emanuel. *The History of Biological Theories*. Trans. E. J. Hatfield. London: Humphrey Milford (Oxford University Press) 1930, 408. The author asserts on p. 372 that from the 1890's on, the authority of Darwinism waned and "decadents and mystics—followers of F. Nietzsche and Bergson—grew rank and luxurious amidst the ruins of the scientific edifice." On pp. 275-376 he concludes that Bergson's philosophy did not directly influence evolutionary theories: "But indirectly it was of considerable importance, for it added to the growing scepticism with which the Darwinian ideas were viewed.

1942   Rey, Abel. "L'Opinion de M. Abel Rey." *Documents de la Vie Intellectuelle*, 2, No. 5, 20 février 1930, 254-256. This essay is drawn from Janet's and Séailles' history of philosophy, 1928, 204-206.

1943   Roland-Gosselin, Marie-Dominique. "Peut-on parler d'un intuition intellectuelle dans la philosophie thomiste?" in *Philosophia Perennis: Abhandlungen zu ihrer Vergangenheit und Gegenwart*. Vol. 2. Regensburg: Josef Habbel, 1930, 709-730.

1944   Rutkeiwics, Bodhan. "L'Antimécanisme biologique." *Revista di filosofia neoscolastica* 22, No. 3-4, 1930. This is a translation of chapter III of a book published in Poland entitled *L'Antimécanisme biologique et les bases du finalisme*, Lublin, 1929. The author defends finalism and intellectualism in biology against Bergson's criticisms.

1945   Scheifley, William H. "Bergson and his Sway." In *Essays in French Literature*. Los Angeles: Wetzel, 1930, 379-386.

1946   Schilpp, Paul Arthur. *Commemorative Essays in Celebration of the First Publication of Darwin's "Origin of the Species" and of the Seventieth Birthday of Henri Bergson, Edmond Husserl, John Dewey*. Stockton, California: California Private Publications, 1930, 47.

1947   Simon, P. "Wissenschaftsideal und Philosophie mit bes. Berücks. von Bergson." *Philosophia perennis*. Vol. 2, Regensburg, Germany: Habbel, 1930, 351-376.

1948   Spirito, Ugo. *L'idealismo italiano e i suoi critici: Durata reale e intuizione*. Firenze: Le Monnier, 1930, 266.

1949   Standing, Herbert F. *Spirit in Evolution: From Amoeba to Saint*. New York: The Dial Press, 1930, 312. The author states in his introduction: "Students of Bergson will see how much I am indebted in some parts of this study to his work on *Creative Evolution*" p. 12. This is an unusually clear-headed "vitalist" account of biology.

1950   Styx, Pierre-Maurice de. "Où J. Benda rencontrerait Henri Bergson." *Nouvelle Revue*, 110 (3e Livraison), No. 440 (Quatrième série), 1930, 184-197.

1951   Tilgher, Adriano. *Work: What it has Meant Through the Ages*. Trans. Dorothy Canfield Fisher. New York: Harcourt, Brace and Co., 1930, 225. Bergson's influence is found throughout this study of the part which work has played in the evolution of the human race.

1952   Vloemans, Antoon. "De philosophie van H. Bergson." *De Ploeg*, 12, 1930.

1953   Wallon, Henri. "Le Problème biologique de la conscience." *Nouveau Traité de psychologie*. Vol. 1. Ed. Georges Dumas. Paris: Félix Alcan, 1930, 293-331.

On pp. 303-305 the author dismisses Bergson's contention that consciousness can not be measured as irrelevant. Knowledge of the conditions under which a phenomenon occurs is the key to science.

1954　Weiss, Konrad. *Die Reine Wahrnehmung im psychophysischen Problem Bergsons.* Diss., Berlin, Humboldt-Universität, 1930, 75; Ilsenburg-Harz, Germany: Ruland, 1930, 75.

1955　Wickham, Harvey. *The Unrealists: James, Bergson, Santayana, Russell, Dewey, Alexander, and Whitehead.* New York: Dial, 1930, 314. A thoroughly critical, equally superficial account of Bergson's philosophy is given on pp. 68-93.

1931

1956　*Anthologie des philosophes français contemporains.* Ed. Arnaund Dandieu. Paris: Edition du Saggitaire, 1931, 533. Twenty-two philosophers, including H. Poincaré, E. Durkheim, Bergson, and E. Meyerson, are presented in this anthology.

1957　Bellon, L. "De tweebronnen van den Godsdienst volgens H. Bergson." *Studia Catholica,* 8, 1931-1932.

1958　Charpentier, Jacques. "Henri Bergson." *Mercure de France,* 229, 15 juillet 1931, 369-372.

1959　Crutcher, Roberta. *Personality and Reason.* London: Favil Press, 1931, 178. The preface is by H. Wildon Carr. The author combines Bergson's vitalism with Carr's monadology to produce a theory of personality.

1960　Carrel, Alexis. "The New Cytology," *Science,* 73, No. 1890, 1931, 297-303. The author, one of the first in French biology to accept Bergson's ideas, describes the conceptual shift necessary to the creation of a new cytology. "Time," he states, "is really the fourth dimension of living organisms. It enters as a part into the constitution of a tissue. Cell colonies, or organs, are events which progressively unfold themselves. They must be studied like history. A tissue consists of a society of complex organisms which does not respond in an instantaneous manner to the changes of the environment... The temporal extension of a tissue is as important as its spatial existence" (p. 298). The author discusses the application of such ideas to the study of cell cultures "in vitro", through the manipulation of the intercellular medium. He mentions discoveries resulting from this method, involving the problem of ageing and the nature of cancer.

1961　Carrel, Alexis. "Physiological Time." *Science,* 74, No. 1929, December 18, 1931, 618-621. The author concludes: "Such a knowledge is indispensable to a real understanding of the constitution of the body, which is composed of organs, bones, lymph and blood, but also of duration."

1962　Demiashkevich, Michael John. "The Educational Implications of Bergson's Theory of Knowledge." *Educational Administration and Supervision,* 17, February 1931, 128-138.

1963　Dwelshauvers, Georges. "Intuition du spirituel." *Revue de Philosophie,* 31, No. 1931, 327-394.

1964　Emmens, Wilko. *Das Raumproblem bei H. Bergson.* Leiden: Brill, 1931, 223.

1965　Feuling, D. "Bergson, Henri." *Lexikon für Theologie und Kirche.* Vol. 2. Freiburg im Breisgau: Herder and Co., 1931, 190.

1966   Friedman, G. "A Propos d'un livre sur Bergson." *Europe*, 27, 1931, 281-285.

1967   Jankĺévitch, Vladimir. *Bergson*. Paris: Félix Alcan, 1931, 300. Instead of confining himself to a simple exposition, the author tries to recover the genesis and framework of Bergson's thought by a reconstruction of ideas. He places special emphasis on the critical interpretation of concepts of matter.

1968   Jolivet, Régis. "Critique de la critique bergsonienne de l'idée du néant exposée dans l'ouvrage de Le Roy, *Le Problème de Dieu.*" *Archives de Philosophie*, 8, No. 2, 1931, 75-83.

1969   Klemperer, Victor. *Geschichte der französischen Literatur*. Vol. 5. Leipzig: Teubner, 1931, 382. Chapter X, entitled "Bergson: Die gewahrte Form," appears on p. 190.

1970   Klemperer, Victor. *Geschichte der französichen Literatur. Vol. 3. Der Ausgleich*. Leiden, Germany: Teubner, 1931, 190. This study contains seventy pages devoted to Bergson.

1971   Lenoir, Raymond. "Bergson, à propos d'un ouvrage récent." *Revue de Synthèse*, 1, No. 2, 1931, 257-263. This is a review of Jankélévitch's *Bergson*.

1972   Lovejoy, Arthur Oncken. "The Paradox of the Time-Retarding Journey." *Philosphical Review*, 60, No. 1, January 1931, 48-68; No. 2, April 1931, 152-167. In this essay Lovejoy concurs with Bergson's criticisms of both the general and special theories of relativity and defends Bergson against Arthur d'Abro.

1973   Mangold, F. "Bergsons Begriff d. Komischen erarbeitet a. Molières Komödien." *Zeitschrift für französische Sprache und Literatur*, 30, No. 1, 1931, 1-11.

1974   Mounier, Emmanuel, Péguy, Marcel, and Izard, Georges. *La Pensée de Charles Péguy*. Paris: Plon, 1931, 424. Mounier's section of this work deals with Péguy's Bergsonism.

1975   Rey, Abel. "Philosophy in France, 1929." *Philosophical Review*, 40, No. 1, January 1931, 1-31. The author states that French philosophy continues to try to determine, through the transformation wrought by Bergson, the manner in which our intelligence apprehends reality. A trend towards earlier, classical philosophies is evident.

1976   Sassen, Ferdinand. "De ethiek von Bergson." *Studia Catholica*, 8, 1931-1932, 321-334.

1977   Schottlaender, Felix. "Henry Bergsons Gedächtnistheorie im Lichte er Psychoanalyse." *Psychoanalytische Bewegung*, 3, 1931, 250-273. The lack of mutual interest shown by philosophy and psychoanalysis is unfortunate. The author attempts to show that each has value for the other. There are similar points of interest in Bergson's thought-system and Freud's psychoanalysis. Bergson recognizes two of the Freudian fundamentals, the unconscious and repression, but fails to recognize the place of sexuality. Psychoanalysis begins where Bergson's philosophical construction ends. The author discusses the place of the theory of freedom of the will and the relationship between conscience and consciousness. A. B. Herring in *Psychological Abstracts*, 6, No. 1, 1932, p. 32.

1978   Simon, Yves René. "La Philosophie bergsonienne: Etude critique." *Revue de Philosophie*, 31, No. 7, juillet 1931, 281-290.

1979 Thibaudet, Albert. "Péguy et Bergson." *Nouvelle Revue Française*, 19, No. 211, avril 1931, 580-592.

1980 Vial, Fernand. "Méconnaissance du temps." *Revue des Sciences Philosophiques et Théologiques*, 20, No. 3, août 1931. A. Uchenko, Bergson, and B. Russell are all wrong, according to the author. Time is not a movement, but its measure.

1981 Wilson, Edmund. *Axel's Castle: A Study in the Imaginative Literature of 1870-1930*, New York: Charles Scribner's Sons, 1931, 319. On p. 157 the author alludes to Bergson's "profound influence" on Marcel Proust.

1932

1982 Algar, Thorold. "Review of *Les Deux Sources de la morale et de la religion* by Henri Bergson." *Criterion*, 12, No. 46, 1932, 124-128.

1983 Atkinson, J. Brooks. "Laughter." *New York Times*, 81, No. 27,168, June 12, 1932, pt. 10, p. 1:1. This is a comic essay on Bergson's essay on laughter.

1984 Audard, Jean. "Review of *Le Deux Sources de la morale et de la religion* by Henri Bergson." *Cahiers du Sud*, 19 Année, No. 141, Juin, 1932, 400-403. This is a joint review of *The Two Sources* and Freud's *The Future on an Illusion*. The author declares Freud's views useful and plausible, Bergson's less so: "Autant le livre de Bergson ne pouvait apporter de solution que banal à la crise moral actuelle, autant *l'Avenir d'une Illusion*, écrit sincère et précis, parvient à développer jusqu'au bout un diagnostique raisonnable." p. 402.

1985 Bachelard, Gaston. *L'Intuition de l'instant*. Paris: Stock, 1932, 129. The author opposes the conceptions of Roupnel to those of Bergson, arguing that "instant" and "duration" are not incommensurate.

1986 Baldwin. "Mysticism and Mechanics." *The Journal of Philosophy*, 43, No. 24, 1932, 680-681. This is an abstract of a talk on Bergson's *The Two Sources of Morality and Religion*.

1987 Baruzi, Jean. "Le Point de recontre de Bergson et de la mystique." *Recherches Philosophiques*, 2, 1932-1933, 301-316. This essay is written by a Bersonian thinker who is also a historian of religion.

1988 Benrubi, Isaac. "Eucken und Bergson." *Technik*, 3, No. 1, 1932, 26-27. This article was published under the name Jacques Benrubi.

1989 Benrubi, Isaac. "Review of *Quellen der Moral und der Religion* by Henri Bergson." *Deutsche-Französische Rundschau*, 5, 1932, 773-778. This is a review of *Les Deux Sources*.

1990 Bergmann. "Review of *Les Deux Sources de la morale et de la religion* by Henri Bergson." *Jüdische Rundschau*, 37, 1932, 378f.

1991 Berl, Emmanuel. "Les Sources de la morale et de la religion." *Europe*, 19, No. 114, 1932, 318-323. This is a highly critical review of *Les Deux Sources*.

1992 Berl, Heinrich. "Bergson." *Menorah*, 10, N. 7-8, 1932, 317-318. This is an account of a visit with Bergson.

1993 Berton, Jean. "Review of *Les Deux Sources de la morale et de la religion* by Henri Bergson." *Etudes Théologiques et Religieuses*, 7e Année, No. 4, 1932, 325-326.

1994 Blondel, Charles. *La Psychographie de Marcel Proust*. Paris: Vrin, 1932, 195. Bergson and Proust are discussed on pp. 166-191.

1995   Bogdanovitch, R. "L'Idée de durée chez Bergson et chez Marcel Proust." *Notre Temps*, 3 juillet 1932, 208-213.

1996   Bois, Elie-Joseph. "A La Recherche du temps perdu." *Le Temps*, No. 19124, 13 novembre 1932, 2. Bois' article contains M. Proust's denial of Bergson's influence.

1997   Borne, Etienne. "Spiritualité bergsonienne et spiritualité chrétienne." *Etudes Carmélitaines*, 17, No. 2, octobre 1932, 157-184. This article contains a critique of *Les Deux Sources*. The author holds that Bergson brings over into the realm of morals and religion ideas which have no value except in aesthetics.

1998   Brisbois, Ed. "Review of *Les Deux Sources de la morale et de la religion* by Henri Bergson." *Revue des Questions Scientifique*, 2, No. 4, 1932, 174-176. The author regrets that Bergson's philosophy of religion is not consistent with orthodox Catholicism, but commends *Les Deux Sources* as among the most remarkable and beneficial works of contemporary philosophy.

1999   C., M. F. "Review of *Les Deux Sources de la morale et de la religion* by Henri Bergson." *Rivista di psicologia*, 28, 1932, 347.

2000   Camus, Albert. "La Philosophie de la siècle." *Sud*, 2, No. 7, juin, 1932, 125-130. In this article (written when the author was 18) Camus expresses his disappointment with *Les Deux Sources de la morale et de la religion*. *Sud* was a short-lived Algerian journal.

2001   Cattaui, Georges. "Bergson and Mysticism." *Spectator*, 149, No. 5435, 1932, 264. This is a highly laudatory brief survey of the main themes of *Les Deux Sources de la morale et de la religion*.

2002   Chevalier, Jacques. "M. Bergson et les sources de la morale." *Revue des Deux Mondes*, 8e Sér., 9, No. 10, 15 mai 1932, 384-395. This is a review of *Les Deux Sources de la morale et de la religion*.

2003   Chevalier, Jacques. *L'Idée et le réel*. Grenoble: Arthaud, 1932, 173. This book consists of four articles previously published in *La Nouvelle Journée*, *Les Annales de l'Université de Grenoble*, *Les Mélanges Hauriou*, and *Proceedings of the Aristotelian Society*

2004   Chevalier, Jacques. "La Morale de Bergson." *Le Van*, No. 169, mai 1932, 28-29. This is a review of *Les Deux Sources*. It is included in Chevalier's *Bergson*.

2005   Chevalier, Jacques. *La Vie de l'esprit*. Grenoble: Arthaud, 1932, 96.

2006   Dal Sasso, A. "Le sorgenti della morale e della religione in Bergson." *Rivista di filosofia neoscolastica*, 23, No. 6, 1932. This is a review of *Les Deux Sources*.

2007   Delattre, Floris. "La Durée bergsonienne dans le roman de Virginia Woolf." *Revue Anglo-américaine*, 9, No. 2, 1932, 97-108. The author argues that both Bergson and William James influenced Woolf.

2008   Delattre, Floris. *Le Roman psychologique de Virginia Woolf: Essais d'art et de philosophie*. Paris: J. Vrin, 1932, 268. The author finds Bergson's influence throughout Virginia Woolf's stream of consciousness novels.

2009   Deman, Th. "Review of Ch. 1, *Les Deux Sources de la morale et de la religion* by Henri Bergson." *Revue des Sciences Philosophiques et Théologieques*, 21, No. 4, 1932, 636-641.

2010   "Review of *Les Deux Sources de la morale et de la religion* by Henri Bergson." *Journal des Débats*, 39, Pt. 1, 8 avril 1932, 557-559.

2011   "Review of *Les Deux Sources de la morale et de la religion* by Henri Bergson."
        Al Machrig, Revue catholique oriental, 30, 1932, 472f. This article is in Arabic.

2012   "Review of *Les Deux Sources de la morale et de la religion* by Henri Bergson."
        Études Théologiques et Religieuses, 7, 1932, 325-326.

2013   "Review of *Les Deux Sources de la morale et de la religion* by Henri Bergson."
        Rassegna Italiana, 15, Giugno 1932, 546.

2014   "Review of *Les Deux Sources de la morale et de la religion* by Henri Bergson."
        Revue de Métaphysique et de Morale, 39, No. 2, 1932, 1. This is a brief and
        laudatory notice, which announces that a more detailed review will appear in a
        later issue of the *Revue*.

2015   Dhanis, E. "Review of *Les Deux Sources de la morale et de la religion* by Henri
        Bergson." *Civiltà cattolica*, 83, No. 3, 1932, 470-476.

2016   Dopp, Joseph. "Review of *Les Deux Sources de la morale et de la religion* by
        Henri Bergson." *Revue Neo-Scolastique de Philosophie*, 34, No. 36, 1932,
        521-526.

2017   Dubray, Paul. "Bergson et son influence sur la littérature contemporaine."
        Zeitschrift für Französichen und Englischen Unterricht, 31, No. 5, 1932, 269-
        274.

2018   Ducassé, Pierre. "Review of *Les Deux Sources de la morale et de la religion* by
        Henri Bergson." *Revue de Synthèse*, 4, octobre 1932, 173-182.

2019   Groethuysen, B. "Review of *Les Deux Sources de la morale et de la religion* by
        Henri Bergson." *Deutsche Literatur-Zeitung*, 3, 1932, 1875-1879.

2020   Gsell, Paul. "La Conversion de Bergson au mysticisme." *Revue Mondiale*, 208,
        No. 1, 1932, 25-36.

2021   Guy-Grand, Georges. "M. Bergson et la civilisation moderne." *Mercure de France*,
        Sér. moderne 236, 15 juin 1932, 513-531. This article is a review of *Les Deux
        Sources*.

2022   Haldane, John Burdon Sanderson. *The Causes of Evolution*. London and New
        York: Longmans, Green and Co., 1932, 234. Bergson is discussed on pp.
        166-168.

2023   Harpe, Jean de la. "Review of *Les Deux Sources de la morale et de la religion*
        by Henri Bergson." "Revue de Synthèse, N.S. 24, 1932, 122-147.

2024   Hersch, Jeanne. "Les Images dans l'oveure de M. Bergson." *Archives de
        Psychologie*, 23, No. 90, 1932, 97-130. Images provide an invaluable means
        of understanding Bergson's thought. The author studies the different sorts of
        imagery used in each of Bergson's major works to date. An appendix gives
        several examples of images.

2025   Hurst, Charles Chamberlain. *The Mechanism of Creative Evolution*. Cambridge:
        At the University Press, 1932, 365. On pp. xii-xv the author briefly describes
        Bergson's "charming literary account of evolution" and points out that: "While
        neither accepting nor rejecting Bergson's vitalistic and orthogenetic theory of
        Élan vital but regarding it as redundant, many biologists have recognized that
        Bergson's description of evolution as 'creative' is a true and apt expression of
        the biological fact." (p. xiv) The author will use Bergson's term, but wishes to
        give it a more scientific meaning. (Evolution is creative when it gives rise to
        new genetical species.)

2026   Jacques, R. S. "The Significance of Bergson for Recent Political Thought and Movements in France." *Royal Society of Canada Proceedings and Transactions*, 3rd Series, 26, 1932, Section ii, 5-12. This concerns Bergson and G. Sorel. It concludes with syndicalism's concepts of the consumer and the general strike.

2027   Jaensch, E. R. and Kretz, Adalbert. "Strukturpsychologische Erläuterungen zur philosophischen Zeitlehre, insbesondere bei Bergson und Proust." *Zeitschrift für Psychologie und Physiologie der Sinnesorgane I. Abtlg.: Zeitschrift für Psychologie*, 124, No. 1, 1932, 55-92.

2028   Jolivet, Régîs. *Essai sur le bergsonisme*. Paris: Vitté, 1931; Lyon: Vitté, 1932, 162.

2029   Jolivet, Régîs. "Le Nouveau Livre de M. Berson: *Les Deux Sources de la morale et de la religion*." *Revue Apologétique*, 54, No. 561, juin 1932, 641-662.

2030   Keeling, Stanley V. "The Latest Phase of M. Bergson's Philosophy." *Philosophy (Journal of Philosophical Studies)*, 7, No. 27, July 1932, 327-331. This is a largely expository account of *Les Deux Sources*.

2031   Krakowski, Edouard. "L'Avènement du bergsonisme: Génie et tradition." *Grande Revue*, 137, No. 3, février 1932, 566-574; 138, No. 3, mars 1932, 57-72; No. 4, avril 1932, 267-282; No. 5, mai 1932, 428-450.

2032   Krause, Franz. "Wo sucht Bergson die beiden Quellen der Moral und der Religion." *Die Drei*, 15, No. 1, 1932, 27-32.

2033   Lacroix, Marcel. "M. Bergson et les origines de la morale et de la religion." *Le Correspondant*, 104e Année, No. 1672, 25 mai 1932, 481-491. Tis is a review of *Les Deux Sources*.

2034   La Dow, Stanley V. "Bergson's View of Mysticism." *Theosophy Quarterly*, 30, No. 118, October 1932, 108-119. This is a review of *Les Deux Sources*.

2035   Lambercier, M. R. "Abstract of 'Les Images dans l'oeuvre de Bergson' by Jenne Hersch." *Psychological Abstracts*, 6, No. 7, 1932, 351-352. This abstract states: "The objective comprehension of a literary work does not suffice; to understand it throughly one must think subjectively with the author. This is why images, and in general all figures of speech which serve to give to ideas a more tangible form, will be found to be a valuable means of comprehending the thought of Bergson. The author considers successively the roles of visual image, auditory images, olfactory, gustatory, motor, intellectual, and affective images in Bergson's four principal works (*Essai sur les Données Immédiates de la Conscience, Matière et Mémoire, Le Rire, L'Evolution Créatrice*). In the *Essai* only a restrained use of imagery is evident, which is due to the fact that for Bergson the life of the deeper self is itself highly concrete. But to apprehend successfully this deeper self one must listen, as it were—whence the greater relative importance of auditory imagery in this than in the other works. The image of melody as an expression of pure duration is fundamental here. In *Matière et Mémoire* the function of imagery is much more to explain, to heighten the clarity of the exposition, than to convey an impression. *L'Évolution Créatrice* is characterized by the abundance and variety of its imagery, chiefly of the visual and motor sort, which serves to express the epic of vital energy.

2036   Lang. "Review of *Les Deux Sources de la morale et de la religion* by Henri Bergson." *Schweitzer Monatshefte für Politik und Kultur*, 12, 1932, 288.

2037 Laporte, Jean. "La Philosophie religieuse de Bergson." *Revue Politique et Littéraire, Revue Bleue*, 70e Année, No. 23, 3 décembre 1932, 719-726. This is a review of *Les Deux Sources*.

2038 Laporte, Jean. "A Travers l'actualité philosophique: La Mentalité primitive d'apreès M. Lévy-Bruhl et d'après M. Bergson." *Revue de France*, 12, 1 avril 1932, 754-761. The author notes passages in *Les Deux Sources* in which Bergson responds suggestively to recent anthoropological controversies in France. Bergson and L. Lévy-Bruhl agree on the distinction primitive-civilized.

2039 Lasbax, Emile. "Daniel Essertier et les sources du bergsonisme sociologique." *Revue Internationale de sociologie*, 40, Nos. 3-4, 1932, 183-191. The author describes the efforts of Daniel Essertier (1889-1930) to apply Bergson's philosophy to sociology, beginning with Essertier's teachers at Bordeaux and his doctoral theses at the Sorbonne (1928), "Les Formes inferieurs de l'explication" and "Psychologie et sociologie: Essai de bibliographie critique." The author states, "avec le don de mesure qui était le trait le plus frappant de son jugement, il se montrait par-dessus tout soucieux de réserver les droits de la psychologie en face de ceux de la sociologie, afin de ménager une entente durable et sûre entre ces deux disciplines" (p. 190). This is an account of the intellectual development of the Bergsonian sociologist Daniel Essertier.

2040 Léon, P. "Review of *Les Deux Sources de la morale et de la religion* by Henri Bergson." *Mind*, 39, No. 164, October 1932, 485-495. This is a critical but appreciative review.

2041 Le Roy, Edouard. *Bergson*. Trans. Carlos Rahola. Barcelona: Ed. Labor, 1932, 204.

2042 Lersch, Philipp. *Lebensphilosophie der Gegenwart*. Berlin: Junker und Dünnhaupt, 1932, 98. Bergson, W. Dilthey, M. Scheler, G. H. Keyserling, and their philosophies are discussed in the study of the "Philosophy of Life."

2043 Le Senne, René. "Le Bergsonisme et la morale." *Revue de Paris*, 39, No. 14, 15 juillet 1932, 411-422. This is a review of *Les Deux Sources*.

2044 Linn, Pierre. "Return of Bergson." *Commonweal*, 17, No. 1, November 2, 1932, 14-17. This is a review of *Les Deux Sources*.

2045 *Livre jubilarie du Collège de France: 1530-1930*. Paris: Presses Universitaires de France, 1932, 420.

2046 Lovecchio, A. "E. Bergson e la sua ultima opera." *Ricerche filosofiche*, Anno 2, No. 3-4, 1932. This is a review of *Les Deux Sources*.

2047 Mac Callum, H. R. "Review of *Bergson* by V. Jankélévitch." *International Journal of Ethics*, 42, No. 4, 1932, 501-503. This is a clear, insightful review. It is largely expository.

2048 Madaule, Jacques. "Le Dernier Livre de M. Henri Bergson." *Revue Hebdomadaire*, 41, No. 47, 1932, 350-362. This is a review of *Les Deux Sources*.

2049 Maes, J.-D. "Bergsons Godsdienstphilosophie." *Thomistisch Tijdschrift*, 2, 1932.

2050 Maeztu, Ramiro de. "La moral de Bergson." *La Prensa*, 11 septiembre 1932, Sec. II, Col. 1 (Suppl.).

2051 Marble, Annie Russell. "Henri Bergson: Thinker and Teacher." *Nobel Prize Winners in Literature, 1901-1931*. New York: Appleton-Century, 1932, 313-326.

2052 Marcel, Gabriel. "Henri Bergson et le problème de Dieu." *L'Europe Nouvelle*, 15, No. 742, 30 avril 1932, 558-559. This is a review of *Les Deux Sources*.

2053   Masson-Oursel, Paul. "Review of *Les Deux Sources de la morale et de la religion* by Henri Bergson." *Mercure de France*, 238, 1 septembre 1932, 394-397.

2054   Mazzantini, Carlo. "La morale e la religione secondo Bergson." *Convivium*, 4, No. 5, 1932. This is a review of *Les Deux Sources*.

2055   Metz, André. "L'Ame et le coprs d'après Bergson." *Revue de Philosophie*, 32, No. 1, janvier 1932, 7-35. The author examines Bergson's theory of mind-body interaction. He concludes that Bergson is right to deny that images and representations can be found in the brain, wrong to place the distinction between mind and body where he does. The brain itself is what calls up or excludes images. Perception and memory are not so different as Bergson makes them appear.

2056   Meyerson, Ignace. "Les Images." In *Nouveau traité de psychologie*. Vol. II. Ed. Georges Dumas. Paris: Félix Alcan, 1932, 541-606. Bergson, William James, and the concept of the image are discussed here on pp. 554-557.

2057   Millot, Albert. *La Théorie bergsonienne de l'obligation morale et ses conséquences pédagogiques*. Paris: Editions des Cours Jarach, 1932, 16. This essay was first published in *Littérature, Philosophie, Pdagogie*, July 1932.

2058   Morente, Manuel Garcia. "Las Dos Fuentes de la religión y de la morale." *Revista de Occidente*, 37, No. 111, 1932, 270-284.

2059   Morris, Charles William. *Six Theories of Mind*. Chicago: University of Chicago Press, 1932, 337. Chapter I is entitled "Mind as Process: Hegel, Bradley, Bosanquet, Bergson, Gentile."

2060   Mourgue, Raoul. *Neurobiologie de l'halucination: Essai sur une variété particulière de désintégration de la fonction*. Bruxelles: Lamertin, 1932, 416. "Lettre-préface d'Henri Bergson."

2061   Muirhead, J. "M. Bergson's New Work on Morals and Religion." *Hibbert Journal*, 31, No. 1, October 1932, 1-11. This is a summary, with critical remarks, of *Les Deux Sources*.

2062   Nizan, Paul. *Les Chiens de garde*. 3e Ed. Paris: Les Éditions Rieder, 1932, 285. This is an attack on the French philosophical establishment, which the author terms unrealistic and bourgeoise. Directed especially at L. Brunschvicg, it also strikes out at H. Bergson. Cf. pp. 129-130, 192-193, 228-229.

2063   Ouy, Achille. "Review of *Les Deux Sources de la morale et de la religion* by Henri Bergson." *Revue Internationale de Sociologie*, 40, 1932, 550-552. The author compliments Bergson for his new book, but states that Bergson's method involves certain dangers.

2064   Pallière, Aimé. *Bergson et le judaisme*. Paris: Félix Alcan, 1932, 43. Conference fait à l'Association 'Chema Israel' à Paris, le 11 décembre 1932.

2065   Parmentier, Georges. "L'Originalité du Bergsonisme." *La Nouvelle Revue*, 119, No. 476, 1932, 220-225. This is a review of *Les Deux Sources de la morale et de la religion* by Henri Bergson.

2066   Pénido, Maurillo T. "La Morale et la religion bergsonienne." *Nova et Vetera*, 7, No. 3, juillet-septembre 1932, 249-279.

2067   Pierre-Quint, Léon. "Review of *Les Deux Sources de la morale et de la religion* by Henri Bergson." *Revue de France*, 12e Année, No. 10, 15 mai 1932, 324-347. This is a very personal and laudatory review.

2068   Prévost, Jean. "Review of *Les Deux Sources de la morale et de la religion* by Henri Bergson." *Nouvelle Revue Française*, 29, No. 226, 1932, 113-118.

2069   Quartier, Charles. "Review of *Les Deux Sources de la morale et de la religion* by Henri Bergson." *Revue métapsychique*, 39. 1932, 222-226.

2070   R., G. d. "Review of *Les Deux Sources de la morale et de la religion* by Henri Bergson." *La Critica*, 30, 1932, 296-300. The reviewer is Guido de Ruggiero.

2071   Rideau, Emile. *Le Dieu de Bergson: Essai de critique religieuse.* Paris: Félix Alcan, 1932, 135.

2072   Rideau, Emile. *Les Rapports de la matière et de l'esprit dans le bergsonisme.* Paris: Félix Alcan, 1932, 182.

2073   Rochedieu, Edmond. "L'Univers: Une Machine à faire des dieux." *Revue de Théologie et de Philosophie*, N.S. 20, No. 3, juillet 1932, 165-190. This is a review of *Les Deux Sources.*

2074   Romeyer, Blaise. "Morale et religion chez Bergson." *Archives de Philosophie*, 9, No. 3, 1932, 283-317. The author holds that Bergson "...manque à chercher la raison suffisante de cette valeur qui ne peut être que l'absolu subsistant, Dieu."

2075   Rostand, Jean. *L'Evolution des espèces: Histoire des idées transformistes.* Paris: Hachette, 1932, 205. (Le roman de la science) The author states in his conclusion that science, as such, can not explain evolution. It is necessary to have recourse "...à un interprétation métaphysique, telle que l'élan vital de Bergson." (pp. 196-197) Cf. also p. 183.

2076   Roure, Lucien. "Review of *Bergson* by V. Jankélévitch." *Etudes par des Pères de la Compagnie de Jésus*, 210, 5 mars 1932, 617-618.

2077   Row, T. V. Seshagiri. *New Light on Fundamental Problems, Including Nature and Function of Art: A Critical and Constructive Study of the Problems of Philosophy from the New Point of View of Henri Bergson.* Madras, India: University of Madras, 1932, 273.

2078   Sertillanges, Antonin Gilbert. "Morale et religion d'après M. Bergson." *La Vie Intellectuelle*, 15, No. 2, 10 Mai 1932, 224-245. This is a review article concerning *Les Deux Sources.*

2079   Sertillanges, Antonin Gilbert. "Questions à M. Bergson." *La Vie Intellectuelle*, 15, No. 3, 10 juin 1932, 356-385.

2080   Smith, Marshall P. *Criticism of Philosophical Method in Henri Bergson and John Dewey.* Honors Thesis. Harvard University, 1932.

2081   Sosset, M. "A Propos du dernier livre de Bergson: *Les Deux Sources.*" *Revue de l'Université de Bruxelles*, 37, 1932, 489-509.

2082   Sujol, A. "Le Dieu calviniste et le dieu bergsonien." *Christianisme Social*, 45e Année, No. 3, mai 1932, 333-346. This is a review of *Les Deux Sources.*

2083   Szende, P. "Henri Bergson, d. Metaphysiker d. Gegenrevolution." *Wirtschaftswissenschaftliche Gesellschaft*, 7, No. 2, 1932, 542-568.

2084   T., G. "De un buen estilo filosófico." *Criterio*, 5, No. 242, 20 octubre 1932, 58-59. This is a review of *The Two Sources of Morality and Religion.*

2085   Tilgher, Adriano. *Filosofi e moralisti del novecento.* Roma: Bardi, 1932, 234. This study contains a chapter on Bergson.

2086   Tonquédec, Joseph de. "La Clef des *Deux Sources.*" *Etudes par des Pères de la Compagnie de Jésus*, 208, 5 décembre 1932, 516-534; 20 décembre 1932, 667-683.

2087   Troy, William. "Virginia Woolf: The Novel of Sensibility." *The Symposium*, 3, No. 1, 1932, 55-63; No. 2, 1932, 153-166.
2088   Vloemans, H. "Review of *Les Deux Sources de la morale et de la religion* by Henri Bergson." *Gids*, 96, No. 3, 1932, 302-315.
2089   Wahl, Jean. *Vers le concret: Études d'histoire de la philosophie contemporaine*. Paris: J. Vrin, 1932, 269. (Bibliothèque d'Histoire de la Philosophie) For Bergson's influence on Wm. James Cf. "L'Empirisme radical: L'Influence de M. Bergson," 90-97, and 'l'Anti-intellectualism.' La Lecture de *L'Evolution creatrice*. Le 'Pluralistic Universe', 113-120. For relations between the thought of Bergson and A. N. Whitehead Cf. pp. 133-134, 117, 148, 151, 169, 174-175, 190.

1933

2090   Bachelard, Gaston. *Les Intuitions atomistiques*. Paris: Boivin et Cie., 1933, 162.
2091   Baudoin, Charles. "Review of *Les Deux Sources de la morale et de la religion* by Henri Bergson." *Scientia*, 53, 1933, 367-369.
2092   Becker, H. "Review of *Les Deux Sources de la morale et de la religion* by Henri Bergson." *Annals of the American Academy of Political and Social Science*, 164, 1933, 270.
2093   "Review of *Die Beiden Quellen der Moral und der Religion* by Henri Bergson." *Die Hilfe*, 39, 1933, 576.
2094   "Review of *Die Beiden Quellen der Moral und der Religion* by Henri Bergson." *Jüdische Rundschau*, 38, 1933, 294f.
2095   "Review of *Die Beiden Quellen der Moral und der Religion* by Henri Bergson." *Theologie der Gegenwart*, 38, 1933, 156.
2096   Benrubi, Isaac. *Les Sources et les courants de la philosophie contemporaine en France*. 2 vols. Paris: Félix Alcan, 1933, 1058. Bergson is discussed in Vol. 2, on pp. 741-938.
2097   "Bergson's New Message on Dynamic Religion." *Literary Digest*, 116, August 19, 1933, 18.
2098   Bouquet, A. C. "Review of *Les Deux Sources de la morale et de la religion* by Henri Bergson." *Cambridge Review*, 56, 1933-1935, 308-310.
2099   Carbonara, Cleto. "Morale e religione nella filosofia di H. Bergson." *Logos*, 16, Nos. 2, 3, e 4, 1933. This is a review article concerning *Les Deux Sources*.
2100   Casares, Carlos Alberto. *Leyendo a Bergson: Al margen del libro Les Deux Sources de la morale et de la religion*. Buenos Aires: Imprenta Amorrortu, 1933, 53.
2101   Cattaui, Georges. "Bergson, Kierkegaard and Mysticism." Trans. A. Dru. *Dublin Review* 192, No. 1, January 1933, 70-78.
2102   Cattaui, Georges. "Marcel Proust and the Jews" *Jewish Review*, No. 3, December 1932-March 1933, 66-75.
2103   Chevrillon, A. *Taine: Formation de sa pensée*. Paris: Plon, 1932, vii, 415. The author discusses resemblances between Bergson and Taine on pp. 135-147.
2104   Citoleux, Marc. "Le Bergsonisme et l'expérience mystique." *Revue Universitaire*, 42e Année, No. 1, janvier 1933, 35-41. This is a review of *Les Deux Sources*.

2105 "Creative Religion." *The London Times Literary Supplement*, No. 1576, April 14, 1932, p. 260. This is a review of *Les Deux Sources*. The reviewer provides an unusually accurate, insightful account of Bergson's philosophy of religion.

2106 Dehove, Henri Charles. *La Théorie bergsonienne de la morale et de la religion*. Lille, France: S.I.L.I.C., 1933, 105. This consists of five lectures on Bergson's philosophy of religion.

2107 De Rouville, M. "Review of *Les Deux Sources de la morale et de la religion* by Henri Bergson." *Vragen van den Dag*, 48, 1933.

2108 "Review of *Les Deux Sources de la morale et de la religion* by Henri Bergson." *Biblioteca Sacra*, 91, No. 3 octubre 1933, 456-460.

2109 "Review of *Les Deux Sources de la morale et de la religion* by Henri Bergson." *Journal of Nervous and Mental Disease*, 77, No. 4, March 1933, 452-454. This review contains some interesting comparisons of Bergson and Freud.

2110 "Review of *Les Deux Sources de la morale et de la religion* by Henri Bergson." *Sophia*, 1, Nos. 3-4, 1933, 478-480.

2111 Dubray, Paul. "Bergson et son influence sur le néo-catholicisme littéraire." *Zeitschrift für Französischen und Englischen Unterricht*, 32, No. 3, 1933, 131-136.

2112 Dumas, Georges. "Les Expressions préalables." *Nouveau Traité de psychologie*. Vol. 3. Ed. Georges Dumas. Paris: Félix Alcan, 1933, 84-292. Bergson's theory of laughter is discussed on pp. 256-258 and 269-271.

2113 Dumas, Georges. "L'Expressions des émotions. Réactions émotionelles communes." In *Nouveau Traité de la psychologie*, Vol. 3. Ed. Georges Dumas. Paris: Félix Alcan, 1933, 210-292.

2114 Emmet, Dorothy M. "Some Reflections Concerning M. Bergson's 'Two Sources of Morality and Religion'." *Proceedings of the Aristotelian Society*, N.S. 34, 1933-1934, 231-248.

2115 "Entretien avec Bergson." *La Vie Catholique*, 10, 7 janvier 1933, 432.

2116 Fatone, Vincente. "Review of *Les Deux Sources de la morale et de la religion* by Henri Bergson." *Verbum*, 26, No. 83, 1933, 107-110.

2117 Festugière, A. J. "Religion statique et mysticisme en Grèce d'après un ouvrage récent." *La Vie Spirituelle*, 34, Suppl., 1933, 89-102.

2118 Finnbogason, G. "Kenning Bergson's um trúarbrögdin." *Skirnir*, 107, 1933, 1-23. This article is written in Icelandic.

2119 Flewelling, Ralph Tyler. "Bergson and Personalism." *Personalist*, 14, No. 2, April 1933, 81-92. The author argues that Bergson's philosophy has a close affinity with personalism. The author here reverses an earlier opinion (1920).

2120 Flewelling, Ralph Tyler. "The Culmination of *L'Évolution créatrice*." *Personalist*, 14, No. 2, 1933, 134-136. This is a review of *Les Deux Sources de la morale et de la religion* by Henri Bergson. The reviewer concludes, "Personalists will hail this marked advance in Professor Bergson's thinking as definitely aligning them with the personalist position and to them *Les Deux Sources de la morale et de la religion* will seem to bring the culmination of his thought" (p. 136).

2121 Forest, Aimé. "La Réalité concrète chez Bergson et chez Saint Thomas. *Revue Thomiste*, N.S. 16, No. 77, mai-juin 1933, 368-398.

2122   Galli, Luis Alejandro. "Materialismo y espiritualismo." *Criterio*, 6, No. 303, diciembre 1933, 374.

2123   Gally, Henriette. *Ruskin et l'esthétique intuitive*. Paris: Vrin, 1933, 353. Chapter three concerns J. Ruskin and Bergson.

2124   Garnett, A. Campbell. "Review of *Les Deux Sources de la morale et de la religion* by Henri Bergson." *International Journal of Ethics*, 63, No. 2, January 1933, 232-233.

2125   Ginsburg, Benjamin. "Bergson's Creative Ethics." *Nation*, 136, No. 3537, April 19, 1933, 452-453. This is an account of Bergson's position in *Les Deux Sources*.

2126   Gottlieb, N. "D'Une Erreur fondamentale dans *Les Deux Sources* de M. Bergson." *Revue des Etudes Juives*, 96, No. 1, 1933, 1-22.

2127   Guerrero, Eustaquio. "Review of *Les Deux Sources de la morale et de la religion* by Henri Bergson." *Estudios Ecclesiásticos*, 1933, 250-267.

2128   Guerrero, F. "Review of *Les Deux Sources de la morale et de la religion* by Henri Bergson." *Estudios Ecclesiásticos*, 12, No. 2, abril 1933, 251-268.

2129   Harris, Marjorie S. "Bergson and the Art of Life." *Personalist*, 14, No. 2, April 1933, 107-118.

2130   Harris, Marjorie S. "Bergson's Conception of Freedom." *Philosophical Review*, 62, No. 5, September 1933, 511-520.

2131   Hauriou, Maurice. *Aux sources du droit: Le Pouvoir, l'ordre et la liberté*. Paris: Bloud et Gay, 1933, 217. (Cahiers de la nouvelle journée) This book contains a supplement involving Paul Archambault, René Aigrain, and Marc Scherer, in which Bergson's philosophy of religion is discussed.

2132   Hausheer, Herman. "Thought Affinities of Bergson and Schelling." *Personalist*, 14, No. 2, April 1933, 93-106. Bergson and Schelling show close affinities, according to the author. Bergson adds an empirical foundation to Schelling's speculations.

2133   Herbertz, R. "Ueber die sog. 'fausse reconnaissance." *Psychologische Rundschau* (Swiss), 4, 1933, 223-228; 1933, 251-257. The author finds Bergson's treatment of "dèja vu" to be the "deepest and the best" of those he has examined.

2134   Hess, Gerhard. *Französische Philosophie der Gegenwart*. Berlin: Junker und Dünnhaupt, 1933, 95. This study of recent French philosophy begins with a section on Bergson.

2135   Jankélévitch, Vladimir. "Les Deux Sources de la morale et de la religion d'après Bergson." *Revue de Métaphysique et de Morale*, 40, No. 1, 1933, 101-117. This is a highly appreciative review.

2136   Joad, Cyril Edward Mitchinson. *Great Philosophies of the World*. New York: Robert M. McBride and Co., 1933, 79. Bergson is discussed in Chapter VI, "The Philosophy of Change," 114-123.

2137   Jolivet, Régîs. "De L'Evolution créatrice aux Deux Sources." Revue Thomist, N.S. 16, No. 77, mai-juin 1933, 347-367.

2138   Jolivet, Régîs. "L'Intuition intellectuelle de Bergson considerée du point de vue thomiste," in *Sbornik Mezinarodnich Thomistickych Konferenci v Praze, 1932*. Ed. M. Haban. Olomouc: Slovenska, 1933, 173-187.

2139   Kayser, Rudolf. "Der neue Bergson." *Neue Rundschau*, 46, Pt. 2, 1933, 141-143.

2140   Kinkel, H. "Geist und Seele: Die Grundlagen der Anthropologie bei Ludwig
         Klages." *Philosophisches Jahrbuch der Görresgesellschaft*, 46, No. 3, 1933,
         175-200. Section b of this essay "Die Unerfassbarkeit der Wirklichkeit, Klages
         und Bergson" appears on pp. 178-181. The author is concerned with "philosoph-
         ical" anthropology.

2141   König, R. "Review of *Les Deux Sources de la morale et de la religion* by Henri
         Bergson." *Zeitschrift für Sozialforschung*, 2, 1933, 450-451.

2142   Krakowski, Edouard. "Bergson et les philosophers de l'héroisme." *Mercure de
         France*, 247, novembre 1933, 513-528.

2143   Lachelier, Jules. *Oeuvres*. Paris: Félix Alcan, 1933, I, 219; II, 244.

2144   Lacombe, Roger-E. *La Psychologie bersonienne: Etude critique*. Paris: Félix Alcan,
         1933, 324. Cf. lengthy review, *Revue de Métaphysique et de Morale*, 61, No.
         1, 1934, 7-9. "The author denies that the arguments and facts brought forward
         by Bergson support the conception of life which he proposes. Bergson has not
         succeeded in justifying the two central theses of his psychology. His critique of
         parallelism is not convincing and his conception of the deeper mental life has
         not been established." Henri Pieron in *Psychological Abstracts*, 8, No. 7, 1934,
         270.

2145   Lelièvre, Charles. "Bergson et les deux bases de la morale." *Christianisme Social*,
         46e Année, No. 1, janvier-février 1933, 55-72. This is a review of *Les Deux
         Sources*.

2146   Lemaître, Charles. "Bergsonisme et métaphysique." *Revue Néo-scolastique de
-2156   Philosophie*, 2e Sér., 35, No. 40, novembre 1933, 516-538; 36, No. 42, mai
         1934, 5-28; No. 43, août 1934, 153-177. This essay deals with Bergson and
         Aquinas. It would be natural for Bergson to infer God's existence from the
         contingency of nature, but Le Maître holds the *Les Deux Sources* disappoints
         us in this respect.

2157   Lewkowitz, Albert. *Das Judentum und die geistigen Strömungen des 19ᵉ Jahrhun-
         derts: Grundriss der Gesamtwissenschaft des Judentums*. 3 vols. Breslau: Mar-
         cus, 1933, 570.

2158   Lida, Raimundo. "Bergson: Filósofo del lenguaje." *Nosotros*, 27, No. 282, sep-
         tiembre 1933, 5-49. Cf. Bergson's highly affirmative response to this article,
         1933.

2159   Loisy, Alfred. *Y a-t-il deux sources de la religion et de la morale?* Paris: Nourry,
         1933, 204. This is a clear, powerful critique of Bergson's position in *The Two
         Sources of Morality and Religion* by a prominent historian of religion. Essentially,
         the author argues that Bergson's sharp distinctions (open-closed, aspiration-social
         pressure, etc.) can not be defended and his dualisms portray two different aspects
         of the same thing.

2160   Lubac, Henri de. "Deux thèses de doctorat sur Bergson." *Etudes*, 216, 5 août
         1933, 306-313. This is a largely favorable review of Rideau's *Les Rapports de
         la matière et de l'esprit dans le bergsonisme* and his *Le Dieu de Bergson*.

2161   Magnin, E. "Un Colloquio con H. Bergson." *Rivista di filosofia neoscolastica*,
         25, No. 1, enero 1933, 109-114. This article recounts a conversation between
         Magnin and Bergson concerning *The Two Sources of Morality and Religion*. It
         contains some interesting comments on philosophical method.

2162 Magnin, E. "Entretien avec M. Bergson." *Vie Catholique*, 10, No. 432, 7 janvier 1933, 1-2.

2163 Maire, Gilbert. *William James et le pragmatisme religieux.* Paris: Denoël et Steele, 1933, 287. (Les Maîtres de la pensée religieuse)

2164 Masson-Oursel, Paul. "L'Inde n'a-t-elle connu qu'un mysticisme incomplet? (*Les Deux Sources* et la mystique indienne)." *Revue de Métaphysique et de Morale*, 60, No. 3, juillet-septembre 1933, 355-362. The author holds, against Bergson, that certain varieties of Indian mysticism deserve to be called "complete."

2165 Mead, Hunter. *The Relation of the Philosophy of William James to that of Henri Bergson, An Essay.* University of Southern California, School of Philosophy, William James Prize Essay 1933/34. This manuscript is in the Hoose Library of Philosophy, U.C.L.A.

2166 Meisner, E. "Henri Bergson: Philosoph." *Geisteskultur*, 42, 1933, 72-77.

2167 Mentré, F. "Une Nouvelle Philosophie de la sensation." *Revue de Philosophie*, 33, Nos. 1-2, janvier-février 1933, 76-84. This study concerns the works of M. Pradines, "le disingué disciple de Bergson."

2168 Mesnard, Paul. "Catholicisme et bergsonisme." *Revue Apologétique*, 55, Nos. 4-5, avril-mai 1933, 546-557.

2169 Messaut, Jourdain. "Author des *Deux Sources*." *Revue Thomiste*, N.S. 16, No. 77, 1933, 466-502.

2170 Metz, André. *Bergson et le bergsonisme.* Paris: Vrin, 1933, 253. The author is highly critical of both Bergson and Bergsonism.

2171 Millet, Raymond. "Révision de quelques jugements sur la pensée de Bergson." *Le Temps*, No. 26323, 23 septembre 1933, 4.

2172 Minkowski, Eugène. *Le Temps vécu: Etudes phénoménologiques et psychopathologiques.* Paris: s'Arthey, 1933.

2173 Montcheuil, Y. de. "Review of *Le Dieu de Bergson* by Emile Rideau." *Revue Apologétique*, 55, No. 7, août 1933, 129-143.

2174 Montcheuil, Y. de. "Une Thèse de philosophie religieuse sur Bergson." *Revue Apologétique*, 56, No. 6, juillet 1933, 5-25.

2175 Motte, A. R. "Review of *Les Deux Sources de la morale et de la religion* by Henri Bergson." *Revue des Sciences Philosophiques et Théologiques*, 22, No. 2, 1933, 95-104.

2176 "Review of *Neurobiologie de l'hallucination* by Raoul Mourgue." *Journal of Nervous and Mental Disease*, 77, No. 3, 1933, 321-323. The reviewer commends this work but criticizes the author for remaining on physiological grounds and not venturing into "an important precinct" of psychological defense dynamics.

2177 Parodi, Dominique. "M. Bergson et la morale." *Enseignement Public*, 102, No. 1, janvier 1933, 1-20. This is a review of *Les Deux Sources*.

2178 Penido, Maurilio Teixeira-Leite. "Réflexions sur la théodicée bergsonienne." *Revue Thomiste*, N.S. 16, No. 77, mai-juin 1933, 426-452.

2179 Perry, Ralph Barton. "William James et M. H. Bergson: Lettres, 1902-1910." *Revue des Deux Mondes*, 8e Sér., 17, No. 20, 15 octobre 1933, 783-823.

2180 Petrovici, J. "Le Dynamisme contemporain." *Revue Politique et Littéraire, Revue Bleue*, 71e Année, No. 12, 17 juin 1933, 356-359; No. 13, ler juillet 1933, 401-405.

2181   Piddington, Ralph. *The Psychology of Laughter: A Study in Social Adaptation.*
        London: Figurehead, 1933, 228. This study analyzes the philosophical theories
        of Laughter developed by Immanuel Kant, G. W. F. Hegel, Harald Höffding,
        and Henri Bergson.

2182   Pomar, Felipe C. del. "Los 'ismos' en la pintura contemporánea." *Cursos y Con-
        ferencias,* 3, No. 5, noviembre 1933, 451.

2183   Rabeau, Gaston. "L'Expérience mystique et la preuve de l'existence de Dieu."
        Revue Thomiste, N.S. 16, No. 77, mai-juin 1933, 453-465.

2184   Rageot, Gaston. "Henri Bergson: L'Intuition." *Conferencia,* 2, octobre 1933, 423-
        435.

2185   Ravaisson-Mollien, Félix. *Testament philosophique et fragments précédés de la
        notice lue en 1904 par Henri Bergson.* "Texte revu et présenté par Charles
        Devivaise." Paris: Boivin, 1933, 197.

2186   Rees, R. "Review of *Les Deux Sources de la morale et de la religion* by Henri
        Bergson." *Adelphi,* 10, 1933, 117-126.

2187   Rice, C. "M. Bergson, Mystic." *Blackfriars,* 92, No. 3, March 3, 1933, 201-203.
        This is a review of *Les Deux Sources.*

2188   Rignano, Eugenio. "Ce qu la biologie doit à Bergson." *Documents de la Vie
        Intellectuelle,* 1, No. 4, 20 janvier 1933, 65-66. This article originally appeared
        in *Nouvelles Littéraires,* 1928.

2189   Rivaud, Albert. "Remarques sur la durée." *Recherches Philosophiques,* 3, 1933-
        1934, 19-33.

2190   Rivaud, Albert. *Remarques sur la durée.* Paris: Boivin, 1933-1934, 15. This article
        appeard originally in *Recherches Philosophiques.*

2191   Romeyer, Blaise. "Autour du problème de la philosophie chrétienne." *Archives de
        Philosophie,* 10, No. 1, 1933, 45-64.

2192   Romeyer, Blaise. "La Liberté humaine d'après Bergson." *Revue Néo-scolastique
        de Philosophie,* 35, No. 2, mai 1933, 190-219. The author argues that the *Essai*
        is "seulement une analyse expérimentale suggestive et pénétrante." It is not a
        metaphysics of liberty and hence cannot be opposed to "la vraie métaphysique
        spiritualiste."

2193   Romeyer, Blaise. "Spiritualité et survie d'après Bergson." *Revue de Philosophie,*
        33, No. 2, mars-avril 1933, 117-156.

2194   Rubi, Basili di. "Dues deus de la moral i de la religio segons Bergson." *Criterion,*
        9, No. 34, ottobre-decembre 1933. This is a critical appreciation of *Les Deux
        Sources.*

2195   Ruyssen, Théodore. "M. Bergson." *Eveil des Peuples,* ler janvier 1933. This is a
        review of *Les Deux Sources.*

2196   Sérouya, Henri. *Initiation à la philosophie contemporaine.* Paris: Renaissance du
        Livre, 1933, 312. Chapter III, entitled "Le Bergsonisme." is on pp. 35-81.

2197   Sertillanges, Antonin Gilbert. *Dieu ou rien.* Paris: Flammarion, 1933, 19.

2198   Singer, Edgar A. Jr. "Review of *Les Deux Sources de la morale et de la religion*
        by Henri Bergson." *Journal of Philosophy,* 30, No. 1, 1933, 14-23.

2199   Steffes, J. P. "Review of *Les Deux Sources de la morale et de la religion* by Henri
        Bergson." *Zeitschrift für Missionswissenschaft,* 23, 1933, 365f.

2200 Taymans d'Eypernon, Fr. *Le Blondelism.* Louvain: Museum Lessianum, 1933, 188. (Museum Lessianum, Section philosophique, No. 15) Cf. Ch. 4.

2201 Thibon, Gustave. "La Notion de conscience d'après Bergson." *Revue Thomiste*, N.S. 16, No. 77, mai-juin 1933, 399-423. The author criticizes Bergson's concept of consciousness from a Thomistic standpoint. He concludes with an exposition of the Thomistic theory of the different kinds of consciousness, from God through man to the animals, which scarcely deserve to be termed "conscious."

2202 Tilgher, Adriano. "Il tempo." *Logos*, 16, No. 4, 1933. The author argues that time is one with consciousness and is nothing outside of consciousness.

2203 Tonquédec, Joseph de. "Le Contenu des *Deux Sources.*" *Etudes par des Pères de la Compagnie de Jésus*, 214, 20 mars 1933, 641-668; 215, 5 avril 1933, 26-54.

2204 Voisine, F. "Obligation morale et pression sociale." *Revue de Philosophie*, 33, No. 4, 1933, 384-390. This is a critique of *Les Deux Sources.* This is a careful exposition of Bergson's concept(s) of moral obligation. The author criticizes some common misunderstandings of Bergson's position. Though Bergson's position seems to contrast strongly with traditional Christian moral philosophy, his ideas on moral obligation can be reconciled with Catholic orthodoxy.

2205 Whitehead, Alfred North. *Adventures of Ideas.* New York: Macmillan, 1933, 392. The author describes the "dogmatic fallacy," and on p. 287 notes types of reactions against it. "Another type of reaction is to assume, often tacitly, that if there can be any intellectual analysis it must proceed according to some one discarded dogmatic method, and thence to deduce that intellect is intrinsically tied to erroneous fictions. This type is illustrated by the anti-intellectualism of Nietzsche and Bergson, and tinges American Pragmatism."

1934

2206 Alderisio, Felice. "Review of *Les Deux Sources de la morale et de la religion* by Henri Bergson." *Nuova Rivista Storica*, 18, 1934, 629-633.

2207 Altmann, Bruno. "Judentum und Christentum: Henri Bergson und der Kirchenhistoriker, Loisy." *Jüdische Rundschau*, 29, No. 23, 1934, 6ff.

2208 B., G. "Review of *La Pensée et le mouvant* by Henri Bergson." *Journal of Philosophy*, 31, No. 21, October 11, 1934, 694. The reviewer states: "There would seem to be nothing new in this volume—except the historical information on Ravaisson—for students of Bergson, but the old doctrines of *durée réelle*, intuition and change, are all defended and sometimes restated in ways which may be unfamiliar to contemporary readers." The similarity between Bergson's philosophy and the ideas of certain modern physicists is particularly striking.

2209 Barrett, Clifford. Review of *Les Deux Sources de la morale et de la religion* by Henri Bergson. *Philosophical Review*, 43, No. 3, 1934, 301-305. The reviewer notes with surprise Bergson's "deep indebtedness" to M. Lévy-Bruhl for anthropological data, and chides Bergson for failing—here, of all places—to make his concept of God intelligible. The reviewer concludes, "Yet one can not feel that the book, taken as a whole, is disappointing, but rather that is is not systematically complete" (p. 305).

2210   Bauhofer, O. "Review of *Die Beiden Quellen der Moral und der Religion* by Henri Bergson." *Der Katholische Gedanke*, 7, 1934, 178f.

2211   Bauhofer, Oskar. "Review of *Les Deux Sources de la morale et de la religion* by Henri Bergson." *Theologie der Gegenwart*, 38, 1934, 156.

2212   "Bergsonismo y Cristianismo." *Estudios*, No. 24, Noviembre, 1934, 29-30.

2213   Berteval, W. "Réflexions sur quelques points de la philosophie de M. Bergson." *Revue de Théologie et de Philosophie*, 22, No. 90, 1934, 34-50.

2214   Blondel, Maurice. "Confusion à prévenir sur le concret et sur l'intuition." in *La Pensée*. Vol. 2. Paris: F. Alcan, 1934, 430-433. Cf. also pp. 74, 75, 530.

2215   Blondel, Maurice. "Sur l'élan vital." in *La Pensée*. Vol. 1, Paris: F. Alcan, 1934, 300-311.

2216   Bovet, Pierre. "Review of *Les Deux Sources de la morale et de la religion* by Henri Bergson." *Archives de Psychologie*, 24, No. 96, 1934, 378. The reviewer cites some Swiss anticipations of Bergson's *Les Deux Sources*, including an article he himself published in the *Année psychologique* in 1912, distinguishing between two inner experiences "correspondant aux deux idées de Bien et de Devoir" and describing factors capable of evoking the feeling of Duty independently of the impression of Good. The reviewer's article was followed by Jean Piaget's *Le Jugement moral chez l'enfant*, which might have been titled *Les Deux Sources de la morale chez l'enfant*. It is extremely interesting that for Piaget the admiration of the young for the hero generates a morality based on authority and social life opens up a moral progress with indefinite perspectives while for Bergson the opposite is the case: social pressure creates a static morality while the appeal of the hero creates a dynamic morality. "Aux analyses approfondies de demain à resoudre la contradiction apparente."

2217   Carbonara, Cleto. *Morale e religione nella filosofia de Enrico Bergson*. Napoli: Perella, 1934, 69.

2218   Cardone, Domenico Antonio. "Tempo obbietivo e tempo unico nella filosofia di H. Bergson." *Logos*, 17, No. 1, 1934, 1-16. The author compares Bergson's position with I. Kant's.

2219   Castellano, Torres F. "La crisis del idealismo." *Criterio*, 7, No. 324, 17 mayo 1934, 60.

2220   Copleston, Frederick Charles. "Bergson and Intuition." *Modern Schoolman*, 11, No. 3, March 1934, 61-65. This is an analysis of Bergson's concept of "intuition." Several different meanings of the term are defined.

2221   Corday, Michel. *The Paris Front: An Unpublished Diary: 1914-1918*. New York: E. P. Dutton & Co., Inc., 1934, 395. An entry for April 12, 1916, states, "...C...has tried to persuade the philosopher Bergson to write a letter to Balfour suggesting that the present Allies should at once form a confederation to come into force when peace is declared. Bergson seemed attracted by the idea" (p. 158).

2222   Decorte, Marcel. "Les Origines ravaissoniennes du bergsonisme." *New Scholasticism*, 8, No. 2, April 1934, 103-151.

2223   Delacroix, Henri. *Les Grandes Formes de la vie mentale*. Paris: Félix Alcan, 1934, 187. The author's psychology is influenced by Bergson, especially his theory of the function of the body and his theory of memory. Cf. pp. 108, 126, 171-172, 181.

2224   Deshayes, Marius Louis. *Dialogues bergsoniens*. Niort, France: Imp. Soulisse-Martin, 1934, 85.

2225   "Review of *Les Deux Sources de la morale et de la religion* by Henri Bergson." *Monist*, 44, No. 1, 1934, 158.

2226   "Review of *Les Deux Sources de la morale et de la religion* by Henri Bergson." *Rivista di Psicologia*, 28, 1934, 347f.

2227   Dhorme, Edouard. "Review of *Les Deux Sources de la morale et de la religion* by Henri Bergson." *Revue de l'Histoire des Religions*, 109, 1934, 220-227. This is an "étude critique."

2228   Dollard, Stewart E. "Bergsonian Metaphysics and God." Diss., St. Louis, 1934.

2229   Dumas, Georges. "La Symbolisation." *Nouveau Traité de Psychologie*. Vol. 4. Ed. Georges Dumas. Paris: Félix Alcan, 1934, 264-338. This (pp. 306-311) is an exposition of Bergson's concept of symbolism, with brief applications to the arts.

2230   Dwelshauvers, Georges. *Traité de psychologie*. Paris: Payot, 1934, 606. Bergson and Wm. James are discussed on p. 17; Bergson and introspective psychology on pp. 34-35; Bergson and J. B. Watson on p. 39; Bergson and F. Ravaisson on habit on pp. 134-138; "durée psychologique" on pp. 399-400 and 407-408; and Bergson on memory on pp. 431, 542, 570-581, and 589.

2231   Eliot, Thomas Stearns. "A Commentary." *The Criterion*, 13, No. 52, April, 1934, 451-452. The author, looking back on the "intellectual desert" of England and America in the "first decade and more" of the twentieth century, asserts the importance of France as a source of ideas and inspiration for English-speaking thinkers. Among the most important of these sources was Bergson's philosophy, whose metaphysics "was apt to be involved with discussion of Matisse and Picasso."

2232   Ellwood, Charles A. "Review of *Les Deux Sources de la morale et de la religion* by Henri Bergson." *American Journal of Sociology*, 39, No. 4, 1934, 540. This is a very brief review. The author concludes, "it is a masterly summing up of the social philosophy of religion which has been gradually taking shape in the minds of psychologists, anthropologists, and sociologists..." (p. 540).

2233   Fernandez, Ramon. "Review of *La Pensée et le mouvant* by H. Bergson." *Nouvelle Revue Française*, 22, No. 250, 1er juillet 1934, 135-136.

2234   Forest, Aimé. "La Méthode idéaliste." *Revue Néo-scolastique de Philosophie*, 2e Sér., 37, No. 43, août 1934, 178-201. This study concerns the problem of contemporary French idealism. It deals with the debt of Bergson and E. Boutroux to F. Ravaisson.

2235   Fort, Joseph Barthélemy. *Samuel Butler (1835-1902): Etude d'un caractère et d'une intelligence*. Bordeaux: Imprimerie Bière, 1934, 515. The author deals with Bergson and Butler in this study.

2236   Giusso, Lorenzo. "La conquista dell'assoluto in Bergson." *Giornale d'Italia*, 34, 1 aprile 1934.

2237   Giusti, Roberto Fernando. "Una amistad entre filósofos." *La Pensa*, 7 enero 1934, Sec. II. This is a comment on the Wm. James-Bergson correspondence.

2238   Gouhier, Henri. "Autour du bergsonisme." *Revue d'Histoire de la Philosophie et d'Histoire Générale de la Civilisation*, N.S. N. 7, 15 juillet 1934, 279-285.

This is a review of books on Bergson by Jolivet, Rideau, Penido, Metz, and Lacombe.

2239 Hirsch, L. "Kämpfer gegen Materialismus und Intellectualismus für das 75. Jahr Bergsons." C. V. *Zeitung Blätter für Deutschtum und Judentum*, 13, No. 41, 1934.

2240 Honigsheim, Paul. "Bergson et Neitzsche dans la nouvelle littérature française." *Zeitschrift für Sozialforschung*, 3, 1934, 409-415.

2241 Horkheimer, Max. "Zur Henri Bergsons Metaphysik der Zeit." *Zeitschrift für Sozialforschung*, 3, 1934, 321-342.

2242 Jäckel, Kurt. *Bergson und Proust: Eine Untersuchung über die weltanschaulichen Grundlagen von "A La Recherche du temps perdu."* Breslau: Priebatsch, 1934, 129. (Sprache and Kultur der germanischen and romanischen Völker, 10)

2243 Jacks, Lawrence Pearsall. "M. Bergson as Liberator." *Hibbert Journal*, 33, No. 1, October 1934, 55-68. This is a review of *La Pensée et le mouvant* by Henri Bergson.

2244 Jolivet, Régîs. "L'Intuition intellectuelle et le problème de la métaphysique." *Archives de Philosophie*, 11, 1934, No. 2, 97-111.

2245 Jung, Carl Gustav. "The Meaning of Psychology for Modern Man." *Collected Works*, 10, 134-156. In this essay, written in 1934, the author likens his own concept of *libido* on p. 147 to Bergson's *élan vital*, Aristotle's *hormé*, and Schopenhauer's "will." He adds skeptically that no concept seems capable of explaining what *libido* is like in itself.

2246 Laird, John. "Review of *La Pensée et le mouvant: Essais et Conférences* by Henri Bergson." *Mind*, 43, No. 172, October 1934, 518-526. This is a thoughtful, penetrating review.

2247 Lalande, André. "Philosophy in France, 1932." *Philosophical Review*, 43, No. 1, 1934, 1-26. Bergson's *Les Deux Sources*, too compact for a résumé, is declared a remarkably rich and original book.

2248 Lalande, André. "Review of *Les Sources et les courants de la philosophie contemporaine en France* by J. Benrubi." *Revue Philosophique de la France et de l'Etranger*, 117, No. 2, 1934, 285-291.

2249 Larrabee, Harold A. "Review of *La Pensée et le mouvant* by Henri Bergson." *International Journal of Ethics*, 45, No. 1, October 1934-1935, 117-118.

2250 Le Roy, Edouard. *L'Expérience de l'effort et de la grâce chez Maine de Biran.* Paris: Boivin et Cie., 1934, 441.

2251 Le Savoureux, H. "Bergsonisme et neurologie." *Nouvelle Revue Française*, 22, No. 251, ler août 1934, 201-227.

2252 Le Savoureux, H. *Bergsonisme et neurologie.* Paris: Nouvelle Revue Française, 1934, 27. The author argues that Professor P. Marie's theories (which are becoming dated anyhow) do not support Bergson's theories. Bergson's theory of aphasia is purely metaphysical and devoid of scientific value.

2253 Loisy, Alfred Firmin. *Y a-t-il deux sources de la religion et de la morale?* 2nd Ed. Paris: Émile Nourry, 1934, 244.

2254 Luard, Trant Bramston. *Incarnation: A Monologue in Verse.* London: Centaur Press, 1934, 22. This work is based on the English translation of Henri Bergson's *L'Evolution créatrice.*

2255 Marc, Alexandre. "Le Temps et la personne." *Recherches Philosophiques*, 4, 1934-1935, 127-149.

2256 Marcel, Gabriel. "Review of *La Pensée et le mouvant* by Henri Bergson." *Europe Nouvelle*, 17, No. 1, 30 juin 1934, 662-663.

2257 McEvoy, P. "Idea of God in the Philosophy of Bergson." *Irish Ecclesiastical Records*, 44, October 1934, 367-379. This is a review of *Les Deux Sources*.

2258 Miroglio, Abel and Yvonne-Delphée. "Rfelxions sur les *Deux Sources de la morale et de la religion.*" *Revue Philosophique de la France et de l'Etranger*, 117, No. 1, janvier-février 1934, 50-103.

2259 Mueller, Gustav. "Review of *Les Deux Sources de la morale et de la religion* by Henri Bergson." *Books Abroad*, 8, No. 4, October 1934, 425. According to the author, Bergson approves of the inevitability of war. This is a cursory, curt review.

2260 Mure, G. R. G. "Change, II." *Philosophy*, 9, No. 36, 1934, 450-464. Bergson and modern physics are discussed on pp. 451-452 and problems in interpreting Bergson on p. 456.

2261 Nabert, Jean. "Les Instincts virtuels et l'intelligence dans *Les Deux Sources de la morale et de la religion.*" *Journal de Psychologie Normale et Pathologique*, 31, 1934, 309-332. This is a penetrating analysis of the function of mystical intuition in Bergson's philosophy of religion. The author examines *Les Deux Sources* from the vantage-point of Bergson's concept of man's "virtual instincts": the "faculté fabulatrice" and "sentiment de présence". He deals with Bergson's concept of the primitive mind, totemism and obligation, paying particular attention to the agreements of Bergson and the anthropologist L. Lévy-Bruhl. His remarks on Bergson's concepts of mystical intuition and history, and the difficulties connected with them, are apt.

2262 Palumbo, Enrique. "La intuición bergsoniana." en "Lógica y metafísica: Una introducción al estudio del problema de la causalidad." *Cursos y Conferencias*, 3, No. 9, marzo 1934, 908-911.

2263 "Review of *La Pensée et le mouvant* by Henri Bergson." *Rassegna italiana*, 17, 1934, 827.

2264 "Review of *La Pensée et le mouvant* by Henri Bergson." *Revue de Métaphysique et de Morale* (Supplément), 41, No. 4, octobre 1934, 1.

2265 "Review of *La Pensée et le mouvant* by Henri Bergson." *Revue Mabillon*, 26, 1934.

2266 Pignato, Luca. "Durata e storia tramonto di Bergson." *Italia letteraria*, Anno 10, No. 80, 1934, 1-2. This is a review of *La Pensée et le mouvant* by Henri Bergson.

2267 Prins, D.-H. "Bergson over het wezen de moral en dat van den godsdienst." *Theosophia*, 1934.

2268 Rabow, Hans. "Bericht über Neuerscheinungen der französischen Philosophie." *Kantstudien*, 39, Nos. 3-4, 1934, 351-352. This is a brief notice concerning *Les Deux Sources*.

2269 Rageot, Gaston. "Una entrevista con Henri Bergson." *La Nación*, 30 septiembre 1934.

2270 Rensi, Giuseppe. *Raffigurazioni: Schizzi di uomini e di dottrine*. Modena, Italy: Guanda, 1934, 156. This study includes a chapter on Bergson containing a vigorous critique of Bergson's distinction between instinct and intelligence.

2271   Robertazzi, M. "Review of *La Pensée et le mouvant* by Henri Bergson." *Convegno*, 15 Anno, 1934, 150-153.

2272   Romer, A. "Review of *Die Beiden Quellen der Moral und der Religion* by Henri Bergson." *Archiv für die gesamte Psychologie*, 96, 1934, 570.

2273   Romeyer, Blaise. "Review of *La Pensée et le mouvant* by Henri Bergson." *Archives de Philosophie*, 10, No. 1, 1934, 36-38.

2274   Ruggiero, Guido de. *Filosofia del novocento*. Bari, Italy: Laterza, 1934, 296. Chapter X, entitled "L'ultimo Bergson," is found on pp. 148-172.

2275   Sarailieff, Ivan V. *Quelques points obscurs dans la philosophie de Bergson*. Sofia: Imprimerie de la cour, 1934, 10pp. (Sofia Universitet. Istoriko-filologicheski fakultet. No. 30) The text of this article is in Bulgarian.

2276   Schönberg, Bernard. "Bergson et Judaïsme. "Revue Juive de Genève, 3, 1934, 115-119.

2277   Seillière, Ernest. "Review of *La Pensée et le mouvant* by Henri Bergson." *Journal des Débats*, 41, Pt. 1, 27 juillet 1934, 1198-1200.

2278   Sever de Montsonis. "Entorn de la filosofia bergsoniana." *Criterion*, 10, 1934, 241-246.

2279   Sirven, Joseph. "Review of *La Pensée et le mouvant* by Henri Bergson." *Polybiblion*, N.S. 188 (Partie littéraire, 3), 1934, 163-164.

2280   Stallknecht, Newton Phelps. *Bergson's Idea of Creation*. Princeton, New Jersey, 1934, 113.

2281   Stallknecht, Newton Phelps. *Studies in the Philosophy of Creation: With Special Reference to Bergson and Whitehead*. Princeton, New Jersey: Princeton University Press, 1934, xii, 170. The author argues that Bergson has two theories of creation, one tenable, one not.

2282   Szemere, S. "Henri Bergson: Zu seinem 75. Geburtstag." *Pester Lloyd*, 30, 1934.

2283   Toynbee, Arnold J. *A Study of History*. Vol. 1. Oxford: Oxford University Press; London: Humphrey Milford, 1934, 476. On p. 434 the author cites Bergson's *Creative Evolution*, pp. 67-92, and concludes that if "the creative power instinct in all life" is able to produce similar structures on widely different evolutionary branches, human cultures ought to be able to do the same thing. Diffusionism is thus a one-sided notion for the historian and anthropologist.

2284   Toynbee, Arnold J. *A Study of History*. Vol. 3 Oxford: Oxford University Press; London: Humphrey Milford, 1934, 551. Bergson's *The Two Sources of Morality and Religion* is cited 18 times in this work. Cf. esp. 231-237.

2285   Truc, Gonzague. *La Pensée: Tableau du XXe siècle 1900-1933*. Paris: Denoël et Steele, 1934, 300.

2286   "Review of *The Two Sources of Morality and Religion* by Henri Bergson." *Modern Languages*, 16, 1934-1935, 162.

2287   Vassallo, Angel. "Henri Bergson: Especialmente ética y filosofía de la religión." *Cursos y Conferencias*, 4, No. 7, noviembre 1934, 707-718.

2288   Verneaux, Roger. "Review of *La Pensée et le mouvant* by Henri Bergson." *Revue de Philosophie*, N.S. 4, No. 3, 1934, 316-319.

2289   Wunderle. "Review of *Die Beiden Quellen der Moral und der Religion* by Henri Bergson." *Jahrbuch der katholischen missionsärztlichen Fürsorge*, 11, 1934, 167f.

1935

2290   Aberly, J. "Review of *Les Deux Sources de la morale et de la religion* by Henri Bergson." *Lutheran Church Quarterly*, 8, 1935, 419-420.

2291   Allemand, J. "Henri Bergson." *Existences*, 1, No. 4, 1935, 5-7.

2292   Baudouin, Charles. "Review of *La Pensée et le mouvant* by Henri Bergson." *Scientia*, 58, No. 12, 1935, 369-437.

2293   Bayet, Albert. "Morale bergsonienne et sociologie." *Annales Sociologiques*, Série C, Fascicule 1, 1935, 1-51. This is an extensive critique of *The Two Sources of Morality and Religion*. Bergson fails to dustinguish convincingly between the "closed" and the "open" society. He fails to attend to historians of religion, and does not grasp the meaning of the evolution of stoicism. Bergson, generally, fails to use sociological methods.

2294   "Bergson Returns to Realism." *America*, 54, No. 2, October 19, 1935, 28.

2295   "M. Bergson's Philosophy." *London Times Literary Supplement*, 34, No. 1744, July 4, 1935, 426. This is a review of *La Pensée et le mouvant*.

2296   Berlin, I. "Impressionist Philosophy." *London Mercury*, Vol. 32, No. 191, September, 1935, 489-490. This is a review of *The Two Sources of Morality and Religion* by Henri Bergson. The reviewer begins by asserting that Bergson, more than any living man, "is responsible for the abandonment of rigorous critical standards and the substitution in their place of casual emotional responses." He Holds that while Bergson is guilty of these crimes, *The Two Sources* is not one of those books in which they are committed. Bergson's concept of the closed society is analyzed, and the reviewer concludes that *The Two Sources* is "a fascinating essay in the phenomenology and natural history of moral and religious experience."

2297   Berteloot, Joseph. "Humanitarisme et 'bergsonisme'." *Etudes par des Pères de la Compagnie de Jésus*, 72e Année, No. 223, 5 avril 1935, 29-47.

2298   Blondel, Maurice. *L'Être et les etres*. Paris: F. Alcan, 1935, 540. (Bibliothèque de Philosophie Contemporaine) Cf. Exc. 2, 253f, 117-123, 440.

2299   Bouglé, Célestin. "Trois Philosophes français: Bergson, Blondel, Brunschvicg." *Revue de Paris*, 42, No, 5, 1935, 214-231.

2300   Braileanu, T. "Review of *Les Deux Sources de la morale et de la religion* by Henri Bergson." *Revista de pedagogia*, 2, Nos. 1-2, 1935, 111-117.

2301   Brereton, Cloudesley. "Bergson on Morality and Religion." *Contemporary Review*, 148, No. 408, 1935, 369-373. This is a review of *The Two Sources* by one of its English translators.

2302   Brunello, Bruno. "Review of *La Pensée et le mouvant* by Henri Bergson." *Giornale critico della la filosofia italiana*, 16, No. 1, 1935, 78-81.

2303   Carrel, Alexis. *L'Homme, cet inconnu*. Paris: Libraire Plon, 1935, 400. See especially Chapitre V, "Le Temps intérieur," pp. 201-214. The author applies Bergson's concept of duration to the problem of biology, especially those of cytological time.

2304   Carrel, Alexis. *Man, the Unknown*. New York: Harper & Bros., 1935, xv, 346.
        See especially Chapter V, "Inward Time," pp. 150-190. See also pp. 199, 202,
        205, and 246.

2305   Catel, Paola. *Péguy e Bergson*. Saggio: Casale Monferrato, 1935, 8.

2306   Cattaui, Georges. *L'Amitié de Proust*. Paris: Libraire Gallimard, 1935, 228. (Les
        Cahiers Marcel Proust, 8) The author finds both parallels between Proust and
        Bergson as well as differences. Cf. esp. 208-211.

2307   Cazamian, Louis. "Bergson on Ethics and Religion." *University of Toronto Quar-
        terly*, 4, No. 2, January 1935, 139-157. The author gives a general account of
        The Two Sources.

2308   Challaye, Félicien. *Metodologiá de las ciencias*. Barcelona: Ed. Labor, 1935, 220.
        Bergson's views are discussed on pp. 148, 166, and 203.

2309   Chandler, A. "M. Bergson's 'Two Sources'." *Theology*, 30, No. 3, March 1935,
        136-146.

2310   Cor, Raphaël. "De La Morale bergsonienne à l'immoralisme." *Mercure de France*,
        258, No. 881, 1935, 225-246. The author feels that Bergson is a dangerous
        freethinker.

2311   Cor, Raphaël. *De La Morale bergsonienne à l'immoralisme*. Paris: Mercure de
        France, 1935, 23.

2312   Delattre, Floris. "Samuel Butler et le bergsonisme: Avec Deux Lettres inédites
        d'Henri Bergson." *Revue Anglo-américaine*, 13, No. 5, 1935-1936, 385-405.
        Significant differences between Bergson and Butler are pointed out here by the
        author. Cf. Henri Bergson, 1935, for Bergson's very high opinion of Samuel
        Butler.

2313   Demianshkevich, Michael John. *An Introduction to the Philosophy of Education*.
        New York: American Book Company, 1935, 449. The educational philosophy
        of Bergson is examined on pp. 149-155. The author concludes that the basic
        principles of Bergson's pedagogy are that intellectual effort must be strong and
        methodical and that it must seek high quality in its results.

2314   Descoqs, Pedro. *Praelectiones Theologiae Naturalis*. Vol. 2. Paris: Beauchesne,
        1935, 725. Section V, Chapter 4 is entitled: "Argumentum ex experientia mystica
        H. Bergson" (375-411). The author argues that Bergson, though a great
        psychologist, was not a great metaphysician.

2315   Dewey, John. "Bergson on Instinct." *New Republic*, 83, No. 1073, 1935, 200-201.
        This is a very brief review of *The Two Sources*. The author states that: "One
        who finds nothing sound in the philosophical foundations may nevertheless learn
        a great deal from Bergson's clear and informed discussion of these matters."
        (201).

2316   Dollard, Stewart E. "Bergson and the Communion of Saints." *America*, 53, May
        25, 1935, 163. This is a review of *The Two Sources*.

2317   Edman, Irwin. "Review of *The Two Sources of Religion and Morality* by Henri
        Bergson." *Journal of Philosophy*, 32, No. 14, 1935, 387-388. The author con-
        cludes that: "Mr. Bergson's book is in the best sense provocative."

2318   Edman, Irwin. "Review of *The Two Sources of Morality and Religion* by Henri
        Bergson." *New York Herald Tribune Books*, April 28, 1935, p. 2.

2319   Fondane, Benjamin. "Bergson, Freud y los dioses." *Sur*, Año 5, No. 15, 1935,
        30-80. This is a reading of Bergson's *The Two Sources of Morality and Religion*

in terms of S. Freud's *The Future of an Illusion*. The author denies Bergson's distinction between the open and the closed society and argues that Freud's scientific, stoic viewpoint is superior.

2320   Geiger, L. B. "Review of *La Pensée et le mouvant* by Henri Bergson." *Revue des Sciences Philosophiques et Religieuses*, 24, 1935, 312.

2321   Gentile, Giovanni. "Review of *La Pensée et le mouvant* by Henri Bergson." *Leonardo*, Anno 6, No. 7-8, 1935, 339-340.

2322   Giorgiantonio, Michele. "Review of *La Pensée et le mouvant* by Henri Bergson." *Sophia*, 3, No. 2, 1935, 259-261.

2323   Goosens, Werner. "La Théodicé de M. H. Bergson: A Propos d'un ouvrage récent." *Collationes Grandavenses*, 22, 1935, 113-118, 172-176.

2324   Gorce, Matthieu-Maxime. "Le Néo-réalisme bergsonien-thomiste." *Sophia*, 3, No. 1, gennaio-febbraio 1935, 35-47, 145-160. The author argues that the philosophies of immanence, as presented by E. Le Roy and M. Blondel, have tried to find in the idealism of Bergson a new apologetic and an attractive way to the heart of Christianity, but they have failed. Bergson is not Aquinas.

2325   Gruber, Ruth. *Virginia Woolf: A Study*. Leipzig: Verlag Von Bernhard Tauchnitz, 1935, 100. (Kölner Anglistische Arbeiten, 24 Band) In this study of the novelist Virginia Woolf many parallels are drawn between Bergson's philosophy and Woolf's novels and short stories. A direct influence by Bergson is claimed: "While in her earlier novels, she had returned to Sir Thomas Browne and the dead philosophers for inspiration, she stands now in the air of her time. It is Bergson's problem and solutions which modulate her thinking and with it her style." (p. 49). Cf. also pp. 37, 38, 50-54, 75.

2326   "Human Morality." *Saturday Review of Literature*, 12, No. 9, June 29, 1935, p. 16. This is a brief review of *The Two Sources* by Henri Bergson.

2327   Hume, Theodore C. "A Philosopher Turns Evangelical." *Christian Century*, 52, No. 45, November 6, 1935, 1415-1416. This is a review of *The Two Sources of Morality and Religion*. The review presents Bergson as solving several important problems faced by modern theology. Bergson presents systematically an alternative to the pessimistic ethics of those who understand only the ethics of the closed society. He provides an absolutely essential metaphysical foundation for the "evolutionary" school of religious thought. He provides an answer to the scientific, rationalistic approach to religion of H. N. Wieman and his followers. And he shows the important place that activism plays in religion. However, Cf. Wm. S. Minor, 1977.

2328   Joad, C. E. M. "Review of *The Two Sources of Morality and Religion* by Henri Bergson." *New Statesman and Nation*, 9, March 9, 1935, 334.

2329   Jolivet, Régîs. "Philosophie chrétienne et bergsonisme." *Revue des Sciences Religieuses*, 15, No. 1, 1935, 28-43.

2330   Joseph, H. W. B. *Essays in Ancient and Modern Philosophy*. Oxford: At the Clarendon Press, 1935, 340. On pp. 311-312 the author criticizes defenders of emergent evolution, urging that émergent" either means "creative" or it does not. If it does simply mean "creative", why not use this—Bergson's—term?

2331   Jung, Carl Gustav. "The Tavistock Lectures (1935)." In C. G. Jung, *Collected Works*, 18, 1-264. On p. 121 of these lectures, Jung describes the "key god

Aion" as an exemplification of Bergson's "durée créatrice."

2332 Kann, Albert. *Henri Bergson und meine Ideen.* Vienna: Selbstverlag, 1935, 246. The author claims to have antedated Bergson's ideas in *The Two Sources.*

2333 Keeling, Stanley V. "Philosophy in France: Some Afterthoughts of M. Bergson." *Philosophy*, 10, No. 39, July 1935, 355-359. This is a review of *La Pensée et le mouvant.* It is largely expository.

2334 Lalande, André. "Philosophy in France, 1933-1934." *Philosophical Review*, 44, No. 1, January 1935, 1-23. This article includes a brief account of *La Pensée et le mouvant.*

2335 Lee, Atkinson. "Review of *The Two Sources of Morality and Religion* by Henri Bergson." *London Quarterly Review*, 160, No. 3, July 1935, 397-399.

2336 Lemasson, Emile. *Histoire de la philosophie: Une Doctrine, le bergsonisme: Exposé historique.* Paris: Beauchesne, 1935, 130.

2337 Maire, Gilbert. *Bergson mon maître.* Paris: Grasset, 1935, 230. The author gives personal recollections of Bergson and traces the development of his own Bergsonism.

2338 Manacorda, Guido, *I contrafforti.* Brescia, Italy: Morcelliana, 1935, 330. A chapter entitled "L'Ultimo Bergson" appears on pp. 241-245.

2339 Mathews, Dean. "Review of *The Two Sources of Morality and Religion* by Henri Bergson." *Fortnightly Review*, N.S. 137, No. 4, April 1935, 495-496. This is a schematic but laudatory review.

2340 Mazzantini, Carlo. "Review of *La Pensée et le mouvant* by Henri Bergson." *Rivista di filosofia neocolastica*, 27, 1935, 544-545.

2341 Mitchell, Arthur. "Review of *La Pensée et le mouvant* by Henri Bergson." *Philosophical Review*, 45, No. 1, 1935, 94-95.

2342 Molina, Enrique. *Proyecciones de la intuicion: Nuevos estudios sobre la filosofía Bergsoniana.* Santiago de Chile: Prensas de la Universidad de Chile, 1935, 99. Indice: I. El método intuitivo. II. Caracteres generales de la filosofía de Bergson. III. Del espíritu. De la libertad. V. De la moral. VI. De la religión. The author concludes: "Tratando de mantener esos estados de espíritu y las actitudes y normas que ellos entrañan, y traduciéndolos a la vez en la vida activa correspondiente, contribuiremos a ir acercándonos a la perfección que por lo menos, existe como ideal humano, perfeccion que puede llamarse la realización de lo divino en la Tierra." (99).

2343 Mourgue, Raoul. "Une Découverte scientifique: La Durée bergsonienne." *Revue Philosophique de la France et de l'Etranger*, 120, No. 4, novembre 1935, 350-367.

2344 Mourgue, Raoul. *Une Découverte scientifique: La Durée bergsonienne.* Paris: Félix alcan, 1935, 18. This is reprinted from *Revue Philosophique de la France et d l'Etranger*, 1935.

2345 Myers, Henry Alonzo. "Analysis of Laughter." *Sewanee Review*, 43, No. 4, October 1935, 452-463.

2346 N., R. "Review of *La Pensée et le mouvant* by Henri Bergson." *Revue Mabillon*, 25, No. 100, octobre-décembre 1935, 1.

2347 Niebuhr, Reinhold. "Henri Bergson on the Nature of Morality and Religion." *New York Times*, 84, No. 28, 218, April 28, 1935, pt. 6, p. 3. This is a largely unfavorable review of *The Two Sources* by Henri Bergson.

2348   Olgiati, Francesco. "La filosofia bergsoniana e il realismo." *Relazioni e comunicazioni al X Congresso nazionale di filosofia.* Milan: Vita e Pensiero, 1935.

2349   Olgiati, Francesco. "La filosofia bergsoniana e il realismo." *Revista di filosofia neoscolastica*, Suppl. 27, 1935, 59-70.

2350   Pacotte, Julian. *La Logique et l' empirisme intégral.* Paris: Hermann and Co., 1935, 56. Views of Bergson and H. Poincaré are discussed in this study.

2351   Palmer, Francis L. "Review of *The Two Sources of Morality and Religion* by Henri Bergson." *Living Church*, 39, No. 7, October 5, 1935, p. 333.

2352   Parodi, Dominique. "Review of *La Pensée et le mouvant* by Henri Bergson." *Revue de Synthèse*, 10, No. 2, 1935, 211-222.

2353   Péguy, Charles. *Note conjointe: Note sur M. Bergson et la philosophie bergsonienne: Note conjointe sur M. Descartes et la philosophie cartésienne.* Paris: Gallimard, 1935, 318.

2354   Péguy, Charles. *Note sur M. Bergson et la philosophie bergsonienne: Note sur Descartes et la philosophie cartésienne.* Paris: Nouvelle Revue Française, 1935, 323.

2355   Pelloux, Dott. Luigi. "L'opera di Maine de Biran e el fenomenismo." *Relazion: X Congresso Nazionale di Filosofia.* Milano: Vita e Pensiero, 1935, 71-78.

2356   Perry, Ralph Barton. *The Thought and Character of William James.* Boston: Little, Brown and Company, 1935, Vol. 1, 825, Vol. 2, 768. In volume one Bergson is discussed on pp. 485, 461, 468, 652, 688. In volume two Bergson is discussed on pp. 201, 386, 404, 437-438, 482, 496, 498, 537-538, 544, 551, 564, 566-568, 576, 581, 589-590, 599-636, 642-643, 650, 654-655, 664, 666, 683, 696, 744, 754, 575, and 762-763. Correspondence between James and Bergson may be found on pp. 605-633.

2357   Reis, Lincoln. "Bergson on Religion." *Nation*, 140, No. 3649, June 12, 1935, 691-692. This is a review of *The Two Sources.*

2358   Roa Rebolledo, Armando. "La filosofía Bergsoniana frente al pensamiento contemporáneo." *Estudios*, No. 37, Diciembre, 1935, 14-36.

2359   Romanell, Patrick. "Le Monisme esthétique de José Vasconcelos." *Revista de Filosofía*, 64, No. 2, abril 1935. The author explains that by renewing neoplatonic Christianity through Bergson, Vasconcelos achieves a religious monism.

2360   Sadlowski, E. L. "Henri Bergson's Approach to God." Master's Thesis, Catholic University of America, 1935.

2361   Salas Edwards, Ramón. "Las ideas de Bergson." *Estudios*, No. 26, Enero, 1935, 16-21.

2362   Sébestyen, K. "Die Gerüchte um Bergson." *Pester Lloyd*, 29, No. 6, 1935.

2363   Segond, Joseph. "La Méthodologie bergsonienne." *Etudes Philosophiques*, 9, No, décembre 1935, 116-134. This is a review of *La Pensée et le mouvant (The Creative Mind)*, dealing especially with the two "introductions" written especially for this volume.

2364   Selbie, W. R. "Review of *The Two Sources of Morality and Religion* by Henri Bergson." *Congregational Quarterly*, 13, 1935, 367-368.

2365   Sokolow, Nahum. *Ishim*. Tel-Aviv, 1935, III, 170-179. Details of Bergson's ancestry are given in this article, which is in Hebrew.

2366   Sommer, Erika. *Bergsons Einfluss auf die französische Schriftsprache: Inaugural-Dissertation*. München: "Polygraph," 1935, xiv, 295.

2367   Teran, Sisto. *Approximaciones a la doctrina tradicional*. Buenos Aires: Juan Roldán y Cía., 1935, 402. Bergson and metaphor are discussed on pp. 124-129; becoming, relativism, and novelty are discussed on pp. 193-213.

2368   Thérive, E. "Review of *Bergson: Mon Maître* by G. Maire." *Europe Nouvelle*, 18, 26 octobre 1935, 1045-1046.

2369   Thorold, Algar. "Review of *La Pensée et le mouvant* by Henri Bergson." *Criterion*, 14, No. 57, 1935, 690-694.

2370   Troude, R. "Review of *La Pensée et le mouvant* by Henri Bergson." *Revue Scientifique*, 73, No. 2, 1935, 772.

2371   "Review of *The Two Sources of Morality and Religion* by Henri Bergson." *American Mercury*, 25, No. 139, 1935, 367-377. This is a very brief, very skeptical review.

2372   "Review of *The Two Sources of Morality and Religion* by Henri Bergson." *Booklist*, 31, No. 10, June, 1935, p. 328.

2373   "Review of *The Two Sources of Morality and Religion* by Henri Bergson." *Catholic World*, 142, No. 847, 1935, 112-113.

2374   "Review of *The Two Sources of Morality and Religion* by Henri Bergson." *London Times Literary Supplement*, No. 1727, March 7, 1935, p. 147. This is a brief report on the English Translation.

2375   Van Der Brugh, Emmanuel Johannes. "Loisy contre Bergson." *Nieuw Theologisch Tijdschrift*, 24, 1935, 302-330.

2376   Van Der Kooij, J. "Het Godsbegrip volgens het Bergsonisme." *Kultuurleven*, 4, 1935, 166-167.

2377   Van Der Kooij, J. "De Methode van H. Bergson." *Kultuurleven*, 6, 1935.

2378   Vassallo, Angel. "Inteligencia y instint: La intuición: Mecanismo creador y devenir creador." *Cursos y Conferencias*, 4, No. 11, marzo 1935, 1175-1191.

2379   Vincent, A. "Les Religions statiques et dynamiques de M. Bergson et l'histoire de religion." *Revue des Sciences Religieuses*, 15, 1935, 44-58. This is a series of reflections on *Les Deux Sources*. In particular, the author opposes the views of the church historian A. Loisy to Bergson's ideas.

2380   Vlastos, Gregory. "Review of *The Two Sources of Morality and Religion* by Henri Bergson and *Mind, Self, and Society* by George Herbert Mead." *Queen's Quarterly*, 42, No. 4, 1935, 563-565.

2381   Weber, Louis. "Review of *La Pensée et le mouvant* by Henri Bergson." *Revue de Métaphysique et de Morale*, 42, No. 1, 1935, 53-75. This is an exposition of Bergson's position in *La Pensée et le mouvant*, with critical comments.

2382   Wingfield-Stratford, Esmé Cecil. "Henri Bergson." in *Men of Turmoil: Biographies by Leading Authorities of the Dominating Personalities of Our Day*. New York: Minton, Balch and Company, 1935, 267-276.

2383   Woodburne, A. S. "Review of *The Two Sources of Morality and Religion* by Henri Bergson." *Crozer Quarterly*, 12, No. 3, July 1935, p. 314.

2384   Wrede, Otto. *Pädagogische Probleme bei Henri Bergson*. Forchheim, Germany: Mauser, 1935, 79.

1936

2385　　Bachelard, Gaston. *La Dialectique de la durée*. Paris: Boivin, 1936, 170. This is a thoroughgoing critique of the Bergsonian concept of duration as "continuous" and "full." The author argues that duration contains discontinuities and is best understood as a dialectic movement between being and non-being. This is an important critique of a basic Bergsonian concept. (Cf. A. Ventura, 1984.)

2386　　Baisnée, Jules A. "Bergson's Approach to God." *New Scholasticism*, 10, No. 2, April 1936, 116-144. The author holds that Bergson, in spite of his virtues, fails to counter the charges of pantheism and agnosticism.

2387　　Bonnard, André. *Le Mouvement antipositiviste contemporain en France*. Thèse de doctorat d'Etat, Grenoble, 1936. Paris: Jel, 1936, 227. Cf. Chapter 4 "La Metaphysique Positive d'Henri Bergson", pp. 134-198. The author treats Bergson as an antisystematic philosopher intent on bringing us to reflect on the richness of concrete experience. Bergson is to positivism as the open is the the closed.

2388　　Bruers, Antonio. *Pensatori antichi e moderni*. Roma: Bardi, 1936, 308. Bergson is discussed on pp. 283-295.

2389　　Bustos-Fierro, Raul. "Spencer en Bergson." *Homenaje a Bergson*. Córdoba, Argentina: Imprenta de la Universidad, 1936, 97-122.

2390　　Butty, Enrique. "La duración de Bergson y el tiempo de Einstein." *Cursos y Conferencias*, Año 5, No. 5, agosto 1936, 449-489; No. 7, octubre 1936, 681-706; No. 8, noviembre 1936, 825-845; No. 10, enero 1937, 1020-1052; No. 11, febrero 1937, 1203-1228; No. 12, marzo 1937, 1327-1362. This examination of the relations between Einstein's and Bergson's concepts of time consists of seven chapters, entitled: 1. Objectividad scientifica; 2. Movimiento, espacio y tiempo; 3. Duración y tiempo; 4. El tiempo físico; 5. El tiempo de la teoría de la relatividad; 6. Los tiempos multiples de Einstein y el tiempo universal; 7. El universo de Minkowski y la duración universal. The author explains Bergson's criticisms of relativity theory but adds little to the debate.

2391　　C., D. H. Review of *The Two Sources of Morality and Religion* by Henri Bergson. *Dublin Magazine*, N.S. 11, No. 2, 1936, 68-69.

2392　　Calderon, Francisco García. "El filósofo francés: Henri Bergson." *Universidad*, 2, No. 9, 1936, 4-5.

2393　　Campbell, Clarence A. "Review of *The Two Sources of Morality and Religion* by Henri Bergson." *Philosophy*, 11, No. 41, January 1936, 98-102. This is a critical, balanced review.

2394　　Cattaui, Georges. "Henri Bergson: His Work and Influence." *Colosseum*, 3, No. 4, December 1936, 272-286.

2395　　Chernowitz, Maurice. "Bergson's Influence on Marcel Proust." *Romantic Review*, 27, No. 1, 1936, 45-60. This is a review of *Bergson and Proust* by Jäckel.

2396　　Chevalier, Jacques. "William James et Bergson." in *Harvard et la France: Recueil d'études*. Paris: Edité par les soins de la Revue d'Histoire Moderne, 1936, 103-116.

2397　　Cuvillier, Armand. "Les Courants irrationalistes dans la philosophie contemporaine." *Cahiers Rationalistes*, 6, No. 35, mars-avril 1936, 45-82.

2398   Dalbiez, Roland. *La Méthode psychoanalytique et le doctrine freudienne*. 2 Vols.
        Pref. Henri Claude. Paris: Desclée de Brouwer, 1936. (Bibliothèque de
        philosophie médicale, 1) This is a careful critique of the claims of Freudian
        psychoanalysis which seeks a balanced judgement of its value. Bergson evidently
        read this work with appreciation. Cf. Jean de La Harpe, 1943. For annotation,
        Cf. Roland Dalbiez, 1948.

2399   Donadille, Marc. *Essai sur le problème moral à propose des "Deux Sources de
        la morale et de la religion" de M. Henri Bergson*. Genève: S.N.D. Ed., 1936,
        160.

2400   Donadille, Marc. "Essai sur le problème moral à propos des'Deux Sources de la
        morale et de la religion'de M. Henri Bergson." Diss., Genève, 1936, 4 (Résumé).

2401   Feldman, Valentin. *L'Esthétique française contemporaine*. Paris: Félix Alcan,
        1936, 139. The romantic realism of V. Basch, "illuminism" of Bergson,
        "rationalistic realism" of E. Souriau, etc. are discussed in this essay.

2402   Flewelling, Ralph Tyler. "Review of *La Pensée et le mouvant* and *The Two Sources
        of Morality and Religion* by Henri Bergson." *Personalist*, 17, No. 1, 1936, 86-88.

2403   Fondane, Benjamin. *La Conscience malheureuse*. Paris: Denoël et Steele, 1936,
        306. Nietzsche, Gide, Bergson, Husserl, Heidegger, Kierkegaard, and Chestov
        are dealt with in this study of the "unhappy consciousness."

2404   Forest, A. "Review of *La Pensée et le mouvant* by Henri Bergson." *Revue Thomiste*,
        N.S. 19, No. 1, 1936, 272-274.

2405   Fragueiro, Alfredo. "El intuicionismo bergsoniano en la filosofía del Derecho."
        Homenaje a Bergson. Córdoba, Argentina: Imprenta de la Universidad, 1936,
        159-178.

2406   Genta, Jordán B. "Comentario sobre el libro *Homenaje a Bergson* editado por el
        Instituto de Filosofía de la Universidad de Córdoba (R.A.)." *Nosotros*, 1, No.
        1, julio 1936, 466-468.

2407   Ghéréa, J. D. "Le Problème de la connaissance et les durées." *Revue de
        Métaphysique et de Morale*, 43, No. 1, janvier 1936, 89-111. The author explains
        his method as follows: "Nous avons commencé, cette fois, par décomposer le
        'temps' en ses durées, et c'est la multiplicité de celles-ci qui est à la base de
        l'analyse aboutissant à la conscience impersonelle... ." (111). The author offers
        many criticisms of intuitionism.

2408   Glasser, Richard. *Studien zur Geschichte des französischen Zeitbegriffes, eine
        Orientierung*. München: M. Heuber, 1936, x, 255. The author deals especially
        with Bergson, M. Proust, and E. Zola.

2409   Gouiran, Emilio. "Un punto de vista sobre la filosofía Bergsoniana: Charles Péguy."
        Homenaje a Bergson. Córdoba, Argentina: Imprenta de la Universidad, 1936,
        54-64.

2410   Habicht, Rob. *Henri Bergson und das deutsche Typenlustspiel*. Leipzig: Heitz,
        1936, 226. This concerns Bergson's concept of laughter and German "comedy".

2411   Heath, Louise Robinson. *The Concept of Time*. Chicago: University of Chicago
        Press; London: Cambridge University Press, 1936, 235. This is a historical study
        of the development of the concept of time, culminating in a discussion of the
        reality of time. References to Bergson are found throughout.

2412   Henle, Robert J. "Review of *The Two Sources of Morality and Religion* by Henri Bergson." *Thought*, 11, No. 4, September, 1936, 333-336.

2413   "La herencia moral de la filosofía Griega." *Criterio*, 9, No. 456, noviembre 1936, 292. This is a comment on a book by Enrique Molina.

2414   Hess, M. Whitcomb. "Bergson and Greek Mysticism." *Personalist*, 17, No. 4, 1936, 377-383. The author uses this essay largely as an opportunity to express his own views. He mentions Bergson's position as an unjustifiable anti-intellectualism and holds that Bergson failed to understand Aristotle, Plotinus, and Greek mysticism generally.

2415   *Homenaje a Bergson*. Córdoba, Argentina: Imprenta de la Universidad, 1936, 189. Instituto de Filosofía.

2416   Jarlot, G. "Personne et humanité: Deux sources?" *Archives de Philosophie*, 12, No. 1, 1936, 1-65. This study concerns *Les Deux Sources de la morale et de la religion* by Henri Bergson.

2417   Jurēvičs, Paulis. *Divi apzinas filosofi: Teichmullers un Bergsons*. Riga: Ramavez apgādés, 1936, 35.

2418   Kaul, C. "Henri Bergson und das Baal Schem." *Der Morgen*, 12, 1936, 307-309. This concerns Bergson's Jewish, Hassidic background and his philosophy of religion.

2419   Laird, John. *Recent Philosophy*. London: Thornton Butterworth, Ltd., 1936, 256. Chapter V is entitled "The Pragmatists and Bergson," 84-107.

2420   Levi, Adolfo. "L'ultime libre di Henri Bergson." *Rivista di filosofia*, 27, No. 2, 1936, 173-176. This is a review of *La Pensée et le mouvant*.

2421   Lindegaard-Petersen, V. "Henri Bergson som religiøs Taenker." *Teologisk Tijdsskrift*, 5, 1936, 1-28.

2422   Loisy, Alfred Dirmin. *George Tyrrell et Henri Bergson*. Paris: Nourry, 1936, viii, 205.

2423   Martiñez Paz, Enrique. "Dios en la filosofía de Henri Bergson." *Homenaje a Bergson*. Córdoba, Argentina: Imprenta de la Universidad, 1936, 123-138.

2424   Martiñez Paz, Enrique. *Dios en la filosofía de Henri Bergson*. Córdoba, Argentina: Imprenta de la Universidad, 1936, 21.

2425   Martinez, Raúl. "El problema de la religión en Bergson." *Homenaje a Bergson*. Córdoba, Argentina: Imprenta de la Universidad, 1936, 179-189.

2426   McFadden, C. J. "The Problem of Religion in *The Two Sources of Morality and Religion*." Master's Thesis, Catholic University of America, 1936.

2427   Mead, George Herbert. *Mouvements of Thought in the Nineteenth Century*. Chicago: University of Chicago Press, 1936, 518. Bergson is discussed on pp. 292-325 and 496-510.

2428   Minkowski, Eugène. *Vers Une Cosmologie: Fragments philosophiques*. 1-2 éds. Paris: Aubier, 1936, 1967, 263.

2429   Mitchell, E. T. "Review of *La Pensée et le mouvant* by Henri Bergson." *Philosophical Review*, 45, No. 1, 1936, 94-95. The reviewer concludes, "While this volume contains few ideas not already familiar to students of Bergson it does throw interesting sidelights on his fundamental theses and makes readily available practically all the journal articles of significance" (p. 95).

2430 Nieva, R. "Notio Synthetica Temporis Apud Henri Bergson." *Homenaje a Bergson*. Córdoba, Argentina: Imprenta de la Universidad, 1936, 139-157.

2431 Orgaz, Raúl A. "Los fundamentos sociológicos de la moral de Bergson." *Homenaje a Bergson*. Córdoba, Argentina: Imprenta de la Universidad, 1936, 33-52.

2432 Orgaz, Raúl A. "La sociología en la moral de Bergson." *Cursos y Conferencias*, Año 4, No. 5, 1936, 449-469. This is an exposition of Bergson's social philosophy, as found in *The Two Sources of Morality and Religion*. The author doubts in concluding, whether "vital necessities" are necessarily ethical, or "spontaneity" is freedom.

2433 Ottaviano, Carmelo. "Bergson e il realismo." *Sophia*, 4, No. 1, 1936, 104-107. This article contains a letter from Bergson to Gorce concerning his agreements with Thomas Aquinas. Cf. Henri Bergson, 1935.

2434 Parkes, Henry Bramford. "The Tendencies of Bergsonism." *Scrutiny*, 4, No. 4, March 1936, 407-424.

2435 Pastuska, J. *Filozofja religje H. Bergsona*. 1936.

2436 Pavlov, Todor (P. Dosev). *Teoria otrazheniya*. Moscow: Socekgiz, 1936, 200. The author attacks the intuitionism of Bergson and N. Lossky, which he presumes are both irrationalisms.

2437 Peghaire, Julien. *Intellectus et ratio selon s. Thomas d'Aguin*. Paris: J. Vrin, 1936, 318. (Publications de l'Institute d'études médiévals d'Ottowa, 6) The author concludes that the Thomistic distinction between "Intellectus" and "Ratio" provides for a harmonius synthesis of Aristotelianism and Neoplatonism, and provides an analogical notion of intuition for Thomism. This starting point allows Thomism to become open to the profound tendencies of the philosophies of H. Bergson and E. Meyerson, and provides for Aristotelianism and Neoplatonism a psychological base.

2438 "Picks 10 'Greatest Jews'." *New York Times*, 85, No. 28, 553, March 28, 1936, p. 17, col. 2. In this article Bergson is named one of the ten greatest living Jews by Ludwig Lewisohn.

2439 "Portrait of Bergson." *Scholastic*, 29, No. 5, October 17, 1936, 21.

2440 Rau, Enrique. "El irracionalismo religioso de José Vasconcelos." *Criterio*, 9, No. 450, 15 octubre 1936, 155, Col. 1a.

2441 Reyles, C. M. "Vida y estructura: El 'Homo Loquax'." *La Nación*, 1936.

2442 Reymond, Arnold. "La Pensée religieuse et la philosophie française contemporaine." *Revue de Théologie et de Philosophie*, N.S. 24, 1936, 252-266.

2443 Richard, René. "Henri Bergson habla y concluye." *La Nación*, 1936.

2444 Taborda, Saúl. "El fenómeno político." *Homenaje a Bergson*. Córdoba, Argentina: Imprenta de la Universidad, 1936, 65-95. The author explores Bergson's *The Two Sources of Morality and Religion* as a "political anthropology". He follows Bergson's account of the development of human societies from their primitive to their present state, adding historical-political data in support to Bergson's argument. This is a valuable study. Cf. E. Kennedy, 1980.

2445 Thielmans, H. "Bergson." *Streven*, 3, 1936, 246-270.

2446 Tilley, Ethel. "The Problem of Identity in Henri Bergson's Philosophy." Diss., Boston, 1936.

2447 Tomeucci, Luigi. *La critica attualista del Bergson*. Messina, Italy, 1936.

2448 Tomisme de Bergson al realismo de Santo Tomás." *Criterion*, 12, 1936. Articles on Bergson by R. Esquerra, J. Sanfelin, Sever de Montsonis, and Augusti de Montclar are included in an issue of this journal in 1936.

2449 Tonquédec, Joseph de. *Sur La Philosophie bergsonienne*. Paris: Beauchesne, 1936, 241. This study consists of five articles published earlier in *Etudes par des Pères de la Compagnie de Jésus* (1905, 1908, 1932, and 1933) and the *Revue Critique des Idées et des Livres* (1913).

2450 "Review of *The Two Sources of Morality and Religion* by Henri Bergson." *Journal of Nervous and Mental Disease*, 84, 1936, 221-223.

2451 Vassallo, Angel. "Bergson y el problema de la metafísica." *Homenaje de Bergson*. Córdoba, Argentina: Imprenta de la Universidad, 1936, 13-31.

2452 Vassallo, Angel. "Las dos fuentes de la moral." *Cursos y Conferencias*, 5, No. 6, septiembre 1936, 603-654.

2453 Vermorel, L. J. "Henri Bergson y su filosofía." *Universidad de Panamá*, 1, No. 3, 1936, 8-16.

2454 Zawirski, Zygmunt. *L'Evolution et la notion du temps*. Kraków: Gebethner and Wolff, 1936, 357.

1937

2455 Allport, Gordon W. *Personality: A Psychological Interpretation*. New York: Henry Holt and Company, 1937, 588. Several references to Bergson are given in the text of this study. The author appears particularly interested in Bergson's distinction between intuition (which he compares to *Verstehen*) and analysis. Cf. pp. 40, 144, 435-436, 536-538.

2456 "Bergson Reported Catholic." *The American Hebrew*, 141, No. 9, July 16, 1937, 18.

2457 "Henri Bergsons Weg zu Thomismus." *Hochland*, 34, No. 2, 1937, 174-175.

2458 Callot, Emile. "Review of *La Dialectique de la durée* by G. Bachelard." *Revue de Philosophie*, 37, No. 2, 1937, 164-170. The author explains that the originality of Bachelard's thought can be seen by comparing it with Bergson's. For Bergson duration is continuous. For Bachelard, duration (conceived as a dialectic between being and non-being) has basic discontinuities.

2459 Capěk, Milič. *Bergson a tendance současné fysiky*. Prague: Facultas Philosophica Universitates Carolinae pragensis, 1937-1938, 160 (Práce z vědeckých ustavu, No. 47). This is a dissertation. The author argues that Bergson's thought coincides with the tendencies of modern physics. Cf. Bergson's response to the author, July, 1938.

2460 Chevalier, Jacques. *Henri Bergson*. Trans. E. Zazo. Pref. Ch. Boyer, Brescia, Italy: Morcelliana, 1937, 173.

2461 Chevalier, Jacques. "De Descartes Bergson et à Maurice Blondel." *Revue Politique et Littéraire, Revue Bleue*, 75e Année, N. 4, 20 février 1937, 131-133.

2462 Cleugh, Mary Frances. *Time and Its Importance in Modern Thought*. London: Metheun, 1937, 308. The author prefaces this study by stating: "Bergson, Alexander, McTaggart, and Dunne have given us something fresh to think about and to take us farther than St. Augustine deemed possible." Bergson is dealt with especially on pp. 108-127.

2463   Coster, Sylvain de. "Bergson et Varendonck." *Revue de l'Université Libre de Bruxelles*, 43, No. 3, 1937-1938, 295-303.

2464   Cronan, Edward P. "Bergson and Free Will." *New Scholasticism*, 11, No. 1, January 1937, 1-57. The author agrees with Bergson that free will is an observable fact, that physical determinism is an unproved assumption, and that the attempt to measure psychic life is too often only a measurement of external causes. But he argues that Bergson's refutation of choice is invalid. Bergson's errors are due to an anti-intellectual prejudice, a mistaken insistence that time and space are mutually exclusive categories, and to the practice of fitting facts to his preconceived idea of duration.

2465   Delmer, Gerrard. *De La Mémoire à l'intuition*. Bruxelles: Ed. de la Phalange, 1937, 285.

2466   Dimitroff, Emanouil P. *Filosofsky Stoudii*. Sofia, 1937, 102. Dimitroff's book includes chapters on Bergson and vitalism.

2467   Dunn, Oliver C. "A Study of Bergson's Theory of Morality." Diss., Cornell, 1937.

2468   "Die einzige mögliche Weltreligion: H. Bergson." *Deutsche Rundschau*, 63 Jahrg., No. 3, 1937, 211.

2469   Fenart, Michel. *Les Assertions bergsoniennes*. Paris: Vrin, 1937, 362.

2470   Gallagher-Parks, Mercedes. "Art et réalité: Etude pour une esthétique psychologique et bergsonienne." *Deuxième Congrès internationale d'esthétique et de science de l'art*. Vol. 1. Paris: Félix Alcan, 1937, 75-79.

2471   Gibson, A. Boyce. "Review of *The Two Sources of Morality and Religion* by Henri Bergson." *Australasian Journal of Psychology and Philosophy*, 15, No. 1, 1937, 65-75. This is a thoughtful, laudatory review.

2472   Guillaume, Paul. *La Psychologie de la forme*. Paris: Flammarion, 1937, 236. Bergson, functionalism, and the "Gestalt" are discussed on pp. 215-218. Bergson's psychology is compared with gestalt psychology on pp. 224-228. The author treats Bergson as a French forerunner of gestalt psychology.

2473   Janet, Pierre. "La Psychologie de la croyance et le mysticisme." *Revue de Métaphysique et de Morale*, 43, No. 4, 1936, 507-532; 44, No. 2, 1937, 369-410.

2474   Jurēvičs, Paulis. "Andrijs Bergsons." *Lielās personības*, 2, 1937, 408-448.

2475   Jurēvičs, Paulis. "Divi apzinas filozofi: G. Teichmullers un H. Bergson." *Celi*, 7, 1937, 21-53.

2476   Kallen, Horace Meyer. "Remarks on R. B. Perry's Portrait of William James." *Philosophical Review*, 41, No. 1, 1937, 68-78. The author descants on Perry's treatment of Bergson's influence on James on p. 74. That James could accept *any* of Bergson's ideas was due to James' unconscious acceptance of his father's religious notions.

2477   Korn, Alejandro. "Bergson en la filosofía contemporánea." *Homenaje a Bergson*. Córdoba, Argentina: Imprenta de la Universidad, 1937, 3-12.

2478   Korn, Alejandro. "Bergson in la Filosofía Contemporánea." In *Filósofos y Sistemas*. Buenos Aires: Colección Claridad, 1937, 182.

2479   Lehrmann, Chanan. *Bergsonisme et judaïsme: Cours professé à l'Université de Lausanne*. Genève: Editions Union, 1937, 120. Cf. Bibliography, pp. 117-118.

2480   Le Roy, Edouard. "Les Paradoxes de la relativité sur le temps." *Revue Philosophique de la France et de l'Etranger*, 62, No. 1-2, 1937, 10-47; No. 3-4, 1937, 194-245. This is a study of the philosophical implications of the special theory of relativity. The author denies, against Bergson, that the multiple times and relative simultaneities of the special theory are fictitious. Bergson's error lay in his treatment of two different definitions of "reality": one based on direct perception, the other on abstraction. Cf. esp. 228-232 and 242-245.

2481   Le Roy, Georges. "Le Dualisme cartesienne et la notion biranienne d'effort." *Travaux de IXe Congrès de Philosophie*, Fasc. 9, 1937, 115-120.

2482   Lersch, Philipp. "Grundsätzliches zur Lebensphilosophie." *Blätter für deutsche Philosophie*, 9, No. 4, 1936; 10, Nos. 1 and 2, 1937. Bergson, pragmatism, and F. Schelling are dealt with in this study.

2483   Levine, Menache. "Al ha' comi o al ha' enouchi." *Haaretz*, 24 December 1937, 10. These are notes on the Hebrew translation of *Laughter*.

2484   Lewis, John. *Introduction to Philosophy*. London: V. Gollancz Ltd., 1937, 94.

2485   Loomba, Ram Murti. *Bradley and Bergson: A Comparative Study*. Lucknow, India: Upper India Publishing House, 1937, 187.

2486   Lyman, Eugene W. "Bergson's Philosophy of Religion." *Review of Religion*, 1, No. 3, March 1937, 249-269. This is an analysis and exposition of *The Two Sources*.

2487   Maquart, F. X. *Elementa Philosophiae*. Vol. 4. Paris: Blot, 1937. Cf. "De existentia Dei ab experientia mysticorum textata, juxta Bergson," 338-343.

2488   Maritain, Jacques. "Santo Tomás y Henri Bergson en los estilos de la ética." *Columna*, No. 8, 1937, 66-67.

2489   Metz, André. *Temps, espace, relativité*. Paris: Beauchesne, 1937, 211. Bergson is discussed on pp. 69, 79, and 82-89.

2490   Miroglio, Abel. "Trois Réfuations du parallélisme psychophysiologique." *Revue Philosophique de la France et de l'Etranger*, 42, Nos. 11-12, novembre-décembre 1937, 215-254. The author examines refutations of mind-body parallelism by Bergson, Blanché and Salzi. Bergson denounces an equivocation in the use of "mind-language" and "matter-language". Blanché (in *La Notion de fait psychique*) presents an idealist refutation; Salzi (in *La Sensation*) provides a refutation based on experimental psychology. The three refutations are treated as complementary and decisive.

2491   Paraf, Pierre. "De Jules Romains à Henri Bergson." *La République*, 12 septembre 1937.

2492   Quevedo, J. F. "Síntesis de filosofia Bergsoniana." *Proa*, julio 1937, 4-5.

2493   Rideau, Emile. "Le Bergsonisme." *Nouvelle Revue Théologique*, 69e Année, No. 6, juin 1937, 621-639; No. 7, juillet-août 1937, 733-754.

2494   Rideau, Emile. "O Bergsonismo perante o mundo contemporâneo." *Brotéria*, 24, No. 2, 1937, 121-127.

2495   Rideau, Emile. *Descartes, Pascal, Bergson*. Paris: Boivin, 1937, 264.

2496   Roa Rebolledo, Armando. "Bergson y el problema del conocimiento." *Estudios*, No. 61, diciembre 1937, 34-43.

2497   Rochedieu, Edmond. "La personalità de Dio in Bergson." *Religio*, 13, No. 5, 1937, 321-332.

2498   Rolland, Edouard. *La Finalité morale dans le bergsonisme.* Paris: Beauchesne, 1937, 181. (Bibliographie des Archives de Philosophie)

2499   Routh, Harold Victor. *Towards the Twentieth Century: Essays in the Spiritual History of the Nineteenth.* Cambridge, England: Cambridge University Press; New York: Macmillan, 1937, 329. Bergson is discussed on pp. 346-366.

2500   Ruyer, Raymond. *La Conscience et la corps.* Paris: Félix Alcan, 1937, 144. (Nouvelle Encyclopédie philosophique) Cf. pp. 4-29 for critiques of Bergson's account of mind-body parallelism and of his theory of perception. The author denies dualistic theories of mind and body and poses an "intellectualist" concept of knowledge. But Cf. "Conscience et organisme," pp. 127-141.

2501   Seidemann, Alfred. *Bergsons Stellung zu Kant.* Endigen-Kaiser-stahl, Germany: Wild, 1937, 98.

2502   Sertillanges, Antonin Gilbert. "Le Libre Arbitre chez Saint-Thomas et chez Bergson." *La Vie Intellectuelle,* N.S. 39, No. 1, 10 avril 1937, 232-267. Bergson's reply to Sertillanges may be found on pp. 268-269. Cf. Henri Bergson, 1937.

2503   Shotwell, James T. *At the Paris Peace Conference.* New York: Macmillan, 1937, 444. On pp. 221-222, the author states, "Friday, March 21, 1919. Luncheon at the Maison Dufayel arranged by the French Government for some of our delegation, with Professor Bergson as the chief lion to meet. He recalled me when M. Monod, who had arranged the luncheon, jogged his memory, but I think his recollection was rather in the nature of an official duty than as an illustration of the 'reality of duration', of which his philosophy makes so much."

2504   Sorokin, Pitirim A. *Social and Cultural Dynamics,* Vol. 1, *Fluctuation of Forms of Art.* New York: American Book Company, 1937, 745. Cf. esp. pp. 160-161, 169.

2505   Sorokin, Pitirim A. and Merton, Robert K. "Social Time: A Methodological and Functional Analysis." *American Journal of Sociology,* 42, No. 5, 1937, 615-629.

2506   Souriau, Michel. *Le Temps.* Paris: F. Alcan, 1937, 178. (Nouvelle Encyclopédie Philosophique) Cf. esp, 35, 57-58, 62-66, 143, 159.

2507   Szathmary, Arthur. *The Aesthetic Theory of Bergson.* Cambridge, Massachusetts: Harvard University Press, 1937, 74. This is a very clear and very suggestive account of Bergson's aesthetics.

2508   Taylor, Alfred Edward. *The Faith of a Moralist:* Vol. 2. *Natural Theology and the Positive Religions.* London: Macmillan, 1937, 437. The author offers various criticisms of Bergson's concepts of intuition, measurement, time, and space on pp. 338-354.

2509   Thonnard, F.-J. *Précis d'histoire de la philosophie.* Paris: Tournai, 1937, 810. Bergson is viewed from a Thomist viewpoint on pp. 707-740.

2510   Troy, William. "Virginia Woolf: The Novel of Sensibility." In *Literary Opinion in America.* Ed. Morton Dauwen Zabel. New York, London: Harper & Bros., 1937, 340-358. On p. 340 the author finds in Virginia Woolf, if not the "exact voice of Bergson" then "at least a very successful imitation."

2511   "Review of *The Two Sources of Morality and Religion* by Henri Bergson." *Nature,* 137, No. 3457, February 1, 1937, 171.

2512   Van Klinken, L. "De Profeet der intuitie." *Paedag. Tijdschrift voor het Christelijk Onderwis,* 29, 1937.

2513   Van Tiegheim, Paul. "Review of *Bergson und Proust* by Kurt Jäckel." *Revue d'Histoire Littéraire de la France*, 44, No. 3, 1937, 444.

2514   Vasconcelos, José. *Historia del pensamiento filosófico*. México: Universidad Nacional Autónoma de Mexico, 1937, 578. This is a history of philosophy containing a chapter on Bergson.

1938

2515   Altmann, Bruno. "Henri Bergson, Stammvater der Naziphilosophie?" *Das Wort*, 3, No. 3, 1938, 119-124.

2516   Barnes, Harry Elmer and Becker, Howard. *Sociological Trends throughout the World*. Vol. II of *Social Thought from Lore to Science*. New York: D. C. Heath and Co., 1938, 193-1178. The author describes the work of Charles Blondel on p. 847 as "a remarkable convergence of the influences of Bergson and Durkheim." On p. 862 he notes Daniel Essertier's Bergsonian criticisms of Durkheim in *Psychologie et sociologie*. On p. 885 he notes a similarity between Bergson's vitalism and that of Wilhelm Dilthey. On p. 947 he notes Bergson's influence on the Swedish philosopher and political leader Gustaf F. Steffen (1864-1929), "Because of the influence of Bergson's philosophy, Steffen rejects the idea that sociology is a natural science, maintaining that it must be based on a sort of intuitive insight that will render possible the understanding of the social actions of others."

2517   Bars, Henri. "Bergson et l'humanité." *L'Eveil des Peuples*, 10 avril 1938.

2518   Bouglé, Célestin. *Les Maîtres de la philosophie universitaire en France*. Paris: Maloine, 1938, 112.

2519   Brambila, Antonio. "Anotaciones críticas sobre el Dios de Bergson." *Luminar*, 2, No. 4, otoño 1938, 22-62.

2520   Bravo, C. "Duración y intuición en la filosofía de Henri Bergson." *Estudios*, 59, No. 321, 1938, 233-254.

2521   Challaye, Félicien R. "L'Evolution, la spiritualisation et la socialization des tendances." In *Nouveau Traité de psychologie*. Vol. VI. Ed. Georges Dumas. Paris: Félix Alcan, 1938, 55-114.

2522   Citoleux, Marc. "La Philosophie de la vie et le bergsonisme." *Mercure de France*, 281, No. 950, 15 janvier 1938, 225-258.

2523   Cohen, Josué. "La Morale bergsonienne." *Revue des Conférences Françaises en Orient*, 2, No. 18, 1938, 593-601.

2524   Coviello, Alfredo. *Critica bibliográfica y análisis cultural*. Tucumán, Argentina: Septentrion, 1938. Bergson is discussed on pp. 24, 40, 101, 104, 115, 117, 143, 280, 293, 301; evolution on p. 101; intuition on pp. 98, 132; and intuitionism on p. 107.

2525   Crooks, Samuel Bennett. "Review of *Bradley and Bergson* by R. M. Loomba." *Dublin Magazine*, N.S. 13, No. 4, October-December 1938, 65-67.

2526   De Burgh, William George. *From Morality to Religion; Being the Gifford Lectures, delivered at the University of St. Andrews, 1938, by W. G. De Burgh...* London: Macdonald and Evans, 1938, xxii, 352.

2527 Draghicesco, Demetrio."Dios y la immortalidad en la filosofía de Bergsón." *Luminar*, 2, No. 4, otoño 1938, 9-21.

2528 Fessard, Gaston. *La Méthode de réflexion chez Maine de Biran*. Paris: Bloud et Gay, 1938, 153.

2529 Frenkian, A. M. "Libertatea si determinismul la Bergson fatâ de stinta modernă." *Revista de Pedagogie*, 1938, 215-243.

2530 Gladen, Karl. "Kommentär des Lachens: Eine Auseinandersetzung mit Bergson über das Problem der Komik." *Philosophisches Jahrbuch der Görresgesellschaft*, 51, No. 4, 1938, 393-413. This is an exposition and criticism of Bergson's theory of laughter.

2531 Grozeff, Grozu. "Intouitziata spored Bergson." *Filossofski Pregled*, 10, No. 3, 1938, 255-266.

2532 Haytschek, Aloisia. "Henri Bergsons Theorie des Komischen." Diss., Wien, 1938, 207.

2533 Heyne, Ranier. "Georges Sorel und der autoritäre Staat des 20. Jahrhunderts." *Archiv des öffentlichen Rechts*, 29, Nos. 2-3, 1938, 129-177, 257-309. Cf. esp. "Henri Bergson. Irrationalismus," pp. 154-158.

2534 Jolivet, Régîs. "Thomisme et bergsonisme." *Studia Catholica*, 14, No. 1, 1938, 43-60.

2535 Kaulins, Jānis. "Vai A. Bergsons, Kā apzinas filozofs, pielīdzinams G. Teichmilleram?" *Celi*, 8, 1938, 406-415. This is a critique of Jurevics' article, "Divi apzinas filosofi." (1937) The author asks if Bergson is really like Teichmüller.

2536 Koort, Alfred. *Kaasaegset filosofiat I*. Tartu, Soviet Union: Akdeemilin Kooperativ, 1938, 127. This book contains a section on Bergson.

2537 Lavelle, Louis. "Le Rythme du temps." *Le Temps*, 77, No. 27547, 1938, 3. This is a review of *Le Temps et la vie* by P. Lecomte du Noüy and *La Dialectique de la durée* by G. Bachelard.

2538 Le Boutillier, Cornelia. *Religious Values in the Philosophy of Emergent Evolution*. New York: Columbia University Press, 1938, 104.

2539 Lenoir, Raymond. "Bergsonisme et sociologie." *Revue de Métaphysique et de Morale*, 45, No. 2, 1938, 255-268.

2540 Léotard, Georges. *En Marge de Bergson: Essai sur la matérialité de la mémoire*. Dilbeck: Editions Marguerite, 1938, 191.

2541 Le Roy, Edouard. *Les Origines humaines et l'évolution de l'intelligence*. Paris: Boivin et Cie., 1938, 375.

2542 Madinier, Gabriel. *Conscience et mouvement: Etude sur la philosophie française de Condillac à Bergson*. Paris: Presses Universitaires de France, 1938, 481.

2543 Maritain, Jacques. *Metafísica de Bergson: Freudismo y psicoanalisis*. Trans. M. A. Berraz. Buenos Aires: Instituto de Filosofía, 1938, 73. (Publ. de filos. contemporáena, 1)

2544 Maritain, Jacques. "Remarques sur l'intuition bergsonienne de la durée." *Miscellanea Philosophica R. P. Josepho Gredt*. Romae: S.A.L.E.R. Herder, 1938, 73-80. This is Vols. 7-8 of *Studia Anselmiana*.

2545 Mead, George Herbert. *The Philosophy of the Act*. Eds. C. W. Morris, J. M. Brewster, A. M. Dunham, D. L. Miller. Chicago: University of Chicago Press, 1938, 696. The author refers to Bergson on pp. 232, 315, 344, 377-378, 506,

517, 529, 638, 644, 645, 59. On pp. 231-232 he gives an essentially Bergsonian treatment of lived-time versus mathematical time. The same distinciton is stressed on pp. 344-346. On pp. 377-378 he criticizes Bergson's mind-body theory. On pp. 644-645 he discusses Bergson's biology.

2546   Metalnikov, S. "Les Facteurs psychiques de l'évolution." *Revue de Synthèse*, 16, No. 2, 1938, 107-119. The author argues for the existence of "creative activity" in organisms and in evolution which accounts for the diversity of biological forms and the individuality of organisms and their behavior.

2547   Moore, John Morrison. *Theories of Religious Experience with Special Reference to James, Otto, and Bergson*. New York: Round Table Press, 1938, 253. On pp. 113-157 the author denies Bergson's contention that Jesus is a typical mystic, as well as his contention that mysticism can be open and dynamic. Bergson absolutizes empirical distinctions.

2548   Quintanilla, Louis. "Bergsonisme et politique." Diss., Johns Hopkins, 1938.

2549   Ralea, Mihail. *Psihologie si vieata*. Bucuresti, Rumania: Fundatia p. lit. si artă, 1938, 298. This work contains a section on Bergson and Einstein.

2550   Richli-Bidal, M.-L. *Après le symbolisme: Retour à l'humain*. Paris: Presses Modernes, 1938, 240. A discussion of Bergson and the "unamiste" movement may be found on pp. 78-91.

2551   Roa, A. "Bergson y el problema del conocimiento." *Estudios*, 59, No. 61, 1938, 34-43.

2552   Roberts, Michael. *T. E. Hulme*. New York: Haskell House; London: Faber and Faber, Lt., 1938, 310. Bergson is mentioned on pp. 13, 16-20, 34, 68, 69, 78 *et seq.*, and throughout. Hulme's translation of Bergson's *Introduction à la Metaphysique* is quoted on pp. 79, 81, 82, and 83. On pp. 79-93 the author explores the similarities and dissimilarities of Hulme's and Bergson's thought. Bergson and G. E. Moore are compared on p. 150.

2553   Rochedieu, Edmond. "La personalidad de Dios según Bergson." *Luminar*, 2, No. 4, otoño 1938, 86-99.

2554   Rouges, Alberto. "Totalidades sucesivas." *Universidad Católica Bolivariana*, 3, Nos. 8-9, 1938-1939, 133-145.

2555   Sanctis, Sante De. "Intuitions in Children." *Journal of Genetic Psychology*, 25, No. 1, 1938, 18-25. The author is at great pain to distinguish his concept of intuition as "immediate cognition" from the Bergsonian conception.

2556   Santos, Delfim. "Una visita a Henry Bergsón." *Luminar*, 2, No. 4, otoño 1938, 3-8.

2557   Schiller, Paul. "A Configurational Theory of Puzzles and Jokes." *Journal of General Psychology*, 18, No. 2, 1938, 217-234. The author develops a theory of jokes and of puzzles by stressing their similarities, and showing how both relate to the *Gestalt* phenomenon of configuration. On pp. 229-231 he criticizes Bergson's theory of laughter. Enjoying a joke, the author holds, is like solving a "puzzle: this joy of reasoning gives rise to laughter as it usually arises through sudden relief from embarrassment. The same joy of reasoning occurs if solving a puzzle" (p. 233).

2558   Torres, Francisco W. *Dos filósofos de la vida: Bergson y Schopenhauer*. Córdoba, Argentina: Imprenta de la Universidad, 1938, 155. The author examines Bergson's basic ideas in metaphysics, ethics, and sociology.

2559   Vivante, Leone. *Il concetto della indeterminazione*. Firenze: Vallecchi, 1938, 231.

2560   Watson, Beatrice. "The Bergsonism of Marcel Proust." Diss., Chicago, 1938.

2561   Wautier d'Aygalliers, A. "El Dios de Bergson." *Luminar*, 2, No. 4, otoño 1938, 63-85.

2562   Wild, K. W. *Intuition*. Cambridge, England: At the University Press, 1938, 240. In chapter one (pp. 3-17) the author deals with Bergson's concept of intuition. Bergson, he states, made "the most strenuous philosophical attempt ever made to establish intuition as an independant mental function." (p. 3) The author does not make the common mistake of identifying Bergsonian intuition with instinct. But he does wrongly identify Bergsonian intuition with imagination—and then denies that we need a new word for such a common capacity. He concludes that while from Bergson we do get the idea of a kind of knowledge different from instinct or reason, "...we do not get a definite, consistent, practicable idea of intuition as differing essentially from either these." (p. 17) From Bergson we get not a new method, only new ideas.

1939

2563   Aberman, Jean. *Curentul antintelectualist francez*. Bucharest, Roumania: Tiparul Universitar, 1939, 340.

2564   Alliegro, Ciro. *Conoscenza di Dio secondo H. Bergson*. Diss., Pnt. Univ. Gregoriana, 1939, 80. Roma: Via Reggio Emila 34, 1939, 80.

2565   "A Monsieur Henri Bergson." *Revue de Métaphysique et de Morale*, 41, No. 4, 1939, 557-558.

2566   Bate, Walter Jackson. *Negative Capability: The Intuitive Approach in Keats*. Harvard Honors Thesis in English, Number 13. Cambridge, Massachusetts: Harvard University Press, 1939, 11-24. Bate compares Keats' distinction between "Imagination" and the "logical faculty" to Bergson's distinction between intuition and intellect.

2567   Bonaparte, Marie. "L'Inconscient et le temps." *Revue Française de Psychanalyse*, 11, No. 1, 1939, 61-105. The author, Sigmund Freud's French translator, criticizes the Freudian contention that the unconscious is timeless.

2568   Burtt, Edwin Arthur. "Some Individual Philosophies and Current Trends." in *Types of Religious Philosophy*. New York and London: Harper and Brothers, 1939, 409-448.

2569   Busch, Joseph F. *Bergson of Betoomd élan rhythme de schepping*. Amsterdam: Bech, 1939, 255.

2570   Busch, Joseph F. "Het gouden jaar van Bergson." *Synthèse*, 4, No. 1, 1939, 42-51. This is a general appreciation of Bergson's philosphy. The title translates, roughly, as "Bergson's Golden Year."

2571   Cahuet, Albéric. "Ceux qui auront connu trois guerres: Les Récents Octogénaires de l'Académie." *Illustration*, 97, No. 5046, 18 novembre 1939, 308.

2572   Calderon, Francisco García. "Bergson: Crítico de la civilización occidental." *La Nación*, 19 novembre 1939, Sec. II, 1, Col. 1.

2573 Chevalier, Jacques. "Bergson et les sources de la morale." *Cadences*. Vol. 1. Paris: Plon, 1939, 374.

2574 Chevalier, Jacques. "Hoe Bergson God heeft gevonden." *Het Schild*, 20, 1939, 372-373.

2575 Coviello, Alfredo. *La essencia de la contradicción*. Tucumán, Argentina: Septentrion, 1939. Bergson is discussed on pp. 75, 76, 81, 85, 87, 88, 97, 105, and 161.

2576 Cresson, André. *Le Problème moral et les Philosophes*. Paris: Armand Colin, 1939, 202. Cf. Conclusions, 189-199.

2577 Davy, Georges. "Les Sentiments sociaux et les sentiments moraux." *Nouveau Traité de psychologie*. Vol. 6. Ed. Georges Dumas. Paris: Félix Alcan, 1939, 153-240. Bergson's views on moral obligation are discussed on pp. 201-203 and also on 235n.

2578 Dhurout, E. *Claude Bernard: Extraits de son oeuvre: Avec un exposé de sa philosophie: Emprunté à l'oeuvre d'H. Bergson*. Paris: Félix Alcan, 1939, 140. Bergson's essay on Claude Bernard is republished in this book on pp. 19-32. Cf. Henri Bergson, 1913, 1934.

2579 Dugas, L. "La Logique des sentiments." *Nouveau Traité de psychologie*. Vol. 6. Ed. Georges Dumas. Paris: Félix Alcan, 1939, 1-114. Bergson and morality are discussed on pp. 107-113. The author follows Bergson ind distinguishing between "closed" and "open" societies and their differing religious functions and spirit.

2580 Feibleman, James K. *In Praise of Comedy*. London: G. Allen and Unwin, 1939, 284. Cf. "Criticism of Modern Theories of Comedy," pp. 123-167.

2581 Ghéréa, J. D. *Le Moi et le monde*. Paris: Vrin, 1939, 475. The author argues that ideas and immediate "durée" are the materials out of which the self and the world are constructed.

2582 Giusti, Roberto Fernando. "Una amistad entre filósofos." *Literatura y vida*. Buenos Aires: Nosotros, 1939, 374. This is a commentary on the James-Bergson correspondence.

2583 Héring, Jean. "La Phénoménologie il y a trente ans." *Revue Internationale de Philosophie*, 1, No. 2, 1939, 367-373. The author notes on p. 368 that when Alexandre Koyré described Bergson's philosophy to the Göttingen circle in 1911 Edmund Husserl proclaimed: "We are the true Bergsonians." This is a general appreciation of Bergson's philosophy.

2584 Korn, Alejandro. "Bergson." *Obras*. La Plata, Argentina: Universidad Nacional de La Plata, 1939, 11-30.

2585 Labadie, Jean. *Aux frontières de l'au-delà*. Paris: Félix Alcan, 1939, 236.

2586 Marache, Theodore Jr. "Bergson and Free Will." *Personalist*, 20, No. 1, 1939, 21-28.

2587 Marcel, Gabriel. "Charles Du Bos: In Memoriam." *Etudes par des Pères de la Compagnie de Jésus*, 240, 5-20 septembre 1939, 449-455. Also in *Hommage à Charles Du Bos*. Paris: Plon, 1945, 165-171.

2588 Maritain, Jacques. *Quatre Essais sur l'esprit dans sa condition charnelle*. Paris: Desclée de Brouwer, 1939, 267. On pp. 31-32 the author urges that Freud's theory of neurosis is the therapeutic refutation of Bergson's theory that habit is to be limited to the physical organism alone. Freud shows us that the mind *itself* can be invaded by habit and automatism. (Bergson, however, concedes this point in the Essai, 1889 (Ed.))

2589 Mason, Joseph Warren Teets. "Las influencias de Bergson en el Japón." *La Prensa*, 12 noviembre 1939, Sec. 111.

2590 Mason, Joseph Warren Teets. "Renacimiento del bergsonismo en Los Estados Unidos." *La Prensa*, 5 mayo 1939, Sec, II.

2591 Mavit, Henri. *L'Intelligence créatrice*. Paris: Presses Universitaires de France, 1939, 155 (Bibliothèque de Philosophie Contemporaine). Mavit's study is permeated with Bergson's ideas.

2592 Moore, John Morrison. "Theories of Religious Experience, with Special Reference to James, Otto, and Bergson." Diss., Columbia 1939, 253.

2593 Muret, Maurice. "La Vie à Paris." *Le Mois Suisse*, 1, No. 8, 1939, p. 77.

2594 Nédeljkovic, Dušan. Анри Бергсон: прилог критици савременог интуиционизма и друштвеног мистицизма. Скопле, "Славија," 1939, 184. (In Serbian).

2595 Paoli, J. *Défilé entre La Bruyère et Bergson*. Göteborg, Sweden. Wettergren and Kerber, 193, 58 (Götesborgs Högskolas arsskrift, No. 2). This study attempts an explanation of certain social ideas in La Bruyère's *Caractères* by reference to Bergson's writings.

2596 Pound, Ezra. "This Hulme Business." *The Townsman*, 2, No. 5, January 1939, 15. The author here notes that the literary critic T. E. Hulme had meetings on Frith Street which were "diluted with crap like Bergson."

2597 Pucciarelli, Eugenio. *Espiritu y materia en Bergson*. 1939.

2598 Rader, Melvin. *No Compromise: The Conflict Between Two Worlds*. New York: Macmillan, 1939, 403. On p. 22 the author asserts that Bergson's theory of the superiority of instinct and intuition is a source of 20th century fascism. But on p. 24 he states: "Bergson does not approve of Fascism. The 'intuition' which he exhalts is 'instinct become disinterested,' and is much more akin to pure esthetic contemplation than to pragmatism." It is G. Sorel who reinterprets Bergson's intuition as a faculty of political action.

2599 Rideau, Emile. "Bergsonisme et catholicism." *Collationes Brugenses*, 39, 1939, 246-250.

2600 Rochedieu, Edmond. *La Personalité divine*. Genève: Editions Labor, 1939, 480. Section one of this work contains a discussion of Bergson's philosophy of religion.

2601 Rojas, Neria. "De Bergson a Freud." *La Nación*, Noviembre 26 de 1939, Sec. 2, p. 3, col. 1.

2602 Rouges, Alberto. "La vida espiritual y la vida de la filosofía." *Sustancia*, Año 1, No. 1, 1939.

2603 Saens, Hayes A. "Homenaje de Francia." *La Prensa*, 24 noviembre 1939.

2604 Samara, Adolfo Menédez. *Dos ensayos sobre Heidegger*. México: Letras de México, 1939, 61. This study contains an essay entitled "La nada en Bergson y Heidegger."

2605 Schwartz, Emanuel K. "Henri Bergson: The Father of Modern Philosophical Thought Will be 80 Years Old Next Week." *American Hebrew*, October 13, 1939, pp, 8, 17. While describing Bergson's life and thought the author notes

Bergson's following among "Romanticists, mystics and pragmatists in England and America." Among these are "William James, Whitehead, Joad, Hoernle and Lloyd Morgan." (p. 17)

2606   Souza, Sibyl de. "Proust and Bergson." *Dublin Magazine*, N.S. 14, No. 2, 1939, 63-65.

2607   Souza, Sibyl de. *La Philosophie de Marcel Proust*. Paris: Rieder, 1939, 176. The influence of Bergson on Proust is discussed on pp. 49-61. Proust found in Bergson the metaphysical foundation J. Ruskin lacked.

2608   Speer, Catherine Ellis. "Bergson's Theory of Individuality and the Self." Diss., Texas, 1939, 97.

2609   Thibaud, Marguerite. "L'Effort chez Maine de Biran et Bergson." Diss., Grenoble, 1939, 199.

2610   Tomeucci, Luigi. *La dottrina della durée e la critica italiana*. Messina, Italy, 1939.

2611   Toynbee, Arnold J. *A Study of History*. Vol. 4. New York, London, Toronto: Oxford University Press, 1939, 656. On p. 122 the author states: "What is the weakness that exposes a growing civilization to this risk of stumbling and falling in the mid-career and losing its Promethean élan?" On p. 123 he cites Bergson's *The Two Sources* in regard to the nature of machinery. On p. 152n he cites Bergson's treatment of modern warfare. Cf. also pp. 156, 259n, 635-636.

2612   Toynbee, Arnold J. *A Study of History*. Vol. 5. London, New York, Toronto: Oxford University Press, 1939, 712. On p. 79n the author cites, and agrees with, Bergson's distinction between closed, tribal and open, "human" religion. On p. 558 he quotes a paragraph from Bergson's *The Two Sources* dealing with the above distinction. On p. 563n he notes Bergson's distinction between the active saint and the uninvolved philosopher. Cf. also pp. 419-420n for a brief discussion of Bergson's concepts of "chance" and "order".

2613   Toynbee, Arnold J. *A Study of History*. Vol. 6. New York, London, Toronto: Oxford University Press, 1939, 633. Citing Bergson's *Les Deux Sources*, the author describes Bergson's thesis that "...there is no terrestrial road along which man can make the transit from a primitive Ishmaelitish tribalism to an oecumenical concord of all Mankind." Cf. also pp. 13, 115, 166n. On 166n the author cites Vol. 5, C. (1) (d) 7, pp. 12-13 and "Part VII, below" for Bergson's contention that only the love of God can separate man from tribalism.

2614   Van der Meersch, Joseph. "Bersonisme et catholicisme." *Collationes Brugenses*, 39, No. 1, 1939, 60-82; No. 2, 1939, 154-162.

2615   Vialatoux, Joseph. *De Durkeim à Bergson*. Paris: Bloud et Gay, 1939, 200. (Coll. La nouvelle journée, No. 5) The author proposes a Bergsonian sociology in place of the sociology of E. Durkheim, for which "l'homme individuel n'est pas une réalité mais une pure abstraction." (p. 16) Durkheim has not explained the true nature of the social tie.

2616   Vivante, Leone. *Indétermination et création: L'indéterminism dans ses rapports avec l'imagination créatrice et l'activité morale*. Trans. Lorenzo Ercole Lanza. Paris: Fernand Sorlot, 1939, 270. Bergson's concept of duration is discussed on pp. 97 and 130.

2617   Wheeler, Leonard Richmond. *Vitalism: Its History and Validity*. London: J. F. and G. Witherby, 1939, 275. This study contains references to Bergson throughout. The author deals with *Matter and Memory* on pp. 182-185.

1940

2618   "Bergson Declines Relief From Vichy French Laws." *New York Times*, 90, No. 30271, December 10, 1940, p. 14, col. 3. Bergson is here reported as declining an offer from the Vichy French government to exempt him from a law forcing Jews to resign from state positions.

2619   "Dr. Bergson Wins Gold Prize." *New York Times*, 89, No. 30071, May 24, 1940, p. 17, col. 3. This article notes the award to Bergson by Columbia University of the Nicholas Murray Butler Gold Medal for his *The Two Sources of Morality and Religion*.

2620   Bonaparte, Marie. "Time and the Unconscious." *International Journal of Psycho-Analysis*, 21, No. 4, 1940, 427-468. The author objects to the Freudian notion that the unconscious mind subsists unchanged by the passage of time, as well as to the idea that space and time are mere forms of human perception. Various references to Henri Bergson and to Pierre Janet are found in this article.

2621   Bujeau, L.-V. *L'Oeuvre de J.-H. Fabre et la psychologie de l'insecte*. Paris: Presses Universitaires de France, 1940, 98. Bergson's definition of instinct is discussed on p. 3; the association of ideas (images) in animals on p. 48; animal intelligence on p. 54; insect intelligence on p. 56; insect language on p. 57. See also pp. 59, 65, and 75.

2622   Crottwell, C.F.M.F. *A History of the Great War, 1914-1918*. 2nd ed. Oxford: The Clarendon Press, 1940, 655. The author states, "In the years immediately preceding the war, however, the generation which knew not 1870 was soaked in the doctrine of immediate and brutal offensive, the efficacy of which was preached with almost mythical fervor. It appears to have been partly inspired by the Philosophy of Bergson, then so popular in France, of which the effect was to exhalt instinct and intuition above the intellectual process of reasoning. It was also supported by the more material and solid consideration that the French field gun, the famous '75,' was greatly superior both in rapidity and accuracy of fire to anything the Germans could produce" (p. 10).

2623   Cuervo, M. "La postrera obra de Bergson." *Ciencia Tomista*, 25, 1940, 209-214.

2624   De Kadt, J. "Bergson." *De Fakkel*, 1940.

2625   Deustua, Alejandro O. *Los Sistemas de Moral*. Vol. 2. Callao, Perú: Empresa Editora de "El Callao", 1940, 505.

2626   Dollard, Stewart E. *Bergsonian Metaphysics and God*. Ann Arbor, Michigan: University Microfilms, 1940, 236.

2627   Dewey, John. "Time and Individuality." in *Time and its Mysteries: Four Lectures Given on the James Arthur Foundation*. Ed. D. W. Hering. New York: New York University Press, 1940, 85-109. The author here credits Bergson with being the first to take time seriously and to show its relations to individuality.

2628   Fitch, Girdler B. "The Comic Sense of Flaubert in the Light of Bergson's *Le Rire*." *Publications of the Modern Language Association of America*, 55, No. 2, June 1940, 511-531.

2629   Fleury, René-Albert. *Bergson et la quantité.* Paris: Copy-Odéon, 1940, 8.

2630   "France Permits Jews to Remain in Army." *New York Times*, 90, No. 30,375, December 14, 1940, p. 6, col. 4. Bergson is reported here as resigning his honorary position at the Collège de France.

2631   Free, Lincoln Forrest. "The Philosophical and Educational Views of Henri Bergson." Diss., New York, 1940, 284.

2632   Gotschalk, D. W. *Metaphysics in Modern Times: A Present-Day Perspective.* Chicago: The University of Chicago Press, 1940, 110. The author refers at several points to Henri Bergson as a proponent of a recent metaphysical position. The author describes Bergson not as anti-scientific but as anti-Platonic: "Once this Platonism is rejected, once the empirical discoveries of the sciences are ranked above their artificial constructions, the sciences, according to Bergson, offer philosophers invaluable data from which to proceed to metaphysical insights." (p. 7) The author cites F. H. Bradley's philosophy as in these respects being far more anti-scientific than Bergson's. For other references to Bergson Cf. pp. 6-12, 17, 61-62, 71, 99.

2633   Hertrich, Charles. *Le Génie de Bergson.* St.-Etienne: Edit. des Flambeaux, 1940, 14.

2634   Houwens Post, Hendrik. *Bergson: De Philosophie der Intuitie.* Den Haag, Netherlands: Leopolds Uitg. Maatsch., 1940, 95.

2635   Iliev, Athanasse. *Le Bergsonisme: Une Philosophie prospective.* Sofia: "L'Essor bulgare," 194?, 166.

2636   Jurēvičs, Paulis. "Deux Philosophes de la conscience: Teichmüller et Bergson." *Archiv für spiritualistische Philosophie und ihre Geschichte*, 1, 1940, 273-307.

2637   Lévy-Bruhl, Henri. "Histoire et bergsonisme." *Revue de Synthèse*, 19-59, 1940-1945, 141-149.

2638   Marmy, Emile. "Hommage à Henri Bergson." *Monatsschrift d. Schweiz. Studentverein*, 85, 1940-1941, 267.

2639   McKenzie, Sherry. "Bergson, Henri Louis." *The Universal Jewish Encyclopedia*, 2, 1940, 201-202.

2640   Merleau-Ponty, Maurice. "Discours sur Bergson." *Bulletin de la Société Française de Philosophie*, 54, No. 1, 1940, 35-45.

2641   Milet, Albert. "Les Cahiers du P. Marechal: Sources, doctrines et influences subies." *Revue Néo-scolastique de Philosophie*, 2e Sér., 43, No. 67-68, 1940-1945, 225-251. Bergson is discussed on pp. 238-241.

2642   Montague, William Pepperell. "Substance, Potentiality, and Cause: A Positivistic Theory of Rationalistic Categories." in *The Ways of Things.* New York: Prentice-Hall, 1940, 408-417.

2643   "Nicholas Murray Butler Medal Awarded to Henri Bergson in Recognition of his *Two Sources of Morality and Religion*." *Journal of Philosophy*, 37, No. 13, June 20, 1940, 364.

2644   Parodi, D. "Philosophy in France, 1938-1939." *Philosophical Review*, 49, No. 289, January, 1940, 1-24. On p. 14 the author notes Bergson's influence on Konczewski's *Pensée préconsciente*.

2645   Pereira Rodriguez, José. *Páginas escogidas de filosofía: Platón, Kant, Bergson; noticias bio-bibliográficas.* Montevideo: A. Monteverde y cía, 1940, 115.

2646   Pos, Hendrick Josephus. *Uren met Bergson.* Baam, Netherlands: Hollandia, 1940, 192.

2647   Rein'l, Robert Lincoln Coffin. "Intuition and Analysis in Bergson's Theory of Knowledge." Diss., Harvard, 1940, 284.

2648   Romero, Francisco. "Temporalismo." *Nosotros*, 5, No. 50-51, 1940, 329-355. W. Dilthey, E. Husserl, Bergson, and M. Heidegger are examined in this study.

2649   Romero, Francisco. "Temporalismo." *Nueva Democracia*, 21, Nos. 11 and 12, 1940, 26-28, 20-24; 22, No. 1, 1944, 16-18. This article is reprinted from *Nosotros*, 1940.

2650   Sunden, Hjalmar. *La Théorie bergsonienne de la religion.* Trans. J. Nougé and M. Bouvier. Uppsala: Almquist et Wiksells Boktryckeri: 1940, 319. This study contains an exchange of letters between Bergson and N. Söderblom. It is written from the vantage-point of a historian of religion, and details Bergson's readings leading to *The Two Sources of Morality and Religion* and his contacts with ministers of various faiths.

2651   Vassallo, Angel. "Para una visión y juicio del tiempo presente." *Sur*, 10, No. 65, febrero 1940, 77-86.

2652   Vial, Fernand. "Bergson et Proust: L'Idée de Temps." *Publications of the Modern Language Association of America*, 55, No. 4, 1940, 1191-1212.

2653   Wodehouse, Helen. "Bergson and World-Loyalty; Based on *The Two Sources of Morality and Religion.*" *Hibbert Journal*, 38, No. 4, July 1940, 457-468. This essay also appears in *Menorah Journal*, 29, April 1941, 125-137.

2654   Yépes, Gumersindo. "Henri Bergson, su vida y su obra." *Revista del Colegio Nacional Vicente Rocafuerte*, 17, No. 52, 1940.

1941

2655   Alquie, Ferdinand. "Bergson et la *Revue de Métaphysique et de Morale.*" *Revue de Métaphysique et de Morale*, 47, No. 4, 1941, 315-328. The author is largely critical of Bergson.

2656   Alzamoa Valdez, Mario. "Bergson o el renacimiento de la sabiduria." *Mercurio Peruano*, 23, No. 168, marzo 1941, 111-114.

2657   Alzamoa Valdez, Mario. "La filosofía de Bergson." *Universidad Pontificia Bolivariana*, 9, 1941, 144-161.

2658   Anquin, Nimio de. "El bergsonismo: Analogía de la experiencia." *Sol y Luna*, Año 4, No. 6, julio 1941, 13-62.

2659   Anshen, Ruth Nanda. "The Legacy of Henri Bergson." *Decision*, 1, No. 2, 1941, 60-62.

2660   Arslan, Emin. "Un recuerdo de Bergson." *El Mundo*, (Buenos Aires) enero 1941.

2661   "The Author of 'Creative Evolution'." *Spectator*, 166, No. 5871, January 10, 1941, 27. This is an obituary article.

2662   Avord, René. "Réflexions sur la philosophie bergsonienne." *France Libre*, 2, No. 7, mai 1941, 42-54. This is a Résistance publication.

2663   B., E. "Review of *Henri Bergson: Essais et témoignages inédits* by Albert Beguin et Pierre Thevenaz." *Revue Philosophique de la France et de l'Etranger*, 131, Nos. 9-12, 1941, 469-470.

2664   Banhos, Alfonso. "Bergson e o pensamento moderno." *Etudios*, febrero-marzo 1941.

2665   Baralt, Luis A. "Bergson y la muerte." *Sustancia*, 2, Nos. 7-8, septiembre 1941, 344-346.

2666   Barth, Hans. "Bergson und Sorel." *Jahrbuch der Schweizerischen Philosophischen Gesellschaft*, 1, 1941, 66-67.

2667   Barzin, Betty, "Bergson et Vichy." *Nation*, 152, No. 8, February 22, 1941, 223. This article discusses relations between Bergson and the Vichy government and E. Husserl and the German government.

2668   Barzin, Betty. "Reply to D. Cairns." *Nation*, 152, No. 13, March 29, 1941, 392.

2669   Bayer, Raymond. "L'Esthétique de Bergson." *Revue Philosophique de la France et de l'Etranger*, 131, Nos. 3-4, mars-août 1941, 244-318. This is a well-known inquiry into Bergson's aesthetics, stressing both the strengths and weaknesses of Bergson's position. Bergson, according to the author, fails to stress the place of technical elements in art. Cf. Fabre-Luce de Gruson, Franciose, 1959.

2670   Berger, Gaston. "La Philosophie d'Henri Bergson." *Cahiers du Sud*, No. 233, mars 1941, 165-171.

2671   "Bergson Died a Roman Catholic." *Christian Century*, 58, No. 5, January 29, 1941, 139-140. This article comments favorably on Raissa Maritain's claims concerning Bergson's baptism.

2672   "Bergson Dies in Paris." *Christian Century*, 58, No. 3, January 15, 1941, 76-77.

2673   "Bergson est mort." *France*, No. 113, 6 janvier 1941, 1, 4.

2674   "Henri Bergson." *London Times Literary Supplement*, 40, No. 2033, January 18, 1941, 27, 36. This is an obituary.

2675   "Henri Bergson." *Sustancia*, 2, No. 6, 1941, 305-306.

2676   Betancour, Cayetano. "Henri Bergson." *Universidad Católica Boliviarana*, 6, Nos. 19-20, 1941, 177-208.

2677   Broglie, Louis de. "Les Conceptions de la physique contemporaine et les idées de Bergson sur le temps et le mouvement." *Revue de Métaphysique et de Morale*, 48, No. 4, 1941, 241-257. This article is translated, with an introduction, in *Bergson and the Evolution of Physics*, (1969) Ed. P. A. Y. Gunter, 45-62. The author, the originator of the wave theory of matter, holds that Bergson's philosophy foreshadows later developments of quantum physics. These anticipations include close analogies with Heisenberg's principle of indeterminacy and Bohr's wave-particle duality.

2678   Burkill, T. A. "Henri Bergson." *Nature*, 147, February 8, 1941, 168-169. This is an obituary notice.

2679   Carrasquilla, Tomas. "Punctos de vista: Bergson." *Atenea*, Año 18, No. 187, enero 1941, 1-3.

2680   Cassirer, Ernst. "Henri Bergsons etik och religionsfilosofi." *Judisk Tidskrift*, 14, No. 1, 1941, 13-18.

2681   Ceriani, Grazioso. "Enrico Bergson." *Civiltà cattolica*, 92, No. 2, 1941, 113-126.

2682   Ceriani, Grazioso. "Henri Bergson (+ 1941)." *Scuola catolica*, 69, No. 2, 1941, 112-126; No. 3, 243-259. This is an obituary notice.

2683   Chaumeix, André. "Henri Bergson." *Revue des Deux Mondes*, 111, 8e période, No. 61, 1er février 1941, 345-355. This essay is a tribute to Bergson written soon after his death.

2684   Chaumeix, André. "Le Souvenir d'Henri Bergson." *Candide*, 27, No. 2, 15 janvier 1941.

2685   Chávez, Ezequiel. "El pensamiento filosófico de Enrique Bergson con referencia a los acontecimientos culminantes de la época y el momento actual de la vida en el mundo." *Luminar*, 2, No. 4, 1941.

2686   Chevalier, Jacques. "Bergson." *el Escorial*, 2, 1941, 317-318.

2687   Chevalier, Jacques. "Chevalier parle de Bergson." *Esprit*, 9, No. 97, février 1941, 259.

2688   Chevalier, Jacques. "Enrique Bergson (1859-1941)." *La ciencia Tomista*, 60, 1941, 146-147.

2689   Chevalier, Jacques. "El pensamiento frances." *Mercurio Peruano*, 23, No. 176, 1941, 595-604.

2690   Conte, Alberto. "O mundo objectivo na filosofía intuicionista de Bergson." *Sustancia*, 2, Nos. 7-8, septiembre 1941, 334-343.

2691   Copleston, Frederick Charles. "Henri Bergson." *The Month*, 177, No. 1, January-February 1941, 47-57.

2692   Coviello, Alfredo. "Henri Bergson." *Sustancia*, Año 2, No. 6, marzo 1941, 305-306.

2693   Coviello, Alfredo. "Bibliographia bergsoniana." *Sustancia*, 2, Nos. 7-8, 1941, 394-440.

2694   Coviello, Alfredo. "La influencia de Bergson in America." *Sustancia*, Nos. 7-8, septiembre 1941, 375-393.

2695   Coviello, Alfredo. *El proceso filosófico de Bergson y su bibliografía*. Tucumàn, Argentina: La Raza, 1941, 119. This is a biographical-critical sketch and bibliography formerly published in *Sustancia*. This version contains additional materials.

2696   Cresson, André. *Bergson, sa vie, son oeuvre: Avec Un Exposé de sa philosophie*. Paris: Presses Universitaires de France, 1941, 160. This work contains passages from Bergson's writings.

2697   Cresson, André. *H. Bergson: Liste des articles et des oeuvres*. Paris: Presses Universitaires de France, 1941, 158.

2698   Croce, Benedetto. *History as the Story of Liberty*. Trans. Sylvia Sprigge. New York: Norton; London: G. Allen and Unwin, 1941, 324. Cf. pp. 132, 139.

2699   D'Arcy, M. C. "Henri Bergson." *Tablet*, 177, January 11, 1941, 29.

2700   Davy, Georges. "Henri Bergson: 1859-1941." *Revue Universitaire*, 9, No. 4, 1941, 243-255; No. 5, 1941, 321-336.

2701   Delattre, Floris. "Les Dernières Années d'Henri Bergson." *Revue Philosophique de la France et de l'Etranger*, 131, Nos. 2-3, mars-août 1941, 125-138. This is a series of glimpses into the concerns which occupied Bergson's later years. The philosophies of Samuel Butler and Wm. James are dealt with.

2702   Delle Piane, Arístides L. "Henri Bergson." *Revista Nacional Literatura-Arte-Ciencia*, 13, No. 39, marzo 1941, 364-411.

2703   Delle Piane, Arístides L. *Henri Bergson*. Montevideo: Talleres gráficos de institutos penales, 1941, 57.

2704   Deustua, Alejandro O. "Libertad y axiologia." *Sustancia*, 2, Nos. 7-8, septiembre 1941, 327-328.

2705   Dingle, Reginald J. "Henri Bergson." *Nineteenth Century*, 129, No. 768, February 1941, 128-134. This is an obituary article.

2706   "Les Disparus de la science et des lettres: Henri Bergson." *L'Illustration*, No. 5107, 25 Janvier 1941, 92. Of Bergson's death the author states: "Ce départ effacé n'est pas dénué de grandeur. Il faut peut-être beaucoup de courage de vivre. Il en faut davantage pour savoir mourir à la manière d'Henri Bergson."

2707   Dj., M. "Necrolog: Henri Bergson." *Analeli Facultatii de drept*, Annul 2, Nr. 2-3-4, 1941, 3pp. This article was published in Bucharest.

2708   Dooley, Lucille. "The Concept of Time in Defense of Ego Integrity." *Psychiatry*, 4, No. 1, 1941, 13-23. The author footnotes Bergson and Alexis Carrel, and studies the ego's use of "time" as a defense mechanism, i.e., a means by which the ego maintains its own integrity. Case histories in which this defense is misused are presented. The author fails to distinguish clearly between duration and clock-time.

2709   Dujovne, León. "Bergson o el discípulo de su propra filosofía." *La Nación*, 9 febrero 1941.

2710   Dujovne, León. "Moral, religión y arte en la obra de Bergson." *La Nación*, 9 marzo 1941.

2711   Dujovne, León. "El problema de la personalidad en Bergson." *Logos*, (Argentina) Año 1, No. 1, 1941, 105-117.

2712   E., P. "En días de dolor para Francia se apagó la vida del gran filósofo Henri Bergson." *La Gaceta*, 6 enero 1941.

2713   "Editorial." *New York Times*, January 7, 1941, 22, col. 2.

2714   Edman, Irwin. "Henri Bergson." *Nation*, 152, No. 3, January 18, 1941, 76-77. This is an obituary article. It was used as a preface to the Modern Library edition of *Creative Evolution*.

2715   Edman, Irwin. "Henri Bergson." *Sustancia*, 2, Nos. 7-8, septiembre 1941, 329-333.

2716   Edman, Irwin. "Lo que nos ha dejado Bergson." *Ultra*, marzo 1941 (Havana). This is a Castillian version of an article in *Nation*, January 1941.

2717   "Etudes bergsoniennes." *Revue Philosphique de la France et de l'Etranger*, Nos. 3-4, mars-août 1941, 121-342.

2718   "Falleció en Paris el concocido filósofo Henri Bergson." *La prensa*, Enero 5, 1941.

2719   Fernandez, Ramon. "Henri Bergson." *Nouvelle Revue Française*, 55, No. 325, 1941, 470-473.

2720   Flewelling, Ralph Tyler. "Bergson: A Philosopher of Freedom." *Personalist*, 22, No. 2, April 1941, 189-190.

2721   "Floris Delattre on Bergson's Catholicism." *New York Times*, December 7, 1941, 33, col. 3.

2722   Franchesi, Gustavo J. "En la muerte de Enrique Bergson." *Criterio*, Año 13, No. 678, 27 febrero 1941, 197-201.

2723   Gabriel, José. "De Socrates à Bergson." *Argentina Libre*, 2, 23 enero 1941.

2724   Gaos, Joaé. "Bergson, ségun su autobiografía filosófica." *Homenaje a Bergson*. Imprenta Universitaria México, 1941, 7-48.

2725   Gibson, A. Boyce. "Review of *Bradley and Bergson* by R. Loomba." *Australasian Journal of Psychology and Philosophy*, 19, No. 1, 1941, 76-78.

2726   Gómez Robledo, Antonio. "Reflexiones sobre Bergson." *Abside*, 5, Nos. 4-5, abril 1941, 223-242.

2727   Gouhier, Henri. "La Conversion de Maine de Biran au platonisme." *Revue des Sciences Philosophiques et Théologiques*, 2, 1941.

2728   Gouhier, Henri. "L'Esprit du bergsonisme." *Rencontres*, 1, No. 5, 1941, 87-103.

2729   Gouiran, Emilio. "Henri Bergson: Precisiones." *Sustancia*, 2, Nos. 7-8, septiembre 1941, 357-358.

2730   Gregh, Fernand. "Bergson et Proust." *Journal de Genève*, 27 juillet 1941.

2731   Grunsky, Hans Alfred. "Bergson." *Das Reich*, 2, No. 21, 1941, 13.

2732   Guthrie, Hunter. "Bergson Sought the Truth and Found it Before the End." *America*, 64, No. 16, January 25, 1941, 427-428.

2733   "Ha fallecido el filósofo francés, M. Henri Bergson." *La nacion*, Enero 5, 1941.

2734   Hansen, Valdemar. "Henri Bergson: Et Tilbageblik." *Nordisk Tidskrift*, 17, No. 4, 1941, 264-269.

2735   Hendel, Charles W. "The Achievement of Bergson." *University of Toronto Quarterly*, 10, No. 3, April 1941, 269-282. This is a highly affirmative assessment of Bergson's philosophy.

2736   Hocking, William E. "Whitehead on Mind and Nature." In *The Philosophy of Alfred North Whitehead*. Ed. Paul A. Schilpp. Evanston and Chicago: Northwestern University Press, 1941, 381-404. (Library of Living Philosophers, 3) The author finds various similarities between Whitehead and Bergson. On p. 386 he notes the similarities between Bergson's and A. N. Whitehead's concepts of action; on p. 400 he notes a similarity between Bergson's and Whitehead's concepts of explanation.

2737   *Homenaje a Bergson*. México: Imprenta Universitaria, 1941, 188. Universidad Nacional Autonoma de México, Centro de Estudios Filosoficos de la Facultad de Filosofía y Letras.

2738   Iberico, Mariano. "La filosofía de Bergson." *Sustancia*, 2, Nos. 7-8, septiembre 1941, 351-356.

2739   Iberico, Rodrígues Mariano. "La filosofía de Bergson." *Letras*, No. 20, 1941, 307-316.

2740   Iberico, Mariano. "La filosofía de Bergson." *Letras* (Lima), 7, 1941, 307-316.

2741   Iriarte, Joaquín de. "El sentido espiritualista de la filosofía de Bergson." *Razón y Fe*, 122, No. 2, 1941, 196-210.

2742   Irwin, Jean McQueen. "Bergson and Gestalt Psychology: Corollary Critiques of Scientific Method in Psychology." *Psychological Bulletin*, 38, No. 8, October 1941, 739. This is an abstract of a paper given at the twenty-first meeting of the Western Psychological Association.

2743   Joad, Cyril Edward Mitchinson. "Henri Bergson." *New Statesman and Nation*, 21, No. 516, January 11, 1941, 33-34. This is an obituary notice.

2744   Jolivet, Régîs. "Bergson et le bergsonisme." *L'Année Théologique*, 2, 1941, 253-264.

2745 Jules-Bois, H. A. "Bergson the Magician." *Catholic World*, 152, No. 912, March 1941, 673-681. The author concludes that: "The fundamentals of Bergson's philosophy are neo-Platonic or Eleatic, in no way Christian or Catholic." (674).

2746 Junco, Alfonso. "La conversión de Bergson." *America Español*, 12, No. 42-43, 1941, 291-295.

2747 Lacroix, Jean. "Henri Bergson." *Esprit*, No. 96, janvier 1941, 182-184.

2748 Lacroix, Jean. "La Pensée engagée." *Esprit*, 9, No. 96, 1941, 182-184.

2749 Lalo, Charles. "Promesses et carences de l'esthétique bergsonienne." *Revue de Metaphysique et de Morale*, 47, No. 4, 1941, 301-314. The author states: "...Bergson ne s'est jamais arrêté devant ces difficultés inhérentes à son système—sauf en matière d'esthétique. De cette surprenante exception nous avons tenté de donner ici quelques raisons principales." (314).

2750 Latanzi, Lamberto. "Un sabio, un articulo y un libro." *Criterio*, Año 14, No. 682, 27 marzo 1941, 299-302.

2751 Lavelle, Louis. "Bergson: El hombre y el filósofo." *La Nación* (Buenos Aires), 6 abril 1941, Sec. II, pág. 4, Col. 1. Also in *Le Temps*, 7 January 1941.

2752 Lavelle, Louis. "Henri Bergson." *France Libre*, 1, No. 4, 1941, 347-353. Also in *Le Temps*, 7 January 1941.

2753 Lavelle, Louis. "Henri Bergson: L'Homme et le philosophe." *Le Temps*, 7 janvier 1941.

2754 Lavelle, Louis. "La Pensée religieuse de Bergson." *Revue Philosophique de la France et de l'Etranger*, 131, Nos. 3-8, mars-août 1941, 139-174.

2755 Lazareff, Pierre. "French Spirit vs. Nazi Peace." *Decision*, 1, No. 3, March 1941.

2756 Le Senne, René. "L'Intuition morale d'après Bergson." *Revue Philosophique de la France et de l'Etranger*, 131, Nos. 2-3, mars-août 1941, 219-243.

2757 Le Senne, René. *Traité de caractérologie*. Paris: Presses Universitaires de France, 1941, 523.

2758 Lewis, Clarence Irving. "The Categories of Natural Knowledge." *The Philosophy of Alfred North Whitehead*. Ed. Paul A. Schilpp. La Salle, Illinois: Open Court Publishing Co., 1941, 701-744. (Library of Living Philosophers, 3).

2759 Loomba, Ram Murti. "Henri Bergson." *Prabuddha Bharata* (Calcutta), August 1941, 347-352.

2760 M., F. "Henri Bergson é morto cattolico?" *La Civiltá cattolica*, 92, No. 3, 1941, 537-538.

2761 Malloy, Joseph I. "Death of Noted French Philosopher." *Catholic World*, 152, No. 911, February 1941, 620-621.

2762 Maritain, Jacques and Raissa. "Notre Maître perdu et retrouvé." *Revue Dominicaine*, 47, No. 2, février 1941, 61-68.

2763 Maritain, Raissa. "Henri Bergson." *Commonweal*, 33, No. 13, January 17, 1941, 317-319. In this article Raissa Maritain makes controversial claims concerning Bergson presumed conversion to Catholicism.

2764 Maritain, Raissa. "Henri Bergson." *Catholic Digest*, 5, No. 3, March 1941, 7-10. This is a short version of articles and discussions in *Commonweal*, 1941.

2765 Maritain, Raissa. "Henri Bergson." *La Relève*, 5ᵉSer., 6ᵉCahier, mars 1941, 161-167. This is a French version of the author's article which appeared in *The Commonweal*, January 1941.

2766   Maritain, Raissa. "Communications: Bergson." *The Commonweal*, 34, No. 19, August 29, 1941, 446-447. This is a note concerning Bergson's presumed conversion to Catholicism.

2767   Maritain, Raissa. "Concerning Henri Bergson: Madame Maritain's Reply." *The Commonweal*, 33, No. 20, March 7, 1941, 493-494.

2768   Maritain, Raissa. "Discussion of Bergson." *Commonweal*, 33, No. 20, March 7, 1941, 492-494; No. 24, April 4, 1941, 601.

2769   Maritain, Raissa. *Les Grandes Amitiés: Souvenirs*. Paris: Desclée de Brouwer, 1941, 228.

2770   Maritain, Raissa. "Souvenirs." *La Relève*, Sér., 5 mars 1941, 161-187. This article is republished in *Henri Bergson*, edited by Béguin and Thévenaz, (1943), 349-356.

2771   Maritain, Raissa. "Henri Bergson." *Nova et Vetera*, 14e Année, No. 1, 1941, 3-12.

2772   "Maritain on Bergson's Catholicism." *New York Times*, January 13, 1941, p. 18, col. 8.

2773   Massis, Henri. "Les Cours du Collège de France." *Candide*, 27, No. 2, 14 janvier 1941.

2774   Masson-Oursel, Paul. "Henri Bergson et l'Inde." *Revue de l'Histoire des Religions*, No. 123, mars-juin 1941, 193-200. The author states that: "Notre conclusion sera que Bergson, malgré les allusions qu'il y a faites dans les *Deux Sources*, prêta peu d'intérêt à l'expérience indienne." (200).

2775   Masson-Oursel, Paul. "Mystique et logique! I. Ingénuité naturelle ou torsion? II. Logique bergsonienne." *Revue Philosophique de la France et de l'Etranger*, 131, Nos. 3-8, mars-août 1941, 176-181.

2776   Masur, Gerhard. "Bergson y la evolución creadora." *Educación*, Ser. 1-2, No. 1, julio-agosto 1941, 25-31.

2777   Maurois, André. *Etudes littéraires*. Vol. 1. New York: Edit. de la Maison Française, 1941. P. Valéry, A. Gide, M. Proust, Bergson, P. Claudel, and C. Péguy are discussed in this study.

2778   McGovern, Wm. M. *From Luther to Hitler: The History of Fascist-Nazi Political Philosophy*. Boston and New York: Houghton Mifflin Company, 1941, 638. The author explains on pp. 404-408 that Bergson is an "irrationalist." His explanation, however, does not justify the use of this term.

2779   Ménégoz, Fernand. "Études critiques. La Théorie bergsonienne de la religion par Hjalmar Sunden." *Revue d'Histoire et de Philosophie Religieuses*, 21, No. 3, 1941, 225-248. This is a careful analysis of Sunden's doctoral thesis in theology, published in 1940 in Uppsala, Sweden.

2780   Millot, Albert. "L'Intérêt pédagogique de la doctrine de Bergson." *Revue Philosophique de la France et de l'Etranger*, 131, Nos. 3-8, mars-août 1941, 218-243.

2781   Monod, Wilfred. *Quelques Philosophes de France*. Libourne, France: Gélix, 1941, 55. A chapter on Bergson is included in this book.

2782   Mounier, Emmanuel. "Henri Bergson." *Temps Nouveau*, 17 janvier 1941. This is apparently a Résistance publication published in Moscow.

2783	"La Muerte de Henri Bergson." *Filosofía y Letras, Universidad Autónoma de México*, No. 1, enero-marzo 1941.

2784	Mullen, Mary Domenica. *Essence and Operation in the Teaching of St. Thomas and in some Modern Philosophies*. Washington, D.C.: Catholic University of America Press, 1941, 119. (Philosophical Studies, No. 58)

2785	Nabert, Jean. "L'Intuition bergsonienne et la conscience de Dieu." *Revue de Métaphysique et de Morale*, 48, No. 4, 1941, 283-300.

2786	Newman, Rabbi L. I. "Tribute to Bergson." *New York Times*, January 19, 1941, 34 col. 8.

2787	Nicol, Eduardo. "La marcha de Bergson hacia lo concreto: Mysticismo y temporalidad." *Homenaje a Bergson*. Imprenta Universitaria México, 1941, 49-80.

2788	Nicol, Eduardo. "La marcha de Bergson hacia lo concreto: Misticismo y temporalidad." *Filosofía y Letras*, 1, No. 2, 1941, 217-237.

2789	Northrop. F.S.C. "Whitehead's Philosophy of Science." *The Philosophy of Alfred North Whitehead*. Ed. Paul A. Schilpp. Evanston and Chicago: Northwestern University Press, 1941, 167-207 (Library of Living Philosophers, 3). The author holds that Whitehead's philosophy of science has been produced by three factors: (1) Bergson's emphasis upon the all-sufficiency of immediate intuition and the primacy of process, (2) the epistemological difficulties into which the scientist's bifurcation of nature led modern philosophers, and (3) the reconstruction in the fundamental concepts of contemporary science made necessary especially by Einsteinian relativity.

2790	Noulet, Emilie. "Bergson y Valéry." *Homenaje a Bergson*. Imprenta Universitaria México, 1941, 81-106.

2791	"Obituary." *American Journal of Sociology*, 56, No. 6, March 1941, 734.

2792	"Obituary." *Current Biography Yearbook*. New York: Wilson, 1941, 976, 73.

2793	"Obituary." *Publisher's Weekly*, 139, No. 3, January 11, 1941, 148.

2794	"Obituary." *School and Society*, 53, No. 1359, January 11, 1941, 50.

2795	"Obituary." *Time*, 37, No. 2, January 13, 1941, 32.

2796	"Obituary." *Wilson Library Bulletin*, 15, No. 2, February 1941, 454.

2797	"Obituary." *New York Times*, January 6, 1941, 15, col. 1.

2798	Oko, A. S. "Concerning Henri Bergson." *Commonweal*, 33, No. 20, March 7, 1941, 492-493. This is a letter to the editor. The author questions Bergson's supposed conversion to Catholicism and baptism, as reported by Raissa Maritain in the January 17, 1941 issue of *The Commonweal*: "I submit, with all due respect, that Madame Maritain's inferences as to Bergson's Catholicism are highly speculative and far outrun the evidence adduced by her." (p. 493)

2799	Oldewelt, H. M. J. "De psychologische ondergrond van Bergson's wijsbegeerte." *Synthèse*, 3, No. 2, 1941, 49-61. A résumé of this article, in French, may be found in vol. 3, No. 3 of *Synthèse* on pp. 99-100.

2800	Olgiati, Francesco. "La morte di Henri Bergson." *Revista di filosofia neoscolastica*, Anno 33, No. 1, 1941, 86-94.

2801	Parker, DeWitt H. *Experience and Substance*. Ann Arbor, Michigan: University of Michigan Press, 1941, 371. Bergson is discussed on pp. 22, 26, 67, 136, 138-139, 145, and 171n.

2802   Parkes, Henry Bramford. *Pragmatic Test: Essays in the History of Ideas.* San Francisco, California: Colt Press, 1941, 240. This study includes an essay on Bergson.

2803   Parodi, Dominique. "La Durée et la matière." *Revue de Métaphysique et de Morale*, 48, No. 4, 1941, 258-265.

2804   Parpagnoli, Guido. "Henri Bergson." *Argentina Libre*, 2, enero 1941.

2805   Paulus, Jean. *Le Problème de l'hallucination et l'évolution de la psychologie d'Esquirol à Pierre Janet.* Paris: Droz, 1941, 198 (Bibliothèque de la Faculté de philosophie et lettres de l'Université de Liège, Fasc. 91). Bergson is discussed on pp. 14n, 19, 66, 110, 117, 141, 151n, 143, 155, 163, and 164. The author states: "La psychologie académique en France reste fidèle au point de vue de Ribot, mais tout ce qui s'y fait de fécond révèle l'influence tres différent de Bergson et de Janet." p. 19.

2806   "Philosopher in Eclipse: Henri Bergson and the Jet of Life." *London Times Literary Supplement*, No. 2033, January 18, 1941, 27-36. This is an obituary notice.

2807   Polimeni, E. "Bergson and the Church." *Tablet*, 177, 22 February 1941, 156.

2808   Polimeni, E. "Bergson and Péguy." *Tablet*, 177, February 15, 1941, 136.

2809   Polimeni, E. "Call to Heroism: The Tribute of Charles Péguy to Henri Bergson." *The Month*, 178, Nos. 9-10, September-October 1941, 462-466.

2810   Poortman, J. J. "H. Bergson en die parapsychologie." *Tijdschrift voor Parapsychologie*, 13, 1941, 51-66.

2811   Pradines, Maurice. "Spiritualisme et psychologie chez Henri Bergson." *Revue Philosophique de la France et de l'Etranger*, 131, Nos. 3-8, 1941, 182-217.

2812   Price, H. H. "Henri Bergson." *Proceedings of the Society for Psychical Research*, 46, Part 164, June 1941, 271-276. Bergson's theories of mind-body relations, of immortality, and of extra-sensory perception are discussed in this essay.

2813   Pucciarelli, Eugenio. "Bergson y la experiencia metafísica." *Sustancia*, 2, Nos. 7-8, septiembre 1941, 363-374.

2814   Pucciarelli, Eugenio. *Bergson y la experiencia metafisica.* Tucumán, Argentina: Editorial La Raza, 1941, 14. This pamphlet is reprinted from the September 1941 issue of *Sustancia*.

2815   Ramos, Samuel. "Concepto de la filosofía según Bergson." *Homenaje a Bergson.* Imprenta Universitaria México, 1941, 107-122.

2816   Rao, P. Nagaraja. "Bergson and Sankara." *Aryon Path*, 12, No. 4, April 1941, 174-177.

2817   "Report of Bergson's Funeral." *New York Times*, January 16, 1941, 21, col. 2.

2818   Richardson, W. "The Jet of Life." *Modern Churchman*, 31, No. 3, 1941, 442-446.

2819   Ricour, Pierre. "Aux Sources vives du bergsonisme: Qu'est-ce que philosopher?" *Bulletin des Etudes Françaises*, 1, No. 1, avril 1941, 39-50.

2820   Rivaud, Albert. "La Pensée de Bergson et sa place dans l'histoire des idées." *Revue des Deux Mondes*, 111, 8e période, No. 65, 15 juillet 1941, 158-184. This is an account of the development of Bergson's thought.

2821   Roa Rebolledo, Armando. "Bergson." *Estudios*, No. 97, Enero, 1941, 38-43.

2822   Robbers, H. "Henri Bergson." *Studien's Hertogenbosch*, 1941, 135.

2823   Robbers, H. "Henri Bergson: 18 octobre 1859-5 janvier 1941." *Studiën*, 73, février 1941, 134-144.

2824   Robles, Oswaldo. "Breve nota sobre la psicología y la antropología de Mr. Henri Bergson." *Homenaje a Bergson*. Imprenta Universitaria México, 1941, 123-132.

2825   Romero, Francisco. *La Filosofía Contemporánea: Estudios y Notas*. Buenos Aires: Editorial Losada, 1941, 211.

2826   Romero, Francisco. "Temporalismo en 'Filosofia Contemporánea'." *Losada*, 1941.

2827   Rougés, Alberto. "La duración de Bergson, el tiempo físico y el acontecer físico." *Sustancia*, 2, Nos. 7-8, septiembre 1941, 317-326. The author argues that Bergson failed to understand physical time as a real time and never examined the possibility of a scientific conception of time different from that of mechanism.

2828   Saboia de Madieros, R. "Bergson: La Tragedia de su vitalismo." *Revista Javeriana*, 16, No. 78, 1941, 171-177.

2829   Salomaa, J. E. *Filosofian probleema ja*. Helsinki: Porvoo, 1941, 238.

2830   Schneider. "Les Cours de Bergson au Collège de France." *Le Temps*, 9 février 1941.

2831   Schnittkind, Henry T. and Dana L. *Living Biographies of Great Philosophers* New York: Garden City Publishing Co., 1941, 335. Cf. pp. 309-22.

2832   "Secret of Henri Bergson." *Newsweek*, 22, No. 4, January 27, 1941, 59. This is a brief mention of Bergson's relations with Catholicism.

2833   Serrus, Charles. "La Pensée symbolisée et la pensée pure." *Revue de Metaphysique et de Morale*, 48, No. 4, 1941, 268-282. The author concludes: "L'oeuvre de Bergson nous a présenté ainsi une théorie profonde et complète du symbolisme, dont la séméiologie tient aujourd'hui le plus grand compte et dont elle tire en même temps le plus grand profit." (282).

2834   Sertillanges, Antonin Gilbert. *Avec Henri Bergson*. Paris: Gallimard, 1941, 50 (Collection Catholique).

2835   Sertillanges, Antonin Gilbert. *Henri Bergson et le catholicisme*. Paris: Flammarion, 1941, 151.

2836   Skard, Bjarne. "Henri Bergson: 1859-1941." *Syn og segn*, 47, No. 1, 1941, 49-60.

2837   Sneyers, Germain. *Les Romanciers d'entre les deux guerres*. Paris: Desclée de Brouwer, 1941, 326. See pp. 22-30 for a discussion of Bergson's intuitive method.

2838   Solages, Bruno de. "Bergson, témoin du spirituel." *Bulletin de Littérature Ecclesiastique*, Octobre-Decembre, 1941, 181-189.

2839   Sousa, Filho J. B. "Bergson y la inteligencia." *Sustancia*, 2, Nos. 7-8, septiembre 1941, 359-362.

2840   Stallknecht, Newton P. "Intuition and the Traditional Problems of Philosophy." *Philosophical Review*, 50, No. 4, July 1941, 396-409. The author offers many apt insights into the relations between intuition and intellect in Bergson's philosophy. Intuition not only keeps us from semantic excesses, it is the source of new forms of rationality.

2841   Stebbing, Lizzie Susan. "Henri Bergson." *World Review*, 10, Pt. 1, March 1941, 35-38.

2842   Tavares, Lima Rossine de. "Libre arbitro e determinismo na filosofia Bergsoniana." *Sustancia*, 2, Nos. 7-8, septiembre 1941, 347-350.

2843   Taylor, Alastair MacDonald. "Vitalistic Philosophy of History: What Can Bergsonism Contribute to Historiography?" *Journal of Social Philosophy*, 6,

No. 1, January 1941, 137-150.

2844 Thomas, Henry and D. L. Thomas. *Living Biographies of Great Philosophers.* Garden City, New York: Garden City Publishing Co., 1941, viii, 335. An essay on Bergson's philosophy appears here on pp. 307-322.

2845 Toryho, Jacinto. "Bergson en anécdotas." *Argentina Libre*, 2, 1941.

2846 Urban, Wilbur Marshall. "Whitehead's Philosophy of Language and its Relation to his Metaphysics." *The Philosophy of Alfred North Whitehead.* Ed. Paul A. Schilpp. Evanston and Chicago: Northwestern University Press, 1941, 301-327. (Library of Living Philosophers) The author notes Bergson's realization of the difficulties and centrality of a philosophy of language in a process philosophy on pp. 303-304. On pp. 304-305 he describes Whitehead as being influenced by both Bergson's and Bertrand Russell's theories of language. On p. 307 he speculates that Whitehead's concept of experience was derived from that of Bergson and William James. On p. 308 he reflects on the Bergsonian distinction between scientific and philosophical language. Other references to Bergson's philosophy of language occur on pp. 312, 313, 319-320, 321-322.

2847 Valdez Alzamora, Mario. "La filosofía de Bergson." *Revista de la Universidad Católica del Perú*, 9, 1941, 144-161.

2848 Valeriu, Martin. "Das Verhältnis der Religion zur Gesellschaft in der neuesten französischen Philosophie." Diss., Jena, 1941.

2849 Valéry, Paul. "Allocution à l'occasion du décès de M. Henri Bergson prononcée à la séance tenue par l'Académie française, le 9 janvier 1941." *Revue Philosophique de la France et de l'Etranger*, 131, Nos. 3-8, mars-août 1941, 121-124. This is a powerful funeral oration by France's premier poet. The author praises Bergson as a very elevated and dispassionate intellectual.

2850 Valéry, Paul. "Henri Bergson: Allocution prononcée à l'Académie frančaise le 9 janvier 1941." *Suisse Contemporaine*, juin 1941.

2851 Valéry, Paul. "Henri Bergson: Allocution prononcée à l'Académie française le 9 janvier 1941." *Henri Bergson.* Ed. Béguin and Thévenaz, (1943) 19-23.

2852 Valéry, Paul. "Discours sur la mort de Bergson." *Lettres Françaises* (Buenos Aires), 1re Année, No. 2, 1er octobre 1941, 5-8.

2853 Vasconcelos, José. "Bergson en México." *Homenaje a Bergson.* Imprenta Universitaria México, 1941, 135-158.

2854 Vasconcelos, José. "Bergson en México: Dedicatoria." *Filosofia y Letras*, 1, No. 2, 1941, 239-253.

2855 Vassallo, Angel. "En la muerte de Henri Bergson." *Sur*, 10, No. 76, enero 1941, 7-13.

2856 Vestdijk, J. "De beeldende philosoof." *Groot-Nederland*, 1, No. 4, 1941, 269-280. This is an obituary article.

2857 Vial, Fernand. "Henri Bergson: Spiritual and Literary Influence." *Thougth*, 16, No. 61, June 1941, 241-258.

2858 Waelhens, Alphonse de. "Over Bergson en het Bergsonisme." *Tijdschrift voor Philosophie*, 3, No. 1, 1941, 185-195.

2859 "Was Bergson a Catholic?" *Tablet*, 177, February 15, 1941, 128.

2860 Waterhouse, E. S. "Henri Bergson." *Religions*, April, 1941.

2861 Waterhouse, E. S. "Obituary." *London Quarterly Review*, 166, No. 2, April 1941, 127-137.

2862 Watkin, E. I. "Philosophy of Henri Bergson: With a Summary of his *Two Sources of Morality and Religion.*" *Dublin Review*, 209, No. 3, July 1941, 7-22.

2863 Wright, William Kelley. *A History of Modern Philosophy.* New York: Macmillan, 1941, 633. Bergson is discussed on pp. 560-577.

2864 Xirau, Joaquín. "La plenitude orgánica." *Homenaje a Bergson.* Imprenta Universitaria México, 1941, 159-189.

2865 Zaragüeta, Juan. *La intuición en la filosofía de Henri Bergson.* Madrid: Espasa-Calpe, 1941, 320.

2866 Zaragüeta, Juan. "La libertad en la filosofía de Henri Bergson." *El Escorial*, 4, Junio 1941, 91-116.

1942

2867 Baker, Alberto E. *Inicación a la filosofía: Desde Sócrates a Bergson.* Ed. and Pref. F. Susanna. 7 Ed. Barcelona: Apollo, 1942, 180.

2868 Benrubi, Isaac. *Bergson: Estudio sobre su doctrina: Selección de textos.* Trans. Demetrio Yañez. Buenos Aires: Ed. Sudamericana, 1942, 225. This book was published under the name Jacques Benrubi. (Breviarios del pensamiento filosófico)

2869 Benrubi, Isaac. *Souvenirs sur Henri Bergson.* Paris: Delachaux et Niestle, 1942, 135. The author recounts the substance of numerous conversations with Bergson over the course of many years. This is an important source of insights into Bergson's life and thought.

2870 Berteval, W. "Bergson et Einstein." *Revue Philosophique de la France et de l'Etranger*, 132, No. 1, 1942-1943, 17-28. This is an attempt to reconcile Bergson and Einstein. It is translated, with an introduction, in *Bergson and the Evolution of Physics*, Ed. P. A. Y. Gunter, (1969), 214-227. Bergson and A. Einstein both reject absolute rest, try to deal adequately with what happens between the beginning and the end of motion, hold that physics starts with a "moving" reality. Both derive mechanical reality from a more complex reality.

2871 Binswanger, Ludwig. *Grundformen und Erkenntnis Menschlichen Daseins.* Zürich: Max Niehans Verlag, 1942, 726. Cf. 542-544, 650-653.

2872 Boer, Jesse De. "A Critical Study of Bergson's Theory of Change, Duration, and Causality." Diss., Harvard, 1942.

2873 Bornecque, Jacques-Henry. "Une Source du *Rire* de Bergson." *Revue Universelle*, N.S. 42, 25 septembre 1942, 304-311.

2874 Cannabrava, Euryalo. *Descartes e Bergson.* São Paulo: Editôra Amigos do Livra, 1942, 208. This was first published in 1932.

2875 Celtus. "Bergson et la politesse." *Le Figaro*, 117, No. 46, 24 février 1942, 1.

2876 Copleston, Frederick Charles. *Friedrich Nietzsche: Philosopher and Culture.* London: Burnes and Oates, 1942, 205-213. Copleston compares Bergson's mysticism and Nietzsche's superhumanism.

2877 Cuénot, Lucien. *Invention et finalité en biologie.* Paris: Flammarion, 1942, 259. Cf. esp. pp. 156-159, 192-193 for an appreciative treatment of Bergson's concept of evolutionary convergence.

2878   Delattre, Floris. "Les Dernières Années de Bergson." *Etudes Bergsoniennes*. Paris: Presses Universitaires de France, 1942, 5-18.

2879   Delay, Jean. *Les Dissolutions de la mémoire*. Pref. Pierre Janet. Paris: Presses Universitaires de France, 1942, xx, 152. Bergson's concept of memory is discussed on pp. 5 and 8-13; Bergson's concept of amnesia on 43-75. Bergson's "durée" is characterized as mere "temps autistique" on pp. 99-100 and 111-113.

2880   Dollard, Stewart E. "Bibliographic Footnote." *Modern Schoolman*, 20, No. 1, November 1942, 27-36.

2881   Dollard, Stewart E. "A Summary of Bergsonism." *Modern Schoolman*, 20, No. 1, November 1942, 27-36. The author produces a succinct summary of Bergson's thought with suitable Thomistic criticisms.

2882   Duhamel, Georges. "Un Entretien sur la vie." *Le Figaro*, 117e Année, No. 81, 4-5 avril 1942, 3.

2883   Dumani, Georges. "Henri Bergson ou un philosophe entre deux défaites." *Revue du Caire*, 5e Année, No. 48, novembre 1942, 17-32.

2884   Duque, Baldomero Jiménez. "El problema mistico." *Revista Española de Teleogía*, 2, No. 4, octubre-diciembre 1942, 617-647.

2885   Fauré-Fremiet, Ph. "L'Effort réalisateur de la conscience." *Revue Philosophique de la France et de l'Etranger*, 133, Nos. 7-9, 1942-1943, 34-67.

2886   Hertrich, Charles. "Qu'est-ce que la vie? d'après Bergson. St.-Etienne: Edit. des Flambeaux, 1942, 24.

2887   Iyer, V. Subrahmanya. "V. Subrahmanya's Last Interview With Bergson." *Philosophy*, 17, No. 68, November, 1942, 382-383. The author recounts an interview with Bergson in 1937. Bergson agreed with the basic goals of Indian philosophy as explained by the author: "To sum up: He appeared to agree fully with the Indian thinkers in the view that the first thing to do in 'Philosophy' is to make the meaning of Truth clear, and then to show wheter one's interpretations of life of existence harmonize with it or not. If Truth be the same to all, there can be but one *Philosophy* in the world." (p. 383).

2888   Laberthonnière, Lucien. *Esquisse d'une philosophie personnaliste*. Paris: Vrin, 1942, xvii, 724. (Oeuvres)

2889   Lachance, Louis, "The Philosophy of Language." *Thomist*, 4, No. 4, 1942, 547-588.

2890   Larkin, Oliver. "The Art of Chiroco." *Saturday Review of Literature*, 25, No. 12, March 21, 1942, 16. This is a review of *From Cubism to Surrealism in French Literature* by G. Lemaitre.

2891   Lavelle, Louis. *Leçon inaugurale faite au Collège de France, le 2 décembre 1941*. Paris: L'Artisan du Livre, 1942, 52.

2892   Lavelle, Louis. *La Philosophie française entre les deux guerres*. Paris: Aubier, 1942, 275. Bergson is discussed on pp. 89-112.

2893   Lazzeroni, V. "La psicologia di Henri Bergson." *Sophia*, 10, No. 2-3, 1942, 275-289; No. 4, 1942, 424-439. This very careful study of Bergson's psychology is republished in *Studi e ricerche di psicologia attuale*, edited by a. Marzi e collaboratori. Firenze: Instituto de Psicologia dell'Universita di Firenze, 1947. The author concludes that Bergson has done more than any other to formulate basic questions of psychology correctly—especially questions concerning psychological development. But Bergson then turns towards cosmic, abstract philosophical principles, and fails to solve the basic psychological problems.

2894   Léotard, Georges. *Etudes philosophiques: Introduction au bergsonisme ou l'univers de Monsieur Henri Bergson.* Bruxelles: Editions Marguerite, 1942, 88.

2895   Maritain, Raissa. *We Have Been Friends Together.* Trans. J. Kernan. New York and Toronto: Longman's, Green and Co., 1942, 208. Bergson is discussed on pp. 79-103.

2896   Martins, Diamantino. "De la intuición filosófica, a la intuición mistica en Bergson." *Manresa*, 14, 1942, 70-76.

2897   Martins, Diamantino. "A memoria de Bergson." *Broteria*, 34, No. 3, março 1942, 241-248.

2898   Masin, Jacques. "Sur un hommage à Bergson." *Cahiers du Sud*, 3, No. 242, 1942, 45-53.

2899   Masson-Oursel, Paul. "Mystique et logique: I. Ingénuité naturelle ou torsion? II. Logique bergsonienne." *Etudes Bergsoniennes.* Paris: Presses Universitaires de France, 1942, 55-61.

2900   Masui, Jacques. "Sur Un Hommage à Bergson." *Cahiers du Sud*, No. 242, janvier 1942, 43-53.

2901   Matisse, Georges. *L'Eternelle Illusion: Les Métaphysiques de la vie et de l'esprit.* Paris: Editions d'Art et d'Histoire, 1942, 771.

2902   Merlan, Philip. "A Certain Aspect of Bergson's Philosophy." *Philosophy and Phenomenological Research*, 2, No. 4, June 1942, 529-545. "Bergson's great discovery is, that it is not only with our instincts, that we serve, but that even our intellectual life is service..." Merlan's article contains interesting comments on the sources of Bergson's optimism.

2903   Meyerson, Emile. *Identity and Reality.* Trans. Kate Loewenberg. New York: Dover Publications, 1942, 495. Bergson is discussed on pp. 131, 153, 257, 292, 295-296, 307, 354-357, 361, 366, 378, 384, 433, and 436. Cf. Bergson's review of this work, 1909.

2904   Millot, Albert. "L'Entérêt pédagogique de la doctrine de Bergson." *Etudes Bergsoniennes.* Paris: Presses Universitaires de France, 1942, 199-222.

2905   Muirhead, John Henry. *Reflections by a Journeyman in Philosophy on the Movements of Thought and Practice in his Time.* Ed. John W. Harvey. London: George Allen & Unwin Ltd., 1942, 215. The author's remarks on Bergson are found on pp. 149-152. This is an abridged form of the author's reminiscences published in *Philosophy*, November, 1942.

2906   Muirhead, John Henry. "Some Reminiscences by the Late J. H. Muirhead." *Philosophy*, 17, No. 68, November 1942, 334-350. On pp. 342-346 the author recounts his acquaintance with Bergson on the occasion of the Huxley Lectureship at Birmingham University. Bergson's Huxley Lecture was a great success, unlike the Huxley Lecture of Emile Boutroux. While in Birmingham Bergson met Samuel Alexander. Bergson stayed while in Birmingham with Oliver Lodge, the physicist-spiritualist. Bergson criticized the spiritualist argument for survival, arguing that only a novel creative idea from the spiritualist would convince him that the spiritualist was in contact with a departed soul. The author notes a remarkable similarity between Bergson's appearance and that of John Stuart Mill.

2907   Palacios, Leopoldo Eulogion. "Disertación sobre la filosofía contemporánea del tema general. La personalidad humana." *A. C. N. de P.*, Año 18, No. 283, 1 febrero 1942, 1-4.

2908   Papadopoulo, Alexandre. *Un Philosophe entre deux défaites: Henri Bergson entre 1870 et 1940.* Le Caire, Egypt: Editions de la Revue du Caire, 1942, viii, 420.

2909   Papini, Giovanni. *Bli amanti di sofia: 1902-1918.* Firenze: Vallecchi, 1942, 365.

2910   Przyluski, Jean. *L'Evolution humaine.* Paris: Presses Universitaires de France, 1942, 268.

2911   Pucciarelli, Eugenio. "Espíritu y materia en Bergson." *Revista de Pdagogía*, Año 1, Nos. 4 y 5, 1942.

2912   Raymond, Marcel. *Génies de France.* Neuchâtel, Switzerland: La Baconnière, 1942, 247. This study contains a section entitled "Bergson et la poésie récente"

2913   Rolland, Romain. "Unpublished letter to Jean-Pierre Dubois, 31 March 1942." A copy of this letter is retained in the archives of Mme. Romain Rolland. The letter concerns C. Péguy's Bergsonism.

2914   Rousseau, André. "Péguy, Bergson et Proust." *Fontaine*, 4, No. 22, juin 1942, 123-127.

2915   Ryan, Arthur H. "Henri Bergson." *Studies*, 31, No. 3, June 1942, 193-201.

2916   Sciacca, Michele Federico. *Il secolo XX: Parte I: Dal pragmatismo allo spiritualismo cristiano: Parte II: Storici ed eruditi.* Milano: Bocca, 1942, 768, 263. (Storia Della Filosofia Italiana, 23)

2917   Sheldon, Wilmon Henry. *America's Progressive Philosophy.* New Haven: Yale University Press, 1942, 232. (Powell lectures on Philosophy at Indiana University, No. 7) The author proposes that a process-oriented philosophy is typical of the American viewpoint. He cites Bergson as a prominent representative of process philosophy. (pp. 1, 2) On pp. 59-61 he examines Bergson's doctrine of intuition, denies that intuition is a special faculty. On pp. 118-119 he quotes from *Creative Evolution*. On p. 157 he notes Bergson's pragmatic conception of the function of intellect.

2918   "A travers la presse: Hommage à Bergson." *France*, No. 468, 27 février, 1942, 3.

2919   Valéry, Paul. "Allocution à l'occasion du décès de M. H. Bergson." *Etudes Bergsoniennes*. Paris: Presses Universitaires de France, 1942, 1-4.

2920   Valéry, Paul. "L'hommage de Paul Valéry à Bergson." *Figaro*, 117 Année, No. 3, Janvier 3-4, 1942, 3.

2921   Verdene, Georges. *Bergson le révolté ou l'ascension d'une âme.* Genève: P.-F. Perret-Gentil, 1942, 224.

2922   Zaragüeta, Juan. "Henri Bergson (1859-1941)." *Revista de Filosofía*, 1, No. 1, 1942, 167-174.

1943

2923   Bachelard, Gaston. *L'Air des songes: Essai sur l'imagination du mouvement.* Paris: Librairie José Corti, 1943, 307. Cf. "Philosophie cinématique et philosophie dynamique," 289-302. The author holds that:"...d'autres images, prises dans leurs aspects matériels et dans leurs aspects dynamiques, pourraient offrir au bergsonisme des motifs d'explication plus appropriés." (290).

2924 Balthasar, Hans Urs Von. "La Philosophie de la vie chez Bergson et chez les Allemands modernes." *Henri Bergson*. Ed. Béguin and Thévenaz, 264-270. The author explores the profound influence of Bergson on the German "Philosophers of Life," especially M. Scheler and L. Klages.

2925 Bayer, Raymond. *L'Esthétique de Bergson*. Paris: Presses Universitaires de France, 1943, 75.

2926 Bayer, Raymond. "L'Esthétique de Bergson." *Etudes Bergsoniennes*. Paris: Presses Universitaires de France, 1943, 124-198.

2927 Béguin, Albert. "Note conjointe sur Bergson et Péguy." *Henri Bergson*. Ed. Béguin and Thévenaz, 321-327.

2928 Béguin, Albert and Thévenaz, Pierre. "Avant-propos." *Henri Bergson*. Ed. Béguin and Thévenaz, 7-12. The authors cite points of similarity and difference between Bergson and C. Péguy. Péguy was more "Christian" than Bergson and did not share the latter's optimism.

2929 Benrubi, Isaac. "Un Entretien avec Bergson: Fragment de journal." *Henri Bergson*. Ed. Béguin and Thévenaz, 365-371. The author describes a visit with Bergson in December, 1934. The significance of Bergson's essay "Le Posible et le réel" is discussed, along with Bergson's intellectual development.

2930 Berger, Gaston. "Le Progrès de la réflexion chez Bergson et chez Husserl." *Henri Bergson*. Ed. Béguin and Thévenaz, 257-263. The author compares Bergson and E. Husserl, both of whom he characterizes as Cartesian. According to the author, Bergson's and Husserl's thought both end in insurmountable difficulties. Bergson is left with the untenability of a purely felt present, and Husserl with the inaccessibility of an absolute verity.

2931 *Henri Bergson: Essais et témoignages*. Ed. Albert Béguin and Pierre Thévenaz. Neuchâtel: La Baconnière, 1943, 373 (Les Cahiers du Rhône).

2932 Blanchot, Maurice. *Faux pas*. Paris: Gallimard, 1943, 366. M. Proust, A. Camus, S. Mallarmé, Bergson, and others are discussed in this book.

2933 Blondel, Maurice. "La Philosophie ouverte." *Henri Bergson*. Ed. Béguin and Thévenaz, 73-90. The author examines Bergson's philosophical method and concept of intuition. He is both respectful and critical of the conclusions to which Bergson's method leads, particularly as concerns religious philosophy.

2934 Bopp, Léon. "Bergson et Thibaudet." *Henri Bergson*. Ed. Béguin and Thévenaz, 341-348. The author examines both the Bergsonian and the non-Bergsonian aspects of the literary criticism of Albert Thibaudet.

2935 Borne, Etienne. "Simples Notes de poétique bergsonienne." *Henri Bergson*. Ed. Béguin and Thévenaz, 135-140. The author holds that Bergson's philosophy contains a recognizable poetic. He claims that for Bergson art is neither a servile imitation of reality nor an escape into illusion, but a kind of knowledge. For Bergson the beautiful is an allusion to an invisible reality of which nature is the visible symbol.

2936 Brunschvicg, Léon. "La Vie intérieure de l'intuition." *Henri Bergson*. Ed. Béguin and Thévenaz, 181-186. The author discusses the often surprising, always creative development of Bergson's thought. We must study Bergson, he holds, by avoiding the temptation to enclose Bergson's thought in a system.

2937   Canguilhem, Georges. "Commentaire au 3e chapitre de *L'Evolution créatrice.*" *Bulletin de la Faculté des Lettres de Strasbourg*, 21, No. 5-6, 1943, 126-143; No. 8, 199-214. This is an excellent, very careful analysis of the third chapter of *Creative Evolution*, relating Bergson's thought to recent biology.

2938   Cattaui, Georges. "Témoignage." *Henri Bergson*. Ed. Béguin and Thévenaz, 120-131. The author gives an account of talks with Bergson 1932-1938, concerning such topics as Charles Péguy, Jacques Maritain, Marcel Proust, Hyppolite Taine, Christianity, and the future of Europe.

2939   Chevalier, Irénée. "L'Expérience mystique." *Henri Bergson*. Ed. Béguin and Thévenaz, 105-120. The author considers Bergson's theory of mysticism in its relations to the concept of the "élan vital" and the teachings of the Christian mystics.

2940   Chevalier, Jacques. "Comment Bergson a trouvé Dieu." *Henri Bergson*. Ed. Béguin and Thévenaz, 91-96. The author traces the development of Bergson's thought to its culmination in a philosophy of religion. Letters to the author from Bergson dealing with the terms "classic" and "Greco-Latin" are quoted in part.

2941   Christoflour, Raymond. "Bergson et la conception mystique de l'art." *Henri Bergson*. Ed. Béguin and Thévenaz, 157-169. The author examines passages in *Laughter* and *The Two Sources of Morality and Religion* for their implications for Bergson's concept of art. He concludes that for Bergson art, like other basic human activities, has a religious goal.

2942   Dami, Aldo. "L'Intelligence et le 'discontinu'." *Henri Bergson*. Ed. Béguin and Thévenaz, 233-238. The author concludes that Bergson is an essentially literary figure whose ideas are in no way confirmed by modern physics and mathematics. He concedes, however, that Bergson did maintain some interest in the exact sciences.

2943   Davenson, Henri. "Bergson et l'histoire." *Henri Bergson*. Ed. Béguin and Thévenaz, 205-213. The author explores the influence of Bergson's philosophy on the philosophy of history in France. In one respect, he explains that Bergson's philosophy has been felt as liberating his contemporaries from a preoccupation with history. Yet Bergson's philosophy leads us to view history as a living discipline which can enrich our present and future.

2944   De Carvalho, A. Mosca. "O paradoxo fundamental do tempo e a filosofia de H. Bergson." *Estudos*, 3, No. 1-2, 1943, 32-38.

2945   Fernandez, Ramon. *Itinéraire français*. Paris: Editions du Pavois, 1943, 480. The influence of Bergson on A. Thibaudet is discussed on pp. 36-55.

2946   Frank, Simon. "L'Intuition fondamentale de Bergson." *Henri Bergson*. Ed. Béguin and Thévenaz, 187-195.

2947   Gagnebin, Samuel. "Note sur la méthode dans la philosophie de Bergson." *Henri Bergson*. Ed. Béguin and Thévenaz, 222-226. The author discusses Bergson's philosophical method, which he terms "experimental." Because he did not sufficiently realize the importance of the intellect, the author holds, Bergson is not able to resolve his sharp oppositions between quality and quantity, duration and space, memory and perception.

2948   Ganne, Pierre. "Bergson et Claudel." *Henri Bergson*. Ed. Béguin and Thévenaz, 294-301. The author compares Bergson and Paul Claudel at length, terming Bergson a "poet" and Claudel a "philosopher." He finds their ideas and personal development to be basically similar.

2949   Gurvitch, Georges. "La Philosophie sociale de Bergson." *Renaissance*, 1, No. 2, 1943, 81-94.

2950   Heroux, Jean. "La Liberté humaine dans Bergson." *Le Canada Français*, 31, No. 6, 1943-1944, 430-443.

2951   Hersch, Jeanne. "L'Obstacle du langage." *Henri Bergson*. Ed. Béguin and Thévenaz, 214-221. The author examines and criticizes Bergson's conception of the function of language and concludes that Bergson's philosophical language is not sufficiently "profoundly created."

2952   Huxley, Julian. *Evolution: The Modern Synthesis*. New York and London: Harper & Bros., 1943, 645. This is an important restatement, and presumed validation, of the principles of neo-Darwinism. On p. 28 the author states, "it is with this reborn Darwinism, this mutated phoenix risen from the ashes of the pyre kindled by men so unlike as Bateson and Bergson, that I propose to deal in succeeding chapters of this book." On pp. 457-458 he remarks, "How has adaption been brought about? Modern science must rule out special creation or divine guidance. It cannot well avoid frowning upon entelechies and purposive vital urges. Bergson's *élan vital* can serve as a symbolic description of the thrust of life during its evolution but not as a scientific explanation. To read *L'Évolution Créatrice* is to realize that Bergson was a writer of great vision but with little biological understanding, a good poet but a bad scientist. To say that an adaptive trend towards a particular specialization or towards all-round biological efficiency is explained by an *élan vital* is like saying that the movement of a railway train is explained by the *élan locomotif* of the engine." On pp. 474-475 the author uses R. A. Fisher's dictum that natural selection is a mechanism for generating a high degree of improbability to demonstrate the inevitability of the formation of the human eye starting with the pigment-spot of one-celled creatures, including the case of the convergent evolution of the eye in man and the cephalopods. He refers to J.B.S. Haldane, *The Causes of Evolution*, (London, 1932), on this point. Cf. also R. A. Fisher, 1950.

2953   Iracheta, M. Cardenal. "Henri Bergson: 1859-1941." *Revista de Ideas Estéticas*, 1, No. 3, 1943, 127-142; No. 4, 1943, 109-116. This is a collection of passages from Bergson's writings dealing with aesthetics.

2954   Iturrioz, J. "El cristianismo de Bergson." *Razón y Fe*, 43, No. 127, 1943, 243-256.

2955   Jacks, L. P. "The Brain-Myth." *The Hibbert Journal*, 41, No. 2, January, 1943, 103-114. This is a wordy critique of both idealist and materialist concepts of brain function, followed by an account of Bergson's theory of mind-brain interaction.

2956   Jankélévitch, Vladimir. "De La Simplicité." *Henri Bergson*. Ed. Béguin and Thévenaz, 170-178. The author describes Bergson's thought as an attempt to attain an ultimately simple insight, and thereby overcome the complexities which the intelligence has artificially introduced.

2957   Jetté, Emile. "La Perception chez Bergson." Diss., Laval, 1943, 147.

2958   Junod, Robert. "Roses de Noël." *Henri Bergson*. Ed Béguin and Thévenaz, 49-55. The author praises Bergson, comparing his inspiration with the laborious methods of the associationist H. Taine. Bergson's philosophy, he concludes, will endure.

2959   Kubitz, O. A. "Eduardo Nicol's Situational Psychology." *Philosophy and Phenomenological Research*, 3, No. 3, 1943, 303-312. The author notes on pp. 305-306 passages in Nichol's *Psicología de las situaciones vitales* (pp. 22-56) in which Nicol criticizes Bergson's concept of the self. The author summarizes Nicol's views as follows: "Bergson was right in regarding the self as temporal, but wrong in maintaining the dualism of perceptual and intellectual functions. If it is admitted that intellectual and perceptual functions are never distinct, it is possible to find temporal and spatial characters, memory, and spirit all cooperating in an immediate present experience..." (p. 306).

2960   Lacroix, Jean. "L'Intuition, méthode de purification." *Henri Bergson*. Ed. Béguin and Thévenaz, 196-204. The author examines Bergson's conceptions of intuition and of philosophical method. He rejects anti-intellectual interpretations of Bergson's intuition and concludes that Bergson's method involves a laborious effort to transcend conventional concepts.

2961   La Harpe, Jean de. "Souvenirs personnels." *Henri Bergson*. Ed. Béguin and Thévenaz, 357-364. The author describes a visit with Bergson in September 1936. Among the subjects discussed were: the influence of A. Cournot and others on Bergson; the significance of certain of Bergson's critics; and the import of psychoanalysis. Bergson, in particular, mentions Rolland Dalbiez' critique of Freud (1936) with enthusiasm.

2962   Lavelle, Louis. "L'Homme et le philosophe." *Henri Bergson*. Ed. Béguin and Thévenaz, 39-48. The author considers various respects in which both the openness of the future and the memory of the past combine to constitute Bergson's "duration." The author concludes that Bergson's criticisms of the intelligence are directed only against abstractions which distance us from life.

2963   Lavelle, Louis. "La Pensée religieuse d'Henri Bergson." *Les Études bergsoniennes*. Paris: Presses Universitaires de France, 1943, 19-54.

2964   Le Senne, René. "L'Intuition morale d'après Bergson." *Etudes Bergsoniennes*. Paris: Presses Universitaires de France, 1943, 98-123.

2965   Luchaire, Julien. *Confession d'un Français moyen*. Marseille: Editions du Saggitaire, 1943, 303.

2966   Madaule, Jacques. *Reconnaissances*. Paris: Desclée de Brouwer, 1943, 111, 422. L. Bloy, A. Fournier, Rivière, Bergson, and Martin du Gard are discussed in this book.

2967   Marcel, Gabriel. "Grandeur de Bergson." *Henri Bergson*. Ed. Béguin and Thévenaz, 29-38. The author stresses the openness of Bergson's thought and its emphasis on authentic experience. He suggests that Bergson's intuition achieves its true value only through the dialectic by which it is tested. This is a basic theme in the author's evaluation of Bergson. However, Cf. P. Gunter, 1969, 1978.

2968   Maritain, Jacques. *Ransoming the Time*. Trans. H. Binsse. New York: Scribner's, 1943, 322. Chapter 2 is entitled "The Metaphysics of Bergson."

2969   Maritain, Raissa. "Henri Bergson: Souvenirs." *Henri Bergson*. Ed. Béguin and Thévenaz, 349-356. The author recounts reports concerning Bergson during his later years. She claims that Bergson was baptised sometime after 1932. (But Cf. J. Wahl, 1944.) She also recounts a visit with Bergson in 1936 or 1937.

2970 Martins, Diamantino. "Bergson ante la mística cristiana." *Manresa*, 15, No. 2, 1943, 97-106.

2971 Martins, Diamantino. *Bergson: La intuición como método en la metafísica.* Trans. José H. López. Madrid: Bolanos y Aquilar, 1943, xv, 322.

2972 Martins, Diamantino. "La filosofía bergsoniana." *Revista de Filosofía*, 2, No. 3, 1943, 315-346.

2973 Mercanton, Jacques. "La Philosophie bergsonienne et le problème de l'art." *Henri Bergson.* Ed. Béguin and Thévenaz, 149-156. The author asserts that Bergson's philosophy is ideally suited to explicating the nature of art. He examines aspects of Bergson's thought that lend themselves to such explications.

2974 Millot, Albert. *Etudes Bergsoniennes. L'Intérêt pédagogique de la doctrine de Bergson.* Paris: Presses Universitaires de France, 1943, 24. This article was first published in the *Revue Philosophique de la France et de l'Etranger*, 1941.

2975 Mounier, Emmanuel. "Péguy: Médiateur de Bergson." *Henri Bergson.* Ed. Béguin and Thévenaz, 311-320. The author examines Péguy's advocacy of Bergson's philosophy. Péguy's originality, the author holds, lay in applying Bergson's philosophy beyond the limits of the university "ivory tower."

2976 Muller, Herbert J. *Science and Criticism.* New Haven, Connecticut: Yale University Press, 1943, 495. Cf. the author, 1956.

2977 Muller, Maurice. "Un Aspect de la théorie bergsonienne de la physique." *Henri Bergson.* Ed. Béguin and Thévenaz, 227-232. The author concludes that the physical theories encountered by Bergson in the course of his career do not constitute an essential part of his philosophy.

2978 Oulmont, Charles. *Bergson.* Trans. José Marinho. Lisboa: Editorial Inquérito, 1943, 70. (Cuadernos "Inquerito", Sér. C, Filosofia e religião, 12)

2979 Paliard, Jacques. "Note sur la poésie bergsonienne." in Béguin et Thévenaz, *Henri Bergson*, 141-148.

2980 Paulus, Jean. "Les Deux Direction de la psychologie bergsonienne et la méthode introspective de l'*Essai*." *Tijdschrift voor Philosophie*, 5, No. 1, 1943, 85-140. The author effects an excellent analysis of Bergson's psychology, which, he concludes, points both towards introspection and behaviorism. Cf. the author 1944 for successor to this article.

2981 Péguy, Charles. "Un Témoignage inédit de Péguy." *Henri Bergson.* Ed. Béguin and Thévenaz, 13-15.

2982 Pierre-Quint, Léon. "Bergson et Marcel Proust: Fragments d'une étude." *Henri Bergson.* Ed. Béguin and Thévenaz, 328-340. The author argues that Marcel Proust simply transposed Bergson's vision of the world into literature.

2983 Pradines, Maurice. "Spiritualisme et psychologie chez Henri Bergson." *Etudes Bergsoniennes.* Paris: Presses Universitaires de France, 1943, 62-97.

2984 Raymond, Marcel. "Bergson et la poésie récente: Notes pour une étude." *Henri Bergson.* Ed. Béguin and Thévenaz, 281-293. The author examines the influence of Bergson on the poets C. Péguy and P. Valéry.

2985 Reymond, Arnold. "Henri Bergson et Maine de Biran." *Henri Bergson.* Ed. Béguin and Thévenaz, 248-256. The author compares Bergson and Maine de Biran. He explains that the thought of the two philosophers developed similarly. Both end by finding support for the activity of the individual self in the divine will.

2986   Rougés, Alberto. *Las Jerarquías del Ser y la Eternidad*. Tucumán, Argentina: Universidad Nacional, Facultad de Filosofía y Letras, 1943, 155. The author faults Bergson for not giving a sufficient account of the future.

2987   Rousseaux, André. "De Bergson à Louis de Broglie." *Henri Bergson*. Ed. Béguin and Thévenaz, 271-280. Bergson's philosophy, the author asserts, finds confirmation in the discoveries of twentieth-century physics. The author compares Bergson's philosophy of science to that of the physicist Max Planck.

2988   Scharfstein, Ben-Ami. "Roots of Bergson's Philosophy." Diss., Columbia, 1943, 156.

2989   Scharfstein, Ben-Ami. *Roots of Bergson's Philosophy*. New York: Columbia University Press, 1943, 156. The author holds that Bergson's ideas were largely borrowed from other thinkers and that Bergson exhibited intellectual originality in only a few instances, chiefly in his mind-body theory.

2990   "Se convirtío Bergson?" *Revista Javeriana*, 20, No. 99, 1943, 176-177.

2991   Segond, Joseph. "Schématisme bergsonien et schématisme kantien." *Henri Bergson*. Ed. Béguin and Thévenaz, 241-247. The author considers Bergson's and Immanuel Kant's conceptions of schematism and attempts to unify them.

2992   Sertillanges, Antonin Gilbert. "Bergson apologiste." *Henri Bergson*. Ed. Béguin and Thévenaz, 57-72. The author views Bergson as an apologist for Christianity, but an apologist "from without." Bergson's philosophy, he holds, is not Christian but comes close to Christianity in many respects.

2993   Sertillanges, Antonin Gilbert. *Lumière et périls du bergsonisme*. Paris: Flammarion, 1943, 64.

2994   Sorokin, Pitrim A. *Sociocultural Causality, Space, Time*. Durham, North Carolina: Duke University Press, 1943, 246. Cf. "Sociocultural Time", Ch. IV. esp. pp. 162-167, 200-201n.

2995   Thévenaz, Pierre. "Refus du réel et spiritualité." *Henri Bergson*. Ed. Béguin and Thévenaz, 97-104. The author considers Bergson's puzzling call to freedom for people who are, on his terms, already free. Difficulties in Bergson's concept of mystical intuition are also stressed.

2996   Wahl, Jean. "Présence de Bergson." *Henri Bergson*. Ed. Béguin and Thévenaz, 25-28. The author discusses Bergson's thought in the context of the history of Western philosophy and mentions a brief visit with Bergson in November 1940.

1944

2997   Asthana, H. S. "Bergson's Ethical Outlook." *Philosophical Quarterly* (India), 20, No. 3, July 1944, 149-152.

2998   Bard, Joseph. "Tradition and Experiment." *Royal Society of Literature of the United Kingdom, London, Essays by Diverse Hands*, N.S. 21, 1944, 103-124. Bergson and Proust are dealt with in this essay.

2999   Bonhomme, Mary Bernard. *Educational Implications of the Philosophy of Henri Bergson*. Washington, D. C.: Catholic University of America Press, 1944, xv, 208. "In the light of Catholic educational philosophy, one conclusion is unavoidable. Despite its many fine qualities and the genuine good will of its author, Bergsonism, like all modern philosophies, is exclusivistic. It is not based on a complete conception of reality." (183). The author gives a very general, rather minimal account of Bergson's philosophy of education.

3000   Bonhomme, Mary Bernard. "Educational Implications of the Philosophy of Henri Bergson." Diss., Catholic University of America, 1944, 184.

3001   Brightman, Edgar Sheffield. "Review of *Las Jerarquías del Ser y la Eternidad* by Alberto Rougés. *Philosophic Abstracts*, 3, Nos. 13-14, 1944, p. 32.

3002   Brasillach, Robert. *Les Quatre Jeudis: Images d'avantguerre.* Paris: Edit. Balzac, 1944, 519. Bergson is discussed on pp. 62-69.

3003   Brunschvicg, Léon. "Evolution de la pensée française." *La Nef*, 1, No. 2, août 1944, 36-54.

3004   Cassirer, Ernst. *An Essay on Man.* New Haven, Connecticut: Yale University Press, 1944, 237. Bergson is discussed on pp. 88, 89ff, 102ff, and 107.

3005   Copleston, Frederick Charles. "Review of *Roots of Bergson's Philosophy* by Ben-Ami Scharfstein." *Hibbert Journal*, 42, No. 167, 1944, 286-288.

3006   Dumontet, Georges. "Morality and Religion in the Philosophy of Henri Bergson: Exposition and Critique." Diss., Harvard, 1944, 320.

3007   Enver, Ishrat Hasan. *The Metaphysics of Iqbal.* Lahore, W. Pakistan: Muhammad Ashraf, 1944, 91.

3008   Iturrioz, J. "El cristianismo de Bergson." *Estudios*, No. 132, 1944, 9 *et seq.*

3009   Jérome, J. "L'Intelligence et intuition chez Bergson et St. Thomas." *L'Année Theologique*, 5, No. 3, 1944, 476-487.

3010   Jiminez Luque, Baldomero. "El valor noético del misticismo bergsoniano." *Spes Nostra*, 1, No. 1, 1944, 25-36.

3011   Jung, Carl Gustav. *Psychological Types: Or the Psychology of Individuation.* Trans. H. Godwin Baynes. London: Kegan Paul, Trench, Trubner & Co.; New York: Harcourt, Brace & Co., 1944, 654. There are numerous references in this study, first published in 1920, to Bergson. On pp. 398-399 the author criticizes Bergsonian intuition as incomparably inferior to Nietzsche's. On p. 400 he indicates that German intuition is far superior to French and American versions. On p. 568 he likens Bergsonian and Spinozist concepts of intuition. On p. 246 he likens a state of Brahmin to "durée créatrice;" on p. 265 he identifies "durée créatrice" with the Tao. *Psychological Types* is republished in C. G. Jung's *Collected Works*, 6.

3012   Keleher, James F. "The Search for the Intelligible Good." *Thomist*, 7, No. 4, 1944, 492-504. On p. 501 the author briefly discounts "Bergsonian vitalism" as being unable to distinguish living things from non-living.

3013   Maritain, Jacques. *De Bergson à Thomas d'Aquin: Essais de métaphysique et de morale.* New York: Edit. de la Maison Française, 1944, 269.

3014   Maritain, Raissa. *Les Grandes Amitiés: Les Aventures de la grâce.* Paris: Desclée de Brouwer, 1944, 262.

3015   Markrich, William Louis. "Hay Bergsonismo en la filosofía de José Enrique Rodó?" *University of Washington Abstracts of Thesis and Faculty Bibliography*, 8, 1944, 58.

3016   Meyer, François. *Pour connaître la pensée de Bergson.* Grenoble: Bordas, 1944, 124. (Coll ‹‹Pour connaître...››)

3017 Mirabent, F. "A Propósito de Bergson." *Revista de Ideas Estéticas*, 2, No. 8, 1944, 77-89.

3018 Nahm, Milton C. "Review of *The Roots of Bergson's Philosophy* by Ben-Ami Scharfstein." *Philosophic Abstracts*, 3, No. 13-14, 1944, 25-26. The reviewer is skeptical of the author's "narrow" methods.

3019 Noulet, Émilie. "Una doctrina de la vida." *Cuadernos Americanos*, 13, No. 1, Enero-Febrero, 1944, 86-96.

3020 Paulus, Jean. "Les Deux Directions de la psychologie bergsonienne: Behaviorisme et introspection dans *Matière et mémoire.*" *Tijdschrift voor Philosophie*, 6, Nos. 3-4, 1944, 297-332. This is a very penetrating analysis of Bergson's theory of mind-body interaction. Cf. the author 1943 for the predecessor of this article.

3021 Reulet, Aníbal Sánchez. "Review of *Las Jerarquías del Ser y la Eternidad* by Alberto Rougés." *Philosophic Abstracts*, 3, Nos. 15-16, 1944, 3-4.

3022 Sciacca, Michele Federico. *Il problema di Dio e della religione nella filosofia attuale.* Brescia, Italy: Morcelliana, 1944, 379. Bergson is discussed on pp. 29-47.

3023 Silva Garcia, Mario A. *Plenitude y degradación a propósito del Bergsonismo.* Montevideo, 1944.

3024 Tillich, Paul. "Existential Philosophy." *Journal of the History of Ideas*, 5, No. 1, January 1944, 44-70.

3025 Valéry, Paul. "In Memory of Henri Bergson." *Partisan Review*, 11, No. 1, Winter 1944, 18-21.

3026 Wahl, Jean. "Concerning Bergson's Relation to the Catholic Church." *Review of Religion*, 9. No. 1, November 1944, 45-50. In this brief article the author points out that though Bergson was, in the end, very close to Catholicism, he was never baptised. The obstacles which separated Bergson from this decisive act of union were, however, profound and permanent, and not temporary as some (Père Sertillanges) would have it. The author reproduces the "essentials" of Mme. Bergson's September 9, 1941 letter to *La Gazette de Lausanne* concerning her husband's attitude towards Catholicism.

3027 White, John S. "The Character and Development of Ernest Psichari: A Study on Fascism in France." *Psychiatry*, 7, No, 4, 1944, 409-423. Bergson's influence on Psichari is mentioned on pp. 417-418.

3028 Xirau, Joaquín. *Vida, pensamiento y obra de Bergson.* México: Edit: Leyenda, 1944, 157 (Col. Atalaya, 4).

1945

3029 Beer, François-Joachim. "Souvenir sur Henri Bergson." *Arts*, No. 20, 15 juin 1945, 3.

3030 Benda, Julien. *La France Byzantine; ou, le triomphe de la littérature pure, Mallarmé, Gide, Valéry, Alain, Giraudoux, Suarès, les surréalistes: Essai d'une psychologie originelle du littérature.* Paris: Gallimard, 1945, 291. The author cites Marcel Proust several times as a disciple of Bergson. Proust, Bergson and many others from S. Mallarmé to J. P. Sartre are roundly criticized here for their failure to adhere to Cartesian rationalism.

3031 Benda, Julien. "De la mobilité de la pensée selon une philosophie contemporaine." *Revue de Métaphysique et de Morale*, 50, No. 3, juillet 1945, 161-202.

3032 "Bergson au Panthéon." *Le Figaro*, 99, No. 127, 13 janvier 1945, 2. This article describes a dispute ouver whether Bergson's remains should be placed in the Panthéon.

3033 Bertocci, Peter A. "A Reinterpretation of Moral Obligation." *Philosophy and Phenomenological Research*, 6, No. 2, 1945, 270-283. On pp. 280-281 the author rejects Bergson's view that the experience of moral obligation is derived from social pressure.

3034 Billy, André. "Réorganisons le Panthéon." *Le Figaro*, 119, No. 133, 20 janvier 1945, 1. This article concerns a suggestion that Bergson's remains be buried in the Panthéon.

3035 Bisson, L.-A. "Proust, Bergson, and George Eliot." *Modern Language Review*, 40, No. 2, April 1945, 104-114. The author discusses the influence of Bergson as well as George Eliot on M. Proust.

3036 Blanchot, Maurice. "Quelques réflexions sur le surréalisme." *Arche*, 2, No. 8, 1945, 98-104.

3037 Bofill, Jaime. "La redención bergsoniana." *Cristiandad*, 2, 1945, 427-429.

3038 Bréhier, Emile. *Histoire de la philosophie*: Vol. 2. *La Philosophie moderne: 2e Partie*. Paris: Presses Universitaires de France, 1945, 1206. Bergson is discussed on pp. 1023-1034.

3039 Cantin, Stanislaus. "H. Bergson et le problème de la liberté." *Laval Théologique et Philosophique*, 10, No. 1, 1945, 71-102.

3040 Cantin, Stanislaus. *Henri Bergson et le problème de la liberté*. Quebéc: Ed. de l'Université Laval, 1945, 31. This is a Thomistic critique of Bergson's theory of "free will" in *Time and Free Will*. Bergson makes free will mere spontaneity, exclusive of the intellect.

3041 "Close to Catholicism." *Ave Maria*, 61, April 7, 1945, 210.

3042 Cotnarneanu, Léon, Ed. *Suites françaises: Par Henri Bergson, le duc de Broglie, Jules Cambon*. New York: Brentano's, 1945. This is a collection of articles from *Le Figaro*.

3043 Descaves, Pierre. "De Bergson à Valéry." *Gavroche*, 3, 13 septembre 1945.

3044 Dive, Pierre. *Les Interprétations physiques de la théorie d'Einstein*. "2e édition, revue et augmentée." Paris: Dunod, 1945, 80. "Préface de M. Ernest Esclangon. Avec le facsimile d'un autographe d'Henri Bergson." The author defends Bergson's interpretation of relativity theory.

3045 Fleming, William. "The Newer Concepts of Time and Their Relation to the Temporal Arts." *Journal of Aesthetics and Art Criticism*, 4, No. 2, December 1945, 101-106. Cf. esp. 104-105.

3046 Frondizi, Risieri. *El Punto de partida del filosofar*. Buenos Aires: Editorial Losada, 1945, 162. (Biblioteca Filosofica) The author states in his preface: "Cabe tan sólo destacar la resonancia que dejaron en el espiritu del autor las reiteradas lectuaras de Bergson, Husserl y Whitehead..." (p. 9).

3047 Gaos, José. *Dos exclusivas del hombre: La mano y et tiempo*. México: Fondo de Cultura Econoómica, 1945, 189. This book consists of five lectures developing the thesis that the human hand and human time are unique in nature.

3048   Gauthier, E. "Is Bergson a Monist?" *Philosophical Quarterly*, 19, No. 4, 1945.

3049   George, André. "Bergson et la déshumanisation de la science." *Nouvelles Littéraires*, No. 957, 6 décembre 1945, 5. This article recounts the proceedings of the first meetings of "Les Amis de Bergson." The basic subject discussed was the danger to man posed by his technology, as symbolized by the recently exploded atomic bomb. L. De Broglie, E. Le Roy, G. Marcel, and others entered into the discussion. Bergson, it was concluded, remains an optimist about technology.

3050   Guerin, Pierre. "Aristote, Bergson et Brunschvicg vus par Laberthonnière." *Revue de l'Histoire de la Philosophie Religieuse*, 25, No. 1, 1945, 52-70.

3051   Hersch, Jeanne. "Souplesse bergsonienne." *Labyrinthe: Journal Mensuel des Lettres et des Arts*, 2, No. 13, 6 août 1945.

3052   Iswolsky, Hélène. *Au Temps de la lumière*. Montréal: Edit. de l'Arbre, 1945, 260.

3053   Iturrioz, J. "El cristianismo de Bergson." *Vida Contemporáneo*, 6, No. 113, 1945.

3054   Kahn, Sholom J. "Henri Bergson's Method." *Antioch Review*, 5, No. 3, 1945, 440-441.

3055   Lacroix, Maurice. "Rolland, Péguy, Bergson." *Résistances*, 13 janvier 1945.

3056   Lavelle, Louis. *Du Temps et de l'éternité*. Paris: Editions Montaigne, 1945, 447. (Coll. Philosophie de l'esprit, 37)

3057   Marcel, Gabriel. "En Mémoire de Bergson." *Temps Présent*, 9, No. 21, 12 janvier 1945, 6.

3058   Maritain, Jacques. *Von Bergson zu Thomas von Aquin*. Cambridge, Mass.: Schönhof, 1945, 296.

3059   Maritain, Raissa. *Adventures in Grace: Sequel to 'We Have Been Friends Together.'* New York and Toronto: Longmans, Green and Co., 1945, 262.

3060   Maritain, Raissa. *Les Grandes Amitiés: We Have Been Friends Together*. 2nd ed. Trans. J. Kernan. New York: Longmans, Green and Co., 1945, 208.

3061   Mercanton, Jacques. "Une Visite à Bergson." *Labyrinthe. Journal Mensuel des Lettres et des Arts*, 2, No. 13, 13 octobre 1945, 6.

3062   Merleau-Ponty, Maurice. *Phénoménologie de la perception*. Paris: Editions Gallimard, 1945, 531. (Bibliothèque des idées) Cf. esp. the author's criticism of Bergson's conception of memory and the past on pp. 472-488. The cumulative nature of Bergson's duration must be rejected as not essential to true temporality.

3063   N., M. "Les Derniers Moments de Bergson." *Le Figaro Littéraire*, 119, No. 121, 6 janvier 1945, 2.

3064   Naville, Pierre. "Après Bergson." *Cahiers du Sud*, No. 271, 1945, 319-366.

3065   Paraf, Pierre. "H. Bergson et V. Basch." *Fraternité*, 12 janvier 1945.

3066   "A Paris et ailleurs: Sous la Coupole: Renfort pour le dictionnaire: Peur des mots: Bergson et la politesse: Bergson et Rembrandt." *Nouvelles Littéraires*, No. 951, 25 octobre 1945.

3067   Piechaud, Louis. "La Maison de Bergson." *Nouvelles Littéraires*, No. 927, 10 mai 1945.

3068   Raymond, Marcel. "Sur une définition de poésie" in *Paul Valéry: Essais et témoignages inédits*. Ed. Marc Eigeldinger. Neuachtêl: A la Baconnière, 1945, 37-47.

3069   Riess, Curt. "Notes on a Visit to France: How the Cultural Resistance Movement Operated." *Saturday Review of Literature*, 28, No. 15, April 14, 1945, 16-17,

72-73.

3070 Roig Gironella, Juan. "La sumisión de los místicos al dogma enjuiciada por Bergson." *Manresa*, 17, No. 1, 1945, 44-56.

3071 Romeyer, Blaise. *Le Problème moral et religieux*. Paris: Bloud et Gay, 1945.

3072 Russell, Bertrand. *A History of Western Philosophy*. New York: Simon and Schuster, 1945, 895. "Bergson" occurs on pp. 791-870. This article is reprinted from the *Monist*, 1912.

3073 Slochower, Harry. *No Voice is Wholly Lost*. New York: Creative Age Press, 1945, 404. On pp. 170-181 the author deals with Marcel Proust. He points up differences between Proust's notion of essences and Bergson's philosophy.

3074 Sokolow, Nahum. "Henri Bergson's Old-Warsaw Lineage." In *Jewish Frontier Anthology, 1933-1944*. New York: Jewish Frontier Associates, 1945, 345-359.

3075 Solonitsi, Tatiana. "A personalidade de Bergson." *Alio*, No. 17, 1945-1946, 5.

3076 Tharaud, Jérôme and Jean. "Encore le Panthéon." *Le Figaro*, 119, No. 134, 21-22 janvier 1945, 1-2.

3077 Valéry, Paul. *Henri Bergson: Allocution prononcée à la séance de l'Académie du jeudi 9 janvier 1941*. Paris: Domat-Montchrestien, 1945, 11 (Collection "Au Voilier").

3078 Vial, Fernand. "Le Bergsonisme de Paul Claudel." *Publications of the Modern Language Association of America*, 60, No. 2, June 1945, 437-462. Claudel's is an integral Bergsonism.

3079 Wahl, Jean. "Au Sujet des relations de Bergson avec l'Eglise catholique." *Nouvelle Relève*, 4, No. 1, avril 1945, 1-11.

3080 Widart, H. "A Propos de la philosophie bergsonienne." *Collectanea Mechliniensia*, N.S. 15, No. 1, février 1945, 15-60; No. 5-6, novembre 1945, 503-529.

3081 Xirau, Joaquin. "Time and its Dimensions." *Philosphy and Phenomenological Research*, 6, No. 3, 1945, 381-399. Trans. W. D. Johnson.

1946

3082 Adolphe, Lydie. *La Philosophie religieuse de Bergson*. Préf. Emile Brehier. Paris: Presses Universitaires de France, 1946, 236. The author demonstrates the unity of Bergsonism, relating it particularly to Taoism and Hinduism.

3083 Allers, Rudolf. "On Darkness, Silence, and the Nought." *Thomist*, 9, No. 4, 1946, 515-572. Bergson's treatment of nothingness is examined here on pp. 552-565. The author contends that Bergson's views are mistaken.

3084 Aubrun, Charles-Vincent. "La Critique littéraire et Bergson." *Mélanges littéraires et historiques*. Poitiers: Publications de l'Université, 1946, 232-239.

3085 Balcar, A. "Zaklady Bersonovy filosoficike soustavy." *Filosoficka revue*, 19, No. 3, 1946, 74-78; No. 4-5, 1946, 112-115. This essay surveys the foundation of Bergson's system from a Thomist viewpoint.

3086 Benda, Julien. "Le Procès du rationalisme." *La Pensée*, N.S. 7, avril-juin 1946, 100-103.

3087 Berger, Gaston. "The Different Trends of Contemporary French Philosophy." *Philosophy and Phenomenological Research*, 7, No. 1, 1946, 1-11. Bergson is discussed on pp. 2 and 6.

3088 "Henri Bergson." *Synthèses*, 5, No. 4-5, 1946, 244-247.

3089 Bonnet, Christian L. "Review of *The Creative Mind* by Henri Bergson." *Modern Schoolman*, 23, No. 4, May 1946, 222-223.

3090 Bordeaux, Henry. "Dernière Visite à Bergson." *L'Académie française en 1914: Histoire d'une candidature*. Paris: Edit. d'histoire et d'art, 1946, 78-86.

3091 Bréhier, Emile. "L'Idéalisme de L. Brunschvicg." *Revue Philosophique de la France et de l'Etranger*, 136. Nos. 1-3, 1946, 1-7. Bréhier stresses similarities between Brunschvicg and Bergson.

3092 Bréhier, Emile. *Notice sur la vie et les oeuvres de M. Bergson*. Paris: Firmin-Didot, 1946, 31.

3093 Casaubon, Juan A. *Aspectos del bergsonismo*. Buenos Aires, 1946.

3094 Chaumeix, André and Le Roy, Edouard. *Séance de l'Académie française du 18 octobre 1945: Discours de réception de M. Edouard Le Roy: Réponse de M. André Chaumeix*. Paris: Perrin, 1946, 63.

3095 Cuvillier, Armand. "Bergson et le message de l'Orient." *Nouvelle Littéraires*, No. 1005, 7 novembre 1946.

3096 Descaves, Pierre. "Autour des 'posthumes' de Valéry et de Bergson." *Erasme*, 1re Année, 1946, 411-413.

3097 Duboîs-Dumée, J.-P. "Péguy: Ecrivain bergsonien." *La Nef*, 3, No. 23, décembre 1946, 75-83.

3098 Esser, P. H. *Levensaspecten: Essays Over Bergson, Pascal, Kierkegaard en Dostoievsky*. Zutphen: Ruys, 1946, 130.

3099 Fernandat, René. "Bergson et Valéry." *Vie Intellectuelle*, 14, Nos. 8-9, août-septembre 1946, 122-146.

3100 Ferrater Mora, José. *Introducción a Bergson*. Buenos Aires: Ed. Sudamericana, 1946, 64.

3101 Frost, S. E., Jr. *Masterworks of Philosophy: Digests of 11 Great Classics*. Garden City, New York: Doubleday, 1946, 757. Selections from *Creative Evolution* are quoted on pp. 725-757.

3102 Garcia Bacca, Juan David. "Bergson o el tiempo creador." *Cuadernos Americanos*, 26, No. 2, marzo-abril 1946, 89-128.

3103 Gironella, Juan Roig. "Ensayo de filosofía religiosa." *Revista de Filosofía*, 4, No. 1, enero-marzo 1945, 197-203.

3104 Groot, M. "'La Durée' een sleutel tot de filosofie van Bergson." *Brandpunt*, 1, 1946.

3105 Groot, M. "Einstein, Bergson, Freud." *Het Baken*, 2, 1946.

3106 Hershey, John J. "Bergson's Influence in Latin America." *Latin American Thought*, 1, No. 2, January 1946, 1-2.

3107 Houf, Horace T. "Review of *The Creative Mind* by Henri Bergson." *Christian Century*, 43, No. 10, March 6, 1946, 305.

3108 Iberico, Mariano. *El Sentimiento de la Vida Cósmica*. Buenos Aires: Editorial Losada, 1946, 122.

3109 Joad, Cyril E. M. *Guide to Philosophy*. New York: Dover, 1946, 592.

3110 Knox, Israel. "Review of *The Creative Mind* by Henri Bergson." *Comment*, 2, 1946, 96.

3111   Krakowski, Edouard. *La Philosophie: Gardienne de la cité, de Plotin à Bergson.* Paris: Ed. du Myrtle, 1946, 292.

3112   Larrabee, Harold A. "Review of *The Creative Mind* by Henri Bergson." *Ethics,* 56, No. 3, April 1946, p. 233.

3113   Le Roy, Edouard and Chaumeix, André. *Séance de l'Académie française du 18 octobre 1945: Discours de réception de M. Edouard Le Roy: Réponse de M. André Chaumeix.* Paris: Perrin, 1946, 63.

3114   Lefèvre, Frédéric. *Ce Vagabond (Henri Bergson).* Moutins: Beffroi, 1946, 263.

3115   Madaule, Jacques. *Reconnaissainces III.* Paris: Desclée de Brouwer, 1946, 423.

3116   Maritain, Jacques. "The Bergsonian Philosophy of Morality and Religion." *Redeeming the Time.* London: Centenary Press, 1946, 74-100.

3117   Maritain, Jacques. *De Bergson a Santo Tomás de Aquino: Ensayos de metafísica y de moral.* Trans. G. Moteau de Buedo. Buenos Aires: Club de Letores, 1946, 254.

3118   Maritain, Jacques. *De Bergson a Tommaso d'Aquino: Saggio di metafisica e morale.* Trans. R. Bartolozi. Verone, Italy: Mondadori, 1946, 300.

3119   Maritain, Jacques. "The Metaphysics of Bergson." *Redeeming the Time.* London: Centenary Press, 1946, 46-73.

3120   Martins, Diamantino. *Bergson: A intuição como método na metafísica.* Porto: Tavares Martins, 1946, xv, 327.

3121   Moore, Merritt H. "Review of *The Creative Mind* by Henri Bergson." *Philosophical Review,* 55, 1946, 714-715.

3122   "Os Prêmios Nobel de literatura. XXV. Henri Bergson." *Leitura,* 4, No. 39, 1946, 9.

3123   Péguy, Charles. *Nota conjunta sobre Descartes y la filosofía cartesiana sequida de una nota sobre Bergson y la filosofía bergsoniana.* Trans. M. Brugnoli. Buenos Aires: Emecé, 1946, 349. The critical introduction is written by Carmen R. L. de Gándara.

3124   Pos, Hendrick Josephus. "Henri Bergson in memoriam." *Algemeen Nederlands Tijdschrift voor Wijsbegeerte en Psychologie,* 38, Nos. 3-4, 1946, 71-76.

3125   Pouillon, Jean. *Temps et roman.* Paris: Gallimard, 1946, 277. (La Jeune Philosophie)

3126   Radkowski, Tadeusz. "Henryk Bergson." *Tygodnik Warszawski,* 2, No. 3, 1946, 3-4.

3127   Romeyer, Blaise. "Autour du bergsonisme." *Archives de Philosophie,* 16, No. 2, 1946, 1-45 (Supplément).

3128   Romeyer, Blaise. "Le Problème moral et religieux: Maurice Blondel en regard d'Ollé-Laprune et de Bergson." *Hommage à Maurice Blondel.* Paris: Bloud et Gay, 1946, 49-80.

3129   Roustan, Désiré. *La Raison et la vie.* Intro. A. Cuvillier. Paris: Presses Universitaires de France, 1946, 200.

3130   Ruggiero, Guido de. *Filosofías del siglo XX.* Buenos Aires: Abril, 1946, 289.

3131   Scharfstein, Ben-Ami. "Review of *The Creative Mind* by Henri Bergson." *Journal of Philosophy,* 43, No. 10, May 9, 1946, 278. This is a brief, condescending review of the English translation of *La Pensée et le mouvant.*

3132 "Science et humanisme." *La Nef*, 2, No. 15, février 1946, 57-77.

3133 Sousa, Eudoro de. "Leonardo e Bergson, trecho do prefácio a una antologia de Leonardo." *Acçao*, 3, 4 aprile 1946.

3134 Tansey, Anne. "Henri Bergson: Abridged." *Catholic Digest*, 10, No. 9, September 1946, 27-29.

3135 Tansey, Anne. "The Triumph of a Soul." *Context*, 2, No. 2, October 1946, 13-15. This article is a condensation of an article which appeared originally in *The Lamp*.

3136 Tauzin, Sebastian. *Bergson e São Tomás: Conflicto entre a intuição e a inteligencia.* Pref. T. de Athayde. Rio de Janeiro: Desclée de Brouwer, 1946.

3137 Thomas, Henry, and D. L. Thomas. *Living Biographies of Great Philosophers.* Garden City, New York: Blue Ribbon Books, 1946, viii, 335. An essay on Bergson's philosophy appears here on pp. 307-322.

3138 Thyrion, Jacques. "Henri Bergson." *Revue Générale Belge*, 2, 1946, 74-79.

3139 Toupin, Paul. "Bergson et Proust." *L'Action Universitaire*, 13, novembre 1946, 18-30.

3140 Toupin, Paul. "Bergson et Proust." *Amérique Française*, 5, No. 8, novembre 1946, 18-30.

3141 Ushenko, Andrew. "Zeno's Paradoxes." *Mind*, 55, No. 218, April 1946, 151-165. This article examines various attempted refutations of Zeno, including Bergson's, which is likened to J. Wisdom's.

3142 Ushenko, Andrew P. *Power and Events: An Essay in Dynamics in Philosophy.* Princeton, N. J.: Princeton University Press, 1946, 301. On pp. 146-154 the author attempts to "rehabilitate" Bergson's reputation, which, he believes, was done in by the rise of relativity theory in physics. "No sooner had Bergson developed his central idea, that the spatializing schemes of the intellect distort our intuition of the absolute creative time, than Einstein demonstrated that time itself can be incorporated into a geometrical scheme of a four-dimensional world, and that alternative differentiations between time and space within the world are incompatible with the notion of an absolute time." (p. 146) Philosophers and physicists anxious to find a realist interpretation of relativity theory were not impressed with Bergson's *Duration and Simultaneity*, which made relativity theory an operational and not a metaphysical scheme. The advent of operationism as a philosophy of science, moreover, has not removed the stigma. Quantum physics, even if given a realist interpretation, justifies a dynamical (hence Bergsonian) philosophy of nature. An abstract, measurable time is not, for quantum physics, sufficient for the understanding of electronic phenomena. The most important misunderstanding of Bergson's philosophy, however, stems from a failure to see the place played in his philosophy by "power" (i.e., "potentiality").

3143 Vartiovaara, Klaus V. "Nykyaikaisen filosofian johtana aateita." *Volvoga*, No. 3, 1946, 53-58.

3144 Wahl, Jean. *Tableau de la philosophie française.* Paris: Fontaine, 1946, 235. R. Descartes, A. Comte, and Bergson are discussed at length in this study.

3145 Wavre, Rolin. "Les Possibles de Diodora à Bergson." *Alma Mater*, 3, 1946, 223-227.

3146 Xirau, Joaquín. "Crisis: Husserl and Bergson." *Personalist*, 27, No. 3, July 1946, 269-284.

3147   Zunini, G. "Henri Bergson." *Revue de Synthèse*, 5, Nos. 5-6, 1946.

1947

3148   Albert, Ethel. "Review of *The Creative Mind* by Henri Bergson." *Philosophic Abstracts*, 8, No. 25, 1947, 4.

3149   Andreu, Pierre. "Bergson et la théorie des mythes chez Sorel." *La Nef*, 4, No. 32. juillet 1947, 51-58. This article is reprinted from Andreu's *Notre Maître, Monsieur Sorel*, "La Trilogie de l'esprit." Paris: Table Ronde, 1947.

3150   Baratz, Léon. *Deux "Juifs-chrétiens": Henri Bergson et J.-J. Bernard*. Monte Carlo: L'auteur, 7 rue Bel Respiro, 1947, 6.

3151   Beck, Lewis White. "Review of *The Creative Mind* by Henri Bergson." *Philosophy and Phenomenological Research*, 7, No. 4, 1947, 659-661.

3152   Blanché, Robert. "Review of *L'Intellectualisme de Bergson* by Léon Husson." *Journal de Psychologie Normale et Pathologique*, 44, 1947, 246-247. The reviewer commends the author for his accurate examination of the development of Bergson's concept of intuition and for his refutation of the view that Bergson's philosophy is anti-intellectual.

3153   Bochenski, Innocentius M. *Europäische Philosophie der Gegenwart*. Bern: A. Francke Ag. Verlag, 1947, 304. (Sammlung dalp, 50) Bergson is treated here, along with W. Dilthey and the pragmatists, as an exponent of *Lebensphilosophie*.

3154   Bonhomme, Mary Bernard. *Educational Implications of Bergson's Philosophy*." *Catholic Educational Review*, 45, No. 10, December 1947, 615-616. This is an abstract of the author's dissertation, 1944.

3155   Boulanger, Maurice. "Cervantès et Bergson." *Lettres Romanes*, 1, No. 4, novembre 1947, 277-296.

3156   Bremond, A. "Réflexions sur l'homme dans la philosophie de Bergson." *Archives de Philosophie*, 17, No. 1, 1947, 122-148.

3157   Broglie, Louis de. *Physique et microphysique*. Paris: Albin Michel, 1947, 371. "Les Idées de Bergson sur le temps et le mouvement" is found on pp. 191-211.

3158   Brunet, Georges. "Autour de Pascal: II. Une Page retrouvé de Bergson." *Revue d'Histoire Littéraire de la France*, 47, No. 2, 1947, 169-171.

3159   Bruno, Antonio. *Religiosità perenne*. Bari: Laterza e Figli, 1947, 121. Chapter five, entitled "Bergson positiva e negativa dell'attavismo," is found on pp. 76-81.

3160   Burzio, Filippo. "Bergson e il problema della natura." *Agorā*, Anno 2, No. 8, 1947.

3161   Burzio, Filippo. "Scienza e filosofia bergsoniana." *Rassegna d'Italiana*, 2, 1947, 89-93.

3162   C., E. G. "Review of *Bergson e São Tomaz o conflicto entre a intuicāo e a inteligenica* by Sebastian Tauzan." *Sapientia*, 1, No. 3, enero-marzo 1947, 93-96.

3163   Challaye, Félicien Robert. *Bergson*. Nouv. éd. rev et augm. Paris: Mellottée, 1947, 309. (Les philosophes)

3164   Ciardo, Manlio. *Le quattro epoche dello storicismo: Vico, Kant, Hegel, Croce*. Bari: Laterza, 1947. The author compares Bergson and Croce on pp. 202-225, concluding that Bergson is as to Croce as Schelling is to Hegel.

3165   D'Aurec, Pierre. "De Bergson spencérien à l'auteur de l'*Essai.*" *Archives de Philosophie*, 17, No. 1, 1947, 102-121. Bergson's early intellectual development is chronicled in this article.

3166   Delattre, Floris. *Ruskin et Bergson: De L'Intuition esthétique à l'intuition métaphysique.* Oxford: Clarendon Press, 1947, 27. This is the Zaharoff Lecture for 1947. Cf. the author, 1932.

3167   Dolléans, Edouard. "Conversation avec Bergson sur la justice." *La Nef*, 4, No. 32, juillet 1947, 61-62.

3168   Domenach, Jean-Marie. "Essais." *Esprit*, 16e Année, No. 131, mars 1947, 528-530. Péguy and Bergson are discussed in this essay.

3169   Faral, Edmond and Le Roy, Edouard. *Hommage national à Henri Bergson à la Sorbonne, le 13 mai 1947.* Paris: Firmin-Didot, 1947, 10.

3170   Feuer, Lewis S. "Review of *Le Bergsonisme: Une Mystification philosophique* by Politzer." *Philosophy and Phenomenological Research*, 8, No. 3, 1947-1948, 470-472.

3171   Flewelling, Ralph Tyler. "Review of *The Creative Mind* by Henri Bergson." *Personalist*, 28, No. 1, 1947, 91-93.

3172   Forest, Aimé. "L'Existence selon Bergson." *Archives de Philosophie*, 17, No. 1, 1947, 81-101.

3173   Garcia Bacca, Juan David. *Nueve grandes filosofos contemporaneos y sus temas*: Vol 1. *Bergson, Husserl, Unamuno, Heidegger, Scheler, Hartmann.* Caracas: Imprenta Nacional, 1947, 316. Bergson is discussed on pp. 9-51.

3174   Gibson, A. Boyce. "Mystic or Pragmatist?" *Australasian Journal of Psychology and Philosophy*, 25, No. 1. 1947, 81-103. This is a review of *The Creative Mind*. The author draws interesting parallels between Bergson, pragmatism, and positivism.

3175   Gide, André. *The Journals of André Gide.* I, 1889-1913. Ed. and Trans. Justin O'Brien. New York: Alfred A. Knopf, 1947, 380. References to Bergson appear here on pp. 232, 233, and 287.

3176   Gilson, Etienne. "La Gloire de Bergson." *Tribune de Genève*, 29 mai 1947.

3177   Gilson, Etienne. "The Glory of Bergson." *Thought*, 22, No. 87, December 1947, 581-584.

3178   "God's Instrument." *Catholic World*, 165, No. 990, September 1947, 556-557. This is an excerpt from *The Two Sources*, with introductory comments.

3179   Gregh, Fernand. *L'Age d'or: Souvenirs d'efance et de jeunesse.* Paris: Grasset, 1947, 335. The author describes Bergson's visits with the Prousts on pp. 153-158.

3180   Gregoire, Franz. *L'Intuition selon Bergson: Etude critique.* Louvain: Nauwelaerts, 1947, 127.

3181   Gregoire, Franz. "Réflexions sur l'étude critique des philosophies intuitionnistes: Le Cas de l'élan vital chez Bergson." *Revue Philosophique de Louvain*, 3e Sér., 45, Nos. 6-7, mai-août 1947, 169-187. The author explores Bergson's claimed intuition of (1) self, (2) evolutionary factor, and (3) God. He validates 1 and 3, but claims that 2 is an inference.

3182   Guitry, Sacha. *Quatre Ans d'occupation.* Paris: L'Elan, 1947, 555. The author discusses an encounter with Bergson on p. 120.

3183   Havet, Jacques. *Kant et le problème du temps*. 2nd ed. Paris: Gallimard, 1947, 230. (La Jeune Philosophie, 4) See especially Chapter 4, "Le Temps et l'expérience interne."

3184   Husson, Léon. *L'Intellectualisme de Bergson: Genèse et développement de la notion bergsonienne d'intuition*. Paris: Presses Universitaires de France, 1947, 240. This is an important examination of the development of Bergson's concept of intuition. The author argues effectively against anti-intellectual interpretations of Bergson's thought.

3185   Jetté, Emile. "L'Illusion bergsonienne et la perception extérieure." *Carnets Viatoriens*, 12, No. 4, 1947, 266-276. This is a Thomistic exposition and criticism of Bergson's theory of perception. The author depicts Bergson's as an "idealistic theory of perception."

3186   Johnson, Allison H. "A. N. Whitehead's Theory of Intuition." *Journal of General Psychology*, 37, No. 1, 1947, 61-66. The author deals on pp. 63-64 with the distinction between Whitehead's and Bergson's concepts of intuition. Whitehead's intuition, the author states, is not to be distinguished from intelligence, and it is applied to both the physical and the vital. Moreover, Bergson seems to disregard the factor of "subjective form."

3187   Kadt, J. de. "Afscheid van Bergson" in *Verdediging van het westen*. Amsterdam: G. A. van Oorschat, 1947, 188-209.

3188   Kucharski, Paul. "Sur Le Point de départ de la philosophie de Bergson." *Archives de Philosophie*, 17, No. 1, 1947, 56-80.

3189   Lalande, André. *Vocabulaire technique et critique de la philosophie*. Paris: Presses Universitaires de France, 1947, 1280. "Cinquième édition, augmentée d'un grand nombre d'articles nouveaux." Bergson's concept of "immédiat" is discussed on pp. 460-462; "inconnaissable," on 473; "intuition," on 528; and "liberté," on 545.

3190   Lalou, René. *Histoire de la littérature française contemporaine*. Paris: Presses Universitaires de France, 1947, 447. Bergson and Péguy are discussed on pp. 322-323 and 333.

3191   Laporte, Jean. *La Conscience de la liberté*. Paris: Flammarion, 1947, 296. (Bibliothèque de Philosophie Scientifique) There are numerous references to Bergson in this defense of liberty. Cf. esp. pp. 56-62 for comparisons of Bergson's and Leibniz' concepts of freedom and causation; pp. 115-117 for an examination of Bergson's concept of "dynamic schema"; pp. 203-204 and 209-212 for an appreciative criticism of Bergson's concept of "choice".

3192   Lenoir, Raymond. "A Propos d'Henri Bergson." *Synthèses*, 2e Année, No. 7, 1947, 81-84. The author recalls events of Bergson's life from his lectures at the Collège de France through interviews in his later years.

3193   Le Roy, Edouard. "Une Enquête sur quelques traits majeurs de la philosophie bergsonienne." *Archives de Philosophie*, 17, No. 1, 1947, 7-21.

3194   Le Roy, Edouard. "Hommage à Henri Bergson." *La Nef*, 4, No. 32, juillet 1947, 47-50. Bergson "...avait même voulu pratiquer la biologie au laboratoire, en technicien." Bergson's scrupulous scientific preparation is discussed on pp. 47-48.

3195   Le Roy, Edouard and Faral, Edmond. *Hommage national à Henri Bergson à la Sorbonne, le 13 mai 1947*. Paris: Firmin-Didot, 1947, 10.

3196   Levron, Jacques. "Bergson: Professeur de littérature à Angers, 1882-1883." *Nouvelles Littéraires*, No. 1014, 9 janvier 1947, 6. This note concerns Bergson's courses at Angers on Rousseau and on literary criticism.

3197   Lippman, Walter. "Most Dangerous Man in the World." *Saturday Review of Literature*, 30, No. 34, 23 August 1947, 18. This essay is reprinted from *Everybody's Magazine*, July 1912.

3198   López-Morillas, Juan. "Antonio Machado's Temporal Interpretation of Poetry." *Journal of Aesthetics and Art Criticism*, 6, No. 2, 1947, 161-171. The author describes Machado as a "self-avowed disciple of Bergson" (p. 164). On pp. 164-169 he analyzes Bergson's influence on Machado.

3199   Maillard, Pierre. "Henri Bergson." *Philosophisches Jahrbuch der Görresgesellschaft*, 5, 1947, 409-412.

3200   Maire, Gilbert. "Le Bergsonisme dans la pensée sorélienne." *Fédération*, novembre 1947, 17-18.

3201   Marcel, Gabriel. "Les Amis de Bergson." *La Nef*, 4, No. 31, 1947, 176.

3202   Maritain, Jacques. *De Bergson à Thomas d'Aquin: Essais de métaphysique et de morale*. Paris: Hartmann, 1947, 333.

3203   Maurois, André. *Etudes littéraires*. Vol. 1. Paris: S. F. E. L. T., 1947, 248. A study of Bergson's philosophy appears here on pp. 149-181. Cf. also pp. 7-8 for the author's account of a visit to an ailing Bergson.

3204   Mavit, Henri. "Le Message de Bergson." *Culture Humaine*, 9, No. 9, août 1947, 481-501.

3205   Mercanton, Jacques. *Poètes de l'univers*. Paris: Skira, 1947, 230. Bergson is discussed on pp. 209-216.

3206   Meyer, François. *L'Accélération évolutive: Essai sur le rythme évolutive et son intérprétation quantique*. Paris: Librarie des Sciences et des Arts, 1947, 68. The author, who takes his inspiration from Bergson and also Pierre Teilhard de Chardin, finds an over-all regularity in biological evolution. This regularity is accelerative, involving a constant increase in the rate of evolution. The author develops a mathematics which he believes adequately describes, and predicts, the evolutionary advance: including the evident acceleration of the pace of human history.

3207   Michaud, Guy. *Message poétique du symbolisme*. Paris: Nizet, 1947. Vol. 3, *L'Univers poétique*, contains an essay entitled "Bergson philosophe de temps perdu." It appears on pp. 486-492.

3208   Mix, Paolo. "La Poetica Proustiana della penombra." *Letteratura*, 9, No. 1, 1947, 185-197. This article includes a discussion of Proust's relations with Bergson.

3209   Mochulsky, Konstantin V. *Doestoevskii: Zhizn i tvorchestv*. Paris: YMCA Press, 1947, 561. On pp. 243f the author describes F. Dostoevsky's *Crime and Punishment* as the work which most closely approximates Bergsonian "durée réelle."

3210   Morsier, Edouard de. *Silhouettes d' hommes célebres: Bergson, al.* Genève: Editions du Mont-Blanc, 1947, 135.

3211   Mougin, Henri. "The French Origin of Existentialism." *Science and Society*, 11, No. 2, Spring 1947, 127-143. Trans. H. F. Mins, Jr. Cf. esp. pp. 128-130 for Bergson's influence on existentialism.

3212 Moulyn, Adrian C. "Mechanism and Mental Phenomena." *Philosophy of Science*, 14, No. 3, 1947, 242-253. On p. 246 the author states, "According to Henri Bergson, the difference in time relationship between direct contact stimuli and response, and between visual and auditory stimuli and response, allows the animal time for the new function of choice. He points out that where an amoeba is determined by the stimuli which affect its surface, higher animals become 'centers of non-determination' as the distance increases between the object which causes the stimulus and the body of the animal. This means that a new factor, different from pure mechanisms, has been introduced."

3213 Muller, Maurice. *De Descartes à Marcel Proust: Essais sur la théorie des essences, le positivisme et les méthodes dialectique et reflexive*. Neuchâtel: Editions de la Baconnière, 1947, 161. The author states on p. 56, "L'influence de Bergson sur Proust est une influence diffuse, quoique tant de résultats abtenus par Proust dans sa recherche du Temps perdu sont comparables (et, peut-on dire, analogues) aux thèmes bergsoniens. C'est probablement grâce à Bergson que Proust s'est dégagé d'une psychologie conceptualle où la trop grande rigidité des notions laisse echapper la réalité mouvant du moi."

3214 Nance, John. "Are we Developing a New Faculty, the Awareness of Becoming?" *Hibbert Journal*, 45, No. 2, January 1947, 147-152.

3215 Nance, John. "Are We Developing a New Faculty?" *The Hibbert Journal*, 45, No. 177, January, 1947, 147-152. The "new faculty" of which the author speaks is the awareness of duration, and awareness first explicitly described by Henri Bergson around the turn of the century. The author notes (on p. 150) similarities between Bergson's world-view and the world described by twentieth century physics. "Somewhere there has entered into the field of human intuition an attitude which was never there before and which is the awareness of becoming. So that man today has an added faculty..." (pp. 151-152) Pressed to deal with this new situation, modern man lacks a sense of security.

3216 Oesterreicher, John M. "Henri Bergson and the Faith." *Thought*, 22, No. 87, December 1947, 635-678.

3217 Ortegat, Paul. *Intuition et religion*. Louvain: Institut supérieur de philosophie à l'Université catholique, 1947, 248. The author lumps Bergson, E. Le Roy, and the existentialists together under the same heading (intuitionism). He is higly critical of "intuitionism."

3218 Patri, Aimé. "Actualité ou déclin du bergsonisme." *Paru*, No. 32, 1947, 93-94.

3219 Politzer, Georges. *Le Bergsonisme: Une Mystification philosophique*. 2e éd. Paris: Editions Sociales, 1947, 112.

3220 Quiles, Ismael. "La filosofía de la religión según Bergson." *Ciencia y Fe*, 3, No. 3, julio-diciembre 1947, 36-43.

3221 Raymond, Marcel. *De Baudelair au Surrealism*. Paris: Librarie José Corti, 1947, 368. The author states concerning Bergson: "...une étude de son influence, au propre sens du mot, sur le mouvement poétique contemporaine serait parmi les plus difficiles qui soient...les analogies que preśente l'oeuvre du philosophe avec celles des poètes attestent dans la majorité des cas une partenté de la pensée speculative et de la littérature, sans qu'il soit permis de conclure à un rapport de cause à conséquence." (p. 70) Bergson's thought and the Zeitgeist thus developed on parallel trajectories. The author finds this parallelism in the writings of Lèon-Paul Fargue and O.-V. de Milosz, on pp. 124-127; in a mystical tendency among many French turn-of-the-century writers, on pp. 188-192. See also pp. 69, 194-195n, 222 and 357.

3222   Ricour, Aimé. "Morale et nature dans la philosophie morale de Bergson." *Archives de Philosophie*, 17, No. 1, 1947.

3223   Romeyer, Blaise. "Caractéristiques religieuses du spiritualisme de Bergson." *Archives de Philosophie*, 17, No. 1, 1947, 22-55.

3224   Roustan, Desirée. *Psychologie*. Nouv. ed. entièrement refondue par P. Burgelin. Paris: Delagrave, 1947, 519. (Leçons de philosophie)

3225   Sertillanges, Antonin Gilbert. "La Critica bergsoniana e la creazione 'ex nihilo'." *Quaderni di Roma*, 1, No. 2, marzo 1947, 101-110.

3226   Sorel, Georges. "Bergson et Pascal: Lettre inédite du 8 avril 1913." *La Nef*, 4, No. 32, juillet 1947, 59-60.

3227   Stark, Werner. "Diminishing Utility Reconsidered." *Kyklos*, 1, No. 2, 1947, 321-344. The author uses Bergson's critique of psychophysics in *Time and Free Will* to criticize the utilitarian quantification of pleasures which underlies classical economics.

3228   "Ein Streit um Bergson." *Abendland*, 2, No. 3, 1947, 89-90.

3229   Stur, Svätopluk. "Henri Bergson." *Tvorba*, 1, Nos. 1-2, 1947, 30-31. The author criticizes Bergson's dualism of intelligence and intuition.

3230   Thyrion, Jacques. "Bergson devant le désordre contemporain." *Revue Générale Belge*, No. 17, mars 1947, 703-709.

3231   Tindall, William York. *Forces in Modern British Literature, 1885-1946*. New York: Alfred A. Knopf, 1947, xiii, 386. Bergson is mentioned often in this study of recent British literature. "Classicist" objections to Bergson and his followers (for example, by Wyndham Lewis) are mentioned on pp. 105, 106, 108, and 109. Bergson's influence on George Bernard Shaw is noted on pp. 192-193. Bergson's influence on T. E. Hulme and British "imagism" is explained briefly on p. 264. Bergson's influence on the stream of consciousness novel is briefly touched on in pp. 284-285. Virginia Woolf's novels are said by the author to be more representative of the ideal of William James and Henri Bergson than those of James Joyce (p. 300); "Bergson's disciple Proust" is said to have influenced Woolf's later writing (p. 304n); that Woolf had not read Bergson but was familiar with him through the Bloomsbury group is asserted (p. 305).

1948

3232   Alexander, Ian W. "Review of *Ruskin et Bergson: De L'Intuition esthétique à l'intuition métaphysique* by Floris Delattre." *French Studies*, 2, No. 1, 1948, 98-99.

3233   Beauchataud, G. and Le Senne, René. "Le Caractère et l'écriture d'Henri Bergson." *Graphologie*, No. 30, avril 1948, 3-11.

3234   Blondel, Charles. *La Personnalité*. Paris: Presses Universitaires de France, 1948, 40. (*Nouveau Traité de Psychologie*, 7, No. 3, 1948, 97-137) The author concludes, on pp. 132-133, that Bergson's theory of the self is profounder than that of William James. Cf. also pp. 97, 121, 124.

3235   Boviatsis-Deschamps, Renée. "Le Bergsonisme est-il un humanisme?" Diss., Montpellier, 1948, 195. The author holds that Bergson envisaged man as capable, by his own capacities, of becoming semi-divine.

3236   Bréhier, Emile. "Liberté et métaphysique." *Revue Internationale de Philosophie*, 2, No. 5, 1948, 1-13. Bergson and others are treated in this study.

3237   Charlier. "Compte rendu de l'intellectualisme de L. Husson." *L'Education Nationale*, 2, No. 5, 29 janvier 1948, 14. This is a brief review.

3238   Claessens, François. "Bergson en Proust: Wijsgeer en dichter." *Streven*, 2, No. 1, 1948, 318-320. This is on Delattre's *Bergson et Proust*.

3239   Dalbiez, Rolland. *Psychoanalytical Method and the Doctrine of Freud*. Vol. 1. Trans. T. F. Lindsay. Intro. E. B. Strauss. New York: Longmans, Green and Co., 1948, 415. On pp. 100-101 the author criticizes Bergson's concept of negation; on p. 200 he claims that Bergson limits the sphere of habit to the body, denies (unlike Freud) that the mind can become habituated. Cf. pp. 210-223 for differences between Bergson and Freud that follow from this.

3240   Dalbiez, Rolland. *Psychoanalytical Method and the Doctrine of Freud*. Vol. 2. Trans. T. F. Lindsay. New York: Longmans, Green and Co., 1948, 331. Cf. p. 43 for "intuitive" recovery of memory, pp. 88-89 for distinction of two kinds of memory, pp. 233-234 for treatment of mind-brain relations. Cf. J. de La Harpe, 1943, for Bergson's very high opinion of this work.

3241   Delattre, Floris. "Bergson et Proust, accords et dissonances." *Etudes Bergsoniennes*, 1, 1948, 1-127.

3242   Derins, François. "En Marge du bergsonisme." *La Nef*, 5, No. 41, avril 1948, 135-136. The author discusses problems with Mlle. Lafranchi's thesis on Bergson at the Sorbonne.

3243   Derins, François. "Hommage national à Henri Bergson." *Etudes Bergsoniennes*, 1, 1948, 177-179. This article was originally published in *La Nef*, June 1947.

3244   Deshayes, Marius Louis. *La Foi bergsonienne*. Compiègne, France: Imprimerie de Compiègne, 1948, 37.

3245   Desternes, Jean. "Grèce: Kazantzakis nous parle de Bergson et d'Istrati." *Nouvelles Littéraires*, No. 1068, 13 février 1948, 5. Kazantzakis speaks here of Bergson's influence on him.

3246   Dimitroff, Emanouil P. *Estetikata na Bergsona*. Sofia: Kameñ del, 1948, 92. This book surveys Bergson's aesthetics.

3247   Dolléans, Edouard. "Review of *Ruskin et Bergson: De L'Intuition esthétique à l'intuition méataphysique* by Floris Delattre." *Etudes Bergsoniennes*, 1, 1948, 188-200. This review is laudatory.

3248   Drouin, Marcel. "Fragments philosophiques de la mémoire, du jugement, de l'action: Ribot, Bergson, Hamelin." *Revue de Métaphysique et de Morale*, 53, No. 1, 1948, 1-25. Hamelin gives us a better concept of "l'esprit" than does Bergson, according to the author.

3249   Du Bos, Charles. *Journal: 1924-1925*. Paris: Corrêa, 1948, 460. Bergson is discussed on pp. 63-68. This item first appeared in *Revue de Paris*, October, 1946.

3250   Eliot, Thomas Stearns. *Sermon Preached in Magdalene College Chapel, 7, March 1948*. Cambridge, 1948, 7. Here Eliot asserts that his "only conversion, by the deliberate influence of any individual, was a temporary conversion to

Bergsonism" (p. 5).

3251   *Etudes Bergsoniennes*. Vol. 1. Paris: Albin Michel, 1948, 220. Bergson and Proust, Bergson and Maine de Biran are discussed in this issue.

3252   *Etudes Bergsoniennes*. Paris: Albin Michel, 1949, Vol. 2, 273. Bergson's Latin thesis, Bergson and Plotinus, Bergson and England, and Bergson and existentialism are discussed in this isse.

3253   Gide, André. *The Journals of André Gide. II. 1914-1927*. Ed. and Trans. Justin O'Brien. New York: Alfred A. Knopf, 1948, 462. Gide asserts on p. 348 (March 1, 1924): "Thibaudet on Bergsonism; after having taken a great interest in the preface (all the greater since I know almost nothing of Bergson), I am losing contact. What I dislike in Bergson's doctrine is all I already thought without his saying it, and everything in it that is flattering, even caressing to the mind. Later on, his influence on our epoch will be thought to be seen everywhere, simply because he himself belongs to the epoch and constantly yields to the trend. Whence his *representative* importance." On p. 406 (July 18, 1927) Gide notes that he is having great difficulty reading Bergson's *Time and Free Will*.

3254   Gouhier, Henri. "Maine de Biran et Bergson." *Etudes Bergsoniennes*, 1, 1948, 131-173.

3255   Gouhier, Henri. "Les Rapports de Dieu et le monde dans la philosophie d'Henri Bergson." *Der Mensch vor Gott: Festschrift für Theodor Steinbüchel zu seinem 60. Geburtstag*. Düsseldorf: Patmos-Verlag, 1948, 291-302.

3256   Gurvitch, Georges. "La Philosophie sociale de Bergson." *Revue de Métaphysique et de Morale*, 53, No. 3, 1948, 294-306.

3257   Gusdorf, Georges. "Le Sens du présent." *Revue de Métaphysique et de Morale*, 53, No. 3, 1948, 265-293. H. Piéron, Pierre Janet, and Bergson are discussed in this article.

3258   Henry, André. *Bergson, maître de Péguy*. Paris: Editions Elzévir, 1948, 328. (Les Jeunes Etudes philosophiques)

3259   Hladki, Zygmunt. "An Approach to Bergson." *Hibbert Journal*, 47, No. 1, October 1948, 71-78.

3260   Kanters, Robert. "De Bergson à Bourvil." *Table Ronde*, 1re Année, No. 5, mai 1948, 840-843.

3261   Koppnang, Ole. "Etiske verdieri Henri Bergsons filosofi." *Spektrum*, 3, No. 2, 1948, 30-37.

3262   Lafranchi, Geneviève. "La Méthode de Bergson: De La Position du problème métaphysique." Diss., Paris, 1948.

3263   Lalou, René. "Review of *Bergson et Proust* by Floris Delattre." *Nouvelles Littéraires*, No. 1087, ler juillet 1948, 8.

3264   Landré, L. "Henri Bergson et l'Angleterre." *Langues Modernes*, 42, No. 2, 1948, 174-177.

3265   Lapique, Charles. "Espace de la peinture et espace de la nature." in *La Profondeur et le rythme*. Paris: B. Arthaud, 1948, 7-28.

3266   Laprade, Jacques de. "Autour de Bergson." *Arts*, No. 176, 23 juillet 1948, 2.

3267   Laprade, Jacques de. "Review of 'Bergson et Proust' by Floris Delattre." *Arts: Beaux-Arts, Littérature, Spectacles*, 6 août 1948, p. 2. This is a highly critical review.

3268   Lash, Kenneth. "A Theory of the Comic as Insight." *Journal of Philosophy*, 45, No. 5, February 1948, 113-121.

3269   Lazarev, Adolf-M. *Vie et connaissance: Essais traduits du russe par B. Schloezer*. Pref. Nicolas Berdiaeff. Paris: Vrin, 1948, 136.

3270   Le Senne, René and Beauchataud, G. "Le Caractère et l'écriture d'Henri Bergson." *Graphologie*, No. 30, avril 1948, 3-11. This article contains an analysis of Bergson's handwriting.

3271   Long, Wilbur. "Heterodoxy of Henri Bergson." *Personalist*, 29, No. 1, January 1948, 60-72.

3272   Magnat, G.-E. "Portraits graphologiques: Deux Philosophes: Henri Bergson et Louis Lavelle." *Une Semaine Dans le Monde*, 26 juin 1948. This article contains an analysis of Bergson's handwriting.

3273   Maire, Gilbert. "Review of 'Bergson et bergsonisme'. *Archives de Philosophie*, 17, Cahier I." *Etudes Bergsoniennes*, 1, 1948, 200-213. This is a review of an issue of the *Archives de Philosophie* dedicated to Bergson, his thought and influence. E. Le Roy, B. Romeyer, P. Kucharski, A. Forest, P. d'Aurec, A. Bremond, and A. Ricour contributed to the issue. The reviewer explains that the issue testifies to a remarkable effort by Catholic philosophy to grasp the essentials of Bergson's thought.

3274   Marcotte, Marcel. "Histoire de la philosophie: Bergson." *L'Enseignement Secondaire au Canada*, 28, No. 4, octobre 1948, 47-55.

3275   Maritain, Jacques. "Bergsons Metaphysik und Moral." *Philosophisches Jahrbuch der Görresgesellschaft*, 58, No. 3, 1948, 179-210. This is a translation from *De Bergson à Thomas d'Aquin*.

3276   Mayoux, Jean-Jacques. "Le Temps et la destinée chez William Faulkner." in *La Profondour et le rythme*. Paris: B. Arthaud, 1948, 303-331.

3277   Monroe, D. S. Warner. "The Vital Impulse as a Basis for Morality: A Critical Development of Bergson's Position." Diss., Washington at Seattle, 1948.

3278   Mossé-Bastide, Rose-Marie. "L'Intuition bergsonienne." *Revue Philosophique de la France et de l'Etranger*, 138, Nos. 4-6, avril-juin 1948, 195-206. Several aspects of intuition are discussed by the author.

3279   Noulet, Emilie. "Bergson et Valéry." *Lettres Françaises*, 1, No. 3, janvier 1948, 31-51.

3280   Papini, Giovanni. *Passato remoto: 1885-1914*, Firenze: L'Arco, 1948, 279. Bergson, R. de Gourmont, C. Péguy, R. Rolland, G. Sorel, LeCardonnel, and others are mentioned in this book.

3281   Pastori, Paolo. "Bergson e Sorel." *Dialoghi*, Anno 16, No. 4-5, 1948, 129-169.

3282   Pierre-Quint, Leon. "Un Effort pour dominer l'absurde." *Revue de Paris*, 75, No. 4, 1948, 68-78.

3283   Polin, Raymond. "Review of *L'Intellectualisme de Bergson* by Léon Husson." *Etudes Bergsoniennes*, 1, 1948, 214-217. The author is critical of Husson's definition of "intellect."

3284   Poussa, Narciso. *Bergson y el problema de la libertad*. Buenos Aires: Editorial Schapire, 1948.

3285   Prabhavananda, Swami. "Buddha and Bergson." *Vedanta for the Western World.* Ed. Christopher Isherwood. Hollywood, California: Marcel Rodd Co., 1948, 288-293.

3286   Prevost, Jean. *Les Caractères.* Paris; Albin Michel, 1948, 346. M. Barrès, Bergson, P. Bourget, P. Claudel, and others are discussed in this book.

3287   Rand, Benjamin, Ed. *Modern Classical Philosophers.* Boston: Houghton Mifflin Co., 1948, 892. This book includes selections from Bergson.

3288   Rangel Frias, Raúl. "Bergson." *Armas y Letras*, 5, No. 5, mayo 1948, 5.

3289   Salvan, Jacques L. "Des Conceptions bergsonienne et sartrienne de la liberté." *French Review*, 22, No. 2, 1948, 113-127. This essay contains interesting comparisons of Bergson and Sartre, particularly as concerns their concepts of temporality.

3290   Sartre, Jean-Paul. *The Psychology of Imagination.* New York: Philosophical Library, 1948, 285. Part One of this work, "The Certain", deals with images and imagery. The author cites Bergson here on pp. 9, 37-38, and 60-62. On pp. 85-89 he criticizes (while accepting in part) Bergson's concept of the "dynamic schema".

3291   Schluter-Hermkes, Maria. "Bergsons Verhältnis zum Christentum." *Hochland*, 42, No. 2, 1948-1950, 105-118.

3292   Sciacca, Michele Federico. "Review of *L'Intellectualisme de Bergson* by Léon Husson." *Giornale di metafisica*, 2, No. 3, 1948, 25-28.

3293   Sciacca, Michele Federico. "Review of *La Philosophie religieuse de Bergson* by Lydie Adolphe." *Giornale de metafisica*, 2, No. 3, 1948, 258.

3294   Smith, Norman Kemp. "Bergson's Manner of Approach to Moral and Social Questions." *Proceedings of the Aristotelian Society*, N.S. 47, 1948, 1-13. The author describes the dualistic character of Bergson's moral and social philosophy. Bergson holds "...that non-moral, natural necessities, give rise to a type of obligation upon which a static morality is based, and that the spiritual values give rise to a different type of obligation, upon which a creative morality is based." (p. 10) It follows, then, that there exist values "which can be determined in complete abstraction from natural necessities of every kind." (p. 10) While the author has profound sympathy for Bergson's views, he denies Bergson's sharp dualism: "*all* moral choices, not merely certain of them, are in some measure *forced* choices; and that all choices, *however forced*, are at the same time based on appreciation of values." (p. 11)

3295   Spitzer, Leo. "Patterns of Thought in the Style of Albert Thibaudet." *Modern Language Quarterly*, 9, No. 3, 1948, 259-272; No. 4, 1948, 478-491. The author denies that Thibaudet was a follower of Bergson.

3296   Sundén, Hjalmar. *La Théorie bergsonienne de la religión.* Trans. J. Nogué and M. Bouvier. Paris: Presses Universitaires de France, 1947, 319.

3297   Wahl, Jean. "Présence de Bergson." *Poésie, pensée, perception.* Paris: Calmann-Lévy, 1948, 116-118. (Cf. also pp. 113-115)

3298   Wavre, Rolin. "La Vie de l'esprit dans les mathématiques." *Synthese*, 6, Nos. 1 and 2, 1947, 11-24. The author describes three tendencies in the interpretation of mathematics: Platonism, Bergsonism, and Empiricism. Cf. pp. 14-17.

3299   Weber, Alois. *Der Begriff Intuition bei Descartes, Pascal und Bergson.* Luzern, Switzerland, 1948, 67 (Jahresber. d. Kanton höheren Lehranstalten 1947/1948).

3300   Wiener, Norbert. *Cybernetics: Or Control and Communication in the Animal and*
        the Machine. New York: Wiley & Sons; Paris: Hermann et Cie, 1948, 194. In
        Chapter I, titled "Newtonian and Bergsonian Time," the author concludes that
        organisms as well as cybernetic machines exist in an irreversible and to this
        extent Bergsonian time.

1949

3301   Adès, Albert. *Adès chez Bergon: Reliques inconnues d'une amitié.* Paris: N. Fortin
        et ses fils, 1949, 159. This is a republication of three articles published in 1918.
        It includes an account of an interview with Bergson in March 1918, and an
        exchange of letters concerning this interview. Bergson's political and social
        view are expressed.

3302   Adolphe, Lydie. "Emile Bréhier, 'Images plotiniennes, images bergsoniennes'
        (Discussion)." *Etudes Bergsoniennes,* 2, 1949, 215-222.

3303   Alexander, Ian W. "Review of *Les Etudes Bergsoniennes,* Vol. 1. Floris Delattre:
        Bergson et Proust. Henri Gouhier: *Maine de Biran et Bergson." French Studies,*
        3, No. 2, April 1949, 175-176.

3304   Alexander, Ian W. "Review of *Les Etudes Bergsoniennes,* Vol. II, 1949." *French*
        Studies, 3, No. 4, 1949, 373-374.

3305   Andreu, Pierre. "Bergson et Sorel." *Etudes Bergsoniennes,* 2, 1949, 225-226. The
        author examines G. Sorel's interpretation of Bergson as an essentially religious
        philosopher. This article is followed by an unpublished passage by Sorel, "La
        Trilogie de l'esprit."

3306   "Background to Bergson: A Study in Genealogy." *Tablet,* 194, No. 5712, November
        12, 1949, 313.

3307   Baruzi, Jean. "Emile Bréhier, 'Images plotiniennes, images bergsoniennes'."
        Etudes Bergsoniennes, 2, 1949, 215-222. The author participates here with
        several philosophers in a discussion of Bergson and Plotinus.

3308   Baruzi, Joseph. "Jean Hyppolite, 'Henri Bergson et l'existentialisme'." *Etudes*
        Bergsoniennes, 2, 1949, 208-215. The author participates here with several
        philosophers in a discussion of Bergson and existentialism.

3309   Battaglia, Otto Forst de. "Les Origines d'Henri Bergson." *Le Figaro Littéraire,*
        4, No. 193, 31 décembre 1949, 6.

3310   Bechara Hernandez, J. "La filosofía de Bergson." *Universidad de Antioquia* (Col-
        umbia), Ser. 6, Año 15, Nos. 94-95, 1949, 209-220.

3311   Bemol, Maurice. *Paul Veléry.* Paris: Les Belles Lettres, 1949, 454. Bergson and
        Valéry are discussed on pp. 426-427.

3312   Benda, Julien. *La Crise du rationalisme.* Paris: Edit. du Club Maintenant, 1949,
        125.

3313   Benda, Julien. "Un Phénomène moderne: La Volonté conciliatrice." *Etudes*
        Philosophiques, N.S. 4, No. 3 juillet-décembre 1949, 310-318.

3314   Bertocci, Angelo Philip. *Charles Du Bos and English Literature: A Critic and his*
        Orientation. New York: Columbia University Press, 1949, 285. This study
        contains many references to Bergson and Du Bos.

3315   Bibes, Jacques. "Contrainte sociale et vocation spirituelle dans la philosophie morale de Bergson." *Revue universitaire*, 58, 1949, 134-144.

3316   Blanchot, Maurice. "Symbolism and Bergson." *Yale French Studies*, 2, No. 2, 1949, 63-66.

3317   Bonnet, Henri. *Le Progrès spirituel dans l'oeuvre de Marcel Proust*: Vol. 2. *L'Eudémonisme esthétique de Proust*. Paris: Vrin, 1949, 293. Bergson and Proust are discussed on pp. 212-236.

3318   Bréhier, Emile. "Emile Bréhier. 'Images plotiniennes, images bergsoniennes'." *Etudes Bergsoniennes*, 2, 1949, 215-222. This is a discussion between Bréhier and several other philosophers of his article, "Images plotiniennes, images bergsoniennes."

3319   Bréhier, Emile. "Henri Gouhier. 'Maine de Biran et Bergson'." *Etudes Bergsoniennes*, 2, 1949, 198-199. The author argues that Bergson and Maine de Biran are entirely different in their approach and conclusions.

3320   Bréhier, Emile. "Hommage à Bergson." *Revue des Deux Mondes*, N.S. 2, No. 10, 15 mai 1949, 368-370.

3321   Bréhier, Emile. "Images plotiniennes, images bergsoniennes." *Etudes Bergsoniennes*, 2, 1949, 107-128.

3322   Breton, Stanislas. "La Notion de puissance et la critique contemporaine." *Sofia*, 17, No. 3-4, 1949, 290-293. The author cites criticisms of the concept of potential ("puissance") by Bergson, O. Hamelin, N. Hartmann, J.-P. Sartre, and L. Lavelle.

3323   Cairola, Giuseppi. "Bergson e Spinoza." *Rivista di filosofia*, 40, No. 4, 1949, 406-418. This article is republished in the author,s *Scritti*, Torino, 1954, 67-82.

3324   Cantin, Stanislas. "Henri Bergson et le problème de la liberté." Diss., Laval, 1949, 102.

3325   Chaumeix, André. "Hommage à Bergson." *Revue des Deux Mondes*, N.S. 2, No. 10, 15 mai 1949, 371-375.

3326   Church, Margaret. "Bergson's 'durée' in Modern English and American Literature." Diss., Duke, 1949.

3327   Clouard, Henri. *Histoire de la littérature française: Du Symbolisme à nos jours (1885-1914)*. Paris: Albin Michel, 1949, 665. The chapter entitled "Bergson libérateur" is an appreciative account of Bergson as a writer and of his literary influence.

3328   Costa de Beauregard, Oliver. "Le Principe de la relativité et la spatialisation du temps." *Revue des Questions Scientifiques*, 5e Série, No. 1, 1949, 38-65. The author concludes that, in spite of the success of Einstein's spatialized time, the Bergsonian aspects of time remain to be treated by science. Physicists should study Bergsonian duration as a challenge. This article is translated, with an introduction, in *Bergson and the Evolution of Physics*, (1969) Ed. P. A. Y. Gunter, 227-250.

3329   Cotranei, Giulio. "Henri Bergson e il pensiero biologico." *Idea*, 1, No. 24, 1949, 4.

3330   Delattre, Floris. "Review of *Approach to Metaphysics* by E. W. F. Tomlin." *Etudes Bergsoniennes*, 2, 1949, 265-269. Delattre is critical of Tomlin's dismissal of Bergson.

3331   Delattre, Floris. "Floris Delattre, 'Henri Bergson et l'Angleterre' (Discussion)." *Etudes Bergsoniennes*, 2, 1949, 199-208. This is a résumé of Delattre's previous article on Bergson and Great Britain, with additional insights. Bergson knew Britain as Victorian Britain.

3332   Deledalle, Gerard. *L'Existentiel: Philosophes et littératures de l'existence*. Paris: Lacoste, 1949, 291.

3333   Delhomme, Jean. "Durée et vie dans la philosophie de Bergson." *Etudes Bergsoniennes*, 2, 1949, 131-190.

3334   Devivaise, Charles. "Présence de Bergson." *Etudes Philosophiques*, N.S. 4, 1, janvier-mars 1949, 45-49.

3335   Dolléans, Edouard. "L'Influence d'Henri Bergson à travers les lettres françaises." *Etudes Bergsoniennes*, 2, 1949, 228-237. This essay examines the influence of Bergson on Charles Du Bos, Joseph Baruzi, and others.

3336   Dolléans, Edouard. "Review of *L'Intelligence créatrice* and 'Le Message de Bergson' by Henry Mavit." *Etudes Bergsoniennes*, 2, 1949, 257-264.

3337   Dresden, Samuel. *Bezonken avonturen: Essays*. Amsterdam: Meulenhoff, 1949, 189. Bergson, M. Proust, P. Valéry, and A. Camus are discussed in this work.

3338   Duggan, G. H. *Evolution and Philosophy*. Wellington, New Zeland: A. H. and A. W. Reed, 1949, 227. The first section (of three) contains criticisms of Bergson's evolutionary theories.

3339   *Etudes Bergsoniennes*. Vol. 2. Paris: Albin Michel, 1949, 273. Bergson's Latin thesis, Bergson and Plotinus, Bergson and England, Bergson and existentialism are discussed in this volume.

3340   Faville, A. "Review of *L'Intellectualisme de Bergson* by Léon Husson." *Revue Philosophique de Louvain*, 3e Série, 4, No. 4, novembre 1949, 527-529.

3341   Filloux, Jean-Claude. *La Mémoire*. Paris: Presses Universitaires de France, 1949, 128. Bergson is discussed on pp. 6-7, 15, 24, 34-36, 44-45, 72-73, 100, and 107-120. On pp. 110-121 the author criticizes Bergson's concept of memory: 1. Bergson reduces memory to an inferior aspect of itself, the conservation of images. 2. Bergson's concept of the image as a (static) photograph is now universally rejected. 3. Bergson's concept of "mémoire pure" is unintelligible. 4. Bergson's pragmatism is unacceptable.

3342   Galeffi, Romano. *La filosofia di Bergson*. Roma: Instituto Statele dei Sordomuti, 1949, viii, 191.

3343   Gauss, Charles Edward. *The Aesthetic Theories of French Artists 1885 to the Present*. Baltimore: Johns Hopkins Press, 1949, 111.

3344   Gide, André. *The Journals of André Gide. III. 1928-1939*. Ed. and Trans. Justin O'Brien. New York: Alfred A. Knopf, 1949, 450. On p. 244 (July 19, 1932) Gide speaks of Paul Nizan, who, he states, would not attack art and philosophy for fear of losing some of his allies, the scoffers. "The scoffers would no longer be on his side, not those who are delighted to see him make fun of Bergson or Brunschvicg because ratiocination bores them."

3345   Giusso, Lorenzo. *Bergson*. Milano: Bocca, 1949, 239.

3346   Gouhier, Henri. "Bergson et l'histoire des idées." *Revue Internationale de Philosophie*, 3, No. 10, 1949, 407-433.

3347   Gouhier, Henri. "Review of 'L'Intuition bergsonienne' by R.-M. Mossé-Bastide." *Etudes Bergsoniennes*, 2, 1949. 250-251.

3348 Gouhier, Henri. "Review of *La Théorie bergsonienne de la religion* by Hjalmar Sunden." *Etudes Bergsoniennes*, 2, 1949, 244-250. The author takes issue with supposed "influences" on Bergson. In general, he is appreciative.

3349 Green, Frederick Charles. *The Mind of Proust: A Detailed Interpretation of "A La Recherche du temps perdu."* Cambridge, England: Cambridge University Press, 1949, 546. Bergson's influence on Proust is discussed on pp. 494-546.

3350 Gregoire, Franz. "La Collaboration de l'intution et de l'intelligence." *Revue Internationale de Philosophie*, 3, No. 3, 1949, 392-406.

3351 H., D. Z. "Thibaudet, or, the Critic as Mediator." *Yale French Studies*, 2, No. 3, 1949, 74-78. The influence of Bergson on Thibaudet is discussed on pp. 77-78.

3352 Hage, Kamal el. "La Valeur du langage chez Henri Bergson: Exposé et critique." Diss., Paris: 1949, 206.

3353 "Hommage à Bergson: Allocution de Stanislas Sicé, Emile Bréhier, André Chaumeix." *Revue des Deux Mondes*, N.S. 2, No. 10, 15 mai 1949, 364-375.

3354 Hubert, Judd D. "the Influence of H. Bergson on Contemporary Esthetics (in France)." Diss., Columbia, 1949.

3355 Hulme, Thomas Ernest. *Speculations: Essays on Humanism and the Philosophy of Art.* Ed. Herbert Read. London: Routledge and Kegan Paul, Ltd., 1949, 271. The foreward is by Jacob Epstein. The following chapters on Bergson occur on the following pages: "Bergson's Theory of Art," 143-169; "The Philosophy of Intensive Manifolds," 173-214.

3356 Husson, Léon. "Les Aspects méconnus de la liberté bergsonienne." *Actes du 4e Congrès des Sociétés de Philosophie de Langue Française.* Neuchâtel, Switzerland: La Baconnière, 1949, 373-391.

3357 Husson, Léon. "Renée Boviatis-Deschamps. Le Bergsonisme est-il un humanisme? Thèse présentée à la Faculté des Lettres de Montpellier, 195 pages dactylographiées, 1948." *Etudes Bergsoniennes*, 2, 1949, 251-256. This is an appreciative review, which, however, criticizes the author's failure to deal with the step by step development of Bergson's thought. Bergson did not intend men to become "gods."

3358 Hyppolite, Jean. "Aspects divers de la mémoire chez Bergson." *Revue Internationale de Philosophie*, 3, No. 10, 1949, 373-391. The author deals with the distinction between past and present in Bergson: a distinction which he holds in far more basic than that between image memory and habit memory. Past (contemplation) and present (action) are separate, but are bound together by "living memory." Pure memory is not a collection of images, but a profound unity of "virtual" imagery.

3359 Hyppolite, Jean. "Du Bergsonisme à l'existentialisme." *Universidad National. Cuyo, Actas primero Congreso nacional de Filosofía*, 1, 1949, 442-455.

3360 Hyppolite, Jean. "Emile Bréhier, 'Images plotiniennes, images bergsoniennes'." *Etudes Bergsoniennes*, 2, 1949, 215-222. The author participates here with several philosophers in a discussion of Bergson and Plotinus.

3361 Hyppolite, Jean. "Jean Hyppolite, 'Henri Bergson et l'existentialism'." *Etudes Bergsoniennes*, 2, 1949, 208-215. The author participates here with several philosophers in a discussion of Bergson and existentialisme.

3362   Hyppolite, Jean. "Vie et philosophie de l'histoire chez Bergson." *Universidad nacional. Cuyo, Actas primero Congreso nacional de Filosofía*, 2, 1949, 915-921.

3363   Iriarte, Joaquín de. "Review of *Nueve grandes filósofos contemporáneos y sus temas* by J. David García Bacca." *Razón y Fe*, 140, No. 620-621, 1949, 235.

3364   Jones, Joseph. "Emerson and Bergson on the Comic." *Comparative Literature*, 1, No. 1, 1949, 63-72.

3365   Jurēvičs. Paulis. *Henri Bergson: Eine Einführung in seine Philosophie*. Freiburg, Germany: Alber, 1949, 268.

3366   Kahn, Sholom J. "Isms in Art." *Saturday Review of Literature*, 32, No. 49, December 3, 1949, 66-67. This is a review of *The Aesthetic Theories of French Artists* by C. E. Gauss.

3367   Koestler, Arthur. *Insight and Outlook*. London and New York: Macmillan, 1949, xiv, 442. Detailed analyses of Freud's and Bergson's theories of humor are contained in Appendix II of this book.

3368   Larrabee, Harold A. *Selections From Bergson*. New York: Appleton-Century-Crofts, 1949, xix, 160.

3369   Leibrich, Louis. "Iphigénie en Tauride à la lumière de la philosophie d'aujourd'hui." *Etudes Germaniques*, 4e Année, No. 2-3, avril-septembre 1949, 129-138. This essay deals with Bergson and several other contemporary philosophers.

3370   Le Senne, René. *Introduction à la philosophie*. Pref. L. Lavelle. Paris: Presses Universitaires de France, 1949, xii, 476. O. Hamelin, Bergson, and others are discussed in this study.

3371   Lion, Ferdinando. *Lebensquellen französischer Metaphysik: Descartes, Rousseau, Bergson*. Trans. R. Gillischewski. Hamburg: Claasen and Goverts; Zürich: Europa-Verlag, 1949, 128.

3372   Lion, Fernand. *Cartesio, Rousseau e Bergson: Saggio di storia vitalista della filosofia*. Trans. L. Anceschi. Milano: Bompiani, 1949, 183.

3373   Lowe, Victor. "The Influence of Bergson, James, and Alexander on Whitehead." *Journal of the History of Ideas*, 10, No. 2, 1949, 267-296. The author argues that very little influence was exerted by Bergson on A. N. Whitehead.

3374   Maire, Gilbert. "Les Années de Bergson à Clermont-Ferrand." *Glanes*, 2, mars-avril 1949.

3375   Maire, Gilbert. "Les Années de Bergson à Clermont-Ferrand avant les *Données immédiates de la conscience*." *Proceedings of the Tenth International Congress of Philosophy*. Amsterdam: North-Holland Publishing Company, 1949, 1207-1209.

3376   Maire, Gilbert. "Bergsonisme et fédéralisme." *Fédération*, décembre 1949.

3377   Maire, Gilbert. "Jean Hyppolite. 'Henri Bergson et l'existentialisme'." *Etudes Bergsoniennes*, 2, 1949, 208-215. The author participates here with several philosophers in a discussion of Bergson and existentialism.

3378   Maire, Gilbert. "Un Jugement littéraire récent sur Henri Bergson." *Etudes Bergsoniennes*, 2, 1949, 238-243. This is a review of Clouard, *Histoire de la littératrue française*. "Pour la première fois, à ma connaissance, un philosophe est dignement étudiè dans une oeuvre strictement littéraire et par un pur littérateur." (243).

3379   Marcel, Gabriel. "Floris Delattre, 'Henri Bergson et l'Angleterre'." *Etudes Bergsoniennes*, 2, 1949, 199-208. The author participates here with several philosophers in a discussion of Bergson and Great Britain.

3380   Maritain, Raissa. *Souvenirs*. Vol. i of *Les Grandes Amitiés*. 2nd ed. Paris: Desclée de Brouwer, 1949, 439. Bergson is discussed here on pp. 77-97.

3381   Mayer, Hans. "Welt und Wirkung Henri Bergsons." *Literatur der Übergangszeit: Essays*. Wiesbaden, Germany: Limes Verlag, 1949, 98-116.

3382   Mayer, Hans. *Literatur der Übergangszeit*. Wiesbaden: Limes Verlag, 1949, 255. A section of this work titled "Welt und Wirkung Henri Bergson" may be found on p. 98 and following.

3383   Meyer, Hans. "Die Lebensphilosophie in Frankreich: Henri Bergson." *Geschichte der abendländischen Weltanschauung. Vol. 5. Die Weltanschauung der Gegenwart*. Würzburg, Germany: Schöningh, 1949, 245-266.

3384   Millas, Jorge. "Goethe en Bergson." *Asomante*, 5, No. 4, 1949, 104-116.

3385   Monroe, Warner. "The Vital Impulse and Spiritual Aspiration." *Ethics*, 59, No. 3, April 1949, 201-210.

3386   Mossé-Bastide, Rose-Marie. "Bergson et Spinoza." *Revue de Métaphysique et de Morale*, 54, No. 1, 1949, 67-82.

3387   Müller, Claus G. "Henri Bergson." *Das jüdische Gemeindeblatt*, 4, No. 42, 1949, 7.

3388   Osuegada, Raul. *El problema de la libertad y personalidad en la temática bergsoniana*. Guatemala: Universidad de San Carlos de Guatemala, Facultad de Humanidades, 1949, 80. The author argues as follows. Bergson holds that reason is capable of comprehending extension or substance but that duration or becoming can only be understood intuitively. The conclusions of reason are deterministic, while those of intuition are vitalistic or creative. Although indeterminacy or incipient creativity is characteristic of all life, it is only in man that it is coupled with the ability to react in terms of past experience. This reaction in terms of the totality of one's experience is personality.

3389   Poulet, Georges. *Etudes sur le temps humain*. Edinburgh: University Press, 1949, 407. Bergson's influence is found throughout this study of man's sense of time.

3390   Rose, Mary C. "Three Hierarchies of Value: A Study in the Philosophies of Value of Henri Bergson, Alfred North Whitehead, and Søren Kierkegaard." Diss., Johns Hopkins, 1949, 310.

3391   Rosenbloom, Joseph. "The Internal Structure of Bergson's Philosophy." Diss., Chicago, 1949.

3392   Rousseaux, André. "Etudes Bergsoniennes." *Le Figaro Littérarie*, 4 juin 1949.

3393   Salinas Quiroga, Genaro. "Bergson y la moral." *Armas y Letras*, 6, No. 8, agosto 1949, 1. 6.

3394   Schwiesselman, Martin. "Henri Bergson." *Neuphilosophische Zeitschrift*, 1, No. 3, 1949, 1-8.

3395   "Review of *El Sentimiento de la Vida Cósmica* by Mariano Iberico." *Philosophic Abstracts*, 11, No. 32, Summer, 1949, 31.

3396   Sicé, Stanislas. "Hommage à Bergson." *Revue des Deux Mondes*, N.S. 2, No. 10, 15 mai 1949, 364-367.

3397   Sorel, Georges. "La Trilogie de l'esprit." *Etudes Bergsoniennes*, 2, 1949, 226-227. This is a previously unpublished passage by Sorel concerning the religious import of Bergson's thought.

3398 Stark, Werner. "Henri Bergson: A Guide for Sociologists." *Revue Internationale de Philosophie*, 3, No. 10, 15 octobre 1949, 407-443. The author argues that sociology has not yet overcome two 19th-century legacies: the concept of society as a great organism and the concept of society as a great machine. He offers in their place Bergson's *The Two Sources of Morality and Religion*: "It is Bergson's outstanding importance for the sociologist that his philosophy offers annihilating criticisms of both these theoretical tendencies, and thus clears the way for a sounder system of social analysis" (p. 408) The author notes articles in *Kylos*, 1947 and yet to come (1950) in which he brings Bergson's ideas to bear on similar weaknesses of modern economics.

3399 Sunden, Hjalmar. "Bergson en Suède." *Revue Internationale de Philosophie*, 3, No. 10, 1949, 445-458.

3400 Torres, J. V. "El primado de la temporalidad." *Actas del Primero Congreso Nacional de Filosofía de Argentina*, 2, 1949, 858-864.

3401 Ward, Anne. "Speculations on Eliot's Time-World: An Analysis of *The Family Reunion* in Relation to Hulme and Bergson." *American Literature*, 21, No. 1, March 1949, 18-34. The author explores the extent to which the poet T. S. Eliot was influenced by Bergson through the thought of T. E. Hulme.

1950

3402 Alavoine, Maurice. "Quelques Remarques sur une origine commune de la magie et de la religion selon Bergson." *Revue de la Méditerranée*, 8, No. 4, 1950, 421-440; No. 5, 1950, 553-371; No. 6, 1950, 694-716. The author denies Bergson's contention that magic and religion have a common origin. Magic developed earlier than religion and has nothing to do with an alienation deriving from the use of human intelligence, while religion is specifically derived from that alienation. Magic has purely instinctive origins.

3403 Aliotta, Antonio. *Le origini dell'irrazionalismo contemporaneo*. 2nd ed. Napoli: Libreria scientifica editrice, 1950, xxxvii, 326, (Filosofia e pedagogia).

3404 Benda, Julien. *De Quelques Constantes de l'esprit humaine: Critique du mobilisme contemporain. (Bergson, Brunschvicg, Boutroux, Le Roy, Bachelard, Rougier)*. Paris: Gallimard, 1950, 213.

3405 Berndtson, Arthur. "Chapter Thirty. Vitalism." in *A History of Vitalism*. Ed. Virgilius Ferm. New York: Philosophical Library, 1950, 375-386. The author describes F. Nietzsche and Bergson as the foremost proponents of vitalism. He discusses Bergson on pp. 380-385, noting his powerful influence on three Latin American philosophers: Alejandro Korn (Argentina), Jose Vasconselos and Antonio Caso (Mexico).

3406 Bourloud, Albert. *De la psychologie a la philosophie*. Paris: Hachette, 1950, 238. On pp. 26-31 the author argues that though psychology may not agree with Bergson's conclusions, it must employ Bergson's *method* in search of the immediate data of consciousness. Cf. also pp. 78-89, 93-94, 104-107, 172-175.

3407 Cambon, G. "L'ombra di Bergson e la letteratura contemporanea." *L'ultima*, Anno 5, maggio-giugno 1950.

3408   Čapek, Milič. "Stream of Consciousness and 'durée réelle.'" *Philosophy and Phenomenological Research*, 20, No. 3, March 1950, 331-353. The author provides a very clear and very perceptive analysis of the similarities and differences between Bergson and William James concepts of psychological time.

3409   Castellani, Leonardo. "Bergson." *Humanidades* (Salta), Año 3, No. 7, 1950, 26-32.

3410   Cavarnos, Constantine. *A Dialogue Between Bergson, Aristotle and Philologus.* Cambridge, Massachusetts: The Author, 1950, 60. Perennial problems of change, knowledge and the structure of reality are approached in this book at an introductory level.

3411   Cesselin, Félix. *La Philosophie organique de Whitehead.* Paris: Presses Universitaires de France, 1950, 248. Bergson's and Whitehead's similarities are discussed on pp. 64-65, 88-89, 104-105, 128-129, 172-173, 178-179, 200-201, 204, and 205.

3412   Cohen, Robert Joseph. *Morale individualiste ou morale sociale: Henri Bergson ou Josué Jéhouda.* Pref. Henri Baruk. Paris: La Colonne Verdôme, 1950, 47.

3413   Cornu, Auguste. "Bergsonisme et existentialisme." In *La Philosophie française*, Vol. II of *L'Activité philosophique contemporaine en France et aux Etats-Unis.* Ed. Marvin Farber. Paris: Presses Universitaries de France, 1950, 164-183.

3414   Datta, Dhirendra Mohan. *The Chief Currents of Contemporary Philosophy.* Calcutta: Calcutta University Press, 1950, 541.

3415   Dejardin, André. "Bergson aux frontières du catholicisme." *Synthèse*, 4, No. 47, avril 1950, 192-195.

3416   Delattre, Floris. *Feux d'automne: Essais choisis.* Paris: Didier, 1950, 284."

3417   Du Bos, Charles. "Begegnung mit Bergson." *Merkur*, 4, No. 8, 1950, 854-861.

3418   Fauconnet, Charles-André. "Review of *Bergson* by Félicien Challaye." *Erasmus*, 3, No. 17-18, 1950, 547-550.

3419   Fisher, Ronald A. *Creative Aspects of Natural Law.* The Fourth Arthur Stanley Eddington Memorial Lecture. Cambridge: The University Press, 1950, 23. The author, one of the founders of recent evolutionary theory, argues that philosophers such as Henri Bergson, Jan Christian Smuts, and Alfred North Whitehead have been correct to stress the creative character of evolution. Creative causality is inextricably linked with indeterminism, which is a fundamental feature of 20th century physics. "Bergson's title *L'Évolution créatrice* was therefore well justified, and well in advance of his time. The biological thought of his age *was* impeded and constricted by the assumption of completely deterministic causation; the so-called 'Mutation theory,' as a contribution to evolutionary thought, seems to me to be typical of the relative sterility of the epoch. Bergson, with striking originality, broke away from this assumption." (pp. 6-7). Bergson's error lay in his failure to distinguish clearly between determinism and mechanism, and his consequent introduction of the *élan vital*, a spiritual being whose mode of operation is "magical"(p. 10).

3420   Forest, Aimé. "Histoire de la philosophie." *Revue Thomiste*, 50, No. 1, 1950, 231-241. The author reviews books on Bergson by L. Husson and H. Gouhier.

3421   Forsyth, T. M. "Creative Evolution in its Bearings on the Idea of God." *Philosophy*, 25, No. 94, July 1950, 195-208. The author holds: "Foundational for the whole doctrine of Creative Evolution is the philosophy of Bergson, and the principle has been one of the most prominent in philosophy, ever since the publication of his epoch-making book bearing that title." (195).

3422   Fowlie, Wallace. *Age of Surrealism*. Bloomington, Indiana: Indiana University Press, 1950, 215. The influence of Bergson on surrealism is discussed on pp. 19-20, 86, and 104.

3423   Gregoire, Franz. *L'Intuition selon Bergson: Fasc. 2. Complément sur la fidélité de Bergson aux documents mystiques*. Louvain: Université, 1950, 106.

3424   Grozev, Grozyu P. *Bergsonizŭm i dialekticheski materializŭm*. София: Наука и изкуство, 1950, 145. Bergson's psychology is viewed by the author as a "form of bourgeois subjective-idealist psychology" and his views of heredity and development are seen as "idealistic and anti-scientific." The psychology of Pavlov is in decisive opposition to the Bergsonian introspective, subjective concept of consciousness. According to Pavlov consciousness is the highest neural activity, conditioned by the action of the external world. (I. D. London. *Psychological Abstracts*, 27, No. 1, 1953, p. 2)

3425   Guitton, Jean. "Souvenirs sur les relations de M. Loisy et de M. Bergson." *Mémorial J. Chaine*. Lyon: Facultés Catholiques, 1950, 187-202.

3426   Gurvitch, Georges. *La Vocation actuelle de la sociologie*. Paris: Presses Universitaires de France, 1950, 607. "La Théorie sociologique de Bergson" is discussed on pp. 554-567; "La Thèorie de la magie chez Bergson," pp. 436-442.

3427   Guyot, Charly. "Péguy et Bergson." *Revue d'Histoire de Philosophie Religieuse*, 13e Année, No. 2, 1950, 273-289.

3428   Heintz, Joseph-Walter. "La Notion de conscience chez William James et Henri Bergson." Diss., Paris, 1950.

3429   Hengstenberg, Hans Eduard. "Henri Bergson in Deutschland." *Die Besinnung*, 5, 1950, 248-254.

3430   Henry, André. "Du vrai sérieux vécu par Péguy et sérieux inauthentique décrit par l'existentialisme athée." *Amitié Charles Péguy, Bulletin Trimestriel*, 18, 1950, 1-17. The author uses the concept of "seriousness" to distinguish between Péguy's Bergsonian position and the existentialist attitude.

3431   Husson, Léon. "Y a-t-il de l'intellectualisme chez Bergson? Réponse à M. J. Benda." *Etudes Philosophiques*, N.S. 5, No. 2, avril-juin 1950, 233-239.

3432   Jeanson, Francis. *Signification humaine du rire*. Paris: Editions du Seuil, 1950, 213. Bergson's concept of laughter is discussed on pp. 33-41 and throughout. The author criticizes Bergson's concept of laughter for its dualistic basis, which renders laughter inhuman, humans *per se* incapable of laugher.

3433   Johannet, René. *Vie et mort de Péguy*. Paris: Flammarion, 1950, 474 pp. (Les Grandes Biographies) Chapter thirtyfour of this work (pp. 387-398) is titled "A la rescousse de Bergson. A la rencontre de Nietzsche." The author deals primarily with Bergson and Péguy's Catholicism.

3434   Keeton, Morris T. *The Philosophy of Edmund Montgomery*. Dallas: University Press in Dallas, 1950, xi, 386.

3435   Maurentius, F. "Du Caractère humanisant de l'éducation artistique." *Nouvelle Revue Pédagogique*, 5, No. 7, 1950, 409-411.

3436   Melzi, Giuseppe. "L'imortalità dell'anima nella filosofia di H. Bergson." *Rivista di filosofia neoscolastica*, 42, No. 3, 1950, 238-255. The author concludes that

Bergson's reflections on immortality are insufficient. His philosophy can only establish an impersonal immortality.

3437   Minkowski, Eugène. "Sur Le Chemin d'une psychologie formelle." *Tijdschrift voor Philosophie*, 12, No. 3, 1950, 504-530. Minkowski holds that a new category ("le vécu") should be added by psychology to its categories "conscient" and "inconscient." This essay was originally written in 1938.

3438   Montague, William Pepperell. *Great Visions of Philosophy: Varieties of Speculative Thought in the West From the Greeks to Bergson*. La Salle, Illinois: Open Court, 1950, 484 (Paul Carus Lectures, 4th Series). Chapter 23, entitled "Bergson and a World on the March," appears on pp. 412-426.

3439   Moulyn, Adrian C. "The Limitations of Mechanistic Methods in the Biological Sciences." *Scientific Monthly*, 71, No. 1, July, 1950, 44-49.

3440   Nicholson, John Angus. *Philosophy of Religion*. New York: Ronald Press, 1950, viii, 419.

3441   Nicol, Eduardo. *Historicismo y existencialismo: La temporalidad del ser y la razón*. México: Colegio de México, 1950, 375. Bergson, G. Marcel, J.-P. Sartre, and others are discussed in this study.

3442   Petrucciano, Mario, "Intuizionismo ed ermetismo." *Idea*, 2, No. 41, 1950, 2.

3443   Poulet, Georges. *Etudes sur le temps humain*. Paris: Plon, 1950, 409.

3444   Riefstahl, Hermann. "Henri Bergsons *Zeit und Freiheit*." *Philosophischer Literaturanzeiger*, 3, No. 2, 1950, 67-71.

3445   Riese, Walther and Hoff, Ebbe C. "A History of the Doctrine of Cerebral Localization: Sources, Anticipations, and Basic Reasoning." *Journal of the History of Medicine and Allied Sciences*, 5, 1950, 49-71. The author, in the course of a discussion of mind-body theories, predominantly in Descartes and Kant, points out on pp. 66-68 Bergson's contributions to theories of cerebral location. Bergson touched on still basic difficulties in experimental work on localization, and developed a fruitful theory of the relationship of thought to behavior.

3446   Rossani, Wolfgango. "Le suggestioni di Bergson." *Fiera Letteraria*, 5, No. 22, 1950, p. 5.

3447   Saisset, Frédéric. *Qu'est-ce que la métaphysique? D'après Richet, Bergson et Osty*. Paris: Editions Nicolaus, 1950, 112.

3448   Schutz, Alfred. "Language, Language Disturbances, and the Texture of Consciousness: Philosophical Interpretations of Language Disturbances: Henri Bergson." *Social Research*, 17, No. 3, September 1950, 374-378.

3449   Siegfried, André. "Orateurs que j'ai connus: Silhouettes." *Revue Générale Belge*, No. 52, février 1950, 505-524. Bergson, F. Brunetière, and G. Sorel are discussed in this article.

3450   Smith, Vincent. *Idea-Men of Today*. Milwaukee: Bruce, 1950, 434, Cf. "A Reaction Against Scientism," 213-237.

3451   Smith, Vincent Edward. "Jurēvičs: Eine Einführung in seine Philosophie." *Renascence*, 3, No. 1, 1950, 66-67.

3452   Sorel, Georges. *Reflections on Violence*. Trans. J. Roth. Glencoe, Illinois: Free Press, 1950, 311.

3453   Stahl, Roland. "The Influence of Bergson on Whitehead." Diss., Boston, 1950.

3454   Stark, Werner. "Stable Equilibrium Re-examined." *Kyklos*, 4, No. 1, 1950, 218-232. The author uses Bergson's *Creative Evolution* to criticize the economists' concept of stable equilibrium. The concept is too static, and assumes that cause and effect are equivalent.

3455   Taymans, Adrien c. "Tarde and Schumpeter: A Similar Vision." *Quarterly Journal of Economics*, 64, No. 4, August 1950, 611-622. The author explains: "I venture to say that the idea of dynamic development, so fully expressed by Bergson, the philosopher, and by Schumpeter, the economist, had first been crystallized by Gabriel Tarde (1834-1904), the French sociologist..." (611).

3456   Wavre, Rolin. *La Figure du monde: Essai sur le problème de l'espace des Grecs à nos jours*. Neuchâtel, Switzerland: La Baconnière, 1950, 170. This study contains sections on Bergson's and J.-P. Sartre's concepts of space.

3457   Winston, Alexander P. "The Concept of Human Freedom in Bergson and James." Diss. Washington, 1950, 176.

1951

3458   Adolphe, Lydie. "La Contemplation créatrice (Aristote, Plotin, Bergson)". Diss., Paris (Sorbonne): 1951, 157.

3459   Adolphe, Lydie. *La Dialectique des images chez Bergson*. Paris: Presses Universitaires de France, 1951, 308. (Bibliothèque de philosophie contemporaine. Psychologie et sociologie).

3460   Ahlberg, Alf. *Psychologiens historia: D. 2. Fran Spinoza till Bergson*. Stockholm: Natur und Kultur, 1951, 133. (Natur och Kulture, 163)

3461   Bachelard, Gaston. *L'Activité rationaliste de la physique contemporaine*. Paris: Presses Universitaires de France, 1951, 223. Bergson's concept of motion is examined and criticized on pp. 54-58.

3462   Bense, Max. *Die Philosophie*. Frankfurt am Main: Suhrkamp, 1951, 466. *Zwischen den beiden Kriegen*. 1. Bd. Bergson, J. Benda, and E. Mounier are discussed in this section.

3463   Bertocci, Peter A. *Introduction to the Philosophy of Religion*. New York: Prentice-Hall, 1951, 565.

3464   Blanché, Robert. "Psychologie de la durée et physique du champ." *Journal de Psychologie Normale et Pathologique*, 44, No. 3, 1951, 411-424. This article is translated with introduction in *Bergson and the Evolution of Physics*, Ed. P. A. Y. Gunter, 105-120. The author argues that Bergson establishes an absolutely sharp distinction between duration and space, the inner and the outer worlds. His psychology thus stressed continuity and failed to do justice to discontinuity. It can not be reformulated to take in new discoveries.

3465   Bochénski, Innocentius M. *La Philosophie contemporaine en Europe*. Trans. F. Vaudon. Paris: Payot, 1951, 252.

3466   Bross, John Robert. "The Role of Creativity in Metaphysics and Religion." Diss. Columbia, 1951, 205. The author deals with the concept of freedom as it is treated by H. Bergson and A. N. Whitehead. He concludes: "Not every creative process results in good. Whether the outcome is good or evil depends upon the use to which the creation is put. In religion all creative processes aim at good and will result in good if the three elements of good are present and work together for a compromise course of action." *Dissertation Abstracts*, 12, No. 1, 1952, 75-76.

3467   Cardone, Domenico Antonio. "La disindividualizzione nella cultura moderna e il problema della civiltà morale, alla memoria de H. Bergson." *Richerche filosofiche*, 5, No. 1, 1951, 4-15.

3468   Chastaing, Maxime. *La Philosophie de Virginia Woolf*. Paris: Presses Universitaires de France, 1951, 196. (Bibliothèque de philosophie contemporaine) On pp. 147-150 the author objects to attempts to "Bergsonize" Virginia Woolf.

3469   Chevalier, Jacques. "Comment Bergson a trouvé Dieu." *Revue des Deux Mondes*, N.S. Année 4, No. 20, 15 octobre 1951, 604-618.

3470   Chevalier, Jacques. "Comment Bergson a trouvé le Dieu." *Cadences II*. Paris: Plon, 1951, 70-88.

3471   Claudel, Paul. "Lettre à Andreé Suarez. 25 juillet 1907." *André Suarès et Paul Claudel: Correspondance, 1904-1938*. 5ᵉ éd. Paris: Gallimard, 1951, 105-106. The author notes that he has just read Bergson's *L'Evolution Créatrice* and that any similarity between his ideas and Bergson's are due to the *Zeitgeist*. He criticizes Bergson's biology as being too much like the old doctrine of successive creations. Cf. p. 216.

3472   Contri, Sirro. "Ciò che manca ad Aristotele." *Fiera Letteraria*, 6, No. 37, 1951, p. 2.

3473   D'Amore, Benedetto. "La filosofia davanti al problema dell'esistenza di Dio ne *Les Deux Sources* di Enrico Bergson." *Sapienza*, 4, No. 2, 1951, 248-263.

3474   De Francesco, Dian Angelo. "La 'Professione del tragico'." *Letteratura moderne*, 1, No. 1951, 94-98.

3475   Deschoux, Marcel. "Brunschvicg et Bergson." *Revue Internationale de Philosophie*, 5, No. 15, 1951, 100-114.

3476   De Stefano, R. "Metafisica e scienza positiva in Bergson." *Richerche filosofiche*, 5, No. 1, 1951, 16-30.

3477   Distello, A. "Hamelin, Bergson e Brunschvicg." *Richerche filosofiche*, 5, No. 1, 1951, 31-34. It is argued here that Bergsonism is a kind of historicism.

3478   Fabre-Luce, Alfred. *Journal 1951*. Paris: Amiot-Dumont, 1951, 420. This entry deals with Bergson, among others.

3479   Filiasi Carcano, P. "Review of *Bergson* by Lorenzo Giusso." *Giornale critico della filosofia italiano*, 5, No. 1, 1951, 145-152. This is a detailed, highly attentive review. The reviewer concludes that the author, who is relativistic and anti-metaphysical, fails to see the true significance of Bergson's philosophy. Bergson has reshaped the problematic of philosophy.

3480   Foulquié, Paul et Deledalle, Gérard. *La Psychologie Contemporaine*. Paris: Presses Universitaires de France, 1951, 438. Pages 152-179 of this book are titled "William James et Bergson." The authors find the intellectual temperaments and conception of the inner life of the two thinkers to be extremely similar. Their treatment of Bergson concludes: "La psychologie bergsonienne n'est donc pas dépassé. Ce qui est dépassé c'est la condition humaine telle que la concevait Bergson." (p. 179) On pp. 178-179 the authors describe Bergson as having prepared the way for existentialism. On pp. 292-328 the authors mention the "psycho-biological current" which in French psychology includes such figures as M. Pradines, A. Bourloud, R. Ruyer, and in Anglo-American psychology, William McDougall. This tendency, to couple consciousness with life and psychology with biology, was already fully present, the authors note, in Bergson.

3481   Francia, Ennio. "Caratteri della 'recherche' nella letteratura francese." *Humanitas*, Anno 6, No. 7, luglio 1951, 752-765. This study is concerned with Bergson, A. Gide, F. Mauriac, and M. Proust.

3482   Gallegos Rocafull, J. M. "De Bergson a Tomás de Aquino." *Latino-américa*, 3, 1951, 457-459. This is a review of J. Maritain's *De Bergson à Thomas d'Aquin*

3483   Gide, André. *The Journals of André Gide. IV. 1939-1949*. Ed and Trans. Justin O'Brien. New York: Alfred A. Knopf, 1951, 341. On p. 127 (October 13, 1942) Gide states: "Then made another vain effort to try to penetrate Bergson's thought; hard at *Matière et mémoire* for five days without succeeding in understanding or really getting interested." On p. 236 (February, 1944) he lauds Bergson's preface to *Lucretius*."

3484   Gueroult, Martial. "Bergson en face des philosophes." *Revista Brasileira de Filosofia*, 1, No. 3. 1951, 239-254.

3485   Gusdorf, Georges. *Mémoire et personne*: Vol. 1. *La Mémoire conrèete*. Paris: Presses Universitaires de France, 1951, 258. Bergson is discussed on pp. 17-21, 27-28, 32-36, 77-81, 98-99, 144-145, and 248-249. The author proposes largely Bergsonian categories for the interpretation of experience and personality, but both criticizes and attempts to "complete" these categories. In this volume he particularly attempts to transform Bergson's concept of the present, which he deems too pragmatic and too intellectualist.

3486   Gusdorf, Georges. *Mémoire et personne*: Vol. 2. *La Dialectique de la mémoire*. Paris: Presses Universitaires de France, 1951, 280. Bergson is discussed on pp. 300-301, 308, 352-357, 439-441, 462-463, 464-468, 490-491, and 541-544. The author deals particularly with Bergson's concepts of forgetting (as an active, not a passive process), E. Minkowski's psychiatry, Bergson's two sorts of memory, concepts of "déjà vu," psychopathology, faults in Bergson's concept of memory. This study is valuable for both its criticisms and its bibliography.

3487   Guyot, Charles. "Péguy et Bergson." Unpublished lecture given at the University of Strasbourg. Summary in *Amitié Charles Péguy*, No. 22, Juillet, 1951, 25.

3488   Hessen, Johannes. *Die Philosophie des 20. Jahrhunderts*. Rottenburg, Germany: Bader, 1951, 190. Bergson and existentialism are discussed in this history of twentieth century philosophy.

3489   Jankélévitch, Vladimir. "L'Optimisme bergsonien." *Evidences*, No. 16, janvier 1951, 1-4.

3490   Kahl-Furthmann, G. "Henri Bergson: Das Lachen." *Philosophischer Literaturanzeiger*, 3, No. 3, 1951, 103-105.

3491   Kalif, George. *A Critical Survey and Evaluation of Hegel's Dialectic and Bergson's Intuition*. Bowdoin Prize. Harvard University, 1951, 55.

3492   Kaplan, Francis. "Le Christianisme de Bergson." *Evidences*, No. 19, mai-juin 1951, 12-17.

3493   Kopper, Joachim. "Review of *Pour connaître la pensée de Bergson* by Fançois Meyer." *Philosophischer Literaturanzeiger*, 3, No. 6, 1951, 262-266.

3494 Lapierre, J. W. "Vers Une Sociologie concrète." *Esprit*, 19e Année, No. 184, novembre 1951, 720-730. C. Levi-Strauss and Bergson are discussed in this essay.

3495 Larroyo, Francisco. *El existencialismo: Sus fuentes y direcciones.* México: Editorial Stylo, 1951, 227. (Voces universitarias) Bergson, M. Blondel, J.-P. Sartre, G. Marcel, and others are dealt with in this study.

3496 Lerch, Eugen. "Henri Bergson." *Das Buch*, 3, No. 2, 1951, 5-16.

3497 Levasti, Arrigo. *Bergson e la religione.* Roma: Edizion del Tripode, 1951, 20. This essay was published originally in *Tripode*, No. 12, settèmbre 1951.

3498 Lewis, Clarence Irving. "The Categories of Natural Knowledge." *The Philosophy of Alfred North Whitehead.* Ed. Paul A. Schilpp. New York: Tudor Publishing Co., 1951, 701-744. On p. 729 the author asserts that the "point of closest affinity" of Whitehead and Bergson lies in their acceptance of "the direction of creative advance as the time-dimension." See also pp. 743-744.

3499 Lossky, N. O. *History of Russian Philosophy.* New York: International Universities Press, 1951, 416. On p. 161 the author notes Bergson's influence on L. M. Lopatin. On p. 252-253 he states similarities and differences between his own views and Bergson's.

3500 Maire, Gilbert. "Le Philosophe Bergson tel que je l'ai connu." *France Illustration*, 7, No. 279, 17 février 1951, 190.

3501 Mathieu, Vittorio. "Il duale in Bergson." *Filosofia*, 2, No. 2, 1951, 229-252.

3502 Mayer, Charles L. *Man: Mind or Matter?* Trans. and Pref. by Harold A. Larrabee. Boston: Beacon Press, 1951, 200. Criticisms of Bergson's position in *Matter and Memory* are developed on pp. 86-88.

3503 Morgan, Charles. *Liberties of the Mind.* New York: The MacMillan Company, 1951, 252. Pages 209-216 of this book, titled "Bergson and the Maritains or Liberty From Materialism," is a review of the English translation of Raissa Maritain's *We Have Been Friends Together* (1942). The authors discussion essentially concerns the Maritains.

3504 Mossé-Bastide, Rose-Marie. Review of *Études bergsoniennes*, Vol. 1, 1948; of *La Théorie bergsonienne de la religion by Hj. Sunden; of L'Intellectualisme de Bergson* by L. Husson. *Revue Philosophique de la France et de l'Étranger*, 141, No. 1, 1951, 107-118.

3505 Nyquist, Finn. "Evolusjonen etter Bergson og sporsmalet transcendens." *Samtiden*, 69, No. 10, 1951, 672-680. This study explores the concept of evolution according to Bergson and the problem of transcendence.

3506 O'Neill, James C. "An Intellectual Affinity: Bergson and Valéry." *Publications of the Modern Language Association*, 66, No. 2, March 1951, 49-64. There are similarities, but no influences, between Bergson and Valéry, according to the author.

3507 Plinval, Georges de. "Il y a dix ans mourait Henri Bergson." *Ecrits de Paris*, janvier 1951, 91-96.

3508 "Portrait of Bergson." *United Nations World*, 5, No. 4, April 1951, 42-43. Bergson is discussed in this article on the French mentality.

3509 Pugliesi, Anna. "Henri Bergson tra Cattolici e Communisti." *Richerche filosofiche*, 5, No. 1, 1951, 35-39. The author doubts Bergson's conversion to Catholicism and stresses similarities between the doctrines of *Les Deux Sources* and Communism.

3510   Raudive, Konstantin. *Der Chaosmensch und seine Überwindung.* Memmingen: Dietrich, 1951, 400.

3511   Read, Herbert. *Collected Essays in Literary Criticism.* London: Faber and Faber, 1951, 381.

3512   Read, Herbert Edward. *Art and the Evolution of Man*: Lecture Delivered at Conway Hall, London, on April 10, 1951. London: Freedom Press, 1951, 51.

3513   Ruth-Adelaide. "Charles Du Bos: Fils de Bergson." *Revue de L'Université d'Ottawa*, 5, 1951, 857-863.

3514   Schutz, Alfed. "Choosing Among Projects of Action." *Philosophy and Phenomenological Research*, 12, No. 2, 1951, 161-184.

3515   Seaman, Francis Chester. "The Impact of the Theory of Relativity on Some Recent Philosophers." Diss. Michigan, 1951, 204, This dissertation considers the impact of relativity theory on four philosophers: Ernest Cassirer, Samuel Alexander, Henri Bergson, and Alfred North Whitehead. The author's abstract concludes, "Henri Bergson's philosophy was developed before relativity. In it there was an elegant symmetry between the self and the universe; a symmetry which was one recommendation of his scheme. But relativity theory with its alternative time systems disrupted this symmetry. Bergson never adequately reworked his system... Whitehead's later philosophy, as expressed in *Process and Reality*, envisions the universe as composed of atomic actualities in process. Whitehead argues that relativity confirms that the real is atomic rather than one large continuous process. This provides a cue as to the resolution of Bergson's difficulty. By putting his 'vital' inside events, both the self and the universe can be conceived as growing by finite increments. Thus, through Whitehead, a resolution of Bergson's problem is achieved." (See *Dissertation Abstracts*, 11, No. 1, 1951, 387.)

3516   Stefano, R. "Metafisica e scienza positiva in Bergson." *Richerche filosofiche*, 5, No. 1, 1951, 16-30.

3517   Stolpe, Sven. "Henri Bergson och kyrkan." *Credo* (Sweden), 32, No. 3, 1951, 138-141.

3518   Stolpe, Sven. "Henri Bergson und die katholische Kirche." *Stimmen der Zeit*, 149, No. 3, 1951-1952, 143-145.

3519   Troy, William. "Virginia Woolf: The Novel of Sensibility." In *Literary Opinion in America*. 2nd ed. New York, London: Harper and Brothers, 1951, 324-327.

3520   Vogt, Fritz J. "Review of *Henri Bergson: Eine Einführung in seine Philosophie* by Paulis Jurēviŝ." *Philosophischer Literaturanzeiger*, 3, No. 1, 1951, 17-22.

3521   Watanabé, Satosi. "Le Concept du temps en physique moderne et la durée de Bergson." *Revue de Métaphysique et de Morale*, 56, No. 2, 1951, 128-142. Translated, with an introduction, in *Bergson and the Evolution of Physics*, Ed. P. A. Y. Gunter, 67-77. The introduction to this essay is by Louis de Broglie. The author relates quantum physics, thermodynamics, and Bergsonian duration. He argues that the increase of entropy is due to human cognitive processes, which are rooted in our irreversible, subjective duration. (It is not clear that this is Bergson's position. Cf. Čapek, *Process Studies*, 1972)

3522 Wenger, Marguerite. "Bibliographie der Schriften von und über Bergson." *Das Buch*, 3, No. 2, 1951, 64-70.

3523 Williams, D. C. "The Myth of Passage." *Journal of Philosophy*, 58, No. 15, 1951, 457-472. The author criticizes various modern concepts of "passage."

1952

3524 Adolphe, Lydie. "Bergson et l'élan vital." *Etudes Bergsoniennes*, 3, 1952, 79-138.

3525 Béguin, Albert. "Péguy et Bergson." *Feuillets de l'Amitié Charles Péguy*, No. 30, octobre 1952, 3-7.

3526 Biagioni, L. "Giovanni Papini: Begegnung mit Henri Bergson." *Zeitschrift für Religion und Geistesgeschichte*, 4, No. 4, 1952, 371-374.

3527 Bréhier. Emile. "Review of *Bergson, maître de Péguy* by André Henry." *Etudes Bergsoniennes*, 1952, 3, 213-214.

3528 Buber, Martin. "The Silent Question: About Henri Bergson and Simone Weil." *Judaism*, 1, No. 2, April 1952, 99-105.

3529 Canguilhem, Georges. "Réflexions sur la création artistique selon Alain." *Revue de Métaphysique et de morale*, 57, No. 2, 1952, 171-186. The author opposes Alain's esthetics to Plato's, likens it to Bergson's and Kant's.

3530 Čapek, Milič. "La Genèse idéal de la matière chez Bergson; la structure de la durée." *Revue de Métaphysique et de Morale*, 57, No. 3, 1952, 325-348. This is an account of Bergson's philosophical cosmogony. It is also an analysis of the structure of duration. Cf. Gunter, 1971.

3531 Cattaui, Georges. *Marcel Proust*. Paris: Julliard, 1952, 287. Bergson and Proust are discussed here. Cf. esp. pp. 181-188, 205-208.

3532 Chevalier, Jacques. "Comó Bergson encontró a Dios." *Revista de Filosofía* (Madrid), 11, No. 11, No. 43, 1952, 539-557.

3533 Cojazzi, Antonio. "Il Croce de fronte a Socrate e a Bergson." *Città de vita*, 7, 1952, 654-661.

3534 Costa de Beauregard, Olivier. "Quelques aspects de l'irréversibilité du temps dans la physique classique et quantique." *Revue des Questions Scientifiques*, 5e Série, No. 2, 20 avril 1952, 171-191. The author argues that while microscopic physical processes are reversible, macroscopic physical processes, like those of biology and psychology, are not. He suggests that in other respects the relations between past, present and future are symmetrical. (Past, present and future may exist simultaneously.)

3535 Delattre, Floris. "Review of *La Liberté* by Léon Husson." *Etudes bergsoniennes*, 3, 218-219.

3536 Delhomme, Jean. "Review of 'Les Rapports de Dieu et le monde dans la philosophie de Bergson' by Henri Gouhier." *Etudes Bergsoniennes*, 3, 215-217.

3537 Delhomme, Jeanne. "L'Exercice de la pensée et ses conditions dans la philosphie d'Henri Bergson." *Etudes Bergsoniennes*, 3, 152-158. This is a résumé of a talk by Delhomme followed by a discussion between Delhomme and several other philosophers.

3538   Dresden, Samuel. "Het religieuze spiritualisme von Henri Bergson." *Algemeen Nederlands Tijdschrift voor Wijsbegeerte*, 45, No. 2, 1952, 89-104.

3539   *Etudes Bergsoniennes*. Paris: Albin Michel, 1952, Vol. 3, 219. Bergson's concept of evil and his relations with G.Sorel and L. Dauriac are discussed in this issue.

3540   Ferro, Carmelo. "Bergson davanti a Cristo." *Vita e pensiero*, 35, No. 1, gennaio 1952.

3541   Fiser, Emeric. *Le Symbol littéraire: Essai sur la signification du symbole chez Wagner, Baudelaire, Mallarmé, Bergson et Marcel Proust*. Paris: Corti, 1952, 225. This is a dissertation, completed 1941.

3542   Forsyth, Thomas Miller. *God and the World*. London: Allen and Unwin, 1952, 160.

3543   Gouhier, Henri. "Bergson et le Fonds Dauriac de la Bibliothèque Victor Cousin." *Etudes Bergsoniennes*, 3, 195-198. The author examines the relations between Bergson and L. Dauriac.

3544   Gouhier, Henri. "le Bergsonisme et l'histoire de la philosophie (Position de questions)." L'Homme et l'Histoire *(Actes du VIe Congrès des Sociétés de Philosophie de Langue Française)*. *Paris: Presses Universitaires de France, 1952, 385-388.*

3545   Hastoupis, A. P. "Bergson and his Religious Philosophy." Θεολογια (Athens), 23, 1952, 596-603.

3546   Heidsieck, François. "Bergson et l'histoire de la philosophie." *L'Homme et l'histoire* (Actes du Vie Congrès des Sociétés de Philosophie de Langue Française). Paris: Presses Universitaires de France, 1952, 389-394.

3547   Hogarth, Henry. "Bergson's Spiritual Pilgrimage." *Hibbert Journal*, 51, No. 200, October 1952, 63-66. Bergson is Catholicized in this article.

3548   Husson, Léon. "Le Dévelopment de la conception de l'intelligence chez Bergson." *Bulletin Ecole Pratique de Psychologie et de Pédagogie*, 6, No. 4, 1952, 301-313.

3549   Kaufman, Alvin H. "Elan Vital, Nisus and Creativity as Treated in the Thought of Henri Bergson, S. Alexander, and A. N. Whitehead." Diss., Boston, 1952.

3550   Lachieze-Rey, Pierre. "Blondel et Bergson." *Etudes Philosophiques*, 7, No. 5, 1952, 383-386. It is argued here that M. Blondel substituted an "élan spirituel" for Bergson's "élan vital."

3551   Llera, Humberto Pinera. *Filosofía de la vida y filosofía existencial: Ensayos*. Cuba: La Havane, 1952, 228.

3552   Martin, Auguste. "Correspondance Péguy-Bergson." *Feuillets de l'Amitié Charles Péguy*, No. 30, Octobre, 1952, 8-12.

3553   Mathieu, Vittorio. "La durata." *Filosofia*, 3, No. 1, 1952, 3-32.

3554   Mathieu, Vittorio. "La memoria e il profoundo." *Filosofia*, 3, No. 4, ottobre 1952, 507-528.

3555   Mavit, Henri. "Bergson et l'existence créatrice." *Etudes Bergsoniennes*. 3, 141-148.

3556   Mendilow, Adam Abraham. *Time and the Novel*. Intro. J. Isaacs. London: Peter Nevill, 1952, 244.

3557   Mossé-Bastide, Rose-Marie. "Reviews of *H. Bergson: Eine Einführung in Seine Philosophie* by P. Jurēvičs; *Bergson maître de Péguy* by A. Henry." *Revue Philosophique de la France et de l'Étranger*, 143, Nos. 1-3, 1952, 95-102.

3558   Moubray, G. a. de C. de. "Bergson and Swedenborg." *New Church Magazine*, 71, No. 2, April-June 1952, 23-26. The author finds Bergson's and Emmanuel

Swedenborg's concepts of the relations between mystical intuition and social action to be very closely similar. He concludes that Bergson borrowed ideas from Swedenborg.

3559   Moulyn, Adrian C. "The Functions of Point and Line in Time Measuring Operations." *Philosophy of Science*, 19, No. 2, 1952, 141-155. The author analyzes the part played by the concepts of solids, planes, lines, and points in the measurement of time. In the series solid, plane, line, and point there is "an ever increasing abstraction from and limitation of movement" as we move from solid to geometrical point (p. 142). There is nevertheless a profound logical gap between the concept of the line and that of the point: "The concept 'straight line' must include temporal facets because movement is a factor within the concept of straightness. But the definition of the geometric point excludes any temporal qualities because movement is excluded from the geometric point" (p. 144). The author conludes that line point and instant are required by time-measurement, which also requires a subjective temporal experience. The notions of temporal interval and temporal instant are derived, from the "precious present" of subjective time.

3560   Moulyn, Adrian C. "Reflections on the Problem of Time in Relation to Neurophysiology and Psychology." *Philosophy of Science*, 19, No. 1, 1952, 33-49. This paper is a sequel to the author's "Mechanism and Mental Phenomena," which appeared in 1947 in the same journal. In the present article the author analyzes the "mental triad" posited in the earlier article to account for the non-physical element in conditioned reflexes. The "triad" in question is the threefold structure of temporality; past, present and future. The author analyzes "movement" as investigated by physics and biology. In physics, motion is derived from the past; in biology, it refers to the future. Physics thus deals with Causality; biology with foresight, i.e., purpose. Physics need not deal with "inner time" but the biological sciences must.

3561   Mueller, Gustav E. "Review of *Time and Free Will* and *Matter and Memory* by Henri Bergson." *Personalist*, 33, No. 3, 1952, 290. The reviewer feels that Bergson's struggle with materialism is *depasée*.

3562   Newman, Pauline. *Marcel Proust et l'existentialisme*. Paris: Nouvelles Editions Latines, 1952, 170. On pp. 26-41, the author discusses Bergson's and Proust's concepts of time and memory. On p. 36 she states, "Le Reflect de la théorie bergsonienne sur l'oeuvre de Proust est incontestable." On p. 41 she states, "Si l'acheminement progressif de Marcel Proust vers une conception essentialiste du monde marque une tendance qu'il partage avec Ruskin, c'est en même temps le produit de l'enseignement bergsonien." See, howerver, pp. 106-107 where the author tends to oppose Proust's thought to that of Bergson.

3563   Oesterreicher, John M. *Walls are Crumbling: Seven Jewish Philosophers Discover Christ*. New York: Devin-Adair, 1952, 393.

3564   Papini, Giovanni. "Begegnung mit Henri Bergson." *Zeitschrift für Religion und Geistesgeschichte*, 4, No. 4, 1952, 371-374.

3565   Pichl, K. "Bergson und seine Nachfolger." *Wissenschaft und Weltbild*, 5, No. 9, 1952, 304-314.

3566   Polin, Raymond. "Henri Bergson et le mal." *Etudes Bergsoniennes*, 3, 7-40. According to the author, evil is for Bergson a positive reality and coincides with matter.

3567   Polin, Raymond. "Henri Bergson et le mal." *Etudes Bergsoniennes*, 3, 180-191. This is a résumé of Polin's talk followed by a discussion, with several philosophers, of Bergson's concempt of evil.

3568   Poulet, Georges. "La Distance intérieure. Paris: Plon, 1952, 357.

3569   Priddin, Deidre. *The Art of the Dance in French Literature from Théophile Gautier to Paul Valéry*. London: Black, 1952, xvi, 176.

3570   Rauch, William Rufus. "The Personal Universe: Forword to the Paperback Edition." in Emmanuel Mounier, *Personalism*. Trans. Philip Mairet. Notre Dame & London: University of Notre Dame Press, 1952, 132. Rauch notes Bergson as one of Mounier's philosophical sources on p. viii. He describes Mounier's encounter with Bergson's disciple Charles Péguy, on pp. ix-x, as one of two great shaping events in Mounier's life.

3571   Romanell, Patrick. *Making of the Mexican Mind*. Lincoln, Nebraska: University of Nebraska Press, 1952, 213.

3572   Romero, Francisco. *Sobre la filosofía en América*. Buenos Aires: Raigal, 1952, 135.

3573   Rusconi, N. "L'esperienza cristiana di Bergson." *Osservatore romano*, No. 17, 1952, 3.

3574   Santonastaso, Giuseppe. "Sorel e Bergson." *Mondo*, 4, No. 44, 1952, 6.

3575   Sassen, Ferdinand. *Van Kant tot Bergson*. Antwerp: Standaard-boekhandel, 1952, 232.

3576   Savioz, Raymond. "Intellectualisme et intuition bergsonienne." *Revue Philosophique de la France et de l'Etranger*, 142, Nos. 4-6, 1952, 187-195.

3577   Sciacca, Michele Federico. *La filosofia oggi*. Vol. 2, 2nd ed. Milano e Roma: Fratelli Bocca, 1952, 485. "Il contingentismo di E. Boutroux e l'intuitionismo d. E. Bergson" appears on pp. 48-58.

3578   Tomlin, E. W. F. *The Great Philosophers: Vol. 1 The Western World*. New York: A. A. Wynn, Inc., 1952, 282. On pp. 263-273 the author provides an enthusiastic survey of Bergson's life and thought. He is unusually well acquainted with Bergson's biography.

3579   Tonquedec, Joseph de. "Les Lettres de Bergson sur Dieu." *Revue des Deux Mondes*, N.S. Année 5, No. 14, 15 juillet 1952, 232-263.

3580   Valéry, Paul. *Lettres à quelques-uns*. Paris: Gallimard, 1952, 256, 162-166. This book contains a letter by Valéry denying Bergson's influence on him. It was published previously in the preface to Martin Gillet, *Paul Valéry et la métaphysique*. Paris: La Tour d'Ivoire, 1927, 187.

3581   Vassallo, Angel. "Bergson y nosotros." *Ciencia y Fe*, 8, Nos. 31-32, 1952, 41-55.

3582   Vernet, Maurice. *La Vie et la mort*. Paris: Flammarion, 1952, 298. (Bibliothèque de Philosophie Scientifique) Cf. esp. pp. 165-181.

3583   Voegelin, Eric. *New Science of Politics*. Chicago: University of Chicago Press, 1952, 193. Bergson is discussed on pp. 26, 60, and 61; Bergson's philosophy of history, on pp. 79-80.

3584   Wagner, Robert Dean. "The Last Illusion: Examples of the Spiritual Life in Modern Literature." Diss. Columbia, 1952, 264. "The first chapter briefly summarizes the two major forms that the spiritual life has taken in the past—the balanced idealism of theistic religion or (as in the philosophy of Bergson) the anti-idealism of a pantheistic worship of nature." Neither form can sustain the spiritual life, however. The second chapter analyzes Proust's literature as "the most successful literary realization of a philosophy of disillusion." *Dissertation Abstracts*, 12, No. 5, 1952, 624-625.

3585   Walters, F. P. *A History of the League of Nations*. Vol. 1. London: Oxford University Press, 1952, 463 pp. On pp. 190-194 the author discusses the work work of the Committee on Intellectual Cooperation of the League of Nations.

1953

3586   Bahm, Archie J. *Philosophy: An Introduction*. New York: John Wiley and Sons, 1953, 441; Ch. 11, "Intuitionism," 142-151. This is an exposition of Bergson's philosophy, primarily his epistemology, with comparisons to naive realism.

3587   Boer, Jesse De. "A Critique of Continuity, Infinity, and Allied Concepts in the Natural Philosophy of Bergson and Russell." *The Return to Reason*, Ed. John Wild. Chicago: Henry Regnery Company, 1953, 373, 92-124. This paper presents an analytical and critical study of the Bergson-Russell conflict. It deals with Bergson's treatment of Zeno's paradoxes, Russell's critique of Bergson, and Russell's concepts of time and motion.

3588   Bouvier, Robert. "Review of *Les Etudes Bergsoniennes*. Vol. III." *Erasmus*, 6, Nos. 13-14, 1953, 449-452.

3589   Bréhier, Émile. "Ch. 7, Le Spiritualisme d'Henri Bergson." *Histoire de la philosophie*, Vol. 2, *La Philosophie moderne*, 4, *Le XIXe Siècle après 1850, Le XIXe Siècle*, 4 ed. Paris: Presses Universitaires de France, 1953, 1023-1034. The author notes in succeeding chapters several thinkers who were influenced by Bergson.

3590   Breurs, A. "La conversione di Bergson." *Osservatore romano*, No. 3, 1953, 3.

3591   Buber, Martin. *Hinweise: Gesammelte Essays*. Zürich: Manesse Verlag, Conzett und Huber, 1953, 220-228. This was first published in 1943. It contains a chapter on Bergson titled "Zu Bergson's Begriff der Intuition." (See the author, 1957, for annotation.)

3592   Callot, Emile. *Von Montaigne zu Sartre*. Meisenheim und Wien: Westkulturverlag Von Hain, 1953, 206.

3593   Čapek, Milič. "La Théorie bergsonienne de la matière et la physique moderne." *Revue Philosophique de la France et de l'Etranger*, 143, Nos. 1-3, janvier-mars 1953, 28-59. This article is translated, with an introduction, in *Bergson and the Evolution of Physics*, (1969) Ed. P. A. Y. Gunter, 297-330. It is the best brief general survey of Bergson's philosophy of physics. The author argues that Bergson's physical ideas were very close to the basic concepts of classical quantum physics. Bergson's material duration strongly resembles the world of relativity theory—more than he realized.

3594   Carnus, J. "The Rise of French Personalism." *Personalist*, 34, No. 3, 1953, 261-268. This article discusses the relations between Bergson, Maine de Biran, and personalism, as represented by E. Mounier.

3595 Ciardo, Manilo. "Croce e Bergson nel Pensiero Contemporaneo." in *Benedetto Croce*. Ed. Francesco Flora. Milano: Malfasi Editore, 1953, 381-395.

3596 Ciusa, Niso. *Inchiesta sul bergsonismo*. Sassari, Italy: Tip. Gallizzi, 1953, 111.

3597 Collin, Lucien. "Mon Maître, Bergson." *Amérique Française*, 11, No. 3, mai-juin 1953, 35-37.

3598 Daval, Roger. *Histoire des idées en France*. Paris: Presses Universitaires de France, 1953, 128. (Que sais-je?) This study includes a section on Bergson.

3599 Dresden, Samuel. "Het religieuze spiritualisme van Henri Bergson." *Annalen van het Genootschap voor Wetenschappelijke Philosophie*, 22, 1953, 27-42. This essay was first printed in *Algemeen Nederlands Tijdschrift voor Wijsbegeerte*, 1952.

3600 Elsasser, Walter M. "A Reformulation of Bergson's Theory of Memory." *Philosophy of Science*, 20, No. 1, 1953, 7-21. This is a restatement of Bergson's theory of memory by a prominent quantum physicist. The author argures that "pure" long-term memories are not stored in the brain, but depends on a capacity to generate past "reverberatory patterns." A generalized principle of complementarity is necessary to explain the nature of these patterns.

3601 Gomulicki, Bronislaw R. "The Development and Present Status of the Trace Theory of Memory." *British Journal of Psychology Monograph Supplements*, 29, 1953, 94. Bergson's influence on Wm. McDougall is discussed on pp. 30-31; his concepts of habit memory and pure memory on p. 61.

3602 Gray, Christopher. *Cubist Aesthetic Theories*. Baltimore: Johns Hopkins Press, 1953, 190. Cf. esp. 65, 69-71, 85-88 for the relations between Bergson and cubism.

3603 Grünbaum, Adolf. "Relativity and the Atomicity of Becoming." *Review of Metaphysics*, 4, No. 2, 1953, 143-186. The author examines and criticizes Bergson's "radically phenomenological theory of change" on pp. 150-155. Bergson is wrong in holding that mathematics is built on spatial concepts and that a Cantorian continuum of events can not define movement. The author defends B. Russell's thesis of 1912.

3604 Gueroult, Martial. "Perception, idée, object, chose chez G. Berkeley: La Formule bergsonienne." *Revue Philosophique de la France et de l'Etranger*, 143, No. 2, avril 1953, 181-200. This article examines Bergson's interpretation of George Berkeley's philosophy.

3605 Gurko, Leo. *Heroes, Highbrows and the Popular Mind*. Indianapolis and New York: The Bobbs-Merrill Company, In., 1953, 319. (Charter Books) The author deals with Bergson (and Edouard von Hartmann, William James and others) in Chapter 10, "Intuition and Kindred Matters", pp. 201-223. This chapter provides an interesting example of the general attitute towards "intuition" among English-speaking scholars. Intuition is here said to "inhabit the persons of women, children, animals and geniuses" (p. 203) and to be exhibited in "numerology, phrenology, the playing of hunches, spiritualism..." (p. 205) and the trade in good luck charms and "superstitious tokens."

3606 Hulme, T. E. "Bergson's Theory of Art." in *The Problems of Aesthetics*. Eds. E. Vivas and M. Krieger. New York: Rinehart, 1953, 125-138.

3607 Husson, Léon. "Signification et limites de la critique de l'intelligence chez Bergson." *Actes du XIe Congrès internationale de philosophy. XIII. Histoire de la philosophie moderne et contemporaine.* Louvain: Nauwelaerts; Amsterdam: North-Holland Publishing Co., 1953, 174-179.

3608   Jaloux, Edmond. *Avec Marcel Proust.* Paris et Genève: La Palatine, 1953, 153. The influence of Bergson on Proust is discussed on pp. 19-20 and 23.

3609   Jamil, Khwija Moinud-Din. "Nietzsche and Bergson in the Domain of Moral Philosophy." Diss., Paris, 1953, 133.

3610   Kremer-Marietti, Angèle. *Les Formes du mouvement chez Bergson.* Le Puy, France: Cahiers du Nouvel Humanisme, 1953, 126.

3611   Laurent, Jacques. "Mèches à vendre." *La Parisienne*, No. 9, septembre 1953, 1304-1337. This study deals with Bergson, Courteline, Giraudoux, and others.

3612   Leroy, André-Louis. "Influence de la philosophie berkleyenne sur la pensée continentale." *Hermathena*, 82, No. 2, novembre 1953, 27-48.

3613   Macedo, Sílvio de. *Filosofía de linguagem e ciência jurídica.* Maceió, Brazil: Livraria Ramalho, 1953. This work contains a chapter titled "A filosofía bergsoniana como filosofía liberadora."

3614   Mahadevan, T. M. P. *Time and Timeless.* Madras: Upanishad Vihar, 1953, 88.

3615   Mathieu, Vittorio. "Il tempo ritrovato: Bergson e Einstein." *Filosofia*, 4, No. 4, 1953, 625-656.

3616   Merleau-Ponty, Maurice. "Bergson se faisant." *Eloge de la philosophie et autres essais.* Paris: Gallimard, 1953, 288-308.

3617   Merleau-Ponty, Maurice. *Eloge de la philosophie: Leçon inaugurale faite au Collège de France, le 15 janvier 1953.* Paris: Gallimard, 1953, 93.

3618   Niso, Ciusa. *Inchiesta sul bergsonismo.* Sassari, Italy: Galizzi, 1953, 111.

3619   Péguy, Charles. "Deux Lettres à Bergson." *Esprit*, 21e Année, No. 200, février 1953, 337-338.

3620   Pemberton, Harrison J. "The Problem of Personal Identity with Special Reference to Whitehead and Bergson." Diss., Yale, 1953.

3621   Queiroz, Amaro Xisto de. "A estética de Bergson." *Kriterion*, 6, Nos. 25-26, 1953, 315-319.

3622   Quintanilla, Louis. *Bergsonismo y política.* México and Buenos Aires: Fondo de Cultura Económica, 1953, 205. The introduction is by Samuel Ramos. This study concerns primarily Bergson and Georges Sorel.

3623   Reulet-Sanchez, Aníbal. "Review of *Bergsonismo y política* by L. Quintanilla." *Américas*, 5, No. 7, July 1953, 36-37. The author observes: "For more than a quarter of a century, Bergson was the European philosopher most influential in the Spanish American countries. But so far as I know, outside of a small sphere of intellectual anarchists Bergsonian philosophy found its warmest welcome among liberal and democratic elements... An in Mexico, around 1910, it was the ideological battering ram used to start the attack on the Porfirio Diáz dictatorship..." (37).

3624   Rideau, Emile. *Paganisme et christianisme.* Tournai, France: Casterman, 1953, 254. This study treats of Bergson, along with many others.

3625   Sánchez-Reulet, Aníbal. "A Philosophy and its Consequences." *Américas*, 5, No. 7, July 1953, 36-37.

3626   Schilder, Paul. *Medical Psychology*. Trans. David Rapaport. New York: International Universities Press, Inc., 1953, 428. This book appeared originally, in German, in 1923. Its seventh section, "Affect and Experience," is excluded by the translator. On p. 141 the author notes, against Bergson's concept of memory, that sensory and motor phenomena are to a certain extent independent of each other; on pp. 144-145 he states that the functional theory of aphasia and agnosia is securely founded, and cites Bergson's proof that no images are destroyed by these maladies; on p. 159 he cites a mind-brain theory similar to Bergson's; on pp. 162-163 he illustrates Bergson's distinction between pure remembering and remembering which serves a specific purpose.

3627   Servais, Yvonne. *Charles Péguy: The Pursuit of Salvation*. Westminster, Maryland: The Newman Press, 1953, 401. The author treats Péguy as an "instinctive Bergsonian" (p. 9) a "Bergsonian" before having read Bergson. She notes Péguy's sense of intellectual discomfort on hearing Jean Jaurès expound "the whole of Bergson's philosophy in less than thirteen minutes." (p. 110) Péguy did not accept, the author holds on pp. 206-212, 290-294, the whole of Bergson's philosophy. But Bergson's philosophy led Péguy back to Catholicism.

3628   Tresmontant, Claude. *Essai sur la pensée hebraique*. Paris: Editions du Cerf, 1953, 169. (Lectie devine, 12) An essay titled "Le Neo-Platonisme de Bergson" appears here on pp. 155-164.

3629   Virieux-Reymond, Antoinette. "Review of *Les Etudes Bergsoniennes*, vol. III." *Revue de Théologie et de Philosophie*, 3e Série, 3, No. 1, 1953, 75-76.

3630   Willoch, Helga Aubert. "Bergson." *Edda*, 40, bind 53, No. 1, 1953, 110-130.

3631   Xirau, José R. "Filosofía y pólitica." *Revista Interamericana de Bibliografía*, 2, No. 2, mayo-agosto 1953, 141-145. This is a review of *Bergsonismo y política* by Quintanilla.

1954

3632   Ancelot-Hustache, Jeanne. *Een doopsel van begeerte: Henri Bergson, 1859-1941*. Antwerpen: Hoogland, Frankrijklei, 1954, 16. "Vertaald door Kor. Van Miert."

3633   Bayer, Raymond. *Epistémologie et logique depuis Kant jusqu'à nos jours*. Paris: Presses Universitaires de France, 1954, 365 pp. (Philosophie de la matière). On p. 95 the author compares the vitalism of A. A. Cournot with the vitalism of Bergson, which he describes as an irrationalism; on pp. 118-119 the author draws a parallel between certain of Cournot's moral theories and ideas developed in Bergson's *The Two Sources*; on p. 120 he holds that Cournot was on of the first to conceive the idea of a "philosophy of religion" (before E. Boutroux, H. Höffding, Bergson and others).

3634   Billy, André. "M. Pouget, Bergson et l'enfer." *Le Figaro Littéraire*, 30 octobre 1954, 2.

3635   Bridoux, André. *Le Souvenir*. Paris: Presses Universitaires de France, 1954, 90. The author's research is Bergsonian in inspiration, though he criticizes many of Bergson's central ideas, including those of the memory-image and the unconscious.

3636   Cepeda I, Manuel Eduardo. "La teoriá filosófica de Bergson." *Annales Universidad Central del Ecuador*, 83, No. 338, 1954, 65-73.

3637   Challaye, Félicien. "Bergson vu par les Soviets." *Preuves*, 4, No. 44, octobre 1954, 62-63.

3638   Challaye, Félicien. *Péguy socialiste*. Paris: Amiot-Dumont, 1954, 334, Cf. p. 74f.

3639   Chevalier, Jacques. *Bergson et le père Pouget*. Préf. François Mauriac. Paris: Plon, 1954, 80.

3640   Clement, André. "La Conception du hasard chez Lévy-Bruhl et la critique qui en fit Bergson." Diss., Laval, 1954, iii, 306.

3641   Collins, James. *A History of Modern European Philosophy*. Milwaukee: Bruce, 1954, 954. Bergson is discussed on pp. 809-848.

3642   Delhomme, Jean. *Vie et conscience de la vie: Essai sur Bergson*. Paris: Presses Universitaires de France, 1954, 195. This is a study of Bergson's biological epistemology. The author characterizes Bergson's theory of knowledge as breaking with the Cartesian cogito and its spectator theory of knowledge. He describes the dialectic of Bergson's philosophy as a struggle between self and other, not between affirmation and negation.

3643   Favager, Charles. "Review of *La Dialectique des images chez Bergson* by Lydie Adolphe." *Revue de Théologie et de Philosophie*, 3e Série, 4, No. 1, 1954, 84-85.

3644   Friedell, Egon. *A Cultural History of the Modern Age*. Vol. 3, Trans. C. F. Atkinson. New York: A. A. Knopf, 1954, 489. On pp. 372-373 the author characterizes Bergson as "by far the most influential French philosopher since Comte", and gives a very general description of his philosophy, which he terms an "irrationalism."

3645   Gemelli, Agostino and Zunini, Giorgio. *Introduzione alla psicologia*. 4th Ed. Milano: Società Editrice «Vita e Pensiero», 1954, 490. (Pubblicazioni dell'Università Cattolica del Sacro Cuore, N.S. Vol. 20) Cf. 61, 75-79, 176-177, 390.

3646   Gouhier, Henri. "Bergson et l'actualité de l'histoire." *Actualité de l'Histoire*, No. 8, May, 1954, 3-4.

3647   Guzzo, Agosto. "Bergson: Il profonde e la sua espressione." *Archivo di filosofia*, 23, No. 1, 1954, 257-259. This is a review of V. Mathieu's *Bergson*.

3648   Hafley, James. *The Glass Roof: Viginia Woolf as Novelist*. Berkeley and Los Angeles: University of California Press, 1954, 195. The author sees Virginia Woolf proceeding from a Bergsonian philosophy in her earlier novels to a philosophy emphasizing "public as well as personal values" in her later novels. The author mentions Woolf's short story "Kew Gardens" as a literary application of Bergsonian biology.

3649   Halski, Czesaw R. "Michal Bergson." *Grove's Dictionary of Music and Musicians*. Fifth Ed. 1954, Vol. 1, p. 643. This is a brief biographical sketch of the pianist-composer Michal Bergson (1820-1898) the father of Henri Bergson.

3650   Harris, Errol E. *Nature, Mind and Modern Science*. London: George Allen and Unwin Ltd., 1954, 455. On pp. 393-399 the author discusses Bergson's philosophy as "the most typically modern philosophy." He describes Bergson's attempt to create a conception of nature radically different from that devised by 17th century thinkers as seriously incoherent. This incoherence arises from Bergson's "zeal to get rid of matter" (p. 395), his unwillingness to admit that matter exists. (The author commits the common error of supposing that for Bergson matter has no duration. On this point Cf. Milič Čapek, *Bergson and Modern Physics*

(1971) 189-222.)

3651   Joussain, André. "Le Testament de Bergson." *Ecrits de Paris*, novembre 1954, 75-77.

3652   Kelley, John Joseph. "Bergson's Mysticism: A Philosophical Exposition and Evaluation of Bergson's Concept of Mysticism." Diss., Fribourg, 1954, 151.

3653   Kelley, John Joseph. *Bergson's Mysticism: A Philosophical Exposition and Evaluation of Bergson's Concept of Mysticism.* Fribourg, Germany: Saint Martin's Press, 1954, 151.

3654   Kumar, Shiv Kumar. "Bergson and the Stream of Consciousness Novel." Diss., Cambridge, 1954.

3655   Lafille, Pierre. *André Gide, romancier.* Paris: Hachette, 1954, xxii, 595. A comparison of Bergson and Gide is found on pp. 402-405.

3656   La Selle, Mgr. H. de. *Un Duel à quatre: Saint Thomas, Kant, Bergson, Sartre.* Vion, France: La Chapelle du Chêne, 1954, 62.

3657   Lewis, John. *Introduction to Philosophy.* 2nd ed. London: Watts, 1954, 236. This is a much enlarged version of an original edition published in 1937. It presents historically-important philosophers from Plato through Henri Bergson and Alfred North Whitehead.

3658   Macedo, Sílvio de. *A Epistemología Bergsoniana.* Maceió, Brazil: Livraria Ramalho, 1954.

3659   McFarland, Horace Neill. "Theories of the Social Origin of Religion in the Tradition of Émile Durkheim." Diss., Columbia, 1954, 309. The author argues that Bergson was influenced by Durkheim in developing his notion of the closed morality and static religion, but concludes that Bergson's "stress upon intuition and the creative role of individual mystical experience removed him to the periphery of the Durkheimian tradition and rendered him less a follower than a critic of its essential features." *Dissertation Abstracts*, 14, No. 9, 1954, 1470.

3660   Maritain, Raissa. *Die grossen Freundschaften: Begegnungen mit Henri Bergson, Léon Bloy, Jacques Maritain, Pierre van der Meer de Walcheren, Charles Péguy.* Trans. B. Schluter and G. G. Meister. Heidelberg: Kerle, 1954, 451.

3661   Mathieu, Vittorio. *Bergson: Il profundo e la sua espressione.* Torino: Edizione di Filosofia, 1954, 292. The essential idea of this study is that of conceptualizing Bergson's intuitions in order to render them technically useful and to submit them, in a certain fashion, to experimental tests. The author argues that Bergson showed great originality in arguing that intuition is "testable."

3662   Mathieu, Vittorio. "Schemi e simboli." *Filosofia*, 5, No. 2, 1954, 173-190.

3663   Meyer, François. *Problématique de l'évolution.* Paris: Presses Universitaires de France, 1954, 284. (Bibliothèque de philosophie contemporaine) The author argues that a new orientation is necessary for biology, involving new questions and new fields of research. The result of this reorientation is a mathematics of the creative advance of evolution, one which confirms Bergson's ideas but not his belief that the human intellect must fail to understand evolution.

3664   Minkowski, Eugène. *La Schizophrénie: Psychopathologie des schizoides et des schizophrènes.* Paris: Desclée de Brouwer, 1954, 254. This was originally published in 1927.

3665   Meerloo, Joost a. M. *The Two Faces of Man: Two Studies on the Sense of Time and on Ambivalence.* New York: International Universities Press, 1954, 237. Cf. Part 1, The Psychology of Time Sense, esp. Ch. 3 "Spatialization of Time"; Ch. 5 "The Sense of Duration and Continuity." The author views time from the vantage point of a psychotherapist.

3666   Moruzzi, G. "Bergson e la scienza." *Studium,* 50, No. 1, 1954, 3-10.

3667   Myers, Frederic William Henry. *Human Personality, and its Survival of Bodily Death.* Vol. I. New York, London, Toronto: Longmans, Green & Co., 1954, 477-479. This is a response to and criticism of Bergson's article (*Revue philosophique* November, 1886) concerning a supposed case of clairvoyance. The subject, Bergson discovered, could read letters reflected on the cornea of his hypnotizer. He was unaware of this capacity, thus providing an instance of "simulation inconscient." Myers points out that other facts alleged by Bergson may be hard to believe: "Bergson says that he showed the boy a microscopic photograph of twelve men, its longest diameter 2mm., and that the boy saw and imitated the attitude of each man. Also that he showed the boy a microscopic preperation, involving cells not greater than .06 mm. in diameter and the boy saw and drew these cells" (p. 478). Myers speculates, perhaps under hypnosis a muscular spasm can change the shape of the eye, turning it into a sort of "microscope." Myers had discussed Bergson's at length in the January, 1887, issue of *Mind.* He mentions an exchange of letters between Bergson and himself. (This book was first published in 1902.)

3668   Oesterreicher, John M. *Muren storten in: Zeven Joodse filosofen de weg naar Christus.* Haarlem: Standaardboekerij, 1954, 411.

3669   Pfister, Karin. *Zeit und Wirklichkeit bei Thomas Wolfe.* Heidelberg: C. Winter, 1954, 193. The author relates the prose of the novelist Thomas Wolfe to the writings of Marcel Proust and Henri Bergson.

3670   Pradines, Maurice. "L'Evolution du problème de la sensation au XXe siècle." *Journal de Psychologie Normale et Pathologique,* 51, No. 1, 1954, 43-68. Cf. pp. 43-44. Bergson introduced and propagated the notion that a sensation is more an instrument of adaptation than a mode of cognition.

3671   Read, Herbert. "Art and the Evolution of Consciousness." *Journal of Aesthetics and Art Criticism,* 13, No. 3, 1954, 143-155. The author confesses himself to be "an unregenerate Bergsonian" on the question of whether art is an offspring of magic, religion, science, philosophy. To the contrary he holds that art is "the mainspring, the mental faculty without which none of these other graces of mankind would have had a chance of coming into existence..." (p. 151). He uses Bergson's "synoptic" views and those of Lancelot Law Whyte to defend the biological centrality of the artist's perceptions.

3672   Revel, Jean-François. *Pourquoi des philosophes?* Paris: Pauvert, 1954, 184. This study deals with Bergson, J.-P. Sartre, M. Merleau-Ponty, and C. Lévi-Strauss.

3673   Romanell, Patrick. *La formación de la mentalidad mexicana.* Pref. José Gaos. México: Colegio de México, 1954, 238. References to Bergson may be found throughout this study of the Mexican mind.

3674   Roqué, Horacio E. *El Tema de Dios en Bergson.* Córdoba: Dirección general de publicidad de la Universidad nacional de Córdoba, Republica Argentina, 1954, 71.

3675 Scheler, Max. *The Nature of Sympathy.* Trans. Peter Heath. Intro. W. Stark. London: Routledge & Kegan Paul, 1954, 274. On p. 62 the author states: "The only people who are entitled, and obligated, to look for a *metaphysical* concept of fellow-feeling are those who agree with Schopenhauer, Bergson and myself in regarding it in its purest form as a primary act, whose presentative function is essentially one of carrying us *beyond* our own welfare-situation." Cf. also pp. 26-30, 46-47, 56-57, 74-75.

3676 Slater, Mary White. *The Vision of Bergson: An Essay.* New York: Exposition Press, 1954, 45.

3677 Stallknecht, Newton P. and Brumbaugh, Robert S. *The Compass of Philosophy: An Essay In Intellectual Orientation.* New York: Longmans, Green, 1954, 258.

3678 Suckling, Norman. *Paul Valéry and the Civilized Mind.* London: Oxford University Press, 1954, 285. Chapter VII of this book (pp. 199-236) is titled "The Answer to Bergson." In it the author argues not only that Valéry was in no way influenced by Bergson, but that Bergson's and Valéry's philosophies are totally different, Bergson's ideas being anti-rational, biological and activist, Valéry's being intellectualist, passivist, humanistic.

3679 Susman, Margarete. *Gestalten und Kreise.* Zürich: Diana Verlag, 1954, 365.

3680 T., C. "Le Testament de Bergson." *Preuves*, 4, No. 41, juillet 1954, 61-62.

3681 Visentin, Giovanni. "Testimonianza." *Idea*, 6, No. 35, 1954, 3.

3682 Waelhens, Alphonse de. "Notes on Some Trends of Contemporary Philosophy." *Diogenes*, No. 5, Winter 1954, 39-56. Similarities between Bergson and G. W. F. Hegel, K. Marx, S. Kierkegaard, and F. Nietzsche are pointed out by the author.

3683 Wahl, Jean. "M. Jean Wahl apporte du nouveau sur Bergson." *Le Figaro Littéraire*, 22 mai 1954, 9. This concerns hitherto unpublished portions of Bergson's will, which forbid publication of previously unpublished manuscripts and urge response to attacks by his enemies.

3684 Werner, Charles. *La Philosophie moderne.* Paris: Payot, 1954, 326. A section on the reaction against rationalism in this study contains discussions of F. Nietzsche, Bergson, and existentialism.

3685 Wild, John. "The New Empiricism and Human Time." *Review of Metaphysics*, 7, No. 4, June 1954, 537-557. The author discusses Bergson's opposition between lived time and spatial extension on pp. 541-542.

1955

3686 Adolphe, Lydie. *L'Univers bergsonien.* Paris: Edit. du Vieux Colombier, 1955, 353. This work is an exposition of Bergson's philosophy of the sciences. It primarily emphasizes the natural sciences. Cf. pp. 29-58 for Bergson's response to the biologist F. Le Dantec; pp. 159-253 for reflections on the philosophical background involved in Bergson's critique of relativity physics, and for comparisons of Bergson's approach to physics with those of A. Eddington, N. Bohr, L. de Broglie, A. Einstein.

3687 "A La Recherche de l'esthétique à travers les oeuvres de Bergson, Proust, Malraux." *Arts*, No. 509, 1955, 3. This is a review of André and Jean Brincourt, *Les Oeuvres et les lumières.*

3688   Alvarez de linera, Antonio. "Galeria de conversos: El caso extraño de Bergson."
        Revista de Espiritualidad, 14, 1955, 373-384.

3689   Baratz, Léon. *Bergson et ses rapports avec le catholicisme et le judaisme*. Monte
        Carlo: L'auteur, 7 rue Bel Respiro, 1955, 4.

3690   Barthélemy, Madeleine. "Esquisse d'une étude sur la philosophie bergsonienne et
        la vocation de l'unité." *Revue de Métaphysique et de Morale*, 60, No. 1-2,
        1955, 58-68.

3691   Brincourt, André and Jean. *Les Oeuvres et les lumières: A La Rechereche de
        l'esthétique à travers Bergson, Proust, Malraux*. Paris: La Table Ronde, 1955,
        222.

3692   Broglie, Louis de. *Physics and Microphysics*. New York: Pantheon Books, 1955,
        282. "Concepts of Contemporary Physics and the Ideas of Bergson on Time
        and Motion" occurs in abridged form on pp. 186-193.

3693   Caminos, Irene Enriqueta. "La libertad como problema psicológico: Bergson y
        Santo Tomás." *Actas del Primer Congreso Argentino de Psicologia*, 1, 1955,
        177-184.

3694   Canguilhem, Georges. *La Formation du concept de réflex aux XVIIe et XVIIIe
        siècles*. Paris: Presses Universitaires de France, 1955, 206. (Bibliothèque de
        Philosophie Contemporaine: Logique et Philosophie des Sciences) On pp. 74-75
        the author cites passages from Bergson and Wm. James which express the
        viewpoint of Thomas Willis (1621-1675), pioneering English neurologist and
        physiologist.

3695   Cazamian, Louis François. *A History of French Literature*. Oxford: The Clarendon
        Press, 1955, 462. The ideas and influence of Bergson are discussed on pp.
        405-408; Bergson's influence on Proust is discussed on p. 431.

3696   Copleston, Frederich Charles. "Bergson on Morality." *Proceedings of the British
        Academy*, 41, 1955, 247-266.

3697   Cuvillier, Armand. "Préface." Émile Durkheim, *Pragmatisme et sociologie: Cours
        inédit prononcé à la Sorbonne en 1913-1914 et restitué par Armand Cuvillier
        d'après des notes d'étudiants*. Paris: Librarie Philosophique J. Vrin, 1955, 7-26.
        The author compares Durkheim and Bergson on pp. 12, 13-14, and 18.

3698   Devaux, Philippe. *De Thales à Bergson*. Liège, Belgium: Sciences et Lettres,
        1955, 607. Bergson is discussed on pp. 560-573.

3699   Durkheim, Emile. *Pragmatisme et sociologie: Cours inédit prononce à la Sorbonne
        en 1913-1914 et restitué par Armand Cuvillier d'après des notes d'étudiants*.
        Préface Armand Cuvillier. Paris: Librarie Philosophique J. Vrin, 1955, 211. On
        pp. 41-42 the author notes that Henri Bergson and Henri Poincaré have been
        described by William James as pragmatists. The author, however, is skeptical
        concerning such claims. On p. 71, while criticizing the pragmatic critique of
        intellectualism, the author notes that William James derived some of his best
        arguments against the intellect from Bergson. On p. 74 the author asserts James'
        indebtedness to Bergson for the arguments of Chapter VI of *A Pluralistic Uni-
        verse*. On pp. 74-81 he examines these arguments and discounts them as having
        any effect against a rationalism which accepts, and does not try to rule out,
        change. On pp. 107-107 the author notes the similarity between James' idea of
        the "concept" and Bergson's concept of the "dynamic schema." On p. 189 the

author examines the pragmatist's claim that the true and the real are "heterogen-ous." He considers that in doing so he will also be examining the objections which pragmatism has, at this point, borrowed from Bergson. This examination is carried out on pp. 190-197. There are some fascinating comparisons here of Bergson's concept of *élan vital* in biology and Durkheim's notion of social development from primitive to more sophisticated societies. The author con-cludes, "Ajoutons que la verité, en même temps que chose sociale et humaine, est aussi chose *vivante*" (p. 196).

3700   Einstein, Albert. "Foreword." Louis de Broglie. *Physics and Microphysics*. New York: Pantheon Books, 1955, 7. Einstein states: "If found the consideration of Bergson's and Zeno's philosophy from the point of view of the newly acquired concepts highly fascinating."

3701   Enver, Ishrat Hasan. *The Metaphysics of Iqbal*. 2nd Ed., Lahore W. Pakistan: Muhammad Ashraf, 1955, 91.

3702   Ferrater Mora, José. "Introducción a Bergson." *Cuestiones disputadas: Ensayos de filosofía*. Madrid: Revista de Occidente, 1955, 113-150.

3703   Friedmann, Melvin. "William James and Henri Bergson: The Psychological Basis." *Stream of Consciousness: A Study in Literary Method*. New Haven, Connecticut: Yale University Press; London: Geoffrey Cumberlege, Oxford University Press, 1955, 74-98.

3704   Gagnebin, Samuel. "Hommage á Edouard Le Roy." *Revue de Théologie et de Philosophie*, 3e Sér., 5, 1955, 202-217.

3705   Gex, M. "A Propos de la pensée philosophique de Gustave Mercier." *Revue de la Mediterranée*, 15, No. 70, 1955, 641-643.

3706   Green, F. C. *Jean-Jacques Rousseau: A Critical Study of His Life and Writings*. Cambridge: University Press, 1955, 376. The author argues that Bergson was influenced by Rousseau and that much of the ground for Bergson's theories was broken by Rousseau.

3707   Heidsieck, François. "La Notion d'espace chez Bergson." Diss., Paris, 1955, 196.

3708   Hulme, Thomas Ernest. *Further Speculations*. Ed. Sam Hynes. Minneapolis, Min-nesota: University of Minnesota Press, 1955, 226. The editor discusses Hulme's Bergsonism on pp. xii-xiv; Hulme's notes on Bergson are given on pp. 28-63.

3709   Joussain, André. "Bergson et la pensée juive." *Ecrits de Paris*, septembre 1955, 75-81.

3710   Marietti, Angèle. "Le Bergsonisme dans la perspective d'une théorie du même et autre." *Revue Moderne des Arts et de la Vie*, 56, No. 11, ler novembre 1955, 21-22.

3711   Maritain, Jacques. *Bergsonian Philosophy and Thomism*. Trans. Mabelle L. Andison with J. Gordon Andison. New York: Philosophical Library, 1955, 383.

3712   Meyerhoff, Hans. *Time in Literature*. Berkeley and Los Angeles: University of California Press, 1955, 160. The author uses Bergson's philosophy to explore concepts of duration and memory in the work of many recent writers, including Thomas Wolfe, Virginia Woolf, James Joyce, Marcel Proust. He mistakenly holds that Bergson had no concept of duration in nature and that William James took his concept of the specious present from Bergson. (Cf. pp. 17, 28)

3713   Minkowski, Eugène. "Zum Problem der erlebten Zeit." *Studium Generale*, 8, No. 10, 1955, 601-607.

3714   Mossé-Bastide, Rose-Marie. *Bergson éducateur*. Paris: Presses Universitaires de France, 1955, 465. This book is an excellent study of Bergson's concept of education, in the broadest sense. It is also a detailed account of Bergson's life and opinions.

3715   Mossé-Bastide, Rose-Marie. "Bibliographie des questions d'enseignement et d'éducation." *Bergson éducateur*. Paris: Presses Universitaires de France, 1955, 449-450. This bibliography contains references to articles and books in which Bergson's educational ideas are discussed. It is very brief.

3716   Nuñez, E. "O sentido do tempo no homen." *Journal Brasileiro Psiquiatria*, 4, No. 2, 1955, 198-212. The author discusses the experience of time in E. Minkowski, L. Binswanger, Bergson, M. Heidegger, and modern psychiatry.

3717   Oesterreicher, John M. *Sept Philosophes juifs devant le Christ*. Paris: Cerf, 1955, 616. Bergson, B. Spinoza, L. Brunschvicg, and other Jewish thinkers are analyzed by the author in terms of their attitudes towards Christ and Christianity.

3718   Poulain, Dorothy. "Monsieur Pouget: A Christian Socrates." *Catholic World*, 181, No. 1085, August 1955, 326-331.

3719   "A la rechereche de l'esthétique." *Arts*, No. 509, 1955, 3. This is a review of *Les Oeuvres et les lumières: A la rechereche de l'esthétique...*by André and Jean Brincourt.

3720   Santayana, George. *The Letters of George Santayana*. Ed. and Intro. Daniel Cory. New York: Scribner, 1955, xxxi, 451. Santayana remarks on p. 121 that he has written "reams on Bergson." (Much of what Santayana wrote was never published, and remains in manuscript, in a Columbia University library. See Morris Grossmann, "Santayana as Dramatist and Dialectician.")

3721   Scharfstein, Ben-Ami. "Bergson and Merleau-Ponty: A Preliminary Comparison." *Journal of Philosophy*, 52, No. 14, 1955, 380-386.

3722   Stahl, Roland. "Bergson's Influence on Whitehead." *Personalist*, 36, No. 3, 1955, 250-257. Whitehead was deeply indebted to Bergson, according to the author.

3723   Torchia Estrada, J. *La filosofía del siglo XX*. Buenos Aires: Atlantida, 1955, 346.

3724   Untermeyer, Louis. *Makers of the Modern World: The Lives of Ninety-two Writers, Artists, Scientists, Statesmen, Inventors, Philosophers, Composers, and Other Creators Who Formed the Pattern of Our Century*. New York: Simon and Schuster, 1955, 809.

3725   Valensin, Auguste. *Regards sur Platon, Descartes, Pascal, Bergson, Blondel*. Intro. André Blauchet. Paris: Aubier, 1955, 327.

3726   Vax, Louis. "Du Bergsonisme á la philosophie première." *Critique*, 11, No. 92, 1955, 36-52. This is a study of Jankélévitch's *Bergson*.

3727   Wagner, Geoffrey. "Wyndham Lewis and Bergson." *Romantic Review*, 46, No. 2, 1955, 112-124. Lewis owed an inadvertent debt to Bergson, according to the author.

3728   White, Morton. "Time, Instinct, and Freedom." *The Great Ages of Western Philosophy: The Age of Analysis—20th Century Philosophers*. New York: New American Library, 1955, 253. An introduction and readings from Bergson are on pp. 65-81.

3729   Whitehead, Alfred North. *The Concept of Nature: Tarner Lectures Deilvered in Trinity College, November 1919*. Cambridge: The University Press, 1955, 202. This work was originally published in 1920. On p. 54 the author states, "The process of nature can also be termed the passage of nature. I definitely refrain at this stage from using the word 'time,' since the measurable time of science and civilized life generally merely exhibits some aspects of the fundamental fact of the passage of nature. I believe that in this doctrine I am in full accord with Bergson, though he uses 'time' for the fundamental fact which I call the 'passage of nature.' Also the passage of nature is exhibited equally in spatial transition as well as in temporal transition." The author uses the term "duration" on pp. 37, 53, 55, and 186. On pp. 59, 73, and 190 he uses the phrase "families of durations."

3730   Wyrick, Green D. "Hemingway and Bergson: The Elan Vital." *Modern Fiction Studies*, 1, No. 3, August 1955, 17-19. Parallels between Bergson and Hemingway are sought after in this article.

1956

3731   Acker, Leonardo van. "Structure épistémologique et méthodologique de la métaphysique bergsonienne." *Revista da Universidade Católica de São Paulo*, 10, Nos. 18-19, 1956, 125-163. The author deals with Bergson's substantialism and with the complementarity which Bergson establishes between intuition and intellect. This study is published in the author's *A filosofia bergsoniana*.

3732   Acker, Leonardo van. *Structure épistémologique et méthodologique de la métaphysique bergsonienne*. São Paulo: Ed. de Revista da Universidade Católica de São Paulo, 1956.

3733   Alain. *Propos*. Ed. Maurice Savin. Paris: Gallimard, 1956, 1370. Bergson is discussed on p. 614.

3734   Alves, Garcia J. "O dualismo metodologico na psicología contemporánea." *Revista Portuguesa de Filosofia*, 12, No. 1, 1956, 14-28. The author argues that for Bergson a dualism of objects and of methods need not lead to a dualism of kinds of knowledge.

3735   Anselme, F. "Review of *Bergson éducateur* by R.-M. Mossé-Bastide." *Nouvelle Revue Pédagogique*, 11, 1956, 334-340.

3736   Antoni, Carlo. "Henri Bergson." *Vite de pensatoir*. Torino: Ediz. Radio Italiana, 1956, 96.

3737   Arbour, Roméo. *Henri Bergson et les lettres françaises*. Paris: Corti, 1956, 456.

3738   Ardao, Arturo. *La filosofía en el Uruguay en el siglo XX*. México and Buenos Aires: Fondo de Cultura Economica, 1956, 193. Bergson is discussed on pp. 56-60, 88-89, and 167-170.

3739   Aron, Raymond. "Note sur Bergson et l'histoire." *Etudes Bergsoniennes*, 4, 1956, 41-51.

3740   Baillet, Dom Louis. "Lettres de Dom Louis Baillet à Joseph Lotte, présentées par C.-Th. Quoniam." *Feuillets de l'Amitié Charles Péguy*, No. 54, septembre 1956, 19-36.

3741 Bordeaux, Henry. *Histoire d'une vie*: Vol. 3. *La Douceur de vivre menacée 1909-1914*. Paris: Plon, 1956, 367.

3742 Camon Aznar, José. *La idea del tiempo en Bergson y el impresionismo: Contestación de S. Zuazo Ugalde*. Madrid: Aguirre, 1956, 69.

3743 Chahine, Osman Eissa. "La Durée créatrice dans la philosophie de Bergson." Diss., Paris, 1956, 190.

3744 Chaix-Ruy, Jules. "Bergson et ses critiques italiens." *Études Bergsoniennes*, 4, 1956, 205-266. This article contains a bibliography, pp. 225-226.

3745 Cocking, J. M. *Proust*. London: Bowes and Bowes, 1956, 80. The author discusses Bergson's influence on Proust on pp. 21-25.

3746 Deleuze, Gilles. "Bergson (1859-1941)." *Les Philosophes célèbres: Ouvrage publié sous la direction de Maurice Merleau-Ponty*. Paris: Editions d'Art Lucien Mazenod, 1956, 292-299.

3747 Deleuze, Gilles. "La Conception de la différence chez Bergson." *Etudes Bergsoniennes*, 4, 1956, 77-112.

3748 Dresden, Samuel. "Les Idées esthétiques de Bergson." *Etudes Bergsoniennes*, 4, 1956, 55-75.

3749 Durand, R. L. "Review of *Regards sur Platon, Descartes, Pascal, Bergson, Blondel* by A. Valensin." *Revista Nacional de Cultura*, 18, No. 115, 1956, 197.

3750 *Etudes Bergsoniennes*. Paris: Presses Universitaires de France, 1956, Vol. 4, 254. Bergson's philosophy of history, Bergson's aesthetics, and Bergson and Péguy are discussed in this issue.

3751 Favarger, Charles. "Review of *L'Univers bergsonien* by Lydie Adolphe." *Revue de Théologie et de Philosophie*, 3e Série, 6, No. 2, 1956, 147-149.

3752 Francastel, Pierre. "Bergson et Picasso." *Mélanges 1945*: Vol. 4. *Etudes philosophiques*. Paris: Les Belles Lettres, 1946, 200-213.

3753 Frye, Robert Edward. "Pragmatism in Recent Non-Pragmatic Systems: Santayana, Bergson, Whitehead." Diss. Indiana, 1956, 168. While Santayana, Bergson, and Whitehead each recognize that the mind has a pragmatic function, each, the author states, takes a different view of its limitations. Santayana criticizes pragmatism for failing to give an account of the mind's purely contemplative capacities. The author criticizes Santayana for failing to show the relevance of man's purely speculative capacities to action, which Santayana describes as being based on "animal faith" and needing no coherent world view. The author examines Bergson's critique of reason, concluding that while Bergson attempts to safeguard speculation by showing reason's pragmatic bias, he ends by rendering intuition—and creativity—entirely blind. He can not account for the discipline of reason in his own work. Whitehead is able, by contrast, to show that speculative reason is both transcendent and orderly, and that intuition is a form of reason. Whitehead's extension of pragmatic doctrines allows him to accept Bergson's appeal to experience without negating the claims of reason. (See *Dissertation Abstracts International*, 17, Nos. 1-4, 1957, 377.)

3754 Fulton, James Street. "Bergson's Religious Interpretation of Evolution." *Rice Institute Pamphlet*, 43, No. 3, 1956, 14-27. This essay discusses Bergson's position in *The Two Sources of Morality and Religion*. The author argues that in this book Bergson no longer describes evolution as a mere emergence of novelty, but as the increase of value, progress, and spiritual significance. The author provides a brief but penetrating account of moral obligation and static religion.

3755 Garcia, J. Alvez. "O dualismo metodologico na psicologia contemporânea." *Revista Portuguesa de Filosofia*, 12, No. 1, 1956, 14-20. Bergson is one of several figures discussed. (E. Husserl, K. Jaspers, W. Kohler...). The discussion of Bergson (pp. 20-23) is brief, critical.

3756 Giboulot, G. "Expérience ésthetique et expérience religieuse de Bergson." Diss. Paris 1956, 269.

3757 Graham, J. W. "A Negative Note on Bergson and Virginia Woolf." *Essays in Criticism*, 6, No. 1, 1956, 70-74.

3758 Hamilton, G. H. "Cezanne, Bergson and the Image of Time." *College Art Journal*, 16, No. 1, 1956, 2-12.

3759 Henry, André. "Quelques Aspects du bergsonisme de Péguy d'après les notes de 1914." *Etudes Bergsoniennes*, 4, 1956, 113-115.

3760 Husson, Léon. "Les Aspects méconnus de la liberté bergsonienne." *Etudes Bergsoniennes*, 4, 1956, 157-201.

3761 Iacono, Gustavo. "La Perception de la durée." *Journal de Psychologie Normale et Pathologiques*, 53, No. 3, 1956, 307-314. The author has devised a new method for the measurement of experienced duration, which differs from the traditional method of the reproduction of brief temporal intervals. The author hopes to discover whether the notion of duration is rooted in perceptual experience or derives from a sort of spatialized duration.

3762 Jacques, E. "Review of *L'Univers bergsonien* by Lydie Adolphe." *Revue Philosophique de Louvain*, 3e Sér., 54, No. 43, 1956, 508-509.

3763 Joussain, André. "Bergsonisme et marxisme." *Ecrits de Paris*, No. 137, avril 1956, 50-55. The author argues that Bergson is neither a revolutionary like Sartre nor, as certain Russian commentators insist, a reactionary conservative. Unlike the revolutionary, Bergson believes in the conservation of the past and tradition. Unlike the reactionary, he believes in creativity and the openness of the future.

3764 Krieger, Murray. *The New Apologists for Poetry*. Minneapolis: University of Minnesota Press, 1956, 225. On pp. 33-45 the author explains the nature and extent of Bergson's influence on the literary critic T. E. Hulme.

3765 Lahbabi, Mohamed Aziz. *Liberté ou libération?: A Partir des libertés bergsoniennes*. Préf. M. de Gandillac. Paris: Editions Montaigne, 1956, 254. The author argues that Bergson's identification of liberty with subjectivity makes it impossible to understand how liberty can be active in a social context. Real liberty has as its conditions both supports in human reality and a location in external liberty.

3766 Maiorana, María-Teresa. "Comentarios deshilvanados a una lectura de Bergson: *Las dos fuentes de la religión y la moral*." *Criterio*, 29, Nos. 1266-1270, 1956, 769-772.

3767 Maire, Gilbert. "Un Ami d'Henri Bergson: Joseph Desaymard." *Etudes Bergsoniennes*, 3, 158-159. This is a résumé of Maire's talk on Bergson and Desaymard, followed by a discussion.

3768 Maitra, S. K. *The Meeting of the East and the West in Sri Aurobindo's Philosophy*. Pondicherry: Sri Aurobindo Ashram, 1956, 451.

3769 Mikumo, Natsumi. "Essay on the Moral and Religious Philosophy of Bergson and Blondel." *Philosophy*, No. 32, 1956, 4-6. This article is in Japanese.

3770 Millet, Louis. "La Chaire de Bergson au Collège de France." *Études Bergsoniennes*, 4, 1956, 230-233.

3771 Millet, Louis. "Lettres et entretiens de Bergson." *Études Bergsoniennes*, 4, 1956, 233-239.

3772 Millet, Louis. "Note pour une bibliographie bergsonienne." *Études Bergsoniennes*, 4, 1956, 243-254.

3773 Minkowski, Eugène. "L'Éphemère, durer et avoir une durée, l'éternal." *Revue de Métaphysique et de Morale*, 61, Nos. 3-4, 1956, 217-241.

3774 Morgan, Charles. "Bergson und die Maritains oder die Freiheit vom Materialismus." *Von der Freiheit des Geistes: Essays*. Ed. Gerd van Bebber and Ernst Sander. Stuttgart: Dt. Verl.-Anst., 1956, 173-180.

3775 Moschetti, Andrea Mario. "S. Agostino e il bergsonismo." *S. Agostino e le grandi correnti della filosofia agostiniana: Atti del Congresso Italiano di Filosofia Agostiniana, Roma 20-23 ottobre 1954*. Macerata, Italy: Edizioni Agostiniane, 1956, 271-277.

3776 Muller, Herbert J. *Science and Criticism*. New York: George Braziller, Inc., 1956, 303. Bergson is discussed on pp. 246-250 and 260 under the heading "Purport of Scientific Humanism."

3777 Niel, André. "Vers Un Humanisme cosmologique: De Bergson à Teilhard de Chardin et J. Huxley." *Critique*, 11e Année, No. 106, 1956, 220-229. This is a review of books by P. Teilhard de Chardin, A. Vandel, M. Gex, A. Varagnac, J. Huxley. The author views these works as examples of a philosophy of nature begun by Bergson. In these more recent works Bergson's inner time becomes cosmic time.

3778 Niess, Robert J. *Julien Benda*, Ann Arbor, Michigan: University of Michigan Press, 1956, x, 361. The author discusses Benda's fourty-year personal vendetta against Bergson on pp. 95-143.

3779 Polin, Raymond. "Y a-t-il chez Bergson une philosophie de l'histoire?" *Etudes Bergsoniennes*, 4, 1956, 7-40.

3780 Poulet, Georges. *Studies in Human Time*. Baltimore, Maryland: Johns Hopkins Press, 1956, 323.

3781 Révész, F. *The Origins and Prehistory of Language*. Trans. J. Butler. New York: Longman's, Green and Co., 1956, 240. On p. 92 the author concurs with Bergson on the importance of stone tools for the dating of the evolutionary emergence of man and of human language. On pp. 174-177 he uses Bergson's concept of duration and the "cinematic" nature of imagery to deal with the relation between continuity and discontinuity in speech and in biological evolution. The author cites the imperative as the most primitive form of speech and suggests a "contact" theory of the development of language.

3782 Ribiero, Alvaro. "Bergson au Portugal." *Etudes Bergsoniennes*, 4, 1956, 227-229.

3783 Russell, Bertrand. *Portraits from Memory and Other Essays*. New York: Simon and Schuster, 1956, 247. Russell says of Whitehead, "He had always had a leaning toward Kant, of whom I thought ill, and when he began to develop his own philosophy he was considerably influenced by Bergson" (pp. 100-101). "It used to be the custom among clever people to say that Shaw was not unusually vain, but only unusually candid. I came to think later that this was a mistake. Two incidents at which I was present convinced me of this. The first was a luncheon in London in honor of Bergson, to which Shaw had been invited as an admirer, along with a number of professional philosophers whose attitude to Bergson was more critical. Shaw set to work to expound Bergson's philosophy in the style of the preface to Methusela. In this version, the philosophy was hardly one to recommend itself to professionals, and Bergson mildly interjected, 'Ah, no-o! It is not qvite zat!' But Shaw was quite unabashed, and replied, 'Oh, my dear fellow, I understand your philosophy much better than you do.' Bergson clenched his fists and nearly exploded with rage; but with a great effort, he controlled himself, and Shaw's expository monologue continued" (p. 78). "Butler's influence on Shaw was much greater than most people realized. It was from him that Shaw acquired his antipathy to Darwin, which afterward made him an admirer of Bergson" (p. 79).

3784   Seyppel, Joachim H. "A Criticism of Heidegger's Time Concept with Reference to Bergson's 'durée'." *Revue Internationale de Philosophie*, 10, No. 4, 1956, 503-508.

3785   Sypher, Wylie. "Appendix: The Meanings of Comedy." in *Comedy*. Garden City, New York: Doubleday and Company, Inc., 1956, 193-258. The author explores the history of the concept of comedy and argues that Bergson's notion of comedy is incomplete.

3786   Sypher, Wylie. "Introduction" in *Comedy*. Garden City, New York: Doubleday and Company, Inc., 1956, vii-xvi. The author gives general accounts of George Meredith's *An Essay on Comedy* and Henri Bergson's *Laughter*, which are co-published in this volume.

3787   Taminiaux, Jacques. "De Bergson à la phénoménologie existentielle." *Revue Philosophique de Louvain*, 54, No. 1, février 1956, 26-85.

3788   Tissier, A. "Il y a 15 dans mourait Bergson." *France-Asie*, 12, No. 117, 1956, 647-676.

3789   Veatch, Henry. "Review of *Bergsonian Philosophy and Thomism* by Jacques Chevalier." *Speculum*, 31, No. 3, July, 1956, 532-534.

3790   Voelke, A. "Les Thèmes fondamentaux de la métaphysique de Raymond Ruyer." *Revue de Théologie et de Philosophie*, 6, No. 1, 1956, 11-28. The author explains: "Partant de travaux scientifiques, Ruyer a formulé une philosophie que l'on peut rapprocher de celle de Bergson."

1957

3791   Abel, Darrel. "Frozen Movement in *Light in August*." *Boston University Studies in English*, 3, No. 3, September, 1957, 32-44. The author uses Bergson's distinctions between intuition and intellect, duration and space (frozen movement) to explore the vision of the American novelist William Faulkner.

3792   Alexander, Ian W. *Bergson: Philosopher of Reflection*. London: Bowes and Bowes Publishers Limited; New York: Hillary House, 1957, 109 (Studies in Modern European Literature and Thought). This is an excellent short study of Bergson's philosophy. It draws parallels between Bergson's thought and behaviorism and phenomenology, and argues against irrationalist interpretations of Bergson.

3793 Battaglia, Felice. "Bergson e la storia." *Giornale di metafisica*, 12, No. 2, 1957, 180-182. This is a note on articles by Polin and Aron in *Etudes Bergsoniennes*, 4 (1956).

3794 Bausola, A. "Review of *Bergson éducateur* by R.-M. Mossé-Bastide." *Rivista di filosofia neoscolastica*, 49, No. 5-6, 1957, 559-561.

3795 Boaz, George. *Dominant Themes of Modern Philosophy*. New York: Ronald Press Co., 1957, 660. The author discusses Bergson's philosophy in connection with that of Félix Ravaisson on pp. 620-628. The general title for this section of the author's book is "The Acceptance of Time."

3796 Bruch, Jean-Louis. "Die Bergson-Forschung in Frankreich." *Antares*, 5, No. 2, 1957, 31-32.

3797 Buber, Martin. "Bergson's Concept of Intuition." in *Pointing the Way: Collected Essays*. Ed. and Trans. Maurice Friedman. London: Routledge and Kegan Paul, 1957. The author, highly critical, argues that in intuition as Bergson describes it one could only know the immediate past (p. 82), that the effort to achieve intuition must disturb and hence distort the reality known (p. 82), that intuition can not achieve a unified "absolute" viewpoint (pp. 83-84), that intuition, as instinct, can not know life as a whole, but only in particular cases (pp. 84-86). In general the author wishes to restrict "intuition" to I-Thou relationships.

3798 Challaye, Félicien. "Immortalité et existentialisme." *Synthèses*, No. 128, janvier 1957, 286-296.

3799 Chauvy, Michel. *Intériorité: Trois Cheminements vers l'intériorité: Plotin, Saint Augustin, Bergson*. Montreux, Suisse: Payot, 1957, 28.

3800 Czoniczer, Elisabeth. *Quelques antécédents de <<A la recherche du temps perdu>>: Tendances qui peuvent avoir contribué à la cristallisation du roman proustien*. Genève: E. Droz, 1957, 224. Sec especially pp. 103-109. On p. 109 the author states, "Car, bien plus certes qu'entre Freud et Proust, bein plus qu'entre Bergson et Proust, il semble y avoir des correspondances entre Proust et Frédéric Paulhan."

3801 Delfgaauw, Bernard. *Die Wijsbegeerte van de 20e Eeuw*. Baarn, Holland: Uitgeverij het Wereldvenster, 1957, 198.

3802 Duckworth, Colin. "Albert Thibaudet: Poète bergsonien." *Revue des Sciences Humaines*, N.S. No. 88, 1957, 461-468.

3803 Dujovne, León. *La filosofía de la histoira de Neitzsche a Toynbee*. Buenos Aires: Edición Galatea-Nueva Visión, 1957, 203. The author maintains that Bergson, with Spengler, constituted the all-important influence on Toynbee.

3804 Garcez, Maria Dulce Nogueira. *Do significado da contribuição de Bergson para e a educação contemporâneas*. Univ. de S. Paulo, Faculd. de Filosofia, 1957, 242. (Boletim n. 184, Psicologia educacional n. 4) On pp. 239-242 English and French language summaries are provided. The author states (p. 241) "The purpose of this work is to make a synthesis and a critical study of Bergson's system, in so far as it concerns Psychology and Education." She applies Bergson's ideas to physical as well as intellectual education (literature, science, philosophy, art).

3805 Heidsieck, François. *Henri Bergson et la notion d'espace*. Paris: Le Cercle du Livre, 1957, 196. This is a careful analysis of Bergson's concept of space: its origins, development, and function in Bergson's philosophy. The author argues that the concept of space is dialectically bound up with that of genesis or creation. Bergson did not at all points adversely criticize the notion of space. "...Mais non! C'est bien plus un 'revelateur'. (p. 14) The author's analysis of the relations between philosophy and science in Bergson is particularly perceptive, as is his treatment of Bergson and relativity physics.

3806   Hellman, Winfried. "Der Begriff der Zeit bei Henri Bergson." *Philosophia Naturalis*, 4, No. 1, 1957, 126-139.

3807   Horne, James R. "Bergson's Mysticism Compared with *Agape* and *Eros*." *Hibbert Journal*, 55, No. 4, July 1957, 363-372. The author argues that Bergson tried to fit Agape into a metaphysical system too limited to appropriate it.

3808   Jankélévitch, Vladimir. "Bergson et le judaisme." *Mélanges de philosophie et de littérature juives*. Vol. 1. Paris: Presses Universitaires de France, 1957, 64-94.

3809   Kermode, Frank. *Romantic Image*. New York: MacMillan, 1957, 171. The author explores Bergson's influence on the Imagism of T. E. Hulme on pp. 120-136 and on the Vorticism of Wyndham Lewis on pp. 133-135.

3810   King, Clifford. "The Laughter of Marcel Proust." *Adam*, 25, No. 260, 1957, 126-129. This is an analysis of Proustian comedy in terms of Bergson's theory of laughter.

3811   Kumar, Shiv Kumar. "Bergson and Stephen Dedalus' Aesthetic Theory." *Journal of Aesthetics and Art Criticism*, 16, No. 1, 1957-1958, 124-127.

3812   Kumar, Shiv K. "Space-Time Polarity in *Finnegan's Wake*." *Modern Philosophy*, 54, No. 4, 1957, 230-233. The author asserts on p. 230 that "in the work of James Joyce, as in the entire thought of Bergson, space and time are presented as contraries, with durational flux as the only true reality." The author denies, however, that Joyce is consciously influenced by Bergson.

3813   Kumar, Shiv Kumar. *Virginia Woolf and Bergson's 'durée'*. Hoshiarpur, India: Vishveshvaranand Book Agency, 1957, 17.

3814   Lehmann, Gerhard. *Geschichte der Philosophie*: Vol. 10. *Die Philosophie im ersten Drittel des XX. Jahrhunderts*. Berlin: de Gruyter and Co., 1957, 128. Bergson is discussed in this book under the heading "Irrationalismus und Intuitionismus."

3815   Leròy, André-Louis. "A Propose du cône bergsonien." *Revue Philosophique de la France et de l'Étranger*, 147, No. 1, 1957, 65-68.

3816   Mathieu, Vittorio. "Bergson, Henri-Louis." *Enciclopedia Filosofia*, Vol. 1, 643-651.

3817   Maurois, André. "Bergson." In *Les Grandes Ecrivains du demi siècle*. Paris: Club du Livre du Mois, 1957, 101-123.

3818   Mayer, Hans. "Welt und Wirkung Henri Bergsons." *Deutsche Literatur und Weltliteratur Reden und Aufsätze*. Berlin: Rütten und Loening, 1957, 517-530.

3819   Mossé-Bastide, Rose-Marie, Ed. *Ecrits et paroles*. Paris: Presses Universitaires de France, 1957-1959, 3 vols., 665 (Bibliothèque de Philosophie Contemporaine). This is a relatively complete collection of talks, reports, letters, and other short writings by Bergson.

3820   Mossé-Bastide. Rose-Marie. "Introduction à la traduction, *Quid Aristoteles de Loco Senserit* par Henri Bergson." *Etudes Bergsoniennes*, 2, 1949, 9-25.

3821   Mossé-Bastide, Rose-Marie. "Review of *La Dialectique des images chez Bergson* by Lydie Adolphe." *Revue Philosophique de la France et de l'Étranger*, 147,

No. 1, 1957, 95-96.

3822   Moulyn, Adrian C. *Structure, Function and Purpose: An Inquiry into the Concepts and Methods of Biology from the Viewpoint of Time.* Pref. Yervant H. Krikorian. New York: Liberal Arts Press, 1957, 198. The author states: "Biology in the wider sense needs a dynamic time concept like the precious present" (p. 117). Only man and some higher organisms share in this dynamic present, however.

3823   Oddino, Montiani. *Bergson e il suo umanismo integrale.* Padua: A. Milani, 1957, 306. (Il Pensiero moderno)

3824   Pró, Diego F. "La realidad espiritual y ontología." *Alberto Rouges.* Argentina: Valles Calchaquiés, 1957, 386.

3825   Rideau, Emile. "En relisant *Les Deux Sources.*" *Etudes par des Pères de la Compagnie de Jésus*, 294, octobre 1957, 3-16.

3826   Rossi, Carlo. *Fenomeno e contenuto della conscienza.* Milano: C. Marzorati, 1957, 123.

3827   Sartre, Jean-Paul. *The Transcendence of The Ego: An Existentialist Theory of Consciousness.* Trans., Ann. with Intro. Forrest Williams and Rbt. Kirkpatrick. New York: Noonday Press, 1957. The author criticizes Bergson for having made the ego an object (an *en soi*), illicitly projecting into it the pure spontaneity of transcendental consciousness (a *pour soi*). Cf. esp. pp. 80-85.

3828   Scharfstein, Ben-Ami. "Review of *Bergsonian Philosophy and Thomism* by Jacques Maritain." *Journal of Philosophy*, 54, No. 3, 1957, 76-78.

3829   Smith, Colin. "The Philosophy of Vladimir Jankélévitch." *Philosophy*, 32, No. 123, 1957, 315-324.

3830   Wagner, Geoffrey. "Wyndham Lewis and James Joyce: A Study in Controversy." *South Atlantic Quarterly*, 56, No. 1, 1957, 57-66. This is a study of the critic Wyndham Lewis and his indictment, in *Time and Western Man, The Childremass*, and elsewhere, of James Joyce's presumably Bergsonian and Einsteinian views. The author claims that after all [after all the endless controversy] Joyce was not Bergsonian.

3831   Webb, Clifford Wellington. "Space and Time in the Philosophies of Kant and Bergson." Diss. Toronto 1957, 137.

3832   Wieman, Henry Nelson. "Intellectual Autobiography" Unpublished Manuscript. Carbondale: Southern Illinois University, Archives, 1957. On p. 11 Wieman states of the period of his pastorate (prior to his entering graduate school in philosophy at Harvard): "I read Bergson and found him exciting. Bergson gave to my thinking a direction which deflected the influence of Harvard and caused me to reinterpret my teachers as I would not otherwise have done. Ever since those days of private study in Davis my thinking has been deeply influenced by Bergson's idea of Creativity, although my interpretation is somewhat different from his." Concerning the influence on him at Harvard of the idealist philosophies of Josiah Royce and William Ernest Hocking, Wieman also states: "Bergson had already intervened to turn me away from the metaphysics of idealism..." (p. 11)

3833   Wolff, Edgar. "La Théorie de la mémoire chez Bergson." *Archives de Philosophie*, 20, No. 1, 1957, 42-77. The author holds that: "Il faut repenser *Matière et mémoire* à travers *L'Effort intellectuel* et *L'Evolution créatrice.*" In *Matter and*

Memory Bergson defines memory as the preservation of a multiplicty of recollections; in *Creative Evolution* he developes a different hypothesis, which relates memory to the concept of duration. The author reinterprets Bergson in terms of a concept of schematism developed in his thesis, *La Sensation et l'image* (Toulouse, 1943). Cf. the author, 1959.

1958

3834   Alain. *Les Arts et les dieux*. Ed. Georges Bénézé. Paris: Gallimard, 1958, 1488. Bergson's disciples are discussed on pp. 63 and 1195.

3835   Barisch, Theodor. "Henri Bergson und das Problem des Komischen: Eine Vorstudie." *Beitrag zur deutschen und nordischen Literatur*. Berlin: Akademie Verlag, 1958, 377-391. "Festgabe für Leopold Magon zum 70. Geburtstag."

3836   Barrett, William. *Irrational Man: A Study in Existential Philosophy*. New York: Doubleday and Company, Inc., 1958, 278. Bergson as a source of French existentialism is discussed on pp. 13 and 100.

3837   Bordeaux, Henry. "Les Dernières Années d'Henri Bergson." *Revue des Deux Mondes*, N.S. Année 11, No. 22, 15 novembre 1958, 220-226.

3838   Bruning, Walter. "La filosofia irracionalista de la historia en la actualidad." *Revista de Filosofía*, 5, No. 2, 1958, 3-17. F. Nietzsche, Bergson, and L. Klages are discussed in this study of irracionalist philosophies of history.

3839   Champigny, Robert. "Temps et reconnaissance chez Proust et quelques philosophes." *Publications of the Modern Language Association of America*, 73, No. 1, March 1958, 129-135. According to the author Proust differed with Bergson at many points.

3840   Colin, Pierre. "Bergson et l'absolu." *Recherches de Philosophie*, 3-4, 1958, 113-124.

3841   Chandra, S. Subhash. "The Reign of Time in Contemporary Thought." *The Philosophical Quarterly*, 31, No. 1, April 1958, 49-56."

3842   Cornu, A. "Der Bergsonismus." In *Im Dienste der Sprache: Festschrift für Victor Klemperer zum 75. Geburtstag*. Ed. Horst Heintze and Erwin Silzer. Halle: Niemeyer, 1958, 152-156.

3843   Decloux, S. "Review of *Bergson: Il profondo e la sua espressione* by Vittorio Mathieu." *Revue Philosophique de Louvain*, 3e Série, 56, No. 51, août 1958, 525-526. The reviewer comments on the author's treatment of *Duration and Simultaneity* and of the "stratified" and "prospective" aspects of Bergson's universe.

3844   Deshayes, M.-L. "L'Esthétique bergsonienne." *Les Humanités. Classes de lettres. Sections modernes*. CI. 341, décembre 1958, 21-26.

3845   Ferrater Mora, José. *Diccionario de filosofía*. 3e ed. Buenos Aires: Ed. Sudamericana, 1958, 1047.

3846   Friar, Kimon. "Introduction." *The Odyssey: A Modern Sequel* by Nikos Kazantzakis. Trans. Kimon Friar. New York: Simon and Schuster, 1958, ix-xxviii. Bergson's influence on Kazantzakis is discussed here on pp. xvi-xvii. The translator states on p. xxi that "Perhaps the deepest influence on Kazantzakis' thought has been that of Bergson."

3847 Galeffi, Romano. "O cômico em Bergson." *Revista Brasileira de Filosofia*, 8, No. 32, 1958, 416-444. This is an analysis of Chapter I, *Le Rire*.

3848 Groot, Herko. *Het mysterie van de tijd*. Assens, Denmark: Van Gorcum, 1958, 100. This essay includes a discussion of Kant and Bergson.

3849 Hampshire, Stuart. "Philosophy in France." *New Statesman*, 55, No. 1402, January 25, 1958, 109-110.

3850 Henry, André. "Review of *Henri Bergson et les lettres françaises* by Romeo Arbour." *Feuillets de l'Amitié Charles Péguy*, No. 65, juin 1958, 35-36.

3851 Hughes, Henry Stuart. *Consciousness and Society: The Reorientation of European Social Thought, 1890-1930*. New York: Alfred A. Knopf, 1958, 433. "Bergson and the Uses of Intuition" are discussed here on pp. 113-125. The author argues that the conceptual and pragmatic fruitfulness of intuition, as Bergson understood it, were not understood by his conservative French contemporaries, but might have been understood by German thinkers.

3852 Iberico, Mariano. *Perspectivas sobre el tema del tiempo*. Lima: Universidad Nacional Mayor de San Marcos, 1958, 195.

3853 Journet, C. "Autour d'Henri Bergson." *Nova et Vetera*, 33, No. 4, 1958, 262-278. J. Chevalier, A. Sertillanges, and the Maritains are dealt with in this study.

3854 Levi, Albert William. "Substance, Process, Being: A Whiteheadian-Bergsonian View." *Journal of Philosophy*, 55, No. 18, August 29, 1958, 749-761.

3855 Long, Wilbur, "Review of *Mémoire et vie* by Gilles Deleuze." *Personalist*, 39, No. 2, 1958, 220.

3856 Marcel, Gabriel. "Bergsonism and Music." *Reflections on Art*. Ed. Susanne K. Langer. Baltimore, Maryland: Johns Hopkins Press, 1958, 142-151.

3857 Mathieu, Vittorio. "Review of *Ecrits et paroles* by Henri Bergson." *Filosofia*, 9, No. 3, 1958, 500-501.

3858 Mathieu, Vittorio. "Tempo, memoria, eternità: Bergson e Proust." *Archivio di filosofia*, 21, No. 1, 1958, 161-173.

3859 Mathieu, Vittorio. "Tempo, memoria, enternità: Bergson e Proust." *Il Tempo*. Padova: Cedam, 1958, 256.

3860 Moreau, Pierre. "Review of *Henri Bergson et les lettres françaises* by Roméo Arbour." *Revue d'Histoire Littéraire de la France*, 58, No. 2, avril-juin 1958, 249-259.

3861 Niebuhr, Reinhold. "Thinkers and Thought." *New York Times*, 107, No. 36, 695, July 13, 1958, pt. 7, p. 4. This is a very short review of I. Alexander's *Bergson*, which is termed "compact and competent".

3862 Noon, William t. "Modern Literature and the Sense of Time." *Thought*, 33, No. 131, 1958-1959, 571-603. The author includes S. Beckett, Bergson, and M. Proust in his survey of temporalist literature.

3863 Pierre-Quint, Léon. "Entretien avec Bergson." *Revue de Paris*, 65, No. 8, septembre 1958, 120-129.

3864 Plekhanov, Georges. "Sur *L'Evolution créatrice* d'Henri Bergson (Trad. par Jean Deprun)." *Pensée*, N.S. No. 80, juillet-août 1958, 103-107.

3865 Pugliesi, Anna. "Le Bergsonisme en Italie." *Collaboration philosophique*. Bologna: Mareggiani, 1958, 59-78.

3866   Reymond, Arnold. "Notes sur Carnot et Bergson." *Revue Philosophique de la France et de l'Etranger*, 83, No. 3, 1958, 371-372.

3867   Rudy, Zvi Hirsch. *Hogi u-be'ayet hem.* Tel Aviv, 1958, 335. An essay on Bergson appears here on pp. 183-212.

3868   Scholl, Klaus. "Henri Bergson auf dem Wege zur Kirche." *Begegnung*, 13, 1958, 229.

3869   Shklar, Judith. "Bergson and the Politics of Intuition." *Review of Politics*, 20, No. 3, October 1958, 634-656. Faith in "creativity" and the "life force" is not a sufficient basis for a political theory.

3870   Stewart, Allegra. "The Quality of Gertrude Stein's Creativity." *American Literature*, 28, No. 4, January 1957, 488-506. *American Literature*, 28, No. 4, January 1957, 488-506. This essay deals with Stein in relation to G. Marcel and Bergson.

3871   Tremblay, Jacques. "La Notion de philosophie chez Bergson." *Laval Théologique et Philosophique*, 14, No. 1, 1958, 30-76.

3872   Vandel, Albert. *L'Homme et l'evolution.* 13th ed. Paris: Gallimard, 1958, 311. (L'Avenir de la science, No. 28). The author develops views of the nature of evolution which at many points parallel those of Bergson. On pp. 21-22, he stresses Bergson's claim that change is "the law of nature;" on p. 47 he notes Bergson as the first to stress the manner in which the great phyla of the animal kingdom evolve through "dichotomy" (splitting); on pp. 70-71 he states the irreversibility of evolution as a fundamental biological law; on pp. 96-97 he describes the development of the nervous system and consciousness as the fundamental tendencies of animal evolution; on pp. 100-101 he quotes Bergson (and Teilhard) on the reality of biological time; on pp. 122-123 he defends Bergson's biology against the criticisms of Julian Huxley.

3873   Vedaldi, Armando. *Cinque profili di filosofi francesi: Montaigne, Pascal, Comte, Bergson, Blondel.* Torino: Taylor, 1958, 267. The author gives a pantheistic interpretation of Bergson on pp. 127-253.

3874   Wahl, Jean. "Henri Bergson." *From the N.R.F.* Ed. Justin O'Brien. New York: Farrar, Straus and Cudahy, 1958, 282-284, 383.

3875   Watnough, J. R. "Anti-Intellectualism." *The Hibbert Journal*, 56, No. 223, July 1958, 352-360. The author opposes "anti-intellectualism".

1959

3876   Acker, Leonardo van. *A filosofia bergsoniana: Gênese, evolução e estrutura gnoseológica do bergsonismo.* São Paulo: Livraria Martins Editõra, 1959, 200.

3877   Adolphe, Lydie. "Bergson et la science d'aujourd'hui." *Etudes Philosophiques*, N.S. 14, No. 4, 1959, 479-488. According to the author, Bergson's philosophy is consistent with contemporary science. This is particularly true of quantum physics.

3878   Agosti, Vittorio. "Di alcune pubblicazioni del centenario bergsoniano." *Humanitas*, 14, No. 11, 1959, 837-842.

3879   Alavoine, Maurice. "Signification actuelle de Bergson." *Revue de la Méditerranée*, 19, Nos. 4-5, juillet-octobre 1959, 272-287.

3880   Alessandri, A. "Review of *Liberté ou libération?* by M. A. Lahbabi." *Revue Philosophique de la France et de l'Etranger*, 84, No. 3, 1959, 416-417.

3881   Amado-Levy-Valensi, Eliane. "Bergson et le mal: Y a-t-il un pessimisme bergsonien?" *Actes du Xe Congrès des Sociétés de Philosophie de Langue Française* (Congrès Bergson). Paris: Armand Colin, 1, 1959, 7-11. This study deals with Bergson's conception of the problem of evil, both in those works in which it is treated explicitly and in those in which it is approached but not designated as such. The author concludes with an analysis of the pessimism-optimism contrast at the heart of Bergson's thought.

3882   Amado-Levy-Valensi, Eliane. "Table ronde: Morale." *Actes du Xe Congrès des Sociétés de Philosophie de Langue Française* (Congrès Bergson). Paris: Armand Colin, 2, 1959, 237-257.

3883   Ambacher, Michel. "Intelligence physicienne de la matieère et expérience philosophique de la matérialité dans la philosophie naturelle de Bergson." *Actes du Xe Congrès des Sociétés de Philosophie de Langue Française* (Congrès Bergson). Paris: Armand Colin, 1, 1959, 13-16. The problem of matter is often obscured in Bergson's philosophy by the brilliance which surrounds his treatment of life, evolution, and religion. Nonetheless, the problem is approached in *The Two Sources, Matter and Memory*, and elsewhere. The author suggests an interpretation of Bergson's concept of matter.

3884   Ancelot-Hustache, J. "Un Baptisé de désir: Bergson." In *Convertis du 20ᵉ siècle*. Vol. III. Ed. F. Lelotte. Paris, Tournai: Casterman; Bruxelles: Foyer Notre-Dame, 1959, 7-22.

3885   Arbour, Roméo. "Le Bergsonisme dans la littérature française." *Revue Internationale de Philosophie*, 13, No. 2, 1959, 220-248. This article is an analysis of the aesthetic latent in Bergson's works. It deals with the fortuitous convergence of Bergson and symbolism and the literary polemics circa 1910. Bergson's influence is diffuse and enduring. His disciples included C. Péguy, M. Proust, Ch. Du Bos, and A. Thibaudet.

3886   Axelos, K. "Review of *L'Univers bergsonien* by Lydie Adolphe." *Revue Philosophique de la France et de l'Etranger*, 84, No. 3, 1959, 411.

3887   Barata Vianna, Sylvio. "Bergson e a duração real." *Kriterion*, 12, Nos. 49-50, 1959, 310-326.

3888   Barthélemy-Madaule, Madeleine. "Actualité de Bergson." *Etudes Philosophiques*, 14, No. 4, 1959, 479-488.

3889   Barthélemy-Madaule, Madeleine. "Introduction à la méthode chez Bergson et Teilhard de Chardin." *Actes du Xe Congrès des Sociétés de Philosophie de Langue Française* (Congrès Bergson). Paris: Armand Colin, 1, 1959, 211-216. Bergson and Teilhard de Chardin felt, from the beginning, the same need to return to the great metaphysical questions, to discover a being ("être") which does not deceive. The author analyzes the direction and the method which each philosopher utilized.

3890   Barthélemy-Madaule, Madeleine. "Table ronde: Vie et évolution." *Actes du Xe Congrès des Sociétés de Philosophie de Langue Française* (Congrès Bergson). Paris: Armand Colin, 2, 1959, 91-117.

3891   Barzin, Marcel. "L'Intuition bergsonienne." *Académie Royale de Belgique. Bulletin de la Classe des Lettres et des Sciences Morales et Politiques*, 45, Nos. 10-11, 1959, 527-534.

3892   Barzin, Marcel. "Table ronde: Matière, causalité, discontinu." *Actes du Xe Congrès des Sociétés de Philosophie de Langue Française* (Congrès Bergson). Paris: Armand Colin, 2, 1959, 121-142.

3893   Bastide, Georges. "Table ronde: Esthétique." *Actes du Xe Congrès des Sociétés de Philosophie de Langue Française* (Congrès Bergson). Paris: Armand Colin, 2, 1959, 193-210.

3894   Bastide, Georges. "Table ronde: Unité, unicité, dialogue." *Actes du Xe Congrès des Sociétés de Philosophie de Langue Française* (Congrès Bergson). Paris: Armand Colin, 2, 1959, 281-302.

3895   Battaglia, Félice. "Introduction: Synthèse des travaux du congrès." *Actes du Xe Congrès des Sociétés des Philosophie de Langue Française* (Congrès Bergson). Paris: Armand Colin, 2, 1959, 305.

3896   Baudouin, Charles. "Epiméthée et Prométhée: Recherche d'un dénominateur commun entre les diverses bipolarités bergsoniennes." *Actes du Xe Congrès des Sociétés de Philosophie de Langue Française* (Congrès Bergson). Paris: Armand Colin, 1, 1959, 17-22. According to the author, all the polarities inherent in Bergson's philosophy (mathematical time and lived time, intelligence and intuition, etc.) can be likened to the opposition between two brothers, Prometheus (the inspired soul) and Epimetheus (the conformist mind).

3897   Baudouin, Charles. "Table ronde: Liberté." *Actes du Xe Congrès des Sociétés de Philosophie de Langue Française* (Congrès Bergson). Paris: Armand Colin, 2, 1959, 167-189.

3898   Baudouin, Charles. "Table ronde: Psychologie, phénoménologie, intuition." *Actes du Xe Congrès des Sociétés de Philosophie de Langue Française* (Congrès Bergson). Paris: Armand Colin, 1959, 2, 15-37.

3899   Beck, L. J. "Henri Bergson." *Thought* (Delhi), 11, No. 47, November 21, 1959, 10-11.

3900   Belin-Milleron, Jean. "Dynamique de la différenciation et équivalence: En marge de la fabulation et de l'élan vital." *Actes du Xe Congrès des Sociétés de Philosophie de Langue Française* (Congrès Bergson). Paris: Armand Colin, 1, 1959, 23-25. Bergson urges us to enlarge the schemas by which we translate reality. To enter into the path opened by Bergson is to construe the results of our observations under the heading of the multiple and the cosmic. The author presents the results of an inquiry into collective thought, then observations on the dynamic of natural forms.

3901   Belin-Milleron, Jean. "Table ronde: Matière, causalité, discontinu." *Actes du Xe Congrès des Sociétés de Philosophie de Langue Française* (Congrès Bergson). Paris: Armand Colin, 2, 1959, 121-142.

3902   Beltrán de Heredia, Benito. "Henri Louis Bergson: Un príncipe del espíritu: Resonancias de un centenario." *Verdad y Vida*, 17, 1959, 729-746.

3903   Bénézé, Georges. "Bergson et la mémoire-image." *Actes du Xe Congrès des Sociétés de Philosophie de Langue Française* (Congrès Bergson). Paris: Armand Colin, 1, 1959, 27-29. This is a critical study of Bergson's theories of habit memory and memory image, a distinction used by him to prove the existence of a psychological unconscious.

3904 Bénéze, Georges. "Table ronde: Durée et meémoire." *Actes du Xe Congrès des Sociétés de Philosophie de Langue Française* (Congrès Bergson). Paris: Armand Colin, 2, 1959, 41-61.

3905 Berger, Gaston. "Discours inaugural du Congrès." *Actes du Xe Congrès des Sociétés de Philosophie de Langue Française* (Congrès Bergson). Paris: Armand Colin, 2, 1959, 9-11.

3906 Berger, Gaston. "Table ronde: Matière, causalité, disontinu." *Actes du Xe Congrès des Sociétés de Philosophie de Langue Française* (Congrès Bergson). Paris: Armand Colin, 2, 1959, 121-142.

3907 "Bergson Centenary, 1859-1959." *Discovery*, 12, December 1959, 507.

3908 "Bergson devant cinq philosophes d'aujourd'hui." *Nouvelles Littéraires*, No. 1677, 22 octobre 1959, 1 et 5-6. Jean Brun, Gaston Berger, Gabriel Marcel, Henri Gouhier, and Dominique Janicaud discuss Bergson and his present relevance.

3909 *Bergson, Henri, exposition du centenaire. Paris 2 mai-juillet 1959.* S. Pétremont et G. Willemetz. Préf. J. Cain. Paris: Bibliothèque Nationale, 1959, 56.

3910 Berl, Emmanuel. "Cinquante ans après." *Nouvelles Littéraires*, No. 1677, 22 octobre 1959, 6.

3911 Berne-Joffroy, A. "Valéry et les philosophes." *Revue de Métaphysique et de Morale*, 44, No. 1, 1959, 72-95. The author argues on pp. 91-95 that Valéry and Bergson differ profoundly.

3912 Bevilacqua, Giulio. "Bergson e l'esperienza mistica." *Humanitas*, 14, No. 11, 1959, 771-778.

3913 Bibesco. "L'Anémone et l'asphodèle." *Nouvelles Littéraires*, No. 1677, 22 octobre 1959, 1 et 6.

3914 Billy, André. "La Conversion de Bergson." *Le Figaro Littéraire*, 17 octobre 1959, 4.

3915 Blanchard, Pierre. "Philosophie et vie spirituelle." *Actes du Xe Congrès des Sociétés de Langue Française* (Congrès Bergson). Paris: Armand Colin, 1, 1959, 31-34. The author argues that Bergson's philosophy is prophetic. With almost Biblical accents, it recalls man to his destiny and humanity to its function.

3916 Blanchard, P. "Review of *Bergson et Plotin* by R.-M. Mossé-Bastide." *Bulletin des Facultés catholiques de Lyon*, 26, janiver-juin, 1959, 69.

3917 Blanco, J. E. "Cinco lecciones sobre Bergson." *Studium*, 3, Nos. 7-8, 1959, 149-160. This article contains an introduction, a short biography of Bergson, and a bibliography.

3918 Bloch, Marc-André. "Sens et postérité de l'*Essai*." *Actes du Xe Congrès des Sociétés de Philosophie de Langue Française* (Congrès Bergson). Paris: Armand Colin, 1, 1959, 35-38. With the *Essai*, the author holds that French philosophy assigned itself for the first time to the task of recovering what Bergson termed "les données immédiates de la conscience," or what his successors would call "expérience préobjective" or "expérience à l'état naissant." Bergson provided a model of a style of philosophizing which is still felt in a sector of French philosophy.

3919 Bloch, Marc-André. "Table ronde: Sources et histoire du bergsonisme." *Actes du Xe Congrès des Sociétés de Philosophie Française* (Congrès Bergson). Paris: Armand Colin, 2, 1959, 213-233.

3920 Bloch-Michel, Jean. "Review of 'Bergson aujourd'hui' by Émile Rideau." *Preuves*, 9, No. 103, 1959, 90-91.

3921 Boaz, George. "Bergson (1859-1941) and His Predecessors." *Journal of the History of Ideas*, 20, No. 4, October 1959, 503-514. According to the author, Bergson's originality lies in the use he made of his predecessor's ideas.

3922 Bonnet, Henri. "Bergson et Proust." *Actes du Xe Congrès des Sociétés de Philosophie de Langue Française* (Congrès Bergson). Paris: Armand Colin, 1, 1959, 39-43. The author argues that the analogies between Bergson and Proust are most numerous at the level of the exploration of the unconscious mind. This is not a matter of influence. Both seek felt experience. Both have a similar starting point. They differ at the level of interpretations and conceptions.

3923 Bonnet, Henri. "Table ronde: Durée et mémoire." *Actes du Xe Congrès des Sociétés de Philosophie de Langue Française* (Congrès Bergson). Paris: Armand Colin, 2, 1959, 41-61.

3924 Boyer, Charles. "Bergson et l'immortalité de l'âme." *Giornale di metafisica*, 14, No. 6, novembre-dicembre 1959, 753-758. For Bergson experience renders probable the independence of the soul with respect to the body, after whose dissolution it (the soul) could continue to subsist—though it is not possible to prove the soul's immortality. Bergson rests his case primarily on the retention and recall of memories.

3925 Boyer, Charles. "Il pensiero religioso di Bergson." *Humanitas*, 14, No. 11, 1959, 779-784.

3926 Brisson, Pierre. *Vingt ans de Figaro: 1938-1958*. Paris: Gallimard, 1959, 273. Bergson and many others are treated in this book.

3927 Brophy, Liam. "The Anguish of Henri Bergson." *Social Justice Review*, 53, August 1959, 110-119. According to the author a conflict between Jewish background and Catholic faith is evident in Bergson's later years.

3928 Brunner, Fernand. "Table ronde: Morale." *Actes du Xe Congrès des Sociétés de Philosophie de Langue Française* (Congrès Bergson). Paris: Armand Colin, 2, 1959, 237-257.

3929 Burgelin, Pierre. "Le Social et la nature chez Bergson." *Actes du Xe Congrès des Sociétés de Philosophie de Langue Française* (Congrès Bergson). Paris: Armand Colin, 1, 1959, 45-47. Bergson's reticence and use of metaphor make interpretation of his text a delicate matter. A case in point is the term "nature" in *Les Deux Sources*, which Burgelin attempts to define.

3930 Burgelin, Pierre. "Table ronde: Morale." *Actes du Xe Congrès des Sociétés de Philosophie de Langue Française* (Congrès Bergson). Paris: Armand Colin, 2, 1959, 237-257.

3931 Burkill, T. A. "L'Attitude subjectiviste et ses dangers de Descartes à Bergson." *Revue Philosophique de la France et de l'Etranger*, 149, No. 3, 1959, 325-337. The author argues that Bergson's reduction of all really to pure duration seems as arbitrary as Descartes' logico-mathematical cosmology.

3932 Busch, Joseph F. "Einstein et Bergson, convergence et divergence de leurs idées." *Proceedings of the Tenth International Congress of Philosophy*. Amsterdam: North-Holland Publishing Co., 1959, 872-875. This abstract of a talk is translated in *Bergson and the Evolution of Physics*, (1969) Ed. P. A. Y. Gunter, 208-214. The author seeks to use the concept of "positionality," taken from H. Plessner, to combine Bergson's qualitative, Einstein's quantitative viewpoints.

3933 Cadin, Francesco. "Heidsieck e la dottrina bergsoniana dello spazio." *Revista di filosofia neoscolastica*, 51, Nos. 5-6, 1959, 529-534.

3934 Cain, Julien. "Bergson à la Nationale." *Nouvelles Littéraires*, 65, No. 1655, 21 mai 1959, p. 7. The author, an acquaintance of Bergson, describes Bergson's career, and the difficulties of putting together an exhibit on his life and writings at the Bibliothèque Nationale.

3935 Canivez, André. "Bergson et Lagneau." *Actes du Xe Congrès des Sociétés de Philosophie de Langue Française* (Congrès Bergson). Paris: Armand Colin, 1, 1959, 49-52. The author stresses both the points of contact and the differences between Bergson and Lagneau. Neither proposed doctrines. Each proposed a kind of difficult philosophical life, Lagneau with rudeness, Bergson with art and finesse.

3936 Canivez, André. "Table ronde: Unité, unicité, dialogue." *Actes du Xe Congrès des Sociétés de Philosophie de Langue Française* (Congrès Bergson). Paris: Armand Colin, 2, 1959, 281-302.

3937 Čapek, Milič. "Bergson et l'esprit de la physique contemporaine." *Actes du Xe Congrès des Sociétés de Philosophie de Langue Française* (Congrès Bergson). Paris: Armand Colin, 1, 1959, 53-56. This study outlines the basic ideas behind Bergson's concept of matter and shows remarkable agreements between these and the spirit of recent physics.

3938 Čapek, Milič. "Process and Personality in Bergson's Thought." *Philosophical Forum*, 18, 1959-1960, 25-42. "If the dynamic and incomplete universe is the only place in which human action can be meaningfully called 'action,' then certain polarity within the universe is necessary to save ethical judgments from becoming inconsequential emotive reactions." (41-42). The author argues that Bergson's philosophy provides a framework in which moral judgements and moral action have meaning.

3939 Čapek, Milič. "Table ronde: Physique." *Actes du Xe Congrès des Sociétés de Philosophie de Langue Française* (Congrès Bergson). Paris: Armand Colin, 2, 1959, 65-87.

3940 Čapek, Milič. "La Théorie biologique de la connaissance chez Bergson et sa signification actuelle." *Revue de Métaphysique et de Morale*, 64, No. 2, 1959, 194-211.

3941 Cardone, Domenico Antonio. "Ce que je dois à Bergson." *Actes du Xe Congrès des Sociétés de Philosophie de Langue Française*, (Congrès Bergson). Paris: Armand Colin, 1, 1959, 57-58. The encounter with Bergson's thought revealed to Cardone the means of attaining the absolute. Cardone claims that man can become the God of our planet in realizing a community of love and through this community attain the secret reason of creative evolution.

3942 Chaix-Ruy, Jules. "Bergson parvient-il à éliminer toute réference au néant?" *Actes du Xe Congrès des Sociétés de Philosophie de Langue Française* (Congrès Bergson). Paris: Armand Colin, 1, 1959, 59-62. Bergson's critique of the idea of nothing seems decisive. But has Bergson completely exorcized this concept? Can it be eliminated by philosophical reflection? The author ponders these questions.

3943   Chaix-Ruy, Jules. "L'Exigence morale dans la philosophie d'Henri Bergson."
        Giornale di metafisica, 14, No. 6, 1959, 766-783. An increasing moral exigency
        constitutes, the author holds, one of the most marked traits of Bergson's thought.
        At the level of human history, Bergson teaches in *The Two Sources* that we
        assist in an evolution of the law which culminates in Christian morality, the
        most open morality in existence.

3944   Chaix-Ruy, Jules. "I molteplici orientamenti della filosofia bergsoniana."
        Humanitas, 14, No. 11, 1959, 800-821.

3945   Chaix-Ruy, Jules. "Table ronde: Néant et existentialisme." *Actes du Xe Congrès
        des Sociétés de Philosophie de Langue Française* (Congrès Bergson). Paris:
        Armand Colin, 2, 1959, 145-164.

3946   Champigny, Robert. "Position philosophique de la liberté." *Revue de Métaphysique
        et de Morale*, 64, No. 2, 1959, 225-235. Bergson, R. Ruyer, and J.-P. Sartre
        are compared.

3947   Chattelun, Maurice. "De L'Expérience musicale à l'essentialisme bergsonien."
        Actes du Xe Congrès des Sociétés de Philosophie de Langue Française (Congrès
        Bergson). Paris: Armand Colin, 1, 1959, 63-66. The author evokes Bergsonian
        views which a musician could be led to consider.

3948   Chattelun, Maurice. "Table ronde: Esthétique." *Actes du Xe Congrès des Sociétés
        de Philosophie de Langue Française* (Congrès Bergson). Paris: Armand Colin,
        2, 1959, 193-210.

3949   Chauchard, Paul. "Evolution matérialiste et fixisme ontologique dans la création
        évolutive." *Actes du Xe Congrès des Sociétés de Philosophie de Langue Fran-
        çaise* (Congrès Bergson). Paris: Armand Colin, 1, 1959, 67-70. If, on the
        scientific level, one cannot be a "fixiste" in the classical sense of the word, the
        author holds, at the level of philosophy the fact of evolution agrees equally well
        with either an evolutionary explanation or a certain "fixiste" thesis. Until
        Bergson, evolution appeared a purely mechanistic concept.

3950   Chauchard, Paul. "Table ronde: Vie et évolution." *Actes du Xe Congrès des Sociétés
        de Philosophie de Langue Française* (Congrès Bergson). Paris: Armand Colin,
        2, 1969, 91-117.

3951   Chevalier, Jacques. "Bergson nous parle..." *Le Figaro Littéraire*, 14, No. 680, 2
        mai 1959, 1, 7; No. 681, 9 mai 1959, 1, 5-6, 8.

3952   Chevalier, Jacques. "Bergson vu par Jacques Chevalier." *Nouvelles Littéraires*,
        No. 1677, 22 octobre 1959, 2.

3953   Chevalier, Jacques. *Bergson y el Padre Pouget*. Trans. José A. Míguez. Madrid:
        Aguilar, 1959, 92.

3954   Chevalier, Jacques. "Ciò che la filosofia deve a Bergson." *Humanitas*, 14, No.
        11, 1959, 785-791.

3955   Chevalier, Jacques. "Comment Bergson échappa à l'Index." *Le Figaro Littéraire*,
        9 mai 1959, 5-6.

3956   Chevalier, Jacques. "Entretiens avec Bergson." *Table Ronde*, No. 137, mai 1959,
        9-28.

3957   Chevalier, Jacques. *Entretiens avec Bergson*. Paris: Plon, 1959, 315. This records
        personal records of conversations and correspondence with Bergson over the
        course of many years. It is an important source of information about Bergson's
        ideas, associates, and personal life, but perhaps is colored by the author's own

social and political views.

3958 Chevalier, Jacques. "Entretiens avec Bergson: Extraits du volume du même titre." *Humanitas*, 14, No. 11, 1959, 843-852.

3959 Colin, Pierre. "Bergson et l'absolu." *De La Connaissance de Dieu*. Paris and Bruges: Desclée de Brouwer, 1959, 113-124.

3960 Collins, James. "Darwin's Impact on Philosophy." *Thought*, 34, No. 133, 1959, 185-248. Section 4 of this article (pp. 220-224) is titled "Bergson and the Methodology of Evolutionism." Bergson's view, the author states, "remains closer to the biologist's approach to nature and to the actual shifts in evolutionary theories, without surrendering the human significance of the genesis of life" (p. 220).

3961 Conche, Marcel. "Sur La Critique bergsonienne de l'idée de néant." *Actes du Xe Congrès des Sociétés de Langue Française* (Congrès Bergson). Paris: Armand Colin, 1, 1959, 71-75. It is argued in this article that the metaphysical concept of "nothing" is a pseudo-idea.

3962 Conche, Marcel. "Table ronde: Néant et existentialisme." *Actes du Xe Congrès des Sociétés de Philosophie de Langue Française* (Congrès Bergson). Paris: Armand Colin, 2, 1959, 145-164.

3963 Costa de Beauregaard, Olivier. "Essai sur la physique du temps: Son Equivalence avec l'espace; son irréversibilité." *Actes du Xe Congrès des Sociétés de Philosophie de Langue Française* (Congrès Bergson). Paris: Armand Colin, 1, 1959, 77-80. The author deals with the law of equivalence between space and time and its apparent antinomy, so deeply felt by Bergson. He deals with, in particular, the problem of the insertion of minds into the material cosmos and the problem of the irreversibility of time.

3964 Costa de Beauregaard, Olivier. "Table ronde: Physique." *Actes du Xe Congrès des Sociétés de Philosophie de Langue Française* (Congrès Bergson). Paris: Armand Colin, 2, 1959, 65-87.

3965 Cruz-Hernandes, Miguel. "Bergson et Unamuno." *Actes du Xe Congrès des Sociétés de Philosophie de Langue Française* (Congrès Bergson). Paris: Armand Colin, 1, 1959, 81-83. Bergson was for Unamuno the greatest contemporary philosopher. In the midst of positivistic scientism Bergson's thought involved a spiritualistic restoration which merited the supreme title "quixotic."

3966 Dambska, Izydora. "Sur Quelques Idées communes à Bergson, Poincaré et Eddington." *Actes du Xe Congrès des Sociétés de Philosophie de Langue Française* (Congrès Bergson). Paris: Armand Colin, 1, 1959, 85-89. Sir Arthur Eddington is often very close to Bergson, the author holds, when it comes to questions of methodology concerning the structure of science. Eddington is close to the moderate conventionalism of H. Poincaré, and it is through this that he rejoins Bergson's concept of science.

3967 Dambska, Izydora. "Table ronde: Physique." *Actes du Xe Congrès des Sociétés de Philosophie de Langue Française* (Congrès Bergson). Paris: Armand Colin, 2, 1959, 65-87.

3968 Davies, John C. "Thibaudet and Bergson." *Journal of the Australaian Universities Language and Literature Association*, No. 9, 1959, 48-59. This article presents A. Thibaudet's debt to Bergson. It includes a bibliography.

3969   Decreus, J. "Dynamisme et bergsonisme dans *L'Amoureuse Initiation.*" *Le Bayou*, 23, No. 78, 1959, 366-371. This is the study of Bergson's influence on a work by O. V. de L. Milosz. The author states on p. 370, "Pour Pinamonte comme pour le mystique en extase le temps et l'espace n'existent plus. Sous ce rapport, *L'Amoureuse Initiation* garde visiblement l'empreinte du Bergsonisme déclinant de 1910."

3970   Delay, Jean. "Table ronde: Durée et mémoire." *Actes du Xe Congrès des Sociétés de Philosophie de Langue Française* (Congrès Bergson). Paris: Armand Colin, 2, 1959, 41-61.

3971   Delay, Jean. "Table ronde: Psychologie, phénoménologie, intuition." *Actes du Xe Congrès des Sociétés de Philosophie de Langue Française* (Congrès Bergson). Paris: Armand Colin, 2, 1959, 15-37.

3972   Delfgaauw, Bernard. "Bergson et la philosophie existentielle." *Actes du Xe Congrès des Sociétés de Philosophie de Langue Française* (Congrès Bergson). Paris: Armand Colin, 1, 1959, 91-96. Existential philosophers, the author holds, have in general a very low opinion of Bergson. Nonetheless their philosophies are very close to Bergson's on at least three points: the importance of choice, the unity of time, and affectivity.

3973   Delfgaauw, Bernard. "Table ronde: Néant et existentialisme." *Actes du Xe Congrès des Sociétés de Philosophie de Langue Française* (Congrès Bergson). Paris: Armand Colin, 2, 1959, 145-164.

3974   Delhomme, Jeanne. "Le Problème de l'intériorité: Bergson et Sartre." *Revue Internationale de Philosopie*, 48, No. 2, 1959, 201-219. The author argues that Bergson and Sartre bypass the Kantian distinction between matter and form to recover the unity of the empirical and the transcendental, of consciousness and self, and of experience and thought. But Bergson identifies consciousness and spirit ("esprit"), conceiving philosophy as metaphysics. Sartre conceives consciousness as the negative dimension of the being of the subject and as the starting-point of an ontology of nothingness.

3975   Devaux, André-A. "A L'Occasion du centenaire de la naissance d'Henri Bergson: Signification et exigences de la vocation philosophique chez Bergson." *Revue de Synthèse*, 3e Série, 80, Nos. 13-14, janvier-juin 1959, 3-30.

3976   Devaux, André-A. "La Connexion entre liberté et vocation dans la philosophie de Bergson." *Actes du Xe Congrès des Sociétés de Philosophie de Langue Française* (Congrès Bergson). Paris: Armand Colin, 1, 1959, 97-101. For Bergson liberty is a fact, and can be known without proofs, simply by the experience we have of ourselves. The author attempts to show that this fact reveals another, that of "personal vocation" felt as an appeal to each man to realize the ideal self which he bears within him.

3977   Devaux, André-A. "La Destination de l'homme selon Bergson." *Afrique*, No. 271, 1959, 19-26.

3978   Devaux, André- A. "Le Mystique et le philosophe selon Bergson." *Giornale di metafisica*, 14, No. 6, 1959, 766-783. Bergson holds, according to the author, that in the mystical experience the person coincides with supra-intellectual emotion without losing his own identity. The universe is renewed by the mystics, who are the conscious instruments of God.

3979   Devaux, André-A. "Table ronde: Liberté." *Actes du Xe Congrès des Sociétés de Philosophie de Langue Française* (Congrès Bergson). Paris: Armand Colin, 2,

1959, 167-189.

3980 Devaux, Philippe. "Table ronde: Sources et histoire du bergsonisme." *Actes du Xe Congrès des Sociétés de Philosophie de Langue Française* (Congrès Bergson). Paris: Armand Colin, 2, 1959, 213-233.

3981 Devivaise, Charles. "Table ronde: Psychologie, phénoménologie, intuition." *Actes du Xe Congrès des Sociétés de Philosophie de Langue Française* (Congrès Bergson). Paris: Armand Colin, 2, 1959, 15-37.

3982 D'Hautefeuille, François. "La Critique par Henri Bergson de l'idée de néant." *Revue de Métaphysique et de Morale*, 64, No. 2, 1959, 212-224.

3983 D'Hautefeuille, François. "Le Développement de la philosophie de Bergson et la poésie contemporaine." *Ecrits de Paris*, février 1959, 73-78.

3984 D'Hendécourt, Marie-Madeleine. "Métaphysique et mystique chez Bergson et Laberthonnière." *Actes du Xe Congrès des Sociétés de Philosophie de Langue Française* (Congrès Bergson). Paris: Armand Colin, 1, 1959, 149-152. This essay explores the spiritual initiatives of Bergson and Laberthonnière, stressing the analogies between Bergsonian intuition and the "laborious intuition" of charity of Laberthonnière.

3985 D'Hendécourt, Marie-Madeleine. "Table ronde: Religion." *Actes du Xe Congrès des Sociétés de Philosophie de Langue Française* (Congrès Bergson). Paris: Armand Colin, 2, 1959, 261-278.

3986 Doumic, René. "Bergson vu par René Doumic." *Nouvelles Littéraires*, No. 1677, 22 octobre 1959, 2.

3987 Drago, G. Review of *Fenomeno e contenuto della conscienza* by C. Rossi. *Giornale di metafisica*, 14, No. 1, 1959, 123-124.

3988 Du Bos, Charles. "Bergson vu par Charles Du Bos." *Nouvelles Littéraires*, No. 1677, 22 octobre 1959, 2.

3989 Ellenberger, Henri F. "A Clinical Introduction to Psychiatric Phenomenology and Existential Analysis." in *Existence* Ed. Rollow May, Ernest Angel and Henri F. Ellenberger. New York: Basic Books, Inc., 1959, 92-124. On p. 95 the author notes Charles Blondel's *La Conscience morbide* as a poineering work in psychiatric phenomenology. On p. 102 he notes Bergson's influence on Eugene Minkowski and Minkowski's poineering work in the clinical study of phenomenological time. Cf. pp. 102-108.

3990 Etcheverry, Auguste. "La Durée bergsonienne." *Actes du Xe Congrès des Sociétés de Philosophie de Langue Française* (Congrès Bergson). Paris: Armand Colin, 1, 1959, 103-106. The theory of duration, the author holds, is at the heart of Bergson's doctrine; it is on this foundation that his entire metaphysics rests. The awareness of lived time constitutes the ultimate source of his intuitive method.

3991 Etcheverry, Auguste. "Table ronde: Durée et mémoire." *Actes du Xe Congrès des Sociétés de Philosophie de Langue Française* (Congrès Bergson). Paris: Armand Colin, 2, 1959, 41-61.

3992 Fabre-Luce de Gruson, Françoise. "Actualité de l'esthétique bergsonienne." *Actes du Xe Congrès des Sociétés de Philosophie de Langue Française* (Congrès Bergson). Paris: Armand Colin, 1, 1959, 107-110. This essay is a reply to R. Bayer's article on Bergson's theory of art (1941). Bergson systematically eliminated all technical considerations from the nature of art, while for Bayer art is above all a matter of "technique."

3993   Fabre-Luce de Gruson, Françoise. "Sens commun et bon sens chez Bergson." *Revue Internationale de Philosophie*, 13, No. 2, 1959, 187-200. According to the author, Bergson's dialectic between common sense ("sens commun") and good sense ("bon sens") presupposes a primary dissociation of their functions, according to which the judiciary element of good sense makes up for the mistakes of common sense. Bergson attempts to elicit again the agreement of minds at the level of good sense. While common sense bases itself on the prejudices natural to the intelligence, good sense appropriates the pure apprehensions of intuition. To make good sense prevail over common sense is to affirm the superiority of the immediate, of movement, and of progress over their contraries.

3994   Fabre-Luce de Gruson, Françoise. "Table ronde: Esthétique." *Actes du Xe Congrès des Sociétés de Philosophie de Langue Française* (Congrès Bergson). Paris: Armand Colin, 2, 1959, 193-210.

3995   Fataud, Jean-Marie. "Roman Ingarden: Critique de Bergson." *For Roman Ingarden: Nine Essays in Phenomenology*. Ed. Anna-Teresa Tymieniecka. S-Gravenhage: Martinus Nijhoff, 1959, 7-28.

3996   Fouks, Léon. "Note sur la dialectique bergsonienne et le judaisme." *Actes du Xe Congrès des Sociétés de Philosophie de Langue Française* (Congrès Bergson). Paris: Armand Colin, 1, 1959, 111-113. During his last years Bergson found himself increasingly attracted to Christianity and, by contrast, seems to have ignored Judaism. Nonetheless, the author holds, there are striking analogies between his conceptions and those of Israel, whose unique faith is an ardent quest for God.

3997   Fouks, Léon. "Table ronde: Durée et mémoire." *Actes du Xe Congrès des Sociétés de Philosophie de Langue Française* (Congrès Bergson). Paris: Armand Colin, 2, 1959, 41-61.

3998   Fouks, Léon. "Table ronde: Morale." *Actes du Xe Congrès des Sociétés de Philosophie de Langue Française* (Congrès Bergson). Paris: Armand Colin, 2, 1959, 237-257.

3999   Fouks, Léon. "Table ronde: Religion." *Actes du Xe Congrès des Sociétés de Philosophie de Langue Française* (Congrès Bergson). Paris: Armand Colin, 2, 1959, 261-278.

4000   Fraenkl, Pavel. "Bergsons betydning for europeisk litteratur i vart arhundre: Et idéhistorisk panorama." *Samtiden*, 68, No. 8, 1959, 485-496.

4001   Gagnabin, Samuel. "A L'Occasion du centenaire de Bergson (18 octobre 1859-3 janvier 1941)." *Studia Philosophica*, 19, 1959, 87-118. This article concerns the Bergson conference of the Société romande de philosophie (Swiss) held 12-13 September 1959.

4002   Gagnabin, Samuel. *A L'Occasion du centenaire de Bergson (18 octobre 1859-3 janvier 1941)*. Bâle, Switzerland: Verlag für Recht und Gesellschaft, 1959, 32. *This article appeared originally in Studia Philosophica, 1959.*

4003   Galimberti, Andrea. "Au Sujet d'un mot de Bergson." *Actes du Xe Congrès des Sociétés de Philosophie de Langue Française* (Congrès Bergson). Paris: Armand Colin, 1, 1959, 115-117. In explicating a sentence asserted by Bergson in 1911 ("No philosopher has had more than one idea.") The author examines the way in which Bergson conceives his theory of man's world and his civilization, and the part which he assigns there to ideas.

4004   Galimberti, Andrea. "Table ronde: Unité, unicité, dialogue." *Actes du Xe Congrès des Sociétés de Philosophie de Langue Française* (Congrès Bergson). Paris: Armand Colin, 2, 1959, 281-302.

4005   Gilson, Etienne. "Souvenir de Bergson." *Revue de Métaphysique et de Morale*, 64, No. 2, avril 1959, 129-140.

4006   Gilson, Etienne. "Table ronde: Religion." *Actes du Xe Congrès des Sociétés de Philosophie de Langue Française* (Congrès Bergson). Paris: Armand Colin, 1959, 2, 261-278.

4007   Gilson, Etienne. "Table ronde: Sources et histoire du bergsonisme." *Actes du Xe Congrès des Sociétés de Philosophie de Langue Française* (Congrès Bergson). Paris: Armand Colin, 2, 1959, 213-233.

4008   Givord, Robert. "L'Idée de néant est-elle une pseudo-idée?" *Actes du Xe Congrès des Sociétés de Philosophie de Langue Française* (Congrès Bergson). Paris: Armand Colin, 1, 1959, 119-122. This is an analysis of Bergson's critique of the idea of nothingness. In spite of Bergson's critique, the author holds that if one considers only the logical universe of significations, the idea of nothingness exists mentally just as well as other ideas. Moreover, Bergson did not see the entire significance of his critique and did not understand that metaphysics, in the last analysis, is nothing but this critique taken to the limit.

4009   Givord, Robert. "Table ronde: Néant et existentialsme." *Actes du Xe Congrès des Sociétés de Philosphie de Langue Française* (Congrès Bergson). Paris: Armand Colin, 2, 1959, 145-164.

4010   Gonzalo Casas, Manuel. "Bergson y el sentido de su influencia en América." *Humanitas*, 8, No. 12, 1959, 95-108. A Latin American Bergson bibliography is given on pp. 103-108.

4011   Gonzalo Casas, Manuel. "Bibliographia bergsoniana in Spagna e nell'America latina." *Giornale di metafisica*, 14, No. 6, 1959, 866-872.

4012   Gouhier, Henri. "Le Bergsonisme dans l'histoire de la philosophie fançaise." *Revue des Travaux de l'Académie des Sciences Morales et Politiques*, 4e Sér., 112e Année, ler semestre, 1959, 183-200.

4013   Gouhier, Henri. "Table ronde: Esthétique." *Actes du Xe Congrès des Sociétés de Philosophie de Langue Française* (Congrès Bergson). Paris: Armand Colin, 2, 1959, 193-210.

4014   Gouhier, Henri. "Table ronde: Liberté." *Actes du Xe Congrès des Sociétés de Philosophie de Langue Française* (Congrès Bergson). Paris: Armand Colin, 2, 1959, 167-189.

4015   Gouhier, Henri and Robinet, André, Eds. *Henri Bergson: Oeuvres: Edition du centenaire*. Paris: Presses Universitaires de France, 1959, 1602. Professor Robinet's "Apparat critique" and "Notes historiques" are found on pp. 1485-1539 and 1541-1578 respectively. Professor Gouhier's *Introduction" is found on pp. vii-xxx. This centennial edition contains French-language editions of Laughter, Creative Evolution, Mind-Energy, The Two Sources of Morality and Religion* and *The Creative Mind*.

4016 Grappe, André. "Bergson et le symbole." *Actes du Xe Congrès des Sociétés de Philosophie de Langue Française* (Congrès Bergson). Paris: Armand Colin, 1, 1959, 123-129. No aspect of Bergson's philosophy has been more disparaged than his symbolism. Is this attitude valid? The author analyzes Bergson's concept of symbolism and compares it with Bergson's concept of the image.

4017 Grappe, André. "Table ronde: Psychologie, phénoménoligie, intuition." *Actes du Xe Congrès des Sociétés de Philosophie de Langue Française* (Congrès Bergson). Paris: Armand Colin, 2, 1959, 15-37.

4018 Grenet, Paul. "Racines bergsoniennes de l'existentialisme." *Actes du Xe Congrès des Sociétés de Philosophie de Langue Française* (Congrès Bergson). Paris: Armand Colin, 1, 1959, 131-134. The author holds that Bergson's philosophy contains several positions very close to those of the existentialists: the priority of existence over possibility, the identification of existence with liberty, and the separation of reality into two zones: the in-itself, identical, inert, passive, and the for-itself, always other, free, empty. Nonetheless, Bergson is not an existentialist. He possesses a conviction which transfigures these propositions: the refusal of all real negativity.

4019 Grenet, Paul. "Table ronde: Néant et existentialisme." *Actes du Xe Congrès des Sociétés de Philosophie de Langue Française* (Congrès Bergson). Paris: Armand Colin, 2, 1959, 145-164.

4020 Groot, H. "Review of *Henri Bergson* by Günther Pflug." *Mens en Kosmos*, 15, No. 6, 1959, 283-284. This is a brief, critical review.

4021 Groot, H. "Van de redactie." *Mens en Kosmos*, 15, No. 6, 1959, 249-251. This is an editorial comment on the accompanying Bergson number of *Mens en Kosmos*. It includes a general assessment of Bergson's epoch and his contemporary significance.

4022 Guitton, Jean. "Bergson et Loisy." *Actes du Xe Congrès des Sociétés de Philosophie de Langue Française* (Congrès Bergson). Paris: Armand Colin, 1, 1959, 135-137. The author evokes some memories and offers some thoughts concerning the relations between Bergson and A. Loisy, in particular their positions with regard to the religious problem and Christianity.

4023 Guitton, Jean. "Bergson et Loisy." *Revue de Paris*, 66e Année, No. 12, décembre 1959, 27-39.

4024 Guitton, Jean. "Dieu et le temps." *Études Philosophiques*, 14, No. 3, 1959, 283-290.

4025 Guitton, Jean. "Table ronde: Religion." *Actes du Xe Congrès des Sociétés de Philosophie de Langue Française* (Congrès Bergson). Paris: Armand Colin, 2, 1959, 261-278.

4026 Guy, Alain. "El Congreso Bergson: París, 17-20 de mayo de 1959." *Espíritu*, 8, No. 1959, 194-195.

4027 Guy, Alain. "O Congresso 'Bergson'—17-20 de maio de 1959." *Revista Portugesa di Filosofia*, 15, 1959, 417-419.

4028 Guy, Alain. "José Vasconcelos et Bergson." *Actes du Xe Congrès des Sociétés de Philosophie de Langue Française* (Congrès Bergson). Paris: Armand Colin, 1, 1959, 139-143. The author holds that the aesthetic and Christian monism of the Mexican philosopher Vasconcelos is an original and audacious "refraction" of Bergsonism. Vasconcelos thought he had surpassed Bergson at more than one point.

4029   Guy, Alain. "Table ronde: Sources et histoire du bergsonisme." *Actes du Xe Congrès des Sociétés de Philosophie de Langue Française* (Congrès Bergson). Paris: Armand Colin, 2, 1959, 213-233.

4030   Guyot, Charly. "Notes sur Bergson et les lettres françaises." *Revue Internationale de Philosophie*, 13, No. 2, 1959, 249-271. The author holds that C. Péguy transposed certain "simple ideas" of Bergson onto the sociological and historical level. M. Proust is nearer to Bergson than Péguy, thanks to a common Ruskinian affiliation.

4031   Hearsolte, R. A. V. van. "Enkele raakpunten van Bergson met de exacte wetenschappen." *Algemeen Nederlands Tijdschrift voor Wijsbegeerte en Psychologie*, 52, No. 1, 1959-1960, 12-23. Bergson reproaches the devotees of natural science for not having sufficiently taken account of duration. But he was wrong to transpose onto an ontological level the superiority of "lived time" over "time-space." The author considers the resolution of the paradox of Achilles in the light of this distinction.

4032   Hayen, André. "La Réflexion est dialogue." *Actes du Xe Congrès des Sociétés de Philosophie de Langue Française* (Congrès Bergson). Paris: Armand Colin, 1, 1959, 145-147.

4033   Hayen, André. "Table ronde: Liberté." *Actes du Xe Congrès des Sociétés de Philosophie de Langue Française* (Congrès Bergson). Paris: Armand Colin, 2, 1959, 167-189.

4034   Hayen, André. "Table ronde: Unité, unicité, dialogue." *Actes du Xe Congrès des Sociétés de Philosophie de Langue Française* (Congrès Bergson). Paris: Armand Colin, 2, 1959, 281-302.

4035   Heidsieck, François. "Table ronde: Physique." *Actes du Xe Congrès des Sociétés de Philosophie de Langue Française* (Congrès Bergson). Paris: Armand Colin, 2, 1959, 65-87.

4036   Howlett, Jacques. "Fragilité bergsonienne." *Lettres Nouvelles*, 7e Année, No. 14, 3 juin 1959, 2-4.

4037   Howlett, J. "L'Art de faire parler Bergson." *Les Lettres Nouvelles*, 7, No. 30, 18 novembre 1959, 20-22.

4038   Huisman, Denis. "Bergson existe-t-il?" *Carrefour*, No. 767, 27 mai 1959, 21.

4039   Huisman, Denis. "Y a-t-il une esthétique bergsonienne?" *Actes du Xe Congrès des Sociétés de Philosophie de Langue Française* (Congrès Bergson). Paris: Armand Colin, 1, 1959, 153-155. Bergson did not write a treatise on aesthetics. Nonetheless, it can be said that the eight volumes of his work are eight books on the philosophy of art. The author holds that intuition is for Bergson aesthetic in all its manifestations. Bergson's thought is a vast aesthetic of perception.

4040   Husson, Léon. "le Centenaire d'Henri Bergson." *Cahiers Français*, 13, No. 44, 1959, 8-13.

4041   Husson, Léon. "La Portée lointaine de la psychologie bergsonienne." *Actes du Xe Congrès des Sociétés de Philosophie de Langue Française* (Congrès Bergson). Paris: Armand Colin, 1, 1959, 157-162. In studying Bergson's theory of pure memory the author wishes to show how Bergson's psychology surpasses the formulas within which psychology is usually imprisoned and how it can still renew the reflections of contemporary thinkers.

4042 Husson, Léon. "Table ronde: Durée et mémoire." *Actes du Xe Congrès des Sociétés de Philosophie de Langue Française* (Congrès Bergson). Paris: Armand Colin, 2, 1959, 41-61.

4043 Husson, Léon. "Table ronde: Liberté." *Actes du Xe Congrès des Sociétés de Philosophie de Langue Française* (Congrès Bergson). Paris: Armand Colin, 2, 1959, 167-189.

4044 Husson, Léon. "Table ronde: Matière, causalité, discontinu." *Actes du Xe Congrès des Sociétés de Philosophie de Langue Française* (Congrès Bergson). Paris: Armand Colin, 2, 1959, 121-142.

4045 Husson, Léon. "Table ronde: Morale." *Actes du Xe Congrès des Sociétés de Philosophie de Langue Française* (Congrès Bergson). Paris: Armand Colin, 2, 1959, 237-257.

4046 Husson, Léon. "Table ronde: Psychologie, phénoménologie, intuition." *Actes du Xe Congrès des Sociétés de Philosophie de Langue Française* (Congrès Bergson). Paris: Armand Colin, 2, 1959, 15-37.

4047 Hyppolite, Jean. "Du Bergsonisme à l'existentialisme." *Mercure de France*, 306, No. 2, mai-août 1959, 403-416.

4048 Hyppolite, Jean. "Table ronde: Néant et existentialisme." *Actes du Xe Congrès des Sociétés de Philosophie de Langue Française* (Congrès Bergson). Paris: Armand Colin, 2, 1959, 145-164.

4049 Hyppolite, Jean. "Table ronde: Unité, unicité. dialogue." *Actes du Xe Congrès des Sociétés de Philosophie de Langue Française* (Congrès Bergson). Paris: Armand Colin, 2, 1959, 281-302.

4050 Ingarden, Roman. "L'Intuition bergsonienne et le problème phénoménologique de la constitution." *Actes du Xe Congrès des Sociétés de Philosphie de Langue Française* (Congrès Bergson). Paris: Armand Colin, 1, 1959, 163-166. The author examines the analogies between Bergson's intuition of pure duration and the theories of I. Kant and above all E. Husserl. Differences between these philosophers are also made apparent.

4051 Ingarden, Roman. "Table ronde: Psychologie, phénoménologie, intuition." *Actes du Xe Congrès des Sociètès de Philosophie de Langue Française* (Congrès Bergson). Paris: Armand Colin, 2, 1959, 15-37.

4052 Ingarden, Roman. "Table ronde: Unité, unicité, dialogue." *Actes du Xe Congrès des Sociétés de Philosophie de Langue Française* (Congrès Bergson). Paris: Armand Colin, 2, 1959, 281-302.

4053 Irairte, Joaquín de. "El mistico gesto de Bergson." *Razon y Fe*, 160, Nos. 738-379, 1959, 25-38.

4054 Isaye, Gaston. "Bergson et Teilhard de Chardin." *Actes du Xe Congrès des Sociétés de Philosophie de Langue Française* (Congrès Bergson). Paris: Armand Colin, 1, 1959, 167-169. The author studies the role of Bergson's intuition (conceived as both reflective and synthesizing intuition) in three of Teilhard de Chardin's affirmations: the question of the "within," the question of finality, and the question of "ultra-reflexion."

4055 Isaye, Gaston. "Table ronde: Liberté." *Actes du Xe Congrès des Sociétés de Philosophie de Langue Française* (Congrès Bergson). Paris: Armand Colin, 2,

1959, 167-189.

4056   Isaye, Gaston. "Table ronde: Vie et évolution." *Actes du Xe Congrès des Sociétés de Philosophie de Langue Française* (Congrès Bergson). Paris: Armand Colin, 2, 1959, 91-117.

4057   Jacobi, Jolande. *Complex/Archetype/Symbol in the Psychology of C. G. Jung.* Trans. Ralph Manheim. Princeton: Princeton University Press, 1959, 236. On p. 52 the author notes that Carl Gustav Jung liked to refer to his archetypes using Bergson's phrase "les éternels incrées."

4058   Jamil, Khwija Moinud-Din. *Nietzsche and Bergson.* Rajshahi, Pakistan: International Printing Firm, 1959, xxii, 173.

4059   Jankélévitch, Vladimir. *Henri Bergson.* Paris: Presses Universitaires de France, 1959, 299. (Les Grands Penseurs) This is a thoroughgoing revision of the author's earlier *Bergson* (1931). It is one of the best general works on Bergson. The author adds two chapters (5 and 7) concerning Bergson's philosophy of religion and an appendix on Bergson and Judaism.

4060   Jankélévitch, Vladimir. "N'écoutez pas ce qu'ils disent, regaredez ce qu'ils font." *Revue de Métaphysique et de Morale*, 64, No. 2, 1959, 161-162. The author claims that central to Bergson's philosophy is the necessity "s'engager."

4061   Jolivet, Régîs. "Réflexions sur le déclin du bergsonisme dans les années d'après-guerre." *Actes du Xe Congrès des Sociétés de Philosophie de Langue Française* (Congrès Bergson). Paris: Armand Colin, 1, 1959, 171-175. The author argues that the decline of Bergsonism is due to criticisms of Bergson's psychology and to the emergence of existential doctrines. Bergson combined existential elements in his doctrine, but these never went beyond the abstract level of a conceptual analysis.

4062   Joussain, André. "Le Conscient, l'inconscient dans leur rapport avec de durée pure chez Bergson." *Archives de Philosophie*, 22, No. 1, janvier-mars 1959, 5-23. This is a criticism of Bergson's concept of the self. Bergson neglected the permanence of the conscious self. His treatment of the unconscious mind, as memory and as *élan*, shows many hesitations and inconsistencies.

4063   Kinnen, Edouard. "Le Bergsonisme et les fondements philosophiques d'une civilisation humaniste." Diss., Paris, 1959, 280. For a short résumé Cf. *Annales de l'Université de Paris*, 29e Année, No. 4, octobre-décembre 1959, 693-695.

4064   Korn, Alejandro. *De San Augustin a Bergson.* Intro. J. C. Torchia Estrada. 2nd ed. Buenos Aires: Nova, 1959, 154.

4065   Kremer-Marietti, Angèle. "Bergson métaphysicien de la matière." *Actes du Xe Congrès des Sociétés de Philosophie de Langue Française* (Congrès Bergson). Paris: Armand Colin, 1, 1959, 177-181. The function of "matter" in Bergson's philosophy cannot be resolved simply by distinguishing living from non-living matter. The author discusses criteria given by Bergson for an integral knowledge of matter and his theories concerning perception, which is the insertion of spirit in matter.

4066   Kremer-Marietti, Angèle. "Table ronde: Matière, causalité, discontinu." *Actes du Xe Congrès des Sociétés de Philosophie de Langue Française* (Congrès Bergson). Paris: Armand Colin, 2, 1959, 121-142.

4067   Kudielka, E. "Der 'andere' Bergson: Zum Gedenken anlässlich der 100. Wiederkehr seines Geburtstages." *Wissenschaft und Weltbild*, 12, No. 4, 1959, 622-628.

4068   Kumar, Shiv Kumar. "Bergson and Proust's 'Souvenir involuntaire'." *Canadian Modern Language Review*, 16, No. 2, 1959, 7-10.

4069   Kumar, Shiv Kumar. "Dorothy Richardson and Bergson's 'Mémoire par excellence'." *Notes and Queries*, 6, No. 1, 1959, 14-19.

4070   Kumar, Shiv Kumar. "Dorothy Richardson and the Dilemma of Being Versus Becoming." *Modern Language Notes*, 74, No. 6, June 1959, 494-501. Parallels and disagreements between Richardson and Bergson are analyzed in this article.

4071   Kumar, Shiv Kumar. "Joyce's 'Epiphany' and Bergson's 'L'Intuition philosophique'." *Modern Language Quarterly*, 20, No. 1, March 1959, 27-30.

4072   Lafranchi, Genevieve. "Du Niveau psychologique de l'intuition bergsonienne." *Actes du Xe Congrès des Sociétés de Philosophie de Langue Française* (Congrès Bergson). Paris: Armand Colin, 1, 1959, 183-184. The author holds that it is possible, thanks to reference points of a psychological order, for Bergson to pass from a metaphysical intuition to a lucidly controlled mystical or contemplative intuition.

4073   Lafranchi, Geneviève. "Table ronde: Psychologie, phénoménologie, intuition." *Actes du Xe Congrès des Sociétés de Philosophie de Langue Française* (Congrès Bergson). Paris: Armand Colin, 2, 1959, 15-37.

4074   Lameere, Jean. "Table ronde: Esthétique." *Actes du Xe Congrès des Sociétés de Philosophie de Langue Française* (Congrès Bergson). Paris: Armand Colin, 2, 1959, 193-210.

4075   Lantieri, Simon. "Table ronde: Esthétique." *Actes du Xe Congrès des Sociétés de Philosophie de Langue Française* (Congrès Bergson). Paris: Armand Colin, 2, 1959, 193-210.

4076   Laragueta, J. "La Liberté dans la philosophie d'Henri Bergson." *Actes du Xe Congrès des Sociétés de Philosophie de Langue Française* (Congrès Bergson). Paris: Armand Colin, 1, 1959, 339-342. Is there for consciousness a causality which is, the author asks, not only contingent and open to variability but also free in the sense of a possible option between different directions? What is Bergson's position in this regard? The definition of liberty has its reality in human life.

4077   Larbaud, Valéry. "Charles Péguy: A Propos de son cahier sur M. Bergson et la philosophie bergsonienne." *Feuillets de l'Amitié Charles Péguy*, No. 72, juin 1959, 2-5. This is a translation of an article from *The New Weekly*, 4, July 1914.

4078   Lattre, Alain De. "Une Ontologie de la précarité: Jeanne Delhomme." *Revue Philosophique de la France et de l'Etranger*, 149, No. 3, 1959, 381-394. This article includes a discussion of the relations between Delhomme and Bergson."

4079   Lazzarini, Renato. "Bergson e noi: X Congresso della Società di filosofia di lingua francese, Parigi, 17-19 maggio 1959." *Filosofia*, 10, No. 4, 1959, 642-643.

4080   Lazzarini, Renato. "Intention et intuition dans la méthodologie philosophique de Bergson." *Actes du Xe Congrès des Sociétés de Philosophie de Langue Française* (Congrès Bergson). Paris: Armand Colin, 1, 1959, 189-195. One finds in Bergson, the author holds, a double methodological procedure: "méthodique des choses," in which mind adapts itself to things in oder to manipulate them, and the "méthodique propre au sujet spirituel," in which the mind enters into the essences of things conceived as so many durations.

4081 Lazzarini, Renato. "Table ronde: Psychologie, phénoménologie, intuition." *Actes du Xe Congrès des Sociétés de Philosophie de Langue Française* (Congrès Bergson). Paris: Armand Colin, 2, 1959, 15-37.

4082 Lazzarini, Renato. "Table ronde: Sources et histoire du bergsonisme." *Actes du Xe Congrès des Sociétés de Philosophie de Langue Française* (Congrés Bergson). Paris: Armand Colin, 2, 1959, 213-233.

4083 Lechat, Paul-Hubert. "Influence de Bergson sur l'évolution de la pensée contemporaine." *Actes du Xe Congrès des Sociétés de Philosophie de Langue Française* (Congrès Bergson). Paris: Armand Colin, 1, 1959, 191-194. Bergson's influence, the author holds, is felt in diverse fields (psychology, literary criticism). In metaphysics itself a Bergsonism of intention, if not of fact, is paralleled by intellectualist philosophies.

4084 Lechat, Paul-Hubert. "Table ronde: Sources et histoire du bergsonisme." *Actes du Xe Congrès des Sociétés de Philosophie de Langue Française* (Congrès Bergson). Paris: Armand Colin, 2, 1959, 213-233.

4085 Lee, Harold N. "Bergson's Two Ways of Knowing." *Tulane Studies in Philosophy,* 8, 1959, 50-59. Bergson's most important contribution to philosophy, the author holds, is his insistence on the continuity of concrete duration. Bergson's distinction between intellect and intuition, however, downgrades the intellect. The author reinterprets the meanings of intellect and intuition so as to escape anti-intellectualism.

4086 Lefebvre, Henri. "Sur Proust, Bergson et Gide." In *La Somme et le reste* by Henri Lefebvre. Paris: La Nef de Paris, 1959, 381-388.

4087 Lefevre, Frédéric. "Table ronde: Esthéthique." *Actes du Xe Congrès des Sociétés de Philosophie de Langue Française* (Congrès Bergson). Paris: Armand Colin, 2, 1959, 193-210.

4088 Lenoir, Raymond. "Henri Bergson au Meeting d'Oxford." *Revue Philosophique de la France et de l'Etranger,* 149, No. 3, 1959, 339-343.

4089 Leroy, André-Louis. "Review of *Bergson* by I. W. Alexander." *Revue Philosophique de la France et de l'Etranger,* 149, No. 3, 1959, 412-415.

4090 Leroy, André-Louis. "Le Congrès Bergson (17-20 mai 1959)." *Revue Philosophique de la France et de l'Etranger,* 149, No. 3, 1959, 379-380. The author states that the method of "table ronde" was a happy innovation and that the discussion of Bergson's philosophy of religion at the Congrès Bergson was impassioned.

4091 Le Roy, Edouard. "Bergson vu par Edouard Le Roy." *Nouvelles Littéraires,* No. 1677, 22 octobre 1959, 2.

4092 Le Roy, Georges. "La Pensée bergsonienne et le christianisme." *Actes du Xe Congrès des Sociétés de Philosophie de Langue Française* (Congrès Bergson). Paris: Armand Colin, 1, 1959, 195-199. Bergson's philosophy cannot be counted, the author holds, among the specifically Christian philosophies; too many difficulties prevent this.

4093 Le Roy, Georges. "Table ronde: Religion." *Actes du Xe Congrès des Sociétés de Philosophie de Langue Française* (Congrès Bergson). Paris: Armand Colin, 2, 1959, 261-278.

4094   Leveque, Raphael. "Retour sur 'l'intellectualisme bergsonien'." *Actes du Xe Congrès des Sociétés de Philosophie de Langue Française* (Congrès Bergson). Paris: Armand Colin, 1, 1959, 201-204. Bergson is not an "intellectualist," the author holds. For, from the intellectualist perspective, philosophy is a laborious effort. For Bergson, however, philosophy has an intrinsic grace. Once we have mounted to the source, we have only to consent to the movement with which we are impelled.

4095   Levi, Albert William. *Philosophy and the Modern World*. Bloomington, Indiana: University of Indiana Press, 1959, 591.

4096   Lévy-Bruhl, Lucien. "Bergson vu par L. Lévy-Bruhl." *Nouvelles Littéraires*, No. 1677, 22 octobre 1959, 2.

4097   Lovejoy, Arthur Oncken. "Schopenhauer as an Evolutionist." In *Forerunners of Darwin*. Ed. Bentley Glass, Owsei Temkin, and William L. Straus. Baltimore: Johns Hopkins Press, 1959, 415-437. The author argues that Schopenhauer did not, at the beginning of his philosophical activity, "put an evolutionistic construction on the conception of the will..." (p. 418). Such a view of the will increasingly forced itself on him, however. Bergson's criticisms of Spencer's concept of evolution are noted on p. 433. Schopenhauer is treated as a precursor of Bergson on pp. 435-437. The author states, "there can be no doubt that in Schopenhauer we find the first emphatic affirmation of the three conceptions most characteristic of the biological philosophy of *L'évolution créatrice*" (p. 436). These three conceptions are (1) the repeated production of absolute novelties, (2) the criticism of finalism, and (3) the concept of "blind purpose." (This article was first published in *The Monist*, 21 (1911).)

4098   Lucques, Claire. "Le Présent supplément d'âme." *Actes du Xe Congrès des Sociétés de Philosophie de Langue Française* (Congrès Bergson). Paris: Armand Colin, 1, 1959, 205-209.

4099   Lucques, Claire. "Table ronde: Morale." *Actes du Xe Congrès des Sociétés de Philosophie de Langue Française* (Congrès Bergson). Paris: Armand Colin, 2, 1959, 237-257.

4100   Maiorana, María-Teresa. "Bergson et les penseurs ibéro-américains." *Actes du Xe Congrès des Sociétés de Philosophie de Langue Française* (Congrès Bergson). Paris: Armand Colin, 1, 1959, 217-220. The author recounts the situation in Spanish-American philosophy at the time of Bergson's influence and indicates briefly those authors who felt Bergson's influence and contributed to independent philosophical thought in Latin America.

4101   Maire, Gilbert. "Bergson et l'élan vital." *Age Nouveau*, 13, No. 2, février-mars 1959, 71-75. This is a discussion of Bergson's biology, including his theory of instinct and his comparative psychology.

4102   Maire, Gilbert. "Henri Bergson et la défense de la civilisation." *Civilisation*, 1, No. 1, 1959, 10-12.

4103   Maire, Gilbert. *Une Régression mentale, de Bergson à J.-P. Sartre*. Paris: Grasset, 1959, 212. Cf. esp. "Intuition et phénoménologie," 101-111.

4104   Mañach, Jorge. "En el centenario de Bergson." *Revista de la Biblioteca Nacional Jose Martí*, 1, Nos. 1-4, 1959, 18-41.

4105   Mandel, A. "Bergson et la question." *Monde Juif*, 14e Année, No. 85-86, 1959.

4106   Maritain, Jacques. "Sur L'Ethique bergsonienne." *Revue de Métaphysique et de Morale*, 64, No. 2, 1959, 141-149. The author argues that Bergson's error was to term "moral" a system of social pressures which is infra-moral.

4107   Marquet, Urbain. "Bergson, novitas florida..." *Actes du Xe Congrès des Sociétés de Philosohpie de Langue Française* (Congrès Bergson). Paris: Armand Colin, 1, 1959, 221-223. The author holds that the intellectualist climate in which Bergson lived and wrote excluded from thought a function of reason which can be termed inspiration. Inspiration can be defined through its contrast with external pressure. In his "novitas florida" Bergson introduces us to a renewed fecundity.

4108   Marquet, Urbain. "Table ronde: Psychologie, phénoménologie, intuition." *Actes du Xe Congrès des Sociétés de Philosophie de Langue Française* (Congrès Bergson). Paris: Armand Colin, 2, 1959, 15-37.

4109   Massis, Henri. "A L'Ocasion du centenaire de la naissance d'Henri Bergson: Proust et Bergson." *Revue de la Méditeranée*, 19, No. 4-5, juillet-octobre 1959, 263-271.

4110   Matchinski, Mathias. "Image scientifique de monde: Son caractère 'Cinématographique' d'après Bergson et principe de causalité." *Actes du Xe Congrès des Sociétés de Philosophie de Langue Française* (Congrès Bergson). Paris: Armand Colin, 1, 1959, 225-228. What attitude should a scientist or philosopher have towards Bergson's celebrated critique of the cinematographic, atomizing scientific mind? The author argues that the sciences can approach the ideal of continuity presented by Bergson and that the problem of the cinematographic image of the world is bound up in science with the problem of causality.

4111   Matchinski, Mathias. "Table ronde: Matière, causalité, discontinu." *Actes du Xe Congrès des Sociétés de Philosophie de Langue Française* (Congrès Bergson). Paris: Armand Colin, 2, 1959, 121-142.

4112   Matchinski, Mathias. "Table ronde: Physique." *Actes du Xe Congrès des Sociétés de Philosophie de Langue Française* (Congrès Bergson). Paris: Armand Colin, 2, 1959, 65-87.

4113   Mathieu, Vittorio. "Review of *Henri Bergson* by G. Pflug." *Philosophische Rundschau*, 7, Nos. 3-4, 1959, 242-246.

4114   Mathieu, Vittorio. "Review of *Bergson et Plotin* by Rose-Marie Mossé-Bastide," *Filosofia*, 10, No. 4, 1959, 674-676.

4115   Mathieu, Vittorio. "Review of *Bergson: Quellen und Konsequenzen einer induktiven Metaphysik* by Günther Pflug." *Giornale di metafisika*, 14, 1959, 854-856.

4116   Mathieu, Vittorio. "Bergson technicien." *Revue Internationale de Philosophie*, 13, No. 48, 1959, 173-186. The author argues that Bergson employs an entirely conceptual technique in order to attain a non-conceptual object. This technique involves the realization that concepts and images are equally metaphorical. Images, however, manage through their plurality to suggest a reality beyond all images. Bergson's thought is an exemplary testimony to the effort to surpass intelligence by means of the intelligence itself.

4117   Mathieu, Vittorio. "Bibliographia bergsoniana in Francia (1945-1959)." *Giornale di metafisica*, 14, No. 6, 1959, 835-852.

4118   Mathieu, Vittorio. "Bibliografia bergsoniana in Germania (1945-1959)." *Giornale di metafisica*, 14, No. 6, 1959, 853-856.

4119   Mathieu, Vittorio. "Interpreti vecchi e nuovi di Bergson." *Humanitas*, 14, No. 11, 1959, 822-836.

4120   Mathieu, Vittorio. "Scienza e metafisica in Bergson." *Giornale di metafisica*, 14, No. 6, 1959, 784-798. For Bergson, the author argues, science and philosophy study different aspects or reality. Their methods are therefore different. Philosophy, possessing its own method and object, will be scientific and will be able to progress indefinitely like science. Bergson's thought in this regard shows originality.

4121   Maurois, André. "Un Grand Vivant." *Nouvelles Littéraires*, No. 1677, 22 octobre 1959, 1 et 5. Maurois' visits with Bergson are discussed in this article.

4122   Mavit, Henri. "Bergson et le langage du philosophe." *Vie et Langage*, 8e Année, No. 86, mai 1959, 257-260.

4123   Mavit, Henri. "Table ronde: Esthétique." *Actes du Xe Congrès des Sociétés de Philosophie de Langue Française* (Congrès Bergson). Paris: Armand Colin, 2, 1959, 193-210.

4124   May, Henri F. *The End of American Innocence: A Study of the First Years of Our Own Time, 1912-1917*. New York: Knopf, 1959, 412. The author distinguishes three popular movements at the beginning of the 20th century: naturalism, desparing aestheticism, and vitalism: "The most convincing spokesman of the third movement, vitalism or cheerful neomysticism, was Henri Bergson, and its most popular prophet H. G. Wells" (p. 169). For Bergson's diverse influence on American intellectuals, Cf. pp. 228-230, 287, 295, 302-305.

4125   Mazzantini, Carlo. "Evidenza e problematicitá dell'iniziativa nella filosofia morale di Enrico Bergson." *Giornale di metafisica*, 14, No. 6, 1959, 799-817. This is a critical interpretation of Bergson's conceptions of intellectual activity, with special emphasis on the problem of "initiative" as it is presented in *The Two Sources*. Bergson considers "initiative" to be the essential attribute of humanity.

4126   Mercier, André. "Table ronde: Physique." *Actes du Xe Congrès des Sociétés de Philosophie de Langue Française* (Congrès Bergson). Paris: Armand Colin, 2, 1959, 65-87.

4127   Merlan, Philip. "Le Problème de l'irrationalisme dans les *Deux Sources* de Bergson." *Revue Philosophique de la France et de l'Etranger*, 149, No. 3, juillet-septembre 1959, 305-319. The author concludes: "Parce qu'il n'y a pas de dualisme dans toutes les autres branches de ses speculations philosophiques. Tout y est harmonie; il en est ainsi de l'intellect et de l'intuition. L'irrationalité elle-même n'est que la rationalité en devenir." (319).

4128   Mesnard, Pierre. "La Doctrine de l'héroisme moral considéré comme clef de voûte de la philosophie bergsonienne." *Actes du Xe Congrès des Sociétés de Philosophie de Langue Française* (Congrès Bergson). Paris: Armand Colin, 1, 1959, 227-233. Bergson's doctrine of moral heroism is the justification of his entire doctrine of liberty, the author holds, since at this level liberty becomes creative of superior ideas.

4129   Mesnard, Pierre. "Table ronde: Morale." *Actes du Xe Congrès des Sociétés de Philosophie de Langue Française* (Congrès Bergson). Paris: Armand Colin, 2, 1959, 237-257.

4130   Metz, André. "Bergson, Einstein et les relativistes." *Archives de Philosophie*, 22, No. 3, juillet 1959, 369-384. The author argues that Edouard Le Roy played a significant role in the error which Bergson made in interpreting relativity. In

1937 Le Roy published an article rectifying Bergson's error. (Cf. E. Le Le Roy, 1937) Moreover, Bergson's conception of duration can be shown to harmonize with Einstein's conception of time and to complete it. But Bergson misunderstood Einstein's conception of time, in part because he confused relativity with relativism.

4131 Metz, André. "Bergson et Meyerson." *Actes du Xe Congrès des Sociétés de Philosophie de Langue Française* (Congrès Bergson). Paris: Armand Colin, 1, 1959, 235-237. The author reviews Meyerson's bibliography and quotes at length from Bergson's review of Meyerson's *Identity and Reality*.

4132 Metz, André. "Table Ronde: Physique." *Actes du Xe Congrès des Sociétés de Philosophie de Langue française.* (Congrès Bergson) Paris: Armand Colin, 1959, 2, 65-87.

4133 Miéville, Henri. "La Philosophie religieuse de Bergson: Questions de méthode." *Studia Philosophica*, 19, 1959, 173-192. The author argues that Bergson's shift from a biological monism to a theistic position involves changes in his methodology.

4134 Miéville, Henri. *La Philosophie religieuse de Bergson: Questions de méthode.* Basel, Switzerland: Verlag für Recht und Ges., 1959, 20. This essay is reprinted from *Studia Philosophica*.

4135 Minkowski, Eugène. "Findings in a Case of Schizophrenic Depression." in *Existence*. Ed. Rollo May, Ernest Angel, Henri F. Ellenberger. New York: Basic Books, 1959, 127-138. Trans. Barbara Bliss. This essay (first published in the *Journal de Psychologie normale et pathologique*, 1923, and later, condensed, in *Le Temps vecú*, 1933) is a pioneering work in the clinical study of phenomenological time. A patient's attitude towards the future, the author found, can be the cause of mental illnes. Basic personal temporal orientation can be the cause of delusions.

4136 Minkowski, Eugène. "L'Irrationnel: Donnée immédiate." *Revue Philosophique de la France et de l'Etranger*, 84, No. 3, 1959, 289-304. The transcendance of becoming, as an immediate datum of consciousness, consists in what is most immanent in it and in what follows from it. The author has reached this conclusion by proceeding along the path traced out by Bergson, though he has deviated from Bergson's thought in part through his adherence to Bleuler. These "infidelities," howerver, are only the expressions of a dialogue.

4137 Minkowski, Eugène. "La Pure Durée et la durée vécue." *Actes du Xe Congrès des Sociétés de Philosophie de Langue Française* (Congrès Bergson). Paris: Armand Colin, 1, 1959, 239-241. The terms "pure duration" and "felt duration" are employed by Bergson in both *Time and Free Will* and *Creative Evolution*. What encompasses these two ideas? How are they related?

4138 Minkowski, Eugène. "Table ronde: Durée et mémoire." *Actes du Xe Congrès des Sociétés de Philosophie de Langue Française* (Congrès Bergson). Paris: Armand Colin, 2, 1959, 41-61.

4139 Minkowski, Eugène. "Table ronde: Morale." *Actes du Xe Congrès des Sociétés de Philosophie de Langue Française* (Congrès Bergson). Paris: Armand Colin, 2, 1959, 237-257.

4140 Minkowski, Eugène. "Table ronde: Psychologie, phénoménologie, intuition." *Actes du Xe Congrès des Sociétés de Philosophie de Langue Française* (Congrès

Bergson). Paris: Armand Colin, 2, 1959, 15-37.

4141   Minkowski, Eugène. "Table ronde: Sources et histoire du bergsonisme." *Actes du Xe Congrès des Sociétés de Philosophie de Langue Française* (Congrès Bergson). Paris: Armand Colin, 2, 1959, 213-233.

4142   Miroglio, Abel. "Table ronde: Matière, causalité, discontinu." *Actes du Xe Congrès des Sociétés de Philosophie de Langue Française* (Congrès Bergson). Paris: Armand Colin, 2, 1959, 121-142.

4143   Moreau, Joseph. "Table ronde: Matière, causalité, discontinu." *Actes du Xe Congrès des Sociétés de Philosophie de Langue Française* (Congrès Bergson). Paris: Armand Colin, 2, 1959, 121-142.

4144   Moreau, Joseph. "Table ronde: Sources et histoire du bergsonisme." *Actes du Xe Congrès des Sociétés de Philosophie de Langue Française* (Congrès Bergson). Paris: Armand Colin, 2, 1959, 213-233.

4145   Mossé-Bastide, Rose-Marie. "Review of *Adès chez Bergson: Reliques inconnues d'une amitié* by A. Adés." *Revue Philosophique de la France et de l'Etranger*, 84, No. 3, 1959, 403-406.

4146   Mossé-Bastide, Rose-Marie. *Bergson et Plotin*. Paris: Presses Universitaires de France, 1959, 422. The author argues that Bergson and Plotinus share the same approach to metaphysics through psychological experience, an indentical concept of creative causality, and the same description of the means of salvation. But for Bergson ecstasy is not a "point of arrival."

4147   Mossé-Bastide, Rose-Marie. "Review of *Bergson: Quellen und Konsequenzen einer induktiven Metaphysik* by Günther Pflug." *Études Philosophiques*, N.S. 14, No. 4, 1959, 556.

4148   Mossé-Bastide, Rose-Marie. "Table ronde: Esthétique." *Actes du Xe Congrès des Sociétés de Philosophie de Langue Française* (Congrès Bergson). Paris: Armand Colin, 2, 1959, 193-210.

4149   Mossé-Bastide, Rose-Marie. "Table ronde: Psychologie, phénoménologie, intuition." *Actes du Xe Congrès des Sociétés de Philosophie de Langue Française* (Congrès Bergson). Paris, Armand Colin, 2, 1959, 15-37.

4150   Mossé-Bastide, Rose-Marie. "Table ronde: Sources et histoire du bergsonisme." *Actes du Xe Congrès des Sociétés de Philosophie de Langue Française* (Congrès Bergson). Paris: Armand Colin, 2, 1959, 213-233.

4151   Mossé-Bastide, Rose-Marie. "La Théorie bergsonienne de la connaissance et ses rapports avec la philosophie de Plotin." *Actes du Xe Congrès des Sociétés de Philosophie de Langue Française* (Congrès Bergson). Paris: Armand Colin, 1, 1959, 243-247. This study stresses the influence of Plotinus' theories concerning the participation of the self in the universality of beings and being on the development of Bergson's thought. Our duration can intensify and enlarge itself so as to coincide with eternity.

4152   Namer, Emile. "Review of *Bergson: Il profondo e la sua espressione* by Vittorio Mathieu." *Revue Philosophique de la France et de l'Etranger*, 84, No. 3, 1959, 411-412.

4153   Namer, Emile. "Le Message de Giordano Bruno et d'Henri Bergson." *Actes du Xe Congrès des Sociétés de Philosophie de Langue Française* (Congrès Bergson). Paris: Félix Alcan, 1, 1959, 250-254. Both Bergson and Bruno, the author holds, were placed at a turning point in history, Bruno at the birth of Copernicus's system, Bergson at the birth of the general theory of relativity. In spite of the disparity between the problems and the times, both ally themselves with the Pythagorean tradition according to which mathematics and science lead both to philosophical intuition and religious thought.

4154 Namer, Emile. "Table ronde: Sources et histoire du bergsonisme." *Actes du Xe Congrès des Sociétés de Philosophie de Langue Française* (Congrès Bergson). Paris: Félix Alcan, 2, 1959, 213-233.

4155 Nédoncelle, Maurice. "Quelques Aspects de la causalité chez Bergson." *Actes du Xe Congrès des Sociétés de Philosophie de Langue Française* (Congrès Bergson). Paris: Félix Alcan, 1, 1959, 255-260. The author studies the idea of cause in Bergson's thought, including its principal aspects (the causality of matter, personal causality, and interpersonal causality) and their significance for a philosophy of intersubjectivity.

4156 Nédoncelle, Maurice. "Table ronde: Matière, causalité, discontinu." *Actes du Xe Congrès des Sociétés de Philosophie de Langue Française* (Congrès Bergson). Paris: Félix Alcan, 2, 1959, 121-142.

4157 Noailles, Anna, Comtesse de. "Bergson vu par Anna de Noailles." *Nouvelles Littéraires*, No. 1677, 22 octobre 1959, 1.

4158 Nyman, Alf. *Evidence logique et évidence géométrique.* Lund, Sweden: Gleerup, 1959, 120. The author explores attempts by F. A. Lange, K. Kroman, and H. Bergson to reduce logic to space.

4159 Oldewelt, H. M. J. "1859-Bergson-1959." *Algemeen Nederlands Tijdschrift voor Wijsbegeerte en Psychologie*, 52, 1, 1959-1960, 1-12.

4160 Ouy, Achille. "Review of *Bergson et Plotin* by Rose-Marie Mossé-Bastide." *Mercure de France*, 337, No. 1154, 1959, 345-348.

4161 Oyarzún, Luis. "La idea de inspiración en Bergson." *Revista de Filosofía*, 6, No. 2-3, 1959, 73-83.

4162 Painter, George Duncan. *Marcel Proust: A Biography.* Vol. I. Boston: Little, Brown; London: Chatto and Windus, 1959, 351. Bergson is mentioned in connection with Proust's character Bergotte on pp. 68 and 279; the author notes Proust's attendance at Bergson's lectures on p. 80.

4163 Papini, Giovanni. "Bergson vu par Giovanni Papini." *Nouvelles Littéraires*, No. 1677, 22 octobre 1959, 2.

4164 Parain-Vial, Jeanne. "Bergson et la 'philosophia perennis'." *Actes du Xe Congrès des Sociétés de Philosophie de Langue Française* (Congrès Bergson). Paris: Armand Colin, 1, 1959, 261-266. Though Bergson often stresses his opposition to traditional philosophy, the author argues, he nonetheless coincides at several points with the 'philosophia perennis.' Three points of coincidence are: the theory of knowledge, the philosophy of being, and moral philosophy.

4165 Parain-Vial, Jeanne. "Table ronde: Unité, unicité, dialogue." *Actes du Xe Congrès des Sociétés de Philosophie de Langue Française* (Congrès Bergson). Paris: Armand Colin, 2, 1959, 281-302.

4166 Parker, George Frederick. "Duration and Method in the Philosophy of Bergson." Diss. Michigan 1959. Cf. *Dissertation Abstacts*, 20, No. 5, November 1959, 1828.

4167   Péguy, Charles. "Bergson vu par Charles Péguy." *Nouvelles Littéraires*, No. 1677, 22 octobre 1959, 1 et 2.

4168   Perelman, Chaim. "Synthèse des travaux du Congrès." *Actes du Xe Congrès des Sociétés de Philosophie de Langue Française* (Congrès Bergson). Paris: Armand Colin, 1959, 305-313.

4169   Petit, Henri. "Review of *Entretiens avec Bergson* by Jacques Chevalier." *Nouvelles Littéraires*, No. 1677, 22 octobre 1959, 2-3.

4170   Pflug, Günther. *Henri Bergson: Quellen und Konsequenzen einer Induktiven Metaphysik*. Berlin: Walter de Gruyter und Ges., 1959, 393. Pages 116-129 are translated, with an introduction, in *Bergson and the Evolution of Physics*, Ed. P. A. Y. Gunter on pp. 190-208 under the title "Inner Time and the Relativity of Motion." The author descants on the weakness in Bergson's own position evoked by his critique of relativity theory. Bergson involves himself in a "strange agnosticism" involving merely represented physical systems. He isolates the consciousness of the individual man. He posits an interpersonal time that is hard to substantiate. (Cf. M. Čapek, 1971.)

4171   Philippe, Oscar. "Table ronde: Néant et existentialisme." *Actes du Xe Congrès des Sociétés de Philosophie de Langue Française* (Congrès Bergson). Paris: Armand Colin, 2, 1959, 145-164.

4172   Piaget, Jean. "Lettre." *Revue de Théologie et de Philosophie*, 9, No. 1, 1959, 44-47. In this letter Jean Piaget, founder of "genetic epistemology," states his early adherence to Bergson's philosophy and theory of biology, which made him see "the possibility of a biological theory of knowledge." His professor at the Gymnasium and later at the University of Neuchâtel, Arnold Reymond, was, however, able to convince the young Piaget (against Bergson) of the "solidarity of logic and biology."

4173   Pina, António Ambrósio. "O problema do método no intuicionismo de Bergson." *Filosofia*, 6, No. 1, 1959, 11-27.

4174   Poulet, Georges. *Studies in Human Time*. Trans. Elliott Coleman. New York: Harper and Bros., 1959, 363. Bergson is discussed throughout.

4175   Prins, D. H. "Review of *Bergson, Philosopher of Reflection* by Ian Alexander." *Mens en Kosmos*, 15, No. 6, 1959, 284.

4176   Pucelle, Jean. "L'Instant: Croisement de séries." *Actes du Xe Congrès des Sociétés de Philosophie de Langue Française* (Congrès Bergson). Paris: Armand Colin, 1, 1959, 267-269.

4177   Raeymaeker, Louis de. "Table ronde: Religion." *Actes du Xe Congrès des Sociétés de Philosophie de Langue Française* (Congrès Bergson). Paris: Armand Colin, 2, 1959, 261-278.

4178   Raymond, Marcel. "Bergson et la Suisse romande." *Actes du Xe Congrès des Sociétés de Philosophie de Langue Française* (Congrès Bergson). Paris: Armand Colin, 1, 1959, 271-274. The author deals with Bergson's visits to French Switzerland, his influence on philosophical thought there, and with the "pre-Bergsonian" character of the thought of Amiel and De Gourd.

4179   Reck, Andrew J. "Bergson's Theory of Duration." *Tulane Studies in Philosophy*, 8, 1959, 27-47.

4180 Regnier, Marcel. "Le Congrès Bergson." *Etudes par des Pèrex de la Compagnie de Jésus*, 302, juillet-août 1959, 128-130.

4181 Reiss, Françoise. "Quelle est la valeur actuelle de la pensée bergsonienne?" *Arts*, No. 724, 27 mai-2 juin 1959, 3.

4182 Reverdin, Henri. "Table ronde: Liberté." *Actes du Xe Congrès des Sociétés de Philosophie de Langue Française* (Congrès Bergson). Paris: Armand Colin, 2, 1959, 167-189.

4183 Reverdin, Henri. "Table ronde: Religion." *Actes du Xe Congrès des Sociétés de Philosophie de Langue Française* (Congrès Bergson). Paris: Armand Colin, 2, 1959, 261-278.

4184 Ricks, C. B. "Frederic Harrison and Bergson." *Notes and Queries*, 6, No. 5, May 1959, 175-178. The author recounts various criticisms of Bergson's *Introduction to Metaphysics* by a British positivist.

4185 Rideau, Emile. "Bergson aujourd'hui." *Etudes*, 302, Nos. 7-8, août 1959, 3-23.

4186 Riefstahl, Hermann. "Review of *Écrits et paroles* by Henri Bergson." *Zeitschrift für philosophische Forschung*, 13, 1959, 637ff; 17 , 1963, 173ff.

4187 Robinet, André. "L'Espérance de la philosophie unique." *Actes du Xe Congrès des Sociétés de Philosophie de Langue Française* (Congrès Bergson). Paris: Armand Colin, 1, 1959, 275-280.

4188 Robinet, André. "Table ronde: Unité, unicité, dialogue." *Actes du Xe Congrès des Sociétés de Philosophie de Langue Française* (Congrès Bergson). Paris: Armand Colin, 2, 1959, 281-302.

4189 Robinet, André and Gouhier, Herni, Eds. *Henri Bergson: Oeuvres: Edition du Centenaire*. Paris: Presses Universitaires de France, 1959, 1602. Professore Robinet's "Apparat critique" and "Notes historiques" are found on pp. 1485-1539 and 1541-1578, respectively. Professor Gouhier's "Introduction" is found on pp. vii-xxx.

4190 Roche, Claude. "La Notion d''autisme' chez Bergson." *Actes du Xe Congrès des Sociétés de Philosophie de Langue Française* (Congrès Bergson). Paris: Armand Colin, 1, 1959, 281-284. By "autisme" is meant the most fundamental and most intimate part of the self. It escapes the common conditions of knowledge. The author discusses how, according to Bergson, it can be revealed and what its principal aspects are.

4191 Ruyer, Ramond. "Bergson et le sphex ammophile." *Revue de Métaphysique et de Morale*, 64, No. 2, 1959, 165-179. The author argues that Bergson's treatment of instinct among the insects has been criticized unfairly. He concludes that: "La conception bergsonienne de l'instinct est donc juste dans l'ensemble. Ses faiblesses tiennent plutôt à ses contacts avec d'autres théories voisines, moins heureuses." (176).

4192 Ruyssen, Théodore. "Table ronde: Liberté." *Actes du Xe Congrès des Sociétés de Philosophie de Langue Française* (Congrès Bergson). Paris: Armand Colin, 1, 1959, 167-189.

4193 Ruyssen, Théodore. "Table ronde: Néant et existentialisme." *Actes du Xe Congrès des Sociétés de Philosophie de Langue Française* (Congrès Bergson). Paris: Armand Colin, 2, 1959, 145-164.

4194 Sancipriano, Mario. "Henri Bergson e Edmund Husserl." *Humanitas*, 14, No. 11, 1959, 792-799.

4195   Sancipriano, Mario. "La 'metafisica induttiva' del Bergson." *Giornale di metafisica*, 14, No. 6, 1959, 818-825. The author holds that Bergson's thought involves the attempt to apply the inductive method to construct a metaphysics which can be presented as a science. This attempt is discovered in the theory of psychological time, in the study of liberty, the substantiality of the soul, and the "élan vital." Bergson's merit was to have brought again essentially empirical problems into the purview of philosophy.

4196   Saulnier, Claude. "Pour Une Compréhension intuitive du rire: Intériorité bergsonienne et intentionnalité axiologique." *Actes du Xe Congrès des Sociétés de Philosophie de Langue Française* (Congrès Bergson). Paris: Armand Colin, 1, 1959, 285-288. In order to study the phenomenon of laughter the author adopts a reformulated introspective method, taking from Bergson the intuitive comprehesion of the act in a state of becoming and from phenomenology the sense of true interiority. Laughter, an aesthetic play ("jeu"), pertains to felt life and verifies the laws of action which Parodi terms axiological laws.

4197   Saulnier, Claude. "Table ronde: Matière, causalité, discontinu." *Actes du Xe Congrès des Sociétés de Philosophie de Langue Française* (Congrès Bergson). Paris: Armand Colin, 2, 121-142.

4198   Saulnier, Claude. "Table ronde: Psychologie, phénoménologie, intuition." *Actes du Xe Congrès des Sociétés de Philosophie de Langue Française* (Congrès Bergson). Paris: Armand Colin, 2, 1959, 15-37.

4199   Schepers, Eugène. "Table ronde: Liberté. *Actes du Xe Congrès des Sociétés de Philosophie de Langue Française* (Congrès Bergson). Paris: Armand Colin, 2, 1959, 167-189.

4200   Schepers, Eugène. "Table ronde: Morale." *Actes du Xe Congrès des Sociétés de Philosophie de Langue Française* (Congrès Bergson). Paris: Armand Colin, 2, 1959, 237-257.

4201   Scherer, René. "Table ronde: Morale." *Actes du Xe Congrès des Sociétés de Philosophie de Langue Française* (Congrès Bergson). Paris: Armand Colin, 2, 1959, 237-257.

4202   Schuhl, Pierre-Maxime. "Carnet de notes." *Revue Philosophique de la France et de l'Etranger*, 84, No. 3, 1959, 371-377. This article contains an account of a visit with Bergson on December 30, 1938, as well as reminiscences of other French philosophers.

4203   Schuhl, Pierre-Maxime. "Une Heure avec Bergson." *Revue Philosophique de la France et de l'Etranger*, 149, No. 3, 1959, 371. Bergson and aesthetics are discussed in this account of an interview with Bergson.

4204   Sciacca, Michele Federico (M. F. S.). "Ommagio a Henri Bergson." *Humanitas*, 14, No. 11, 1959, 769-770.

4205   "Semaine Bergson au Maroc: 20-26 avril 1959." *Etudes Philosophiques*, N.S. 14e Année, No. 3, juillet-septembre 1959, 347-350. The agenda and opening speech of a conference on Bergson are reported in this article.

4206   Sérouya, Henri. "Bergson et la Kabbale." *Revue Philosophique de la France et de l'Etranger*, 149, No. 3, juillet-septembre 1959, 321-324. The author states: "Au cours d'une longue conversation d'avant guerre, relative au mysticisme, Bergson nous a déclaré que, dans sa jeunesse, il avait appris l'hébreu, mais qu'il ignorait la Kabbale." (321). But the basis for his thought according to the author, already existed in the Kabbala.

4207 Sérouya, Henri. "Le Génie de Bergson." *Actes du Xe Congrès des Sociétes de Philosophie de Langue Française* (Congrès Bergson). Paris: Armand Colin, 1, 1959, 289-291. Kant attributed genius only to poets and artists. It is found nonetheless in certain great philosophers whose thought, like Bergson's, has an intuitive character. Bergson possesses to a considerable degree that subjectivity which is the attribute of the artist or poet.

4208 Sérouya, Henri. "Table ronde: Sources et histoire du bergsonisme." *Actes du Xe Congrès des Sociétés de Philosophie de Langue Française* (Congrès Bergson). Paris: Armand Colin, 2, 1959, 213-233.

4209 Sérouya, Henri. "Table ronde: Unité, unicité, dialogue." *Actes du Xe Congrès des Sociétés de Philosophie de Langue Française* (Congrès Bergson). Paris: Armand Colin, 2, 1959, 281-302.

4210 Silbermann, Alphons. "Notizen zu Bergsons hundertstem Geburtstag." *Theater und Zeit*, 7, 1959-1960, 107-111.

4211 Spengler, Boris de. "Table ronde: Physique." *Actes du Xe Congrès des Sociétés de Philosophie de Langue Française* (Congrès Bergson). Paris: Armand Colin, 2, 1959, 65-87.

4212 Stern, Axel. "Morale ouverte = morale rationelle." *Actes du Xe Congrès des Sociétés de Philosophie de Langue Française* (Congrès Bergson). Paris: Armand Colin, 1, 1959, 283-296. We owe to Bergson the distinction between closed and open morality and the revival of the distinction between intelligence and intuition. Rejecting this latter distinction, the author shows that rational morality is open and that morality, in order to be open, must be rational.

4213 Stern, Axel. "Table ronde: Morale." *Actes du Xe Congrès des Sociétés de Philosophie de Langue Française* (Congrès Bergson). Paris: Armand Colin, 2, 1959, 237-257.

4214 Stern, Axel. "Table ronde: Physique." *Actes du Xe Congrès des Sociétés de Philosophie de Langue Française* (Congrès Bergson). Paris: Armand Colin, 2, 1959, 65-87.

4215 Suares, André. "Bergson vu par André Suares." *Nouvelles Littéraires*, No. 1677, 22 octobre 1959, 2.

4216 Takayama, Thakashi. *Ide-forusu no Tetsugaku*. Tokyo, Japan: Yamamoto-shoter, 1959, 300. This is a study of A. Fouillée's philosophy of the "Idea-force." It deals with both Fouillée and Bergson.

4217 Taminiaux, Jacques. "Le Congrès Bergson." *Revue Philosophique de Louvain*, 57, No. 3, août 1959, 438-442.

4218 Tatarkiewicz, Ladislas. "L'Esthétique de Bergson et l'art de son temps." *Actes du Xe Congrès des Sociétés de Philosophie de Langue Française* (Congrès Bergson). Paris: Armand Colin, 1, 1959, 297-302. The author explains that although Bergson had a great deal to say about art and the beautiful in his metaphysical writings, it is difficult to say what actual form of art corresponds to his opinions. The problem is to know what artistic currents influenced his way of viewing art and what artistic developments were influenced by him.

4219   Tatarkiewicz, Ladislas. "Table ronde: Esthétique." *Actes du Xe Congrès des Sociétés de Philosophie de Langue Française* (Congrès Bergson). Paris: Armand Colin, 2, 1959, 193-210.

4220   Thibaudet, Albert. "Bergson vu par Albert Thibaudet." *Nouvelles Littéraires*, No. 1677, 22 octobre 1959, 2.

4221   Tonquédec, Joseph de. "La Conception bergsonienne de Dieu." *Actes du Xe Congrès des Sociétés de Philosophie de Langue Française* (Congrès Bergson). Paris: Armand Colin, 1, 1959, 303-306. The author, who has corresponded with Bergson concerning religion, expresses certain reservations concerning Bergson's concept of God. In spite of Bergson's rejection of a static monism, the evolutionary thesis of *Creative Evolution*, which plunges everything into becoming, has a certain monistic tinge. Further, Bergson's conception of mysticism differs from the Christian conception.

4222   Tonquédec, Joseph de. "Table ronde: Religion." *Actes du Xe Congrès des Sociétés de Philosophie de Langue Française* (Congrès Bergson). Paris: Armand Colin, 2, 1959, 261-278.

4223   Tresmontant, Claude. "Deux Métaphysiques bergsoniennes?" *Revue de Métaphysique et de Morale*, 64, No. 2, 1959, 180-193. The author examines contrary tendencies in Bergson's thought: his "metaphysics of creation" and his "neoplatonism."

4224   Trouillard, Jean. "Review of *Bergson et Plotin* by Rose-Marie Mossé-Bastide." *Études Philosophiques*, N.S. 14, No. 4, 1959, 554.

4225   Trouillard, Jean. "Sagesse bergsonienne, sagesse plotinienne." *Actes du Xe Congrès des Sociétés de Philosophie de Langue Française* (Congrès Bergson). Paris: Armand Colin, 1, 1959, 307-310. Nothing could seem farther from a philosophy of spiritual creation than the common conception of the Platonic Idea. Nonetheless, there is in Bergson a search for a simplicity at once original and creative, whose anteriority, the author holds, can be an excellent way of reinventing the Platonic Idea.

4226   Trouillard, Jean. "Table ronde: Sources et histoire du bergsonisme." *Actes du Xe Congrès des Sociétés de Philosophie de Langue Française* (Congrès Bergson). Paris: Armand Colin, 2, 1959, 213-233.

4227   Tsanoff, Radoslav A. "Evolution, Teleology and History." *Rice Institute Pamphlet*, 46, No. 1, April 1959, 32-51.

4228   Unsoeld, William Francis. "Mysticism, Morality, and Freedom: The Role of the Vital Impulse in Bergson's Theory of Ethics." Diss., Washington (Seattle), 1959, 267.

4229   Urmeneta, Fermín de. "Henri Bergson et l'esthétique de la 'jovialité'." *Actes du Xe Congrès des Sociétés de Philosophie de Langue Française* (Congrès Bergson). Paris: Armand Colin, 1, 1959, 311-314. In *Laughter* one discovers, the author holds, a faith in joviality which is at once conciliatory, objective, and exalting, and which makes Bergson's work such a stimulating incentive for its readers. The author examines the aesthetic categories of the caricature and their closely allied categories.

4230   Urtin, Henri. "Le Fondement de L'intuition." *Actes du Xe Congrès des Sociétés de Philosophie de Langue Française* (Congrès Bergson). Paris: Armand Colin,

1, 1959, 315-318. It is possible to find within ourselves, the author holds, the essentials of intuition, which is basically the original character of our personal law ("statute"å. It is necessary to search for this personal formula which constitutes our originality. Also intuition intervenes necessarily in other domains.

4231 Vandel, Albert. "Fils de Bergson." *Nouvelles Littéraires*, No. 1677, 22 octobre 1959, 6.

4232 Vandel, Albert. "Table ronde: Vie et évolution." *Actes du Xe Congrès des Sociétés de Philosophie de Langue Française* (Congrès Bergson). Paris: Armand Colin, 2, 1959, 91-117.

4233 Versiani Velloso, Arthur. "Centenarios de 1959: Husserl, Bergson..." *Kriterion*, 12, No. 49-50, 1959, 499-156.

4234 Vigone, Lucette. "Quelques Etudes bergsoniennes en Italie." *Actes du Xe Congrès des Sociétés de Philosophie de Langue Française* (Congrès Bergson). Paris: Armand Colin, 1, 1959, 319-326. This is a bibliography of writing concerning Bergson in Italy from 1900-1958. It deals with the more important works.

4235 Vigone, Lucette. "Table ronde: Sources et histoire du bergsonisme." *Actes du Xe Congrès des Sociétés de Philosophie de Langue Française* (Congrès Bergson). Paris: Armand Colin, 1959, 2, 213-233.

4236 Vigone, Luciana. "Bibliografia bergsoniana in Italia (1940-1959)." *Giornale di metafisica*, 14, No. 6, 1959, 853-856.

4237 Vigone, Luciana. "Congresso Bergson (Parigi, 17-19 maggio 1959)." *Rivista di filosofia neoscolastica*, 51, No. 4, 1959, 372-376.

4238 Virieux-Reymond, Antoinette. "A Propos du problème du discontinu dans la philosophie bergsonienne." *Actes du Xe Congrès des Sociétés de Langue Française* (Congrès Bergson). Paris: Armand Colin, 1, 1959, 327-331. In Bergson's thought discontinuities are, the author holds, always displayed against a background of contintuity. What are these discontinuities and how can they be integrated into Bergson's continuist hypotheses? Are they due to the conceptual fragmentation which our intelligence projects onto reality, or do they pertain to reality itself?

4239 Virieux-Reymond, Antoinette. "Réflexions sur la nature du temps: Bergson." *Giornale di metafisica*, 14, No. 6, 1959, 826-834. This is an explanation of Bergson's conception of the nature of time. It deals with time as conceived in Greek philosophy and Zeno's paradoxes. Bergson's duration is seized from within through an act of intuition, the author explains. Heterogeneous in its flow, it is creative and embodies liberty.

4240 Virieux-Reymond, Antoinette. "Table ronde: Esthétique." *Actes du Xe Congrès des Sociétés de Philosophie de Langue Française* (Congrès Bergson). Paris: Armand Colin, 2, 1959, 193-210.

4241 Virieux-Reymond, Antoinette. "Table ronde: Matière, causalité, discontinu." *Actes du Xe Congrès des Sociétés de Philosophie de Langue Française* (Congrès Bergson). Paris: Armand Colin, 2, 1959, 121-142.

4242 Vita, Luís Washington. "O bergsonismo na filosofia latino-americana." *Revista Brasiliense*, 25, set.-out. 1959, 137-145.

4243 Wahl, Jean. "Table ronde: Matière, causalité, discontinu." *Actes du Xe Congrès des Sociétés de Philosophie de Langue Française* (Congrès Bergson). Paris:

Armand Colin, 2, 1959, 121-142.

4244 Wahl, Jean. "Table ronde: Néant et existentialisme." *Actes du Xe Congrès des Sociétés de Philosophie de Langue Française* (Congrès Bergson). Paris: Armand Colin, 2, 1959, 145-164.

4245 Wahl, Jean. "Table ronde: Sources et histoire du bergsonisme." *Actes du Xe Congrès des Sociétés de Philosophie de Langue Française* (Congrès Bergson). Paris: Armand Colin, 2, 1959, 213-233.

4246 Werner, Charles. "Table ronde: Durée et mémoire." *Actes du Xe Congrès des Sociétés de Philosophie de Langue Française* (Congrès Bergson). Paris: Armand Colin, 2, 1959, 41-61.

4247 Werner, Charles. "Table ronde: Liberté." *Actes du Xe Congrès des Sociétés de Philosophie de Langue Française* (Congrès Bergson). Paris: Armand Colin, 2, 1959, 167-189.

4248 Wolff, Edgar. "D'Un Progrès dialectique dans la pensée de Bergson: Changement, mémoire, durée." *Archives de Philosophie*, 12, No. 1, octobre-décembre 1959, 521-528. The author argues that Bergson was driven to assert the paradoxical doctrine of the integral conservation of the past because, having defined the inner life as radical change, he needed a stable vantage-point from which to appreciate change. He found this vantage-point in the extra-temporality of memory, which he could have demanded of the characterological unity of the profound self.

4249 Wolff, Edgar. "Mémoire et durée." *Actes du Xe Congrès des Sociétés de Philosophie de Langue Française* (Congrès Bergson). Paris: Armand Colin, 1, 1959, 333-337. According to the author, in *Matter and Memory* Bergson asserts that pure memory constutites, in the strongest sense of the term, a representation of the past, i.e., an intuitive vision of once-experienced events. This pure memory is the essence of real memory. This interior contemplation of the past permits us, in an instantaneous apprehension, to recover all its elements. The author examines objections to this thesis. (Cf. G. Poulet, 1960.)

4250 Wolff, Edgar. "Table ronde: Durée et mémoire." *Actes du Xe Congrès des Sociétés de Philosophie de Langue Française* (Congrès Bergson). Paris: Armand Colin, 2, 1959, 41-61.

4251 Wolff, Edgar. "Table ronde: Matière, causalité, discontinu." *Actes du Xe Congrès des Sociétés de Philosophie de Langue Française* (Congrès Bergson). Paris: Armand Colin, 2, 1959, 121-142.

4252 Wolff, Edgar. "Table ronde: Morale." *Actes du Xe Congrès des Sociétés de Philosophie de Langue Française* (Congrès Bergson). Paris: Armand Colin, 2, 1959, 237-257.

4253 Xirau, Ramon. *El péndulo y el espiral*. Xalapa, México: Universidad Veracruzana, 1959, 146. This is a study of modern philosophy of history based on *Les Deux Sources*.

4254 Zaalberg, C. A. "Bergson en *De weg van het licht*." In *Miscellanea litteraria in commemorationem primi decennii institui edita*. Studi litteraria rhenotraictina, No. 4. Groningen: Wolters, 1959, 181-184. This is a study of Bergson's influence on a work by A. Verwey.

4255 Zaragüeta, Juan. "La Liberté dans la philosophie d'Henri Bergson." *Actes du Xe Congrès des Sociétés de Philosophie de Langue Française* (Congrès Bergson). Paris: Armand Colin, 1, 1959, 339-342.

4256 Zaragüeta, Juan. "Table ronde: Liberté." *Actes du Xe Congrès des Sociétés de Philosophie de Langue Française* (Congrès Bergson). Paris: Armand Colin, 2, 1959, 167-189.

4257 Zaragüeta, Juan. "Table ronde: Psychologie, phénoménologie, intuition." *Actes du Xe Congrès des Sociétés de Philosophie de Langue Française* (Congrès Bergson). Paris: Armand Colin, 2, 1959, 15-37.

4258 Zephir, Jacques J. *La Personnalité humaine dans l'oeuvre de Marcel Proust: Essai de psychologie littéraire*. Paris: Lettres Modernes, 1959, 331. There are many references to Bergson in this work, which likens Bergson's psychology to that of Marcel Proust.

4259 Zwiebel, Daniel. "Durée de Dieu et imprévisibilité des actes libres chez Bergson." *Actes du Xe Congrès des Sociétés de Philosophie de Langue Française* (Congrès Bergson). Paris: Armand Colin, 1, 1959, 343-346. The author claims that the free act is for Bergson creative and unforseeable. God is for Bergson creative and free, but Bergson's God endures and must be distinguished from the un-temporal Deity of classical theology. But God's duration is not man's, and the descent of God into the soul of the mystic involves the elevation of the human duration to the divine tension.

4260 Zwiebel, Daniel. "Table ronde: Liberté." *Actes du Xe Congrès des Sociétés de Philosophie de Langue Française* (Congrès Bergson). Paris: Armand Colin, 2, 1959, 167-189.

1960

4261 Almeida, Vieira de. "Bergson: Esboço de análise." *Colóquio*, 2, No. 10, 1960, 52-56.

4262 Argan, Giulio Carlo. "Da Bergson a Fautrier." *Aut Aut*, No. 55, gennaio 1960, 10-23.

4263 Arraiza, I. "Dios en la filosofia de Henri Bergson." *Ecclesiastica Xaveriana*, 10, No. 1, 1960, 8-140.

4264 Badi', Amir Mehdi. *L'Illusion de l'extensibilité infinie de la vérité: Vol. 2. Vers une connaissance objective*. Lausanne: Payot, 1960, 159. This study includes criticisms of Bergson and Fichte.

4265 Barthélemy-Madaule, Madeleine. "Author du *Bergson* de M. Jankélévitch." *Revue de Méthapysique et de Morale*, 55, No. 4, 1960, 511-524. This is a highly laudatory review of the second edition of Jankélévitch's *Bergson*.

4266 Barthélemy-Madaule, Madeleine. "Introduction à un rapprochement entre Bergson et Teilhard de Chardin." *Etudes Bergsoniennes*, 5, 1960, 65-85.

4267 Bataillon, Marcel. "Discours au Collège de France." *Bullentin de la Société Française de Philosophie*, 54, No. 1, janvier-mars 1960, 11-20.

4268 Bémol, Maurice. *Essai sur l'orientation des littératures de langue française au XXe siècle*. Paris: Nizet, 1960, 338. The author states that Bergson's influence on French literature was decisive: "L'Apparition de la philosophie bergsonienne, qu'elle fût objet de sympathie ou de réprobation, représentait pour tous un changement irréversible de de l'atmosphère intellectuelle, un depassement du positivisme scientiste, un élargissement du rationalisme qui allaient permettre dans tous les ordres, des efforts et des tentatives inattendus." (p. 19) The author outlines Bergson's influence on Charles Péguy on pp. 51-52; on Marcel Proust on pp. 117-119; on Albert Thibaudet on pp. 226. On pp. 132-137 he summarizes Bergson's role as a "catalyst".

4269   Benavides, C. "Simpatias filosofias de William James." *Pensamiento*, 16, No. 63, 1960, 317-330. This essay discusses the influence on James of several philosophers, including Bergson.

4270   Berger, Gaston. "Discours à la Sorbonne." *Bulletin de la Société Française de Philosophie*, 54, No. 1, janvier-mars 1960, 21-25.

4271   Bergson, Staffan. *Time and Eternity: A Study in the Structure and Symbolism of T. S. Eliot's Four Quartets*. Stockholm: Svenska bokforlaget, 1960, 285. (Studia litterarum Upsaliensia, 1)

4272   Besnier, Charles. "Sur Bergson 'perdu et retrouvé'." *Nouvelle Revue Pédagogique*, 15 mai 1960.

4273   Blanco, J. E. "Cinco lecciones sobre Bergson: Lección segunda." *Studium*, 4, Nos. 9-10, 1960, 3-17. Blanco analyzes Bergson's Latin dissertation *Quid Aristoteles de loco senserit* and the *Essai*.

4274   Brun, Jean. "Review of *Bergson* by Vladimir Jankélévitch." *Cahiers du Sud*, 48, No. 358, 1960-1961, 482-483.

4275   Brun, Jean. "Bergson: Philosophe de la coincidence." *Critique*, 16, No. 157, 1960, 535-552.

4276   Cain, Julien. "Bergson président de la Commission internationale de coopération intellectuelle." *American Philosophical Society Proceedings*, N.S. 104, No. 4, August 1960, 404-407.

4277   Camilucci, Marcello. "La madre di Bergson." *L'osservatore romano*, 28 settèmbre 1960.

4278   Chaix-Ruy, Jules. "Vitalité et élan vital: Bergson et Croce." *Etudes Bergsoniennes*, 5, 1960, 143-167.

4279   Chanyshev, A. N. Философия Анри Бергсона. Москва: Издательстфо Московского университета, 1960, 54. (Pamphlet).

4280   Chevalier, Jacques. *Conversaciones con Bergson*. Trans. José A. Miguez. Madrid: Aguilar, 1960, 420.

4281   Chevalier, Jacques. "Le Souvenir de Bergson." *Ecrits de Paris*, octobre 1960, 103-112. "Entretien à la radio canadienne, avec Odette Lutgen."

4282   Ciudad, Mario. *Bergson y Husserl: Diversidad en coincidencia*. Ediciones de los Anales de la Universidad de Chile, Serie Negra, No. 8, 1960, 43.

4283   Core, Nicholas. *Pierre Teilhard de Chardin: His Life and Spirit*. New York: Barrie and Rockliff, 1960. The author quotes Chardin as stating, "I remember clearly having read *Creative Evolution* with avidity at this time. But although I didn't very well understand at this period what exactly Bergson's Durée meant—and in any case it was not sufficiently convergent to satisfy me—I can see clearly that the effect of these passionate pages on me was merely, at the right moment and in a flash, to stir up a fire that was already burning in my heart and mind" (p. 10). The "time" referred to is 1912. This is one of the few recorded remarks of Pierre Teilhard de Chardin concerning Bergson.

4284 Costa, João Cruz. "O itinerário de Bergson." *Kriterion*, 13, No. 51-52, 1960, 1-8.

4285 Crastre, Victor. "Review of *La Vocation de Bergson* by Jean Guitton." *Cahiers du Sud*, 48, No. 358, 1960-1961, 483-484.

4286 Cuzacq, René. "Bergson et Jacques Chevalier à Dax et aux Pyrenées." *Pyrénées*, No. 43, 1960, 166-167.

4287 Debidour, V. H. "Review of *Entretiens avec Bergson* by Jacques Chevalier." *Bulletin des Lettres*, 22e Année, No. 216, 15 mars 1960, 103-104.

4288 De Gaulle, Charles. *The Edge of the Sword*. Trans. G. Hopkins. New York: Criterion Books, 1960, 128. Bergson is discussed on pp. 16-17 and 20-21.

4289 Delhomme, Jeanne. "Nietzsche et Bergson: La Représentation de la vérité." *Etudes Bergsoniennes*, 5, 1960, 39-62.

4290 Deshayes, M.-L. "La Morale bergsonienne." *Les Humanités. Classes de lettres. Sections modernes*. CI. 367, Avril 1960, 22-25.

4291 Devaux, André-A. "Aspects de la pédagogie de Bergson." *Synthèses*, 15e Année, No. 171, août 1960, 44-56.

4292 D'Hautefeuille, François. "Bergson et Spinoza." *Revue de Métaphysique et de Morale*, 65, No. 4, 1960, 463-474.

4293 Diaz, D. "Review of *Une Régression mentale, de Bergson à J.-P. Sartre* by Gilbert Maire." *Revista de Filosofía*, 19, Nos. 73-74, 1960, 297.

4294 Dyserinck, Hugo. "Die Briefe Henri Bergsons an Graf Hermann Keyserling." *Deutsche Vierteljahrschrift für Literaturwissenschaft und Geistesgeschichte*, 34, No. 1, 1960, 535-552; No. 2, 1960, 169-188.

4295 Emery, Léon. "Vers de Point oméga?" *Polarité du symbole*. Paris: Les Etudes Carmélitaines chez Desclée de Brouwer, 1960, 75-93. The author deals in this essay with Bergson and Teilhard de Chardin.

4296 *Etudes Bergsoniennes*. Paris: Presses Universitaires de France, 1960, Vol. 5, 220. P. Valéry, F. Nietzsche, P. Teilhard de Chardin, Edouard Le Roy, B. Croce, I. Kant, and others are discussed in this issue in relation to Bergson.

4297 Fabre-Luce de Gruson, Françoise. "Bergson: Lecteur de Kant." *Etudes Bergsoniennes*, 5, 1960, 171-190.

4298 Favarger, Charles. "Durée et intuition." *Revue de Théologie et de Philosophie*, 3e Série, 10, No. 3, 1960, 169-187. This talk was given at the Congrès Bergson of the Société romande de philosophie.

4299 Favarger, Charles. "Review of *Henri Bergson* by Günther Pflug." *Revue de Théologie et de Philosophie*, 3e Série, 10, No. 3, 1960, 257-258.

4300 Frutos, Eugenio. "El primer Bergson en Antonio Machado." *Revista de Filosofía*, 19, Nos. 73-74. 1960, 117-168. The influence of Bergson on the poet Machado is discussed in this article.

4301 Galeffi, Romano. "Presença de Bergson." *Anais do III Congresso Nacional de Filosofia*. São Paulo: Instituto Brasileiro de Filosofia, 1960, 425-445.

4302 Gilson, Etienne. *Le Philosophe et la théologie*. Paris: Fayard, 1960, 263. (Cf. the author, 1962)

4303 Gonzales Sanchez, Gustavo. "Bergson y nosotros." *Revista Javeriana*, 54, No. 269, 1960, 638-645; No. 270, 1960, 714-719; 55, No. 271, 1961, 41-46.

4304   Gouhier, Henri. "Bergson et la philosophie du christianisme." *Revue de Théologie et de Philosophie*, 3e Sér., 10, No. 1, 1960, 1-22.

4305   Gouhier, Henri. "Vingt Ans après." *Nouvelles litteraires*, No. 1677, 4 février 1960, 4. This is a review of Bergson's *Oeuvres* and *Ecrits et paroles* and Jankélévitch's *Bergson*.

4306   Grossman, Morris. "Santayana as Dramatist and Dialectician: A Critical Estimate Made with the Help of Unpublished Manuscripts." Diss. Columbia 1960, 293. The author briefly discusses unpublished manuscripts by George Santayana in which Bergson is roundly, if not vehemently, criticized. (See *Dissertation Abstracts*, 21, No. 4, 1960, 925-926.)

4307   Gueroult, Martial. "Bergson en face des philosophes." *Etudes Bergsoniennes*, 5, 1960, 9-35.

4308   Guitton, Jean. "Esquisse pour un portrait d'Henri Bergson." *Table Ronde*, No. 145, 1960, 57-71. This sketch of Bergson begins from personal reminiscences. Bergson had great charm, but was by no means a "conversationalist." Irony, modesty, and economy were basic to his character. Candor and ingenuity appeard to him to be dispositions towards genius.

4309   Guitton, Jean. "La Mère de Bergson." *Le Figaro Littéraire*, 28 mai 1960, 4.

4310   Guitton, Jean. *La Vocation de Bergson*. Paris: Gallimard, 1960, 263. (Vocations, 9)

4311   Gurvitch, Georges. "Deux Aspects de la philosophie de Bergson: Temps et liberté." *Revue de Métaphysique et de Morale*, 65, No. 3, 1960, 307-316.

4312   Hofmann, H. "Review of 'World of Dreams' by Henri Bergson." *Harvard Divinity Bulletin*, 25, No. 10, October 1960, 26-27.

4313   Hyppolite, Jean. "Discours à l'Ecole Normale Supérieure." *Bulletin de la Société Française de Philosophie*, 54, No. 1, janvier-mars 1960, 7-9.

4314   Jagu, Chanoine Armand. "Hommage à Bergson: Le Savant, l'écrivain, l'artiste." *Mémoires de l'Académie des Sciences, Belles-Lettres et Arts d'Angers*, 1960.

4315   Jankélévitch, Vladimir. "Avec L'Ame toute-entière." *Bulletin de la Société Française de Philosophie*, 54, No. 1, janvier-mars 1960, 55-62.

4316   Jolivet, Régîs. "Bergson et le bergsonienne." *Doctor Communis*, 13, No. 1, 1960, 49-75.

4317   Jones, Alun R. *The Life and Opinions of T. E. Hulme*. Boston: Beacon Press, 1960; London: Victor Gollancz, 1960, 233. Chapter 4, titled "Bergson" appears here on pp. 57-67.

4318   Jouhaud, Michel. "Edouard Le Roy, le bergsonisme et la philosophie réflexive." *Etudes Bergsoniennes*, 5, 1960, 87-139. This is a review of Le Roy's *Essai d'une philosophie première*. Part 1 is entitled "The Structure of Le Roy's Thought" and Part 2, "Le Roy and Bergson." The author concludes: "...si la *matière* de l'oeuvre reste bergsonienne, sa *forme*, c'est-à-dire son mouvement d'ensemble, s'inspire davantage de Lachelier." (129).

4319   Joussain, André. "Le Possible et le réel chez Bergson." *Archives de Philosophie*, 23, No. 4, octobre-décembre 1960, 512-521.

4320   Kinnen, Edouard. "La filosofía social de H. Bergson." *Revista de Filosofía*, 7, No. 1-2, 1960, 57-74.

4321 Kohl, Marvin. "The Unanimity Argument and the Mystics." *The Hibbert Journal*, 58, No. 230, April 1960, 268-275. This article is a criticism of Bergson's defense of mysticism in *The Two Sources of Morality and Religion*. The author denies that intuition can produce knowledge, or that the mystics have produced verification of the devine existence. He uses arguments put forward by William James to undermine Bergson's thesis.

4322 Kumar, Shiv Kumar. "Bergson's Theory of the Novel." *Modern Fiction Studies*, 6, No. 4, Winter 1960, 325-336.

4323 Kumar, Shiv Kumar. "Memory in Virgina Woolf and Bergson." *University of Kansas Review*, 26, No. 3, Spring 1960, 235-239.

4324 Kumar, Shiv Kumar. "Virginia Woolf and Bergson's 'Mémoire par excellence'." *English Studies*, 41, No. 5, October 1960, 313-318.

4325 Lacroix, Jean. "La Philosophie: Ravaisson et Bergson." *Le Monde*, No. 7877, 13 mai 1960, 16. Also in *Le Monde hebdomadaire*, No. 1128, 4-10 juin 1970, 13.

4326 Lea, Frank Alfred. *The Life of John Middleton Murry*. New York: Oxford University Press, 1960, 378 pp. The biographer notes on p. 20 Murry's determination to study under Bergson in Paris and his reading of *L'Évolution créatrice*. On pp. 24-25 he prints a letter from Murry to Philip Landon in which Murry proposes to use his new magazine, *Rhythm*, as a vehicle for Modernism as well as Bergsonism: "Modernism means, when I use it, Bergsonism in Philosophy—that is a really *Creative* Evolution with only in the end an Intuition to put the individual at its heart roots..." (p. 24).

4327 Le Brun, P. "The Influence of Bergson on Some Modern Critics." Diss. Oxford 1960-1961.

4328 Lins, Ivan. "Bergson: Un filósofo da 'Belle-époque'." *Revista do Livro*, 50, No. 19, 1960, 19-33.

4329 Long, Wilbur. "Review of *Dreams* by Henri Bergson." *Personalist*, 41, No. 1, 1960, 91.

4330 Marcel, Gabriel. "Discours sur Bergson." *Bulletin de la Société Française de Philosophie*, 54, No. 1, janvier-mars 1960, 27-32.

4331 Maritain, Jacques. *La Philosophie morale: Examen historique et critique de grandes systemes*. Paris: Gallimard, 1960, 588. Chapter 14 of this work, pp. 518-560, is titled: "L'Ethique bergsonienne et le problème de la supra-morale."

4332 Marneffe, J. de. "Bergson's and Husserl's Concepts of Intuition." *Philosophical Quarterly*, 23, No. 3, 1960, 169-180. The author argues that we must use Husserl's method while maintaining Bergson's realism.

4333 Massis, Henri. "Un Art de vivre." *Arts*, No. 776, 25-31 mai 1960, 1, 3.

4334 Mavit, Henri. "Présence de Bergson." *L'Age Nouveau*, No. 109, 1960, 115-117.

4335 Meland, Bernard Eugene. "From Darwin to Whitehead: A Study in the Shift in Ethos and Perspective Underlying Religious Thought." *Journal of Religion*, 40, No. 4, 1960, 229-245. On pp. 234-237 the author discusses the function of Bergson (and also of William James) in transforming 19th century mechanistic categories, and the relationships between this transformation and recent theological concepts. He suggests ways in which Bergson's and Whitehead's categories complement and correct each other. He describes Bergson's *élan vital* as a regulative concept—a way of looking at evolution.

4336 Merleau-Ponty, Maurice. *Signes.* Paris: Gallimard, 1960, 439. "Bergson se faisant" is on pp. 221-249.

4337 Millet, Louis. "Review of *Bergson* by Vladimir Jankélévitch. 2nd ed." *Études Philosophiques*, N.S. 15, No. 2, 1960, 287.

4338 Minkowski, Eugène. "Imagination?" *Revue Internationale de Philosophie*, 14, No. 51, 1960, 3-31.

4339 Minkowski, Eugène. "Position bergsonienne et typologie contemporaine." *Cahiers du Groupe François Minkowska*, April 1960, 25-30.

4340 Morandi, F. "Il Congresso dellà Società di Filosofia di Lingua Francesi: Bergson et Nous." *Gregorianum*, 41, No. 1, 1960, 78-79.

4341 Morrow, Carolyn. "An Analysis of 'Poema de un dia': The Philosophy of Bergson in Machado's Concept of Time." *Romance Notes*, 11, No. 2, 1960, 149-153. The author discusses the influence of Bergson on Machado.

4342 Mueller, Fernand-Lucien. *Histoire de la psychologie, de L'Antiquite à nos jours.* Paris: Payot, 1960, 444. Chapter nine of this history, "De Maine de Biran a Bergson," is found on pp. 329-345. On pp. 342-344 the author discusses Bergson's two concepts of memory. On pp. 344-345 depicts Bergson's influence on subsequent psychology. Though Bergson's dualisms call for correctives, the author concludes, "son rôle de ferment est loin d'être épuisé" (p. 345).

4343 Navarte, Cástor. "Razón y vida en el pensamiento de Bergson." *Razón y Fe*, 7, No. 1-2, 1960, 27-56.

4344 Polin, Raymond. "Bergson philosophe de la création." *Etudes Bergsoniennes*, 5, 1960, 193-213.

4345 Poulet, Georges. "Bergson et le thème de la vision panoramique des mourants." *Revue de Théologie et de Philosophie*, 10, No. 1, 1960, 23-41. Bergson's psychology of attention is analyzed in this searching study. Bergson achieved a consistent treatment of phenomena of panoramic vision of the past in those threatened with sudden death.

4346 Revel, Jean-François. "D'Un Nouvel Eclectisme." *Cahiers des Saisons*, No. 19, Hiver 1960, 387-392.

4347 Rideau, Emile. "Matière et esprit chez Bergson." *Revue Nouvelle*, 16e Année, 31, No. 4, 15 avril 1960, 337-354. According to the author, matter is, for Bergson generally, anything which disintegrates, analyses, and dissociates.

4348 Riefstahl, Hermann. "Die Philosophie Henri Bergsons und das Denken des 20. Jahrhunderts." *Universitas*, 15, No. 9, 1960, 981-988.

4349 Robinet, André. "Le Passage à la conception biologique: De La Perception, de l'image et du souvenir chez Bergson: Notes pour un commentaire du chapitre 11 de *Matière et Mémoire*." *Etudes Philosophiques*, N.S. 15, No. 3, 1960, 375-388. The author studies the way in which Bergson, in *Matter and Memory*, prepares for the biological reflections of *Creative Evolution*.

4350 Rocha, Zeferino. "O misticismo na filosofia de Henri Bergson." *Symposium*, 1, Nos. 2-3, 1960, 105-120.

4351 Romanell, Patrick. "Bergson in Mexico: A Tribute to José Vasconcelos." *Philosophy and Phenomenological Research*, 21, No. 4, 1960-1961, 501-513. This study examines the Bergsonian period in Mexican philosophy (1910-1925) and the influence of Bergson on Vasconcelos.

4352   Romanell, Patrick. "Bergson en Mexico: Un tributo a José Vasconcelos." *Humanitas*, 1, No. 1, 1960, 247-266. Trans. Alberto Garciá Gómez.

4353   Romanell, Patrick. "Bergson no México: Um tribute a José Vasconcelos." *Revista Brasileira de Filosofia*, 10, No. 3, 1960, 373-383.

4354   Rutten, Christian. "La Méthode philosophique chez Bergson et chez Plotin." *Revue Philosophique de Louvain*, 58, No. 3, août 1960, 430-452.

4355   Ryan, John K. "Aristotle's Concept of Place." *Ancients and Moderns*. Ed. John K. Ryan. Washington: Catholic University of America Press, 1960, 12-72. This is a translation of Bergson's Latin thesis, *Quid Aristoteles de Loco Senserit*.

4356   Sandre, Yves. "Review of *La Vocation de Bergson* by Jean Guitton." *Europe*, 38, No. 379-380, 1960, 301-302.

4357   Schuhl, Pierre-Maxime, ed. "Lettres à Félix Ravaisson: 1846-1892." *Revue de Métaphysique et de Morale*, 45, No. 2, 1960, 173-202. This article contains a letter by Bergson (2 novembre 1892).

4358   Sipriot, P. "Review of *Entretiens avec Bergson* by Jacques Chevalier." *La Table Ronde*, No. 145, 1960, 156-158.

4359   Slatoff, Walter J. *Quest for Failure*. Ithaca, New York: Cornell University Press, 1960, 275. The author describes similarities between Bergson and Wm. Faulkner on pp. 242-248. Motion, tension, insight derived from experience, and "irrationalism" are basic to both.

4360   Smith, Colin. "Philosophical Survey: Philosophy in France." *Philosophy*, 25, No. 134, July 1960, 265-271. Bergson and Jankélévitch are discussed in this article.

4361   Soucy, Claude. "Technique et philosophie." *Recherches et Débats*, No. 31, juin 1960, 109-123. Various references to Bergson are included in this article.

4362   "Le Souvenir de Bergson." *Écrits de Paris*, Octobre 1960, 103-112. This concerns an interview of Jacques Chevalier by Odette Lutgen on Canadian radio.

4363   Spiegelberg, Herbert. *The Phenomenology Movement*. Vol. 1. The Hague: Martinus Nijhoff, 1960, 391. The author notes that Martin Heidegger, in *Sein und Zeit*, "...rejects Bergson's ideas with surprising violence." p. 336. Cf. Martin Heidegger, 1962.

4364   Stepelevich, Lawrence S. "Benda's Attack on Bergson." *New Scholasticism*, 34, No. 4, October 1960, 488-498.

4365   Teixeira, Lívio. "Bergson e a história da filosofia." *Kriterion*, 13, Nos. 51-52, 1960, 9-20.

4366   Valéry, Paul. "Deux Lettres à Henri Bergson." *Etudes Bergsoniennes*, 5, 1960, 3-7. Cf. P. Valéry, 1932, 1934.

4367   Valéry, Paul. "Lettre à Henri Bergson, 8 mars 1932." *Les Etudes Bergsoniennes*, 5, 1960, 3-4. The author thanks Bergson for a copy of *Les Deux Sources de la morale et de la religion*.

4368   Valéry, Paul. *Lettre à Henri Bergson, 25 juin 1934."* *Les Etudes Bergsoniennes*, 5, 1960, 5-7. The author thanks Bergson for a copy of *La Pensée et le mouvant (The Creative Mind)*.

4369   Vandel, Albert. "L'Importance de *L'Evolution créatrice* dans la genèse de la pensée moderne." *Revue de Théologie et de Philosophie*, 9, No. 2, 1960, 85-108. The author deals with the philosophy of evolution since Lamarck and Bergson's contribution to the philosophy of evolution. He also deals with Bergson's influence on F. Leenhardt, G. Mercier, and P. Teilhard de Chardin.

4370　　Van Peursen, C. A. "Henri Bergson: Phénoméonologie de la perception." *Revue de Métaphysique et de Morale*, 65, No. 3, 1960, 317-326.

4371　　Viggiani, Carl. "Albert Camus' First Publications." *Modern Language Notes*, 75, No. 7, November, 1960, 589-596. This article includes a brief analysis of Camus' review of Bergson's *Les Deux Sources*. Cf. A. Camus, 1932.

4372　　Violette, René. "Review of *Henri Bergson* by Vladimir Jankélévitch." *Revue Philosophique de la France et de l'Etranger*, 85, No. 4, octobre-décembre 1960, 501-504.

4373　　Virtanen, Reino. *Claude Bernard and his Place in the History of Ideas*. London: University of Nebraska Press, 1960, 156. The author refers to Bergson on pp. 1, 13, 63, 84, 97, 101, 110-112, 113-114, 116, 130-131, and 132. He concedes Claude Bernard's influence on Bergson but states, "It is striking to find Bernard's imprint on a philosophy as remote from his characteristic rationalist and determinist position as is the intuitionism of Bergson" (p. 110). Bernard's concept of the internal environment (*milieu intérieur*) is found in Bergson's *Creative Evolution*.

4374　　Vita, Luís Washington. "O bergsonismo na filosofia latino-americana." *Revista Brasileira de Filosofia*, 10, No. 4, 1960, 536-542.

4375　　Wahl, Jean. "Discours sur Bergson." *Bulletin de la Société Française de Philosophie*, 54, No. 1, janvier-mars 1960, 49-52.

1961

4376　　Abbagno, Nicolo. "Whitehead e il concetto della ragione." *Revue Internationale de Philosophie*, 15, Nos. 3-4, 1961, 204-216. This is an exposition and criticism of A. N. Whitehead's *The Function of Reason*. It contains comparisons of Whitehead's and Bergson's philosophy on pp. 205-207, and 212.

4377　　Acker, Leonardo van. "Centenário de Bergson: Depoimento." *Revista Brasileira de Filosofia*, 11, No. 41, 1961, 108-110. The author discusses the articles and books which he has written on Bergson, as well as those aspects in which he conceives Bergson's thought to be valuable. He concludes by mentioning studies of Bergson published in Brazil.

4378　　Arregui, Cristina. "Cuatro filósofos contempráneos frente al problema de la immortalidad: H. Bergson, Max Scheler, Louis Lavelle, A. Wenzl." *Cuadernos Urugayos de Filosofía*, 1, No. 1, 1961, 109-137.

4379　　Azm, Sadik Jalal. "The Moral Philosophy of Henry Bergson." Diss. Yale 1961, 143.

4380　　Bigelow, Gordon E. "A Primer of Existentialism." *College English*, 23, No. 3, December 1961, 171-178. This study treats of Bergson along with many other thinkers (Sartre, Camus, Marcel, etc.).

4381　　Bonnet, Henri. *Alphonse Darlu: Le Maître de philosophie de Marcel Proust*. Paris: Nizet, 1961, 139. "Darlu et Bergson" are discussed on pp. 79-82.

4382　　Bruch, Jean-Louis. "Vingt Ans après la mort de Bergson." *Culture Française*, No. 5, octobre-décembre 1961.

4383　　Buytendijk, Frederick Jacobus Johannes. *Pain*. Trans. Eda O'Shiel. London, Hutchinson, 1961, 190. On pp. 115-120 the author examines, and concurs with, Bergson's concept of pain as a "motor tendency": a local reaction of the organism.

(The author notes that he subscribes to this view throughout the section of this book on the physiology of pain, pp. 42-70.) Bergson holds that (1) pain is an effort of the affected part of the organism (2) the sensation must suddenly turn into an "emotional impression" and the experience of pain appear suddenly (3) the difference between perception and affection is one of essence, not degree. (p. 118)

4384   Campanale, Domenico. "Scienza e metafisica nel pensiero di H. Bergson." *Problemi epistemologici da Hume all'ultimo Wittgenstein*. Bari: Adriatica Editrice, 1961, 424. Bergson is discussed on pp. 156-198.

4385   Čapek, Milič. *The Philosophical Impact of Contemporary Physics*. New York: Van Nostrand Company, Inc., 1961, 414. Bergson and modern physics are discussed throughout. The author concludes that Bergson's concepts of matter, energy, motion and duration are consistent with major developments in 20th century physics. Cf. esp. the author, *Bergson and Modern Physics*, 1971.

4386   Castillo-Arráez, Albert. *El espiritualismo bergsoniano: ensayo*. Caracas, Venezuela: Edicion del Instituto Pedagógico, Dirección de Cultura, 1961, 191.

4387   Crescini, Angelo. "La molteplicità nella filosofia del Bergson." *Rivista de filosofia neoscolastica*, 53, No. 5, 1961, 414-419. This article considers the problem of the one and the many in Bergson.

4388   Cresson, André. *Bergson, sa vie son oeuvre avec un exposé de sa philosophie*. Paris: Presses Universitaires de France, 1961, 160.

4389   De Gennaro, Angelo A. *The Philosophy of Benedetto Croce*. New York: Citadel Press, 1961, 103. On pp. 12-14 the author notes that Croce considered Bergson as a precursor of his own philosophy. Both philosophers belong to the "economic-scientific" school, for which scientific concepts are useful, but relative, logically strict but manipulative. But while for Bergson scientific practicality conflicts with the immediacy of intuition, for Croce it conflicts with the theoretical activity of the intellect.

4390   Dènes, Tibor. "Bergson et Proust." *Bulletin de la Société des Amis de Marcel Proust et des Amis de Combray*, No. 11, 1961, 411-417.

4391   Devaux, Philippe. "Le Bergsonisme de Whitehead." *Revue Internationale de Philosophie*, 15, Nos. 56-57, 1961, 217-236.

4392   Dubois, Jacques. "Trois Interprétations classiques de la définition aristotélicienne du temps: 3. Un Dialogue avec Kant et Bergson: Henri Carteron." *Revue Thomist*, 61, No. 3, 1961, 399-429. The first two sections of this article appeared in earlier issues of the *Revue Thomiste* and are not concerned directly with Bergson.

4393   Eckstein, Jerome. "Interestedness and non-Interestedness: Two Approaches to Knowledge." Diss., Columbia, 1961.

4394   Ellacuria, Ignacio. "Religión y religiosidad en Bergson: II. La religión estática, sus formas: Crítica." *Revista de Orientación y Cultura*, 16, No. 159, 1961, 205-212.

4395   *Etudes Bergsoniennes*. Paris: Presses Universitaires de France, 1961, Vol. 6, 212. Several of Bergson's essays are published here: "La Conscience et la vie," "Fantômes de vivants," "Le Rêve," "L'Effort intellectuel," "Le Posible et le réel," and "La Perception du changement." The table of contents of the *Edition du Centenaire* also appears here.

4396   Filho, Candido Mota. "Centenário de Bergson: Depoimento." *Revista Brasileira de Filosofia*, 11, No. 41, 1961, 106-107. The author describes Bergson's influence on his philosophy and mentions articles which he has written concerning Bergson.

4397   Fleischmann, Wolfgang B. "Conrad's *Chance* and Bergson's *Laughter*." *Renascence*, 14, No. 2, Winter 1961, 66-71.

4398   Galeffi, Romano. *Presença de Bergson*. Salvador, Brazil: Publicações da Universidade da Bahia, 1961, 82.

4399   Galy, R. "Le Temps et la liberté chez Kant et chez Bergson." *Etudes Philosophiques*, 16, No. 3, juillet-septembre 1961, 281-284.

4400   Gasparini, Duilio. "Maritain e Bergson: Trent-anni dopo." *Studia patavina*, 8, No. 4, 1961, 490-500.

4401   Gouhier, Henri. *Bergson et le Christ des Evangiles*. Paris: Fayard, 1961, 222. The author relates Bergson's religious philosophy to his earlier psychological and evolutionary theories. He explains the philosophical method which Bergson uses to study the teachings of the mystics. Cf. esp. Chapitre V and Conclusion for a a profound treatment of Bergson's Christology. The author also examines the influence of H. Delacroix and Wm. James on Bergson.

4402   Guitton, Jean. "Jeanne Bergson." *Le Figaro*, 7 décembre 1961.

4403   Hamlyn, D. W. *Sensation and Perception: A History of the Philosophy of Perception*. London: Routledge & Kegan Paul; New York: The Humanities Press, 1961, 210. On pp. 164-171 the author discusses the philosophies of Henri Bergson and William James as part of a pronounced general reaction to sensationalism around the turn of the century. In the thought of these two philosophers the issues under debate emerged with the greatest clarity. On p. 186 he notes that the distinction between sensation and perception has rarely been made: "It was made by Reid and Bergson, but by few others." The author believes this distinction is of greatest importance.

4404   Hill, Thomas English. *Contemporary Theories of Knowledge*. New York: Ronald Press, 1961, 583. Cf. pp. 250-254 for concepts of intuition.

4405   Horowitz, Irving Louis. *Radicalism and the Revolt Against Reason: The Social Theories of George Sorel*. New York: The Humanities Press, 1961, 264. Part II, Section 3 (pp. 39-56) of this study of Sorel's "irrationalist" philosophy is titled "Henri Bergson: The Liberation of Will From Intelligence." The author regards Bergson's philosophy as a backward-looking petit-bourgeoise rationalization, which saw in the machine an instrument of dehumanization. William James' pragmatism saved Sorel from Bergson's negativism.

4406   Hubscher, Arthur. "Bergson." *Von Hegel zu Heidegger*. Stuttgart: Reclam, 1961, 278.

4407   Jankélévitch, Vladimir. "Henri Bergson: Totalidades orgánicas." *La Palabra y el Hombre*, 20, No. 4, 1961, 561-581.

4408   Johannet, René. "De Tardieu à Bergson." *Ecrits de Paris*, No. 189, janvier 1961, 45-57.

4409   Jones, Ernest. *Years of Maturity*. Vol. II of *The Life and Work of Sigmund Freud*. New York: Basic Books, Inc., 1961, 512. "As early as 1909 Jung was complaining to Freud about his difficulty in explaining to his pupils the concept of libido and begged him for a fuller definition. Freud tersely replied that he could give no clearer one than he had already. Only two years later Jung equated the concept with Bergson's *élan vital*, with life energy in general, and thus robbed it of its distinctive sexual connotation" (p. 283).

4410 Khatchadourian, Haig. "On Time." *Philosophy and Phenomenological Research*, 21, No. 4, 1961, 456-466. This article contains an extensive analysis and criticism of Bergson's concept of duration.

4411 Kingston, F. Temple. *French Existentialism: A Christian Critique*. Toronto: University of Toronto Press, 1961, 221. Bergson and existentialism are discussed on pp. 13, 81, 82, 93, 146, 159, and 195.

4412 Kumar, Shiv Kumar. "Bergson's Theory of the Novel." *Modern Language Review*, 56, No. 2, April 1961, 172-179. The author argues that Bergson provides a theoretical basis for the stream of consciousness novel.

4413 Kumar, Shiv Kumar. "Joyce and Bergson's 'mémoire pure'." *Osmania Journal of English Studies*, 1, No. 1, 1961, 55-60.

4414 Lazzarini, Renato. "Internationalism and Contemporary Currents of Spiritualist Philosophy." *International Philosophy Quarterly*, 1, No. 2, 1961, 301-332. A section titled "Spiritualism and Intentionalism in Scholastic Intellectualism and in Bergson, Blondel, and Lavelle" is found on pp. 322-325.

4415 Lovejoy, Arthur Oncken. *The Reason, the Understanding, and Time*. Baltimore, Maryland: Johns Hopkins Press, 1961, 210. See especially "Bergson on 'Real Duration'," 185-202, for a letter from Bergson and criticisms of "real duration." Bergson's views are discussed at several points in this study.

4416 Macedo, Sílvio de. "Centenário de Bergson: Depoimento." *Revista Brasileira de Filosofia*, 11, No. 41, 1961, 112-113. The author states the reasons that led him to study Bergson. He explains the basic concepts covered in his writings and the nature of Bergson's influence on Brazilian philosophy.

4417 Maiorana, María-Teresa. "Bergson y el misticismo cristiano." *Criterio*, 33, No. 1373, 1961, 94-96.

4418 Marsak, Leonard M., ed. *French Philosophers from Descartes to Sartre*. New York: World Publishing Co., 1961, 502. Sections from *Creative Evolution* and *An Introduction to Metaphysics* are presented on pp. 412-421 and 422-437, respectively. A brief synopsis of Bergson's philosophy is presented on pp. 411-412. "Though the vital impulse is irrational," the author concludes, "intuition is not, difficult as it is to reason about" (p. 412).

4419 Massis, Henri. *Maurras et notre temps: Entretiens et souvenirs*. Paris: Plon, 1961, 452. "Edt. définitive augm. de documents inédits."

4420 Mathieu, Vittorio. "Intorno a Bergson: Filosofo della religione." *Studia Patavina*, 8, No. 1, 1961, 79-93.

4421 Meyerhoff, Hans. "Translator's Introduction." in *Man's Place in Nature*, by Max Scheler. New York: Noonday Press, 1961, vii-xxxv. The translator notes that two main, and conflicting, contemporary influences shaped Scheler's thought, the phenomenological movement and the philosophy of life, for which F. Nietzsche, H. Bergson and W. Dilthey were the most prominent spokesmen. On p. xxvii he notes Scheler's use of a concept corresponding to *élan vital* to explain early evolutionary development. On p. xxix he asserts that Scheler is indebted to Bergson, Nietzsche, and *Gestalt* biologies and psychologies.

4422 Misiak, Henry K. *The Philosophical Roots of Scientific Psychology*. New York: Fordham University Press, 1961, 142. Bergson's criticisms of associationism are mentioned on p. 99; the influence of Bergson on psychology is mentioned on pp. 116-118 and 123.

4423 Nery, José de Castro. "Centenário de Bergson: Depoimento." *Revista Brasileira de Filosofia*, 11, No. 41, 1961, 111-112. The author briefly considers the influence of Bergson on his thought.

4424 Osmun, George F. "Review of *The Philosophy of Poetry* by Henri Bergson." *Personalist*, 42, No. 1, 1961, 109-110.

4425 Pellé-Douel, Yvonne. "Bergson und unser Jahrhundert." *Stimmen der Zeit*, 168, No. 5, Mai 1961, 116-127.

4426 Piazza, Elena. "Il problema morale e religioso in H. Bergson." *Sapienza*, 13, Nos. 5-6, 1961, 459-478.

4427 Pinto, Luigi. "Introduction" to the Italian translation of *Les Deux Sources de la morale et de la religion*. Napoli: Ediz. Claux, 1961, 141.

4428 Poortman, J. J. "Henri Bergson en die parapsychologie." *De grondparadox en andere voordrachten en essays*. Assens, Denmark: Van Gorcum, 1961, 38-53.

4429 Rolland, Edouard. "Le Dieu de Bergson." *Sciences Ecclésiastiques*, 14, No. 1, 1961, 83-98.

4430 Sandre, Yves. "Review of *Bergson*, 2nd ed., by Vladimir Jankélévitch." *Europe*, 39, No. 381, 1961, 143-144.

4431 Smidt, Kristain. *Poetry and Belief in the Works of T. S. Eliot*. New York: Humanities Press, 1961, 258. This is a completely revised version of the study first published in 1949 by the Norwegian Academy of Science and Letters. Cf. "Bergson, and the Problem of Time," 165-181.

4432 Toynbee, Arnold J. *A Study of History*. Vol. 12. *Reconsiderations*. New York, London, Toronto: Oxford University Press, 1961, 740. On p. 149n the author notes his agreement with Bergson concerning the creative individual as "superhuman": "Here I was echoing—but in the act, exaggerating—Bergson's dictum that 'the apparition of each of these souls has been like the creation of a new species'." Cf. also 253, 568n. Cf. pp. 252-254 for parallels in the author's and Bergson's concept of creativity.

4433 Urmeneta, Fermín de. "La estética en el 'Congreso Bergson'." *Revista de Ideas Estéticas*, 19, No. 74, 1961, 135-138.

4434 Vuillemin, J. "Review of *Henri Bergson: Quellen und Konsequenzen einer induktiven Metaphysik* by G. Pflug." *Archiv für Geschichte der Philosophie*, 43, No. 3, 1961, 323-324.

4435 Yamamoto, Seisaku. "The Philosophy of Pure Experience." Diss. Emory 1961, 178. The author attempts to account for "pure experience" by examining and criticizing such philosophers as W. James, A. N. Whitehead, H. Bergson, and M. Heidegger. He explains what is meant by "pure experience" and analyzes it. He draws attention to basic epistemological problems involved in this notion. (See *Dissertation Abstracts International*, 23, Nos. 10-12, 1961, 4385.)

1962

4436 Adams, Richard P. "The Apprenticeship of William Faulkner." *Tulane Studies in English*, 12, 1962, 113-155. On pp. 152-155 the author argues that the novelist Faulkner had read Bergson's *Creative Evolution, Laughter*, and *An Introduction to Metaphysics*.

4437 Andreu, Pierre. "Bergson et Sorel." *Etudes Bergsoniennes*, 3, 1962, 43-78.

4438 Andreu, Pierre. "Discussion of 'Bergson et Sorel'." *Etudes Bergsoniennes*, 3, 1962, 170-180.

4439 Barrett, William. "Introduction to Part Four: Phenomenology and Existentialism." In *Philosophy in the Twentieth Century: An Anthology*. Vol. III. Ed. William Barrett and Henry D. Aiken. New York: Random Houst, 1962, 125-169. On pp. 138-141 the author briefly examines Bergson's philosophy, treating its significance as being primarily limited to its phenomenological content. He describes Bergson as anticipating the existentialists.

4440 Bataillon, Marcel. "A Tribute to Bergson on the Occasion of the Bergson Centennial in Paris, 1959." *The Bergsonian Heritage*. Ed. Thomas Hanna. New York and London: Columbia University Press, 1962, 105-118. This is a discussion of Bergson as a teacher.

4441 Behler, Ernst. "Der Beitrag Henri Bergsons zur Gegenwartsphilosophie." *Hochland*, 55, No. 5, 1962-1963, 417-429.

4442 Berger, Gaston. "A Tribute to Bergson on the Occasion of the Bergson Centennial in Paris, 1959." *The Bergsonian Heritage*. Ed. Thomas Hanna. New York and London: Columbia University Press, 1962, 119-123. The author holds that Bergson's message prepares us to meet our present technological problems.

4443 "Review of *Bergson and the Stream of Consciousness Novel* by Shiv Kumar." *Modern Fiction Studies*, 8, No. 2, Summer 1962, 195.

4444 Borne, Etienne. *Passion de la vérité*. Paris: Fayard, 1962, 251. (Les Idées de la vie) The second chapter of this work concerns B. Pascal, Bergson, and M. Blondel.

4445 Bunge, Mario. *Intuition and Science*. Englewood Cliffs, New Jersey: Prentice-Hall, Inc., 1942. The author criticizes Bergson's concept of intuition on pp. 12-17.

4446 Callen, Shirley Parker. "Bergsonian Dynamism in the Writings of William Faulkner." Diss. Tulane 1962, 183.

4447 Čapek, Milič. "La Signification actuelle de la philosophie de James." *Revue de Métaphysique et de Morale*, 67, No. 3, 1962, 291-321. Section V of this article is entitled "James et Bergson: Les Influences réciproques," 308-315.

4448 Champigny, Robert. "Proust, Bergson and Other Philosophers." *Proust: A Collection of Critical Essays*. Ed. René Girard. New Jersey: Prentice-Hall, Inc., 1962, 122-131. This was published originally as "Temps et reconnaissance chez Proust et quelques philosophes," PMLA, 1958.

4449 Chappell, Vere C. "Time and Zeno's Arrow." *Journal of Philosophy*, 59, No. 8, April 12, 1962, 197-213. This article is republished, with an introduction, in *Bergson and the Evolution of Physics*, (1969) Ed. P. A. Y. Gunter, 253-274. The author argues that *reductio ad absurdam* arguments against Zeno fail, by themselves, to establish any particular theory of time. He describes Bergson as holding the view that time (duration) is radically continuous. Cf. a powerful response to this claim by D. A. Sipfle, 1969.

4450 Church, Margaret. *Time and Reality: Studies in Contemporary Fiction.* Chapel Hill: University of North Carolina Press, 1962, vi, 302. The first chapter of this work (pp. 3-20) deals with the ideas of Bergson and Marcel Proust, and, secondarily, with Bergson's influence on Proust. Bergson's influence on James Joyce's *Finnegan's Wake* is suggested on pp. 63-65; his influence on Virginia Woolf is discussed briefly on pp. 69 and 98-99; his rejection by Aldous Huxley is noted on pp. 105 and 112; his relationship to William Faulkner is examined on pp. 228-230; his relations to Jean-Paul Sartre are examined on pp. 254-256.

4451 Collin, Lucien. "Bergson: Un Homme de chrétienté." *Amérique Française*, 10, No. 6, 1952, 58-60.

4452 Devaux, André-A. "La Métaphysique de Bergson et le christianisme." *Table Ronde*, No. 172, mai 1962, 105-115. This article concerns Gouhier's *Bergson et Le Christ des Evangiles.*

4453 Doubrovsky, Serge. "The Ethics of Albert Camus." In *Camus: A Collection of Critical Essays.* Ed. Germaine Bree. Englewood Cliffs, New Jersey: Prentice-Hall, 1962, 182, (71-84). "It is perhaps worth recalling here young Camus' vivid interest in Plotinus. His experience is the very opposite of Sartre's nausea...in Camus we detect a Bergsonism but without teleology. Though life, in Camus' work no longer moves in an ascending and reassuring direction, it still has impetus; though it has lost its finality it has preserved, so to speak, its vitality" (p. 74).

4454 Dunbar, Harry B. "The Impact of the Ecole Normale Supérieure on Selected Men of Letters of France." *Dissertation Abstracts*, 23, No. 2, August 1962, 630.

4455 Durant, Will. *Van Sokrates tot Bergson: Hoofdfiguren uit de geschiedenis van het denken.* "Vert. door Helena C. Pos (Herdruk III: Van Spencer tot Bergson)." Amsterdam: Em Querido, 1962, 191.

4456 Fasel, Ida. "Spatial Form and Spatial Time." *Western Humanities Review*, 16, No. 3, Summer 1962, 223-234. The author attacks the notion that "spatial time" (dead, flat, motionless) can serve as the basis for literature, which requires a living, moving real time (duration). Of the novels of William Faulkner the author holds that the tragedy of the characters, with a few exceptions, is that they can not break into the stream of becoming. They are in bondage to the past through a failure of connection with true time. They move blindly in a world where vision and values are both possible. The author imputes much of Faulkner's success, particularly in *The Sound and the Fury*, to his Bergsonism.

4457 Gabriel, Leo. "Evolution und Zeitbegriff von H. Bergson zu Teilhard de Chardin." *Wissenschaft und Weltbild*, 15, 1962, 31-36.

4458 Gardner, Martin. *Relativity for the Million.* New York: Macmillan, 1962, 182. The author discusses Bergson and Einstein on pp. 120-125.

4459 Gilson, Etienne. "L'Itinéraire d'Henri Bergson." *Nouvelles Littéraires*, No. 1795, 25 janvier 1962, 1 et 9. This is a review of *Bergson et le Christ des Evangiles* by Henri Gouhier.

4460 Gilson, Entienne. *The Philosopher and Theology.* New York: Random House, 1962, 237. Bergsonians and war are discussed on pp. 23-24 and 44-46; "The Bergson Affair" on pp. 107-131; and Bergson and Thomism on pp. 155-173. Bergson is declared not to be a Christian on pp. 133-152.

4461 Glendenning, Nigel. "The Philosophy of Henri Bergson in the Poetry of Antonio Machado." *Revue de Littérature Comparée*, 36, No. 1, 1962, 53-70.

4462 Goldberg, Harvey. *The Life of Jean Jaurès*. Madison, Wisconsin: University of Wisconsin Press, 1962, 590. On pp. 16 and 22 the author notes the rivalry between Bergson and Jaurès at the École Normale Supérieure; on pp. 68-69 he mentions Jaurès' negative attitude towards Bergson's newfound religiousness; on p. 210 he notes Bergson's Jewishness; on p. 379 he describes Bergson as a tool used in the critique of traditional French socialism; on p. 400 he mentions Bergson's philosophy as an instrument of those in France contemptuous of reason, democracy, and "weakness".

4463 Hagstrand, Yngve. *Forskande filosofi det Bergsonska tänkandet och den moderna fysiken*. Pref. Alf Nyman. Lund, Sweden: Gleerup, 1962, 141.

4464 Hanna, Thomas, ed. *The Bergsonian Heritage*. New York: Columbia University Press, 1962, viii, 170. This book is a collection of papers presented during the American and French Bergson centennial celebrations, October 16, 1959, and May 19, 1959. It includes papers by E. Morot-Sir, J. Pelikan, and E. Starkie; from Paris by J. Hyppolite, M. Bataillon, G. Berger, G. Marcel, M. Merleau-Ponty, J. Wahl, V. Jankélévitch.

4465 Hanna, Thomas. "The Bergsonian Heritage." *The Bergsonian Heritage*. Ed. Thomas Hanna. New York and London: Columbia University Press, 1962, 1-31. The author concludes that interest in Bergson's philosophy, already curtailed to a minimum, is destined to fade away.

4466 Heidegger, Martin. *Being and Time*. Trans. John Macquarrie and Edward Robinson. New York and Evanston: Harper and Row, 1962, 589. On pp. 500-501 the author characterizes Bergson's concept of time as based on Aristotle. He then dismisses this concept. On p. 382 he adds that commonsense clock time is a real, not an illusory phenomenon. Cf. Herbert Spiegelberg, 1960.

4467 Henry, Mary. "Péguy's Debt to Pascal." *L'Esprit créateur*, No. 2, 1962, 55-65.

4468 Hyppolite, Jean. "A Tribute to Bergson on the Occasion of the Bergson Centennial in Paris, 1959." *The Bergsonian Heritage*. Ed. Thomas Hanna. New York and London: Columbia University Press, 1962, 103-106. This essay discusses Bergson's contribution to the Collège de France.

4469 Jankélévitch, Vladimir. *Henri Bergson*. Trans. F. Gonzales Arambura. Xalapa, México, 1962, 379.

4470 Jankélévitch, Vladimir. "A Tribute to Bergson on the Occasion of the Bergson Centennial in Paris, 1959: With the Whole Soul." *The Bergsonian Heritage*. Ed. Thomas Hanna. New York and London: Columbia University Press, 1952, 155-166. The author insists that: "Bergsonism is a maximalist philosophy... For Bergson there are only utter totalities, organic totalities; no vacuum comes to deplete the positive fullness in which we live; all that exists is complete, viable, all-sufficient to itself." (156).

4471 Jerphagnon, Lucien. "Entre La Solitude et la banalite: Philosophie bergsonienne du banal." *Revue de Métaphysique et de Morale*, 67, No. 3, 1962, 322-329.

4472 Johnson, Allison Heartz. *Whitehead's Theory of Reality*. New York: Dover Publications, Inc., 1962, 267. The author compares Bergson and Whitehead on pp. 132-135.

4473 Lefevre, Jules. "*L'Evolution créatrice* de Bergson: Notes critiques de biologie." *Pensée Catholique*, No. 81, 1962, 18-58. This is a thoroughgoing criticism of Bergson's biology, written 1943-1944 by a biologist. The author defends human intelligence against Bergson's reproaches.

4474 Lentin, A. "Review of *La Philosophie organique de Whitehead* by F. Cesselin." *Pensée*, 45, 1962, 141.

4475 Levi, Albert William. *Literature, Philosophy and the Imagination*. Bloomington, Indiana: University of Indiana Press, 1962, 346.

4476 Levi-Strauss, Claude. *Le Totémisme aujourd'hui*. Paris: Presses Universitaires de France, 1962, 156. Bergson is discussed on pp. 92-103.

4477 Lissarague, Salvador. "El perfil de la convivencia en Bergson." *Revista Internacional de Sociología*, 20, 1962, 149-157.

4478 Love, Howard Louis. "Gerald Heard's Natural Theology in Relation to the Philosophy of Henri Bergson." Diss. Boston 1962, 272.

4479 Lowe, Victor. *Understanding Whitehead*. Baltimore, Maryland: Johns Hopkins Press, 1962, 398. The influence of Bergson on Whitehead is discussed on pp. 257-263.

4480 Marcel, Gabriel. "A Tribute to Bergson on the Occasion of the Bergson Centennial in Paris, 1959." *The Bergsonian Heritage*. Ed. Thomas Hanna. New York and London: Columbia University Press, 1962, 124-132. According to the author, Bergson is distinguished through his attachment to "authentic experience."

4481 Mazzantini, Carlo. "Il tempo come slancio vitale nell'intuitionismo di Bergson." *Il Tempo*, Anno 18, 1962, 43-54.

4482 Mein, Margaret. *Proust's Challenge to Time*. Manchester, England: Manchester University Press, 1962, 144. References to Bergson are found throughout this work, especially on pp. 78-93.

4483 Meissner, W. W. "The Problem of Psychophysics: Bergson's Critique." *Journal of General Psychology*, 66, No. 2, 1962, 301-309. The author examines Bergson's critique of psychophysics in *Time and Free Will*, on pp. 308-309 suggests its relevance to recent psychophysics: "Rather, it seems to me, the whole force of Bergson's critique ought to be felt in the posing of an honest question: Precisely what is the relation between the qualitative and quantitative aspects of physical measurement and what are the evidences which can be brought to bear in the examination of that relation?"

4484 Meland, Bernard E. *The Realities of Faith: The Revolution in Cultural Forms*. New York: Oxford University Press, 1962, 368.

4485 Merleau-Ponty, Maurice. "A Tribute to Bergson on the Occasion of the Bergson Centennial in Paris, 1959." *The Bergsonian Heritage*. Ed. Thomas Hanna. New York and London: Columbia University Press, 1962, 133-149. This is a general, highly appreciative survey of Bergson's thought.

4486 Morot-Sir, Edouard. "What Bergson Means to us Today." *The Bergsonian Heritage*. Ed. Thomas Hanna. New York and London: Columbia University Press, 1962, 35-53. The author suggests points at which Bergson's philosophy can have future impact on biological and sociological thought and on psychology.

4487 Moutsopoulos, E. "La Critique de la philosophie platonicienne chez Bergson." "Αθηνα, 66, 1962, 192-284.

4488   Pelikan, Jaroslav. "Bergson Among the Theologians." *The Bergsonian Heritage.* Ed. Thomas Hanna. New York and London: Columbia University Press, 1962, 54-73. Pelikan's essay recounts the influence of Bergson on church historians H. Richard Niebuhr and Alfred Loisy.

4489   Peyre, Henri. "The Legacy of Proust." In *Proust: A Collection of Critical Essays.* Ed. René Girard. Englewood Cliffs, New Jersey: Prentice-Hall, Inc., 1962, 28-41. On pp. 38-39 the author compares Bergson and Marcel Proust, insisting that Proust's writings are independent of Bergson's philosophy. "Proust may more convincingly be presented as the Christ heralded by Bergson the Baptist" (p. 38).

4490   Philibert, M. "Les Conceptions métaphysiques de Lagneau et Bergson." *Revue de l'Enseignement Philosophique*, 12, No. 4, 1962, 1-14.

4491   Pierola, Raul Alberto. "Imaginación y conciencia artística en la filosofía de Bergson." *Philosophia*, 25, No. 25, 1962, 55-58.

4492   Ricoeur, Paul. "L'Humanité de l'homme: Contribution de la philosophie française contemporaine." *Studium Generale*, 5, 1962, 309-323. The author deals especially with Bergson, J. P. Sartre, and M. Merleau-Ponty.

4493   Roberts, James Deotis. *Faith and Reason: A Comparative Study of Pascal, Bergson, and James.* Boston: Christopher Publishing House, 1962, 98.

4494   Rueckert, William H. "Review of *Bergson and the Stream of Consciousness Novel* by Sh. K. Kumar." *Journal of English and Germanic Philosophy*, 61, No. 4, 1962, 941-942.

4495   Salvan, Jacques L. *To Be and Not To Be: An Analysis of Jean-Paul Sartre's Ontology.* Detroit: Wayne State University Press, 1962, 155. Bergson's influence on existentialism is considered on pp. xx, xxi, xxix, xxxiv, and xxxv.

4496   Schuhl, Pierre-Maxime. *L'Imagination et le merveilleux: La Pensée et l'action.* Paris: Flammarion, 1962, 242. Aymé, L. Lévy-Bruhl, Bergson, P. Valéry, and others are discussed in this book.

4497   Starkie, Enid. "Bergson and Literature." *The Bergsonian Heritage.* Ed. Thomas Hanna. New York and London: Columbia University Press, 1962, 74-99. The author studies the influence of Bergson on his literary contemporaries: Gide, Proust, etc.

4498   Stephenson, Ralph. "Space, Time and Montage." *British Journal of Aesthetics*, 2, No. 3, July 1962, 249-258. Marcel Martin, Jean Epstein, Bergson, and Resnais are discussed in this article.

4499   Tatarkiewicz, Wladyslaw. "Abstract Art and Philosophy." *British Journal of Aesthetics*, 2, No. 3, July 1962, 227-238.

4500   Taylor, Harold. "A Philosophy for Modern Man." *Texas Quarterly*, 5, No.1, Spring 1962, 150-161.

4501   Thibaudet, Albert. "Bergson, Henri." *Encyclopedia Britannica.* Chicago: Benton, 1962, Vol. 3, 505-506.

4502   Thomas, Henry. "Henri Bergson (1859-1941)." in *Understanding the Great Philosophers.* Garden City, New York: Doubleday, 1962, 292-299.

4503   Thornhill, John. "The Philosophical Assumptions, Implicit and Explicit, of Arnold J. Toynbee's Philosophy of History." *Thomist*, 25, No. 2, 1962, 201-251. The author holds that Toynbee was influenced by Bergson's philosophy in developing his basic concepts of history. The author nontheless claims that Toynbee's philosophy is independent of Bergson's.

4504 Tuchman, Barbara Wertheim. *The Guns of August.* New York: Macmillan, 1962, 511. Bergson's influence on French military strategy is discussed on pp. 21 and 436.

4505 Tymieniecka, Anna-Teresa. *Phenomenology and Science in Contemporary European Thought.* Pref. I M. Bochenski. New York: Noonday Press, 1962, 198. The author notes the similarities between Bergson's and Husserl's concepts of time (p. 106); she notes Bergson's influence on phenomenological anthropology (p. 136); on pp. 139-159 she notes Bergson's influence on Eugène Minkowski, and examines Minkowski's concepts of psychopathology; she notes Bergson's theory of dreams (p. 158).

4506 Uscatescu, George. *Profetas de Europa.* Madrid: Editoria Nacional, 1962, 172.

4507 Veloso, A. "Bergson e la libertação do pensamiento." *Broteria,* 75, 1962, 505-515.

4508 Voronov, Albert Ivanovich. *Intuitivna filosofia Bergsona.* НЗа-во "Знание," 1962, 47. The title of this work is *Bergson's Intuitive Philosophy.*

4509 Wahl, Jean. "A Tribute to Bergson on the Occasion of the Bergson Centennial in Paris, 1959." *The Bergsonian Heritage.* Ed. Thomas Hanna. New York and London: Columbia University Press, 1962, 150-154. Bergson, for all his optimism, retains "a profound disquiet about this life," according to the author.

4510 Weber, Eugen. *Action Française: Royalism and Reaction in Twentieth-Century France.* Standford, California: Stanford University Press, 1962, 594. Bergson and P. Claudel are discussed as disruptive issues within the reactionary Action française on p. 82.

4511 Winsnes, Andreas Hofgaard. "Henri Bergson." In *Fra Marx til Sartre.* Vol. III of *Vestens tendere fra antikken til vare dager.* Ed. Eiliv Skard and Andreas Hofgaard Wisnes. Oslo: Aschehoug, 1962, 329.

4512 Wolf, R. "Der Einfluss Bergsons auf Péguy." Diss. Graz, 1963, iv, 114.

4513 Young, Kenneth. *Arthur James Balfour.* London: G. Bell & Sons, Ltd., 1963, 516. Lord Balfour's meeting with Bergson in 1911 is discussed on p. 319; his article on Bergson's philosophy is discussed on pp. 322-323.

1963

4514 Ahmad, Hafizuddin. "The Second Line of Kant's Influence." *Pakistan Philosophical Congress Publication,* 10, 1963, 222-229.

4515 Arabi-Darkaoui, Assad. *Essai sur l'idée de pureté chez Bergson.* Damas, Syria: Impr. de l'Université, 1963, 178.

4516 Baron, Roger. "Intuition bergsonienne et intuition sophianique." *Etudes Philosophiques,* 18, No. 4, 1963, 439-442.

4517 Bars, Henri. *La Littérature et sa conscience.* Paris: Grasset, 1963, 380.

4518 Barthélémy-Madaule, Madeleine. "Bergson adversaire de Kant: Étude critique de la conception bergsonienne du Kantisme suivi d'une bibliographie Kantienne." Diss. Paris 1963, 214. This is a "thèse complementaire."

4519   Barthélémy-Madaule, Madeleine. "Bergson et Teilhard de Chardin." Diss. Paris
        1963. This is the author's "thèse principal."

4520   Barthélémy-Madaule, Madeleine. *Bergson et Teilhard de Chardin*. Paris: Editions
        du Seuil, 1963, 685.

4521   Church, Margaret. *Time and Reality: Studies in Contemporary Fiction*. Chapel
        Hill: University of North Carolina Press, 1963, 302. This work was first published
        in 1949. Chapter one of this work (pp. 3-20), "The Birth of an Idea: Bergson
        and Proust", is a compendium of opinions on the Proust-Bergson relationship.

4522   Cimadevilla, Cándido. "La caida en el orden, según Bergson." *Atlántida*, 1, No.
        2, 1963, 180-191.

4523   Costa de Beauregard, Olivier. *La Notion du temps: Equivalence avec l'espace*.
        Paris: Herman, 1963, 207. The author urges that Einstein has opened the way
        toward a reconciliation of physics' time-quantity and Bergson's time-quality.

4524   Costa de Beauregard, Olivier. *Le Second Principe de la science du temps*. Paris:
        Editions du Seuil, 1963, 152. The author argues for a dualism of matter, as
        investigated by physics, and mind, as discerned by psychology and evolutionary
        biology. Matter is "timeless," i.e., its past, present and future exist simultane-
        ously. Mind is dynamic and creative, just as Bergson held, and is therefore
        easily and entirely distinguishable from matter. The author argues that both
        relativity and quantum physics describe a timeless physical universe. "Negen-
        tropy" and "information" describe a creative *élan*. Cf. esp. pp. 120-144.

4525   Costello, Harry Todd. *Josiah Royce's Seminar, 1913-1914: As Recorded in the
        Notebooks of Harry T. Costello*. Ed. Grover Smith. Essay on the philosophy of
        Royce: Richard Hocking. New Brunswick, New Jersey: Rutgers University
        Press, 1963, 209.

4526   Datta, A. H. "An Introduction to the Study of Samuel Alexander (1859-1938)."
        Pakistan Philosophical Congress Publication, 10, 1963, 230-240.

4527   Déguy, Michel. "Essai de prolongement du *Rire*." *Nouvelle Revue Française*, 11,
        No. 1, janvier 1963, 177-180.

4528   De Miro D'Ajeta, Vittorio. *Il drama del pensiero nella filosofia de Enrico Bergson*.
        Napoli: Tip. Laurenziana, 1963, 85.

4529   Emmet, Dorothy, "The Concept of Freedom With Reference to Open and Closed
        Societies." in *The Concept of Freedom in Anthropology*. Ed. David Bidney.
        The Hague: Mouton & Co., 1963, 91-105. The author describes three senses
        in which a society may be said to be "open" or "closed": 1. having freedom of
        entry (Max Weber) 2. open-minded (Karl Popper) and 3. open-hearted (Bergson).

4530   *Eucken (Rudolph), Bergson (Henri) en Russell (Bertrand): Filosofische
        Gegenschriften*. Haarlem: De Toorts, 1963, 397. "Ingeleid door R. F. Beerling
        en B. Delfgaauw. Vert. van Henri Bergson: Gerard Wijdeveld en A. Moreno."
        (Pantheen der winnars van de Nobelprijs voor literatur)

4531   Fernandez, Julio César. "Henri Bergson's Message: A Philosophy for Today."
        Américas, 15, No. 8, August 1963, 10-12.

4532   Fraisse, Paul. *The Psychology of Time*. Trans. Jennifer Leith. New York: Harper
        and Row, Publishers, 1963, 343. The author finds, on pp. 7-8, that Bergson's
        treatment of the unity of subjective time remains valid, and is defended today
        by phenomenology; he notes (p. 13) that Bergson's distinction between time-lived
        and time-thought is found today in all psychological treatises; on p. 14 he

indicates, while keeping this distinction, that his own view requires that our notions of the significance of this distinction must change. Cf. also pp. 70-71, 78-80, 84-85, 282-283, 288. In general, the author utilizes the notion of "conditioning to time" and takes up the question of the nature of this conditioning. He thus puts the organism into time, yet makes the experience of time depend upon adaptation. His approach might be termed quasi-Bergsonian.

4533   Gallagher, Idella J. "Moral Obligation in the Philosophy of Henri Bergson." Diss., Marquette, 1963, 197.

4534   George, André. "La Confrontation Teilhard-Bergson." *Nouvelles Littéraires*, No. 1878, 29 août 1963, 3.

4535   Guitton, Jean. *The Guitton Journals 1952-1955*. Trans. Frances Forrest. London: Harvill Press, 1963, 320. "Bergson's House" is discussed on pp. 260-264 and "Bergson's Testament" on pp. 224-226.

4536   Gunter, Pete Addison Yancey. "Nietzscheans Laughter." *Sewanee Review*, 76, No. 3, Summer 1963, 493-506. This article contains criticisms of Bergson's theory of laughter.

4537   Gunter, Pete Addison Yancey. "The Unity of Intuition and the Understanding in Bergson." Diss., Yale, 1963, 269. The author argues that: "Intuition and discursive understanding must be conceived to constitute a functioning unity, a unity in which these two modes of judgment work together to create a continual 'expansion' of knowledge."

4538   Gurvitch, George. "Social Structure and the Multiplicity of Times." *Sociological Theory, Values, and Sociocultural Change: Essays in Honor of Pitirim a. Sorokin*. Ed. A. Tiryakian. New York: Free Press of Glencoe; London: Collier-Macmillan, 1963, 161-184. Cf. esp. pp. 172-173.

4539   Guy, Alain. "Le Bergsonisme en Amérique latine." *Caravelle: Cahiers du Monde Hispanique et Luso-brésilien*, 1, No. 1, 1963, 121-139.

4540   Hehlmann, Wilhelm. *Geschichte der Psychologie*. Stuttgart: Kröner, 1963, 464. (Kröners Taschenausgabe, No. 200) The author deals with several thinkers under the heading "Psychology in 1900." These are L. Klages, Pierre Janet, Wm. McDougall, F. Brentano, S. Freud, A. Adler, C. G. Jung, Bergson, W. Dilthey, K. Jaspers, E. Husserl, and Wm. James. The author deals with Bergson on pp. 250-251. On p. 227 he notes Bergson's influence on Pierre Janet. On pp. 281-283 he defines Bergson as equally a phenomenologist and a psychologist.

4541   Horne, Alistair. *The Price of Glory*. New York: St. Martin's Press, 1963, 371. Bergson and French militarism are discussed on p. 11.

4542   Hyppolite, Jean. *Sens et existence dans la philosophie de Merleau-Ponty*. Oxford: Clarendon University Press, 1963, 26. References to Bergson and Merleau-Ponty are found in this study.

4543   Ingarden, Roman. "Intuicja i inteleck u Henryka Bergsona." *Z badań nad filosofia współczena*. Warzawa: Pánstwowe Wydawnictwo Naukowe, 1963, 664.

4544   Joussain, André. "Schopenhauer et Bergson." *Archives de Philosophie*, 26, No. 4, octobre-décembre 1963, 71-89.

4545   Kinnen, Edouard. "Bergson et nous." *Revue Internationale de Philosophie*, 14, No. 1, 1963, 68-91. This article consists of reflections inspired by the 1959 Congrès Bergson.

4546 Kumar, Shiv Kumar. *Bergson and the Stream of Consciousness Novel*. London: Blackie, 1962; New York: New York University Press, 1963, ix, 174.

4547 Lacombe, Olivier; Gouhier, Henri; Barthélémy-Madaule, Mme.; and Le Blond, R. P. "Bergson et le Christ des Evangiles." *Recherches et Débats*, No. 43, juin 1963, 161-196.

4548 Levi-Strauss, Claude. *Totemism*. Trans. R. Needham. Boston: Beacon Press, 1963, 116. Bergson, totemism, and intuition as method in anthropology are discussed in chapter V, "Totemism From Within," which appears on pp. 92-104.

4549 Lotte, Joseph. "Henri Bergson: L'Evolution créatrice." *La Renaissance catholique au début du XXe siècle*. Ed. L.-A. Maugendre. Paris: Beauchesne, 1963, 89-92. This article is reprinted from *Messager de la Vendée*, 11 and 18 August 1907.

4550 Lotte, Joseph. "Une Philosophie de la vie." *La Renaissance catholique au début du XXe siècle*. Ed. L.-A. Maugendre. Paris: Beauchesne, 1963, 294, 119-128. This article is reprinted from *Journal de Coutances*, 6 and 26 July 1910.

4551 Lovejoy, Arthur Oncken. *The Thirteen Pragmatisms*. Baltimore, Maryland: Johns Hopkins Press, 1963, 290. Bergson's influence on William James is discussed in "William James as Philosopher" on pp. 105-188. The essay was first published in *International Journal of Ethics*, 1911.

4552 Macquarrie, John. *Twentieth-Century Religious Thought*. New York and Evanston, 1963, 415. Vitalism and Bergson are discussed on pp. 170-173.

4553 Masur, Gerhard. *Prophets of Yesterday: Studies in European Culture 1890-1914*. London: Weidenfeld and Nicholson, 1963, 482. Cf. "The Confident Years," pp. 252-297.

4554 Mathieu, Vittorio. "Storicismo e bergsonismo." *Cultura e scuola*, No. 7, marzo-maggio 1963, 151-157.

4555 Maurois, André. *Choses nues: Chroniques*. Paris: Gallimard, 1963, 278. Bergson and many others are discussed in this book.

4556 Meland, Bernard Eugene." The Root and Form of Wieman's Thought." in *The Empirical Theology of Henry Nelson Wieman*. Ed. Robert W. Bretall. Carbondale and Edwardsville: Southern Illinois University Press; London and Amsterdam: Feffer and Simons, 1963, 44-68. On pp. 53-54 and elsewhere the author notes Bergson's influence on H. N. Wieman. On pp. 44-48 the author credits Bergson with initiating "process thinking as it bears on the problem of God", and with inspiring among British philosophers and scientists an "organismic philosophy".

4557 Moreau, Pierre. "Review of *Henri Bergson et les lettres françaises* by Roméo Arbour." *Revue de Littérature Comparée*, 37, No. 3, 1963, 480-483.

4558 Morra, Gianfranco. "Morale della pressione e morale dell'aspirazione secondo Bergson." *Ethica*, 2, No. 1, 1963, 41-53.

4559 O'Brien, James F. "Zeno's Paradoxes of Motion: Analysis of Aristotle, Russell, Bergson." *Modern Schoolman*, 40, No. 1, January 1963, 105-137.

4560 O'Dea, Thomas F. "Sociological Dilemmas: Five Paradoxes of Institutionalization." in *Sociological Theory, Values, and Sociocultural Change: Essays in Honor of Pitirim A. Sorokin*. Ed. E. A. Tiryakian. New York: Free Press of Glencoe; London: Collier-MacMillan, 1963, 71-89. The author offers five dilemmas ("structured sets of ambivalences") as fundamental to religious life and the history of religions. In all of them, he states, "...we are dealing with varied expressions of the problem of spontaneity versus stability, of creativity versus continuity. This problem—the Bergsonian problem, it may appropriately be called,—we may state with bleak economy..." (p. 88)

4561   Pasquali, Antonio. *Fundamentos gnoseológicos para una ciencia de la moral: Ensayo sobre la formación de una teoría del conocimiento moral en las filosifías de Kant, Lequier, Renouvier y Bergson.* Caracas: Universidad Central de Venezuela, 1963, 150. (Colección Temas)

4562   "Review of *The Philosophy of Poetry* by Henri Bergson." *Classical Bulletin*, 39, No. 1, January 1963, 46.

4563   Picon, Gaëtan. *Lecture de Proust.* Paris: Mercure de France, 1963, 216. The author concludes (154n) that there is no Bergsonism in the writings of Marcel Proust.

4564   Popper, Karl Raimund. *The Open Society and its Enemies.* Vol. 1. *The Spell of Plato.* 4th Ed. Princeton, New Jersey: Princeton University Press, 1963, 351. On pp. 202-203, 294, and 314-315 the author (who concedes that Bergson was the first to use the dinstinction) distinguishes his use of the terms "open society" and "closed society" from Bergson's. For Bergson an open society is one founded on mystical intuition (which the author treats as essentially reactionary) while for the author it is founded on human intelligence.

4565   Popper, Karl Raimund. *The Open Society and its Enemies.* Vol. 2. *The High Tide of Prophecy: Hegel, Marx, and the Aftermath.* Princeton, New Jersey: Princeton University Press, 1963, 420. In general the author describes Bergson as an irrationalist who, along with Hegel and the majority of German philosophers, brought the "closed society" to Europe. Cf. pp. 228-229, 258, 307, 315, 316, 361.

4566   Poulet, Georges. *L'Espace Proustien.* Paris: Gallimard, 1963, 183. The author sharply distinguishes Bergson's "durational" viewpoint from that of M. Proust, who "juxtaposes" reality in an "aesthetic space." Cf. esp. "Bergson. Le Thème de la vision panoramique des movrants et la juxtaposition," 137-177.

4567   Reck, Andrew J. "The Philosophy of A. O. Lovejoy (1873-1962)." *Review of Metaphysics*, 17, No. 4, 1963, 257-285.

4568   "Résumé of *Bergson et Teilhard de Chardin* by Madeleine Barthélémy-Maudale." *Annales de l'Université de Paris*, 33, 1963, 246-248.

4569   Riby, Jules. "Lettres à Joseph Lotte: I. Avant-propos et notes par Théo Quoniam." *Feuillets de l'Amitié Charles Péguy*, No. 98, janvier 1963, 11-33.

4570   Riby, Jules. "Lettres à Joseph Lotte: IV. Avant-propos et notes par Théo Quoniam." *Feuillets de l'Amitié Charles Péguy*, No. 102, août 1963, 2-19.

4571   Riby, Jules. "Lettres à Joseph Lotte: V. Avant-propos et notes par Théo Quoniam." *Feuillets de l'Amitié Charles Péguy*, No. 104, 25 décembre 1963, 17-36.

4572   Riefstahl, Hermann. "Neue Bergson-Literatur." *Zeitschrift für philosophische Forschung*, 17, No. 1, 1963, 173-179.

4573   Roberts, James Deotis. "Bergson as a Metaphysical, Epistemological, and Religious Thinker." *Journal of Religious Thought*, 20, No. 2, 1963-1964, 105-114.

4574   Rochot, B. "Sur Deux Livres d'Henri Bergson." *Revue de Synthèse*, 33, No. 4, octobre-décembre 1963, 502-509.

4575   Sanctis, Nicola de. "Note su Bergson e l'esistenzialismo dal non-essere al nulla." *Studi urbinati di storia*, Anno 37, N.S. (B) No. 1, 1963, 135-142.

4576   Sandoz, Ellis. "Myth and Society in the Philosophy of Bergson." *Social Research*, 30, No. 2, Summer 1963, 171-202. This study deals largely with *The Two Sources*, the part played by myth in Bergson's thought, and Bergson's immanentism and tendency towards pantheism.

4577   Shukla, J. P. "The Concept of Mind in Evolutionism." *University of Jabalpur Journal of Philosophy*, No. 2, April, 1963, 26-44. On pp. 27-31 the author describes Bergson's "vitalistic monism." On p. 31 he asserts that Bergson influenced C. Loyd Morgan's concept of emergent evolution.

4578   Simon, W. M. *European Positivism in the Nineteenth Century*. Ithaca, New York: Cornell University Press, 1963, 384. This study deals with many thinkers of whom Bergson is only one. Bergson is discussed on pp. 108-110.

4579   Spector, Robert D. "Review of *Bergson and the Stream of Consciousness Novel* by Sh. K. Kumar." *Modern Language Quarterly*, 24, No. 3, 1963, 308-310.

4580   Stepelevich, Lawrence S. *Henri Bergson's Concept of Man: An Exposition and Critique*. Washington, D.C.: Catholic University of America Press, 1963, 172. (Microfilm).

4581   Taccone Gallucci, Nicola. *Introduzione all'etica del Bergson e dello Scheler*. Lecce, Italy: Ediz. Milella, 1963, 70.

4582   Takeuchi, Yoshirō. *Jitsuzonteki Jiyū no Bōken*. Tokyo: Gendai-shichōsha, 1963, 414. The English title of this book is *The Adventure of Existential Freedom from Nietzsche to Marx*. It contains articles on F. Nietzsche, Bergson, J.-P. Sartre, and K. Marx.

4583   Torrevejano, Mercedes. "Bergson: En busca de una experiencia de Dios." *Revista de la Institución Teresiana*, agosto-septiembre 1963, 4-5.

4584   Trevisan, Armindo. "Essai sur le problème de la création chez Bergson." Diss., Fribourg, Germany, 1963, 194.

4585   Violette, René. "Empirisme de demonstration et avenement de la spirtiualité dans la philosophie de Bergson." 3 vols. Thèse 3ᵉ cycle. Lettres. Montpellier, 1963, 520pp.

4586   Weitz, Morris. *Philosophy as Literature*. Detroit, Michigan: Wayne State University Press, 1963, 116. On pp. 71-78 the author considers Proust's *Remembrance of Things Past* as a philosophical novel. He describes Proust's concept of time as Lockean, not Bergsonian, but denies that Proust's notion of "essence" is Platonic.

4587   Zac, Sylvain. "Review of *Bergson et le Christ des Evangiles* by Henri Gouhier." *Revue de Synthèse*, 84, No. 32, 1963, 502-509.

4588   Zaragüeta, Juan. "La intuición y la inteligencia en la filosofía de Henri Bergson." *Estudios filosóficos*. Madrid: Instituto "Luis Vives" de Filosofía, C.S.I.C., 1963, 375-383.

4589   Zubiri, Xavier. "Bergson." *Cinco lecciones di filosofía*. Madrid: Sociedad de Estudios y Publicaciones, 1963, 163-211.

1964

4590   Alain. *Cahiers de Lorient*. Vol. 2. Paris: Gallimard, 1964, 332.

4591   Ames, Van Meter. "Review of *Time and Reality: Studies in Contemporary Fiction* by Margaret Church." *Journal of Aesthetics and Art Criticism*, 23, No. 2, 1964, 280-281.

4592   Ames, Van Meter. "Kumar: Bergson and the Stream of Consciousness Novel." *Journal of Aesthetics and Art Criticism*, 22, No. 3, 1964, 347. This is a review.

4593   Barthélémy-Madaule, Madeleine. "Bergson et Teilhard de Chardin." *Annales de l'Université de Paris*, 34, No. 2, 1964, 246-248.

4594   Barthélémy-Madaule, Madeleine. "Bergson et Teilhard de Chardin." *La Parole attendue*. Ed. Pierre Teilhard de Chardin *et al*. Paris: Editions du Seuil, 1964, 116-131 (Cahiers de Pierre Teilhard de Chardin, No. IV).

4595   Bergeron, André. "L'Autoposition du moi par la conscience morale." *Dialogue*, 97, No. 11, 1964, 105-111. L. Brunschvicg, L. Lavelle, M. Blondel, J.-P. Sartre, Bergson, and others are discussed in this study of the development of the human self.

4596   Bergier, Jacques, and Pawels, Louis. *The Morning of the Magicians*. New York: Stein and Day, 1964, 145. The authors note on p. 145 that S. L. Mathers, Grand Master of the Golden Dawn, married Henri Bergson's daughter. Mathers was succeeded in office by William Butler Yeats.

4597   Bordeaux, Henry. *Histoire d'une vie*: Vol. 10. *Voyages d'un monde à l'autre: 1931-1936*. Paris: Plon, 1964, 354.

4598   Brettschneider, Bertram D. *The Philosophy of Samuel Alexander: Idealism in "Space, Time and Deity"*. New York: Humanities Press, 1964, 177. The author states Alexander's belief that Bergson did not take space seriously enough: "Here the contradiction develops: Alexander protests the degradation of Space and yet in his own ontological system Time is the ordering principle. That which is ordered is Space; the principle of order is Time. Moreover, Time is not only the principle of order, but also the principle of creativity in the universe. The same agent thus serves the functions of ordering and creativity." (p. 20)

4599   Campanale, Domenico. "Scienza e metafisica nel pensiero di Henri Bergson." *Rassegna di scienze filosofiche*, 7, No. 2, 1964, 137-167; Nos. 3-4, 1964, 306-333.

4600   Čapek, Milič. "Memini, ergo fui?" in *Memorias del XIII Congreso Internacional de Filosofía*, Mexico, 1964, Vol. 5, 415-426. The author examines the problem of memory and its veracity. Classical theories of memory approach this problem on the assumption that past and present are mutually external. The problem can only be solved, however, on the assumption that present and past are profoundly interrelated. This is Bergson's position.

4601   Čapek, Milič. "Simple Location and Fragmentation of Reality." *Monist*, 48, No. 2, 1964, 195-218. "Whitehead's criticism of the fallacy of simple location in space and time is nothing but another name for the rejection of the doctrine of external relations, i.e., fragmentation of reality into mutually external units. Long before Whitehead's criticism the reaction against the atomization of reality took place in psychology under the name of *Gestalt* Theory, even before that some outstanding physicists, such as Faraday and Maxwell, pointed out that the concept of isolated particle is a result of artificial abstraction since, as Mach later pointed out, 'to neglect the rest of the universe is impossible.' However, Whitehead went too far in holding that 'everything is present everywhere;' this view would lead to another version of 'the block universe' and is contrary to the present empirical evidence." *The Philosopher's Index: A Retrospective Index to U. S. Publications from 1940.* Vol. III, p. 1229.

4602 Čapek, Milič. "Simple Location and Fragmentation of Reality." in *Process and Divinity.* Eds. William L. Reese and Eugene Freeman. La Salle, Illinois: Open Court, 1964, 79-100.

4603 Catherine-Nollace, Jeanne. *Le Cinéisme.* Paris: Edit. Universitaires, 1964, 203.

4604 Chapelan, Maurice. "Le Fonds Bergson à la bibliothèque Doucet." *Le Figaro Littéraire,* 19, No. 945, 28 mai 1964, 10. This concerns the creation of a Bergson library in Paris.

4605 Chevalier, Jacques. "Henri Bergson." *Les Grands Courants de la pensée mondiale contemporaine: IIIe Partie: Portraits. I.* Paris: Fischbacher, 1964, 820. See pp. 123-152.

4606 Colletti, Giovanni. *I fondamenti logico-metafisici del Bergsonismo, e altri scritti.* Padova: Cedam, 1964, 104.

4607 Colletti, Giovanni. "Psicologia o filosofia in Bergson?" *Sophia,* 32, Nos, 3-4, 1964, 320-331.

4608 Daiches, David. "Time and Sensibility." *Modern Language Quarterly,* 25, No. 4, 1964, 486-492. This is a review of *Time and Reality: Studies in Contemporary Fiction* by Margaret Church and *The Lyrical Novel: Studies in Hermann Hesse, André Gide, and Virginia Woolf* by Ralph Freedman.

4609 D'Armagnac, Christian. "De Bergson à Teilhard: La Nature, l'homme et Dieu." *Etudes,* 320, février 1964, 167-177. This is a review of R.-M. Barthélémy-Madaule, *Bergson et Teilhard de Chardin* and H. Gouhier, *Bergson et le Christ des Evangiles.*

4610 Decaudin, Michel. *Henri Bergson.* Guilde du Livre, 1964, 402.

4611 Denat, A. "Note sur Bergson, Teilhard et Camus." *Synthèses,* No. 216, 1964, 134-137.

4612 Devaux, André-A. "Bergson et Teilhard de Chardin." *Cahiers Universitaires Catholiques,* No. 2, novembre 1964, 116-120.

4613 Fleming, Rudd. "Review of *Time and Reality: Studies in Contemporary Fiction* by Margaret Church." *Modern Language Journal,* 48, No. 5, 1964, 315.

4614 Fornasari, Archimedes. "A Critical Study of Henri Bergson's *Two Sources of Morality and Religion.*" This is an unpublished work written in 1964 at the Catholic University of America. The author defends Bergson against charges of anti-intellectualism and pantheism, but criticizes his notion of final cause.

4615 Foster, Steven. "Bergson's 'Intuition' and Whitman's 'Song of Myself'." *Texas Studies in Literature and Language,* 6, No. 3, 1964, 376-387.

4616 Garrity, Robert John. "Finality in the Philosophy of Henri Bergson." Diss., Duquesne, 1964, 255.

4617 Gorsen, Peter. "Ahnherr des modernen Denkens: Der lange missverstandene Philosoph Henri Bergson." *Die Welt der Literatur,* 1, No. 19, November 26, 1964, 641. This is a review of *Materie und Gedächtnis* by Henri Bergson. The reviewer recommends Bergson's form of *Lebensphilosophie.*

4618 Grossman, Morris. "A Glimpse of Some Unpublished Santayana Manuscripts." *Journal of Philosophy,* 61, No. 1, 1964, 61-69. Comments on Bergson constitute, the author states, "the largest single corpus in the Columbia collection" (p. 64). "Hasty hostility and capsule refutation" were gradually transformed in Santayana's unpublished writings, the author holds, into the more measured and restrained statements in *Winds of Doctrine*.

4619 Gurvitch, Georges. *The Spectrum of Social Time*. Dordrecht, Netherlands: Reidel, 1964, 152. Bergson's social philosophy is discussed on pp. 18-25 and Bergson's influence on Gurvitch, on pp. ix-x.

4620 Gurwitsch, Aron. *The Field of Consciousness*. Pittsburgh, Pennsylvania: Duquesne University Press, 1964, 427. Bergson's concept of qualitative multiplicity is discussed on pp. 140-143. For other references, see the index.

4621 Hawkins, David. *The Language of Nature*. San Francisco: W. H. Freeman and Co., 1964, 372. On pp. 222-224 the author examines Bergson's conception of time. On pp. 222-223 the author states, "The thermodynamic point of view is much more congenial to Bergsonian *metaphor* than is the conceptual framework of dynamics, particularly eighteenth-century dynamics (where many philosophers have stopped)." He notes the agreement of H. Reichenbach and Bergson concerning the unreality of the future.

4622 Hudson, David. "Three French Philosophers." *Circle Magazine*, No. 1, January 1964, 10.

4623 Ingarden, Roman. *Time and Modes of Being*. Trans. H. R. Michejda. Springfield, Illinois: Charles C. Thomas, 1964, 170.

4624 Jeune, S. "Review of *Bergson and the Stream of Consciousness Novel* by S. K. Kumar." *Revue de Littérature Comparée*, 38, 1964, 456-458.

4625 Levi, Albert William. "Bergson or Whitehead?" In *Process and Divinity*. Ed. W. L. Reese and E. Freeman. La Salle, Illinois: Open Court Publishing Co., 1964, 139-159. The author concludes that for Whitehead, the Platonist, the analysis of reality requires both actual entities and eternal objects. For Bergson, who uses biological concepts, it is sufficient that there is matter and life.

4626 Maritain, Jacques. "Bergsonian Morality and the Problem of Supra-Morality." *Moral Philosophy*. New York: Scribner's, 1964, 418-447.

4627 Maurois, André. *De Proust à Camus*. Paris: Perrin, 1964, 346. Henri Bergson is discussed on pp. 45-64.

4628 Maurois, André. *Von Proust bis Camus*. München und Zürich: Droemer, 1964, 304. This study contains a section on Bergson.

4629 Merleau-Ponty, Maurice. *Sense and Non-Sense*. 3rd Ed. Trans. H. L. and Patricia A. Dreyfus. Evanston, Illinois: Northwestern University Press, 1964, 97n. The author asserts that in his understanding of the manner in which scientific formulas are separated by "a margin of indetermination" from the data they are intended to explain, Bergson "has perfectly defined the metaphysical approach to the world." However, he reproaches Bergson for not being entirely true to his own method.

4630 Merleau-Ponty, Maurice. *Signs*. Trans. Richard C. McCleary, Evanston: The Northwestern University Press, 1964, 355. The essay "Bergson in the Making," 182-191, appeared originally in *Bulletin de la Société Française de Philosophie*."

4631 Minkowski, Eugène. "Métaphore et symbole." *Cahiers Internationaux de Symbolisme*, No. 5, 1964, 47-55. This essay deals with the function of symbolism in Bergson and G. Bachelard. The symbol is capable of expressing the human experience profoundly while metaphors, as a function of language, is not. The problem of symbolism is bound up with the problem of expression, including the *biology of expression*.

4632 Morse, Samuel French. "Wallace Stevens, Bergson, Pater." *ELH*, 31, No. 1, March 1964, 1-34.

4633 Mourélos, Georges. *Bergson et les niveaux de la réalité*. Paris: Presses Universitaires de France, 1964, 256. The author demonstrates that Bergson's philosophy consists of two levels, one ruled by a mechanical causality which limits the concepts of science, the other by an organic causality. The author introduces the notion of "causal field" to characterize the transition from one level to the other. He relates his study to contemporary psychology, sociology, biology.

4634 Noulet, Emilie. "Une Doctrine de vie." *Alphabet critique: 1924-1964*. Vol. 1. Bruxelles: Presses Universitaires de Bruxelles, 1964, 106-114. The original version, in Spanish, was published in *Cuadernos Americanos*, January-February 1944.

4635 Parsons, Edmund. *Time Devoured: A Materialistic Discussion of Duration*. London: George Allen and Unwin, 1964, 132. Bergson is discussed on pp. 94-97.

4636 Pernot, C. "Spiritualisme et spiritisme chez Bergson." *Revue de l'Enseignement Philosophique*, 14, No. 3, 1964, 1-24. This is a study of Bergson's attitude towards psychical research.

4637 Philonenko, Alexis. "Bergson: *Le Rêve*: Etude d'un texte de *L'Energie spirituelle*." *Cahiers de Philosophie*, 2, No. 7, 1964, sans pagination." "Edités par le Groupe d'études de philosophie de la Faculté des lettres de Paris."

4638 Piccioto, Robert S. "Meditaciones rurales de una mentalidad urbana: El tiempo, Bergson y Manrique en un poema de Antonio Machado." *Torre*, 12, Nos. 45-46, 1964, 141-150.

4639 Raúl Vallejos, M. A. "El mundo especulativo de Henri Bergson." *Universidad de San Carlos*, No. 62, enero-abril 1964, 113-119.

4640 Reinehr, Merle Jerome. "Self Creative Self in Henri Bergson." Diss., St. Louis, 1964.

4641 Riby, Jules. "Lettres à Joseph Lotte: VI. Avant-propos et notes par Théo Quoniam." *Feuillets de l'Amitié Charles Péguy*, No. 105, 25 février 1964, 5-31.

4642 Ricoeur, Paul. "Le Symbolisme et l'explication structurale." *Cahiers Internationaux de Symbolisme*, No. 4, 1964, 81-96. This is an explication and critique of structuralism and the structuralist concept of language, which the author holds is too static, lacking a concept of history. Cf. pp. 91-92, 94-96.

4643 Ryan, John K. "Henri Bergson: Heraclitus Redivivus." *Twentieth-Century Thinkers*. Ed. John K. Ryan. New York: Alba House, 1964, 13-36.

4644 Sanctis, Nicola de. "Bergson l'estistenzialismo e il problema della libertà come 'souci de soi'." *Studi urbinati di storia*, Anno 38, N.S. (B) No. 1-2, 1964, 164-197.

4645 Sartre, Jean-Paul. *The Words*. Greenwich, Connecticut: Fawcett Publications, Inc., 1964, 18. The author remarks in passing: "My grandfather has crossed Lake Geneva with Henri Bergson. 'I was wild with enthusiasm,' he would say. 'I hadn't eyes enough to contemplate the sparkling crests, to follow the shimmering of the water. But Bergson sat on his valise and never once looked up.' He would conclude from this incident that poetic meditation was preferable to philosophy."

4646   Sciacca, Michele Federico. *Philosophical Trends in the Contemporary World.* Trans. A. Salerno. South Bend, Indiana: Notre Dame Press, 1964, 656. A section entitled "Contingentism of E. Boutroux and Intuitionism of H. Bergson" may be found on pp. 29-36.

4647   Smith, Colin. *Contemporary French Philosophy.* New York: Barnes and Noble, 1964, 266. The content and influence of *Les Deux Sources* are discussed on pp. 143-161.

4648   Staudenmaier, John Michael. "Bergson's Latin Thesis: A Textual Study." Diss., St. Louis, 1964.

4649   Van Holk, L. J. "Van William James naar Henri Bergson." *Wijsgerig Perspectief of Maatschappij en Wetenschap*, 5, No. 2, 1964-1965, 101-110.

4650   Vial, Fernand. "Review of *The Bergsonian Heritage*. Ed. Thomas Hanna." *French Review*, 37, No. 5, April 1964, 594-596.

4651   Vita, Luís Washington. *Momentos decisivos do pensamento filosófico.* São Paulo: Melhormentos, 1964, 518. Bergson is discussed on pp. 355-366.

4652   Vogely, Maxine Arnold. "Some Applications of Bergsonian Philosophy to the Concept of 'Self' in *Á la recherche du temps perdu*." M. A. Thesis, University of Southern Illinois at Carbondale, 1964, 80.

4653   Wright, Sewall. "Biology and the Philosophy of Science." in *Process and Divinity.* Eds. William L. Reese and Eugene Freeman. La Salle, Illinois: Open Court, 1964, 101-125. On p. 112 the author cites Bergson as a philosopher who has given "appealing philosophical support" for a vitalistic philosophy of biology. On p. 116 he notes that his reading of Bergson's *Creative Evolution* as a young man has lead to a shaking of his previous mechanistic philosophy of biology— though he was unable to accept Bergson's philosophy of science "as a whole." The author is one of the founders of population theory, and (hence) of "Darwinism, the modern synthesis."

4654   Zaslawsky, Denis. "Bergson, le finalisme et la philosophie analytique." *Revue de Théologie et de Philosophie*, 3e Série, 14, No. 6, 1964, 335-347.

1965

4655   Arbelet, Claire. *Magnificat du soir: Journal.* Paris: Beauchesne, 1965, 138.

4656   Banfi, Antonio. *Studia sulla filosofia del novecento.* Roma: Editori Riuniti, 1965, 570. This study includes an essay on Bergson's "pragmatic idealism."

4657   Baylis, Charles A. "Tranquility is not Enough." *Philosophy Forum (Pacific)*, 3, No. 4, 1965, 84-95. The author criticizes Professor Paul Wienpahl's "neo-Bergsonian" epistemology, holding on p. 85 that: "There is no intelligible truth about a particular which we are unable to state." (p. 85)

4658   Bentley, Eric. *The Life of Drama.* London: Methuen, 1965, 371.

4659   Berl, Emmanuel. *Mort de la morale bourgeoise, 1929.* Paris: Pauvert, 1965, 175.

4660   Boros, Ladislas. *The Moment of Truth: Mysterium Mortis.* London: Bruns and Oates, 1965, 201. The author treats of death in Bergson, M. Blondel, G. Marcel, and others.

4661 Bréhier, Emile. "Notice sur la vie et les travaux d'Henri Bergson." *Etudes de philosophie moderne*. Paris: Presses Universitaires de France, 1965, 129-144. The author examines Bergson's practical philosophy in the context of a very perceptive account of his life. He explores Bergson's concepts of war, industrialism, idealism, internationalism.

4662 Browning, Douglas. *Philosophers of Process*. Intro. Charles Hartshorne. New York: Random House, 1965, 346. A selection from Bergson is presented on pp. 2-56.

4663 Burgers, Antoon. "De houding van Bergson en Merleau-Ponty t.o.v. de wetenschappen." *Tijdschrift voor Filosofie*, 27, No. 2, June 1965, 262-297.

4664 Carles, Jules. *Le Transformisme*. 4th ed. Paris: Presses Universitaires de France, 1965, 126. (Que sais-je? No. 502.) The author views Bergson's philosophy as a modern version of the philosophy of ancient stoicism. He credits Bergson with teaching a Nietzschean doctrine of eternal recurrence. See also pp. 87-90.

4665 Chaix-Ruy, Jules. *Le Surhomme: De Nietzsche à Teilhard de Chardin*. Paris: Editions du Centurion, 1965, 349.

4666 Colombo, Yoseph. "Un concetto bergsoniano in antichi testi ebraici." *Studi di letteratura, storia e filosofia in onore di Bruno Revel*. Firenze: Leo S. Olschki editore, 1965, 201-205.

4667 Dan, C. "Determinism and Creation in Bergson's Philosophy." *Revista de Filozofie*, 12, No. 12, 1965, 1587-1603. This article is in Rumanian.

4668 Dayan, Maurice. "L'Inconscient chez Bergson." *Revue de Métaphysique et de Morale*, 70, No. 3, 1965, 287-324. This is a careful and valuable study.

4669 Dédéyan, Charles. "Bergson et Du Bos." *Table Ronde*, No. 208, mai 1965, 79-90. This is a chapter from the author's book on C. Du Bos. It traces certain influences on Du Bos by Bergson.

4670 Dewey, John. "Spencer and Bergson." Ed. with a French translation by Gérard Deledalle. *Revue de Métaphysique et de Morale*, 70, No. 3, 1965, 325-333. In this article Dewey analyzes the close relations between H. Spencer's and Bergson's thought.

4671 D'Hautefeuille, François. "Schopenhauer, Nietzsche et Bergson." *Archives de Philosophie*, 28 No. 4, octobre-décembre 1965, 553-556.

4672 Dingle, Herbert. "Introduction." *Duration and Simultaneity*. Indianapolis, Indiana: Bobbs-Merrill, 1965, xv-lxii. The author defends Bergson's criticism of relativity theory while rejecting Bergson's "psychological" starting-point.

4673 Duployé, Pie. *La Religion de Péguy*. Paris: Editions Klincksiek, 1965, xliv, 693. Cf. p. 374 for anti-semitic attacks on Bergson by the right wing Action française.

4674 Eckstein, Jerome. "Bergson's Views on Science and Metaphysics: Reconsidered." *Philosophical Quarterly* (Indiana), 38, No. 3, 1965, 163-179. Bergson's attitude towards science has been misunderstood. The author compares Bergson and Dewey and stresses their similar approaches towards science.

4675 Emery, Léon. *De Montaigne à Teilhard de Chardin via Pascal et Rousseau*. Lyon: Cahiers Libres, 1965, 144.

4676 Ferrater Mora, José. "Bergson, Henri (1859-1941)." *Diccionario de Filosofía*. 5th Ed. (Vol. 1) Buenos Aires: Editorial Sudamericana, 1965, 193-202.

4677   Ferrater Mora, José. "Bergsonismo." *Diccionario de Filosofía*. 5th ed. Vol. 1. Buenos Aires: Editorial Sudamericana, 1965, 202-203.

4678   Fieschi, Pascal. "Le Temps perdu est retrouvé." In *Proust, Génies et réalités*. Paris: Hachette, 1965, 243-273. The author concludes that Marcel Proust was an "unorthodox Bergsonian:" "Si la vision de Proust a des traits encontestablement bergsoniens, il s'en faut de beaucoup que Proust soit un bergsonien orthodoxe" (p. 244).

4679   Fowlie, Wallace. *André Gide: His Life and Art*. New York: Macmillan, 1965, 217. On pp. 7-8 the author notes Bergson's influence on André Gide.

4680   Garcia Caffarena, Judit G. "Bipolaridad: Leit Motiv bergsoniano." *Universidad de Santa Fe*, 64, No. 1, 1965, 127-138.

4681   Grappe, André. "Pardines et Bergson." *Revue Philosophique de la France et de l'Etranger*, 155, No. 1, 1965, 103-110; 156, No. 4, 1966, 478-496; 158, No. 3, 1967, 371-384.

4682   Hale, Nathan George, Jr. "The Origins and Foundations of the Psychoanalytic Movement in America, 1909-1914." Diss. California at Berkeley 1965, 495. The author details the "Bergson vogue" in the United States on pp. 355-359. Bergson appealed to a remarkably wide group, "liberal congregationalists, socialists and syndicalists, Theodore Roosevelt, society belles, feminists and rebellious young intellectuals" (p. 355). On p. 380, "Bergsonian vitalism" is described as one of the four determining factors in the early psychoanalytic movement in the United States. The other three were the medical orientation of the movement, a strong moral emphasis, and an optimistic view of human nature. Bergson's influence on James Jackson Putnam is noted on pp. 408-409 and 435-439. Bergson's influence on William Allanson White is noted on pp. 408 and 450-451. Bergson's influence on Smith Ely Jeliffe is noted on p. 408.

4683   Hamilton, George Rostrevor. "Divine Philosophy 1921." in *Rapids of Time: Sketches From the Past*. London: Heinemann, 1965, 106-111. Bergson. In 1921 (under the pen-name George Rostrevor) the author published a book, *Bergson and Future Philosophy*, in which he defended Bergson's concept of duration but attacked Bergson's distinction between intuition and analysis, arguing that both intuition and analysis are intellectual activities. Bergson, who had been given a copy of the author's study, responded with "an eight page manuscript letter" much of which the author reproduces. (Cf. H. Bergson, 1921.) In this letter Bergson agrees that there is no *serious* harm in asserting that intuition is intellectual; but if one does, one will be likely to confuse two different ways of thinking. Bergson concludes: "Employer le même terme dans les deux cas est s'exposer à des confusions." (p. 109) One will also tend, if one fails to make this distinction, to fail to understand the all-important distinction between instinct and intelligence. The author also notes Bergson's frustration at the views of physicists, few of whom, he believes, understand the relations between his philosophy and physics. The author also notes a visit at Bergson's home by the Dutch physicist H. A. Lorentz. This is a precise, charming, informative account of Bergson's relations to a younger philosopher.

4684   Howarth, Herbert. *Notes on Some Figures Behind T. S. Eliot*. London: Chatto and Windus, 1965, 396.

4685   Jacobson, Leon. "Translator's Preface." *Duration and Simultaneity*. Indianapolis, Indiana: Bobbs-Merril, 1965, 190, v-xi.

4686   Jerphagnon, Lucien. *De La Banalité: Essai sur l'Ipséité et sa durée vécue: Durée personnelle et co-durée*. Paris: Vrin, 1965, 426.

4687   Lanson, Gustave. "Sur Le Rire de Bergson." *Essais de méthode, de critique et d'histoire littéraire*. Paris: Hachette, 1965, 497, 459-462.

4688   Lichtigfeld, A. "The Survival of the Soul: 1. A Reflection about the Survival of the Soul in the Thought of Macmurray, Bergson, Jaspers. 2. The Survival-Hypothesis in Modern Thought." *Filosofia*, 16, Suppl. al No. 4, november 1965, 753-762.

4689   Liiceanu, G. "On Intellectualist Interpretations of Bergson's Intuitionism." *Revista de Filozofie*, 13, No. 6, 1965, 795-801. The author holds that the richness of the real leads Bergson to transcend the conditions of elementary logic; but he is wrong to search for the solution in a zone opposed to reason. This article is in Rumanian.

4690   Malinow, Carlos A. "Finalidad y determinismo en los sistemas evolutivos de Pierre Teilhard y Henri Bergson." *Diàlogos*, 2, No. 4, 1965, 111-131.

4691   McMahon, C. Patrick. "The Concept of Matter in the Metaphysics of Bergson." Diss. Saint Louis 1965, 255. The author poses the following question: If matter, for Bergson, is the antithesis of duration, how can it function in his mature metaphysics of duration? The author describes Bergson's reformulation of his concept of matter in *Matter and Memory* and *Creative Evolution*. When matter is no longer the antithesis of duration, but rather its lowest degree, the problems of its inclusion in a metaphysics of duration and of its interaction with spirit can be resolved. (See *Dissertation Abstracts International*, 26, Nos. 7-8, 1965, 4731-4732.)

4692   Mendilow, Adam Abraham. *Time and the Novel*. New York: Humanitas Press, 1965, 245. Bergson, M. Proust, A. Gide, and others are discussed in this study.

4693   Meissner, W. W. "The Function of Memory and Psychic Structure." *Journal of Existentialism*, 6, No. 21, Fall, 1965, 41-52. The author explains Bergson's theory of mind-body interaction and relates it to Freud's theory of memory. Bergson's theory of the unconscious may prove closer to the concept of psychic structure towards which psychoanalysis is now moving.

4694   Metz, André. "Bergson et la notion d'espace." *Archives de Philosophie*, 28, No. 3, 1965, 439-444. This is a review of F. Heidsieck's *Henri Bergson et la notion d'espace* stressing the importance of relativity theory.

4695   Minkowski, Eugène. "Les Idées de bergson en psychopathologie." *Recueil d'articles 1923-1965*. Paris: Librairie Le Livre Psychologique; Lille, France: Librairie Le Foret du Nord, 1965, 43-46.

4696   Mole, Jack. *The Time of Our Lives*. London: Epworth Press, 1965, 164. A chapter titled "Duration" appears in this book on pp. 33-38.

4697   Murillo, Roberto E. "Bergson y el problema de la educación." *Revista de Filosofía de la Universidad de Costa Rica*. 4, Nos. 15-16, 1965, 351-359.

4698   Murillo Zamora, Robert. *Communicación y lenguaje en la filosofía de Bergson*. San José, Costa Rica: Ciudad universitaria Rodrigo Facio, 1965, 129.

4699   Painter, George Duncan. *Marcel Proust: A Biography*. Vol. 2. Boston: Little, Brown; London: Chatto and Windus, 1965, 424. On p. 8 the author notes

Bergson's review, before the Académie des Sciences Morales et Politiques, of Proust's translation of *La Bible d'Amiens*; on pp. 52-53 the author describes Proust's response to a psychiatrist who, Proust felt, did not understand Bergson; on p. 325 he cites Bergson's introduction of Proust to his Swedish translator, Algot Ruhe.

4700   Ravera, Rosa María. "Las ideas estéticas de Bergson." *Universidad*, 31, No. 1, enero-marzo 1965, 127-150. (Philosophes de tous les temps, 21)

4701   Ribiero, Alvaro. *Escritores doutrinados*. Lisboa: Sociedade de expansão cultural, 1965, 245. An essay on Bergson's philosophy of language is included in this book.

4702   Riby, Jules. "Lettres à Joseph Lotte: X. Avant-propos et notes par Théo Quoniam." *Feuillets de l'Amitié Charles Péguy*, No. 112, février 1965, 11-35.

4703   Riby, Jules. "Lettres à Joseph Lotte: XI. Notes par Théo Quoniam." *Feuillets de l'Amitié Charles Péguy*, No. 113, avril 1965, 4-22.

4704   Robinet, André. *Bergson et les métamorphoses de la durée*. Paris: Seghers, 1965, 192. (Philosophes de tous les temps) The author explores the manner in which both the concept of intuition and the concept of duration are transformed as Bergson's thought develops. Both concepts were enriched and broadened in the course of Bergson's investigations.

4705   Robinson, J. "Valéry critique de Bergson." *Cahiers de l'Association International des Études Françaises*, 17, 1965, 203-215. For a discussion of the author's views, see pp. 293-296.

4706   Ryan, John Kenneth, ed. *Twentieth-Century Thinkers: Studies in the Work of Seventeen Modern Philosophers*. Staten Island, New York: Alba House, 1965, 405. Cf. "Henri Bergson: Heraclitus Redivivus" appears on pp. 13-25.

4707   Santos, Jessy. "A influencia de Bergson no Brasil." *Revista Brasileira de Filosofia*, 15, No. 58, 1965, 237-244.

4708   Sartre, Jean Paul. "A Candid Conversation." *Playboy*, 12, No. 5, May, 1965, 69-76. On p. 70 the author states of himself at age 16: "My ambition was to become a professor of literature. The I came across a book by Henri Bergson in which he describes in a concrete way how time is experienced in one's mind. I recognized the truth of this in myself. A little later I discovered 'phenomenology'. That is, I learned that one could talk in a concrete way about any subject whatever..."

4709   Turner, Merle B. *Philosophy and the Science of Behavior*. New York: Appleton-Century-Crofts, 1965, 539. Bergson and psychology are discussed on pp. 286, 292, 297-298. "Now it is important to note that Bergson does not dismiss science and retreat into irrationalism. Rather one brings intuition to focus on the same experience that we symbolize and conceptualize within the language of science" (p. 297). The author notes the similarities between Bergson's philosophy and more recent writings by Michael Scriven and William Kneale.

4710   Urmeneta, Fermín de. "Louis Vives: Peldaño ideológico entre San Agustin y Enrique Bergson." *Revista de Filosofía*, 24, No. 94-95, 1965, 373-383.

4711   Wahl, Jean. *Bergson*. Paris: Centre de documentation universitaire, 1965, 161. These are the lecture notes from a course on Bergson at the Sorbonne.

1966

4712 Albert, F. "Lettre du ministre de l'Instruction publique et des Beaux-Arts au Président de la Commission Internationale de Coopération Intellectuelle. 24 juillet 1924." *Journal of World History*, 10, No. 1, 1966, pp. 239-241. In this letter to Henri Bergson, President of the Commission for International Intellectual Cooperation, M. Albert presents the offer of the French government to establish an Institute for International Intellectual Cooperation in Paris: "L'Appel que vous avez dernieèrement lancé, au nom de la Commission de coopération intellectuelle, et ou vous demandez le secours de toutes les nations pour l'oeuvre enterprise par la Commission a éte, je l'espère, entendu." p. 239.

4713 Angeli, A. M. de. "L'influsso della filosofia di Bergson sull'estetica Proustiana." Diss., Universita cattolica del Sacre Cuore de Milan, 1966.

4714 Antonelli, Maria Teresa. "La filosofia in Henri Bergson." *Rivista rosminiana*, 60, No. 1, 1966, 37-67.

4715 Arapura, John G. *Radhakrishnan and Integral Experience*. New York: Asia Pub. House, 1966, 211.

4716 Arruda, Aniz de. "Review of *Matière et mémoire* and *Duration and Simultaneity* by Henri Bergson." *Revista Portuguesa de Filosofia*, 22, 1966, 212-213. This is a review of the English translation of *Duration and Simultaneity* and the 72nd printing of *Matière et mémoire*.

4717 Barlow, Michel. *Henri Bergson*. Paris: Editions Universitaires, 1966, 128 (Classiques du XXe Siècle, 83). This is an account of Bergson's thought for the general reader.

4718 Barthélémy-Madaule, Madeleine. *Bergson: Adversaire de Kant: Etude critique de la conception bergsonienne du kantisme, suivie d'une bibliographie kantienne.* Pref. Vladimir Jankélévitch. Paris: Presses Universitaires de France, 1966, 276.

4719 Benge, Frances. "Bergson y Prado." *Cuadernos Americanos*, 147, No. 4, 1966, 116-123.

4720 Benjamin, A. Cornelius. "Ideas of Time in the History of Philosophy." In *The Voices of Time*, ed. Julius Thomas Fraser. New York: George Braziller, 1966, 710. Bergson's concepts of time, duration, and freedom are discussed by the author on pp. 23-25. He states that, for Bergson, outside the Self there is no duration. Bergson and Samuel Alexander are compared on pp. 26-27.

4721 Beth, Evert W. and Piaget, Jean. *Mathematical Epistemology and Pyschology*. Trans. W. Mays. Dordrecht-Holland: D. Reidl; New York: Gordon and Breach, 1966, 326. With regard to G. Mannoury's psycho-linquistics ("significs") as a procedure for disentangling formal logic from psychology, Beth asserts: "His remarks on the dual character of negation have to a certain extent been anticipated by Bergson and Wundt, who, however, have not gone into the question as deeply." (p. 35) In a section titled "Temporal Intuition: Kant, Bergson, Brouwer and De Groot", Beth singles out Bergson as one of the rare philosophers "who have thought deeply about the problem of temporal intuition." (p. 106) On p. 131n Piaget states "...when I was at the lycee, I believed, under Bergson's influence, in the irreducible nature of biological processes in relation to logico-mathematical structures, but later reflections on the concept of 'species' and on biological classification in general, and especially the application of biometrical methods to the variability of land molluscs, convinced me of the close relationship between organic and logical or mathematical structures." Piaget, "deconverted" from philosophical speculation, decided henceforth to have confidence only in experimentation and calculation. He then devoted himself to the study of embryos. In a section titled "Intuition of Time" (pp. 209-213) Piaget criticizes Bergson's concept of duration.

4722   Biddle, Bruce J. and Thomas, Edwin J., Eds. *Role Theory: Concepts and Research*. New York: Wiley, 1966. On pp. 4-5 the authors cite Bergson as an early precursor of "role theory."

4723   Bonnet, Henri. "La Société des Nations et la Coopération intellectuelle." *Journal of World History*, 10, No. 1, 1966, 198-209. This is a brief account of the genesis of the Commission for Intellectual Cooperation and of its later offshoot, the Institute for International Intellectual Cooperation, headquartered in Paris. (The author was one of the most important leaders of the latter.) The author stresses the opposition of the British to the Commission and the Institute and the general disinterest of the League: "Riche d'idées, elle ne disposait d'aucun moyen de les réaliser. Il etait pathétique de voir Henri Bergson, frêle, modeste et persuasif, venir lu-même plaider en vain devant l'Assemblée sourd à ses accents la cause de cette parente pauvre, la Société des Esprit." p. 201.

4724   Canguilhem, Georges. "Le Concept et la vie." *Revue Philosophique de Louvain*, 64, T.S. No. 82, mai 1966, 193-223.

4725   Cattaui, Georges. "Ce Bergson qui fut des nôtres." *Journal de Genève*, 26-27, février 1966.

4726   Cavadi, Rosa. "L'apprendimento genuino del tempo nella metafisica de H. Bergson." *Teoresi*, 21, No. 1, 1966, 45-96.

4727   Cavagna, Giordano Bruno. *La dottrina conoscenza in Enrico Bergson*. Napoli: Instituto Edit. del Mezzogiorno, 1966, 317.

4728   Chevalier, Jacques. *Histoire de la pensée*: Vol. 4. *La Pensée moderne de Hegel à Bergson*. Paris: Flammarion, 1966, 756. "Texte posthume revu et mis au point par Léon Husson."

4729   Dédéyan, Charles. *Le Cosmopolitisme littéraire de Charles Du Bos: La Maturité de Charles Du Bos (1914-1927)*. Vol. 2. Paris: Société d'Edit. d'Enseignement Supérieur, 1966, 732.

4730   De Donadio, Delia M. "Acerca de las nociones de posibilidad y de nada en Bergson." *Diálogos*, 3, No. 5, 1966, 83-99.

4731   Deleuze, Gilles. *Le Bergsonisme*. Paris: Presses Universitaires de France, 1966, 120. (Initiation Philosophique, 76) The author carefully examines Bergson's concept of philosophical method, arguing that it is extremely elaborate. He analyzes the rules of this method, whose goal is to rediscover real differences of kind. Particular attention is payed here to the concept of "multiplicity."

4732   Doggett, Frank. *Steven's Poetry of Thought*. Baltimore: The Johns Hopkins Press, 1966, 223. The author uses Bergson's philosophy to explain many passages in the poetry of Wallace Stevens.

4733   *Etudes Bergsoniennes*. Paris: Presses Universitaires de France, 1966, Vol. 7, 231. Summaries of "The Nature of the Soul" and "The Nature of Personality," lectures by Bergson delivered in Britain in 1911 and 1914, are published in this issue, along with articles on Bergson's philosophy of religion and his relations with

Albert Thibaudet.

4734   Fabre-Luce de Gruson, Françoise. "Bergson et Proust." In *Entretiens sur Marcel Proust*, ed. Georges Cattaui and Philip Kolb. Paris: Mouton et Co., 1966, 234-246. The author finds many similarities between Bergson and M. Proust.

4735   Fabris, Matteo. *La filosofia sociale di Henri Bergson*. Bari, Italy: Resta, 1966, 262.

4736   Fressin, Augustin. "La Perception chez Bergson et chez Merleau-Ponty." Diss. Paris 1966. This is a "thèse, 3ᵉ cycle."

4737   Gandillac, Maurice de. "‹‹Scission›› et ‹‹co-naissance›› d'après l'‹‹art peétique›› de Claudel." *Revue de Métaphysique et de Morale*, 71, No. 4, 1966, 412-425. Cf. esp. 413.

4738   Gauss, Charles Edward. *The Aesthetic Theories of French Artists From Realism to Surrealism* Baltimore: Johns Hopkins Press, 1966, 111.

4739   Genette, Gérard. *Figures: Essais*. Paris: Edit. du Seuil, 1966, 269.

4740   Gilson, Etienne H. "Maine de Biran's French Posterity." in *Recent Philosophy, Hegel to the Present*, Ed. E. H. Gilson, Thos. Langan and A. A. Maurer. New York: Random House, 1966, 290-317.

4741   Gilson, Etienne. "Review of *Bergson et le Christ des Evangiles* by Henri Gouhier." *Etudes Bergsoniennes*, 7, 1966, 221-227. This essay was first published in *Les Nouvelles Littéraires*, 25 January 1962, under the title "L'Itinéraire d'Henri Bergson." It is an extremely favorable review, which cites Chapter V, "Une Christologie philosophique," as a masterpiece.

4742   Gorsen, Peter. *Zur Phänomenologie des Bewusstseinsstroms: Bergson, Dilthey, Husserl, Simmel und die lebensphilosophischen Antinomien*. Bonn: Bouvier, 1966, 243.

4743   Gramont, Elisabeth de. *Souvenirs du monde 1890 à 1940*. Paris: Grasset, 1966, 452.

4744   Guiney, Mortimer. *La Poésie de Pierre Reverdy*. Geneva: Georg, 1966, 261. The author places certain of Reverdy's poems in a broad cultural and philosophical context, and suggests rapprochments between Reverdy's ideas and those of A. Camus, Bergson, C. G. Jung and others.

4745   Guitton, Jean. *Justification du temps*. 3ᵉ ed. Paris: Presses Universitaires de France, 1966, 123. (Initiation Philosophique, No. 49)

4746   Guitton, Jean. *Tre saggi: Il problema di Gesu Cristo. Ateismo ed ecumenismo. Bergson e Teilhard de Chardin*. Trans. C. Di Zoppola. Brescia: Morcelliana, 1966, 91. (Universale moderna Morcelliana, 26)

4747   Guitton, Jean. *La Vocation de Bergson*. In Jean Guitton, *Portraits*, Vol. I of *Oeuvres complètes*. Paris: Desclée de Brouwer, 1966, 565-677.

4748   Gunter, Pete Addison Yancey. "Bergson's Reflective Anti-intellectualism." *Personalist*, 47, No. 1, 1966, 43-60. The author defends Bergson against the dual charges of anti-intellectualism and an anti-scientific attitude. Bergson's intuition is reflection and is intended to be scientifically fruitful.

4749   Gunter, Pete Addison Yancey. "Whitehead, Bergson, Freud: Suggestions Toward a Theory of Laughter." *Southern Journal of Philosophy*, 4, No. 2, 1966, 55-60. This article contains criticisms of Bergson's concept of laughter.

4750   Jackson, Elizabeth R. *L'Évolution de la mémoire involuntaire dans l'oeuvre de Marcel Proust*. Paris: Nizet, 1966, 280. The author makes may comparisons of Bergson and Proust on pp. 238-251, stressing the profoundly different attitudes of each towards time.

4751 Jacob, André. "Review of *Bergson adversaire de Kant* by Madeleine Barthélémy-Madaule." *Études Philosophiques*, 21, No. 3, 1966, 403.

4752 Jacob, Jean and Weiler, Maurice. *Ecrivains français du vingtième siècle: Textes choisis*. Paris: Belin, 1966, 375.

4753 Janicaud, Dominique. "Ravaisson et Bergson." Diss. Paris 1966, iii, 372. This is a "thèse, 3ᵉ cycle."

4754 Jha, A. "Notes on the Nature of Comic Laughter." *Calcutta Review*, 180, No. 1, July 1966, 62-69. S. Beckett, Bergson, and E. Ionesco are discussed in this essay.

4755 Joll, James. "Le Président Soleil." *New York Review of Books*, 7, No. 8, November 17, 1966, 18. Bergson's influence on Charles DeGaulle is mentioned in this article.

4756 Klawitter, Robert. "Henri Bergson and James Joyce's Fictional World." *Comparative Literature Studies*, 3, No. 4, 1966, 429-437.

4757 Klimov, Alexis. "Une Initiation à la philosophie de Bergson." *Revue de l'Université Laval*, 21, No. 1, 1966, 71-74.

4758 Kremer-Marietti, Angèle. "L'Explication bergsonienne." *Etudes Bergsoniennes*, 7, 1966, 184-192. The author asserts that: "L'Explication métaphysique, dans l'esprit du bergsonisme, au contraire, au lieu d'identifier rationalité et réalité, *impliquerait* l'objet et tendrait en le recouvrant tout entier à ne laisser aucun vide entre la pensée et la réalité." (182).

4759 Kümmel, Friedrich. "Time as Succession and the Problem of Duration." In *The Voices of Time*, ed. Julius Thomas Fraser. New York: George Braziller, 1966, 710. The author states that Bergson's attempt to understand duration in its vitality marked an advance in the philosophy of time. But, on pp. 46-49, he criticizes Bergson's concept of duration for its inability to deal with the reality of, and the relations between, the "three times:" past, present, and future.

4760 Kurris, Frans. "Le Bergsonisme d'Albert Thibaudet." *Etudes Bergsoniennes*, 7, 1966, 139-178. The author studies the influence of Bergson on the most important French literary critic "d'entre les deux guerres." Thibaudet, however, was not in all respects Bergsonian.

4761 Lafrance, Guy. "Inspiration biologique et pensée sociale chez Bergson." Diss. Caen, 1966, 299.

4762 Larock, V. "Les Deux Morales selon Bergson." *Synthèses*, 20, Nos. 236-237, 1966, 13-22.

4763 Lattre, Alain de. "Remarques sur l'intuition comme principe régulateur de la connaissance chez Bergson." *Etudes Bergsoniennes*, 7, 1966, 195-215. "De l'intuition comme retour à une intimité inédite et secrète, il n'est pas une fois question; l'intuition, constante dans *Matière et Mémoire*, n'intervient qu'à titre de principe directeur, de règle et de référence permanente par rapport à quoi peut être discerné le *sens* des analyses qui sont effectuées par ailleurs et dont les résultats sont consignés." (210). An excellent treatment of *Matter and Memory* is given on pp. 211-214.

4764 La Via, Luigi. "Possibilità di sviluppi tra dualismo e concreto nella considerazione bergsoniana del tempo e della conscienza." *Teoresi*, 21, 1966, 194-237.

4765 Lecointe, Michel. "La Matière biblique dans la *Note sur M. Bergson et la philosophie bergsonienne* et la *Note conjointe sur M. Descartes et la philosophie cartesienne.*" Diss. Aix-en-Provence 1966, 167. This is a "mémoire pour l'obtention du Diplôme d'Études supérieures."

4766 Lecuyer, Maurice. "Ionesco, ou la précédence du verbe." *Cahiers de la Compagnie Madeleine Renaud-Jean Louis Barrault*, 53, 1966, 3-34.

4767 Loreis, Hector-Jan. "De wortels van de nieuwe roman." *Nieuw Vlaams Tijdschrift*, 19, 1966, 397-408. The author finds Bergson (along with Vian and Queneau) to be one of the roots of the "new novel."

4768 Macedo, Sílvio de. *Intuição e linguagem em Bergson e Heidegger*. Maceió, Brazil, 1966, 112.

4769 Maurois, André. "Il y a ving-cinq mourait Bergson." *Historia*, No. 230, 1966, 108-112. This is a general account of Bergson's influence on his generation and of his central philosophical conceptions. It includes an account of Bergson's death. (See *Index Analytique*, 1, 1966, A-0038.)

4770 McMahon, C. Patrick. "The Concept of Matter in the Metaphysics of Bergson." Diss., St. Louis. *Dissertation Abstracts*, 26, No. 8, February 1966, 4731.

4771 Meissner, W. W. "The Temporal Dimension in the Understanding of Human Experiance." *Journal of Existentialism*, 7, No. 26, 1966-1967, 129-161. The author relates Bergson's theory of duration, as developed in *Time and Free Will*, to the ideas of I. Pavlov, C. Hull, K. Lewin, E. Minkowski.

4772 Moon, H. Kay. "Alejandro Casona and Henri Bergson." *Symposium Unamuno*, 55, 1966, 345-359.

4773 Muller, Peter J. "Review of *Duration and Simultaneity* by Henri Bergson." *Review of Metaphysics*, 9, No. 4, 1965-1966, 804-805.

4774 Munk, Arthur W. "Was Bergson an Irrationalist?" *Calcutta Review*, 180, No. 2, 1966, 89-93.

4775 Murillo Zamora, Roberto. "La Notion de causalité dans la philosophie de Bergson." Diss., Strasbourg, 1967, 196.

4776 Passmore, John. *A Hundred Years of Philosophy*. Baltimore, Maryland: Penguin Books, 1966, 640. Bergson and James are discussed on pp. 104-107; Bergson and Sorel on p. 119; Bergson, James and instrumentalism on p. 174; Bergson's influence on Ralph Barton Perry on p. 262; Bergson and Lloyd Morgan on p. 270; Bergson and Samuel Alexander on p. 271.

4777 Pignato, Luca. "Durata e storia nel pensiero de Bergson." *Dialogo*, 3, No. 1, 1966, 109-117.

4778 Quoniam, Théodore. "Review of *Le Bergsonisme* by Gilles Deleuze." *Études Philosophiques*, 21, No. 4, 1966, 545-546.

4779 Quito, Emérito S. "The Philosophy of Henri Bergson." *Unitas*, 39, No. 1, 1966, 3-29.

4780 Raimond, Michel. *La Crise du Roman: Des lendemains du Naturalisme aux années vingt*. Paris: J. Corti, 1966, 541. The author makes many comparisons of Bergson's philosophy and Proust's novels.

4781 Riverso, Emanuele. "Alfred North Whitehead Oggi." *Giornale Critico Della Filosofia Italiana*, 20, No. 2, 1966, 274-277.

4782 Robinet, André. "Le Fonds Bergson de la Bibliothèque Doucet." *Etudes Bergsoniennes*, 7, 1966, 219-220. The author explains that a collection of certain of Bergson's letters, notes, manuscripts, and his personal library has been deposited in the Bibliothèque Doucet in Paris.

4783 Robinet, André and Martine. "Henri Bergson et l'Angleterre." *Etudes Bergsoniennes*, 7, 1966, 5-136. This article contains a partial summary of "The Nature of the Soul" (a series of lectures presented by Bergson at the University College, London, October, 1911) with press clippings, as well as a complete summary of "The Problem of Personality" (The Gifford Lectures, given by Bergson at Edinburgh, April-May, 1914, but never completed) with press clippings. An interview with Bergson appears on pp. 131-136.

4784 Rumayor Aguirre, Alicia. *La conciencia: Psicofenómeno e intencionalidad: Revision del tema a traves de Henri Bergson*. Monterrey, México, 1966, 87. Tesis (Maestra en psicología) Universidad Labastida.

4785 Sach, Nathan. *Zeman v'rythmus eitsel Bergson unvashirah hamodernit (Time and Rhythm in Bergson and Modern Poetry)*. Tel Aviv: Alef, 1966. In Hebrew.

4786 Sanmartin Grau, Juan. "Bergson: La liberación del espíritu." *Annales de la Universidad de Cuenca*, 22, Nos. 3-4, 1966, 589-595.

4787 Sauvegeot, Aurelian. "Rappel et souvenir." *Vie et Langage*, No. 166, 1966, 39-40. This is a response to an article by Felicien Mars which appeared in the August 1965, number of *Vie et Langage*. The author reexamines Bergson's distinction between "se souvenir" and "se rappeler." (See *Index Analytique*, 1, 1966, A-0038.)

4788 Scott, Nathan A. *The Broken Center: Studies in the Theological Horizon of Modern Literature*. New Haven, Connecticut, and London: Yale University Press, 1966, 237.

4789 Stodieck, Henrique. *Bergson e outros temas*. Florianópolis, Brazil: Rotiero, 1966, 117. This study contains a chapter on Bergson and sociology.

4790 Stromberg, Roland N. *An Intellectual History of Modern Europe*. New York: Appleton-Century-Crofts, 1966, 487. Bergson is dicussed on pp. 340-343.

4791 Temple, Mary Lyons. "Proust and Bergson: The Relation of Relatives." in *Papers on Proust*. Ed. Louis D. Rubin. Hollins College, Virginia: Hollins College, 1966, 55-56.

4792 Tuchman, Barbara Wertheim. *The Proud Tower: A Portrait of the World Before the War, 1890-1914*. New York: Macmillan, 1966, 528. Bergson and social psychology are discussed on pp. 383-384.

4793 Tymieniecka, Anna-Teresa. *Why is there Something Rather Than Nothing? Prolegomena to the Phenomenology of Cosmic Creation*. Assen: Van Gorcum & Comp., 1966, 1960. This volume is dedicated "To the memory of my mother Maria-Ludwika de Lanval Tymieniecka with whom I first read Bergson." The author agrees with Bergson that, in raising the question "Why is there something rather than nothing?" we should not presume that Being is *ipso facto* a "conquest over nothingness". She also agrees that "'nothing' is merely (to repeat Bergson)" a word that symbolizes a concept. "This concept does not possess a distinctive denotation but draws all its content from the reality which it means to negate." (p. 10) To say this much is, however, not to agree with Bergson that the question of why there is something rather than nothing is a pseudo-question. The first half (Part I) of this very thoughtful study is to a significant degree a debate with Bergson. The author's arguments are, however, deeply flawed by her contention that for Bergson reality is "chaotic and inarticulate, purposeless and unaccountable", (p. 11) that is, formless.

4794   Vloemans, Antoon. "Terugblik op Bergson." *Nieuw Vlaams Tijdschrift*, 19, No. 6, 1966, 603-610.

4795   Wahl, Jean; Jankélévitch, Vladimir; Trotignon, Pierre; and Mazars, Pierre. "Cet invisible Bergson que nous portons." *Le Figaro Littéraire*, No. 1048, 19 mai 1966, 10, 11. This "table ronde" contains discussions of Bergson's philosophical system, his influence on literature and music, and his disciples.

4796   Wallis, Robert. *Le Temps, quatrième dimension de l'esprit: Etude de la fonction temporelle de l'homme du point de vue physique, biologique et métaphysique.* Pref. O. Costa de Beauregard. Paris: Flammarion, 1966, 288. The author notes: "Avec Henri Bergson, nous pouvons nous demander s'il est vrai que 'le temps est création ou il n'est rien du tout'." (29). References to Bergson may be found throughout.

4797   Weiler, Maurice and Jacob, Jean. *Ecrivains français du vingtième siècle: Textes choisis.* Paris: Belin, 1966, 375.

4798   Zacks, Hanna. "Perception and Action in Henri Bergson and Allied Philosophers." Diss. Columbia 1966, 181. The author contends that Bergson's theory of knowledge has as its main objective to prove that science and metaphysics are both possible. In approaching this objective, however, Bergson vacillates between two opposing standpoints both in his metaphysics and his theory of perception. The author traces the roots of this inconsistency to basic ontological, epistemological and anthropological assumptions. He examines Bergson's theory of perception and contrasts it with the pragmatic account of perception, as well as with the theories of Stuart Hampshire and Maurice Merleau-Ponty. (See *Dissertation Abstracts International*, 27, Nos. 1-4, 1966, 803A.)

1967

4799   Albanese, Vincenzo. "H. Bergson e la renascita religiosa." *Studia Patavina*, 14, 1967, 427-435.

4800   Anderson, James F. "Bergson, Aquinas, and Heidegger on the Notion of Nothingness." *The Nature of Philosophical Enquiry. Proceedings of the American Catholic Philosophical Association.* Ed George F. McLean and V. Voorhies. Washington, D.C.: Catholic University of America, 1967, 143-148.

4801   Barthélémy-Madaule, Madeleine. *Bergson.* Paris: Éditions du Seuil, 1967, 189. (Ecrivains de toujours). This is a popular presentation of Bergson's life, times, ideas.

4802   Bissondoyal, Mauritius B. "India in Mauritian Literature." *Indo-Asian Culture*, 16, No. 1, 1967, 38-49.

4803   Blanch, Robert J. "The Synchronized Clocks of Bergson and Thoreau." *Revue des Langues Vivantes*, 33, No. 5, 1967, 489-492.

4804   Brucker, Ted J. "Finality in the Philosophy of Henri Bergson." Diss., St. Louis, 1967.

4805   Burnham, John C. *Psychoanalysis and American Medicine: 1894-1918.* New York: International Universities Press, 1967, 249. For appropriation of Bergsonian ideas by S. E. Jeliffe and Beatrice M. Hinkle, Cf. pp. 114, 131-132 respectively.

4806 Čapek, Milič. "Change." *Encyclopedia of Philosophy*, Vol. 2, 75-79. This is a historical overview of the development of the concept of change from the pre-Socratics through contemporary process philosophy. A bibliography is presented on pp. 79.

4807 Čapek, Milič. "Time and Eternity in Royce and Bergson." *Revue Internationale de Philosophie*, 79-80, Nos. 1-2, 1967, 22-45. The American philosopher Josiah Royce's ultimate failure to "take time seriously" and his abortive attempts to do so are discussed in this article, which includes many comparisons of Royce and Bergson.

4808 Chenu, J. "Review of *Le Bergsonisme* by Gilles Deleuze." *Études Philosophiques et Littéraires*, 1, No. 1, 1967, 47-50.

4809 Culum, Jovan. "Svet-memorija Anrija Bergsona." *Letopis Matice srpske*, 143, No. 4, 1967, 298-324.

4810 Dansel, Michel. "Bergson." In *Les Nobel français de littérature*. Paris: Bonne, 1967, 107-120. (Les Grands Documentaires illustrés)

4811 Delpech, L.-J. "Review of *Bergson adversaire de Kant* by Madeleine Barthélémy-Madaule." *Revue de Synthèse*, 88, 1967, 265-266.

4812 Dietschy, Marcel. *Le Cas André Suarès*. Neuchâtel: À la Baconnière, 1967, 364. (Langages, Documents) Cf. pp. 84, 92, 160, 183, 282, 292, 301-304.

4813 "Doctoral Disserations, 1969." *Review of Metaphysics*, 23, No. 1, 1969, 189.

4814 Epperson, Gordon. *The Musical Symbol: A Study of the Philosophic Theory of Music*. Ames, Iowa: Iowa State University Press, 1967, xvii, 323.

4815 Étiemble, René. "Proust et la crise de l'intelligence." In *C'est le bouquet!* Vol. V of *Hygiène des lettres*. Paris: Gallimard, 1967, 150-212. The author (whose essay was written 1944-1945) finds profound oppositions between Bergson and Marcel Proust at all points except the concept of language. His discussion of Bergson and Proust begins on p. 190, and contains many bibliographic references.

4816 Fabre-Luce de Gruson. "Bergson et Proust" in *Entretiens sur le temps*. Eds. Jeanne Hersch et René Poirier. Paris, La Haye: Mouton, 1967, 234-246. (Décade du Centre culturel international de Cerisy-la-Salle. Nouvelle série. 5)

4817 Fioroli, E. "Review of *La filosofia sociale di Henri Bergson* by M. Fabris." *Culture Française*, 14, 1967, 16-17.

4818 Fressin, Augustin. *La Perception chez Bergson et chez Merleau-Ponty*. Paris: Société d'Editions d'Enseignement Supérieure, 1967, 399.

4819 Friedman, Maurice. "Bergson and Kazantzakis." *To Deny Our Nothingness: Contemporary Images of Man*. London: Victor Gollancz, Ldt., 1967, 63-79.

4820 Gallager, Idella J. "Bergson, Henri Louis." *New Catholic Encyclopedia*, Vol. II, 1967, 323-325.

4821 Gilson, Etienne. *Hommage public à Henri Bergson, Panthéon, le...11 mai 1967*. Paris: Firmin-Didot, 1967, 6.

4822 Gilson, Etienne. "Le Privilège de l'intelligence." *Nouvelles Littéraires*, No. 2071, 11 mai 1967, 3. This is an address delivered at the dedication of the Bergson plaque at the Panthéon.

4823 Goudge, T. A. "Bergson, Henri." *The Encyclopedia of Philosophy*, Ed. Paul Edwards. Vol. I. New York: Macmillan, 1967, 287-295.

4824 Hagan, Robert Alfred. "The Person and Bergson's Metaphysics." Diss., St. Louis, 1967.

4825 Halbfass, Wilhelm. "Review of *Bergson adversaire de Kant* by Madeleine Barthélémy-Madaule." *Erasmus*, Vol. 19, No. 9-10, 1967, 257-259.

4826 Hirofugi, T. "A Study of Mind and Matter in Bergson's Philosophy." *Mem. Osaka Kyoiku University*, 10, 1967, 135-140. The text of this article is in Japanese.

4827 James, William. "The Experience of Activity." In *Essays in Radical Empiricism: A Pluralistic Universe*. 1943; rpt. Gloucester, Massachusetts: Smith, 1967, 155-188.

4828 Kerr, Walter. *Tragedy and Comedy*. New York: Simon and Schuster, 1967, 355. Bergson is discussed on pp. 152, 175, 186, 196, 198, 243, 244, 246, and 272.

4829 Lamblin, M. "'Le Rire' de H. Bergson: 'Hippias Majeur' de Platon." *Bulletin Psychologique*, 20, 1967, 1382-1394.

4830 Le Brun, Philip. "T. S. Eliot and Henri Bergson." *Review of English Studies*, 18, No. 70, 1967, 149-161; No. 71, 1967, 172-286. Bergson exercised an unacknowledged influence on Eliot, according to the author.

4831 Madinier, Gabriel. *Conscience et mouvement: Etude sur la philosophie française de Condillac à Bergson*. Louvain: Nauwelaerts; Paris: Béatrice-Nauwelaerts, 1967, 482.

4832 Matthews, Fred Hamilton. "The Americanization of Sigmund Freud: Adaptations of Psychoanalysis before 1917." *Journal of American Studies*, 1, No. 1, April, 1967, 39-62. Cf. p. 43.

4833 Mathieu, Vittorio. "Studi bergsoniani dal 1945 a oggi." *Cultura e Scuola*, 6, No. 23, 1967, 88-92. This is a bibliographic essay. It details literature in Italy devoted to Bergson from 1945 through 1966.

4834 Maurois, André. *De Proust a Camus*. Trans. D. Pruna. Barcelona: Ediciones G. P., 1967, 307.

4835 Maurois, André. *From Proust to Camus: Profiles of Modern French Writers*. London: Weidenfeld and Nicholson, 1967, 368. Cf. pp. 30-46.

4836 Meissner, W. W. "Spirit and Matter: The Psychological Paradox." *Journal of Existentialism*, 8, No. 30, 1967-1968, 179-202.

4837 Ménard, Philippe. "Le Temps la durée dans les romans de Chrétien de Troyes." *Le Moyen Age*, 73, Nos. 3-4, 1967, 375-401.

4838 Merleau-Ponty, Maurice. *La Structure du comportement*. 6 ed. Pref. A. de Waelhens. Paris: Presses Universitaires de France, 1967, 248. Cf. esp. pp. 176-180 and following. The author compares Bergson's theory of perception with *Gestalt* theories. (This work appeared originally in 1942).

4839 Milhaud, Jean. *A Bergson: La Patrie reconnaissante*. Paris: Imprimerie nationale, 1967, 78. "Texte précédé d'une lettre de M. André Maurois...à Jean Milhaud. Post-face de M. Jean Guitton." This is an account of successful efforts to place a plaque dedicated to Bergson in the Panthéon. This item also contains many interesting observations concerning the relations between Bergson and M. Proust, P. Valéry, A. Malraux, and others. It also contains an essay by Jean Guitton, "Bergson au Panthéon" taken from *Le Figaro* 11 mai 1967.

4840   Min, Anselm Kyongsuk. "An Evolutionary View of Religion: Henri Bergson."
        Diss., St. Louis, 1967.

4841   Minkowski, Eugène. "Imagination?" Trans. Nathaniel Lawrence. in *Readings in
        Existential Phenomenology*. Ed. N. Lawrence and D. O'Connor. Englewood
        Cliffs, New Jersey: Prentice-Hall, 1967, 75-92.

4842   Morkovsky, Theresa Clare. "Freedom in Henri Bergson's Metaphysics." Diss. St.
        Louis. *Dissertation Abstracts*, 27, No. 9, March 1967, 3084A.

4843   Neisser, Ulrich. *Cognitive Psychology*. New York: Appleton-Century-Crofts, 1967,
        351. (Century Psychology Series) On pp. 94-95 the author notes that "the view
        that perception is basically a constructive act rather than a receptive or simply
        an analytic one" goes back to Brentano, Bergson, and William James. On pp.
        190-191 and following he examines new "analysis-by-synthesis" models of
        speech perception, noting their similarity to Bergson's "motor theory" of percep-
        tion.

4844   Njog-Mouelle, Ebénézer. "Bergson et l'idée de profondeur." Diss., Paris: 1967,
        213. (Thèse 3ᵉ Cycle. Lettres)

4845   Pange, Jean de. *Journal: 1931-1933*. Paris: Grasset, 1967, 412.

4846   Pire, François. *De l'imagination poétique dans l'oeuvre de Gaston Bachelard*.
        Paris: J. Corti, 1967, 221.

4847   "Une Plaque Bergson au Panthéon." *Le Monde*, No. 6856, 27 janvier 1967, 8.

4848   Rabil, Albert. *Merleau-Ponty: Existentialist of the Social World*. New York and
        London: Columbia University Press, 1967, 331. Bergson's concept of the func-
        tion of the body is discussed on pp. 24-25; Merleau-Ponty, on pp. 180-187;
        Merleau-Ponty's theory of perception, on pp. 180-182. The author states:
        "Hence, two years before the writing of his first book, Merleau-Ponty apparently
        looked to Bergson's theory of perception as one aiming at that 'ambiguous'
        world to which his own thinking was directing him." (183). (Cf. F. Heidsieck,
        1971, No. 5164)

4849   Riccaboni, Joseph J. "Bergson's Metaphysical Intuition and Science." *Journal of
        the History of Philosophy*, 5, No. 2, April 1967, 159-161. The author argues
        that Bergson's intuition is "metaphysical" and therefore not intended—as Mario
        Bunge insists—to be scientifically fruitful.

4850   Rideau, Émile. "Actualité de Bergson." *Études*, No. 326, 1967, 638-651. "Influ-
        ence actuelle de Bergson: (1) L'affirmation de la liberté contre les conditionne-
        ments intérieurs et les déterminismes du monde; (2) L'affirmation de l''*élan
        vital*' évolutif et de la 'finalité' interne des organismes: question toujours posée
        à une biologie, tentée de reduire la Vie à des méchanismes matériels; (3) La
        reconnaissance du courant religieux axial de l'histoire, qui à travers Israel aboutit
        aux au Christ et aux mustiques chrétiens, et qui resurgit dans tous les revivals
        religieux; (4) L'invitation à accorder, pour le salut même de l'humanité, le
        travail sur le monde et les 'énergies spirituelles'." *The Philosophers Index*, 13,
        No. 1, 1979, 104.

4851   Robinet, André. "Le Bon Roi Dagobert est-il Jaurès?" *Feuillets de l'Amitié Charles
        Péguy*, No. 135, 1967, 29-30. This is a passage quoted from the author's *Péguy
        entre Juarès, Bergson, et l'Eglise*.

4852   Salvan, Jacques L. *The Scandalous Ghost: Sartre's Existentialism as Related to
        Vitalism, Humanism, Mysticism, Marxism*. Detroit: Wayne State University

Press, 1967, 216.

4853 Sándor, Pál. *Bergson.* Budapest: Gondolat, 1967, 180.

4854 Schlumberger, Jean. "Trois Grands Hommes et une soeur abusive." *Revue de Paris,* 74e Année, Nos. 7-8, juillet-août 1967, 93-96. Bergson and P. Valéry are discussed in this article.

4855 Tison-Braun, Micheline. *La Crise de l'humanisme: Le Conflit de l'individu et de la société dans la littérature française moderne.* Paris: Nizet, 1967, 468.

4856 Trethowan, Dom Illtyd. "Bergson and the Zeitgeist: With Excerpts from *The Two Sources of Morality and Religion.*" *Downside Review,* 85, No. 2, April 1967, 138-147; No. 3, July 1967, 262-273.

4857 Vassallo, Angel. *Bergson.* Buenos Aires: Centro Editor de America Latina, 1967, 116.

4858 Vloemans, Antoon. *Bergson.* Den Haag: Kruseman, 1967, 144. (Helden van de geest)

4859 Wahl, Jean. "L'Espèce à part." *Nouvelles Littéraires,* No. 2071, 11 mai 1967, 13. This is an address delivered at the dedication of a Bergson plaque at the Panthéon.

4860 Wahl, Jean. "Les Hommages à Henri Bergson (11 mai 1967)." *Annales de l'Université de Paris,* 37, 1967, 571-573.

4861 Wellek, René. "French 'Classical' Criticism in the Twentieth Century." *Yale French Studies,* No. 38, 1967, 47-71. The author deals here with various criticisms of Bergson and Bergsonism by French neo-classicists. Among these critics are Pierre Laserre (p. 56), Henri Massis (p. 50), and Julian Benda (pp. 65-66). The attitudes of T. S. Eliot and T. E. Hulme towards Bergson are mentioned on pp. 69-70.

4862 Weyembergh, Maurice. "La Personnalité charismatique chez M. Weber et le héros chez Bergson." *Morale et Enseignement, Bulletin de l'Institut de Philosophie,* 16, 1967, 121-175.

4863 Whitehead, Alfred North. *Science and the Modern World: The Lowell Lectures, 1925.* New York: The Free Press, 1967, 212. On pp. 51-52 the author states, "The simple location of instantaneous material configurations is what Bergson has protested against, so far as it concerns time and so far as it is taken to be the fundamental fact of concrete nature. He calls it a distortion of nature due to the intellectual 'spatialization' of things. I agree with Bergson in his protest: but I do not agree that such distortion is a vice necessary to the intellectual comprehension of nature. I shall in subsequent lectures endeavor to show that his spatialization is the expression of more concrete facts under the guise of very abstract logical constructions. There is an error; but it is merely the accidental error of mistaken the abstract for the concrete. It is an example of what I will call the 'Fallacy of Misplaced Concreteness'." On pp. 147-148 the author describes Bergson as the most characteristic philosopher of his epoch, at least as concerns Bergson's relations to the science of his times: "Bergson introduced into philosophy the organic conceptions of physiological science. He has most completely moved away from the static materialism of the seventeenth century." The author notes that Bergson's protest against the spatialization of time is directed against taking Newtonian ideas as anything but abstractions. "His so-called 'anti-intellectualism' should be construed in this sense."

1968

4864   Amidou, Philip R. "Memory and Duration in Bergson: A Study of Terminology in *Matter and Memory* and Introduction to Metaphysics." Diss., St. Louis, 1968.

4865   Austermann, Maria. "Die Entwicklung der ethischen und religionsphilosophischen Gedanken bei Bergson." Diss. Münster (Westf.) 1968, 225.

4866   Barlow, Michel. *El pensamiento de Bergson*. Trans. María Martínez Peñaloza. México: Fondo de Cultura Economica, 1968, 149. (Brevarios, No. 202) This is an anthology of Bergson's writings.

4867   Barron, Frank X. *Creativity and Personal Freedom*. Princeton, New Jersey: D. Van Nostrand, 1968, 322. On p. 233 the author notes the similarities between Bergson's and Freud's conceptions of the manner in which life and entropy are opposed.

4868   Barthélémy-Madaule, Madeleine. *Bergson*. Paris: Presses Universitaires de France, 1968, 122. This is a more academic treatment of Bergson than the author's earlier *Bergson*, published in 1967.

4869   Barthélémy-Madaule, Madeleine. "Lire Bergson." *Etudes Bergsoniennes*, 8, 1968, 85-120. This is a criticism of Gilles Deleuze (*Le Bergsonisme*, P.U.F., 1966) concerning intuition as a method of "division," memory as "virtual coexistence," and the distinction between "superhuman" and "inhuman."

4870   Bayer, Raymond. "Recent Esthetic Thought in France." *Philosophic Thought in France and the United States*. Ed. Marvin Faber. Albany, New York: State University of New York Press, 1968, 267-278. Bergson is discussed on pp. 271-272.

4871   Becker, Ernest. *The Structure of Evil: An Essay on the Unification of the Science of Man*. New York: George Braziller, 1968, 430. The author refers to Bergson very briefly on pp. 13, 113, 127, 147, 232 and 252. On p. 252 he states, "We noted earlier that Bergson saw the innovator as the instrument of evolution itself, nature working against encrusted social forms. Max Weber too held a similar view, and assigned a very important place in his thought to the charismatic person, the radical innovator who reworks all meanings and cuts through all the 'routinized' cultural forms."

4872   Cattaui, Georges and Madaule, Jacques, Eds. *Entretiens sur Paul Claudel*. Paris and La Haye: Mouton, 1968, 333.

4873   Chaix-Ruy, Jules. *El superhombre: De Nietzsche a Teilhard de Chardin*. Trans. D. R. Duch. Salamanca: Ed. Síguene, 1968, 311.

4874   Chevalier, Jacques. *Historia del pensamiento: El pensamiento moderno de Hegel a Bergson*. Trans. and Preface José A. Miquez. Madrid: Aguilar, 1968, 733. This posthumous text was edited by Léon Husson.

4875   Cluny, Claude Michel. "Le Temps de Bergson." *Lettres Françaises*, No. 1249, 18-24 septembre 1968, 13.

4876   Cornu, Auguste. "Bergsonianism and Existentialism." *Philosophic Thought in France and the United States*; Ed. Marvin Farber. Albany, New York: State University of New York Press, 1968, 813. See pp. 151-168. Cornu provides a Marxist interpretation of Bergson.

4877 Deleuze, Gilles. *Le Bergsonisme*. 2nd ed. Paris: Presses Universitaires de France, 1968, 124. (Initiation philosophique, No. 76)

4878 Deleuze, Gilles. *Différence et répétition*. Paris: Presses Universitaires de France, 1968, 411. (Bibliothèque de Philosophie contemporaine) The author explores two directions of research, the first concerning the concept of difference without negation, the second concerning the concept of repetition of the same. It is impossible, he states, to think either concept without the other. The author opposes his essentially Bergsonian viewpoint to those of G. W. F. Hegel and contemporary "Hegelians." (Cf. also J. Lebacqz, 1968)

4879 Deprun, Jean. *L'Union de l'âme et du corps chez Malebranche, Biran et Bergson: Notes prises au cours de Merleau-Ponty à l'Ecole normale supérieure: (1947-1948)*. Paris: Vrin, 1968, 131.

4880 Devaux, André-A. "Michel Lecointe: La Matière biblique dans la 'Note sur M. Bergson et le philosophie bergsonienne' et la 'Note conjointe sur M. Descartes et la philosophie cartésienne' de Charles Péguy." *Feuillets de l'Amitié Charles Péguy*, No. 138, 15 février 1968, 26-27.

4881 Dobzhansky, Theodosius Grigorievich and Boesiger, Ernest. *Essais sur l'évolution*. Paris: Masson et Cie., 1968, 182 (Collection "Les Grands Problèmes de la Biologie," No. 9). Bergson is discussed on pp. 2, 6, and 145-148. Chapter 7, which is entitled "L'Evolution créatrice," appears on pp. 145-165. The authors reject Bergson's vitalism but argue the evolution is "creative."

4882 "Doctoral Dissertations, 1968." *Review of Metaphysics*, 22, No. 1, 1968, 201.

4883 Ebacher, Roger. *La Philosophie dans la cité technique: Essai sur la philosophie bergsonienne des techniques*. Québec: Laval University Press; Paris: Bloud et Gay, 1968, 242. The author applies Bergson's philosophy, particularly as expressed in *The Two Sources of Morality and Religion*, to the question of the place of philosophy in a technological society. The final section of this study traces parallels between Bergson and Karl Marx.

4884 Eslick, Leonard J. "God in the Metaphysics of Whitehead." in *New Themes in Christian Philosophy*. Ed. Ralph M. McInerny. Notre Dame, Indiana: University of Notre Dame Press, 1968, 64-81. The author criticizes A. N. Whitehead's concept of God and of finite entities from an essentially Bergsonian viewpoint, urging that on Whitehead's terms only God has causal efficacy.

4885 *Etudes Bergsoniennes*. Paris: Presses Universitaires de France, 1968, Vol. 8, 175. Lettres between Bergson and Péguy are published in this issue, which also contains an essay on Spinozist themes in Bergson's thought and various talks given at the unveiling of a Bergson plaque at the Panthéon.

4886 Farber, Marvin (Ed.). *Philosophic Thought in France and the United States*. Albany: State University of New York Press, 1950, Second Edition, enlarged, 1968, 813. Bergson and Blondel are dealt with on pp. 3-30; Bergson's influence, 35-36; Bergson and existentialism, 151-168; and religion, 259-261; and aesthetics, 271-272.

4887 Gallagher, Idella J. "Bergson on Closed and Open Morality." *New Scholasticism*, 42, No. 3, Winter 1968, 48-71. This is a thoughtful analysis of Bergson's two kinds of morality.

4888 Galperine, Charles. "Conversation sur Claudel et Bergson." *Entretiens sur Paul Claudel*. Ed. Georges Cattaui and Jacques Madaule. Paris and La Haye: Mouton, 1968, 141-152.

4889   Gilson, Etienne. "Bergson: Le Privilège de l'intelligence." *Etudes Bergsoniennes*, 8, 1968, 170-173.

4890   Gouhier, Henri. "Bergson et Claudel." Ed. Georges Cattaui and Jacques Madaule. *Entretiens sur Paul Claudel*. Paris and La Haye: Mouton, 1968, 135-140.

4891   Gouhier, Henri. *Bergson e il Cristo dei Vangeli*. Trans. S. Marzorati. Milano: I.P.L., 1968, 220. (Studi e opinioni)

4892   Guitton, Jean. *Journal*. Vol. 1. Paris: Plon, 1968, 315. The following articles on Bergson appear here: "Prix Nobel," 60-65; "Sur La Mère de Bergson," 152-155; "Le Testament de Bergson," 227-228; "La Maison de Bergson," 261-265; and "Bergson, Bréhier, Brunschvicg," 268-273.

4893   Guitton, Jean. *Regards sur la pensée française, 1870-1940: Leçons de captivité*. Paris: Beauchesne, 1968, 253.

4894   Guyot, Charly. "Notes sur Bergson et les lettres françaises." In *De Rousseau à Marcel Proust: Recueil d'essais littéraries* by Charly Guyot. Préf. M. Raymond. Neuchâtel: Ides et Calendes, 1968, 159-172.

4895   Guyot, Charly. "Péguy et Bergson." In *De Rousseau à Marcel Proust: Recueil d'essais litteraires* by Charly Guyot. Préf. M. Raymond. Neuchâtel: Ides et Calendes, 1968, 173-183.

4896   Gunnel, John C. *Political Philosophy and Time*. Middletown, Connecticut: Wesleyan University Press, 1968, 314. Cf. esp. pp. 18, 254-255.

4897   Hart, Thomas N. "God in the Ethico-religious Thought of Henri Bergson." *Thomist*, 32, No. 3, July 1968, 333-365. The author argues that Bergson opposes a supra-human to an infra-human ethic. The ordinary ethic is bypassed.

4898   Havet, Jacques. "French Philosophical Tradition Between the Two Wars." *Philosophic Thought in France and the United States*. Ed. Marvin Farber. Albany, New York: State University of New York Press, 1968, 3-30. Bergson and M. Blondel are discussed on pp. 5-8.

4899   Herman, D. J. "Finality in the Philosophy of Henri Bergson." Diss. Northwestern. *Dissertation Abstracts International*, 29, No. 7, 1968, 2302A.

4900   James, William. *Le Pragmatisme*. Trans. E. Le Brun. Paris: Flammarion, 1968, 251. This book contains an introduction by Henri Bergson.

4901   Jonçich, Geraldine. *The Sane Positivist: A Biography of Edward L. Thorndike*. Middletown, Connecticut: Wesleyan University Press, 1968, 634. "The mood of the age is symbolized by Henri Bergson's *Creative Evolution*, a runaway best-seller in intellectual circles and popularized by everyone else. When Bergson comes to New York City to lecture at Columbia University in 1913, the city is strangled in perhaps the first traffic jam of the brand new automotive age, as people fight to reach Morningside Heights to hear one called the day's most influential thinkers." p. 334.

4902   Kazantzakis, Helen. *Nikos Kazantzakis: A Biography Based on his Letters*. New York: Simon and Schuster, 1968, 589. Bergson's relations to Kazantzakis are discussed on pp. 58, 400, 444, 459, 490, and 561.

4903   Kolakowski, Leszek. *The Alienation of Reason: A History of Positivist Thought*. Trans. Norbert Buterman. Garden City, New York: Doubleday, 1968, vi, 230. The author refers to Bergson on pp. 77, 78, 126, 131, 132, 135, 148, 152-153, and 217. On p. 78 he notes that Bergson, Husserl, and Heidegger take for granted the separation of the objects of science and of philosophy; on pp. 131-132 he compares Bergson's and Husserl's epistemologies; Bergson, conventionalism, and Edouard Le Roy are discussed by the author on pp. 135-137 and 148, as well as on pp. 152-153, where the author holds that Le Roy showed that Bergson's intuitionism is compatible with positivism. pp. 217-218.

4904   Kremer-Marietti, Angèle. "Intuition et durée quelques ouvrages récents sur Bergson." *Etudes Bergsoniennes*, 8, 1968, 159-167. This is a review of *Bergson et les métamorphoses de la durée* by André Robinet; *Bergson et les niveaux de la réalité* by Georges Mourelos; and *Bergsonisme* by Gilles Deleuze.

4905   Krieger, Murray. "Ekphrasis and the Still Movement of Poetry: Or Laokoon Revisited." in *Perspectives on Poetry*. Ed. James L. Calderwood and Harold E. Toliver. New York: Oxford University Press, 1968, 323-348. The author sums up his position on pp. 345-346, where he urges that a Bergsonian and merely phenomenological aesthetics is insufficient, and can not do justice to form. (P. Douglass, 1983.)

4906   Kümmel, Friedrich. "Time as Succession and the Problem of Duration." in *The Voices of Time*. Ed. J. T. Fraser. London: Allen Lane, The Penquin Press, 1968, 31-55. The author criticizes Bergson's concept of duration on pp. 48-51, urging that Bergson can not provide a satisfactory account of the past as past or the future as future. Bergson's *durée* fuses these "times" and thus can not distinguish them.

4907   Kurris, Frans. *Kerngedachten van Henri Bergson*. Roermond, Netherlands: Romen, 1968, 129. (Kerngedachten, 6)

4908   Lafrance, Guy. "Continuité et absolue nouveauté dans la durée bergsonienne." *Dialogue*, 7, No. 1, June 1968, 94-101. The author states his intentions as follows: "Comment, en effet, Bergson réussit-il à concilier, au sein d'une même réalité, deux éléments en apparence aussi opposés que la continuité et l'absolue nouveauté? Telle est la question que nous voulons élucider dans cet article." (98).

4909   Lebacqz, Joseph. *De l'identique au multiple: Le Problème des universaux reconsidéré à lumière du bergsonisme et des philosophies existentialistes*. Louvain: Éditions Nauwelaerts; Paris: Béatrice-Nauwelaerts, 1968, 164. (Bibliothèque de la Faculté de philosophie et de lettres de Namur, fasc. 43) Cf. also G. Deleuze, 1968)

4910   Lebacques, Joseph. *De l'identique au multiple. Le Problème des universaux reconsidéré à la lumière du bergsonisme et des philosophes existentialistes*. Louvain: Éditions Nauwelaerts; Québec: Les Presses de l'Université Laval, 1968. 162.

4911   Lindsay, Alexander Dunlap. *The Philosophy of Bergson*. 1911 rpt. New York: Kennikat Press, 1968, 247.

4912   Linschoten, Hans. *On the Way Toward a Phenomenological Psychology: The Psychology of William James*. Ed. Amedeo Giorgi. Pittsburgh: Duguesne University Press, 1968, 319. (Duguesne Studies, Psychological Series, 5) In general the author uses Bergson's philosophy to help explain various of James' ideas. On pp. 111-112 he discusses Bergson's ideas concerning social life and reality; on pp. 116 and 120-121 he compares James' and Bergson's concepts of the limitations of language; on pp. 148 and 173 he compares their notions of "transitivity."

4913   Madaule, Jacques and Cattaui, Georges, Eds. *Entretiens sur Paul Claudel*. Paris and La Haye: Mouton, 1968, 333.

4914   Maritain, Jacques, *Bergsonian Philosophy and Thomism*. New York: Greenwood Press, 1968, 383.

4915   Margolin, Jean-Claude. "Review of *Bergson* by Madeleine Barthélémy-Madaule." *Etudes philosophiques*, 23, No. 2, 1968, 218-219.

4916   Martin, Auguste. "Le Dossier Bergson-Péguy." *Etudes Bergsoniennes*, 8, 1968, 3-60. This article contains correspondence between Bergson, Péguy, Joseph Lotte, and others. It also contains the account of an interview of Bergson with J. Lotte.

4917   May, William Eugene. "The Reality of Matter in the Metaphysics of Bergson." Diss. Marquette 1968, 269. The author points out that the problem of the reality of matter arises naturally from Bergson's philosophy. He concludes that for Bergson matter is real because it is "within concretely enduring realities, a genuine tendency not to endure." This tendency can not succeed; it can only approach non-duration as a limit. Matter is, however, in no way independently real since it depends on spirit, with which it is permeated, in order to endure. (See *Dissertation Abstracts International*, 29, Nos. 7-9, 1969, 3184A.)

4918   McInerny, Ralph M., Ed. *New Themes in Christian Philosophy*. Notre Dame: Notre Dame University Press, 1968, 416.

4919   Mehl, Roger. "The Situation of Religious Philosophy in France." *Philosophic Thought in France and the United States*. Ed. Marvin Farber. Albany, New York: State University of New York Press, 1968, 249-264. Bergson is discussed on pp. 259-261.

4920   Meriwether, James B., and Michael Millgate. *Lion in the Garden: Interviews with William Faulkner*. New York: Random House, 1968, xvi, 298. On p. 70 William Faulkner describes his theology, "'Naturally,' he continued, 'I'm not talking about a personified or a mechanical God, but a God who rests both in eternity and in the now.' When I asked if he were thinking of the God of Bergson, he said, 'Yes, a diety very close to Bergson's. Listen, neither God nor morality can be destroyed.' I repeated this remark to myself, for he had said it with great emphasis." Cf. also p. 72.

4921   Merleau-Ponty, Maurice. *Résumés de cours: Collège de France, 1952-1960*. Ed. C. Lefort. Paris: Gallimard, 1968, 182. Bergson's philosophy of nature is discussed on pp. 109-111.

4922   Merleau-Ponty, Maurice. *L'Union de l'âme et du corps chez Malebranche, Biran et Bergson: Notes prises au cours de Maurice Merleau-Ponty à l'Ecole normale supérieure (1947-1948)*. Ed. Jean Duprun. Paris: Vrin, 1968, 136.

4923   Merleau-Ponty, Maurice. *The Visible and the Invisible: Followed by Working Notes*. Ed. Claude Lefort. Trans Alphonso Lingis. Evanston, Illinois: Northwestern University Press, 1968, 282. (Northwestern University Studies in Phenomenology and Existential Philosophy) Cf. especially "Interrogation and Intuition", pp. 105-129, for criticisms of Bergson's concept of intuition.

4924   Meyerhoff, Hans. *Time in Literature*. Berkeley and Los Angeles, University of California Press, 1968, 160. The author cites Henri Bergson's notion of time "given as an immediate datum of consciousness" as the key to the notion of time in modern literature: "Yet it is so easy to understand why Bergson's philosophy has exercised so profound an influence on literature: the literary treatment of time, as we shall see, has always been 'Bergsonian' in the sense of analyzing time as an immediate datum of consciousness and as it enters into human lives and actions rather than 'into mechanics and physics'" (p. 10). Bergson's duration is employed by the author as a technical term on p. 14 *et seq*. See also pp. 36-37, 67, 76-77, and 153n.

4925   Murillo Zamora, Roberto. "La notion de causalité dans la philosophie de Bergson." *Revista de Filosofía de la Universidad de Costa Rica*, 7, No. 23, 1968, 1-127. The author assembles all the remarks which Bergson has made on the notion of causality, concluding that Bergson espouses a polarity consisting of two sorts of causation, psychological and physical. A third, biological, results from the interaction of these two.

4926   Murillo Zamora, Robert. *La Notion de causalité dans le philosophie de Bergson*. San José, Costa Rica: Ciudad universitaria, 1968, 127. This is reprinted from *Revista de Filosofía de la Universidad de Costa Rica*, 1968.

4927   Nabi, Muhammad Noor. "Islam and Science Not Opposed to Each Other. The Muslim Philosopher Ibm Tufayl (d. 1185 C.E.), Darwin and Bergson." *Islamic Review*, 56, No. 4, 1968, 6-9.

4928   Naess, Arne. *Four Modern Philosophers: Carnap, Wittgenstein, Heidegger, Sartre*. Chicago: University of Chicago Press, 1968, 367. The author states on p. 155n, "it is difficult to feel that Wittgenstein's *Investigation* and works with a similar orientation constitute a violent break with earlier philosophy, particularly for someone who has already felt the powerful impact of the pragmatic *Lebensform*-theoretical positions of William James, Bergson, and Georg Simmel."

4929   Nelson, Alvin F. *The Development of Lester Ward's World View*. Fort Worth, Texas: Branch-Smith, Inc., 1968, 67. Similarities between Ward and Bergson are discussed on pp. 65-67.

4930   Pepper, Stephen C. "The Development of Contextual Aesthetics." *Antioch Review*, 28, No. 2, 1968, 169-185.

4931   Quoniam, Théodore. "Review of *La Perception chez Bergson et chez Merleau-Ponty* by Augustin Fressin." *Études Philosophiques*, 23, No. 1, 1968, 68-69.

4932   Reboul, Olivier. "La Création en art: Artiste et artisan: Alain, Bergson et Valéry." *L'Homme et ses passions d'après Alain*: Vol. 2. *La Sagesse*. Paris: Presses Universitaries de France, 1968, 69-74.

4933   Rideau, Émile. "Bergson gegen den Materialismus." *Dokumente*, 24, 1968, 452-463.

4934   Robinet, André. "Le Drapeau noir de Péguy." *Nouvelles Littéraires*, 46, No. 2132, 1 août 1968, 4. This is a review of Vol. 8 of *Les Études Bergsoniennes*, which concentrates on the relations between Bergson and Charles Péguy.

4935   Robinet, André. *Péguy entre Jaurès, Bergson, et l'Eglise: Métaphysique et politique*. Paris: Seghers, 1968, 351.

4936   Robinet, André. "Péguy, lecteur de Bergson: Première rencontre." *Etudes Bergsoniennes*, 8, 1968, 63-81. This study is a description of the initial influence of Bergson on Péguy, with some interesting comments on the relations between both men and J. Jaurès.

4937   Sanmartin Grau, Juan. "Bergson." *Annales de la Universidad de Cuenca*, 24, Nos. 1-2, 1968, 204-211.

4938   Schlumberger, Jean. "Bergson." *Recontres*. Paris: Gallimard, 1968, 133-135.

4939   Schoubourg, Gary. "Bergson's Intuitional Approach to Free Will." *Modern School-man*, 45, No. 1, January 1968, 123-144.

4940   Singerman, Ora. "The Relation Between Philosophy and Science: A Comparison of the Positions of Bergson and Whitehead." *Iyyun*, 9, No. 2, April 1968, 65-91. This article is in Hebrew. The sociologies of Whitehead and Bergson are discussed in this article.

4941   Slosson, Edwin Henry. *Major Prophets of Today*. Rpt. 1914. Freeport, New York: Books for Libraries Press, 1968, 299.

4942   Strozewski, Władysław. "History of the Problems of Negation: Part 2,: Ontological Problems of Negation in John Scotus Erigena and Henri Bergson." *Studia mediewistyczne*. Eds. Jan Legowicz and Stefan Swiezawski. Wroctaw-Warzawa: Ossolineum, 1968, 306.

4943   Thompson, W. R. "Evolution and Some Philosophers." in *Melanges à la mémoire de Charles de Koninck*. Québec: Les Presses de L'Université Laval, 1968, 363-378. The author examines Bergson's philosophy of biology appreciatively on pp. 366-368. He uses it to criticize the biological philosophy of Teilhard de Chardin. He notes (p. 366) that biologists George Gaylord Simpson and H. W. B. Joseph agree with Bergson on important issues in the interpretation of evolution.

4944   Tilliette, X. "Review of *Bergson* by M. Barthélémy-Madaule." *Études*, No. 329, 1968, 168.

4945   Topcu, Nurettin, *Bergson*. Istanbul: Hareket Yayinlari, 1968, 116.

4946   Touchard, Pierre-Aimé. *Le Théâtre et l'angoisse des hommes*. Paris: Edit. du Seuil, 1968, 221. S. Beckett, Bergson, P. Claudel, J. Cocteau, and others are discussed in this study.

4947   Trotignon, Pierre. *L'Idée de vie chez Bergson et la critique de la métaphysique*. Paris: Presses Universitaires de France, 1968, 336. (Épiméthée)

4948   Turquet-Milnes, Gladys Rosaleen. *Some Modern French Writers: A Study in Bergsonism*. 1921 rpt. Freeport, New York: Books for Libraries Press, 1968, xiii, 302.

4949   Valensin, Auguste. *Profili: Platone, Cartesio, Pascal, Bergson, Blondel*. Milano: IPL, 1968, 343. (Studi e opinioni, 15)

4950   Valéry, Paul. "Bergson: Extracts from the Notebooks." *Masters and Friends* (Coll. works, IX). London: Routledge and Kegan Paul, 1968, 342-349.

4951   Valéry, Paul. "Funeral Address on Bergson." *Masters and Friends*. (Coll. works, IX) London: Routledge and Kegan Paul, 1968, 302-306.

4952   Vassallo, Angel. *Retablo de la filosofía moderna: Figuras y fervores*. Buenos Aires: Universidad Nacional de la Pista, 1968, 140. This history of philosophy includes sections on Leonardo, Spinoza, Blondel, and Bergson.

4953   Violette, René. *La Spiritualité de Bergson: Essai sur l'élaboration d'une philosophie spirituelle dans l'oeuvre d'Henri Bergson*. Toulouse: Privat, 1968, 575. (Nouvelle Recherche)

4954   Vuarnet, Jean-Noël. "Bergson vu par Madeleine Barthélémy-Madaule." *Lettres Françaises*, No. 1258, 20-26 novembre 1968, 17.

4955   Wahl, Jean. "L'Espèce à part." *Etudes Bergsoniennes*, 8, 1968, 173-175.

4956   Wahl, Jean. "The Present Situation and the Present Future of French Philosophy."
        Philosophic Thought in France and the United States. Ed. Marvin Farber.
        Albany, New York: State University of New York Press, 1968, 35-49. The
        influence of Bergson is discussed on pp. 35-36.

4957   Westcott, Malcom R. *Toward a Contemporary Psychology of Intuition*. New York:
        Holt, Rinehart and Winston, Inc., 1968, 228. Bergson is discussed on pp. 6-11,
        19-21, 75-77, and elsewhere. The author criticizes Bergson's concept of intuition,
        but argues that intuition is a valid and distinctive mode of thought.

4958   Wiriath, Marcel. *Notes du soir*. Paris: Plon, 1968, 201.

4959   Zac, Sylvian. "Les Thèmes spinozistes dans la philosophie de Bergson." *Etudes
        Bergsoniennes*, 8, 1968, 123-158. This is a thoughtful comparison of Bergson
        and Spinoza. It suggests interesting similarities between the two philosophers.

1969

4960   Aichele, Ronald B. "Russell on 'The Theory of Continuity'." *Dianoia*, 5, Spring
        1969, 1-11. The author discusses the mathematical theory of motion, Bergson's
        objections to it, and Russell's defense.

4961   Alvarez Arroyo, Jesús. "La sustancialidad del tempo en Bergson." *Salmanticensis*,
        16, 1969, 299-327. This is a segment of the author's thesis, "El tiempo en
        Bergson."

4962   Alexander, Stephan Toth, Jr. "Joyce-Bergson Correspondences in the Theory of
        Time Structure of 'Dubliners,' 'A Portrait,' and 'Ulysses.'" Diss. Southern
        California 1969, 208.

4963   Atkinson, John Keith. "Les Caves du Vatican and Bergson's *Le Rire*." *Publications
        of the Modern Language Association of America*, 84, No. 2, March 1969,
        325-328. The author argues that Gide's attitude towards comedy in his one great
        comic work is remarkably similar to Bergson's approach to comedy. For Gide's
        relations to Bergson Cf. Pierre Lafille, 1954.

4964   Barreau, Hervé. "Bergson et Zénon d'Elée." *Revue Philosophique de Louvain*, 3e
        Sér., 67, No. 94, mai 1969, 267-284; No. 95, août 1969, 389-430. Bergson
        successively presented four reports of Zeno's argument, especially of the Achil-
        les. His interpretation differs from that of the neo-Kantians (Renouvier, Evellin)
        and from that of the historians of mathematics (Tannery, Milhaud) who were
        his contemporaries. It is metaphysical and proceeds in opposing space that is
        divisible and duration and motion that are indivisible. Zeno is right, according
        to Bergson, in denouncing the contradictions of common sense and scientific
        thought. Both agree in attributing indivisible unity to true beings. Bergsonism
        is hence an Eleatism, not an Eleatism of rest (Parmenides) but an Eleatism of
        motion.

4965   Becker, Kenneth L. "Review of *Duration and Simultaneity* by Henri Bergson."
        Modern Schoolman, 47, No. 1, 1969, 121.

4966   Berl, Emmanuel. *A Contretemps*. Paris: Gallimard, 1969, 215.

4967   Bloch, Bernard G. "Koncepcja ewolucja zycia u H. Bergson i P. Teilharda de
        Chardin." *Studia philosophiae christianae*, 5, No. 1, 1969, 217-228.

4968   Bréhier, Emile. "Ch. 7, The Spiritualism of Henri Bergson." *The History of Philosophy*. Trans. Wade Baskin. Chicago and London: University of Chicago Press, 1969, 119-131.

4969   Chaix-Ruy, Jules. *The Superman: From Nietzsche to Teilhard de Chardin*. Notre Dame and London: University of Notre Dame Press, 1969, 229.

4970   Chevalier, Jacques. *Henri Bergson*. Trans. L. Clare, 1928; rpt. Freeport, New York: AMS Press, 1969, 351.

4971   Chóron, Jacques. "Bergson, Klages, Simmel: La Mort et les 'philosophies de la vie'." *La Mort et la pensée occidentale*. Trans. M. Manin. Paris: Payot, 1969, 181-183.

4972   Crescenzo, Giovanni de. "Review of *L'Idée de vie chez Bergson et la critique de la métaphysique* by Pierre Trotignon." *Rivista di filosofia*, 40, No. 2, 1969, 217-220.

4973   Cysarz, Herbert. "Descartes und Bergson: Französischer Rationalismus und Irrationalismus in Deutschland." *Schopenhauer-Jahrbuch*, 50, 1969, 38-55.

4974   Da Matta, Roberto. "Letter Concerning Professor Evans-Pritchard's Concept of Primitive Notions of Causality." *Man*, N.S. 4, No. 3, September 1969, 455-456. The author points out close similarities between Bergson's and E. E. Evans-Pritchard's concepts of primitive man's notion of causality. Both Bergson (*Les Deux Sources*) and Evans-Pritchard (*Witchcraft, Oracles and Magic Among the Azande*. Oxford, 1937) saw that primitive man is aware of physical causes, but may superimpose on them causes of a magical nature when these have "significance for social behavior", i.e. when they concern human affairs. The author ponders whether Professor Evens-Pritchard was influenced by Bergson. (See Evans-Pritchard's response, in *Man*, 1970, p. 131).

4975   David, André. *Paroles d'or: Les Coulisses des "Conférences des Ambassadeurs."* Paris: La Table Ronde, 1969, 290.

4976   Delfgaauw, Bernard. *Twentieth-Century Philosophy*. Trans. N. D. Smith. Albany, New York: Magi Books, 1969, 172. Bergson is discussed in "The Philosophy of Evolution," 93-102.

4977   Delòrme, Albert. "Review of *Péguy entre Jaurés, Bergson et l'église* by André Robinet." *Revue de Synthèse*, 90, Nos. 53-54, 1969, 181-184.

4978   Duméry, Henry. "Review of *Péguy entre Jaurès, Bergson et l'église* by André Robinet." *Études Philosophiques*, 24, No. 2, 1969, 259. The reviewer concludes: "Ouvrage pour lecteurs qui consentent à se laisser bousculer."

4979   Ebacher, Roger. "Existence historique et temporalité selon Bergson." *Laval Théologique et Philosophique*, 25, No. 2, 1969, 208-233.

4980   Foulquie, P. "Étude de texte." *École des Lettres*, 2e cycle, 60, No. 17, 1969, 901-902. The author descants on the relations between science and philosophy in Bergson. (See *Index Analytique*, 4, 1969, A-26.)

4981   Gagey, Jacques. *Gaston Bachelard ou la conversion à l'imaginaire*. Paris: Rivière et Cie., 1969, 303.

4982   German, Terence Joseph. "Bergson's Individual-Communal Morality." Diss., St. Louis, 1969.

4983   Gillouin, René. "Les Dernières Années d'un sage: Bergson vivant." *Ecrits de Paris*, No. 279, mars 1969, 55-62.

4984   Gillouin, René. "Un Humaniste de notre temps." *Ecrits de Paris*, No. 279, février 1969, 48-57.

4985 Goldschmidt, Victor. "Le Vide pythagoréan et le nombre chez Bergson." *Revue Philosophique de la France et de l'Etranger*, 94, No. 2, 1969, 259-266.

4986 Gouhier, Henri. "Bergson et Claudel." in *Entretiens sur Paul Claudel*. Eds. Georges Cattaui et Jacques Madaule. Paris, La Haye: Mouton, 1969, 135-140. (Décades du Centre culturel international de Cerisy-la-Salle, N.S. 11)

4987 Goyard-Fabre, Simon. "Trois thèses de doctorat sur Bergson." *École des Lettres*, 2ᵉ cycle, 61, No. 7, 1969, 29-30.

4988 Guillaume, Henri. "Face à Juarès, Bergson et l'Eglise: Peu à peu, Péguy s'éclaire." *Le Monde des Livres*, No. 7482, ler février 1969, 1-2.

4989 Guisan, Gilbert, *et al.*, Eds. "Hommage à Arnold Reymond, 1874-1958." *Etudes de Lettres*, 3e Sér., 11, 1969, 74-126.

4990 Guitton, Jean. *Profils parallèles*. Paris: Fayard, 1969, 496. Pierre Teilhard de Chardin and Bergson are discussed on pp. 401-457.

4991 Gunter, Pete Addison Yancey, Ed. and Trans. *Bergson and the Evolution of Physics*. Knoxville, Tennessee: University of Tennessee Press, 1969, 348. This is a collection of essays concerning Bergson's philosophy of physics. It is introduced by the editor's essay on Bergson's philosophical method, which, it is argued, is *pro* and not *anti*-scientific.

4992 Janicaud, Dominique. *Une Généalogie du spiritualisme français: Aux Sources du bergsonisme: Ravaisson et la métaphysique*. The Hague: Martinus Nijhoff, 1969, 276. This excellent study traces the sources of Bergson's thought in Ravaisson. A bibliography occurs on pp. 277-285.

4993 Karczewska-Markiewicz, Zofia. "Roman-autoportrait: Eléments bergsoniens dans *Jean Christophe*." *Zagadnienia rodzajow literackich*, 21, 1969, 100-123. A résumé of this article, is given, in Polish, on pp. 124-125.

4994 Konczewski, C. "La Pensée inverbale ralentie et accélérée (De la mémoire créatrice)." *Revue de Métaphysique et de Morale*, 74, No. 1, Janvier-Mars 1969, 91-105. The author, whose ideas and terminology are Bergsonian (though he cites Bergson only twice), explores the relationships between memory, personal duration and creativity. All memories, he holds, are preserved, though most are necessarily forgotten. The perpetual reorganization which goes on among our memories is a necessary part of our personal and intellectual autobiography, making possible our personal and intellectual creativity, which are an expression of our intuition.

4995 Lacroix, Jean. "Henri Bergson." *Le Monde*, No. 1102, 4-10 décembre 1969, 11.

4996 Lebrec, Jean. *Joseph Malègue romancier et penseur: Avec des documents idédits*. Paris: Dessain et Tolra, 1969, 462.

4997 Magaña Esquivel, Antonio. "Análisis de conciencia." *Hispano Americana*, 54, No. 1398, 1969, 46. This item concerns Jean Guitton and Emmanuel Mounier.

4998 Malter, R. "Review of *La Perception chez Bergson et chez Merleau-Ponty* by A. Fressin." *Philosophischer Literatur-Anzeiger*, 22, 1969, 162-167.

4999 Martin, A. "Review of *Péguy entre Jaurès, Bergson et l'église* by André Robinet." *Feuillets Mensuels d'Informations de l'Amitié Charles Péguy*, No. 154, 1969, 41-45.

5000 May, William Eugene. "The Reality of Matter in the Philosophy of Henri Bergson." Diss. Marquette. *Dissertation Abstracts*, 29, No. 9, March 1969, 3184A. (Cf.

the author, 1970.)

5001   Milner, G. B. "Siamese Twins, Birds and the Double Helix." *Man: The Journal of the Royal Anthropological Institute*, N.S. 4, No. 1, March 1969, 5-23. The author demonstrates that Bergson's concept of intuition (which he interprets as as aesthetic, rather than an emotional or an intellectual faculty) can be used to account for data investigated by anthropologists. Intuition allows "primitive" societies to produce symbols in which "the demands of both emotion and intellect seem to be integrated, harmonized, and expressed to the complete and enduring satisfaction not only of a given individual, but in the case of religious and political symbols, of entire social groups." (p. 6) The author defends his avowedly Bergsonian standpoint against Raymond Firth, who wishes to take "emotional" factors into account in anthropological explanation, and Claude Lévi-Strauss, who utilizes an exclusively intellectual approach.

5002   Montiero Pacheco, Maria Cândida de Costa Reis. "A dimensão temporal definidora duma antropologia em S. Grégorio de Nissa e Bergson." *Revista Portuguesa de Filosofia*, 25, Nos. 3-4, 1969, 153-164.

5003   Oppler, Ellen Charlotte. "Fauvism Reexamined." Diss. Columbia, 1969, 465. Bergson's philosophy, among many other cultural trends, is explored here for its influence on Fauvism. Cf. *Dissertation Abstracts International*, 33, No. 4, 1972, 1616A.

5004   Osorio Osorio, Alberto. "Ideas sobre el humanismo espiritualista de Bergson." *Lotería*, 14, No. 161, 1969, 19-21.

5005   Paquette, Guy. "Le Fait social chez Bergson." Diss., Paris, 1969, 394.

5006   Pariente, Jean-Claude. "Bergson et Wittgenstein, discussion" *Revue Internationale de Philosophie*, 23, Nos. 88-89, 1969, 183-204. Cf. the author, 1973.

5007   Quoniam, Théodore. "Review of *La Conscience de la durée et le concept de temps* by Jean Theau." *Études Philosophiques*, 24, No. 3, 1969, 425-426.

5008   Quoniam, Théodore. "Review of *La Critique bergsonienne du concept* by Theau." *Études Philosophiques*, 24, No. 3, 1969, 424-425.

5009   Quoniam, Théodore. "Review of *Péguy entre Jaurès, Bergson et l'église* by André Robinet." *Études Philosophiques*, 24, No. 2, 1969, 259-260.

5010   Quoniam, Théodore. "Review of *La Spiritualité de Bergson* by René Violette." *Études Philosophiques*, 24, No. 3, 1969, 426-427.

5011   Rocheblave-Spenlé, Anne-Marie. *La Notion de rôle en psychologie sociale.* 2nd ed. Paris: *Presses Universitaires de France*, 1969, 534. Bergson is classed among the French precursors of the study of social roles on pp. 19-20. On pp. 22-23 Bergson's influence on Charles Blondel's concept of social role is outlined. Bergson's influence on the social psychology of Pierre Janet is examined within pp. 24-30; his influence on Max Scheler on p. 31. Cf. also pp. 91-92.

5012   Ross, Stephen D. *Literature and Philosophy: An Analysis of the Philosophical Novel.* New York: Appleton-Century-Crofts, 1969, 221.

5013   Rotenstreich, Nathan. "The Changing Concept of Intuition and Bergson." *Iyyun*, 20, January-October 1969, 1-13. This article is in Hebrew.

5014   Rózza, E. "Observations sur l'éthique de Henri Bergson." *Studia Universitatis Babes-Bolyai*, 14, 1969, philosophy section, 63-78.

5015 Ruggiero, Guido de. "The Bergsonian School." In *Modern Philosophy*. Trans. A. Howard Hannay and R. G. Collingwood. Westport, Connecticut: Greenwood Press, 1969, 181-184. The author mentions Édouard Le Roy and Georges Rémacle as followers of Bergson. He passes them off as naive primitives. All fail to transcend a naturalistic conception of fact.

5016 Ruggiero, Guido de. "The Philosophy of Intuition: Bergson." In *Modern Philosophy*. Trans. A. Howard Hannay and R. G. Collingwood. Westport, Connecticut: Greenwood Press, 1969, 171-181. The author criticizes Bergson's philosophy for its reliance on intuition, which is described as an insufficiently dialectical approach to reality: "Now, intuition presupposes its object and does not create it: hence thought is for Bergson a mere observing..." (p. 180)

5017 Saigusa, Mitsuyoshi. "Henri Bergson and Buddhist Thought." Trans. J. R. McEwan. *Philosophical Studies of Japan*, 9, 1969, 79-102.

5018 Sipfle, David A. "Henri Bergson and the Epochal Theory of Time." *Bergson and the Evolution of Physics*. Ed. and Trans. with Intro. P. A. Y. Gunter, 275-294. Contrary to general opinion, the author holds, Bergson held the view that time (i.e., "durée") is epochal and occurs in quasi-discontinuous rhythms or pulsations. This is a penetrating and important study.

5019 Spiegelberg, Herbert. *The Phenomenological Movement: A Historical Introduction*. 2nd Ed. Vol. I. The Hague: Martinus Nijhoff, 1969, 391. For accounts of Bergson's influence on Max Scheler, Cf. pp. 235-236, 240, 242, 265. The author notes that Heidegger rejects Bergson's ideas "with almost surprising violence." (p. 336) Cf. also 226.

5020 Spiegelberg, Herbert. *The Phenomenological Movement: A Historical Introduction*. 2nd Ed. Vol. 2. The Hague: Martinus Nijhoff, 1969, 374. On pp. 398-399 the author notes the role of Bergsonism in the introduction of phenomenology into France. Cf. p. 402 for Bergson's relations with Max Scheler. Cf. pp. 105, 430, 461-462 for Bergson's ideas and the philosophies of E. Minkowski, G. Marcel, and J. P. Sartre respectively.

5021 Theau, Jean. *La Conscience de la durée et le concept du temps*. Toulouse: Privat, 1969, 311. The author wishes to deny Bergson's dichotomy of "real duration" (with its dynamic creativity) and "homogeneous time" (with its mechanical repetition). This denial, though it involves going beyond Bergson's metaphysics, remains faithful to his basic aim, that of founding a "philosophy of creation."

5022 Troland, Leonard T. *The Principles of Psychophysiology: A Survey of Modern Scientific Psychology*, Vol. 1. *The Problems of Psychology and Perception*. New York: Greenwood Press, 1969, 429. This is a reprint of the 1929 first edition. The author feels obliged to refute or dismiss Bergson's philosophy at several points, as simply an obstacle to scientific psychology. He provides, thus, examples of classic misunderstandings of Bergson's thought. Cf. esp. 197f.

5023 Wall, Bernard. *Headlong into Change: An Autobiography and a Memoir of Ideas Since the Thirties*. London: Harvill Press, 1969, 288. P. Claudel, A. Gide, P. Desjardins, Ch. Du Bos, J. Maritain, P. Valéry, and Bergson are discussed in this book.

1970

5024 Alain. *Propos 1906-1936*. Vol. 2, Ed. S. S. de Sacy. Paris: Gallimard, 1970, 1408.

5025 Barthélémy-Madaule, Madeleine. *Bergson und Teilhard de Chardin: Die Anfänge einer neuen Welterkenntnis.* Trans. L. Hafliger. Olten and Freiburg im Breisgau: Walter, 1970, 783.

5026 "Review of *Bergson and the Evolution of Physics.* Ed. P. A. Y. Gunter." *Choice,* 7, No. 7, September 1970, 887.

5027 "Review of *Bergson and the Evolution of Physics* by P. A. Y. Gunter." *Science Books,* 6, No. 1, 1970, 28.

5028 "Bergson-Péguy Correspondence (1902-1914). Présentations et commentaires par Auguste Martin." *Amitié Charles Péguy. Feuillets Mensuels,* No. 155, 1970, 7-57.

5029 Bernard-Maître, Henri. "Autour de la pensée d'Henri Bergson." *Revue de Synthèse,* 91, No. 57-58, janvier-juin 1970, 133-135.

5030 Bjelland, Andrew George. "The Foundations of Bergson's Metaphysics: An Essay on Henri Bergson's Early Metaphysical Dualism." Diss. Saint Louis 1970, 433. The author examines the "dialectical character of Bergsonian metaphysics" within the context of Bergson's mind-body dualism. Central to the understanding of Bergson's philosophy is his description of the "endosmotic tension" between two tendentially differentiated aspects of experience, the awareness of heterogeneous duration and the concept of homogeneous space. These notions, developed originally in *Time and Free Will,* are elaborated further in *Matter and Memory,* where the notions of spirit and matter are reformulated as modes of duration, the reality of spirit is stressed, and an account is presented of "the on-going interpenetration of the two." In the concluding chapter the author provides a critical exposition of Bergson's mitigation of the concepts of traditional dualism. (See *Dissertation Abstracts International,* 31, Nos. 7-8, 1971, 4212A.)

5031 Califano, Joseph J. "Bergson's Concept of Motion." *Thomist,* 34, No. 4, 1970, 555-567. The author argues that Bergson's concept of motion is distinct from his concept of duration and close to that of Aquinas.

5032 Carr, Herbert Wildon. *Henri Bergson: The Philosophy of Change.* 1912; rpt. Port Washington, New York: Kennikat, 1970, 91.

5033 Chahine, Osman Eissa. *La Durée chez Bergson.* Publié sous l'égide de Structures nouvelles; diffusion: Paris: H. Boucher, 1970, 104.

5034 Chambers, Connor John. "Henri Bergson and the Reality of the Physical World." Diss. Saint Louis 1970, 212. The author wishes to quarrel with those who conceive of Bergson's physical universe as "richly fluid," i.e., as embodying creative duration. Bergson's ultimate refusal to move beyond a temporal standpoint, his methodological identification of physics with mathematics, his confinement of the physicist within a psychologistic perspective prevent him from doing justice to physical reality. The author concludes with the suggestion that, had Bergson realized the full usefulness of his notion of extension and allowed the physicist greater methodological independence, his "common frontier" of metaphysics and science could have been much more adequately described. In particular, it would have been possible to do justice to the "real spatial diversity of the physical universe." (See *Dissertation Abstracts International,* 31, Nos. 7-8, 1971, 4231A.)

5035 Chandra, S. Subhash. "Henri Bergson's Approach to Freedom." *Aryan Path,* 41, No. 1, 1970, 12-18.

5036   Chandra, Subhash. "Intuition et instinct chez Schopenhauer et Bergson." *Thèse univ. Lettres*. Paris, 1970, 249pp.

5037   Chevalier, Jacques. *Henri Bergson*. Auth. trans. Lilian A. Clare. 1928; rpt. Freeport, N. Y.: Books for Libraries Press, 1970, xxi, 351.

5038   Christensen, M. T. "L'humour Gidien dans *Les Caves du Vatican*." *Theoria*, 34, 1970, 57-76.

5039   Clancy, Bonnie Ruth Aarons. "Thought at an Impasse: A Case Study of Philosophical Mysticism." Diss. Michigan, 1971, 169. The author concludes: "Hence the central problem generated by Bergson's irrationalist metaphysics is the problem of expressing the results of intuition. This problem ("the translation problem" as we term it) attends each one of Bergson's theses and continually threatens to condemn him to silence. Unless a justification for philosophical discourse can be found, Bergson's use of language will be inconsistent with his critique. To seek a way out of the translation problem, we propose that a role be assigned to language consistent with its constraints." *Dissertation Abstracts International*, 32, No. 7, 1972, 4059-4060A.

5040   Coates, Wilson Havelock, and White, Hayden V. *Since the French Revolution*. Vol. II of *The Ordeal of Liberal Humanism: An Intellectual History of Western Europe*. New York: McGraw-Hill, 1970, 499. The author notes the influence of the physics of Clerk Maxwell on the thought of E. Mach, B. Croce, Bergson, S. Alexander, and A. N. Whitehead on p. 121. On pp. 278 and 279 he relates the thought of Freud to that of both W. Dilthey and Bergson. The author compares the thought of Bergson with that of B.Croce on pp. 285, 287, and 288. On pp. 417-418 he notes Bergson's influence on Georges Sorel. On p. 449 he states, "Bergson proved in the end to be irrelevant if not hostile to liberal humanism..." On pp. 270-278 the author examines Bergson's philosophy, treating Bergson as the closest French counterpart to German thinkers like W. Dilthey and M. Weber.

5041   Corvez, M. "Bulletin de philosophie: Bergson. Blondel. Sciences humaines, structuralisme." *Revue Thomiste*, 70, No. 2, 1970, 335-343.

5042   Costa de Beauregard, Olivier. "On Time, Information and Life." In *Evolution in Perspective: Commentaries in Honor of Pierre Lecomte du Noüy*. Eds. George N. Schuster and Ralph E. Thorson. Notre Dame and London: University of Notre Dame Press, 1970, 193-210. The author considers, from a physicist's viewpoint, the two fundamental concepts of time, i.e., time as a measurable magnitude and time as irreversible. Concepts of temporal irreversibility have, the author believes, close ties to metaphysics, especially with questions of finalism and causality. The world of non-living matter (the "Carnot" world) contrasts with the world of living things. The Carnot world allows prediction but not retrodiction. Cf. p. 209.

5043   Cristiani, Aldo Horacio. "Duración y tiempo en Bergson." *Cuadernos de Filosofía*, 10, No. 1, 1970, 121-135. This is a discussion of Bergson's theory of duration, with special reference to Einstein's theory of relativity.

5044   Curtis, Charles J. *Contemporary Protestant Thought*. New York: Bruce Publishing Company, 1970. On pp. 58-59 the author notes Bergson's influence on Alfred North Whitehead's *Process and Reality*; on p. 64 he notes the influence of Bergson on Whitehead and Pierre Teilhard de Chardin, especially on the latter's concept of evolutionary energy; on pp. 76 and 81 he again notes Bergson's influence on Teilhard de Chardin.

5045   De Burgh, William George. *From Morality to Religion*. The Gifford Lectures, 1938. 1938; rpt. Port Washington, New York: Kennikat Press, 1970, xxii, 352.

5046   "Doctoral Dissertations, 1970." *Review of Metaphysics*, 24, No. 1, September 1970, 190.

5047   Dyserinck, Hugo. *Graf Hermann Keyserling und Frankreich, Ein Kapitel deutsch-französischer Geistesbeziehungen im XX. Jahrhundert*. Bonn: H. Bouvier & Co., 1970, 157. This book examines G. H. Keyserling's relations with several French thinkers during the years 1925 and 1935, including Henri Bergson.

5048   Ellenberger, Henri F. *The Discovery of the Unconscious*. New York: Basic Books, 1970, 932. Bergson's knowledge of hypnotism is discussed on p. 168; his critique of thought-reading under hypnosis on p. 172; his similarities with Von Schubert on p. 262; Bergson's prophecies on research into the unconscious mind on p. 321; his relationships with Pierre Janet on pp. 336, 354-355, 376, 394, and 400; his relationships with Alfred Binet on p. 355; his similarities to Alfred Adler on p. 624; his relationship to Paul Haberlin on p. 623; and his relations with C. G. Jung on p. 818. For other references see the index.

5049   *Etudes Bergsoniennes*. Paris: Presses Universitaires de France, 1970, Vol. 9, 232. Bergson's mission to Spain in 1916, talks given in Madrid entitled "L'Ame humaine" and "La Personnalité" are presented here, along with materials pertaining to Bergson and Charles Du Bos.

5050   Evans-Pritchard, E. E. "Bergson and Witchcraft." *Man*, N.S. 5, No. 1, March 1970, p. 131. This is a reply to Professor Roberto Da Matta's letter in a previous edition of *Man* (N.S. Vol. 4, pp, 455-45). Professor Da Matta had noted the similarity of what Professor Evans-Pritchard had written concerning primitive notions of causality, in his *Witchcraft, Oracles and Magic Among the Azande* (1937) to what Bergson had written in *The Two Sources* (1932). Professor Evans-Pritchard agrees on the similarity in question and is happy to find himself in such eminent company. However, his ideas had already been published in 1929.

5051   Filali-Ansary, Mohammed Abdou. "La Notion d'intuition chez Spinoza et chez Bergson." Thèse. Univ. Dijon. Lettres, 1970, 301.

5052   Fraisse, Simone. "Review of *Péguy entre Juarès et l'église* by André Robinet." *Revue d'Histoire Littéraire de la France*, 70e Année, No. 1, 1970, 153-155.

5053   Freire, Antonio. "O pensamento de deus de Nikos Kazantzakis." *Revista Portuguesa de Filosofia*, 26, No. 1, 1970, 92-109.

5054   Gaidenko, P. P. "Bergson, Henri." *Great Soviet Encyclopedia*, Vol. 3, 190-191.

5055   Gallagher, Idella J. *Morality in Evolution: The Moral Philosophy of Henri Bergson*. The Hague: Martinus Nijhoff, 1970, 112.

5056   Gidley, N. "One Continuous Force: Notes on Faulkner's Extra-Literary Reading." *Mississippi Quarterly*, 23, No. 3, 1970, 299-314.

5057   Gobar, Ash. "The Phenomenology of William James." *Proceedings of the American Philosophical Society*, 114, No. 4, August 20, 1970, 294-309. The author describes William James as an indigenous American thinker whose philosophy provides a native source of phenonemology. On p. 304, he cites with approval a passage from Bergson's introduction to the French translation of James' *Prag-*

matism, in which Bergson describes the pragmatist *via* the metaphor of a sailboat. A steamboat, Bergson holds, proceeds by its internal combustion engine, while a sailboat, at least in part, is driven by winds external to itself. The true pragmatist steers a sailboat, not a steamboat; he is constrained by a real world with which he is in contact.

5058   Gouhier, Henri. "Introduction to a Debate on Philosophical Exigence." In *Evolution in Perspective: Commentaries in Honor of Pierre Lecomte du Noüy*. Ed. George N. Schuster and Ralph E. Thorson. Notre Dame and London: University of Notre Dame Press, 1970, 123-131.

5059   Grieder, Jerome B. *Hu Shih and the Chinese Renaissance: Liberalism and the Chinese Revolution, 1917-1937*. Cambridge, Massachusetts: Harvard University Press, 1970, 420. Bergson is mentioned in this study of the Chinese response to western ideas on pp. 133, 138, 157, 158, and 167. Concerning the "neot-raditionalist" Liang Ch'i-ch'ao, the author states on p. 133, "Liang turned to Bergson with particular enthusiasm, for he discovered in the Bergsonian idea of 'creative evolution' a means of salvaging the faith in evolutionary progress that had lain close to his heart since the early days of his association with K'ang Yu-wei." On pp. 156-157 he asserts, "Liang Ch'i-ch'ao, though he had at best a traveler's acquaintance with Europe, had spent time there on several occasions since the turn of the century, and in the course of his tour in 1919 he had called upon Bergson and Eucken. A few years earlier Chang Chun-mai had studied under both men."

5060   Gunter, Pete Addison Yancey. "The Heuristic Force of *Creative Evolution*." *Southwest Journal of Philosophy*, 1, No. 3, 1970, 111-118. The author argues that Bergson's biological theories remain potentially fruitful and suggest mathematical interpretations of evolutionary processes. (Cf. Marcus Ford, 1982.)

5061   Halda, Bernard. "Bergson et Du Bos." *Etudes Bergsoniennes*, 9, 1970, 157-200.

5062   Hasley, Louis. "Humor in Literature: a Definition." *The CEA Critic*, 32, No. 5, February 1970, 10-11.

5063   Heaton, David M. "Two French Philosophical Sources of T. W. Hulme's Imagism." *Dissertation Abstracts International*, 31, 1970, 759A.

5064   Jourdan-Laforte, Maurice. "Les Éléments anthropologiques de la pensée bergsonienne." *Thèse*, 3ᵉ cycle. Lettres. Paris. 1970, 275.

5065   Kayatta, George Nayef. "Comic Elements in Montaigne's Essays in the Light of Bergson's *Le Rire*." Diss. Case Western Reserve 1970, 329. The author uses Bergson's theory of comedy to analyze the "nature, purpose, span and expression" of the comic elements in Montaigne's *Essays*. Like Bergson, Montaigne views the universe as in constant flux and unpredictable. This similarity provides a basis for the comparison of Montaigne's views with Bergson's notion that the comic is simply a form of mechanization imposed on the living. The author examines both Montaigne's use of the simpler and the more complex forms of the comic. (See *Dissertation Abstracts International*, 32, No. 1, 1971, 408A.)

5066   Kremer-Marietti, Angèle. "Bibliographie: Une Idéologie bergsonienne." *Etudes Bergsoniennes*, 9, 1970, 209-227.

5067   Lachenmeyer, Charles W. "Experimentation: A Misunderstood Methodology in Psychological and Socio-Psychological Research." *American Psychologist*, 25, No. 7, July, 1970, 617-624. The author argues against a "narrow" concept of experimentation prevalent in the behavioral sciences, and offers in its place a broader view. "On p. 620 he notes Bergson's assertion (in *Duration and Simultaneity*) that in physics Einstein's and Maxwell-Lorenz's relativity theories exist side by side. He also cites Herbert Dingle's introduction to the English translation of *Duration and Simultaneity* as proof that the Michelson-Morley experiment may not have been the *experimention crucis* it is supposed to have been. He concludes: "...the social scientific conceptualization of experimentation as a monolithic entity is grossly over simplified." (p. 620)

5068   Le Senne, René. *Introduction à la philosophie*. Paris: Presses Universitaires de France, 1970, 604. "Cinquième édition augmentée et mise au jour par Edouard Morot-sir et Paule Levert." Chapter three, "L'Intuitionisme bergsonien," appears on pp. 178-223.

5069   Maire, Gilbert. "Rencontre de Bergson." *Etudes Bergsoniennes*, 9, 1970, 201-208.

5070   Martin, Auguste. "Bergson-Péguy." *Feuillets de L'Amitié Charles Péguy*, No. 155, Janvier, 1970, 5-57. This correspondence between and concerning Bergson and Péguy was published originally in *Les Études bergsoniennes*, 8, 1968.

5071   Martin, Wallace. "The Sources of the Imagist Aesthetic." *Proceedings of the Modern Language Association*, 85, No. 2, 1970, 196-204.

5072   Mauriac, François. *Le Dernier Bloc-notes, 1968-1970*. Paris: Flammarion, 1970, 354. This study contains passages concerning Bergson, along with passages relating to many other literary and philosophical figures.

5073   May, William Eugene. "The Reality of Matter in the Metaphysics of Bergson." *International Philosophical Quarterly*, 10, No. 4, 1970, 611-642. The author holds that a detailed examination of both Bergson's text and his Plotinian heritage reveals that matter, though entirely dependent on spirit in order to endure, is real in the sense that it is an authentic meontic principle within enduring principles.

5074   McDermott, Robert. "The Religion Game: Some Family Resemblances." *Journal of the American Academy of Religion*, 38, No. 4, 1970, 390-400. The author holds that the search for the "illusive essence of religion" should give way to the description of religion "in terms of how the game is played." (p. 391) He cites William James' *The Varieties of Religious Experience* and Bergson's *The Two Sources* as investigations which conform to this latter approach. Cf. pp. 400-401.

5075   Melges, Frederick T,; Tinklenberg, Jared R.; Hollister, Leo E.; and Gillespie, Hamp K. "Temporal Disintegration and Depersonalization During Marihuana Intoxication." *Archives of General Psychiatry*, 23, No. 3, September 1970, 204-210. The authors report the statements of marihuana users concerning "temporal disintegration" and "depersonalization". By temporal disintegration the authors mean mental indcoordination, in which "the individual had difficulty in retaining, coordinating, and serially indexing those memories, perceptions, and expectations that are relevant to the goal he is pursuing." (p. 204) By depersonalization they mean "the experience of the self as strange und unreal." (p. 204) Experiments with eight subjects produced the following results: 1. Marihuana ingestion produces pronounced temporal disintegration. 2. Evidence indicates that temporal disintegration and depersonalization are closely linked. 3. Patterns of emotive response vary widely among individuals. The authors cite Eugène

Minkowski's "I-here-now" distinction and quote a statement of Bergson's on the "continuous progress of the past which gnaws into the future"—the sense of which is lost to marihuana users.

5076   Melges, Frederick T.; Tinklenberg, Jared R.; Hollister, Leo E.; and Gillespie, Hamp K. "Marihuana and Temporal Disintegration." *Science*, 168, No. 3935, May 20, 1970, 1118-1120.

5077   Metzel, Nancy. "Translator's Introduction," *Lived Time: Phenomenological and Psychopathological Studies* by Eugène Minkowski. Evanston, Illinois: Northwestern University Press, 1970, xv-xxxvi. In this essay Minkowski's debt to Henri Bergson as well as his criticisms of Bergson are examined. Bergson, according to Minkowski, failed to give sufficient attention to "lived space." In real life, time and space are never sharply separated.

5078   Milet, Jean. *Gabriel Tarde et la philosophie de l'histoire*. Paris: Vrin, 1970, 410. For the relations between Tarde and Bergson, see especially pp. 386-389 and 391.

5079   Minkowski, Eugéne. *Lived Time: Phenomenological and Psychological Studies*. Trans. Nancy Metzel. Evanston, Illinois: Northwestern University Press, 1970, 455. This is an application of Bergsonian ideas—with certain additional insights—to the problems of psychopathology.

5080   Moed, H. K. W. "Constancy and Contrast, IIIc." *Acta Psychologica*, 34, No. 4, 1970, 525-645. Cf. pp. 604-605.

5081   Moutsopoulos, E. "La Critique du platonisme chez Bergson." *Etudes Bergsoniennes*, 9, 1970, 123-156.

5082   Muraret, Ion. "Paul Valéry, Henri Bergson et Georges Opresco la liga natiunilor." *Analele Universitătii Bucuresti. Literatură Universală şi comparată*, 19, No. 1, 1970, 171-183. A resume of this article is given here on p. 183 under the title "L'Activité de Paul Valéry, de Henri Bergson et de Georges Opresco à la Société des Nations."

5083   Muratore, Margherita. "Review of *Péguy entre Juarès, Bergson et l'église* by André Robinet." *Studi francesi*, No. 40, 1970, 119-121.

5084   Muret, T. "L'Intuition comme principe d'une raison concrété et d'une philosophie de l'histoire dans l'oeuvre de Bergson." Diss., Paris, 1970.

5085   Nédoncelle, Maurice. "Quelques Aspects de la causalité chez Bergson." *Explorations personnalistes*. Paris: Aubier Montaigne, 1970, 243-249. This article appeard originally in *Actes du Xe Congrès des Sociétés de Philosophie de Langue Française* (Congrès Bergson), 1959.

5086   Oger, Erik. "Review of *L'Idée de vie chez Bergson et la critique de la métaphysique* by Pierre Trotignon." *Tijdschrift Voor Filosofie*, 32, No. 2, 1970, 342-345.

5087   Oulmont, Charles. *En écoutant et en lisant Bergson: Souvenirs personnels*. Strasbourg: Istra, 1970, 42. (Coll. des oeuvres complétes de Ch. Oulmont, No. 6)

5088   Palacios, Juan-Miguel. "L'Accueil fait à Bergson par la presse espagnole." *Etudes Bergsoniennes*, 9, 1970, 114-121. This essay describes Bergson's reception by the Spanish press during his mission to Spain in 1916.

5089   Palacios, Juan-Miguel. "Circonstances du voyage espagnol." Trans. Michel Gauthier. *Etudes Bergsoniennes*, 9, 1970, 7-10.

5090   Palacios, Juan-Miguel. "Traductions en espagnol d'oeuvres d'Henri Bergson." *Etudes Bergsoniennes*, 9, 1970, 122. This is a bibliography of the Spanish translations of Bergson's writings.

5091 Pascal, Georges. *L'Idée de philosophie chez Alain*. Paris: Bordas, 1970, 414. (Coll. Études supérieures, serie verte)

5092 Patel, Aster Mira Verma. "Étude comparée des philosophies de Sri Aurobindo et de Bergson." Diss. Paris 1970, vii, 453.

5093 Philonenko, Alexis. "Bergson et la philosophie: Etude critique sur l'interprétation de P. Trotignon." *Archives de Philosophie*, 33, No. 1, 1970, 73-95. This is a study of P. Trotignon's *L'Idée de vie chez Bergson et la critique de la métaphysique*.

5094 Piclin, Michel. "Angoisse et espérance dans le bergsonisme, de Bergson à l'existentialisme." Diss. Paris 1970, 247. This is a "thèse complementaire."

5095 Piclin, Michel. "Bergson et la transcendance." *Revue Philosophique de la France et de l'Etranger*, 95, No. 4, 1970, 445-469. This article considers Bergson's concept of the transcendance of God, contrasting Bergson's position with that of classical Christian theology. The transcendance of God, according to Bergson, is a transcendence "vis a tergo." The unity of God is situated behind us, in the past, not in the future.

5096 Prajs, Lazare. *Péguy et Israël*. Intro. Pierre Moreau. Paris: Nizet, 1970, 217.

5097 Pucciarelli, Eugenio. "Dos actides frente al tiempo." *Cuadernos de filosofía*, 10, No. 1, enero-junio 1970, 7-48. This article considers the relationship between time and man's participation in eternity. Bergson, G. Bachelard, L. Lavelle, J. Guitton, and several other philosophers are discussed.

5098 Pucciarelli, Eugenio. *El tiempo en la filosofia actual*. Universidad de Buenos Aires: Facultad de Filosofía y Letras, 1970, 47.

5099 Robinet, André. *Bergson et les métamorphoses de la durée*. 3rd ed. Paris: Seghers, 1970, 191. (Philosophes de tous les temps, No. 21)

5100 Schlagel, Richard H. "Review of *Bergson and the Evolution of Physics*, Ed. and Trans. with Intro. P. A. Y. Gunter." *Isis*, 61, No. 4, 1970, 548-549.

5101 Schmidt-Radefelt, Jurgen. *Paul Valéry linguiste dans les Cahiers*. Paris: Edit. Klincksieck, 1970, 262. (Bibliotheque française et romane. Série C: Études littéraires, 27) The author deals especially with Bergson, S. Mallarmé, A. Rimbaud and F. de Saussure.

5102 Sgro, Serafino. *La filosofia di E. Bergson e le sue implicanze pedagogiche*. Regio, Calabria: Leo, 1970, 150.

5103 Smith, Michael. "Considering a Poetic." *Lace Curtain*, No. 3, Summer 1970, 45-50. The author deals with M. Proust, S. Beckett, and Bergson.

5104 Solomon, Joseph. *Bergson*. 1911 rpt. Port Washington, New York, and London: Kennikat Press, 1970, 128.

5105 Sulzberger, Cyrus L. "Entretiens avec le général de Gaulle: II. De Bergson à Staline." *Le Monde*, No. 8003, 7 octobre 1970, 10.

5106 Szathmary, Arthur. "Bergson, Henri (1859-1941)." *Encyclopedia Americana* Vol. 3, 1970, 580-582.

5107 Tadié, Jean-Yves. *Introduction à la vie littéraire du XIXe siècle*. Paris et Montréal: Bordas, 1970, 146. This study in literary history contains references to Bergson as well as to many other literary and political personages.

5108 Terzi, Carlo. "Henri Gouhier: *Bergson e il Cristo del Vangeli.*" *Filosofia*, Anno 21, No. 4, ottobre 1970, 573-576. This is a review.

5109 Torre, Guillermo de. *Doctrina y estetica literaria.* Madrid: Edic. Guadarrama, 1970, 810.

5110 Vansina, F. "Review of Vol. 8, *Les Études bergsoniennes.*" *Tijdschrift Voor Filosofie*, 32, No. 4, 1970, 794.

5111 "Le Voyage espagnol d'Henri Bergson (avril-mai 1916): Documents rassemblés par Juan-Miguel Palacios: Traduction Michel Gauthier." *Etudes Bergsoniennes*, 9, 1970, 7-122.

5112 Weiss, Donald H. "Modern Materialism and the Evolution of Self-Consciousness." *Southwestern Journal of Philosophy*, 1, No. 3, 1970, 38-44. On pp. 39-40 the author uses Bergson's *Creative Evolution* as an aid in understanding "self-directed evolution."

5113 Wickham, Harvey. *The Unrealists: James, Bergson, Santayana, Einstein, Bertrand Russell, John Dewey, Alexander, and Whitehead.* 1930; rpt. Freeport, New York: Books for Libraries, 1970, 314.

5114 Wylie, Laurence and Begue, Armand, in collaboration with Begue, Louise. *Les Français.* Englewood Cliffs, New Jersey: Prentice-Hall, Inc., 1970, 444. The authors discuss Bergson's concept of laughter and the comedies of Molière on pp. 392-394, 397, and 402.

5115 Yamaguchi, Minoro. *The Intuition of Zen and Bergson: Comparative intellectual approach to Zen: Reason of divergences between East and West.* Tokyo: Enderle Bookstore, 1970, 235. The author concludes that Bergson has created a synthesis of Eastern ("introverted") and Western ("extroverted") thought.

5116 Zambelloni, Franco. "Bergson e la filosofia italiana (1900-1915)." *Filosofia*, Anno 21, No. 3, luglio 1970, 331-360. The author discusses the reception of Bergson's thought in Italy during the first years of this century. In general Bergson's thought was not understood correctly and as a whole. Papini and Prezzolini described Bergson's thought as a "magical pragmatism." Croce used Bergson against the positivists.

1971

5117 "Against Rationalism." *London Times Literary Supplement*, No. 3610, May 7, 1971, 530. This is a review of *Bergson and the Evolution of Physics*, Ed. P. A. Y. Gunter.

5118 Aigrisse, Gilbert. "10. Une Manière de narcissisme." In *Les Critiques de notre temps et Valéry.* Ed. Jean Bellemin-Noël. Paris: Éd. Garnier Frères, 1971, 119-132.

5119 Amado Lévy-Valensi, Elaine. "Review of *Bergson éducateur* by R. M. Mossé-Bastide." *Revue Philosophique de la France et de l'Etranger*, 161, No. 4, 1971, 446-447.

5120 Amado Lévy-Valensi, E. "Review of *Écrits et paroles* by Henri Bergson." *Revue Philosophique de la France et de l'Étranger*, 161, No. 4, 1971, 442-443.

5121 Barlow, Michel. *Le Socialisme d'Emmanuel Mounier.* Toulouse: Privat, 1971, 174. Bergson and many other French intellectual leaders are mentioned in this study.

5122   Barreau, Hervé. "Pourquoi Bergson s'est-il trompé dans l'interprétation de la théorie de la relativité restreinte?" In *IVe Congrès International de logique, méthodologie et philosophie de la science: Abstracts*. Bucarest: Centre d'Informat. et de Document. des Sciences Politiques et Sociales, 1971, 231-232.

5123   Barthélémy-Madaule, Madeleine. "Review of *Bergson et le Christ des Évangiles* by Henri Gouhier." *Revue Philosophique de la France et de l'Étranger*, 161, No. 4, 1971, 448-451.

5124   Bastaire, Jean. "Sur le livre de André Robinet." *Feuillets de l'Amitié Charles Péguy*, No. 173, 1971, 21-22. This is a review of *Péguy entre Jaurés, Bergson et l'Eglise* by André Robinet.

5125   Beyer, Victor. "En Lisant Charles Oulmont." *Saisons d' Alsace*, No. 38, 1971, 3 (no pagination). This is a review of Oulmont's *En écoutant et en lisant Bergson: Souvenirs personnels*.

5126   Birx, H. James. "Pierre Teilhard de Chardin's Philosophy of Evolution." Diss. New York at Buffalo 1971, 235.

5127   Blanché, Robert. "Review of *Bergson and the Evolution of Physics*. Ed. and Trans. with Intro. P. A. Y. Gunter." *Journal de Psychologie Normale et Pathologique*, 68, No. 1, janvier-mars 1971, 106-107.

5128   Bodenheimer, Edgar. "Philosophical Anthropology and the Law." *California Law Review*, 59, No. 3, May 1971, 653-682. The author argues for the pragmatic value of philosophical anthropology for the "analysis and elucidation" of legal phenomena. He concludes by citing Bergson's test of the "good" society. Having experienced it, would men be willing to return to previous societies?

5129   Brumbaugh, Roberts S. "Cosmography." *Review of Metaphysics*, 25, No. 2, 1971, 337-347. The author seeks "transformation rules" relating basic philosophical systems, rules which may reveal unsuspected isomorphisms between systems, explain past controversies, and suggest supplemental insights from one system to strengthen another. On pp. 345-346 he explores Bergson's contention that his philosophy of duration is an "inverted Platonism". By reversing Plato's index of reality and index of multiplicity one creates a Bergsonian universe; and *vice versa*.

5130   Brun, Jean. "Review of *Une Genealogie du spiritualisme française* by Dominique Janicaud." *Etudes philosophiques*, No. 1, 1971, 125.

5131   Čapek, Milič. *Bergson and Modern Physics*. New York: Humanities Press; Dordrecht, Holland: Reidel Publishing Company, 1971, 414 (Vol. 7, Boston Studies in the Philosophy of Science, Synthese Library). This is the most complete analysis of Bergson's insights into the problems and basic concepts of contemporary physics. It includes analyses of Bergson's biological theory of knowledge, his prophetic insights into quantum physics and contemporary scientific cosmology, his critique of relativity theory. It also contains a concluding section on B. Russell's "hidden bergsonism."

5132   Čapek, Milič. "The Fiction of Instants." *Studium Generale*, 24, No. 1, 1971, 31-43. The author argues that, on the basis of the nature of "phenomenal continua," it is possible to deny the reality of instants without accepting the self-contradictory "atomization" of time.

5133 Caponigri, A. Robert. *Philosophy from the Age of Positivism to the Age of Analysis.* Vol. V of *A History of Western Philosophy.* Notre Dame, Indiana: University of Notre Dame Press, 1971, xv, 365. This work contains a section on Henri Bergson.

5134 Chambers, Connor J. "Henri Bergson, Zenon, y la disensión académica." *Diálogos,* 7, No. 4, 1971, 17-38.

5135 Clark, Ronald W. *Einstein: The Life and Times.* New York: T. Y. Crowell, 1971, 718. On p. 287 the author notes that Bergson attended Einstein's lecture in Paris March 31, 1922; on p. 353 he cites the International Committee on Intellectual Cooperation as Bergson's "brainchild"; on pp. 291-294 he describes Einstein's relations with the Committee; on pp. 355, 359, 360 he cites Bergson's relations to Einstein. On p. 362 he cites Gilbert Murray's statement: "Bergson once said of (Einstein) that he had made discoveries at a greater distance from the ordinary organs of human knowledge than any other man in history."

5136 Cloutier, Paul Philip. "A Bergsonian Analysis of the Humor of Anatole France." Diss. Wisconsin 1971, 592. The author uses the "optic" of Henri Bergson's *Le Rire* to explore the diverse forces constituting the (sadly neglected) "comicality" of Anatole France. The author concludes that France placed great emphasis on the important role played by laughter in human life and lamented the recent demise of laughter under the impact of the new mediocrity. (See *Dissertation Abstracts International,* 32, No. 2, 1971, 911A-912A.)

5137 Davis, William H. "Review of *Bergson and the Evolution of Physics.* Ed. and Trans. P. A. Y. Gunter." *Southern Humanities Review,* 5, No. 1, Winter 1971, 88-89.

5138 de Andrés Hernansanz, Teodoro. "El Discurso Bergsoniano del Metodo." *Crisis; Revista Española de Filosofía,* 18, No. 72, 1971, 291-319. This is a step-by-step examination of Bergson's philosophical method, primarily as it is presented in *An Introduction to Metaphysics.* Cf. the author's continuation of this article, 1972.

5139 Delfor Mandrioni, Hector. *Hombre y poesía.* Buenos Aires: Editorial Guadalupe, 1971, 175. (El Hombre en el tiempo)

5140 Devaux, André-A. "André Robinet: 'Péguy lecteur de Bergson, première recontre.'" *Feuillets de l'Amitié Charles Péguy,* No. 173, 1971, 16.

5141 Devaux, André-A. "Auguste Martin: 'Le Dossier Bergson-Péguy'." *Feuillets de l'Amitié Charles Péguy,* No. 173, 1971, 14-15.

5142 Doob, Leonard William. *The Patterning of Time.* New Haven: Yale, 1971, 472. On pp. 92-93 the author states, "Bergson made duration the key concept in his philosophical system and has had an important effect not only upon philosophy but also upon psychiatry; in addition his analysis is said to have 'brought about a new conception of character in much modern fiction' (Mendilow, 1952, p. 149), to which—in my opinion—film could be appended." The reference is here to A. A. Mendilow, *Time and the Novel.*

5143 Freitag, Emil. "Kontinuität bei Henri Bergson und in Hermann Stehrs Dichtung." In *Wangener Beiträge zur Stehrforschung: Jahresschrift des Hermann-Stehr-Archivs Wangen im Allgäu für 1971-1972.* München: Delp, 1971, 5-27.

5144 Freud, Sigmund. "Letter to James Jackson Putnam, July 8, 1915." In *James Jackson Putnam and Psychoanalysis.* Ed. Nathan G. Hale, Jr. Cambridge, Mass.: Harvard University Press, 1971, 188-191. On p. 189 Freud remarks, "What I have seen of religious-ethical conversion has not been inviting. Jung, for example, I found sympathetic so long as he lived blindly, as I did. Then came his religious-ethical crisis with higher morality, 'rebirth,' Bergson, and at the very same time, lies, brutality and antisemitic condescension towards me. It has not been the first or last experience to reinforce my disgust with saintly converts" (p. 189). The German version of this letter appears on pp. 375-377. The editor points out on p. 191n that this passage was omitted from previously published versions of this letter.

5145 Fürstenberg, Hans. *Dialektik des einundzwanzigsten Jahrhunderts; Ein Diskurs. Der neue Weg des Denkens von der Atomphysik bis zu den Wissenschaften vom Menschen.* Düsseldorf: Econ-Verlag, 1971, 127. This essay deals with the concept of dialectic, with Max Planck, Henri Bergson, and the philosophy of science.

5146 Gagnebin, Samuel. "Pour comprendre Bergson." In *A la recherche d'un ordre naturel* by Samuel Gagnebin. Neuchâtel: La Baconnière, 1971, 361-391.

5147 Garcia, Ofelia. "Montaigne and Bergson: A Comparison." *Rackham Literary Studies*, 1, No. 1, 1971, 27-34.

5148 Gastañazatorre Echano, Luciano de. "Marcel Proust y Henri Bergson (Reflexion ante un Centenario) 1871-1971" *Arbor*, 80, No. 312, Diciembre 1971, 339-352. The author briefly discusses Proust's life and personality, and his relations with Bergson. He finds that Proust, while diverging significantly from Bergson, did owe him a philosophical debt.

5149 Gaubert, Serge. "Proust et le jeu de l'alphabet" *Europe*, 49, No. 502-503, février-mars 1971, 68-83.

5150 Gilson, Etienne. *D'Aristote à Darwin et retour: Essai sur quelques constants de la biophilosophie.* Paris: J. Vrin, 1971, 254. (Essais d'art et de philosophie) (Cf. the author, 1984.)

5151 Giroux, Laurent. "Review of *Bergson and the Evolution of Physics* by Pete A. Y. Gunter." *Review of Metaphysics*, 25, No. 1, 1971, 140-141.

5152 Giroux, Laurent. "Bergson et la conception du temps chez Platon et Aristote." *Dialogue*, 10, No. 3, 1971, 479-503. The author agrees with Bergson's account of Plato's concept of time but criticizes Bergson's account of Aristotle's account of time. An analysis of Book Four of Aristotle's *Physics* shows that units of time, not units of space, are Aristotle's means of measuring time. Moreover, for Aristotle time varies according to the kind of motion which is to be measured.

5153 Giroux, Laurent. *Durée pure et temporalité: Bergson et Heidegger.* Paris: Tournai, Desclée; Montréal, Ballarmin, 1971, 136. (Recherches publiées par les Facultés S. J. de Montréal, Philosophie, No. 4)

5154 Goyard-Fabre, Simon. "Le Corps-image selon Bergson." *Ecole des Lettres*, 2e cycle, 62, No. 13, 1971, 37-41. The author examines Bergson's rehabilitation of the imagination in *Matter and Memory* through his treatment of the body-image. (See *Index Analytique*, 6, 1971-1972, A-51.)

5155 Grimaldi, Nicholas. *Le Désir et le temps.* Paris: Presses Universitaires de France, 1971, 507. (Bibliothèque de Philosophie Contemporaine: Histoire de Philosophie et Philosophie générale) Cf. esp. pp. 129-151 for the author's criticisms of Bergson's vitalism in terms of the author's own "ontologie du desir." Bergson tried to explain halts and divisions of life *via* the opposition of "life" and "matter". The author argues that life is "désir" and "désir" contains "dissociation" within itself. Bergson has refused to take negativity seriously. (p. 141)

5156 Grimaldi, Nicholas. "Matière et tradition." *Revue de Métaphysique et de Morale*, 76, No. 2, avril-juin 1971, 167-195. Matter is an "attribute of time"; it is a resistance to the future and a conservation of the present. This essay includes an interpretation of both Bergson's and Leibniz' concept of matter.

5157 Guillén, Claudio. *Literature as System; Essays Toward The Theory of Literary History*. Princeton, New Jersey: Princeton University Press, 1971, 528.

5158 Gunter, Pete Addison Yancey. "Bergson's Theory of Matter and Modern Cosmology." *Journal of the History of Ideas*, 32 No. 4, October-December 1971, 525-542. According to the author, Bergson's theory of matter foreshadows developments in contemporary cosmology. Bergson's cosmology is a cosmogony, contains the concepts of the expansion of space and the creation of matter. Traces of both "steady state" and "big bang" theories are present in his thinking. Cf. M. Čapek *Bergson and Modern Physics*, 1971, Appendix III.

5159 Gunter, Pete Addison Yancey. "Temps biologique et dévelopment biologique." *Cahiers de l'Association Lecomte du Noüy*, 3, Spring 1971, 16-22. The author argues that new discoveries in embryology suggest the validity of Bergson's and Lecomte du Noüy's concepts of biological time.

5160 Hage, Kamal e. *La Valeur du langage chez Bergson*. Beyrouth, Lebanon: Publications de l'Université Libanaise, 1971, 146. This is a continuation of the author's thesis.

5161 Hale, Nathan G. Jr. *James Jackson Putnam and Psychoanalysis*. Cambridge, Mass. Harvard University Press, 1971, 384. On pp. 48-49 and 56 the author describes Putnam's interest in Bergson's philosophy, and Bergson's influence on Putnam's approach to psychoanalysis. On p. 94 a letter from Putnam to Sigmund Freud is printed, in which Putnam urges Bergson's views on the founder of psychoanalysis. On pp. 96-97 Freud's reply to Putnam is given: "I make bold to say, that from the very beginning I have agreed with Bergson's logical view of the matter. I have made it mine." Other references to Bergson may be found on pp. 106-107, 108, and 345.

5162 Harder, Worth Travis. *A Certain Order: The Development of Herbert Read's Theory of Poetry*. The Hague: Mouton, 1971, 165. (De propietatibus litterarum. Series Practica, 26)

5163 Heidsieck, François. "Review of *Bergson et les niveaux de réalité* by Georges Mourelos." *Review Philosophique de la France et de l'Étranger*, 161, No. 4, 1971, 447-448.

5164 Heidsieck, François. *L'Ontologie de Merleau-Ponty*. Bibliothèque de philosophie contemporaine. Paris: Presses Universitaires de France, 1971, 140. (Bibliothèque de philosophie contemporaine). The author argues that Merleau-Ponty conjoins phenomenology and ontology throughout his writings. The concept of "ambiguity" is thus not at the center of Merleau-Ponty's philosophy. The author makes numerous references to Bergson. On pp. 24-52 he deals with Merleau-Ponty's attitude towards Bergson and Jean-Paul Sartre: "L'explication la plus simple consisterait a dire; Merleau-Ponty, d'abord phenomenologue, existentialiste, ami de Sartre, est devenu tout autre chose, philosophe d l'*en soi*, attentif a l'invisible, ami de Bergson" (p. 25).

5165   Hesse, Herman. *Mein Glaube: Eine Dokumentation*, Pref. S. Unseld. Frankfurt
        am Main: Suhrkamp Verlag, 1971, 152.

5166   Hyppolite, Jean. *Figures de la pensée philosophique: Écrits de Jean Hyppolite*
        (1931-1968). Vol. I. Ed. Dina Dreyfus. Paris: Presses Universitaires de France,
        1971, vii, 512. (Epiméthée) The first volume of this history of philosophy
        contains several sections on Bergson: Ch. VII, 1, "Du Bergsonisme à l'existen-
        tialisme," 443-458; 2, "Vie et philosophe de l'histoire chez Bergson," 459-467;
        3, "Aspects divers de la mémoire chez Bergson," 468-488; 4, "Vie et existence
        d'après Bergson: Faiblesse et grandeur de l'intelligence," 489-498. This last
        section, a lecture given at Leyden in 1950, is published here for the first time.

5167   Kassan, Shalom. "Louis Dembitz Brandeis: In Memoriam." *Israel Law Review*,
        6, No. 4, 1971, 447-466. The author concludes his eulogy of U. S. Supreme
        Court Justice Brandeis by a quotation from *The Two Sources* in which Bergson
        finds the source of our modern conception of Justice in the Prophets of Israel.
        This same "almost militant insistence on righteousness" can be found in the
        opinions of Justice Brandeis.

5168   Kayatta, George N. "Comic Elements in Montaigne's *Essais* in the Light of
        Bergson's *Le Rire.*" Diss. Case Western Reserve. *Dissertation Abstracts Inter-
        national*, 32, 1971, 408A.

5169   Klein, Elise. "Esthétique et métaphysique chez Bergson et Vasconcelos." Diss.
        Toulouse 1971, xii, 191. This is a "thèse, 3ᵉ cycle."

5170   Koenig, Thomas. *The Philosophy of Georges Bastide*. The Hague: Martinus Nijhoff,
        1971, xiii, 224.

5171   Lafrance, Guy. "La Communication dans la philosophie bergsonienne." *La Com-
        munication. Actes du XVᵉ Congrès de l'Association des Sociétés de Philosophie
        de Langue Française*. Montréal: Éd. Montmorency, 1971, 30-34.

5172   Lakshmana Rao, Ayyagari. *Metaphysical Psychology of Henri Bergson: A Critical
        Study*. Waltair: Andhra University, 1971, 203.

5173   Levine, Israel. *Faithful Rebels: A Study in Jewish Speculative Thought*. 1922; rpt.
        Port Washington, N. Y. & London: Kennikat Press, 1971, 146. Bergson is
        discussed on pp. 101-119. The author likens him, especially, to Spinoza. He
        concludes "There seems no reason to doubt that in its ultimate purport the creed
        of Bergson is in harmony with that Jewish attitude to life and the world we have
        now traced from Biblical times down almost to the present day." (p. 119)

5174   Mangy, Claude-Edmonde. *Littérature et critique*. Pref. M. A. Burke. Paris: Payot,
        1971, 452.

5175   Maiorana, Maria-Teresa. "Bergson et le rayonnement de sa pensée (Compte rendu
        sommaire)." *Revue de Synthèse*, 92, Nos. 63-64, 1971, 319-321. This is a
        review of *Bergson* by Madeleine Barthélémy-Madaule, *La Durée chez Bergson*
        by Osman E. Chahine, and Vol. IX of *Les Études Bergsoniennes*.

5176   Maristany, J. "La fantasía en Sartre, Freud y Bergson." *Convivium*, No. 36, 1971,
        45-82.

5177   Martin, Auguste. "Review of *Péguy entre Juarès, Bergson et l'Eglise* by André
        Robinet." *Feuillets de l'Amitié Charles Péguy*, No. 173, 1971, 17-21.

5178   Mathieu, Vittorio. *Bergson, Il profundo e la sua espressione*. Napoli: Guida Editori,
        1971, 453. (Esperienzi, No. 9). This study of Bergson's theory of knowledge

and its application to scientific knowledge (first published in 1954) contains an appendix discussing recent work on Bergson in France, Italy, and Germany.

5179 McInnes, Neil. "The Young Marx and the New Left." *Contemporary History*, 6, No. 6, 1971, 141-159. The author seeks the sources of the "new left" in contemporary political theory. Particularly he is concerned with the neo-Marxist "Critical Theory of Society". He finds one important source of the new left to lie in Bergson's contrast between the fluidity of reality and the rigidity of scientific and technological thought. (pp. 157-153) Bergsonism, however, was but a brief fad; only in Germany did anti-scientific views (H. Rickert, G. Simmel) take over after the First World War, and flower finally in Fascism and anti-intellectual Marxism. Cf. also pp. 155, 157.

5180 McMahon, Francis E. "Maritain: Was It Possible to Update Aquinas?" *New York Times Book Review*, November 14, 1971, 60-61. This article deals with the religious and metaphysical conceptions of Jacques Maritain, Charles Péguy, Henri Bergson, and Léon Bloy.

5181 Merleau-Ponty, J. "Review of *Duration and Simultaneity* by Henri Bergson." *Revue Philosophique de la France et de l'Étranger*, 161, No. 4, 1971, 445-446. This is a review of the Leon Jacobson translation of *Durée et simultanéité*. The reviewer finds Jacobson's translation satisfactory, and states concerning *Duration and Simultaneity*, "C'est un beau livre. Les erreurs qu'il contient, les vues discutables qui y sont présentées sur la théorie de la Relativité n'empêchent pas qu'il ne mette en pleine lumière des problèmes dont le triomphe d'Einstein a sûrement modifié les données, mais qu'il n'a pas fait disparaître: une ontologie qui voit le devenir à la source des etres est compatible avec la Physique relativiste, sans qu'on doive donner de cette Physique l'interprétation douteuse de Bergson, ni admettre avec lui une veritable discontinuité épistémologique entre la Philosophie et le Science? Le lecture de *Durée et simultanéité* ne peut éviter de se poser ces questions" (p. 446).

5182 Meyer, François. *Pour connaître la pensée de Bergson*. 1944; rpt. Genève: Edito-Service, 1971, 127.

5183 *Miguel angel Asturias, Jacinto Benavente and Henri Bergson*. New York: A. Gregory, 1971, 378. (Nobel Prize Library) This volume contains Henri Bergson's Nobel Prize acceptance speech, an excerpt form *Creative Evolution*, and an account of his life and work.

5184 Minkowski, Eugène. *Die gelebte Zeit*, Vol. I, *Über den zeitlichen Aspekt des Lebens*. Trans. Meinrad Perrez and Lucien Kayser. Salzburg: Otto Müller, 1971, 175. (Neues Forum, Das Bild des Menschen in der Wissenschaft, No. 11)

5185 Morán, Francisco José and Matías Díez Alonzo. *Historia de los premios Nobel: Literatura*. Léon (España): Editorial Everest, 1971, 334.

5186 Morkovsky, Mary Christine. "Bergson's Exorcism of the Phantom of Nothingness." *Modern Schoolman*, 48, No. 2, 1971, 135-150. The ideas of nothing and of possibility are necessary for practical knowledge. But, the author holds, intellectualist philosophies that reach reality only by passing through them reduce spontaneity to rearrangement and freedom to determinism. Negation, possibility, and necessity are for Bergson always subordinate to and derived from creatively evolving duration.

5187 Morkovsky, Mary Christine. "Crystallized Creativity: Bergson's view of Customs." *Humanitas*, 7, No. 1, Spring 1971, 37-48. The author argues that for Bergson, creativity generates customs. The view that customs generate or account for creativity is false.

5188 Pardo Martínez, Jesés. "Bergson: praxis y filosofia." *Estudios de Metafísica*, No. 2, 1971-1972, 245-252.

5189 Parr, Susan Dale Resneck. "'And by Bergson, Obviously': Faulkner's *The Sound and the Fury, As I Lay Dying* and *Absalom, Absalom!* From a Bergsonian Perspective." Diss. Wisconsin. *Dissertation Abstracts International*, 32, 1971, 6996A. The author, pointing out Faulkner's stated indebtedness to Bergson, shows that Bergsonian concepts explain much in Faulkner's writings.

5190 Piclin, Michel. "Review of *Une Généalogie du spiritualisme française* by Dominique Janicaud." *Revue Philosophique de la France et de l'Étranger*, 161, No. 4, 1971, 451-453.

5191 Pilkington, A. E. "A Study of Bergson in Relation to Péguy, Valéry, Proust and Benda." Diss. Oxford 1971-1972.

5192 Prigogine, I. "Evolution of Physics." *Nature*, 234, 19 November 1971, 159-160. This is a review of *Bergson and the Evolution of Physics*, Ed. P. A. Y. Gunter.

5193 Pringle-Pattison, Seth. *The Idea of God in the Light of Recent Philosophy*. Aberdeen, Scotland: University Press, 1917, 423. Bergson is discussed on pp. 366-385.

5194 Rao, Ayyagari Lakshmana Rao. *Metaphysical Psychology of Henri Bergson: A Critical Study*. Foreword K. Satchidananda Murthy. Waltair: Andhra University, 1971, 203. A bibliography is given here on pp. 201-203.

5195 Reichenbach, Hans. *The Direction of Time*. Ed. Maria Reichenbach. Berkeley, Los Angeles, London: University of California Press, 1971, 280. The author refers to Bergson on pp. 16 and 17. He states that Bergson's attitude towards time (i.e., Becoming), though emotionally rewarding, cannot replace logical investigation. Bergson, moreover, has said that the physicist has misunderstood time by treating it as a mere dimension of space. But, he replies, "It is a hopeless enterprise to search for the nature of time without studying physics" (p. 17). We cannot tell whether an intuition is true simply by appeal to another intuition. Cf. M. Čapek, 1971.

5196 Riefstahl, Hermann. "Review of *Bergson et Teilhard de Chardin* by Madeleine Barthélémy-Madaule." *Philosophischer Literaturanzeiger*, 24, 1971, 352-355.

5197 Robberechts, Ludovic. *Essai sur la philosophie reflexive*. Vol. 1. *De Biran à Brunschvicg*. Namur: Secrétariat des Publications, Facultés universitaires; Gembloux: J. Duculot, 1971, 376. (Bibliothèque de la Faculté de philosophie et lettres de Namur, No. 48)

5198 Rycroft, Charles. *Wilhelm Reich*. New York: Viking, 1971, 115. The author notes on p. 17 that in the early 1920's Reich read "a lot of Bergson" an in the autobiographical chapter of the 1942 version of *The Function of the Orgasm* Reich states that he always wanted to resolve the vitalist-mechanist antithesis by finding some tangible thing in which the life force could be located. Cf. also p. 75.

5199 Schmidt, Paul F. "Review of *The Intuition of Zen and Bergson* by M. Yamaguchi." *Philosophy East and West*, 21, No. 1, 1971, 92-93.

5200   Schottlaender, Rudolf. "Henri Bergson, der «Biophile» par exellence. Zur dreis-sigsten Wiederkehr seines Todestages am 4. Januar 1971." *Zeitschrift für Philosophische Forschung*, 25, No. 2, 1971, 260-275.

5201   Solomon, Lawrence N. "Humanism and the Training of Applied Behavioral Scientists." *Journal of Applied Behavioral Science*, 7, No, 5, 1971, 531-547. The author argues that a philosophy of humanism provides a valuational base for the activities of applied behavioral scientists. On p. 541 he suggests Bergson's *élan vital* as one basis for a model of personal growth. He points on pp. 542-543 to Bergson as one who's views were "prophetic in an anticipation of humanistic psychology."

5202   Somville, Leon. *Devanciers du surréalisme: Les Groupes d'avant-garde et le mouvement poétique 1912-1925.* Genève: Librarie Droz, 1971, 215.

5203   Spanos, William V. "Modern Drama and the Aristotelian Tradition: The Formal Imperatives of Absurd Time." *Contemporary Literature*, 12, No. 3, 1971, 345-372. This study deals primarily with Bergson, J.-P. Sartre, M. Proust and E. Ionesco.

5204   Togeby, Knud. "Bergson." In *Kapitler af fransk litteraturhistorie: 20 arhundrede: Kronik og kritik.* Uudvalg ved Hans Boll Johansen. Copenhagen: Akademisk forlag, 1971, 7-11. (Kapitler af fransk litteraturhistorie, No. 1)

5205   Tonnelat, Marie-Antoinette. *Histoire du principe de relativité.* Paris: Flammarion, 1971, 561. Bergson and Zeno's paradoxes are discussed here on p. 211; Bergson and relativity theory on pp. 212, 219; Bergson and Ernst Mach are discussed on p. 271; Bergson's criticisms of relativity theory are examined on pp. 280-293. The author concludes that Bergson's critique of relativity theory should not be accused of naiveté or anthropomorphism. Bergson's errors were based on "Textes elliptiques, incomplets, pu comprehensibles et certainement mal compris" of certain writers on relativity. This is an excellent, very important study.

5206   Violette, René. "Review of *Henri Bergson: Quellen und Konsequenzen einer induktiven Metaphysik* by Günther Pflug." *Revue Philosophique de la France et de l'Étranger*, 161, No. 4, 1971, 443-445.

5207   Walker, Marshall. "Shakespeare's Comedy (or Much Ado About Bergson)." *Interpretations*, 3, No. 1, 1971, 1-12.

5208   Whyte, Lancelot Law. "Review of *Bergson and the Evolution of Physics*, Ed. and Trans, with Intro. P. A. Y. Gunter." *British Journal for the Philosophy of Science*, 22, No. 1, February 1971, 75-76.

5209   Wickham, Harvey. *The Unrealists: William James, Bergson, Santayana, Einstein, Bertrand Russell, John Dewey, Alexander and Whitehead.* 1930; rpt. Port Washington, New York: Kennikat Press, 1971, 264.

5210   Williams, Robert C. "Concerning the German Spiritual in Russian Art: Vasilii Kandinskii." *Journal of European Studies*, 1, No. 4, 1971, 325-336. The author notes the similarity of Bergson's philosophy with post-impressionist art on pp. 329-330. On p. 335 he states that Kandinskii agreed with Bergson that in a material world and materialistic society the spiritual is hidden from us, "veiled."

5211   Younoszai, Barbara. "El tiempo de Bergson en la obra de Jorge Luis Borges." Diss. Minnesota. *Dissertation Abstracts International*, 32, 1971, 2715A. The author explores similarities between Bergson's and Borges' concepts of time.

1972

5212   Anderson, James F. "Teilhard's Christianized Cosmology." *Heythrop Journal*, 13, No. 1, January 1972, 63-67. The author casts light on Teilhard de Chardin's evolutionism by referring to two philosophers, M. Blondel and Bergson, who influenced him.

5213   Antonio-Miguez, José. "Review of *La filosofía de Bergson*, by Manuel García Morente." *Arbor*, 83, Nos. 321-324, 1972, 139-143.

5214   Bachelard, Gaston. *La Dialectique de la durée (H. Bergson)*. Paris: Presses Universitaires de France, 1972, 150.

5215   Barthélémy-Madaule, Madeleine. *L'Ideologie du hasard et de la nécessité*. Paris: Editions du Seuil, 1972, 219. This book deals with the concept of evolution as viewed by Henri Bergson and Pierre Teilhard de Chardin, in relation to the "reductionist" ideas of biologist Jacques Monod.

5216   Bayonas, August. "Review of 'La Critique de la philosophie platonicienne chez Bergson' by E. Moutsopoulos." *Revue Philosophique de la France et de l'Étranger*, 162, No. 1, 1972, 44-49. Cf. Moutsopoulos' article, 1962 and 1970.

5217   Bhattacharya, A. C. *Sri Aurobindo and Bergson: A Synthetic Study*. Gyanpur, India: Jagabandhu Prakshan, 1972, 282.

5218   Bien, Peter. *Nikos Kazantzakis*. New York and London: Columbia University Press, 1972, 48. (Columbia Essays on Modern Writers, No. 62) The author states: "Much has been said, and quite rightly, about Kazantzakis' debt to Nietzsche, very little about his debt to Bergson. Yet it is clear that, of the two, Bergson played a much greater role in Kazantzakis' intellectual life..." (p. 11)

5219   Birx, H. James, *Pierre Teilhard de Chardin's Philosophy of Evolution*. Springfield, Illinois: Thomas, 1972, xxii, 1963. (American Lecture Series, No. 852)

5220   Bourbon Busset, Jacques de. *Le Jeu de la constance*. Paris: Gallimard, 1972, 180. (Voies ouvertes)

5221   Cassel, Eric J. "On Educational Changes for the Field of Aging." *Gerontologist*, 12, No. 3, 1972, Part I, 251-256. The author argues on p. 253 against overly spatial concepts of time and on p. 254 uses Bergson's epistemology to argue against an overly analytical, hence reductionist, view of man. A new mode of education—more holistic, intuitive, and intellectual—is necessary for those who deal with aging.

5222   Cattaui, Georges. *Proust et ses métamorphoses*. Paris: Nizet, 1972, 300. The author holds (see p. 73) that Marcel Proust opposes the Bergsonian temporal flux and that his work tends towards the abolition of time altogether.

5223   Čapek, Milič. "Review of *Bergson and the Evolution of Physics*, Ed. and Trans. with Intro. P. A. Y. Gunter." *Process Studies*, 2, No. 2, Summer 1972, 149-159.

5224   Carbonara, Cleto. *Pensatori moderni: L. Brunschvicg, H. Bergson, B. Croce, A. Aliotta*. Napoli: Libreria Scientifica Editrice, 1972, 290. Bergson's philosophy of religion is discussed on p. 121-210.

5225   Charlton, D. G. *France: A Comparison to French Studies*. London: Methuen, 1972, 613.

5226   Crane, John K. "Golding and Bergson: The Free Fall of Free Will." *Bulletin of the Rocky Mountain Modern Language Association*, 26, 1972, 136-141. The novels of William Golding are studies of free will. In *Free Fall* Golding employs

Bergson's psychology, depicting his hero as freely giving up his powers of volition and rendering himself morally impotent. (See 1972 *MLA Abstracts*, 2, p. 22.)

5227 de Andrés Hernansanz, Teodoro. "Algunas Repercusiones Importantes del'Discurso Bergsoniano del Metodo." *Crisis; Revista Española de Filosofía*, 19, Nos. 75-76, 1972, 243-270. The author here developes further his exposition of Bergson's concept of philosophical method in an earlier issue (1971) of this journal. He notes that for Bergson intuition leads to clear and distinct concepts, that intuition and clarity increase after initial obscurity. The author also deals with Bergson's concept of language and (at length) with his concept of the relations between philosophy and science.

5228 Dédéyan, Charles. "Henri Bergson." In *Spleen, révolte et idéal dans la littérature européenne, 1889-1914*, Vol. I of *Le Nouveau mal de siècle de Baudelaire à nos jours*. Paris: SEDES, 1972, 24-29.

5229 Delaney, C. F. "Bergson on Science and Philosophy." *Process Studies*, 2, No. 1, Spring 1972, 29-43. The author analyzes the differences between and the interdependence of science and philosophy in Bergson's philosophy by comparing Bergson's position with Kant's. He concludes by suggesting criticisms by C. S. Pierce of the concept of intuiton.

5230 DuPlessis, Samuel I. M. *The Compatibility of Science and Philosophy in France, 1840-1940*. Cape Town: A. A. Balkema, 1972, 300.

5231 Farrugia, Edward George. "Did Bergson's Moral Philosophy Undergo Radical Development?" Diss. St. Louis, 1972, 478. The author concludes: "...the present dissertation hopes to provide both a commentary on certain neglected aspects of Bergson's thinking and a discussion of the ethical theme, ultimately independent of Bergson, of the shift from the impersonal to the personal in ethics." *Dissertation Abstracts International*, 34, No. 9, 1974, 6041-6042A.

5232 Ferreira, A. Lopes. "Henri Bergson: A religiâo dinámica e S. Francisco de Assis." *Brotéria*, 94, 1972, 256-259.

5233 García Morente, Manuel. *La filosofía de Henri Bergson*. Selección intro. Pedro Muro Romero. Madrid: Espasa-Calpe, 1972, 147. (Colección Austral, No. 1495)

5234 Giambalvo, Epifania. *La metafisica come esigenza nel Bergson e l'esigenza della metafisica nel Fazio-Allmayer*. Pref. Bruno Fazio-Allmayer. Palermo: Tumminelli, 1972, vi, 107. (Università di Palermo. Collana di studi etico-pedagogoci, 1)

5235 Glasser, Richard. *Time in French Life and Thought*. Trans. C. G. Pearson. Manchester: Manchester University Press; Totowa, New Jersey: Rowman and Littlefield, 1972, 306. This is a translation of the 1936 edition. The author deals especially with Bergson, M. Proust, and E. Zola.

5236 Gosztonyi, Alexander. "Bergson und Teilhard." *Perspektiven der Zukunft*, 2, 1972, 7-9.

5237 Gouhier, Henri. "Avant-propos." *Henri Bergson: Mélanges*. Paris: Presses Universitaires de France, 1972, vii-xxiii.

5238 Gouhier, Henri. "Review of *Henri Bergson: Mélanges* by André Robinet and others." *Revue des Travaux de l'Académie des Sciences Morales et Politiques*, 125, No. 1 (ler semestre), 1972, 335-337.

5239   Govinda, Lama Anagarika. "The Two Aspects of Reality." *Main Currents*, 28, No. 4, 1972, 125-130. On p. 127 the author, a leading interpreter of Tibetan Buddhism, uses Bergson's ideas to illustrate the future-oriented vector of experienced time and the preservation of the past in memory. The author states: "...the entire past has to be raised into the light of consciousness, before the control of desire, will and action can be achieved and perfect enlightenment can be attained."

5240   Goyard-Fabre, Simom. "Gaston Bachelard, critique de Bergson." *École des Lettres*, 2ᵉ cycle, 63, No. 10, 1972, 31-34. The author discusses the opposition between Bergson, the philosopher of continuity and the plenum, and Gaston Bachelard, the philosoher of discontinuity. (See *Index Analytique*, 6, 1971-1972, A-51.)

5241   Goyard-Fabre, Simon. "Le Temps et la durée selon Bergson." *École des Lettres*, 2ᵉ cycle, 63, No. 9, 1972, 31-34. The author discusses the problem of temporality, the heart of Bergson's philosophy. He examines several Bergsonian antinomies: consciousness and science; continuity and discontinuity, quality and quantity. He notes Bergson's denunciation of Zeno's paradox. (See *Indes Analytique*, 6, 1971-1972, A-51.)

5242   Hall, D. L. "Abstract of 'Bergson's Theory of Matter and Modern Cosmology' by P. A. Y. Gunter." *Process Studies*, 2, No. 2, Summer 1972, 172. This article is more a review than an abstract.

5243   Jaki, Stanley L. "Review of *Bergson and the Evoluiton of Physics*. Ed. P. A. Y. Gunter." *Zygon*, 7, No. 2, June 1972, 138-139.

5244   Ladrille, G. "Review of *La Conscience de la durée et le concept du temps* by Jean Theau." *Archives de Philosophie*, 35, No. 4, 1972, 691-692.

5245   Ladrille, G. "Review of *La Critique bergsonienne du concept* by Jean Theau." *Archives de Philosophie*, 35, No. 4, 1972, 690-691.

5246   Larock, Victor. "Le Socrate oriental de Bergson." *Réseaux*, No. 18-19, 1972, 47-57.

5247   Lattre, Alain de. "Perception et réfléxion chez Descartes et chez Bergson." *Études Philosophiques*, 27, No. 2, 1972, 179-199. "'Percevoir, dit Bergson, finit par n'être plus qu'une occasion de se souvenir.' De se souvenir ou de réflćhir? De Descartes à Bergson, toute la différence est la. Et, rétablies dans leur juridiction, elles nous forcent de penser d'autre façon de que l'intelligence seule imaginait de concevoir. Du côté de Descartes comme dans celui de Bergson, la philosophie se presente alors l'effort pour composer un équilibre entre ces deux postulations adverses, celle de la perception et celle de la réfléxion: (author's résumé, p. 179)."

5248   Lestienne, R. "Caractères de la durée physique." *Scientia*, 107, 1972, 77-89. The author examines the relations between the time of consciousness and that of physical processes. He distinguishes two kinds of physical time and raises the question whether physical time is irreversible.

5249   Maritain, Jacques. *Ransoming the Time*. Trans. Harry Lorin Binsse. New York: Gordian Press, 1972, xii, 322.

5250   Miguez, José Antonio. "La Filosofía de Henri Bergson." *Arbor*, 82, No. 321-322, 1972, 139-143. This is a review of a book by Manual García Morente.

5251   Monge, Jean. *Temps et mémoire: Le Problème reversiblité-irreversibilité*. Préf. Jean Ullmo. Paris: Editions Horvath, 1972, 199.

5252   Monod, Jacques. *Chance and Necessity: An Essay on the Philosophy of Modern Biology.* New York: Vintage Books, 1972, 199. On pp. 26-27 Monod briefly discusses Bergson's "metaphysical vitalism" as a "metaphorical dialectic bare of logic but not of poetry." On pp. 115-117 the indeterminism in Bergson's account of evolution is seen to be very close to that involved in the contemporary view of evolution.

5253   Morkovsky, Mary Christine. "Intellectual Analysis in Bergson's Theory of Knowing." *Journal of the History of Philosophy,* 10, No. 1, January 1972, 43-54. For Bergson, intellectual analysis is a necessary condition of the most valuable kind of knowledge, the intuition of duration. The author examines Bergsonian analyses of the human self and life. These follow a brief outline Bergson gives of his method in *Creative Evolution.*

5254   Nanajivako, Bhikklau. "Karma: The Ripening Fruit." *Main Currents,* 29, No. 5, September-October 1972, 28-36. Karma (activity) designates in Indian philosophies the "ripening fruit" of vital processes. It corresponds to the need of a new categorial term in modern philosophy for phenomena inadequately interpreted through mechanical activity. Bergson speaks of the free action as ripening fruit. Heidegger continues to extend the range of its existential significance.

5255   P., R. d. "Review of *Bergson and Modern Physics* by Milič Čapek." *Review of Metaphysics,* 26, No. 2, 1972, 355.

5256   Pardo-Martínez, Jesús. "Intuición y duración real (Nota sobre Bergson)." *Estudios de Metafísica,* No. 3, 1972-1973, 133-139; No. 4, 1973-1974, 187-211.

5257   Paulin, Hillewi. "Levertin och Bergson's idévärld." *Edda,* 72, No. 4, 1972, 201-219.

5258   Paumen, Jean. *Temps et choix.* Bruxelles: Éd. de l'Université de Bruxelles, 1972, 238. Chapter II of this book ("Le Choix du temps," pp. 35-69) contains critical reflections on Bergson's philosophy.

5259   Pavan, A. "Maritain e Bergson." *Revista di filosofia neo-scolastica.* 64, aprile-junio 1972, 265-287.

5260   Pinera, (Llera), Humberto. *Las Grandes Intuiciones de la Filosofía.* Madrid: Editorial Oscar, 1972, 387, Chapter VIII of this book, "Bergson: e Ser como 'evolución'," appears on pp. 257-308.

5261   Poulakidas, Andreas K. "Kazantzakis and Bergson: Metaphysic Aestheticians." *Journal of Modern Literature,* 2, No. 2, 1972, 267-283. "It is an established fact that Kazantzakis knew the philosophical outlook of Bergson. Kazantzakis introduced into *Freedom or Death* such Bergsonian concepts as *la durée, mémoire involuntaire,* and free will which develop his novel's stream of consciousness, themes, and his literary impressionistic style. Also, Kazantzakis' translation of Bergson's *Laughter: An Essay on the Meaning of the Comic* in 1915 aided him in devising and developing his minor characters. Above all, Bergson's theory of creative evolution recalled for Kazantzakis an ancient Christian belief, clothed by the name of metousiosis (transubstantiation), the crux of Kazantzakis' philosophy. What Eastern Orthodox theology preaches, regarding the Mystery of the Holy Eucharist, and what Bergsonian philosophy taught in *Creative Evolution* and *The Two Sources of Morality and Religion,* Kazantzakian philosophy synthesized. Metousiosis is the culminating point of a dynamic theology just as creative evolution is the undetected process of an intuitive science." (A.K.P. in 1972 *MLA Abstracts*, 2, 77-78.)

5262   Price, Connie Barnett Crank. "Consciousness and History in Bergson's Philosophy." Diss. Pennsylvania State 1972, 149. The author sets out to show that for Bergson consciousness is ultimate and irreducible, and is the ground of human experience. Though it is the "irreducible component of experience," consciousness is itself constituted by "unique and significant experiences." Bergson's concept of duration is a further conformation that consciousness is a ground. Duration involves creativity, and Bergson proposes that human creativity is the standard of history. The author concludes that "certain arbitrary postulations of exclusiveness from the movement of history" kept Bergson's theory of history from being as pervasive as his theory of consciousness. (See *Dissertation Abstracts International*, 23, No. 3, 1972, 1323A.)

5263   Pucelle, Jean. *Le Temps*. 5th Ed. Paris: Presses Universitaires de France, 1972, 109. (Le Philosophe, 16) Cf. especially Ch. 1, "Le Temps vecú."

5264   Reck, Andrew J. *Speculative Philosophy: A Study of Its Nature, Types and Uses.* Albuquerque: University of New Mexico Press, 1972, 284. The author examines Bergson's concept of duration on pp. 201-207. He raises difficulties concerning the rational coherence of Bergson's thought on pp. 206-207. Other references to Bergson are found throughout.

5265   Rivera de Ventosa, Enrique. "Henri Bergson y M. de Unamuno: Dos filósofos de la vida." *Cuadernos de la Catédra de Unamuno*, 22, 1972, 99-125.

5266   Rotenstreich, Nathan. "Bergson and the Transformations of the Notion of Intuition." *Journal of the History of Philosophy*, 10, No. 3, July 1972, 335-346.

5267   Rousseau, Richard W. "Secular and Christian Images of Man." *Thought*, 47, No. 185, 1972, 165-200. The author discusses the image of man in Bernanos, Bergson, Sartre, Camus, Teilhard de Chardin and others. Bergson is treated here as a proponent of "man in motion." The author concludes, "This image of creative movement as always upward and the identification of ultimate reality has one weakness. It is unrelated or insufficiently realted to the concrete individual and his relationship to the world of men and things. And the experience of history has shown us the disasterous results of uncontrolled energy" (p. 170).

5268   Saint-Yves, Roland de. "Entre Bergson et Monod: Matérialisme, évolutionisme, et théologie de l'évolution." *Resurrection*, No. 37, 1972, 29-32.

5269   Salet, Georges. *Hasard et certitude: Le Transformisme devant la biologie actuelle.* Paris: Editions scientifiques Saint-Edme, 1972, xxxvii, 454. The author denies that the theory of biological evolution is consistent with recent biological discoveries, "en revelant l'extraordinaire complexité des êtres vivants, même les plus simples, la Biologie a rendu de plus en plus invraisemblable l'explication de la vie et l'évolution par le hasard" (p. 128). Part 8 of this study contains quotes from Bergson, L. Cuenot, and Vialleton.

5270   Sartre, Jean-Paul. *Imagination: A Psychological Critique.* Trans. with Intro. Forrest Williams. Ann Arbor, Michigan: Ann Arbor Paperbacks, 1972, 162. Chapters 4 and 5 (pp. 37-64) of this work, titled respectively "Bergson" and "Bergsonism", contain a critique of Bergson's concepts of images and consciousness. Bergson's concept of the image, the author holds, can not explain the existence of consciousness or of the self (pp. 40-42). Nor can Bergson explain how an "image" becomes a "memory-image" (pp. 42-51). This is a concerted, careful critique of basic theses in *Matter and Memory*. The author concludes that Bergson retained the concept of "image" proposed by H. Taine and T. Ribot. On p. 81 the author chides contemporary psychology (*circa* 1936) for its merely eclectic notion of images, which retains the old mechanistic notions under a vague "Bergsonian penumbra" of duration and continuity.

5271   Sawnor, Edna A. "Borges y Bergson." *Cuadernos Americanos*, 185, No. 6, 1972, 247-254. The author argues that critics who have sought to find the philosophical master of the writer, Jorge Luis Borges in David Hume, George Berkeley, or Arthur Schopenhauer are mistaken. Henri Bergson is the "verdadero filósofo de Borges" (p. 247). Bergson influenced Borges during the latter's student days in Europe, from 1914 until 1921.

5272   Sazbon, José. "Sobre algunas premisas comunes a Saussure y sus contemporáneos." *Cuadernos de filosofía*, 12, No. 2, julio-diciembre 1972, 279-286.

5273   Simon, John K. Ed. *Modern French Criticism From Proust and Valéry to Structuralism.* Chicago and London: University of Chicago Press, 1972, 405.

5274   Sipfle, David A. "Abstract of 'Bergson's Theory of Matter and Modern Physics' by Milič Čapek." *Process Studies*, 2, No. 2, Summer 1972, 169-170. This is an abstract of a translation of Čapek's article in *Bergson and the Evolution of Physics*, Ed. and Trans. with Intro. P. A. Y. Gunter.

5275   Spiegelberg, Herbert. *Phenomenology in Psychology and Psychiatry.* Evanston, Ill.: Northwestern University Press, 1972, 411. The author refers to Bergson's coeditorship of the *Zeitschrift für Pathopsychologie* on p. 93; to Bergson's influence on E. Minkowski and the journal *L'Évolution psychiatrique* on p. 114; to Bergson and Henri Ey on pp. 117-118; to Bergson and L. Binswanger on p. 202; to Bergson and Eugène Minkowski on pp. 234-235, 237, 241, and 245-247.

5276   Sroufe, L. Alan and Wunsch, Jane Picard. "The Development of Laughter in the First Year of Life." *Child Development*, 43, No. 4, December, 1972, 1326-1344. The authors use Bergson's analysis of laughter as part of the theoretical background for clinical studies of laughter. Cf. pp. 1327, 1339, 1343.

5277   T., R. "Review of *El tiempo en la filosofía francesa del siglo XX* by the Faculty of Arts and Lettres, University of Buenos Aires." *Diálogos*, 3, No. 23, 1972, 243.

5278   Tatarkiewicz, Wladyslaw. *Droga przez estetyk.* Warszawa: Panstwowe Wydawnictwo Naukowe, 1972, 482. This volume (Vol. 2 of the author's works) contains an essay on Bergson's aesthetics and the art of his time.

5279   *El tiempo en la Filosofía francesa del siglo XX.* Cuadernos de Filosofía. Facultad de Filosofía y Letras. Universidad de Buenos Aires. Año 10, No. 13, 1970, 239. This volume, published in 1972, deals with the problem of time as developed in twentieth century French philosophy. Among the thinkers considered are Paul Ricouer, Gabriel Marcel, Maurice Merleau-Ponty, Jean-Paul Sartre, Louis Lavelle, Henri Bergson and Olivier Costa de Beauregard. It is preceded by an overview, "Two Attitudes Towards Time" ("Dos actitudes frente al tiempo") by Eugenio Puciarelli.

5280   Uritus, Ronald Michael. "Cognition and Action in Bergson's Ethics." Diss. Saint Louis 1972, 283. This study focuses on the problem of the extent and presence of cognitive activities—both analytic and intuitive—in Bergson's account of moral philosophy and moral action. The author concludes, after examining the role of cognitive elements for Bergson in practical, creative, and moral activity, that while Bergson admits the need for various sorts of cognition in moral activities, in many instances these are subordinated to affective factors. (See *Dissertation Abstracts International*, 34, No. 9, 1972, 6052A.)

5281   Vassilie-Lemeny, S. T. "Les Sens du Néant." *Sapienza*, 25, No. 4, 1972, 419-429.

5282   Winther, Truls. *Tausheten og Ordet*. Oslo: Gyldendal norsk forlag, 1972, 101. This work, which deals with problems in recent aesthetics, contains an essay on Bergson titled "Henri Bergson og Kunsten".

5283   Zaniello, Thomas Anthony. "The Moment of Perception in Nineteenth and Twentieth Century Literature." Diss. Stanford, 1972, 236. This is a study of the role of perception in the work of selected ninteenth and twentieth century authors. Bergson's concept of the "cinematographic" mechanism of thought is examined as a widespread modern basis for the understanding of perception. *Dissertation Abstracts International*, 33, No. 8, 1973, 4373A.

1973

5284   Adams, Richard P. "The Apprenticeship of William Faulkner." In *William Faulkner: Four Decades of Criticism*. Ed. Linda Welshimer Wagner. East Lansing, Michigan: Michigan State University Press, 1973, 7-44. On pp. 39-41 the author discusses the influence of Bergson's concepts of God, Time, and laughter on Faulkner's thought and writing.

5285   Alberini, Coriolano. *Escritos de Metafisica*. Ed. Diego F. Pro. Mendoza, Argentina: Universidad Nacional de Cuyo, 1973, 260. (Historia de la Filosofía Argentina)

5286   Ansbacher, Heinz L. "Adler's Interpretations of Early Recollections: Historical Accounts." *Journal of Individual Psychology*, 29, No. 2, 1973, 135-145. This paper discusses a central tenet of Adlerian psychoanalysis, the importance of early childhood memories as a key to personality. Adler's concept of memory was influenced by Bergson, through the work of Paul Schrecker, a young Viennese who had studied under Bergson in Paris in 1911. Cf. P. Schrecker, 1912.

5287   Barreau, Hervé. "Bergson et Einstein. A propos de *Durée et simultanéité*." *Études Bergsoniennes*, 10, 1973, 73-134.

5288   Bejenaru, Cornelia. "Influente bergsonienne in literatura franceza contemporana." *Analele Universității București, Filosofie*, 22, No. 2, 1973, 129-135. The author provides a résumé of his article in French.

5289   "Review of *Bergson: Vie et morte de l'homme et de dieu* by Georges Levesque." *Bulletin Critique du Livre Français*, 28, No. 331, juillet 1973, 889.

5290   "Review of *Bergson and Modern Physics* by Milič Čapek." *Choice*, 10, No. 1, 1973, 398-399. This is a brief, highly affirmative review. The author concludes, "Čapek gets inside Bergson, brilliantly defending his relevance to contemporary physics with a mastery of recent developments. Highly recommended in its own right and as a sequel to Čapek's *The Philosophical Impact of Contemporary Physics*, 1961."

5291   Berning, Vinzent. *Das Wagnis der Treue: Gabriel Marcels Weg zu einer konkreten Philosophie des Schöpferischen*. Freiburg/München: Karl Alber, 1973, 404.

5292   Biancucci, Duilio. *Henri Bergson en los umbrales de la moral.* Buenos Aires: Editorial Guadalupe, 1973, 153. (Hombres y sus ideas, No. 8)

5293   Biondi, A. "Teilhard and Bergson." *Teilhard Review*, 8, No. 3, 1973, 82-85.

5294   Bretonneau, G. "L'Idée de Création dans la philosophie de Bergson." Diss. Université de Lille, 1973, 843. This work contains three sections: 1. Creation and Freedom 2. Creation and Intuition 3. Creation and Aspiration. "A look at creativity and the idea of aspiration as a participation in the divine conclude this thesis." *Dissertation Abstracts International*, 37, No. 1, Sec. c, 1976, p. 25.

5295   Brun, Jean. "Review of *Bergson and Modern Physics* by Milič Čapek." *Études Philosophique*, 28, No. 2, 1973, 229-231.

5296   Carrabino, Victor. "Robbe-Grillet and Phenomenological Time." *Research Studies* (Washington State University), 41, 1973, 42-51. "Although 20th-century stream-of-consciousness novelists have made wide use of the Bergsonian duration, phenomenological time still remains to be explored in modern narrative. While Bergson understands the mind as a living organism, the phenomenologist conceives the perceiving consciousness as an entity devoid of psychology, for he is interested in 'primitive formations' of time-consciousness. Merleau-Ponty, for example, reduces time to pure subjectivity. For him the subject is temporality. He states, 'Time...arises from my relation to things... We are the upsurge of time.' Alain Robbe-Grillet—the most represen..ative figure in the New Novel movement—has adopted the phenomenological time in his novels where the narrator acts as the only subjective time-consciousness. In his novels mechanical time gradually disappears. He presents a narrator who acts as a subject-temporality, hence time is created as the novel is created." (*1974 MLA Abstracts*, 2, 39.)

5297   Cavarnos, Constantine. *A Dialogue between Bergson, Aristotle, and Philologos.* 2nd ed. Belmont, Mass.: Institute for Byzantine and Modern Greek Studies, 1973, 62.

5298   Clark, Terry Nichols. *"Prophets and Patrons: The French University and the Emergence of the Social Sciences.* Cambridge, Mass." Harvard University Press, 1973, 282. The author notes Theodule Ribot, Gabriel Tarde, and Henri Bergson on p. 58 as representatives of French social philosophy; on p. 80n he describes the Bergson enthusiasts who met with Georges Sorel and Charles Péguy at the Cahiers de la Quinzaine as having failed to create a "cluster;" he describes Bergson's thesis (*L'Essai*) on p. 83 as a "classical monument of scholarship;" on p. 192 he notes briefly Bergson's relations with Gabriel Tarde; on pp. 192-193 he characterizes Bergson's lectures at the Collège de France; he notes the increasing popularity of Bergson's ideas in France after 1905 on p. 215; he notes Bergson's support of chairs of sociology and of economic and social sciences on p. 219n; he notes on p. 222 Bergson's participation, in 1923, in curriculum revision; he notes Bergson's influence on Daniel Essertier and Emile Lasbax on p. 224. See also pp. 88n and 166.

5299   Daetwyler, Jean-Jacques. "Review of *Bergson and Modern Physics* by Milič Čapek." *Erasmuns*, 25, No. 11, 1973, 330-331.

5300   Dagognet, François. *Ecriture et iconographie.* Paris: Librairie Philosophique Vrin, 1973, 170. (Problèmes et controverses)

5301   d'Entreves, Allesandro Passarin. "Obbligo politico e società aperta." *Rivista Internazionale di Filosofia del Diritto*, 50, No. 3, 1973, 765-770.

5302   Devaux, André-A. "Bergson en son temps." *Études Philosophiques*, 28, No. 2, 1973, 199-202. This is an appreciative review of *Mélanges*, a collection of Bergson's writings, letters, and lectures.

5303   Devaux, André-A. "D'un malentendu entre Péguy et Bergson." *Revue d'Histoire littéraire de la France*, 73, No. 2-3, 1973, 281-299.

5304   Devaux, André-A. "René Le Senne face à Henri Bergson." *Études Bergsoniennes*, 10, 1973, 135-169.

5305   Dewey, John. *Lectures in China, 1919-1920*. Ed. and trans. Robert W. Clopton and Tsuin-Chen Ou. Honolulu: University Press of Hawaii, 1973, 337. The editors point out on p. 8 that while in China, Dewey gave a series of lectures concerning William James, Henri Bergson, and Bertrand Russell titled "Three Contemporary Philosophers." Copies of these lectures can be purchased from the University of Hawaii. On p. 326 the editors note that Dewey devoted two lectures each to James, Bergson, and Russell. On p. 101, in a talk titled "Economics and Social Philosophy," Dewey stated, "Recently the French philosopher Henri Bergson has preferred the definition of man as the tool-making animal—a peculiarly apt definition, in my opinion. Bergson's definition directs attention to man's ability to devise from the materials of nature instrumentalities for the satisfaction of his desires—a characteristic which lower orders of animals do not possess, and which is therefore unique to man."

5306   "Doctoral Dissertations, 1973." *Review of Metaphysics*, 27, No. 1, September, 1973, 203, 205, 208.

5307   Eile, Stanisław. *Swiatopoglad powiesci*. Wrocław, Warzawa, Craków, Gdansk: Zaklad Narodowy Imiena Ossonlinskih, 1973, 258. (Polska adademia nauk. Komitet nauk o literaturze polskiej)

5308   Erickson, John D. "The Proust-Einstein Relation: A Study in Relative Points of View." In *Marcel Proust: A Critical Panorama*. Ed. Larkin B. Price. Urbana: University of Illinois Press, 1973, 247-276.

5309   *Études Bergsoniennes*, Vol. 10. Paris: Presses Universitaires de France, 1973, 196. This volume contains an article on Bergson and Einstein by H. Barreau, a bibliography on Bergson's part in history by A. Kremer-Marietti, an article on Bergson and Plotinus by J. Foubert, a study of Bergson and René Le Senne by A.-A. Devaux, and an article on H. Rickert's critique of Bergson by A. Métraux.

5310   Foubert, Jean. "Mystique plotinienne, mystique bergsonienne, I. De la contemplation à l'union. L'Un plotinien. II. La Mystique selon Bergson." *Les Études bergsoniennes*, 10, 1973, 6-71.

5311   Fraisse, Simone. *Péguy et le monde antique*. Paris: Armand Colin, 1973, 561.

5312   Gaidamavičiene, Irena. "A Bergsonas: Intuityvistinés filosofijos kūrejas." *Problemos*, 1, No. 1, 1973, 91-98.

5313   Gandillac, Maurice de. "Le Plotin de Bergson." *Revue de Théologie et de Philosophie*, 23, No. 2, 1973, 173-183. "Sans evisager l'ensenble des problèmes posés par l'influence de Plotin sur Bergson, l'auteur analyse, sur les notes prises par un auditeur, un cours professé par Bergson au Collège de France. Il montre Bergson trop attaché à l'idée d'un Plotin 'adossant la temporalité à un bloc immobile d'éternité, sous-estimant l'immanence active des idées dans le cosmos. La lecture bergsonienne des textes sur l'âme reste inflechie en un sens 'psychologiste' et porte la trace du pessimisme hartmannien. Et elle bergsonise Plotin par reference a la doctrine de l'élan vital, avec ses 'ratés' et ses 'percées'?"

5314   Gidley, M. "One Continuous Force: Notes on Faulkner's Extra-Literary Reading." In *William Faulkner: Four Decades of Criticism*. Ed. Linda Welshimer Wagner. East Lansing, Michigan: Michigan State University Press, 1973, 54-68. On p. 56 the author notes various critics who have held that Bergson influenced Faulkner. On pp. 61-62 he briefly explores the influence of Elie Faure's *History of Art* on Faulkner. The author asserts that Faure was probably helped to his notions of dynamism by Bergson.

5315   Giroux, Laurent. "'Matière et mémoire' de Henri Bergson." *Dialogue* (Canada), 12, No. 4, 1973, 670-675. The author examines Bergson's mind-matter dualism, his theories of memory and perception. Various difficulties in Bergson's position are stressed and a new starting point is suggested, based on a concept developed by existentialism.

5316   Gerrard, Charlotte F. "Bergsonian Elements in Ionesco's *Le Piéton d l'air.*" *Papers on Language and Literature*, 9, No. 3, 1973, 297-310. The author concludes, "*Le Piéton de l'air* is not a parody, bitter like Adamov's *La Grande et la petite maneuvre*, but an outright *féerie*. Rather than representing the mixed genres of Ionesco's absurdist plays and even his later ones, *Le Piéton de l'air* is pure fantasy and laughter. Even the apocalypse reported by Berenger does not destroy the underlying mood of the comic. After all, such masters as Moliere and Shaw allowed serious thoughts to enter their theatre without writing tragedy or philosophy. No bow to these latter dramatic categories is in order, so much as is a curtain call for Henri Bergson." (p. 310).

5317   González, Juan de Dios. *El símbolo en la filosofía de Henri Bergson*. Guatemala, 1973, vi, 88. Thesis (lincenciatura en filosofía) Universidad de San Carlos de Guatemala.

5318   Greene, Maxine. "Cognition and Consciousness: Humanities and the Elementary School Teacher." *Philosophic Exchange*, 1, No. 3, 1973, 43-62.

5319   Hamilton, James Jay. "Georges Sorel and the Inconsistencies of a Bergsonian Marxism." *Political Theory*, 1, No. 3, 1973, 329-340. Sorel tried to revise orthodox Marxism by means of Bergson's vitalist epistemology. Sorel applies Bergson's psychology of the free, creative man *via* his own concept of social myth, in which the rational and irrational merge. But there can by no coherent synthesis of Marxism's deterministic economic and social analysis with the individualist, intuitionist, anti-rationalist philosophy of Bergson. Social regularity frustrates Bergson's defense of individual freedom. Hence Sorel's doctrine of freedom becomes untenable, which invalidates the justification for revolution.

5320   Jerphagnon, Lucien, Ed. *Dictionnaire des grandes philosophies*. Toulouse: Privat, 1973, 397. This work deals especially with existentialism, Bergson, Maurice Blondel.

5321   Johnson, Patricia J. "Bergson's *Le rire: Game Plan for Camus' L'Étranger?*" *French Review*, 47, No. 1, 1973, 46-56. "Camus's surprising declaration that critics have neglected the comic theme in his work suggests the re-examination of one of his major works, *L'Étranger*, to determine how the author's judgment is justified. A search among Bergsonian principles is less an automatic gesture than it is a compelling examination of laughter studies by a philosopher whom Camus admired and knew very well: Bergson as source for Camus's comic elements is justifiable and critically sound, especially with respect to the comedy of form, of movement, of language, and of situation. Only the application of Bergson's theories concerning the comedy of character is blocked by *L'Étranger*'s first person narration. This emphasis on an individual point of view, rather than that of society, creates in turn a bizarre feeling of absurdity rather than outright laughter." (Abstract by author in *1973 MLA Abstracts*, 2, 20-21.)

5322   Jones, Louisa. "The Comic as Poetry: Bergson Revisited." *Nineteenth Century French Studies*, 2, Nos. 1 and 2, 1973-1974, 75-85. The author states, "I would like to show here firstly, how close Bergson came to making the connection between poetry and humor and in what ways; secondly, what assumptions held him back; thirdly...three distinctive types of humor in contemporary literature which are quite at home in a lyrical context" (pp. 75-76).

5323   Jung, Carl Gustav. "Letter to Alice Raphael Eckstein, September 16, 1930." In C. G. Jung *Letters*, Vol. I. Eds. Adler and Aniela Jaffe. Princeton, New Jersey: Princeton University Press, 1973, 596. Jung states, "Bergson is quite right when he thinks of the possibility of a relatively loose connection between the brain and consciousness, because despite our ordinary experience the connection might be less tight than we suppose. There is no reason why one shouldn't suppose that consciousness could exist detached from a brain" (p. 76).

5324   Kremer-Marietti, Angèle. "Bibliographie: Bergson dans l'histoire." *Études Bergsoniennes*, 10, 1973, 189-195.

5325   Le Breton, Maurice. "Les Romanciers américains et la personne." In *Problèmes de la personne*. Ed. Ignace Meyerson. Paris: Mouton, 1973, 305-311. The author deals with those (recent) novelists who have boldly probed beneath the "social self" to reveal the deeper, non-rational self: a programme which, he states, was first envisaged by Bergson in 1888 (*Les Données immédiates de la conscience*, Ch. II). In France Marcel Proust moved in this direction; in England James Joyce, Virginia Woolf and Aldous Huxley also have transformed the methods of the novelist in order to accomodate the new psychology of flux. The American novel from 1920-1930 underwent a similar development.

5326   Lee, Harold Newton. *Percepts, Concepts, and Theoretic Knowledge: A Study in Epistemology*. Memphis, Tennessee: Memphis State University Press, 1973, 257. The author states those respects in which his philosophy is indebted to Bergson (pp. 31n and 208).

5327   Leforte, Claude, Ed. *The Prose of the World*. Trans. John O'Neill. Evanston: Northwestern University Press, 1973, xlvi, 154. (Northwestern University Studies in Phenomenology and Existential Philosophy)

5328   Levesque, Georges. *Bergson; vie et mort de l'homme et de Dieu*. Paris: Les Éditions du Cerf, 1973, 136. (Horizon philosophique) The author argues that Bergson proposes a radical critique of the "God of the philosophers" and of static religions. On Bergson's terms the question of God is precisely that of the birth and death of man.

5329   Lobrot, Michel. *L'Intelligence et ses formes: Esquisse d'un modèle explicatif*. Paris-Brussels-Montreal: Dunod, 1973, vii, 336. The author criticizes both Bergsonian and structuralist views of intelligence.

5330   McMorris, M. N. "Time and Reality in Eliot and Einstein." *Main Currents*, 29, No. 3, 1973, 91-99. Likening the poet T. S. Eliot's Eleatic concept of time to

Einstein's, the author also shows Eliot's rejection of Bergson's duration.

5331   Megay, Joyce N. "La Question de l'influence de Bergson sur Proust." Diss. Neb-
        raska 1973, 246; Paris 1976. The author unites a critical analysis of the literature
        from 1913 to 1973 dealing with Bergson's supposed influence on Proust with
        her own analysis of the writings of Bergson and Proust. She concludes not only
        that Bergson did not influence Proust, but that at most essential points they
        stand in profound disagreement: "In their critical attitudes towards the superficial
        self, voluntary memory, intelligence, and language, Bergson and Proust are in
        essential agreement; but they part paths over the nature of the deep self,
        psychological time, involuntary memory, the positive role of intelligence, the
        nature of the real, and the power of poetic expression." (See *Dissertation
        Abstracts International*, 34, No. 12, Part 1, 1974, 7767A-7768A.) Cf. Jean-Paul
        Weber, 1973. (Also Cf. the author, 1976.)

5332   Megay, Joyce N. "La Queston de l'influence de Bergson sur Proust." *Bulletin of
        the Rocky Mountain Modern Language Association*, 27, No. 1, 1973, 53-58.
        (The journal in which this article appears is now titled *Rocky Mountain Review
        of Language and Literature*.)

5333   Metraux, Alexandre. "Heinrich Rickert, critique de Bergson." *Études Bergsonien-
        nes*, 10, 1973, 135-169.

5334   Mitsuo, Nakato. "Le Rôle de la notion de valeur dans le bergsonisme." Diss. Paris
        1973.

5335   Nicholas, Sister Joan Dunston. "Bergson's Theory of the Unity of the Person."
        Diss. Saint Louis, 1973, 277. The author criticizes Bergson's theory of person-
        ality on the basis that his epistemology is faulty, his dualism divides the person
        from the body, and his notion of duration provides an insufficient notion of
        substance. Cf. *Dissertation Abstracts International*, 35, No. 5, Sec. A, 1974,
        3060-3061.

5336   Pariente, Jean-Claude. *Le Langage et l'individu*. Paris: A. Colin, 1973, 304. The
        first chapter of this work develops insights first approached in "Bergson et
        Wittgenstein," *Revue International de Philosophie*, 1969.

5337   Paulhan, Jean. "La Terreur trouve son philosophe." in *Les Fleurs de Tarbs ou La
        Terreur dans les lettres: Suivi d'un dossier etabli par Jean-Claude Zylberstein*.
        Paris: 1973, 58-61.

5338   Prasad, B. K. "Bergson's *élan vital* and Ramanuja's Brahman." *Indian Philosophy
        and Culture*, 18, No. 2, 1973, 190-199.

5339   Prévost, Claude M. *Janet, Freud et la psychologie clinique*. Paris: Payot, 1973,
        213. (Petite Bibliothèque Payot, 228) The author relates Bergson's psychology
        at several points to those of S. Freud and P. Janet (pp. 128, 136-137, 164-165,
        175-176, 193). On p. 203n he states that, in conformity with tradition and
        popular mode, he compared Janet and Freud. A systematic confrontation of
        Bergson and P. Janet—much richer and more difficult—is called for.

5340   Prévost, Claude M. *La Psycho-philosophie de Pierre Janet: Economies mentales
        et progrès humain*. Paris: Payot, 1973, 348. Cf. esp. "Les Paradoxes de l'évolu-
        tion" pp. 71-77 for a comparison of Bergson's and Janet's psycho-philosophies,
        particularly with regard to Janet's *L'Evolution de la mémoire et de la notion de
        temps* (1928). Cf. also pp. 116, 123, 238-239, 249, 289, 312 and throughout.

5341   Robinet, André, Ed. *Henri Bergson: Mélanges*. Paris: Presses Universitaires de
        France, 1973, 1692. "Notes des éditeurs" are found on pp. 1599-1629. This
        collection of Bergson's writings was edited by Professor Robinet in collaboration
        with Rose-Marie Mossé-Bastide, Martine Robinet, and Michel Gauthier. It
        includes *Aristotle's Concept of Place, Duration and Simultaneity*, essays and
        talks which appear in *Mind-Energy* and *The Creative Mind*, and extensive cor-
        respondence.

5342   Rodríguez Echeverría, Alvaro A. "La intuicion Bergsoniana." *Logos: Revista de
        Filosofía*, 1, No. 3, 1973, 319-357. The author concludes: "Por eso, la intuición
        bergsoniana es eminentemente creadora, pues es una intuición de la vida en toda
        su amplitud, de la duración y del devenir."

5343   Rossi, Patrizio. "Bergson and Pirandello's *Il Giuoco della Parti.*" *Rivista di lett-
        erature moderne e comparate*, 26, No. 1, 1973, 61-71.

5344   Rossi, Patrizio. "La filosofia di Bergson in *Sei personaggi in cerca d'autore.*"
        Proceedings: Pacific Northwest Conference on Foreign Languages, 20, 1973,
        163-168.

5345   Sales, M. "Review of *Henri Bergson: Mélanges* by André Robinet and others."
        Archives de Philosophie, 36, No. 1, 1973, 168-169.

5346   Schmidtke, Charles Raymond. "Bergson's Meaning of Continuity." Diss. Tulane
        1973, 260. The author investigates Bergson's concept of continuity and the
        manner in which he orients philosophy towards the resolution of the problem
        of continuity. Though Bergson hopes to resolve the problem of continuity through
        the experience of life itself, this approach is not anti-intellectual, nor does it
        "destroy analysis" as some critics have claimed. The mathematical concept of
        continuity, as analyzed by Dedekind and Huntington, provides support for
        Bergson's concept of continuity. A satisfactory examination of the nature of
        continuity requries an investigation of the relationship between the theories of
        the mathematicians and Bergson's metaphysics. This dissertation compares and
        contrasts various aspects of the mathematical concept of continuity with
        Bergson's notion. The author believes that he has added "another dimension"
        to Bergson's method. (See *Dissertation Abstracts International*, 34, No. 5,
        1973, 2707A.)

5347   Schneider, Herbert W. "Review of *A History of Western Philosophy* by Ralph M.
        McInerny and A. Robert Caponigri." *Journal of the History of Philosophy*, 11,
        No. 1, 1973, 107-109. The reviewer notes of Vol. V of this history of philosophy,
        "Significant, I suppose, is the fact that in all this welter Bergson stands out
        alone, and yet central."

5348   Schrecker, Paul. "Individual Psychological Significance of First Childhood Recol-
        lections." *Journal of Individual Psychology*, 29, No. 2, 1973, 146-156. This is
        a translation of "Die individual-psychologische Bedeutung der ersten Kindheit-
        serinnerungen" by P. Schrecker, *Zbl. Psychoanal. Psychother.*, 4, 1913-1914,
        121-130. The author develops a theory of the psychoanalytic importance of
        early childhood memories based on the insights of Bergson and Alfred Adler.
        Adler was to incorporate these ideas in his own system of dynamic psychiatry.
        Cf. H. Ansbacher, 1973; the author, 1912.

5349   Schubert, Venanz. *Plotin: Einführung in sein Philosophieren*. Freiburg, München:
        K. Alber, 1973, 177. (Kolleg Philosophie) The author begins his study of
        Plotinus' thought with a brief analysis of the role played by Plotinus' philosophy

in the thought of Goethe, Schelling, Hegel, and Bergson.

5350   Smirnov, Alexandrovich. *Problems of the Psychology of Memory.* Trans. Samuel
        A. Corson. New York and London: Plenum Press, 1973, 338. This book was
        published originally in Moscow in 1966. It contains several criticisms of
        Bergson's concept of memory. These appear in Chapter 6, "Reflective Activity,"
        Section 2, "Meaningful Points of Support and their Separation," pp. 172-187.
        Bergson fails to point out that we must deal with a logical chain of ideas: with
        several points of support. Also Bergson suspiciously fails to mention the necessity
        of dividing the material into meaningful parts, although "it is this process which
        is the basis for understanding the logic of the material" (p. 1973). The author
        concludes by criticizing Bergson's concept of the "dynamic schema" as the basic
        point of support. This is the old "idea-force," a notoriously idealistic notion.
        He cites several experiments against Bergson.

5351   Ştefănescu, Cornelia. *Momente ale romanului.* Bucureşti: Eminescu, 1973, 338.

5352   Street, Eduard Arnold. "From Proust to Richard: French Thematic and
        Phenomenological Criticism," Diss. Yale, 1973, 246. The author, in tracing the
        development of contemporary French literary criticism, cites G. Bachelard's
        methods as "close to Bergsonian intuitionism." *Dissertation Abstracts Interna-
        tional*, 34, No. 6, 1973, 3433-3434A.

5353   Tallon, Andrew. "Memory and Man's Composite Nature According to Bergson."
        New Scholasticism, 47, No. 4, 1973, 483-489. This is a study of the interrelations
        between Bergson's two sorts of memory.

5354   Tamás, Miklós Gaspar. "Bergson a Módszerről." *Magyar Filozofiai Szemle*, 17,
        1973, 112-140. This article concerns Bergson's philosophical method.

5355   Theau, Jean. "La Conception bergsonienne de la philosophie." *La Philosophie et
        les philosophes.* 2. *De Nietzsche à nos jours.* Montréal: Bellarmin; Paris-Tour-
        nai,: Duclée, 1973, 65-81. The author points out that for Bergson philosophy
        is not merely a game, but a serious quest, which can bring us joy. Joy, however,
        is for Bergson dependent on knowledge, i.e., "connaissance intérior", "intui-
        tion". Intuition, however, requires analysis as its necessary condition; in turn,
        intuition can transform our modes of analysis.

5356   Trouillard, Jean, Maurice P. Grandillac, and others. *Études néoplatoniciennes, par
        J. Trouillard, Pierre Hadot, Heindrick Dorrie, Fernand Brunner, et Maurice
        P. de Grandillac.* Neuchâtel: Ed. La Beconnière, 1973, 126. (Languages) This
        is a collection of talks given at the University of Neuchâtel, 1971-1972, and
        published originally in the *Revue de Theologie et de Philosophie* (No. 2, 1973).
        It contains an article by Maurice P. de Grandillac titled "Le Plotin de Bergson."

5357   Verdenal, René. "La Philosophie de Bergson." In *La Philosophie du monde scien-
        tifique et industriel (1860-1940).* Vol. VI of *Histoire de la philosophie: Idées,
        Doctrines.* Ed. François Chatelet. Paris: Hachette, 1973, 349.

5358   Weber, Jean-Paul. "Bergson and Proust." In *In Search of Marcel Proust: Essays
        from the Marcel Proust Centennial Colloquium Held at Claremont Colleges,
        on Nov. 12, 13, 14, 1971.* Ed. Monique Chedfor. Claremont, California: Scripps
        College and the Ward Ritchie Press, 1973, 55-77. The author concludes that
        Proust was influenced by Bergson's concepts of memory and duration. He holds
        that Bergson is, to a large extent, the model for Ralph Savaie, a comic character
        in Proust's incomplete early novel *Jean Santeuil*. While arguing for Bergson's

influence on Proust, however, he is careful to point out the many differences in the viewpoints of the two men.

5359   Wells, David F. "George Tyrrell: Precursor of Process Theology." *Scottish Journal of Theology*, 26, No. 1, 1973, 71-84. The author discusses G. Tyrrell as one of the European Catholic Progeny of Bergson. (The other important set of Bergson's progeny are categorised as American Protestants.) (See Review by J. G. Janzen in *Process Studies*, 3, No. 2, 1973, 135.)

5360   Wilson, Barrie A. "Review of *Mélanges* by Henri Bergson." *Modern Schoolman*, 50, No. 2, 1973, 311-312.

5361   Wyss, Dieter. *Psychoanalytic Schools from the Beginning to the Present*. Trans. Gerald Onn. Intro. Leston L. Havens. New York: Jason Aronson, Inc., 1973, 568. This is a translation of the author's *Die Tiefenpsychologischen Schulen von den Anfängen bis zur Gegenwart* (1961). On p. 105 the author discusses the final phase of Freud's thought, resulting in "that irrational mythology of drives, which established the work of the strictly scientific founder of psychoanalysis as being closely akin to the related, modern (irrational) enquiries of *Bergson* and a *Klages*, to the inroads made by the irrational in Surrealism and Existentialism, and even to the writings of *C. G. Jung*, but which failed to grasp the true nature of the irrational." On p. 282 the author notes that Harry Stack Sullivan's concept of "empathy" is taken from Bergson.

5362   Zaner, Richard M. "The Subjectivity of the Human Body." *Main Currents*, 29, No. 1, January-February 1973, 117-120.

1974

5363   Ando, Takatura. *Metaphysics: A Critical Survey of its Meaning*. The Hague: Martinus Nijhoff, 1974, 158. Section 1 (pp. 95-103) of Chapter V ("Metaphysics in Recent Philosophy") concerns Bergson. The author concludes: "It was Bergson's fervent desire, just as it was Kant's, to save metaphysics from the despotism of science. But the divorce was not an easy task, as had been at first imagined. Metaphysics was like a gallant who, being weary of a sterling housewife "Understanding," yet without the brilliant wit necessary to become intimate with a lady "Reason," has found comfort in a street girl "Intuition," but, to avoid scandal, has begged forgiveness from the wife he has betrayed." (p. 103)

5364   Baldino, Pasquale. *L'Arte nella concezione di Bergson*. Napoli: A. De Frede, 1974, 22.

5365   Berl, Emmanuel. "Quand Bergson me parlait de télépathie." *Figaro Littéraire*, No. 1476, 31 août 1974, I, 9.

5366   Birch, Charles. "Chance Necessity and Purpose." in *Studies in the Philosophy of Biology: Reduction and Related Problems*. Ed. Francisco Jose Ayala and Theodosius Dobzhansky. Berkeley and Los Angeles: University of California Press, 1974, 224-238. On p. 236 the author states: "Sewall Wright (1953-1964), starting from the recognition of his own 'stream of consciousness', derives matter from mind, not the other way around. His earlier mechanistic viewpoint was shaken by reading Bergson's *Creative Evolution*, thought he was unable to accept this as a philosophy of science. But it was a result of reading Karl Pearson's *Grammar of Science* that he emerged a convinced panpsychist..." The author footnotes Wright's "Gene and Organism". *The American Naturalist*, 87, 1953, 5-18 and "Biology and the Philosophy of Science" in *Process and Divinity* (Ed. W. L. Riese and E. Freeman) La Salle, Illinois, 1964.

5367 Bjelland, Andrew G. "Bergson's dualism in *Time and Free Will*." *Process Studies*, 4, No. 2, 1974, 83-106.

5368 Böhme, Gernot. *Studien zur Zeittheorie bei Platon, Aristoteles, Leibniz und Kant.* Frankfurt: V. Klostermann, 1974, vii, 281. (Philosophische Abhandlungen, 45) "Diese historischen Untersuchungen sind von dem systematischen Interesse geleitet, jene Unterscheidungen zwischen physikalischer, und erlebter Zeit zu überwinden, die sich seit Bergson und Heidegger entfaltet hat." Otto Pöggeler, *Bibliographie de la Philosophie*, 25, No. 4, 1978, 293.

5369 Bonnes, Jean-Paul. "Actualité de Bergson." *Monde Moderne*, No. 8, 1974-1975, 203-206.

5370 Brennan, Joseph John. "The Comic in the Plays of Eugene O'Neill: The Use of Characterization, Situation, and Language in Relation to Bergson's Theory of Comedy." Diss. New York 1974, 504. The author utilizes Bergson's concept of comedy to investigate comic characterization, situation, and language in the plays of Eugene O'Neill. Bergson's *Laughter* is utilized, the author states, because it is more complete than any other treatment of the comic. O'Neill, as he matured, made progressively greater use of comedy. (*Dissertation Abstracts International*, 35, No. 2, 1974, 1088A.)

5371 Canivez, André. "Henri Bergson." In *Historie de la philosophie*. Vol. III of *Du XIXe Siècle à nos jours*. Ed. Yvon Belaval. Paris: Gallimard, 1974, 283-306.

5372 Chambers, Connor J. "Zeno of Elea and Bergson's Neglected Thesis." *Journal of the History of Philosophy*, 12, No. 1, 1974, 63-76. The author contends that Henri Bergson's neglected Latin Thesis is not a defense of Kant's theory of space, as has been supposed. In this thesis Bergson's debt to Zeno is twofold. First, Zeno's paradoxes provide Bergson with a basic set of problems. Second, taking his theses before a predominantly Kantian faculty, Bergson cleverly illustrates in the Latin work his mastery of Zeno's classical method of academic protest, illustrating the weakness of Kant's theory of space no less than Aristotle's.

5373 Claudel, Paul. *Correspondance Paul Claudel/Jean-Louis Barrault*. Préf. Jean-Louis Barrault. Intro. Michel Lioure. Paris: Gallimard, 1974, 410.

5374 Colum, Jovan. *Дневник са Атлатика и други есеяи*. Београд: Нолит, 1974, 166. The romanized title of this work is *Dnevnik sa Atlantika i drugi esejf.*

5375 Copleston, Frederic. *A History of Philosophy*. Vol. 9, *Biran to Sartre*. New York: Newman Press, 1974, 480. Chapters 9 and 10 of this history of philosophy discuss Henri Bergson's philosophy. The first chapter (pp. 178-201) states Bergson's general position; the next (pp. 202-215) deals with Bergson's moral and religious philosophy.

5376 Cullen, John Charles."The Unity of René Le Senne's Philosophy." Diss. St. Louis, 1974, 301. The author explores Le Senne's critique of Bergson's concept of the unimpeded continuity of duration. Bergson is one of several authors treated. *Dissertation Abstracts International*, 35, No. 5, 1974, 3050A.

5377 Danielou, Jean. *Et qui est mon prochain? Mémoires*. Paris: Stock, 1974, 250. This book deals with many figures in French intellectual life, including Bergson.

5378   Delattre, Floris. *Ruskin et Bergson; et l'intuition esthétique à l'intuition metaphysique*. 1947; rpt. Folcroft, Pa: Folcroft Library Editions, 1974, 27.

5379   Dessoughi, Kamal. *'Ilm al-nafs wa dirasat al tawafug*. Bereut: Dar an-Nahda al-'Arabiyya, 1974, 420. The title of this work is translated as *Psychology and the Study of Adaptation*. The author is critical of concepts like *élan vital*, suggests the concept of "need" in their place.

5380   Devaux, André-A. "Charles Du Bose, Jacques Maritain et Gabriel Marcel ou peut-on aller de Bergson a Saint Thomas d'Aquin?" *Cahiers Charles Du Bos*, No. 18, 1974, 87-103.

5381   "Doctoral Dissertations, 1974." *Review of Metaphysics*, 28, No. 1, 1974, 183.

5382   Edwards, William Sterling, and Edwards, Peter D. *Alexis Carrel: Visionary Surgeon*. Foreword Charles A. Lindbergh. Springfield, Illinois: Charles C. Thomas, 1974, 143. In 1913, "at a large dinner in Paris at the home of the philosopher, Henri Bergson, the guests were discussing the epidemics that were decimating the French army in Morocco. Crudel asked, 'But how can we let the soldiers die without remedy?' Metchinikoff responded, 'The vaccines are inefficient.' Coudert turned to Carrel and asked, 'What does Dr. Carrel think about this?' 'They are too ignorant in France to plan for the future,' he replied from the end of the table. These words fell in a dismayed silence" (p. 61). (This was just after Carrel was given the Nobel Prize for surgery)

5383   Felt, James W. "The Temporality of Divine Freedom." *Process Studies*, 4, No. 4, 1974, 252-262. In this essay the author attempts to correct A. N. Whitehead's concept of God through an examination of Bergson's concept of freedom. The non-temporal freedom of Whitehead's "primordial" aspect of deity must be joined with a temporal freedom, as suggested by Bergson. This temporal freedom must find its place in Whitehead's "consequent" aspect of deity. Only thus can God's love for individuals, and not just *types* of *kinds* of individuals, be understood.

5384   Feuer, Lewis S. *Einstein and the Generations of Science*. New York: Basic Books, 1974, 374. In "Louis Victor, Prince de Broglie, Aristocratic Revolutionist," pp. 200-236, the author discusses Bergson's influence on de Broglie's physics, terming Bergson "de Broglie's pilot wave."

5385   Fiddian, R. W. "Unamuno-Bergson: A Reconsideration." *Modern Language Review*, 69, No. 4, 1974, 787-795. "The theories of *intrahistoria* and *durée* ⸯ Unamuno and Bergson can fruitfully be compared and contrasted. Both thinkers postulate the existence of an autonomous cosmic force in which qualitative timelessness transcends the quantitative framework of historical time. But Bergson's dynamic and monistic view of mind and matter as homogeneous activity is at variance with Unamuno's quietist and dualist interpretation of reality as a combination of opposites such as mobility and stasis, time and eternity. In addition, whereas the two systems accommondate the notions of humanity and God, Unamuno's admission of teleological consciousness, plenitude and transcendence in *intrahistoria* differs from Bergson's immanentist philosophy of *durée* which denies the purposive faculty of mind, diverges from the conventional idea of God, and sees the temporal structure of the world as open-ended." (1974 MLA Abstracts, 2, 62.)

5386 Flint, F. S. "Contemporary French Poetry." in *The Road From Paris: French Influence on English Poetry, 1900-1920*. ed. Cyrena N. Pondrom. Cambridge: At the University Press, 1974, 86-145. This is reprinted from *The Poetry Review* (1912). Cf. the editor's remarks pp. 84-85 for Flint's use of Bergson.

5387 Gale, Richard M. "Bergson's Analysis of the Concept of Nothing." *Modern Schoolman*, 51, No. 2, 1974, 269-300.

5388 Goulet, Jean. "*Matière et mémoire* (1896) aujourd'hui." *Revue de l'Université d'Ottowa*, 44, No. 2, 1974, 224-258.

5389 Grogin, Robert C. "Bergson and the French Catholic Revival: 1900-1914." *Thought*, 49, No. 3, 1974, 311-322. The author explores Bergson's impact on Teilhard de Chardin, Charles Péguy, the Maritains, Édouard Le Roy, Joseph Lotte, Paul Claudel, and others. "Bergsonism, after all was never a school which set guidelines for its members, but rather a tendency in pre-war France, where men could call themselves Bergsonians and still be their own masters" (p. 322).

5390 Guitton, Jean. *Ecrire comme on se souvient*. Paris: Fayard, 1974, 382. This study particularly concerns Bergson, A. Loisy and P. Teilhard de Chardin.

5391 Hammer, Felix. *Leib und Geschlecht: Philosophische Perspektiven von Nietzsche bis Merleau-Ponty und phänomenologisch-systematischer Aufriss*. Bonn: Bouvier, 1974, viii, 1974. (Abh. zur Philosophie, Psychologie und Pädagogik, 91) Bergson is treated here with Dilthey, Simmel, Klages and Ortega, as an exponent of *Lebensphilosophie*.

5392 Heilbron, J. L. "Review of *Einstein and the Generations of Science* by Lewis S. Feuer." *Science*, 185, No. 4153, 1974, 777-778. The reviewer dismisses as "fantasy" Feuer's thesis that Bergson's metaphysics influenced L. de Broglie's physics.

5393 Hesse, Herman. "Henri Bergson." in *My Belief*. Ed. Th. Ziolkowski. Trans. D. Lindley. New York: Farar Straus and Giroux, 1974, 364-365.

5394 Hulme, Terence Ernest. "Review of *L'Attitude de lyrisme contemporaine* by T. de Visan." in *The Road From Paris: French Influence on English Poetry 1900-1920*. Ed. Cyrena N. Pondrom. Cambridge: At the University Press, 1974, 58-60. This article, reprinted from *New Age* (1911), appears in a section titled "Bergson and the Theory of Modern French Poetry."

5395 Jones, Deborah. *The Reactions of Bergson and Piaget to the Theory of Special Relativity*. James Bryant Conant Prizes. Harvard University, 1974.

5396 Jous, Dominique. "La Notion de creation dans «L'Évolution créatrice» d'Henri Bergson." Diss. Liege 1974. This work is listed as a "mémoire de licence."

5397 Lafrance, Guy. "Review of *Les Études Bergsoniennes*, Vol. 10." *Dialogue*, 13, No. 2, June, 1974, 419-423.

5398 Lafrance, Guy. *La Philosophie sociale de Bergson*. Ottawa, Canada: Éditions de l'Université d'Ottawa, 1974, 148. (Collection "philosophica", Vol. 3) The author finds many similarities between Bergson's social philosophy and that of Émile Durkheim. Cf. J. Theau's review, 1975. He also finds many close connections between Bergson's biology and his ideas in *The Two Sources*.

5399 Lee, Harold Newton. "Process and Pragmatism." *Tulane Studies in Philosophy*, 23, 1974, 87-97. The relations between Bergson's "process philosophy" and pragmatism are examined here on pp. 87-89.

5400 Lefèvre, L. J. "Nos actes nous suivent: Notes sur Descartes et sur Bergson." *Le Pensée Catholique*, 28, No. 151, 1974, 67-97.

5401 Levesque, Georges *Bergson, vida y muerte del hombre y de Dios*. Trans. Alejandro Estaban Lator Ros. Barcelona: Herder, 1974, 152.

5402 Lubkicki, Narcyz. "Roman Ingarden's Philosophical Profile." *Dialectics and Humanism*, 1, No. 3, 1974, 157-177.

5403 Margolin, Jean-Claude. "Henri Bergson." *Revue de Synthèse*, 95, No. 73-74, 1974, 95-96. This is a review of *Bergson* by Vittorio Mathieu.

5404 Margolin, Jean-Claude. "Du nouveau sur Bergson." *Revue de Synthèse*, 95, No. 75-76, 1974, 323-324.

5405 Megay, Joyce N. "Bibliographie critique sur la question de l'influence de Bergson sur Proust." *Proust Research Association Newsletter*, No. 12, 1974, 14-21. The bibliographer deals here only with major studies devoted to the relationships between Marcel Proust and Bergson. Additional related bibliographic sources are presented by the author in the next number of the *Proust Research Association Newsletter*.

5406 Mehlmann, Jeffrey. "Proust's Counterplot." in *A Structural Study of Autobiography: Proust, Leiris, Sartre, Levi-Strauss*. Ithaca, New York: Cornell University Press, 1974, 20-64.

5407 Milet, Jean. *Henri Bergson et le calcul infinitésimal: ou, La Raison et le temps*. Préf. Jean Ullmo. Paris: Presses Universitaires de France, 1974, 184. (Bibliothèque de philosophie contemporaine) The author argues that Bergson's concept of intuition was formed through his study of calculus, and that his philosophy can be conceived as a "dynamic rationalism." Cf. J. Ullmo, 1974.

5408 Morot-Sir, Edouard. "Review of *Morality in Evolution: The Moral Philosophy of Henri Bergson* by Idella J. Gallagher." *Journal of the History of Philosophy*, 12, No. 3, 1974, 410-411. The author states, "Then I would emphasize, more than Mrs. Gallagher has done, the deep opposition to Kant, and consider that one of the most important intentions in writing *The Two Sources of Morality and Religion* was to sweep out the Kantian influence which pervades French official values after 1870 and continues today, in spite of Henri Bergson's gallant fight" (p. 411).

5409 Murry, John Middleton, "Art and Philosophy." in *The Road From Paris: French Influence on English Poetry, 1900-1920*. Ed. Cryena J. Pondrom. Cambridge: At the University Press, 1974, 54-57. This article, reprinted from *Rhythm* (1911), appears here in a section titled "Bergson and the *Avant Garde*."

5410 Nedelijkovič, Dušan. *Интуиционизам И дияалекика*. Београд: Научно Дело, 1974, 184. Both Henri Bergson and A. O. Lovejoy are discussed in this work, whose romanized title is *Intuicionizam i dijalektika*.

5411 Panou, Stavros. "The Logic of Nothingness." *Philosophia*, 4, 1974, 59-67. This article is in Greek.

5412 Piclin, Michel. *Schopenhauer, ou le tragédien de la volunté*. Paris: Seghers, 1974, 176. This study of Schopenhauer contains a comparison of his philosophy with Bergson's.

5413 Piguet, Jean-Claude. "Le Philosophe devant le monde aujourdhui." *Études de Lettres*, S. 3, Vol. 7, No. 2, 1974, 15-26.

5414 Pondrom, Cyrena N. *The Road From Paris: French Influence on English Poetry, 1900-1910*. Cambridge: At the University Press, 1974, 334. The author traces the influence of French literature and philosophy on English poetry. She notes the influence of Bergson on F. S. Flint, John Middleton Murry, and T. E. Hulme, among others, and reprints English-language articles *circa* 1910 concerning Bergson's philosophy and its relations to poetry. Cf. esp. pp. 1, 13-18, 54-60, 81-86.

5415 Porter, Burton F. *Philosophy: A Literary and Conceptual Approach*. New York: Harcourt, Brace, Jovanovich, 1974, 514. Chapter I, "The Concept of Self," contains selections from Bergson's *An Introduction to Metaphysics*.

5416 Rivera de Ventosa, Enrique. "San Buenaventura y Henri Bergson: Estudio comparativo de dos anthoropologías." *Salmanticensis*, 21, 1974, 27-67.

5417 Rossi, Patrizio. "Tempo e memoria bergsoniani nell' *Enrico IV* di Luigi Pirandello." In *Proceedings: Pacific Northwest Conference on Foreign Languages*, ed. Walter C. Kraft, Vol. 25, Part I: *Literature and Linguistics*. Corvallis: Oregon State University Press, 1974, 296. "Bergsonian philosophical schemes are use in *Enrico IV* where dramatic tension is constructed on the relation between memory and time. By comparing the development of the plot of *Enrico IV* with the ideas exposed in *Materia e memoria*, *Enrico IV* is seen as one of the best plays by Pirandello, although critics often point out that Pirandello is dealing with abstract ideas and not with emotions and feelings which are truly human." (*1974 MLA Abstracts*, 2, 47.)

5418 Rosso, Corrado. *Inventari e postile: Letture francesi, divagazioni europee*. Pisa: Editrice Libreria Goliardica, 1974, 404. Cf. pp. 59-62 for a study of idealism and romanticism in Bergson, Proust and Goethe. This article concerns Vittorio Mathieu's *Bergson*. It appeared originally in *Convivium*, March-April, 1955.

5419 Sancipriano, Mario. "The Activity of Consciousness: Husserl and Bergson." *Analectica Husserliana*, 3, 1974, 161-167.

5420 Santelli, Lusia. *Problemi pedagogici in Henri Bergson*. Padove: Liviana, 1974, vi, 166. A bibliography is given here on pp. 161-164.

5421 Santos, J. "Review of *Henri Bergson: A Bibliography* by P. A. Y. Gunter." *Revista Brasiliera de Filosofia*, 24, 1974, 499-501.

5422 Seidenberg, Roderick. *Posthistoric Man: An Inquriy* 1950: rpt. New York: Viking, 1974, 244. The author utilizes throughout this strange study a distinction between instinct and intelligence drawn from *Creative Evolution*. He sees, however, instinct becoming totally eclipsed by intelligence in a final, perfectly mechanized state of mankind, in which all inward, personal values will be eclipsed, and consciousness itself disappear. (Cf. pp. 186-189) He rejects A. Toynbee's and Bergson's views of a spiritual resolution of man's present dilemmas. (Cf. pp. 200-226.)

5423 Soreil, Arsene. "Retour au «Faber»." In *Thèmes de saison: Art et culture*, Bruxelles: La Renaissance du Livre, 1974, 25-32.

5424 Sorrell, Martin R. M. "Le Grand Meaulnes: A Bergsonian View of the *fête étrange*." *Australian Journal of French Studies*, 11, No. 2, 1974, 182-187. The author finds parallels with many of Bergson's ideas in a novel by Alain-Fournier.

5425 Suances Marcos, Anselmo Manuel. *Los Fundamentos de la moral en Bergson*. Madrid: S.E.R.E.S.A., 1974, 36. (Velazquez, 17)

5426　　Suances Marcos, Anselmo Manuel. "La libertad como maduración en la filosofía bergsoniana." *Razon y Fe*, 190, No. 922, 1974, 328-341. This is an exposition of Bergson's concept of freedom.

5427　　Stevens, Richard. *James and Husserl: The Foundation of Meaning*. The Hague: M. Nijhoff, 1974, viii, 191. (Phaenomenologica, 60) The author relates James' ideas to Bergson and considers Bergson's influence on Wm. James.

5428　　Ullmo, Jean. "Préface." *Henri Bergson et le calcul infinitesimal* by Jean Milet. Paris: Presses Universitaires de France, 1974, 5-11. The author, himself a mathematician, commends Jean Milet for his study of the part which mathematics played in the development of the thought of Henri Bergson. Milet has shown, correctly, that the concept of the infinitesimal calculus played a central role in Bergson's philosophy. By means of his interpretation of the calculus, Bergson was able to show that mathematics is able to describe motion: not by spatializing and fragmenting motion but by taking it as an indivisible "whole." Once the "whole" of motion is given, its constituent "parts" can be derived. This root conception is one which Bergson was able to apply prophetically to other sciences, notably to quantum physics.

5429　　Whitehead, Alfred North. "Reflections on Time and Endurance." *Southern Journal of Philosophy*. 12, No. 1, 1974, 117-126. This is a classroom lecture delivered by Whitehead in 1934, as part of a course titled "Cosmologies Ancient and Modern." Whitehead compares Bergson's concept of duration with Descartes' concept of "perpetual perishing" and Epicurus' view of time as an "accident of accidents." Whitehead likens his own position to Bergson's and twice commends Bergson for the "tremendous service" he has performed for philosophy. He also criticizes Bergson's concept of the intellect and its function. (These notes were originally transcribed, and subsequently edited and published, by Joseph Gerard Brennan.)

5430　　Winance, E. "Review of *Bergson and Modern Physics* by Milič Čapek." *Journal of the History of Philosophy*, 12, No. 1, 1974, 130-131. This review, which is written in French, is balanced and informative.

5431　　Winther, Truls. *Paul Claudel og det skapende ord*. Oslo: Universitet i Oslo, 1974, 343. This is a criticism and interpretation of the work of Paul Claudel.

5432　　Yu, Pauline. "Georges Poulet and the Symbolist Tradition." *Criticism*, 16, No. 1, Winter, 1974, 39-57. This article deals with Poulet in connection with M. Proust, Bergson and S. Mallarmé.

1975

5433　　Adam, Michel. "Review of *Bergson: Vie et mort de l'homme et de Dieu* by George Levesque." *Revue Philosophique de la France et de l'Étranger*, 165, No. 3, 1975, 360-361.

5434　　Adam, Michel. "Review of *La Philosophie sociale de Bergson* by Guy Lafrance." *Revue Philosophique de la France et de l'Étranger*, 165, No. 3, 1975, 361.

5435　　Amato, Joseph. *Mounier and Maritain: A French Catholic Understanding of the Modern World*. University, Alabama: University of Alabama Press, 1975, 215. (Studies in the Humanities: Philosophy, 6) The author recounts the influence of

Bergson (through Jacques Chevalier) on E. Mounier.

5436   Baron, Frank. "The Needs for Order and for Disorder as Motives in Creative Activity." In *Scientific Creativity: Its Recognition and Development*. Ed. Calvin W. Taylor and Frank Baron. Huntington, New York: Robert E. Krieger Publishing Co., 1975, 153-160. The author uses Bergsonian ideas to explain the psychology of creative people, including especially creative scientists. Bergson has shown, he states, how the human intellect attempts to discern the repetitive and the foreseeable in experience; Bergson has also shown that man's *creative intellect makes new classifications and new modes of prediction. To complete the philosophy of creative evolution, however, it is necessary to explain why creative people prefer relatively disorderd geometric figures to simply ordered figures—a fact which the author's research makes clear. Creative people, the author concludes, have learned to prefer a "disorder" which can be transformed into a new vision of order to a simply-established order based on concepts which are already old.*

5437   Berndtson, Arthur. "A Theory of Radical Creativity." *The Modern Schoolman*, 53, No. 4, 1975, 1-18. The author evaluates Nietzsche's, Bergson's and Whitehead's theories of creativity before detailing his own theory of creativity. He finds Bergson's philosophy has several weaknesses: its life force is "a parochialism of post-Darwinian thought," its concept of matter is unaccounted for, its concept of intuition can not be extended beyond the individual, and its transcendence of nihilism leads to a too-easy optimism.

5438   Bjelke, Johan Fredrik. *Den Europeiske Filosofi: Fra Thomas Aquinas til Henri Bergson*. Oslo: Univ.-Forlaget, 1975, 213.

5439   Blanché, Robert. "Review of *Henri Bergson et le calcul infinitésimal* by Jean Milet." *Revue Philosophique de la France et de l'Étranger*, 165, No. 2, 1975, 358-362.

5440   Bretonneau, Gisèle. *Création et valeurs éthiques chez Bergson*. Paris: Société d'Edition d'Enseignement Supérieur, 1975, 319.

5441   César, Constança Marcondes. "A crítica de Bachelard à duração bergsoniana." *Reflexão*, 1, No. 2, 1975-1976, 9-16.

5442   Chandra, S. Subhash. "Bergson's Philosophy of Nature: I." *The Aryan Path*, 42, No. 2, 1975, 60-65.

5443   Chevrier, Pierre, Ed. *Antoine de Saint-Exupéry: Carnets*. Paris: Gallimard, 1975, 284.

5444   Chiari, Joseph. *Twentieth-Century French Thought: From Bergson to Levi-Strauss*. New York: Gordian Press, 1975, 207. Chapter I, titled "Henri Bergson," appears here on pp. 21-59.

5445   Conte, Arthur. *Le ler janvier 1900*. Paris: Plon, 1975, xiii, 346. This book deals with Bergson, P. Claudel, E. Durkheim, A. Gide, C. Péguy and many others.

5446   Copleston, Frederick. *A History of Philosophy: Volume IX, Maine de Biran to Sartre*. Paramus, New Jersey: Newman Press, 1975, 480. Chapters nine and ten (pp. 178-215) of this work are devoted to Bergson. In general the author gives an accurate and even-handed account of Bergson's philosophy. His account of Bergson's "influence" is lamentably brief, and one feels that his lamentations over the "looseness" and "imprecision" of Bergson's language spring in part from a failure to penetrate to Bergson's actual meanings. The author is accurate without being perceptive.

5447 Dhavernas, Marie-Josèphe. "Abstract of *Bergson et le calcul infinitésimal* by Jean Milet." *Bibliographie de la Philosophie*, 22, No. 2, 1975, 164.

5448 Dolgov, K. M. "The Philosophy and Aesthetics of Maurice Merleau-Ponty." *Soviet Studies in Philosophy*, 14, No. 1, 1975-1976, 67-92.

5449 Dominguez Rey, Antonio. "Lenguaje y conocimiento poético de Antonio Machado." *Estafeta Literaria*, No. 569-570, 1-15 agosto 1975, 4-6. Bergson's influence on Machado is discussed in this essay.

5450 Douglas, Charlotte. "Suprematism: The Sensible Domain." *The Russian Review*, 34, No. 3, July, 1975, 266-281. The author examines the influence of Bergson's philosophy on suprematism, a rigorously abstract form of painting developed in Russia by Kazimir Malevich beginning around 1913-1914. Russian suprematists believed that they, and not futurism, really understood Bergson.

5451 Downer, Shirley. "Une Vue de la comédie sauvage selon les théories du rire de Bergson." *Chimères*, 9, No. 1, 1975, 32-42. The phrase "comédie sauvage" has been suggested by Professor Kenneth White to describe a new type of comic theater, in which violence is at the base of the comic situation. The author uses Bergson's theory of laughter to explore the "comédie sauvage," which includes works by Alfred Jarry, Louis Aragon, and Tristan Tsara.

5452 Eisely, Loren. "The Coming of the Giant Wasps." *Audubon Magazine*, 77, No. 5, September 1975, 35-39.

5453 Eisely, Loren. "The Coming of the Giant Wasps." in *All The Strange Hours: The Excavations of a Life*. New York: Charles Scribner's Sons, 1975, 243-254. The author, a well-known paleontologist and historian of science, asserts his belief that "In the world there is nothing to explain the world." (p. 245) He notes that biological scientists are in the end forced, by trying to explain nature, into metaphysical positions reflecting their temperamental bent. Some are reductionists like Jacques Loeb, others vitalists like Henri Bergson. The author argues that Bergson's treatment of the instincts of the solitary wasps in *Creative Evolution* touched on problems which have not yet been resolved. How the wasp can have innate ideas of its prey's nervous system, for example, is hard to explain through natural selection.

5454 Fizer, John. "Ingarden's Passes, Bergson's Durée Réelle, and William James' Stream: Metaphoric Variants of Mutually Exclusive Concepts on the Theme of Time." *Dialectics and Humanism* (Italy), 2, No, 3, 1975, 23-48. "The intent of this article is to give an analytical view of Roman Ingarden's understanding of temporality of intentionally contingent objects, particularly those of the work of literary art, and to juxtapose it with the views of Henri Bergson and William James. According to Ingarden, due to the ontological and structural complexity of these objects there exist three distinct possibilities of time in them. First, when their intentionality is bracketed from the lived experience, they become purely spatio-temporal phenomena; second, when they are conceived as artistic objects, their temporal sequence is given simultaneously; and third, when they are treated as aesthetic objects, their temporal phases exist serially through our experienced presentification. Bergson's, James' and Ingarden's positions on time reveal some resemblance but also substantial differences which are to be understood respectively in terms of their differing philosophies, vitalism, radical empiricism and phenomenology." (*Philosopher's Index*, 10, No. 1, 1976, 62.)

5455 Fizer, John. "Fazy ingardena, durée réelle bergsona, strumien williama jamesa." *Studia filozoficzne*, No. 10, 1975, 27-44.

5456 Garcia Astrada, Arturo. "Alberto Rougés y el problema del tiempo." *Cuadernos de Filosofia* (Argentina), 15, No. 22-23, 1975, 59-67.

5457 Glyn, P. Norton. *Montaigne and the Introspective Mind*. The Hague: Mouton, 1975, 219.

5458 Grau, Joseph A. *Morality and the Human Future in the Thought of Teilhard de Chardin: A Critical Study*. Rutherford: Fairleigh Dickinson University Press, 1975, 389. The author holds that Teilhard, like Bergson, distinguishes between a closed morality of equilibrium and an open morality.

5459 Gunter, Pete A. Y. "Review of *Bergson and Modern Physics* by Milič Čapek." *Southwestern Journal of Philosophy*, 6, No. 1, 1975, 155-156. (Cf. Čapek's response, 1978.)

5460 Haakonsen, Daniel. "Henri Bergson og norsk litteratur." In *Fransk I Norge: Festskrift til Gunnar Host*. Ed. Anne-Lisa Amadou and others. Oslo: Aschehoug, 1975, 202.

5461 Hara, Shôji. "Bergson et l'ésthetique." Thèse, Université de Paris-I, 1975, 175.

5462 Hausman, Carl R. *A Discourse on Novelty and Creation*. The Hague: Martinus Nijhoff, 1975, 159. The author argues on pp. 81-84 that Bergson's arguments concerning the limits of discursive analysis and the need for non-abstractive, non-discursive knowledge can not be ignored. Cf. also pp. 140-141, 152.

5463 Heidegger, Martin. *Die Grundprobleme der Phenomenologie*. Ed. F.-W. von Herrman. Frankfurt am Main: V. Klostermann, 1975, x, 473. This is the third section of the first volume of *Sein und Zeit*. Here the author in part recants his criticisms of Bergson as Aristotelian. Cf. M. Heidegger, 1982.

5464 Heidsieck, François. "Bergson et la physique contemporaine." *Revue de Métaphysique et de Morale*, 80, No, 4, 1975, 528-540. This is a review of Milič Čapek's *Bergson and Modern Physics*.

5465 Hendricks, C. Davis and Hendricks, Jon. "Historical Development of the Multiplicity of Times and Implications for the Analysis of Aging." *The Human Context*, 8, No. 1, 1975, 117-129. The authors explore the history of the two sorts of time, "mechanistic" and "subjective." The subjective notion of time runs from St. Augustine through Bergson and Einstein. On pp. 121-122 the authors state Bergson's view of time, implying that he had no concept of objective time and that his concept of duration is purely subjective.

5466 Hesse, Hermann. "Henri Bergson. 1916" in *My Belief: Essays on Life and Art*. Trans. D. Lindley. New York: Farrar, Straus and Giroux, 1975, 364-365. The author draws attention to the German edition of Bergson's works, and commends his writings to the German reading public. Bergson is, like Nietzsche, an anti-Kantian. He concludes: "...the more we recognize his work as not yet completed, as needing many editions, many sequels, to just that extent we must treasure him as a source of the greatest inspiration."

5467 Jankélévitch, Vladimir. *Henri Bergson*. 2nd ed. Paris: Presses Universitaires de France, 1975, 299. (Les Grands Penseurs)

5468   Johnson, Richard E. *In Quest of a New Psychology: Toward a Redefinition of Humanism*. New York: Human Sciences Press, 1975, 348. The author proposes a "new heuristic model for psychology" based on the philosophy of Henri Bergson. Humanistic psychology, lacking such a foundation and, hence, lacking a scientific base, will soon fade and dissolve. The author states concerning Bergson, "I have tried to make the basic tenets of his philosophy directly relevant to contemporary issues in psychology and readily available to all those persons concerned about the modern crisis in human and social evolution" (p. 19).

5469   Jones, William Thomas. *The Twentieth Century to Wittgenstein and Sartre*. Vol. V. of *A History of Western Philosophy*. 2nd ed. New York: Harcourt, Brace, Jovanovich, Inc., 1975, 435. Chapter II is titled "Three Philosophies of Process: Bergson, Dewey and Whitehead." The author finds, on pp. 17-34, that Bergson's metaphysics was crippled by his destructive criticism of the human intellect. On p. 34 the author states that Bergson's "activism" played a role in the development of pragmatism.

5470   Lachance, Paul Francis. "The Imagery of Generations in French Public Opinion on the Eve of the World War One." Diss. Wisconsin, 1975, 635. The author deals with the "new generation" which emerged, or was thought to emerge, in France around 1910. He deals with Bergson's philosophy as one of several which influenced this generation. *Dissertation Abstracts International*, 35, No. 11, 1975, 7226A.

5471   Levesque, Georges. *Bergson: Vida y muerte del hombre de Dios*. Barcelona: Herder, 1975, 110.

5472   Llapaset, José. "La Quête des données immédiates, Bergson et J.-J. Rousseau." Thèse 3ᵉ cycle Université de Montpellier-III, 1975, 171.

5473   Maritain, Jacques. *Oeuvres (1912-1939)*. Ed. Henry Bars. Paris: Desclée de Brouwer, 1975, 1928. (Bibliothèque européenne) This book contains: "Les Deux Bergsonismes", "Bergsonisme et metaphysique", Pref. to 2nd ed. *La Philosophie Bergsonienne*.

5474   McLean, Jeanne Priley. "Immediate Experience and the Problem of Expression: A Study in the Philosophy of Bergson." Diss. Loyola of Chicago 1975, 151. The author states that the problem of expression in Bergson is closely bound up with his distinction between intuition and intellect, while this distinction is in turn rooted in his metaphysics of duration. In the first chapter the author examines Bergson's metaphysics and in the second the relationships between intellect, intuition and reality. If the intellect deforms our intuitions of a fluid reality, is there any alternative way in which our intuitions can achieve valid expression? In chapter three the author examines those texts in which Bergson asserts that language, music, and art can provide a more fluid, hence more accurate description of duration. In the final chapter the author examines Bergson's proposal that philosophy employ an intuitive method and develops the implications of this proposal for philosophical discourse and method. (See *Dissertation Abstracts International*, 31, No. 4, 1975, 2260-A-2261A.)

5475   McMahon, Joseph John. "Bergson's Theistic Evolutionism." Diss. St. John's, 1975, 229. The author argues that Bergson's position in *The Two Sources of Morality and Religion* is not the natural outgrowth of his position in *Creative Evolution*. Bergson's duration does not require God and his intuition does not see God. *Dissertation Abstracts International*, 36, No. 9, 1976, 6148-6149A.

5476   Megay, Joyce N. "Bibliographie critique sur la question de l'influence de Bergson
        sur Proust." *Proust Research Association Newsletter*, No. 13, 1975, 17-20.

5477   Megay, Joyce N. "Proust et Bergson, en 1909." *Bulletin de la Société des Amis
        de Marcel Proust*, No. 25, 1975, 89-96. The author concludes, "Toujours est-il
        que les faits que nous venons de relever indiquent assez clairement que Bergson
        n'était pas au Centre des préoccupations de Proust au moment où celui-ci se
        mettait à composer le premier volume de *La Recherche*" (p. 96).

5478   Míguez, José Antonio. "Bergson y Edith Stein: Dos Caminos hacia la mistica."
        Arbor, 92, Nos. 357-358, 1975, 15-31.

5479   Nakamura, Yumiko. "De la Conception du bon sens chez Bergson." *Études de
        Langue et Littérature Françaises*, No. 25-26, 1975, 70-88. (Published by La
        Société Japonaise de langue et Littérature Françaises.) The author identifies
        Bergson's concept of intuition with his concept of "good sense," and discusses
        the necessary ambiguity of intuition, with its reference both to reflection and to
        practical applications. She states, "le bon sens consiste a faire effort pour remonter
        la pente dont la base est le *sens commun* (le *tout* fait) et dont le sommet est
        l'intuition, en essayant de coincider avec le se faisant" (p. 71).

5480   Peiretti, Antonio. *Della critica del positivismo ad oggi*. Milano: Marzorati editore,
        1975, 590. (Storia del pensiero occidentale. Volume sesto.)

5481   "Philosophy." *Choice*, 12, No. 9, 1975, 1184. This is a review of *Mounier et
        Maritain* by J. Amato.

5482   Pickens, Michele. "Bergsonian Comic Elements in Franz Kafka's *The Trial*." M.
        A. Thesis: Stephen F. Austin State University, 1974, 63. The author uses
        Bergson's concept of comedy to search for the comic in Kafka. *Master's
        Abstracts*, 13, No. 1, 1975, 27.

5483   Rahman, Fazlur. *The Philosophy of Mulla Sadra*. Albany: State Univ. of New
        York Press, 1975, vii, 277. The author compares Sadra's use of Plotinus' to
        Bergson's.

5484   Reck, Andrew J. "Process Philosophy, A Categorial Analysis." *Tulane Studies in
        Philosophy*, 24, 1975, 58-91. The author examines the categories of process
        philosophy, suggesting ten categories as essential. S. Alexander, A. N.
        Whitehead, J. Dewey, G. H. Mead, Wm .James, Bergson, C. Hartshorne, A.
        Ushenko, S. Pepper, and J. H. Randall are among the process philosophers
        whose views are discussed.

5485   Reix, A. "Review of *Création et valeurs éthiques chez Bergson* by Gisèle Breton-
        neau." *Revue Philosophique de la France et de l'Étranger*, 165, No. 4, 1975,
        450.

5486   Reix, A. "Review of *Henri Bergson et le calcul infinitésimal* by Jean Milet." *Revue
        de Métaphysique et de Morale*, 80, No. 3, 1975, 389-390. The reviewer states
        that Milet's fook is important, that Milet has demonstrated the centrality of
        calculus and the problem of the continuum in Bergson's thought. Bergson's
        philosophy is "un rationalisme du temps."

5487   Ricoeur, Paul. *La Métaphore vive*. Paris: Éditions du Sevil, 1975, 414.

5488   Riefstahl, Hermann. "Review of *Henri Bergson: Mélanges* by André Robinet;
        Bergson et le calcul infinitésimal by Jean Milet; and *La Philosophie sociale de
        Bergson* by Guy Lafrance." *Philosophischer Literaturanzeiger*, 28, No. 5, 1975,

286-288.

5489 Rotenstreich, Nathan. "Reflection and Philosophy." *Ratio*, 17, No. 2, 1975, 1-7.

5490 Sandon, Leo. "H. Richard Niebuhr's Principles of Historiography." *Foundations*, 18, No. 1, January-March 1975, 61-74.

5491 Santos-Escudero, Ceferino. "Budismo Zen y Bergson." *Pensamiento*, 31, No. 1, 1975, 55-68; No. 2, 1975, 167-177.

5492 Sarale, Nicolino. *Domanda sull'uomo: La ricerca del senso della vita in Simon Weil, Henri Bergson, Luigi Pirandello, Giacomo Leopardi.* Torino Leumann: Elle Di Ci, 1975, 93. (Itinerari, No. 1)

5493 Schmidtke, Charles R. "A Crossroads for Process Philosophy." *Tulane Studies in Philosophy*, 24, 1975, 92-100. (*Studies in Process Philosophy II*) "Two different strands in process philosophy are explored, the one originating from Bergson's notion of an intuitive comprehension of the universe, the other stemming from Whitehead's approach, which aims to achieve a coherent account of the universe through logical construction. Schmidtke illustrates the difference between these two forms of process philosophy pursuing the analysis of continuity in the two philosophers. The logical difference between their two approaches turns, he thinks, on the priority given by Bergson to his vision of a continuous unity of creative energy, whereas Whitehead emphasizes atomic entities and portrays the extensive continuum as merely potential. One evidence of the difference is in the question 'whether time is to be considered epochal or durational.' Schmidtke asks if it is not possible to synthesize these two traditions within process philosophy; speaking as a Bergsonian, he seems to hold that such a synthesis is not possible, because he regards Whitehead's concept of continuity as fundamentally deficient. In particular, he holds that Whitehead's treatment of continuity in terms of 'indefinite divisibility' fails to provide a sufficient condition for continuity." (J. Gilmour, *Process Studies*, 6, No. 4, 1976, 301)

5494 Sears, John F. "William James, Henri Bergson, and the Poetics of Robert Frost." *New England Quarterly*, 48, No. 3, 1975, 341-361. The author states, "Frost understood that time is real and makes a difference. Perhaps he learned this first from nature, but it must have been confirmed by his reading of Bergson's *Creative Evolution* and particularly by Bergson's effort to express it through metaphor" (p. 354). Frost's "vitalism"is discussed here on pp. 354-361.

5495 Sherover, Charles M. *The Human Experience of Time: The Development of its Philosophic Meaning.* New York: New York University Press, 1975, 603. On p. 163 the author holds (the only such claim in the entire literature) that Bergson "built on" the thought of R. Lotze; on p. 167 he claims both Bergson and S. Alexander depended on Lotze; on pp. 168-174 he gives a general account of Bergson's philosophy; on pp. 179-181 he compares Bergson's and Alexander's concepts of "instant," "specious present," and "causality;" on pp. 218-238 he presents Ch. 3 of *Duration and Simultaneity*.

5496 Skarga, Barbara. *Kłopoty intelektu: między Comté'em a Bergsonem.* Warsawa: Panstwowe Wydawm. Naukowe, 1975, 505. The table of contents in this book is given in both Polish and French.

5497 Smith, Colin. "Maîtres à penser." *Times Literary Supplement*, No. 3839, October 10, 1975, 1216. This is a review of *Twentieth Century French Thought from Bergson to Levi-Strauss* by J. Chiari and *A History of Philosophy*, Vol. 9, by

F. Copleston.

5498   Stern, Alfred. *Filosofía de la risa y del llanto*. 2nd Ed. Trans. Julio Cortazar. San Juan, Puerto Rico: Ed. Universitaria, 1975, 204. (Mente y Palabra)

5499   Stone, Charles. "Two Types of Knowledge in Bergson and Buber." *Pakistan Philosophical Journal*, 13, 1975, 77-81. "The epistemologies set forth by Buber in *Ich und Du* and Bergson in *An Introduction to Metaphysics* entail a dualism through the manner in which man knows reality: on the one hand it can be perceived through its individual qualities or attributes whereby the subject is always distinct from its object of knowledge; on the other—and for both this was the more important perspective—reality can be known in its inexhaustible wholeness whereby no dichotomy exists between subject and object." (*Philosopher's Index*, 9, No. 4, 1975, 123.)

5500   Stumpf, Samuel Enoch. *Socrates to Sartre: A History of Philosophy*. 2nd Ed. New York: McGraw Hill, 1975, 527. This work includes discussions of Bergson, existentialism.

5501   Suances Marcos, Manuel. "Naturaleza del misticismo y la función del héroe en la moral abierta." *Arbor*, 90, No. 350, 1975, 17-32.

5502   Theau, Jean. "Review of *La Philosophie sociale de Bergson* by Guy Lafrance." *Dialogue*, 14, No. 4, 1975, 700-704. The reviewer states, "Guy Lafrance, servi justement pas sa double compétence et, fait plus rare mais encore plus heureux, par sa double sympathie, établit d'une facon quasi dirimante que Bergson a mis en pratique dans le domaine de la sociologie la règle qu'il avait adoptée dans celui de la physique, de la psychologie et de la biologie: se rendre docile aux enseignements de science contemporaine lorsqu'on s'aventure sur son terrain" (p. 702).

5503   Theau, Jean. "Le Rapport Quantité-Qualité Chez Hegel et Chez Bergson." *Philosophiques*, 2, No. 1, 1975, 3-21. "If we read *Time and Free Will* and *The Science of Logic*, we are struck by more than a few similar phrases about number, quantity, and mathematics in general. These similarities are even more striking as the two stand so far from each other. Nevertheless, if we analyze the developments which both have devoted to number, quantity, and mathematics in general, we see that the similitudes in language are not accidental: they arise from an analogy in the ordering of the notions. In Bergson as well as in Hegel, quantity follows quality and is opposed to it by a kind of negative process. But after we have emphasized the correspondences between the two doctrines, we better perceive their differences: for in Bergson the negative process, which is a reversal, is not at all an "Aufhebung," which could be conceived by a logical dialectic: it must be studied empirically." (*Philosopher's Index*, 9, No. 3, Fall 1975, 97.)

5504   Trotignon, Pierre. "Review of *Bergson and the Evolution of Physics* by Pete A. Y. Gunter." *Revue Philosophique de la France et de l'Étranger*, 165, No. 3, 1975, 361-362.

5505   Trotignon, Pierre. "Review of *La Conscience de la durée et le concept de temps* by Jean Theau." *Revue Philosophique de la France et de l'Étranger*, 165, No. 3, 1975, 358.

5506   Trotignon, Pierre. "Review of *La Critique bergsonienne du concept* by Jean Theau." *Revue Philosophique de la France et de l'Étranger*, 165, No. 3, 1975, 357-358.

5507   Viard, Jacques. "Péguy, Pierre Leroux et la vrai chrétienté." *Feuillets de l'Amitié Charles Péguy*, No. 201, 1975, 2-30.

5508   Winther, Truls. *Paul Claudel og det skapende ord.* Oslo: Gyldendal, 1975, 156. This is an enlarged version of the first part of the author's thesis.

5509   Yew-Kwang, N. "Bentham or Bergson? Finite Sensibility, Utility Functions and Social Welfare Functions." *Review of Economic Studies*, 42, No. 132, 1975, 545-569.

1976

5510   *Approches littéraires: Français, 2nd cycle. 1. Les thèmes. Textes choisis et présentés par Pierre Brunel, Daniel Couty, Lionel Archer, et Jean Maurice.* Paris: Bordas, 1976, 385. (Collection Brunel-Couty)

5511   Baumli, Marion Francis. "Laughter, Comedy and Morals: A Bergsonian Synthesis." Diss. Missouri, 1976, 224. "...Bergson's theory is similar to the sensory variety of the incongruity theory, and to both types of the superiority theory with a predeliction for the personal variety. Bergson does not incorporate phsysiological analysis or the ambivalence and play varieties of the incongruity theory. "The author concludes by exploring possibilities of overcoming Bergson's pessimism concerning laughter." *Dissertation Abstracts International*, 37, No. 9, Sec. A, 1977, 5881-5882.

5512   Becco, Anne. "Leibniz, Bergson et le Language." *Études Bergsoniennes*, 11, 1976, 9-24. The author finds that Bergson's and Leibniz's views of the nature and importance of language are not incompatible. She examines the works by Leibniz in Bergson's private library.

5513   Beer, F.-J. "Du nouveau sur Bergson, 3 janvier 1941-3 janvier 1976: Il y a trente ans mourait Henri Bergson sans s'être converti." *Amitiés France-Israël*, No. 227, 1976, 43, 45, 47, 49.

5514   Blumenthal, Henry. *American and French Culture, 1800-1900: Interchange in Art, Science, Literature, and Society.* Baton Rouge, Louisiana: Louisiana State University Press, 1976, 554.

5515   Boboc, Alexandru. "Bergson si bergsonismul: In jurul semnificatiei unei filosofii a continuitatii." *Analele Universitatii Bucuresti. Filozofie*, 25, 1976, 19-30.

5516   Bradbury, Malcom, and McFarlane, James, Eds. *Modernism.* Harmondsworth, Middlesex: Penguin Books, 1976, 683.

5517   Brun, Jean. "Bergsonisme et coincidence." *Etudes Bergsoniennes*, 11, 1976, 25-33. The author explains Bergson's concept of intuition through Bergson's use of the word "coincidence" and similar words.

5518   Cariou, Marie. *Bergson et le fait mystique.* Paris: Aubier Montaigne, 1976, 267. The author holds that Bergson, rather than negating Kant, extends the Kantian search for categories in a new direction. Bergson's quest ends in fresh insights into religion and mysticism. The author distinguishes mysticism in Bergson's sense from pathological mysticisms. She places emphasis on the heuristic role of science in his philosophy.

5519   Cocking, J. M. "Memorial Distinctions." *London Times Literary Supplement*, 75, No. 3889, 1976, 1214. This is a review of Joyce N. Megay,'s *Bergson et Proust*. The reviewer congratulates Megay for her contribution to the debate over the relations between Bergson and Proust, but states, "Whatever the importance of Proust's encounter with Bergson it was not absorption but dialogue. In general the evidence suggests that Proust was clearly aware of what he had in common with Bergson and afraid that others, seeing it just as clearly, would underrate his own originality."

5520 Copleston, Frederick C. "Bergson on Morality." *Philosophers and Philosophies.* London: Search Press; New York: Barnes and Noble, 1976, 131-147.

5521 Curtis, James M. "Bergson and Russian Formalism." *Comparative Literature,* 28, No. 2, 1976, 109-121. The author states on p. 109, "This paper suggests that, to a considerable extent, Russian formalism did succeed in creating 'an epistemologically based aesthetics,' for a conceptual paradigm which derives from the thought of Henri Bergson informs the criticism of the two principle theoreticians of formalism, Viktor Shklovsky and Yury Tynianov."

5522 Delessert, André. "Review of *Henri Bergson et le calcul infinitésimal* by Jean Milet." *Dialectica* (Swiss), 30, No. 1, 1976, 105-106.

5523 Delhomme, Jeanne. "Le Sens Interne." *Études Bergsoniennes,* 11, 1976, 35-65. The author examines the Kantian "Categories of the Understanding" from a Bergsonian point of view. The examination leads to Bergsonian "categories."

5524 "Directions For Criticism: Structuralism and its Alternatives." *Contemporary Literature,* 17, No. 3, 1976, 297-435.

5525 "Doctoral Dissertations, 1976." *Review of Metaphysics,* 30, No. 1, 1976, 185.

5526 Druet, Pierre-Philippe. "Review of *Les Études Bergsoniennes,* Vol. 10." *Revue Philosophique de Louvain,* 74, No. 22, 1976, 287.

5527 Ebacher, Roger. "Review of *Henri Bergson et le calcul infinitésimal* by Jean Milet." *Laval Théologique et Philosophique,* 32, No. 1, 1976, 107-108.

5528 Feuer, Lewis S. "Recollections of Harry Austryn Wolfson." *American Jewish Archives,* 28, No. 1, 1976, 49-50.

5529 Fizer, John. "Ingarden's Phases, Bergson's Durée réele, and W. James' Stream. Metaphoric Variants or Mutually Exclusive Concepts on the Theme of Time." In *Ingardenia: A Spectrum of Specialized Studies Establishing the Field of Research.* Ed. Anna-Teresa Tymieniecka. Dordrecht; Boston: D. Reidel Publishing Co., 1976, 121-139. (Analectica Husserliana, No. 4)

5530 González Bedoya, Jesús. *Teoría del hombre en Bergson.* Madrid: Autor (C. M. Casa del Brasil), 1976, 324.

5531 Goulet, J. "Review of *La Philosophie Sociale de Bergson, Sources et Interpretation* par Guy Lafrance." *Philosophiques,* 3, No. 1, 1976, 81-92. "Utile contribution à la connaissance 'sociologique' de Bergson, contemporain de l'École française. On regrette toutefois que l'auteur ait laisse passer l'occasion de montrer en quoi le bergsonisme social, meme quand il s'allie a la science, se refuse—en vertu de son unité—a toute réduction et a toute interpretation autre que métaphysique." (*The Philosopher's Index,* 10, No. 4, 1976, 66.)

5532 Greenberg, Louis M. "Bergson and Durkheim as Sons and Assimilators: The Early Years." *French Historical Studies,* 9, No. 4, 1976, 619-634. This article deals with the early personal histories of Henri Bergson and Émile Durkheim. It touches, particularly, on "certain failings of their fathers."

5533   Guitton, Jean. *Journal de ma vie*: Vol. 2. *Avenir du présent*. Paris: Desclée de Brouwer, 1976, 381.

5534   Guitton, Jean. *Journal de ma vie*: Vol. 1. *Présence du passé*. Paris: Desclée de Brouwer, 1976, 357.

5535   Gunter, Pete A. Y. "Review of *Henri Bergson et le calcul infinitésimal* by Jean Milet." *Journal of the History of Philosophy*, 14, No. 2, 1976, 244-246.

5536   Halbwachs, Maurice. *Les Cadres sociaux de la mémoire*. Pref. Fr. Châtelet. Paris-La Haye: Mouton, 1976, xiv, 298. This is a "réédition" of the first edition (1925) of this work. The author, initially a Bergsonian, came to treat memory as a social and not a personal phenomenon. He provides evidence that individual memories depend on social existence.

5537   Hall, Dorothy Judd. "The Height of Feeling Free: Frost and Bergson." *Texas Quarterly*, 19, No. 1, 1976, 128-143. The author describes the lasting impact of Henri Bergson on the American poet Robert Frost. This influence was occasioned in 1911 when Frost read the English translation of Bergson's *Creative Evolution*, and can be found in such poems as "The Grindstone," "West-Running Brook," and "Kitty Hawk," among others.

5538   Harris, Geoffry. "Bergson and Catholic Thought." *Month*, 2nd N.S., 9, No. 12, 1976, 414-417. This is a review and criticism of A. E. Pilkington's *Bergson and His Influence: A Reassessment*. The reviewer defends Bergson against many of Pilkington's criticisms, and reviews Bergson's influence on French Catholic thought in the early decades of the 20th century.

5539   Harris, Geoffrey. "Copleston and Chevalier on French Metaphysics." *Downside Review*, No. 314, January, 1976, 47-59.

5540   Hartmann, Lorraine Obuchowski. "Review of *Henri Bergson: A Bibliography* by P. A. Y. Gunter." *French Review*, 50, No. 1, 1976, 167.

5541   Holder, Keith. "Elements of Henri Bergson's *Creative Evolution* in the Stream of Consciousness Novels of Virginia Woolf." Master's Thesis, Midwestern State, 1976, 78. The author holds that though Virginia Woolf was not influenced by Bergson, many aspects of her novels are Bergsonian. He attributes this similarity to the *Zeitgeist*. The author concludes his study with an original short story which, he believes, embodies Bergsonian ideas.

5542   Huett, Richard. "Nietzsche and Bergson, A Discursive Dialogue." *Midwestern Journal of Philosophy*, 4, No. 1, 1976, 30-34. "An attempt, through a brief, imaginary encounter, to point up some of the principal themes of the two philosophers, wherein they are similar and where they differ. The fundamental identification between the two, however, is that 'Essentially, nevertheless, we affirmed the multiplicity of existence, the creativity of the universe, the novelty that continues to emerge. We called Heraclitus father and disowned Parmenides.' In addition, it is suggested that there is a relationship between style and content." (*Philosopher's Index*, 10, No. 2, 1976, 81.)

5543   Hurley, Patrick J. "Bergson and Whitehead on Freedom." *Proceedings of the American Catholic Philosophical Association*, 50, 1976, 107-117. "Both H. Bergson and A. N. Whitehead hold that freedom is an ubiquitous factor in the world, yet the two approach the subject from different perspectives. Bergson, to avoid any trace of mechanism, insists that the free act is creative of radical novelty. Whitehead, observing that significant freedom involves vision, postulates a realm of eternal forms which convey to the free agent information about the corresponding environment. The two positions are thus at odds with each other. A modification of Whitehead's position is suggested which might allow it to retain its own distinctive advantages yet avoid the charges of mechanism from the Bergsonian camp." (*Philosopher's Index*, 11, No. 4, 1977, 68.)

5544 Jous, Dominique. "Le Souffle de Dieu dans *L'Évolution créatrice.*" *Études Bergsoniennes*, 11, 1976, 67-76. The author studies the Biblical, especially the Jewish, elements in Bergson's philosophy.

5545 Kaspi, André. *Le Temps des Américains: Le Concours américain à la France en 1917-1918.* Paris: 17, rue de la Sorbonne, 1976, 375. Bergson's diplomatic missions in the United States during World War I are discussed by the author on pp. 11-12 and 16. On p. 11n the author notes the existence, in the United States and France, of papers concerning Bergson's diplomatic activities.

5546 Kremer-Marietti, Angèle. "Tendances des recherches actuelles." *Études Bergsoniennes*, 11, 1976, 115-122. The author lists books and theses on Bergson published since 1970.

5547 Lafrance, Guy. "Lire Bergson (réponse à J. Goulet)." *Philosophiques*, 3, No. 2, 1976, 279-284. "This article is a controversy on reading Bergson. It is in part a reply by the author to a criticism of his book *La philosophie sociale de Bergson, Sources et interpretation.* In his reply the author demonstrates the necessity for an accurate understanding of Bergson's social philosophy, to situate Bergson's thought within its intellectual climate which was one of confrontation with the sciences and in particular with the social sciences and social ideas of his time. The main trend of the author's book was to make explicit how Bergson was well informed of the questions discussed by the anthropologists and the sociologists of his time and how his social thought was seriously taking into account those discussions." (*Philosopher's Index*, 11, No. 2, 1977, 94.)

5548 Levert, Paule. "Passé-Durée-Présent." *Études Bergsoniennes*, 11, 1976, 77-86. The author studies Bergson's concepts of memory, of the past, and of the present, relating Bergson's thought to that of Louis Lavelle. Mention is made of a similarity between Bergson's philosophy and the associationism of David Hume.

5549 Lucas, Thierry. "Review of *Henri Bergson et le calcul infinitésimal* by Jean Milet." *Revue Philosophique de Louvain*, 74, No. 22, 1976, 285-286. The reviewer concurs with the author's claim that Bergson saw the infinitesimal calculus as having introduced time into mathematics, thus making possible a new "rationalité du temps." He regrets that the author does not examine the view of contemporary mathematicians, particularly those who espouse "non-standard analysis."

5550 Megay, Joyce N. *Bergson et Proust: Essai de mise au point de la question de l'influence de Bergson sur Proust.* Paris: Vrin, 1976, 170. The author denies that Henri Bergson's philosophy influenced the novels of Marcel Proust. This is a very careful and detailed study, which examines the history of attempts to relate the thought of Proust and Bergson.

5551 Morkovsky, Mary Christine. "Henri Bergson on Freedom without Antecedent Possibility." *Proceedings of the American Catholic Philosophical Association*, 50, 1976, 99-106. "Henri Bergson maintained that freedom described or defined in terms of possibility negates the dynamism of real duration. He also claimed that free choice involves conceiving several possible actions. The article summarizes definitions of freedom unacceptable to Bergson and the metaphysical implications of his view of possibility. It concludes that his views on human freedom are consistent. Creative duration enhances antecedent reality rather than adding to antecedently existing possibility. Conceptual possibility is an immobilization and intellectual product, rather than a source of continuous, ongoing evolution." (*Philosopher's Index*, 11, No. 4, 1977, 76.)

5552   Morot-Sir, Edouard. "Vases communicants: Twentieth-Century Franco-American Dialogue." *The French Review*, 99, No. 6, 1976, 1072-1088. The author discusses the common conceptions of Bergson and William James and their influence on the novel, particularly on the novels of Henry James and Marcel Proust, and ultimately those of William Faulkner and André Malraux.

5553   Mueller, Fernand-Lucien. *Histoire de la psychologie*. Vol. I: *De l'Antiquité à Bergson*; Vol. II: *La Psychologie contemporaine*. 4ᵉ éd. Paris: Payot, 1976, 562. (Bibliothèque scientifique)

5554   Novikov, A. V. *От позитивизма к интуитиву: критические очерки бурЖуауазнои астетикн.*Москва: Искусство, 1976, 253. The romanized title of this Russian-language work is *Ot pozitiviszma k intuitivizmu*. It contains addresses, essays, and lectures on 19th and 20th century aesthetics and on the philosophy of Bergson.

5555   Pemán, José Manuel. "Henri Bergson and the Open Society: A Study of the Philosophical Roots and Implications of Bergson's Social Thought." Diss. Virginia, 1976, 428. The author explores Bergson's now-popular distinction between the open and the closed society. He argues that "...the Bergsonian paradigms of openess and closure can not be said to be based upon 'a kind of religious distinction,' since they are the result of an exacting application of Bergson's theory of man to the human experiences that generate our social symbols." *Dissertation Abstracts International*, 37, No. 5, Sec. A, 1976, 3159.

5556   Phoba-Mvika, J. "Bergson et la théologie morale." Diss. Université d'Amiens, 1976, 523. The ambitious second Vatican council project of rebalancing the ethical and the religious aspects of moral theology arrived at conflicting results. "Bergsonian thought provides a synthesis of morals and religion which can serve as a force for renewal in moral theology." *Dissertation Abstracts International*, 39, No. 4, Sec. C, 1979, 590.

5557   Piclin, Michel. "Bergson, La Transcendance et le Kantisme." *Études Bergsoniennes*, 11, 1976, 87-113. The author examines Bergson's and Kant's conceptions of time. Kant's notion of the aesthetic (artistic) object is closely similar to Bergson's "durée."

5558   Pilkington, Anthony Edward. *Bergson and His Influence: A Reassessment*. Cambridge: Cambridge University Press, 1976, viii, 253. The author examines the degree of Bergson's influence on four thinkers: Charles Péguy, Paul Valéry, Marcel Proust, and Julien Benda. He illustrates Péguy's indebtedness to Bergson as well as his intellectual independence. He finds any relations of influence by Bergson on Valéry difficult to trace and any clearcut and simple conclusions difficult to formulate. His conclusions concerning the relations between Bergson and Proust are highly complex. He is in any case clear that there are many important divergences between the philosopher and the novelist over the concepts of memory and of time. The author's analysis of Benda's lifelong campaign against Bergson and Bergsonism is extremely perceptive. The author examines Benda's arguments, showing many to be merely "verbal."

5559   Pipa, Hirshi. "L'Influence de Boutroux et de Bergson sur Montal." *Revue des Études Italiennes*, N.S. 22, No. 3, 1976, 193-204. The author studies the influence of the philosophies of Bergson and Boutroux on the poetry of Montal.

5560   Ringold, Francine. "the Metaphysics of Yoknapatawpha County: 'Airy Space and Scope for your Delirium'." *Hartford Studies in Literature*, 8, 1976, 223-240. The author describes Bergson's influence on the novelist William Faulkner.

5561   Proust, Marcel. "Letter to Antoine Bibesco: 9 Août 1902." in *Correspondence*. Vol. 3. *1902-1903*. Ed. Philip Kolb. Paris: Plon, 1976, 83. Here Proust notes that Henri Bergson has not answered a plea by Proust's mother. He also appears to have given a letter by Bergson to Bibesco.

5562   Robert, Jean-Dominique. "Review of *Mélanges* by Henri Bergson." *Revue Philosophique de Louvain*, 74, No. 22, 1976, 284-285.

5563   Robinet, André. "Documentation Bergsonienne." *Études Bergsoniennes*, 11, 1976, 5-8. Professor Robinet lists letters between Bergson and Harald Höffding and between Bergson and Dr. John Landquist. A brief note from Bergson to Edmund Husserl is mentioned.

5564   Roche de Coppens, Peter. "The Rediscovery of Bergson's Work. Its Implications for Sociology in General and the Sociology of Religion in Particular." *Revista Internacional de Sociologia*, 34, No. 17, 1976, 133-160. The author proposes that Bergson's work, now long neglected, is due for rediscovery. He describes Bergson's *milieu* and the development of his philosophy, claiming that several figures in recent history are directly or indirectly in Bergson's debt, including William James, Carl Jung, Pitrim Sorokin, Arnold Toynbee, Mircea Eliade, Roberto Assaglioli, and others. Bergson's great merit, the author holds, is to make us rethink our received opinions about what is real and important. His greatest contribution can be to our understanding of human nature. Bergson makes this possible by showing (1) valid knowledge stems not only from the senses and the intellect but also from *lived human experience*; (2) man is not only a biosocial and a psychological but also a spiritual being; (3) to fully actualize himself man must turn towards and take into account his spiritual nature.

5565   Russo, F. "Review of *Henri Bergson et le calcul infinitésimal* by Jean Milet." *Archives de Philosophie*, 39, No. 2, 1976, 337-338.

5566   Salas, Carlo Gonzalez. "Dios y las pruebas de su existencia en la filosofia." *Humanitas* (Mexico), 17, 1976, 41-78.

5567   Sancipriano, Mario. "Ingarden et le 'vrai' bergsonisme." In *Ingardenia: A Spectrum of Specialized Studies Establishing the Field of Research*. Ed. Anna-Teresa Tymieniecka. Dordrecht; Boston: D. Reidel Publishing Co., 1976, 141-148. (Analectica Husserliana, Vol. 4)

5568   Shaw, David. "Review of *Henri Bergson: A Bibliography* by P. A. Y. Gunter." *The Library* 5th Ser., 31, No. 4, 1976, 417.

5569   Sonnenfeld, Albert. "Review of *Bergson et Proust* by Joyce N. Megay." *French Review*, 50, No. 2, 1976-1977, 349. The reviewer states, "In other words, Megay's thesis ['un abîme les sépare, en ce qui concerne leur vision du monde'] is not a constant in a relentlessly overstated polemic but a conclusion reached after judicious presentation of textual evidence..." The reviewer, however, does question the author's literal-mindedness.

5570   Soulez, Philippe. "Lorsque Bergson parle de Freud." *Psychanalyse à l'Universite*, 2, No. 5, 1976, 145-165. The author utilizes lecture notes from Bergson's course on "The Theory of the Person." (1910-1911) to examine Bergson's reading of and reaction to Freud. Bergson's reading of Freud involved conflicts between the views of Freud and Pierre Janet. Bergson sided with Freud at several points. Cf. the author, 1977.

5571   Stearns, J. Brenton. "Becoming: A Problem for Determinists?" *Process Studies*, 6, No. 4, 1976, 237-248. "A doctrine of central importance to process metaphysics (especially to Bergson, Čapek, and Hartshorne, and probably also to James, Weiss, and Whitehead) is that the determinist contradicts himself when talking about a fully determinate future. Since actuality adds nothing to an entity's definiteness, to say that a future event is definite now is to say it is actual now—a contradiction. I argue in reply that a determinist can consistently believe in an authentic future and that process metaphysics itself provides conceptual apparatus for thinking about the asymmetries of time without grounding itself on a flimsy refutation of determinism." (*Philosopher's Index*, 11, No. 2, 1977, 111.)

5572   Stern, Alfred. *Problemas filosóficos de la sciencia*. San Juan, Puerto Rico: Ed. Universitaria, 1976, 203. (Mente y Palabra) In the last chapter of this work the author examines the concept and the critics of vitalism. He explores Bergson's vitalism.

5573   Teilhard de Chardin, Pierre. "Letter to Pierre Leroy. April 6, 1952." in *Letters From My Friend. Teilhard de Chardin, 1948-1955, Including Letters Written During His Final Years in America*. Collected and Introduced by Pierre Leroy. Trans. Mary Lukas. New York: Paulist Press, 1976, 125-127. Teilhard states on p. 126: "It's interesting to see how much, as much on the right as on the left, the finest minds can not bring themselves to see in the universe, and especially in Man, this extraordinary—I might say blinding—phenomenon, which Bergson (clearly although not too scientifically) saw: a Noogenesis rising through the play of chance."

5574   Theau, Jean. "Review of *Bergson et le calcul infinitésimal* by Jean Milet." *Dialogue*, 15, No. 1, March, 1976, 169-173.

5575   Weinstein, Michael A. *The Polarity of Mexican Thought: Instrumentalism and Finalism*. University Park and London: The Pennsylvania State University Press, 1976, 128. The author mentions on p. 1 the part played by Bergson in undermining Mexican turn-of-the-century Positivism, which supported the Porfirio Díaz dictatorship. Bergson's influence on Alejandro Korn is noted on p. 17; Bergson's influence on Alejandro Deustua is noted on pp. 17-18; Bergson's influence on José Vasconcelos is noted on pp. 23-24.

5576   Weisman, Peter Franklin. "The Broken Mirror: A Study of the Poetics of French Symbolism and Anglo-American Imagism (1870-1920)." Diss. Berkeley, 1976, 605. The author deals with Bergson's influence on the imagism of T. E. Hulme. *Dissertation Abstracts International*, 37, No. 1, 1976, 287A.

5577   Zwart, P. J. *About Time: A Philosophical Inquiry into the Origin and Nature of Time*. Amsterdam and Oxford: North-Holland Publishing Co.; New York: American Elsevier Publishing Co., Inc., 1976, 266. The author adopts a view "in which time is regarded as a concept based on the primitive relation of before-and-after" (p. 1). He states, "In any case time works, it is active, and consequently it is real. The efficacity of time constitutes its reality" (p. 4). Bergson's distinction between physical and psychological time is mentioned on p. 44; Bergson's refutation of Zeno's Achilles paradox is refuted on pp. 210-211, on the basis that Bergson refers only the special case of discontinuous motion; Bergson's attempted resolution of Zeno's paradoxes is examined on pp. 224-226. The author examines and argues against the concept of physical time-reversal on pp. 140-160.

1977

5578   Alderman, Harold. "The Place of Comedy." *Man and World*, 10, No. 2, 1977, 152-172. The author compares Bergson's "subjective" theory of comedy with James K. Feibleman's "Object-oriented" view. On p. 169 he states, "In summary, comedy, as we have seen, is reducible neither to an objective property (Feibleman) nor to a subjective response (Bergson)."

5579   Appan Ramanujam, A. "Bergson's Philosophy of Laughter." *Indian Philosophical Quarterly*, 4, No. 2, 1977, 7-17. "The aim of this article is to highlight a particular form of logic at work in the phenomenon of laughter—the logic of imagination. In my estimation the interpretations offered by Bergson follow naturally from his metaphysical standpoint. The article opens with an introduction emphasizing the importance of laughter as a specifically human phenomenon. It is followed by a brief statement of Bergson's metaphysical position and his concept of imagination which is a key to his work on laughter. The rest of this article is devoted to show how in Bergson's hands laughter ceases to be an elusive phenomenon." (*Philosopher's Index*, 11, No. 4, 1977, 53.)

5580   Armour, Leslie. "Review of *Bergson and his Influence* by A. E. Pilkington." *Library Journal*, 102, No. 2, 1977, 205.

5581   Bailey, Ninette. "Review of *Bergson and His Influence* by A. E. Pilkington." *Journal of European Studies*, 7, No. 4, 1977, 295.

5582   Bailey, Ninette. "Disciples and Adversaries." *Times Higher Education Supplement*, No. 283, March 25, 1977, 20. This is a review of *Bergson and His Influence* by A. Pilkington.

5583   Barthélemy-Madaule, Madeleine. *Bergson*. Réimpr. avec remise à jour. Paris: Le Seuil, 1977, 192 pp. (Ecrivains de toujours, 77).

5584   Baumer, Franklin L. *Modern European Thought: Continuity and Change in Ideas, 1600-1950*. New York: Macmillan; London: Collier Macmillan, 1977, 541.

5585   Bertini, M. "Review of *Bergson et Proust* by Joyce Megay." *Studi francesi*, 21, 1977, 352-353.

5586   Bertman, Martin A. "Bergson and the Hierophantic Arts." *Diotoma*, 5, Part 1, 1977, 193-199.

5587   Bonnet, Henri. "Review of *Bergson et Proust* by Joyce N. Megay." *Bulletin de la Société des Amis de Marcel Proust*, No. 27, 1977, 539-542.

5588   Bruaire, C. "Le Droit du concept chez Blondel et Bergson." In *Journées d'études (9-10 november 1974): Blondel-Bergson-Maritain-Loisy*. Ed. Claude Troisfontaines. Louvain: Institut Supérieur de Philosophie; Louvain: Éditions Peeters, 1977, 31-36. For a résumé of a discussion of Bergson and Blondel, see pp. 37-38.

5589   Cain, Julien. "Henri Bergson." In *Écrivains et artistes*. Eds. François Chapon, Pierre Georgel, Jean Prinet, Jacques Suffel. Paris: Éds. du Centre National de la Recherche scientifique, 1977, 137-141. This article appeared originally as a preface to *Catalogue de l'Exposition Henri Bergson* (Paris: Bibliothèque National, 1959).

5590   Čapek, Milič. "Immediate and Mediate Memory." *Process Studies*, 7, No. 2, 1977, 90-96. In this essay Čapek replies to criticisms of his view of Bergson's concept of memory, criticisms posed in David Sipfle's review of Čapek's *Bergson and Modern Physics*.

5591   Čapek, Milič. "La Pensée de Bergson en Amérique." *Revue Internationale de Philosophie*, 121-122, Nos. 3-4, 1977, 229-350. The author analyzes the influence of Bergson on several American philosophers: William James, Charles Sanders Peirce, Horace Meyer Kallen, Ralph Barton Perry, John Dewey, George Santayana, Josiah Royce, Arthur Oncken Lovejoy, and Ralph Tyler Flewelling. His analysis of the relations between Bergson and James (pp. 330-340) shows the close affinities of the two thinkers, as well as their very important mutual influences.

5592   Colomb, G. G. "Roman Ingardon and the Language of Art and Science." *Analectica Husserliana*, 35, No. 1, 1976, 7-13.

5593   Devaux, André-A. "DuBos disciple de Bergson?" *Cahiers Charles Du Bos*, 21, 1977, 47-63. A discussion follows on pp. 64-67. The author explores Bergson's profound influence on the literary critic Charles Du Bos. While detailing this influence, however, he very carefully notes Du Bos' reservations concerning Bergson's philosophy. The discussion of Bergson and Du Bos contains extremely interesting dialogues between the author and Gabriel Marcel, as well as between the author and Georges Poulet.

5594   Devaux, André-A. "Nature et rôle de l'Attention chez Simone Weil," *Giornale de Metafisca*, 32, No. 2, 1977, 217-227.

5595   Emmet, Dorothy. "Language and Metaphysics: Introduction to a Symposium." *Theoria to Theory*, 11, No. 3, 1977, 49-56.

5596   "Le Feuillet envolé. Pages oubliées: Grèce—Kazantzakis nous parle de Bergson et d'Istrati." *Cahiers des Amis de Panait Istrati*, No. 8, December, 1977, 21-22.

5597   Flewelling, Ralph Tyler. "Letter to Henri bergson, 1919." In Daniel S. Robinson's "The Bergson-Flewelling Correspondence, 1914-1940." *Coranto*, 10, No. 2, 1977, 23. In this letter Flewelling replies to Bergson's response to criticisms contained in the manuscript to the first half of Flewelling's *Bergson and Personal Realism* (1920). The criticisms which he has posed, Flewelling states, are more tentative than they may at first appear. He urges Bergson to read the second half of his manuscript before coming to any conclusions.

5598   Flewelling, Ralph Tyler. "Letter to Henri Bergson, 1920." In Daniel S. Robinson's "The Bergson-Flewelling Correspondence, 1914-1940." *Coranto*, 10, No. 2, 1977, 24. In this letter, sent along with a copy of the first issue of *The Personalist*, Flewelling invites Bergson to respond to criticisms posed in the second half of the manuscript to Flewelling's *Bergson and Personal Realism* (1920).

5599   Flewelling, Ralph Tyler. "Letter to Henri Bergson, October 8, 1920." In Daniel S. Robinson's "The Bergson-Flewelling Correspondence, 1914-1940." *Coranto*, 10, No. 2, 1977, 25. In this letter Flewelling re-extends an invitation to Bergson to lecture at the University of Southern California.

5600   Flewelling, Ralph Tyler. "Letter to Henri Bergson, December 1, 1920." In Daniel S. Robinson's "The Bergson-Flewelling Correspondence, 1914-1940." *Coranto*, 10, No. 2, 1977, 26. In this letter Flewelling thanks Bergson for agreeing to lecture at the University of Southern California, on any occasion in which he might come to America again.

5601   Flewelling, Ralph Tyler. "Letter to Henri Bergson, August 18, 1921." In Daniel s. Robinson's *The Bergson-Flewelling Correspondence, 1914-1940.*" *Coranto*, 10, No. 2, 1977, 26-27. In this letter Flewelling introduces Bergson to President William Arnold Shanklin of Wesleyan University, who wishes to extend an invitation to Bergson to give a course of lectures.

5602   Flewelling, Ralph Tyler. "Letter to Henri Bergson, April 16, 1932." In Daniel S. Robinson's "The Bergson-Flewelling Correspondence, 1914-1940." *Coranto*, 10, No. 2, 1977, 27-28. In this letter Flewelling thanks Bergson for an autographed copy of his book, *Les Deux Sources de la morale et de la religion*, and promises to review it in *The Personalist*. He states that, in spite of past criticisms, his own position has moved closer and closer to Bergson's, thanks in part to conversations with H. Wildon Carr. (Flewelling's review appears in *The Personalist*, Vol. 14, 134-136.)

5603   Flewelling, Ralph Tyler. "Letter to Henri Bergson, March 29, 1933." In Daniel S. Robinson's "The Bergson-Flewelling Correspondence, 1914-1940." *Coranto*, 10, No. 2, 1977, 28-29. With this letter Flewelling encloses two copies of the Bergson issue of *The Personalist*. He wishes Bergson well and hopes Bergson will find the issue to his liking.

5604   Flewelling, Ralph Tyler. "Letter to Henri Bergson, June 6, 1933." In Daniel S. Robinson's "The Bergson-Flewelling Correspondence, 1914-1940." *Coranto*, 10, No. 2, 1977, 30. In this letter Flewelling thanks Bergson for his warm response to the Bergson issue of *The Personalist*. He encloses with his letter a letter of introduction to L. J. Hopkins, an American philosopher who wishes to meet Bergson.

5605   Gentile, Luigi. "Origini, Funzioni e Natura del Linguaggio Nella Filosofia di H. Bergson." *Aquinas*, 20, 1977, 417-418. "The author has written this article because he is firmly convinced that the knowledge of the origin, nature and function of language in Bergson's thought helps a thorough understanding of it. After pointing out that human communication is deeply linked to human nature and to social structure, the author analyzes the connections between instinct, intelligence, intuition and language. He proceeds to call attention to the connections between language and 'durée,' language and thought. To explain these connections means to clear up such problems as causality, freedom and the human person. The author concludes by saying the word must always serve the idea and not vice versa." (*Philosopher's Index*, 12, No. 3, 1978, 101.)

5606   Hartshorne, Charles. "The Neglect of Relative Predicates in Modern Philosophy." *American Philosophical Quarterly*, 14, No. 3, 1977, 308-318.

5607   Harmon, William. *Time in Ezra Pound's Work*. Chapel Hill: The University of North Carolina Press, 1977, 165. The author speculates concerning an early

Bergsonian influence on Pound by T. E. Hulme on p. 8. He examines Wyndham Lewis' attack on Bergson on pp. 130-134.

5608   Harris, Geoffrey. "Review of *Bergson and His Influence* by A. E. Pilkington." *Downside Review*, No. 319, April 1977, 150-151.

5609   Herbert, G. S. "The Concept of Future in Bergson and Heidegger: A Comparative Study." *Indian Philosophical Quarterly*, 4, No. 3, 1977, 597-604. "The Concept of the Future is important in any philosophy of time and the aim of this paper is to show that there can be more than one view of future and of time. Bergson and Heidegger hold that real time is self-generic and cannot be quantified. Both of them distinguish between two types of time, but with a difference—Bergson: pure time and alloyed time; and Heidegger: authentic and inauthentic time. For Bergson future is open, indefinite and infinite. For Heidegger future is limited, definite and finite. This difference arises because Bergson thinks in terms of creative evolution, whereas Heidegger thinks on the basis of authentic Dasein. Any point of view is equally possible and justifialbe from the standpoint of a philosopher." (*Philosopher's Index*, 11, No. 4, 1977, 67.)

5610   Johnston, William M. "Review of *Twentieth-Century French Thought from Bergson to Levi-Strauss* by Joseph Chiari." *The French Review*, 50, No. 5, 1977, 794-795. The reviewer criticizes the author for treating so many diverse philosophers as if they were in agreement.

5611   Jouhaud, M. "Bergson et Blondel: Cosmologie et philosophie de la destinée." In *Journées d'études (9-10 novembre 1974). Blondel-Bergson-Maritain-Loisy*. Ed. Claude Troisfontaines. Louvain: Institute Supérieur de Philosophie; Louvain: Éditions Peeters, 1977, 7-29. For a résumé of a discussion of Bergson and Blondel, see pp. 37-38.

5612   Kennedy, Ellen Lee. "'Freedom' and 'the Open Society': Henri Bergson's Contribution to Political Philosophy." London University, 1977, 278. This is an unpublished thesis, listed in the *London Bibliography of the Social Sciences*.

5613   Lacroix, Jean. "La Philosophie: Le 'Visage' de Bergson." *Monde (Aujourd'hui)*, No. 9984, 6-7 mars 1977, 15.

5614   Ladrière, Jean. "La Philosophie et son passé: Durée et simultanéité." *Revue Philosophique du Louvain*, 75, No. 26, 1977, 332-357. The author critiques theories of the history of philosophy whether prospective or retrospective, based on a linear concept of time: "But the time of history should be conceived as a duration, made of succession *and* simultaneity. This duration is a field of creativity, which gives rise unceasingly to new particular forms..." (Author's abstract, p. 357.)

5615   Lasine, Stuart. "Sight, Body and Motion in Plato and Kafka: A Study of Projective and Topological Experience." Diss. Wisonsin-Madison 1977, 731. The author distinguishes two basic modes of knowledge. The first, based on the biological process of metabolic exchange, involves a fluid world in topological space. The second, based on the model of sight at a distance, keeps the fluid world at a distance at the cost of the possibility of intercourse with it. The comparison of these two modes of knowing creates a "model for textual analysis." In the first two chapters texts by Lucretius, A. Schopenhauer, S. Freud, Bergson, and J.-P. Sartre dealing with the problems of sight and body are examined. In the last two chapters, Plato and Kafka are examined. Both Plato and Kafka prefer sight to intercourse with the fluid world. The author concludes with an examination of the distorting effect of "detached beholding." (*Dissertation Abstracts International*, 38, No. 12, 1978, 7314A.)

5616   Levitt, Morton P. "The Companions of Kazantzakis: Nietzsche, Bergson, and Zorba the Greek." *Comparative Literature Studies*, 14, No. 4, 1977, 368-380.

5617   Llewelyn, J. E. "Review of *Henri Bergson: A Bibliography* by P. A. Y. Gunter." *Modern Language Review*, 72, No. 1, 1977, 207-208.

5618   Llewelyn, J. E. "Joseph Chiari: Twentieth Century French Thought: From Bergson to Lévi-Strauss." *Modern Language Review*, 72, No. 2, April 1977, 457-458.

5619   Lutzow, Thomas H. "The Structure of the Free Act in Bergson." *Process Studies*, 7, No. 2, 1977, 73-89. "The study shows that Bergson's thought can be interpreted axiomatically with indetermination accepted in a Cartesian-like fashion as the most basic indubitable fact. Accepting indetermination from the start, Bergson lists each of the mental and physical structures, e.g., conscious perception, memory, affection, intellect, space, the organic and inorganic fields, as its necessary conditions. This approach is clearly opposed to mechanism as well as Kantian phenomenalism in that these latter views take the experience of freedom to be an illusion. In the end, Bergson offers us a finalism that has the present level of human freedom as in intermediate goal in evolutionary process with the structures listed above as necessary consequents supportive of that goal." (*Philosopher's Index*, 12, No. 3, 1978, 116.)

5620   Marcel, Gabriel. "Disscussion à la suite de cet exposé." *Cahiers Charles Du Bos*, 21, 1977, 47-63. In the course of a discussion with André-A. Devaux concerning Devaux' article "Du Bos disciple de Bergson?" Marcel ponders Bergson's early emphasis on the philosophy of Herbert Spencer, and his influence on Marcel's philosophical development.

5621   Margolin, Jean-Claude. "Review of *Création et valeurs éthiques chez Bergson* by Gisèle Bretonneau." *Revue de Synthèse*, 118, No. 85-86, 1977, 122.

5622   Megay, Joyce N. "Review of *Bergson and his Influence* by Anthony Edward Pilkington." *Bulletin de la Société des Amis de Marcel Proust*, No. 27, 1977, 558. The reviewer criticizes Pilkington for not pressing further in his comparison of Proust and Bergson.

5623   Megay, Joyce N. "Review of *Bergson and His Influence: A Reassessment* by A. E. Pilkington." *The French Review*, 41, No. 2, 1977, 307. The reviewer states that Pilkington's book is "a reassessment of affinities and divergencies, rather than of the direct influence of Bergson's thought."

5624   Mijuskovic, Ben. "The Simplicity Argument and Time in Schopenhauer and Bergson." *Schopenhauer-Jahrbuch*, 58, 1977, 43-58.

5625   Minafra, Vincenzo. "Intuizione e filosofia negativa in Henri Bergson." *Raccolta di Studi e Richerche* (Bari, Italy), 1, 1977, 231-239.

5626   Minor, William Sherman. *Creativity in Henry Nelson Wieman*. Foreword by Bernard E. Meland. Metuchen, New Jersey and London: Scarecrow Press, Inc. and American Theological Library Association, 1977, 231 pp. (ATLA Monograph Series, No. 11). On pp. 4-6 the author describes the influence of Bergson on Henry Nelson Wieman's philosophy as one of four basic influences. On pp. 71-86 Chapter 5, "Creativity in Wieman as a Response to Bergson's and Whitehead's Organismic Philosophy" the author concludes: 1. Wieman's study of *Creative Evolution* was his first introduction to the "bio-mystical process philosophy", which was to be a "continuing influence" on his thought. 2. Bergson's influence caused Wieman to reinterpret his teachers at Harvard. 3. Bergson's influence on Wieman preceded A. N. Whitehead's.

5627   Mitchell, Bonner. "Review of *Bergson and His Influence* by Anthony Edward Pilkington." *World Literature Today*, 51, No. 3, 1977, 411. The reviewer states, "All serious students of Proust, including erudite specialists, should now consult (Pilkington's) thirty-two dense pages on the subject. The other studies are equally lucid and convincing."

5628   Mitchell, Timothy. "Bergson, Le Bon, and Hermetic Cubism." *Journal of Aesthetics and Art Criticism*, 36, No. 2, 1977, 175-183. The author discusses the influence of the ideas of Henri Poincaré, Henri Bergson, and Gustav Le Bon on cubism. He proposes a re-evaluation of hermetic cubism in the light of the notions of science and philosophy confronting artists in the first decade of the 20th century in France. On p. 176 he states, "Bergson's philosophy is as important to the development of cubism as Schelling's Nature Philosophy was to German romantic painting."

5629   Mittler, Sylvia. "Le Jeune Henri Pourrat: De Barrès et Bergson à l'âme rustique." *Travaux de Linguistique et de Littérature Publiés par le Centre de Philologie et de Littératures Romanes de l'Université de Strasbourg*, 15, No. 2, 1977, 193-215.

5630   Montefoschi, Paola. "Bergson e la poetica di Ungaretti." *L'Approdo Letterario*, 77-78, 1977, 172-182.

5631   Morkovsky, Mary Christine. "L'Accomplisement de l'homme dans sa rencontre avec Dieu." *Communion* (Taizeé), No. 15-16, 1977, 65-73. The author deals from a Bergsonian perspective with the problem of human fulfillment through the encounter with God. "Quand il est co-créateur avec Dieu, et quand tout comme son Père céleste il a à coeur d'eveiller et d'etendre la vie, l'homme trouve son accomplissement" (p. 71).

5632   Nakata, Mitsuo. *Bergson Tetsugaku: Jitsuzai to Kachi*. Tokyo: Tokyo Univ. Press, 1977, 572. "The author wishes to respond to the question 'Is it possible to find out ethics in the philosophy of Bergson?' The A. deepens, universalizes and puts the question on the possibility to find out the problem of value in Bergsonism." Kenichi Sasake. *Bibliographie de la Philosophie*, 26, No. 2, 1979, 227.

5633   Neuenschwander, Ulrich. *Gott im neuzeitlichen Denken, II: Henri Bergson, Ernst Bloch, Martin Buber, Hermann Cohen, Ludwig Feuerbach, Johann Gottlieb Fichte, Georg Friedrich Wilhelm Hegel, Martin Heidegger, Karl Jaspers, Sören Kierkegaard, Karl Marx, Friedrich Nietzsche, Jean-Paul Sartre, Max Scheler, Friedrich Wilhelm Joseph Schelling*. Gütersloh: Gütersloher Verlagshaus Mohn, 1977, 244. (Gütersloher Taschenbücher Siebenstern, No. 244)

5634   Pacholski, Maksymillian. *Florian Znaniecki: Spoteczna dinamiki Kultury*. Warsaw: Państwowe Wydawnictwo Naukowe, 1977, 304. "Philosophe et sociologue, Znaniecki a concentré ses recherches sur les problèmes de la méthode des sciences humaines, de la théorie de la culture et de la sociologie. L'A. reconstruit et expose les résultats de ces recherches en montrant leurs rapports avec les idées de Dilthey, Bergson et du pragmatisme." Isydora Dambska, *Bibliographie de la Philosophie*, 25, No. 3, 1978, 189.

5635   Peden, Creighton. "Wieman's Empirical Process Philosophy. Intro. William S. Minor. Washington, D. C.: University Press of America, 1977, 140 pp. On p. 2 Professor Minor points out that the transition of the American thinker, Henry Nelson Wieman (1884-1975) from theology to the study of philosophy was occasioned by Wieman's reading of Henri Bergson's *Creative Evolution*. On p. 17 the author states of Wieman: "Under the influence of Bergson, Wieman began his Ph. D. studies at Harvard University." On p. 106, in an interview, Wieman states that under the influence of *Creative Evolution* he moved away from his earlier personalism prior to going to Harvard to study philosophy.

5636   Péguy, Charles. *Cartesio e Bergson*. Trans. Angelo Prontero and Mario Petrone. Pref. Jacques Viard. Lecce: Milella, 1977.

5637   Phalen, Adolf. *Ur efterlämnade manuskript, 8: Några riktningar i nyare Kunskaplära*. Stockholm: Natur O. Kultur, 1977, 235. The title of this work translates as *From Posthumous Manuscripts: Some Movements in Later Theories of Knowledge*.

5638   Phoba, Mvika. *Bergson et la théologie morale*. Lille: Atelier Reprod. des Thèses Université de Lille, III; Paris: H. Champion, 1977, xi, 512.

5639   Pinto, Luigia de. "Tempo reale e tempo matematico in Henri Bergson." *Raccolta di Studi e Richerche* (Bari, Italy), 1, 1977, 177-210.

5640   Pipa, Arshi. "L'Influence de Boutroux et de Bergson sur Montale." *Revue des Études Italiennes*, 22, 1977, 193-204.

5641   Poulet, Georges. *Proustian Space*. Trans. Elliott Coleman. Baltimore and London: Johns Hopkins University Press, 1977, 113. The author recalls Bergson's protest against the "spatialization of time," but argues that Marcel Proust, who has so often been taken to be a disciple of Bergson, takes a position diametrically opposed to Bergson. "To the bad juxtaposition, to the intellectual space condemned by Bergson, there is opposed a good juxtaposition, an aesthetic space, where, in ordering themselves, moments and places form the work of art, altogether memorable and admirable." (p. 4) Cf. especially pp. 105-106.

5642   Pruche, Benoit. *Existant et acte d'être*. Vol. 1. *Critique existentielle*. Vol. 2. *Analyse existentielle*. Paris: Tournai; Montreal: Desclee/Bellarmin, 1977 and 1980, 216, 280. (Philosophie, Recherches, Nos. 18 and 19) "D'Abondantes notes critiques sont consacrées á S. Thomas (l'auteur le plus utilisé), Kant, Descartes, Bergson, Sartre, etc." Jean-Louis Dumas. *Bibliographie de la Philosophie*, 27, No. 4, 1980, 284.

5643   Robinson, Daniel S. "The Bergson-Flewelling Correspondence, 1914-1940." *Coranto*, 10, No. 2, 1977, 21-37. The author presents, and comments on, a series of letters between Henri Bergson and Ralph Tyler Flewelling, an American personalist who was the founder of the School of Philosophy at the University of Southern California and of the journal *The Personalist*. These letters begin with discussions of Flewelling's vivid criticisms of Bergson in his *Bergson and Personal Realism* (1920) and conclude with Flewelling's acceptance of Bergson's philosophy as expressed in *The Two Sources of Morality and Religion* (1932).

5644   Russell, Bertrand. *The Philosophy of Bergson*. 1912; rpt. Folcroft, Pennsylvania, Folcroft Library Editions, 1977, 36.

5645   Soulez, Philippe. "Lorsque Freud parle de Bergson." *Psychanalyse à l'Université*, 3, No. 9, 1977, 93-109. In this article, the second of two devoted to the topic of the relations between Bergson and Freud, the author examines the two known references by Freud to Bergson: (1) The passages in *Wit and its Relations to the Unconscious* in which Freud critiques, and in part utilizes, Bergson's theory of comedy, and (2) Freud's letter of 1910 to James Jackson Putnam, leader of the early psychoanalytic movement in the United States. Freud, the author concludes, doubtless read Bergson's *Matter and Memory* (1896). He and Bergson clearly agreed (1) that the unconscious can not be reduced to brain mechanisms, and (2) that all memories are stored in the unconscious; none are lost. The author, in establishing this dual thesis, mentions Bergson's lectures *circa* 1892 and his close contact with Marie Bonaparte, Freud's French translator. Cf. the author, 1976. These two articles (1977 and 1976), though brief, constitute the most complete comparisons of Freud and Bergson done so far.

5646   Shillingsburg, Miriam and Peter, and Takaes, Zoltan. "Theses and Dissertations Within the SCMLA Region, 1976." *South Central Bulletin*, 37, No. 1, 1977, 14-21.

5647   St. Aubyn, F. C. *Charles Péguy*. Boston: Twayne Publishers, 1977, 175.

5648   Tanigawa, Atsuchi. "Genèse et structure de l'esthétique d'Etienne Souriau." *Bigaku*, 28, No. 4, 1977, 56. (In Japanese) "E. Souriau est philosophe avant d'être estheticien et e'est le problème de la connaissance qui l'a amené à mediter sur l'art et non inversement. Dans la première oeuvre, 'Pensée vivante et perfection formelle', qui date des 1925 et constitue l'un des premiers documents de la réaction contre le bergsonisme, Soriau cherchant à réhabiliter le rationnel comme instrument d'une connaissance de l'ontique, demande au sentiment ésthetique d'une perfection formelle de justifier la realité objective de cette connaissance. Mais cette perfection n'est pas une donnée toute faite en dehors de l'esprit, et pour ainsi dire passive et statique. Il préfére placer la perfection dans la creation ou l'*instauration*. De ce point de vue, le seul et le meilleur moyen de saisir l'être sur le vif, c'est de le creer soi'même sous le signe de la perfection, Voila pourquoi l'activité instauratrice de l'artiste est le la révélation mètaphysique des realités absolues, et pourquoi c'est bien l'esthétique qui est le modèle d'un accomplissement de l'idéation en connaissance ontologique." (*Philosopher's Index*, 12, No. 2, 1978, 97.)

5649   Theau, Jean. *La Philosophie française dans le première moitié du XXe siècle*. Ottowa: Ed. de l'Univ. d'Ottowa, 1977, 205. (Philosophes) Cf. "Les Etapes de la méditation bergsonienne," Ch. 3, pp. 79-100.

5650   Thinés, Georges. *Phenomenology and the Science of Behavior: An Historical and Epistemological Approach*. London: George Allen & Unwin, 1977, 174. "The peculiar nature of subjective time was first stressed in an explicit manner by Bergson; it was not primarily a phenomenological issue. However, in contrasting the continuous time-flow of consciousness with the discontinuity of measurable physical time, Bergson inaugurated, concurrently with William James, a new approach to the nature of consciousness which had major consequences in phenomenology and psychology" (p. 51). The question of psychological time was later raised indirectly and in new terms by "purposive machines" which were, for a time, "Hastily endowed with temporal characteristics similar to those of the living subject" (p. 52). The author rejects this identification on pp. 52-55. He refers to F. J. J. Buytendijk, *Prolegomena to an Anthropological Physiology*,

Pittsburgh: Duquesne University Press, 1974, 223-224, where Buytendijk states, "Thus the modern automaton exists in the same sort of Bergsonian time as the living organism." This is only *apparently* the case."

5651 Tulving, Endel. "Cue-Dependent Forgetting." In *Current Trends in Psychology: Readings from the American Scientist.* Ed. Irving L. Janis. Los Altos, California: William Kaufmann, Inc., 1977, 142-150. The author begins his exposition of contemporary theories of memory with a quote from *Creative Evolution: "We trail behind us, unawares, the whole of our past; but our memory pours into the present only the odd recollection or two that in some way complete our present situation."* He defends the theory that forgetting is *"cue-dependent," i.e., that forgetting involves not the loss of memory-traces but the failure to retrieve the correct memory. By providing the correct "cue," it is often possible to retrieve a memory which is supposedly lost. The author defends this theory of memory against the theory that memory is "trace-dependent."*

5652 Tummolo, Giovanni. *Reincarnazione e magia. La scommessa de Pascal. I tre volti di Bergson.* Trieste: Editrice Tip. Triestina, 1977, 73.

5653 Wagner, Helmut R. "The Bergsonian Period of Alfred Schutz." *Philosophy and Phenomenological Research*, 38, No. 4, 1977, 187-199. "The article discusses the attempt which Schutz made in 1925 to link Weber's Sociology of Under-standing to Bergson's philosophy. The major unfinished essay analyzed is devoted to a preliminary construction of a theory of the ego, comprising six 'life-forms' ranging from pure duration to the thinking I. The author suggests that Schutz gave up this attempt, realizing that Bergson's 'pure duration' remained inaccessible to experience and introspection. Therefore, he turned to Husserl who contributed the main phenomenological support to his fundamental study of *Der Sinnhafte Aufbau der Sozialen Welt.*" (*Philosopher's Index*, 12, No. 2, 1978, 99.)

5654 Waszkinel, Romuald. "O zrodlach filozofii Bergsona." *Roczniki Filozoficzne*, 25, No. 1, 1977, 111-140. This article concerns the sources of Bergson's philosophy. The author includes a résumé, in French.

1978

5655 Aguirre, J. M. "La Voz a ti debida: Salinas y Bergson." *Revue de Littératrue Comparée*, 52, No. 7, 1978, 98-118. The author states, "El objeto del presente arículo es establecer la coherencia metafísica de *La voz a ti debida* (1933), tratando de demonstrar la estrecha relacíon existente entre el poema de Pedro Salinas y la filosofía de Bergson, así como el grave problema que la adherencia inicial a la misma supuso para el poeta" (p. 98).

5656 Alexander, Ian W. "Review of *Bergson and His Influence: A Reassessment* by Anthony Edward Pilkington." *French Studies*, 33, No. 4, 1978, 478-479.

5657 Barreau, Hervé. "Review of *Bergson et le fait mystique* by Marie Cariou." *Revue Internationale de Philosophie*, 32, Nos. 2-3, 1978, 409-413.

5658 Benassi, Stefano. "Proust e Bergson: dell'indifferenza grado zero dell'entropia." *Studi di Estetica*, No. 5, 1978-1980, 145-198.

5659 Bochner, Jay. *Blaise Cendrars: Discovery and Recreation.* Toronto, Buffalo, London: University of Toronto Press, 1978, 311. Bergson is dealt with here as one among many twentieth century artistic and intellectual figures.

5660 Bush, Clive. "Toward the Outside: The Quest for Discontinuity in Gertrude Stein's *The Making of Americans*: Being the History of a Family's Progress." *Twentieth Century Literature*, 24, No. 1, 1978, 27-56.

5661 Cahm, E. "Bergson and his Influence: A Reassessment." *History*, 63, No. 207, February 1978, 163. This is a brief review of *Bergson and his Influence* by A. E. Pilkington.

5662 Čapek, Milič. "Bergson, Nominalism, and Relativity." *Southwestern Journal of Philosophy*, 10, No. 3, 1978, 127-133. This is a response to a review of the author's *Bergson and Modern Physics* by Pete A. Y. Gunter in an earlier issue of the *Southwestern Journal of Philosophy* (6, No. 1, 1975). The author deals with two issues raised in the review: the question of Bergson's supposed nominalism and the question of the relations of quantum and relativity theories. Bergson, in spite of received opinions, is not a nominalist; he is instead a conceptualist. The author denies Gunter's contention that relativity and quantum physics are distinct, incompatible theories. He also denies that relativity theory permits velocities faster than light, or particles "travelling into the past." Cf. Gunter 1978.

5663 Cariou, Marie. *L'Atomisme: Gassendi, Leibniz, Bergson et Lucrèce*. Paris: Aubier Montaigne, 1978, 234.

5664 Coffey, Rebecca Kathryn. "A Comparison-Contrast of *Laughter* to *An Italian Straw Hat* and *The Bald Soprano*." Thesis, Cal. State at Long Beach, 1978, 93. The author applies Bergson's concept of laughter to two comic plays differing radically in style. Bergson's concept of laughter applies well to *An Italian Straw Hat*, and less well to *The Bald Soprano* (only insofar as inversion and repetition are concerned). *Masters Abstracts*, 17, No. 1, 1979, 96.

5665 Collins, James. "Review of *Journée d'Études 9-10 novembre 1974: Blondel-Bergson-Maritain-Loisy*. Ed. Claude Troisfontaines." *Modern Schoolman*, 55, No. 2, 1978, 205-206.

5666 Cruickshank, John. "Review of *Bergson and his Influence* by Anthony Edward Pilkington." *Modern Language Review*, 73, No. 3, 1978, 647.

5667 Dąmbska, Izydora. "Review of *Kłopoty intelektu: Między Comtéem a Bergsonom* by Barbara Skarga." *Revue Philosophique de la France et de l'Étranger*, 103, No. 2, 1978, 201-202.

5668 Devaux, André-A. "La Rencontre entre Péguy et Bergson." in *Péguy vivant: Atti del Convegno Internazionale "Péguy vivant" svoltosi presso l'Università degli Studi di Lecce dal 27 al 30 aprile 1977*. Eds. Jean Bastaire, Angelo Prontera, Giuseppe A. Roggerone. Lecce: Milella, 1978, 561-566.

5669 Doumic, René. "A Normal Supérieure: Juarès et Bergson." *Nouvelle Revue des Deux Mondes*, No. 4, Avril 1978, 86-91. The author characterizes Jean Juarès and Henri Bergson as "normaliens." In particular, he describes their mutual competition as debaters and their (very distinctive) personalities.

5670 Dunaway, John. *Jacques Maritain*. Boston: Twayne Publishers, 1978, 174.

5671 Epperly, Bruce. "Abstract of 'Bergson's Philosophical Method and its Applications to the Sciences' by Pete A. Y. Gunter." *Process Studies*, 8, No. 1, 1978, 65.

5672   Ermath, Michael. *Wilhelm Dilthey: The Critique of Historical Reason.* Chicago: University of Chicago Press, 1978, xiv, 414. The author deals with Dilthey's relations with Bergson, among many others.

5673   Favre, Yves-Alain. *La Recherche de la grandeur dans l'oeuvre de Suarès.* Paris: Klincksieck, 1978, 490.

5674   Freinberg, Leonard. *The Secret of Humor.* Amsterdam: Rodopi, 1978, 218.

5675   Felt, James W. "Abstract of 'Bergson and Whitehead on Freedom' by Patrick J. Hurley," *Process Studies*, 8, No. 1, 1978, 65-66.

5676   Felt, James W. "Abstract of 'Henri Bergson on Freedom without Antecedent Possibility' by Mary C. Morkovsky." *Process Studies*, 8, No. 1, 1978, 66-67.

5677   Felt, James W. "Philosophic Understanding and the Continuity of Becoming." *International Philosophical Quarterly*, 18, No. 4, 1978, 375-393. "This studies two different modes of philosophic understanding, Bergson's emphasizing intuition, and Whitehead's emphasizing intellection, brought to bear on a single problem, the analysis of becoming. Bergson's conclusion that becoming is fundamentally continuous, Whitehead's that it is epochal or episodic, are apparently antithetical. It is argued, however, that the intuitive and intellectual methods are in fact mutually interrelated, the latter ancillary to the former, so that the respective conclusions are seen as mutually complimentary rather than antithetical. The two modes of analysis stand in need of one another, and intuition, properly understood, must be taken seriously as a philosophic method." (*Philosopher's Index*, 13, No. 1, 1979, 84.)

5678   Gabel, Joseph. *Idéologies II: Althusserisme et Stalinisme.* Paris: Éditions Anthropes, 1978, 167. In Chapter III of this work the author notes the influence of Bergson on the Hungarian philosopher Lukacs. Thanks to Lukacs, Bergson was in a dominant position in Budapest prior to the First World War.

5679   Gallagher, Edward J. "A Checklist of Nineteenth Century French Titles on the *Index Librorum Prohibitorum.*" *Romance Notes*, 19, No. 2, 1978, 196-205.

5680   Gillet, Marcel. *L'Homme et sa structure: Essai sur les valeurs morales.* Pref. Jean Guitton. Paris: Téqui, 1978, 772. Bergson is dealt with here along with many other French intellectuals.

5681   Gilson, Bernard. *L'Individualité dans la philosophie de Bergson.* Paris: J. Vrin, 1978, 87. (Bibliothèque d'histoire de la philosophie)

5682   Greaves, Anthony A. *Maurice Barrès.* Boston: Boston: Twayne, 1978, 168.

5683   Groggin, Robert. "The French Academy Elections of 1914 and the French Right." *Humanities Association Review*, 29, No. 1, 1978, 61-72.

5684   Gunter, Pete A. Y. "Bergson, Conceptualism, and Indeterminancy: A Rejoinder to Čapek." *Southwestern Journal of Philosophy*, 9, No. 3, 1978, 135-137. This is a reply to Milič Čapek's response to the author's previous review (*Southwestern Journal of Philosophy*, 6, No. 1, 1975) of Čapek's *Bergson and Modern Physics.* The author agrees with Čapek that Bergson is not a nominalist, but urges that the question of nominalism be pursued in an ontological and not merely an epistemological context. Only the most basic features of duration should, on Bergson's terms, be viewed as universals. The author agrees with Čapek that relativity and quantum physics do not really allow for "particles travelling backward in time." He disagrees, however, concerning the complete compatibility of relativistic determinism and quantum indeterminism.

5685   Gunter, Pete A. Y. "Bergson's Philosophical Method and its Applications to the Sciences." *Southern Journal of Philosophy*, 16, No. 3, 1978, 167-181. "Henri Bergson has often been interpreted as anti-intellectual and anti-scientific because his philosophical method, with its polarity of intuition and intelligence, has been misunderstood. The interaction of philosophical intuition and scientific intelligence is understood by Bergson as being fruitful for both terms. Intuition, a form of reflection and not mere "feeling," is awakened by the fragmentary and static concepts of scientific intelligence. In turn, intuition of the dynamisms of nature can provoke new, more supple scientific concepts. Intuition and intelligence thus constitute the terms of a dialectic. Bergsonian method continues to apply, e.g., to thermodynamics and chronobiology." (*Philosopher's Index*, 14, No. 2, 1980, 98.)

5686   Gunter, Pete A. Y. "Review of *In Quest of a New Psychology: Toward a Redefinition of Humanism* by Richard E. Johnson." *Philosophy and Phenomenological Research*, 29, No. 2, 1978, 293-295.

5687   Hale, Nathan G., Jr. *L'Introduction de la Psychanalyse aux États-unis: Autour de James Jackson Putnam*. Trans. Catherine Cullien. Paris: Gallimard, 1978.

5688   Heidegger, Martin. "The Concept of Time in the Science of History." Trans. Harry S. Taylor and Hans W. Uffelman. *Journal of the British Society for Phenomenology*, 9, No. 1, January 1978, 3-10. Cf. the author, 1916, for annotation.

5689   Herbert, G. S. *Time: A Metaphysical Study*. Trivandrum, India: College Book House, 1978, 144.

5690   Holland, Norman N. "What Can a Concept of Identity Add to Psycholinguistics?" In *Psychiatry and the Humanities*, Vol. III of *Psychoanalysis and Language*. Ed. Joseph E. Smith. New Haven and London: Yale University Press, 1978, 171-234. The author quotes Bergson's *Matter and Memory* (p. 136, Macmillan, 1911) to the effect that listening is an active process. The author adds, "Perhaps the most useful term for this scanning process is Halle and Steven's 'analysis-by-synthesis.' They propose 'a recognition model for speech' in which 'patterns are generated internally in the analyzer according to a flexible or adaptable sequence of instructions until a best match with the input signal is obtained;' in other words, an analysis 'achieved through active internal synthesis of comparison signals'." The author footnotes M. Halle and K. N. Stevens, "Speech Recognition: A Model and a Program for Research," in Eds. J. A. Fodor and J. Katz' *The Structure of Language*, Englewood Cliffs: Prentice-Hall, 1964, 604.

5691   Hughes, James M. "Webster, Poulet, and Bergson: A Note on M. M. Khan's 'Intuition of Time, Eternity, and Immortality' (*Higginson Journal*, 14)." *Dickinson Studies*, No. 34, December 1978, 38-41.

5692   Humes, Joy Nachod. *Two Against Time: A Study of the Very Present Worlds of Paul Claudel and Charles Péguy*. Chapel Hill: North Carolina Studies in the Romance Languages and Literature, University of North Carolina Department of Romance Languages, 1978, 171. In Chapter III, "...And Time Again" (pp. 80-100), the author examines Bergson's influence on Charles Péguy, an influence which, she states, "would be difficult to exaggerate" (p. 80).

5693   Johnson, Ragnar. "Joking Relationships." *Man*, N.S. 13, No. 1, 1978, 130-132. The author includes Bergson, S. Freud, A. Koestler and others among those proposing "bisociation" theories of joking. (The joke, on this theory, is a social form which mediates between social and anti-social order.) The debate over joking begun by Griaule and Radcliffe-Brown was correctly seen by Mary Douglas (*Man*, 1968) as part of a greater debate on the social sciences begun by Bergson and Freud.

5694   Jung, Hwa Yol. "Democratic Ontology and Technology: A Critique of C. B. Macpherson." *Polity*, 11, No. 2, 1978, 247-269. The author states on p. 248 that he is guided by H. Bergson and M. Heidegger in his description of Macpherson as a "systematic" thinker. Macpherson fails to take account of the "antihumanistic" characteristics of technology.

5695   Kellner, Georg. "Péguys Apologie der Bergsonschen Dauer." Diss. Vienna, 1978, v, 165.

5696   "Review of *Klopoty intellektu* by I. Dambska." *Revue Philosophique de la France et de l'Etranger*, 103, No. 2, 1978, 201-202.

5697   Koestler, Arthur. *Janus: A Summing Up*. New York: Vintage Books, 1978, 354. On pp. 115, 116n, 123, 128, and 137, the author cites Bergson's (and Freud's) theories of laughter. On pp. 224 and 269 he equates Schrodinger's "negentropy" with Bergson's *élan vital*. On p. 226 he quotes a passage summing up the value of vitalism from Bergson's *Creative Evolution*.

5698   Marquit, Erwin. "Dialectics of Motion in Continous and Discrete Spaces." *Science and Society*, 42, No. 4, 1978-1979, 410-425. On pp. 421-422 the author likens Bergson's treatment of motion to G. W. F. Hegel's. Both deny that a moving body is *at* a place *at* an instant.

5699   Mataix, Carmen. "Review of *Bergson and Modern Physics* by Milič Čapek." *Annales del Seminario del Metafisica*, 13, 1978, 88-91.

5700   Merleau-Ponty, Maurice. *L'Union de l'âme et du corps chez Malebranche, Biran et Bergson*. Paris: Vrin, 1978, 137. (Bibliothèque d'Histoire de la Philosophie) This new edition, edited by Michel Jouhaud, contains previously unpublished materials.

5701   Meyer, M. "La Notion bergsonienne de néant, la conception de Sartre et le paradoxe de la conscience." *Filosofia Oggi*, 1, No. 4, 1978, 356-363. "L'Auteur soutient la thèse que la redevance de *l'Etre et le néant*, à Hegel-Husserl-Heidegger, n'est pas incompatible avec l'idée que Sartre pensait clairement à Bergson au moins autant qu'à Heidegger. Sartre part de Bergson et avant tout de sa conception du néant pour en tirer de conclusions opposées." *Bulletin signalétique: Philosophie*, 34, No. 1, 1980, p. 15.

5702   Mijuskovic, Ben. "The Simplicity Argument and the Freedom of Consciousness." *Idealistic Studies*, 8, No. 1, 1978, 62-74.

5703   Omesco, Ion. *La Metamorphose de la tragédie*. Paris: Presses Universitaires de France, 1978, 275.

5704   Patout, Paulette. *Alfonso Reyes et la France*. Paris: Klincksieck, 1978, 687. (Témoins de l'Espagne et de l'Amerique latine: Série historique, 8.)

5705   *Philosophie: époque contemporaine: Bergson-Jaspers-Austin*. 2 Vols. Bruxelles: Presses Universitaires de Bruxelles, 1978.

5706   Pilkington, Anthony Edward. "Review of *Bergson et Proust: Essai de mise au point de la question de l'influence de Bergson sur Proust* by Joyce N. Megay." *French Studies*, 33, No. 4, 1978, 480-483.

5707　　Pilkington, Anthony Edward. "Review of *Henri Bergson: A Bibliography* by P. A. Y. Gunter." *French Studies*, 33, No. 4, 1978, 479-480.

5708　　Prontera, Angelo. "Wilhelm Reich, Bergson e Péguy." *Quaderno filosofico*, 2, 1978, 207-216.

5709　　Riggs, Mickey Ray. "The Other Tiger: Bergsonian Philosophy in Henry Miller's Early Novels." M. A. Thesis. Stephen F. Austin State University, 1978, 100. The author argues that Miller's first three published novels embody three recurrent ideas from Bergson's philosophy: the idea of order, automatism, nothingness. *Master's Abstracts*, 16, No. 4, 1978, 232.

5710　　Roberts, Michael. *T. E. Hulme*. 1938; rpt. New York: Haskell House Publishers, Ltd. 1978, 310.

5711　　Romyn, Herms. *Het slapend en dromend bewustzijn: Hersenonderzoek, psychanalyse, parapsychologie*. Baarn: Ambo, 1978, 103. The title of this work translates into English as: *Consciousness as Sleep and Dream: Researches in Brain, Psychoanalysis, Parapsychology*. The author uses the ideas of Bergson as well as C. G. Jung, S. Freud, P. Teilhard de Chardin, M. Merleau-Ponty.

5712　　Rotman, Brian. *Jean Piaget: Psychologist of the Real*. Ithaca: Cornell University Press, 1978, 200.

5713　　Russell, Bertrand. *The Philosophy of Bergson*. 1912; rpt. Norwood, Pennsylvania: Norwood Editions, 1978, 36.

5714　　Sarcella, Cosimo. *Il pensiero di Jacques Maritain*. Manduria: Lacaita Editore, 1978, 387. (Biblioteca di Studi Moderni, 14.)

5715　　Sibley, Jack R., and Pete A. Y. Gunter. *Process Philosophy: Basic Writings*. Pref. Charles Hartshorne. Washington: University Press of America, 1978, xvii, 579. This anthology contains, along with writings by many other authors, passages from Bergson's *Creative Evolution* and *An Introduction to Metaphysics*, with introductory sections on each. It also contains numerous references to Henri Bergson and the part which he has played in the history of process philosophy.

5716　　Smrcka, Antonin Klement Josef. "A Study of Humor from Henri Bergson to the Present Time." Diss. New Mexico, 1978, 364. Cf. *Dissertation Abstracts International*, 39, No. 7, 1979, 4116A.

5717　　Srubar, Ilja. "Schütz's Perception of Bergson as Reconstructed from as yet Unpublished Writing: The Consequences for the Concept of Meaning." Diss. University of Konstanz, Federal Republic of Germany, 1978. With regard to Schütz's first published manuscript, *Der Sinnhafte Aufbau der sozialen Welt (The Meaningful Creation of the Social World*, Vienna, 1952) the author concludes: (Schütz's) concept of meaning is a result of his attempt to reformulate M. Weber's problem of meaningful action in the framework of Bergson's philosophy. The attempt to do so generated consequences which molded Schütz's theoretical procedure even before he was influenced by phenomenological considerations." *Sociological Abstracts*, 26, 1978, ISA Supplement No. 82-II, p. 2311.

5718　　Svas'ian, Karen Araevich. *Esteticheskaia sushnost' intuitivnoi filosofi Bergsona*. ЕреВаН: Изд-во Ан Армянскои ССР, 1978, 118.

5719　　Taylor, Stanley W. "Pascal, Bergson et *Notre Patrie*." in *Péguy vivant: Atti del Convegno Internazionale*. Eds. J. Bastaire, Angelo Prontero, Giuseppe A. Roggerone. Leccee: Milella, 1978, 561-566.

5720   Theau, Jean. "Henri Bergson." in *Les Littératures de langues européennes au tournant du siècle. Lectures d'aujourd'hui.* Cahiers V-VI, pp. 15-24. This is a selective bibliography of writings on Bergson, 1965-1978, plus a commentary on the fate of Bergson's philosophy in the post war decades. He describes the emergence of a continuing and vital interest in Bergson's philosophy in the 1970's.

5721   Urdánoz, Teófilo. *Historia de la Filosofía:* Vol. 6. *Siglo XX: De Bergson al final del existencialismo.* Madrid: La Edition Católica, 1978, xvi, 775. (Biblioteca de Autores Cristianos, 398)

5722   Wainwright, William J. "Bergson, Henri. The Two Sources of Morality and Religion." In *Philosophy of Religion: An Annotated Bibliography of Twentieth-Century Writings in English* by William J. Wainwright. New York and London: Garland Publishing, Inc., 1978, 370-371. This includes a brief characterization of Bergson's philosophy of religion.

5723   Waszkinel, Romuald. "Bergsona Koncepcja Liczby a Jego Metafizyka." *Roczniki Filozoficzne,* 26, No. 1, 1978, 113-129. This is a study of Bergson's philosophy of mathematics. The author pays particular attention to the concepts of unity, multiplicity, space, and mental acts.

5724   Weinstein, Michael A. *Meaning and Appreciation: Time and Modern Political Life.* West Lafayette, Ind.: Purdue University Press, 1978, ix, 155. The author claims to use a Bergsonian method in this book. He defines the essence of politics as the control over space, and proposes an "appreciative logic" for today's man who can no longer direct his life through meaningful action.

5725   Whitehead, Alfred North. *Process and Reality: An Essay in Cosmology.* Corrected ed. Ed. David Ray Griffin and Donald W. Sherburne. New York: The Free Press, 1978, 413. The author refers to Bergson on pp. xii, 33, 41, 82, 107, 114, 209, 220, 280, and 321. No significant corrections have been made in these passages over the 1929 or other subsequent editions.

5726   Whiting, Charles G. *Paul Valéry.* London: University of London, the Athlone Press, 1978, 147. (Athlone French Poets.)

5727   Winther, Truls. *Des skapende menneske: Om Henri Bergsons filosofi.* Oslo, Bergen, Trømso: Universitets-forlaget, 1978, 143. (Tankerers: Serie i filosofi, s amfunns- og miløspørsmal, No. 4)

5728   Zima, Pierre. *Pour une sociologie du texte littéraire.* Paris: Union Générale d'Editions, 1978, 372.

1979

5729   Appan Ramanujam, A. "A Study in the Development of the Philosophy of Henri Bergson." Diss. Annamalai (India) 1979. The goal of this study is to analyze the shift in Bergson's thought between *Creative Evolution* (1906) and *The Two Sources of Morality and Religion* (1932). In the first part the author examines the historical roots of Bergson's thought. In the second part he deals with Bergson's earlier and later concepts of God, intellect, and intuition. In *Creative Evolution* God is the impersonal and undetermined "push" behind evolution. In *The Two Sources of Morality and Religion* God becomes both personal and purposeful. The third part examines the shift in Bergson's thought in greater detail. The author finds basic inconsistencies in Bergson's thought. Mystical intuition is portrayed by Bergson as both practical action and as absorption in God. But it is hard to see how it can be both.

5730	Astroh, Michael. "Review of *L'Atomisme: Gassendi, Leibniz, Bergson et Lucrèce* by Marie Cariou." *Revue Philosophique de Louvain*, 77, No. 35, 1979, 414-417.

5731	Barron, Frank. *The Shaping of Personality: Conflict, Choice, and Growth.* New York: Harper and Row, 1979, 359. In Chapter 25 ("The Conflict of Connected Opposites," pp. 295-306), the author examines Bergson's distinction between intellect and intuition and relates this distinction to recent theories of brain lateralization. (In the process he describes Bergson as the "mentor" of the most significant contributor to cognitive psychology, Jean Piaget.) The author believes that Bergson's attempt to distinguish mind from brain *via* data drawn from the study of the aphasias shows much naiveté, but concludes that work done on hemispheric specialization bears out Bergson's distinction between two opposed principles of mental functioning. In this connection he notes, "modern theorists such as Joseph Bogen (the neurosurgeon who first performed the split-brained operation in human beings) and R. W. Sperry, who had earlie initiated such experiments with cats, have found Bergson's ideas useful in understanding some of these new observations concerning the functioning of the human brain" (p. 297). Cf. Intellect and Intuition, pp. 295-298.

5732	Battail, Jean François. *Le Mouvement des idées en Suède à l'age du bergsonisme.* Paris: Lettres Modernes, 1979, 413. (Bibliothèque nordique, 5)

5733	Blasucci, Savino. *Il problema dell'intuizione in Cartesio, Kant e Bergson.* Bari: Edizioni Levante, 1979, 189 pp.

5734	Borzym, S. "The Transformations of Bergson's Ideas: *Sorel and Brzozowski.*" *Archiwum Historii Filozofii i Myśli Spolecznej*, 25, 1979, 247-273. This article is written in Polish. "Convergence des idées de S. Brzozowski avec celles de Sorel pour qui est de la réception de la philosophie bergsonienne." *Bulletin Signalétique: Philosophie*, 34, No. 4, 1980, p. 16.

5735	Brée, Germaine. "Review of *Bergson and his Influence* by A. E. Pilkington." *Revue d'Histoire Littéraire de la France*, 79, No. 5, 1979, 876-878.

5736	Brincourt, André. *Les Ecrivains du XXe siècle: Un Musée imaginaire de la littér-ature mondiale.* Paris: Editions Retz, 1979, 735. (Les encyclopédies du savoir moderne.)

5737	Brisson, Mary Jo T. Landiera. "The Presence of Henri Bergson in Antonio Machado." Diss. North Carolina 1979, 243. The author analyses the direct relationships between Bergson and the poet Antonio Machado in four areas: personality, pedagogics, poetry and language, and the comic. She concludes that the similarities are least pronounced in the case of the comic. These similarities may be traced, the author concludes, to the *Zeitgeist* rather than to direct influence. (*Dissertations Abstracts International*, 40, No. 8, 1980, 4619A.)

5738	Callot, Emile. *La Philosophie de la science et de la nature: Essais dialectiques et critiques sur la forme et le contenu de la connaissance de la réalité.* Paris: Ed. Ophrys, 1979, 268. "Un dernier chap. conclut sur le temps à partir de Kant et Bergson, prennant en considération son objectivation biologique, son universalization sociale et les figures qu'il revêt dans la physique classique, dans la mécanique et dans la mécanique relativiste. Temps senti et temps conçu auxquels la philosophie de la nature, comme idéalisme objectif, peut conferer une certaine unité." Marcel Deschoux. *Bibliographie de la Philosophie*, 27, No. 4, 1980, 279.

5739 Castellano, Enrique. "El rechazo de la filosofía en Goethe y en Bergson." *Plural*, 9, 2a, época, No. 97, 1979, 25-27.

5740 Colletti, Lucio. *Marxism and Hegel*. London: Verso, 1979. In Chapter Ten, "From Bergson to Lukacs" (pp. 157-198) the author characterizes Bergson's philosophy as the high point of the convergence between the modern idealistic reaction against science and certain major themes of romantic philosophy, and stresses similarities between Bergson and F. Engels. On the surface this chapter would seem to be an examination of Bergson's influence on the Marxist philosophy of George Lukacs. In fact, the author merely takes the occasion to argue the superiority of "Western Marxism" over Russian "dialectical materialism". Cf. *The Philosopher's Index*, 15, No. 1, 1981, 94 for the author's abstract.

5741 Dedola, Rossana. "*La Voce* e i *Cahiers de la Quinizaine*: una messa a punto." *Giornale Storico della Letteratura Italiana*, 156, No. 496, 1979, 548-563.

5742 Escribar, Wicks, Ana. "Crisis moral contemporánea. Sus causas. Análisis y diagnóstico, basados en las tesis bergsonianas." *Revista de Filosofía* (Chile), 17, 1979, 47-61.

5743 Faune, Jean-Pierre. "Le Temps de Bergson à Einstein." *Europe*, 57, No. 602-603, juin-juillet 1979, 191-204. This essay deals primarily with Jean Piaget.

5744 Gentile, Luigi. "Relatività Assolutezza Della Filosofia in Henri Bergson." *Aquinas*, 22, No. 1, 1979, 94-117. "Gentile considers fundamental the clarification of the essence and the method of the 'philosophy' as they result from the whole philosopher's work... Bergson succeeds, through his 'positive metaphysics,' in escaping the pernicious dilemma of either dogmatism or scepticism." *Philosopher's Index*, 13, No. 4, 1979, 102)

5745 Georgopoulos, N. "Kazantzakis, Bergson, Lenin, and the 'Russian Experiment'." *Journal of the Hellenic Diaspora*, 5, No. 4, 1979, 32-34. The author argues that the philosophy of Bergson gave to the ever-changing thought of Nikos Kazantzakis a certain "encompassing and integral character."

5746 Griese, Anneliese. "Zeit—Bewegung—Entwickling: Philosophische Aspekte des Zeitproblems in der Physik." *Deutsche Zeitschrift für Philosophie*, 27, No. 2, 1979, 191-202.

5747 Hernandez, Gustavo R. "Theses and Dissertations for 1977." *South Atlantic Bulletin*, 44, No. 2, May, 1979, 104-129.

5748 Harris, Jane Gary. *Mandelstam: The Complete Critical Prose and Letters*. Ann Arbor, Michigan: Ardis, 1979, 725. On pp. 19, 615-616n, 618, 619, 220, 639, 685 the author explores Bergson's influence on the Russian poet and critic, Osip Mandelstam.

5749 Hartshorne, Charles. "Whitehead's Revolutionary Conception of Prehension." *International Philosophical Quarterly*, 19, No. 3, 1979, 253-263.

5750 Jalfen, Louis Jorge. *La amenaza de las ideologías*. Buenos Aires: Galerna, 1979, 192. "Aunque en este trabajo se soslaya cierta influencia de Heidegger, se podría afirmar, no obstante, que en sus conclusiones—mas que en su planteamiento methodológico—el A. parece estar próximo a ciertos rasgos de la filosofía de Bergson." S. A. J. Dolgopol. *Bibliographie de la Philosophie*, 28, Nos. 2-3, 1981, 106.

5751		Kouassi, A. *Bergson et Gabriel Marcel: Profil d'un rencontre*. Thèse de doct. de 3e cycle Octobre 1979, 264 pp. Université de Poitiers. Faculté de sciences humaines.

5752		Kumar, Shiv Kumar. *Bergson and the Stream of Consciousness Novel*. 1962; rpt. Westport, Connecticut: Greenwood Press 1979, 174 pp.

5753		Langer, Suzanne K. *Feeling and Form: A Theory of Art Developed from Philosophy in a New Key*. New York: Charles Scribner's Sons, 1979, 431. Chapter VII of this study in aesthetic theory ("The Image of Time," pp. 104-119) discusses Bergson's theory of real duration as fundamental to a satisfactory musical aesthetics, and a satisfactory theory of musical aesthetics as fundamental to all aesthetic theory. The author criticizes Bergson, however, for his rejection of symbolism in metaphysics and his repudiation of space. According to Professor Langer, for Bergson duration is "formless."

5754		Mandelstam, Osip. "On the Nature of the World." in *Mandelstam: The Complete Critical Prose and Letters*. Ed. Jane Gary Harris. Ann Arbor, Michigan: Ardis, 1979, 117-132. On pp. 117 and 118 of this essay the author gives his opinion of the significance of Bergson's philosophy for literature, especially Russian Literature.

5755		Margolin, Jean-Claude. "Du nouveau sur Bergson." *Revue de Synthèse*, Nos. 93-94, janvier-juin 1979, 115-116. This is a review of *Bergson et le fait mystique* by Marie Cariou."

5756		McCool, Gerald A. "Maritain's Defence of Democracy." *Thought*, 54, No. 3, 1979, 132-142.

5757		Minic, Janet Barnett. "An Interdisciplinary Study of the Early Works of Gertrude Stein in the Context of Cubism." Diss. S.U.N.Y. at Binghamton, 1979, 251. "This study of Gertrude Stein uses an interdisciplinary approach to examine the development of her writings from 1904 to 1919 in the context of Cubism and the philosophical theories of time and perception of Henri Bergson and William James." *Dissertation Abstracts International*, 40, No. 5, 1979, 2666-A.

5758		Morujão, Manuel. "O Problema De Existencia De Deuz Em Bergson." *Revista Portuguesa de Filosofia*, 35, No. 4, 1979, 362-405.

5759		Namer, E. "Review of *Bergson et le fait mystique* by Marie Cariou." *Revue de Métaphysique et de Morale*, 84, No. 3, 1979, 420.

5760		Navali, Mahmoud. "Les Origines de la philosophie de Bergson et la tradition philosophique." Thèse, Université de Toulouse-Le-Mirail, 1979.

5761		Nye, Mary Jo. "The Boutroux Circle and Poincaré's Conventionalism." *Journal of the History of Ideas*, 40, No. 1, 1979, 107-120. On p. 120 the author, after arguing for the influence of Émile Boutroux and his circle of Henri Poincaré, notes, "Paradoxically for his conservative aims, Boutroux's philosophy provided an opportunity for the budding of philosophical and scientific relativism, and Poincaré was to spend long hours defending conventionalism against this skeptical variant. The relativistic offshoot took root in Paris in Bergson's intuitionism, and, in reaction, the French scientific community, including Poincaré himself, may well have sought defensively to emphasize more than ever experimentalism and the dependence of science on observed experimental data, rather than to take risks in speculative metaphysical approaches." Cf. also 107n, 118.

5762   O'Neil, L. Thomas. *Towards the Divine Life: Sri Aurobindo's Vision*. New Delhi: Manohar, 1979, 103. On pp. 13-17 the author discusses the relationships between the philosophy of Bergson and the philosophy of Sri Aurobindo. Aurobindo attacks Bergson's concept of evolution for its lack of a concept of teleology. He attacks Bergson's notion of intuition for its dualistic bias. The author concludes, "Thus, Aurobindo finds in Bergson a system which man must go beyond. Bergson has just scratched the surface of an analysis of evolution and does not go deeply enough into it" (p. 17).

5763   Rader, Melvin. *A Modern Book of Esthetics: An Anthology*. 5th ed. New York: Holt, Rinehart, and Winston, 1979, 563. Chapter III of this book, titled "Intuition-Expression" (p. 71-87), contains excerpts from Bergson's *Laughter* and Benedetto Croce's article "Aesthetics." The selection from *Laughter* (pp. 73-80) is titled "The Individual and the Type."

5764   Reix, André. "Review of *Bergson et la théologie* by Mvika Phoba." *Revue Philosophique de Louvain*, 77, No. 36, 1979, 582-583.

5765   *Roczniki Filozoficzne*. Vol. 25, No. 1: *Metafizyka, Logika, Historia Filozofii*. Lublin: Towarzyystwo Naukowe K.U.L., 1979, 158. This journal contains an essay by R. Waszkinel on the sources of Bergson's philosophy.

5766   *Roczniki Filozoficzne*. Vol. 26, No. 1: *Metafizyka, Logika, Historia Filozofii*. Lublin: Towarzystwo Naukowe, K.U.L., 1979, 262. This journal contains an essay by R. Wazkinel on the concept of number and of metaphysics in Bergson.

5767   Schalk, David L. *The Spectrum of Political Engagement: Mounier, Benda, Nizan, Brasillach, Sartre*. Princeton, New Jersey: Princeton University Press, 1979, 187.

5768   Shalvey, Thomas. *Claude Levi-Strauss: Social Psychotherapy and the Collective Unconscious*. Amherst: Univ. of Massachusetts Press, 1979, xii, 180. The author deals with the influence of Bergson—and many others—on Levi-Strauss.

5769   Shinohara, Motoaki. "La Mémoire dans le Bergsonisme" (In Japanese) *Bigaku*, 30, No. 4, 1979, 1-11. "Dans le bergsonisme, la mémoire est présentée sous deux aspects: mémoire-souvenir et mémoire-contraction. La mémoire-souvenir concerne la conservation du passé. La mémoire contraction concern l'épaisseur du présent et fait venir le futur qui est imprévisible." Abstract, edited, *Philosopher's Index*, 14, No. 3, 1980, 169.

5770   Soulez, Philippe. "Review of *L'Introduction de la psychanalyse aus Etats-unis: Autor de James Jackson Putnam* by Nathan G. Hale, Jr." *Psychanalyse à l'Université*, 4, No. 14, 1979, 353-357.

5771   Vergotte, Antoine. "L'Articulation du temps." *Revue Philosophique de Louvain*, 77, No. 34, 1979, 219-232. According to the author, time consists of the articulation of natural processes by the chronothetic act of language in the present. The idea of objective time is therefore a derived concept. In its dialectical relations with the past and future, the present, as a bringing forth, also establishes the possible. Finally, in discussion with Bergson and Husserl, the author examines the two inseparable and opposed characteristics of time: discontinuity and continuity or synchrony in diachrony. The difference between active and passive repetition illustrates the analysis of time presented here. The author attacks Bergson's (presumed) view that time is entirely continuous. On this point Cf.

D. Sipfle, 1969.

5772   Weinstein, Michael A. *Structure of Human Life: A Vitalist Ontology*. New York and London: New York University Press, 1979, 188. The author's "critical vitalism" is to be distinguished from the "classical vitalism" of Bergson. Critical vitalism does not support Bergson's concept of an eternal creative process; instead it reveals "embodied experience" to be a complex of conflicting tendencies incapable of final resolution.

5773   Wohl, Robert. *The Generation of 1914*. Cambridge, Massachusetts: Harvard University Press, 1979, 307.

1980

5774   Annan, Noël. "Grand Disillusions." *New York Review of Books*, 27, No. 5, 1980, 11-15. This is a review of *The Generation of 1914* by Robert Wohl.

5775   Balestra, Dominic J. "The Mind of Jean Piaget: Its Philosophical Roots." *Thought*, 55, No. 219, 1980, 412-427. "The article highlights the early sources of Jean Piaget's ideas in order to reveal their permanent role in shaping his mature thinking. In particular, it shows that Piaget had sought to integrate biological and philosophical standpoints on the problem of the growth of knowledge primarily as a consequence of the influence of four thinkers—Henri Bergson, Arnold Raymond, Emile Meyerson, and Immanuel Kant. The result is seen to be an early intimation toward a dynamic theory of the equilibration of structures, characterized by an unmistakable Kantian inheritance." *Philosopher's Index*, 15, No. 2, 1981, p. 89.

5776   Bédé, Jean-Albert and Edgerton, William B., Eds. *Columbia Dictionary of Modern European Literature*. London, New York: Cambridge University Press, 1980, 895.

5777   Boboc, A. *Filosofia Contemporană*. Bukarest: Didaktische u. Pedagogische Verlag, 1980, 228. Bergson is treated here as a proponent of neo-romanticism and *Lebensphilosophie*.

5778   Bonnet, Henri. *Roman et poésie: Essai sur l'esthétique des genres; La littérature d'avant-garde et Marcel Proust*. Paris: A. G. Nizet, 1980, 294. Bergson and many other intellectual figures are dealt with in this study.

5779   Boudot, Maurice. "L'Espace selon Bergson." *Revue de Métaphysique et de Morale*, 85, No. 3, juillet-septembre, 1980, 332-356. The author is highly critical of Bergson's treatment of the concept of space, which he regards as thoroughly incoherent.

5780   Boyer, Charles. "Bergson y el catolicismo." Trans. Ricardo Ibinarriaga. *Revista de Filosofía* (México) 13, No. 2, 1980, 193-200.

5781   Butler, Robert James. "Christian and Pragmatic Visions of Time in the Lonigan Trilogy." *Thought*, 55, No. 219, December 1980, 641-475. The author argues that several allied philosophical sources shaped the novels of the American writer James T. Farrell. Among these are the philosophies of William James, Henri Bergson, and George Herbert Mead. Each of these philosophies contrasts the ongoing, creative duration of life with static, closed, and cyclic concepts of time.

5782 Čapek, Milič. "Ce qui est vivant et ce qui est mort dans la critique bergsonienne de la relativité." *Revue de synthèse*, Sèrie générale Vol. 101, Troisième Série Nos. 99-100, juillet-décembre 1980, 313-344. Those aspects of Bergson's interpretation of relativity physics which remain valid derive from the essentials of his philosophy, those which are mistaken drive from concepts less central to his thought. Bergson wrongly identified the "appearance" of moving relativistic systems with their "unobservability," turning such systems into virtual "window-less monads." He wrongly held that the purely referential character of relativistic effects—valid in the special theory—also holds in the general theory. Bergson inconsistently accepted the constant velocity of light while attempting to retain absolute simultaneity. He was right to hold that the relation "at rest with regard to oneself" is a real, "absolutist" feature of relativity, and to hold that contemporaneous but metrically discordant times presuppose a unified time which contains tem. "Finally, in correctly rejecting static interpretations of Einstein's space-time, he did not give them the dynamic interpretation which was the only justified one; but this does not prevent us from discovering the remarkable affinity between the structure of relativistic space-time and the "extensive becoming" of *Creative Evolution*." (p. 344)

5783 Delhomme, Jeanne. "Savoir lire? Synchronie et diachronie (Bergson)" in *Textes pour E. Levinas*. Ed. François Laruelle. Paris: Jean-Michel Place, 1980, 151-165.

5784 de Lucas, F. J. "Henri Bergson: La justicia entre presión social y *élan d'amour*." *Anuario Filosófico* (Pamplona) 13, No. 2, 1980, 27-65.

5785 Descombes, Vincent. *Modern French Philosophy*. Trans. L. Scott-Fox and J. M. Harding. Cambridge: Cambridge University Press, 1980, 192. Noting the changes in French mentality in the 1930's, the author states: "There is no clearer sign of the changes in mentality—the revolt against neo-Kantianism, the decline of Bergsonism—than the triumphal return of Hegel." (p. 9) On pp. 25-26 the author describes Bergson's attempted "annihilation of nothingness"; He states of Bergson's attempted annihilation: "For the Kantians as for Bergson, the origin of nothingness is negation; but what is the origin of negation? The Bergsonian explanation has all the characteristics of a conjuring trick in which the negative is not eliminated, as was promised, but, simply palmed." The question then becomes (since Bergson traces the origin of negation to "desire") whether desire is, itself, positive or negative. This question was to be raised by Gilles Deleuze's "philosophy of desire". The debate about the nature of desire" ...is more a settling of accounts between Deleuze, as disciple of Bergson, and the Hegelians (primarily Sartre and Lacan), than a conflict between Nietzsche and Plato." (p. 26) Cf. also p. 49, 66-67.

5786 Duffin, Kathleen E. "Arthur O. Lovejoy and the Emergence of Novelty." *Journal of the History of Ideas*, 61, No. 2, 1980, 267-328. The author argues that A. O. Lovejoy's advocacy of the genetic method of historical analysis and his temporalism both spring from his concept of emergent evolutionary process. On pp. 274-275 he examines Lovejoy's lectures on Bergson's philosophy: "While Lovejoy casts a critical eye on parts of Bergson's scheme of creative evolution, he finds that much of what Bergson expresses echoes his own ideas about the inadequacy of idealist thought, and the supremacy of the temporal" (p. 275).

5787 Dumas, Jean-Louis. "Bergson (1859-1941)." in *Histoire des grandes philosophies*. Toulouse: Privat, 1980, 354.

5788   Edward S. Casey. "Piaget and Freud on Childhood Memory." in *Piaget Philosophy
        and the Human Sciences*. Ed. Hugh J. Silverman. New Jersey: Humanities Press;
        Sussex: Harvester Press, 1980, 174, 63-102. The author notes, on pp. 73-74,
        Piaget's distinction between three main types of memory: recognition, reconstruc-
        tion, and recall (évocation). He notes Piaget's insistence on the importance of
        "reconstruction", which bridges the gap between Bergson's two types of memory
        (habitual and recollective). On pp. 84-86 the author distinguishes Piaget's theory
        of memory from that of Pierre Janet and that of Sigmund Freud and Henri
        Bergson. For Janet, memory is simply retrospective narration ("conduit du
        recit"), and hence a form of behavior in the present. Piaget thinks that experi-
        mental evidence disqualifies this view. Piaget describes Bergson and Freud as
        holding a conservationist model of memory—that 'the entire past is recorded
        and conserved in the unconscious'. (MI, 17) "On this view, the only changes
        are quantitative ones: we may retain more or less information, or forget more
        or less. But if the acquisition and extinction rates may thus vary, neither the
        content nor the mechanisms by which this content is remembered can change."
        (p. 84) Piaget argues in opposition to this model that it is too static. The author
        doubts, however, whether this static, 'conservationist' theory of memory is
        actually held by Freud and Bergson. He footnotes *Matter and Memory* (pp.
        22-23, 119-123, 173-174), pointing out that Bergson's accent on the 'virtuality'
        of memory prevents him from holding a "thesis of constant conservation."

5789   Cotta, S. "Meaning of Politics in Works of Hegel and Bergson." *Cahiers Vilfredo
        Pareto*, 18, No. 52, 1980, 193-206.

5790   Devaux, André-A. "Bergson aujourd'hui." *Filosofia oggi*, 3, 1980, 189-193.

5791   Fiser, Emeric. *Le Symbole littéraire: Essai sur la signification du sumbole chez
        Wagner, Baudelaire, Mallarmé, Bergson et Marcel Proust*. 1952; rpt. New
        York: AMS Press, 1980, 223.

5792   Fondane, Benjamin. "Bergson, Freud et des dieux." in *La Conscience malheureuse*,
        by Benjamin Fondane. New York: Garland Publishers, 1980, xxv, 306.
        (Phenomenology, Background, Foreground and Influences, 5)

5793   Gillois, André. *Ce siècle avait deux ans*. Paris: Pierre Belfond, 1980, 380. Bergson
        is discussed here along with many other 20th century French thinkers.

5794   Herman, Daniel J. *The Philosophy of Henri Bergson*. Washington, D.C.: University
        Press of America, 1980, 102. The author tackles the difficult problem of the
        relations between mechanism and finalism in Bergson's philosophy. He argues
        that the passages in *Creative Evolution* in which Bergson criticizes final causes
        are really directed at a narrow and mechanical conception of final causality, and
        that in *The Two Sources of Morality and Religion* Bergson clearly and unmistak-
        ably utilizes a finalistic argument. Human social evolution for Bergson points
        toward an ultimate harmonious convergence of otherwise conflicting tendencies.
        The "open society" is the final cause of the evolutionary process. (Cf. M.
        Morkovsky, 1981.)

5795   Jerphagnon, Lucien, Ed. *Histoire des grandes philosophers*. Toulous: Privat, 1980,
        355.

5796   Kallen, Horace Meyer. *William James and Henri Bergson: A Study in Contrasting
        Theories of Life*. 1914; rpt. New York: AMS Press, 1980, 248 pp.

5797   Kennedy, Ellen. "Bergson's Philosophy and French Political Doctrines: Sorel,
        Maurras, Péguy and de Gaulle." *Government and Opposition*, 15 No. 1, 1980,

75-91. The author argues that Bergson is neither "a right nor a left radical" but, instead, as a representative of 20th-century liberalism. She concludes: "Bergson's appeal rests on a sometimes incongruous blend of political ideas. He combines individual freedom with criticism of social division and classes; he affirms the value of community and tradition, but encourages change and innovation in society. Finally, Bergson tries to reconcile man's need for religious and spiritual values, with his achievements in technology and science. This does not lead him to the extremist politics of Sorel, much less Maurras, but to a new liberalism." (p. 90)

5798   Kennedy, Ellen. "Bergson's Political Doctrines." *Literature of Liberty*, 3, No. 2, 1980, 54. The diversity of Bergson's beliefs explains the diversity of his disciples.

5799   Lawson, Lewis A. "Walker Percy's *The Moviegoer*: The Cinema as Cave." *Southern Studies*, 19, Winter, 1980, 331-354. The author argues on pp. 347-354 that the novelist Percy is strongly influenced by Bergson's concepts of duration and of the cinematographic fallacy.

5800   Lefranc, J. "Rire est-il diabolique?" *Revue de l'Enseignement Philosophique*, 30, No. 3, 1980, 18-25. "Approche de l'essence du rire; Bergson et Freud. Mais c'est Baudelaire qui a saisi dans le rire les parages du mal, de la mort et du non-sens." *Bulletin Signalétique: Philosophie*, 34, No. 3, 1980, p. 16.

5801   Limongi, Salvatore. "Analectica bergsoniana, I: Riflessioni e note sul «Saggio»." *Annali dell'Intstituto di Filosofia (Firenze)*, 2, 1980-1981, 71-95.

5802   MacDonald, Angus George. "The Philosophy of Religion of Jacques Maritain and Henri Bergson." Diss. Columbia Univ. 1980, 221. Cf. *Dissertation Abstracts International*, 41, No. 7, 1981, Sec A, 3141.

5803   Maritain, Jacques. *Da Bergson a Tommaso d'Aquino: Saggi di Metafisica e di morale*. Trans R. Bartolozzi. Intro. Vittorio Possenti. Milano: Vita e Pensiero, 1980, 270.

5804   Moutsopoulos, E. *La Critique du platonisme chez Bergson*. Athènes: Société hellénique des études philosophiques, 1980, 75. («Recherches», 3)

5805   Robinson, Fred M. "The Comedy of Language." in *The Comedy of Language: Studies in Modern Comic Literature*. Amherst: University of Massachusetts Press, 1980, 1-24.

5806   Rossie, Susana. "La filosofía religiosa de Bergson." *Convivium*, 23, No. 6, 1980, 38-53.

5807   Russo, F. "Review of *Atomisme* by Marie Cariou." *Archives de Philosophie*, 43, No. 2, 1980, 303-304.

5808   Salgado, Cesareo Lopez. "Presencia y Lugar De La Nada En La Filosofia Del Ser." *Sapientia*, 35, 1980, 217-238.

5809   Scharfstein, Ben-Ami. *The Philosophers: Their Lives and the Nature of Their Thought*. New York: Oxford University Press, 1980, 486. On pp. 63-64 the author notes that Wittgenstein and Bergson, both unusually sensitive to music, commented on the "importance of what may be called the musicality of language". Thus Wittgenstein asserted "Sometimes a sentence can be understood only when one reads it in the correct tempo. My sentences should all be read *slowly*." (p. 64) "Bergson's respect for the musicality of language was so great that he insisted that full understanding of a philosopher was impossible without sensitivity to the philosopher's rhythms." (p. 64) Cf. also pp. 259, 352-353.

5810   Skolimowski, Henryk. "Evolutionary Illuminations." *Alternative Futures*, 3, No. 4, 1980, 3-34. "The Western scientific view of the world is no longer adequate to cope with new realities. The historic conflict between science and religion is coming to an end, and can be seen as part of the same spectrum of human knowledge and human experience. The imperative for our times is the formulation of a world view based on humane survival. This imperative has long been understood by philosophers and theologians such as Bergson, Whitehead and Teilhard de Chardin. Evolutionary illuminations in the work of these and other thinkers are summarized. Proposed is an ecological theory of mind that emphasizes cosmic and human unity and in which human purpose is congruent with the elan of evolution." *Sociological Abstracts*, 30, Part 1, No. 1, 1982, 154.

5811   Tomlinson, David. "T. S. Eliot and the Cubists." *Twentieth Century Literature*, 26, No. 1, 1980, 64-81.

5812   Vanni Rovighi, S. *Storia della filosofia contemporanea*. Brescia: La Scoula, 1980, 753. This history of philosophy contains a section on The Critique of Science in France and H. Bergson.

5813   Walicki, Andrzej, Ed. *Archiwum historii filozofii i myśli społecznej*. Vol. 26. Warsaw: Osilineum, 1980, 375. This journal contains an essay in Polish by M. Kepczynska titled "The Alienated Cogito: The Concept of Psychology in Bergson and Jung."

5814   Wojnar, Irena, Ed. *Antologia współczesnej estetyki francuskiej*. Pref. W. Tatarkiewicz. Warsaw: Państwowe Wydawnictwo Naukowe, 1980, 574. The title of this work translates into English as *Anthology of Contemporary French Aesthetics*. Bergson's views are examined in part one of this book.

1981

5815   Austermann, Maria. *Die Entwicklung der ethischen und religionsphilosophischen Gedanken bei Henri Bergson*. Frankfurt a. M.: R. G. Fisher, 1981, 223.

5816   Bjelland, Andrew G. "Čapek, Bergson, and Process Proto-Mentalism." *Process Studies*, 11, No. 3, 1981, 180-189. The author analyzes and comments on Henri Bergson's proto-mentalism (the ascription of mental states to non-living physical nature) as explained by Milič Čapek in *Bergson and Modern Physics*. Bergson's concept of proto-mentalism is similar in most but not all respects to Whitehead's panpsychism. For Bergson matter is not "unconscious" but is a low-level consciousness; for Whitehead, matter is unconscious—a notion the author believes Bergson would find inconsistent. The author concludes: "...Bergson's proto-mentalism, as interpreted by Čapek, is perhaps best viewed as a generalized theory of agency erected upon a phenomenology of experienced succcession. Each physical event *is* in virtue of its interior agency—an agency analogous to memory as an active synthesis." (p. 185).

5817   Borzym, Stanisław. "Bergson i Leśmian: Światopoglad filozofa światoglas poety." *Studia Liturgica*, Nos. 7-8, 1981, 145-182.

5818   Borzym, Stanisław. "Ingardenowska Krytyka bergsonizmu jako teorii pozmania." *Studia Filozoficzne*, No. 11, 1981, 23-42.

5819   Bryant, Jennings; Brown, Dan; Parks, Sheri L. "Ridicule as an Educational Correc-
        tive." *Journal of Educational Psychology*, 73, No. 5, 1981, 722-727. Starting
        from Bergson's notion that ridicule is an effective social corrective. (*Le Rire*,
        1901) the authors determine that insult and ridicule are effective educational
        techniques.

5820   Čapek, Milič. "Philosophy and Classical Determinism: Their Incompatibility."
        Process Studies, 11, No. 3, 1981, 190-195. In this article (a response to J.
        Brenton Stearns' "Becoming: A Problem for Determinists?" in the previous
        volume of *Process Studies*) the author argues that "becoming" and strict deter-
        minism are incompatible. Strict determinism bifurcates reality, supposing a
        world of timelessly valid propositions and a world in which these propositions
        are successively embodied. Still worse, determinism can give no reason as to
        why these propositions come to be embodied successively. Rather than providing
        a reason, determinists must surreptitiously appeal to experience, which shows
        events occurring one after the other.

5821   Curtis, James M. "McLuhan: The Aesthete as Historian." *Journal of Communica-
        tion*, 31, No. 3, 1981, 144-152. On pp. 147-148 the author asserts that the
        Canadian historian Marshall McLuhan derived his "historical paradigm" from
        G. W. F. Hegel and H. Bergson. McLuhan, specifically, derived his concept
        of technology from Bergson.

5822   Douglas, Malcom Paul. "In and Out of Time: Eliot, Faulkner, and the Legacy of
        Bergson." Diss. Univ. of California, Los Angeles, 1981, 384. "Bergson influ-
        enced twentieth century literature mainly by asserting the intuited flux of inner
        life against intellect's 'artificial immobilizations.' But popularizations of his
        philosophy have exaggerated his aversion to science. For Bergson, inner life
        demanded scientific exploration, and the artist is an advanced scout in a 'new
        empiricism' to be founded on 'the immediate data of consciousness.' This study
        shows how Bergson's Intuition, Duration, and Creative Evolution influenced
        American writers, especially T. S. Eliot and William Faulkner." Cf. *Dissertation
        Abstracts International*, 42, No. 8, 1982, 3599A.

5823   Dumoncel, Jean-Claude. "Popper et Bergson." *Revue de l'Enseignement
        Philosophique*, 32, No. 3, 1981-1982, 37-48.

5824   Finance, Joseph de. "L'Échelle des consciences chez Bergson et chez saint
        Thomas." in *Scritti in onore di N. Petruzzellis*. Napoli: Giannini Editore, 1981,
        93-103.

5825   Graham, Loren R. "Bergson, Monod, and France." in *Between Science and Values*.
        New York: Columbia University Press, 1981, 136-158.

5826   Gunter, Pete A. Y. "Henri Bergson: A Bibliography, 1911-1980." *Philosophy
        Research Archives*, 7, No. 2, 1981, 172 pp. "This is a 1,039-item update and
        extension of *Henri Bergson: A Bibliography*, published by the Philosophy
        Documentation Center in 1974. While it concentrates on bibliographic items
        that have appeared in the 1970's, this bibliography contains items both by and
        about Bergson which were published prior to the 1970's. The present work is
        admittedly incomplete; but it attempts a more complete annotation than was
        available in the 1974 bibliography." *Philosopher's Index*, 15, No. 2, 1981, p.
        109.

5827   Günther, Sigl. "Das Problem der Methode in Bergsons Denken sub specie
        durationis." Thesis, Universität Innsbruck, 1981, 207.

5828   Hahn, G. "Instante y Duración: Polémica Entre Bachelard y Bergson." *Stromata*, 37, Julio-Diciembre, 1981, 173-195.

5829   Hellmann, John. "Jacques Chevalier, Bergsonism, and Modern French Catholic Intellectuals." *Biography*, 4, No. 2, 1981, 138-153.

5830   Henry, Anne. *Marcel Proust: Théories pour une esthétique*. Paris: Klincksieck, 1981, 392. The author denies Bergson's influence on Proust, explores Proust's knowledge of F. Schelling.

5831   Lauer, Robert H. *Temporal Man: The Meaning and Uses of Social Time*. New York: Praeger, 1981, 179. The author, who believes that the "fact of temporality is the essence of human life" (p. 2), cites Bergson as one of a group of thinkers who have "recognized and argued that social time must be distinguished from clock time." (p. 21) On pp. 21-23 the author cites studies which establish the difference between clock time and social time.

5832   Lawson, Lewis A. "The Allegory of the Cave and the *Moviegoer*." *South Carolina Review*, 13, No. 2, 1981, 10, 14-18. On pp. 17-18, the author argues that the novelist Walker Percy has been influenced by Bergson's critique of the cinematographic fallacy.

5833   Lisciani-Petrini, Enrica. "*Durée e Image*: Il problema del tempo in Bergson." *Cannocchiale*, No. 1-3, 1981, 180-191.

5834   Manganelli, Maria. *Il linguaggio nel pensiero di H. Bergson*, Milano: Marzorati Ed., 1981, 71. (Pubblicazioni dell'Instituto di Filosofia. Facolta di Magistero dell'Università di Genova, 30).

5835   Morkovsky, Mary Christine. "Review of *The Philosophy of Bergson* by Daniel J. Herman." *Philosophical Topics*, 12, No. 1, Spring, 1981, 254-258. The reviewer denies the author's contention that finality is an essential feature of Bergson's later, but not of his earlier, philosophy. Bergson's treatment of finality in *The Two Sources of Morality and Religion* (1932) does not differ radically from his treatment of finality in *Creative Evolution* (1970): "But, if finality in any being, including God, is tendency to promote free action—an aim that can be achieved even in the present thought by its very nature it can never be accomplished in such a way that there will be no further liberation—then Bergson's later views appear more to extend and enrich than to contrast with his earlier ones." (p. 257.)

5836   Najder-Stefaniak, Krystyna. "Kategoria pickna w estetyczne koncepeji bergsona." *Studia Liturgica*, No. 11, 1981, 43-48.

5837   Ramanujam, A. Appan. "Emotion and Mysticism in Bergson's Philosophy." *Indian Philosophical Quarterly*, 9, October 1981, 6-10 (Supplement). "Bergson explains 'Creations' by both man and God in *The Two Sources*. 'Emotion is used in a much wider sense than 'inspiration' and is of two kinds: (1) the infra-intellectual and (2) the supra-intellectual. Man's creation through supra-intellectual emotion resembles God's creation through love. It is synonymous with the sublime love which is for the mystic the very essence of God. The burning of emotional content, after melting, solidifies to frame into moral and scientific laws." *Philosopher's Index*, 16, No. 2, 1982, 148.

5838   Roberts, Don D. "The Labeling Problem." in *Pragmatism and Purpose: Essays Presented to Thomas a. Goudge*. Edited by L. W. Sumner, Toronto: University of Toronto Press, 1981, 75-87. "What I call 'the labeling problem' is the problem of determining how *in practice* we come to apply certain labels that we use.

This article concerns the label knowledge and asks two philosophers the question 'What criteria did you employ to convince *yourself* that this thing you talk about is 'knowledge'? The question is asked of Euthyphro, who represents the view that we *can* have philosophical knowledge even though we may not be able to express it, and Bergson, who represents the view that there are non-cognitive, non-symbolic routes to philosophical knowledge." *Philosopher's Index*, 15, No. 3, 1981, p. 124.

5839   Robinson, Christopher. "New Perceptions." in *French Literature in the Twentieth Century*. Devon, England: Newton Abbot; Totowa, New Jersey: Barnes and Noble, 1981, 7-51.

5840   Santos, Jessy. *Filosofia e humanismo*. São Paulo: Livraria Duas Cidades, 1981, 152. Part 2 of this work consists of a revised section of the author's *Instinto, razao e intuição*, Livraria Martins, 1950.

5841   Schütz, Alfred. *Theorie der Lebensformen: Frühe Ms. aus d. Bergson-Periode*. Ed. and Intro. Ilja Srubar. Frankfurt a. M.: Suhrkamp, 1981, 341, pp. (Suhrkamp-Taschenbuch Wissenschaft, 350)

5842   Sellars, Wilfrid. "Naturalism and Process." *The Monist*, 64, No. 1, 1981, 37-65. The author, who defends a "Heraclitean" viewpoint, asserts on p. 57: "I shall conclude this lecture with some variations on themes from Bergson, and in particular, on the sin of spatializing time."

5843   Sheldrake, Rupert. "Three Approaches to Biology: II, Vitalism." *Theoria to Theory*, 14, No. 2, 1981, 227-240. "In modern works on biology, vitalism is usually treated as if it were a kind of superstition which has been swept away by the advance of modern science. This is far from being the case. Vitalists such as Hans Driesch and Henri Bergson raised questions over 70 years ago about the development of form in living organisms which still resist explanation in mechanistic terms. Vitalism has not been rendered invalid by advances in mechanistic biology, but has rather been superseded by the potentially more radical holistic or organismic approach." *Philosopher's Index*, 15, No. 2, 1981, 137.

5844   Sleczka, Kazimierz, Ed. *Z zagadnień dialektyki i świadomosci społecznej*. Katowice: Uniwersytet Slaski, 1981, 135. This anthology contains an article by J. Bańka, "L'Intuition en tant que méthode de la critique dialectique chez Henri Bergson." The title of this anthology may be translated as *Problems of Dialectic and Social Conscience*.

5845   Stehlen, Catherine. "Jarry, le cours Bergson et la philosophie." in *Alfred Jarry*, Paris: Europe, 1981, 34-51. This is No. 323-324 of the journal *Europe*, March-April, 1981.

5846   Tison-Braun, Micheline. *L'Introuvable Origine: Le Problème de la personnalité au seuil du XXe siècle: Flaubert, Mallarmé, Rimbaud, Valéry, Bergson, Claudel, Gide, Proust*. Genève: Droz, 1981, 257. (Histoire des idées et critique littéraire, 199) The author examines Bergson's concept of personality on pp. 139-158.

5847   Verschaffel, B. "Abstract of 'La Pensée de Bergson en Amérique' by Milič Čapek." *Process Studies*, 11, No. 3, 1981, 217-218.

5848   Webb, Ronald G. "Political Uses of Humor." *ETC: A Review of General Semantics*, 38, No. 1, 1981, 35-50. The author notes that Bergson is among those who take the less frequent but equally important social or historical approach to laughter. Bergson's is a conservative theory of the uses of humor. Conservative humor corrects deviations from society's norms. The author points out that there is also "radical" humor.

1982

5849   Benjamin, A. Cornelius. "Essay-Review of *An Introduction to Metaphysics* by Henri Bergson." in *World Philosophy: Essay-Reviews of 225 Major Works*. Vol. 4. *1896-1932*. Eds. Frank N. Magill and Ian P. McGreal. Englewood Cliffs, New Jersey: Salem Press, 1982, 1582-1587.

5850   Bertolini, Mara Meletti. "Il Pensiero morale e religioso di Henri Bergson e la sociologia." (1982) Cf. No. 5873.

5851   Bor, J. and Teppema, S. Eds. *25 eeuwen filosofie*. Meppel: Boom, 1982, 303. This anthology, (titled *25 Centuries of Philosophy*) contains a brief selection from Bergson.

5852   Boydston, Jo Ann. *John Dewey's Personal and Professional Library: A Checklist*. Carbondale and Edwardsville: Southern Illinois University Press, 1982, 119. This checklist contains, on p. 9, a list of books by Bergson in Dewey's personal library. These are: *Dreams*, Trans. with Intro. Edwin E. Slosson. New York: B. W. Huebsch, 1914. (Inscribed by Slosson to Dewey.); *Matter and Memory*, Trans. Nancy Margaret Paul and Scott Palmer. London: Swan and Sonnenschein; New York: Macmillan Co., 1911. (Library of Philosophy) Much underlining and annotation, autographed by Dewey. *The Two Sources of Morality and Religion*, Trans. R. Ashley Audra and Cloudesly Brereton. New York: Henry Holt and Co., 1935. (Some annotation, much underlining, and corners of pages folded over by Dewey.)

5853   Brinton, Alan. "Bergson on Determinism and Determinacy." *Dialogos*, 17, No. 2, November, 1982, 71-82." "Bergson's views about possibility and the nature of the past provide the basis for a rejection of logical determinism. Its view that the future is determined depends upon the assumption that the future is determinate, an assumption which begs the question. If the future is indeterminate, there can not be determinate true statements about it, except to the effect that it is indeterminate." *Philosopher's Index*, 17, No. 3, 1983, 62.

5854   Chessick, Richard D. "Critique: Proust's Way." *American Journal of Psychotherapy*, 36, No. 2, 1982, 272-274. This is a review of a new translation of Proust's *Remembrance of Things Past*. The author says of Proust's theories of *Time and Memory*: "I have explained these theories and examined the philosophical view point of Bergson upon which they are based (in spite of the fact that Proust denied it) in a forthcoming publication. A knowledge of Bergson's philosophy greatly enhances the understanding of Proust." (p. 273) The author footnotes his *The Search of the Authentic Self in Bergson and Proust*, in press.) The author's viewpoint contrasts strongly with that of Joyce N. Megay (*Bergson et Proust*, Paris, 1976) who finds Proust uninfluenced by Bergson.

5855   Cruickshank, John. "Saying the Unsayable: Problems of Expression." in *Variations on Catastrophe: Some French Responses to the Great War*. Oxford: Oxford University Press, 1982, 27-41.

5856   Csenqeri, K. E. "T. E. Hulme's Borrowings From Freud." *Comparative Literature*, 34, No. 1, 1982, 16-27.

5857   Faurot, Jean. "Essay-Review of *The Two Sources of Morality and Religion* by Henri Bergson." in *World Philosophy: Essay-Reviews of 225 Major Works*. Eds. Frank N. Magill and Ian P. McGreal. Englewood Cliffs, New Jersey: Salem Press, 1982, 2013-2018.

5858   Filion, Richard. "Durée et liberté. Une étude du premier Bergson." in *Verité et ethos*. Recueil commemoratif dédié à Alphonse-Marie Parent sous la direction de Jaromir Danek. Québec: Les Presses de l'Université Laval, 1982, 233-244.

5859   Ford, Marcus. "Exposition of Chapter 3, *Winds of Doctrine* by Geroge Santayana." in *World Philosophy: Essay-Reviews of 225 Major Works*. Vol. 4. Eds. Frank N. Magill and Ian P. McGreal. Englewood Cliffs, New Jersey: Salem Press, 1982, 1624-1625.

5860   Ford, Marcus. "Exposition of an Essay on Bergson by Albert William Levi (*Philosophy and the Modern World*, Pt. 2)" in *World Philosophy: Essay-Reviews of 225 Major Works*. Vol. 3. *1726-1896*. Eds. Frank N. Magill and Ian P. McGreal. Englewood Cliffs, New Jersey: Salem Press, 1982, 1490-1491.

5861   Ford, Marcus. "Exposition of *Henri Bergson* by Jacques Chevalier." in *World Philosophy: Essay-Reviews of 225 Major Works*. Eds. Frank N. Magill and Ian P. McGreal. Englewood Cliffs, New Jersey: Salem Press, 1982, 1621-1623.

5862   Ford, Marcus. "Exposition of 'The Heuristic Force of Creative Evolution' by Pete A. Y. Gunter." in *World Philosophy: Essay-Reviews of 225 Major Works*. Vol. 4. Eds. Frank N. Magill and Ian P. McGreal. Englewood Cliffs, New Jersey, Salem Press, 1982, 1623-1625.

5863   Ford, Marcus. "Exposition of *Lectures on Bergson* by Harold Höffding." in *World Philosophy: Essay-Reviews of 225 Major Works*. Vol. 3. *1729-1896*. Eds. Frank N. Magill and Ian P. McGreal. Englewood Cliffs, New Jersey: Salem Press, 1982, 1487-1488.

5864   Ford, Marcus. "Exposition of *The Philosophy of Bergson* by Bertrand Russell." in *World Philosophy: Essay-Reviews of 225 Major Works*. Vol. 3. *1726-1896*. Eds. Frank N. Magill and Ian P. McGreal. Englewood Cliffs, New Jersey: Salem Press, 1982, 1488-1490.

5865   Frieden-Markevitch, Natalie. *La Philosophie de Bergson: Aperçu sur un stoicisme inconscient*. Fribourg: Eds. Universitaires, 1982, 277. (Studia Friburgensia, N. S. 59).

5866   Gabaude, Jean-Marc. "*Review of La Critique de platonisme chez Bergson* by Evanghélos Moutsopoulos." *Revue Philosophique de la France et de l'Etranger*, 172, No. 1, 1982, 70-71.

5867   Germino, Dante L. *Political Philosophy and the Open Society*. Baton Rouge and London: Louisiana State University Press, 1982, 190 pp. On pp. 148-169 (Ch. IX. "Henri Bergson's *Two Sources of Morality and Religion: The Initial Formulation of the Open Society Theory*.") The author examines Bergson's treatment of the tension between the closed and the open societies. His discussion of Bergson's description of the "opening of the soul", mysticism, the "natural society", and of Bergson's understanding of the prospects for achieving an open society in the modern world are clear and adequate. On pp. 166-169 he criticizes Bergson's social and religious philosophy, utilizing the (similar) ideas of Eric Voegelin: "In his overemphasis on activist mysticism, Bergson comes close to espousing an innerworldly millenium, or perfect realm of one thousand years, to be ruled by the saints. To the degree that this is so, Bergson fails to perceive the full implication of his own discovery: *viz.*, the eschatological character of the open society symbol. In terms of Voegelin's analysis, Bergson failed to recognize the qualitative distinction between universality and ecumenicity and the open society thus becomes a project to be achieved in the future rather than an ever-present spiritual reality." (p. 168) Cf. also pp. 66-71 for the author's discussion of the "axis-time" in human history, a concept common to Lewis Mumford and Karl Jaspers which is also found (though not under that name) in Bergson's *The Two Sources*. On p. 68 he notes that while Mumford mentions his indebtedness to Bergson, Jaspers does not.

5868   Ghālib, Mustafá. *Hayghil ta'līf Mustafá Ghālib.* 3 vols. Beirut: Dār wa-Maktabat al-Hilāl, 1982, 153, 159, 155.

5869   Gishman, Murray. "Letter to Robert Bruce Williams. May 31, 1970." in Robert Bruce Williams. *John Dewey: Recollections.* Washington, D.C.: University Press of America, 1982, 63-64. The author mentions his correspondence with Dewey: "There was one letter which I believe to be of great import, since in it Dewey contrasts his philosophy with that of Bergson and in which he points out quite fundamentally the distinction between Bergson's intuitive approach to living and mental realities and Dewey's approach. In this respect, Bergson was contrasting living and mental realities to the scientific and logical approach to the physical world. Dewey emphasized in his letter that conceptual structures were necessary in both domains." p. 63.

5870   Heidegger, Martin. *The Basic Problems of Phenomenology.* Trans. Albert Hofstadter. Bloomington: Indiana University Press, 1982, 396. This is the third division of the first volume of *Sein und Zeit* (1927). It was published by the author in 1975 as *Die Grundprobleme der Phenomenologie.* On pp. 320-321 he changes his interpretation of Bergson's "durée," asserting that Bergson *opposes* Aristotle's concept of time, and attempts "to surpass the traditional concept of time." Cf. also p. 244.

5871   Lisciani Petrini, Enrica. "L'immaginazione infinita in Bergson: dalla psicologia alla ontologia." *L'Uomo, un Segno*, 5, No. 1, 1982, 71-108.

5872   McFadden, George. "The Modern Comic Ethos: Bergson's Laughter." in *Discovering the Comic*. Princeton, New Jersey: Princeton University Press, 1982, 111-130.

5873   Meletti Bertolini, Mara. "Il pensiero morale e religioso di Henri Bergson e la sociologia." *Filosofia*, 33, No. 1, 1982, 11-25. This is primarily a comparison of the sociologies of Bergson and E. Durkheim.

5874   Melges, Frederick T. *Time and the Inner Future: A Temporal Approach to Psychiatric Disorders.* New York: J. Wiley and Sons, 1982, 365.

5875   Meyer, Rudolf N. "Bergson in Deutschland: Unter besonderer Berücksichtigung seiner Zeitauffassung." *Phänomenologische Forschung*, No. 13, 1982, 10-64.

5876   Miller, Leonard. "Essay-Review of *Creative Evolution* by Henri Bergson." in *World Philosophy: Essay-Reviews of 225 Major Works. Vol. 4. 1896-1932.* Eds. Frank N. Magill and Ian P. McGreal. Englewood Cliffs, New Jersey: Salem Press, 1982, 1616-1621.

5877 Rossi, L. S. "La filosofia de Bergson y el misticismo Cristiano." *Stromata*, 38, Julio-Diciembre, 1982, 391-400. The author considers interpretation of Bergson by G. Levesque, E. Rideau, M. Cariou.

5878 Roth, John K. "Exposition of an Essay on Bergson by F. C. Copleston (*A History of Philosophy*, Vol. 10)." in *World Philosophy: Essay-Reviews of 225 Major Works*. Vol. 4. *1896-1932*. Eds. Frank N. Magill and Ian P. McGreal. Englewood Cliffs, New Jersey: Salem Press, 1982, 1590-1591.

5879 Roth, John K. "Exposition of 'Introduction' by Thomas A. Goudge to Bergson's *An Introduction to Metaphysics*." in *World Philosophy: Essay-Reviews of 225 Major Works*. Vol. 4. *1896-1932*. Eds. Frank N. Magill and Ian P. McGreal. Englewood Cliffs, New Jersey: Salem Press, 1982, 1587-1589.

5880 Roth, John K. "Exposition of 'Kant to Wittgenstein and Sartre' by W. T. Jones." in *World Philosophy: Essay-Reviews of 225 Major Works*. Vol. 4. *1896-1932*. Eds. Frank N. Magill and Ian P. McGreal. Englewood Cliffs, New Jersey: Salem Press, 1982, 1589-1590.

5881 Rusinko, E. "Acmeism, Post-Symbolism, and Henri Bergson." *Slavic Review*, 41, No. 3, 1982, 494-510. "It is not difficult," the author states, "to see the impact of Bergsonism on Russian modernist poetry, Symbolist, Futurist, and Imaginist, as well as Acmeist." (p. 504) The author, however, limits himself to exploring the relations between Bergson's philosophy and the major Acmeist writers, Nikolai Gumilev (leader of the Acmeist movement) and Osip Mandel'shtam, relationships which were extremely important to the formulation of the Acmeist aesthetic. A monograph on Bergson's impact on Mandel'shtam, and on Russian poetry and culture in the first two decades of this century is, according to the author "sorely wanting." (p. 505n)

5882 Skarga, Barbara. *Czas i trwanie: Studia o Bergsonie*. Warszawa: Państwowe Wydawnictwo Naukowe, 1982, 291. "Les Etudes recueilles dans ce livre, ne pretendent pas exposer l'ensenble des idées philosophiques de Bergson. L'Auteur fait choix en se concentrant sur les problèmes qu'elle trouve importants ou pour l'époque, ou pour Bergson lui-même, ou pour la philosophie de notre temps. Elle se penche donc sur la critique bergsonienne du transcentalisme kantien, sur les problèmes de la durée, de la rationalité, du néant et de la plénitude, de la perception et de la mémoire, de l'intuition et de l'experience mystique." Izidora Dambska in *Bibliographie de la Philosophie*, 30, No. 3, 1983, 295.

5883 Smithson, Isaiah. "Time and Irony in T. S. Eliot's Early Poetry." *Massachusetts Studies in English*, 8, No. 2, 1982, 39-52. The author examines sources of Eliot's concept of time in Bergson and S. Kierkegaard.

5884 Sontag, Frederick. "Essay-Review of *Time and Free Will* by Henri Bergson." in *World Philosophy: Essay-Reviews of 225 Major Works*. Vol. 3. *1726-1896*. Eds. Frank N. Magill and Ian P. McGreal. Englewood Cliffs, New Jersey: Salem Press, 1982, 1484-1487.

5885 Theau, Jean. "Henri Bergson." in *Les Littératures de langues européennes au tournant du siècle: La Perspective critique française*. Serie A, Cahier V-VI. Ed. Clive Thompson. Ottowa, Ontario: Georges Riser, 1982, 15-24.

5886 Wasserstrom, William. "Kenneth Burke, 'Logology', and the Tribal No." in *Representing Kenneth Burke*. Hayden White and Margaret Brose, Eds. Baltimore: Johns Hopkins University Press, 1982, 92-118. The author examines negation and victimization in America, compares the views of Bergson and Michel

Foucault.

5887   Yandell, Keith E. "Exposition of 'Bergson on Morality' by F. C. Copleston." in *World Philosophy: Essay-Reviews of 225 Major Works*. Eds. Frank N. Magill and Ian P. McGreal. Englewood Cliffs, New Jersey: Salem Press, 1982, 2018-2020.

5888   Yandell, Keith E. "Exposition of *Morality in Evolution* by Idella J. Gallagher." in *World Philosophy: Essay-Reviews of 225 Major Works*. Eds. Frank N. Magill and Ian P. McGreal. Englewood Cliffs, New Jersey: Salem Press, 1982, 2021-2023.

1983

5889   Čapek, Milič. "Temps-espace plutot qu'espace-temps." *Diogène*, No. 123, 1983, 31-52. The author argues that while the phrase "space-time" accurately characterizes the world model of classical Newtonian physics, it does not apply to that of relativity physics, which presupposes a dynamic world model more accurately described through the phrase "time-space". The dynamic character of relativity physics rests on its (a) negation of the simultanéité of distant events (b) non-elimination of the successive character of the physical world (c) the absolute character of succession of causal transmissions in any given reference system. Attempts to avoid this interpretation lead to a dualism far more extreme than Descartes'.

5890   Douglass, Paul. "The Gold Coin: Bergsonian Intuition and Modernist Aesthetics." *Thought*, 58, No. 229, 1983, 234-250. "Challenges the view typified my Murray Krieger that Bergson's philosophy yeilds an aesthetic theory unable to give approaches to 'form' in art and particularly in twentieth century British and American literatrue. Establishes Bergson's use of a Kantian vocabulary to distinguish between scholastic and intuitive logic, posits a literary form that would result from Bergson's belief in the immutability of 'truth of experience', and demonstrates close parallels between Bergsonian theory and the artistic practice of Pound, Woolf, and others." *Philosopher's Index*, 16, No. 4, 1983, 82. (Cf. M. Krieger, 1968.)

5891   Field, Richard W. "William James and the Epochal Theory of Time." *Process Studies*, 13, No. 4, 1983, 260-274. "William James, in his later works, developed a theory of time that closely resembles the epochal theory of time offered by A. N. Whitehead in *Process and Reality*. In this article the development of James' theory is traced through his works, and it is compared to the 'intuitive 'theory of time offered by Bergson." *The Philosopher's Index*, 19, No. 1, 1985, 90.

5892   Fourastié. Jean. "Reflections on Laughing." *Diogenes*, No. 121, Spring 1983, 126-141. The author characterizes Bergson's *Laughter* in the following way: "eighty years after its publication, the book is by far, in every language in the world, the most read, the most famous and the most sold (again by far) of all books published on laughter. However, its thesis is false; moreover, its restrictive nature makes it profoundly destabilizing." (p. 127) Bergson's thesis that laughter springs from a perception of "mechanical" behavior in nonmechanical (human) beings has prevented further serious examinations of laughter: of our *need* for laughter, of the role of laughter in ordinary life. Laughter, the author holds, involves "the participation of instinctive forces in conceptual thinking." (p. 129) One who laughs is in a "situtation of creativity" (p. 129). Laughter, according to the author, springs from a perception of the failure of determinism and hence of a conflict between sense and nonsense. He refers to his book *Le Rire, suite*, to be published by Denoël, Paris. Cf. the author's abstract of this article, *Philosopher's Index*, 17, No. 4, 1983, 84.

5893 Haghi, Syyed Mohammad. "Matter Life Consciousness: The Interrelation of Science, Religion, and Reality in the Philosophy of Bergson." Diss. Harvard, 1983, 390. Bergson's overall response to questions of man's nature, origin and destiny reflects, the author states, an integration of science, religion and reality from the viewpoint of both ontology epistemology. "Bergson credits intuition for what is best, original, and most genuine in the realm of science, metaphysics and religion." *Dissertation Abstracts International*, 44, No. 6, 1983, 1815A.

5894 Hartocollis, Peter. *Time and Timelessness: Or, The Varieties of Temporal Experience*. New York: International Universities Press, 1983, 261. Cf. esp. Ch. 2, "Time and the Self: From Bergson and Heidegger to Piaget," 15-30.

5895 Howe, Lawrence Westerby. "The idea of Endosmosis in Bergson's Philosophy." Diss. Missouri, 1983, 146. "Ultimately this dissertation supports the view that endosmosis is a feature of Bergson's method for criticizing some concepts pertaining to theory of knowledge and metaphysics. Emphasis is placed on Bergson's belief that the task of philosophy is to disentangle interpretive elements from the data of immediate experience." *Dissertation Abstracts International*, 44, No. 12, 1984, Part I, 3713A.

5896 Lowe, Sue Davidson. *Stieglitz: A Memoir/Biography*. New York: Farrar Straus Giroux, 1983, 456. The author states concerning the American critic, editor, and photographer Alfred Stieglitz: "The first and perhaps strongest philosophic thread derived from the metaphysical constructions of Henri Bergson... ...Possibly Alfred knew Bergson's works already in Berlin; certainly he knew them later. *Creative Evolution* dominated many of the Round Table discussions of the Photo-Secssionists and the *Camera Workers*—with most of the dissenters lined up with Steichen on the side of Maeterlinck—as well as the painters and writers. Alfred and Dove, at least, were spurred to further explore philosophies congenial to Bergson, notably those built on Eastern thought," p. 210.

5897 Lucas, George R. Jr. *The Genesis of Modern Process Thought: A Historical Outline With Bibliography*. Metuchen, New Jersey and London: Scarecrow Press and American Theological Library Assn., 1983, 231. (ATLA Bibliography Series, 7) This is primarily an annotated bibliography organized to show the development of philosophies of process, including Bergson's. (Cf. pp. 60, 68-71, 165, and throughout.)

5898 May, Rollo. "Chapter Ten. Of Time and History", in *The Discovery of Being: Writings in Existential Psychology*. New York and London: W. W. Norton and Company, 1983, pp. 133-142. The author, a leader of the existential psychotherapy movement, briefly explores the relevance of temporality to therapy. He shows how Eugene Minkowski discovered, through a reading of Bergson, the relevance of the "time dimension" to psychotherapy. In dealing with a paranoid patient, Minkowski concluded that the patient's problems stemmed from a "profound disorder in his attitude towards the future." (p. 134) Some therapists would have said that this disorder stemmed from the patient's delusions; Minkowski reversed this relationship, arguing that the patient's problem was his "distorted attitude towards the future, while his delusions were only one of its manifestations." (p. 135) The author adds to Minkowski's insights: "That is, I discovered with some surprise that if we can help the severely anxious or depressed patient to focus on some point in the future when he will be *outside* his anxiety or depression, the battle is half won." (p. 135)

5899   Poggi, Stefano. "Il Tormento Della Distingione E. Il Flusso Della Coscienza: Bergson, Spencer E I Fatti Della Psiche." *Rivista di Filosofia*, 73, No. 3, 1983, 122-169.

5900   Stroda, Magdalena. "Moral Duty and Inspiration in the Philosophy of Henri Bergson." *Etyka*, 20, 1983, 23-44. This article, which describes the basic duality in Bergson's ethics, is written in Polish.

5901   Sullivan, Kevin. "The Relation Between Duration and the Critique of the Idea of Nothing in Bergson's Thought." *De Philosophia*, 4, 1983, 75-86.

5902   Wagner, Helmut R. *Alfred Schutz: An Intellectual Biography*. Chicago and London: The University of Chicago Press, 1983, 357. (The Heritage of Sociology) The author contends that Schutz approached Bergson's writings in the hope of finding there a key to understanding the concept of *Verstehen* in Weber's sociology. Schutz found Bergson's key concept of duration "inaccessible", however, and turned to E. Husserl for guidance: "While Husserl claimed the center of Schutz's phenomenological-psychological work, Bergson supplemented the latter substantially." (pp. 273). Cf. esp. pp. 273-284.

1984

5903   Bandy, Thomas G. "Tillich's Limited Understanding of the Thought of Henri Bergson as 'Life Philosophy'." in *Theonomy and Autonomy: Studies in Paul Tillich's Engagement with Modern Culture*. Ed. John J. Carey. Macon, Georgia: Mercer University Press, 1984, 3-33. The author deals particularly with Bergson's and Paul Tillich's concepts of "participation". The author mentions Bergson's influence on the British philosopher Andrew Seth.

5904   Čapek, Milič. "Particles or Events?" *Physical Sciences and History of Physics*. Eds. R. S. Cohen and M. W. Wartofsky. Dordrecht, Boston, Lancaster: D. Reidel, 1984, 259. (Boston Studies in the Philosphy of Science, 82) The autor states: "... the view of the particle as a *string of imageless events* seems to me the only one that is free of the epistemological crudities of visual mechanistic models." (p. 22) Cf. Patrick A. Heelan's response, 1984.

5905   Casey, Edward S. "Habitual Body and Memory in Merleau-Ponty." *Man and World*, 17, 1984, 279-298.

5906   Davis, Harold Eugene. "Alejandro Deustua (1849-1945): His Critique of the Aesthetics of Jose Vasconcelos." *International Philosophical Quarterly*, 24, No. 2, March 1984, 69-78.

5907   Gidley, Mick. "The Later Faulkner, Bergson, and God." *Mississippi Quarterly*, 37, No. 3, 1984, 377-383. The author argues that the novelest William Faulkner's concept of God was very close to that of Bergson.

5908   Gilson, Etienne. *From Aristotle to Darwin and Back Again: A Journey in Final Causality, Species, and Evolution.* Trans. John Lyon. Notre Dame, Indiana: University of Notre Dame Press, 1984, 209. Cf. esp. Ch. IV, "Bergsonism and Teleology," pp. 90-104. The author credits Bergson with opening the way towards a new "finalism," while having himself failed to understand the nature of finalism, through his failure to understand Aristotle.

5909   Hartshorne, Charles. *Creativity in American Philosophy.* Albany: State University of New York Press, 1984.

5910   Heelan, Patrick A. "Commentary on 'Particles or Events?'" *Physical Sciences and History of Physics.* Eds. R. S. Cohen and M. W. Wartofsky. Dordrecht, Boston, Lancaster: D. Reidel, 1984, 259. (Boston Studies in the Philosophy of Science, 82)

5911   Klaric, Arlette. "Arthur G. Dove's Abstract Style of 1912: Dimensions of the Decorative and Bergsonian Time." Diss. Wisconsin, 1984.

5912   Mish'Alani, James K. "Threats, Laughter, and Society." *Man and World,* 17, 1984, 143-159.

5913   Sagal, Paul T. "Review of *Bergson and Modern Physics* by Milič Čapek." *Journal of the British Society for Phenomenology,* 15, No. 1, 1984, 103-105.

5914   Ventura, Antonino. "Il Tempo Nel Pensiero Di Gaston Bachelard." *Rivista di Filosofia Neo-Scolastica,* 76, No. 1, 1984, 98-121. "This work focuses on Bachelard's thought concerning the notion of time, in order to stress the evolution of it and bring out the ontological meaning. The conclusions show that the thesis on temporal discontinuity in Bachelard's first phase is improved later, in the works about the imaginary, by a concept of temporality close to Bergsonism and metaphysically useful." *The Philosopher's Index,* 19, No. 1, 1985, 130.

5915   Wallon, Henri. "Psychology: Natural or Human Science?" Trans. D. Nicholson-Smith. in *The World of Henri Wallon.* Ed. Gilbert Voyat. New York and London: Jason Aronson, 1984, 179-203. On pp. 189-192 the author introduces and criticizes Bergson's attempt to make the intuition of duration the basis of psychology. He suggests Charles Blondel's approach instead, then criticizes all "psychologies of consciousness." (This article was published originally in *Revue de Synthèse,* 1931.)

5916   Wallon, Henri. "the Psychological and Sociological Study of the Child." Trans. D. Nicholson-Smith. in *The World of Henri Wallon.* Ed. Gilbert Voyat. New York and London: Jason Aronson, 1984, 205-223. On pp. 205-208 the author cites associationist and Bergsonian psychologies as "individualist", offering "an individual closed in upon himself." He cites Maurice Halbwachs (*Les Cadres sociaux de la memoire*) as a psychologist who, starting as a Bergsonian, joined Durkheim's school and tried to show that so-called personal memories are determined by social factors. On pp. 211-212, he discusses Ch. Blondel's recourse to Bergson's individual durée, impenetrable to language. The author then offers his own concept of the sociability of the "self". This article appeared originally in *Cahiers internationaux de sociologie,* 1947.

5917   Zazzo, René. "Who is Henri Wallon?" Trans. D. Nicholson-Smith. in *The World of Henri Wallon.* Ed. Gilbert Voyat. New York and London: Jason Aronson, 1984, 7-14. The author notes that Wallon, a critic of Piaget, introduces the concept of duration into psychology. Duration is for Wallon the creative evolution of the individual, yet Wallon denied to duration any existence over and above the things which endure.

1985

5918   Cohen, I. Bernard. *Revolution in Science*. Cambridge, Massachusetts: The Belknap
       Press of Harvard University Press, 1985, 711. In "A Bergsonian Revolution?",
       pp. 555-558, the author rejects out of hand the notion that there was, around
       the turn of the century, a Bergsonian revolution in science. (So far as this
       bibliographer knows, no one has ever claimed that such a revolution existed,
       in science.)

5919   Mijuskovic, Ben. *Contingent Immaterialism: Meaning, Freedom, Time, and Mind*.
       Amsterdam: B. R. Grüner, 1984, 214. Cf. esp. Ch. 4, pp. 66-85, "The Simplicity
       Argument and Time in Schopenhauer and Bergson." The author argues against
       Bergson's attempt, in *Matter and Memory*, to relate mind intimately with matter.

5920   Pannenberg, Wolfhart. "Atom, Duration, Form: Difficulties With Process Philos-
       ophy." Trans. J. C. Robertson and G. Vallée. *Process Studies*, 14, No. 1,
       Spring 1985, 21-30.

5921   Wagner, Helmut R. *A Bergsonian Bridge to Phenomenological Psychology, Current
       Continental Research*. Lanham, Maryland: University Press of America, 1985,
       192. This study deals with an early phase (1924-1928) in the life work of Alfred
       Schutz, social science scholar who contributed to the movement of international
       phenomenology. Schutz utilized Bergson's ideas to "radicalize" the sociology
       of Max Weber.

Fragments Without Dates

5922   Deustua, Alejandro O. "El Orden y la Libertad." in *La Filosofía Latino-americana
       Contemporánea*. Ed. Aníbal Sánchez Reulet. Washington D. C.: Union
       Panamericana, n. d., p. 64. In this essay a prominent Argentinian philosopher
       argues that creative freedom is necessary to explain order. The principle of
       freedom, hidden for centuries, has been made obvious in Bergson's philosophy,
       which shows that liberty, conceived as creative activity, is 'free by being free,
       by not repeating its effects as does mechanical activity.' There is, moreover, a
       structure to creative activity.

5923   Gide, André. *Journal, 1923-1931*. Vol. 3. Americ=Edit. On p. 16 (ler Mars,
       1924) the author states of Bergson's influence: "Plus tard, on croira découvrir
       partout so influence sur notre époque, simplement parce que lui-même est de
       son époque et qu'il cede sans cesse au mouvement. D'oú son importance repré-
       sentative." On p. 90 (18 Juillet) he notes is difficulty in understanding *Time
       and Free Will*.

5924   Gide, André. *Journal, 1932-1939*. Vol. 4. Americ=Edit. On p. 56 (19 Juillet
       1932) the author chides Paul Nizan, who, he states, would not attack art an
       philosophy for he would lose his following of scoffers. However, in his *Chiens
       de Garde*, Nizan attacks Bergson and Brunschvicg.

5925   Grond, Gertrud. "Über den Gegensatz der empirisch naturwissenschaftlich fun-
       dierten und der aus metaphysischer Intuition entspringenden Theorien des

organischen Lebens mit besonderen Berücksichtigungen der Lebenstheorien Schopenhauers und Bergsons." This item appears in a Bergson bibliography published in 1957 in *Das Buch*. No date, place of publication or publisher are given.

5926 Harley, J. A. *Syndicalism* London: T. C. & E. C. Jack; New York: Dodge Publishing Co., n. d., 94pp. (The People's Books) Cf. pp. 54, 56, 67.

PART IV

SOURCES USED IN COMPILING
THIS BIBLIOGRAPHY

1. Bergson Bibliographies

"Bibliografia bergsoniana." *Giornale di metafisica*, 14, No. 6, 1959, 835-872. 1945-1959, France, Italy, Spain, Latin America.

Centre nationale de bibliographie. Les Bibliographies (Bruxelles), 6. Henri Bergson, 1966, 24 pp.

A Contribution to a Bibliograpy of Henri Bergson. New York: Columbia University Press, 1913, 56.

Coviello, Alfredo. "Bibliografía bergsoniana." *Sustancia*, 11, No. 7-8, septiembre 1941, 394-440.

Coviello, Alfredo. *El processo filosófico de Bergson y su bibliografía*. Tucumán, Argentina: Revista Sustancia, 1941, 117.

Dossier Henri Bergson. Salle des imprimés. Bibliothèque nationale. (Several review articles and expositions of Bergson's philosophy.)

Gonzalo Casas, Manuel. "Bibliografia bergsoniana in Spagna e nell'America Latina." *Giornale di metafisica*, 14, No. 6, 1959, 866-872.

Gonzalo Casas, Manuel. "Bibliografía hispanoamericana de Bergson." *Humanitas*, 7, No. 12, 1959, 103-108.

Lameere, J. "Bibliographie de Bergson." *Revue Internationale de Philosophie*, 3, No. 10, 15 octobre 1949, 459-478.

Martins, Diamantino. *Bergson: La intuicion como método en la metafísica*. Trans. J. J. López. Madrid: Bolanos y Aguilar, 1943, 303-320.

Mathieu, Vittorio. "Bibliografia bergsoniana in Francia (1945-1959)." *Giornale di metafisica*, 14, No. 6, 1959, 835-852.

Mathieu, Vittorio. "Bibliografia bergsoniana in Germania (1945-1959). *Giornale di metafisica*, 14, No. 6, 1959, 853-856.

Meckauer, Walter. "Literaturverzeichnis." *Der Intuitionismus und seine Elemente bei Henri Bergson*. Leipzig: Meiner, 1917, 160, ix-xiv.

Mossé-Bastide, Rose-Marie. "Bibliographie de Bergson." *Bergson éducateur*. Paris: Presses Universitaires de France, 1955, 359-379.

Mossé-Bastide, Rose-Marie. "Bibliographie générale des études sur le bergsonisme. *Bergson éducateur*. Paris: Presses Universitaires de France, 1955, 381-448.

Mourélos, Georges. *Bergson et les niveaux de la réalité*. Paris: Presses Universitaires de France, 1964, 256.

References on Henri Bergson. Washington, D.C.: Library of Congress, 1913, 3.

"Séminaire Bergson de Louvain, bibliographie de Bergson." *Revue Internationale de*

Philosophie, 4, No. 13, 15 juin 1950, 341-350.

Vigone, Luciana. "Bibliografia bergsoniana in Italia." *Giornale di metafisica*, 14, No. 6, 1959, 857-865.

Wenger, Marguerite. "Bibliographie der Schriften von und über Bergson." *Das Buch*, 3, No. 2, 1961, 64-70.

2. Issues of Journals, Reviews, etc. Dedicated to Bergson

Actes du Xe Congrès des Sociétés de Philosophie de Langue Française (Congrès Bergson). Paris: Armand Colin, 1959, 355 (*Bulletin de la Société Française de Philosophie*, 53e Année, 1959. Numéro spécial).

Archives de Philosophie, 17, No. 1, 1947, 1-172 (Bergson et bergsonisme).

Bégin, Albert and Thévenaz, Pierre, Eds. *Henri Bergson: Essais et témoignages*. Neuchâtel, Switzerland: La Baconnière, 1943, 373 (Les Cahiers du Rhône, hors série, août 1943). An earlier edition of this collection of articles appeared in 1941 at Neuchâtel.

Bulletin de la Société Française de Philosophie, 10, No. 1, 1960, 2-108. This issue contains talks given in September, 1959 at the Congrès Bergson of the Société romande de philosophie.

Criterion, 11, 1936 (Tomismo de Bergson al realismo de Santo Tomàs).

Etudes Bergsoniennes. Paris: Presses Universitaires de France, 1942, 222 (Tiré à part de la *Revue Philosophique*).

Giornale di metafisica, 14, No. 6, novembre-dicembre 1959, 753-872.

Homenaje a Bergson. Córdoba, Argentina: *Imprenta de la Universidad, 1936, 191*.

Homenaje a Bergson. México: Imprenta Universitaria, 1941.

Humanitas, 14, No. 11, 1959, 769-852 (Ommagio a Henri Bergson).

Kriterion, 13, No. 1, 1960, 1-20.

Luminar, 2, No. 4, 1938, 1-99 (Homenaje a Bergson).

Mens en Kosmos, Vol. 15, No. 6, November, 1959.

La Nef, 4, No. 32, juillet 1947 (Bergson et la justice).

Nouvelles Littéraires, No. 322, 15 décembre 1928. This issue was dedicated to Bergson on the occasion of his receiving the Nobel Prize for literature.

Nouvelles Littéraires, No. 1677, 22 octobre 1959. This issue is dedicated to Bergson on the centennial of his birth.

The Personalist, 14, No. 2, April 1933.

Revista brasileira de filosofia, 11, 1961, 106-113 (Centenário de Bergson. Depoimentos).

Revue de Métaphysique et de Morale, 48, No. 4, 1941 (Controverses bergsoniennes).

Revue de Métaphysique et de Morale, 64, No. 2, 1959, 129-256 (Pour le centenaire de Bergson).

Revue de Théologie et de Philosophie, 54, No. 1, janvier-mars 1960, 1-63 (Hommage solonnel à Bergson).

Revue Internationale de Philosophie, 13, No. 2, 1959, 171-290.

Revue Philosophique de la France et de l'Etranger, 131, No. 3-8, mars-août 1941, 121-342 (Hommage à Henri Bergson).

Revue Philosophique de la France et de l'Etranger, 149, No. 3, juillet-septembre 1959

(Autour de Bergson).

Revue Thomiste, N.S. 16, No. 77, mai-juin 1933, 347-502. This issue is devoted to Bergson's philosophy of religion.

Richerche filosofiche, 5, No. 1, 1951.

Sustancia. Revista de Cultura Superior, Año 2, No. 7-8, septiembre 1941, 317-439.

3. General Bibliographic Sources

American Journal of Psychology. 1900-1929.

American Yearbook. 1910-1919.

Archiv für Begriffsgeschichte: Band 5. *Eine Begriffsgeschichte deutscher Hochschulschriften von 1900-1955.* Bonn: Bouvier und Ges., Verlag, 1960, 718. Henri Bergson: 127ff, 1094, 1267f, 3850ff, 4089, 4099, 4422ff, 4584, 4604f, 6477, 8828, 8900, 9176, 9400.

Arnold, Albert James. *Paul Valéry and his Critics: A Bibliography.* Charlottesville: University Press of Virginia, 1970, 617.

ATLA Index to Religious Periodical Literature. 1949-1977.

Bancroft Library, University of California at Berkeley. Catalogue of Printed Books, Vol. 2. First Supplement Vol. I; Second Supplement, Vol. I.

"*Biblio.*" 1-37, 1934-1970.

Bibliografía Argentina de Filosofía. La Plata, Argentina: Ministerio de Educación. 2-4, 1960-1962.

Bibliografia filosofica italiana. Dal 1900 al 1950. Roma: Edizioni Delfino, 1950, 298. Vol. 1, 116-118.

Bibliographia General de la Revista Estudios. (Chile) 1932-1957.

Bibliographie de la Littérature française du Moyen Age à nos jours. Années 1967, 1969.

Bibliographie de la Philosophie. 1937-1983.

Bibliographie der deutschen Zeitschriften-Literatur. Ergänzungsband. 1899-1917.

Bibliographie der deutschen Zeitschriften-Literatur. New York: Kraus Reprint, 1961. Orig. Osnabrück: Verlag Dietrich, 1896-1944 (1); 1944-1946 (2); 1947-1949; 1950 (Abt. A)-1963 (1).

Bibliographie der Französischen Literaturewissenschaft. 1956-1982.

Bibliographie der Rezensionen und Referat (IBZ). 1900-1943.

Bibliographisches Handbuch der Deutschen Literaturwissenschaft, 1945, Vols. 1 and 2.

Biblioteca Nacional Argentina. 1919.

Biblioteca Nazionale Centrale Firenze: Catologo Cumulativo: 1886-1957. New York: Kraus Reprint. Vol. 5, 103-104.

Bibliothèque nationale. Catalogue matières, ouvrages entrés de 1894-1959, et depuis 1960.

The Book Review Digest. Ed. Mertice James and Dorothy Brown. New York: H. W. Wilson Company, 1905-1983.

Books Abroad. 2-24.

Bourke, Vernon J. Thomistic Bibliography, 1920-1940. St. Louis, Missouri: The Modern Schoolman, 1945, 311. (Supplement to Vol. 21, *The Modern Schoolman*).

Brie, G. A. de. *Bibliographica Philosophica.* Bruxelles, Editiones Spectrum, 1950, 1954.

2 vols. (Esp. Vol 1, 546-551.)

British Humanities Index. 1969-1984 (No. 2).

British Museum, General Catalogue of Printed Books. London: Trustees of British Museum, 1965, Vol. 15.

British Museum, General Catalogue of Printed Books. Five-Year Supplement, 1966-1970, Vol. II.

Bulletin Analytique de Philosophie. 1947-1960. This publication is continued as *Bulletin Signalétique: Sciences Humaines: Philosophie*.

Bulletin Signalétique: Sciences Humaines: Philosophie, 1961-1970, 1980.

Catalogo General de la Librería Española, 1931-1950, Vol. I.

Catalogo General de la Librería Española e Hispanoamericana, 1901-1930. Autores, Vol. I.

Catalogue of the Latin American Collection: University of Texas Library: Austin. Vol. 4. Bergson: 144-145.

Catholic Periodical Index. 1930-1936; 1939-1968.

Catholic Periodical and Literature Index. 1968-1983.

Combined Retrospective Index to Book Reviews in Scholarly Journals, 1886-1974.

Combined Retrospective Index to Book Reviews in Humanities Journals, 1902-1974.

Comprehensive Dissertation Index, 1861-1972. pp. 21, 131, 516.

Comprehensive Index to English-Language Little Magazines, 1890-1970. Series One. Vol. 1, 330-331.

Comprehensive Index to Little Magazines, 1890-1970. Vol. 1, 330-331.

A Critical Bibliography of French Literature. Vol. 6. *The Twentieth Century*. Eds. Douglas W. Alden and Richard A. Brooks. Syracuse, New York: Syracuse University Press, 1980, 2073.

Cumulative Subject Index to Psychological Abstracts, 1927-1960; First Supplement, 1961-1965; Second Supplement, 1966-1968.

Dictionaire de Biographie Française. Vol. 6, 13-15.

Dissertation Abstracts International, 1969-1984.

Dissertations in Philosophy Accepted at American Universities, 1861-1975. Ed. Thomas C. Bechtle and Mary F. Riley. New York and London: Garland Publishing, Inc., 1978, 537.

Dreher, S. and Rolli, M. *Bibliographie de la littérature française: 1930-1939*. Genève: Droz, 1948, 438. Successor to H. P. Thieme's bibliography.

Drevet, Marguerite L. *Bibliographie de la littérature française: 1940-1949*. Genève: Droz, 1954, 644. Successor to H. P. Thieme's bibliography.

Educational Literature, 1907-1932. Intro. Malcom Hamilton. London and New York: Bowker, 1977.

Essay and General Literature Index. 1900-1954, 1960-1983.

William Faulkner, a Bibliography of Secondary Works. Ed. Beatrice Ricks. Metachin, New Jersey and London: Scarecrow Press, 1981, 657.

French 7 Bibliography. 1949-1968.

French 20 Bibliography. 1969-1983.

Gallagher, Donald and Idella. *The Achievement of Jacques and Raissa Maritain: A Bibliography, 1906-1961*. New York: Doubleday and Co., 1962, 256.

Gesamtverzeichnis des deutschsprachigen Schrifttums 1911-1965. Vol. 11, pp. 457-458.

Gomez, Luis Martínez. *Bibliografía Filosófica: Española e Hispanoamericana (1940-1958)*. Barcelona: Juan Flors, 1961, pp. 119, 163-165, 186-188, 443, 234-235.

Gropp, A. E. *A Bibliography of Latin American Bibliographies Published in Periodicals*. V. I. Metuchin, New Jersey: Scarecrow Press, 1976, p. 210.

Guerry, Herbert. *A Bibliography of Philosophical Bibliographies*, pp. 23, 121.

Handbook of Latin American Studies. Nos. 5-26, 28, 30, 32, 1939-1970.

Hebrew Union College. *Dictionary Catalogue of the Klau Library*, Vol. 3, pp. 398-406.

Hispanic American Periodicals Index, 1975-1980.

Humanities Index, 1974-1984 (No. 1).

Index Analytique, 1966-1972.

Index to American Little Magazines, 1900-1919, Vol. 1, 105.

Index to Commonwealth Little Magazines, 1964-1975.

Index to Jewish Periodicals, Vols. 1-20 (No. 2), 1963-1982.

Index to Latin American Periodical Literature: 1929-1960. Boston: Hall and Co., 1962. Vol. 1.

Index to Latin American Periodicals: Humanities and Social Sciences. 1-10, 1961-1970, Nos. 1 and 2.

Index to Little Magazines, 1920-1939; 1943-1947.

Index Translationum 1932-1940 (Nos. 1-31); N.S. 1948-1978 (Vols. 1-31).

International Bibliography of Social Sciences, 1960-1980.

International Bibliography of Sociology, 1955-1959.

International Index to Periodicals. 1907-1965. This publication is continued, as concerns philosophy, in the *Social Sciences and Humanities Index*.

Internationale Bibliographie der Zeitschriften Literatur, 1965-1983, Part 1.

Isis Cumulative Bibliography, 1913-1965: Personalities. Vol. 1.

The John Crerar Library Author-Title Catalogue, Vol. 4.

Journal of Abnormal Psychology, Vols. 1-16, 1907-1922.

The Journal of Philosophy: A Bibliography of Philosophy for 1933.

Koehler und Volckmar Fachbibliographien Philosophie und Grenzgebiete. 1945-1964. Bergson: 29, 70, 305, 327.

Lapointe, Francis and Claire. *Jean-Paul Sartre and his Critics: An International Bibliography* (1938-1975).

Library of Congress Catalogue. Books: Subjects. 1950-1977.

Library of Congress Catalogue of Printed Cards, Vol. 13, pp. 96-98.

Library of Congress Catalogues, National Union Catalogue, 1973-1976.

Library of Congress and National Union Catalogue Author Lists, 1942-1962. A Master Cumulation, Vol. 14.

Lineback, Richard H., ed. *The Philosopher's Index: A Retrospective Index to Non-U. S. English Language Publications From 1940*. 3 Vols. Bowling Green, Ohio: Philosophy Documentation Center, Bowling Green State University, 1980, 1265.

A London Bibliography of the Social Sciences, 1929-1983.

Maïre, Gilbert. *Henri Bergson: Son Oeuvre*. Paris: Nouvelle Revue Critique, 1928, 52-71.

Manuel de la recherche documentaire en France: Tome II, 1re Partie, 7e Section. Philosophie

(Sous la direction de Raymond Bayer). Paris: Vrin, 1950, 417. Bergson: 27, 60, 65, 70, 96, 121, 147, 158, 190, 225.

Miethe, Terry L. and Bourke, Vernon J. *Thomistic Bibliography, 1940-1978*. Westport, Connecticut: Greenwood Press, 1980, 318.

Miller, Joan M. *French Structuralism: A Multidisciplinary Bibliography*. New York and London: Garland Publishing, Inc., 1981, 553.

MLA International Bibliography, 1970-1982.

National Union Catalogue Author List, 1952-1972.

National Union Catalogue, Pre-1956 Imprints, Vol. 48, 496-510.

New York Public Library Slavonic Collection Catalogue. Boston: Hall and Co., 1959. Vol. 2.

Palau y Dulcet, Antonio. *Manuel del Librero Hispanoamericano*. Barcelona: Librería Palau, 1949, 494. Bergson: 180.

Philosophen-Lexikon. Berlin: Walter de Gruyter und Ges., 1949, I, 700, Brief article on Bergson with bibliography.

The Philosopher's Index, 1968-1984.

The Philosopher's Index: A Retrospective Index to U. S. Publications from 1940.

Philosophic Abstracts. 1939-1954.

Die Philosophie des Ausländers vom Beginn des 19. Jahrhunderts bis auf die Gegenwart. Berlin: Mittler, 1928, 431. Bergson: 21, 35, 53, 56ff, 78, 195, 240, 396, 418.

Philosophische Dokumentation aus dem Philosophischen Institut der Universität Düsseldorf. Gesamtregister zur Zeitschrift für philosophische Forschung 1-21 (1946-1967). Meisenheim am Glan: Verlag Anton Hain, 1968, 618. Bergson: 130.

The Present State of French Studies: A Collection of Research Reviews. Ed. Charles B. Osburn. Metuchen, New Jersey: Scarecrow Press, 1971, 995.

Psychoanalytic Review. 1913-1929.

Psychological Review. 1898-1919.

Reader's Guide to Periodical Literature 1900-1971.

Répertoire bibliographique de la philosophie. 1949-1984 (Nos. 1 and 2).

Sader, Marion. *Comprehensive Index to English-Language Little Magazines*. Series One. Vol. 1.

Sass, Hans-Martin. *Martin Heidegger: Bibliography and Glossary*. Bowling Green, Ohio: Philosophy Documentation Center, 1982, 513.

Skrupskelis, Ignas K. *William James: A Reference Guide*. Boston: G. K. Hall, 1977, 250.

Social Science Abstracts, 1929-1932.

Social Sciences and Humanities Index. 1965-1973.

Social Sciences Index. 1974-1983 (No. 3).

Sociological Abstracts, 1953-1984.

A Subject Bibliography of the First World War: Books in English, 1914-1978. Ed. A. G. S. Enser. London: A. Deutsch, 1979, 485.

Subject Index to Periodicals (American and Englishå. 1915-1961.

Taylor, Russell. *Marcel Proust and His Contexts: A Critical Bibliography of English-Language Scholarship*. New York and London: Garland Publishing, Inc., 1981, 235.

Theau, Jean. "Henri Bergson." in *Les Littératures de langues européennes au tournant du siècle. Lectures d'aujourd'hui*. Cahiers V-VI, pp. 15-24.

Thieme, Hugo Paul. *Bibliographie de la littérature française de 1800 à 1930*. Paris: Droz, 1933, i, 1061. Bergson: 185-189.

Thils, Gustave. *Theologica e Miscellaneis*. Louvain: Warny, 1960, 434 (Festschriften and memorial volumes since World War I). Bergson: 1630, 2244, 2340, 2700, 3107, 3614.

Tijdschrift voor Philosophie. Bibliographisch Repertorium. 1939-1956; 1964-1967.

Turner, Mary C. *Libros an Venta en Hispanoamérica y España*. New York: Bowker, 1964, 1891. Bergsonismo: 1276.

Varet, Gilbert. *Manuel de bibliographie philosophique*. Paris: Presses Universitaires de France, 1956, 2 vols., 1058. Bergson: 153n, 260, 448, 605, 674, 744, 869, 894-895.

Watson, Robert I. *Eminent Contributions to Psychology*. Vol. 1. *A Bibliography of Primary References*, 26-27.

Watson, Robert I. *Eminent Contributions to Psychology*. Vol. 2. *A Bibliography of Secondary References*, 60-64.

Widener Library Shelflist. Philosophy and Psychology. Vol. 2. Author and Title Listing, pp. 49-50.

Woodbridge, Barry A. *Alfred North Whitehead: A Primary-Secondary Bibliography*. Bowling Green: Philosophy Documentation Center, 1977, 405.

PART V

INDEXES

Index: Works By Bergson

Index: Works Concerning Bergson

Coviello, Alfredo: 2524, 2575, 2690, 2692, 2693, 2694.

Creative Evolution: 119, 124, 132, 135, 138, 140, 142, 143, 147, 154, 157, 164, 166, 169, 178, 179, 183, 184, 188, 197, 199, 206, 207, 208, 209, 221, 225, 233, 235, 334, 335, 341, 342, 345, 354, 356, 357, 358, 359, 360, 361, 368, 406, 424, 450, 459, 464, 465, 493, 494, 500, 513, 514, 560, 561, 564, 579, 580, 622, 649, 681, 688, 699, 703, 756, 776, 790, 791, 798, 872, 892, 1035, 1355, 1382, 1599, 1883, 1907, 1924, 1949, 2137, 2254, 2937, 3454, 3864, 4137, 4349, 4369, 4549, 4653, 4881, 4901, 5060, 5112, 5253, 5366, 5395, 5452, 5453, 5475, 5541, 5544, 5729, 5862, 5876.

The Creative Mind: 2208, 2233, 2243, 2246, 2249, 2256, 2263, 2264, 2265, 2266, 2271, 2273, 2277, 2279, 2288, 2292, 2295, 2302, 2320, 2321, 2322, 2333, 2334, 2340, 2341, 2346, 2352, 2363, 2369, 2370, 2381, 2402, 2404, 2420, 2429, 3089, 3107, 3110, 3112, 3121, 3148, 3151, 3171, 3174.

Creativity: 1547, 1768, 2280, 2281, 2591, 3225, 3336, 3458, 3466, 3549, 3555, 4223, 4344, 4560, 4584, 4640, 4667, 4932, 4994, 5187, 5294, 5395, 5436, 5437, 5440, 5462.

Crémieux, B.: 1517, 1819.

Crescini, Angelo: 4387.

Cresson, André: 2576, 2694, 2695, 4388.

Cristiani, Aldo Horacio: 5043.

Croce, Benedetto: 518, 744, 1081, 1224, 1226, 1250, 1401, 1620, 1820, 2698, 3164, 3533, 3595, 4278, 4389, 4554, 5040.

Cubism (*see also* Picasso): 5628, 5757, 5811.

Cuénot, Lucien: 2877.

Cuvillier, Armand: 2397, 3095, 3697.

D'Abro, Arthur: 1662, 1663.

Dalbiez, Roland: 2398, 2961, 3239, 3240.

Dandieu, Arnaud: 1903.

Darwin, Charles: 649, 699, 1433, 5150.

Dauriac, Lionel: 39, 819, 944, 945, 3539, 3543.

Dayan, Maurice: 4668.

Death, Concept of: 2528, 2665, 2812, 2906, 3436, 3798, 3924, 4378, 4660, 4688, 4971.

De Broglie, Louis: 2677, 2987, 3049, 3157, 3521, 3692, 3700, 5384, 5392.

Decoster, Paul: 1272, 1729.

De Gaulle, Charles: 4288, 4755, 5105, 5797.

Dehove, Henri Charles: 2106.

Dejà vu (*see* False Recognition).

Dejardin, André: 3415.

Delacroix, Henri: 2223, 4401.

Delage, Yves: 1273.

Delattre, Floris: 1412, 1462, 1520, 1664, 1689, 2007, 2008, 2701, 2721, 2878, 3166, 3232, 3241, 3263, 3267, 3330, 3331, 3379, 3416, 3535, 5378.

Delay, Jean: 2877, 3970, 3971.

Delbos, Victor: 1135.

Deledalle, Gerard: 3322, 3840.

4923, 4957, 4991, 5013, 5039, 5084, 5227, 5239, 5253, 5256, 5266, 5342, 5355, 5363, 5401, 5436, 5437, 5479, 5517, 5554, 5677, 5685, 5731, 5733, 5840.

Ionesco, Eugene: 4766, 5203, 5316, 5664.

Iriarte, Joaquín: 2741, 3363, 4053.

Irrationalism (*see* Instinct, Intellect, Intuition).

Isaye, Gaston: 4054, 4055, 4056.

Italy (*see also* Allioto, Croce, Gentile, Papini): 3744, 3865, 4234, 4833, 5116, 5178.

Iturriouz, J.: 3008, 3053.

Jacks, Lawrence Pearsall: 287, 2243, 2955.

Jaeckel, Kurt: 2513.

Jaensch, Erich B.: 2026.

James, William (*see also* Pragmatism): 101, 105, 106, 172, 232, 240, 252, 263, 268, 289, 290, 291, 292, 293, 296, 303, 308, 313, 341, 350, 371, 381, 400, 408, 421, 441, 442, 563, 613, 674, 756, 864, 922, 982, 983, 1039, 1100, 1108, 1125, 1360, 1438, 1462, 1506, 1512, 1520, 1573, 1625, 1849, 2056, 2089, 2163, 2165, 2179, 2230, 2237, 2356, 2396, 2476, 2582, 2592, 2701, 2846, 3234, 3373, 3408, 3427, 3480, 3694, 3699, 3703, 4269, 4321, 4401, 4405, 4447, 4493, 4551, 4649, 4776, 4827, 4900, 4912, 5057, 5427, 5454, 5455, 5494, 5552, 5564, 5591, 5757, 5891.

Janet, Pierre: 77, 101, 110, 976, 1398, 1405, 1742, 2473, 2805, 3257, 5011, 5048, 5339, 5340, 5570.

Janicaud, Dominique: 3908, 4753, 4992, 5130, 5190.

Jankélévitch, Vladimir: 1526, 1743, 1841, 1914, 1967, 2076, 2135, 2956, 3489, 3726, 3808, 3829, 4059, 4060, 4265, 4274, 4305, 4315, 4337, 4358, 4372, 4407, 4430, 4469, 4470, 4718, 4795, 5467.

Japan: 1749, 2589.

Jarry, Alfred: 5451, 5845.

Jaspers, Karl (*see also* Existentialism): 790, 5867.

Jaurès, Jean: 4462, 4851, 4935, 5669.

Jeliffe, Smith Ely: 791, 1095, 4805.

Jerphagnon, Lucien: 4471, 4686, 5320, 5795.

Jetté, Emile: 2957, 3185.

Joad, C. E. M.: 2328, 2743, 3109.

Johnson, Allison H.: 3186, 4472.

Johnson, Richard E.: 5468, 5686.

Johnstone, James: 797, 978, 1249, 1527.

Jolivet, Régis: 1744, 1968, 2028, 2029, 2137, 2138, 2238, 2244, 2329, 2534, 2744, 4061, 4316.

Jones, Ernest: 244, 1096, 4409.

Joseph, H. W. B.: 2330.

Joyce, James: 1758, 3712, 3811, 3812, 3830, 4071, 4450, 4756, 4962.

Jourdain, Philip E. B.: 799.

Jous, Dominique: 5395, 5544.

Joussain, André: 402, 403, 586, 587, 1381, 3651, 3709, 3763, 4062, 4319, 4544.

Judaism: 727, 795, 874, 934, 1155, 2064, 2102, 2157, 2207, 2276, 2418, 2438, 2479, 2639, 3150, 3216, 3412, 3528, 3563, 3629, 3668, 3689, 3709, 3717, 3808, 3927, 3996, 4059, 4105, 4206, 4666, 5096, 5173, 5544.

Jung, Carl Gustav (*see also* Freud, Pierre Janet, Psychopathology, Unconscious): 113, 800, 801, 802, 973, 976, 980, 981, 984, 1151, 1152, 1467, 1745, 1746, 2126, 2245, 2331, 3011, 4057, 4409, 5048, 5323, 5564, 5813.

Junod, Robert: 2958.

Jurevics, Paulis: 1916, 2417, 2474, 2475, 2535, 2636, 3365, 3451, 3520, 3557.

Kallen, Horace Meyer: 293, 296, 588, 982, 1097, 1100, 1108, 1427, 2476, 5591, 5796.

Kant, Immanuel: 69, 73, 86, 355, 528, 585, 696, 732, 733, 832, 838, 1515, 1529, 2218, 2501, 2991, 3183, 3529, 3831, 3848, 4297, 4392, 4399, 4514, 4518, 4718, 4825, 5229, 5372, 5408, 5518, 5523, 5619, 5733.

Kazantzakis, Nikos: 3245, 3846, 4819, 4902, 5053, 5218, 5261, 5596, 5616, 5745.

Keats, John: 2566.

Keller, Adolph: 1152.

Kennedy: Ellen Lee: 5612, 5797, 5798.

Keyserling, Graf Hermann: 590, 1437, 4294, 5047.

Kierkegaard, Soren: 1737, 2102, 3097, 3390, 5883.

Kinnen, Edouard: 4063, 4320, 4545.

Klages, Ludwig: 2140, 2924, 3838, 4971.

Klimov, Alexis: 4757.

Knowledge, Theory of: 139, 143, 157, 200, 205, 211, 376, 457, 466, 563, 675, 744, 864, 1048, 1260, 1369, 1587, 2496, 2647, 2775, 3410, 3633, 3658, 3731, 3732, 3805, 3940, 4085, 4151, 4172, 4389, 4393, 4404, 4435, 4537, 4561, 4573, 4727, 4843, 4991, 5499, 5637, 5690, 5838, 5895.

Knudsen, Peter: 1747.

Koestler, Arthur: 3367, 5697.

Konczewski: 2644, 4994.

Korn, Alejandro: 1675, 1917, 2477, 2478, 2584, 3405, 4064, 5575.

Koyré, Alexander: 1429, 2583.

Krakowski, Edouard: 1844, 1845, 1918, 1919, 2031, 2142, 3111.

Kremer-Marietti, Angèle: 3610, 3710, 4065, 4066, 4758, 4904, 5066, 5324, 5546.

Kucharski, Paul: 3188.

Kumar, Shiv: 3654, 3811, 3812, 3813, 4068, 4069, 4070, 4071, 4412, 4413, 4443, 4494, 4546, 4579, 4624, 5752.

Laberthonnière, Lucien: 2888, 3050, 3984.

Lachelier, Jules: 1445, 2143, 4318.

Lachieze-Ray, Pierre: 3550.

Lacombe, Roger-E.: 2144, 2238.

Lacroix, Jean: 4325, 4995.

Lafrance, Guy: 4761, 4908, 5171, 5396, 5434, 5488, 5502, 5531, 5547.

Lafranchi, Geneviève: 3262, 4072, 4073.

Lagneau, J.: 128, 3935, 4490.

5405, 5418.

Mathematics (*see also* Intellect, Intuition, Space): 1, 15, 38, 43, 94, 123, 155, 352, 458, 556, 663, 664, 728, 799, 1080, 1164, 1584, 2629, 2942, 3298, 3603, 4158, 4176, 4721, 4985, 5034, 5060, 5346, 5407, 5428, 5493, 5503, 5549, 5723, 5766.

Matière et mémoire (*see Matter and Memory*).

Matisse, Georges: 2901.

Matter (*see also Creative Evolution, Duration and Simultaneity,* Lucretius, Mathematics, *Matter and Memory,* Physics, Space): 749, 1241, 1759, 1967, 2072, 2803, 3530, 3566, 3567, 3593, 3650, 3883, 3892, 3901, 3906, 4044, 4065, 4066, 4142, 4143, 4156, 4197, 4347, 4691, 4770, 4917, 5000, 5034, 5073, 5131, 5156, 5158, 5248, 5816.

Matter and Memory (*see also* Aphasia, Attention, Matter, Memory, Mind-Body Problem, Perception, Psychopathology, Unconscious): 14, 17, 19, 21, 22, 24, 25, 26, 29, 66, 210, 255, 280, 305, 310, 341, 342, 345, 368, 376, 406, 415, 416, 417, 418, 419, 424, 441, 457, 500, 524, 541, 545, 589, 623, 756, 1072, 1196, 1568, 3020, 3502, 3561, 4349, 4716, 4763, 4864, 5030, 5154, 5270, 5315, 5388.

Mauriac, François: 3639, 5072.

Maurois, André: 2777, 3203, 3817, 4121, 4555, 4627, 4628, 4769, 4834, 4835.

Maurras, Charles: 1596, 4419, 5797.

Mavit, Henri: 2591, 3204, 3335, 3555, 4122, 4123, 4334.

May, Rollo: 5898.

May, W. E.: 4917, 5000, 5073.

Mayer, Hans: 3381, 3382, 3383.

Mazzantini, Carlo: 2054, 2340, 4125, 4481.

McDougall, William: 306, 1297, 1436, 1507.

McLean, Jeanne Priley: 5474.

McLuhan, Marshall: 5821.

McMahon, C. Patrick: 4691, 4770.

Mead, George Herbert: 1534, 2427, 2545.

Meerloo, Joost A.: 3665.

Megay, Joyce: 5331, 5332, 5405, 5476, 5477, 5519, 5550, 5569, 5585, 5587, 5622, 5706, 5845.

Meissner, W. W.: 4483, 4693, 4771.

Meland, Bernard: 4335, 4484, 4556.

Melges, Frederick T.: 5075, 5076, 5874.

Memory (*see also* Aphasia, Duration, *Matter and Memory,* Marcel Proust, Psychopathology, Unconscious): 245, 421, 441, 624, 656, 668, 778, 863, 1039, 1076, 1156, 1233, 1297, 1389, 1460, 1522, 1615, 1670, 1684, 1742, 1977, 2230, 2465, 2540, 2879, 3062, 3248, 3341, 3358, 3485, 3486, 3554, 3600, 3601, 3626, 3636, 3815, 3833, 3903, 3904, 3923, 3924, 3970, 3997, 4041, 4042, 4138, 4248, 4249, 4323, 4324, 4345, 4600, 4693, 4750, 4787, 4864, 4994, 5251, 5270, 5286, 5350, 5353, 5536, 5548, 5590, 5651, 5749, 5769, 5788, 5905.

Mercanton, Jacques: 2973, 3205.

Mercier, Gustave: 3705, 4369.

Merlan, Philip: 2902, 4127.

Schrecker, Paul: 668, 863, 944, 5287, 5348.

Schuhl, Pierre-Maxime: 4202, 4203, 4357.

Sciacca, Michele Federico: 3022, 3292, 3293, 3577, 4204, 4646.

Science (*see also* Biology, Mathematics, Physics, Psychology, Psychopathology, Physics): 30, 40, 43, 47, 57, 355, 471, 505, 530, 534, 1065, 1390, 1459, 1710, 1865, 2308, 2632, 3049, 3161, 3194, 3476, 3516, 3666, 3776, 3877, 4031, 4120, 4384, 4537, 4599, 4629, 4663, 4674, 4748, 4849, 4883, 4980, 5067, 5145, 5227, 5229, 5502, 5572, 5685, 5812, 5893, 5918.

Schutz, Alfred: 3448, 3514, 5653, 5717, 5841, 5903, 5921.

Scott, J. W.: 1036, 1256, 1295.

Segond, Joseph: 445, 670, 867, 944, 1207, 1257, 1258, 1549, 2363, 2991.

Seillière, Ernest: 869, 1208, 2277.

Self (*see* Personality).

Sellars, Wilfrid: 5842.

Sensation (*see* Perception).

Serini, Paulo: 1445, 1495.

Serouya, Henri: 2196, 4206, 4207, 4208, 4209.

Serrus, Charles: 2833.

Sertillanges, A. G. (*see also* Catholicism, Thomism): 1792, 2078, 2079, 2197, 2502, 2834, 2835, 2992, 2993, 3026, 3225, 3853.

Shakespeare: 1843, 5207.

Shaw, George Bernard: 3231, 3783.

Shklovsky, Viktor: 5521.

Sicé, Stanislaus: 3353, 3396.

Simmel, Georg (*see also* Philosophy of Life): 1040, 1116, 1433, 1446, 4971.

Sipfle, David A.: 5018, 5274, 5590.

Sirven, Joseph: 2280.

Smith, Colin: 3829, 4647.

Smith, Norman Kemp: 200, 673, 1261, 3294.

Social Philosophy: 389, 472, 489, 547, 559, 711, 806, 1256, 1490, 1534, 1728, 1735, 2204, 2233, 2405, 2444, 2515, 2516, 2522, 2595, 2848, 2949, 3111, 3170, 3256, 3294, 3301, 3315, 3402, 3412, 3467, 3637, 3638, 3929, 4320, 4394, 4442, 4477, 4531, 4538, 4576, 4661, 4735, 4761, 4817, 4883, 4982, 5005, 5128, 5171, 5179, 5187, 5188, 5298, 5319, 5398, 5502, 5547, 5717, 5831.

Sociology (*see also* Durkheim, Essertier, Gurvitch, Lasbax, Schutz, Sorokin): 284, 489, 502, 1086, 2233, 2293, 2431, 2432, 2504, 2505, 2539, 2577, 2848, 3398, 3426, 3455, 3494, 3659, 4538, 4560, 4619, 4709, 4722, 4789, 4793, 4940, 5011, 5187, 5298, 5398, 5536, 5548, 5564, 5650, 5717, 5738, 5831, 5850, 5873, 5916.

Socrates: 707, 5246.

Söderblom, N.: 1792, 2650.

Sorel, Georges (*see also* Social Philosophy, Syndicalism): 14, 143, 201, 243, 244, 284, 325, 326, 453, 616, 935, 1172, 1430, 1735, 2533, 2548, 2666, 3149, 3200, 3226, 3281, 3305, 3397, 3449, 3452, 3539, 3622, 3633, 4405, 4438, 4776, 5319, 5734, 5797.

Soulez, Philippe: 5570, 5645.